THE BOOK OF GOLFERS

THE BOOK OF GOLFERS

A Biographical History of the Royal & Ancient Game

Daniel Wexler

SMG
SPORTS
MEDIA
GROUP

All inquiries should be addressed to:
Sports Media Group
An imprint of Ann Arbor Media Group LLC
2500 S. State Street
Ann Arbor, MI 48104

Printed and bound at Edwards Brothers, Inc., Ann Arbor, Michigan, USA.

09   08   07   06   05   1   2   3   4   5

Wexler, Daniel.
    The book of golfers : a biographical history of the royal & ancient game / Daniel Wexler.
        p. cm.
    Includes bibliographical references.
    ISBN-13: 978-1-58726-190-9 (hardcover : alk. paper)
    ISBN-10: 1-58726-190-1 (hardcover : alk. paper)
    1. Golfers—Biography—Dictionaries. I. Title.

GV964.A1W39 2005
796.352′092′2—dc22
2005012390

ISBN-13: 978-1-58726-190-9
ISBN-10: 1-58726-190-1

For my mother Roberta—simply the greatest!

Contents

Introduction

This is a big book—but not without good reason.

The game of golf has, for nearly three centuries, provided us with one of the sporting world's richest rosters of people: an impressive list of players, course architects, writers, impresarios, caddies, and general hangers-on who, in all manner of ways, have contributed to this uniquely wonderful worldwide pastime. The goal of this book, then, is to profile nearly 1,300 of these people, providing a record of their accomplishments and, where possible, assessing their place within 300 years of golfing history.

Is this an entirely original concept? Not quite. Several previous titles have at least partially taken up the task, and I must quickly acknowledge both Donald Steel and Peter Ryde's *Shell International Encyclopedia of Golf* and Peter Alliss' *Who's Who in Golf* as fine resources with which to begin one's research.

But *The Book of Golfers* is different.

To begin with it is contemporary, whereas the above-mentioned titles date from 1975 and 1982, respectively. But even more important, its scope is one of unparalleled broadness, for not only does it cover nearly 1,000 of the game's all-time finest players but also more than 140 architects, 40 journalists, and numerous others whose impacts have ranged from amusing to highly significant. Further, an expansive appendix provides considerable data with which to compare the game's all-time greats, including a wide variety of performance tables for both players and architects, a bibliography for all profiled writers, and my own carefully considered rankings of the top 50 men and top 25 women golfers of all time. It is my belief, then, that there have been few more comprehensive or detailed volumes in this field than *The Book of Golfers*. Between its covers there is much for anyone interested in the game to digest.

Though all entries are consistent in style and appearance, several important differences do exist. Beyond their varying lengths (determined by an individual's overall significance), one notable distinction lies in dates and places of birth and death. For deceased Hall of Fame–caliber greats, detailed specifics are provided just beneath the person's name atop the entry. For everyone else, this information is worked into the text, often in less detail (e.g., years only, instead of exact dates). This approach, unfortunately, reflects the difficulty with which such information is often found, especially since many of the game's less famous have died in relative obscurity. Though not all of the blanks have been filled in, my efforts in this regard have included the exhaustion of my personal library, countless old magazines dating to 1900, detailed searches of the archives of the *New York Times* and the *Los Angeles Times*, the Social Security Death Index, several genealogical sites, and a number of additional online resources. In most cases, at least a year of birth has been determined, but the reader should not assume that a person remains alive simply because no date of passing is indicated ("born 1855" proving this point conclusively).

Several things must also be noted with regard to the many tournaments and tours referenced within. To begin with, since the PGA and European Tours as we know them date back only to 1970, a good deal of historical record-keeping has been done after the fact, with the American Tour in particular retroactively recognizing what are now deemed "official" victories dating to 1916. In this light the phrase "PGA Tour event" is used rather loosely for, in truth, the Tour itself did not yet exist at the time many were played. Similarly, the Champions Tour (the former Senior Tour) and Nationwide Tour (ex-Hogan and Buy.com Tours) have only been so-named of late, yet all of their past events are referred to under these current titles for the sake of simplicity. The same can be said for events like the British Ladies (officially the Ladies British Open Amateur Championship), which are also referred to colloquially for reasons of space. Finally, American readers may find "Open" or "Closed" to be odd modifiers in the names of many old overseas events. Such largely outdated phrasing was used to indicate whether foreign players were allowed into a given field, with, for example, only an Irishman being eligible for the Irish Closed Amateur, but any and all being welcomed into its Open counterpart—an important consideration when evaluating strengths of fields in many small-country events.

Regarding international team play I, like many others before me, have placed a good deal of emphasis on a player being selected to compete in the Curtis, Walker, Ryder, and/or Presidents Cups. This is not because a particular three-day match generally means very much within the whole of a career but rather because being chosen represents one of the few merit badges awarded in golf; it is a recognition of top-level play over the preceding two years and, thus, a barometer of career success like few others.

All of which brings us to the individual profiles themselves. They are, by and large, straightforward, reporting on backgrounds, achievements, statistics, and matters of historical importance, with prominent tournament victories in boldface. For the more prominent entries, however, some additional information is provided that readers hopefully will find helpful. In the case of top architects, for example, I have included a listing of famous courses designed, its size determined by an architect's overall prominence, its boldfaced entries representing courses presently nationally ranked or of particular historical significance.

For players, however, there is a bit more added material. For them our definition of prominent must be clearly defined. To make this grade, a full-time PGA Tour player will have won at least 10 official Tour events, while regulars on the slightly less competitive European and LPGA Tours require 12 victories each. Male amateurs will have claimed at least seven important titles, female amateurs eight, and both must have at least one British or American national championship on their résumé. Events from the Japan, Australasian, South African, and South American Tours do not count toward these totals, except in cases where they are cosponsored by the European Tour.

The significance of meeting these qualifications is that such players (plus a handful of historically important others) will have beneath their entries a ledger resembling Figure A in the Key to Tables. This ledger represents a summary of their career record, highlighting important victories both at home and abroad, and listing years of participation in the above-mentioned international team matches. While further details are provided beneath Figure A, one point requiring amplification is the choice of tournaments included under "PGA Tour Wins" and "Intn'l Wins." Specifically, as it is spatially impossible to list each player's complete record of victories, those which do appear have been culled from a preselected roster of tournaments designated the most important/prestigious of their eras. This list (which is detailed in Key to Tables, Figure D) offers a balance of new and old events both in America and worldwide, for men and women, professional and amateur. It has been formulated with a high degree of geographic distribution and, with the exception of the Masters and two match-play titles, includes only full-field events. The amateur lists have been similarly crafted, though it will be noted that only players who have spent extended careers in the amateur ranks have such events listed; those who quickly turned professional do not.

Players' victories in these designated events appear chronologically in their ledgers, with Major championships (the modern professional Grand Slams plus pre–World War II men's and women's U.S. and British Amateurs) highlighted in boldface. Due to their inherent newsworthiness, any nondesignated events won on three or more occasions are also noted. Lastly, as many professional tournaments undergo frequent sponsor-oriented name changes, I have, for the sake of clarity, listed each designated event under a single, easily recognized title, as detailed in Figure D.

A final informative feature—though one limited primarily to Hall of Fame–caliber players—is the inclusion of a table providing Major championship results throughout a player's legitimately competitive years. These tables (as illustrated in Figure C) appear at the end of the player's entry and are largely self-explanatory, their ups and downs providing a fascinating supplement to any assessment of a competitive golfing life.

A final word on the accuracy of *The Book of Golfers*: In any volume this size errors are inevitable. In certain cases these mistakes may be mine; in others they are the result of bad information published elsewhere. The reader may rest assured, however, that whenever possible multiple sources have been referenced to confirm the facts and to resolve questions or discrepancies. Further, materials whose validity I am skeptical of generally have been presented as such, often with signal phrases like "it is reported that..." as a red flag. Our statistics (which run through August 2004) enjoy a similar degree of reliability; most are rock-solid, but older PGA and LPGA Tour numbers, for example, are, by the Tours' own admissions, not 100 percent accurate.

Use these tools wisely—as guideposts, not good-to-the-decimal-point guarantees—and a remarkable perspective can be gained on the game's long and splendid history. In this light, it is my sincere hope that you will experience as much enjoyment from reading *The Book of Golfers* as I did from writing it.

Daniel Wexler
Los Angeles, 2005

Key to Tables

Experienced followers of competitive golf likely will need little explanation of the following, but for everyone else...

Figure A

(Player career ledgers)

PGA Tour Wins (12): 1967 & '72 Greensboro; 1969 Bing Crosby; **1969 Masters;** 1971 San Diego; 1972 Los
    Angeles; and 3 Memphis Classics
Intn'l Wins (7): 1978 World Match Play; 1983, '84 & '87 Japan Open
Champions Tour Wins: 19 (1989–2000)
Ryder Cup: 1987–91, '93 (c) (4); 2002 Capt

    "PGA Tour Wins" and **"Intn'l Wins"** are as explained in the introduction, with the complete list of events designated for inclusion detailed in Figure D. Where applicable, **"Champions Tour Wins"** simply summarizes a player's senior record, providing his total number of wins and the time frame in which they were accomplished.

    International team listings (e.g., **Ryder Cup**) detail the years in which a player participated, with consecutive appearances lumped together (1987–91) to save space. Readers will remember that such events are biennial, thus 1987–91 reflects three events played and not five. When more than one appearance has been made, the total number of matches participated in also appears in parentheses. Finally, a **(c)** represents a playing captaincy, while a **Capt** indicates a nonplaying one, the latter type being listed separately at the end of the entry.

Figure B

(Architect's course ledgers)

Notable Courses: Dornick Hills G&CC, Oklahoma; Old Town C, North Carolina; **Prairie Dunes CC (9),
    Kansas;** Southern Hills CC, Oklahoma

    As explained in the introduction, these brief listings appear beneath the profiles of the game's important architects, their length determined by the designer's historical significance. Those shown in boldface are presently nationally ranked or of particular historical significance, and all courses are of 18 holes unless followed by **(9)**, **(27)**, or **(36)**. Layouts followed by **(NLE)** are no longer in existence while those labeled **(BO)** have been built over, essentially replaced by a new course on the same site.

Figure C

(Major championship record)

Tiger Woods

	95	96	97	98	99	00	01	02	03	04
Masters	T41	MC	1	T8	T18	5	1	1	T15	T22
US Open	WD	T82	T19	T18	T3	1	T12	1	T20	T17
British	T68	T22	T24	3	T7	1	T25	T28	T4	T9
PGA	-	-	T29	T10	1	1	T29	2	T39	T24

Major championship tables run from a player's first appearance (often as an amateur) through the end of his/her legitimately competitive years. Events are consistent for all male professionals (the Masters, U.S. Open, British Open and PGA) and early amateurs (U.S. Amateur and/or British Amateur), though a particular tournament may be omitted entirely if it did not exist during the player's competitive years. Tables for LPGA players universally include the LPGA Championship and the U.S. Women's Open, plus the Dinah Shore (today's Kraft Nabisco Championship) for anyone competing later than 1982. For those whose competitive years extended beyond 1978, a fourth Major, the du Maurier Classic, appears—though as it, in turn, was replaced by the Women's British Open in 2001, players who competed throughout this period will have "dM/Brit" appear as their fourth event.

The tables simply list the place in which a player finished in each event, each year. A blank space indicates that the event did not take place (e.g., the Masters, pre-1934). Additional symbols are as follows:

T	=	player tied for that position (e.g., T45).
MC	=	player missed the 36-hole cut.
WD	=	player withdrew after entering.
DQ	=	player was disqualified after the start of play.
-	=	player did not participate in the event.

Note: The U.S. Amateur (save from 1965 to 1972), the British Amateur, and, from 1916 to 1957, the PGA Championship are/were contested at match play. Consequently, their results break down as follows.

1	=	champion.
2	=	lost in final.
T3	=	lost in semifinals.
T5	=	lost in quarterfinals.
T9	=	lost in round of 16.
T17	=	lost in round of 32.
T33	=	lost in round of 64.

Figure D

The following lists the tournaments designated among the most prestigious/important of their eras; those which may appear on the career ledgers of prominent players. Most have been selected based on their widely acknowledged standing within the game, though on the LPGA side, the historical scarcity of long-term events has required some emphasis on simple longevity. While not all of those chosen were ultra-prestigious, they did stick around long enough to provide a representative sample. The amateur events, not surprisingly, have changed the least.

Because of the ever-shifting sponsorship landscape in professional golf, many tournaments have existed under several names throughout their lifetimes. The most prominent of these alternative monikers appear just below the event's current name, though in the interest of brevity I have listed only the primary past sponsor and not every single incarnation/name change. The left-hand column provides the event's official name, the right how it will appear within a player's ledger.

MEN WORLDWIDE

TOURNAMENT NAME(S)	APPEARS AS:
The Masters	Masters
U.S. Open	U.S. Open
The Open Championship	British Open
PGA Championship	PGA
WGC-Accenture Match Play	WGC-Match Play
WGC-NEC Invitational	World Series
World Series of Golf (1976–98)	

PGA TOUR

MODERN	APPEARS AS:
Buick Invitational	San Diego
San Diego Open (1952–85)	
Shearson Lehman... (1986–91)	
AT&T Pebble Beach Pro-Am	Bing Crosby
Bing Crosby Pro-Am (1937–85)	
Nissan Open	Los Angeles
Los Angeles Open (1926–94)	
Ford Championship at Doral	Doral
Doral Open (1962–2000)	
Genuity Championship (2001–02)	
Players Championship	Players Championship
MCI Heritage	Heritage
EDS Byron Nelson Championship	Byron Nelson
Dallas Open (1944–67)	
B of A Colonial	Colonial
Memorial Tournament	Memorial
Buick Classic	Westchester
Westchester Classic (1967–89)	
Western Open	Western Open
Canadian Open	Canadian Open

EARLY	APPEARS AS:
Metropolitan Open (through 1940)	Metropolitan
World Championship of Golf	World Championship
North & South Open	North & South
Phoenix Open (through 1970)	Phoenix
Texas Open (through 1970)	Texas
Greater Greensboro Open (through 1970)	Greensboro
Houston Open (through 1970)	Houston

OVERSEAS

EUROPEAN TOUR

Volvo PGA Championship
Volvo Masters Andalucia
Benson & Hedges International
HSBC World Match Play
Trophée Lancôme
Dubai Desert Classic
News of the World Match Play (1903–79)
Dunlop British Masters
Omega European Masters*
Johnnie Walker Classic

*The Swiss Open became the European Masters in 1983.

APPEARS AS:

Volvo PGA
Volvo Masters
Benson & Hedges
World Match Play
Trophée Lancôme
Dubai
PGA Match Play
British Masters
European Masters
Johnnie Walker

SOUTH AFRICA

South African Open
Dunhill Championship
    South African PGA (through 1999)

APPEARS AS:

South African Open
South African PGA

AUSTRALIA

Australian Open
Australian PGA

APPEARS AS:

Australian Open
Australian PGA

NATIONAL OPENS

Belgian Open
Dutch Open
French Open
German Open
Hong Kong Open
Irish Open
Italian Open
Japan Open
Mexican Open
Portuguese Open
Scottish Open
    Loch Lomond... (1996–2001)
Spanish Open
Swiss Open (through 1982)

APPEARS AS:

Belgian Open
Dutch Open
French Open
German Open
Hong Kong Open
Irish Open
Italian Open
Japan Open
Mexican Open
Portuguese Open
Scottish Open

Spanish Open
Swiss Open

WOMEN

MAJOR CHAMPIONSHIPS	APPEARS AS:
U.S. Women's Open	U.S. Women's Open
McDonald's LPGA Championship	LPGA Championship
Kraft Nabisco Championship	Dinah Shore
Dinah Shore (1972–99) (Major from 1983)	
Weetabix Women's British Open	Women's British Open
(Major since 2001)	
du Maurier Classic	du Maurier
(1973–2000) (Major from 1979)	
Titleholders Championship (1937–72)	Titleholders
Women's Western Open (1937–67)	Western Open

LPGA MODERN	APPEARS AS:
Welch's/Circle K Championship	Welch's
Arizona Copper Classic (1981–82)	
Tucson Conquistadores Open (1983–84)	
Safeway International	Safeway
Portland Classic (1972–85)	
Ping... (1986–95)	
Sybase Classic	Wykagyl
Girl Talk Classic (1975–77)	
Golden Lights Championship (1978–81)	
Chrysler-Plymouth Charity Classic (1982)	
Mastercard International (1984–87)	
Corning Classic	Corning
Wegman's Rochester International	Rochester
Bankers Trust (1977–78)	
Sarah Coventry (1979–81)	
Rochester International (1982–97)	
State Farm Classic	State Farm
Jerry Lewis Muscular Dystrophy (1976–77)	
Rail Charity Classic (1978–92)	
State Farm Rail Classic (1992–2000)	
Samsung World Championship	Samsung WC
Chevrolet World Championship of Women's Golf (1980–84)	
Nestle World Championship (1985–89)	
Trophee Urban—World Championship of Women's Golf (1990)	
Daikyo World Championship of Women's Golf (1991)	
World Championship of Women's Golf (1993–94)	

LPGA EARLY	APPEARS AS:
Tampa Open (1950–60)	Tampa
Babe Zaharias Open (1953–67)	Babe Zaharias
Orange Blossom Classic (1954–89)	Orange Blossom
Dallas Civitan Open (1956–78)	Dallas Civitan
World Championship of Golf (1948–57)	World Championship
Sea Island Open (1954–63)	Sea Island
Peach Blossom (1953–66)	Peach Blossom

AMATEURS

MEN	APPEARS AS:
U.S. Amateur	U.S. Amateur
British Amateur	British Amateur
Western Amateur	Western Amateur
North & South Amateur	North & South
Metropolitan Amateur	Metropolitan
Southern Amateur	Southern
Trans-Mississippi Amateur	Trans-Miss
Pacific Northwest Amateur	Pacific NW

WOMEN	APPEARS AS:
U.S. Women's Amateur	U.S. Women's Amateur
Ladies British Open Amateur	British Ladies
Women's Western Amateur	Western Amateur
North & South Amateur	North & South
Southern Amateur	Southern
Trans-Mississippi Amateur	Trans-Miss
(aka Trans-National Amateur)	
Eastern Amateur	Eastern

A

Tommy Aaron (USA)

Following a runner-up finish at the 1958 U.S. Amateur, victory at the 1960 **Western Amateur,** and a Walker Cup appearance in between (1959), former University of Florida star Tommy Aaron (b. Gainesville, Georgia, 2/22/1937) enjoyed a solid PGA Tour career, winning three times and remaining among the top 60 money winners from 1961 to 1973. His first victory came in 1969, when a sparkling final-round 64 set up an 18-hole play-off triumph over Sam Snead at the **Canadian Open.** After winning France's **Trophée Lancôme** and rising to ninth on the PGA Tour money list in 1972, Aaron then achieved his competitive zenith in 1973 when a closing 68 helped capture the **Masters,** defeating J. C. Snead by one.

Unfortunately, Aaron is perhaps equally well remembered for having mismarked playing partner Roberto de Vicenzo's scorecard at the 1968 Masters, resulting in the popular Argentinean signing for (and being stuck with) a 66 instead of a 65, costing de Vicenzo a chance at a play-off for the Green Jacket. Ironic then that it was at Augusta, five years later, that Aaron reached his high watermark, and that he also stands as the oldest player to make the cut there, doing so in 2000 at age 63.

Margaret Abbott (USA)

Margaret Abbott holds the unique distinction of being the only woman ever to win an Olympic gold medal in golf, a feat she accomplished in 1900 in Paris during the game's sole appearance in a women's Olympiad. Of course, the victory also gave Abbott the rather more substantial honor of being the first American woman to win *any* gold medal—though history fails to record whether her winning nine-hole score of 47 had anything to do with golf's imminent disappearance from the games.

John Abercromby (UK)

Though not quite of championship caliber, Felixtowe, England's John F. Abercromby (1861–1935) was a fine late-nineteenth-century amateur before becoming involved in the design of Worplesdon GC in 1908. With his work there

well received, "Aber" took to architecture full-time, working almost exclusively on the sandy heathland west of London. Having consulted on occasion with the famous Willie Park Jr., he eventually joined a firm operated by Herbert Fowler, Tom Simpson, and Arthur Croome, though his most memorable design—36 holes for the Addington GC—was entirely a solo affair.

Serving for many years as Addington's benevolent dictator (where he supposedly coined the phrase "*I am the suggestion box*" when in receipt of "constructive" criticism), Abercromby was a consummate architectural naturalist whose use of natural terrain and rejection of formalized plans are revered among students of design. His portfolio, however, is a relatively small one, further reduced by the losses of an early design for the Netherlands' Haagsche GC as well as one of his best, the New course at Addington, which was subdivided after the war.

Notable Courses: Addington GC; Coombe Hill GC (with W. Park Jr.); Liphook GC (with A. Croome)

Perry Adair (USA)

Several years older than his childhood friend Bobby Jones, Oliver Perry Adair (1900–1953) was known as "The Boy Wonder of Dixie" for his early golfing exploits, which included defeating his father George in the semifinals of the 1914 Southern Amateur before getting clobbered in the final, 13 and 12. Adair would eventually win the **Southern** twice (1921 and '23) but is perhaps best remembered as one of the "Dixie Kids," the famous 1918 Red Cross fund-raising tour that featured himself, Jones, their fellow Atlantan (and reigning Women's Amateur champion) Alexa Stirling, and Chicago's Elaine Rosenthal. Though ultimately Jones' playing career would considerably exceed Adair's, it is difficult to overestimate the impact of both Adair and his highly supportive father on the immortal Bobby's formative years.

Rhona Adair (Northern Ireland)

Though an 1899 issue of the *Irish Golfer* suggested that Rhona Adair (1878–1961) was actually born four years later than generally credited, most accounts cite her age as 17 when first entering the British Championship in 1895, an event played over her home links at Royal Portrush. Whatever her true age, Adair became far more than a youthful footnote by eventually winning the **British Ladies** twice, first in 1900 at Westward Ho, then again in 1903 back at Portrush. Despite constantly battling her friendly local rivals, the Hezlet sisters, Adair also enjoyed a splendid four-year run in the **Irish Ladies,** winning it from 1900 to 1903.

Widely chronicled for her prodigious hitting, Adair had a long, wide swing and great balance, though she routinely throttled back to three-quarters in windy conditions. Her pleasing personality also helped to make her a fine draw, leading to a 1903 tour of the United States in which she reportedly took 16 victories in 17 contests, an achievement that helped to further advance golf's ever-expanding popularity among American women. Adair married a West Yorkshire army Captain in 1907, apparently quitting competitive golf thereafter to raise two children. Widowed during World War I, she remained active in women's golfing affairs (serving as president of the Irish Ladies Golf Union) until her death in 1961.

James Adams (UK)

Cited by Henry Longhurst for his "long, flowing 'St. Andrews' swing" and "magnificent putter," Troon's Jimmy Adams (1910–1986) was twice a serious contender in the Open Championship. In 1936, at Hoylake, he finished one off Alf Padgham's winning total of 287 when his 30-foot putt at the 72nd lipped out just before Padgham holed a 15-footer to win. Two years later, at Royal St. George's, Adams led by one going into the final 36 but in a windstorm strong enough to flatten the merchandise tent managed only a pair of closing 78s to finish two behind Reg Whitcombe.

A native of Troon, where as a youth he caddied for 1883 Open Champion Willie Fernie, Adams went on to become one of Britain's stronger post-war campaigners, appearing in four Ryder Cups (1947–53) and winning national Opens in **Belgium** (1949), the **Netherlands** (1949), and **Italy** (1951). He claimed several notable domestic victories as well, including a tie with Bobby Locke for the inaugural **British Masters** in 1946.

Kathy Ahern (USA)

A three-time winner on the LPGA Tour, Kathy Ahern (1949–1996) reached her peak in 1972 when she claimed her lone Major, the **LPGA Championship,** at Massachusetts' Pleasant Valley CC. Beating native New Englander Jane Blalock by six shots, Ahern continued her hot play two weeks later in capturing the **George Washington Classic** in Horsham, Pennsylvania. Though never again a tour winner, Ahern generally remained among the LPGA's top 50 money winners for the remainder of the decade. She passed away of cancer at age 47.

Ray Ainsley (USA)

A little-known Santa Barbara, California professional, Ray Ainsley (1901–1986) set a well-nigh unbreakable record by carding a spectacular 19 at Cherry Hills CC's 397-yard 16th hole during the 1938 U.S. Open. This he managed by flailing away repeatedly at a ball drifting in a greenside creek, leading to the surely apocryphal story of a child in the gallery observing, at adventure's end, that "it must be dead now, he's stopped hitting it."

Rokuro Akaboshi (Japan)

Followed closely by his brother Shiro, Rokuro Akaboshi was Japan's first native-born golfing star, competing successfully during his college years at Princeton, then winning the inaugural **Japan Open** in 1927. A respected instructor who played a large role in advancing the game among his countrymen (particularly after its virtual death during World War II), Akaboshi was also active in course design, with more than 60 layouts to his credit throughout Japan and Southeast Asia. He was heavily influenced by the famous 1930–31 visit of English architect C. H. Alison, after which he followed so many American designers of the period by making a pilgrimage to Scotland to study the characteristics and quirks of the grand old links.

With the great majority of Japan's prewar courses wiped out during the conflict, little of Akaboshi's early work remains in play today. Regardless, he can justly be cited as both a Japanese golfing icon and pioneer.

Notable Courses: Fujigaya CC (with C. H. Alison) (NLE); Sagami CC

Amy Alcott (USA)

Hall of Famer Amy Alcott (b. 2/22/1956) was born in Kansas City, Missouri but raised in Southern California where, as a 17-year-old, she won the 1973 **USGA Junior Girls** title. Turning professional without benefit of extended amateur or collegiate competition, she quickly made her presence felt by winning in just her third LPGA start (the 1975 **Orange Blossom Classic**) and was named Rookie of the Year at season's end.

So began a 12-year run that saw Alcott take her place among the elite of the women's game, recording 29 victories, three Major championships (the 1979 **du Maurier Classic**, the 1980 **U.S. Women's Open,** and the 1983 **Dinah Shore**), and only a single season (1977) outside of the top 10 in official earnings. Her U.S. Open victory is especially worth recalling, for it came by a stunning nine shots over three-time champion Hollis Stacy in sweltering heat at Nashville's old Richland CC. By this time, Alcott was also responding impressively to Nancy Lopez's explosive 1978 arrival by posting her own best years in 1979 and 1980, winning four times in each campaign and logging back-to-back career-best thirds on the money list. She would again win four times in 1984 and thrice the following year, though none of these were Major championships. All told, Alcott won 8.4 percent of her starts during these 12 years, a total exceeded only by Lopez over the same period.

A quiet but highly competitive sort, Alcott was long a favorite with writers (if not always her fellow players) for being both thoughtful and forthright in the press tent. Though she would claim only three additional titles after 1986, two came at the **Dinah Shore,** raising her career Major total to five. Following her final victory at the 1991 Dinah, Alcott only once cracked the top-50 on the money list (35th in 1994) before scaling back her schedule substantially in the new millennium. In 1999, she was inducted into both the LPGA and World Golf Halls of Fame.

LPGA Wins (29): 1975 Orange Blossom; **1979 du Maurier; 1980 U.S. Women's Open;** 1983, **'88 & '91 Dinah Shore;** 1985 Welch's; 1985 Samsung WC

1975-1994

	75	76	77	78	79	80	81	82	83	84
Dinah									1	T10
LPGA	MC	MC	T34	2	3	T10	9	T5	T26	T52
US Open	18	T5	T4	T12	T37	1	T19	T13	T11	T3
du Maur					1	T10	T25	WD	T13	T10

	85	86	87	88	89	90	91	92	93	94
Dinah	T31	T14	T11	1	T62	T34	1	T32	T56	T58
LPGA	T8	T15	T9	2	T14	T46	10	T10	MC	T7
US Open	11	T5	T12	T41	T26	T9	3	T13	T26	T6
du Maur	3	T8	T14	T4	T4	MC	T44	MC	T25	14

Janet Alex (USA)

Pennsylvanian Janet Alex (b. West Sunbury, 3/10/1956) climbed the ladder steadily in women's professional golf, joining the LPGA Tour in 1978, winning Rookie of the Year in 1978, reaching the top 25 on the money list in 1980, then finishing 16th in 1981. But 1982 would clearly mark her competitive peak when a final-round 68 left the field in the dust at July's **U.S. Women's Open** in Sacramento, giving Alex a six-shot victory (her first as a pro). This success would prove fleeting, however, for Alex (who also played under her married name of Anderson) would never again win on the LPGA Tour.

Skip Alexander (USA)

Lexington, North Carolina, product Stewart "Skip" Alexander (1918–1987) might well be recalled as a poor man's Ben Hogan, not so much for his legion of victories (the 1941 **North & South Amateur** and three modest PGA Tour wins) as his ability to come back from life-threaten-

ing injury. Having played in the 1949 Ryder Cup at Ganton, Alexander was involved in a light plane crash soon thereafter, breaking his ankles and suffering burns to both his hands. Reportedly having asked his doctors to shape his badly damaged left hand into a position resembling a golf grip, Alexander made it back in time to play in the 1951 Ryder Cup, roundly defeating John Panton 8 and 7 at singles. He later received the 1959 Ben Hogan award in recognition of his comeback.

Helen Alfredsson (Sweden)

A former six-time national champion in Sweden, Helen Alfredsson (b. Goteborg, 4/9/1965) graduated from San Diego's U.S. International University in 1988, was the LPGA Tour's 1992 Rookie of the Year, then won her lone Major championship, the **Dinah Shore** (while tying for second at the U.S. Women's Open) a year later. She drew further Major attention by firing an Open record 63 in the first round at Indianwood in 1994, before ultimately tying for ninth. Since then, Alfredsson has managed four more victories including two (the **Office Depot** and the **Welch's/Circle K**) in 1998 and one (the **Longs Drugs Challenge**) in 2003. She has also established herself as a veteran of international competition, appearing in the first seven Solheim Cup matches (1990–2002), missing her first in 2003.

C. H. Alison (UK)

Born: Preston, England, 3/5/1883 **Died:** Cape Town, South Africa, 10/20/1952

One of golf architecture's more underrated talents, Charles Hugh Alison began his golfing life as a fine amateur player, touring America with the Oxford & Cambridge Golfing Society in 1903. Following school, Alison signed on as secretary at the Stoke Poges GC, soon aiding architect H. S. Colt in the course's design and construction, then eventually assisting Colt on a number of pre–World War I English and Irish designs. Following the war, Alison became a full partner in Colt's high-profile firm, which later included J. S. F. Morrison and, at least until 1921, Dr. Alister MacKenzie.

Alison and Colt would remain partners for the rest of their lives, buoyed by a symbiotic work relationship that saw Colt handle most of the firm's British and European projects while Alison, 14 years the younger, traveled the world. He made an extended visit to America in the 1920s, opening offices in New York and Detroit, and designing or redesigning approximately 30 courses in both the United States and Canada. Though nearly all of these were contractually completed by Colt & Alison (with, in some earlier cases, MacKenzie's name thrown in), virtually all represented Alison's solo work.

In 1930 Alison traveled to Japan where, in conjunction with several of that nation's earliest golfers, he completed seven projects that would set a lasting standard for Asian design. Their influence was so profound that his steep-walled style of bunkering became known, after translation issues, as "Arisons." In 1947, with Colt effectively retired, Alison made his second visit to South Africa, once again engaging in a number of influential designs. Though never taking a permanent African residence, there is little evidence to suggest that Alison had any intention of ever returning to England. He passed away in Johannesburg at age 69.

Notable Courses: Fresh Meadow GC, New York; Glendower CC, S. Africa; **Hirono GC, Japan; Kawana Hotel GC, Fuji Course, Japan;** Kirtland CC, Ohio; Sea Island GC, Georgia (BO); **Timber Point GC, New York (BO)**

A. J. Travers Allan (UK)

To quote Bernard Darwin, Scotland's Jack Allan (1875–1898) "was one golfer whose exact status in golfing history will always be a question for argument." For having won the 1897 **British Amateur** at Muirfield at the ripe old age of 22, he contracted a lung disease and passed away before even having a chance to defend. A largely unknown contestant and a bit of a free spirit, Allan trained down from Edinburgh each morning of the championship, biked several miles to the course, then played in both street clothes and spikeless shoes. Having only known the game for five years (and never under the spotlight of championship play) his victories over Laurie Auchterlonie, Leslie Balfour-Melville, and, finally, James Robb were stunning. His loose, confident playing style and unfortunately early demise were nearly equally so.

Fulton Allem (South Africa)

Known as one of golf's streakiest, most aggressive, and certainly most colorful players, Fulton Allem (b. Kroonstadt, 9/15/1957) recorded a remarkable 18 runner-up finishes on the South African Tour before finally claiming his first of 14 homeland victories in 1985. Following a surprise second-place finish at the 1987 World Series of Golf, Allem joined the PGA Tour, playing more than 20 events a year and gaining the first of three wins in 1991. Two years later a closing 67 defeated Greg Norman by one at **Colonial,** returning Allem once more to the **World Series** where a scorching final-round 62 won both the title and a 10-year exemption in America. A captain's pick for the inaugural 1994 Presidents Cup, Allem more recently has suffered from a degenerative back condition as his exemption expires.

Sir Peter Allen (UK)

Sir Peter Allen (b. 1905) was the chairman of Royal Dutch Shell and an amateur golfer of, by his own description, "no more than moderate skill." His writing talents, however, were quite considerable, making his two guidebooks, *Famous Fairways* (Stanley Paul, 1968) and *Play the Best Courses* (Stanley Paul, 1973), essential reading for fans of the genre. A truly eloquent lover of the game, Allen played the finest courses on five continents and for some time held the distinction of being Augusta National's lone non-American member.

Robert Allenby (Australia)

A leader among a generation of fine young Australian players, long, lean Robert Mark Allenby (b. Melbourne, 7/12/1971) scored multiple victories on the Australasian, European, and American tours prior to his 30th birthday. Following stellar junior and amateur careers in his native Victoria, he began winning professionally in 1992 and has seldom stopped, save for time spent recovering from injuries suffered in a 1996 car accident in Spain. Though not yet a Major champion at the time of this writing, Allenby has garnered 16 worldwide titles including **Australian, English,** and **French Opens;** two **Australian PGAs;** an **Australian Masters;** and, in America, the prestigious **Western** and **Los Angeles Opens.** At the latter, in 2001, he won a memorable six-man play-off by making birdie at Riviera's famed 451-yard 18th, lashing a 3-wood through an icy rain to five feet. With shots like that, it is perhaps not surprising that Allenby stands a perfect 7-0 in professional play-offs.

PGA Tour Wins (4): 2000 Western Open; 2001 Los Angeles
Intn'l Wins (12): 1994 Australian Open; 1996 British Masters; 1996 French Open; 2000 & '01 Australian PGA
Presidents Cup: 1994, '96, 2000 & '03 (4)

Buddy Allin (USA)

A native of Bremerton, Washington, Brian "Buddy" Allin (b. 10/13/1944) played collegiate golf on the same Brigham Young team as Johnny Miller before serving 16 months in Vietnam where he was four times decorated as an artillery officer. Standing all of 5′9″ and weighing 135 pounds, Allin qualified for the PGA Tour in 1970 and was a regular top-60 money winner for most of the 1970s. He took five titles on Tour (all between 1971 and 1976) with his finest season coming in 1974 when he captured the **Doral Open** and the **Byron Nelson Classic,** and finished ninth on the money list. Though capable of going very low (he won the 1973 **Florida Citrus Open** by eight with a 23-under-par 265), Allin retired from the Tour in the early 1980s, returning for a single 1997 victory on the Champions Tour after turning 50.

Percy Alliss (UK)

Perhaps best recognized by modern readers as the father of the iconic Peter Alliss, Percy (1897–1975) was a fine player in his own right, representing Great Britain on four pre–World War II Ryder Cup teams, scoring six top-five finishes at the Open Championship, and twice winning the old *News of the World* match play, Britain's second most important period event. A native of Sheffield, England, he captured no less than 16 professional titles throughout Europe, including five **German Opens**—a seemingly incongruous total until one realizes that he served as professional at Berlin's Wannsee Club for a number of years before the war. Returning to the United Kingdom before the outbreak of hostilities, Alliss held several more club jobs, his last a long stint at Ferndown in Dorset. Among his distinctions, he also set a 72-hole record for a national championship by posting a 262 in Italy, a record that would stand alone until matched by Lu Liang Huan at the 1971 French Open.

Intn'l Wins (16): 1926, '27, '28, '29 & '33 German Open; 1927 & '35 Italian Open; 1933 & '37 PGA Match Play
Ryder Cup: 1929, 1933–37 (4)

Peter Alliss (UK)

The son of well-known professional Percy, Peter Alliss (b. Berlin, 2/28/1931) has loomed large in the international golfing world for more than half a century, first as a player, then as a club professional, writer, broadcaster, and course architect. An elegantly powerful swinger, he followed in his father's footsteps by capturing numerous Continental titles (including the 1958 **Spanish, Portuguese,** and **Italian Opens** in succeeding weeks) but also held firm at home, claiming three **Volvo PGA** titles. Never seriously contending for an Open Championship and missing a crucial putt in his 1953 Ryder Cup debut were career low points, but a remarkable eight total Cup appearances (plus nine World Cup selections between 1954 and 1967) are a testimonial to the consistency and longevity of his talent.

With stops at Parkstone and Moor Allerton, Alliss maintained a strong working résumé, though his greatest nonplaying fame would surely come as a broadcaster for both the BBC and American television. Blessed with an uncommon wit and great facility with the English language, he has also authored or coauthored more than 20 books including three prominent autobiographies, *Alliss Through the Looking Glass* (Cassell, 1963), *Peter Allis: An Autobiography* (Collins, 1981), and *My Life* (Hodder & Stoughton, 2004). His golf course design business, generally in partnership with either Dave Thomas or Clive Clark, has been similarly prolific, fashioning courses in the United Kingdom, Europe, South America, and Africa.

It is doubtful that the game has seen a more capable, all-around talent.

Intn'l Wins (21): 1956 & '58 Spanish Opens; 1957, '62 & '65 Volvo PGA; 1958 Portuguese Open; 1958 Italian Open
Ryder Cup: 1953, 1957–69 (8)

Stephen Ames
(Trinidad & Tobago)

The first touring professional ever to emerge from the Southern Caribbean islands of Trinidad and Tobago, Stephen Ames (b. 4/28/1964) has plied his trade internationally since 1990, initially spending three seasons on the Nationwide Tour before heading off to Europe in 1993. Twice a winner on the European Tour (including the 1996 **Benson & Hedges International**), he began to play the PGA Tour regularly in 1998 where, through 2003, he quite consistently ranked between 83rd and 46th on the money list. Frequently a contender yet winless over his first 165 Tour starts, Ames finally broke through at the 2004 **Western Open** in Chicago, where a third-round 64 sparked a two-stroke victory, the centerpiece of what was easily his finest year as a professional. Already age 40, however, how much more of the mountain is Ames likely to climb?

Danielle Ammaccapane
(USA)

The 1985 winner of both the **USGA Public Links** and the **NCAA** individual championship while at Arizona State, Danielle Ammaccapane (b. Babylon, New York, 11/27/1965) began her professional career solidly, finishing 44th and 23rd on the money list before climbing to 9th, 6th and 3rd from 1990 to 1992. She won three times in 1992, her career-best year, with titles at the **Standard Register PING,** the **Centel Classic,** and the **Lady Keystone Open.** A combined three more wins would follow in 1997 and '98, though a slump in 1999 and 2000 saw her fall completely from the top 100 money winners. Not one of the LPGA's more powerful hitters, Ammaccapane has struggled somewhat on longer Major championship courses, resulting in only four top-10 finishes in 65 Major starts. She was, however, a Curtis Cup player in 1986 and a Solheim Cupper in 1992.

David Anderson (UK)

David Anderson ("Old Da'") was a mid-nineteenth-century greenkeeper at St. Andrews who, later in life, turned to caddying and, from available evidence, clubmaking. Eventually allowed to operate a ginger beer stall near the Old Course's ninth hole, he was a traditionalist who was critical of, among other things, the removal of the whins that once made today's mile-wide layout quite a bit narrower. Anderson was also the father of four golfing sons, of whom Jamie won the Open Championship thrice in succession and David Jr. started one of the largest clubmaking outfits in St. Andrews.

James Anderson (UK)

The son of David, St. Andrews' clubmaker Jamie Anderson (1842–1905) became the first player after Young Tom Morris to win the **Open Championship** in three consecutive years, from 1877 to 1879. A fast but not terribly powerful player, he was likened by Bernard Darwin to J. H. Taylor "in an almost incredible accuracy and in mastery of the pitching shot."

On the occasion of his first title, at Musselburgh, Anderson triumphed rather mundanely, defeating Bob Pringle by two. Save for playing on his home links at St. Andrews, his third win offered little greater drama. The middle championship, however, contested over 36 holes at Prestwick in 1878, was truly one for the ages.

Aware that he needed to play the final four holes in 17 strokes to defeat an already-finished J. O. F. Morris, Anderson holed a full iron shot for three at the 33rd, then drained a sizeable putt for four at the 34th. At the short 35th, his approach flew slightly long before kicking back off a mound and rolling straight into the cup for the first known ace in competitive golf history. A routine five at the 36th brought Anderson in four strokes better than Morris — though a late-finishing Bob Kirk actually had a chance to tie at the last before three-putting.

Though Anderson would still contend on several occasions, his days as a champion were over, quickly replaced by Musselburgh native Robert Ferguson who himself would capture three straight Claret Jugs. The two played several memorable challenge matches in later years, though Anderson's primary focus became his clubmaking business, with wooden putters considered to be his finest product.

John Anderson (USA)

Though a winner of the **French Amateur** on two occasions, Clinton, Massachusetts, native John G. Anderson (1884–1933) was one of those players who frequently came close in bigger events, only to fall just shy. He twice lost in the final of the U.S. Amateur, for example, first to Jerry Travers at Garden City in 1913, then to Robert Gardner at the Detroit CC two years later. He also bears mention as the great Walter Travis' final victim, losing the 1915 Metropolitan Amateur to the then-53-year-old "Old Man" when Travis sunk a 40-footer on the last green at Apawamis — and then promptly retired. A powerful hitter who once scored a 328-yard ace at Massachusetts' Brae Burn CC, Anderson may well have been the first person to spot the greatness of the young Francis Ouimet, for in the 1913 Massachusetts Amateur, Anderson led Ouimet two up with six to play, then could do little more than watch as the soon-to-be U.S. Open champion finished with six consecutive threes. Also an avid golf writer, Anderson is remembered at Winged Foot, his home club, by the annual Anderson Memorial tournament.

Peter Anderson (UK)

A tall and lanky man, Peter Corsar Anderson (1873–1955) was a 20-year-old student at St. Andrews University—and little known beyond the city's confines—when he came out of nowhere to capture the 1893 **British Amateur** at Prestwick. Lest anyone view the victory as a fluke, it will be noted that Anderson defeated S. Mure Fergusson in the semifinals, then dispatched two-time champion J. E. Laidlay two up in the final. Obviously of the Old School, Anderson won the title with only six clubs and did not carry a golf bag. He later emigrated to Australia in 1896 (reportedly for health reasons) where he became a schoolmaster and an influential golfer, playing at Royal Melbourne and finishing second in the 1902 Australian Amateur. He would later move to Western Australia and design several courses before passing away in 1955.

Tip Anderson (UK)

In some ways the last of a much-romanticized breed, James Garvie "Tip" Anderson (1932–2004) was a fine golfer before becoming perhaps the most prominent of St. Andrews' modern-day caddies. His first major job was looping for a local man, Laurie Ayton, in the 1957 Open Championship, played over the Old Course. Though Ayton finished back in the pack, Anderson would soon win three Opens, first with Arnold Palmer in 1961 and '62 (at Royal Birkdale and Royal Troon), then over the Old Course in 1964 with the popular American Tony Lema. An unsurpassed expert on St. Andrews, Anderson cowrote *How to Play the Old Course* (Newport Press, 2000) with architect Desmond Muirhead.

Willie Anderson (UK/USA)

Born: North Berwick, Scotland, 10/21/1879 **Died:** Chestnut Hill, Pennsylvania, 10/25/1910

Among the most intriguing of all golfers, Willie Anderson, though born in Scotland, was the first dominant profes-

sional to reside on American shores. A slight, physically unimpressive youth, Anderson emigrated with his father in the mid-1890s and was contending at the highest level, the U.S. Open, almost immediately. Indeed, had it not been for Joe Lloyd's remarkable three at the Chicago GC's 466-yard finisher, Anderson would have been playing off for an Open title as early as 1897, at age 17. He would, however, claim the 1901 **Open,** then, following a tie for fifth in 1902, reel off three straight from 1903 to 1905. Anderson's winning scores on these victorious occasions were 331 (the highest ever recorded), then 307, 303 and 314, large numbers to be sure but wholly in line with the primitive playing conditions of the day. A full century later, then, it is still commonly asked: Just how good was Willie Anderson relative to the Hall of Fame champions later to follow?

Beyond noting that a number of his contemporaries, including the long-lived Fred McLeod, considered Anderson largely the equal of men like Jones and Hogan, we must certainly concede that, with the largest Open field he defeated comprised of only 89 players, the depth of Anderson's competition clearly was limited. His swing, we are told, was notably flat by today's standards and hardly aesthetically pure. Yet Anderson's overall record in the Open is really quite something, for in addition to his four wins, he managed seven additional top-five finishes between 1897 and 1909, giving him an impressive 11 top-fives in 13 tries. Similarly, at the only other contemporaneous event of national scope, the **Western Open,** Anderson won four times in seven tries and was never out of the top five. It is also worth noting that his success straddled the line between gutta-percha and rubber balls, an adjustment the magnitude of which cannot be overestimated.

Though his stoic on-course demeanor allowed Anderson frequently to be portrayed as the gruff, dour Scot, he was, by most accounts, fairly popular among his fellow competitors. That he held professional jobs at 10 different clubs over a 14-year span may (or may not) speak to his general congeniality, but he seemed to fit in well enough at New York's esteemed Apawamis Club, where he was employed during his three consecutive Open victories. In the end even Anderson's death was somewhat intriguing for despite appearing in perfect health, he died of arteriosclerosis in Philadelphia at age 31—though many learned observers have suggested that at so young an age, alcohol may well have been the true cause.

Professional Wins (8): 1901, '03, '04 & '05 U.S. Open; 1902, '04, '08 & '09 Western Open

1897-1910

	97	98	99	00	01	02	03	04	05	06	07	08	09	10
US Open	2	3	5	T11	1	T5	1	1	1	5	15	4	T4	11
British	-	-	-	-	-	-	-	-	-	-	-	-	-	-

Billy Andrade (USA)

Former Wake Forest star and Walker Cupper Billy Andrade (b. Bristol, Rhode Island, 1/25/1964) has put together a solid professional career over 15 plus seasons, winning nearly $9 million and four PGA Tour titles since the late 1980s. Growing up three years behind longtime friend Brad Faxon amidst a New England climate not generally supportive of budding golf champions, the 5'8", 155-pound Andrade has never been one to overpower the ball, though his putting, reliable left-to-right game, and engaging personality have long stood him in good stead. His peak season came in 1991 when he won his first two Tour events, the **Kemper Open** and the **Westchester Classic**, in back-to-back weeks and went on to finish 14th on the money list. He also claimed the **Canadian Open** in 1998, beating upstart Bob Friend in sudden death.

Donna Andrews (USA)

Long before joining the LPGA Tour, Lynchburg, Virginia, native Donna Andrews (b. 4/12/1967) was well known in the Mid-Atlantic region, winning five consecutive **Virginia Amateur** titles from 1985 to 1989, as well as Pinehurst's prestigious **North & South Amateur** in 1988. Following an All-American career at North Carolina, she has enjoyed a solid professional run, claiming six LPGA victories and twice representing the United States in Solheim Cup play (1994 and '98). Andrews' best year to date was 1994 when she logged three wins including her first Major at the **Dinah Shore**, though 1998, which saw four consecutive runner-up finishes, a win at the **Longs Drugs Challenge**, and a third-place money finish, certainly ran it close. A very straight driver who is regularly among the LPGA leaders in greens in regulation, it is only Andrews' putter that has kept her from winning more often.

Alfinso Angelini (Italy)

After losing several toes to frostbite during World War II, Alfonso Angelini emerged as one of Italy's top post-war players, capturing his nation's closed **PGA Championship** (for natives only) 11 times between 1947 and 1969 and appearing in the 1964 Masters. A small man who, like the contemporary Italian Emanuele Canonica, still managed to drive it with the best, Angelini also competed quite successfully around the Continent, winning a **Dutch Open** (1955), two **Swiss Opens** (1957 and '66), and two **Portuguese Opens** (1962 and '66). He did not, however, win an Italian Open, his best showing being a play-off loss to countryman Ugo Grappasonni in 1950.

Jody (Rosenthal) Anschutz (USA)

Minneapolis' Jody Rosenthal (b. 10/18/1962) turned professional in 1986 with a glittering amateur résumé, having been an AJGA All-American, a four-time collegiate All-American at the University of Tulsa, and twice runner-up for the NCAA individual title. A 1986 LPGA Tour Rookie-of-the-Year selection suggested good things to come, as did a spectacular 1987, which included a first victory in Virginia, then a Major championship at July's **du Maurier Classic**, where Rosenthal beat Ayako Okamoto by two. With top-10 finishes in all four Majors and fifth place on the money list, Rosenthal thus looked poised for a superstardom that simply never came. A winless 1988 saw her fall to 23rd on the money list and from there her game drifted steadily downward, the occasional strong round or top-10 finish popping up but seldom consistently. Rather inexplicably, she was out of the top 100 by 1993, never to reappear.

Veronica Anstey (UK)

Obviously something of a golfing natural, Veronica Anstey (b. 1/14/1935) was capable, little more than a year after taking up golf, of representing England in international competition. In 1955, at age 20, she joined a team of British juniors who toured Australia and New Zealand, making an unprecedented splash during the brief visit by capturing three prominent titles. The largest was the **Australian Ladies** where, at the old Australian GC, she crushed Joan Fletcher 10 and 9 in a one-sided final. Also claiming the **Victorian Ladies** crown, she added the **New Zealand Amateur** title by winning the last three holes to defeat her traveling teammate Gillian Atkinson one up. She would later marry John Beharrell, himself a young phenom who won the 1956 British Amateur at age 18.

Isao Aoki (Japan)

With due respect to men like Takaaki Kono and Pete Nakamura, Isao Aoki (b. Chiba, 8/31/1942) must surely be considered the first Japanese player capable of regularly competing at golf's highest international levels, claiming victories on four professional tours—the Japan, Australasian, European, and PGA—prior to becoming a world-class senior. Measuring 6'0" and weighing 185 pounds, Aoki stands taller than the average Japanese and his technique is even more anomalous, his full swing looking rather like a Sunday player's overly wristy pitch shot, his putting stroke famous for having the club resting on its heel, toe angled nearly 45 degrees upward.

Of course, for all of that, Aoki has long been one of the game's very finest putters, and his career victory ledger must be similarly envied. Though not even entering the top ranks of his homeland tour until his early 30s, Aoki would ultimately win nearly 60 times in Japan, racking up countless lesser events but also three **Japan Opens** (1983, '84, and '87) and four professional **Match Play** titles, plus multiple victories in two events frequented by Western players, the **Chunichi Crowns** (1973, '75, '78, and '79) and the **Casio World Open** (1989 and '92). Even more impressively, he twice proved his worth on the European Tour by winning the 1978 **World Match Play** at Wentworth (3 and 2 over Simon Owen) and the 1983 **European Open** where he bested Ballesteros, Faldo, and Norman (among others) at Sunningdale.

Though Aoki won only once on the PGA Tour, it was with great style, holing a 100-yard approach at the 72nd to capture the 1983 **Hawaiian Open** by one over Jack Renner. Even more memorable, perhaps, was his dogged pursuit of Jack Nicklaus in the 1980 U.S. Open at Baltusrol, where Aoki's 274 broke the previous Open scoring record, yet still finished two strokes back. More recently, Aoki has been a highly successful senior both at home and on the Champions Tour, where he won nine times between 1992 and 2002 and pocketed nearly $10 million.

PGA Tour Win: (1)
Intn'l Wins (57): 1978 World Match Play; 1983, '84 & '87 Japan Open; and 4 Chunichi Crowns and 4 Japan Professional Match Play
Champions Tour Wins: 9 (1992–2002)

Eric Apperly (Australia)

The first native of New South Wales to win the **Australian Amateur** (in 1920 at the Australian GC), Eric Apperly (1899–1961) was a tall, somewhat unathletic-looking sort who also claimed five **New South Wales Amateurs** between 1912 and 1930. Apperly is perhaps best remembered today, however, as an architect, his unique creative skills allowing him to design both courses and clubhouses. Such work was largely confined to his home state and included courses such as Newcastle, Avondale, and a late lamented 18 at the Lakes GC in Sydney. On this portfolio alone Apperly might remain only of local note, but his name took on an international standing when he completed (and later altered) Dr. Alister MacKenzie's famous New South Wales GC, one of Australia's very finest.

Stuart Appleby (Australia)

Long-hitting Stuart Appleby (b. Cohuna, 5/1/1971) is something of a rarity among Australian players in that he has played relatively little in Europe, instead marching straight off to America in his mid-20s. A former Australian Rules footballer, Appleby spent 1995 finishing fifth on the Nationwide Tour money list, then struggled for one season on the PGA Tour (130th in the 1996) before winning the 1997 **Honda Classic** and soaring to 18th in official earnings. Despite the tragic death of his wife Renay in London in 1998, Appleby has never fallen below 55th place in America while adding wins at the **Kemper Open** (1998), the **Houston Open** (1999), and, after a four-year Stateside drought, the 2003 **Las Vegas Invitational**. He also captured the 2001 **Australian Open** at The Grand GC, a primary goal of any player from Down Under.

More recently a winner of the 2004 and 2005 **Mercedes Championships,** Appleby is a player whose power, skills, and competitive grit would seem to make him the ideal sort for Major championship play. But to date his record has been inconsistent, making only a few more cuts than he's missed, yet also closing the 2002 Open Championship at Muirfield with a wonderful 65 before losing to Ernie Els on the last hole of a four-hole, four-man play-off. Though a three-time International player in the Presidents Cup (1998, 2000, and '03), Appleby has long resided in Orlando, Florida.

Javier Arana (Spain)

The late Peter Dobereiner once wrote that architect "Javier Arana has never received the international recognition that his genius deserved, mainly because he worked exclusively in his native Spain," an opinion echoed frequently among the golfers of Continental Europe. A former three-time **Spanish Amateur** champion (1928, '33, and '34) from Bilbao, Arana (1904–1975) began designing courses in 1936, though his practice did not hit full stride until many years after the war. Perhaps his first top-notch effort was 1954's El Prat, a former Spanish Open site situated just south of Barcelona. But the Arana name is most generally identified with El Saler, a 1968 seaside design near Valencia that is constantly ranked among the top 100 in the world. Arana's nephew Alvaro has carried on the family business since his uncle's death in 1975.

Notable Courses: Campo de Golf El Saler; Golf Rio Real; Golf Guadalmina (36); **Real Club de Golf El Prat**

George Archer (USA)

Aside from standing 6′6″ in a game thought better suited to men half a foot smaller, San Francisco native George William Archer (b. 10/1/1939) will always be remembered as one of golf's all-time finest putters. Indeed, at one time he held the PGA Tour record for fewest putts over 72 holes (95, at the 1980 Heritage Classic) and longtime observer Peter Alliss has ranked him behind only Bobby Locke and Bob Charles among the very best since World War II.

Archer joined the Tour in 1964 and after several solid seasons recorded four top-10 finishes on the money list between 1967 and 1972. Ironically, 1969 was not one of these, though it was surely his finest year with wins at the **Bing Crosby** (after finishing the third round with double- and triple-bogies) and, most prominently, at the **Masters.** There he survived a joust with the pond fronting the 69th green to hang on for a one-shot victory over Tom Weiskopf, George Knudson, and third-round leader Billy Casper.

Though hampered by seven major surgeries throughout his career (including back, wrist, shoulder, and hip), Archer managed 12 Tour wins before becoming a force on the Champions Tour, racking up 19 victories and over $10 million in senior earnings. He also won three events overseas and, once upon a time, was the 1963 **Trans-Mississippi Amateur** champion.

PGA Tour Wins (12): 1967 & '72 Greensboro; 1969 Bing Crosby; **1969 Masters;** 1971 San Diego; 1972 Los Angeles
Intn'l Wins: (3)
Champions Tour Wins: 19 (1989–2000)

Ben Arda (Philippines)

Originally from the island of Cebu, Ben Arda (b. 1929) remains, as of this writing, the finest competitive golfer yet produced by the Philippines. After turning professional at age 23, he worked his way steadily up the Asian ladder, eventually taking two **Philippines Opens** (1960 and '63) as well as national titles in **Singapore** (1967 and '73), **India** (1969), **Malaysia** (1970), and **Japan** (1973). Becoming one of Asia's first internationally prominent players, Arda appeared in the 1962 Masters as well as the 1972 Open Championship at Muirfield. American fans may also recall Arda from the four appearances he made during the 1960s on *Shell's Wonderful World of Golf.* Standing 5′5″, he was frequently known, in homage to Hogan, as "Bantam Ben."

Tommy Armour (UK/USA)

Born: Edinburgh, Scotland, 9/24/1894 **Died:** Larchmont, New York, 9/12/1968

Thomas Dickson Armour, the "Silver Scot," must rank among the most famous of golfers, a man whose legend has grown to the point of perhaps outdistancing his actual accomplishments. Growing up in Edinburgh, Armour was a strong enough player to claim the 1920 **French Amateur** but hardly a man marked for professional greatness, a circumstance undoubtedly due to both a propensity for three-putting and the loss of an eye while fighting in World War I. Traveling with the first Walker Cup team, he emigrated to America in 1922 where he initially worked in a non-golfing capacity at the newly opened Westchester Biltmore (today's Westchester CC), before turning professional at mid-decade and serving at such clubs as Congressional, Chicago's Tam O'Shanter, and Medinah.

A fascinating and much overlooked aspect of the Armour story is the huge, almost magical improvement that transformed his game once in America. The primary reason for this blossoming (at least according to Armour) was instruction he received from the cultishly famous Douglas Edgar, though others have suggested such things as the greater practice regimens generally favored Stateside, putting confidence gained from better agronomical conditions, and the enhanced competitive experience provided by the PGA's annual winter tour. Whatever the answer, Armour was soon a big winner who gained a reputation as an elite iron player (particularly with the longer clubs), though he himself counted driving as his best skill. His putting—even the improved American brand—would forever rate something of a liability, however, particularly in middle age.

All told, Armour won 25 events recognized today by the PGA Tour (tied for 21st all-time), a list that included three **Canadian Opens** (1927, '30, and '34), the 1928 **Metropolitan Open,** and the 1929 **Western Open** (an eight-shot rout of Horton Smith). Most prominent, however, are his three Major championships, the 1927 **U.S. Open,** the 1930 **PGA,** and the 1931 **British Open.** Armour won the 1927 U.S. Open at Oakmont after a famous 3-iron to 10 feet at the 72nd set up a tying birdie, paving the way for a successful play-off against Harry Cooper. The PGA was claimed at New York's old Fresh Meadow CC with a 15-foot putt at the 36th to edge the club's home pro Gene Sarazen one up. Meanwhile the Open Championship required a record-tying 71 in the final round at Carnoustie, followed by the good fortune of Argentina's José Jurado laying up at the par-5 72nd in the erroneous belief that he needed a five to tie when, in fact, a four was required.

It has been widely stated that Armour was the rare man to play against the United States as a Walker Cupper, then for them in the Ryder Cup, but strictly speaking neither tale is true. The "Walker Cup" referred to was actually an informal 1921 match at Hoylake pitting a team of British players against a visiting American squad, a contest that predated the actual Walker Cup by a year. Similarly, Armour competed for America in the 1926 professional match at Wentworth that inspired Samuel Ryder to donate his cup, not the real thing that debuted in 1927 (and for which Armour was ineligible to represent America, having been born overseas).

Retired from active competition, Armour spent many years as one of America's most sought-after teachers, summering at Winged Foot and wintering at Boca Raton. He authored the huge-selling *How to Play Your Best Golf All the Time* (Simon & Schuster, 1953) as well as *A Round of Golf with Tommy Armour* (Simon & Schuster, 1959) and *Tommy Armour's ABC's of Golf* (Simon & Schuster, 1967). Yet beyond all of his playing, teaching and writing accomplishments, Armour's fame likely benefited most from something he had little to do with: several decades' worth of top-shelf MacGregor golf clubs bearing his name. The Armour woods in particular were long coveted by top players and collectors, though they were actually designed (like virtually all of MacGregor's best period equipment) by Toney Penna.

PGA Tour Wins (25): 1927 U.S. Open; 1927, '30 & '34 Canadian Open; 1928 Metropolitan; 1929 Western Open; **1930 PGA Championship; 1931** British Open

1920-1942

	20	21	22	23	24	25	26	27	28	29	30	31
Masters												
US Open	T48	-	-	-	T13	T38	T9	1	16	T5	6	T46
British	-	-	-	-	-	-	13	-	MC	10	-	1
PGA	-	-	-	-	-	T5	-	T5	T17	WD	1	T5

	32	33	34	35	36	37	38	39	40	41	42
Masters		-	T37	T20	T8	T12	-	38	38	T28	
US Open	T21	T4	T50	WD	T22	MC	23	T22	T12	MC	
British	T17	-	-	-	-	-	-	-			
PGA	-	-	T9	2	T33	T33	-	-	-	-	-

Tommy Armour III (USA)

Grandson of the Silver Scot, Denver, Colorado, native Tommy Armour III (b. 10/8/1959) has long been better known for his bloodlines and his celebrity friends than for his golf that, prior to 2003, had yielded only one win (the 1990 **Phoenix Open**) in 15 years on the PGA Tour. That all changed, however, at the 2003 **Texas Open** when the 43-year-old Armour fired rounds of 64-62-63-65, his 254 total setting an all-time record for lowest 72-hole competitive score, beating both Mark Calcavecchia's 256 (shot at the 2001 Phoenix Open) and Englishman Peter Tupling's longstanding 255, done under highly favorable conditions in the 1981 Nigerian Open.

Arjun Atwal (India)

The verdict remains out at the time of this writing as to how effective Arjun Atwal (b. Asansol, 3/20/1973) will be on the PGA Tour, but he has already made history as the first Indian to gain full American playing privileges. This he did the old-fashioned way (at the 2003 Tour Qualifying Tournament), though European Tour victories at the 2002 **Singapore Masters** and the 2003 **Malaysian Open** have certainly proven him a capable international performer. Atwal spent two high school years competing in the United States and his Malaysian win came at the expense of Retief Goosen, but only time will tell how effectively he and countryman Jeev Milka Singh will adjust to the deeper fields prevalent in America.

Laurie Auchterlonie (UK)

The younger brother of famed St. Andrews' clubmaker Willie, Laurie Auchterlonie (1868–1948) joined the pack by emigrating to America shortly before the turn of the twentieth century. Having reached the semifinal of the 1895 British Amateur at St. Andrews (where he lost to Leslie Balfour-Melville at the 19th), Laurie became professional at Chicago's Glen View GC while contending regularly at a number of early **U.S. Opens**. Five times in seven years he would finish among the top five, with victory coming in 1902 at Garden City, where he routed Stewart Gardner and Walter Travis (both members of the host club) by six. Though this would prove Auchterlonie's only important win, it also earned him the distinction of becoming the first player in Open history to break 80 during all four rounds of the championship.

Willie Auchterlonie (UK)

A lifetime resident of St. Andrews, William Auchterlonie (1872–1963) made his bones in 1893 by capturing the **Open Championship** at Prestwick. This he did by two strokes over Johnny Laidlay and three over Sandy Herd, all the while carrying only seven homemade clubs and using only five. Though a regular Open competitor for several years thereafter, Auchterlonie became far more dedicated to his famous club manufacturing business, which has now flourished, just yards from the home green of the Old Course, for over a century. In 1935 Auchterlonie succeeded the recently deceased Andra Kirkaldy and Old Tom Morris as head professional to the R&A, a position that was given to his son Laurie (named after his U.S. Open champion brother) upon his death. By all accounts a perfectionist and an old-school taskmaster, Auchterlonie was made an honorary member of the R&A in 1950.

Debbie Austin (USA)

Former Rollins College standout Debbie Austin (b. Oneida, New York, 2/1/1948) joined the LPGA Tour in 1968 and quickly established herself as a reliable top-40 money winner, with regular visits to the top 20. Winless over her first nine seasons, however, she suddenly exploded in a stunning 1977 that included five victories (three coming in a span of four mid-summer weeks) and sixth place on the money list. An unofficial victory at the **Australian Open** added a late-season flourish, and another win early in 1978 seemed to suggest that 1977 had been no fluke. But Austin soon eased back into the pack, continuing to earn good money but only winning once more, at the 1981 **Mayflower Classic.**

Mike Austin (UK/USA)

One of golf's less documented, more eccentric characters, English-born (1910) and American-raised Mike Austin is widely believed to have been the game's longest-ever hitter, a title backed by the *Guinness Book of World Records,* which credits him with a drive of 515 yards in 1974. A fantasy? Perhaps—except that the blast in question took place during the U.S. National Seniors Open (a forerunner to the USGA's U.S. Senior Open) and claimed as a witness Austin's playing partner former PGA Tour star Chandler Harper. Never good enough to make a living on Tour, Austin was still a well-known commodity in his day, though his boldly offbeat personality makes it difficult to discern fact from fiction when assessing his many golf-related claims. Wheelchair-bound and in his mid-90s, Austin remains a driving range pro in Studio City, California, at the time of this writing.

Mya Aye (Myanmar)

Myanmar (formerly Burma) has hardly shown itself a breeding ground for world-class golfers. Indeed, when the nation's best ever, Mya Aye (b. 1940), was at his peak, he was one of only three professionals in the entire country. But Aye, an ex-caddie, did prove himself at least regionally competitive, winning the 1976 **Indonesian Open,** the 1979 **Philippine Masters,** the 1981 **Singapore Open,** and several smaller titles. He also finished fourth in the 1976 Japan Open (against somewhat stiffer competition) and participated in the 1980 Open Championship at Muirfield where his 80-74 missed the cut.

Paul Azinger (USA)

Holyoke, Massachusetts, native Paul William Azinger (b. 1/6/1960) ranks among the latest blooming of golf's contemporary stars, seldom even breaking 80 as a youth, much less establishing a strong amateur record. But with a desire that would ultimately make him one of the game's grittiest competitors, Azinger "dug it out of the dirt," attending Florida State and developing a swing that, if not altogether artistic, has proven both effective and repeating. A low-ball hitter with perhaps the strongest grip in modern golf, Azinger's deadly short game and steady putting stroke have also helped make him both a big money winner and a Major champion.

Azinger first served notice in 1987 with three victories and second place on the PGA Tour money list. This would prove the first of seven consecutive seasons with at least one victory, the last coming in 1993 when he won the **Memorial** (by holing a 72nd-hole bunker shot), the **New England Classic,** and, in sudden death with Greg Norman, a memorable **PGA Championship.** But only four months later, at the very peak of his career, Azinger was diagnosed with lymphoma in his right shoulder blade, forcing him to miss nearly all of 1994, burdened by chemotherapy and radiation treatments. After beating the cancer (and receiving the Golf Writers' 1995 Ben Hogan Award for his efforts) he embarked on six years of steady play that culminated with his 12th and most popular Tour victory, the 2000 **Hawaiian Open.**

Long respected as a big-game competitor, Azinger defeated Seve Ballesteros in singles during his first Ryder Cup (1989), though his overall Cup record of 5-7-3 may surprise some. Still, Azinger remains capable of dramatics on the biggest of stages, as illustrated by his holed bunker shot at the last to halve a key 2002 Ryder Cup singles match with Sweden's Niclas Fasth.

PGA Tour Wins (12): 1991 Bing Crosby; 1993 Memorial; **1993 PGA Championship**
Intn'l Wins: (2)
Ryder Cup: 1989–93 & 2002 (4); **Presidents Cup:** 2000

B

Doug Bachli (Australia)

An outstanding swimmer who took up golf after his family moved to Canberra in his early teens, Albert Park native Douglas William Bachli (1922–2000) initially made waves by winning **Capital Territory Amateur** titles in 1946 and '48. The latter year also saw him break through in the **Australian Amateur,** soundly defeating P. F. Heard in the final 7 and 6 at Victoria's Metropolitan GC. Though a second national title would follow at age 40 in 1962, Bachli is far better remembered as the only Australian ever to capture the **British Amateur,** a feat accomplished at Muirfield in 1954. On that occasion he defeated the heavily favored American Bill Campbell 2 and 1, winning the 32nd and 33rd holes to take the lead after trailing by one. Not an especially powerful hitter, Bachli wore down the longer Campbell by utilizing the age-old match-play tactic of playing his approach shots first, ratcheting up the pressure by constantly sticking them close.

Aaron Baddeley (USA/Australia)

Few golfers have burst onto the world scene more memorably than Aaron Baddeley (b. 3/17/1981) whose closing 69 outdueled Greg Norman, Colin Montgomerie, and Nick O'Hern to win the 1999 **Australian Open** as a previously unheralded 18-year-old amateur. Having thus stood the golfing world on its collective ear, the streaky youngster managed to repeat the trick, defending his title by two strokes over compatriot Robert Allenby in 2000. Subsequent professional efforts in America have thus far been a tad less successful, however, though a play-off loss to Ernie Els at the PGA Tour's 2003 Hawaiian Open and a 2001 win at Australia's **Holden International** seem to suggest a bright future.

Born in Lebanon, New Hampshire, where his father served as chief mechanic for legendary auto racer Mario Andretti, Baddeley moved with his family to Australia when he was two, residing there ever since.

Marisa Baena (Colombia)

A native of Pereira, Colombia, Marisa Baena (b. 6/1/1977) is one of the finest professional prospects ever produced in South America, though her initial wanderings on the LPGA Tour, while solid enough, have been decidedly unspectacular. The 1996 **NCAA** individual champion at Arizona, Baena was a three-time All-America from 1996 to 1998, and also a 2 and 1 loser to Kelli Kuehne in the final of the 1996 U.S. Women's Amateur. She has yet to win an LPGA event at the time of this writing, however, nor has she ever bettered 33rd on the Tour money list.

Hugh Baiocchi (South Africa)

Johannesburg product Hugh Baiocchi (b. 8/17/1946) was the amateur champion of **Brazil** and **South Africa** before turning professional in 1971, eventually claiming some 20 victories both at home and in Europe. His tenure among South Africa's best extended from 1973 to 1989 but peaked near the middle with a 1978 **South African Open** title as well as 1980 wins at the **South African PGA** and the **Zimbabwe Open.** In Europe Baiocchi was twice **Swiss Open** champion (1973 and '79) with the former anchoring his career-best season, a third-place finish on the Order of Merit. Eligible for the Champions Tour in 1997, Baiocchi quickly established himself as a regular presence, winning once in 1997 and twice in '98, and remaining reasonably competitive well past the millennium.

Ian Baker-Finch (Australia)

Few golfers of the modern era have peaked as high, then swooned so low, as the popular Queenslander Ian Baker-Finch (b. Nambour, 10/24/1960). Following a steady 1980s rise that saw him win 10 international events plus the PGA Tour's 1989 **Colonial Invitational,** the 6′4″ Baker-Finch found the big time when his closing rounds of 64-66 catapulted him to the 1991 **Open Championship** at Royal Birkdale, defeating countryman Mike Harwood by two strokes. Birdies at five of Sunday's first seven holes served as a springboard to a victory that, save for Greg Norman in 1986, was the first by an Australian in the Open since Peter Thomson's halcyon days of the 1950s and '60s.

Though Baker-Finch would win twice more in Australia, his game took a precipitous plunge during the 1990s, resulting in a 167th–place finish on the 1994 PGA Tour money list, 29 consecutive missed cuts during 1995 and '96, and, finally, an early retirement following an opening-round 92 in the 1997 Open Championship at Royal Troon. The ever-pleasant Baker-Finch took it all in stride, however, parlaying his personality and goodwill into a successful commentary career on American television and a golf course design business around the world.

PGA Tour Wins (2): 1989 Colonial; **1991 British Open**
Intn'l Wins (12): 1993 Australian PGA

Al Balding (Canada)

A leading Canadian professional in the decades following World War II, Toronto native Albert Balding (b. 1924) holds the distinction of being the first Canadian to win an official PGA Tour event, that being the 1955 **Mayfair Inn Open**. Balding would also win three times in 1957, in Miami Beach, West Palm Beach, and Havana, giving him four American triumphs all told. Considered a smooth, efficient swinger, he enjoyed even greater success at home, winning **Canadian PGAs** in 1955, '56, '63, and '70 and **Canadian Match Play** titles on four occasions. Largely quiescent following a **Mexican Open** title in 1963, Balding emerged for one last hurrah at the 1968 **World Cup**, capturing medalist honors with a 14-under-par performance while teaming with George Knudson to give Canada its first win in the event originally known as the Canada Cup.

A. J. Balfour (UK)

No more a golfer of championship caliber than his presidential counterparts in the United States, statesman/politician Arthur James Balfour (1848–1930) was a crucial figure in golf's late nineteenth-century explosion in Great Britain. Initially as secretaries to Scotland and Ireland, then later as prime minister, Balfour was perhaps the game's most prominent early booster, regularly playing at North Berwick, serving as captain of the R&A in 1894, and generally garnering unprecedented exposure for the fledgling pastime. Though born to a golfing family in Lothian, Scotland, Balfour didn't take up the game until age 36, leading him to lament belonging to "that unhappy class of beings forever pursued by remorse, who are conscious that they threw away in their youth the opportunity of beginning golf."

L. M. Balfour-Melville (UK)

Edinburgh's Leslie Balfour-Melville (1854–1937) was the product of a golfing background, his father James having written the historic *Reminiscences of Golf on St. Andrews Links* (David Douglas, 1887). An attorney by trade, Leslie was an excellent all-around athlete and a highly competitive golfer, and served as captain of both the Honourable Company of Edinburgh Golfers and the R&A. He was five times a semifinalist in the **British Amateur** but, like several of his contemporaries, bore the ill fortune of competing against that greatest of U.K. amateurs, John Ball. Balfour-Melville did, however, break through to capture the title once, in 1895, defeating Ball on the 19th hole at St. Andrews. Ironically, this would be the same year that Leslie's brother Robert won the second Australian Amateur, making for a remarkable family double half a world apart.

John Ball (UK)

Born: Hoylake, England, 12/24/1861 Died: Holywell, Wales, 12/2/1940

In America it is taken for granted that the greatest amateur of all time *must* be the Grand Slam–winning Bobby Jones, but those whose knowledge casts a wider net may not judge so quickly. The reason for debate is one John Ball, son of a prominent Hoylake innkeeper/golfer and generally referred to as John Ball Jr. (or Johnny) despite actually being the third generation of his family so named (references to "John Ball tertius" appear).

An uncommonly quiet and modest man who shunned publicity, Ball surely inherited his talents from his father, a fine player who reached the semifinals of the British Amateur in 1887. A long, full swinger, Johnny's attractive style was especially favored by Darwin, who observed: "I have derived greater aesthetic and emotional pleasure from watching John Ball than from any other spectacle in any other game." A consummate tee-to-green player whose putting, alas, was of a somewhat lesser standard, Ball was also decidedly old school when it came to equipment and shotmaking, generally adjusting the distance of his iron shots by turning down the clubface for a longer draw or opening it for a shorter fade. With little issue of club selection and only a handful to carry, a caddie's dream!

Ball's career record was actually hurt by his timing, for most accounts have him playing much of his best golf for several years prior to the British Amateur's birth, actually tying for fourth in his lone early Open Championship appearance (1878) as a 16-year-old at Prestwick. Perhaps as the result of an amateur-status flap over his pocketing of minor prize money on this occasion, Ball would not return to the Open until 1890, by which time the Amateur existed and his status was well set.

Johnny Ball's record at the **British Amateur** is unique in the annals of golf, for he won it a remarkable eight times. It began in 1888 at Prestwick with a 5 and 4 victory over John Laidlay and continued, like clockwork, in the alternating years of 1890, '92, and '94. His fifth crown came in 1899, once again back at Prestwick, and this time there was high drama. Ball fell 5 down to the legendary Freddie Tait after 14 holes by struggling on the greens, took a putting lesson from Harold Hilton over lunch, then clawed his way back in the afternoon to stand one up at the 35th. There, at the famous Alps, Tait blasted close from accumulated water within the eponymous fronting bunker (he would draw relief today), a splendid feat promptly matched by Ball's subsequent blast from perilously close to the hazard-fronting sleepers. A clutch three at the last drew Tait back to even but Ball's three at the 37th, culminated by a tricky 10-foot putt, ultimately ended it.

Both Tait and Ball packed off to the Boer War shortly thereafter and while Tait would never return, Ball had only a seven-year gap between titles for his troubles. In 1907 he was a winner once more at St. Andrews, then in 1910—now approaching age 50—he routed C. C. Aylmer 10 and 9 on his home turf at Hoylake to claim number seven. Ball's eighth and final triumph came in 1912, at age 52, when he twice mounted improbable comebacks in the early rounds before defeating a young Abe Mitchell over 38 holes in

the final at Westward Ho!—a play-off made possible only by Mitchell missing a four-footer to clinch at the 36th.

Ball had further boosted his amateur credentials by the occasional venture west, looting the **Irish** title in 1893, '94 and '99. But like all great amateurs he gave added measure of his worth by beating the professionals at their own game, becoming the **Open Championship's** first amateur winner in 1890, once again at Prestwick. On this occasion his rounds of 82-82 defeated Willie Fernie and Archie Simpson by three, a performance he would back up with a tie for second (three behind Hilton) at Muirfield two years later and a tie for eighth in 1893. Yet these, along with his precocious 1878 debut, would be Ball's only top-10 Open finishes in 17 tries—the key difference that indeed allows us to place Bobby Jones safely ahead of him on the all-time amateur ledger.

Like most great players with smooth, rhythmic swings, Ball remained competitive for many years, actually reaching the fifth round of the championship in 1921 (at age 60) and losing in the second to Dr. William Tweddell in 1927, both times at Hoylake. After giving up competitive golf, Ball eventually retired to his brother-in-law's home in North Wales, dying there, as one of the game's most talented and revered figures, at age 79.

Major Amateur Wins (9): 1888, '90, '92, '94, '99, 1907, '10 & '12 British Amateur; 1890 British Open

1878-1912

	78	79	80	81	82	83	84	85	86	87	88	89	90	91	92	93	94	95
Brit Am								T3	T3	2	1	T3	1	T17	1	T9	1	2
British	T4	-	-	-	-	-	-	WD	-	-	-	-	1	T11	T2	T8	T13	T18

	96	97	98	99	00	01	02	03	04	05	06	07	08	09	10	11	12
Brit Am	T5	T33	T5	1	-	-	T33	T5	T9	T125	T33	1	T65	T65	1	T17	1
British	-	17	-	T25	-	-	T15	-	18	-	T35	T15	T13	-	T19	-	-

Ted Ball
(Australia)

A well-known character in Australia as both an amateur and professional, New South Wales' Edward Arthur "Ted" Ball (b. 1939) was widely hailed as one of the world's best from 60 yards and in—and equally noted for possessing one of the fastest swings on record. The Hornsby native arrived in 1960, capturing both the **New South Wales Amateur** and the **Australian Amateur,** the latter played in Western Australia at Lake Karrinyup. A year later Ball

turned professional and eventually went on to win a fair number of regional events between 1964 and 1972, including the 1964 **Singapore Open** and **Wills Masters.** After a one-year sabbatical, he won the **Wills** event again in 1973 and '74, the latter over reigning Masters and British Open champion Gary Player at The Australian GC.

Unfortunately, the cigarette-puffing Ball is often best remembered for refusing to play in 1976 when, in a promotional stunt that was a quarter-century ahead of its time, the Victorian Open allowed a dozen women players into its field.

Tom Ball (UK)

A distant relative to the vastly more famous Johnny, fellow Hoylake native Tom Ball (1882–1919) was a short, skinny man with a decidedly odd swing, yet a fine player frequently cited both for his great length and excellent putting. Competing head-on against the Triumvirate, Tom managed a runner-up finish at the 1908 Open Championship (albeit eight in arrears of James Braid), then third place the following year, six behind J. H. Taylor. He was not without his triumphs, however, capturing back-to-back **Belgian Opens** in 1913 and '14 and gaining his greatest victory at the 1909 *News of the World* match play when he took down Sandy Herd at Walton Heath. Though perhaps past his competitive prime, Tom Ball died relatively young while fighting in World War I.

Jimmy Ballard (USA)

One of golf's most prominent nonplaying figures in the 1970s, Jimmy Ballard was the forerunner of today's high-profile swing coaches, working with a cadre of PGA Tour stars that included Johnny Miller, Curtis Strange, Sandy Lyle, Hal Sutton, and many, many others. Laying out his thoughts in the popular *How to Perfect Your Golf Swing* (Golf Digest, 1981), he was among the first to advocate the use of the body's larger muscles in the golf swing ("connection") and facilitated substantial improvement in a number of high-profile games. Ballard has long given credit for his ideas to ex–New York Yankee outfielder and PGA Tour player Sam Byrd, Ballard's own mentor in the early 1960s.

Severiano Ballesteros (Spain)

Golf is a strange game indeed, for as Pedreña native Seve Ballesteros (b. 4/9/1957) came into his late teens as one of four golfing brothers and nephews of the fine Spanish pro Ramon Sota, he was generally viewed as being far less a prospect than his older sibling Manuel. Having learned the game using a cut-down 3-iron on the beach near Santander, the young Seve was thought way too wild for top-level play—a judgment that, were he any other player, would surely have proven correct. But Seve, as the golf world soon came to see, was definitely *not* any other player.

Regular European observers noticed Ballesteros sooner than most, for as an 18-year-old he finished 26th on the 1975 Order of Merit. For the rest of the universe, however, Ballesteros exploded onto the scene at the 1976 Open Championship at Royal Birkdale, where rounds of 69-69-73 had the 19-year-old two strokes ahead with 18 to play. A closing 75, combined with Johnny Miller's splendid 66, left the young Spaniard in the dust, six back and tied with Jack Nicklaus for second. But proving himself of resilient stuff, Seve came back to finish third in his next two starts, then gained his first European Tour victory at the **Dutch Open** (by eight shots over Howard Clark) in August. He later teamed with Manuel Piñero in Palm Springs to win Spain's first-ever **World Cup**, a title he would defend with Antonio Garrido the following year in Manila.

Now locked and loaded, Ballesteros proceeded to finish first, first, first, and second in the Order of Merit from 1976 to 1979, claiming a total of 11 victories, the last being the 1979 **Open Championship** at Royal Lytham & St. Annes. This triumph (by three over Nicklaus and Crenshaw) was at once one of golf's most thrilling and controversial, for it categorically proved the experts correct: Ballesteros *was* too wild, routinely driving the ball into everything but his own fairway, yet scrambling with remarkable confidence and dexterity to win going away. It also set a tone for the many dramatic victories to follow, making the dashing Spaniard arguably the most intimidating presence on the world scene as he marched inexorably toward his ultimate victory total of 87.

Having already won the 1978 **Greater Greensboro Open** during a rare visit to the United States, Ballesteros next claimed the American Major championship best suited to his game, the **Masters,** in 1980. His victory was epic in its way and not without excitement, for after cruising to the 64th tee with a stunning 10-shot lead, Seve fell apart, only to steady himself over the closing holes to hold on and win by four.

Now capable of standing toe-to-toe with Nicklaus and Watson on the world stage, Ballesteros ran into the sort of attitude-based problems that would frequently pop up throughout his career. In Europe there were issues of appearance money, with Seve not yet being eligible to receive it and thus refusing to play more than eight events there (winning three) in 1981. Consequently he was ignored by the Ryder Cup selectors, making 1981 his sole absence from the event over a 16-year period. Several years later he would also clash with PGA Tour Commissioner Deane Beman over the Tour's requirement that members play a minimum of 15 events, which Ballesteros flatly refused to do. Frequent problems with caddies, even more frequent charges of gamesmanship—these sorts of issues followed Seve throughout his career, though whether such things hurt him or simply fired him up to play better is an interesting question.

Ballesteros would take his second **Masters** in 1983 (beating Crenshaw and Kite by four), then another **Open Championship** in 1984 at St. Andrews when his birdie at the 72nd—made just as Watson was taking five at the Road hole behind him—denied the American his sixth Claret Jug by two. A loss of confidence inevitably followed a blown chance at the 1986 Masters (a smothered 4-iron finding water at the 69th) yet Ballesteros still managed to place first in the Order of Merit in 1986, '88 and '91. The middle year in particular might be cited as his best, for he won five times at home, took his sixth (and final) PGA Tour victory at **Westchester,** and, most important, claimed his third **Open Championship** with a final-round 65, winning a classic duel with Nick Price at Royal Lytham & St. Annes.

Though he would win twice in Europe in both 1992 and '94, Seve was surely on the downside now, but there was still his cause of causes, the Ryder Cup. He would ultimately play in eight matches, logging an overall record of 20-12-5 that included an 11-2-2 record when paired with his friend and semi-protégé José Maria Olazábal. More important, Seve's presence, which began with the addition of European players in 1979, was likely the single most important factor in revitalizing the biennial event, his desire to win, which at times has seemed almost disturbed, driving his side to an eight-match record of 3-4-1 after decades of American dominance. He also captained his team to victory in Spain in 1997, though again not without incident. Wanting the otherwise absent Olazábal on the team, Seve basically forced Spaniard Miguel Angel Martin, an automatic qualifier based on the European Tour point system, out of the competition by demanding he take a physical for a wrist injury. Ballesteros got his way and Martin's career has never been the same, but Europe won the Ryder Cup so for some the end justified the means.

In recent years, bothered by a bad back and arthritis, Ballesteros' game has plummeted dramatically, an occur-

rence rued by some and seen as poetic justice by others. Yet love him or hate him, there is simply no denying that aside from being the finest player ever produced by Continental Europe, Seve was as important a figure as international golf has ever seen. At his peak, his mix of awesome power and world-class scrambling was as effective as it was exciting, causing Nick Price to observe that "In his day, [Seve] had the ability to do anything, and I mean *anything*. The guy could snap-hook his way around the golf course off the tee and still shoot 65." Yet perhaps the most revealing quote about Ballesteros came from his own lips when, following Bernhard Langer's miss of a 6-foot putt to cost Europe the 1991 Ryder Cup, he said: "No one in the world can make that putt. It is too much pressure for anyone. Not even Jack Nicklaus in his prime will make that putt... Not even me!"

A little confidence can go a long way.

PGA Tour Wins (9): 1979, '84 & '88 British Open; 1980 & '83 Masters; 1983 & '88 Westchester
Intn'l Wins (78): 1976, '80 & '86 Dutch Open; 1976, '83, '86 & '88 Trophée Lancôme; 1977, '82, '85 & '86 French Open; 1977, '78 & '89 Swiss Open; 1977 & '78 Japan Open; 1978 & '88 German Open; 1981, '85 & '95 Spanish Open; 1981, '82, '84, '85 & '91 World Match Play; 1981 Australian PGA; 1983 & '91 Volvo PGA; 1983, '85 & '86 Irish Open; 1986 & '91 British Masters; 1992 Dubai; 1994 Benson & Hedges
Ryder Cup: 1979, 1983–95 (8) and 1997 Capt

1978-1995

	75	76	77	78	79	80	81	82	83	84	85
Masters	-	-	T33	T18	T12	1	MC	T3	1	MC	T2
US Open	-	-	-	T16	MC	DQ	T41	MC	T4	T30	T5
British	MC	T2	T15	T17	1	T19	T39	T13	T6	1	T38
PGA	-	-	-	-	-	-	T33	13	T27	5	T32

	86	87	88	89	90	91	92	93	94	95
Masters	4	T2	T11	5	T7	T22	T59	T11	T18	T45
US Open	T24	3	T32	T43	T33	MC	T23	MC	T18	MC
British	T6	T50	1	T77	MC	T9	MC	T27	T38	T40
PGA	MC	T10	MC	T12	MC	T23	-	-	MC	MC

Charles Banks (USA)

After graduating from Yale in 1906, Amenia, New York, native Charles Henry "Josh" Banks (1883–1931) returned to his preparatory alma mater, Connecticut's Hotchkiss School, where he would go on to teach English and coach track for 15 years. As a member of the committee appointed to oversee construction of the school's new nine-hole golf course, he worked closely with the famous

architect Seth Raynor, developing enough interest and aptitude in the design field to accept Raynor's offer of employment in 1921. Abandoning academia, Banks was soon assisting both Raynor and *his* mentor, the great Charles Blair Macdonald, on such well-known projects as Mid Ocean, Deepdale, and Yale. In 1925 he became Raynor's partner.

Sadly Raynor would die unexpectedly in early 1926, leaving Banks to complete 10 of the firm's unfinished projects before continuing in solo practice. Not surprisingly, his design style followed the Macdonald/Raynor lead of mixing strategic original holes with replicas of famous British classics, each adapted to suit the particulars of a site. Banks also expanded upon Raynor's deep, grass-faced bunkering style, creating some of the most severe hazards of his day—and in the process being nicknamed "Steamshovel," in deference to his massive excavations. Having worked up and down the East Coast, and as far south as Venezuela and Colombia, Banks too died young, suffering a fatal heart attack in 1931.

Notable Courses: Castle Harbour GC, Bermuda (BO); CC of Bogotá, Colombia (NLE); Essex County CC, West Course, New Jersey; **The Knoll CC, New Jersey; Whippoorwill CC, New York**

James Barber (UK/USA)

A native of Liverpool, England, James Barber made his fortune in America where his Barber Steamship Lines developed into one of the world's largest, serving the six inhabited continents. A devout practitioner of the royal & ancient game, he began wintering in Pinehurst early in the twentieth century, leading a local golfing group known as the Tin Whistles and building what many believe to have been the world's first miniature course on his estate. In 1927 Barber commissioned Donald Ross to design an equally private regulation 18 that, according to most accounts, was completed in 1928. At 6,478 yards, it stood among the best—and shortest-lived—in the Sandhills region, expiring with the onset of the Depression.

Jerry Barber (USA)

Standing only 5'5" and of no more than average build, Woodson, Illinois, native Carl Jerome "Jerry" Barber (1916–1994) was physically one of the least imposing players on the PGA Tour. Yet with diligent practice and a world-class putting stroke, he managed to win seven times between 1953 and 1963, including the 1961 **PGA Championship,** captured at Olympia Fields at age 45. On that memorable occasion, Barber holed putts of 20, 40 and 60 feet on the final three greens to catch Don January, before defeating the veteran Texan by one in an 18-hole playoff. Primarily on the strength of this win, Barber (who had already played in the 1955 Ryder Cup) was chosen as playing captain of the 1961 team that was victorious at Royal Lytham & St. Annes. His other notable victories came at the 1960 **Tournament of Champions** (where his record score of 268 stood for 26 years) and thrice in the old **Azalea Open Invitational.**

In later years Barber served as professional at Los Angeles' 36-hole Griffith Park facility where he could often be found on the putting green, rather anonymously working on his stroke. He also kicked up a bit of controversy by utilizing his lifetime PGA Tour exemption to participate in the Los Angeles Open well into his 70s, not out of a desire to compete but rather to protest the fact that he was *not* exempt where he really belonged, on the budding Champions Tour.

Miller Barber (USA)

Long known as "Mr. X" for playing behind dark sunglasses, Miller Barber (b. Shreveport, Louisiana, 3/31/1931) also bore one of golf's most recognizable swings, a looping outside-to-in motion that featured a right elbow flying far beyond classically accepted parameters. The key to any golf swing, however, is not its appearance but rather one's ability to repeat it, a task accomplished by Barber with a consistency few contemporaries could match.

Indeed, after attending the University of Arkansas, serving in the Air Force, and working as a club pro at New York's venerable Apawamis, Barber joined the PGA Tour in 1959 and by the mid-60s was regularly logging top-25 finishes on the money list. He would win 11 times overall, never more than once in a season, yet managing to land his one every year from 1967 to 1974 (a streak matched only by Jack Nicklaus). In 1969 Barber finished in the top 10 of all four Major championships and his victory at the 1971 **Phoenix Open** featured a scorching total of 261, the Tour's lowest four-day score since Mike Souchak's 257 in 1955.

Barber managed to maintain form better than many his age, tying the Masters record of 64 in 1979 at age 48. Joining the Champions Tour in 1981, he became one of its best-ever performers, winning 24 titles including a record three **U.S. Senior Opens** in 1982, '84, and '85.

PGA Tour Wins (11): 1968 Byron Nelson
Champions Tour Wins: 24 (1981–1989)
Ryder Cup: 1969 & '71 (2)

Herbert Barker (UK/USA)

The 1906 **Irish Open Amateur** champion, Kirkburton, England, native Herbert H. Barker elected to try his luck competing in the United States, emigrating in 1908. Serving as professional at New York's Garden City GC until 1911, he never won an American event but soon developed a second career remodeling and upgrading a number of early, rudimentary courses. After leaving Garden City, Barker settled in Birmingham, Alabama, laying out several prominent Southern facilities (including Atlanta's Capital City Club and Druid Hills) before returning to Britain in 1915 to fight in World War I. Though surviving the conflict, Barker never made good on a promise to return to America in its aftermath.

Al Barkow (USA)

Born and raised in Chicago, Al Barkow played golf on an NAIA national championship team at Western Illinois University and was good enough to once qualify for the U.S. Amateur. Building a career as a prominent journalist, he served as chief writer for the *Shell's Wonderful World of Golf* TV series and also as an editor at *Golf* and *Golf Illustrated* magazines. An author or coauthor of numerous books, he has especially distinguished himself as a chronicler of golf's past where his oral history of the American professional game, *Gettin' to the Dance Floor* (Atheneum, 1986), and his engaging story of the PGA Tour, *Golf's Golden Grind* (Harcourt Brace Jovanovich, 1974), are widely quoted standards. A third title, *The History of the PGA Tour* (Doubleday, 1989), is equally important for its research and resulting aggregations of the playing records of many old professionals who toiled long before the era of mass media coverage.

Nonna Barlow (Ireland/USA)

After emigrating from Ireland in 1898 with her ex-military husband, Nonna Barlow (b. 1866) was a dominant figure in early Philadelphia-area women's golf, joining the then–Merion Cricket Club and eventually winning six **Philadelphia Women's** championships. A solid all-around player, Barlow was twice a U.S. Women's Amateur finalist, losing 3 and 2 to Scotland's Dorothy Campbell in 1909 (on her home turf at Merion), then falling to Margaret Curtis by the same margin in 1912 at Massachusetts' Essex Country Club. Barlow was also a three-time **North & South Amateur** champion (1915, '16, and '19) and a remarkable six-time winner of the **Eastern Amateur,** claiming that title from 1911 to 1913, then thrice more in succession from 1919 to 1921. Her 1912 victory, scored close to home at the Philadelphia Cricket Club, came by a record 23-stroke margin.

Brian Barnes (UK)

A large and colorful man who turned professional shortly after winning the **British Youths** title in 1964, England's Brian Barnes (b. Addington, 6/3/1945) was coached by 1951

Open champion Max Faulkner, whose daughter he would eventually marry. Utilizing a short backswing followed by a powerful rush downward, Barnes has captured the *News of the World* match play (1976) and the national Opens of **The Netherlands, France, Spain, Portugal,** and **Italy,** while also winning Down Under (the 1970 **Australian Masters**) and in Africa (one **Kenyan** and two **Zambian Opens**). He even managed to win medalist honors at the 1970 PGA Tour qualifier, though he never did come over to play full time. Not surprisingly, Barnes was the foundation of six Ryder Cup teams, going a respectable 10-14-1 on mostly losing sides and twice defeating Jack Nicklaus on the same day in 1975—both times at singles.

As a senior, Barnes' fortunes have been decidedly mixed. He began swimmingly, winning the **Senior British Open** at Royal Portrush in 1995, then defending his title at the same venue a year later. In 1998 at the U.S. Senior Open, however, a two-stroke penalty at the 65th hole (for failing to properly replace his marked ball) derailed what was shaping into an heroic charge, leading to a disappointing tie for fourth. More recently, a bout with arthritis has turned Barnes into a regular voice for the BBC.

Intn'l Wins (14): 1974 Dutch Open; 1975 French Open; 1976 PGA Match Play; 1978 Spanish Open; 1979 Portuguese Open; 1979 Italian Open

Ryder Cup: 1969–79 (6)

Jim Barnes (UK/USA)

Born: Lelant, England, 4/8/1886 **Died:** East Orange, New Jersey, 5/24/1966

Surprisingly overlooked among golf's all-time greats, James M. "Long Jim" Barnes stood 6'4" by the time he left Cornwall for America in or about 1905. A fine all-around talent who was particularly skilled with a driver, Barnes initially held a succession of high-end club jobs throughout America while developing his game to a world-class level. His first major rumblings were heard upon winning the 1916 **North & South Open,** getting far louder when he defeated fellow émigré Jock Hutchison one up to capture that season's first-ever **PGA Championship** at Siwanoy. The PGA would take the next two years off due to World War I but when it returned in 1919 Barnes was there again, routing Fred McLeod 6 and 5 at Long Island's Engineers CC to defend his title. Twice more a PGA finalist in 1921 and '24, he would lose on both occasions to five-time champion Walter Hagen, a common enough occurrence in that period for anyone meeting the Haig at match play.

Though regularly finishing in the top five from 1913 onward, Barnes broke through to win the **U.S. Open** in 1921 at Maryland's Columbia CC, his 72-hole total of 289 standing a record nine shots ahead of both Hagen and McLeod. It only remained then for Barnes to capture an **Open Championship** and after several top-10 finishes and a tie for second (one behind Hagen) in 1922, he eventually broke through at Prestwick in 1925. Here fortune smiled upon Barnes who played his final round early, away from the massive gallery (estimated as large as 15,000) that turned out to root third-round leader and Carnoustie native Macdonald Smith home. Going quietly about his business, Barnes shot 74, while Smith, who was rattled by the chaos, ballooned to an 82. In the end, it was Archie Compston and Ted Ray whom Barnes edged by one.

Thus the taciturn, unassuming Barnes won all three Major championships available to him, the Masters not arriving on the scene until 1934. For those wishing to see professional Majors strictly in groups of four, however, we can always factor in what was, by universal acclaim, the next largest title of the era, the **Western Open,** which Barnes captured three times.

PGA Tour Wins (20): 1914, '17 & '19 Western Open; 1916 & '19 North & South; **1916 & '19 PGA Championships; 1921 U.S. Open; 1925 British Open**

1912-1930

	12	13	14	15	16	17	18	19	20	21	22	23	24	25	26	27	28	29	30
US Open	T18	T4	T13	T4	3			T11	T6	1	T24	T12	-	T29	MC	T24	T36	T21	T39
British	-	-	-						6	T6	T2	-	*	1	T18	T16	T6	7	T6
PGA			1					1	T9	2	T17	T5	2	-	T17	-	T9	-	-

*Result unverified—made cut but finished outside top 30.

Dave Barr (Canada)

Canada's top player throughout virtually all of the 1980s, Kelowna, British Columbia, native Dave Barr (b. 3/1/1952) won more than a dozen events on his home tour and twice in America, in 1981 at **Quad Cities** (in a five-way play-off over eight holes!) and in 1987 at **Atlanta** (with a 23-under-par total of 265). An Oral Roberts graduate and a winner on the Champions Tour in his second season (2003), Barr at one time held a virtual monopoly over Canadian **World Cup** representation, playing in the annual international two-man event 10 times between 1977 and 1990, claiming medalist honors in 1983.

Olivier Barras (Switzerland)

Though undeniably a big fish in one of golf's smaller ponds, Olivier Barras (1932–1965) stands, without much competition, as the finest male golfer ever produced by tiny, mountainous Switzerland. When playing solely against his countrymen, Barras was dominant, winning the **Swiss Closed Amateur** an impressive nine times between 1950 and 1964. Facing a larger **Open Amateur** field, however, he managed only a single title in 1963, plus a runner-up in 1958. With the Olivier Barras Memorial Tournament a regular stop on Europe's Alps minitour and several relatives still important in Swiss golfing circles, the Barras name remains among that nation's most prominent.

Valentin Barrios (Spain)

Shortly before there was Seve Ballesteros, Spanish golf was largely led by Valentin Barrios (b. 4/7/1942), a former bullfighter who topped the Continental Order of Merit in 1967, '69, and '73. A tremendously long hitter, Barrios won a variety of smaller tournaments on the Iberian peninsula but perhaps showed his talent best in several events he did not win, such as the 1973 Trophée Lancôme where he finished second to U.S. Open champion Johnny Miller. Barrios' best finish on the Major stage was a tie for 49th at the 1971 Open Championship (level with an aging Bobby Locke, among others) and he bears the odd distinction of being Bing Crosby's final playing partner, Crosby suffering a fatal 1977 heart attack at the La Moraleja GC where Barrios has long served as professional.

Herman Barron (USA)

Long noted as America's top Jewish golf professional when such things were somehow considered relevant, Port Chester, New York, native Herman Barron (1909–1978) very nearly won the 1946 U.S. Open at Canterbury, when bogies at the 71st and 72nd left him one stroke off the historic three-way, 36-hole play-off between Lloyd Mangrum, Byron Nelson, and Vic Ghezzi (won by Mangrum). Overall, Barron won four times on Tour, his biggest title being the 1942 **Western Open,** which he claimed in Phoenix. He also finished fifth in the 1941 U.S. Open at Colonial and played on the 1947 Ryder Cup team, pairing with Byron Nelson to win the lone match in which he appeared. Long considered one of the Tour's smoothest swingers, Barron served as golf professional at New York's Fenway GC for over 40 years beginning in 1935, and passed away shortly after retiring.

A. Gordon Barry (UK)

Cornwall's Gordon Barry (1885–1942) was a 19-year-old student at St. Andrews University when he became the youngest-ever winner of the **British Amateur** in 1905, beating Michael Scott 3 and 2 at Prestwick. Bernard Darwin described Barry as a confident youngster possessing "a huge swing, to be rigidly cut down later in life." Of course, Barry would only manage a couple of Army titles in the years ahead, prompting Darwin to further note of his Amateur win that "If this was something of a flash in the pan it was a very bright flash."

Pamela Barton (UK)

Dying young tends to substantially enhance one's legacy but in the case of Pam Barton (1917–1943), recalled to this day as an icon of British women's golf, the adulation seems appropriate. A remarkable talent at a young age, the engaging and attractive Londoner first served notice by winning the 1934 **French Ladies** championship at age 17, also reaching the final of the British Women's Amateur (where she lost to Helen Holm and Wanda Morgan) in both that year and the next.

During 1935, Barton starred on a British team that played 14 matches throughout Australia, setting new course records at Royal Melbourne and Royal Canberra en route. Perhaps toughened by the international competition, she finally broke through to win the **British Ladies** in 1936 at Southport and Ainsdale (defeating Bridget Newell 5 and 3), then became only the second woman ever to take the **U.S. Women's Amateur** in the same season (following Dorothy Campbell Hurd) by defeating Mrs. John D. Crews 4 and 3 at Canoe Brook. Curtis Cup appearances in 1934 and '36 added to the ledger, as did a second **British Amateur** triumph in 1939, this time over Mrs. T. Marks at Royal Portrush.

Tragically, Barton died in a wartime plane crash while serving in the Women's Auxiliary Air Force. Only 26 at the time, there is no telling how many postwar titles her powerful, exciting game might have won, and British golf was much affected by her loss. She was remembered on the American side by a series of "Pam Barton Days," fundraisers that helped the financially strapped British Curtis Cup team to make it across for the 1950 contest.

Ralph Barton (USA)

A native of Newport, New Hampshire, Ralph Martin Barton (1875–1941) was first a mathematics teacher at the University of Minnesota, then, after 1921, an employee of noted golf course architect Seth Raynor. Though Barton would never approach the prominence of fellow hiree (and ex-academician) Charles Banks, he did create some controversy when, after both Raynor and Charles Blair Macdonald were dead, he claimed to have played a major role in their designs of both Yale and Mid Ocean—a claim not substantiated by any known source.

Barton's solo work was generally more sporty than distinguished, a reality to which he was apparently oblivious. For while building a pseudo-executive resort nine in rural New Hampshire in 1938, he wrote that "I am now engaged in the building of a course ... at the Mountain View House [in] Whitefield which promises to rank with Yale and Mid Ocean." Perhaps, then, it is not surprising that Barton was working for the New Hampshire Department of Highways when he passed away in 1941.

Alice Bauer (USA)

A founding member of the LPGA, Eureka, South Dakota, native Alice Bauer (1927–2002) is probably best remembered as one of golf's first glamour girls, teaming with her younger sister Marlene (*see* Marlene Hagge) to steal the postwar limelight from all but the great Babe Zaharias. Though only 22 when the LPGA was formed, Bauer played regularly for just a few short years, ultimately preferring to raise her two children in a less transient lifestyle. Though Bauer never achieved the championship standing of her sister (indeed, she never even logged an official LPGA victory), she was gutsy enough to attempt to qualify for the men's 1949 Los Angeles Open. Unlike Zaharias, however, who successfully made the L.A. field in 1945, Bauer missed by nine shots.

Beth Bauer (USA)

Though just beginning her professional career, North Carolinian Beth Bauer (b. Largo, Florida, 3/15/1980) goes into battle with elite credentials, having assembled one of the finest junior and amateur records of her time. A remarkable six-time AJGA All-American and two-time Player of the Year, she attended Duke University for two years, winning a team National Championship and being named an NCAA All-American twice. Following two Curtis Cup appearances in 1998 and 2000, she initially failed LPGA qualifying and so instead dominated the Futures Tour with a four-win, Player of the Year season in

2001. In 2002, she was named the LPGA's Rookie of the Year.

Laura Baugh (USA)

Mostly famous today for her bouts with alcoholism and for *not* winning an LPGA tournament, one-time glamour girl Laura Baugh's golfing skills have, to a large degree, taken a bad rap. For while Baugh (b. Gainesville, Florida, 5/31/1955) did indeed go winless over a professional career spanning some 27 years, she became the youngest (16) ever to claim the **U.S. Women's Amateur** in 1971, was a two-time **Southern Amateur** winner (1970 and '71), a 1972 Curtis Cup player, and 1973 LPGA Rookie of the Year. Further, she finished in the top 25 on the money list in her first four full seasons, logging 32 top-10 finishes over that time, including 13 in 1974. Having cashed in nicely on her good looks, Baugh was never very popular with her LPGA peers and, with an expanding family and growing personal problems, was seldom a serious factor after 1986.

Rex Baxter (USA)

Though a professional career that saw only one PGA Tour win (the 1963 **Cajun Classic**) must be considered a disappointment, Amarillo's Rex Baxter (b. 1936) was one of America's elite young players during the 1950s, initially making his mark by winning the **USGA Junior Boys** title in 1953. At the University of Houston he was instrumental in starting coach Dave Williams' Cougar dynasty, leading the school to its first NCAA titles as a junior and senior (1957 and '58) and becoming its first individual **NCAA** champion in 1957. That same year he won the **Trans-Mississippi** and reached the semifinals of the U.S. Amateur at The Country Club of Brookline, losing to eventual champion Hillman Robbins 2 down. In addition to the Cajun Classic, Baxter also won the 1966 **Brazilian Open** and, after leaving the Tour, the 1970 **PGA Club Professional** title.

George Bayer (USA)

Standing 6'5" and weighing as much as 275 pounds, Bremerton, Washington, native George Bayer (1925–2003) was a football star at the University of Washington, blocking, during his senior year, for future NFL Hall of Famer Hugh McElhenny. After briefly playing professional football with the Washington Redskins, Bayer turned to golf full time in 1954. Not surprisingly, Bayer was among the very longest hitters of his or any other era, routinely driving the ball over 300 yards, recording several tee shots measured at over 400 and—according to unverified leg-

end—once driving it over 500 yards at an event in Australia. A remarkably supple man for one so powerfully built, Bayer's biggest of three career wins came at the 1957 **Canadian Open** where he defeated Texan Bo Wininger by two at the Westmount G&CC. His best Major championship finish was third, at the 1962 PGA at Aronimink.

Andy Bean (USA)

Born in Lafayette, Georgia, before moving to Lakeland, Florida, during his teens, Thomas Andrew Bean (b. 3/13/1953) was a top player on the PGA Tour from the mid-1970s through the mid-80s, winning 11 times and logging five top-10 money finishes before being slowed by tendonitis in his wrist. Standing 6'4" and weighing 225 pounds, Bean was a hard-to-miss figure on the golf course, but was equally well known as a pleasant and generous sort. With such size, he was obviously capable of hitting it a long way, though to his credit Bean was far better known for hitting greens in regulation and possessing a fine short game. Like many players who spend their youths on Bermudagrass, he was especially tough in Florida, winning thrice at **Doral** (1977, '82 and '86) and once at **Bay Hill**. His biggest Tour victory, however, came at the 1978 **Western Open** (in sudden death over Bill Rogers at Butler National GC), though his 1979 win in **Atlanta** might be better remembered as it included a 61 and an eight-shot margin of victory.

Bean was an All-American at the University of Florida, winning both the **Eastern** and **Western Amateurs** before turning pro. He also won the 1978 **Dunlop Phoenix Open** in Japan and claimed a 4-2 record with the 1979 and '87 Ryder Cup teams. More recently, Bean has played two moderately successful Champions Tour seasons at the time of this writing.

PGA Tour Wins (11): 1977, '82 & '86 Doral; 1978 Western Open; 1986 Byron Nelson
Intn'l Win: (1)
Ryder Cup: 1979 & '87 (2)

Frank Beard (USA)

Often portrayed as a dull, mechanical player, Frank Beard (b. Dallas, Texas, 5/1/1930) was certainly one of the PGA Tour's more consistent stars during the latter half of the 1960s, winning 11 times between 1963 and 1971 while logging five top-10 money finishes. Always known as a fine putter, the University of Florida graduate's decline began in 1971 when he began trying to turn his fade into a draw, resulting in three mediocre years before a steady slide out of the limelight. He did make one final cameo, however, leading the 1975 U.S. Open at Medinah through 54 holes before finishing third, one stroke out of the John

Mahaffey–Lou Graham play-off. Beard also made his mark with *Pro* (World Publishing, 1970), a detailed book recounting life on the PGA Tour, as well as by winning the one-and-only **Frank Sinatra Invitational** in 1963.

PGA Tour Wins (11): 1965 Texas; 1967 Houston; 1969 Westchester
Ryder Cup: 1969 & '71 (2)

Chip Beck (USA)

In few competitive arenas can one fall from championship-caliber grace more swiftly or mysteriously than golf, and among modern professionals few have suffered such a decline more prominently than Fayetteville, North Carolina's, Charles Henry "Chip" Beck (b. 9/12/1956). A collegiate star at the University of Georgia and a four-time PGA Tour winner between 1988 and 1992, Beck looked for all the world like a player whose solid, accurate game would serve him long term in the manner of a Jay Haas or Scott Hoch, particularly following a second-place finish on the money list in 1988. In 1991 Beck became only the second player in Tour history to shoot 59 (in the third round of the Las Vegas Invitational), though unlike his predecessor Al Geiberger, Beck did not hold on to win the tournament. He was also a highly successful Ryder Cup player in 1989, '91 and '93, fashioning an overall record of 6-2-1.

In the eyes of some, Beck's undoing began on Sunday of the 1993 Masters when, trailing Bernhard Langer by three, he elected not to go for the 15th green in two from 240 yards. In reality, the decision seems a reasonable one (particularly since many of those criticizing his "conservativeness" would have been the first to lambaste him had he overswung on a 3-wood and blown himself to bits), and, at any rate, it wasn't until 1995 that the wheels really began to come off. Winless and relegated to minitours, Beck has been trying to put them back on ever since.

John Beck (UK)

Englishman John Beaumont Beck (b. 1899) represented Great Britain—though only in a losing foursomes effort—at the 1928 Walker Cup matches in Chicago. He also twice served as Walker Cup captain in the war-bracketing matches of 1938 and '47, both played at St. Andrews. The former event holds a special significance, for it was the scene of Britain's first Walker Cup triumph, a 7-4 victory that led Henry Longhurst to lavishly credit Beck "who imbued into a miscellany of individuals of varying temperament, age, occupation, and nationality a unity of spirit which proved invincible."

Rich Beem (USA)

Though not perhaps among golf's truly great longshots, New Mexico State's Rich Beem (b. Phoenix, Arizona, 8/24/1970) certainly surprised many with his victory at the 2002 **PGA Championship,** a hard-fought one-stroke win over Tiger Woods at the Hazeltine National GC. Of course, Beem had won just the week before, at the Stableford-oriented **International,** but with only a 1999 **Kemper Open** win and two subsequent lean years on his résumé, his courageous handling of Woods certainly seemed epic—at least until Ben Curtis happened along at the Open Championship a year later. Having returned from a self-imposed exile from the game in the mid-1990s, Beem has certainly made good at golf's highest level. However, only time will tell if his stellar 2002 represents a step upward, or if he will join that long list of players whose Major championship total is a single PGA.

Notah Begay III (USA)

A Walker Cup player, three-time collegiate All-American and former teammate of Tiger Woods at Stanford, Notah Begay III (b. Albuquerque, New Mexico, 9/14/1972) became only the second Native American to win a PGA Tour event at the 1999 **Reno-Tahoe Open,** a full quarter-century after Rod Curl's 1974 victory at Colonial. Of course, Begay followed his breakthrough with a same-season win at **Kingsmill** (in a play-off over Tom Byrum), then back-to-back victories at **Memphis** and **Hartford** in 2000, placing himself none too far behind the streaking Woods as the new millennium picked up steam. Unfortunately, a pair of torn discs limited him to 12 starts in 2001 and has continued to slow him since, at least temporarily derailing a highly promising career.

Being half Navajo, one-quarter San Felipe, and one-quarter Isleta, Begay has conducted junior clinics on Indian reservations and welcomed the challenge of being a role model to younger Native Americans. Interestingly, Begay is also that rare player who is completely ambidextrous with his putter, allowing him to switch sides at will and thus avoid more difficult away-breaking putts entirely.

John Beharrell (UK)

A native of Warwickshire, England, John Charles Beharrell (b. 1938) grabbed his piece of history by winning the 1956 **British Amateur** at Troon, breaking Gordon Barry's previous record as the championship's youngest-ever winner. Though he beat a solid field without benefit of any freakish weather or apparently flukish play, Beharrell would seldom be heard from in future years, save for marrying another young English phenom of the period, Ms. Veronica Anstey.

Max Behr (USA)

One of the unsung heroes of Golden Age American golf, New York native Max Howell Behr (1884–1955) was a graduate of New Jersey's Lawrenceville School and, in 1905, Yale University. A talented player, Behr starred on a 1905 NCAA Championship team that was coached by Scottish émigré Robert Pryde (the first of nine consecutive NCAA team titles captured by the Bulldogs). Behr also maintained a keen (if lopsided) competitive rivalry with four-time U.S. Amateur champion Jerome Travers, to whom he lost the final of the 1908 U.S. Amateur; in fact, Travers defeated him on all but one occasion (the final of the 1910 **New Jersey Amateur**).

In 1914, Behr's influence on the game expanded tenfold when he became editor of the new magazine *Golf Illustrated.* Steering the publication toward the wide-ranging coverage for which it is well remembered, he also wrote a good deal of copy before stepping down in 1918, following the death of his wife. Behr then moved to California where golf's popularity was exploding, settling into a life of philosophizing about the game and designing courses. Though his architectural output was numerically small and geographically limited, it boasted several important entries, not the least of which was the Lakeside GC of Hollywood. There, on essentially flat and barren ground, he incorporated both the Los Angeles River and some man-made sand dunes to create a layout that his friend Dr. Alister MacKenzie called "one of the best in the world."

A traditionalist who, at the same time, advocated such oddities as a floating ball, Behr passed away in Los Angeles at age 71.

Notable Courses: Lakeside GC, California; Rancho Santa Fe GC, California

Andrew Bell (USA)

The son of a Scottish-born Burlington, Iowa, merchant, Andrew Bell was sent to study the ministry at the University of Edinburgh in approximately 1880. Upon returning to Burlington in the summer of 1883, he laid out a rudimentary four-hole course upon his father's land, the third earliest documented case of the modern game of golf being played on American soil. History tells us that Bell was something more than a neophyte too, for according to Joseph Davis, a Chicago writer who interviewed him late in life, he possessed several clubs supposedly given to him by Willie Park Jr. and Freddie Tait, and later briefly pursued a career as a golf professional. His four-hole course,

however, disappeared upon his autumn return to Scotland in 1883.

George Bell (Australia)

Though never a top-shelf professional competitor, club pro George Bell was famous throughout Australia during the 1970s and '80s as a long driver of great repute. Standing large (but not huge) at 6'2", he was frequently known to drive it close to 400 yards in a time before unchecked technology rendered such things semi-common. In a particularly memorable feat, he once hit a 2-wood across Penrith's Nepean River, an estimated carry of 320 yards. Such prodigious hitters frequently are not the best of course managers, yet we must acknowledge that on this occasion Bell was evidently in tune enough to recognize that he simply didn't need a driver.

Judy Bell (USA)

Though perhaps most recognized as the USGA's first female president (1996–97), Wichita, Kansas, native Judy Bell (b. 1937) made her name as a top amateur performer of the 1950s and '60s, three times winning the **Kansas Women's** title and competing in the 1950 U.S. Women's Open at age 14. Twice an NCAA individual runner-up while attending Wichita State, Bell also claimed three **Broadmoor Invitationals** and the 1963 **Trans-Mississippi,** twice appeared on winning Curtis Cup teams (1960 and '62), and, in 1964, firing a third-round 67 at the U.S. Women's Open that would remain the event's standard for 14 years. Also a Curtis Cup captain in 1986 and '88, Bell holds the rare distinction of coaching a male national team at the 2000 World Amateur Team event in Germany in addition to being the first woman member of the USGA Executive Committee.

Peggy Kirk Bell (USA)

Findlay, Ohio's, Margaret Anne Kirk (b. 10/28/1921) was a Rollins College graduate and a three-time **Ohio Ladies** champion who went on to capture the 1949 **North & South Amateur,** the 1950 **Eastern Amateur,** and, most impressively, the 1949 **Titleholders,** an LPGA Major championship in which she finished two ahead of the legendary Babe Zaharias. An easy choice for the 1950 Curtis Cup team (where she defeated Jeanne Bisgood in singles), Kirk turned professional soon thereafter and was a charter member of the LPGA. However, her future would lay far more in teaching and, after marrying Warren Bell, in owning/operating North Carolina's Pine Needles Resort, the two-time U.S. Women's Open site where the Bells have held court since 1953. A winner of countless major awards for her service to golf, Mrs. Bell was a groundbreaking female instructor as well as a pioneer in the development of resort golf schools, of which Pine Needles stood among the earliest.

William F. Bell (USA)

The son of Golden Age architect William P. Bell, the younger Billy Bell (1918–1984) joined the family business after graduating from the University of Southern California, eventually taking over the firm upon the elder's 1953 passing. Though not quite the equal of his father in terms of style and creativity, he nonetheless established himself by the late 1950s as *the* name in postwar California design, completing more than 75 Golden State courses including such name venues as Torrey Pines, Industry Hills, and the Canyon CC in Palm Springs. Following eerily in his father's footsteps, William F. died of a heart attack in Pasadena, California, in his mid-60s.

William P. Bell (USA)

A former agricultural student in Pittsburgh, Canonsburg, Pennsylvania, native William Park Bell (1886–1953) moved to Southern California in 1911, becoming caddie master at the Annandale CC, then greenkeeper at Pasadena GC. He entered the field of golf course architecture by working as a construction foreman on several of Willie Watson's Southern California designs, then eventually started his own practice in 1920.

By any definition Bell was successful in his own right, chalking up more than 75 new designs, primarily in California. What complicates our assessment, however, is the loose partnership that he formed with that giant of Golden Age architecture, Captain George C. Thomas Jr., during the 1920s. For beginning with the redesign in 1925 of Santa Barbara's La Cumbre CC, Bell would collaborate on Thomas' final eight projects, with the exact nature of his input occasionally uncertain. Bell, for example, has frequently received solo credit for the 1930 Stanford University GC, though evidence suggests that he actually only performed construction of an ailing Thomas' plans.

Perhaps because of Thomas' iconic status, Bell has often been portrayed as little more than his construction man, but this is not entirely fair. For if nothing else, early photographs illustrate conclusively that the famous "Thomas bunkering style" was far more rooted in Bell's pre-collaboration form than Thomas' own—and this in itself is no small legacy.

Notable Courses: Arizona Biltmore GC, Adobe Course, Arizona (BO); **El Caballero CC, California (NLE); Royal Palms CC, California (NLE);** Tijuana CC (neé Agua Caliente), Mexico

Deane Beman (USA)

Though far better known to some readers as Tim Finchem's predecessor as PGA Tour Commissioner, Deane Beman (b. Washington, D.C., 4/22/1938) was one of the finest amateurs of his time and, eventually, a fairly successful professional. Hesitant to leave a highly successful insurance brokerage in Bethesda, Maryland, Beman initially resisted playing for pay, instead winning the 1959 **British Amateur** (beating fellow American Bill Hyndman at Royal St. George's), the 1960 **U.S. Amateur** (routing R. W. Gardner 6 and 4 at the St. Louis CC), and the 1963 **U.S. Amateur** (over R. H. Sikes at Iowa's Wakonda Club). He was also a member of four consecutive Walker Cup teams between 1959 and 1965, recording an 8-2-2 overall record and going undefeated in singles.

Finally turning professional in 1969, Beman would go on to win four times on the PGA Tour including, as a rookie, the 1969 **Texas Open.** He also tied for second at the '69 U.S. Open, one stroke behind improbable winner Orville Moody. But standing only 5'5", Beman had difficulty keeping up on an increasingly power-oriented PGA Tour and on March 1, 1974, replaced Joseph C. Dey in the office of the commissioner. During his 20-year watch, the Tour experienced unprecedented growth, gaining much wider television exposure and launching both the Champions (née Seniors) Tour in 1980 and the developmental Nationwide (née Hogan) Tour a decade later. Beman also was instrumental in the development of Tournament Players Clubs, the nationwide chain of "stadium" courses, few of which have lived up to Pete Dye's spectacular original in Ponte Vedra Beach, Florida.

PGA Tour Wins (4): 1969 Texas
Major Amateur Wins (4): 1959 British Amateur; 1960 & '63 U.S. Amateur; 1960 Trans-Miss
Walker Cup: 1959–65 (4)

Maurice Bembridge (UK)

One of a handful of touted British professionals to emerge during the late 1960s, Worksop, England's, Maurice Bembridge (b. 2/21/1945) has achieved a fair degree of success on several continents, winning in New Zealand, Zambia, and thrice in the **Kenyan Open** (1968, '69, and '79) in addition to seven official European Tour victories. Among the latter, the 1971 **British Masters** and 1979 **Benson & Hedges International** likely stand the tallest, though Bembridge also holds the distinction of capturing the *News of the World* match play in 1969, an event of great import dating back to the days of the Triumvirate. Bembridge was also a four-time Ryder Cupper (1969–75) with a 6-8-3 ledger and appeared in four Masters, for 12 years holding a piece of the Augusta National course record after shooting 64 in the 1974 final round.

Tom Bendelow (UK/USA)

History has perhaps been less kind to Tom Bendelow (1868–1936) than his pioneering role in American golf deserves. A native of Aberdeen, Scotland, and a skilled amateur player, Bendelow moved to the United States at age 24 where he worked as a typesetter with the old New York *Herald*. Three years later, he answered an advertisement to teach golf to an affluent Long Island family upon whose estate he soon laid out several primitive holes. Bitten anew by the golfing bug, Bendelow soon built several more rudimentary layouts around the New York area, then became manager of Van Cortlandt Park, the nation's first municipal course, which he renovated and expanded to 18 holes.

As an employee of the A. G. Spalding sporting goods company, which he joined in the mid-1890s, Bendelow traveled much of America, laying out countless rather primitive early courses with a technique that was mockingly dubbed "Eighteen-stakes-on-a-Sunday-afternoon." Only by 1920, when he replaced William Langford as lead golf course designer for Chicago's American Park Builders, did Bendelow elevate his technique to a more refined and modern standard. Utilizing drawings, plaster models, and the like, he not only completed the best of his work in this period but also lectured and wrote about golf architecture extensively. Never one whose design portfolio might be confused with that of a MacKenzie or Tillinghast, Tom Bendelow was, nevertheless, one of American golf's most important apostles.

Notable Courses: Dyker Beach GC, New York; Medinah CC, No. 3, Illinois (BO); Olympia Fields CC, South Course, Illinois; **Van Cortland Park GC, New York (BO)**

Jim Benepe (USA)

One of the great lightning bolts in the history of the PGA Tour, Sheridan, Wyoming, native Jim Benepe (b. 10/24/1963) was the rare modern player to win his first-ever Tour start, the 1988 **Western Open** at Chicago's Butler National GC. In the field on a sponsor's exemption, Benepe, a former All-American at nearby Northwestern University, was tied for the lead before three-putting the 72nd hole to fall one behind popular veteran Peter Jacobsen. Jacobsen, however, then fired a 6-iron over the home

green and into a creek, handing the shocked Benepe the title. Benepe would disappear from the top 125 a year later, with the 1988 Western being his sole moment in the limelight.

Harry Bentley (UK)

A native of Manchester, England, Harry Geoffrey Bentley (b. 1907) was a capable career amateur who made his living with his brother Arnold (also a fine player) in a paper manufacturing concern. Though never a winner of the British Amateur, Bentley won the **English, French, German,** and **Italian** titles and twice appeared in Walker Cup play. On the first occasion, in 1938 at St. Andrews, he and Ireland's Jimmy Bruen halved their foursomes match with Johnny Fischer and Chuck Kocsis, helping Britain to its first-ever Walker Cup victory.

Patty Berg (USA)

Though equipment changes, agronomical developments, and varying levels of competition make cross-generational comparisons largely subjective, no discussion of golf's greatest female players can proceed very far without considering one Patricia Jane Berg. A native of Minneapolis (b. 2/13/1918) who grew up playing football with the boys and attending the University of Minnesota, Berg was a fine natural athlete who came into golf on the heels of her avid father and brother. Good enough to appear in a 1935 exhibition match with Walter Hagen, Johnny Revolta, and Horton Smith, she was, that same year, a U.S. Women's Amateur finalist, losing to Glenna Collett Vare 3 and 2 at age 17. In 1936 she made the first of her two Curtis Cup appearances before finally winning the **Amateur** in 1938 at Chicago's Westmoreland CC, having again lost in the final a year earlier. Berg would also claim the 1938 **Western Amateur,** the 1938 and '39 **Trans-Mississippi,** and five straight **Doherty Invitationals** (1936–40) before turning professional in 1940, some 10 years ahead of the LPGA's founding.

Assessing Berg's professional record is no easy task, particularly since 22 of her 60 credited victories took place prior to the reliability of LPGA record-keeping. Thus while we cannot be certain as to how many events she actually entered, it surely was far fewer than the all-time LPGA victory queen, 88-time winner Kathy Whitworth. In 1940, for example, only three events were available to women professionals, with two being added, for a grand total of five, in 1941. Also, it must be noted that Berg missed 18 months, beginning in late 1941, after a car accident, and a similar stretch while serving as a Marine recruiter during World War II. Berg, then, certainly gathered her 60 victories over considerably fewer starts—though it is interesting to note that from 1950 to 1968 (the LPGA's first 18 years of existence), her winning percentage of 12.9 percent was only moderately better than Whitworth's career yield of 10.5 percent. And Whitworth, we can be sure, played against somewhat deeper fields.

Major championships, however, are another story, for among Berg's 60 wins, fully one-quarter were events deemed the Majors of the day: seven **Western Opens,** seven **Titleholders Championships** (the first three as an amateur), and the first **U.S. Women's Open** in 1946. While the strength of those early fields is forever an issue, Berg's total of 15 Majors (in 99 career starts) still represents the all-time LPGA mark, a number made even more impressive by the fact that for many of her legitimately competitive years, only three Majors appeared on the schedule (the LPGA Championship not coming into existence until 1955). Further, it is a record unlikely to be broken anytime soon, for even though today's players have four opportunities annually, the closest active pursuer is Annika Sorenstam with eight.

While we cannot reasonably compare Berg's record directly with Whitworth or, for that matter, Mickey Wright, we pretty well can with her contemporary, the great Babe Zaharias, at least for their directly overlapping years of 1950–55. And while Zaharias' 36 victories during this stretch came in roughly 30 percent fewer starts (owing largely to ill health), Berg's 27 period wins are nothing to scoff at. Also, official LPGA records cite the Babe's low competitive round as being a 67—a number Berg trounced, with an improbable 64, at the Richmond (California) CC in 1952.

But beyond all of her numbers, Patty Berg's importance to women's golf was surely greatest as an ambassador, a personality around which the fledgling sport could grow. A tireless traveler, Berg played countless exhibitions and clinics on the payroll of Wilson Sporting Goods, always relying upon her personality and boundless energy to win over golfers and non-golfers alike. The women's game literally grew up around her, particularly after the Babe's tragic illness and untimely death. Indeed Berg was, in her way, the LPGA's Walter Hagen or Arnold Palmer, for as fellow Hall of Famer Betsy Rawls once said: "She has done

Patty Berg, 1941

more to promote golf than any person in the history of the game."

Professional/LPGA Wins (60): 1937, '38, '39, '48, '53, '55 & '57 Titleholders; 1941, '43, '48, '51, '55, '57 & '58 Western Open; 1946 U.S. Women's Open; 1949 Tampa; 1953, '54, '55 & '57 World Championship; 1955 Orange Blossom; 1956 Dallas Civitan

Curtis Cup: 1936 & '38 (2)

1946-1960

	46	47	48	49	50	51	51	53	54	55	56	57	58	59	60
LPGA										-	2	6	-	2	4
US Open	1	9	T4	T4	5	8	9	3	12	5	T3	2	T9	6	17

Also won Western Opens and Titleholders, as listed above.

Roberto Bernardini (Italy)

One of Italy's stronger players in the late 1960s and early 1970s, Rome native Roberto Bernardini (b. 1944) was highly competitive among the best in Continental Europe. He occasionally competed in both the United Kingdom and the United States, twice appearing in the Masters where he tied for 29th in 1969. Closer to home, Bernardini captured two **Italian PGAs** as well as back-to-back **Swiss Opens** in 1968 and '69, the centerpiece of his Continental résumé.

Susie Berning (USA)

The 1963 **Oklahoma Women's Amateur** champion and a veteran of the men's golf team at Oklahoma City University, Susie Maxwell Berning (b. Pasadena, California, 7/22/1941) was truly of that rare breed who save their best competitive golf for the biggest stages. Indeed, of Berning's 11 career LPGA victories, four came in Major championships, including three **U.S. Women's Opens** between 1968 and 1973 and the 1965 **Western Open**. Berning's game was obviously well suited to the USGA's peculiar style of championship golf for beyond her victories, she logged five additional top-10 finishes in the Open, a particularly impressive number considering the relatively limited schedule Berning played (owing to family responsibilities) into the 1970s.

Silvia Bertolaccini (Argentina)

The finest female international player yet produced by Argentina, Silvia Bertolaccini (b. Rafaela, 1/30/1950) surprisingly won only one national title in her homeland before packing off to the LPGA Tour in 1975. A frequent top-20 money winner for the duration of the decade, Bertolaccini won four official tour events including two **Colgate Far East** titles (in Singapore, then Manila) in 1977 and '79. A long hitter who once carded a record-tying 29 for nine holes, Bertolaccini's form slipped a bit into the 1980s, though she proved herself still capable by winning the **Mazda Classic** in 1984.

Harry Berwick (Australia)

A career amateur until the ripe old age of 53, Mascot, Victoria's, Henry W. "Harry" Berwick (b. 1923) bore the powerful hands of one who began his working life as a bricklayer, his great strength helping to make him one of the finest drivers and long-iron players of his day. Berwick won two **Australian Amateurs** (1950 and '56), one **New Zealand Amateur** (1952), a **New Zealand Open** (1956), and four **New South Wales Amateur** titles, eventually becoming, in 1957, the sole Australian amateur ever to be invited to the Masters—though he declined to travel, apparently for economic reasons. Widely admired as a gracious competitor, Berwick surprised observers by turning professional at age 53, though his impact would prove considerably less than during his best amateur days.

Al Besselink (USA)

One of the all-time great characters in golf, Albert Cornelius Besselink (b. 6/10/1922) hailed from humble beginnings in Merchantville, New Jersey, riding an odd, looping swing and a ton of self-confidence to the University of Miami, then onto the PGA Tour. A handsome, dashing sort, Besselink ran with a colorful (if not altogether savory) crowd, claiming to have made far more money gambling than he ever did in prize money—no small boast given that he was a seven-time Tour winner and a top-10 finisher at the Masters in 1953 and '54.

Still, his gambling ruses tell a far more interesting story. In one favored ploy, Besselink would tank his closing third-round holes if he knew he was out of the running, placing himself among the earliest starters for the finale. He'd then bet his score against the top 10 leaders, inevitably winning when his playing conditions (no spike marks, gallery distractions, or pressure) proved vastly easier than those his "opponents" would face several hours later.

A protégé of Jimmy Demaret, who developed a similarly colorful fashion sense, Besselink once played his second shot at Augusta's famed 12th from a sand bar in Rae's Creek—then, in a Hagen-like stunt, requested a rake to fix his footprints. But in the end, Besselink could certainly play. Indeed, one of his biggest hauls came from laying $500 on himself, at 25-1, to win the inaugural **Tournament of Champions** in 1953. He did, and laughed all the way to the bank.

Franco Bevione (Italy)

The dominant force in Italian men's amateur golf for more than three decades, Franco Bevione (b. 1922) won the **Italian Closed Amateur** some 14 times between 1940 and 1971, as well as the larger-field **Open Amateur** in 1952, '56 and '57. The brother of the equally dominant Isa Goldschmid (née Bevione), he was an aggressive player of limited style, yet clearly capable of delivering high-level golf. His sole prominent wins outside of Italy were the 1956 **Swiss Amateur** and the 1959 **Scandinavian Amateur**.

Count Gustav Bielke (Sweden)

Long before Sweden began producing talented world-class golfers (particularly women) at roughly the same rate with which they churn out Volvos, Count Gustav Adolf Bielke (b. 1930) was something of an anomaly. He captured his country's **Junior** championship at age 18 but also ventured boldly throughout the Continent, winning national Junior crowns in **Belgium, Germany, Italy, Norway,** and **France.** As an adult, he would win the **Swedish Open Amateur** in 1951 and the **Scandinavian Open Amateur** (into which the Swedish title was absorbed) in 1956. He would also represent Sweden internationally nearly 30 times, including twice, as an amateur, at the World Cup.

Ray Billows (USA)

A capable competitor on the national level, seven-time **New York Amateur** champion Ray Billows is best recalled as a man unable to break through in the U.S. Amateur—though in finishing second on three occasions he surely came close. In 1937, Billows lost to 1933 U.S. Open champion Johnny Goodman in Portland, Oregon. Two years later it was two-time Amateur champion Bud Ward delivering the coup de grâce, this time at the North Shore CC in Chicago. Some nine years later in 1948, Billows returned to the final, only to lose 2 and 1 at the Memphis CC to another two-time winner Willie Turnesa. Billows also appeared on victorious Walker Cup teams in 1938 and '49.

Jeanne Bisgood (UK)

Born of good golfing stock, England's Jeanne Mary Bisgood (b. 8/11/1923) spent many years in various administrative capacities after a first-class postwar playing career. Doing most of her damage during the 1950s, Bisgood won **English Ladies** titles in 1951, '53, and '57, and supplemented them with a run of Continental Ladies crowns that included **Sweden** (1952), **Germany** (1953), **Italy** (1953), **Portugal** (1954), and **Norway** (1955). She was a three-time Curtis Cup participant between 1950 and 1954 as well as the nonplaying captain of the 1970 team that lost at Brae Burn.

Don Bisplinghoff (USA)

Orlando, Florida, product Donald M. Bisplinghoff (b. 1935) was the 1952 **USGA Junior Boys** champion as well as four-time **Florida Amateur** winner between 1953 and 1968. He also scored notable victories at the 1955 **North** & South (defeating Bill Campbell 5 and 4) and in three **Florida Opens** (1955, '61 and '62), where he beat primarily professional fields. Though never making major noise at the U.S. Amateur, Bisplinghoff is recalled for his visit to the 1955 British Amateur where a 78-year-old Bernard Darwin had difficulty remembering his tricky last name. "Bisplinghoff, Bisplinghoff, Bisplinghoff," Darwin repeated solemnly. "It's like putting. Some days you have it, and some days you don't."

Thomas Björn (Denmark)

Already firmly established as Denmark's best-ever golfer, Thomas Björn (b. Silkeborg, 2/18/1971) is a two-time Ryder Cup and three-time World Cup player with 10 strong international victories at the time of this writing. Though many will first recall his late collapse at the 2003 Open Championship (where a double bogey at the 70th and bogey at the 71st left him one behind winner Ben Curtis), Björn has frequently distinguished himself under pressure, particularly at the 2001 **Dubai Desert Classic** where he outgunned a hot Tiger Woods head-to-head. He also defeated Sergio Garcia in a play-off for the 1999 **Dunlop Phoenix Open** in Japan and counts the 1996 **Loch Lomond World Invitational,** the 1998 **Spanish Open,** and a pair of **BMW Internationals** among his European wins.

An occasionally recurring neck injury and the psychological damage inflicted by so prominent an Open collapse may hinder Björn, but the Dane has repeatedly proven himself a strong, powerful player with reserves of confidence and resilience. Yet to win on the American PGA Tour, he accepted fully exempt status there for the first time in 2004.

Ted Blackwell (UK)

Edward B. H. Blackwell (b. 1866) was the best known of four golfing brothers from St. Andrews, though a good deal of his legacy stems from being the homeland's last, doomed line of defense during Walter Travis' looting of the British Amateur in 1904. There, as everywhere, Blackwell stood out for his prodigious power, for as Darwin wrote: "His name will always be synonymous with colossal driving and he was not only immensely powerful but had a swing which for combined grace and fury of hitting was glorious to behold." Blackwell was also captain of the R&A in 1925–26 and, though never a national champion, is reported once to have driven an old gutty ball from St. Andrews' 18th tee onto the R&A clubhouse steps, a nearly 350-yard blast that, like Jack Nicklaus' similar feat decades later, was surely at least somewhat wind-assisted.

Jane Blalock (USA)

Despite credentials as an outstanding player, Portsmouth, New Hampshire, native and Rollins graduate Jane Blalock (b. 9/19/1945) is perhaps best remembered for an untoward bout of litigation with the LPGA after being suspended for "actions inconsistent with the code of ethics" in 1972. Accused by fellow players of not correctly replacing her ball after marking it at the Bluegrass Invitational in Louisville, she fought the year-long suspension by filing a $5 million antitrust lawsuit, then continuing to play throughout the proceedings with her winnings being held in escrow. In 1973 a U.S. District Court sided with Blalock, she was reinstated and awarded the nearly $44,000 in interim winnings.

Beyond this regrettable interlude, Blalock's career shined, beginning with being named 1969's LPGA Rookie of the Year and proceeding, through 27 career wins, right on into the mid-1980s. All told, Blalock amassed 11 top-10 finishes on the official money list, including a run of 10 straight from 1971 to 1980. Twenty-four of her victories came during this stretch (during which she won more than 9 percent of her starts), and she managed four wins in a single season on four separate occasions (1972, '74, '77, and '79). Another example of Blalock's remarkable consistency was a streak of 12 years, beginning in 1969, without missing a single cut. Unfortunately, she is also the not-so-happy holder of the LPGA record for the most wins without a Major championship, though she did capture the inaugural **Dinah Shore** event in 1972, some 11 years before it would be granted official Major status.

LPGA Wins (27): 1972 Dinah Shore; 1972 & '76 Dallas Civitan; 1979 Rochester; 1978 & '79 Orange Blossom; 1978 Wykagyl

Homero Blancas (USA)

A hometown product who starred at the University of Houston, Homero Blancas (b. 3/7/1938) was the 1965 PGA Tour Rookie of the Year and a member of the victorious 1973 Ryder Cup team, as well as a winner of five PGA Tour events, primarily during the 1970s. Prior to turning pro, Blancas was twice an All-American and also gained lasting fame by shooting the lowest competitive score ever recorded in the United States, a stunning 55 over a 5,002-yard course in Longview, Texas, during a 1962 collegiate event. Though his professional career went downhill following late-season knee surgery in 1974, Blancas did count one particularly memorable event among his victories, a one-stroke triumph over Lee Trevino and Gene Littler at the 1970 **Colonial** after which Trevino was heard to quip: "Bring on the champagne. We've never had a Mexican winner *and* runner-up."

John Bland (South Africa)

One of the straightest hitters in all of golf, Johannesburg's John Bland (b. 9/22/1945) was a 20-time winner of professional events in his native South Africa and also tasted success on the European Tour, particularly at the 1983 **Benson & Hedges International** where his 273 total was enough to defeat Bernhard Langer by one. With Bland's next most prominent victory being the 1977 **South African PGA,** however, he was largely viewed as something of a journeyman prior to reaching the Shangri-la of senior golf at age 50. Henceforth he won the 1995 **London Masters** in his first senior start, then went to America for a win in **Los Angeles,** and, a year later, four more Champions Tour titles. He has since claimed back-to-back **South African Senior Opens** (1997 and '98) and three second-place finishes in the Senior British Open, maintaining a busy schedule on multiple continents.

P. J. Boatwright (USA)

A native of Augusta, Georgia, Purvis James Boatwright (1927–1991) made a name for himself as a competitive golfer after World War II, winning both the **North Carolina Amateur** (1951) and **Open** (1957), and qualifying for four U.S. Amateurs and the 1950 U.S. Open at Merion (where he made the cut). Having served as executive secretary of the Carolinas Golf Association beginning in 1955, Boatwright moved on to the USGA in 1959, eventually succeeding Joe Dey as executive director a decade later. He maintained this position until 1980, when succeeded by Harry Easterly.

Tommy Bolt (USA)

There are names that all golfers know: Nicklaus, Hogan, Jones, and several other immortals. And while Tommy Bolt (b. Haworth, Oklahoma, 3/31/1918) may not be quite as famous as those three legends, he truly isn't very far behind. The shame of it, of course, is that Bolt's notoriety comes for all the wrong reasons. For while many a Bolt story has been exaggerated, and men like Lefty Stackhouse, Ivan Gantz, and Don Cherry were far more out of control, Thomas Henry Bolt has for many years served as golf's poster child for a burning, uncontrollable temper.

Bolt stories, of course, are legion. Heaving his favorite driver in a lake. Advising players never to break their drivers and putters during the same round. Being told by his caddie to use a 2-iron where a 9 would suffice, as the 2 was the lone serviceable club left in the bag. Such tales have grown exponentially over the years, often making Bolt seem more of a caricature than the tough, competitive, and tremendously talented player that he was. Yet here was a man who, upon missing a short putt, really did glare skyward and painfully intone: "Why don't You come on down here and play me one time?"

Coming on Tour at the ripe old age of 34, the dapper Bolt was a winner right away, first at Pinehurst's old **North & South Open,** then, in years to come, in virtually every corner of the country. All told he would capture 15 PGA Tour victories with the biggest, by far, being the 1958 **U.S. Open** at Tulsa's Southern Hills CC. There, playing in stifling heat, Bolt defeated a 22-year-old Gary Player by four, reaching the peak he had always dreamed of and, by his own admission, losing a bit of competitive edge thereafter.

There are those who will say that given his remarkable talent, Bolt was something of an underachiever, and perhaps there is some truth to that. His swing, after all, was generally rated second only to Snead's, he was a superb driver of the ball who could move it either direction with ease, and his irons landed softer than anyone save Hogan. It was a package that would keep Bolt at the top of his game for many years, allowing him very nearly to win the 1971 PGA (where he eventually finished third) at age 55. There is little question also that Bolt was the best 60- and 70-year-old player in the world in his day, though he came along just a bit too soon to display his wares on the modern, big-money Champions Tour.

Bolt, for his part, learned to have fun with his tempestuous reputation, even writing a book entitled *How to Keep Your Temper on the Golf Course* (David McKay, 1969). But after all the hyperbole and legend, there was still the competitive, super-talented golfer, a man who, upon losing interest in Dan Jenkins' explanation of Clyde Barrow and Bonnie Parker, interrupted with: "Well, son, why don't you just go out and round up them two, and Old Tom'll play their low ball."

PGA Tour Wins (15): 1951 North & South; 1952 Los Angeles; 1953 & '55 San Diego; 1958 Colonial; **1958 U.S. Open**
Ryder Cup: 1955 & '57 (2)

1950-1971

	50	51	52	53	54	55	56	57	58	59	60
Masters	-	-	T3	T5	T12	T22	T8	MC	T32	T30	T20
US Open	MC	T29	T7	MC	T6	T3	T22	WD	1	T38	WD
British	-	-	-	-	-	-	-	-	-	-	-
PGA	-	-	-	T17	T3	T3	T64	T9	T5	T17	T57

	61	62	63	64	65	66	67	68	69	70	71
Masters	T4	MC	T37	MC	T8	T17	T26	-	-	-	-
US Open	T22	MC	MC	-	-	-	MC	-	-	MC	-
British	-	-	-	-	-	-	-	-	-	-	-
PGA	-	T30	-	WD	-	-	-	-	MC	-	3

Angela Ward Bonallack (UK)

The longtime wife of Michael Bonallack, the former Angela Ward (b. 1937) has herself enjoyed an exceptional amateur career, beginning with a **British Girls** title in 1955, then highlighted by **English Ladies** championships in 1958 and '63 (with runner-up finishes in 1960, '62 and '72). Also a two-time finalist in the British Ladies, Ms. Bonallack frequently ventured onto the Continent in her early competitive years, winning the Ladies titles of **Sweden** (1955), **Germany** (1955), **Scandinavia** (1956), and **Portugal** (1956). An obvious candidate for the Curtis Cup, she appeared in six straight matches between 1956 and 1966, amassing a respectable overall record of 6-8-1. Ms. Bonallack also competed in the occasional professional field, finishing as low amateur at the 1975 and '76 LPGA Colgate European Ladies Opens contested at Sunningdale.

Michael Bonallack (UK)

A 2000 inductee into the World Golf Hall of Fame, Chigwell, England's, Sir Michael Bonallack, O.B.E. (b. 12/31/1934), is, without question, the finest career amateur produced by Great Britain in the modern era. His record of achievement both on and off the course is a massive one, ranging from five **British Amateur** and five **English Amateur** victories to captaining the R&A in 2000 and serving as its all-important secretary from 1983 to 1999.

Graced with an iconoclastic swing but a world-class short game and putting stroke, Bonallack first came to notice in 1952 as the **British Boys** champion. He made use of his military time by winning the 1955 **Army** title, then took several more years to find his stride at the highest reaches of amateur golf. He took his first **British Amateur** in 1961, defeating Jimmy Walker 6 and 4 at Turnberry, then won again in 1965, this time at Royal

Porthcawl over Clive Clark. But Bonallack's greatest run would come at the end of the decade when he would capture three Amateurs in succession, from 1968 to 1970. In the first, at Troon, he dismissed good friend Joe Carr in the final while in the later two, played at Hoylake and Royal County Down, he defeated American Bill Hyndman.

Though the British was obviously the marquee event, Bonallack saved some of his most spectacular golf for the **English Amateur,** particularly in 1968 at Ganton where he defeated David Kelley 12 and 11, a runaway in which Bonallack shot an eye-popping 61 in the morning round. In a demonstration of an altogether different sort of talent, he won the 1963 English final at Burnham and Berrow by getting up-and-down an incredible 22 times in 36 holes, absolute proof of his short game supremacy.

The remainder of Bonallack's golfing accomplishments could fill a page, but especially worth mentioning are two low amateur finishes in the Open Championship, playing in every Walker Cup match from 1957 to 1973, captaining the team in 1971 and '73, and representing England in more international matches by far than any other man. The kingpin of a prominent golfing family, Bonallack's wife is six-time Curtis Cup player Angela Ward, while his sister Sally Barber saw Curtis Cup action in 1962.

Aubrey Boomer (UK)

A native of the golf-loving Channel Islands, Aubrey Basil Boomer (1897–1989) was the son of Grouville schoolmaster George Boomer—the very gentleman who taught local youths such as Harry Vardon and Ted Ray to read and write. Aubrey followed in the golfing footsteps of his older brother Percy, though his own playing skills certainly ranked higher, counting five **French,** three **Dutch,** one **Italian,** and two **Belgian Opens** among his trophies, as well as a 1927 victory in Argentina and two late-1920s appearances in the Ryder Cup. A consistent threat at the Open Championship, Aubrey bore the bad luck of peaking during the period in which Bobby Jones won the Claret Jug thrice in five years; his best finish was joint second—behind Jones—at St. Andrews in 1927. Boomer also set an all-time single-round scoring record by shooting 61 in a French PGA event, the field of which included a visiting American Ryder Cup team. This memorable round took place at Golf de St. Cloud, where the genial Aubrey joined the staff of brother Percy in 1914, just before enlisting for service in World War I.

Intn'l Wins (22): 1921, '22, '26, '29 & '31 French Open; 1922 & '26 Belgian Open; 1924, '25 & '26 Dutch Open; 1932 Italian Open
Ryder Cup: 1927 & '29 (2)

Percy Boomer (UK)

The older brother of the highly successful Aubrey, Grouville's Percy Boomer (1886–1949) was himself a player of note, winning the 1923 **Belgian Open** (following Aubrey, who'd won it in 1922), as well as later **Swiss** and **Dutch Opens.** Percy, however, would become far better known as a teacher, taking up residence in 1913 at France's exclusive Golf de St. Cloud where he worked with, among others, fellow Jersey islanders Harry Vardon and Ted Ray. Boomer also authored *On Learning Golf* (John Lane, 1942), a classic instructional volume that spells out his belief that the game is far more about developing the overall feel of the swing than its various mechanics, a task accomplished, he stated, through repetitive motion.

Julius Boros (USA)

Born: Fairfield, Connecticut, 2/31/1920 **Died:** Ft. Lauderdale, Florida, 5/28/1994

An accountant by trade and a kindly, unassuming sort by nature, Julius Nicholas Boros was a thickly built man of Hungarian descent who at first glance appeared among the least likely of golfing champions. Nicknamed "The Moose," Boros' gait was languid and his technique so syrupy smooth as to leave galleries shocked by the power it consistently generated. He was, by his own estimation, only a moderately good putter, but he seldom missed a fairway and was widely viewed as the finest wedge player in the game.

A fascinating golfing story, Boros had little interest in the competitive game well into his 20s, only turning professional at age 30. Even then there might have been questions as to his dedication but after the tragic death of his wife during childbirth, he poured himself wholeheartedly into the game. Considering his obvious lack of competitive seasoning, the results were astounding.

An 18-time winner on the PGA Tour, Boros' first victory came at the 1952 **U.S. Open** where a third-round 68 keyed a four-stroke victory over Ed "Porky" Oliver. He would continue to win consistently in the decade to follow, tacking on eight more titles before a career-best 1963 saw him win thrice. The third victory, another **U.S. Open,** was particularly impressive as the 43-year-old Boros had to go an extra 18 to beat Jacky Cupit and Arnold Palmer in a play-off at the Country Club. But even this paled in comparison to his penultimate win, the 1968 **PGA Championship,** where the now 48-year-old Boros became golf's oldest-ever Major winner by edging Palmer and Bob Charles in San Antonio. Asked later that same year, after his final victory at the **Westchester Classic,** if he planned to retire, Boros replied: "Retire to what? I already play golf and fish for a living."

Boros was a two-time Player of the Year (1952 and '63) and a four-time Ryder Cupper, amassing a 9-3-4 overall record. A man not given to a heavy practice regimen, he once wrote an instructional volume entitled *Swing Easy, Hit Hard* (Harper & Row, 1965)—and one doubts if any book, in this or any other discipline, has ever been more aptly titled.

PGA Tour Wins (18): 1952 & '63 U.S. Open; 1952 & '55 World Championship; 1960 & '63 Colonial; 1964 Greensboro; 1967 Phoenix; **1968 PGA Championship;** 1968 Westchester
Ryder Cup: 1959, 1963–'67 (4)

1950-1974

	50	51	52	53	54	55	56	57	58	59	60	61	62
Masters	T35	17	T7	T10	T16	T4	T24	MC	T39	T8	5	MC	T11
US Open	9	T4	1	T17	T23	T5	T2	T4	3	T28	T3	MC	-
British	-	-	-	-	-	-	-	-	-	-	-	-	-
PGA	-	-	-	-	-	-	-	-	T5	T44	T24	MC	T11

	63	64	65	66	67	68	69	70	71	72	73	74
Masters	T3	MC	MC	T28	5	T16	T33	T23	MC	MC	MC	T26
US Open	1	MC	T4	T17	WD	T16	T13	T12	T42	T29	7	WD
British	-	-	-	15	-	-	-	-	-	-	-	-
PGA	T13	T21	T17	T6	T5	1	T25	T26	T34	WD	MC	-

Pat Borthwick (Australia)

A hairdresser by trade, Sydney's Patricia Borthwick (b. 1926) is one of only four women to capture four **Australian Ladies** titles, winning in 1948, '49, '53 and '56 over four vastly different types of courses in four separate states. Considered a superior iron player whose top form compared her favorably with Australia's all-time best, the tall, athletic Borthwick also took six **New South Wales** titles between 1948 and 1958 (including five of six from 1948 to 1953) and regularly represented her country internationally through 1960.

Jocelyne Bourassa (Canada)

One of the finest all-around female athletes in Quebec history, Shawinigan-Sud product Jocelyne Bourassa (b. 5/30/1947) starred in sports as varied as track and volleyball at the University of Montreal while already a three-time provincial junior golf champion. She would also win four **Quebec** and two **Canadian Ladies** titles (the latter in 1965 and '71) before embarking on a short but not-unproductive LPGA Tour career. Bourassa initially was named Rookie of the Year in 1972 and the following season claimed her lone tour victory at Montreal's **La Canadienne Championship,** making her the only native ever to claim an LPGA event on Canadian soil. She later served as women's golf coach at Arizona from 1979 to 1980.

Dale Bourn (UK)

A great character and surely a bit eccentric, England's Thomas Arundale "Dale" Bourn (b. 1904) was a charmed sort who, in Henry Longhurst's words, "would drive into some impenetrable golfing jungle and not only find his ball teed-up but confidently expect to do so." Thus noted as a master of the grand recovery shot, he was surely best suited for match play in which he won the 1928 **French Amateur** and 1930 **English Amateur,** though he could do no better than runner-up at the larger British Amateur, a result he accomplished in 1933. Hardly a dedicated practicer, he was at once endearing and maddeningly annoying. Longhurst, once more: "There was only one Dale Bourn—perhaps there was only room for one—but there will never be another." He was killed during the scourge of his generation, World War II.

Ken Bousfield (UK)

A quiet, genial man whose inner toughness was revealed by his wartime service as a Royal Marine Commando, Marston Moor, England's, Ken Bousfield (1919–2000) won no less than 19 titles in the United Kingdom and Europe, mostly during the 1950s. A relatively short hitter who was impressively accurate, his best year may well have been 1955 when he won the inaugural **Volvo PGA** (then a closed British event), the first of two **German Opens,** and the old *News of the World* match-play title. Along with several more national Opens, Bousfield also took the 1957 **Dunlop Tournament,** a grueling 90-hole test that was in many ways a battle of attrition. A six-time Ryder Cup pick with a 5-5 overall record, he also gained some notoriety by teaming with John Jacobs in a 1956 stakes game against Harry Weetman and Arthur Lees, a £400 affair that represented a true throwback to the grand challenge matches of yesteryear.

Intn'l Wins (19): 1955 Volvo PGA; 1955 & '59 German Open; 1955 PGA Match Play; 1958 Belgian Open; 1958 Swiss Open; 1960 & '61 Portuguese Open
Ryder Cup: 1949, '51, 1955–61 (6)

Nanci Bowen (USA)

Tifton, Georgia, native and two-time University of Georgia All-American Nanci Bowen (b. 3/31/1967) has only one victory in nearly 15 full seasons on the LPGA Tour but it was a Major, the 1995 **Dinah Shore** where she edged Susie Redman by one. The win anchored a career-best 25th-place finish on the tour money list, a ranking she would closest approach in 1997 when she finished 38th. Despite having earned over $1 million, Bowen only cracked the top 60 on one other occasion, a 58th–place finish in 1996.

Jimmy Boyd (South Africa)

A native of Middleburg on the Eastern Transvaal, James Ramsey Boyd (b. 1916) was one of the great amateurs in South African history, winning regional, club, and provincial titles far too numerous to mention. A wartime pilot in the SAAF, Boyd is one of a small handful of players who have won both the **South African Amateur** and **Open,** the former in 1946 at Royal Johannesburg and 1958 at Bloemfontein (with additional runner-ups in 1949 and '53), the latter in 1953 at Royal Cape in a play-off over Otway Hayes. Seldom competing further from home than Rhodesia (Zimbabwe) and Mozambique, Boyd's career numbers were somewhat suppressed by the war, which consumed the prime playing years of his late 20s.

Auguste Boyer (France)

Widely viewed as the finest Continental player of the interwar period, Auguste Boyer (1896–1956) won an impressive 19 national titles throughout Europe between 1926 and 1936. Though surprisingly little has been recorded of his feats, he is reported to have possessed fine tempo, a tremendous short game, and an admired ability to maintain concentration for the entirety of an event. Naturally Boyer was successful at home, capturing **French Closed** titles in 1931, '33, '34 and '36. But he also dominated the 1930s ledger in Italy, Switzerland, and Germany at a time when British competition, though not at its best, generally did include Henry Cotton. Unfortunately, unlike his famed French predecessor Arnaud Massy, Boyer chose seldom to challenge the British on their home turf, leaving some question as to his rank in the larger scheme of things.

Intn'l Wins (19): 1930, '34 & '35 Swiss Open; 1930 & '31 Italian Open; 1930, '32, '35 & '36 German Open; 1932 Dutch Open; 1933 & '36 Belgian Open

Hugh Boyle (Ireland/UK)

Though a native of County Louth, Ireland, Hugh Boyle (b. 1936) was raised primarily in Birmingham, England, where, like so many others, he initially came to the game as a caddie. He first crashed the professional limelight in 1965 by firing an eye-popping 61 over the East course at Dalmahoy during the Senior Service Festival, though he would only tie for second in the event. Boyle did enjoy several European victories, however, as well as becoming the first British player ever to win in Japan, at the 1966 **Yomiuri Open.** He made one Ryder Cup appearance, in 1967 in Houston, where he went winless in three matches.

Pat Bradley (USA)

A native of Westford, Massachusetts, Pat Bradley (b. 3/24/1951) learned the game of golf just across the state line in Nashua, New Hampshire, before migrating to Florida International University for an All-American collegiate career. A natural athlete who was also an excellent skier, Bradley's powerful, rhythmic swing and smooth putting stroke assured her of a fine professional future—a point hammered home by her 12th-place finish at the 1973 Burdines Invitational while still an amateur.

After taking the LPGA Qualifying Tournament in 1974, Bradley finished 39th and 14th on the money list in her first two seasons despite going winless. Her breakthrough victory came in year three when she defeated Judy Rankin, Bonnie Lauer, and Sandra Post in sudden death to claim the 1976 **Girl Talk Classic** (Wykagyl), jump-starting one of the finest careers in modern women's golf. For over an 11-year span running from 1976 to 1986, Bradley would only once fail to finish among the top-10 money winners (11th, in 1982) while amassing 21 victories, including six Major championships. The pinnacle was reached in 1986 when she finished first on the money list and nearly won the

Grand Slam, capturing the **Dinah Shore,** the **LPGA Championship,** and the **du Maurier,** but tying for fifth at the U.S. Women's Open in Dayton, Ohio. Additional wins at the **S&H Golf Classic** and the **Nestle World Championships** (Samsung) cemented one of women's golf's all-time greatest seasons, which also included Player of the Year honors and a Vare Trophy.

But then, after a one-victory follow-up year in 1987, Bradley suddenly plunged to 109th on the money list in a futile 1988 that saw her make only eight cuts and fail to post even a single top-10 finish. Seeking medical attention, she was eventually determined to be suffering from hyperthyroidism, the same malady that had so adversely affected Masters champion Ben Crenshaw several years earlier. Following treatment, Bradley came back strong with fourth-, fifth-, and first-place money rankings and a total of eight wins from 1989 to 1991, the final year including four victories, plus another Vare Trophy and Player of the Year selection. Soon thereafter, however, Bradley,

who was now in her 40s, began slipping back into the upper reaches of the pack. Though always remaining among the top 30 money winners until 1997, and recording a final victory at the 1995 **Healthsouth Inaugural,** she would, by the millennium, be largely a part-time player.

A three-time Solheim Cup participant between 1990 and 1996, Bradley captained a losing American team in 2000 at Loch Lomond, then returned in 2002 to regain the cup on home soil, at historic Interlachen. A 1992 inductee into the LPGA Hall of Fame, Bradley was accompanied by the bell that her mother would ring on the family's back porch—regardless of hour—to celebrate another of her daughter's 31 career wins.

LPGA Wins (31): 1976 Wykagyl; 1977 & '85 Rochester; 1978 & '91 State Farm; **1980, '85 & '86 du Maurier; 1981 U.S. Women's Open; 1986 Dinah Shore; 1986 LPGA Championship;** 1986 Samsung WC, 1987 & '90 Safeway; 1990 Corning
Solheim Cup: 1990, '92 & '96 (3); 2000 & '02 Capt

1971-1996

	71	72	73	74	75	76	77	78	79	80	81	82	83
Dinah													T15
LPGA	-	-	-	T22	T26	-	T2	T54	T10	T15	T24	T12	T6
US Open	MC	-	-	-	T15	T17	T4	T12	T26	T16	1	T21	T8
du Maur									T19	1	T2	T38	T5

	84	85	86	87	88	89	90	91	92	93	94	95	96
Dinah	2	6	1	3	T74	6	9	T3	T17	T12	T19	T16	T23
LPGA	T2	T3	1	T21	-	T4	T9	T2	T15	MC	T3	T8	T51
US Open	T13	T12	T5	MC	MC	T3	T9	2	T29	T4	T25	T3	T3
du Maur	T19	1	1	T25	T39	T2	T8	T23	-	MC	T52	MC	T53

Harry Bradshaw (Ireland)

One of golf's more engaging fellows, Delgany, Ireland's, Harry Bradshaw (1913–1990), the son of a golf pro, developed into one of his nation's best and most popular postwar competitors. A portly man with a rhythmic three-quarter swing and a first-class short game, Bradshaw utilized one of golf's more unique grips, overlapping three fingers of his right hand so that only his right thumb and forefinger actually touched the shaft.

Bradshaw is famous for an unfortunate incident during the 1949 Open Championship at Royal St. George's where, during the second round, his drive at the fifth finished amidst the remains of a broken beer bottle. With the rules not yet allowing free relief (they would soon change), Bradshaw had little choice but to flail away, moving his first attempt all of 30 yards and ending up with a six. He would eventually tie Bobby Locke at 283, then get lambasted by 12 in the ensuing 36-hole play-off, leaving

historians to debate ever since the degree to which the beer bottle may have cost him the title.

Bradshaw did, however, prove himself a top-flight player on other occasions, most notably becoming the only native-born player to twice win the **Irish Open,** in 1947 at Portmarnock and '49 at Belvoir Park. He was also a two-time champion of the prestigious **British Masters** (1953 and '55), captured the 1958 **Volvo PGA,** and led the Irish to their sole **World Cup** triumph, at the 1958 contest in Mexico City. He was also a three-time Ryder Cup player, going 2-2-1 from 1953 to 1957. A true golfing legend of the Emerald Isle, Bradshaw spent many years as professional at Portmarnock after retiring from tournament play.

Mike Brady (USA)

Among the first American-born professionals to challenge the playing supremacy of the British immigrants,

Brighton, Massachusetts', Michael Joseph Brady (1887–1972) is rather ruefully recalled as a man who, particularly in U.S. Open play, generally came up one round shy. In 1911, for example, he joined a three-way play-off at the Chicago GC with Johnny McDermott and George Simpson but his 82 allowed McDermott to achieve immortality as the Open's first native-born winner. The following year, at the old CC of Buffalo, McDermott defended his crown successfully—but only after Brady, leading the field by four, ballooned to a final-round 79. And then there was 1919 at Brae Burn, where Brady led Walter Hagen by five after 54 holes, shot 80, then was summoned from the clubhouse to watch Hagen miss an eight-footer to win at the last. Unruffled, Hagen came back the next day and, after a controversial ruling at the 17th, won the play-off 77-78.

Brady did win nine official events on the PGA Tour, including the 1917 **North & South Open** and the 1922 **Western Open,** the latter considered virtually a Major championship in its day. But with three so crushing U.S. Open losses, it is inevitable that Brady will forever be recalled far more for his failures than for his not-insignificant successes.

James Braid (UK)

Born: Earlsferry, Scotland, 2/6/1870 **Died:** Tadworth, England, 11/27/1950

A quiet, modest, and decidedly kindly man, James Braid was the son of a Scottish ploughman who neither played golf nor approved of it as a vocation for his son. Thus apprenticed as a carpenter, Braid initially played strictly as an amateur while recovering from having gotten lime in his eyes, the lingering effects of which would bother his eyesight, in varying degrees, throughout his life. Standing comfortably over 6'0" with a long, lanky frame, Braid was by all accounts a curiously short hitter during his early days, and one of golf's more popular myths suggests that he literally awoke one morning suddenly able to drive the ball out of sight. In truth, it would appear that Braid simply acquired for himself a better-fitting driver that allowed his previously cramped and upright swing room to expand to a much fuller arc. Thereafter he was indeed one of the game's longer hitters, utilizing a smooth, powerful move once described by Horace Hutchinson as possessing "a divine fury."

Eventually deciding to ignore his father's wishes, Braid turned professional in 1893 after a childhood friend landed him a job as an apprentice clubmaker for the Army and Navy Stores in London. Playing weekend golf around the capital, he soon developed enough of a reputation to enter the Open Championship upon its first visit to England (at Royal St. George's) in 1894. An opening 91 made 10th place a decent finish, and soon enough a challenge match was arranged with the Open winner J. H. Taylor. When Braid emerged from the contest with a halve, his name and confidence were fully established, and it became simply a matter of time.

But quite a bit of time as it turned out, for despite finishing second to Harold Hilton in 1897 and a distant third to Taylor at St. Andrews in 1900 (where his putting did him in), Braid would end up waiting a total of six years before finally claiming the **Open Championship** in 1901 at Muirfield. On that breakthrough occasion, a third round of 74 set him five ahead of Vardon, allowing a "safe" 80 in difficult conditions to ultimately carry the day.

From this point forward, perhaps aided by the advent of the rubber ball, Braid went on to accomplish the unique feat of taking five **Open Championships** within a single decade, claiming the title again in 1905, '06, '08 and '10. Impressively, none of these victories were particularly close, all coming by at least four strokes and most made to appear closer by a bad hole or two while Braid played conservatively down the stretch. His Open record for the years 1901–10 thus reads as follows: 1st, 2nd, 5th, 2nd, 1st, 1st, 5th, 1st, 2nd, and 1st, an extraordinary stretch that was later approached by Thomson (finishing in the top two from 1952 to 1958) and bettered by Watson (five wins in only nine years, from 1975 to 1983).

There were, of course, precious few high-level tournaments in Braid's day, particularly as he suffered badly from sea sickness, making the trip across to Europe uncomfortable and the prospect of visiting America beyond consideration. He did, however, establish a formidable record in Britain's number two event, the old *News of the World* match play, which he won four times, beating Ted Ray in the event's 1903 inaugural, Tom Vardon in 1905, J. H. Taylor in 1907, and Ray again in 1911. Of nearly equal note, however, was his later reaching the 1927 final at age 57, where he was beaten by that most robust of younger men, Archie Compston.

The 1903, '11, and '27 Match Plays were all contested at Walton Heath, one of England's legendary clubs and the place Braid called home from its opening in 1904 right up until his death in 1950. It is doubtful that another club and professional of such high standing have ever enjoyed so long a relationship, and there is no question that each burnished its reputation greatly by its association with the other.

Braid was generally viewed as a man solely about golf, having only limited outside interests and playing virtually every day, even in old age. In this light it is hardly surprising that he developed a thriving trade as a golf course architect, eventually totaling nearly 200 designs or redesigns, virtually all within Great Britain. Among his standout creations were the Kings and Queens courses at Gleneagles and expansion/redesigns of Southport and Ainsdale (site of the 1933 Ryder Cup) and Scotland's Boat of Garten. He also performed renovations at Carnoustie, St. Enoduc, Nairn, Royal Troon, and numerous others, as well as a thorough redesign—relying exclusively upon a topographical map—of New York's historic St. Andrew's GC in 1930.

In his later years Braid evolved into an elder statesman of truly epic status, his tall, courtly presence and silver mustache leading to the famous observation that "No one could be as wise as James Braid looks."

Intn'l Wins (10): 1901, '05, '06, '08 & '10 British Open; 1903, '05, '07 & '11 PGA Match Play; 1910 French Open

1894-1921

	94	95	96	97	98	99	00	01	02	03	04	05	06	07
US Open	-	-	-	-	-	-	-	-	-	-	-	-	-	-
British	T10	-	6	2	T10	T5	3	1	T2	5	T2	1	1	T5

	08	09	10	11	12	13	14	15	16	17	18	19	20	21
US Open	-	-	-	-	-	-	-					-		
British	1	T2	1	T5	3	T18	T10						T21	T16

Johnnie Bramston (UK)

A native of Winchester, England, and the son of a golfing minister, J. A. T. "Johnnie" Bramston was a top young amateur who starred at Oxford and represented England in the first England-Scotland international match in 1902. Bramston, alas, was struck down by illness at a young age, before ever having the opportunity to strike gold in major events such as the British Amateur. Darwin, however, sung his posthumous praises, noting that "he had the power and the style and all the shots, together with the boyish confidence," while the great J. H. Taylor, who knew him well, observed: "It is my sound belief that if Johnnie had lived his golfing record would have rivaled that of the other Johnnie—Ball, and I can pay no higher tribute to his potentialities than that."

Gordon Brand Jr. (UK)

A winner of six national junior or amateur titles (including the **English, Scottish, Swedish,** and **Portuguese Open Amateurs**) before turning professional, Kirkcaldy, Scotland's, Gordon Brand Jr. (b. 8/19/1958) arrived with a bit more advanced billing than his solid, eight-victory European Tour career has perhaps lived up to. He won twice as a rookie in 1982—in the process setting rather a high bar for himself—and though the victory pace soon lessened, Brand twice has won the **European Open** (1984 and '93) as well as the 1987 **Dutch Open** and the 1989 **Benson & Hedges International.** Also a Ryder Cup pick in 1987 and '89, he managed a 2-4-1 record—respectable enough in the dark days but perhaps a bit less so in matches that saw European teams go 1-0-1.

Jeff Brauer (USA)

A University of Illinois graduate, architect Jeff Brauer (b. 1955) cut his teeth between 1977 and 1983 with the Chicago firm run by Ken Killian and Dick Nugent. Forming his own company in 1984, he is perhaps best known for a series of courses, both domestic and international, that he codesigned with three-time Major champion Larry Nelson beginning in 1990.

John Bredemus (USA)

Flint, Michigan, native John Bredemus (1883–1946) graduated from Princeton rather late (in 1912) with a degree in civil engineering. Having established himself as a superior track-and-field athlete and varsity football player, Bredemus finished second to Jim Thorpe in the 1912 AAU all-around track-and-field competition, ultimately receiving the first-place medal when Thorpe was so egregiously stripped of it.

Bredemus soon took up golf and was competing around the New York City area by 1914, turning pro two years later. Following World War I he moved to San Antonio where he worked as a high school principal, slowly drifting into the field of golf course architecture on the side. He designed his first course at nearby Del Rio in 1920, then became a full-time architect and golf professional soon thereafter. A cofounder of the Texas PGA and a pioneering agronomist, Bredemus' most recognizable design was surely the Colonial CC in Ft. Worth, which, after the replacement of three of his original holes, hosted the U.S. Open (won by Craig Wood) in 1941.

By the end of the 1930s Bredemus was living in Mexico, reportedly as the result of an income tax dispute with the

Gay Brewer

federal government. Building six more courses south of the border, he eventually returned to the Unites States, dying in Big Spring, Texas, of heart problems, at age 62.

Notable Courses: Colonial CC, Texas; Ridglea CC, North Course, Texas

Murle (Lindstrom) Breer (USA)

One of those not-so-rare players for whom the **U.S. Women's Open** has been a first professional victory, St. Petersburg, Florida, product Murle Lindstrom (b. 1/20/1939) took the prestigious title at Myrtle Beach's Dunes GC in 1962, defeating Ruth Jessen and Jo Anne Prentice by two. Though her career would eventually be slowed by the responsibilities of motherhood, Lindstrom (who later played under her married name of Breer) did win three more official LPGA events, perhaps the most important being 1962's season-ending **San Antonio Civitan,** for it quickly proved her Open crown no fluke. Amusingly, Breer only turned professional in 1957 upon being mistakenly introduced as one during her first significant competition—a process that has become somewhat more involved today.

Gay Brewer (USA)

Owing to a childhood elbow injury, Middletown, Ohio's Gay Brewer (b. 3/19/1932) possessed what for many years

was likely the PGA Tour's most eccentric swing, looping the club high to the outside going away, then changing planes comprehensively on the way down. But whatever observers might have felt about such a move, they cannot call it unsuccessful, for Brewer won 10 times on Tour and remained a solid money earner for more than two full decades.

No event figured more prominently in Brewer's career than the **Masters,** first in a heartbreaking way when, in 1966, he three-putted the final green to fall into a play-off with Jack Nicklaus, a contest he would lose by eight strokes. A year later, however, coming off of a scorching win at the **Pensacola Open,** Brewer rode a hot putter to a closing 67 and a one-shot victory over Bobby Nichols for his only Major championship. In 1972, Brewer would suffer a near-fatal ulcer on Wednesday of Masters week, an only slightly odder occurrence than the shocking first-round 72 he fired—at age 66—on a newly toughened layout in 1998. By this time, however, Brewer's putter had long gone jittery, resulting in a quieter Champions Tour career than might otherwise have been expected.

PGA Tour Wins (10): 1967 Masters; 1972 Canadian Open
Ryder Cup: 1967 & '71 (2)

Jock Brews (UK/South Africa)

The older brother of the great South African professional Sid, Blackheath, England, native Jock Brews (1892–1955) came to the Cape to work for his uncle Clarry Moore, the professional at the Pretoria CC. Upon replacing Moore in 1912, Jock convinced brother Sid to journey from England to be his assistant, thus setting the stage for the first great era of South African professional golf. Though Jock was never Sid's competitive equal, he did manage to claim four **South African Opens** in his own right (1921, '23, '26 and '28) and also finished second on five further occasions.

Sid Brews
(UK/South Africa)

The son of the golf professional at England's oldest club, Royal Blackheath, Sidney Francis Brews (1899–1972) initially went to South Africa in 1914 to work for his brother Jock at the Pretoria CC. Returning to England to join the war effort, Sid was taken prisoner in 1918 but survived that brief ordeal to return to a job at the Durban CC, and soon was to dominate South African golf as nobody had before him.

Though the competition wasn't as stiff as that back in England, we must still be impressed not only with Brews' eight **South African Open** titles but also the period over which he won them, an expansive 27 years. Some may suggest that he was beating little more than his brother during the late 1920s but by the time of his last two titles, Bobby Lock, Ronnie Glennie, Clarence Olander, and a good many others had joined the fray. Brews also won six **South African PGAs,** eight **Transvaal Opens,** and four **Natal Opens,** plus both the **Dutch** and **French Opens** in 1934 and '35 and, on a rare visit to America, the 1935 **Philadelphia Open.** His closest brush with immortality came in the 1934 Open Championship where, despite closing rounds of 71-70-71, he finished second to Henry Cotton at Royal St. George's. Three years later, in July of 1938, Brews and a young Bobby Locke lost a £1,000 challenge to Cotton and Reg Whitcombe over 72 holes at Walton Heath, perhaps the last really great stakes match on record.

For more than 30 years the professional at Johannesburg's Houghton CC, Brews dabbled in both golf course architecture and agronomy, laying out several well-known South African courses and developing a heat-resistant grass known as Brewsia.

PGA Tour Win: (1)
Intn'l Wins (40): 1925, '27, '30, '31, '33, '34, '49 & '52 South African Open; 1929 Belgian Open; 1934 & '35 Dutch Open; 1934 & '35 French Open

Jerilyn Britz (USA)

A native of Minneapolis, Minnesota, Jerilyn Britz (b. 1/1/1943) was a high school and college teacher before dedicating herself to golf, only turning professional at age 30. This bold move proved a sound decision, however, for six years later she made her first career victory the 1979 **U.S. Women's Open** at Connecticut's Brooklawn CC, where an even-par total of 284 was enough to beat Debbie Massey and Sandra Palmer by two. Though Britz would only win once more on tour (at the 1980 **Mary Kay Classic**), she did land two second places in the LPGA Championship, in 1979 and 1981, and pocketed over a half-million dollars in career earnings.

John Brodie (USA)

An athlete of obvious stature, San Francisco native John Brodie (b. 8/14/1935) was an All-American quarterback at Stanford before starring for his hometown 49ers from 1957 to 1973, winning league MVP honors in 1970. Long a fine golfer, Brodie worked as a television commentator until turning 50 when he joined the Champions Tour, several times finishing among the top 40 on the money list. His high point, to be sure, was a play-off victory over Chi Chi Rodriguez and George Archer at the 1991 **Security Pacific Classic,** a triumph that placed him alongside former New York Yankee Sam Byrd as that rare major-sport athlete capable of actually winning at the highest levels of professional golf. Brodie suffered a severe stroke in 2000, however, effectively ending his competitive career at age 65.

Mark Brooks (USA)

A three-time All-American at the University of Texas and former **Trans-Mississippi** (1979) and **Southern** (1981) Amateur champion, Ft. Worth, Texas, native Mark Brooks (b. 3/25/1961) enjoyed 12 relatively fruitful years on the PGA Tour before breaking through with a career season in 1996. After winning the **Bob Hope** in his second start, Brooks later holed a 50-foot birdie putt to defeat Jeff Maggert in a play-off at the **Houston Open.** Then in August, a 72nd-hole birdie at the Valhalla GC lifted Brooks into a play-off with Kenny Perry for the **PGA Championship,** whereupon another birdie at the same hole cemented his first Major championship, his seventh career win, a 1996 Presidents Cup berth, and a career-best third place on the money list.

Not an especially long hitter, Brooks has long relied on his shotmaking and putting skills to remain competitive among the game's elite. Following a modest post-PGA slump between 1997 and 2000, he nearly earned a second Major at the 2001 U.S. Open at Southern Hills, losing an 18-hole play-off to South African Retief Goosen after both men memorably blew chances of winning the event outright by three-putting the 72nd green.

Al Brosch (USA)

Al Brosch (1915–1975) was the first professional at New York's Bethpage State Park and a 10-time winner of the **Long Island Open** between 1939 and 1959. An occasional winter player on the PGA Tour, he etched himself permanently into the record book on February 10, 1951, when he fired the Tour's first-ever 60 during the Texas Open at San Antonio's Brackenridge Park. The venue, of course, was hardly Pine Valley. Just four years later, Mike Souchak would equal Brosch's mark en route to his record four-round total of 257, a record that stood on Tour for 46 years.

David Brown (UK/USA)

A slater by trade, David Brown (b. 1860) generally entered big events only on those occasions when they visited his hometown of Musselburgh, Scotland. The 1886 **Open Championship** was one such opportunity and with a 36-hole total of 157, he beat Willie Campbell by two. It was an ill-timed title, of course, somewhat lost between an earlier era of the Morrises, the Parks, Jamie Anderson, and Bob Ferguson, and the great Triumvirate whose arrival remained a decade off. Still, after emigrating to America, Brown succeeded in validating the win by reaching a play-off at the 1903 U.S. Open at Baltusrol, ultimately losing to the great Willie Anderson by the uninspired totals of 82-84.

Eric Brown (UK)

For nearly two decades a dominant force in Scottish professional golf, Edinburgh's Eric Chalmers Brown (1925–1986) was one of the game's toughest competitors, a status gained both by skill and a volatile temperament. A right-to-left player whose full swing extended noticeably beyond parallel, Brown enjoyed fine success at medal play, taking **Swiss, Italian, Irish,** and **Portuguese Opens,** the 1957 **British Masters,** and numerous Scottish and Northern Scottish Professional titles. He also twice finished third in the Open Championship, where he managed six top 10s overall and a then-record round of 65 in 1958.

But clearly it was the head-to-head nature of match play that brought out Brown's best, as he won the 1946 **Scottish Amateur** and, at the end of the line, the old *News of the World* match play twice (1960 and '62.) And then there was the Ryder Cup. Selected four consecutive times from 1953 to 1959, Brown's overall ledger was 4-4, but his singles record was a clean 4-0, defeating, in order, Lloyd Mangrum, Jerry Barber, Tommy Bolt, and Dr. Cary Middlecoff. The Bolt match, as one might imagine, was a hotly contested affair, prompting Jimmy Demaret, upon seeing neither man ready at the appointed time, to sug-gest: "They're out there on the practice tee, throwing clubs at each other from fifty paces."

Brown later served twice as Ryder Cup captain, first in a 1969 tie at Royal Birkdale, then, two years later, in a relatively narrow British loss in St. Louis. He also represented Scotland in the World Cup on 11 occasions between 1954 and 1967.

Intn'l Wins (25): 1951 Swiss Open; 1952 Italian Open; 1953 Irish Open; 1953 Portuguese Open; 1957 British Masters
Ryder Cup: 1953–59 (4) and 1969 & '71 Capt

Francis H. I. Brown (USA)

Generally considered Hawaii's "Mr. Golf," Francis Hyde I'i Brown (1892–1976) was a widely respected figure throughout the islands, a sportsman/philanthropist who helped to develop Waialae CC (home of the Hawaiian Open) and served in both the House of Representatives and the U.S. Senate. Beyond his ample administrative and political skills, Brown was also a golfer of genuine renown, winning Hawaii's prestigious **Manoa Cup** (awarded to the state's amateur champion) a record nine times between 1914 and 1926. A world traveler, the long-hitting Brown was the **Japanese Amateur** champion of 1929, the **California Amateur** winner in 1930, and, perhaps most impressively, the owner of a record-setting 67 at St. Andrews, shot during a practice round for the 1924 British Amateur.

Ken Brown (UK)

Though a native of Harpenden, England, Ken Brown (b. 1/9/1957)—like Brian Barnes and Sandy Lyle—considered himself a Scot and represented only Scotland in World Cup play. He was also, as many may recall, one of the more iconoclastic players in British history, gaining reputations for surliness and slow play, and putting with a wooden-shafted relic that might well have come over from the Low Countries. Perhaps more important, though a fine talent, he was also an underachiever, winning only four European Tour events (including **Irish** and **Dutch Opens**) between 1978 and 1985. Brown was a five-time Ryder Cup player, however, appearing between 1977 and 1987 (missing only 1981) and compiling a 4-9 overall record. He is today a relatively staid broadcaster for the BBC.

Pete Brown (USA)

One imagines that even among knowledgeable golfers, the question "Who was the first black player to win an official PGA Tour event?" will draw one overwhelming answer: Charlie Sifford. But the trailblazing Sifford was actually only the first black to gain full Tour playing privileges. The first to actually win an event was Jackson, Mississippi, native Pete Brown (b. 2/2/1935) who captured the **Waco Turner Open** in 1964. A former two-time winner of the **Negro National Open,** Brown later validated his success by defeating the reigning British Open champion Tony Jacklin in sudden death to take the 1970 **San Diego Open.** All told, Brown remained on Tour for 17 seasons, finished a career-best 35th on the 1970 money list, and did much to pave the way for future stars Calvin Peete, Jim Thorpe, and Tiger Woods.

Mary K. Browne (USA)

A member of the International Tennis Hall of Fame, Californian Mary Kimball Browne (1891–1971) won U.S. singles, doubles, and mixed doubles titles from 1912 to 1914, later becoming the first American woman to turn professional in order to capitalize on lucrative exhibition opportunities. By the early 1920s, she was equally devoted to golf and pulled a unique double in 1924, reaching the semifinals of the American championships in both sports. At tennis she lost to Helen Wills but in golf she actually defeated five-time champion Glenna Collett (at the Rhode Island CC) before losing in the final to three-time winner Dorothy Campbell 7 and 6. A quarter-finalist the following year in St. Louis, Browne never again reached the top rungs but was an active player in Southern California nearly until her death.

Robert Browning (UK)

A native of Glasgow, Scotland, Robert Browning was, for a staggering 45 years, editor of the British magazine *Golfing*. In this capacity, he became one of the game's great repositories of historical knowledge, mining all manner of friends and contacts to piece together many of the more obscure aspects of its early development. As such, Browning's opus, *A History of Golf* (J. M. Dent, 1955), must be considered mandatory reading for any serious student of the game, being called "far and away the finest one-volume history of golf" by no less an authority than Herbert Warren Wind. A quiet, retiring sort, Brown also penned well over 300 club handbooks and British regional golf guides and was a widely published author of verse, generally under the pen name Hara-Kari.

Stanley Bruce (Australia)

The Right Honorable Stanley Bruce (1883–1967) served as Australia's prime minister between 1923 and 1929, and it is doubtful that a more dedicated or pedigreed golfer ever held so powerful an office. The son of Royal Melbourne GC's most influential founder, Bruce spent a good deal of time in the United Kingdom, for he also served as Australian High Commissioner in London and, in 1954, was the first Australian to captain the Royal and Ancient Golf Club. Hardly a championship-caliber player, Bruce palpably reminded everyone of that fact upon the captain's traditional "driving in," where he blasted a particularly memorable tee shot all of 70 yards.

Jimmy Bruen (Northern Ireland)

James O'Grady Bruen Jr. (1920–1972) is one of the great legends of Irish golf, a Belfast insurance broker whose skills were every bit as remarkable as his style was unorthodox. Bruen employed one of the more unique swings in the game's history, a commanding, almost violent action that saw the club loop wildly from outside-to-inside, defying all convention but generating great power. Though frequently wild, he was a splendid scrambler in the Hagen or Ballesteros mold, and his short game and putting were considered among the best of their day.

Truly a youthful prodigy, Bruen won the **British Boys** title at age 16, routing one W. Innes 11 and 9 in the 36-hole final. To this he added an **Irish Open Amateur** in 1938, a pair of **Irish Closed Amateurs** in 1937 and '38, and a leading role (as the youngest-ever participant) on the 1938 Walker Cup team, the first ever to beat the Americans in the event's 16-year history. Having led all qualifiers in the 1939 Open Championship at St. Andrews — as a 19-year-old, we must remember — Bruen was seen in some eyes as ranking among the very finest players in the world while still in his teens.

But if the onset of World War II was a detriment to the careers of numerous golfers, it was positively a disaster for Jimmy Bruen. He emerged from the conflict rusty but still capable (as a victory in the 1946 **British Amateur** will testify) but a recurring wrist problem would dramatically limit his future fortunes. How many major titles might Bruen have won if not for the war, we can never know. But in blazing so brightly and setting a standard for men like Harry Bradshaw, Fred Daly, and Joe Carr to follow, his place in Irish golfing history is forever secure.

Johnny Bulla (USA)

It is entirely conceivable that Newell, West Virginia's, Johnny Bulla (1914–2003) is the finest golfer in history to win only a single PGA Tour event — though at least the

Los Angeles Open, which he claimed at Riviera in 1941, stood among the most prestigious of period titles. Unfortunately, Bulla is far better remembered for so many near misses on the Major championship stage, such as the 1949 Masters, where a pair of closing 69s looked good to win but were bettered by Sam Snead's 67s; the U.S. Open, where, twice finishing in the top five, he led after 54 holes in 1939, only to shoot 76 and drop to sixth; the British Open where he twice finished second, once after having the 54-hole lead; or the PGA championship at which he twice reached the quarter-finals, in 1948 and '51.

On the positive side of the ledger, however, Bulla is also recalled for breaking the mold in several interesting ways. When he captured the L.A. Open, for example, he did so using Walgreen's Po-Do Golf Ball, a knock-off sold for half the price of bigger-name products. He was a licensed pilot who bought his own plane in which to transport fellow touring pros, later flying for Eastern Airlines and starting his own carrier, Arizona Airways. Residing in the Phoenix area for more than 55 years, Bulla won 14 **Arizona Opens** while also dabbling in golf course design, primarily in Arizona and Colorado.

Betty Burfeindt (USA)

Born in New York City, long-hitting Elizabeth Burfeindt (b. 7/20/1945) first stepped to the LPGA forefront in 1972 when she won events in **Birmingham** and **Las Vegas** within a three-week span. Her true moment in the sun, however, came in 1976 when, after finishing second to Judy Rankin at the Dinah Shore some seven weeks earlier, she reversed the tables by defeating Rankin at the year's first Major, the **LPGA Championship,** at Baltimore's Pine Ridge GC. It was the last of Burfeindt's four official LPGA Tour victories.

Billy Burke (USA)

Though a 13-time winner on the PGA Tour, Billy Burke (1902–1972) is largely remembered for his rather remarkable victory at the 1931 **U.S. Open** at Inverness—remarkable because he quite literally had to play two Opens in order to claim the title. Finishing the fourth round in a tie with amateur George Von Elm, the Naugatuck, Connecticut, native (né William Burkauskus) looked to have the 36-hole play-off won until the talented Von Elm birdied the last. So back out they went for 36 more, with Burke only just winning this time, by a single stroke.

Missing part of the fourth finger on his left hand, Burke was a fairly short hitter who relied on accuracy and a deft short game to stay competitive. And competitive he generally was, going 3-0 in two Ryder Cup appearances (1931 and '33), reaching the semifinals of the PGA in 1931, and twice finishing third at the Masters. He also had additional sixth- and seventh-place finishes at the U.S. Open and bears the distinction of being the first player to win the Open using steel shafts.

PGA Tour Wins (13): 1928 North & South; **1931 U.S. Open**
Ryder Cup: 1931 & '33 (2)

Jack Burke Jr. (USA)

The son of a Houston-area golf pro who finished runner-up in the 1920 U.S. Open, Ft. Worth native Jack Burke Jr. (b. 1/29/1923) was obviously raised close to the game, turning professional at age 17. An excellent putter who, like most Texans, was very much at home playing in the wind, Burke didn't try the PGA Tour until 1950, when he began traveling with good friend Jimmy Demaret, a former protégé of his father.

Burke soon proved himself a man who could win regularly, capturing four titles in his first season, then five more (including one red-hot stretch of four in a row) in 1952. The 1952 season witnessed additional milestones including a second–place finish at the Masters (when his closing 69 was the sole sub-70 round recorded in blustery conditions), a near-record score of 260 in winning the **Texas Open** (by six, over Doug Ford), and, at season's end, a Vardon Trophy. Yet all of this notwithstanding, it was in 1956 that Burke would truly stake his claim, winning both the **Masters** and the **PGA Championship** and being named Player of the Year. At Augusta he came from eight strokes behind then-amateur Ken Venturi with a final-round 71, just enough to overtake Venturi's disastrous 80. Three months later, at Massachusetts' Blue Hill CC, Burke beat Ted Kroll 3 and 2 to capture the next-to-last PGA contested at match play.

Though still competing occasionally, Burke largely retired from the Tour following 1956, owing to a hand injury, the desire to be with his family, and, eventually, his partnership with Demaret in the building of Houston's Champions Club. He was, however, a playing captain on the 1957 Ryder Cup team (America's first loser since 1933) and returned as a non-player to lead the victorious 1973 squad. His overall Ryder Cup playing record was an impressive 7-1.

PGA Tour Wins (17): 1950 Bing Crosby; 1952 & '59 Houston; 1952 Texas; **1956 Masters; 1956 PGA Championship**
Ryder Cup: 1951–55 & '57 (c) (4) and 1973 Capt

1949-1965

	49	50	51	52	53	54	55	56	57	58	59	60	61	62	63	64	65
Masters	-	WD	11	2	8	T6	T13	1	T7	MC	T34	T11	T7	T39	MC	MC	MC
US Open	T27	MC	-	T41	T14	T15	T10	MC	-	-	-	-	-	-	T21	-	MC
British	-	-	-	-	-	-	-	-	-	-	-	-	-	-	-	-	-
PGA	T33	-	T5	T17	-	T33	T5	1	T33	4	T17	T29	T52	T17	T34	T44	T8

John Burke (Ireland)

Raised near the great links at Lahinch, John Burke (1900–1972) was a leading player among Irish amateurs for the better part of two decades. A large and powerful man, his pleasant demeanor hid a highly competitive nature that saw him through to eight **Irish Closed Amateur** victories, one **Irish Open Amateur** (in 1947, when he beat a young Joe Carr in the final), and a Walker Cup appearance in 1932. Sadly relegated to a wheelchair in his later years, Burke was at one time so regionally dominant that after winning the **South of Ireland** championship eight times, he was reportedly asked no longer to enter for fear of running off the opposition, killing the economic viability of the event.

Walter Burkemo (USA)

Detroit-born Walter Burkemo (1918–1986) won exactly twice on the PGA Tour—and the 1957 **Mayfair Inn Open** generally holds little interest for contemporary readers. But Burkemo's earlier victory was the 1953 **PGA Championship,** a title he won at hometown Birmingham (Michigan) CC with a dramatic 36th-hole semifinal win over Claude Harmon, then a 2 and 1 victory over Felice Torza in the final. A match-play specialist, Burkemo enjoyed a remarkable 1950s record at the PGA, twice losing in the final (to Sam Snead, 7 and 6, in 1951 and Chick Harbert, 4 and 3, in 1954) and reaching the semifinals in 1957. Clearly a big-game player, Burkemo also managed top-5 finishes in the 1957 and '58 U.S. Opens, though victories, unfortunately, would remain few and far between.

George Burns (USA)

Brooklyn, New York, native George Burns III (b. 7/29/1949) was an excellent all-around athlete who got serious about golf only after playing football at the University of Maryland. Despite standing 6'2" and weighing 210 pounds, Burns' game did not revolve around power, instead relying upon a first-class short game and putting stroke to cap-ture the 1973 **Canadian Amateur,** then the **North & South** and several additional amateur events in 1974.

Turning professional following appearances in the 1975 Masters and Walker Cup, Burns immediately won Ireland's **Kerrygold** tournament and the **Scandinavian Open** before undergoing a four-year learning process on the PGA Tour. Finally in 1979 he partnered with Ben Crenshaw to win the **Walt Disney Team Championship,** then broke through to take the **Bing Crosby** in 1980. Winning twice more in the latter half of that decade, Burns also came terribly close at the 1981 U.S. Open at Merion, where rounds of 69-66-68, followed by a closing 73, might normally have done the trick had Australian David Graham not finished with a superb 67 to claim the title. In recent years Burns has played sporadically on the Champions and European Senior Tours, occasionally contending but not yet winning.

Jack Burns (UK)

Little is recorded of Jack Burns, a St. Andrews plasterer who won the 1888 **Open Championship** over the Old Course, though the event itself is well recalled for the recounting of scores required to verify Burns' one-stroke victory margin over Ben Sayers and David Anderson Jr. As a result of his title, Burns reportedly accepted the professional position at England's newly formed Warwick GC, then gave it up several years later for a platelayer's job on the St. Andrews railway line because, in the words of historian Robert Browning, "he preferred a steady job."

Brandie Burton (USA)

Though slowed substantially since year 2000 by physical problems, San Bernardino, California, native Brandie Burton (b. 1/8/1972) enjoyed an amateur and early professional career that marked her as one of the top prospects of her time. In her teens, Burton won San Diego's **Junior World** in 1987 and '89, the **PGA National Junior** in 1988, and the **USGA Junior Girls** in 1989. In a single season at Arizona State, she claimed six of the seven events she started and was named an All-American. With **North & South** and **Broadmoor Invitational** titles, and a 1990 Curtis Cup appearance to her credit, Burton's amateur résumé lacks only a U.S. Women's Amateur—an event she lost in the final, in 1989, to Pat Hurst.

As a professional, Burton was the 1991 LPGA Rookie of the Year and a five-time winner prior to undergoing multiple surgeries for jaw and shoulder problems. Significantly, two of these wins were Major championships, the 1993 and '98 **du Maurier Classics,** with the former coming in sudden death over Hall of Famer Betsy King. Burton also represented the United States in five consecutive Solheim Cup competitions from 1992 to 2000 but has since gone winless, falling out of the top 50 money winners in both 2002 and '03.

Dick Burton (UK)

A native of Darwin, England, Richard Burton (1907–1974) was described by Longhurst as a "tall and rangy" sort possessing "a beautiful and graceful method for a man of his build." Though a winner of the occasional lesser event, Burton's shining hour came at the 1939 **Open Championship** at St. Andrews where, after holing gutsy putts at the 69th and 70th, he birdied the 72nd for a dramatic two-stroke win over American Johnny Bulla. A three-time Ryder Cupper (1935, '37 and '49), Burton was denied the financial windfall attendant to an Open title by the imminent onset of World War II. One imagines it only small compensation that he enjoyed, by default, the longest reign of any Major champion in history—seven years—before the Open was recommenced in 1946.

Cuthbert S. Butchart (UK/USA)

One of golf's good old-fashioned all-rounders, Cuthbert Strachan Butchart (1876–1955) came from a family of Carnoustie clubmakers and spent several turn-of-the-century years as professional at Northern Ireland's famous Royal County Down. Returning to Scotland, then moving on to Berlin, he continued teaching and making clubs while also widening his talents as a course designer. In 1911 he laid out the Berlin GC, stayed on to serve as its pro, and then won the 1913 **German PGA Championship**—all before being interned in a POW camp for two years upon the outbreak of World War I.

Following the war Butchart found his way to the United States where he soon landed the professional job at the spectacular new Westchester Biltmore CC. For the remainder of his life, he would summer in New York and winter in Florida, manufacturing wooden clubs under the old family name (or in tandem with Gilbert Nicholls) and designing a handful of courses, most of which no longer exist.

Peter Butler (UK)

One of Britain's top professionals during the admittedly lean years of the 1960s, Birmingham's Peter Butler (b. 3/25/1932) was a short but decidedly reliable driver of the ball who managed to win British and European events with some regularity. A professional for fully a decade before trying the tour, Butler's first win came at the 1959 **Swallow-Penfold** tournament, and he would later count the 1963 **Volvo PGA,** the 1968 **French Open,** and pair of **Piccadilly Medal Plays** (1965 and '67) among his more prominent titles. A willing traveler, Butler won the 1975 **Colombian Open** and, more notably, was a regular competitor at the Masters, actually leading at the halfway mark in 1966. Also a four-time Ryder Cup pick, Butler's career record of 3-9-2 was perhaps representative of the period doldrums in British golf.

Intn'l Wins (12): 1963 Volvo PGA; 1968 French Open
Ryder Cup: 1965–73 (4)

Eben Byers (USA)

A wealthy Pittsburgh-area steel manufacturer, Eben M. Byers (1880–1932) competed with some success among the nation's top amateurs during the early years of the last century. In both 1902 and '03 he reached the U.S. Amateur final, only to lose to Louis James (4 and 3 in Chicago) and the great Walter Travis (5 and 4 in New York), respectively. Byers played his way back to the **Amateur** final in 1906, however, this time defeating Canadian champion George S. Lyon at New Jersey's old Englewood GC to get his name etched forever upon the Havemeyer Trophy. Curiously, Byers is one of the very few Americans known to have died from radium poisoning, a condition he developed after consuming large quantities of radium-enriched water on the advice of his physician.

Sam Byrd (USA)

As backup (and eventual replacement) for the great Babe Ruth, Georgia native Samuel Dewey Byrd (1907–1981) was a strong contributor to some great New York Yankee baseball teams, including homering twice on Opening Day, 1932. But in 1935 he was injured, curtailing one professional sports career but opening the door to another. Dedicating himself wholeheartedly to golf, Byrd became a legitimate first-class player, winning six PGA Tour events, losing to Byron Nelson 4 and 3 in the final of the 1945 PGA Championship, and twice finishing in the top five at the Masters. It is worth noting, too, that Byrd's victories were hardly in off-season events against third-rate competition. To wit: At the 1942 **Greater Greensboro Open** he beat Ben Hogan and Lloyd Mangrum by two, while at the 1945 **Texas Open** his tournament-record 268 edged Byron Nelson by one.

Even more overlooked is Byrd's contribution to golf instruction, for it was he who bore the honor of occasionally working with Ben Hogan and who mentored a young Jimmy Ballard, the extremely popular 1970s teacher who credited Byrd with creating Ballard's much-discussed concept of "connection."

Willard Byrd (USA)

A native of Whiteville, North Carolina, who was educated, following World War II naval service, at North Carolina State, Willard Byrd (1919–2004) began working as a landscape designer in Atlanta before eventually switching to golf architecture in the mid-1950s. Credited with the design of roughly 100 new courses from the late 1950s to the early '90s, virtually all of his work was concentrated within the American Southeast, including multiple assignments on Hilton Head Island (Wexford and Planters Row GCs) and sites throughout Florida and North Carolina.

C

Angel Cabrera (Argentina)

A big, broadly built man who can hit it a long way, Angel Cabrera (b. Cordoba 9/12/1969) followed the route of countrymen Eduardo Romero and José Coceres, developing his game in South America before having a go abroad. By 1998 he was highly competitive in Europe, finishing second to Sergio Garcia at the Irish Open and missing a putt that would have put him in a play-off with Mark O'Meara and Brian Watts for the Open Championship. A winner of the 2001 **Argentine Open,** Cabrera tied for 10th at that season's Masters and seventh at the U.S. Open, giving some inkling of what may yet lay ahead. After taking the prestigious 2002 **Benson & Hedges International** (in which he outgunned Colin Montgomerie, Padraig Harrington, and Michael Campbell, among others), Cabrera began splitting time between Europe and the United States, appearing capable of winning on either side.

Mark Calcavecchia (USA)

A winner of over $15 million in 22 full seasons on the PGA Tour, Mark John Calcavecchia (b. 6/12/1960) has remained a fixture among the top 65 money winners every year since 1986. A strong player capable of overwhelming courses with a consistent power fade, Calcavecchia was born in rural Laurel, Nebraska, before getting serious about golf following a childhood move to Florida.

After a fine career at the University of Florida, he joined the PGA Tour in 1982 but initially struggled, only cracking the top 125 in 1986, the year of his first victory at the **Southwest Classic.** Single wins (and top-10 money finishes) would follow in 1987 and '88, with the latter featuring a near miss at the Masters, where only Sandy Lyle's spectacular 72nd-hole birdie denied Calcavecchia a play-off bid. A Major victory came the following summer, however, at the 1989 **Open Championship,** when he defeated Australians Wayne Grady and Greg Norman at Royal Troon in the R&A's first-ever four-hole play-off, the matter being closed with a superb 5-iron to seven feet at the very last.

Thus apparently joining the world's elite, Calcavecchia surprisingly never again made a serious run at a Major, though ties for fourth at the 2001 Masters and PGA certainly indicated continued competitiveness. He would, however, set or tie seven PGA Tour records at the 2001 **Phoenix Open** when his 28-under-par 256 total broke Mike Souchak's 46-year-old aggregate total record of 257 while defeating Rocco Mediate by eight. Calcavecchia is also well remembered for an infamous meltdown during singles play at the 1991 Ryder Cup where, over Kiawah Island's difficult closers, he lost the last four holes (which included two triple bogies) to Colin Montgomerie, allowing Europe to steal a vital half-point. His career Cup ledger of 6-7-1, however, was eminently respectable.

PGA Tour Wins (11): 1989 Los Angeles; **1989 British Open**
Intn'l Wins (4): 1988 Australian Open
Ryder Cup: 1987–91 & 2002 (4) **Presidents Cup:** 1998

Alex "Nipper" Campbell (UK)

Like so many young Scottish golfers of the period, Troon's Alex "Nipper" Campbell (1879–1942) sought his fortune by emigrating to the United States, arriving at the tender age of 19. After competing professionally for a spell (losing the 1907 U.S. Open after his gelatin-centered golf ball decompressed in mid-flight, costing him two strokes), he became the professional at Brookline's storied Country Club in 1899. There he observed the development of a local amateur prospect named Francis Ouimet, then managed to referee the famous 1913 U.S. Open play-off when the 20-year-old upstart shocked the world's two finest players, Harry Vardon and Ted Ray.

As Campbell moved on to professional positions at Baltimore CC, Losantiville CC (in Dayton, Ohio), and ultimately the Moraine CC, he began laying out golf courses as a sideline. Though ultimately credited with more than 30 original designs, few of these garner any great attention today.

Captain Alexander Campbell (UK)

Though not a firmly documented occurrence, ample evidence suggests that Captain Alexander Campbell used homemade clubs and a thoroughly makeshift layout to play golf near Fort Charlotte in Nassau, Bahamas during the late eighteenth century. A Glasgow native, Campbell was the commander of the British garrison in Nassau, thus giving him the necessary authority to use his parade grounds to such effect. Though his efforts predated modern North American golf by a good century, they likely ran concurrent to (or even slightly behind) the early game briefly played along the eastern seaboard as early as 1750.

Bill Campbell (USA)

Perhaps the quintessential modern American amateur, Huntington, West Virginia's William Cammack Campbell (b. 5/5/1923) starred at Princeton in a war-interrupted collegiate career before pursuing the amateur golfer's occupation of choice, brokering insurance. The tall, smooth-swinging Campbell has won literally countless titles, though the most important surely was the 1964 **U.S. Amateur** when he defeated frequent rival Ed Tutwiler one up at Cleveland's Canterbury GC. Surprisingly, this was to be Campbell's sole U.S. Amateur victory despite competing in the event an incredible 37 times between 1938 and 1981. Another testimonial to Campbell's great longevity is his appearance on seven Walker Cup teams between 1951 and 1975, going undefeated in singles play and also captaining a victorious 1955 squad at St. Andrews. He also has competed in 15 U.S. Opens and 18 Masters, and very nearly won the 1954 British Amateur, standing one up on Doug Bachli through 31 holes before the talented Australian rallied to win.

A holy terror in his own region, Campbell is a four-time **West Virginia Open** champion and 15-time **West Virginia Amateur** winner—greater accomplishments than they may at first appear as he frequently had to overcome the talented Tutwiler. Campbell also won Pinehurst's prestigious **North & South** title on four occasions (1950, '53, '57, and '61) and the **Mexican Amateur** in 1956.

Also a prominent golf administrator, Campbell has served twice on the USGA's Executive Committee, first from 1962 to 1965, then again from 1977 to 1984. He was the organization's treasurer in 1978–79, vice-president in 1980–81, and ultimately president in 1982–83. In 1987, he became only the third American to captain the Royal and Ancient Golf Club (following Francis Ouimet and Joe Dey), making Campbell the only man ever to head both of golf's prime governing bodies.

Chad Campbell (USA)

A strong and talented player who is just coming into his own, former Nevada–Las Vegas star David Chad Campbell (b. Andrews, Texas, 5/31/1974) is both long and highly accurate, easily ranking among the PGA Tour's best ball-strikers. Following a 15th-place finish at the 2003 Open

Championship and a solo second at the PGA, Campbell became the first man ever to make the season-ending **Tour Championship** his initial victory, riding a course-record 61 at the Champions GC to a three-stroke victory over Charles Howell III. He followed this up in early 2004 with a resounding six-shot triumph at **Bay Hill,** highlighting a consistent season which generally saw him ranked among the top 25 on the money list and making his initial Ryder Cup appearance. With an all-around game widely respected by his peers, much is expected of Campbell in the years immediately ahead.

Dorothy Campbell Hurd (UK/Canada)

Born: Edinburgh, Scotland, 3/24/1883 **Died:** Yemassee, South Carolina, 3/20/1945

The first female golfer to enjoy great success on both sides of the Atlantic, Dorothy Campbell (later Mrs. J. B. Hurd) grew up at North Berwick where she was taught by the great Ben Sayers. A slender woman with first-class skills from 50 yards in, Campbell began her prime competitive run by capturing **Scottish Ladies** titles in 1905 and '06, then adding a third such win in 1908. That same year she lost a classic British Women's Amateur final over the Old Course at St. Andrews, falling at the 19th to Maud Titterton—an event that nonetheless set the stage for the international greatness soon to come.

In 1909, Campbell became the first woman to win the **British** and **U.S. Women's Amateurs** in the same season, the former at Royal Birkdale (3 and 2 over Florence Hezlet), the latter at the Merion Cricket Club (over Nonna Barlow 3 and 2). Moving to Canada in 1910, she proceeded to defend her American title at Chicago's Homewood CC (2 and 1 over Mrs. G. M. Martin), then added a second British crown in 1911 at Royal Portrush (3 and 2 over Violet Hezlet). Further, three consecutive victories at the **Canadian Amateur** (1910–12) made Campbell the first woman to take the British, U.S., and Canadian titles, a unique distinction until the arrival of Marlene Stewart Streit some four decades later.

Upon getting married in 1913, Campbell is reported to have gone into competitive retirement, only to reemerge during the 1920s with a revamped swing for one last hurrah. She did indeed claim a final **U.S. Amateur** title in 1924 (at age 41), defeating long-hitting ex-tennis champion Mary Brown 7 and 6 at the Rhode Island CC. However, accounts of her retirement were clearly somewhat exaggerated for prior to this comeback, Campbell also had won the 1918, '20 and '21 **North & South Amateurs** at Pinehurst.

Major Amateur Wins (8): 1909 & '11 British Ladies; 1909, '10 & '24 U.S. Womens; 1918, '20 & '21 North & South

Dorothy Campbell Hurd

Sir Guy Campbell (UK/USA)

Born into golfing royalty, Sir Guy Campbell (1885–1960) was the great-grandson of prominent early historian Robert Chambers and a semifinalist in the 1907 British Amateur (where he lost to eight-time champion John Ball). A graduate of St. Andrews University, Campbell served as both a writer and editor for the *Times* of London, also penning countless magazine articles and a popular book, *Golf for Beginners* (C. Arthur Pearson, 1922). His grandest literary contribution, however, came some 30 years later when he contributed sections on early British golf, the development of equipment, and the history of British golf course design for the classic *A History of Golf in Britain* (Cassell, 1952).

Campbell himself began to dabble in architecture after World War I, eventually joining forces with C. K. Hutchison and S. V. Hotchkin in a firm that counted West Sussex and Ashridge GCs, and modifications to North Berwick, among their credits. Following World War II, Campbell worked solo and also teamed with J. S. F. Morrison to facilitate the rebirth of Kent's war-ravaged Prince's GC in 1951. His personal masterpiece, however, must surely be the original Mahoney's Point course at Ireland's Killarney Golf & Fishing Club, a fine design completed for the famed Lord Castlerosse in 1939. Emigrating to America after World War II, Campbell died while constructing his lone non-U.K. design, Virginia's Tides Inn GC, in 1960.

Notable Courses: Ashridge GC (with Hutchison & Hotchkin); Killarney Golf & Fishing Club, Ireland; West Sussex GC (with Hutchison & Hotchkin)

Michael Campbell (New Zealand)

A talented and likeable Maori born in the North Island town of Hawera, Michael Shane Campbell (b. 2/23/1969) is a player who has been knocking on stardom's door for nearly a decade now. The 1992 **Australian Amateur** champion, Campbell leaped to international prominence by leading the 1995 Open Championship at St. Andrews after 54 holes before a closing 76 saw him tied for third, one stroke out of the John Daly–Constantino Rocca play-off. Playing primarily on the European Tour, he finished fifth in the Order of Merit that year before a lingering wrist injury led to a serious three-year loss of form and a return to near-obscurity.

Healthy and refocused by 1998, however, Campbell began a comeback, which has seen him take six official European Tour victories and log four top-15 finishes in the Order of Merit since 2000. His best season came in 2000 when he ranked fourth and won thrice (at the **Johnnie Walker** and **Heineken Classics,** and the **Linde German Masters**), the first two during a red-hot early run, and all three against strong international fields. Campbell successfully defended his **Heineken** crown in 2001 and has since made occasional starts in America, his best PGA Tour finish being second at the 2002 Bay Hill. A three-time World Cup player and an international participant in the 2000 Presidents Cup, Campbell actually has direct Scottish roots in the form of his great grandfather, one Sir Logan Campbell, who emigrated from Edinburgh to New Zealand in 1845.

Patrick Campbell (UK)

Patrick Campbell was both a fine amateur golfer and professional funnyman, playing to a plus-two (with which he made a deep run at the 1949 British Amateur) and serving as a highly thought-of humorist for London's *Sunday Times*. He was also the author of the patently amusing *How to Become a Scratch Golfer* (Anthony Blond, 1963), an easily read volume purporting to guide the beginner through the intricacies of learning the game. Perhaps not on P. G. Wodehouse's level, but recommended reading nonetheless.

Willie Campbell (UK/USA)

A native of Musselburgh, Scotland, professional Willie Campbell (1862–1900) designed a handful of courses in Britain before emigrating to the United States in the early 1890s. In 1894 he finished close behind Willie Dunn in America's first national professional championship—not truly a U.S. Open in the accepted sense because it was contested at match play and, more importantly, because the sponsoring USGA would not come into existence until a year later. Also in 1894, Campbell became the first professional at The Country Club in Brookline, where he laid out the original golf course and presided over its first expansion. Later working at the Essex County Club, Campbell continued designing basic, old-fashioned layouts around the region until his early death at age 38.

José Maria Cañizares (Spain)

Five times a winner of European Tour events over more than 25 years of campaigning, Madrid's José Maria Cañizares (b. 2/18/1947) has long labored within the huge shadows cast by Ballesteros, Olazábal and, of late, Garcia. That these three are so quickly identified as the stars of Spanish golf is curious too, because two of Cañizares' finest moments have come in international play. In 1984, after having won the **World Cup** two years earlier with Manuel Piñero, he teamed with José Rivero to capture Spain's fourth Cup title in Rome, with Cañizares himself taking medalist honors. Then in 1989, at age 42, Cañizares' one up singles victory over Ken Green was the final point needed to secure a tie and European retention of the Ryder Cup following their overseas win of 1987. Twice a winner of the old **Bob Hope British Classic** (1980 and '83) as well as the 1981 **Italian Open,** and four times a top-10 finisher in the Order of Merit, Cañizares has more recently played the Champions Tour, logging one win in 2001.

Emanuele Canonica (Italy)

In some ways a footnote in modern golf, Emanuele Canonica holds the twin distinctions of being the European Tour's shortest player (at 5'2") yet also its longest hitter, having led the Tour's long-driving statistics four times since 1998. On several occasions a runner-up since getting his playing privileges in 1995, Canonica has only once stood among the top 50 on the Order of Merit, that being a 27th-place finish in 2000. But pound for pound, he must surely be among the longest hitters in golfing history.

Donna Caponi (USA)

Something of a cornerstone of the modern LPGA Tour, Donna Caponi (b. Detroit, Michigan, 1/29/1945) turned professional at age 20, finishing 20th on the money list in her rookie season of 1965. A consistent performer whose smooth, even-tempoed swing seemed particularly well suited to Major championship conditions, Caponi would only twice fall from the top 20 over the next 18 seasons, slipping to 24th and 31st in 1967 and '72, respectively. Though not a winner until 1969, once over the threshold she would claim a total of 24 official titles over 13 seasons, including a peak stretch from 1975 to 1981 in which she logged 19 victories, two of her four Major titles, and a winning percentage of 10.1 percent, the highest of the period.

Overall, Caponi's Major championship record is particularly notable, especially as her first career win was the 1969 **U.S. Women's Open** in Pensacola, Florida, where she edged Peggy Wilson by one. A year later she successfully defended the title in Muskogee, Oklahoma, the second of an impressive nine top-10 Open finishes in a 13-year span. Her record in the **LPGA Championship** was of similar quality, with victories in 1979 and '81 (both at King's Island, Ohio) amidst a stretch of nine consecutive top-10 finishes running from 1973 to 1981. It is also worth noting that Caponi won two more titles for which she might well have been given Major credit, the 1976 **Peter Jackson** (later the du Maurier) and the 1980 **Dinah Shore.** Neither event had yet been designated a Major at the time of her victory, yet we cannot help but notice that the LPGA does credit Patty Berg, Betty Jameson, Babe Zaharias, and Louise Suggs with "Majors" for U.S. Women's Opens won prior to its 1950 designation date.

A popular and gregarious player of the fan- and media-friendly Old School, Caponi (who competed under the married name Donna Young from 1971 to 1980) eased slowly from the ranks of the elite in the mid-1980s but today is a frequent presence in the broadcast booth.

LPGA Wins (24): **1969 & '70 U.S. Women's Open;** 1976 du Maurier; **1979 & '81 LPGA Championship;** 1980 Dinah Shore; 1980 Corning

1965-1984

	65	66	67	68	69	70	71	72	73	74	75	76	77	78	79	80	81	82	83	84
Dinah																			T15	T14
LPGA	T15	28	13	11	T6	T26	T23	MC	T4	T10	4	T4	T7	T6	1	T3	1	T28	T57	MC
US Open	20	T18	T23	T23	1	1	T3	T25	T25	T7	T16	MC	8	T6	T8	T4	T6	T21	WD	T50
du Maur														T11	3	T17	T3	T30	T66

John "Fiery" Carey (UK)

Best known as the regular caddie of Willie Park Jr., "Fiery" Carey was one of Scotland's grand old-fashioned loopers, complete with balmoral bonnet and clubs carried beneath the arm in the ancient style. On Park's bag for virtually every important match in which the two-time Open champion engaged, Carey's advice was considered flawless, and it is reported that Park seldom questioned him, simply taking whatever club he was handed. One of the grand old names among golf's colorful proletariat, Carey's nickname is often mistakenly believed to have come from his temper when, in fact, it was based solely upon the ruddy complexion of his weather-beaten skin.

Stig Carlander (Sweden)

Coming along several years behind Count Gustav Bielke, Stig Gunnar Carlander (b. 1937) was widely considered the more talented player, particularly after becoming the youngest-ever **Swedish Amateur** champion, in 1954, at age 16. He was, however, more often the bridesmaid than the bride in major amateur competitions, finishing runner-up in both the Norwegian and Scandinavian Amateurs and never winning a national title beyond his own borders. He did represent Sweden numerous times internationally, however, both on the Continent and in the United Kingdom.

JoAnne (Gunderson) Carner (USA)

There are great amateurs and great professionals, but it is doubtful that in the annals of golf anyone has put together a stronger record on both sides of the fence than the timeless and talented JoAnne Carner (b. Kirkland, Washington, 4/4/1939). Standing 5'7" and notably strong, Carner has always been a power player, overwhelming courses from tee to green while making enough putts to amass a seemingly endless list of amateur and LPGA titles.

Carner first blasted onto the national scene by capturing the 1956 **USGA Junior Girls,** then very nearly pulled off an improbable double when, several weeks later, she stood 4 up with 11 to play in the final of the U.S. Women's Amateur before ultimately losing to Marlene Stewart 2

and 1. From that point forward, the then-Miss Gunderson made the **U.S. Amateur** her personal playground, capturing titles in 1957, '60, '62, 66, and '68, a career total exceeded only by the great Glenna Collett Vare. An undefeated singles player on four Curtis Cup teams (1958–64), Carner would also win **Eastern, Western,** and **Trans-Mississippi** titles by the early 1960s and then, in 1969, the LPGA's **Burdines Invitational,** making her the last amateur to capture an official women's Tour event.

Having run out of nonpaying mountains to climb, Carner turned professional before the 1970 season, embarking on a 43-win career that would include two U.S. Women's Opens, three Player of the Year awards, 30 top-10 finishes in Major championships, and a particularly impressive stretch from 1974 to 1983, which included 37 wins and nine top-5 money finishes. Though not a part of this stellar run, Carner's first **U.S. Women's Open** (at Pennsylvania's Kahkwa CC in 1971) was equally memorable, for her even-par 288 fairly routed the field, leaving runner-up Kathy Whitworth a full seven shots behind! Curiously, despite numerous high finishes, Carner never managed a win in either the Dinah Shore or the LPGA Championship—though in the latter she twice finished second and recorded eight top-6 finishes between 1974 and 1983. Also Carner does not receive "Major" credit for winning the 1975 and '78 **Peter Jacksons** (later the du Maurier), an event which would be knighted to Grand Slam status in 1979.

Since the mid-1980s, Carner has gained attention with one additional quality: longevity. Her last victory, for example, the 1985 **SAFECO Classic,** made her the then-oldest winner in LPGA history at age 46. Further, she logged top-10 finishes well into her 50s and, in 2004, extended her own record as the oldest player ever to make an LPGA cut, doing so at the Dinah Shore, at age 64. The only player ever to win the USGA Junior Girls, the U.S. Women's Amateur, and the U.S. Women's Open, Carner was inducted into the Hall of Fame in 1985.

LPGA Wins (43): 1971 & '76 U.S. Women's Open; 1974 Dallas Civitan; 1975 & '77 Wykagyl; 1975 & '78 du Maurier; 1976 & '81 Orange Blossom; 1981 State Farm; 1983 Samsung WC; 1984 Corning

Major Amateur Wins (8): 1957, '60, '62, '66 & '68 U.S. Women's Amateur; 1959 Western Amateur; 1961 Trans-Miss; 1968 Eastern

Curtis Cup: 1958–64 (4) Solheim Cup: 1994 Capt

1970-1989

	70	71	72	73	74	75	76	77	78	79	80	81	82	83	84	85	86	87	88	89
Dinah														T4	T5	T46	T22	T47	T12	T2
LPGA	T6	39	T12	T47	2	T9	-	T5	4	T6	T3	T5	2	T4	T56	MC	T40	T28	T18	T54
US Open	T21	1	T29	T49	T4	T3	1	3	T2	-	T10	T6	T2	T2	T20	T48	T35	T2	T16	T17
du Maur									-	2	T7	T3	T2	5	T29	T14	-	MC	T10	

Joe Carr (Ireland)

Born: Dublin, Ireland, 2/22/1922 **Died:** Dublin, Ireland, 6/3/2004

Certainly Ireland's best-ever amateur and arguably her best overall player, Joseph Benedict Carr remained competitive for nearly four decades, capturing his first significant title (the **East of Ireland**) in 1941 and still doing battle with the younger set until well into the 1970s. A tall, lanky man with a long swing and powerful hands, Carr was a notably long driver but not always a straight one, yet his powers of recovery were nearly epic. Also a fine iron player, he was slowed only by his balky putter—something he was known to desert altogether (in favor of a 3-iron) when things really went south.

All told, Carr completely dominated affairs on the Emerald Isle, winning the **East** and **West** titles a remarkable 12 times each. He also claimed six **Irish Closed** victories and, perhaps more impressively, four **Open Amateur** crowns between 1946 and 1956. Like any European, however, the acid test for Carr was his record in the United Kingdom and there he truly shined, claiming three **British Amateurs** (1953, '58, and '60) and thrice more reaching the semifinals between 1951 and 1960. The latter two victories (over Alan Thirlwell at St. Andrews and Bob Cochran at Royal Portrush) stand up nicely enough, but it was the 1953 triumph that remains an epic, for there Carr ended a stretch of postwar American dominance by beating defending champion E. Harvie Ward two up at Hoylake.

Though seldom crossing the Atlantic to compete, Carr did enter the 1961 U.S. Amateur at Pebble Beach where, at age 39, he made it through to the semifinal before losing 2 down to upstart Dudley Wysong. He also participated in the Masters from 1967 to 1969, twice making the cut and later becoming the rare foreign member of Augusta National. Further bouts with the professionals resulted in nearly winning the 1959 British Masters at Portmarnock, twice finishing as low amateur at the Open Championship (1956 and '58), and coming home eighth in 1960. Not surprisingly, Carr was also a mainstay of many a Walker Cup side, and his selection for 11 consecutive matches between 1947 and 1967 remains the event standard both for quantity and continuity.

A remarkably popular player both for his style and his rich personality, Carr's widely hailed sportsmanship was acknowledged in 1961 when the USGA presented him with the Bobby Jones Award. It was also observed closer to home when Carr became the first Irishman to serve as captain of the R&A in 1991.

Aldo Casera (Italy)

Though perhaps a shade less successful than his postwar Italian contemporaries Grappasonni or Angelini, San Remo-born Aldo Casera (b. 7/31/1920) was a regular competitor in postwar Europe and an Italian World Cup representative. In 1948 he won both the **Italian Open** and the **Italian PGA,** came back to defend the latter a year later, then won it for a third time in 1956. A quick-tempoed player with a balky putting stroke, Casera's lone major foreign title came in 1950, at the **Swiss Open.**

Paul Casey (UK)

Mirroring the modern trend, Cheltenham, England's Paul Casey (b. 7/21/1977) played American college golf at Arizona State University where, among other accomplishments, he became the only player ever to win three straight Pac 10 conference titles. Twice an **English Amateur** champion (1999 and 2000), the long-hitting Casey also claimed a place in history during Great Britain and Ireland's 1999 Walker Cup victory at Nairn, performing the rare feat of winning all four of his matches without a loss. Today a regular on the European Tour (where he was Rookie of the Year in 2001), Casey, now in his late 20s, has shown steady improvement, particularly in 2003 when he went to Australia to win the **ANZ Classic** at Sydney's New South Wales GC, then later returned to England to capture the **Benson & Hedges International.** Closing the season sixth in the Order of Merit, Casey continued his good play in 2004, qualifying for his first Ryder Cup, tying for sixth at the Masters, and teaming with Luke Donald to win the **World Cup.** Also the winner of the 2001 **Scottish PGA,** Casey now enters his prime years battling Lee Westwood and Ian Poulter for the rank of England's best maturing player.

Tony Cashmore (Australia)

Though hardly a newcomer to the business of golf design, architect Anthony Cashmore is enjoying greater contemporary prominence after completing several fine links-style courses in his homeland, most notably the Dunes GL (on Victoria's Mornington Peninsula) and 36 holes at the Thirteenth Beach GL at Barwon Heads. All told, Cashmore has been involved with upward of 70 design or redesign projects both at home and abroad, though the centerpieces of his portfolio reside exclusively Down Under.

Billy Casper (USA)

With a career record that includes 51 PGA Tour victories (sixth all-time), three Major championships, and a string of eight consecutive Ryder Cup appearances from 1961 to 1975, San Diego's William Earl Casper Jr. (b. 6/24/1931) might well be viewed as the most underrated player of the modern era. The reasons for this are several, though the most obvious is that in not being represented by Mark McCormack, Casper never enjoyed the marketing hype generated for those noted IMG clients Nicklaus, Palmer, and Player. The fact that he was a quiet, conservative sort of golfer surely didn't help, but an examination of the record brings another more legitimate factor to bear: With "only" three Major championships to his credit, Casper's ability to reel in golf's biggest prizes was not on par with Palmer (8), Player (9), or, quite obviously, Nicklaus (20).

All of that said, Casper's record for consistently first-rate performance is among golf's most impressive, for after a 58th-place finish on the money list during his rookie year of 1955, he strung together 16 consecutive seasons inside the top dozen, each of which included at least one victory. Twice the Tour's leading money winner (1966 and '68) and a two-time PGA Player of the Year (1966 and '70), Casper's most impressive feat might well be the claiming of five Vardon Trophies (for lowest scoring average) between 1960 and 1968, a career total thus far matched only by Lee Trevino and Tiger Woods.

Like a young Bobby Locke, Casper spent much of his career playing high-percentage approaches toward the center of greens, a solid tactic given that he is universally ranked among the greatest putters of all time. Nowhere was this style better rewarded than at the 1959 **U.S. Open** at Winged Foot where, over one of golf's most demanding courses, his decidedly wristy stroke was employed only 114 times en route to claiming his first Major title. Casper's second **U.S. Open** victory, however, stands among the most talked-about ever, for in 1966 at the Olympic Club, he trailed Arnold Palmer by seven shots through 63 holes before a final-nine 32 (combined with an epic Palmer collapse) set up an 18-hole play-off. Though trailing early, Casper stormed back to win by four, capping the greatest comeback victory in Major championship history. His final Major came at the 1970 **Masters,** where second- and third-round 68s helped him to tie Gene Littler at 279, with Casper again prevailing in a play-off.

A winner of numerous top-shelf regular Tour events (see below), Casper was also a successful international competitor, taking the 1974 **Trophée Lancôme,** as well as the **Italian** and **Mexican Opens,** a pair of early **Brazilian Opens** (1959 and '60), and the short-lived **Havana Invitational** (1958). He also managed a solid 20-10-7 Ryder Cup record and later captained the 1979 squad to victory at The Greenbrier. Joining the Champions Tour in 1981, Casper went on to record nine victories, including the 1983 **U.S. Senior Open** at Hazeltine National.

PGA Tour Wins (51): 1957 Phoenix; 1958 & '63 Bing Crosby; **1959 & '66 U.S. Open;** 1962 & '64 Doral; 1962 & '68 Greensboro; 1964 & '68 Colonial; 1965, '66, '69 & '73 Western Open; 1966 San Diego; 1967 Canadian Open; 1968 & '70 Los Angeles; **1970 Masters,** and 4 Greater Hartford Opens, 3 Portland Opens & 3 500 Festival Opens

Intn'l Wins (6): 1974 Trophée Lancôme; 1975 Italian Open; 1977 Mexican Open

Champions Tour Wins: 9 (1982–1989)

Ryder Cup: 1961–75 (8); 1979 Capt

1956-1978

	56	57	58	59	60	61	62	63	64	65	66	67
Masters	-	T16	T20	MC	4	T7	T15	T11	T5	T35	T10	T24
US Open	T14	MC	T13	1	T12	T17	MC	-	4	T17	1	4
British	-	-	-	-	-	-	-	-	-	-	-	-
PGA	-	-	2	T17	T24	T15	T51	-	T9	T2	T3	-

	68	69	70	71	72	73	74	75	76	77	78
Masters	T16	T2	1	T13	T17	T17	T37	6	8	T14	MC
US Open	T9	T40	T8	MC	T11	MC	MC	-	-	-	T30
British	4	T25	T17	T7	T40	-	-	-	-	-	-
PGA	T6	T35	T18	2	T4	T35	T63	T5	T51	T31	MC

Lord Castlerosse (UK)

Later the sixth Earl of Kenmare, Killarney, Ireland's Valentine Viscount Castlerosse (1891–1943) was one of golf's greatest-ever personalities, a man described by Henry Longhurst—himself no slouch in this regard—as "the most completely unique character I ever came to know." A prominent pre–World War II columnist for the *Sunday* *Express,* the 275-pound Castlerosse was, quite literally, larger than life, once during a visit to Cannes ordering 12 dozen bottles of hotel mineral water to use for his bath.

As a golfer, he was briefly a scratch player in his early years before a World War I bullet wound to his right elbow, plus years of high living, rendered him a bit less proficient. His great gift to the game, however, has held up far better, for it was Castlerosse who initiated the building of the famous Killarney Golf & Fishing Club upon his ancestral Irish estate. Though his skills deserted him, his Lordship remained an avid player for years, prompting Longhurst to recall one particularly memorable round where Castlerosse, well off his game, topped shot after shot. Finally, at the home hole, when one final swing sent his ball scooting off into the heather, he instructed his caddie to "pick that up, have the clubs destroyed, and leave the course."

He passed away, all too young, in 1943.

Alex Cejka (Czech Republic/ Germany)

The first native of the Czech Republic to earn full PGA Tour playing privileges, Alex Cejka (b. Marienbad, 12/2/ 1970) was actually raised in Germany after fleeing his homeland with his father at age nine. He has won a total of 11 international events on the European and European Challenge Tours (including the 1990 and '92 **Czech Opens** and the 2002 **Trophée Lancôme**) and represented Germany in seven World Cups between 1995 and 2003. Now residing back in Prague, Cejka can be viewed as the top German player since Bernhard Langer or, alternatively, the finest Czech player of all time.

Antonio Cerda (Argentina)

The second world-class player produced by the surprisingly golfing country of Argentina, Tony Cerda (b. 1921) only won his home **Argentine Open** twice (1948 and '56), rather a surprise in an event which has seen homebreds like José Jurado, Vicente Fernandez, and Roberto de Vicenzo make it their personal playgrounds. What Cerda did do, however, was compete successfully abroad, winning back-to-back **German Opens** in 1951 and '52, as well as the 1950 **Spanish** and the 1956 **Dutch** and **Italian**. He also appeared in four Masters tournaments (tying for 24th in 1961) and further demonstrated his world-class skills by teaming with de Vicenzo to win the inaugural 1953 **World Cup** in Montreal (with Cerda taking individual honors), then finishing second and fourth in the ensuing two years. Where Cerda ultimately established himself, however, was at the Open Championship where he cracked the top 5 for five consecutive years (1951–55), twice finishing second. On the first occasion, in 1951, he charged from well back to nipping at leader Max Faulkner's heels before a six at the par-3 14th sealed his fate, while in 1953 Cerda joined the crowd that finished four in arrears of Hogan during his legendary triumph at Carnoustie. A bit of Cerda's Open success might be chalked up to his low, boring ball flight, a style perfect for the wind. But he was also an excellent putter and handy around the greens, a solid championship mix.

Doris Chambers (UK)

For many years a key figure in Britain's Ladies Golf Union, Liverpool's Doris Chambers made her name as the 1923 **British Ladies** champion, her victory at Burnham & Berrow representing the sole break in a string of seven titles claimed by either Cecil Leitch or Joyce Wethered. A semifinalist as far back as 1909, Chambers also captained the 1934, '36, and '48 Curtis Cup sides, as well as several international teams of the 1930s.

Robert Chambers (UK)

The son of a founding brother in Edinburgh's famous W & R Chambers printing and publishing house, Robert Chambers (1802–1871) was a fine amateur player who also wrote one of golf's first-ever books, *A Few Rambling Remarks on Golf.* Really more of a pamphlet at 31 paperback pages, this stylish 1862 work introduced newcomers to the game's rules, equipment, and techniques and would twice be revised and expanded (under the titles *Gymnastics, Golf and Curling* and *Golfing*) later in the century. Chambers was also the great-grandfather of Sir Guy Campbell, a noted player, writer, and course designer of the pre–World War II era, making for an impressive family legacy.

Dick Chapman (USA)

Few amateur golfers of any era can match the international record assembled by Greenwich, Connecticut, socialite Richard Davol Chapman (1911–1978), a dominant American player of the early postwar years. Chapman's résumé included a collection of national amateur titles from five different nations: the **United States** (1940), **Great Britain** (1951), **Canada** (1949), **France** (1939 and '52), and **Italy** (1960). Obviously a man who could afford to travel, Chapman might have found it ironic that his **U.S. Amateur** crown was won at his home club, Winged Foot, where he handsomely thrashed Duff McCullough in the final 11 and 9. The **British Amateur,** on the other hand, required a substantial journey, but once at Royal Porthcawl, Chapman dispatched an elite opponent, fellow American Charlie Coe, in the final by a convincing 5 and 4 margin. He was also champion of the 1958 **North & South.**

A man who tinkered with his swing frequently, Chapman appeared in 19 Masters and represented his country on three Walker Cup teams (1947, '51, and '53), compiling a 3-2 overall record. Oddly, despite capturing events literally the world over, Chapman never managed to win the then-prestigious Metropolitan Amateur—though it was played once at Winged Foot (in 1948) during his peak years.

Bob Charles (New Zealand)

In the many years before Phil Mickelson and Mike Weir, Carterton, New Zealand's Robert James Charles (b. 3/14/1936) was most prominently known, at least in America, as "the best left-handed player" in the game—hardly an unimpressive title, yet one which did a modest disservice to a man who has won over 75 events worldwide, including one Major championship.

Charles first made waves in his homeland at age 18 when he fended off a field that included Peter Thomson to take his first of four **New Zealand Opens.** Surprisingly (again, by American standards) he then waited six years to turn professional before beginning a long playing career throughout Australasia, Europe, and America. Though never a long hitter, Charles was universally known as one of the game's elite putters, frequently ranked behind only Bobby Locke in the postwar era. Naturally this was a key component in his winning six PGA Tour titles between 1963 and 1974 including his greatest triumph, the 1963 **Open Championship** at Royal Lytham & St. Annes, where a clutch five-footer at the 72nd set up the Open's last 36-hole play-off—a one-sided affair in which Charles one-putted 12 of the first 20 greens while routing American Phil Rodgers by eight.

In addition to winning the 1968 **Canadian Open** (by two over Jack Nicklaus), Charles twice finished third in the U.S. Open (1964 and '70), claimed second in the 1968 and '69 Open Championships, and tied for second at the 1968 PGA Championship. Indeed it was only at the Masters that he never seriously contended, owing, perhaps, to his relative lack of length. Charles also added several prominent European titles to his rash of smaller victories, including the 1969 **World Match Play,** the 1972 **British Masters,** and a pair of **Swiss Opens** in 1962 and '74. An occasional visitor to the Cape, he took the **South African Open** in 1973, beating Bobby Cole by three at the famed Durban CC. Not surprisingly, Charles has represented New Zealand nine times in World Cup play.

His velvet putting stroke holding up wonderfully with age, Charles returned to America full time upon turning 50 to tear up the Champions Tour, claiming 23 wins (fourth all-time) and more than $9 million over a 10-year span. He has also won two **Senior British Opens** (1989 and '93) and 10 additional senior titles worldwide.

PGA Tour Wins (6): 1963 Houston; **1963 British Open;** 1968 Canadian Open

Intn'l Wins (23): 1962 & '74 Swiss Open; 1969 World Match Play; 1972 British Masters; 1973 South African Open; and 4 New Zealand Opens & 3 New Zealand PGAs

Champions Tour Wins: 23 (1987–1996)

1958-1987

	58	59	60	61	62	63	64	65	66	67	68	69	70	71	72
Masters	MC	-	-	-	T25	T15	T40	T45	MC	MC	19	T29	17	MC	T22
US Open	-	-	-	-	-	T19	3	MC	MC	MC	T7	MC	T3	T13	MC
British	MC	-	-	MC	5	1	T17	MC	T38	MC	T2	2	T13	T18	T15
PGA	-	-	-	-	-	T13	T19	T41	-	-	T2	T35	T26	T13	T58

	73	74	75	76	77	78	79	80	81	82	83	84	85	86	87
Masters	T29	MC	MC	-	-	-	-								
US Open	T11	MC	-	-	-	-	-								
British	T7	MC	T12	T78	T43	T48	T10								
PGA	-	-	-	-	-	-	-								

Simone Thion de la Chaume (France)

Following in Arnaud Massy's footsteps to become France's second golfer to capture major foreign titles, Paris' Simone Thion de la Chaume (b. 11/24/1908) won the **British Girls** championship in 1924, then the **British Ladies** in 1927, beating the same opponent, Dorothy Pearson, in each final. The possessor of a smoothly repetitive swing, de la Chaume was, naturally, a force on her home turf, winning six **French Ladies Open** titles between 1926 and 1939 and nine **Closed** titles between 1925 and 1938, including a run of six straight from 1925 to 1930. An occasional competitor in America, de la Chaume was far and away France's first top female player, a legacy she seemed intent on bequeathing as she married another great athlete, tennis champion René LaCoste, and gave birth to daughter Catherine, a splendid golfer in her own right.

Don Cherry (USA)

Though long since departed from the competitive golf scene, the wonderfully named Donald Ross Cherry (b. 1924) was a native of Wichita Falls, Texas, who made it big both as a professional singer and a high-class competitive golfer. As a singer, he enjoyed several big hits and once fronted Tommy Dorsey's band, while his record on the links, if not entirely comparable, doesn't miss by much.

Cherry's biggest title was the 1953 **Canadian Amateur,** but he was also a semifinalist at the 1952 U.S. Amateur (where he was eliminated by Al Mengert), a finalist in the 1952 Metropolitan Amateur, and a three-time undefeated Walker Cup player (1953, '55, and '61). Cherry also appeared in nine Masters and eight U.S. Opens, actually having a chance to win the latter in 1960 at Cherry Hills. Having missed short birdie putts at the 69th and 70th, Cherry stood in the par-5 17th fairway, while up ahead Ben Hogan's chance for an epic victory splashed to a famous watery grave. Electing to go for the green in two, Cherry then dunked his approach and ultimately joined Hogan in a tie for ninth.

After years of amateur competition, Cherry actually turned pro in 1962, but made little impact on the PGA Tour. One reason was an explosive temper that, in Cherry's own words, "made Tommy Bolt look like Little Red Riding Hood." Nonetheless, for an entertainer of a genuinely professional level, Cherry's golfing record really was quite remarkable.

Chen Chien-Chung (Taiwan)

The son of Chen King-Shih, a patriarch of Taiwanese golf, Chen Chien-Chung emerged as a highly competitive Far Eastern player in the late 1960s, capturing national titles in **Korea** (1968), **India** (1970), and the **Philippines** (1971). In those early years of the Asian Tour, area professionals could hardly support themselves solely on tournament winnings, nor were club jobs plentiful in Taiwan. Consequently, Chien-Chung spent a number of years employed as a club professional abroad, primarily in Japan.

Chen Ching-Po (Taiwan)

The earliest of Taiwan's talented cadre of postwar golfers—and likely the best known until Lu Liang Huan's famous Open Championship run at Royal Birkdale in 1971—Chen Ching-Po was a consistent winner throughout the Far East, with his biggest title perhaps being the 1959 **Japan Open.** Beginning at Wentworth in 1956, he

was an 11-time World Cup player, though he was no longer representing Taiwan by the time of their historic 1972 triumph at Royal Melbourne. Chen Ching-Po also enjoyed uncommon exposure to American fans by appearing in six Masters (tying for 15th in 1963) and three times on *Shell's Wonderful World of Golf* between 1962 and 1966.

Chen King-Shih (Taiwan)

An important figure in golf's development in Taiwan, Chen King-Shih first discovered the game as a teenage caddie before ultimately turning professional in 1930. With few events in which to compete in those prewar years, and long past his prime by the late-1950s dawning of the Far Eastern circuit, "Old Man Chen" established his name primarily as a teacher. Indeed, it has been suggested that he worked with virtually all of Taiwan's prominent postwar players to one degree or another, especially his very successful son, Chen Chien-Chung.

Cherif El Sayed Cherif (Egypt)

A native of Cairo, the popular Cherif el Sayed Cherif (b. 1923) followed a decidedly Western path into the game of golf, beginning as a caddie, then working as an assistant professional at Egypt's venerable Gezira Sporting Club. A protégé of British expatriate and nine-time Egyptian Amateur champion John Plant, Cherif defeated Hassan Hassanein, his Gezira boss and Egypt's greatest-ever player, by a single shot in the 1955 **Egyptian Professional** championship. So established, he would later add **Egyptian Open** titles in 1959 and '68 before settling into the top professional position at Gezira and, simultaneously, the now-defunct GC of Lebanon.

Frank Chirkinian (USA)

Widely considered the "father of televised golf," Frank Chirkinian served as CBS's golf producer from 1958 to 2000, literally defining the medium as he went. Nicknamed "The Ayatollah" by anchor Pat Summerall for his dictatorial style, Chirkinian introduced many of the cornerstones of modern golf television, including the use of on-course microphones, aerial shots from cranes and blimps, and, most important, the over- and under-par scoring system universally used to keep track of the field. The winner of four Emmys among a plethora of awards, Chirkinian inspired a unique brand of affection among his employees, making him truly one from the Old School.

Willie Chisolm (UK/USA)

One of the countless Scottish professionals who emigrated to America early in the last century, Willie Chisolm achieved lasting fame at the 1919 U.S. Open at Brae Burn by taking an astounding 18 at the par-3 eighth hole during the opening round. This he managed by hitting his tee shot into a rock-filled ravine, then hammering away at it amidst the boulders for an ungodly stretch while playing partner Jim Barnes kept score from a bridge above. Upon finally freeing himself and holing out, Chisolm asked Barnes for a total, then feigned (we hope) shock at hearing 18, reportedly replying "Oh, Jim, that can't be so. You must have counted the echoes."

K. J. Choi (South Korea)

With 2002 victories in **New Orleans** and **Tampa,** Kyoung-Ju "K. J." Choi (b. Wando 5/19/1970) became the first Korean golfer to win an event on the PGA Tour, raising his world ranking from 192nd to 49th in the process. Though winless since, a Presidents Cup berth, his second World Cup appearance, and frequent appearances near the top of some prominent leaderboards have cemented his status as an international player of quality—a standing augmented by six additional victories in Asia and Europe (including the 1996 and '99 **Korean Opens** and the 2003 **Linde German Masters**) since 1996.

Marty Christmas (UK)

England's Martin J. Christmas (b. 1939) was an aggressive player who, at 21, lost the 1960 English Amateur to Doug Sewell in an exhausting 41 holes. Though business commitments soon carried him away from competitive golf, Christmas did make two semifinal appearances in the British Amateur (losing to Michael Bonallack in 1961 and Clive Clark in '64) and twice played in the Walker Cup, being the lone British player to score a point in 1961, in Seattle.

Charlie Chung (USA)

Generally considered the first golf professional of Chinese descent, Hawaii's Charlie Chung began as a caddie at the Oahu CC, learning to play the game with clubs fashioned out of guava sticks. By the mid-1920s he was one of the island's top players, winning the 1924 and '25 **Hawaiian Amateur** (aka the Manoa Cup) and in 1930 becoming the first local to win the **Hawaiian Open.** Though perhaps not to the same extent as black players like Bill Spiller and Ted Rhodes, Chung battled discrimination on many fronts, particularly being denied membership in the PGA of America in Hawaii when he had already been a member while the professional at California's affluent Redlands CC during the mid-1920s.

Stewart Cink (USA)

With four wins and nearly $13 million pocketed in eight full PGA Tour seasons, consistent top-35 money winner Stewart Ernest Cink (b. Huntsville, Alabama, 5/21/1973) has clearly established himself as a solid commodity on the contemporary competitive scene. This is not altogether surprising given his pre-Tour credentials: three-time All-America pick at Georgia Tech, consensus NCAA Player of the Year in 1995, top money winner (with three victories) on the 1996 Nationwide Tour, and a head-to-head defeat of Tiger Woods in a pre-Masters 1995 exhibition. In short, Cink is a classic example of the modern young player who arrives on Tour well seasoned and loaded for bear.

A tall man at 6'4", Cink is neither especially long, nor numbingly accurate. He can, however, keep it in play when conditions demand, as three U.S. Open top 10s since 1998 will testify. A two-time **Mexican Open** winner (1996 and '99), Cink's third Tour victory, the 2004 **Heritage Classic,** was shrouded in controversy when officials allowed him to remove loose impediments from a waste bunker just before winning a sudden-death play-off with Ted Purdy, though Cink's lie appeared clearly to have been improved in the process. He was later a somewhat surprising pick for the 2004 Ryder Cup team (his second appearance) but made Captain Hal Sutton look like a genius by handily winning the **WGC-NEC Invitational** (formerly the World Series of Golf) the very week of his selection.

Bobby Clampett (USA)

Though his career numbers (one win and only $1.4 million earned in 388 events) are indeed modest, forgetful are those who cannot recall the immense buzz that initially surrounded California's Robert Daniel Clampett Jr. (b. 4/22/1960). A native of the charmed Monterey Peninsula, the young Clampett was, quite literally, The Golfing Machine—that is, the walking embodiment of a neoteric, physics-oriented approach to golf outlined by Homer Kelley in his cultish book of the same name. And impressive The Machine was, for in addition to such standard spoils as twice being named NCAA Player of the Year at Brigham Young, winning the 1978 **Western Amateur,** and playing in the 1979 Walker Cup, Clampett wowed even the most seasoned observers with the truly remarkable ball-striking produced by his 5'10", 150-pound frame.

Sadly—and with a bit of mystery about it—The Machine would not last. Perhaps deflated by disappointment at the 1982 Open Championship (where he led by five at the halfway mark, only to finish 77-78, tied for 10th), Clampett slowly disappeared from the ranks of the elite, falling permanently from the PGA Tour's top 100 money winners in 1988 with only the 1982 **Southern Open** on his victory ledger.

Carnegie Clark (UK/Australia)

One of the countless natives of Carnoustie, Scotland, who carried forth the game of golf to the far corners of the planet, Carnegie Clark (1881–1959) was perhaps the single most important component in golf's growth in Australia. Emigrating Down Under in 1895, Clark was originally employed running the golf section of a prominent Sydney sporting goods firm but soon became the first professional at the Royal Sydney GC, a post he would hold for nearly three decades. From this pulpit Clark established himself in all areas of the game, particularly as a player, for his early record included three **Australian Open** titles (1906, '10, and '11) and the 1908 **Australian PGA**. More important, he introduced the primitive Australian scene to cutting-edge items such as wound golf balls and the Vardon grip, establishing a prominent (albeit, one assumes, largely unopposed) reputation as the nation's top teacher. Clark also designed numerous courses, including early layouts at his home club and Royal Queensland, though predictably, little of his original design work remains intact today.

Clive Clark (UK)

Well known on both sides of the Atlantic, England's Clive Clark (b. 1945) initially studied architecture before deciding to make a go of golf, a decision influenced by some unexpectedly fine play in the mid-1960s. Clark was, in 1965, a finalist in both the British and English Amateurs, losing in each (despite leading after the morning rounds) to a peaking and well-nigh unbeatable Michael Bonallack. Splitting the **English Open Stroke Play** title was some consolation that summer, as was a Walker Cup appearance in which Clark holed a gutsy 30-footer at the last to halve both his singles match and the overall cup.

A subsequent professional career was somewhat successful, featuring an invitation to the 1968 Masters and a victory at the 1970 **John Player** tournament. Clark also managed, in 1973, to become that rare man who represents Britain in both Walker and Ryder Cup play. He eventually found work as both a TV commentator and golf course architect.

Gordon Clark (UK)

Englishman Gordon James Clark (b. 1933) was known as a steady, solid player who won the **British Amateur** in 1964, beating the defending champion Michael Lunt on the 39th hole at Ganton. Clark was also a semifinalist in 1967 (losing to American Bob Dickson at Formby) as well as the loser of an epic English Amateur final to Ian Caldwell in 1961. In 1965 he was a member of the Walker Cup team that went to Baltimore but only appeared in one match, a loss at foursomes.

Howard Clark (UK)

One of Britain's more successful pros just before the arrival of the Faldo-Lyle-Woosnam troika, Howard Keith Clark (b. Leeds, 8/26/1954) was the 1971 **British Boys** champion before journeying to Portugal to be coached by the great Henry Cotton. He turned professional following an appearance in the 1973 Walker Cup and enjoyed a fine decade's run, winning 11 times on the European Tour from 1978 to 1988 and playing a stout six times in the Ryder Cup between 1977 and 1995. Clark was also a four-time English representative at the **World Cup,** capturing the individual title in 1985 at La Quinta, California. Though wins at the 1978 **Portuguese Open** and the 1984 **Volvo PGA** represented bona fide quality wins, there are those who feel Clark's raw talent somewhat exceeded his professional success.

Robert Clark (UK)

An Edinburgh printer and avid (if not altogether excellent) golfer, Robert Clark is owed an eternal debt by all those interested in the early history of the game. In 1875, he assembled golf's first epic volume, a 284-page collection of historical documents and records entitled *Golf: A Royal and Ancient Game*. As the book was an attempt at cataloging literally all that had been written about golf prior to that time, it is both thorough and invaluable, preserving for posterity all manner of materials that would otherwise have slipped through the cracks of time. In addition to reprinting this work a number of times through 1899, Clark also published *Famous Scottish Links and Other Golfing Papers*, an historical collection by former R&A captain T. D. Miller, in 1911.

Darren Clarke (Northern Ireland)

An imposing presence on the international scene, Ulsterman Darren Christopher Clarke (b. Dungannon,

8/14/1968) is one of the European Tour's modern stars, placing among the top 10 in the Order of Merit every year but one since 1995. Yet it is perhaps Clark's ability to win around the globe, against quality fields, that is most impressive, an international record exceeded only by the perpetually traveling Ernie Els. Indeed, Clarke has won in the United Kingdom (including three **English Opens**) and Ireland, three European countries, South Africa, Japan, and the United States. And though most of his victories have been noteworthy, few stand out more than the American triumphs as both came in elite-field World Golf Championship events.

In the first, the 2000 **WGC-Match Play,** Clarke defeated World No. 2 David Duval in the semis, then handled No. 1 Tiger Woods 4 and 3 in the final, at San Diego's La Costa CC. In the second, Clarke rode a closing 67 to a four-stroke victory in the 2003 **WGC-NEC Invitational** (formerly the World Series of Golf) at Firestone, becoming only the second player (after Woods) to capture multiple WGC events.

A large, burly figure often given to smoking cigars, Clarke's game is largely about power, particularly off the tee where he ranks among the longer of the world's top players. Consequently, his record in the Majors has been decidedly mixed. The U.S. Open (one top-10 in 10 tries) and PGA (one top-10 and five missed cuts in seven appearances) have been mediocre, while ties for second and third in the 1997 and 2001 Open Championships suggest that a Major breakthrough may still be in the offing. Clarke has also embarked on a more serious fitness regimen of late, perhaps the edge he needs to move his game that one final notch to the elite level.

PGA Tour Wins (2): 2000 WGC-Match Play; 2003 World Series **Intn'l Wins (11):** 1998 Benson & Hedges; 1998 Volvo Masters **Ryder Cup:** 1997–2004 (4)

Mike Clayton (Australia)

Listing the 1978 **Australian** and the 1977 and '81 **Victorian Amateurs** upon his early résumé, Melbourne's Michael Clayton (b. 5/30/1957) turned professional in 1981 before spending some 15 years competing on both the European and Australasian Tours. A one-time winner on the Continent (the 1984 **Timex Open**), he enjoyed greater success at home, listing the 1994 **Heineken** and **Coolum Classics** among six prominent domestic victories, as well as the 1984 **Korean Open** regionally. Having proven himself both an insightful writer (for the *Melbourne Age* and *Golf Australia*) and a skilled television commentator, Clayton has spent the last decade developing his own golf design business, gaining particular notice for his fine restorative work. More recently his collaboration with American Tom Doak on two of Australia's finest new courses, St. Andrews Beach and Barnbougle Dunes, has proven highly successful.

Keith Clearwater (USA)

Few professional careers illustrate the capriciousness of golf better than that of Keith Allen Clearwater (b. Long Beach, California, 9/1/1959). A member of Brigham Young's 1981 national championship team and winner of the 1982 **North & South Amateur,** Clearwater blasted onto the PGA Tour in 1987, winning twice and being named Rookie of the Year. The first victory, at **Colonial,** loomed particularly large, for it included a pair of 64s on a 36-hole Sunday that sparked a three-stroke margin over Davis Love III. But as quickly as Clearwater rose he plummeted, falling out of the top 125 for the next two years and only twice seeing the top 50 since.

Percy Clifford (Mexico)

Something of a throwback to the days of Empire, Percy Clifford (1907–1977) was born to British parents residing in Mexico City and, though educated primarily back in the United Kingdom, would live nearly his entire life south of the border. While Clifford cannot truly be called the father of Mexican Golf (*see* William Townsend), he was certainly its most important contributor, initially making a splash by winning six **Mexican Amateurs,** including a cluster of five in six years from 1928 to 1933.

Toward the end of the 1940s, Clifford enlisted the support of the Mexican government in planning the country's first top-notch facility, the Club de Golf Mexico. Fascinated by the course design process, he soon turned his own career toward architecture, ultimately designing approximately 40 courses—or nearly half of Mexico's nationwide total circa-1980. Hardly the rudimentary type of builder that one might expect to find on the frontier, Clifford frequently created sophisticated layouts of note, including the Club de Golf Vallescondido, a prosperous Mexico City institution whose 18 holes are generally considered among the best in Central and South America. Interestingly, though his work was geared to Mexico's small, affluent golfing class, Clifford was a noted opponent of extravagance in course construction, generally adhering to budgets that would be laughable by contemporary standards.

After retiring to Rancho Santa Fe, California, he died of cancer in Chicago at age 77.

Notable Courses: C de G Bellavista; **C de G Vallescondido;** Pierre Marqués GC

George Cobb (USA)

Savannah, Georgia, native George Cobb (1914–1986) may hold a unique distinction in the annals of golf, likely being the only course designer ever to be commanded into an architectural career by the U.S. Marine Corps. Having enlisted in 1941 when he was a scratch golfer and a practicing landscape architect, Cobb was essentially ordered to build 36 holes at North Carolina's Camp LeJeune—though he would ultimately serve only as construction supervisor after convincing superiors to bring Fred Findlay aboard as primary designer.

Cobb would not enter the design profession full time until 1956 but would then become one of the more successful architects in the Southeast. The builder of roughly 100 courses, he gained a good bit of notoriety by becoming the first consulting architect at Augusta National, frequently implementing changes sought by Bobby Jones and Clifford Roberts, and designing the club's famous par-3 course in 1960. Cobb was assisted in his later years by John LaFoy before passing away in Greenville, South Carolina, at age 71.

José Coceres (Argentina)

With his 2001 victory at the **Heritage Classic,** José Coceres (b. Chaco, 8/14/1963) became the first Argentine to win on the PGA Tour since the great Roberto de Vicenzo in 1968. Clearly something of a late bloomer, Coceres managed only one win outside of his native South America (the 1994 **Heineken Open** in Europe) prior to his 36th birthday. Since that time, however, he has captured the lucrative 2000 **Dubai Desert Classic** (by two over Paul McGinley and Patrick Sjoland) in addition to breaking through twice (at the Heritage and the 2001 **Walt Disney**) in America. Another of golf's modern globe-trotters, the affable Coceres has established himself as the best of Argentina's deepest-ever competitive flock.

Charlie Coe (USA)

Among a strong field of postwar American amateurs, Ardmore, Oklahoma's long, lean Charles R. Coe (1923–2001) might well have been the best. The scion of an affluent oil family, he declined to turn pro following a fine career at the University of Oklahoma, going instead into the family business while saving his elegant swing for golf of a distinctly less-commercial nature. His biggest titles, of course, were a pair of **U.S. Amateur** crowns, won in 1949 and '58. The former, played at Rochester's Oak Hill CC, included a near-record 11 and 10 route of Rufus King in the final, while the latter ended with a 5 and 4 win over University of Florida star Tommy Aaron. A bid for a third title in 1959 fell short by the slimmest of margins: one down to a Jack Nicklaus birdie on the 36th hole at The Broadmoor.

Coe also came close to winning a British Amateur, losing in the 1951 final to fellow American Dick Chapman, but he did claim one **Western Amateur** (1950) and four **Trans-Mississippi** crowns between 1947 and 1956. He was also six times the low amateur at the Masters, including a remarkable tie for second in 1961, just a single stroke behind Gary Player. A fixture on the Walker Cup team, Coe appeared five times, serving as a playing captain in 1959 and compiling an overall mark of 7-2-2. Certainly among the finest career amateurs in American golf history, Coe was paid the supreme tribute by the ultratalented Harvie Ward, who said of him: "He was the only guy that I feared to play."

Major Amateur Wins (7): 1947, '49, '52 & '56 Trans-Miss; 1949 & '58 U.S. Amateur; 1950 Western Amateur
Walker Cup: 1949, '51, '59 (c), '61 & '63 (5)

Jim Colbert (USA)

A former collegiate football player at Kansas State, Jim Colbert (b. Elizabeth, New Jersey, 3/9/1941) was in many ways the consummate journeyman over more than 20 years on the PGA Tour, never posting a top-10 finish on the money list or winning a Major championship but making a good living and capturing eight regular titles. His peak season was 1983, wherein he won both the **Colonial** and the **Texas Open** and finished 15th in money, though he would quickly slip to 64th and 88th in the years immediately to follow. Like many fine athletes, however, Colbert aged well, allowing him to achieve substantial success on the Champions Tour where he won 20 times between 1991 and 2001.

Bobby Cole (South Africa)

Once a teenage phenom touted by Gary Player, Bobby Cole (b. Springs, 5/11/1948) was the **South African Junior** champion at 15 and the youngest-ever **British Amateur** winner in 1966, defeating the redoubtable Ronnie Shade 3 and 2 at Carnoustie. Also the youngest ever to make the cut at the Masters in 1967, Cole enjoyed a fairly successful career at home, capturing the **South African Open** in 1974 and '80 and teaming with Dale Hayes to win the 1974 **World Cup** in Caracas. He managed little headway in Europe or America, however, with the 1977 **Buick Open** being his only victory on either circuit. Long married to former LPGA glamour girl Laura Baugh, Cole played the Champions Tour with limited success for several seasons beginning in 1998.

Neil Coles (UK)

A strong argument can be made that prior to the maturation of six-time Major champion Nick Faldo, London native Neil Chapman Coles, M.B.E. (b. 9/26/1934), was England's finest postwar golf professional. True, he failed to win an Open Championship (a second in 1973 being his best effort) and a fear of flying removed any possibility of establishing himself internationally. Yet the smoothly repetitive Coles has put together quite a record, including 27 European Tour wins, 15 European Senior Tour triumphs, and eight Ryder Cup appearances. He is also the oldest winner (at nearly 68 years) of an officially sponsored major tour event (the 2002 **Lawrence Batley Senior Open**) and the only man to claim an individual professional event in six different decades.

Such are big doings for anyone, never mind a man with a palpably strong grip who turned professional at age 16, while still a 14 handicap! Hard work certainly allowed Coles to develop his game, however, and by the mid-1960s, free of any time-consuming club affiliation, he was regularly cashing winning checks in Britain and around the Continent. He seemed particularly adept at match play, thrice winning the old *News of the World* event and also reaching the final of the first World Match Play, where he lost 2 and 1 to Arnold Palmer in 1964. His then-record 40 Ryder Cup matches—many played during bleak, American-dominated years—resulted in a 12-21-7 record, though twice beating Doug Sanders on the same day in 1967 stands out as a highlight.

Once a bit temperamental on the course, the bald, sideburned Coles later became a model of stoic decorum, quietly going about his business with little outward emotion. It has been suggested that with a bit more drive he might well have been a world beater. But both his fine style of play and massive winning ledger bring to mind the words of Jack Nicklaus who said: "It's amazing sometimes what other people think *you* should do."

Intn'l Wins (27): 1964, '65 & '73 PGA Match Play; 1966 British Masters; 1971 German Open; 1972 Scottish Open; 1973 Spanish Open; 1976 Volvo PGA; and 3 Daks Tournaments
European Sr Tour Wins: 15 (1992–2002)
Ryder Cup: 1961–73 & '77 (8)

Glenna Collett (USA)

Born: New Haven, Connecticut, 6/20/1903 **Died:** Gulfstream, Florida, 2/2/1989

Glenna Collett was a fine young athlete, successfully competing at all manner of games before dedicating herself to golf at age 14. Though naturally a powerful ball-striker (she once hit a measured drive 307 yards), Collett took extensive lessons from two-time U.S. Open winner Alex Smith to develop her all-around skills, much-needed help it seems, for her first tournament entry, the 1918 Rhode Island Ladies, resulted in a medal score of 132!

But with several years of development, Collett had become a polished and dangerous opponent when she arrived at the Greenbrier for the 1922 **U.S. Women's Amateur,** setting a qualifying record score of 81, then passing uneventfully through the field before defeating Mrs. W. A. Gavin 5 and 4 for the title. Over the next 13 years she would win the **Women's Amateur** on five more occasions, a record which, in these days of big-money professionalism, is likely to stand forever. Interestingly, Mrs. Gavin was perhaps the weakest of Collett's final-round opponents, for she would later eliminate such stalwarts as Alexa Stirling (9 and 8 in 1925), Virginia Van Wie (13 and 12 in 1928 and 6 and 5 in 1930), and a young Patty Berg (3 and 2 in 1935). Collett would also batter the great Ada MacKenzie 9 and 8 in the 1924 **Canadian Ladies** (having already won the 1923 Canadian crown more sedately) and for much of the 1920s dominated the links at Pinehurst, taking six **North & South** titles from 1922 to 1930. She was also a six-time **Eastern Amateur** champion.

Though a winner of the 1925 **French Ladies,** Collett failed in several attempts to bring home the British title, most notably after reaching the final in both 1929 and '30. On the former occasion, she lost an epic match to that other great woman of the age, Joyce Wethered, at St. Andrews, this after Wethered had knocked her out at an earlier stage in 1925 at Troon. In 1930 Collett fell victim to 19-year-old Diana Fishwick who upset her, monumentally, at Formby, 4 and 3.

In 1931 Collett wed Edward H. Vare, and it was under her married name that she played and/or captained in the first six Curtis Cups (1932–50). Her name change would also prove highly relevant to the LPGA which, two years after its founding, designated the Vare Trophy to honor the player carrying the year's lowest scoring average in 1952.

Major Amateur Wins (18): 1922, '25, '28, '29, '30 & '35 U.S. Women's Amateur; 1922, '23, '24, '27, '29 & '30 North & South; 1922, '23, '24, '27, '32 & '35 Eastern
Curtis Cup: 1932, '36, '38, '48 (c) (4); 1934 & '50 Capt

Harry Collis (UK/USA)

A London native who starred in soccer as a youth, Harry Collis (1878–1937) came to the United States in 1889, following the standard golfing immigrant route into a greenkeeping job at the Indianapolis CC. Moving on to Chicago's Flossmoor CC in 1906, Collis came up with several agronomical inventions (including a strain of bent grass) and extensively remodeled the golf course, the latter move leading to numerous architectural jobs around the country. Though he occasionally teamed with Olympia Fields professional Jack Daray, most of Collis' more noteworthy work was done solo, including the Phoenix CC in 1919 and a substantial early redesign of Medinah's No. 3 course. He also laid out a soon-defunct course in Annapolis, Maryland, which would later be rebuilt, with alterations by William Flynn, as today's U.S. Naval Academy GC.

Harry S. Colt (UK)

Born: Highgate, England, 8/4/1869 **Died:** East Hendred, England, 11/21/1951

There have been few more prominent figures in the history of golf design than Harry Shapland Colt, an attorney by trade who eventually became as influential a course architect as the game has ever seen. A fine amateur player, Colt captained the team at Cambridge, competed in the Open Championship, was a member of the R&A, and reached the semifinals of the 1906 British Amateur at Hoylake, where he lost 3 and 2 to eventual champion James Robb. He got his first taste of course design in 1894 when he helped professional Douglas Rolland to build a new layout for the Rye GC, stayed on as Rye's secretary, then took a similar position at Sunningdale upon its 1901 opening. He would remain at Sunningdale until 1913, by which time the growing demand for his design services made a full-time architectural career viable.

Having met Dr. Alister MacKenzie while building the Alwoodley GC in 1907, Colt eventually took him on as a partner, though not necessarily with productive results. Relations between the two have long been reported as strained and stories exist of their bidding against each other on the same projects. Although his name would remain on the firm's masthead until 1928, MacKenzie had pretty well drifted off on his own by the early 1920s. More loyal, however, was Captain C. H. Alison, a highly skilled architect at least loosely affiliated with Colt following their meeting at Stoke Poges in 1906. A worldwide traveler, Alison would eventually undertake designs on the firm's behalf in North America, Asia, and South Africa, while Colt handled most of their domestic projects. A later arrival, J. S. F. Morrison, backed up an aging Colt at home while also working throughout the entirety of Europe.

With a list of design and redesign credits that reads like a veritable atlas of British golf, Colt's résumé exceeds capsulized description. We might, however, note that it was Colt to whom turned the St. Andrews Links Trust, in 1913, to build their Eden course; Philadelphian George Crump, to draw initial plans for his renowned Pine Valley; Colt's former employer, Sunningdale, to build their New course in 1922; not less than four clubs in the present Open Championship rota for tournament-related alterations. And the list goes on and on.

Something of a trendsetter in his day, Colt tended to build challenging, full-size courses that were far more in tune with the new Haskell ball than the old gutty. His designs were highly strategic and his bunkers tended to be attractively sculpted and plainly visible. In an era of significantly lower green speeds, he favored heavily contoured putting surfaces that, not coincidentally, tended to drain especially well. He was also an advocate of tree planting and was among the first to actively route golf courses through residential developments. A frequent writer on numerous golf-related subjects, Colt laid out his design concepts, with some help from his partners, in *Golf Course Architecture* (Country Life, 1920), a popular title reprinted in the modern era.

A devout and largely unassuming man, Harry Colt outlived most of his family and friends, dying deaf and lonely at age 82.

Notable Courses: Alwoodley GC (with MacKenzie); Hamilton G&CC, Canada; Moor Park GC (54); **Pine Valley GC (with Crump), USA;** Royal Portrush GC, N. Ireland; St. George's Hill GC (36, 9 NLE); Sunningdale GC, New Course; Swinley Forest GC; Wentworth GC (36)

Andrew Coltart (UK)

A solid if unspectacular player, Andrew Coltart (b. Dumfries, 5/12/1970) is a former **Scottish Boys** champion and Walker Cupper (both in 1991) who has enjoyed varying degrees of success around the world. Primarily a European Tour player, he has also played extensively in Australia where he managed to win the 1998 Order of Merit and has twice captured the **Australian PGA.** His first European win came at the 1998 **Qatar Masters,** a victory which went a long way toward making Coltart a captain's pick for the 1999 Ryder Cup matches.

Archie Compston (UK)

Given to having his caddie tote a toy black cat as a good-luck charm, tall, rugged-looking Archibald Edward Wones Compston (1893–1962) was one of the more compelling figures in inter-war British golf. A powerful and aggressive player, the native of Wolverhampton, England twice won the old *News of the World* match play (the nation's second most important title), as well as a number of smaller events throughout Britain. What Compston could not win, sadly, was the Open Championship, though he certainly had his chances. In 1925, for example, he closed with three straight 75s at Prestwick to tie Ted Ray at 301, one back of

Jim Barnes. An even greater opportunity was squandered in 1930 at Hoylake when a brilliant third-round 68 gave Compston a one-stroke lead before a closing 82 helped Bobby Jones to the second leg of the Grand Slam.

On the positive side of the ledger, however, Compston is equally recalled for one of golf's all-time epic victories, an almost inconceivable 18 and 17 paddling given to a travel-weary Walter Hagen during a 72-hole, £750 challenge match at Moor Park in 1928. This beating—as large a deficit as might be recalled in the history of such things—was certainly comprehensive, yet just a few short days later when the Open Championship came around at Royal St. George's, there was Hagen, back on his feet, taking home the one that really counted, this time by two over Sarazen and three over the hapless Compston.

The winner of two ancient PGA Tour titles (the 1926 **Lakeland Open** and the 1928 **Eastern Open**), Compston was for many years the professional at Coombe Hill, where he was instrumental in the development of the fine amateur Pam Barton and a frequent teacher/playing companion to the Prince of Wales. He later spent many winters as professional at Bermuda's famous Mid Ocean Club, an obviously choice stop.

PGA Tour Wins (2):
Intn'l Wins (13): 1925 & '27 PGA Match Play
Ryder Cup: 1927–31 (3)

Frank Conner (USA)

Born in Vienna, Austria, Frank Conner (b. 1/11/1946) grew up in Belleville, Illinois, where he excelled in tennis, ultimately being named an All-American at Trinity (Texas) University and playing in three U.S. Opens. Realizing that his tennis upside was limited, however, Conner took up golf at age 24 and eventually, several mini-tours and missed Qualifying Schools later, worked his way onto the PGA Tour. Though never a Tour winner, Conner came close, losing the 1982 Heritage Classic in a play-off to Tom Watson. He remains, along with Ellsworth Vines, as the only man to participate in U.S. Opens in both major country club sports.

Sean Connery (UK)

One of Hollywood's best-known and most dedicated golfers (and partial sponsor of ex-PGA Tour player Mike Springer), Edinburgh's Sean Connery, O.B.E. (b. 8/25/1930) also holds the distinction of starring in one of the few meaningful golf scenes ever put to film, the memorable match in the James Bond epic *Goldfinger*. It has often been stated that this was Connery's debut at the game, though he looks entirely too much at home as he clips the

eponymous villain for £5,000 for such an assertion to be entirely true. The sequence was filmed at the Stoke Poges GC, by the way, a fine H. S. Colt layout situated conveniently close to Pinewood Studios.

Joe Conrad (USA)

San Antonio native Joseph W. Conrad (b. 1930) was a strong postwar amateur whose name is perhaps lost among the E. Harvey Wards and Frank Stranahans of the period. A winner of the both the **Southern** and **Trans-Mississippi Amateurs** in 1953 (as well as a second **Southern** in '54), he traveled to St. Andrews with the 1955 American Walker Cup team, split two matches there, then proceeded to win the **British Amateur** at Royal Lytham & St. Annes. He capped off this extended summer visit by returning to St. Andrews to finish as low amateur at the Open Championship, though well back of champion Peter Thomson. Conrad turned professional a year later but proved too short a hitter to enjoy major success on the PGA Tour.

Charles Coody (USA)

After a prominent amateur career in Texas, TCU graduate Billy Charles Coody (b. Stamford, Texas, 7/13/1937) enjoyed a solid professional career which saw long periods of consistent, unspectacular play broken by the occasional dramatic moment. Coody's grandest stage, without a doubt, has been the **Masters** where he bogeyed the final three holes to lose a heartbreaker (by two to George Archer) in 1969, only to come back and win the Green Jacket—his only Major title—when birdies at the 69th and 70th slipped him past a fading Johnny Miller in 1971. He also won twice in Great Britain during the autumn of 1973, including the lucrative **John Player Classic** at Turnberry. A solidly built man standing 6'2", Coody claimed a total of three PGA Tour events and, following his Masters win, made a single Ryder Cup appearance in 1971. He was also a five-time winner on the Champions Tour between 1989 and 1996.

John Cook (USA)

Born in Toledo, Ohio, John Neuman Cook (b. 10/2/1957) grew up in Southern California before returning to the Midwest—recruited by Jack Nicklaus and Tom Weiskopf—to attend college at Ohio State. There he starred on a national championship team, was a three-time All-American, captured the 1978 **U.S. Amateur** (defeating Wake Forest's Scott Hoch 5 and 4 in the final), and nearly defended that title, only losing to Mark O'Meara in the 1979 final. With a father who served as a Tournament Director on the PGA

Tour and a bit of coaching from 1964 U.S. Open champion Ken Venturi, few players have ever been better prepared upon turning pro.

The results, not surprisingly, have been strong, with 11 PGA Tour victories, more than $11 million in career earnings, and occasional scoring outbursts of eye-popping proportion. Most prominent among these was the 1996 **Memphis Classic** where Cook set a 54-hole Tour scoring record by opening 64-62-63, for a 24-under-par total of 189. A closing 72 left him one above Mike Souchak's all-time 72-hole record, but seven strokes ahead of the nearest competition. The following year, trailing by five at the **Bob Hope,** Cook streaked home with 62-63, tying Ron Streck's 36-hole closing record to edge Mark Calcavecchia by one.

Perhaps the sole blemish on the Cook résumé is the lack of a professional Major championship, though second place finishes at the 1992 Open Championship and PGA, and top-5s at the 1994 U.S. Open and PGA prove that he was often in the hunt. An accurate sort who takes the club away against a particularly firm right side, Cook has never been one to overpower a golf course. But when he's been right, the red numbers have flown.

PGA Tour Wins (11): 1981 Bing Crosby; 1983 Canadian Open; 1998 Byron Nelson
Intn'l Wins (2): 1995 Mexican Open
Ryder Cup: 1993

Graham Cooke (Canada)

A native of Toronto, Graham Cooke (b. 1949) was a successful junior and amateur golfer, making honorable mention All-American at Michigan State in 1971, representing Canada seven times in international competition, and twice finishing second in the Canadian Amateur. Also a practicing golf course architect since 1974, Cooke's design work has been primarily confined to his homeland, with roughly half of his 50+ new courses located within the province of Quebec.

Harry Cooper (UK/USA)

Born: Leatherhead, England, 8/4/1904 **Died:** White Plains, New York, 10/17/2000

Given his nickname (for the speed with which he played) by no less than Damon Runyon, "Lighthorse" Harry Cooper was born in England but was raised in Indiana and later Texas, where his father served as professional at Dallas' Cedar Crest CC for many years. Though a winner of 31 official PGA Tour events, Cooper has long been rated among the best players never to have claimed a Major championship, though goodness knows he came close.

In the 1927 U.S. Open at Oakmont, his 301 looked so sure a winner that he was changing clothes in preparation for the presentation ceremony when informed that Tommy Armour had birdied two of the last six holes to force a tie. Armour won the play-off by three the next morning. Then in 1936, a similar scenario played itself out at Baltusrol when Cooper's 284 stood him three clear of the field before Tony Manero's late run to a remarkable 67 once again snatched the trophy from his grasp. Cooper was also a regular contender at Augusta, logging two seconds and two fourths between 1936 and 1940.

But 31 victories is nothing to sneeze at, particularly given the number that were of obvious quality. Cooper, for example, won the inaugural **Los Angeles Open** (by three over George Von Elm) at the Los Angeles CC in 1926, later winning a second L.A. title by five at Griffith Park in 1937. He also twice won the **Canadian Open** (1932 and '37) as well as the 1934 **Western Open,** where he defeated Ky Laffoon in sudden death in Peoria, Illinois. Cooper's best year by far was 1937 when he captured seven official titles as well as the inaugural Vardon Trophy for scoring average, and was the Tour's leading money winner. Yet despite these and other heroics, he was never eligible to represent the United States in Ryder Cup play, having been born in England.

PGA Tour Wins (31): 1926 & '37 Los Angeles; 1932 & '37 Canadian Open; 1934 Western Open; and 3 St. Paul Opens

1923-1942

	23	24	25	26	27	28	29	30	31	32	33	34	35	36	37	38	39	40	41	42
Masters												WD	T25	2	4	T2	T33	T4	T14	T18
US Open	-	-	-	MC	2	MC	T51	4	T15	T7	T29	T3	T28	2	4	T3	T12	MC	-	
British	-																			
PGA	T17	-	T3	T17	T9	-	DQ	T9	-	-	T9	T9	T33	T9	T5	T33	T33	T33	-	T5

Bill Coore (USA)

Golf course architect Bill Coore (b. 1945) grew up near Pinehurst, North Carolina, and played golf at Wake Forest, taking the standard designer-to-be degree in landscape architecture. After working briefly for Pete Dye, Coore became a golf course superintendent and part-time designer in Texas, eventually building his first solo course,

Rockport CC, in 1984. Rockport soon caught the attention of another would-be Texas architect, Masters champion Ben Crenshaw, who engaged Coore in a partnership that is fast approaching its 20th year at the time of this writing.

Never inclined to rush through projects on a profits-first basis, the firm of Coore & Crenshaw has proceeded slowly, initially doing restoration and remodeling jobs for several well-established clubs before producing their first new designs, in 1991, at Barton Creek (Texas) and the Plantation Course at Kapalua (Hawaii). Fourteen more original layouts have followed, always demonstrating the traditional values of strategic options, fascinating green contours, and lots of hole-to-hole variety, all wrapped up in a splendid aesthetic package that gives a Coore & Crenshaw layout a timeless, natural looking quality. Among those projects completed through 2004, two—Nebraska's Sand Hills GC and Long Island's Friar's Head—have garnered extreme acclaim and are quickly taking their places among the world's absolute elite.

Notable Courses: Austin GC, Texas; Cuscowilla GC, Georgia; Friars Head, New York; Hidden Creek GC, New Jersey; Kapalua GC, Plantation Course, Hawaii; Sand Hills GC, Nebraska

Fred Corcoran (USA)

A former caddie from Cambridge, Massachusetts, Fred Corcoran (1905–1977) was the sort of man-about-golf that for many years gave the game color, a flash of the offbeat and, above all, a much-enhanced profile. From 1937 to 1948 he held the title of PGA Tour Tournament Manager, following in the footsteps of fellow promoter Bob Harlow in an ill-defined position that largely amounted to serving as middle man between the players and the PGA, all the while schmoozing sponsors and chambers of commerce *ad nauseum*. While helping grow the Tour substantially in this capacity, Corcoran was also managing the careers of individual players, plus a slate of non-golfers that included Stan Musial and Ted Williams—if nothing else, guaranteeing him fruitful employment once the Tour tired of him.

An entertaining and highly popular sort, Corcoran served as manager (which should not be confused with captain) of several Ryder Cup teams, was involved in the founding of the Golf Writers Association (though he was not himself a professional writer), and also spent time running the LPGA Tour. The author of a semi-autobiographical volume *Unplayable Lies* (Duell, Sloan & Pearce, 1965), Corcoran for many years resided in a familiar white house located just off the 15th green of Winged Foot GC's famous West course.

Kathy Cornelius (USA)

Boston native Kathy Cornelius (b. 10/27/1932) enjoyed a long run on the LPGA Tour, remaining competitive for nearly 20 years beginning in the mid-1950s. Already the 1952 **Southern Amateur** champion and a two-time women's collegiate runner-up, Cornelius won at **St. Petersburg** early in her rookie year of 1956, setting the stage for her only Major championship, the '56 **U.S. Women's Open** at Duluth's Northland CC. There, looking very much a winner, Cornelius was forced to an 18-hole play-off when amateur Barbara McIntire holed a 30-foot putt for eagle at the 72nd hole. The play-off, however, proved anticlimactic with Cornelius' 75 being good enough to win by seven. All told, Cornelius would win six LPGA events, the last coming in **Las Vegas** in June of 1973. Her daughter Kay would eventually win the 1981 USGA Girls Junior, making them the only mother-daughter combination ever to claim USGA titles.

Geoffrey Cornish (Canada/USA)

Prominent Canadian architect Geoffrey Cornish (b. Winnipeg, 8/6/1914) first broke into the design business in the mid-1930s, apprenticing under the legendary Stanley Thompson for four years. Following wartime service in the Canadian army, Cornish briefly rejoined Thompson, then spent several years developing turfgrass at the University of Massachusetts before finally entering the design business on his own in 1952.

What followed was a tremendously prolific career that saw Cornish establish a hegemony of sorts throughout the New England region, building vastly more new courses in Connecticut, Massachusetts, Vermont, and New Hampshire than any architect in history. Taking on associates Brian Silva and Mark Mungeam, Cornish's work has often been described as "functional," for he was most frequently engaged to build public or public-access facilities upon which accommodating a variety of skill levels and speed of play were prime considerations. Perhaps Cornish's greatest legacy to the game, however, has been on paper, for he has written or cowritten not less than five architecturally oriented volumes including the seminal *Architects of Golf* (HarperCollins, 1993) with Ron Whitten, *Eighteen Stakes on a Sunday Afternoon* (Grant, 2002), and *Classic Golf Hole Design* (John Wiley & Sons, 2002), the last with the late Robert Muir Graves.

Notable Courses: The Connecticut GC; International GC, Massachusetts; Stow Acres CC, Massachusetts

C. K. Cotton (UK)

Not related to the great Henry, Englishman Charles Kenneth Cotton (1887–1974) was a latecomer to golf, taking it up after college and before finding employment as a secretary to several British clubs. Becoming involved in the reconstruction of damaged courses following World War II, Cotton soon drifted into the design field full time, both alone and in partnership with the well-traveled John Harris. Though his list of memorable new designs is fairly brief, Cotton did perform renovation work at places like Sunningdale and Royal Lytham & St. Annes, while also helping to shepherd younger designers like Frank Pennink and Donald Steel into the business.

Henry Cotton (UK)

Born: Holmes Chapel, England, 1/26/1907 **Died:** London, England, 12/22/1987

One of the towering figures in British golf, Thomas Henry Cotton, M.B.E., certainly proved his reputation on the course, claiming more than 30 international titles and three Open Championships in a war-interrupted career that lasted roughly two decades. Cotton was also a groundbreaker in a number of off-the-course areas, redefining (particularly in Britain) what a golf professional could and should be.

Cotton, for example, is generally considered the first Briton of means to choose the game for his livelihood. While his professional predecessors had virtually all sprung from the caddie ranks (or had professional fathers), Cotton was an educated fellow who simply decided that golf was to be his chosen route. He is also widely believed to be the first British player for whom voluminous practice was a part of the equation—perhaps the norm today, but rather a groundbreaking concept in the prewar game. Finally, though Walter Hagen was perhaps 15 years ahead of him in America, Cotton was the first Briton since Vardon to use his golfing fame to generate income in areas other than teaching and/or the manufacture and sale of equipment, picking up wide-ranging endorsements and even going so far as to headline his own stage show at the London Coliseum. In short, Cotton was a man who saw many possibilities in golf, then dedicated himself to becoming good enough to make such visions relevant.

After playing the American winter tour in 1929 (converting his fade to a draw at the urging of Tommy Armour) and appearing in that season's Ryder Cup, Cotton's first important win came at the 1930 **Belgian Open,** though his victory in the 1932 *News of the World* match play (over Alf Perry at Moor Park) was of far greater stature. He would go on to claim further *News of the World* crowns in 1940 and '46 while finishing runner-up on two

occasions, but it was in the **Open Championship** that the Cotton legend was truly spawned.

He did not initially enjoy success on the game's oldest stage, failing to contend on several occasions, then blowing himself out of the 1933 event with a closing 79. But in 1934 at Royal St. George's, Cotton opened with 67-65 (the latter being the impetus for Dunlop's famous "65" golf ball), then added a 72 for a seemingly insurmountable 10-shot lead entering the final. Staggering out in 40, he appeared on the verge of an epic collapse before righting the ship to win by five, ending a decade's worth of American Open domination.

Three years later, after a joint third in 1936, Cotton faced a field laced with American Ryder Cuppers at Carnoustie, but closed with a splendid 71 (in a driving rain) to defeat Reg Whitcombe by two, with only Nelson among the Americans managing to crack the top 5. Cotton raised money for the Red Cross during the war after being invalided by the RAF for ulcers, then, having been denied several of his best years, returned to the top of the heap once hostilities ceased. Winning the **French Open** in both 1946 and '47, he finally claimed his third Claret Jug in 1948 at Muirfield where a record second-round 66 sparked a five-shot triumph over Fred Daly.

Always comfortable in warmer climes, Cotton and his colorful Argentinean wife "Toots" spent a good deal of time along the Mediterranean (where he ran a golf school in Monte Carlo) and later retired to a pleasant resort life on the Portuguese Algarve. A prominent course designer in his later years, Cotton also became a coach of top junior players as well as a prolific writer, authoring more than a dozen golf-related works including *This Game of Golf* (Country Life, 1948), *My Golfing Album* (Country Life, 1959), and several general history volumes and guidebooks.

Historically speaking, Cotton's place in the game is an interesting one, ranking as Britain's greatest player between the utter dominance of the Triumvirate and the intercontinental successes of Faldo. But Cotton's era saw limited competition between the Americans and the Europeans, making his merits relative to, say, Hogan, Nelson, and Snead difficult to judge. His 2-4 record in Ryder Cup play offers little to go on and while he certainly handled the Americans at Carnoustie in 1937, Snead easily took his measure (by five) at St. Andrews in 1946. Ironically, during Cotton's two brief excursions to America, his lone win was at the unofficial 1948 **White Sulphur Springs Invitational,** an event hosted by Snead. Cotton also appeared in that season's Masters (where he tied for 25th) nearly 20 years after claiming his only other non-European win, the 1930 **Mar del Plata Open** in Argentina.

Intn'l Wins (32): 1930, '34 & '38 Belgian Open; 1932, '40 & '46 PGA Match Play; **1934, '37 & '48 British Open;** 1936 Italian Open; 1937, '38 & '39 German Open; 1946 & '47 French Open
Ryder Cup: 1929, '37 & '47 (3); 1953 Capt

1927-1958

	27	28	29	30	31	32	33	34	35	36	37	38	39	40	41	42
Masters								-	-	-	-	-	-	-	-	-
US Open	-	-	-	-	MC	-	-	-	-	-	-	-	-	-	-	
British	9	T18	17	8	T9	10	T7	1	T7	T3	1	3	T13			
PGA	-	-	-	-	-	-	-	-	-	-	-	-	-	-	-	-

	43	44	45	46	47	48	49	50	51	52	53	54	55	56	57	58
Masters				-	-	-	-	-	-	-	-	-	-	T68	T63	-
US Open				-	-	-	-	-	-	-	-	-	-	T17	-	-
British				T4	T6	1	-	-	-	4	-	-	T32	T6	T9	T8
PGA	-	-	-	-	-	-	-	-	-	-	-	-	-	-	-	-

Fred Couples (USA)

One of America's most popular contemporary stars, Frederick Steven Couples (b. 10/3/1959) has cast a long shadow over the last 25 years, his rhythmic, highly powerful swing registering 20 professional victories and representing the United States in all manner of international competitions. A native of Seattle, Couples amassed little in the way of prominent amateur titles, yet was an obvious enough talent to be recruited by the powerful University of Houston, where he roomed with broadcaster Jim Nantz and was twice named an All-American.

Like most top-shelf stars, Couples' professional victories have frequently come against high-quality fields. Winning a five-man play-off to capture the 1983 **Kemper Open** was a strong opener, as was his second triumph, a one-shot squeaker over Lee Trevino at the 1984 **Players Championship.** Couples eventually reached his peak in the early 1990s especially during a Player of the Year season in 1992 when he claimed his second **Los Angeles Open,** routed the field by nine at **Bay Hill,** then captured his lone Major title, the **Masters,** by two over Raymond Floyd. In-

dicative of his laid-back playing style was that event's defining moment. His ball hanging precariously above Rae's Creek at the famous 12th, Couples coolly pitched it stiff from the hillside, then casually fished a ball or two from the water with his wedge as if completely oblivious to the final-round pressure cooker around him.

Though a troublesome back knocked him from the summit soon thereafter, Couples remained a mainstay of American Ryder and Presidents Cup teams throughout the 1990s, while also adding further prestige wins at the 1996 **Players Championship** and the 1998 **Memorial.** Finally, following a five-year drought during which he endured family loss, divorce, remarriage, and a reworked swing, the likable Couples surprised observers by capturing the 2003 **Houston Open,** an emotional comeback in a city where he has long maintained his collegiate ties.

PGA Tour Wins (15): 1984 & '96 Players Championship; 1987 Byron Nelson; 1990 & '92 Los Angeles; **1992 Masters;** 1998 Memorial
Intn'l Wins (5): 1995 Johnnie Walker; 1995 Dubai
Ryder Cup: 1989–97 (5) **Presidents Cup:** 1994–98 (3)

1979-2000

	79	80	81	82	83	84	85	86	87	88	89
Masters	-	-	-	-	T32	10	T10	T31	-	T5	T11
US Open	T48	-	-	MC	MC	T9	T39	-	T46	T10	T21
British	-	-	-	-	-	T4	-	T46	T40	T4	T6
PGA	-	-	-	T3	T23	T20	T6	T36	MC	MC	MC

	90	91	92	93	94	95	96	97	98	99	00
Masters	5	T35	1	T21	-	T10	T15	T7	T2	T27	T11
US Open	MC	T3	T17	T16	T16	MC	-	T52	T43	MC	T16
British	T25	T3	MC	T9	-	-	T7	T7	T66	-	6
PGA	2	T27	T21	T31	T39	T31	T41	T29	T13	T26	MC

Gary Cowan (Canada)

A business and family man who refrained from the potential big money of professional golf, Kitchener, Ontario's Gary Cowan (b. 1938) might, by at least one measure, merit consideration for the title of Canada's greatest-ever amateur. While others have won more Canadian national titles, Cowan remains not only the rare Canadian to capture a **U.S. Amateur** crown but also the only non-American to win it twice. His first victory, at Merion in 1966, came in an 18-hole play-off with two-time winner Dean Beman. His second, however, was something of an epic as Cowan holed a 135-yard 9-iron at the 72nd to defeat the promising Eddie Pearce by three at the Wilmington CC (Delaware) in 1971.

Victories in the 1961 **Canadian Amateur** (plus four runners-up), the **Canadian Junior**, the 1970 **North & South Amateur**, and 10 **Ontario Amateurs**, plus appearances on numerous Canadian national teams, are all most impressive. But one suspects that even with such a résumé—and even north of the border—it is the two U.S. Amateurs for which Cowan will be longest remembered.

Whiffy Cox (USA)

Born in Brooklyn, New York, Wilfred H. "Whiffy" Cox (1897–1969) was a mainstay on the American circuit during the 1930s. A nine-time PGA Tour winner, he especially shined in 1931 when he claimed five titles (including the prestigious **North & South Open**), tied for fourth in the U.S. Open (won by Billy Burke at Inverness), and was selected to his only Ryder Cup team. Subsequent top-five U.S. Open finishes in 1932 (at Fresh Meadow) and 1934 (at Merion) are further evidence of his competitiveness.

A short, compact swinger with a wide stance, Cox was initially considered a poor finisher before he hit his championship stride. Perhaps because of these early failures, he spent a number of years as a working professional in Brooklyn (both at New York City's municipal Dyker Beach GC and the old Marine & Field Club) before moving on to Congressional, outside of Washington, D.C., in 1937.

Tom Craddock (Ireland)

The best of four talented golfing brothers from the coastal village of Malahide, Thomas Craddock (b. 1931) was one of Ireland's leading amateurs during the late 1950s, winning the **Open Amateur** in 1958 and the **Closed** in '59, the latter in extra holes over the best of all period Irishmen, Joe Carr. A strong player whose putting was perhaps not entirely on par with the rest of his game, Craddock briefly broke from tournament play in the early 1960s before returning to represent Ireland internationally on numerous occasions (including two Walker Cups) by the end of the decade. In recent years, he has worked with countryman Pat Ruddy designing golf courses.

Jane Crafter (Australia)

Perth native Jane Crafter (b. 12/14/1955) is the product of one of Australia's fine golfing families, her father and uncle both club professionals, her brother a top amateur and golf course architect. A winner of national amateur titles in **New Zealand** (1978) and **Belgium** (1980) and runner-up in Australia (1977) and Canada (1980), Crafter first became a qualified pharmacist before trying the LPGA Tour in 1982, ultimately competing there for the better part of 20 years. Though only a one-time winner (the 1990 **Phar-Mor at Inverrary**), she was 11 times among the top 60 and has won more than $1.6 million. In recent years she has become a familiar voice on LPGA TV broadcasts as well.

Bruce Crampton (Australia)

The son of a Sydney police officer, Bruce Sidney Crampton (b. 9/28/1935) seemed always to have his eye on the money, turning professional at 19 and winning the **New Zealand PGA** almost immediately. The following year, 1955, it was the **New Zealand Open**, and in 1956 the true springboard of his career, the **Australian Open**. Soon thereafter Crampton was off to chase the lucrative purses of America, a long-term raid made successful both by his raw talent and a willingness to play virtually every week in any city.

All told Crampton would win 14 official PGA Tour events with the most significant being the 1971 **Western Open** (by two over Bobby Nichols at Olympia Fields), the 1965 **Bing Crosby** (downing Tony Lema by three), and the 1965 **Colonial**. Always known as a fine putter, Crampton was a top-60 money winner from 1961 to 1975, ranked third in 1970 and second in 1973, and twice won the Vardon Trophy for low scoring average (1973 and '75). Indeed all that's missing from Crampton's résumé is a Major championship, something he might well have won were it not for Jack Nicklaus, behind whom he finished second in a Masters (1972), a U.S. Open (1972), and two PGAs (1973 and '75).

Clearly one of the finest players of his time, Crampton has perhaps been somewhat overlooked due to an occasionally surly demeanor that made him unpopular with both fellow pros and the press. He was, to be sure, a man dedicated to excellence, perhaps showing a single-mindedness that might go unnoticed on today's less colorful PGA Tour. Having retired to a Texas oil business in

1977, Crampton made a highly successful return for the Champions Tour in the late 1980s, winning 20 titles (tied for eighth all-time) and over $6 million.

PGA Tour Wins (14): 1964 Texas; 1965 Bing Crosby; 1965 Colonial; 1970 Westchester; 1971 Western Open
Intn'l Wins (8): 1956 Australian Open
Champions Tour Wins: 20 (1986–93)

Harry "Big" Crawford (UK)

An all-time legend of the caddie ranks, Big Crawford was a regular around North Berwick during the latter years of the nineteenth century, frequently carrying for local hero Ben Sayers or one-time Prime Minister A. J. Balfour, whom he considered a personal friend. A huge fellow with a grand physical presence, Crawford eventually settled down to running a ginger beer stand on the North Berwick links. Also quite friendly with Old Tom Morris, he reportedly made the trip across the Firth of Forth, at no young age, to attend the legendary St. Andrean's funeral, as the two men had a pact that the longer living would see the other off.

Crawford very nearly had a major impact on golfing history when, on the eve of the famous 1899 challenge match between Harry Vardon and Willie Park Jr., he abruptly threw a horseshoe over Vardon's head, narrowly missing the then three-time Open champion. When pressed to explain his actions, Crawford claimed he'd thrown the horseshoe for luck, as he'd backed Vardon with every penny he possessed. And how different might history read if it was Crawford's horseshoe, and not tuberculosis, that waylaid Harry Vardon?

Leonard Crawley (UK)

For all that golfers may know of England's Leonard George Crawley (1903–1981), cricket fans may know more, for Crawley, a great all-around gamesman, was a superstar of the pitch prior to excelling impressively on the links. His midlife career, however, was spent as the longtime golf correspondent for London's *Daily Telegraph* and a frequent contributor to the *Field*, tasks he performed with such skill as to later be viewed "only as a writer." But, like Darwin, Crawley earned his stripes inside the ropes as well, winning the 1931 **English Amateur,** finishing second at the 1937 French Open, and representing the United Kingdom on Walker Cup teams in 1932, '34, '38, and, a bit later, 1947. Crawley actually managed to dent the cup itself with an exceedingly wayward shot in 1932, though he is more rightly recalled as a powerful, elegant player of both of his chosen games.

Paula Creamer (USA)

Pleasanton, California's Paula Creamer (b. 8/5/1986) was for several years a dominant force in American junior golf, earning 2003 AJGA Player of the Year honors as a high school junior and by that time winning 16 national-level junior titles. A 2003 semifinalist at both the USGA Junior Girls and the U.S. Women's Amateur, Creamer twice made cuts in LPGA Tour events during that same season and was a Curtis Cup selection, at age 17, in 2004. Shortly after the international match, Creamer very nearly made history by becoming the first amateur to win a tour event since JoAnne Carner in 1969. At the LPGA's Shop-Rite Classic in Absecon, New Jersey, her 70-64-69 performance came within a missed 10-footer at the 54th (followed by Cristie Kerr's holing from just closer). Turning pro by year's end, she quickly marked herself a star by winning the 2005 **Sybase Classic** (Wykagyl), becoming the first 18-year-old in 53 years to claim an official LPGA event.

Tom Creavy (USA)

Following in the footsteps of another Westchester talent named Gene Sarazen, Tuckahoe, New York, native Tom Creavy (1911–1979) surprised the nation's golfers by capturing the 1931 **PGA Championship** (played at Rhode Island's Wannamoisett CC) at the ripe old age of 20. Having actually caddied for Sarazen and 1928 U.S. Open champion Johnny Farrell as a youth, Creavy seemed undaunted by the PGA's marquee field, eliminating such luminaries as Cyril Walker, Sarazen, and long-hitting Denny Shute en route to victory. A winner of only two other PGA Tour–recognized events, Creavy did make the PGA's semifinals in 1932 and fired a memorable final-round 66 in the 1934 U.S. Open at Merion.

Clifford Ann Creed (USA)

A five-time winner of the **Louisiana Ladies** title (including four straight from 1956 to 1959), Alexandria native Clifford Ann Creed (b. 9/23/1938) was also a two-time **Southern Amateur** winner (1957 and '62) and the 1962 **North & South** champion, as well as a mainstay on the victorious 1962 Curtis Cup team. Turning professional late that season, she joined the LPGA Tour full time in 1963 and proceeded to finish among the top-10 money winners for six consecutive seasons. More a sprinter than a long-distance runner, Creed won three times each in 1964, '65 and '66, then added the last two of her 11 official victories in 1967 before falling slowly back into the pack. Never a major champion, Creed bore the misfortune of peaking at the same time as Mickey Wright and Kathy Whitworth, who between them took 40 titles from 1964 to 1966. She was later honored as the first woman elected to the Louisiana Sports Hall of Fame.

Eric Cremin (Australia)

Widely considered as good a putter as has ever been produced in Australia, Mascot native Eric Cremin (1914–1973) was a slightly built man who relied more on precision and an almost constant ability to hole the long ones than anything resembling a power game. Raised in New South Wales, Cremin's only professional sin was poor timing, as his explosive arrival—in the form of back-to-back **Australian PGAs** in 1937 and '38—came just before the golfless purgatory of wartime. Still, despite losing five peak years outright and playing the limited schedule of events that marked the early postwar years, Cremin managed an impressive 32 career wins, the highlight being the 1949 **Australian Open** in which he defeated Norman Von Nida over the old Alister MacKenzie–designed Australian GC.

The Open win sparked a two-year stretch in which Cremin won 12 times and made his lone trip overseas (to both Britain and the United States) in 1951, meeting with limited success. In later years, however, he did a good deal of traveling about Asia, promoting the fledgling Far East golf circuit and instructing aboard the passenger ship *Canberra*.

Ben Crenshaw (USA)

Born and raised in Austin, Texas, Ben Daniel Crenshaw (b. 1/11/1952) won his first tournament as a fourth grader, studied under Austin CC's longtime professional Harvey Penick, and eventually developed into one of the more highly touted amateurs of his era. Winner of the 1971 and '73 **Southern Amateurs,** the 1972 **Trans-Mississippi,** and the 1973 **Western,** Crenshaw attended hometown University of Texas where he won or shared **NCAA** individual titles in 1971, '72 and '73, was thrice named collegiate Player of the Year, and teamed with Tom Kite to lead the Longhorns to national championships in 1971 and '72.

It may in hindsight seem odd that Crenshaw never won a U.S. Amateur (though he tied for second at stroke play in 1972) but early on he seemed more focused on the PGA tour, even tying for third at the 1972 Heritage Classic while still a collegian. When he finally joined the Tour in 1973, he promptly shot 65 in his first official round, then added 72-66-67 to win the **Texas Open,** making Crenshaw the first man since Marty Fleckman to win his Tour debut. Very much unlike Fleckman, however, Crenshaw would go on to claim 18 more victories in a 23-year span, logging seven top-10 money rankings and establishing himself as one of the finest putters in the history of the game.

Though many of his wins came in marquee events, Crenshaw struggled mightily to claim his first Major championship despite often playing his best golf on these, the biggest stages. Indeed he had seven top-5 Major finishes between 1975 and 1980, tying for third (one out of a play-off) at the 1975 U.S. Open at Medinah after finding water at the 71st, finishing second to Ray Floyd's runaway freight train at the 1976 Masters, logging four straight top-5 finishes in consecutive Open Championships from 1977 to 1980, and losing a heartbreaking play-off to David Graham at the 1979 PGA Championship. Crenshaw's Major ship finally arrived at the 1984 **Masters** where a closing 68 held off Tom Watson by two, though he will be far better remembered for his second Green Jacket, a hugely emotional 1995 victory claimed only days after serving as a pallbearer at the funeral of his mentor Harvey Penick. By this time age 43 and running out of opportunities, Crenshaw again closed with 68 to beat Davis Love III by a single stroke in a stunning, almost magical victory.

Crenshaw's record has at times been inconsistent, partially due to a mid-1980s battle with Graves Disease but equally because of an occasionally volatile temper (which earned him the rather splendid nickname of "Gentle Ben") and sporadic wildness with the driver. A keen student of the game's literature and history, his millennium-era peaks have come in nonplaying roles, both as captain of the 1999 Ryder Cup team (whose epic comeback victory and overdone celebration will be long remembered) and as a golf course architect in partnership with Bill Coore. In the former capacity, he authored the Cup-oriented autobiography *A Feel for the Game* (Doubleday, 2001); in the latter, two Coore & Crenshaw designs, Nebraska's Sandhills GC and Long Island's Friars Head, are widely rated the finest courses to be built in America since World War II.

PGA Tour Wins (19): 1976 Bing Crosby; 1983 Byron Nelson; **1984 & '95 Masters;** 1988 Doral; 1990 Colonial; 1992 Western Open

Ryder Cup: 1981, '83, '87 & '95 (4); 1999 Capt

1970-1997

	70	71	72	73	74	75	76	77	78	79	80	81	82	83
Masters	-	-	T19	T24	T22	T30	2	T8	T37	MC	T6	T8	T25	T2
US Open	T36	T27	-	-	-	T3	T8	T49	MC	T11	T31	T11	T19	MC
British	-	-	-	-	T28	-	-	T5	T5	T2	3	T8	T15	MC
PGA	-	-	-	-	T63	T10	T8	WD	T16	2	T41	MC	MC	T9

	84	85	86	87	88	89	90	91	92	93	94	95	96	97
Masters	1	T57	T16	T4	4	T3	T14	T3	46	MC	T18	1	MC	45
US Open	MC	MC	T6	T4	T12	MC	MC	-	-	-	T33	T71	MC	T65
British	T22	T35	T21	T4	T16	T52	T31	T80	-	MC	T77	T15	T26	-
PGA	MC	T59	T11	T7	T17	T17	T31	WD	T73	T61	T9	T44	T69	MC

Fay Crocker
(Uruguay/USA)

The life of Helen Fay Crocker (b. 1914) must rank among golf's most fascinating of the twentieth century. Born in Montevideo, Uruguay, she was the granddaughter of a New England mariner who'd settled there and, by most accounts, introduced that nation to the game by building an early nine-hole course. Against what clearly was a terribly limited field, Crocker's father became the diminutive country's best player, winning the national championship a reported 37 times. And if the men's field was small, we can only surmise as to the thinness of the women's, where Fay captured the **Uruguayan Ladies** title on 20 occasions. She also crossed the Rio de la Plata often enough to claim 14 **Argentine Ladies** championships, a slightly more established event on the international golfing map.

Big fish in a small pond? Without question, yet Crocker did occasionally venture north to the competitive ocean, participating in several U.S. Women's Amateurs and gaining a bit of attention during a 1950 fourth-round loss to Mae Murray at East Lake, a record-setting affair that went 27 holes with Bobby Jones in attendance. Finally, fast approaching age 40, Crocker turned professional and headed to America full time, eventually logging three wins in 1955, the last being the **U.S. Women's Open,** where she beat Louise Suggs and Mary Lena Faulk by four at the Wichita CC. Crocker would ultimately claim a total of 11 LPGA titles, with her victory at the 1960 **Titleholders Championship** making her, at age 45, the oldest woman ever to win an LPGA Major.

A. C. M. Croome (UK)

One of the finest all-around sportsmen in England, Stroud native Arthur Capel Molyneux Croome (1866–1930) played nearly every sport *but* golf during his days at Wellington and Oxford, not taking up the Royal & Ancient game until employed as a coach and academician at the Radley School. Once bitten by the bug, however, he was not only a capable competitor but also a founding member (and secretary) of the Oxford and Cambridge Golfing Society. To supplement his teaching income, Croome worked as a journalist, covering golf for the *Evening Standard* and the *Morning Post* and later cricket—his best sport—for the *Times.* A friend of J. F. Abercromby, he gradually became involved with golf design, eventually going into partnership with Abercromby, Tom Simpson, and Herbert Fowler. Though mostly involved with the firm's business and publicity efforts, Croome was the primary designer of Liphook GC, a Hampshire heathland course of no small repute.

Claudine Cros (France)

Part of a 1960s spike in French women's golf, Parisienne Claudine Cros (b. 1943) joined Brigitte Varangot and Catherine LaCoste as a mini-triumvirate, dominating domestic play while also competing successfully on the international stage. Challenged as a youth by a pair of talented golfing brothers, Cros developed both a simple, highly rhythmic swing that stood her among the period's best ball-strikers and an elegant style that made her popular with fans and observers. On the whole her record was perhaps not the equal of Varangot or LaCoste, yet Cros was twice the **Ladies Open** champion of France, the first time at age 17 in 1960, then once more in 1968. Also the **German Ladies** champion of 1961 and twice the **French Closed** winner (1964 and '65), Cros twice reached the final of the British Ladies Amateur, losing in 1968 to Varangot (her close friend and roommate for the week) on the 20th hole at Walton Heath and in 1972 to a rampaging Michelle Walker. She frequently played under her married name of Claudine Cros-Rubin.

Bing Crosby (USA)

Few celebrities have been more closely allied with the game of golf than Tacoma, Washington, native Harry Lillis "Bing" Crosby (1903–1977), the popular American singer and actor who, for more than 40 years, hosted what came to be known as the Bing Crosby Pro-Am. Played within the splendid beauty of California's celebrated Monterey Peninsula, the event was famous for its venues (for many years utilizing both Pebble Beach and Cypress Point), its roster of top Hollywood stars, and its famously capricious weather. It is a testimony to the distinction and influence of its founder that more than a quarter-century after his death, and subsequent sponsorship by AT&T, the event is still widely referred to simply as "The Crosby."

Unlike many celebrity golfers, Bing was the real deal, playing, at his peak, to a two handicap and competing in the 1950 British Amateur at St. Andrews. He was a long-time member of Los Angeles' Lakeside GC and, more prominently, of Cypress Point, where he remains one of only a handful of players to ace the terrifying 231-yard 16th. Perhaps fittingly, he died of a heart attack after walking off the 18th green of the La Moraleja GC, just outside of Madrid, at age 73.

Nathaniel Crosby (USA)

The last of crooner Bing Crosby's seven children, Nathaniel Crosby (b. 10/29/1961) was a good—but certainly not great—golfer who rose to one spectacular height, capturing the 1981 **U.S. Amateur** title at the Olympic Club, only a short drive from the family home in Hillsborough. Trailing in four of his six matches, the inspired 19-year-old gamely fought back each time, particularly in the final against fellow Californian Brian Lindley. Here Crosby stood 2 down with 3 to play before squaring things up at the 35th, then claiming the title at the 37th. Though Crosby's only significant title, it was a storybook victory indeed.

Bobby Cruickshank (UK/USA)

Born: Grantown-on-Spey, Scotland, 11/15/1894 **Died:** Delray Beach, Florida, 8/27/1975

Like fellow Scot Tommy Armour, Robert Allan Cruickshank was a strong competitive amateur in his homeland before turning professional and emigrating to America to seek his fortune. Despite standing a slight 5′5″, Cruickshank proved himself most capable, winning 17 PGA Tour events between 1921 and 1936 though none—as history loves to remind us—was a Major championship.

Cruickshank's closest brush with Major glory came at the 1923 U.S. Open at Inwood where, battling a stumbling 21-year-old Bobby Jones, he laced a 2-iron inside of 10 feet at the last, holing the putt to force a play-off. The extra round was an epic, with only three of the first 17 holes being halved and the players reaching the 18th all square. Here Cruickshank hooked his drive badly and was forced to lay up short of a narrow fronting pond. Jones, on the other hand, went for it from 190 yards, knocked his 2-iron to within 6 feet, and won the first of his 13 Major championships. Cruickshank also suffered great U.S. Open disappointment in 1932 at Fresh Meadow when he closed with a splendid 68, only to lose out to Sarazen's stunning 66. There were also third-place finishes in 1934 and '37, the former coming at Merion after a contending Cruickshank tossed his 9-iron happily skyward upon seeing his approach to the 65th bound out of Cobb's Creek and onto the green—only to be knocked woozy when the club beaned him on the way down.

Among Cruickshank's more important wins, he cruised to a six-shot victory in the 1927 **Los Angeles Open** and captured back-to-back **North & South Opens** in 1926 and '27 (the latter over Walter Hagen). Like Armour and the English-born Harry Cooper, Cruickshank lived most of his life Stateside but was ineligible for American Ryder Cup play due to his Scottish birth.

PGA Tour Wins (17): 1926 & '27 North & South; 1927 Los Angeles; 1927 Texas

1921-1942

	21	22	23	24	25	26	27	28	29	30	31
Masters											
US Open	T26	T28	2	T4	-	T49	T11	-	T42	-	T36
British	-	-	-	-	-	-	-	-	6	-	-
PGA	T9	T3	T3	T9	T9	T17	T17	-	-	-	-

	32	33	34	35	36	37	38	39	40	41	42
Masters			T28	T9	T4	17	T18	-	WD	-	T15
US Open	T2	T43	T3	T14	MC	3	T46	T25	MC	-	
British	-	-	-	-	-	T42	-	-			
PGA	T5	T9	-	-	T9	-	-	-	-	-	-

George Crump (USA)

A wealthy Philadelphia hotel owner, George Arthur Crump (1871–1918) was a capable amateur golfer and a founding member of Philadelphia CC before deciding to abandon city life to build his private dream course. Putting together a syndicate of affluent, like-minded friends, he purchased 184 acres of New Jersey pine barren in 1912, moved onto his site, and began the long and arduous process of designing Pine Valley. Enlisting the great British designer H. S. Colt, as well as soliciting ideas from Walter Travis and Philadelphia friends such as Hugh Wilson, George Thomas, and A. W. Tillinghast, Crump had completed 14 holes of his painstakingly detailed construction process when he died suddenly in 1918. Hugh Wilson and his brother Alan (with input from C. H. Alison) would utilize Crump's plans to finish Pine Valley, the result being perhaps the world's most honored, feared, and talked-about golf course.

Carolyn Cudone (USA)

Oxford, Alabama, native Carolyn Cudone (b. 1918) spent much of her life residing in Caldwell, New Jersey, where she won 11 state women's titles in 16 tries beginning in the mid-1950s. She would also take five **Metropolitan Amateurs** between 1955 and 1965, Pinehurst's **North & South Amateur** in 1958, and the **Eastern** title in 1960, though she only once went as far as the semifinals of the U.S. Women's Amateur, that in 1953. A participant (only at foursomes) on the losing 1956 Curtis Cup side, Cudone would later set a record for all USGA events by winning five consecutive **U.S. Senior Women's Amateur** titles between 1968 and 1972, also finishing as runner-up in 1974 and '75.

George Cumming (UK/Canada)

Like so many Scottish golfers, George Cumming (1878–1949), a native of Bridge of Weir, emigrated to North America at a young age, having learned his craft under Willie Campbell at Ranfurly Castle GC and in the clubmaking workshop of Andrew Forgan in Glasgow. Arriving in Ontario in 1900, Cumming became the professional at the Toronto GC, a position he would retain, with great influence, for over 50 years. Though a fine teacher and clubmaker, Cumming is even better remembered as a player, winning the second **Canadian Open** in 1905 while finishing runner-up in the event on four separate occasions. Widely known as the Dean of Canadian pros, he was long a guiding force in the evolution of that nation's

PGA, in addition to turning out several dozen future professionals from his own shop.

Less noticed on the Cumming résumé was an extensive portfolio of course design work that began early and resulted in a list of projects the exact quantity of which has never been verified. What is certain is that in 1920 Cumming joined up with well-known fellow professional Nicol Thompson and his then-anonymous brother Stanley in a design firm known as Thompson, Cumming & Thompson. The concern would be short-lived, however, as Stanley Thompson would eventually go off on his own to achieve Canadian architectural immortality.

Edith Cummings (USA)

Chicago-born Edith Cummings (1899–1992) was perhaps the most glamorous figure of golf's most glamorous age, a skilled player widely chronicled for her beauty, and upon whom the character of Jordan Baker in F. Scott Fitzgerald's *The Great Gatsby* was based. Cummings came from the affluence of suburban Lake Forest and had a brother, Dexter, who won the 1923 and '24 NCAA individual titles for Yale. Edith came close to her own starring role in the 1922 **U.S. Women's Amateur,** losing to eventual champion Glenna Collett in the semifinals. But she would return to claim the title the following year when, in the words of Herbert Warren Wind, she "provided the photographers with a field day when she won the national title," defeating Alexa Stirling at the Westchester Biltmore 3 and 2. A 1924 **Western Amateur** title captured on her home course at Onwentsia (by a thorough 12 and 10 margin over defending champion Miriam Burns) backed up her 1923 success, but following one more run to the semifinals of the 1925 U.S. Women's Amateur, Cummings pulled back from the competitive arena.

Jacky Cupit (USA)

A member of three national championship teams during the halcyon days of the University of Houston's golf program, Longview, Texas, native Jacky Cupit (b. 2/1/1938) went on to a solid four-win career on the PGA Tour. There were times, particularly when he lost a three-way play-off for the 1963 U.S. Open at Brookline, that people foresaw some degree of greatness for Cupit, but his uniquely looping swing perhaps wasn't built to meet such expectations. Still, Cupit logged two particularly fine wins at the 1961 **Canadian** and the 1962 **Western Opens,** and had he somehow gotten past Julius Boros and Arnold Palmer at Brookline, it all might have been different—but then George Fazio, Mike Donald, and Loren Roberts are among a number of Open play-off losers who can make similar claims.

Robert Cupp (USA)

Bob Cupp's (b. 1939) initial exposure to golf course architecture came from the renovation of a public course whose pro shop he was managing, after which he picked up an associate's degree in agronomy from Broward County Junior College and began accepting local commissions. Eventually parlaying this work into a position within Jack Nicklaus' design organization, Cupp produced courses under the Golden Bear masthead while also working with fellow employee Jay Morrish under the name Golforce. Going out on his own in 1985, Cupp has since designed over 100 golf courses worldwide, several in high-profile partnerships with PGA Tour stars such as Jerry Pate, Hubert Green, Fuzzy Zoeller, and Tom Kite. Another frequent partner, 1977 U.S. Amateur champion John Fought, eventually took over the firm's West Coast office in Portland, Oregon.

Despite so large a portfolio, Cupp's most memorable project may turn out to be his 1994 resurrection of the long-abandoned Oakhurst Links, an historic nine-holer in White Sulphur Springs, West Virginia, which dates back to 1884.

Notable Courses: Crosswater GC, Oregon; Old Waverly GC, Mississippi; Pumpkin Ridge GC, Oregon; TPC at Starpass, Arizona

Rod Curl (USA)

Redding, California, native Rod Curl (b. 1/9/1943) didn't take up golf until he was 20, though he was scratch within a year and playing the PGA Tour by age 26. An outgoing, personable sort who, despite standing only 5'5", could drive it toe-to-toe with Jack Nicklaus, Curl's lone win came in 1974, at **Colonial,** where he beat Nicklaus by a shot. With his lineage being three-quarter Wintu Indian, Curl earned the distinction of being the first Native American to win an official PGA Tour event.

Ben Curtis (USA)

Among golf's all-time surprise winners stands young Ben Curtis (b. Columbus, Ohio, 5/26/1977), 26 years old and a reported 500-1 shot on the day he won the 2003 **Open Championship** at Royal St. George's. Of course, as a former collegiate All-American at Kent University and highly ranked amateur, Curtis may not have been floating

as far off golf's radar screen as some have suggested. Further, he birdied six of his first 11 holes on Sunday—no mean feat—though a back-nine stumble necessitated help from Denmark's Thomas Björn (who played the last four holes in 4 over par) before a one-stroke victory was secured. Whether Curtis can eventually repeat such a performance only time will tell, but nothing will change the fact that he was the first man since Francis Ouimet in 1913 to win his first Major championship start.

Harriot Curtis (USA)

Born: Manchester-by-the-Sea, Massachusetts, 6/30/1881 **Died:** Manchester-by-the-Sea, Massachusetts, 10/25/1974

Massachusetts' famous Curtis sisters were born into a prominent Boston family that provided a prime golfing pedigree, their uncle Laurence having been a driving force behind golf's addition at The Country Club of Brookline (later representing the club at the 1894 meeting that founded the USGA) and brother James winning the NCAA individual championship for Harvard in 1898.

The older by two years, Harriot enjoyed less playing success than sister Margaret, though she did win the 1906 **U.S. Women's Amateur** after defeating Mary Adams 2 and 1 at a Boston-area club, Brae Burn. The following year at Illinois' Midlothian CC, she very nearly repeated, reaching the final before meeting Margaret (the only time sisters have ever played at so late a stage) and losing 7 and 6. Though these would prove Harriot's only visits to the summit, she, like Margaret, competed extensively in Great Britain, and it was a friendly match they helped to arrange on the eve of the 1905 British Ladies Championship that would eventually lead to the formation of the eponymous Curtis Cup.

Ultimately retiring to the family home near the famous Essex County Club, Harriot Curtis passed away in the very same room in which she had been born some 93 years before.

Margaret Curtis (USA)

Born: Manchester-by-the-Sea, Massachusetts, 10/8/1883 **Died:** Boston, Massachusetts, 12/24/1965

The younger of the two Curtis sisters, Margaret was without question the superior player, winning the **U.S. Women's Amateur** in 1907, '11, and '12, finishing runner-up in 1900 (at age 17) and '05, and six times either winning or tying for medalist honors. Her first victory was perhaps bittersweet coming against sister Harriot in a not-so-close final at Midlothian, while her second deprived Scotland's Dorothy Campbell of pulling a unique sweep, as Campbell was also the 1911 winner of the British and Canadian championships.

Entering the Amateur as late as age 68, Margaret also enjoyed splendid competitive longevity, perhaps owing to an all-around athletic career that saw her win, for example, the 1908 National Doubles title in lawn tennis. Like Harriot, Margaret was also something of a progressive, supporting the American civil rights movement and serving during World War I with the Red Cross in Paris, ultimately being awarded the Legion d'Honneur by the postwar French government.

While the Curtis sisters' campaign for an international women's golf match and their donation of the eponymous cup are well documented, lesser known was Margaret's willingness to personally underwrite much of the event's cost, having secretly offered to contribute $5,000 per match for the first 10 editions to be applied toward the visiting team's travel expenses. Such a gift was never actually required, though Curtis' organizing of "Pam Barton Day" fundraisers after World War II did help make it possible for the British team to cross the Atlantic in 1950.

D

Marcel Dallemagne
(France)

Many years after the pioneering efforts of Arnaud Massy and Jean Gassiat, Parisian Marcel Dallemagne (b. 1898) established himself, between the wars, as France's next international-class player. A tall, slender man who could hit it a long way, he held a particularly hot hand during the 1930s when he won three straight **French Opens** (1936–1938), as well as the national Opens of the **Netherlands** (1933), **Italy** (1937), **Switzerland** (1931 and '37), and **Belgium** (1927 and '37). Predictably, he was a dominant force in the **French Closed Professional** (for natives only), winning on six occasions between 1930 and 1950. Not so predictably, he enjoyed some real success in Great Britain as well, scoring top-five Open Championship finishes in 1934 and '36.

Fred Daly
(Northern Ireland)

Despite losing the prime golfing years of his early 30s to World War II, Portrush's Fred Daly (1911–1990) was perhaps Ireland's best postwar player and, quite likely, among the very finest in the world circa 1950. A small, lean sort, Daly utilized extra-long clubs and a long, swaying motion in pursuit of added distance, yet he was that rare player who could employ such gimmicks and still hit the ball consistently straight. He was unique in other ways as well, whistling happily along the links and taking, by all reports, countless waggles before pulling the trigger.

Among the top Irish and British players of the immediate postwar years, Daly joined Max Faulkner as the only ones to capture the Holy Grail, the **Open Championship.** For Daly this came in 1947 at Hoylake, when a third-round 78 made it close, necessitating a closing 72 to defeat Reg Horne and Frank Stranahan by one. No flash in the pan, Daly finished second to a great Henry Cotton performance the following year, then added ties for third and fourth, plus a solo third from 1950 to 1952. Further proving his mettle, Daly was a three-time winner of the *News of the World* match play event in 1947, '48 and '52, beating Cotton in the '47 semifinal on his way to becoming

the first to win the Match Play and the Open in the same year since James Braid in 1905.

Daly appeared in the four Ryder Cup matches from 1947 to 1953, accumulating a 3-4-1 record. That history records him as the first Irishman to capture the Open Championship is, one supposes, not so very surprising. That he was the first Irishman to capture the *Irish* Open however—something he did in 1946 at Portmarnock—is another matter altogether.

John Daly (USA)

Though a two-time All-American at the University of Arkansas, John Patrick Daly (b. Carmichael, California, 4/28/1966) burst onto the national stage as an absolute unknown in 1991, stunning the golf world with a three-shot victory in the **PGA Championship** at Indianapolis' Crooked Stick GC. It remains today one of the game's most remarkable arrivals, for Daly began the week as the field's ninth alternate, shot an opening 69 without benefit of a practice round, and left both competitors and galleries amazed at the awesome length of his tee shots. Adding rounds of 67-69-71, he cruised home three ahead of Bruce Lietzke and was soon thereafter named PGA Tour Rookie of the Year.

Despite subsequent wins at the 1992 **B.C. Open** and 1994 **Atlanta Classic,** Daly was already gaining a reputation for off-course problems and unfulfilled potential when lightning struck again, at the 1995 **Open Championship.** There, he thoroughly overpowered the Old Course at St. Andrews, leading after 36 and looking for all the world a champion, before Constantino Rocca rolled in an improbable 65-footer from the famous Valley of Sin to force a play-off. But over four holes Daly's length proved too much and when Rocca took seven at the infamous Road hole, it was all over.

What followed, however, was a long period of personal problems and bizarre incidences, including walking off after 27 holes at the 97th U.S. Open, taking an epic 18 at the par-5 sixth at Bay Hill, and, most disturbingly, batting his ball around like a deranged polo player during the 1999 U.S. Open, racking up an 11 at Pinehurst's par-4 eighth hole. Thrice divorced and facing considerable financial obligations, Daly ultimately plummeted to 299th in the world rankings, apparently derailed beyond hope by alcohol, alimony, and Las Vegas casinos. However, the Daly saga may yet close happily, for he ended a nearly nine-year PGA Tour winless streak at **San Diego** in early 2004, appearing considerably more mature (and no less talented) in the process.

Daly's swing remains entirely unique, a massively long yet surprisingly compact affair that sees the shaft angled nearly vertically at the top of his backswing. Generating immense power, it also requires exceptional timing and balance, and thus has seldom been copied.

Beth Daniel (USA)

A 1999 inductee into the LPGA Hall of Fame, Beth Daniel (b. Charleston, South Carolina, 10/14/1956) entered professional golf with some of the highest expectations in LPGA history. A long, willowy woman of nearly six feet, the Furman graduate possessed length, great ball-striking ability, and a glowing amateur pedigree that included two **U.S. Women's Amateurs** (1975 and '77) and appearances on two victorious Curtis Cup teams (1976 and '78). With Nancy Lopez's nine-win debut in 1978, Daniel's 1979 arrival had fans and media trumpeting her as the remarkable Lopez's obvious rival, a substantial cross for any rookie to bear.

But to a large degree Daniel delivered, for after a one-win Rookie of the Year campaign in 1979, she managed 11 victories over the next three seasons, twice gaining the top spot on the money list and once being named Player of the Year (1980). Then, at the 1982 U.S. Women's Open, holding a one-shot lead during the final round, she penal-ized herself a stroke for having her ball move after being addressed, a violation that Daniel herself was not 100 percent certain had actually occurred. The end result was a disappointing second-place finish, and though Daniel would come back with two wins in the next three weeks, the next five years saw her game slip noticeably, recording only two victories and twice falling out of the top 20 money winners.

In the latter half of the 1980s there were health problems, first a bad back in 1986, then a long bout with mononucleosis in 1988. The time away seemed only to help, however, for over the next three seasons Daniel logged 13 wins, including a career-best seven in 1990, when she was named Player of the Year for the second time. A third such honor came after a four-win 1994, but by 1996 Daniel was turning 40 and seemingly slipping back into the pack, finishing 37th on the Tour money list. Thus largely forgotten as a top-flight contender, she surprised everyone by roaring back to capture the 2003 **Canadian Women's Open,** breaking JoAnne Carner's longstanding record to become the oldest winner in LPGA history at 46 years, eight months, and 29 days.

The lone puzzling aspect of Daniel's career has been the winning of only one Major (the 1990 **LPGA Championship**), particularly as she has nearly 30 top-10 Major finishes and 17 top-5s to her credit. Regardless, Daniel currently sits on 33 career victories, and while that might not match Nancy Lopez's 48, it's been a pretty good run.

LPGA Wins (33): 1980 & '94 Wykagyl; 1980, '81 & '91 Samsung WC; 1982 Safeway; 1989 & '90 State Farm; **1990** LPGA **Championship;** 1994 Corning
Curtis Cup: 1976 & '78 (2) **Solheim Cup:** 1990–96, 2000–03 (7)

1976-2004

	76	77	78	79	80	81	82	83	84	85	86	87	88	89	90
Dinah								T3	4	T11	T7	T2	-	T6	T6
LPGA	-	-	-	T38	T3	T5	T7	T16	T2	T10	T15	T58	-	T14	1
US Open	MC	T24	T53	T20	T10	2	T2	WD	T10	MC	T21	T33	T10	T20	T6
dM/Brit*				T16	5	T17	2	T63	T6	T14	27	MC	T47	T7	3

	91	92	93	94	95	96	97	98	99	00	01	02	03	04	
Dinah	T30	T8	T69	T19	T47	-	MC	72	T43	T47	T55	T14	T5	T40	
LPGA	4	T35	T17	T7	T18	T26	-	T58	MC	T33	T26	2	T3	T39	
US Open	T11	MC	T53	T18	MC	T19	-	T31	T47	8	T24	T7	T20	T27	
dM/Brit*	-	WD	T17	MC	T45	T36	-	T54	T13	T23	MC	T16	T14	T5	

*du Maurier replaced by the Women's British Open in 2001.

Skip Daniels (UK)

Another of Great Britain's famous old-time caddies, Skip Daniels carried for Walter Hagen during the Haig's 1922 Open Championship victory at Royal St. George's, then achieved even greater fame when Hagen "loaned" him to Gene Sarazen for the 1928 event. Sarazen would finish second on that occasion (two shots behind Hagen) but again had Daniels on his bag when he finally broke through four years later at Prince's, taking his lone Claret Jug by five strokes over Macdonald Smith. Writing some 18 years later, Sarazen gave Daniels enormous credit for this long-awaited victory, citing "his brilliant selection of clubs and his understanding of my volatile temperament."

Bettye Danoff (USA)

Largely remembered as one of the 13 founding members of the LPGA, Bettye Mims Danoff grabbed a measure of fame by winning the 1947 **Texas Women's Open,** a victory that broke Babe Zaharias' reported 17-event winning streak. Several additional footnotes attach themselves to Danoff: becoming the tour's first grandmother, taking medalist honors at the 1948 U.S. Women's Amateur, and recording her first tour hole-in-one at the 1962 Austin Civitan. The significance of the latter? That history records the conferring upon her of a most lucrative reward—a case of beer.

Jack Daray (USA)

A native of Louisiana, Jack L. Daray (1881–1958) was 20 years old when he began a career as a golf professional, the lion's share of which was spent at Chicago's Olympia Fields CC. Designing courses on the side beginning in the 1920s, Daray was most active in Illinois and along the Mississippi Gulf Coast, where he wintered for 15 years in Biloxi. His practice slowed to a trickle during the Depression, then revived itself in California following a health-related move in the 1950s. Though his most important work—some modifications made to Olympia Fields' remaining 36 holes in 1946—was not an original design, Daray's résumé does offer a rare combination—charter membership in the PGA of America (1916) and the American Society of Golf Course Architects (1946).

Eamonn Darcy (Ireland)

Though the possessor of one of golf's odder swings—ill-tempoed, elbows bent, but just fine at impact—Eamonn Christopher Darcy (b. Delgany, 8/7/1952) enjoyed a three-decade run on the European Tour, winning four titles and finishing 10 times among the Order of Merit top 20. Curiously, his highest rankings (third in 1975 and second in '76) came during years in which he didn't win any official events, though his victory at the 1983 **Spanish Open** did key an eighth-place finish. Along with a weather-shortened 1987 **Belgian Open** victory over Nick Faldo, Ronan Rafferty, and Ian Woosnam, Darcy has also won lesser events in Australia, New Zealand, and three times in Africa, not to mention at home in Ireland. He was four times a Ryder Cupper with a 1-8-2 record, though the lone victory (one up over Ben Crenshaw in 1987 singles) proved a key point in Europe's first-ever win on American soil.

Bill Darley (Australia)

Though virtually an unknown outside of Australia, Bill Darley (1900–1972) was surely one of golf's most enigmatic figures. Saddled with a leg badly mangled in a childhood encounter with a boar and a speech impediment that he blamed on the same, Darley hobbled around golf courses rather sadly, but often uncorked rounds of almost unbelievable quality. In 1937, for example, he fired a 10-under-par 59 at the Flinders GC (a seaside track redesigned by Dr. Alister MacKenzie) and he once shot a 73 by moonlight to win a bet. But Darley's crowning moment was his teaming with local amateur Tom Graham to route Walter Hagen and Joe Kirkwood in a 1937 exhibition match by the impressive margin of 5 and 4. Apparently the high-profile visitors were rankled by Darley deliberately arriving some 30 minutes late and a few other bits of gamesmanship, tactics that could hardly have been lost on the insouciant Hagen, perhaps the all-time master of the craft.

Bernard Darwin (UK)

Born: Downe, England, 9/7/1876 **Died:** London, England, 10/18/1961

The grandson of the legendary evolutionist Charles, Bernard Richard Meirion Darwin, C.B.E., himself became a legend in the field of golf literature—a field which he almost single-handedly created. A fine player and team captain at Cambridge, Darwin initially pursued a career in law before turning to writing in 1907. He then began simultaneous careers with the *Times* and *Country Life* that would last for nearly half a century, chronicling every great player from the Triumvirate to Hogan, creating in the process a unique archive of historical information which was, in many cases, recorded nowhere else. Beyond this thoroughness, Darwin's writing benefited greatly from two things, an almost visceral knowledge of the game and its myriad pitfalls and splendors, as well as a wonderfully easy

Bernard Darwin, 1922, at Southampton, New York

sively, while covering the inaugural 1922 Walker Cup match at the National GL of America, he was asked, on short notice, to replace team captain Robert Harris who had fallen ill. Darwin obligingly teamed with Cyril Tolley to lose a foursomes match against Francis Ouimet and Jess Guilford, then stepped up in singles to defeat 1910 U.S. Amateur champion William Fownes 3 and 1.

Though deceased for more than four decades now, Darwin's words live on in the form of reprints and new anthologies, one sign, at least, that golf's grand and traditional values have not been completely forgotten.

Baldovino Dassu (Italy)

Baldovino Dassu (b. Florence, 11/3/1952) holds the rare honor of being the only Italian ever to claim a **British Youths** title (1970), soon after which he turned pro and engaged in what was, with one or two exceptions, a journeyman's career. The primary exception, however, was memorable: a three-week stretch in 1976 during which he edged American Hubert Green to capture the prestigious **British Masters,** then scored a runaway eight-shot victory at his home event, the **Italian Open.** A four-time World Cup player between 1976 and 1982, Dassu never again cracked the Order of Merit top 40, though he did tie a European Tour record by firing a 60 during the 1971 Swiss Open.

Laura Davies (UK)

Easily the longest hitter in women's professional golf at the time of her American debut, Coventry, England's former Curtis Cup player Laura Jane Davies, C.B.E. (b. 10/5/1963) won her first Major championship, the 1987 **U.S. Women's Open,** before even being a member of the LPGA. Though already a dominant force on the smaller Women Professional Golfers European Tour (where she won the not-yet-Major 1986 **Women's British Open**), Davies was relatively unknown in the States prior to her dramatic breakthrough, which required the defeat of JoAnne Carner and Ayako Okamoto in an 18-hole playoff at New Jersey's Plainfield CC. On the heels of this win, the LPGA actually amended its constitution to grant the talented Briton immediate membership.

style which managed to convey great detail without losing pace. Raising what previously had been thin and disjointed coverage of golf to an art form, Darwin was not a great golf writer but rather a great writer who happened to write about golf.

Like Henry Longhurst, Darwin was a bit of an old-timer whose traditional values could cause minor altercations, such as when he chastised 1951 Open champion Max Faulkner for interrupting his conversation, saying "Don't you realize, Faulkner, that I am talking to a *gentleman?*" He was also, we are told, the possessor of a daunting on-course temper, though to be sure this never came through in his writing. More than 30 volumes have come to print bearing Darwin's name, most of them anthologies of his newspaper and magazine work. In addition, several of his full-length manuscripts stand out as genuine classics including *Green Memories* (Hodder & Stoughton, 1928), *Golf Between Two Wars* (Chatto & Windus, 1944) and the seminal *Golf Courses of the British Isles* (Duckworth, 1910). Darwin also penned one golf biography, *James Braid* (Hodder & Stoughton, 1952), and was a primary contributor to one of the truly great historical volumes, *A History of Golf in Britain* (Cassell, 1952).

Despite writing voluminously, Darwin remained a fine player for much of his life, twice reaching the semifinals of the British Amateur (1909 and '21). Even more impres-

Davies joined the American tour full time in 1988 and won twice, beginning a six-year stretch of eminently strong, if not spectacular, golf during which she added three more wins, shot a then-record round of 62, and ranged between 13th and 64th on the money list. By the mid-1990s, however, as she reached her 30s, a perhaps more mature Davies took off, enjoying a three-year run that included nine victories, three more Major championships, first- or second-place finishes on the money list, and a Player of the Year award in 1996. Also during 1996, in addition to capturing both the **LPGA Championship** and the **du Maurier,** Davies won the **Standard Register PING** and the **Star Bank LPGA Classic** and lost two sudden-death play-offs. Since that splendid season, however, she has settled back among the mortals, adding five more victories while generally remaining safely among the top 30 on the money list.

Unlike most American-born professionals, Davies has played extensively around the world, nearly tripling her career win total with numerous victories in Europe, Australia, and Asia. Easily England's top contemporary woman golfer and a highly entertaining player, she has appeared in every Solheim Cup to date and was initially awarded an M.B.E. in 1988, then her C.B.E. in 2000.

LPGA Wins (20): 1987 U.S. Women's Open; 1988 Welch's; 1994, '95, '96 & '97 Safeway; **1994 & '96 LPGA Championship; 1996 du Maurier;** 2001 Rochester
Curtis Cup: 1984 **Solheim Cup:** 1990–2003 (8)

1986-2004

	86	87	88	89	90	91	92	93	94	95	96	97	98	99	00	01	02	03	04
Dinah	MC	T33	T21	T42	T44	T23	MC	T12	2	T3	T15	T16	T3	T70	T35	T11	T21	4	T16
LPGA	-	-	MC	T65	-	T51	T52	T45	1	2	1	T4	T44	T7	T6	T6	MC	MC	T42
US Open	T11	1	T50	T7	T26	T44	MC	T11	T12	T24	6	MC	T11	MC	T9	MC	T32	MC	MC
dM/Brit*	-	-	2	T17	MC	T3	T20	-	T38	MC	1	T16	T22	2	73	T25	MC	T19	T8

*du Maurier replaced by the Women's British Open in 2001.

Rodger Davis (Australia)

Colorful Australian Rodger Davis (b. Sydney, 5/18/1951) was for many years a recognizable presence in Europe and Australasia, sporting plus fours well before Payne Stewart discovered them and four times cracking the top 10 on the European Order of Merit between 1986 and 1991. The biggest of Davis' seven European victories came at the 1986 **Volvo PGA** and the 1991 **Volvo Masters,** the latter a defeat of Nick Faldo, Bernhard Langer, and Seve Ballesteros at Valderrama. He would also claim the 1990 **Spanish Open,** as well as 16 more events Down Under, the largest being the 1986 **Australian Open** (a one-stroke triumph at the Metropolitan GC) and the 1979 **Victoria Open.** Davis has represented Australia in four World Cups and is widely remembered for leading the 1979 Open Championship (at Royal Lytham & St. Annes) late in the game before finishing fifth, five behind Ballesteros.

William F. Davis (UK/USA)

William F. Davis (1863–1902) holds a unique place in golf history, for when he left his home in Hoylake, England to accept the pro-greenkeeper position at the Royal Montreal GC in 1881, he became the first of a generation of British pros who headed west to seek their fortunes. Davis' odyssey got off to a shaky start, for he was fired and back in Britain a year later. He would return to Royal Montreal in 1889, however, this time staying for five years before packing off to Rhode Island's pioneering Newport CC in 1894. At Newport, Davis built the members both a nine-hole layout and a shorter beginners' course, with the former serving as the site of the "first" U.S. Opens and Amateurs—both unofficial, then official—in 1894 and '95. By 1896, Davis took the professional position at New York's Apawamis Club, but not before grabbing another piece of history by laying out the original 12-hole course at Long Island's Shinnecock Hills, a job that was for years credited erroneously to another native Scot, Willie Dunn Jr. Davis remained at Apawamis until his untimely death at age 39.

Johnny Dawson (USA)

A native of Los Angeles, John W. Dawson (1903–1986) was a fine amateur player of the late 1920 and '30s, winning the 1936 **Trans-Mississippi,** and reaching the quarter-finals of the 1928 U.S. Amateur (after eliminating Chick Evans) and the semifinals of the 1929 British Amateur at Royal St. George's. But like Francis Ouimet before him, Dawson was employed in the sporting goods business, a grievous sin in the eyes of the USGA, who banished him from amateur competition in 1929. Eventually reinstated, Dawson remained a long-running force in West Coast golf, winning the **Bing Crosby** in 1942 (then still played at Rancho Santa Fe) and losing to Skee Riegel in the final of the 1947 U.S. Amateur at Pebble Beach. Also a Walker Cupper in 1949 and a successful senior competitor,

Dawson played a primary role in the growth of Palm Springs by developing several of the area's earliest country clubs during the 1940s.

David Deas (UK/USA)

A name virtually unknown to most golfers, David Deas is nonetheless of great significance, for according to ancient records at the Port of Leith, Scotland, he was the recipient of a shipment of "8 doz golf clubs, 3 gross golf balls" in May of 1743. The date, of course, is an early one, but what really catches our eye is that Deas resided not in the United Kingdom but in Charleston, South Carolina. Further, it is recorded that his brother John Deas was a ranking member of South Carolina's Freemasons, that quasi-political social society that had so very much to do with golf's early growth in Scotland.

The significance of the Deas brothers' receipt of this equipment is immense, for prior to its discovery, historians generally believed that eighteenth-century "golf clubs" which existed in both Charleston and Savannah, Georgia, were, in fact, social clubs not given to actually playing the game. This seemingly illogical conclusion was not without merit because, though period newspaper accounts verify the clubs' existences, references to courses, tournaments, trophies or annual meetings were essentially nonexistent. The knowledge that a substantial amount of equipment had been shipped to Charleston, however, swings the balance of the argument completely, making it clear that while the game as we know it may not have been played in eighteenth-century America, golf as it was being played contemporaneously in Scotland certainly was.

Interestingly, though no records of similar shipments to Savannah have yet been uncovered, documentation does exist of equipment being sent to Virginia in 1750 and '51 and to Maryland in 1765.

John de Forest (UK)

Playing out of the Addington GC near London, England's John de Forest (b. 1907) lost a heartbreaker in the final of the 1931 **British Amateur** at Westward Ho!, falling 1 down to Martin Smith. Undaunted, he returned the following year to win the crown at Muirfield, where he beat Eric Fiddian 3 and 1. Later titled Count De Bendern, de Forest grabbed a less substantial (but equally memorable) piece of history in the 1953 Masters when, during the third round, his approach to the 13th found the fronting creek. Electing to play his ball from just below the waterline, de Forest stripped off one shoe and a sock and, before an excited crowd, stepped into the creek and took his stance—only to realize that he had removed the wrong shoe.

Jimmy Demaret (USA)

Born: Houston, Texas, 5/24/1910 **Died:** Houston, Texas, 12/28/1983

One of the most amiable, popular, and, above all, talented golfers in history, James Newton Demaret was part of a bumper crop of World War II–era Texas players that also included Ben Hogan, Byron Nelson, Lloyd Mangrum and Ralph Guldahl. Coming from abject poverty, Demaret was working full-time as a barefoot caddie in his early teens before becoming an assistant professional to Jack Burke Sr. at Houston's exclusive River Oaks CC. Thus able to hone his game in a setting conducive to success, Demaret emerged as an elite player, a versatile talent known for a low, wind-cheating ball flight and, more than anything, for his style.

Where Gilbert Nicholls and Walter Hagen had been sharp dressers, Demaret was more a loud one, dazzling galleries with his array of bright, sometimes blinding colors. He was also one of golf's funniest men, a constantly entertaining sort whose never-ending line of quips was entirely original. Also a talented enough singer to perform professionally, Demaret later parlayed his immense likeability into the host position on two TV series, *All-Star Golf* and, most memorably, *Shell's Wonderful World of Golf*. The Demaret touch, quite simply, was magic, for as Sam Snead observed late in life, "I never met one person who said they didn't like Jimmy Demaret."

For all his remarkable popularity, Demaret was a truly great player who, like several of his fellow Texans, lost a number of his best years to wartime. Initially competing primarily in his home state (where he claimed the **Texas PGA** every year from 1934 to 1938), Demaret first tried the winter tour in 1938, then won the following year's **Los Angeles Open** by seven shots over Jug McSpaden. All told he would amass 31 official PGA Tour victories (14th all-time) with the unquestioned highlights being **Masters** titles in 1940, '47 and '50. In both 1940 (when he beat Mangrum by four) and '47, Demaret was among the hottest golfers around, claiming six overall victories in each season. By 1950, however, he was weeks away from turning 40, yet became the Masters' first three-time winner when he slipped past Australian Jim Ferrier by two.

At the U.S. Open Demaret had his chances, missing the famous Nelson-Mangrum-Ghezzi play-off in 1946 by two, breaking the all-time Open scoring record in 1948 at Riviera yet still losing to Hogan, and, most disappointingly, missing out by one on the 1957 Middlecoff-Mayer play-off at Inverness at the ripe old age of 47. He was equally a presence at the PGA where he reached the semifinals on four occasions, yet never advanced to the final. Though not one to travel for the Open Championship (his 1954 tie for 10th was his sole entry), Demaret did venture

Jimmy Demaret, 1940, Houston, Texas

south of the border on occasion, actually winning the **Argentine Open** in 1941.

Demaret also bore the distinction of being Ben Hogan's closest friend in golf, their decidedly opposite personalities seeming to blend beautifully in four-ball play. Like Hogan, Demaret served during World War II but never saw combat, playing a lot of golf with his Navy bosses and later observing: "Every war has a slogan. 'Remember the Alamo' or 'Remember Pearl Harbor.' Mine was 'That'll play, Admiral.'"

In later years Demaret would team with Masters and PGA champion Jack Burke Jr. (his first boss' son) to develop the popular Champions GC in Houston, site of the 1967 Ryder Cup and 1969 U.S. Open. This was Demaret's final home, where he spent most of his free time and generally held court, a place which added much to the warehouse of great Demaret stories. Less frequently reported, however, were his acts of kindness, not only of the financial sort but also those of basic decency, for as disparate a pair as Australia's Peter Thomson and the pioneering black player Bill Spiller both cited Demaret as being particularly supportive. Yet largely lost in all of his popularity, humor, and good works is our sense of just how talented a player Jimmy Demaret really was. For, as Hogan put it with typical succinctness, Demaret "was the most underrated golfer in history."

PGA Tour Wins (31): 1939 Los Angeles; 1940 Western; **1940, '47 & '50 Masters;** 1949 Phoenix; 1952 Bing Crosby; and 4 Inverness Four-Balls
Intn'l Win: 1
Ryder Cup: 1947–51 (3)

1935-1962

	35	36	37	38	39	40	41	42	43	44	45	46	47	48
Masters	-	-	-	-	T33	1	T12	6				T4	1	T18
US Open	-	-	T16	MC	T22	WD	WD					T6	T39	2
British	-	-	-	-	-							-	-	-
PGA	T33	T33	T33	T9	-	T17	T33	T3		-	-	T3	T33	T3

	49	50	51	52	53	54	55	56	57	58	59	60	61	62
Masters	T8	1	T30	WD	T45	T29	-	T34	3	T14	MC	MC	MC	T5
US Open	WD	T20	T14	T15	T4	T29	-	MC	3	WD	-	-	-	-
British	-	-	-	-	-	T10	-	-	-	-	-	-	-	-
PGA	T5	T3	-	-	-	-	-	T33	-	DQ	-	-	-	-

Angel de la Torre (Argentina/Spain/USA)

There remains only limited documentation regarding the early life of Angel de la Torre, a native of Argentina who apparently spent much of his formative time in Spain. What records do exist, however, show that after Arnaud Massy won the inaugural **Spanish Open** in 1915, de la Torre took five of the next six to be played, in 1916, '17, '19, '23, and '25 (the event skipping several years for various reasons), as well as a sixth and final title in 1935. Having also participated in a handful of Open Championships, de la Torre came to the United States during the late 1920s and served as the first professional at Santa Cruz's famed Pasatiempo GC, before returning to a lucrative club job in Madrid. He emigrated permanently to America in 1936, however, taking up long-term residence at Chicago's Lake Shore CC. His son Manuel later established a name for himself as a teacher and professional at the Milwaukee CC.

Jim Dent (USA)

Where men like Pete Brown and Nate Starks drew attention on the PGA Tour largely for the color of their skin, Jim Dent (b. Augusta, Georgia, 5/9/1939), though also black, was noticed for a very different reason. Standing 6′2″ and weighing 225 pounds, the powerful Dent was easily the Tour's longest hitter for most of the 1970s, routinely belting drives far beyond Jack Nicklaus and other mortals. A onetime caddie at Augusta National, Dent never possessed the all-around game to win on the PGA Tour and thus was known almost exclusively for his distance. Upon turning 50 in 1989, however, he found new life on the Champions Tour where he won 12 times between 1989 and 1998.

Helen Dettweiler (USA)

Well known as one of the LPGA's 13 founding members in 1949, Helen Dettweiler (1914–1990) had proven herself a player much earlier by winning the 1939 **Women's Western Open** as a 25-year-old amateur. Of greater interest, however, is Dettweiler's laundry list of accomplishments in other areas. She was, for example, one of the earliest women (behind only Helen Hicks and Patty Berg) to do promotional work for a major equipment manufacturer (Wilson). She would also serve as America's first national female sports reporter (broadcasting Washington Senator baseball games) and held two wartime positions of note in the U.S. military: head cryptographer for the Air Transport Command and, as a member of the Women's Air Force Service Pilots (WASP), a pilot in the ferrying of B-17 bombers. Using her aviation connections, Dettweiler teamed with pioneering flyer Jackie Cochran to also become one of the first female golf course architects, designing a course at Cochran Ranch (today's Indian Palms CC) outside of Palm Springs.

Bruce Devlin (Australia)

The son of a New South Wales plumber, Bruce William Devlin (b. Armidale, 10/10/1937) took up golf as a means of luring his father back onto the links after the latter had lost an arm in a tragic car accident. With father caddying for him during his amateur days, Devlin soon developed into a top prospect, leading Australia to victory at the 1958 **Eisenhower Cup** and winning the **Australian Amateur** in 1959 at Royal Sydney. When he won the 1960 **Australian Open** as an amateur (edging fellow amateur Ted Ball at Lake Karrinyup) it was time to turn professional, and off to America he flew.

For several years Devlin struggled mightily, remaining Stateside partially because he didn't have enough money to leave. But by late 1963 he was back on his feet, first cashing several checks in the States, then getting red-hot en route home, winning thrice in New Zealand before taking four Australia titles (including the **Victoria** and **Queensland Opens**) toward year's end. In 1964 Devlin finally broke through in America (at the **St. Petersburg Open**) and was off to the races, eventually claiming eight PGA Tour victories, the lucrative **Carling World Open** (1966), several more titles of significance in Australia, and, with David Graham, the 1970 **World Cup** in Argentina. He set a period record for consecutive PGA Tour cuts made (36) and even became part of American golfing folklore by jovially taking six swings to extract his ball from the pond fronting the 18th green at Torrey Pines during the 1975 San Diego Open. The result: an epic 10 — and the pond being known as Devlin's Billabong ever since.

An amiable man who enjoyed great popularity worldwide, Devlin eventually moved smoothly into TV work while also designing over 100 golf courses in partnership with American Robert von Hagge.

PGA Tour Wins (8): 1966 Colonial; 1969 Byron Nelson
Intn'l Wins (16): 1960 Australian Open; 1963 French Open

Joe Dey (USA)

Among the most honored of golf's career administrators, Joseph C. Dey (1907–1991) was the longtime executive director of the USGA before resigning in 1969 to become the first commissioner of the PGA Tour. A New Orleans native educated at the University of Pennsylvania, Dey began his working life as a Philadelphia sportswriter before shifting gears, ultimately looming large for many years atop American golf's governing body. He was particularly adroit, it seems, at resolving conflicts, for he numbered among his proudest achievements helping to unify the rules with the R&A in 1951—and his PGA Tour post commenced in the immediate aftermath of the player's acrimonious break with the PGA of America. Dey also bore the distinction of being only the second American (behind Francis Ouimet) to be named captain of the R&A, playing himself in during 1975.

Gardner Dickinson (USA)

Both an admirer and protégé of Ben Hogan, Dothan, Alabama's 5′11″, 140-pound Gardner Dickinson (1927–1998) was a member of Louisiana State's 1947 NCAA championship team before turning professional in 1952. Familiar to period observers for patterning his swing, attire, and mannerisms after Hogan, Dickinson enjoyed only modest early success but eventually blossomed into a seven-time Tour winner, claiming such titles as the 1968 **Doral Open** (by one over Tom Weiskopf), the 1969 **Colonial** (over Gary Player), and his last victory, a sudden-death triumph over Jack Nicklaus at the 1971 **Atlanta Classic**. Dickinson's competitive tenacity was further evidenced during 1967 and '71 Ryder Cup appearances where he posted a thoroughly impressive 9-1 record, including a 5-0 mark when paired with Arnold Palmer in foursomes play. In 1985 he married Judy Clark Dickinson, a four-time winner on the LPGA Tour.

Patric Dickinson (UK)

Patric Thomas Dickinson (1914–1994) was best known as a poet, translator (of Latin) and playwright, with numerous published volumes and several prestigious awards attached to his name. Dickinson, however, was also a fine and avid golfer, playing at Cambridge and authoring a single volume on the game, the classic *A Round of Golf Courses* (Evans Brothers, 1951). Profiling, in depth, 18 of Dickinson's favorite British courses, *A Round of Golf Courses* is enough to make us rue his not choosing a career as a golf scribe. For as Bernard Darwin wrote reverently of Dickinson in the book's foreword, "I feel rather like the man who admired Shakespeare: 'Things come into his head that would never come into mine.'"

Bob Dickson (USA)

Former Oklahoma State star Bob Dickson (b. McAlester, 1/25/1944) enjoyed one of modern golf's most impressive amateur seasons in 1967. In addition to going 3-0 in that summer's Walker Cup victory at Royal St. George's, Dickson captured the **British Amateur** by defeating fellow American Ron Cerrudo 2 and 1 at Formby. Then in September, he edged Vinny Giles by one to capture the stroke-play **U.S. Amateur** at The Broadmoor, thus becoming the first player since Lawson Little in 1935 (and one of only four overall) to win both national Amateurs in the same year. His subsequent PGA Tour career was something of a letdown, though he did claim victory at the 1973 **San Diego Open**.

The Dicksons (UK)

Though their family history remains poorly documented, the Dicksons of Leith, Scotland produced several generations of notable ball and clubmakers, with at least two interesting footnotes attached. In 1629, William and Thomas Dickson were involved in litigation with James Melvill who had, in 1618, been given/sold a Royal monopoly on the making of feathery golf balls by King James I (the Dicksons' emerged victorious in court). The Dickson name appears again in Thomas Mathison's much-reprinted 1743 poem *The Goff*, which reads "... the work of Dickson who in Letha dwells and in the art of making clubs excels." All told, the family, with numerous siblings and offspring, turned out sought-after equipment for roughly 150 years.

William Diddel (USA)

An excellent athlete who managed the distinctive feat of lettering in four different sports at Wabash College, Indianapolis native William Diddel (1884–1985) was a particularly outstanding golfer who won five **Indiana Amateurs** and is believed to have shot his age more than 1000 times. Beginning in architecture by constructing Indianapolis' Highland G & CC (a track routed, but not completed, by Willie Park Jr.) in 1921, Diddel would soon embark on a career that saw him build approximately 100 new courses, primarily in the Midwest. An innovator, Diddel took out a patent on what was surely the first "short" golf ball, a product designed to go roughly half the normal distance, thus saving hugely on overall land and maintenance requirements. He also experimented with an entirely bunkerless layout at Indiana's Woodland CC, molding the ground contours into a test he deemed suitable for a low handicapper. Yet Diddel was also a strong traditionalist, even opposing (according to Pete Dye) the use of artificial irrigation—an okay concept in Indiana perhaps, but a decidedly dicey one in Texas or Arizona.

Notable Courses: Hillcrest GC, Indiana; Hot Springs G&CC, Arlington, Arkansas; Meridian Hills CC, Indiana

Leo Diegel (USA)

Born: Detroit, Michigan, 4/27/1899 **Died:** North Hollywood,
California, 5/8/1951

A 2003 inductee into the World Golf Hall of Fame, Leo
Diegel has long been one of golf's more interesting, yet
sadly overlooked, characters. A wonderful ball-striker who
could hold his own with anyone from tee to green, he was
at best an inconsistent putter who was often seized with
something resembling the yips. His solution, an elbows-
out motion that looked oddly like rocking a baby, apparently served him for a time and was widely copied. Indeed,
Diegel's close friend Gene Sarazen once wrote that "You
could always tell where he had been when you gazed out
on a course and saw the members Diegeling away all over
the place."

Though credited with an impressive 30 PGA Tour wins
(16th all-time), the list of Major championships *not* won
by Diegel tends to get top billing. In the 1929 Open Championship at Muirfield, for example, he headed into the final day with a two stroke lead, shot 82-77, and finished
third. Four years later at St. Andrews, he faced a three-
footer at the last to join Craig Wood and Denny Shute in
a play-off and missed it, by most accounts, nearly a foot
wide. At the U.S. Open he also had his chances, four times
finishing among the top five. But in the face of such disappointments, Diegel did rally to win back-to-back **PGA
Championships** in 1928 and '29, the former being especially significant as it ended Walter Hagen's remarkable
four-year domination of the event, with Diegel himself
retiring the Haig in the semifinals 3 and 2. He also won
Canadian Open titles in 1924, '25, '28 and '29.

A complicated and high-strung man, Diegel constantly
fretted over the state of his game, endlessly theorizing and
torturing himself, as Sarazen put it, "with wild musings
about rounds yet to be played." On one memorable occasion, when Diegel missed a short one to cost him and
Sarazen a four-ball match in Miami, he disappeared for
several days, causing the Squire great concern. But before
the police could be summoned Diegel returned, "tired,
unshaven, apologetic, and wild about a new theory he had
worked out for sinking three-footers."

A participant in all four Ryder Cup matches from 1927
to 1933, Diegel resided for a time in Tijuana, representing

Leo Diegel, 1929, Montreal, Canada, Canadian Open

the Agua Caliente Hotel & CC, a long-defunct 1920s
luxury resort located just over the Mexican border. He
cut back his playing schedule in 1935, apparently as the
result of an ongoing hand problem, and became a well-
regarded teacher for years thereafter.

PGA Tour Wins (30): 1924, '25, '28 & '29 Canadian Open; **1928
& '29 PGA Championship**
Ryder Cup: 1927–33 (4)

1920-1936

	20	21	22	23	24	25	26	27	28	29	30	31	32	33	34	35	36
Masters															T16	T19	-
US Open	T2	T26	7	T8	T25	8	T3	T11	T18	T8	T11	3	4	T17	T17	MC	-
British	-	-	-	T25	-	-	-	-	-	3	T2	-	-	T3	-	-	-
PGA	T17	-	-	-	T17	T5	2	-	1	1	T9	T17	-	T17	T17	-	-

Chris DiMarco (USA)

A solid all-around player, Chris DiMarco (b. Huntington, New York, 8/23/1968) has emerged as one of golf's more consistent performers of the new century, finishing among the PGA Tour's top 20 money winners every year since 2000 and winning single events in 2000, '01, and '02, the last being the **Phoenix Open.** A winless 2003 saw him slip from 11th to 18th in earnings but a fine late-summer stretch in 2004 (including a play-off loss to Vijay Singh at the PGA Championship) had DiMarco once again pushing for the top 10 and making his first Ryder Cup appearance. Also a play-off loser to Tiger Woods at the 2005 Masters, the former University of Florida All-American is widely recognized as the first high-profile user of the "claw" putting grip, an ungainly, hands-split arrangement that has lifted DiMarco from mediocrity to one of the more reliable putters on Tour.

Tom Doak (USA)

Perhaps the first contemporary designer to tailor his educational track exclusively toward becoming a golf course architect, the controversial Tom Doak (b. New York, New York, 3/16/1961) majored in landscape architecture at Cornell before utilizing a postgraduate scholarship to spend a year studying the classic links of the United Kingdom. Following a three-year stint working for Pete Dye, Doak struck out on his own with Michigan's innovative High Pointe GC, an iconoclastically natural creation that bucked numerous modern trends.

Despite this and other design successes, Doak was arguably better known for his outspokenness, particularly in the form of the entertaining *Confidential Guide* (Sleeping Bear, 1996), a collection of the architect's unbridled thoughts on the hundreds of courses he's visited worldwide. A more mainstream volume, *The Anatomy of A Golf Course* (Lyons & Burford, 1992), covered the nuts and bolts of architecture and stands as perhaps the finest book of its type since before World War II.

Though not completing a great number of new designs during the early 1990s, Doak did make a major name for himself as a restorationist, consulting and working at many of America's classic Golden Age courses. Eventually these successes helped pave the way for an expanded roster of new projects with two new-millennium jackpots—Oregon's Pacific Dunes and New Zealand's ultra-spectacular Cape Kidnappers—firmly establishing Doak as one of the game's elite contemporary architects.

Notable Courses: Apache Stronghold GC, Arizona; Barnbougle Dunes GL, Tasmania; **Cape Kidnappers GC, New Zealand; Pacific Dunes, Oregon;** Stonewall GC, Pennsylvania

Peter Dobereiner (USA/UK)

Though born in New York, Peter Dobereiner would spend most of his life residing in Great Britain and, for a period, in India. A law student at Oxford, he eventually followed Darwin's path and gravitated toward writing, making his name primarily as golf correspondent for the *Guardian* and the *Observer*, but also contributing regularly to *Golf Digest* and *Golf World* (UK). Anthologized on several occasions, Dobereiner was also the author of several books, including *The Game with a Hole in It* (Faber & Faber, 1970) and *The Glorious World of Golf* (McGraw-Hill, 1973). His style was certainly unique, mixing legitimate insight with edgy humor, prompting the great golf book collector Joseph Murdoch to suggest that if Dobereiner had "been reporting way back in the sixteenth century, golf would ultimately end up as ancient, but not necessarily royal." He passed away in 1996 at age 70.

Charlotte Dod (UK)

One of the great female athletes in history, Bebington, England's Charlotte "Lottie" Dod (1871–1960) won singles titles at Wimbledon on all five occasions that she entered, was a champion skater, an Olympic silver medal winner for archery, and a skilled hockey and billiards player. Taking to golf after retiring from tennis, she was a semifinalist in the **British Ladies** as early as 1898 and '99, eventually winning the title in 1904 when she defeated May Hezlet one up at Royal Troon. A participant in several of women's golf's earliest international matches, Dod is recalled for her fine recovery play and putting. Given her remarkable record of athletic excellence, it's a good bet she knew a thing or two about the mental aspects of competition as well.

Muriel Dodd (UK)

Crosby, England's Muriel Dodd (b. 1891) pulled a rare double in 1913, winning both the **British** and **Canadian Ladies** titles, at Royal Lytham & St. Anne's and Royal Montreal, respectively. Curiously, she would gain even greater fame a decade later in a British Ladies championship that she failed to win. Prior to losing in the 1923 final to Doris Chambers, Dodd eliminated Joyce Wethered in the semis, the only time anyone other than Cecil Leitch defeated the indomitable Wethered in British national championship play.

Luke Donald (UK)

One of many recent internationals to excel in American collegiate golf, England's Luke Campbell Donald (b.

Hemel Hempstead, 12/7/1977) was an **NCAA** Player of the Year, individual national champion, and a three-time All-American (1999–2001) at Northwestern University. Standing only 5′9″ and weighing 160 pounds, Donald is hardly an overpowering sort, yet he broke through to victory in his first full season on the PGA Tour, winning the rain-shortened 2002 **Southern Farm Bureau Classic** by one over Deane Pappas. Following a winless 2003 that saw him slip to 90th in official earnings, Donald rebounded in 2004, especially in Europe where he claimed the **Scandinavian Masters** and the prestigious **European Masters** (by five over a hot Miguel Angel Jiménez) within a five-week summer stretch, then teamed with Paul Casey to win the **World Cup** in November. A former British Walker Cup star in 1999 and 2001, and a captain's pick for the 2004 Ryder Cup, Donald appears poised for a long and fruitful professional career on both sides of the Atlantic.

Captain Maitland Dougall (UK)

Maitland Dougall was one of a band of early Scottish amateurs widely hailed as the best players of their time who simply lacked an Open or Amateur Championship with which to define themselves. A frequent winner of medals at the R&A, Dougall's shining moment came during 1860 when, in a driving rain, he abandoned a competition mid-course to aid in the rescue of a floundering boat in the bay. Successful, he returned some five hours later and picked up where he had left off, eventually winning with a lead-injected ball that obediently stayed down in the wind. Dougall also represents an additional historical footnote, for having been introduced to the gutta-percha ball for the first time at Blackheath in 1848, he brought some back to St. Andrews for their Scottish debut, whereupon the gutty's quick acceptance signaled impending doom for the age-old feathery.

Dave Douglas (USA)

A native of Philadelphia whose father had emigrated from Scotland, Dave Douglas (1918–1978) was an eight-time winner on the PGA Tour, his biggest title being the 1953 **Canadian Open.** That, combined with a pair of 1952 victories, landed him a spot on the 1953 Ryder Cup team and, unexpectedly, a moment in the spotlight. In the last singles match on the course, Douglas came to the 36th hole 1 down to Bernard Hunt—and absolutely in need of a halve, lest the British snatch the cup for the first time in two decades. Both men found Wentworth's 18th green in three but when Hunt three-putted, Douglas had his halve and America narrowly retained the cup.

Findlay Douglas (UK/USA)

A native of St. Andrews, long-hitting Findlay S. Douglas (1874–1959) emigrated to America in 1896, at age 22. Settling in the New York metropolitan area and playing out of today's Greenwich CC, Douglas soon established himself as a force to be reckoned with, winning the 1898 **U.S. Amateur** at New Jersey's Morris County CC 5 and 3 over Walter B. Smith. Returning to the final the next two years, he would lose first to homebred H. M. Harriman at Chicago's Onwentsia Club when, trailing seven down at lunch, Douglas roared all the way back to square before overshooting the short 16th and losing 3 and 2. Then in 1900, he was beaten two up by Walter Travis as the Australian-born "Old Man," who only took up the game at age 35, was just entering his dominant period. Douglas further filled his trophy case with **Metropolitan Amateur** titles in 1901 and '03, won at Apawamis and Deal respectively.

Yet for all of this on-course success, Findlay Douglas might be better remembered as one of American golf's early organizers, boosters and administrators. A friend and competitive adversary of C. B. Macdonald, he was long involved with the USGA and served as its president in 1929 and '30. Shortly thereafter, he also served a three-year hitch as president of the Metropolitan Golf Association, remaining an influential and highly involved figure throughout his life.

Dale Douglass (USA)

A native of Wewoka, Oklahoma, who attended the University of Colorado, Dale Douglass (b. 3/5/1936) was largely a journeyman on the PGA Tour with the prominent exception of 1969, when he won twice, finished 12th on the money list and was selected to the Ryder Cup team. He remained among the top 30 for two more seasons and won his third (and last) title at the 1970 **Phoenix Open** before slipping from the limelight, only to return as a force on the Champions Tour, ultimately taking 11 titles including the 1986 **U.S. Senior Open.**

Allen Doyle (USA)

The possessor of one of golf's shortest and most ungainly swings, Allen Doyle (b. Woonsocket, RI 6/26/1948) spent the better part of his life competing as an amateur, racking up numerous titles in his adopted home state of Georgia, reaching the semifinals of the 1992 U.S. Amateur and being selected for Walker Cup teams in 1989, '91, and '93. By the middle of the '90s he had turned professional, winning thrice on the then–Nike Tour and becoming the oldest PGA Tour rookie in history, at age 47. This was clearly but a warm-up for Doyle's obvious destination, the Champions Tour. Upon reaching age 50, he became fully exempt in time for the 1999 season and has since gone on to win nine official events, over $10 million and a Player of the Year award in 2001. His swing, he has said, is the product of having practiced in a low-ceilinged room as a youth, and while stylistically nothing to imitate, it has certainly served the 6'3" Doyle long and well.

Norman Drew (Ireland)

A native of Belfast, Norman Vico Drew (b. 1932) enjoyed a strong run of amateur success in the early 1950s, including back-to-back **Irish Open Amateur** wins in 1952 and '53. Earning a Walker Cup spot in the latter year (where he lost in singles to Don Cherry by a lopsided 9 and 7 margin), Drew later turned professional, enjoying enough success to merit a Ryder Cup appearance in 1959. This time he faired better, halving in singles against Doug Ford in Palm Springs. Thus when Drew was selected for the 1960 World (née Canada) Cup, he became the first to represent Ireland in all three major international competitions.

Frank Duane (USA)

A native of the Bronx, New York, Francis J. Duane (1921–1994) was a longtime assistant to architect Robert Trent Jones before eventually going into business on his own in 1963. Wheelchair-bound by Guillame-Barré Syndrome after 1965, his solo practice frequently focused on the modernizing older New York–area courses, with Bethpage State Park, Engineers, Inwood, and Quaker Ridge all availing themselves of his services. During the early 1970s, Duane briefly partnered with Arnold Palmer on several high-profile new designs before retiring toward the close of the decade.

Ed Dudley (USA)

Though recalled today mostly as a past president of the PGA and the longtime professional at Augusta National, sweet-swinging Brunswick, Georgia, native Ed Dudley (1901–1963) was a very successful player during the pre–World War II years, winning 15 PGA Tour events but, alas, never capturing that elusive Major championship. There were close calls of course, particularly at the 1937 U.S. Open at Oakland Hills where Dudley finished fifth after leading through 54, then closing with a 76. He also played his way into the quarter-finals of the PGA Championship on six occasions, yet only once managed to reach the semis.

Still, Dudley's 1931 winning of the **Los Angeles** and **Western Opens** (the latter by four over Walter Hagen) made for an impressive double, and his 3-1 record in three Ryder Cups was more than respectable. In many ways, however, Dudley's best performances were saved for Augusta National, where he finished third in the 1937 Masters, logged six top 10s overall, and, in his teaching capacity, is reported to have cured President Eisenhower's slice.

PGA Tour Wins (15): 1931 Los Angeles; 1931 Western Open; and 3 Philadelphia Opens
Ryder Cup: 1929, '33 & '37 (3)

The Duke of Windsor (UK)

Gaining everlasting fame from his 1936 decision to abdicate the throne and marry American divorcee Wallis Warfield Simpson, the Duke of Windsor was a dedicated—if not altogether successful—golfer who was frequently in attendance at major British events, adding luster to an already golden golfing era. Described by *The Golfer's Handbook* as having "played the game on more widely diversified golf courses in the world than any other golfer," the Duke captained no less than 11 prominent British clubs, including the Royal & Ancient in 1922. On that occasion, however, he foozled the ceremonial first tee shot as the retrieving caddies stood respectfully far afield, allowing one Willie Petrie to rush from Gourlay's fairway-side clubmaking shop to grab both the ball and the traditional gold sovereign reward.

Alexander Duncan (UK)

The son of a professor of philosophy at St. Andrews University and a well-known Freemason, Alexander Duncan bore the relatively rare distinction of being captain, at varying times, of the Honourable Company of Edinburgh Golfers (1771), the Society of Golfers at Blackheath (1766), and the forerunner of the R&A, the Society of Golfers at St. Andrews (1756, '61, and '91). In those days captaincies were generally awarded to the winner of a club's annual tournament and in his third victory (1891) at St. Andrews, Duncan completed play in 99 strokes, making him one of only four men documented to have broken 100 on the Old Course prior to the nineteenth century.

A. D. S. Duncan (New Zealand)

Also a cricket player of real repute, Sri Lanka–born Arthur Duncan Stewart Duncan (1876–1951) was, to most minds, *the* New Zealand golfer from the dawn of the twentieth century well into the 1930s. Referred to by historian G. M. Kelly as "a gentleman of the old school," Duncan "could be aloof, and did not suffer the brash or foolish gladly," yet he served as the very model of the Kiwi game for generations of players.

A slim man with a splendid tempo that allowed him to remain competitive for many years, Duncan won an incomparable 10 **New Zealand Amateurs** between 1899 and 1926, a record that likely will never be approached. He also captured three **New Zealand Opens,** beginning with the inaugural event in 1907, then adding back-to-back crowns in 1910 and '11, with his 295 score of 1910 standing as the tournament record for an impressive 20 years. Such a record, combined with a rigid adherence to the time-honored standards of the game, made Duncan a natural golfing icon in New Zealand, and his presence (which included a bit of architecture and much administrative work) was a massive one.

Colonel Anthony Duncan (UK)

A native of Cardiff, Wales, Colonel Anthony Arthur Duncan, O.B.E. (b. 1914) was an Oxford man and later, for many years, an officer in the British army. Described by Darwin as "one of the shining lights of Welsh golf" and a player of admirable dispatch, Duncan very nearly won the British Amateur of 1939, falling in the final, 2 and 1 to Alec Kyle at Hoylake. Losing the majority of his best golfing years to World War II, Duncan ultimately had to satisfy himself with three **Welsh Amateurs** and six **Army** titles, as well as the captaincy of the 1953 Walker Cup team. Taking his squad to Massachusetts' Kittansett Club, Duncan showed world-class sportsmanship when, after American James Jackson discovered a 15th and 16th club in his bag during foursomes play, he argued against the apparently mandated disqualification of Jackson and his partner Gene Littler. Penalized two holes instead of losing outright, the Americans eventually won the match 3 and 2.

George Duncan (UK)

Born: Methlick, Scotland, 9/16/1883 **Died:** Leeds, England, 1/15/1964

Called "a true golfing genius" by Bernard Darwin, George Duncan joined Abe Mitchell and big Archie Compston as heirs apparent to Britain's great Triumvirate during the inter-war years. Known for his tremendous speed of play, Duncan's style varied greatly throughout his career, for he was ever attempting to improve using a peculiar ability to copy the swings of others without hours of practice. He was also a thoroughly aggressive sort, once described by Henry Cotton as "a player always game to take a risk, because he disliked playing safe." Thus capable of far wider variances of form than most top-flight players, Duncan nonetheless was largely influenced by Harry Vardon, both in terms of his style and the stated desire to carry shots to their target instead of relying upon the time-honored ground game.

Duncan's breakthrough occurred in 1913 at the old *News of the World* match-play event, where he upset James Braid on Braid's home course, Walton Heath. He also captured the 1913 and '27 **French Opens,** as well as the 1927 **Irish Open** at Portmarnock. But then as now, the true test of any British golfer was the **Open Championship,** an event Duncan won in epic style in 1920. Thirteen shots off the lead at the halfway mark, he purchased a new driver in the exhibition tent, came home in 71-72, and beat the 52-year-old Sandy Herd by two. Duncan's overall record at the Open was strong with 12 top-10 finishes between 1906 and 1924, though only in 1910 (when a third-round lead vanished behind a closing 83) and 1922 (when a closing 69 came up one shy of Walter Hagen) was he ever truly in a position to win.

A participant in the first three Ryder Cup matches (1927-31), Duncan bears the distinction of being the only player to defeat Walter Hagen in the event, trouncing him 10 and 8 in 1929. He also appeared in the unofficial 1926 international match and joined Abe Mitchell on several tours of America before turning down job offers there to settle at the Mere GC in Cheshire.

Intn'l Victories (12): 1912 Belgian Open; 1913 PGA Match Play; 1913 & '27 French Open; **1920 British Open;** 1927 Irish Open
Ryder Cup: 1927-31 (3)

Billy Dunk (Australia)

Though virtually a household name to golfers Down Under, New South Wales' Billy Dunk (b. Gosford, 12/10/1938) is largely unknown in America, owing to a dislike of travel that seldom saw him any farther afield than New Zealand or Malaysia. Yet in Australia the highly strung Dunk was a certified legend, a remarkable chipper and putter who won more than 100 domestic events and set over 80 course records. Indeed, the 5'6" Dunk's ability to repeatedly go low was truly impressive, highlighted by an epic 60 at the Merewether GC in 1970 but backed up by a 61 and numerous other rounds at 65 or better. Interestingly, Dunk himself admitted to being somewhat intimidated by the big-name foreign stars, a possible explanation for his never winning the Australian Open which, for decades, has attracted a strong international field. At the closed **Australian PGA,** however, he was explosive, winning in 1962,

'66, '71, '74, and '76. It's a great shame that Dunk could never calm his nerves and travel better for he surely possessed the raw talent to succeed nicely at golf's highest levels.

George Dunlap Jr. (USA)

George T. Dunlap Jr. (b. 1909) was the son of a founding partner of the Grossett & Dunlap publishing house, affording him the sort of lifestyle conducive to high-level amateur golf. A star at Princeton University, Dunlap won team and individual **NCAA** titles in 1930 and a second individual crown in 1931. Already a winter regular at Pinehurst, he captured his first **North & South Amateur** that same year and added six more titles over the next 11. Though never better than semifinalist in the British Amateur (which he accomplished twice, in 1933 and '34), Dunlap did capture the **U.S. Amateur** in 1933 at Ohio's Kenwood CC, routing Max Marston 6 and 5 in the final. He also was a three-time Walker Cup player (1932–36) and won the **Metropolitan Amateur** in 1936, one of the few major events played at Charles Blair Macdonald's legendary Lido GC before its World War II–era demise.

Jamie Dunn (UK)

The identical twin brother of Willie Dunn Sr., Musselburgh's Jamie Dunn (1821–1871) was himself a fine player, though, in the sometimes cold eyes of history, not the equal of his illustrious brother. Some reports have Willie being noticeably taller but the Reverend W. W. Tulloch, in his epic *The Life of Tom Morris*, cites Willie's son Tom in observing that "they were so much alike, and spoke so similarly, that it was a very difficult matter to know the one from the other, unless the individual was very intimately acquainted with them." Perhaps this potentially unnerving twist helps to account for the pair's success in four-ball matches though on the whole, Jamie, who had no children and assisted Willie at most of his club jobs, was inevitably resigned to second-fiddle status.

John D. Dunn (UK/USA)

A member of one of golf's most prominent families, North Berwick–born John Duncan Dunn (1874–1951) — son of Tom Dunn, grandson of Old Willie — served as a professional and greenkeeper in his teens and is rumored to have laid out one or two British courses despite his relative youth. In 1894 he followed his uncle Willie Dunn Jr. to the United States where he initially worked for the Slazenger and Bridgeport Arms sporting goods companies.

In 1897 John replaced Willie as professional at New York's fabulously affluent Ardsley CC.

By 1900, J. D. was wintering as director of golf planning for the Florida West Coast Railway, designing several rather rudimentary courses for the company's early resort hotels in what were then sleepy outposts like Tampa and Winter Park. He also partnered on several designs with the iconic Walter Travis, most notably at Vermont's Ekwanok GC in 1899.

Following World War I, J. D. made his final big move, settling into the pro shop at the Los Angeles CC. There Dunn cemented his reputation as a teacher (giving Babe Zaharias her first golf lessons during the 1932 Olympic Games) while also designing at least a dozen courses, several of which survive today, though in heavily altered states. A capable writer, Dunn authored numerous magazine pieces and several notable instructional books including *Intimate Golf Talks* (G. P. Putnam's, 1920) and *Natural Golf* (G. P. Putnam's, 1931). An important and oft-overlooked contributor to the American game's meteoric pre–World War II growth, Dunn passed away in Los Angeles, at age 77.

May Dunn (UK/USA)

Daughter of Tom Dunn and his wife Isabella Gourlay, and sister of John D. and Seymour, Wimbledon-born May Dunn (1880–1948) was a competitive golfer but, in a world of limited competitive opportunity for female players, not quite a champion. At the onset of World War I, she emigrated to America in search of a golf-related career, initially penning instructional material for the New York *Herald* and, after moving west, becoming the first recorded woman to design golf courses (the Reno and Tahoe Tavern GCs). After serving as professional at each, she married a Californian named Adolph Hupfel and soon retired from the business.

Seymour Dunn (UK/USA)

Son of Tom and younger brother of John D., Seymour Dunn (1882–1959) first came to the United States from his native Prestwick at age 12 to assist J. D., who was then the summer professional at the Stevens Hotel in Lake Placid, New York. Coming of age, Seymour would, during the first decade of the twentieth century, hold numerous professional positions on both sides of the Atlantic, including stops at Connecticut's Griswold Hotel, France's La Boulie and Northern Ireland's famed Royal County Down. In 1908, Dunn finally settled down, becoming director of golf at upstate New York's Lake Placid Club, a position he would retain for 21 years.

A true all-rounder in the old Scottish tradition, Seymour won the **Adirondack Open** 12 years running, established a large mail-order clubmaking business, became a renowned instructor (numbering Hagen, Sarazen, Jim Barnes, and Joe Kirkwood among his students) and designed or redesigned nearly every course in the Adirondack region. Subsequently he and J. D. would found the world's first indoor golf school (at Bournemouth, England) and later still its largest, a massive affair that occupied the rented floor of New York's Madison Square Garden. A further incarnation, the Dunn School of Golf, was located at an even more glamorous New York address, Rockefeller Center. Seymour also wrote several instructional volumes, the most prominent of which, *Golf Fundamentals: Orthodoxy of Style* (printed privately, 1922), has been reissued in the modern era.

Tom Dunn (UK)

The son of Willie Dunn Sr. and father of John D. and Seymour, Blackheath-born Tom Dunn (1849–1902) must stand high upon any Who's Who of nineteenth-century British golf. In addition to being a prominent professional (with stops at Wimbledon, North Berwick, the late Tooting Bec and others) Tom was the first man—with perhaps a gentle nod to Willie Park Sr.—to practice golf course architecture on a large scale.

Of course, the word "architecture" held less grandiose connotations in Dunn's day, a period which lacked both expansive earth-moving equipment and the refined sense of strategy that would appear well after his death. Thus of the 137 courses which Dunn claimed to have built, only a few might have hoped to escape the pejorative tag of "rudimentary," despite the extensive use of forced-carry crossbunkers to lend at least some life to the proceedings. His portfolio included numerous early (and long-altered) efforts for famous clubs, including Broadstone, Saunton, Woking, Ganton, France's Biarritz, and Holland's Haagsche, perhaps making Tom Dunn—should a parallel be necessary—the British equivalent of America's peripatetic Tom Bendelow.

Notable Courses: Golf de Biarritz (with W. Dunn Jr.), France
    (BO); Broadstone GC (BO); Felixstowe Ferry (BO)

Willie Dunn Jr. (UK/USA)

Brother of Tom Dunn and uncle of John D. and Seymour, Musselburgh, Scotland's Willie Dunn Jr. (1865–1952) was serving as professional at the popular French resort of Biarritz (whose course he'd helped Tom build) when, during the winter of 1890-91, he met vacationing Americans William Vanderbilt, Duncan Cryder and Edward Mead. Upon Dunn's demonstration of the basics of golf, the trio returned to the States determined to build their own course in the Long Island summer colony of Southampton. Contrary to what has occasionally been written, it was Scotsman William Davis, and *not* Willie Dunn, who built this, the original 12-hole layout at Shinnecock Hills—though Dunn was hired by Vanderbilt and company as a professional/greenkeeper and eventually rebuilt Davis' track into the club's first 18-hole course in 1896.

That same year Dunn would also lay out a golf course for an even wealthier clientele at Westchester County's Ardsley CC, taking the professional's job upon its completion. Ceding the position to his nephew John in 1897, Willie became a full-time architect and occasional clubmaker, building courses primarily in the Northeast and experiencing several major fluctuations in finance. Eventually moving to St. Louis, then Menlo Park, California, and finally back to Britain at the onset of World War II, Willie's American résumé would ultimately include now-deceased layouts for such famous venues as the Jekyll Island Club (Georgia), Lakewood CC (New Jersey), Balti-

Willie Dunn Jr., 1933

more CC (Maryland), and the Rockaway Hunting Club (New York), in addition to Shinnecock Hills, Ardsley, and some consulting on the original design at Apawamis.

Also remembered as the winner of the first (unofficial) **U.S. Open**—contested at match play, among four professionals at Newport in 1894—Dunn died in Putney, England at age 87.

Notable Courses: Ardsley CC, New York (BO); **Baltimore CC, Roland Park, Maryland (NLE); Shinnecock Hills GC, New York (BO)**

Willie Dunn Sr. (UK)

Willie Dunn Sr. (1821–1878), or "Old Willie" as he came to be known, was the patriarch of one of golf's all-time most legendary families, the Musselburgh clan whose place on the game's stage ranges from some of Scotland's earliest challenge matches to the first U.S. Open championship; from being the first commercial manufacturers of golf clubs to pioneering course design on two continents. Indeed, though ever the silly phrase, there is a good deal of truth to the old golfing aphorism that "If a Dunn hasn't done it, it hasn't been done."

By universal acclaim, Old Willie was among the finest players of his day, a graceful swinger whose prodigious length is forever memorialized by the Dunny bunker, one of the less-famous hazards (at least as compared to the Beardies and Hell) on the 14th at St. Andrews. Lacking any real organized competition during his best years, Willie is instead cited for the high-stakes challenge matches in which he frequently engaged. In perhaps the most memorable, he teamed with his twin brother Jamie to take on the legendary St. Andrews team of Allan Robertson and Old Tom Morris in an 1849 match played at Musselburgh, St. Andrews and North Berwick. The Dunns would eventually lose, two matches to one, after Robertson and Old Tom came from 4 down with 8 to play to capture the rubber game at North Berwick—but not before the twins fairly tanned the St. Andreans by the stately margin of 13 and 12 on the opening day at Musselburgh.

Old Willie spent some 20 years as greenkeeper and professional at England's pioneering Royal Blackheath GC before eventually returning north for stints at Leith, Musselburgh and North Berwick. Dunn also managed to establish himself as one of the very earliest golf course architects, having rebuilt several holes at Blackheath, laid out a handful of short courses on private estates, and built the original Wimbledon course for the London Scottish Regiment in 1865.

He died in North Berwick at age 57.

John Dunsmore (UK/Australia)

A native Scot like virtually all of the world's nineteenth-century golf pioneers, John Dunsmore was by 1850 settled into life as a Sydney, Australia, solicitor. Though opinions differ on an exact date, Dunsmore played golf on land very near today's Concord GC either in 1851 or perhaps a year or two later, the second known demonstration of the game on the Australian mainland. Either way, Dunsmore's example drew few followers—likely due to the almost simultaneous discovery of gold 100 miles west of the city—and like James Graham's ill-fated 1847 experiment in Melbourne, his golfing grounds soon vanished. Dunsmore later donated his original hickory clubs and gutta-percha balls to the Australian GC but, sadly, they burned in a 1931 clubhouse fire.

James Durham (UK)

A member of the Society of Golfers at St. Andrews beginning in 1756, James Durham holds a record that indeed can never be broken. In 1767, he won the organization's Silver Club competition with a score of 94, the first documented occasion of anyone breaking 100 over the Old Course. Inasmuch as such records are accepted as the gospel, the magnitude of this feat is best expressed not in the greater difficulty of the game in those early, unmanicured years but rather by the fact that this record stood unsurpassed for an astounding 86 years, the last six after the invention of the gutta-percha ball. By any measure, a freakishly great performance.

Olin Dutra (USA)

Born and raised in the California golfing hotbed of Monterey, Olin Dutra (1901–1983) grew up caddying and playing with his older brother Mortie and their next-door neighbors, Al and Abe Espinosa, all of whom would eventually blossom into successful touring professionals. So far as official PGA Tour records suggest, Olin won the most substantial titles of the bunch, and his two Major championships certainly lifted him above these and many other players. His first Major came at the 1932 **PGA** where he beat Frank Walsh 4 and 3 at St. Paul, Minnesota's, city-owned Keller GC. Playing well enough to end each match before reaching the 17th tee, Dutra was tabulated to be 19 under par for the run of the event.

Two years later, at the 1934 **U.S. Open** at Merion, a severe stomach ailment forced Dutra to do little more than plod his way through two rounds before closing strongly over the final 36. In the meantime, halfway leader Gene Sarazen was struggling and another contender, Scotland's Bobby Cruickshank, was staggered—quite literally—when the iron he'd tossed jubilantly skyward after a great break at the 65th nearly knocked him cold upon returning to earth. Thus Dutra was afforded the luxury of a bogey-bogey finish to win, his 71-72 performance carrying the day by one.

In 1932, Dutra captured the **Metropolitan Open** at New York's long-lost Lido GC, a legendary layout dubbed "the finest course in the world" by Bernard Darwin.

Dutra's closing 65, which sealed his victory, was a record that would stand into perpetuity, for the Lido was to disappear during World War II. Also a third-place finisher at the 1935 Masters, Dutra held onto his skills for many years, shooting a memorable 61 at the ripe old age of 60 at California's Jurupa Hills CC, his home course.

PGA Tour Wins (10): 1932 Metropolitan; **1932 PGA Championship;** 1934 U.S. Open
Ryder Cup: 1933 & '35 (2)

1928-1941

	28	29	30	31	32	33	34	35	36	37	38	39	40	41
Masters							-	3	-	-	-	-	-	-
US Open	-	-	T25	T21	T7	T7	1	T12	T45	T56	T16	T16	MC	WD
British	-	-	-	-	-	6	-	-	-	-	-	-		
PGA	T17	-	-	-	1	T9	-	-	-	T17	-	-	-	-

Walter Hagen *(right)* chats with Olin Dutra just before driving off
at the Merion Golf Course preparing for the 1934
National Open Golf Championship.

David Duval (USA)

One of modern golf's more enigmatic characters, David Duval (b. Jacksonville, Florida, 11/9/1971) has quite literally seen it all in his 10 years as a professional. The son of a prominent club pro and future Champions Tour player, Duval was the 1989 **USGA Junior Boys** champion and then, while starring at Georgia Tech, a four-time first-team All-American. Appearing in six PGA Tour events as an amateur, Duval nearly made an enormous splash at the 1992 Atlanta Classic, actually holding a two-shot lead after 54 holes before closing with a 79 to tie for 13th.

As a professional Duval initially struggled, failing to secure full-time PGA Tour playing privileges until 1995, then running up an agonizing string of second- and third-place finishes that extended well into 1997. But when Duval finally found his stride, he became, overnight, nearly invincible. Breaking through at **Kingsmill** in late '97, he proceeded to win the following week at the **Walt Disney,** then again at the season-ending **Tour Championship** to finish second on the year's money list. Four more wins, a money title, and a Vardon Trophy would follow in 1998, as would four pre-Masters victories (including the **Players Championship**) in 1999. All told, Duval won a remarkable 11 times in 36 events between October of 1997 and April of 1999, climbing to the top spot in the world rankings and remaining there for 15 weeks. At his peak, he closed with a memorable 59 at the 1999 **Bob Hope,** eagling the 72nd for a one-stroke victory over Steve Pate.

While Duval's play slipped modestly (to seventh- and eighth-place money rankings) in 2000 and 2001, he did manage to break through for his first Major championship, winning the '01 **Open Championship** at Royal Lytham & St. Annes by three over Sweden's Niclas Fasth, cementing his status among the game's elite.

But as quickly as Duval had risen, he suddenly fell. Having worked his body to a lean-yet-muscular extreme, he had first developed back problems by 2000, which over time began to affect his swing. Previously thought of as perhaps golf's best combination of power and accuracy, by 2002 he was struggling with his driver and slipping to 80th on the money list. In 2003 the plummet continued, with a 211th-place money finish and a world ranking which, for the first time, fell out of the top 250. As Duval has long been one of golf's more cerebral types (hinting that early retirement might be an option even during the best of times) questions abound as to his desire to continue. Having sat out the first half of 2004, he made a surprise return at the U.S. Open at Shinnecock Hills (missing the cut), then appeared in several late-season events including another missed cut at the PGA—but can we truly rule out the prospect of a successful comeback from a player of such rare and proven talent?

PGA Tour Wins (13): 1998 World Series; 1999 Players Championship; **2001 British Open**
Intn'l Win: (1)
Walker Cup: 1991 **Ryder Cup:** 1999 & 2002 (2) **Presidents Cup:** 1996–2000 (3)

1990-2004

	90	91	92	93	94	95	96	97	98	99	00	01	02	03	04
Masters	-	-	-	-	-	-	T18	MC	T2	T6	T3	2	MC	MC	-
US Open	T56	-	MC	-	-	T28	T67	T48	T7	T7	T8	T16	MC	MC	MC
British	-	-	-	-	-	T20	T14	T33	T11	T62	T11	1	T22	MC	-
PGA	-	-	-	-	-	MC	T41	T13	MC	T10	-	T10	T34	WD	MC

Alice Dye (USA)

Far more than just the wife of legendary architect Pete Dye, Alice O'Neal Dye (b. 1927) has enjoyed a splendid amateur playing career that included two **USGA Women's Senior** titles, seven **Indiana Women's Amateurs,** the 1968 **North & South Amateur,** the 1972 **Eastern Amateur,** and a spot on the 1970 Curtis Cup team at age 42. From the beginning, she was also an integral part of her husband's design business, initially handling most of the firm's drafting work and often looking after local projects when Pete was on the road. Alice Dye's input on some of Pete's most famous designs (including the famously bulkheaded 13th green at the Harbour Town Golf Links) is well chronicled, though she might equally be celebrated for her advocacy of women's perspectives (e.g., multiple distaff tees) in golf course architecture.

Ken Dye (USA)

A native of San Antonio, the North Carolina State–educated Kenneth Dye Jr. (b. 1953) worked for 15 years with architect Joe Finger, the last six as a full partner. Though much of his work has thus been done in a secondary role, Dye has completed several significant solo designs, most notably Piñon Hills, a desert-style municipal course in Farmington, New Mexico. In the new millennium, he has also found favor performing renovations at several of the New York area's older clubs. He is unrelated to the Pete Dye architectural clan.

P. B. Dye (USA)

The youngest son of Pete and Alice Dye, Paul Burke "P. B." Dye (b. 1955) began his design career working for his father before venturing out on his own in the mid-1980s. A capable player in his youth, P. B. has followed his father's design-it-in-the-field style, and the majority of his best-known jobs have, in fact, been completed in conjunction with the tireless Pete. The well-regarded Loblolly Pines, in Hobe Sound, Florida, stands as a notable exception.

Perry Dye (USA)

The older of Pete and Alice Dye's two sons, Perry (b. 1952) became involved in the family design business in his early teens, eventually joining his father on a number of high-profile projects, a loose partnership that continues to this day. Unlike the rest of his family, however, Perry has also developed a large-scale overseas business, a practice centered primarily in the Far East where he has completed more than 35 courses.

Pete Dye (USA)

Old Tom Morris was among the first to codify it, Willie Park Jr. and H. S. Colt advanced it greatly, C. B. Macdonald gave it Golden Age definition and Robert Trent Jones modernized it worldwide. Yet for all the impact that these men had on golf course design, a strong argument can be made that no one has influenced it more than an insurance broker from rural Urbana, Ohio, one Paul "Pete" Dye.

A fine amateur who competed in one British and five U.S. Amateurs, Dye (b. 12/29/1925) played at Florida's Rollins College where he met and married Alice O'Neal before returning north to sell insurance. In 1959, Dye left the business world to begin designing golf courses, initially creating several low-budget Midwestern layouts hardly demanding of the world's attention. But in 1963, Pete and Alice took a month-long trip to Scotland, where they discovered pot bunkers, unmanicured rough, railroad sleepers shoring up hazards and a far less power-oriented approach to golf. The impact of these things upon the Dyes was immense, and once back in the States Pete blended them into a somewhat modernized hybrid that would soon become the most copied style in the business.

Crooked Stick, a local Indianapolis club completed in 1966, was the first layout to reflect this old/new look, with The Golf Club, a 1967 project in New Albany, Ohio, spreading the word a bit farther. But only in 1969, when Dye teamed with Jack Nicklaus to build Hilton Head Island's Harbour Town Golf Links, was the Dye style widely introduced to the world stage. Initially measuring little more than 6,600 yards, the tight, strategic Harbour Town hosted the PGA Tour's first Heritage Classic in 1969, yielding the highest 36-hole cut of the season with rounds in the 80s outnumbering sub-par scores roughly 2 to 1.

In 1981, Dye would again change the face of architecture with his TPC at Sawgrass, a longer, tougher track built to serve as permanent host of the PGA Tour's Players Championship. With its much-imitated 132-yard 17th elevating the concept of the island green to an entirely new level, the TPC's creative use of waste areas and greens contoured to repel inferior approaches once again captured the design world's attention. Several years later, as advances in equipment began to presage changes in the game's fundamental balance, Dye stepped things up even further, first with the Stadium course at PGA West (1986), then, in 1990, with the windswept Ocean course at Kiawah Island.

It is interesting to note that for most of his career, Pete Dye has charged considerably less for his services than many other big-name architects and, occasionally, has worked essentially for free. Further, he has long built his courses in the oldest of fashions, seldom using maps or even sketches, always improvising and refining in the field. Misunderstood by many but widely observed by all, Pete Dye has surely been postwar golf's most important—and copied—golf course designer.

Notable Courses: Blackwolf Run, River Course, Wisconsin; Casa de Campo GC, Dominican Republic; Crooked Stick GC, Indiana; The Golf Club, Ohio; Harbour Town GL, South Carolina; The Honors Course, Tennessee; Kiawah Island GC, Ocean Course, South Carolina; Long Cove C, South Carolina; Pete Dye GC, West Virginia; PGA West, Stadium Course, California; TPC Sawgrass, Florida; Whistling Straits GL, Straits Course, Wisconsin

Roy Dye (USA)

Younger brother of Pete, Roy Dye (b. 1929) graduated from Yale University with a degree in chemical engineering, a career which he pursued for nearly 20 years before entering the golf design business in 1969. Though often working in conjunction with his brother, Roy has built several very noteworthy layouts of his own, including the spectacular Waterwood National GC (Huntsville, Texas) and the oft-photographed La Mantarraya GC at Mexico's Las Hadas resort. Also of note is his now-deceased Gambel Golf Links in Carefree, Arizona, an unfinished desert track considered by those who played it to be among the most offbeat (and natural) layouts in the history of American golf.

E

Victor East (UK/Australia/USA)

A native of Scotland, Joshua Victor East (1886–1976) was highly representative of just how far the game of golf might carry a man if he had some talent, a bit of drive, and a willingness to travel. Emigrating to Australia by the turn of the century, East became the professional at the Royal Sydney GC from 1901 to 1904, then, after serving as secretary and treasurer of the Australian PGA, at Royal Melbourne from 1915 to 1922. It was during this later stint that East's horizons expanded, beginning with a highly successful venture into golf course design at Victoria's Barwon Heads GC. In 1921, he accompanied talented young Joe Kirkwood to Great Britain, ostensibly serving as Kirkwood's business manager (and human trick-shot prop) while also competing in the Open Championship. Recognizing the potentially green pastures of the budding American market, East then followed Kirkwood to the United States in 1922, settling in as professional at North Carolina's Biltmore Forest CC and dabbling in course design on the side.

East eventually found his greatest success as a golf club designer and executive with both Spalding and Wilson, establishing such a name for himself that Golf Pride's timeless Victory grip was in part named after him. Also well known as a golf writer, East's lifetime involvement in all aspects of the game led Bobby Jones to once observe that "Mr. East possesses knowledge and experience in the game second to no one." East died, at the end of a fascinating golfing life, in Evanston, Illinois at age 90.

Douglas Edgar (UK/USA)

Born: Newcastle-upon-Tyne, England, 9/30/1885 **Died:** Atlanta, Georgia, 8/9/1921

England's John Douglas Edgar has long lingered in the shadows as one of golf's most intriguing and overlooked figures. As a player he achieved his first measure of fame by winning the 1914 **French Open** by six shots over a top field, leading Harry Vardon himself to single Edgar out for future greatness. World War I put a damper on his development, however, and Edgar emigrated to America by 1920. Already in his mid-30s, he soon enjoyed a run of world-class play that included reaching the final of the 1920 PGA Championship (where he lost 1 down to Jock Hutchison upon three-putting the 36th green), winning the 1920 **Southern Open** and capturing back-to-back **Canadian Opens** in 1919 and '20. During his first Canadian triumph, Edgar closed with rounds of 69-66, beating runners-up Bobby Jones and Jim Barnes by a stunning 16 shots while breaking the tournament record by 17!

Edgar was also considered an exceptional teacher and he authored *The Gate to Golf* (privately published, 1920), a cultishly popular volume which stood among the first to advocate an inside-to-out swing. In later years, the great player/teacher Tommy Armour—whose game blossomed after meeting Edgar in America—credited him lavishly, calling his former instructor "the best golfer I ever saw." Edgar's life ended under curious circumstances as he died unobserved on a deserted Atlanta street, the apparent victim of a robbery.

Danny Edwards (USA)

Richard Dan "Danny" Edwards (b. Ketchikan, Alaska, 6/14/1951) was the first of two brothers to find success on the PGA Tour, winning five times and maintaining a spot among the top 125 money winners from 1975 to 1987. Previously a two-time All-American at Oklahoma State, Edwards won the 1972 **North & South Amateur,** was the low amateur at the 1973 Open Championship at Troon and starred on the victorious 1973 Walker Cup team. Among his PGA Tour victories were a pair of **Greater Greensboro Opens** (1977 and '82) and the 1980 **Walt Disney Team Championship,** won with brother David. Edwards has also won in Japan and presently competes part-time on the Champions Tour.

David Edwards (USA)

The other half of this prominent brother act, David Wayne Edwards (b. Neosho, Missouri, 4/18/1956) was also twice an All-American at Oklahoma State before capturing four

PGA Tour victories and carving out a nice living for himself over nearly 20 years. David never finished higher that 20th on the money list but fell out of the top 125 only once between 1979 and 1997, resulting in career earnings in excess of $4.3 million. He also managed to claim several high-end titles such as the 1984 **Los Angeles Open,** the 1992 **Memorial Tournament,** the 1993 **Heritage Classic,** in addition to the above-mentioned **Disney Team** win with brother Danny.

H. Chandler Egan (USA)

Born: Chicago, Illinois, 8/21/1884 Died: Everett, Washington, 4/5/1936

One of the earliest top golfers to emerge from what was then considered the West, Henry Chandler Egan was a Harvard graduate who, during his collegiate years, won the 1902 **NCAA** individual title, three NCAA team titles and, perhaps most important, back-to-back **U.S. Amateur** crowns in 1904 (at Baltusrol) and '05 (at the Chicago GC). Also highly successful winning at home, he won **Western Amateurs** in 1902, '04, '05 and '07, with a final-round loss in 1903 coming at the hands of his cousin Walter.

Essentially retiring from national competition, Egan moved to rural Oregon in 1910 where he initially lived some 300 miles from the nearest golf course and listed his occupation as "fruit grower." Eventually the golf bug returned and in addition to winning five **Pacific Northwest Amateurs** between 1915 and 1932, Egan also took up golf course architecture, producing at least a dozen Oregon courses over a span of 17 years. Thus considered a designer of consequence, he was hired, in 1928, to renovate Pebble Beach in preparation for the 1929 U.S. Amateur. He would institute a handful of changes to the famous layout's routing as well as substantial modifications to many tees, greens, and bunkers, making Egan as responsible as anyone for the golf course we know today. As an interesting aside, he made an unexpected return to competition at the '29 Amateur, playing all the way through to the semifinals at age 45—a remarkable showing that gives pause to consider the sort of record Egan might have amassed had he remained competitive during the previous 20 years.

On the strength of his Pebble Beach redesign, Egan would partner briefly with Dr. Alister MacKenzie and Robert Hunter before returning to solo practice, where his designs at Eastmoreland CC (Oregon) and Indian Canyon GC (Washington) remain prime examples of his work. He died unexpectedly of pneumonia while on a job site at age 51.

Major Amateur Wins (11): 1902, '04, '05 & '07 Western Amateur; 1904 & '05 U.S. Amateur; 1915, '20, '23, '25 & '32 Pacific NW

Gloria Ehret (USA)

A steady performer who was only once out of the LPGA Tour's top 40 money winners throughout her 15-year career, Gloria Ehret played well enough to consistently earn good money but seldom rose high enough to win. She did scale the mountain on two occasions, however, the 1973 **Birmingham Classic** and, far more importantly, the 1966 **LPGA Championship,** a Major title in which she defeated no less than Mickey Wright by three at the old Stardurst CC in Las Vegas.

President Dwight Eisenhower (USA)

General Dwight Eisenhower (1890–1969) made his first trip to the Augusta National GC four years prior to being elected U.S. President, a visit described by longtime Masters chairman Clifford Roberts as: "Ike wanted to play golf, practice golf, or take golf lessons, all day long." An avid player and, ultimately, a longtime Augusta member, the enormously popular Eisenhower was at best an average golfer with a well-above-average slice, yet his widely noted enthusiasm for the game brought it nothing but good publicity in an otherwise quiet postwar period. Eisenhower played regularly while in the White House, making a reported 29 visits to Augusta during the course of his presidency.

Lee Elder (USA)

A one-time sidekick to the legendary hustler Titanic Thompson ("I could probably beat you boys with my chauffeur as a partner..."), Dallas native Robert Lee Elder (b. 7/14/1934) was a hardnosed money player long before becoming the first black to achieve lasting success on the PGA Tour, which he joined in 1967. An utterly dominant force on the minority-oriented United Golf Association circuit, Elder would eventually win four times on Tour, most important at the 1974 **Monsanto Open,** which qualified him as the first black ever to play in the Masters. Saddled with unprecedented media coverage, however, Elder could manage only 72-78 at Augusta, easily missing the cut.

Having also claimed the 1971 **Nigerian Open** (en route to playing in the South African PGA as the groundbreaking guest of Gary Player), Elder's best year on Tour was 1978 when he won twice and finished 13th on the money list. The first victory came in **Milwaukee** where he beat Lee Trevino on the eighth hole of sudden death, soon followed by a one-stroke triumph over Mark Hayes at the lucrative **Westchester Classic.** On the strength of

Lee Elder

these wins, Elder would break another barrier by being selected to the Ryder Cup team in 1979.

Lee Elder's record of accomplishment on the PGA Tour would soon be usurped by Jim Thorpe, Calvin Peete, and, eventually, Tiger Woods. But like Charlie Sifford before him, one wonders just how much more Elder might have won had he not been saddled with the enormous albatross of being a pioneer.

Steve Elkington (Australia)

A native of Inverell, New South Wales, who won the **Australian Junior** title in 1981, Stephen John Elkington (b. 12/8/1962) was among the first foreign players recruited to play collegiate golf in the United States, starring on 1984 and '85 national championship teams at the University of Houston. Blessed with a compact, rhythmic swing that has frequently been held among the modern era's very best, Elkington has been slowed on occasion by his putter, but more frequently by chronically ailing sinuses and a list of assorted injuries.

Something of a tee-to-green specialist, Elkington had one PGA tour win to his credit when he captured the 1991

Players Championship and its associated 10-year exemption. Two more American wins (plus the 1992 **Australian Open**) followed before his career-best year of 1995 when he won the season-opening **Mercedes Championships,** then in August holed a 20-foot birdie putt to defeat Colin Montgomerie in sudden death for the **PGA Championship** at Riviera. Two years later in 1997, he again won twice, taking **Doral** and his second **Players Championship.**

With a total of 10 wins and over $8 million earned between 1988 and 1999, Elkington was, for fully a decade, a top-flight player on the world stage—and when healthy, a genuine threat at any tournament in the world.

PGA Tour Wins (10): 1991 & '97 Players Championship; **1995 PGA Championship;** 1997 & '99 Doral
Intn'l Wins (2): 1992 Australian Open
Presidents Cup: 1994–2000 (4)

Ernie Els (South Africa)

Over three centuries of golf history, it is indeed a short list of players that have possessed the sheer physical talent of Johannesburg native Theodore Ernest Els. Standing 6'4", weighing 230+ pounds, and showcasing a swing that is every bit as effective as it is beautiful, the big blond South African (b. 10/17/1969) can be stunningly long—arguably the longest hitter ever among elite players, even allowing for the boost given by today's unchecked equipment. Yet for all his obvious power, Els also possesses a blue chip short game and a putter which, if not Bobby Locke–like, certainly stands competitive at the world-class level. Throw in a preternaturally calm demeanor and it is no wonder that "The Big Easy" looms as the most believed-in rival to Tiger Woods atop golf's contemporary heap.

A fine all-around athlete, Els won the Eastern Transvaal Junior Tennis Championship at age 13 before turning his complete attention to golf. A scratch player by 14, he made his first international splash in San Diego by capturing the 1984 **Junior World Championship,** defeating a young Phil Mickelson in the process. By 1992 he was, at age 22, the most dominant presence in South Africa since Gary Player, winning six times in his homeland including the **South African Open.** A year later, he became the first player ever to break 70 four times in an Open Championship, finishing joint 6th at Royal St. George's.

Els' major international breakthrough came the following year when, at 24, he won the 1994 **U.S. Open** at Oakmont in a three-way play-off with Colin Montgomerie and Loren Roberts. Though he would later admit to not being ready for the attention and pressures to follow, Els began winning consistently, capturing 38 international and 15 PGA Tour titles by the end of 2004. Prominent on this

Ernie Els at the 2000 PGA Championship at Valhalla
Country Club, Louisville, Kentucky

four-man play-off, eventually defeating Levet in sudden death with a memorable sand save at the historic 18th hole.

For several years now Els has been the hottest player in the world during the winter months, particularly in Hawaii (where he won the 2003 **Mercedes Championships** and the '03 and '04 **Hawaiian Opens**) and Australia (taking the **Heineken Classic** in '02, '03 and '04). He has also proved potent in match play, sweeping the **World Match Play** title at Wentworth in 1994, '95, and '96, then again in 2002, '03, and '04.

Now in the prime of his career, the gifted Els has really hit stride in the new millennium, logging over $12 million in PGA Tour earnings and 10 top-10 finishes in 16 Major championship starts. Despite such lofty standing, he suffered heartbreaking 2004 losses at the Masters (to Mickelson's 72nd-hole birdie), the Open Championship (to Todd Hamilton in a play-off), and the PGA (three-putting the 72nd to miss the Singh-DiMarco-Leonard play-off by one). Yet he certainly ranks among the world's elite at the time of this writing and stands a fine chance of eventually establishing himself among the game's all-time greats.

PGA Tour Wins (15): 1994 & '97 US Open; 1995 Byron Nelson; 1996 & '97 Westchester; 1999 Los Angeles; 2002 Doral; **2002 British Open;** 2004 Memorial

Intn'l Wins (38): 1992, '96 & '98 South African Open; 1992, '95 & '99 South African PGA; 1994 & 2002 Dubai; 1994, '95, '96, 2002 & '03 World Match Play; 1997 & 2003 Johnnie Walker; 2000 Loch Lomond; 2003 Scottish Open

Presidents Cup: 1996–2003 (4)

list was a second **U.S. Open** (at Congressional in 1997) and perhaps his most desired prize, the **Open Championship,** in 2002 at Muirfield. In claiming the Claret Jug, Els joined Steve Elkington, Stuart Appleby and Thomas Levet in a

1989-2004

	89	90	91	92	93	94	95	96	97	98	99	00	01	02	03	04
Masters	-	-	-	-	-	T8	MC	T12	T17	T16	T27	2	T6	T5	T6	2
US Open	-	-	-	-	T7	1	MC	T5	1	T49	MC	T2	T66	T24	T5	T9
British	MC	-	-	T5	T6	T24	T11	T2	T10	T29	T24	T2	T3	1	T18	2
PGA	-	-	-	MC	MC	T25	T3	T61	T53	T21	MC	T34	T13	T34	T5	T4

Devereux Emmet (USA)

Frequently overlooked among the top designers of golf's Golden Age, Devereux Emmet (1861–1934) was the product of a prominent New York family, permitting him a life of leisure in an era well known for its leisurely pursuits. Emmet's family also helped him tangibly as a golf architect, opening doors within New York society that others (with the possible exception of C. B. Macdonald) could do little but envy.

For much of his life, Emmet maintained a pleasant year-round regimen that involved the purchase of young hunting dogs each spring, training them on his Long Island estate over the summer, selling them in Ireland in the fall, then hunting and golfing his winter away in the British Isles and/or the Bahamas. A skilled player himself, Emmet was a founding member of Macdonald's National GL of America, and actually spent one of his British sojourns charting the classic old holes to provide templates for the course's development.

After cutting his teeth with two early layouts on the site of today's Garden City GC, Emmet would go on to design more than 75 courses, roughly two-thirds of which were located in the New York metropolitan area. Among the more prominent were Cherry Valley CC (site of the 1927 U.S. Women's Amateur), PGA Championship venues Pelham CC, Salisbury CC and Pomonok CC, and an early version of the Congressional CC which was substantially altered prior to hosting two U.S. Opens and a PGA. Sadly, more than half of Emmet's designs are no longer, with those that remain often approaching some degree of obsolescence in this era of unregulated equipment. An old-schooler whose designs featured both variety and quirkiness, Emmet remained active until very late in life, winning the **Bahamas Amateur** at age 66 and laying out courses right into 1934, the year of his death.

Notable Courses: Congressional CC, Maryland (BO); **Garden City GC, New York;** Huntington Crescent C, West Course, New York (NLE); **Salisbury CC (nka Eisenhower Park) (90 holes, 72 NLE), New York;** Wee Burn CC, Connecticut

Jim Engh (USA)

American architect Jim Engh (b. 1958) did his fair share of traveling before settling down, initially working in Texas, Illinois, and throughout Europe and Asia, the latter stops under the aegis of the recreational development division of Mark McCormack's IMG colossus. In 1991 Engh returned to the United States, setting up shop in Castle Rock, Colorado, and developing what has thus far been a primarily Western practice. His modern, heavily contoured designs have initially found favor with magazine course raters and photographers, with his highest-profile work to date being The Sanctuary, a private estate course built in Sedalia, Colorado, for real estate magnate Dave Liniger.

Shirley Englehorn (USA)

A product of Caldwell, Idaho, Shirley Englehorn (b. 12/12/1940) was a regional amateur star before commencing a 22-year LPGA Tour career which saw her regularly among the tour's top 10 money winners throughout the 1960s. Seriously injured in a 1965 car accident, Englehorn eventually worked her way back to form, claiming eight of 11 career titles after the crash, including a memorable 1968 triumph over an absurdly difficult layout of nearly 7,000 yards at the **Concord Open.** Englehorn's place in history was truly established in 1970 when, between May 17th and June 13th, she won the four consecutive LPGA events in which she entered. The centerpiece was the **LPGA Championship** at Boston's Pleasant Valley CC, her lone Major championship and one which required extra holes to defeat Hall of Famer Kathy Whitworth. Declining somewhat after this torrid streak, Englehorn slowly eased into a successful teaching career before retiring from the tour in 1981.

Abe Espinosa (USA)

The oldest of seven siblings, six of whom would become golf professionals, Monterey, California, native Abelard G. "Abe" Espinosa (1889–1980) was the one who lit the fuse, becoming a caddie at the new Del Monte golf course at age 10 and earning enough money to entice the rest of the brood to follow. Though brother Al would prove the better player down the road, Abe was the family table-setter, initially working in San Francisco and Sacramento before heading to Chicago, and bigger money, by the mid-1920s. When he won the 1928 **Western Open** at the North Shore GC, he became the first player of Hispanic heritage to win an American title of national scope. That same year, he won the **Illinois** and **Oregon Opens,** proving, if nothing else, that brother Al wasn't the only big-time player in the family.

Al Espinosa (USA)

Abelardus Espinosa (1894–1957) was nicknamed Al at an early age to avoid confusion with his similarly named older brother. He was also the most talented of the golfing Espinosa family, winning a total of nine PGA Tour titles and contending seriously in at least three Major championships. In the 1927 PGA at Dallas' Cedar Crest CC, he reached the semifinals before losing to Walter Hagen on the 37th hole, this after standing one up through 35. A year later, at the Baltimore CC, he went a step farther before losing in the final to Leo Diegel by a healthy 6 and 5 margin. It was in 1929 that Al Espinosa became something of a household name when, over Winged Foot's famed West course, he beat all of the world's best pros over four rounds at the U.S. Open. Unfortunately, there was still an amateur in the mix, one Bobby Jones, and when Jones curled in a difficult 12-footer on the 72nd green, a Sunday play-off became necessary. In a typical act of sportsmanship, Jones requested a later start so Espinosa, a Roman Catholic, might attend church, but divine guidance didn't help. Espinosa blew sky high with 84-80 and lost by a record 23 strokes. Winner of the first four **Mexican Opens** (1944–47), Espinosa appeared on Ryder Cup teams in 1929 and '31, scoring a 2-1-1 record.

Bob Estes (USA)

One of the PGA Tour's better-conditioned athletes, Graham, Texas, native Bob Estes (b. 2/2/56) has been a solid performer since 1989, only once falling out of the top 125 money winners while pocketing over $12 million in career earnings. A medium-length hitter and solid putter who has been known to occasionally uncork a very low number, this former University of Texas star is a four-time Tour winner including twice (at **Memphis** and **Las Vegas**) during a career-best 2001 season. Though a tie for fourth at the 1999 Masters represents his best Major finish, Estes did briefly lead the 1993 PGA Championship during the final round before tying for sixth.

Chick Evans (USA)

Born: Indianapolis, Indiana, 7/18/1890 **Died:** Chicago, Illinois, 11/6/1979

Charles "Chick" Evans Jr. was a seminal figure in American golf, a caddie-turned-amateur superstar who, among his many accomplishments, was perhaps the first native-born American to demonstrate that one didn't have to start from affluence to become a great golfer. A native of Indiana, Evans moved to Chicago in 1898 where, by happenstance, his family's new home backed up to the old Edgewater CC. Recognizing the chance to earn some spending money, Evans became a caddie and, in time, an excellent player, capturing Chicago schoolboy titles and, in 1909, the **Western Amateur** at nearby Flossmoor CC.

An outstanding ball-striker who seldom played with more than seven clubs, Evans followed this up in 1910 by becoming the first amateur to win the **Western Open,** America's second biggest period event, at another Chicago-area course, Beverly CC. Even as he added the 1911 **French Open Amateur** and the **North & South** to his ledger, Evans was gaining a reputation for being unable to win an American national championship, being routed by Jerome Travers 7 and 6 in the 1912 U.S. Amateur final, then finishing one shot behind Walter Hagen at the 1914 U.S. Open. By all accounts it was Evans' putter that was holding him back, leading Travers to observe that "If Evans could putt like Walter Travis, it would be foolish to stage an amateur tourney in this country."

Like all great champions Evans eventually got the pieces into place and in 1916 made history, initially by winning the **U.S. Open** at Minikahda with a 286 total that would remain the tournament record for 20 years. Then some 10 weeks later, he became the first player to take the Open and the **U.S. Amateur** in the same year, claiming the latter at Merion when he defeated two-time champion Robert Gardner 4 and 3 in the final. Evans would add a second **Amateur** crown in 1920 when he beat that other rags-to-riches champion Francis Ouimet 7 and 6 at Long Island's Engineers CC, and he would later lose in the final in 1922 (to Jess Sweetser at The Country Club) and 1927 (to a peaking Bobby Jones at Minikahda). His best subsequent U.S. Open finish was level fourth in 1921, but his regional dominance of the **Western Amateur** was ongoing, for Evans claimed that title a robust eight times

Chick Evans just before winning his first Western Amateur golf championship in 1909

including four in succession from 1920 to 1923. He also enjoyed great longevity, qualifying for the U.S. Open as late as 1953 and the Amateur in 1961 when he was 71!

Generally considered the best player in the United States in the years before Hagen and Jones, Evans chose never to turn professional, supporting himself during the 1920s as a stockbroker, then later as a milk salesman. An affable and immensely popular fellow, he took the earnings from a series of golf instruction records and founded the famed Evans Scholarship Fund, a trust which has helped send generations of young caddies to college. Further, he helped raise thousands of dollars for the Red Cross by playing numerous World War I–era exhibitions and also contributed handsomely to the library of golf by authoring the autobiographical *Chick Evans' Golf Book* (Thos. E. Wilson, 1921).

Major Amateur Wins (13): 1909, '12, '14, '15, '20, '21, '22 & '23 Western Amateur; 1910 Western Open; 1911 North & South; **1916 U.S. Open; 1916 & '20 U.S. Amateur**

1909-1934

	09	10	11	12	13	14	15	16	17	18	19	20	21
US Open	-	-	-	-	-	2	18	1			T9	T6	4
US Am	T3	T3	T3	2	T3	T17	T17	1			T9	1	T3
British	-	-	T49	-	-	-					-	-	-
Brit Am	-	-	T9	-	T17	-					-	-	T33

	22	23	24	25	26	27	28	29	30	31	32	33	34
US Open	16	T14	T10	-	T13	MC	MC	-	T54	-	-	-	-
US Am	2	T17	T17	-	T5	2	T17	-	-	-	T5	T17	T5
British	-	-	-	-	T33	-	-	-	-	-	-	-	-
Brit Am	-	-	-	-	-	-	-	-	-	-	-	-	-

Mary Everard (UK)

Perhaps best known in America as the one-time wife of USGA rules official and LPGA Tour Commissioner John Laupheimer, Mary Everard (b. 10/8/1942) was a dominant Yorkshire golfer who made up in steadiness and toughness what she lacked in raw power. Her biggest victory was the 1972 **English Ladies,** where she defeated Angela Ward Bonallack in the final, though she was also **British Stroke Play** champion in 1970. Prominent near misses came in runner-up finishes at two more British Stroke Plays, the 1964 English Ladies, and the 1977 Women's British Open. Everard was also a four-time Curtis Cup player, appearing on losing sides in 1970, '72, '74 and '78.

Cecil Ewing (Ireland)

After Joe Carr, Rosses Point native Reginald Cecil Ewing (1910–1973) stands as the best of Ireland's twentieth-century amateurs, winning virtually all there was to win in his homeland while also playing on six Walker Cup teams and, on the odd occasion, acquitting himself quite well in Britain. A tall, rather stocky man whose narrow-stanced swing was considered simple and reliable, Ewing first came to prominence by dominating the **West of Ireland** title to a rare degree, winning it nine times between 1930 and 1950. In 1938, making his second Walker Cup appearance, Ewing's singles victory over Ray Billows helped Great Britain and Ireland to their first-ever Cup victory, which fittingly came at St. Andrews. Shortly thereafter, Ewing beat Canadian Sandy Somerville to reach the final of the 1938 British Amateur at Troon, only to fall to American Charlie Yates 3 and 2 in the final.

Ewing clearly lost some prime competitive seasons to World War II but remained successful afterward, winning the **Irish Open** and **Closed Amateurs** twice, including both during a wonderful 1948. At 225 pounds with powerful arms, he was, not surprisingly, a fine wind player whose ability to hit low, driving iron shots was an obvious advantage on the Irish and British links.

Frank Eyre (Australia)

Sydney native Francis Patrick Eyre (b. 1899) was a top Australian professional of the Golden Age, winning the **Australian PGA** in 1926 (6 and 5 over Arthur Le Fevre at Kensington), the 1930 **Queensland Open** and the 1930 **Australian Open** at the Metropolitan GC. A fine all-around sportsman, Eyre served as professional for over 40 years at the Long Reef GC near Sydney while setting numerous course records nationwide. His influence was considerable around New South Wales, and he has been cited as a primary influence by young locals like Norman von Nida and Ossie Pickworth.

Joe Ezar (USA)

American professional Joe Ezar (1909–1978) was of only limited account as a competitive player, instead building his reputation as a trick shot artist in the vein of the famous Joe Kirkwood. Ezar, however, became a timeless footnote in golfing history at the 1936 Italian Open in Sestrières when, responding to a 4,000-lira challenge, he predicted, then produced, a third-round course-record 64. What made the feat so remarkable was that the evening before he had written down on the side of a cigarette box the hole-by-hole scores he planned to achieve, then matched them perfectly, with the only anxious moment coming at the ninth where a 50-yard pitch was holed to make the predicted three. An amazing accomplishment for a man whose career record proves conclusively that he could *not* summon forth a 64 at any time of his choosing.

F

Frank Fairlie (UK)

The son of the very prominent James Fairlie, Major F. A. "Frank" Fairlie was himself a fine player, an innovator and something of a golfing pioneer. As a player, he was cited by Darwin as one of Britain's eight finest amateurs circa 1895, in company that included (albeit higher on the list) John Ball, Horace Hutchinson, and Johnny Laidlay. As an innovator, F. A. invented and produced "Fairlie Irons," a shankless design that, prior to being ruled illegal by the R&A, may indeed have helped cure the dreaded socketing. As a pioneer, he was involved in Britain's earliest golfing adventures in what is today called Sri Lanka, helping to lay out the island's first course—adjacent to a Scottish military garrison, naturally—in 1879. An all-around athlete of repute, Fairlie was Ceylon's tennis champion as well.

James Fairlie (UK)

A resident of Coodham, a small town near Prestwick, James Ogilvy Fairlie (1810–1870) stands among the most overlooked figures of importance in the history of golf. Playing in an era before national championships, Fairlie was generally accorded the title "Champion of Scotland," having won countless medals at St. Andrews, Prestwick and North Berwick, three of the game's earliest epicenters. As a majordomo at Prestwick, he was also responsible not only for organizing the club in 1851 but for luring Old Tom Morris away from St. Andrews to serve as its Keeper of the Green. Morris, in turn, thought enough of Fairlie to name his first son (J. O. F. Morris) after him.

Fairlie was also the man most responsible for organizing the first Open Championship, a task undertaken after his 1857 Great Golf Tournament (a national foursomes event) failed to catch fire. Thus in 1860 Fairlie purchased the soon-to-be-famous championship belt, had Old Tom send out invitations, and the world's oldest golf tournament was soon underway. There is, however, a genuinely fascinating footnote to this genesis, for as history well records, the championship belt became the permanent property of Young Tom Morris upon his winning of a third straight title in 1870, as stipulated by Fairlie's original rules. The Open was then skipped the following year, suppos-edly because a suitable replacement trophy had not yet been located. So strange an explanation seems rather implausible, however, particularly when measured against a more logical alternative: With James Fairlie passing away in 1870, perhaps there simply wasn't anyone else immediately prepared (or interested enough) to take up his leadership role.

Nick Faldo (UK)

A native of Welwyn Garden City, England's Nicholas Alexander Faldo, M.B.E. (b. 7/18/1957) took up the game of golf at age 14 after watching on television Jack Nicklaus capture the 1972 Masters. A precocious talent, he developed his skills quickly, capturing the **British Youths** title in 1975 as well as the **English Amateur,** the latter's youngest-ever winner only eight days past his 18th birthday. Having no delusions about an amateur career, Faldo turned professional in 1976 and didn't wait long to taste success, capturing the relatively minor 36-hole **Skol Lager** event on the 1977 European Tour, then breaking through in a big way at the 1978 **Volvo PGA** (a seven-shot victory over Ken Brown) and placing third on that season's Order of Merit. A disappointing 1979 followed (with only a minor win in distant South Africa) before Faldo strung together Order of Merit finishes of fourth, second, fourth, and first between 1980 and 1983, claiming two more **Volvo PGA** titles in 1980 and '81, and winning five times (including the **French Open** and **European Masters**) in 1983.

Although firmly established as one of Europe's elite, Faldo wasn't satisfied. Standing a wiry 6'3", he was in those days a far longer hitter than contemporary fans might guess, his wide, swaying, leg-driven motion generating enough clubhead speed to have actually won a British Long Driving Championship. Desiring greater consistency, however, he visited instructor David Leadbetter in 1984 and began a two-year process of turning his swing into a compact, highly reliable mechanism that would hold up under fire and allow him to move the ball either direction at will. The result, of course, was a modern approximation of Ben Hogan, a disciplined, machine-like player who would win 26 events worldwide over the next decade, six of them Major championships.

Faldo's Major breakthrough came in 1987 in the **Open Championship** at Muirfield, his 18-par final round of 71 proving just enough when leader Paul Azinger bogeyed both the 71st and the 72nd to lose by one. Two years later Faldo followed Sandy Lyle as the second Briton to claim the **Masters,** riding a Sunday 65 into sudden death with Scott Hoch, then winning at the second extra hole after Hoch missed a 2½-footer to end things at the first. Then in 1990 Faldo proved his Augusta triumph no fluke by defending his title, once again on the second hole of sudden death, only this time against 1976 champion Raymond Floyd. At 47, Floyd was bidding to become the event's oldest-ever winner, but fell away when his pulled approach found the pond next to the 11th green, making Faldo the only man other then Nicklaus (in 1965–66) to take back-to-back Green Jackets. Faldo then added his second Major of the season at St. Andrews, staring down Greg Norman on Saturday before closing with a smooth 71 to take the **Open Championship** by five over Mark McNulty and Payne Stewart.

Still at the top of his game in 1992, Faldo was again in contention at Muirfield, leading by four through 54 holes before stumbling badly on Sunday, getting passed by John Cook and standing two back and fading on the 69th tee. Up ahead Cook missed a three-footer for birdie at the 71st, then bogeyed the last when his approach found the grandstand. Faldo, meanwhile, righted the ship with two clutch birdies and two pars and for the third time the Claret Jug was his.

By 1996, perhaps on the down side but still highly competitive, Faldo entered the final round at the **Masters** running second—a full six shots behind Greg Norman. Norman's collapse to 78 on that fateful Sunday is among golf's most famous disasters, yet it's often forgotten that Faldo didn't just watch Norman stumble; he rocketed forward with the low round of the day, a superb 67, to claim his third Green Jacket and sixth Major championship.

As one of Britain's best before the Ryder Cup absorbed Europe and as perhaps the world's best a bit later, Faldo participated in a record 11 straight Cup matches, also claiming marks for the most individual matches played (46), most points won (25) and most matches won (23). His overall record of 23-19-4 is also impressive, particularly when measured against the 4-6-1 record of his teams during his years of participation.

Now in his late 40s, Faldo has become in international businessman with interests in golf course design, resort academies, pro shops, broadcasting, and an ever-expanding list of quasi-golfing ventures à la Greg Norman. He has also made a determined effort to give back to European golf by founding and underwriting the Faldo Series, a collection of tournaments and tutorials for the region's top young players, a nonprofit enterprise in which Faldo has taken a commendably active role. A future Open champion or two might emerge, and would represent a fine legacy for a man who, with a nod to Henry Cotton, might well be considered the finest British golfer since Harry Vardon.

PGA Tour Wins (9): 1984 Heritage; **1987, '90, & '92 British Open; 1989, '90 & '96 Masters;** 1995 Doral; 1997 Los Angeles

Intn'l Victories (30): 1978, '80, '81 & '89 Volvo PGA; 1983 European Masters; 1987 Spanish Open; 1983, '88 & '89 French Open; 1988 Volvo Masters; 1989 British Masters; 1989 & '92 World Match Play; 1991, '92 & '93 Irish Open; 1993 Johnnie Walker

Ryder Cup: 1977–97 (11)

1976-2003

	76	77	78	79	80	81	82	83	84	85	86	87	88	89
Masters	-	-	-	40	-	-	-	T20	T15	T25	-	-	T30	1
US Open	-	-	-	-	-	-	-	-	T55	-	-	-	2	T18
British	T28	T62	T7	T19	T12	T11	T4	T8	T6	T53	5	1	3	T11
PGA	-	-	-	-	-	-	T14	MC	T20	T54	MC	T28	T4	T9

	90	91	92	93	94	95	96	97	98	99	00	01	02	03
Masters	1	T12	T13	T39	32	T24	1	MC	MC	MC	T28	MC	T14	T33
US Open	T3	T16	T4	T72	MC	T45	T16	T48	MC	MC	7	T72	T5	MC
British	1	T17	1	2	T8	T40	4	T51	T44	MC	T41	MC	T59	T8
PGA	T19	T16	T2	3	T4	T31	T65	MC	T54	T41	T51	T51	T60	-

Johnny Farrell (USA)

Born: White Plains, New York, 4/1/1901 **Died:** Delray Beach, Florida, 6/14/1988

If one buys into the age-old belief that the best way to learn about golf is as a caddie, then one of the game's all-time great finishing schools had to be the old Fairview CC in Elmsford, New York. Out of the Fairview caddie yard came U.S. Open winner Tony Manero, PGA champions Tom Creavy and Jim Turnesa, two-time U.S. Amateur winner William Turnesa and, ahead of them all, Johnny Farrell.

A short, right-to-left hitter with a decidedly elegant swing and, more important, a superb putting stroke,

Farrell won 22 times on the PGA Tour, including a red-hot run in 1926–27 that saw him accumulate 11 titles up and down the Eastern seaboard, plus several unofficial wins as well. The biggest of these victories was the 1927 **Metropolitan Open** at Wykagyl GC, where Farrell overcame a three-stroke deficit with only three to play to edge Bobby Cruickshank at the last. He would only win twice in 1928 but the second occasion was the **U.S. Open,** played at Chicago's Olympia Fields CC. Here Bobby Jones held a lead after 54 holes, then staggered home in 77 to tie Farrell, whose final-round gallery at one point numbered three. Sunday's play-off was a see-saw affair that came down to the 36th, with Farrell ultimately holing a clutch seven footer to win by a single shot.

Though a second-place finisher at the 1929 British Open (a full six behind the rampaging Walter Hagen), Farrell's best competitive days were behind him. In 1934 he became head professional at Baltusrol, a position he would retain for the next 38 years.

PGA Tour Wins (22): 1927 Metropolitan; **1928 U.S. Open;** and 3 Shawnee Opens

Ryder Cup: 1927–31 (3)

1919-1940

	19	20	21	22	23	24	25	26	27	28	29
Masters											
US Open	-	T45	38	T11	T5	T19	T3	T3	T7	1	MC
British		-	-	-	19	-	-	-	-	-	2
PGA	-	T17	-	-	T9	T5	T5	T3	T17	-	2

	30	31	32	33	34	35	36	37	38	39	40
Masters					T36	T37	T29	-	-	39	T14
US Open	8	T10	MC	T9	T58	T52	T22	T40	-	MC	28
British	-	T5	-	*	:	-	-	-	-	-	
PGA	T5	T17	-	T3	T17	-	-	T9	T33	T17	-

*Result unverified—made cut but finished outside top 30.

Mary Lena Faulk (USA)

Born in the panhandle town of Chipley, Florida, Mary Lena Faulk (1926–1995) moved to Thomasville, Georgia, at age 14, winning three **Georgia Women's Amateurs,** the 1953 **U.S. Women's Amateur** (3 and 2 over Polly Riley at the Rhode Island CC) and several regional titles before playing on a victorious 1954 Curtis Cup team. In 1955 she turned professional and joined the LPGA Tour, enjoying an 11-year career which saw her claim 10 victories between 1956 and 1964. Faulk's peak came during a successful June of 1961 when she won the **Western Open,** New York's **Triangle Round Robin,** and the **Eastern Open** in successive weeks, having already captured the **Babe Zaharias Open** back in April. After retiring from the tour in 1965, she taught for many years at two of America's finest resorts, Sea Island, Georgia, and The Broadmoor in Colorado Springs.

Max Faulkner (UK)

For those residing outside of the United Kingdom, Bexhill, England's Max Herbert Gustavas Faulkner, O.B.E. (1916–2005) is generally recalled as the man who won the only **Open Championship** ever played on Irish soil, the 1951 event at Royal Portrush. Such a calling card is certainly fair enough, as was "the only postwar Briton to win the Open" which survived until Tony Jacklin's 1969 triumph at Royal Lytham. But to see Faulkner so narrowly misses a lot, for he was one of the most talented and colorful players produced in modern Britain.

The son of a golf pro, Faulkner flew with the RAF during World War II before ramping up his game in the decade or so that followed it. A flashy dresser in the Jimmy Demaret vein and a famously engaging storyteller, he won a total of 16 significant events around Europe, led by the Open Championship where he defeated Argentina's Antonio Cerda (and an admittedly soft field) by two in Northern Ireland. It is worth noting that stories of Faulkner's signing autographs "1951 Open champion" after 36 holes were greatly exaggerated, as he later admitted to making only one such inscription, this after three rounds and up six strokes—and then only because he was asked to.

The only player to win the Open, the old *News of the World* match play, and the **British Masters,** Faulkner was also a five-time Ryder Cup pick who was honored with his O.B.E. in 2002, at age 85.

Intn'l Wins (16): 1951 British Open; 1951 British Masters; 1952, '53 & '57 Spanish Open; 1953 PGA Match Play; 1968 Portuguese Open

Ryder Cup: 1947–53 & '57 (5)

Brad Faxon (USA)

A former junior star in Rhode Island and an All-American and NCAA Player of the Year at Furman University, Bradford John Faxon Jr. (b. Oceanport, New Jersey, 8/21/1961) has enjoyed a steady 20-year professional career that has seen him win seven PGA Tour events and more than $14 million. Widely considered the best putter in American golf since Ben Crenshaw, Faxon's overall short game is equally lauded by his Tour brethren, and it is teasing indeed to ponder what heights he might have reached were his tee-to-green game of comparable quality.

A high school golf teammate of fellow professional Billy Andrade, Faxon has thrice cracked the top 10 money winners, first in 1992 (when he won twice, at the **New England Classic** and **The International**) and again during 1996 and '97. Perhaps due to his less-reliable ball striking, Faxon's record in Major championships is sketchy, logging only four top 10s in 59 career starts. His single best Major finish, a tie for fifth at the 1995 PGA Championship, saw him shoot a remarkable 28 on Riviera's front nine en route to a closing 63 and a much-coveted spot on the Ryder Cup team.

David Fay (USA)

Since replacing Frank Hannigan as the executive director of the USGA in 1989, David B. Fay has been a highly visible figurehead for golf's governing body, his trademark bow tie suggesting something of a throwback to a different golfing era. Fay himself is a compelling story, growing up in Tuxedo, New York, learning the game as a caddie and on public golf courses, joining the Metropolitan Golf Association after graduating from Colgate and surviving a life-threatening bout with Burkitt's lymphoma in 1986. Amidst the usual ledger of USGA administrative, agronomical and fundraising activities, Fay must be credited with the bold initiative of bringing the U.S. Open to a municipally owned golf course, an idea which came to fruition at Long Island's Bethpage State Park in 2002.

Fay, of course, is hardly autonomous, serving more as a spokesperson for the policies of the organization's 15-member Executive Committee than as a singular decision maker. Nonetheless, it will be his name that is most associated with a new-millennium era that has witnessed membership plunge 20 percent, the organization's signature *Golf Journal* discontinued, and countless classic courses disfigured—at no little expense—as a result of the USGA's abrogation of responsibility regarding the regulation of equipment. Fortunately, Fay is quite well compensated for his trouble.

George Fazio (USA)

Norristown, Pennsylvania, native George Fazio (1912–1986) was a journeyman player on the PGA Tour from the late 1930s through the mid-1950s, claiming the 1946 **Canadian Open** as the bigger of his two victories. Indeed, Fazio is probably more remembered for an event he did not win, the 1950 U.S. Open, in which he and Lloyd Mangrum lost an 18-hole play-off at Merion to Ben Hogan, who claimed the title dramatically only 16 months after his near-fatal car crash. The possessor of one of the game's smoother swings, Fazio seemed to favor more difficult courses, adding top-five Open finishes in 1952 and '53 before easing into competitive retirement toward the end of the decade.

The longtime professional at Pine Valley, Fazio next turned to golf course architecture, a second career in which he became a mainstay. Perhaps because of both his name and his personal popularity, Fazio's firm had a wide-ranging appeal, building courses as far apart as Arizona, the Caribbean and Canada. Perhaps designing toward his own playing strengths, he frequently constructed holes with smaller than average putting surfaces, believing that if a player possessed the skill to hit a green in regulation, they deserved a birdie putt of a reasonable length.

As the longtime site of the Western Open, the Fazio-designed Butler National GC gained an international reputation for its toughness, though also garnering great attention was 1970's Jupiter Hills Club, an oddity among Florida courses with its hilly terrain and occasional Pine Valley-like sand hazards. Fazio also left his mark in one other important way: two of his earliest employees were his nephews, Tom and Jim, both of whom have gone on to prominent design careers of their own.

Notable Courses: Butler National GC, Illinois; Edgewood Tahoe CC, Nevada; **Jupiter Hills C, Hills Course, Florida;** Moselem Springs CC, Pennsylvania

Jim Fazio (USA)

The older of George Fazio's two architect nephews, Jim Fazio (b. 1942) has been considerably less prolific than brother Tom, though in recent years the recurring patronage of real estate mogul Donald Trump has done much to close the gap. Though out of the design business for a number of years, Fazio returned to score big with his Trump contracts, particularly at West Palm Beach's Trump International GC where the hosting of the LPGA's ADT

Championship guaranteed large-scale television exposure. Unfortunately for Fazio, his Trump projects are trivialized among knowledgeable observers due to The Donald's penchant for hyping them to laughably over-inflated levels.

Tom Fazio (USA)

Standing among the biggest names in contemporary golf course architecture, Tom Fazio (b. Norristown, Pennsylvania, 2/10/1945) has been in the design business since 1962 when he began working for his player-turned-architect uncle George. The firm enjoyed a good deal of success as Tom gradually replaced the aging George as its centerpiece, with much of "their" later output more resembling solo designs. Unfortunately prime examples of this work were alterations of Golden Age classics Inverness (1979) and Oak Hill (1980), both Donald Ross–designed Major championship sites upon which Tom constructed multiple new holes which were clearly at odds with the feel and appearance of their older brethren.

Ironically, it would largely be a sense of aesthetics that would establish Fazio as a design superstar, and by the early 1980s he was turning out an assembly line of attractive, often spectacular-looking courses from coast to coast. Frequently appearing more difficult than they actually played, such layouts became a favorite of real estate and resort developers — though a good number of fine private clubs dot the Fazio résumé as well. A strong believer in moving tons of earth, Fazio has long prided himself on being able to build "quality" golf holes on virtually any terrain. It's a philosophy that doesn't come cheap, but it has yielded such layouts as Shadow Creek, casino mogul Steve Wynn's spectacular Las Vegas retreat which, having been built upon a barren desert floor, is surely one of the great accomplishments in the history of golf design.

An overview of Fazio's work yields, however, an interesting dichotomy: While his courses have generally been well-received initially (frequently winning "Best New" honors from various publications), only four managed to crack Golf Magazine's 2003 American Top 100, and none of those were ranked among the nation's top 45. Similarly, only one of golf's four Major championships (the 1987 PGA) has ever been played on a Fazio-designed course. It is an ironic circumstance indeed for a man who has written of the weakness of "the so-called 'classic' era" — or perhaps golf's ratings cognoscenti simply prefer natural topography to another favored Fazio phrase, "total site manipulation."

Notable Courses: Black Diamond Ranch, Quarry Course, Florida; Galloway National GC, New Jersey; The Quarry at La Quinta, California; Shadow Creek GC, Nevada; Victoria National GC, Indiana; Wade Hampton GC; North Carolina; World Woods GC (36), Florida

David Feherty (Northern Ireland)

Due in part to his self-deprecating brand of humor, David Feherty (b. Bangor 8/13/1958) is perhaps not given his proper due as a player, at least on the western shores of the Atlantic. A mainstay on the PGA European Tour throughout the 1980s and early '90s, he tied for fourth in the 1994 Open Championship at Turnberry, ranked among Europe's top 25 money winners seven times, and played on the 1991 European Ryder Cup team. Over 14 years, Feherty amassed 10 victories worldwide, including the 1986 **Scottish** and **Italian Opens**. But after playing the American PGA Tour with only limited success through 1996, he smoothly repaired to the world of television commentary, injecting an irreverent and genuine wit into the proceedings. Feherty has also become a writer, authoring two books and a regular column for America's Golf Magazine.

A. H. Fenn (USA)

A fine all-around athlete, Waterbury, Connecticut-born Arthur H. Fenn (1858–1925) did not take up golf until age 36 but found himself playing to scratch within a year. After laying out a rudimentary course in his hometown of Waterbury in 1895, he became manager of New Hampshire's Waumbek Hotel where his renovation/expansion of a prehistoric nine set him off on a side career in architecture. At his next stop, Maine's famed Poland Spring House, Fenn laid out the resort's original nine holes before staying on as golf professional for 25 years, all the while wintering in Palm Beach.

Generally considered America's first native-born professional, Fenn remained competitive for years, winning the inaugural 1918 **Maine Open** at age 60 and playing with Harry Vardon during the latter's 1900 American tour. Though Fenn would design little more than a dozen documented courses (and largely rudimentary ones at that) these carried no small significance as they were located in New England resort centers that played a major role in golf's early American growth.

Keith Fergus (USA)

A pure ball-striker whose putting occasionally lagged behind, Keith Fergus (b. Temple, Texas, 3/3/1954) was a three-time All-American at the University of Houston, runner-up to Jay Haas for the 1975 NCAA individual title, and, by 10 strokes, the medalist at the 1976 PGA Tour qualifier. After finishing third behind Jack Nicklaus and Isao Aoki at the epic 1980 U.S. Open at Baltusrol, Fergus finally won his first event a year later at **The Memorial**, then added victories in the **Atlanta** and **Bob Hope Classics** in 1982 and '83. Struggling in the mid-1980s, however, he returned to coach Houston's legendary golf program from 1988 to 1994, then re-earned his Tour card for a brief return before joining the Champions Tour in early 2004.

Bob Ferguson (UK)

Musselburgh's Bob Ferguson (1844–1924) is one of only four men ever to win the **Open Championship** three times in succession, doing so immediately after Jamie Anderson, a decade after Young Tom Morris, and roughly 70 years ahead of Australia's Peter Thomson. Having made his bones as a 23-year-old when he borrowed a set of clubs to win an open professional event at Leith, Ferguson was an experienced competitor by the time of his first Claret Jug, which he won in 1880 over his home links in Musselburgh. A year later he defended at Prestwick (defeating Jamie Anderson in a rainstorm of epic proportion), then completed the triple in 1882 at St. Andrews when he beat Willie Fernie by three. Frequently overlooked, however, is that Ferguson came within a whisker of matching Young Tom's four straight titles when, in 1883 at Musselburgh, he finished with three consecutive threes to tie Fernie, forcing a 36-hole play-off. The play-off finish pushed the boundaries of believability and would surely be rejected as a movie script, for Ferguson reportedly came to the last, a 170-yarder, leading by one and proceeded to make a safe four. Fernie, on the other hand, blasted his gutty all the way home, then holed a long putt to steal the victory.

Though a large and extremely powerful man by repute, Ferguson's greatest competitive asset was his mental toughness, for he was said always to be at his best when the wind roared and the rains came. Affected by typhoid shortly after his 1883 loss, Ferguson's game soon fell below championship standard and he died during the First World War while working as a caddie in Musselburgh.

S. Mure Fergusson (UK)

A notable early Scot who was a regular winner of spring and fall events at St. Andrews for roughly four decades, Samuel Mure Fergusson (b. 1855) was twice runner-up in the British Amateur, in 1894 and '98. On both occasions he had the misfortune of running into a well-nigh immovable obstruction, first in the form of John Ball (who won his fourth of eight Amateurs at Fergusson's expense), then the legendary Scotsman Freddie Tait—and it is surely with an eye toward these encounters that many consider Fergusson most unlucky never to have won the big prize.

Fergusson's style was not much to look at and according to Darwin, "he could go very crooked on occasions, but he had a fine dour courage, a great power of recovery, and was a magnificent holer out in a crisis, standing up to the ball and seeming to compel it to go in by sheer force of character." Darwin further rated Fergusson among the eight finest amateurs of the late nineteenth century, grouping him with Leslie Balfour-Melville, a notch behind the cream of the field, Messrs. Hutchinson, Laidlay, and Ball.

Vicente Fernandez (Argentina)

Following in the footsteps of Roberto de Vicenzo, Corrientes, Argentina's Vicente Fernandez (b. 4/5/1946) has been an international golfer for nearly four decades now, regularly winning events in Europe (4) and South America (14) and, after turning 50, in the United States. Standing a lean 5'7", Fernandez will never be confused with John Daly, but his ability to consistently keep the ball in play and hole numerous putts have made him, if not de Vicenzo, a partial facsimile thereof.

After caddying as a youth for Chi Chi Rodriguez at the 1962 World Cup in Buenos Aires, Fernandez first captured his native **Argentine Open** in 1968, defended it in 1969, then went right on winning it at regular intervals until a memorable victory in 2000—at age 54—gave him a total of eight (second only to de Vicenzo's nine). Three **Brazilian Opens** also dot his South American résumé while his biggest European victory came in 1979 at the **Volvo PGA** at St. Andrews, where a level-par performance nipped Gary Player and a host of strong contenders by one. Fourteen times in the Order of Merit top 50, Fernandez was only twice in the top 10, when he finished sixth and ninth in 1974 and '75, respectively.

Upon reaching 50 with his skills largely intact, Fernandez returned to America (where he toiled briefly during the 1970s) to stake his claim on the Champions Tour, winning four tournaments and over $7 million to date.

Willie Fernie (UK)

Though certainly not in the class of Jamie Anderson or Bob Ferguson, the two men who had halved the six preceding titles, St. Andrews–born Willie Fernie (1851–1924) was the winner of the **Open Championship** in 1883 at Musselburgh. Despite a debilitating 10 on his scorecard, Fernie appeared likely to end Ferguson's three-year reign until the homestanding defender carded three straight threes to force a play-off. There, trailing by one, Fernie holed an enormous putt at the 36th for a two which, combined with Ferguson's four, resulted in a rather unlikely one-shot victory.

Also a runner-up on four occasions extending into the 1890s, Fernie worked at Felixstowe and Ardeer before moving to Troon in 1887, where he remained until retirement. He was also a practicing golf course architect who designed or redesigned more than 15 courses throughout the United Kingdom (including a 1900 renovation of Troon) between 1894 and 1909.

Jim Ferrier
(Australia/USA)

Born: Sydney, Australia, 2/24/1915 **Died:** Burbank, California, 6/13/1986

Arguably the finest amateur golfer ever produced by Australia, big, powerful Jim Ferrier was once described by Bernard Darwin as "a magnificent specimen of humanity." Yet ironically it was hardly his long game that drove Ferrier to the heights but rather his skills around the greens which were invariably considered among the finest of all time.

In his youth Ferrier was simply dominant, winning four **Australian Amateurs** between 1935 and 1939, as well as seven state titles beginning in 1931. In that same year, at age 16, he was runner-up at the **Australian Open,** a feat

he repeated in 1933 before winning the title twice (both times over Norman von Nida) in 1938 and '39. He also enjoyed a strong trip to Britain in 1936, losing the British Amateur final at St. Andrews 2 down to Hector Thomson but capturing two smaller titles.

Already making his living primarily as a golf writer, Ferrier emigrated to America in 1940, some said in an attempt at avoiding wartime military service. Upon his Stateside arrival, he found the USGA unwilling to acknowledge his amateur status because he'd profited from authoring a minor Australian instructional book (conveniently ignoring the fact that neither Bobby Jones nor Walter Travis were ever questioned for writing best-sellers). Undaunted, Ferrier turned pro and proceeded to win 18 PGA Tour events from 1944 to 1961, the highlight being the 1947 **PGA Championship,** where he beat Chick Harbert 2 and 1 in Detroit to become Australia's first Major champion. He also claimed back-to-back **Canadian Opens** in 1950 and '51 and finished second at both the 1950 Masters and the 1960 PGA.

PGA Tour Wins (18): 1947 PGA Championship; 1950 & '51 Canadian Open
Intn'l Wins (6): 1938 & '39 Australian Open

1936-1965

	36	37	38	39	40	41	42	43	44	45	46	47	48	49	50
Masters	-	-	-	-	26	T29	T15				T4	T6	T4	T16	2
US Open	-	-	-	-	T29	T30					MC	T6	MC	T23	T5
British	T44	-	-	-							-	-	-	-	-
PGA	-	-	-	-	-	-	-		-	-	T9	1	T17	T3	-

	51	52	53	54	55	56	57	58	59	60	61	62	63	64	65
Masters	7	T3	T16	WD	-	-	-	-	-	-	-	MC	-	T5	MC
US Open	MC	-	MC	-	-	-	-	-	-	MC	T22	-	-	MC	WD
British	-	-	-	-	-	-	-	-	-	-	-	-	-	-	-
PGA	T9	T17	T17	-	-	-	-	-	T38	2	T45	T39	T7	T56	MC

Mike Fetchik (USA)

Yonkers, New York, product Mike Fetchik (b. 1922) was a journeyman on the PGA Tour, save for a memorable 1956 in which he rather suddenly won three times. At the top of this windfall was the **Western Open,** played that year in the shadow of the Golden Gate Bridge at the Presidio GC. There, after tying with Jay Hebert, Don January, and Doug Ford, Fetchik ran away with the 18-hole play-off, winning by five strokes. Decades later Fetchik played in the early days of the Champions Tour where, despite being past his senior prime, he became the oldest winner in

tour history by capturing the 1985 Hilton Head Classic on his 63rd birthday.

Eric Fiddian (UK)

Englishman Eric Westwood Fiddian (b. 1910) nearly pulled an impressive double in 1932, winning the **English Amateur** but losing in the final of the British Amateur at Muirfield to John de Forest, 3 and 1. He also appeared twice in the Walker Cup, going winless during a pair of American drubbings in 1932 and '34. A player who'd demonstrated a great deal of potential, Fiddian stepped away from competition soon thereafter to attend to business and family.

Marta Figueras-Dotti
(Spain)

Though only a one-time winner on the LPGA Tour, Madrid native Marta Figueras-Dotti (b. 11/12/1957) remains, on the strength of her amateur record alone, the finest female golfer thus far produced by Spain. Figueras-Dotti's list of regional titles was a long one, kicked off by two **European Amateurs** while still in her teens (1975 and '77) and anchored by a 1979 season which saw her take the national titles of **Spain, France** and **Italy** while still young enough to claim the **Spanish Junior** as well. Her amateur pinnacle, however, came in 1982 when she bested a field of Europe's top women professionals to take the **Women's British Open** at Royal Birkdale, likely the biggest victory by a female amateur since Catherine LaCoste's triumph at the 1967 U.S. Women's Open. That same year, she was also a collegiate All-American at USC.

Her LPGA victory came at the 1994 **Hawaiian Ladies Open,** during a season in which she finished 43rd on the money list and logged not a single additional top 10. Having been a top-40 finisher in five of her first six campaigns (including 15th in 1984 and 16th in 1988), she was already in decline and never returned to the top 75 thereafter. Figueras-Dotti comes from a golfing family (her father having been president of the Spanish Golf Association) and she was the first Spanish woman ever to make her living as a professional.

Tim Finchem (USA)

A native of Ottawa, Illinois, Tim Finchem (b. 1947) succeeded Deane Beman as commissioner of the PGA Tour in 1994, having served five warm-up years as deputy commissioner and chief operating officer. A graduate of the University of Richmond, Finchem became an attorney and later served as an economic advisor to President Carter before gravitating toward golf. While Finchem has enjoyed much good fortune (including the arrival of Tiger Woods) during his term, he has also done a highly skillful job of keeping the show rolling during the recent economic downturn, riding his unprecedented $800 million TV contract, conjuring up enough sponsors when a shortfall seemed inevitable, and steering the Tour clear of such sideshows as the Martha Burk–Hootie Johnson squabble at the Masters.

Aware that the Tour must balance entertainment value with its competitive integrity, Finchem has voiced concern over both the fan-friendliness of players and the negative effect that unchecked equipment advances are having on

his product. He is in a tricky position on this last point, however, for unlike most sports commissioners who answer to a counsel of owners, Finchem works directly for the players, a group that unfortunately tends to value their endorsement deals well ahead of the overall good of the game.

Alex Findlay (UK/USA)

Born upon a steamer in the North Sea, Alexander H. Findlay (1865–1942) spent his youth in England and Scotland before joining a family friend who had purchased a ranch in Nebraska. Landing on the prairie in the mid-1880s, he became a cowboy while also preaching the gospel of golf, reporting later that he'd laid out a six-hole course in 1887 and, in the early 1890s, an initial track for Omaha's Happy Hollow CC. Eventually Findlay would become associated with the sporting goods firm of Wright & Ditson and serve as "professional golfer-in-chief" for Henry Flagler's Florida East Coast Railway, positions which afforded a great deal of travel. In this context, his oft-reported claim of having played over 2,400 courses seems realistic, and Findlay is well remembered for shepherding the great Harry Vardon around the continent during his celebrated 1900 tour. He also held numerous course records, though there is no record of his ever having competed seriously in any major events.

As a golf course architect, Findlay was prolific yet, truth be told, not particularly distinguished. Like virtually all designers of his day, he produced functional, relatively inexpensive layouts, and like another early missionary, Tom Bendelow, his work did gain a greater level of sophistication as time went by. Though few of his 100 plus designs remain intact today, it is perhaps a commentary on Findlay's talents that a number of these commissions—particularly at resorts like the Greenbrier, the Breakers, the Lake Placid Club, etc.—constituted some of the era's truly plum assignments.

Notable Courses: Aronimink GC, Pennsylvania (NLE); The Greenbrier GC, Lakeside Course, West Virginia, (NLE); Lake Placid C, Mountain Course, New York

James Finegan (USA)

Glenolden, Pennsylvania, native James W. Finegan is a former number-one golfer at LaSalle University, as well as the retired chairman of Philadelphia's Gray & Rogers advertising agency. Having made more than 35 visits to the British Isles, he began writing about them for publications such as *Golf Magazine*, the USGA's defunct *Golf Journal,* and the Philadelphia *Inquirer*. A knowledgeable journalist with an eminently pleasant style, Finegan has also authored four well-regarded books including the comprehensive *A Centennial Tribute to Golf in Philadelphia* (Golf Association of Philadelphia, 1996) and three outstanding travelogue/tour guides for golfers visiting the British Isles (see Appendix).

Joe Finger (USA)

A native of Houston, Joseph S. Finger (b. 1918) majored in engineering at Rice University (where his golf team was coached by one Jimmy Demaret) before receiving a Masters degree from MIT in 1941. Following 15 years in the oil and plastics businesses, Finger became involved in golf course design in the late 1950s, building several local Texas courses as well as layouts for five Air Force bases across the South. All told, Finger laid out approximately 50 new courses (including at least seven built in Mexico), sometimes working solo, sometimes with his eventual partner Ken Dye, and on at least three occasions with the great Byron Nelson. Perhaps the most memorable of Finger's new designs was "The Monster," a nearly 7,700-yard, water-filled beast built for upstate New York's Concord Hotel in 1964.

Dow Finsterwald (USA)

Dow Finsterwald (b. Athens, Ohio, 9/6/29) turned pro in 1950, motivated by the 61 he shot in the St. Louis Open while competing as an amateur. A highly reliable ball-striker and a fine shotmaker in the old-fashioned style, he went on to become one of the PGA Tour's top players of the late 1950s and early '60s, winning 11 times and being named Player of the Year in 1958.

Finsterwald lost a play-off to Doug Sanders at the 1956 Canadian Open, then a year later lost 2 and 1 to Lionel Hebert in the final of the 1957 PGA Championship at Ohio's Miami Valley CC. Bloodied but unbowed, he returned to the **PGA** in 1958 at Pennsylvania's Llanerch CC and defeated Billy Casper by two shots, this being the year that the PGA of America chose to remove all of the event's uniqueness by switching, irrevocably, to stroke play. There would be more brushes with Major titles: a joint third behind Palmer and Nicklaus in the 1960 U.S. Open at Cherry Hills; a tie for fifth at the 1961 Open at Oakland Hills; fourth at the 1959 PGA, and third in the 1963 edition; third in the 1960 Masters (behind Palmer and Venturi); and, in the nearest miss of all, a loss to Palmer (and Gary Player) in a three-way play-off for the 1962 Masters.

A four-time Ryder Cupper who captained the American squad in 1977, Finsterwald scaled back his playing schedule by the early 1970s, settling into a professional job at The Broadmoor Hotel in Colorado Springs.

PGA Tour Wins (11): 1958 PGA Championship; 1959 Greensboro; 1960 Los Angeles

Ryder Cup: 1957–63 (4) and 1977 Capt

1950-1966

	50	51	52	53	54	55	56	57	58	59	60	61	62	63	64	65	66
Masters	-	T50	T46	-	-	-	T24	T7	T17	T18	3	MC	3	T5	T9	T21	T57
US Open	MC	-	MC	-	-	T28	-	T13	-	T11	T3	T6	-	T12	8	MC	-
British	-	-	-	-	-	-	-	-	-	-	-	-	-	-	-	-	-
PGA	-	-	-	-	-	-	-	2	1	4	T15	T41	T11	T3	MC	T63	T12

Ed Fiore (USA)

Long known as "The Grip" for his 10-finger style, Lynwood, California, native Ed Fiore (b. 4/21/1953) played for the powerful University of Houston where he was named an All-American in 1977. Joining the PGA Tour full-time the following year, the 5'7" 190-pound Fiore went on to record four official victories, including the 1981 **Western Open,** the 1982 **Bob Hope** (in a play-off over Tom Kite), and the 1996 **Quad City Classic,** the last being notable both for Fiore's overtaking a young Tiger Woods (a rare time when Woods has been beaten in the late going) and for delaying Fiore's plans to retire and become a charter boat captain. Though plagued by back problems for years, Fiore has been a regular player on the Champions Tour since turning 50, winning an event in 2004.

Johnny Fischer (USA)

One of the most competitive amateurs of his or any other era, Cincinnati native John W. Fischer (1912–1984) made a career-long habit of playing his very best golf when the chips were down. At the University of Michigan, for example, he won the 1932 **NCAA** individual title (contested at match play) by making birdies on three of the last four holes to win 2 and 1. In the 1938 Walker Cup, played at St. Andrews, Fisher was four down to Leonard Crawley after the first 18 holes but rang up seven consecutive threes beginning at the 26th to ultimately prevail 3 and 2.

Having passed on a professional career to become an attorney in his hometown, Fischer's ultimate prize was the **U.S. Amateur,** which he won at New York's famed Garden City GC in 1936. To do so, however, he had to come from 1 down with 3 to play against the talented Scot Jack M'Lean, a task he accomplished by halving the 34th with a stymie, halving the 35th with a birdie, then holing a 12-foot birdie putt at the last to force extra holes. Finally, at the 37th, Fischer coolly rolled in a 20-footer for his third straight birdie and a national championship.

Joan (Lewis) Fisher (Australia)

Raised in an athletic Melbourne family, Joan Fisher (b. 1915) played a variety of sports before taking up golf at age 18. She won the final prewar **Australian Ladies** title (1939) under her maiden name of Lewis, then the first postwar event (1946) as Joan Fisher, later adding a third victory in 1952. A strong all-around player capable of generating great power, Fisher also took eight **Victorian Ladies** titles and was a mainstay of a 1950 Australian team that toured internationally. Her career record, of course, was greatly diminished by the interruption of war.

Diana Fishwick (UK)

Later known as Mrs. A. C. Critchley, London-born Diana Fishwick (b. 4/12/1911) had twice been **British Girls** champion when, at age 19, she reached the final of the Ladies Amateur at Formby, drawing none other than the great American Glenna Collett as her opponent. "What a lark," the amiable Fishwick cheerfully quipped, then went out and dusted off the heavily favored Collett 4 and 3. Later a frequent international competitor who won national titles in **France** (1932), **Germany** (1936 and '38), **Belgium** (1938) and the **Netherlands** (1946), Fishwick demonstrated a similar irreverence at the **English Ladies** championship. There she entered, with virtually no preparation, simply to get a firsthand look at several prospects for the Curtis Cup team she was scheduled to captain in 1950—and promptly won the title. Fishwick also participated in the first two Curtis Cup matches, and both her husband (an army Brigadier) and son were themselves players of note.

Jack Fleck (USA)

Jack Fleck (b. Bettendorf, Iowa, 11/8/1921) has long been the poster boy for the "you never knows" of golf, this because in 1955, with absolutely no reputation and a similar level of pre-tournament confidence, Fleck birdied the 72nd hole of the **U.S. Open** at Olympic to shoot an improbable 67 and tie Ben Hogan for the title. An 18-hole play-off ensued and when the overwhelmingly favored Hogan—attempting to become the first five-time U.S.

Open winner—took six at the 18th, Jack Fleck, of Iowa's Davenport Municipal GC, was America's National Champion.

Fleck did not then disappear as some might have us believe, for he won two additional Tour events, regularly retained his privileges with top-60 money rankings through 1963, and finished in a six-way logjam for third at the 1960 U.S. Open. But he would seldom show the sort of form necessary to compete with the likes of Hogan—just as Hogan would enjoy no better opportunity to capture that elusive fifth U.S. Open.

Marty Fleckman (USA)

Of all professional golf's modern flashes in the pan, Texan Marty Fleckman (b. Port Arthur 4/23/1944) certainly ranks among the elite. The 1965 **NCAA** champion at the University of Houston, Fleckman, while still an amateur, led the 1967 U.S. Open at Baltusrol by one stroke after 54 holes. A Sunday 80 dropped him to 18th but undeterred, Fleckman turned pro, got through the fall qualifying school and promptly won the 1967 **Cajun Classic,** his first Tour event as a professional. And then the dam burst. Fleckman never won again, never placed better than 81st on the money list and, so far as the PGA Tour was concerned, was soon but a distant memory.

Bruce Fleisher (USA)

If living well is indeed the best revenge, then in the world of golf, aging well must surely give it a run for its money. A prime example is Bruce Lee Fleisher (b. Union City, Tennessee, 10/16/1948), the 1968 **U.S. Amateur** champion, 1969 Walker Cupper and all-around young phenom who Eddie Pearced his way off the PGA Tour during the 1970s without ever cracking the top 75 on the money list. After more than a decade as a club professional, Fleisher fought his way back onto the circuit, eventually winning the 1991 **New England Classic** while preparing for professional golf's ultimate mulligan, the Champions Tour. Joining the seniors for the 1999 season, the late-peaking Fleisher immediately began winning and has scarcely looked back, claiming some 18 titles (including the 2001 **U.S. Senior Open**) and banking over $13.5 million in five full seasons. He remains relatively competitive, in his mid-50s, at the time of this writing.

Jack Fleming (Ireland/USA)

A native of County Galway, Ireland, John Francis Fleming (1896–1986) had moved to England and worked his way into a construction foreman's position with Dr. Alister MacKenzie by the age of 24. In 1926 he traveled to California to oversee the building of MacKenzie's Meadow Club layout, then emigrated there permanently after MacKenzie did the same, supervising construction on a number of the Good Doctor's period layouts including Cypress Point. When the Depression arrived, Fleming took a high-ranking job with the San Francisco Parks Department where he would toil for roughly 30 years. As a sidelight he built a number of courses in California, many of them par-three or "executive" designs. He also performed modest renovations at the Olympic Club and added a third nine at city-owned Harding Park.

Steve Flesch (USA)

Joining Phil Mickelson and Mike Weir among prominent left-handed players, Cincinnati native Steve Flesch (b. 5/23/1967) attended the University of Kentucky before taking several years to qualify for the PGA Tour. Since arriving in 1998, however, he has been a highly consistent money winner, never finishing worse than 75th in earnings while peaking with a 13th-place finish in 2000. Now approaching 40, the personable Flesch broke through for his first Tour victory in 2003 at **New Orleans,** then followed it up with a one-shot triumph at the 2004 **Colonial,** only narrowly missing out on a 2004 Ryder Cup spot as a result.

Raymond Floyd (USA)

The son of a career army man who served as the base golf professional at Ft. Bragg, North Carolina, Raymond Loran Floyd (b. Ft. Bragg, North Carolina, 9/4/1942) was a fine athlete who initially concentrated on baseball before a victory in the 1960 **National Jaycees** tournament turned his attentions, such as they were, to golf. A certified lover of the night life, Floyd turned pro in 1961 and joined the PGA Tour in 1963, winning the **St. Petersburg Open** in his 11th start but initially gaining far more attention for his carousing, which included running with Joe Namath and the Chicago Cubs and investing in The Ladybirds, an all-girl musical group billing itself as the first topless rock band.

Despite a lifestyle that made the ability to play with a hangover a necessity, Floyd was talented enough to skate by, often supplementing his inconsistent Tour winnings with high-stakes private games on off days. Despite this strenuous regimen, Floyd somehow had amassed four victories before breaking through at the 1969 **PGA Championship** at Dayton's NCR GC, where rounds of 69-66-67

afforded him the luxury of a closing 74 to beat Gary Player by one. Still, one could find only so much success when struggling to remain vertical, and from the PGA onward, Floyd endured six winless seasons that saw him twice fall below 70th on the money list. His turnaround began in 1974 when he got married and decidedly more focused, working with noted teacher Jack Grout and attempting, for the first time, to reach his potential.

The result was an impressive 18-year run that saw Floyd win 17 times between 1975 and 1992, including three more Major championships, and emerge as one of golf's craftiest and most competitive players. At the 1976 **Masters** he led from wire-to-wire, opening with 65-66 before running away by eight strokes and tying Nicklaus' tournament record at 271. At the 1982 **PGA Championship** at Southern Hills, he opened with a scorching 63, then added 69-68-72 to cruise home three ahead of Lanny Wadkins. But Floyd's crowning achievement came in the 1986 **U.S. Open** at Shinnecock Hills where, with an all-star cast falling by the wayside in the late going, he closed with a flawless 66 to beat Wadkins and Chip Beck by two, becoming, at age 43, the oldest man yet to win the Open. Though never able to complete the career Grand Slam by winning the Open Championship, Floyd came close, three times finishing among the top five, including a tie for second, two behind Nicklaus in 1978 at St. Andrews.

A Hall of Fame inductee in 1989, Floyd served as Ryder Cup captain during that year's tie at the Belfry, then proved his marvelous competitiveness by appearing twice more as a player in 1991 and '93, the last as one of Tom Watson's captain's picks at age 51. On that final occasion, Floyd won twice while partnered with Payne Stewart before providing the Cup clincher with a 2-up victory over José Maria Olazábal at singles, a remarkable display from the oldest Ryder Cup player in history.

Floyd's swing is famously aggressive, though hardly textbook in length or tempo. His short game and ability to score, however, are of an elite standard, leading him to write two fine instructional works, *From 60 Yards In* (Harper & Row, 1989) and *The Elements of Scoring* (Simon & Schuster, 1998). A significant force on the Champions Tour during the 1990s, the semiretired Floyd remains the center of a fine golfing family: his sister Marlene played the LPGA Tour during the late 1970s and '80s, and his son Robert enjoyed a strong amateur career at the University of Florida before a brief run on the PGA Tour.

PGA Tour Wins (22): 1969 & '**82 PGA Championship; 1976
    Masters;** 1977 Byron Nelson; 1980, '81 & '92 Doral; 1981 Players Championship; 1981 Westchester; 1982 Memorial; **1986
    U.S. Open**
Intn'l Wins: 3
Champions Tour Wins: 14 (1992–2000)
Ryder Cup: 1969, '75, '77, '81–'85, '91 & '93 (8) and 1989 Capt

1963-1995

	63	64	65	66	67	68	69	70	71	72	73	74	75	76	77	78	79
Masters	-	-	-	T8	-	T7	T35	MC	T13	MC	54	T22	T30	1	T8	T16	T17
US Open	-	T14	T6	-	T38	-	T13	T22	8	MC	16	T15	T12	13	T47	T12	MC
British	-	-	-	-	-	-	T34	MC	-	-	-	-	T23	4	8	T2	T36
PGA	T57	-	T17	T18	T20	T41	1	T8	MC	T4	T35	T11	T10	T2	T40	T57	-

	80	81	82	83	84	85	86	87	88	89	90	91	92	93	94	95
Masters	T17	T8	T7	T4	T15	T2	MC	MC	T11	T38	2	T17	2	T11	T10	T17
US Open	T45	T37	T49	T13	T52	T23	1	T43	T17	T26	MC	T8	T44	T7	-	T36
British	-	T3	T15	T14	MC	-	T16	T17	MC	T42	T39	MC	T12	T34	-	T58
PGA	T17	T19	1	T20	13	MC	MC	T14	T9	T46	T49	T7	T48	MC	T61	-

William Flynn (USA)

Born: Milton, Massachusetts, 12/25/1890 **Died:** Philadelphia, Pennsylvania, 1/24/1945

Though much overlooked until recently, William Flynn surely ranks among the very finest golf course architects ever produced in the United States. A native of suburban Boston, Flynn was a fine all-around athlete who competed against his childhood friend Francis Ouimet on the golf course and was good enough at tennis to teach professionally. He laid out his first course, a long-forgotten nine in Heartwellville, Vermont, in 1913, but the seeds of his career had already been sown a year earlier, when Hugh Wilson hired him to help build Merion. A planned architectural partnership with Wilson fell through when the latter's health slipped, but Flynn would quickly prove himself capable of great design success on his own.

Initially working primarily in Pennsylvania, Flynn had gone national by the early 1920s, completing three exceptional projects in 1923 (Atlantic City CC, Virginia's Cascades GC, and Denver's Cherry Hills CC). Shortly thereafter, he brought civil engineer Howard Toomey on as a partner, with Flynn handling the actual designs and Toomey overseeing construction, financing, etc. Though often singled out for their superb 1931 rebuild of Shinnecock Hills, the firm completed work of near-comparable quality at numerous other sites from Massachusetts to Florida, including 36 now-deceased holes at the palatial Boca Raton Club. They also built one of the most difficult courses of the day, Albert Lasker's former Chicago-area estate course, Mill Road Farm, and maintained a stranglehold on the Philadelphia market, where not less than nine excellent layouts bear the Flynn imprint.

If there was an identifiable style to Flynn's work, it lay most in his bunkering which was generous, large of scale and usually angled against the line of play, creating interesting strategic possibilities. He was also a bold designer, including the occasional alternate fairway or island green and incorporating vast areas of sandy waste at places like Shinnecock Hills, Atlantic City and Boca Raton. Flynn was also a mentor to several major postwar designers including Dick Wilson, William Gordon and Robert "Red" Lawrence, and left a body of work strong enough to go head-to-head with nearly anyone's.

Notable Courses: Boca Raton Hotel & C, Florida (36, NLE); Cascades GC, Virginia; Cherry Hills CC, Colorado; Indian Creek CC, Florida; **Mill Road Farm GC, Illinois (NLE);** Philadelphia CC, Spring Mill Course, Pennsylvania; **Shinnecock Hills GC, New York;** CC of Virginia, James River Course, Virginia

Pipe Follett (UK/USA)

An Oxford graduate who later emigrated to New York, Wilfred H. "Pipe" Follett (1897–1993) has managed largely to slip through the cracks of American golf history despite spending more than his allotted 15 minutes in its spotlight. His first high-profile position came in the early 1920s when he replaced Max Behr as editor of *Golf Illustrated* after Behr departed for California and the life of a course architect. Follett himself would follow a similar path, though on rather a smaller scale. After helping New York architect Devereux Emmet with his design of the long-deceased Queens Valley CC in 1923, Follett went on to create several area courses of his own, most notably the old Glen Oaks Club, a tricky, wooded design which was sacrificed to real estate development in the early 1970s.

Duncan Forbes (UK)

A prominent jurist in Edinburgh, Duncan Forbes was a founding member of the Gentlemen Golfers of Leith (later the Honourable Company of Edinburgh Golfers), the first documented golf club and writers of the first rules of the game. An inveterate player who repaired to the beach when snows rendered the course unusable, Forbes fought valiantly to diffuse the 1745 Jacobite rebellion and, as an anti-Jacobite, gained lasting golfing fame by using his influence to save his friend and fellow clubmember John Rattray from the post-rebellion gallows. A man much admired for his character, Forbes was glowingly described in Thomas Mathison's poem *The Goff* as "... the great Forbes, patron of the just, the dread of villains and the poor man's trust." He passed away four years after this acclaim, in 1747.

Doug Ford (USA)

Known for his highly compact swing and first-class short game, New Haven, Connecticut, native Doug Ford (b. 8/6/1922) was a force on the PGA Tour throughout the 1950s, his accomplishments during that decade exceeding all but Hogan, Snead, Middlecoff and perhaps Lloyd Mangrum. All told, 15 of Ford's 19 Tour victories came between 1952 and 1959 and at mid-decade he would win three times in three separate years (1953, '55 and '57) while being named Player of the Year in 1955. That was a season in which Ford logged 20 top-10 finishes and won his first Major championship, the **PGA,** where he defeated Middlecoff in a final so well played that Ford shot 66 during the morning 18 and still stood 1 down. He would eventually win 4 and 3.

Ford's second great year came in 1957 when he defeated Jay Hebert by one to win the **Los Angeles Open,** then later took a four-way play-off to capture the **Western Open.** In between, he closed with a then-record 66 (including a holed bunker shot at the 72nd) to overtake Snead and win the **Masters** by three. A year later he would finish second at Augusta, one back of Arnold Palmer, and save for a tie for fifth at the 1959 U.S. Open, that would be it so far as contending in Major championships. Ford's final Tour win overall came at the 1963 **Canadian Open** where, at age 41, he defeated Al Geiberger by one. Though largely retired from competitive play by the mid-1970s, Ford continued to display his game by utilizing his past champion's exemption into the Masters until the ripe old age of 77.

PGA Tour Wins (19): 1954 Greensboro; **1955 PGA Championship;** 1957 Los Angeles; **1957 Masters;** 1957 Western Open; 1959 & '63 Canadian Open; 1962 Bing Crosby

Ryder Cup: 1955–61 (4)

1949-1967

	49	50	51	52	53	54	55	56	57	58	59	60	61	62	63	64	65	66	67
Masters	-	-	-	T21	T21	T33	-	T6	1	T2	T25	T25	T32	T44	T11	T46	T31	T17	T31
US Open	MC	MC	41	T19	T21	T35	T7	T9	T17	34	T5	T33	T6	T8	MC	MC	-	MC	-
British	-	-	-	-	-	-	-	-	-	-	-	-	-	-	-	T24	-	-	-
PGA	-	-	-	-	-	-	1	T17	T9	T11	T11	T7	T5	5	T27	MC	T20	MC	MC

Gerald Ford (USA)

The 38th President of the United States, Gerald R. Ford (b. 7/14/1913) was the most avid golfer among modern presidents, often sneaking away from the White House for a quiet round, frequently playing with many of the top Tour stars of the day. In addition to sponsoring his own Pro-Am event in Vail, Colorado, Ford was a regular in the Palm Springs area, frequently appearing in the Bob Hope Desert Classic. The President, alas, was not nearly so fine a golfer as he was a football player at the University of Michigan, his often-wild tee shots causing Hope to quip that Ford "made golf a contact sport."

Robert Forgan (UK)

A St. Andrews man, Robert Forgan (1835–1900) apprenticed under his uncle Hugh Philp before becoming one of early British golf's most accomplished and celebrated clubmakers. Unlike many more specialized shops, Forgan built both wooden clubs and irons ("cleeks") as well as the occasional gutta-percha ball. His reputation was such that a stint at Forgan's did wonders for one's résumé, assuring a constant supply of talented clubmakers on the payroll. A real craftsman, Forgan is reported to have had an especially fine eye for wood, selecting a supply from the lumberyard, then hammering an R into the chosen timber to be certain he received precisely that which was selected. He was also duly proud of being appointed clubmaker for the Prince of Wales, stamping his product with the Prince's seal (later the royal crown) and advertising the affiliation on his shopfront signage. Though Forgan died in 1900, his son and grandson would carry the firm on into the 1930s when it was ultimately bought out by Spalding.

Ron Forse (USA)

A native of Glen Ridge, New Jersey, with a landscape architecture degree from West Virginia University, Ron Forse (b. 1956) has, since the early 1990s, made a significant name for himself as a top restorer of classic Golden Age courses. Though he has also completed a number of original new designs, Forse's reputation for re-creating old features without attempting to leave his mark has landed all manner of plum assignments including such mainstays as Lawsonia GC (Wisconsin), Indian Creek CC (Florida), Riviera CC (California), and several well-known clubs around Philadelphia.

Keith Foster (USA)

After working for five years with architect Arthur Hills (largely heading up the firm's Phoenix office), Keith Foster (b. 1958) went solo in 1991. Since then he has built a number of new courses primarily in the Western states while also establishing himself as a popular renovator of older facilities. In addition to work done at the historic Baltimore CC, Foster has executed high-profile projects at Oklahoma's Southern Hills (in advance of the 2001 U.S. Open) and the Colonial CC in Ft. Worth, Texas, an annual PGA Tour stop.

George Fotheringham (UK/South Africa/USA)

After learning the game as a caddie and clubmaker at Carnoustie, Kerrimuir native George Fotheringham (1883–1971) emigrated to South Africa in 1903 where he served for 12 years as professional at Royal Durban GC, then for two at the Houghton CC. During this period, he claimed the title of the country's best player from Laurie Waters by winning the **South African Open** in 1908, '10, '11, '12, and '14, and finishing second to his brother Jack in 1909. In his final victory, Fotheringham finished an astonishing 20 shots ahead of runner-up Jock Brews, a margin that will likely never be exceeded. For reasons not recorded, Fotheringham left South Africa for America in 1915, where he would play a bit of competitive golf but mostly focused on club jobs, which would be his primary source of income for many more years.

John Fought (USA)

Within a 10-day period in the late summer of 1977, John Fought (b. Portland, Oregon, 1/28/1954) played on a victorious American Walker Cup team and won the **U.S. Amateur** in a 9 and 8 rout of Doug Fischesser at the Aronimink GC in Philadelphia. After graduating from Brigham Young the following year, he embarked on a PGA Tour career that began red hot with back-to-back wins (at the **Buick Open** and **Anheuser-Busch Classic**) and a

Rookie of the Year award in 1979 before slowly fizzling out over a seven-year span. Never claiming another Tour victory, Fought turned his attention toward golf course design in 1986, teaming with Bob Cupp for a full decade before striking out on his own in 1995. Working primarily in the Western states, Fought has teamed, on occasion, with PGA Tour star Tom Lehman and is engaged in several projects with the 1996 British Open champion at the time of this writing.

James Foulis Jr. (UK/USA)

One of five brothers born to James Foulis, Sr., longtime foreman of Tom Morris' golf shop at St. Andrews, young James (1870–1928) was taught the game by Old Tom and helped to construct several courses designed by the legendary pro. He emigrated to the United States in 1895 to serve as the first professional at Chicago GC and soon proved himself an able competitor by winning the second official **U.S. Open,** defeating Horace Rawlins by three at Shinnecock Hills in 1896. Over the next two decades, James would hold several Chicago-area professional jobs while also developing a very successful club manufacturing concern with his brother David (J & D Foulis Company). He also designed courses as a sideline, the original layout of the Denver CC being perhaps his most recognizable solo effort. In 1917, Foulis became pro-greenkeeper at the brand-new Olympia Fields CC, supervising (though not designing) the building of the club's four famous courses. In 1922, with all four complete, he resigned to pursue architecture full time, working alone until 1927, then partnering with Ralph Wymer until his death at age 58 in Chicago.

Robert Foulis (UK/USA)

Three years younger than his brother James, Robert Foulis (1873–1945) also worked in Old Tom Morris' pro shop as a youth, not playing much competitive golf after suffering two childhood eye injuries. He emigrated to America in 1896, soon assisting his brother, H. J. Tweedie, and H. J. Whigham in the design of the Onwentsia Club (site of the 1899 U.S. Amateur and 1906 U.S. Open). Robert then stayed on as the club's first professional until 1902 when he left to serve at another club that he helped to build, St. Louis' Glen Echo CC. For many years he traveled extensively throughout the Midwest, teaching the game and laying out additional courses, including nine holes at Minnesota's Minikahda Club and the original 18 at Bellerive in St. Louis. Foulis retired in 1942 and died three years later in Orlando, Florida.

Walter Fovargue (USA/Japan)

After serving as professional at Chicago's Skokie CC for 10 years, Walter G. Fovargue moved west where he sold golf equipment, competed successfully as a reinstated amateur, and helped Wilfrid Reid and James Donaldson to lay out the Lakeside G&CC, forerunner of today's Olympic Club. Several years later he moved north to Washington and then, in the early 1920s, across the Pacific to Japan. There he did much to expand the game's growing popularity, and his layout at Yokohama's Hodogaya CC is generally considered Japan's first "modern" design, completed nearly a decade ahead of C. H. Alison's seminal Hirono and Tokyo CC projects.

Herbert Fowler (UK/USA)

Born: Tottenham, England, 5/28/1856 **Died:** London, England, 4/13/1941

William Herbert Fowler, the product of an upper-class English family, had the height (6′4″) and athleticism to make him a force at cricket. Golf didn't enter his life until age 35, though in characteristic fashion, he was playing to scratch and joining both the R&A and the Honourable Company of Edinburgh Golfers with relative dispatch. A banker by trade, Fowler entered the field of golf course design when a group led by his brother-in-law financed the construction of Walton Heath GC in 1904 and, as has frequently been the case, built what many consider to be his best course right out of the box.

More work naturally followed, and Fowler soon formed a partnership with a young Tom Simpson, Fowler handling the British designs, Simpson those throughout the rest of Europe. Easily too old for military service, Fowler spent time in the United States during World War I, becoming involved in a handful of projects. He returned in 1920 when he completed the North course at Los Angeles CC (with George Thomas, who later rebuilt it) and Cape Cod's ultra-natural Eastward Ho! Fowler's British work is considerably more extensive as he continued practicing there well into the 1930s, supplementing original layouts with redesigns of such standards as Saunton, Royal North Devon, Ganton, and Royal Lytham & St. Annes. J. F. Abercromby and A. C. M. Croome would also join Fowler and Simpson, though most of Fowler's designs were completed without their input. Once referred to as "perhaps the most daring and original of all golfing architects" by Bernard Darwin, Fowler was always known as Herbert in golfing circles, yet is listed as Bill in many cricket records..

Notable Courses: Beau Desert GC; **The Berkshire GC (36); Cruden Bay G&CC;** Eastward Ho! GC, Massachusetts; **Walton Heath GC (36)**

Peter Fowler (Australia)

Peter Fowler (b. Sydney, 6/9/1959) looked a potential star when, in his early 20s, he captured the 1983 **Australian Open** by three strokes over Ian Baker-Finch at Kingston Heath. With subsequent wins at the **Queensland PGA** and the **Australian Match Play,** he trundled off to Europe with high hopes but never quite scaled the mountain, placing no higher than 22nd on the Order of Merit, though he was regularly in the top 60. Six times a runner-up, he finally won at the 1993 **BMW International** when a closing 63 beat Ian Woosnam by three. He also partnered Wayne Grady to an Australian **World Cup** win in 1989, claiming individual medalist honors in the process. Though Fowler has struggled since the mid-1990s, of late there have been signs of improvement.

Henry Fownes (USA)

Much like George Crump of Pine Valley fame, Pittsburgh's Henry Clay Fownes (1856–1935) was an affluent businessman and a devout golfer who yearned to build a world-class course. A competitor in the 1901 U.S. Amateur in Atlantic City, Fownes clearly wanted something demanding. Thus, in 1903 he produced Oakmont CC, Pittsburgh's famously difficult track, which will soon be hosting a record eighth U.S. Open. Fownes ran Oakmont for more than 20 years, eventually overseeing the significant 1920 renovation (performed by greenkeeper Emil Loeffler), which shaped most of the layout still in play today.

William Fownes Jr. (USA)

Chicago-born William Clark Fownes Jr. (1877–1950) bears the odd distinction of being a "Jr." whose name differs from that of his father, for he was the son of Henry but named instead after his uncle. In any event, William was a fine player, capturing **Pennsylvania Amateurs** in 1910, '12, '13, and '16, and landing the big prize, the **U.S. Amateur,** at The Country Club of Brookline in 1910. Though often remembered for helping to keep Oakmont the most brutally difficult course imaginable, Fownes was also selected captain of the first American Walker Cup team in 1922 (after leading an unofficial squad to England a year earlier), then returned to play in the 1924 event. He also served as USGA president in 1926 and '27.

Carlos Franco (Paraguay)

Though born into a family of nine living in a one-room home, Carlos Franco (b. Asunción, 5/24/1965) was raised in a golfing environment, for his father was a greenkeeper and caddie while all five of his brothers also became golf professionals. A 19-time winner throughout South America by his late 20s, Franco soon found success in Asia where he won six times beginning in 1994. By 1998 he was a member of the International team in the Presidents Cup, a rare accomplishment in that he'd only played a total of five PGA Tour events up to that point. Fully exempt in America the following year, he wasted little time in winning twice, at **New Orleans** and **Milwaukee,** becoming the first South American to win on the Tour since Roberto de Vicenzo in 1969. A powerful striker of the ball despite standing only 5'9" and weighing 165 pounds, Franco successfully defended his **New Orleans** title in 2000. Then, after three seasons without a victory or a money-list position better than 94th, he won his second **Greater Milwaukee** title during a strong summer of 2004.

Emmet French (USA)

Among the most overlooked American players of all time, Philadelphian Emmet French learned the game as a caddie at Merion, later serving as an assistant professional at that hallowed club before moving on to York CC (Pennsylvania), Youngstown CC (Ohio), and, for a number of years, North Carolina's Southern Pines GC. A three-time winner of what are today deemed official PGA Tour events, the big, burly French was a regular contender in a number of big events during the years after World War I, running second to Hagen at the 1919 Metropolitan Open, tying for second behind Macdonald Smith at the 1925 Western Open (played on his home course at Youngstown), and fifth at the 1921 U.S. Open. His most notable finish was his runner-up to Gene Sarazen at the 1922 PGA at Oakmont, losing 4 and 3 in the final after experiencing a uniquely terrible break: With the match all square, French's second to the par-5 27th hit the metal base of the flagstick on the fly and ricocheted back some 20 yards into a bunker, causing him to lose the hole and much of his momentum. Ironically, he and Sarazen had been roommates in Oakmont's clubhouse all week before separating on the eve of the final. French also served as captain of the American team that engaged in an informal 1926 match with the British at Wentworth, the immediate forerunner of the Ryder Cup.

David Frost (South Africa)

A 1985 arrival on the PGA Tour, David Laurence Frost (b. Cape Town, 9/11/1959) appeared at a time when international players were a bit less common in the United States, though his eventual record of 10 Tour wins and nearly $8.6 million in official earnings certainly proved him to be anything but a novelty. While he was, as former CBS announcer Ben Wright loved to remind us, "a former member of the constabulary," Frost was also teacher David Leadbetter's first high-profile disciple. It was Frost's image (not Nick Price or Nick Faldo's) that illustrated Leadbetter's first book *The Golf Swing.*

Between 1982 and 1999, Frost amassed an impressive 22 overall wins including two **South African Opens,** three **Million Dollar Challenges,** and a **Hong Kong Open** internationally. On the PGA Tour he captured the **World Series of Golf, Canadian Open** and **Colonial,** plus a memorable 1990 **New Orleans Classic** where his holed bunker shot at the 72nd beat a luckless Greg Norman by one.

Like many of Leadbetter's charges, Frost is not overly long but with his sound, compact swing is capable of remarkable precision (and consequent low numbers) when going well. It seems odd then that in 57 Major championship starts, he has logged only seven top-10 finishes—and that his best result, a tie for fifth, came at the 1995 Masters, where length has long been considered a primary component.

PGA Tour Wins (10): 1989 World Series; 1992 Westchester; 1993 Canadian Open; 1997 Colonial
Intn'l Wins (12): 1986 & '99 South African Open; 1993 Hong Kong Open; 1994 South African PGA
Presidents Cup: 1994 & '96 (2)

Kinya Fujita (Japan)

The American-educated son of a wealthy Japanese banking family, Kinya Fujita (1889–1969) discovered the game of golf in the States, joining the Tokyo GC upon returning home. By the late 1920s, Fujita led a group of Tokyo members who broke away to form their own club, Kasumigaseki, whose East course he would design (with help from Shiro Akaboshi) in 1929. Changes would be made to the layout by the visiting C. H. Alison in 1930, and three years later Fujita (this timed aided by a young Seiichi Inouye) would add a West course of comparable stature. Fujita designed several additional prewar Japanese layouts and many more (including numerous reconstructions) afterward. He also fathered the design career of Inouye, who would go on to become Japan's best-known architect.

Pierre Fulke (Sweden)

Though a regular on the European tour since the early 1990s, Sweden's Pierre Fulke (b. Nyköping, 2/21/1971) found his career-best form in 2000, returning from a seven-month layoff (caused by hand problems) to take victories at the **Scottish PGA** and the prestigious **Volvo**

Masters, as well as 12th place on the 2000 Order of Merit. With a runner-up finish to Steve Stricker at the 2001 WGC-Match Play event in Australia and a 2002 Ryder Cup appearance, Fulke appeared ready for a place on golf's center stage. With subsequent drops to 35th and 88th places in the 2002 and '03 Orders of Merit, however, we must now wonder if we have seen his best stuff.

Fred Funk (USA)

A former golf coach at his alma mater, the University of Maryland, popular Fred Funk (b. Takoma Park, Maryland, 6/14/1956) has been a model of consistency on the PGA Tour, winning six times and pocketing nearly $15 million since 1990. His best season may well have been 1995 when he won twice (at **Pleasant Valley** and the **Buick Challenge**) though ironically, his two highest finishes on the money list (1999 and 2002) came in years when he did not record a victory. Frequently the Tour's most accurate driver, Funk boasts the sort of solid, reliable game that has allowed him to continue cracking the top 30 on the money list well into his forties, actually playing his way onto the 2004 Ryder Cup team and winning the 2005 **Players Championship**, both at age 48.

Ed Furgol (USA)

Forever recalled as the man with the withered left arm, Edward J. Furgol (1917–1997) broke the ill-fated limb while growing up in New York Mills, New York, and, upon having it badly set, ended up with a near-70-degree crook at the elbow. Unfazed, he developed a compact, very powerful swing that obviously relied heavily upon both proper body action and a strong right side. The result was a win at the 1945 **North & South Amateur** (where he unceremoniously routed Frank Stranahan 6 and 5 in the final) and, eventually, a much-chronicled winning of the 1954 **U.S. Open** at Baltusrol.

The Open triumph (by a single shot over Gene Littler) was certainly worthy of publicity, but few seem to recall that Furgol was more than a one-hit wonder, winning a total of six PGA Tour events including the 1947 **Bing Crosby** (his first victory), the 1954 **Phoenix Open,** and, in 1957, the old **Agua Caliente Open,** a lucrative event held at a long-defunct resort community in Tijuana. Named Player of the Year in 1954, Furgol appeared on one Ryder Cup team, losing in singles to Dai Rees in 1957.

Marty Furgol (USA)

One of the few things more incredible than Ed Furgol's ability to win a U.S. Open with his damaged left arm is the notion of Marty Furgol (b. 1918) being from the same upstate New York town (New York Mills), being born only a year before Ed, and yet not being related. But so it has long been reported and so, thus far, it remains. For his part Marty never won a Major championship but in taking the 1951 **Western Open** in Davenport, Iowa (edging Dr. Cary Middlecoff) he came fairly close. All told, Marty was a five-time PGA Tour winner, a member of the 1955 Ryder Cup team, and really a rather solid performer in his own right.

Jim Furyk (USA)

The possessor of the PGA Tour's most recognizable swing, former University of Arizona star James Michael Furyk (b. West Chester, Pennsylvania, 5/12/1970) takes the club back almost brushing his right thigh, then appears nearly to loop it twice, outside toward the top, then back inside on the downswing. It is an ungainly move to be sure, yet it produces a reliable power fade that stands Furyk among the game's most accurate drivers. Combined with the highly effective cross-handed putting stroke he has used since childhood, Furyk's methods are enough to make the purist cringe. However, when examining the nine wins and nearly $20 million he has pocketed in 10 years on Tour, one is tempted to wonder why more young players aren't copying him.

Some of Furyk's impressive monetary winnings result from thrice capturing one of the Tour's most lucrative events, the **Las Vegas Invitational.** He has also been a consistent winner, notching a victory a year annually between 1995 and 2002 (save for 1997) and finishing no lower than 33rd on the money list during that span. In 2003 he stepped his game up a notch, winning twice and breaking through at Olympia Fields to capture the **U.S. Open,** for his first Major championship. Played on a golf course weakened by unchecked equipment advances, the Open saw Furyk set 36- and 54-hole scoring records before closing, under tougher conditions, with a fine 72 to tie the all-time Open mark of 272.

Though sidelined for most of 2004's first half with wrist surgery, Furyk was back in time to unsuccessfully defend his Open title and to make his fourth consecutive Ryder Cup appearance (1997–2004). Also a Presidents Cup veteran, Furyk's international experience and past Major championship record (13 top 10s in 34 starts) are enough to suggest that further big-event success lies ahead.

G

Terry Gale (Australia)

Raised on a wheat farm in rural Western Australia, Terry Gale (b. Wyalkatchen, 6/7/1946) first came to note by dominating that state's play in the early 1970s, capturing four **Western Australia Amateurs,** two state **Opens,** and the big prize, the 1974 **Australian Amateur.** As a professional he primarily remained Down Under with the exception of venturing to Britain for the Open Championship, sometimes supplementing it with a handful of surrounding events. Never a winner outside of Australasia, Gale managed 22 regional victories including four more **Western Australian Opens** and the national Opens of **Singapore, Indonesia,** and **Malaysia** (thrice), plus a pair of wins in Japan. Since turning 50, he has played more regularly on the European Senior Tour with some success, notching six titles since 1996.

Bernard Gallacher (UK)

One of the more tenacious competitors among Britain's postwar professional flock, Scotland's Bernard Gallacher, C.B.E. (b. Bathgate, 2/9/1949) was an 11-time winner on the European Tour between 1971 and 1984. Two of his most prominent victories came in 1974 and '75 when he won back-to-back **British Masters,** defeating Gary Player in sudden death in the former, then beating another South African, Dale Hayes, by two at Ganton (with a high total of +5) in the latter. A **Spanish Open** title followed in 1977 and Gallacher again beat a strong field (Faldo and Ballesteros among the top five) at the 1979 **French Open.** He also twice claimed the old **Martini International,** in 1971 and '82.

Currently a competitor on the European Senior circuit, Gallacher is held in the highest esteem for an excellent Ryder Cup record, going 13-13-5 while competing in all eight matches from 1969 to 1983. This record can be better appreciated when we recall that his teams went an anemic 0-7-1 during this stretch—and that Gallacher's successes included singles victories over Lee Trevino (1969), Jack Nicklaus (1977), and Lanny Wadkins (1979).

Angel Gallardo (Spain)

The best of three talented golfing brothers, Barcelona's popular Angel Gallardo (b. 7/29/1943) was the first Spanish professional to compete worldwide, playing on five continents and winning as far away as Colombia and, in 1971, at the **Mexican Open.** In Europe he was a four-time winner including three national Opens, the **Portuguese** (1967), the **Italian** (1977), and his crowning moment, the 1970 **Spanish** at Nueva Andalucia. A former caddie who, like many Europeans, turned professional while still in his teens, Gallardo regularly represented Spain in the World Cup in the pre-Ballesteros years of the early 1970s.

Robert Gamez (USA)

A former Walker Cupper (1989) and collegiate Player of the Year at the University of Arizona, Las Vegas' Robert Gamez (b. 7/21/1968) made a major splash in 1990 as a PGA Tour rookie, winning both the **Tucson Open** and the **Bay Hill,** the latter by holing out a 176-yard 7-iron at the last to victimize Greg Norman by one. He has enjoyed little similar success since, however, logging no more American wins and ultimately falling outside of the top 125 money winners between 1998 and 2001. An 85th-place finish suggested a modest renaissance in 2002, however, followed by a resurgent $1.5 million and 43rd place in 2003, then a somewhat quieter 2004.

Pepe Gancedo (Spain)

A two-time **Spanish Open Amateur** champion and successful businessman, José "Pepe" Gancedo (b. 1938) turned his hand to golf course design in 1975 with Torrequebrada GC, an imaginative but wholly difficult test situated on the Costa del Sol near Marbella. Though very well regarded among modern Continental courses, Torrequebrada became something of a template for Gancedo, with most of his subsequent designs managing, in the words of prominent architect/critic Tom Doak "to toe the line between interesting and crazy." The fact that Gancedo, whose work has appeared almost exclusively in Spain, has been dubbed "the Picasso of golf design" might serve to tilt the scales toward the latter.

Ivan Gantz (USA)

A native of Baltimore, Ivan "The Terrible" Gantz (1907–1990) never made much noise as a PGA Tour player (though many swore he was skilled enough) but he certainly became a golfing legend for his temper. Tales abound—many apocryphal, to be sure—of Gantz hurling himself head-first into bunkers, impaling himself on a cactus, or beating his head against trees, simply overwhelmed with anger at one bad shot or another. Gantz did own up to occasionally braining himself with his putter after missing a short one, though *not*, as is sometimes reported, knocking himself cold. Eventually he smartened up, using his fists instead of a club "so I wouldn't kill myself." Yet Gantz, by most accounts, was otherwise pleasant company. Indeed, Pete Dye, who knew him well, probably summed Ivan Gantz up best by saying: "Everybody liked him. He was everybody's friend. He never hurt anyone else. He only attacked himself."

Jean Garaialde (France)

France's top postwar professional, Ciboune native Jean Garaialde (b. 10/2/1934) was a dominant force when playing amongst his own, winning 16 **French Closed** titles between 1957 and 1975 against, we must admit, limited competition. However he also proved himself competitive around the Continent, particularly in the years just preceding the organizing of the modern European Tour. In 1969, his high watermark, Garaialde took his lone **French Open** (the first native son to win the event in more than two decades) as well as the **Spanish** and **German** titles, the latter being successfully defended in 1970. Appearing in the 1964 and '66 Masters, he also defeated Jack Nicklaus in 1970 in Sweden and played in a record 25 World Cups before scaling back his schedule to only rare appearances by the mid-1980s.

Sergio Garcia (Spain)

Nicknamed "El Niño," Spanish professional Sergio Garcia Fernandez (b. Castellon, 1/9/1980) was a genuine golfing prodigy, winning his club's men's championship at age 12 and making the cut in a PGA European Tour event (the 1995 Turespana Open Mediterranea) only two years later. That same season, he became the youngest-ever winner of the **European Amateur,** a title he matched with a **British Amateur** crown in 1998. All told, Garcia would win 19 titles as an amateur (plus the professional **Catelonian Open**) and make the cut in 12 of 18 European Tour events entered, placing his professional prospects among the most anticipated of recent memory.

In the event, his results have been solid—and really rather more were Garcia not being compared, inevitably, with Tiger Woods. He has, for example, won five times on the PGA Tour and six times internationally, and nearly all of these titles have come in strong-field events of significance. Further, he placed a memorable second to Woods at the 1999 PGA Championship and logged top-10 finishes at all four Majors (plus the Players Championship) of 2002. Tiger or no Tiger, it is a record of which any under-25 player can be rightly proud.

Plagued by occasional inconsistency, however, Garcia undertook major swing changes in 2003, attempting to maintain a more upright posture while reducing the ultra-flat, Ben Hogan–like lag at the start of his downswing. The initial results were sketchy, with only two top 10s and a 95th-place finish (his lowest to date) on the American money list. But by mid-2004 Garcia was back on form, twice winning in America (at the **Byron Nelson** and **Westchester**) and playing in his third consecutive Ryder Cup, where he has already inherited the legacy of his countryman Seve Ballesteros by posting a 10-3-2 record between 1999 and 2004. Also possessing shotmaking skill reminiscent of Ballesteros and fellow Spaniard José Maria Olazábal, Garcia has thus far been able to maintain a comfortable playing balance between Europe and the United States—something which Seve, for one, was never able to master.

Though not yet as consistent as players like Woods, Ernie Els, or Vijay Singh, Garcia's remains a rosy future.

PGA Tour Wins (5): 2001 Colonial; 2001 Westchester; 2004 Byron Nelson; 2004 Westchester
Intn'l Wins (2): 1999 Irish Open; 2001 Trophée Lancôme
Ryder Cup: 1999–2004 (3)

1996-2004

	96	97	98	99	00	01	02	03	04
Masters	-	-	-	T36	T40	MC	8	T28	T4
US Open	-	-	-	-	T46	T12	4	T25	T20
British	MC	-	T29	MC	T36	T9	T8	T10	MC
PGA	-	-	-	2	T34	MC	T10	MC	MC

Robert A. Gardner (USA)

A large figure in World War I–era amateur golf, Hinsdale, Illinois, native Robert Abbe Gardner (1890–1956) was an exceptional all-around athlete (once holding the world pole vault record) who initially made noise as the youngest-ever winner of the **U.S. Amateur** when he defeated H. Chandler Egan in the 1909 final while just a freshman at Yale. Though not a major factor for the duration of his school days, Gardner was back in form in time to capture a second **Amateur** in 1915, defeating John G. Anderson 5 and 4 at the Detroit CC. He then looked good to defend a year later at Merion, only to be dumped 4 and 3 in the final by a streaking Chick Evans.

After serving in the war, Gardner continued to compete, narrowly missing a British Amateur title in 1920 at Muirfield. There, having defeated Michael Scott in the semis, he pulled even with final opponent Cyril Tolley with a birdie at the last, only to lose to Tolley's subsequent birdie at the 37th. Gardner would suffer late-round losses at the U.S. Amateur in 1921 and '23, with his continued good play landing him on the first four Walker Cup teams. Amassing an overall record of 6-2, he served as a playing captain in 1923, '24 and '26.

Ron Garl (USA)

A 1967 graduate of the University of Florida, Ron Garl (b. 1945) entered the golf design profession after only the briefest of apprenticeships, primarily as a field man for veteran designer Joe Lee. Opening his own shop in Lakeland in 1969, he has since become a dominant force in Florida, completing approximately 75 new layouts statewide. A designer of varying styles, Garl has built large championship tests (Bloomingdale Golfers Club and TPC Prestancia), shorter, more user-friendly tracks, and even a course utilizing famous replica holes (Golden Ocala). Developing an international practice in recent years, Garl has undertaken projects in Canada, Costa Rica and the Bahamas, while his Alpine Golf & Sports Club in Bangkok is a recent host of the PGA European Tour's prominent Johnnie Walker Classic.

Antonio Garrido (Spain)

A solid European Tour player for many years, Madrid-born Antonio Garrido (b. 2/22/1944) also bears the distinction of having been, along with Seve Ballesteros, the first Continental Europeans ever to participate in the Ryder Cup, in 1979 at The Greenbrier. This selection came at the height of his powers, when Garrido was in the midst of placing five times in the Order of Merit top 10 between 1976 and 1982, including a career-best third in 1977. Not surprisingly, three of his five official wins came during this period, including the 1977 **Madrid Open,** the inaugural **Tunisian Open** (1982) and Garrido's biggest title, the 1977 **Benson & Hedges International**, where he beat Bob Charles by three. A five-time **Spanish PGA** champion who also teamed with Ballesteros to win the 1977 **World Cup**, Garrido played in the 1978 Masters before later claiming European Senior Tour wins in 1994 and '97.

Ignacio Garrido (Spain)

The son of the highly successful Antonio Garrido, Ignacio (b. Madrid, 3/27/1972) frequently caddied for his father as a youth but would later join him in a more meaningful way, when Ignacio's selection to the 1997 Ryder Cup team made the Garridos only the second father-son pair (after Percy and Peter Alliss) to participate in golf's premier team event. A two-time winner on the European Tour, Ignacio's biggest moment to date came at the 2003 **Volvo PGA** at Wentworth when he closed 66-65, then defeated a hot Trevor Immelman in sudden death.

Philomena Garvey (Ireland)

A retail saleswoman by trade, Drogheda's Philomena Garvey (b. 4/26/1927) dominated Irish women's play for the quarter-century following World War II, winning the **Ladies** championship an amazing 14 times in 18 tries between 1946 and 1963, then tacking on one final victory (following a brief fling with professionalism and an amateur reinstatement) in 1970. Sporting a perfect 15-0 record in Irish finals, Garvey clearly established herself as that nation's finest female player since the early days of Rhona Adair and the Hezlet sisters, thus making her regular assaults on the **British Ladies** title of particular interest.

In the main, Garvey certainly proved her worth by reaching the British final five times, though she was defeated on four occasions, including losses to such international stars as Marlene Streit (1953), Barbara McIntire (1960) and Brigitte Varangot (1963). She did, however, prevail in 1957, defeating Jessie Valentine 4 and 2 at Gleneagles, and thus established herself indelibly as more than just an Emerald Isle phenomenon. As skilled a long iron player as the ladies' game had to that point witnessed, Garvey participated in six Curtis Cup matches between 1948 and 1960 (missing only 1958), though her overall record of 2-8-1 was unspectacular. Partial atonement may have been made, however, during an informal 1951 match against a team of visiting American professionals wherein Garvey took the indomitable Babe Zaharias to the final green—a loss which might well be considered more impressive than any amateur victory.

Jean Gassiat (France)

Biarritz native Jean Gassiat (b. 1883) finished runner-up to Arnaud Massy at the second French Open in 1907, no small accomplishment in that he beat James Braid and a large British contingent in the process. Unfortunately, this result largely symbolized Gassiat's playing career, for Massy, six years older and also from Biarritz, remains, nearly a century later, France's best-ever golfer, with the eminently capable Gassiat generally laboring in his shadow. Gassiat did win the 1912 **French Open** at La Boulie (as well as the lesser **French PGA** title four times) and in 1913 joined Massy, Louis Tellier and Etienne Lafitte on a team that swept American pros Johnny McDermott, Mike Brady, Alex Smith and Tom McNamara in one of the game's early international contests. Gassiat also finished as high as seventh in the Open Championship (1912), and it seems a good bet that, had a larger number of Continental Opens been in existence during his peak years, his name would be far better known today.

Jane Geddes (USA)

Perhaps somewhat overlooked amidst the bigger names that populated the LPGA Tour during the late 1980s and '90s, Jane Geddes (b. Huntington, New York, 2/5/1960) was a highly consistent player who finished among the top 20 money winners 11 times, pocketing over $3 million and 11 tour titles. Significantly, she counted two Major championships among these wins, the 1986 **U.S. Women's Open** (where she beat Sally Little in an 18-hole play-off) and the 1987 **LPGA Championship,** victories which served to anchor fifth- and third–place money finishes over a two-year, seven-win stretch. Geddes remained competitive long enough to participate on the 1996 and 2002 Solheim Cup teams and was assistant captain (to Patty Sheehan) in 2003.

Al Geiberger (USA)

Though the feat has several times been matched in this era of unchecked equipment, former USC star Al Geiberger (b. Red Bluff, California, 9/1/1937) earned the nickname "Mr. 59" in round two of the 1977 **Memphis Classic** when, on a Colonial CC course measuring all of 7,249 yards, he became the first player ever to break 60 in a PGA Tour event. A testing eight-footer was required on the last green to do so and, curiously, Geiberger failed even to break 70 in the other three rounds, though he still managed to win the tournament by three.

Known for his syrupy tempo, Geiberger claimed 10 additional Tour wins, the biggest being the 1966 **PGA Championship** at Firestone CC, where he beat Dudley Wysong by four. He then suffered through a health-related slump between 1969 and 1972 but, recovered and rejuvenated, returned to win seven times between 1974 and 1979. The 1976 **Western Open** was an obvious prize, but Geiberger also scored an odd double at Ft. Worth's Colonial CC, winning the second **Players Championship** there in 1975 (one year before it moved permanently to Florida), then capturing the 1979 **Colonial Invitational** for his final Tour win. Twice a Ryder Cup player (with a 5-1-3 record), Geiberger saw only limited action on the Champions Tour due to continuing health problems.

PGA Tour Wins (11): 1966 PGA Championship; 1975 Players Championship; 1976 Western Open; 1979 Colonial
Ryder Cup: 1967 & '75 (2)

Vic Ghezzi (USA)

Born: Rumson, New Jersey, 10/19/1910 **Died:** Miami, Florida, 5/30/1976

An 11-time winner on the PGA Tour, Vic Ghezzi first found the limelight at the 1935 **Los Angeles Open** where, at age 25, he defeated Johnny Revolta in a play-off at the Los Angeles CC. The following season, looking to step up a notch, he stood among the 54-hole leaders at the U.S. Open at Baltusrol but plummeted to 18th place with a final-round 81. Undaunted, Ghezzi persevered, proving himself a regular winner by amassing eight titles prior to his biggest victory, the 1941 **PGA Championship** at Denver's Cherry Hills CC. On this memorable occasion, Ghezzi defeated Lloyd Mangrum one up in the semifinals, then trailed Byron Nelson by three after 27 holes of the final, before roaring back to force extra holes. At the 38th, with their three-foot par putts too similar to resolve by measurement, a coin was flipped, Nelson won, and promptly missed. Ghezzi then holed his to claim the title.

Ghezzi would only win twice more on Tour, and then not until 1947 and '48, but he did participate in an epic three-way play-off for the 1946 U.S. Open with Lloyd Mangrum and Byron Nelson. Over 18 holes at the Canterbury GC, all three men shot 72s, necessitating a second 18 in which Mangrum's 72 edged Nelson and Ghezzi by one. In a case of terrible timing, Ghezzi never appeared in an actual Ryder Cup match, being selected for the 1939 event (which was cancelled due to World War II), then joining 1941 and '43 teams that existed solely to play war charity fundraisers.

PGA Tour Wins (11): 1935 Los Angeles; 1938 North & South; **1941 PGA Championship;** 1947 Greensboro

1932-1955

	32	33	34	35	36	37	38	39	40	41	42	43
Masters			T25	8	T15	T8	T10	T12	T39	T6	-	
US Open	T45	-	MC	20	T18	T20	T11	T29	15	19		
British	-	-	-	-	-	-	-	-				
PGA	T17	T17	T9	T17	T9	T9	-	-	T17	1	T17	

	44	45	46	47	48	49	50	51	52	53	54	55
Masters			T12	21	T18	T35	T14	WD	T30	WD	T29	T53
US Open			T2	T6	T14	T37	-	-	-	MC	MC	-
British			-	T18	-	-	-	-	-	-	-	-
PGA	-	T5	T17	T3	T33	-	T33	T9	T9	T33	-	T17

Althea Gibson (USA)

Pioneering athlete Althea Gibson (1927–2003) was born to sharecroppers in Silver, South Carolina, but grew up in Harlem and North Carolina, ultimately developing tennis skills that would make her the minority-oriented American Tennis Association's singles champion for 10 consecutive years (1947–56). Eventually becoming the first black to play in mainstream events, she made history by winning both Wimbledon and the U.S. Open in 1957 and '58, as well as the French Open and several Wimbledon doubles titles. Turning to golf soon thereafter, Gibson developed her game quickly, becoming the first black member of the LPGA in 1963. Though never a top-flight Tour player, she was a steady money winner during the latter half of the 1960s and came closest to winning at the 1970 Buick Open, where she and Sandra Haynie both lost in sudden death to Mary Mills.

Gibby Gilbert (USA)

A consistent money winner on the PGA Tour primarily during the 1970s, Chattanooga, Tennessee, native C. L. "Gibby" Gilbert Jr. (b. 1/14/1941) was capable of the occasional low number, as evidenced by his stunning 62 at the 1973 World Open, which bettered the previous Pinehurst No. 2 course record by three strokes. Though a three-time Tour winner and runner-up at the 1980 Masters (four behind Ballesteros), Gilbert was one of many who have found greater success on the Champions Tour, garnering six wins and more than $5.5 million between 1992 and 1997.

Bob Gilder (USA)

A walk-on to an Arizona State team that included Tom Purtzer, Howard Twitty and Morris Hatalsky, Bob Gilder (b. Corvallis, Oregon, 12/31/1950) was eventually named honorable mention All-American before failed attempts at getting his PGA Tour card sent him abroad. He won the 1974 **New Zealand Open** during one such sojourn, notable because he defeated Bob Charles and Jack Newton in a play-off to do it. Finally securing his American playing privileges in 1976, Gilder went on to win some six PGA Tour titles, the first and last coming on familiar ground at the **Phoenix Open** in 1976 and '83.

Gilder's career-best year came in 1982 when he finished sixth on the money list and won the **Byron Nelson,** the **Bank of Boston Classic** and the **Westchester Classic,** the latter long remembered both for his winning total of 261 and a third-round double eagle scored on national television. A Ryder Cup performer in 1983, Gilder remained competitive on Tour throughout that decade before enjoying substantial success on the Champions Tour, winning seven times and over $9 million between 2001 and 2003.

Vinnie Giles (USA)

One of America's top career amateurs of the modern era, Marvin M. "Vinny" Giles (b. Charlottesville, Virginia, 1/4/1943) was a three-time All-American at the University of Georgia before pursuing a career as an investment banker in Richmond, Virginia. Highly competitive at the national level throughout the 1960s and '70s, Giles initially finished second in three consecutive stroke-play U.S. Amateurs, in 1967 at the Broadmoor (losing to Bob Dickson), 1968 at Scioto (one behind Bruce Fleisher), and 1969 at Oakmont (trailing Steve Melnyk). A third-place followed in 1971 before Giles finally claimed the **Amateur** crown in 1972, defeating Mark Hayes by three at the Charlotte CC (North Carolina). Giles cemented his elite status in 1975 by capturing the **British Amateur** at Hoylake, soundly defeating Mark James 8 and 7 in the final. A two-time **Southern Amateur** champion (1967 and '75), seven-time **Virginia Amateur** winner, and low amateur at the 1968 Masters,

Giles was a mainstay of four consecutive Walker Cup teams between 1969 and 1975.

J. Hamilton Gillespie (UK/USA)

Originally hailing from Moffett, Scotland, former Honourable Company member J. Hamilton Gillespie (1852–1923) moved to Sarasota, Florida, in 1885 where he proceeded, in the following year, to carve out a basic two-hole course on land which today sits amidst the city's downtown area. As the game's first authority in the Sunshine State, Gillespie was asked to help design early courses for Henry Plant's resort hotels at Tampa and Clearwater, as well as other layouts as far away as Jacksonville and Havana, Cuba. As an attorney and civic booster of the youthful Sarasota, Gillespie eventually sacked his two-holer for a formal nine, returned to Scotland during World War I, then resettled in Sarasota where, many years after his death, the city named a nine-hole municipal course after him in 1977.

Stewart Ginn (Australia)

Long-haired Melbourne native Stewart Ginn (b. 6/2/1949) topped the Australian Order of Merit in 1973, just two years after turning professional, but seldom regained such heights throughout his under-50 playing career. All told Ginn won nine times in Australia, as well as the national Opens of **Malaysia** (1977), **New Zealand** (1979), and **India** (1992). An occasional visitor to Europe, his sole triumph there was the 1974 **Martini International** in Harrogate, England, where he edged Brian Huggett by one. After turning 50, Ginn came to America and found some success, surprising many observers by capturing the 2002 **Senior Players Championship.**

Bill Glasson (USA)

For a man whose medical history reads more like an NFL linebacker than a professional golfer, Fresno, California, native Bill Glasson (b. 4/29/1960) has enjoyed remarkable success on the PGA Tour, finishing nine times among the top-60 money winners while claiming seven official victories. A two-time All-American at Oral Roberts, Glasson was well known as one of the Tour's longer hitters during his prime years, a status at least somewhat diminished by surgeries to his elbows, knees, sinuses and forearm, plus early 1990s back problems that nearly drove him from the Tour altogether. But healthy and on his game, Glasson often proved himself capable of playing with the best, winning the 1985 **Kemper Open** with a final-round 64, edging Fred Couples for the 1989 **Doral Open,** and again closing with 64 to take the 1994 **Phoenix Open.** Curiously, despite being a strong tee-to-green sort, Glasson logged only one top-10 Major championship finish in 29 starts, that being a tie for fourth at the 1995 U.S. Open at Shinnecock Hills.

Jackie Gleason (USA)

Known theatrically as "The Great One," actor/comedian Jackie Gleason (1916–1987) was another in a long line of golfing celebrities who gave the game great prominence in both their on- and offstage lives. Though not a highly skilled player, the genial and rotund Gleason was certainly avid, particularly after moving his TV show to Florida during the 1960s, and later as host of the PGA Tour's Jackie Gleason Inverrary event (today's Honda Classic). Gleason's hit program *The Honeymooners* featured perhaps the funniest golfing episode in television history, in which Gleason's character Ralph Kramden, picking up a club for the first time, mutters the immortal line: "I can't learn to play golf in two days; it would take at least a week."

George Glennie (UK)

A civil engineer by trade, George Glennie (1818–1886) was an elite golfing talent in the days before national championships, making his mark by winning numerous medals at places like Westward Ho!, Hoylake, and St. Andrews, and especially at Blackheath, where he would spend the last 18 years of his life as club secretary. Among Glennie's many accomplishments, two especially stand out. The first came at the 1855 Autumn meeting of the R&A at which he won the Gold Medal with a splendid 88, setting a new St. Andrews scoring record that would last for 29 years. The second came two years later when Mr. James Fairlie of Prestwick organized what amounted to a forerunner of the Open Championship, a foursomes event contested at St. Andrews among teams representing some 13 prominent clubs. Representing Blackheath, Glennie teamed with another native Scot, Captain J. C. Stewart, to win what proved to be a one-time event, resulting in a small piece of history—as well as lifetime memberships at Blackheath—for both men.

Also a captain of the R&A in 1884, George Glennie would surely be well known today had the British Amateur (which didn't arrive until 1895) been around to provide him with a large enough stage.

Ronnie Glennie (South Africa)

Born in Johannesburg, Ronald William Glennie (b. 1915) was a fine all-around athlete known for both his consistency and great style on the golf course. Winner of the 1949 **South African Amateur** (defeating Jimmy Boyd 3 and 2 at Maccauvlei) and runner-up in 1952, Glennie bore the odd distinction of having earlier won the nation's **Open** title in 1947, a memorable event in that four amateurs finished among the top five. A winner of numerous South African titles who shot a remarkable 62 in 1948, Glennie, a career amateur, was reportedly told by his father that if he ever elected to turn professional, he'd better be ready to change his name.

Bob Goalby (USA)

An excellent all-around athlete and an 11-time winner on the PGA Tour, former University of Illinois star Bob Goalby (b. Belleville, Illinois, 3/14/1929) is undoubtedly best remembered for being involved, albeit peripherally, in one of golf's great tragedies. At the 1968 **Masters,** Goalby lingered within the reach of the leaders for 54 holes before uncorking a superb 66 on Sunday, apparently tying him with popular Argentinean Roberto de Vicenzo at 277. As history sadly records, however, de Vicenzo signed a scorecard incorrectly kept by his partner Tommy Aaron and was thus credited with a 278 total, leaving Goalby, who was essentially an innocent bystander, as a highly unpopular champion.

Goalby's additional accomplishments are quite credible and include being the 1958 Rookie of the Year, a 1963 Ryder Cupper (where he went 3-1-1), the 1961 **Los Angeles Open** champion, and the winner of three additional events in the years following that fateful Masters. He also still holds a piece of the PGA Tour record for consecutive birdies (eight) and, earlier in his career, posted second-place finishes at the 1961 U.S. Open and the 1962 PGA. Yet by failing ever to win another Major championship, Goalby will always be remembered for *l'affaire de Vicenzo.* Considering that stories abound of a bad temper and borderline etiquette breaches early in his career, perhaps, in the end, this is just as well.

PGA Tour Wins (11): 1958 Greensboro; 1961 Los Angeles; 1967 San Diego; **1968 Masters;** 1970 Heritage
Ryder Cup: 1963

Vickie Goetze-Ackerman (USA)

Thus far a journeywoman on the LPGA Tour, Vicki Goetze-Ackerman (b. Michicot, Wisconsin, 10/17/1972) enjoyed one of the contemporary era's finest amateur careers prior to turning professional. An eight-time AJGA All-American and three-time National Player of the Year (1988–1990), she would win two **U.S. Women's Amateurs** (1989 and '92), participate in two Curtis Cups (1990 and '92) and claim the 1992 **NCAA** Championship, all while attending the University of Georgia. But despite this remarkable résumé, Goetze-Ackerman's pronounced lack of length has hindered her at the professional level, resulting, to date, in zero wins and a career-best money ranking of 33rd in 2002.

Lindy (Jennings) Goggin (Australia)

A winner of 18 **Tasmanian Ladies** titles between 1967 and 1990, the athletic Lindy Goggin (b. 1949) has been one of Australia's top female amateurs since her late teens, capturing three national **Ladies** titles in 1971, '77 and '80 while finishing runner-up in 1972 and '82. Not content to simply beat up on the area competition, however, Goggin journeyed to the U.S. Women's Amateur twice in the early 1980s, reaching the final in 1981 after coming back from 4 down to beat future LPGA star Rosie Jones in the semis. The next day, she led defending champion Juli Inkster 1 up with 2 to play before losing to back-to-back birdies—the only birdies either player recorded all day. The next year in Colorado Springs, Goggin returned to the semifinals, this time losing to Cathy Hanlon 6 and 4. A regular Australian team member in international play, Goggin passed on a likely successful professional career abroad in order to raise a family and racehorses at home.

John Golden (USA)

A native of Austria-Hungary who developed his championship skills after emigrating to the New World, Johnny Golden (1896–1936) was one of the more successful players of the 1920s and '30s. Due to his straightness off the tee, he was the twice-requested foursomes partner of Walter Hagen in Ryder Cup matches (1927 and '29) as well as one of the Haig's rare vanquishers at the PGA

Championship, defeating the five-time champion over a then-record 43 holes in 1932. Golden's top individual wins included the 1924 **Texas Open,** the 1931 **Agua Caliente Open,** and the 1932 **North & South Open.** He died of pneumonia in 1936.

Isa (Bevione) Goldschmid (Italy)

Though perhaps the epitome of the big fish in a small pond, Isa Goldschmid (b. 1925) dominated postwar Italian women's golf at a level perhaps unmatched in the game's history, collecting 21 **Italian Closed Ladies** titles, including a run of 15 straight from 1953 to 1967—an impressive streak no matter who the opponents. She also took 10 **Italian Open** titles as well as the national championships of **Spain** (1952) and **France** (1975), the latter coming relatively late in her career and against better competition. Combined with her brother Franco Bevione, the siblings took a total of 35 Italian Closed titles, rather more than Joyce and Roger Wethered's five British championships—but whom would the smart money be betting on?

Mario Gonzalez (Brazil)

Mario Gonzalez (b. 1923) remains the greatest player ever produced by Brazil, having dominated that nation's championships to an unmatched degree. Prior to turning professional, the lean, smooth-swinging Gonzalez won the 1940 **Argentine Open,** the 1947 **Spanish Open,** the Brazilian **Amateur** a record 11 times, and competed in the 1948 Open Championship at Muirfield. He took the **Argentine** title again in 1953 (this time getting paid for it) and quite literally made a habit of winning the **Brazilian Open,** claiming eight titles overall, seven of which fell between 1946 and 1955. Though scarcely challenged when facing his own countrymen, Gonzalez proved himself capable of competing with the best by appearing in three Masters, and by defeating Billy Casper in a 1962 episode of *Shell's Wonderful World of Golf* played at Rio de Janeiro's Gavea G&CC, his home course from 1949 on.

Johnny Goodman (USA)

Few prominent amateurs have come from as impoverished a background as Nebraska's Johnny Goodman (1908–1970), an orphan who traveled in a cattle car to reach the 1929 U.S. Amateur at Pebble Beach—where he sent the great Bobby Jones packing in the opening round. Goodman went on to establish himself as an elite amateur competitor, surely America's best in the years immediately following Jones' retirement in 1930.

Along with Jones, Travers, Ouimet and Evans, Goodman stands among the only men to win both the **U.S. Open** and **Amateur,** capturing the former first in 1933. Playing at Chicago's North Shore GC, Goodman's remarkable second-round 66 staked him to a lead he would not relinquish, though eventual two-time Open winner Ralph Guldahl would creep within a stroke at the close. The U.S. Amateur title came tougher. In 1935 Goodman reached the semifinals and looked every bit a winner before young Lawson Little made four birdies over the final six holes to beat him. A year later he was back in the semis, this time losing 2 and 1 to eventual champion Johnny Fischer. Finally in 1937, at Portland's old Alderwood CC, he defeated Bud Ward one up in the semis, then Ray Billows two up in a close final to capture the Havemeyer Trophy.

Three times a Walker Cupper (1934–38) and winner of the **Trans-Mississippi** in 1927, '31, and '35, Goodman in many ways represents the high watermark of American amateur golf, for he remains the last amateur to win the U.S. Open and, some 70 plus years later, looks very much like staying that way.

Retief Goosen (South Africa)

In a nation where golf has long enjoyed great popularity, it can be argued that only the larger-than-life presence of Ernie Els has stood between Retief Goosen (b. Pietersburg, 2/3/1969) and the role of heir to South African greats Bobby Locke and Gary Player. Indeed, Goosen appears to possess all the requisite qualities for greatness: a rhythmic, rock-solid swing, great length, a putter capable of catching fire and a smooth, measured temperament. He has, however, had to deal with sporadic health problems, including the lingering effects of being struck by lightning during his amateur years.

For many in America, Goosen appeared to come out of left field when he won the 2001 **U.S. Open** at Southern Hills, though in reality he had by this time won the 1990 **South African Amateur,** six professional titles in his homeland (including the 1995 **South African Open**) and four more in Europe, had played in three World Cups, and competed against the Americans in the 2000 Presidents Cup. His victory at Southern Hills came following a bizarre Sunday afternoon in which Goosen, Mark Brooks and Stewart Cink all blew chances of victory by three-putting the 72nd green. Having missed what amounted to a two-foot chance to win the Open, an unruffled Goosen returned Monday to methodically best Brooks by two for both his first Major championship and a spectacular arrival on the American stage.

In the ensuing three years he would win twice more in the States and five times overseas, finish first in the European Order of Merit in 2001 and '02, claim the 2001 **World Cup** title (with Els), log two top-10 finishes on the American money list (each with less than 20 starts), and finish second at the 2002 Masters, three shots behind Tiger Woods. This was a powerful record by any measure, yet Goosen still seemed to surprise many when he emerged from the wreckage of another USGA course set-up debacle to win his second **U.S. Open** in 2004 at Shinnecock Hills, putting the lights out on Sunday before benefiting from a disastrous 71st-hole meltdown by Phil Mickelson.

He followed this with subsequent victories at the **European Open** and, with a closing 64 to overtake Tiger Woods, the season-ending **Tour** Championship, showing that in his mid-30s Goosen is perhaps just entering his prime on both sides of the Atlantic.

PGA Tour Wins (5): 2001 & '04 U.S. Open
Intn'l Wins (17): 1995 South African Open; 1997 & '99 French Open; 2000 & '03 Trophée Lancôme; 2001 Scottish Open; 2002 Johnnie Walker; 2004 European Open
Presidents Cup: 2000 & '03 (2)

1993-2004

	93	94	95	96	97	98	99	00	01	02	03	04
Masters	-	-	-	-	-	MC	-	T40	MC	T2	T13	T13
US Open	-	-	-	-	-	MC	MC	T12	1	MC	T42	1
British	MC	-	-	75	T10	MC	T10	T41	T13	T8	T19	T7
PGA	-	-	-	-	T61	MC	MC	MC	T37	T23	MC	-

William Gordon (USA)

A fine athlete who served in the Navy during World War I, Rhode Island native William Gordon (1893–1973) got into the golf construction business soon thereafter, building courses for several famous architects (including Willie Park Jr., Devereux Emmet and Donald Ross) before being hired by the outstanding Philadelphia designer William Flynn in 1923.

Rather resourcefully going into the business of seeding military installations during World War II, Gordon eventually became a practicing architect in 1950, working primarily in the Northeast and Middle Atlantic regions where he completed more than 50 new designs. Perhaps because Flynn's name appeared so prominently on his résumé, Gordon also landed a number of plum remodeling jobs throughout the region, performing varying degrees of work at places like Canoe Brook (New Jersey), Saucon Valley (Pennsylvania), and several of Flynn's Philadelphia-area classics. He also built nine new holes at New Jersey's prestigious Seaview GC (turning a 1931 Flynn nine into 18) and added six new holes to Flynn's classic Lancaster CC (Pennsylvania).

Notable Courses: Medford Village GC, New Jersey; **The Stanwich Club, Connecticut**

David Gossett (USA)

Though already having one PGA Tour victory to his credit, young David Gossett (b. Phoenix, Arizona, 4/28/1979) is thus far best known for winning the 1999 **U.S. Amateur** at Pebble Beach, playing in that year's Walker Cup, and being named a first-team All-American each of the two years he attended the University of Texas. Generally considered the number one amateur in the country, Gossett turned pro in 2000, shot a 59 at Qualifying School, and, in only his fifth PGA Tour start, won the 2001 **John Deere Classic** by a stroke. He did not, however, finish higher than 68th on the money list during his first three seasons before plummeting badly in 2004.

Isabella Gourlay (UK)

There are few records to consult regarding the golfing prowess of Isabella Gourlay, though she is generally believed to have been the finest woman golfer in a very limited nineteenth-century field. A descendant of the famed ball manufacturers of Musselburgh, Isabella married prominent player/architect Tom Dunn and was the mother of John and Seymour, both of whom found their golfing fortunes in America. But with no recorded events to play in (the British Ladies title not arriving until 1893), Gourlay's great talent must remain unquantified—though, undeniably, much revered.

John Gourlay (UK)

John C. Gourlay (1815–1869) of Musselburgh was a son of the famous feathery ballmaker William Gourlay and the father of Isabella, wife of Tom Dunn. The feathery was virtually synonymous with the Gourlays, its leading manufacturers, so for John the arrival of the gutta-percha ball was an ominous moment indeed. To this point Darwin related a wonderful story wherein Captain Maitland Dougall and James Balfour were playing the first gutty rounds ever seen at Musselburgh: "Gourlay, the chief ball-maker there, came out to watch them: he saw at once that the game was up as far as the poor feathery was concerned, and having a standing order to send Sir David Baird some balls when he had any to spare, sent him six dozen."

Molly Gourlay (UK)

England's Mary Perceval Gourlay, O.B.E. (1898–1990) was one of Britain's better amateur golfers in the years after World War I, capturing the **English Ladies** title in 1926 and '29. In an era when British players routinely competed throughout the Continent, she won three **French Opens** (1923, '28, and '29), three **Swedish Opens** (1932, '36, and '39) and twice in **Belgium,** and participated in the first two Curtis Cup matches—both losses—in 1932 and '34.

Considered a rock-solid ball-striker, Gourlay was a driving force in the founding of both Britain's Ladies Golf Union and the English Ladies Golf Association and was a rules expert of nationwide renown. Interestingly, she was also among the first women to become involved in golf course architecture, assisting the famous Tom Simpson on a handful of projects (including renovation work at Ballybunion and County Louth) during the 1930s.

Jimmy Grace (Australia)

A largely undocumented figure of Golden Age golf, Jimmy Grace was an Australian whose talents were sung by Victor East, the influential professional with whom he spent the 1920s working at North Carolina's Biltmore Forest CC. It was East's contention that Grace, an epileptic, had a superior swing and world-class talent but could not compete because of his affliction, though East related that he had played private matches with both Walter Hagen and Bob Jones. Returning to Australia during the Depression, Grace coached a very young Peter Thomson before eventually dying in Coburg, Victoria in relative anonymity.

Wayne Grady (Australia)

Professional golf has seen a fair number of comets, players capable of successfully competing at the game's highest levels for two or three seasons before slipping, for one reason or another, back into the pack. Queensland's Wayne Grady (b. Brisbane, 7/26/1957) proved himself just such a player when, after a fairly quiet career that included single victories in Australia and Germany, he upset the iconic Greg Norman in a play-off for the 1988 **Australian PGA.** Emboldened, Grady returned to America (where he had previously struggled) to win the 1989 **Westchester Classic,** then, several weeks later, led the Open Championship until the 71st hole before losing (along with fellow Queenslander Norman) in a four-hole play-off to Mark Calcavecchia.

But Grady persevered and a year later became the eighth Australian to win a Major championship by capturing the **PGA** at Shoal Creek, leading after 36 holes and hanging on to win by three. Though a second **Australian PGA** would follow in 1991, Grady had by now seen his best both at home and abroad, and though he continued to play 15 to 20 American events a year, he would never place better than 140th on the money list after 1992. He is today a businessman, broadcaster, and golf course designer in Queensland.

Herb Graffis (USA)

A golf writer and columnist for the Chicago *Sun Times,* Logansport, Indiana, native Herb Graffis (1893–1989) made his largest contribution to the game's American development as a publisher, organizer and general booster of golf. Partnered with his brother Joe, he began his publishing business with the *Chicago Golfer* in 1923, soon following it with the trade publication *Golfdom* (1927) and the more general *Golfing* (1933). The Graffis brothers also were the driving forces behind the National Golf Foundation, the still-active trade organization founded in 1936, and Herb was an original organizer of the Golf Writers Association of America (1946).

A popular and highly entertaining man, Graffis authored several books, ghost wrote numerous others and played a supporting role in producing Tommy Armour's very successful instructional volumes. A 1977 inductee into the World Golf Hall of Fame, he has also been honored by the establishment of the National Golf Foundation's Herb Graffis Award, given for significant contributions to the growth of junior golf.

David Graham (Australia)

Born and raised in the Melbourne suburb of Windsor, Anthony David Graham (b. 5/23/1946) initially took up golf left-handed, playing that way for two years before turning himself around. Against the vehement opposition of his father he was an assistant professional at 14 and, within a few short seasons, the head man at a nine-holer in Tasmania. Always a diligent practicer, Graham developed a solid tee-to-green game that demonstrated marked precision with his irons, catching the attention of American agent Bucky Woy who signed him up in 1969.

Like all top Australian prospects, Graham became a truly international player, spending the northern hemisphere winter competing at home and packing off to Asia, Europe, and America for the duration. A win at the 1970 **French Open** (as well as subsequent victories in Thailand, Venezuela, and Japan) got him his sea legs and when he captured the PGA Tour's 1972 **Cleveland Open** (in a playoff with close friend Bruce Devlin), Graham was truly on the map. In 1976 he rose to eighth on the American money list, largely off wins at **Westchester** and the old **American Golf Classic,** then took one more big step by defeating Hale Irwin over 38 holes at Wentworth to claim the **World Match Play** title.

Though a winner of his native **Australian Open** in 1977, Graham's first Major triumph came at the 1979 **PGA Championship** at Oakland Hills, a more-exciting-than-necessary affair which saw him needing par at the last for a remarkable 63 and a two-shot victory. Blowing his approach long of the green, he staggered to a double-bogey and found himself in sudden death with Ben Crenshaw, a contest Graham won with a birdie at the third after holing from 25 feet at the first just to stay alive. The following year a birdie at the 72nd won Jack Nicklaus' prestigious **Memorial Tournament,** but Graham's greatest triumph would come in 1981, at the **U.S. Open** at Merion. There he trailed 54-hole leader George Burns by three before playing as fine a closing round as the championship had seen, a three-under-par 67 in which Graham hit all 18 greens and won, going away, by three.

By now 35, Graham remained highly competitive for several more seasons while also getting actively involved in both club and course design. Settling primarily in America, he has become something of a forgotten man among his era's best players, though he did reintroduce himself by taking five Champions Tour titles upon turning 50.

PGA Tour Wins (8): 1976 Westchester; **1979 PGA Championship;** 1980 Memorial; **1981 U.S. Open**
Intn'l Wins (18): 1970 French Open; 1976 World Match Play; 1977 Australian Open; 1977 South African PGA; 1980 Mexican Open; 1981 & '82 Trophée Lancôme
Champions Tour Wins: 5 (1997–1999)

1970-1990

	70	71	72	73	74	75	76	77	78	79	80
Masters	-	T36	MC	T29	-	-	-	T6	T9	WD	5
US Open	MC	MC	T47	T58	T18	T29	MC	MC	MC	7	T47
British	T32	T72	-	-	T11	T28	T21	T69	T39	-	T29
PGA	-	-	MC	MC	-	T10	T4	MC	MC	1	T26

	81	82	83	84	85	86	87	88	89	90
Masters	7	19	46	T6	T10	T28	T27	-	-	-
US Open	1	T6	T8	T21	T23	T15	T51	T47	T61	64
British	T14	T27	T14	T71	T3	T11	34	MC	T61	T8
PGA	T43	T49	T14	T48	T32	T7	MC	T17	MC	T66

Jack Graham (UK)

A rather private man dedicated more to his friends and business than to big-time golf, Hoylake's John "Jack" Graham Jr. (1877–1915) was described by Bernard Darwin as "beyond any doubt the finest amateur golfer who never won a championship, and a far, far better player than many who did." By all accounts Graham was a marvelous iron player and an expert in the wind who simply lacked the temperament to survive a solid week's high-pressure golf. "A great runner," Darwin opined, "but a poor racer."

Bound to playing tournament golf by "a sad-eyed loyalty to his admirers," the easygoing Graham reached the semifinals of the British Amateur on four occasions, falling 7 and 5 to Harold Hilton in 1900, 1 down to John L. Low in '01, 1 down to Gordon Barry in '05, and 4 and 3 to H. E. Taylor in 1908. Graham did score victories in numerous regional events, often of the less-involved two-round variety, and it is surely ironic that such a genial, self-effacing man would die leading his troops into battle during the Great War.

James Graham (UK/Australia)

James Graham emigrated from Fife, Scotland, to Melbourne, Australia during the mid-1840s, bringing with him a cache of hickory-shafted golf clubs and old-fashioned feathery balls. In 1847 he enlisted the help of several friends in establishing the Melbourne Golf Club, playing over ground now occupied primarily by the Flagstaff Gardens. Though the club expired in late 1850 (presumably from lack of interest), its documented existence made it Australia's first organized golfing entity. That

Alexander Reid's informal private course in Tasmania predated it by anywhere from five to 25 years likely meant little to the Melbourne crowd as they almost certainly had no inkling of its existence.

Lou Graham (USA)

Those who claim that extreme USGA course setups often bring less-established players into the **U.S. Open** contention have a solid example in Lou Graham (b. Nashville, Tennessee, 1/7/1938), a man who'd never finished better than 19th on the money list and held only two minor victories prior to winning the Open in 1975. Playing at Medinah, Graham, a quiet man from the University of Memphis, trailed a red-hot Tom Watson by 11 at the halfway mark before jumping back into the fray with a third-round 68. A closing two-over-par 73 rather amazingly left Graham in a tie with John Mahaffey before his 71 took the Monday play-off by two strokes. A three-time Ryder Cup player (1973, '75, and '77) Graham enjoyed two other top-five Open finishes and, in 1979, tore his way to three late-career wins in two months at the **Philadelphia** and **Pleasant Valley Classics** and the **Texas Open.**

Grand Duke Michael (Russia)

Grand Duke Mikhail Mikhailovich (1861–1929) was unceremoniously expelled from Russia in 1891 after being blamed for the fatal heart attack suffered by his mother upon hearing of his secretly marrying his longtime mistress. So banished, he came to live in Cannes, then later in England, traveling a great deal and becoming that most un-Russian of creatures, an avid (though not terribly good) golfer. In addition to frequenting courses throughout Britain, Michael (who managed a distinctly royal lifestyle despite his exile) is credited with building at least two layouts in France, a long-deceased nine-holer near Pau as well as the trendy (in 1920) Golf de Cannes Mandelieu. He died in London under some financial strain, his prospects dimming considerably following the Russian Revolution of 1917.

Douglas Grant (USA/UK)

For most, Californian Douglas Grant (1887–1966) is best remembered as the codesigner of the world-renowned Pebble Beach Golf Links, though in truth this represented a relatively minor chapter in a fascinating golfing life. The product of one of the Golden State's wealthiest families, Grant suffered degenerative hearing loss at a young age yet still flourished on the links, winning both the **Northern California** and the **Pacific Amateurs** by the time he

was 22. Sent to the United Kingdom in or about 1910 to broaden his horizons, he married a British girl and spent the remainder of his life shuttling back and forth between the United Kingdom and the Monterey Peninsula, laying out Pebble Beach (in conjunction with local real estate man Jack Neville) during an extended 1916 visit.

When abroad, Grant established himself as one of Britain's finest amateur golfers, winning numerous local and regional events and generally being considered the equal of all but Cyril Tolley and Sir Ernest Holderness. He eventually retired to California, ultimately perishing in a Carmel house fire at age 79.

George Grant (USA)

An 1870 graduate of Harvard Dental School who practiced in the Boston area for decades, George Franklin Grant (1846–1910) was, by all indications, America's first black golfer, likely taking up the game in the mid-1880s and playing primarily in a field adjacent to a property he owned in suburban Arlington Heights. Grant also bears the distinction of first patenting the concept of the golf tee in 1899, though he apparently held no commercial aspirations for his invention and manufactured only enough to give to his friends. Consequently, when New Jersey dentist William Lowell patented his own tee a quarter-century later (and marketed it through the great Walter Hagen), it was he who long received credit as the inventor before historians put the matter right in the early 1990s.

Ugo Grappasonni (Italy)

A temperamental sort who served as club professional first at Villa d'Este and later at the Olgiata CC in Rome, Ugo Grappasonni (b. 5/8/1922) went neck-and-neck with Alfonso Angelini for the title of Italy's best postwar player. By strictly domestic standards, Angelini's 11 **Italian Closed PGAs** (compared to Grappasonni's four) must carry the day. However, if one bases the decision on the demonstrated ability to win against stronger international fields, then Grappasonni stands taller, having captured single **French** (1949), **Moroccan** (1953) and **Dutch** (1954) **Opens** as well as a pair of **Swiss** titles in 1948 and '52. Perhaps most tellingly, Grappasonni twice won the **Italian Open** (1950 and '54) against strong European fields, a feat never managed by Angelini and accomplished only once by lesser rival Aldo Casera.

Robert Muir Graves (USA)

A native of Trenton, Michigan, Robert Muir Graves (1930-2003) stood among a group of postwar American architects (see Arthur Jack Snyder, Gary Roger Baird, etc.) who evidently saw the prominent use of a middle name as an integral aspect of Robert Trent Jones' period dominance. Educated at the University of California–Berkeley, Graves was primarily a West Coast designer, building more than 45 new courses in California, Oregon and Washington, but finding the majority of his work in the remodeling of perhaps four times that many. A lecturer on landscape and golf architecture at several universities, Graves also coauthored (with Geoffrey Cornish) two prominent contemporary works, *Golf Course Design* (John Wiley & Sons, 1998) and *Classic Golf Hole Design* (John Wiley & Sons, 2002).

Notable Courses: Quail Lodge GC, California; La Purisima GC, California

Downing Gray (USA)

One of several prominent American amateurs who chose the insurance business over the chancy prospects of professional golf, Pensacola, Florida, native Albert Downing Gray Jr. (b. 1938) nearly won the 1962 U.S. Amateur at Pinehurst, standing 5 up on Labron Harris Jr. with 15 to play. But at the 22nd hole, he drove under a tree, made double bogey, dropped the next four holes in rapid succession, and ended up losing 1 down. Low amateur in the 1965 Masters, Gray was twice a Walker Cup participant (1963 and '65) and also twice a captain, losing in 1995 at Royal Porthcawl but winning big in 1997 at Quaker Ridge.

Hubert Green

Hubert Green (USA)

Despite being one of modern golf's most unorthodox players—particularly on the putting green where his split-handed stroke with a Depression-era blade defied all convention—Hubert Myatt Green II (b. 12/28/1946) has been extremely successful, winning 19 PGA Tour events, two Major championships, four Champions Tour titles, and two significant events overseas. A native of Birmingham, Alabama, Green was a good all-around athlete who eventually settled on golf, starring at Florida State and twice winning the **Southern Amateur** (1966 and '69) before making it to the Tour full time in 1971. He won as a rookie at the '71 **Houston Open,** then peaked from 1973 to 1979, when he captured 15 titles while finishing no worse than 13th on the money list.

In 1974 Green won four times and in 1976 he performed the rare feat of winning in three consecutive weeks, first at **Doral,** then in **Jacksonville** and at the **Heritage.** But it was in 1977 that Green scored his greatest triumph, winning the **U.S. Open** at Tulsa's Southern Hills CC when he ignored a phoned-in death threat and defeated 1975 Open winner Lou Graham by one. He might well have won the 1978 Masters but for a missed three-footer at the 72nd (which denied him a play-off with Gary Player). After a quiet period in the early 1980s, Green rallied for his second Major, the 1985 **PGA Championship,** by outdueling Lee Trevino at Denver's Cherry Hills CC.

Always good humored and often quotable ("Ninety percent of the putts you leave short don't go in"), Green has long been a fascinating study with his hunched-over outside-to-inside swing and colorful putting style. Upon reaching 50, he would go on to rack up nearly $8 million in Champions Tour winnings between 1997 and 2003 before health problems slowed him dramatically in 2004.

PGA Tour Wins (19): 1976 Doral; 1976 & '78 Heritage; **1977 U.S. Open; 1985 PGA Championship**
Intn'l Wins (2): 1977 Irish Open
Champions Tour Wins: 4 (1998–2002)
Ryder Cup: 1977, '79 & '85 (3)

1969-1990

	69	70	71	72	73	74	75	76	77	78	79
Masters	MC	-	-	T22	T14	T9	T8	T19	T8	T2	T10
US Open	-	-	-	T55	MC	T26	T18	6	1	MC	24
British	-	-	-	-	-	4	T32	T5	3	T29	T41
PGA	-	-	-	T16	DQ	T3	-	T30	T62	T26	T16

	80	81	82	83	84	85	86	87	88	89	90
Masters	4	T11	43	-	-	MC	T36	T35	T19	T34	MC
US Open	T32	T37	MC	T60	T30	MC	T55	MC	MC	T9	MC
British	T6	T23	T77	T19	90	-	77	-	T52	-	-
PGA	T68	T27	MC	MC	T14	1	T41	T56	WD	66	MC

Ken Green (USA)

Despite earning a reputation as an eccentric and a hot-head, Danbury, Connecticut, product Ken Green (b. 7/23/1958) enjoyed a strong run on the PGA Tour during the late 1980s, winning five times, earning over $2 million, and appearing in the 1989 Ryder Cup. Having learned the game in Honduras, where his father was the principal of the American School, Green seemed equally comfortable overseas, winning three substantial events including the 1990 **Hong Kong Open.** Though a winner of the **Canadian** and **Greater Milwaukee Opens** in 1988, Green has since been plagued by injuries and a widely questioned attitude, keeping him well removed from the top 100 money winners since 1993. Still, he continues attempting a comeback—while battling back problems—at the time of this writing.

Tammie Green (USA)

A seven-time winner on the LPGA Tour, 1987 Rookie of the Year Tammie Green (b. Somerset, Ohio, 12/17/1959) experienced her best run during the mid-1990s when she thrice cracked the top-10 money winners over a five-year span, claiming five victories in the process. Her lone earlier triumph was the 1989 **du Maurier Classic,** a Major championship and the cornerstone of her only other top-10 money finish (eighth). A former star at Marshall University, Green is also notable as one of the first ex-Futures Tour players to make it big at the LPGA level, having won 10 events there in the early 1980s before joining the big Tour in 1986. She also appeared on American Solheim Cup teams in 1994 and '98.

Ann (Moore) Gregory (USA)

Before there was Althea Gibson or Renee Powell, there was Ann Gregory (1912–1990), a little-celebrated trailblazer

who was, in fact, *the* barrier-breaker of women's golf. Born in Aberdeen, Mississippi, she took up the game after migrating north to Gary, Indiana, eventually becoming the top female player in the minority-dominated United Golf Association. Gregory's first appearance on the national stage came in 1947 when George S. May invited her to compete in his World Championship of Golf at Chicago's Tam O'Shanter CC, though her most historic entry was the 1956 U.S. Women's Amateur when she became the first black to participate in a USGA-sponsored event. Though never a threat to win the Amateur, Gregory several times advanced into the middle rounds despite having to put up with the sort of senseless harassment (e.g., being barred from the players' dinner at the 1959 Amateur at Congressional) that seldom does anything but motivate a player while leaving an ugly stain on the organization involved.

Malcolm Gregson (UK)

England's Malcolm Gregson (b. Leicester, 8/15/1943) was rated a hot young prospect during the 1960s, particular after his career-best season of 1967 when he won the **Volvo PGA,** tied with Brian Huggett for the **Martini International** and captured the **Daks Tournament** at Wentworth, capping the year with a Vardon Trophy and berths on both the Ryder and World Cup teams. Unfortunately Gregson soon fell off form, defending his **Daks** title in 1968 but failing to win again in Europe thereafter. Since turning 50, however, his luck has proven better on the European Senior tour where he has won four times, most recently in 2003.

Tony Gresham (Australia)

Though neither of his parents were Australian, Anthony Yale Gresham (b. 1940) grew up in Sydney, developing into a career amateur on par with legends Ivo Whitten and Doug Bachli. A consistent performer known especially for his short game, Gresham won the 1977 **Australian Ama-**

teur (in a 40-hole thriller over Christopher Bonython) and was thrice more a finalist in 1973, '76 and '78. He also reached the semifinals of the British Amateur in 1979 and '81 and was a **World Amateur** individual champion in 1972, edging Ben Crenshaw by two in Buenos Aires.

Though one is always skeptical when supporters of an amateur suggest that a great professional career was certain had a different path been chosen, Gresham actually scored a pair of impressive victories over the pros at the 1975 **New South Wales Open** and the 1978 **South Australian Open**. In the latter, he became the event's first-ever amateur winner by an impressive six-shot margin.

Robert Grimsdell (UK/South Africa)

Like so many of golf's early missionaries, Amersham, England's Robert Grimsdell was raised in the United Kingdom before heading abroad, specifically to South Africa, at the ripe young age of 15. After fighting in France during World War I, he returned to Lancashire for a golf professional's job, but went back to the Cape during the 1920s, first serving as pro-greenkeeper at the Mowbray GC, then moving onto the Royal Johannesburg GC in 1926. Here he gradually shifted into full-time course design, initially building Royal Johannesburg's East course in 1933. Performing a good deal of the manual labor himself, Grimsdell was eventually carted off on a stretcher—but not before completing a layout which even today is rated among the best in Africa.

Though firmly rooted in the Golden Age, Grimsdell enjoyed such longevity that he actually built the Maritzburg CC's fine 1935 course, and then its replacement when the club was forced to move some 35 years later. Perhaps most noteworthy among his creations is the Royal Durban GC, a frequent championship venue whose entire facility—clubhouse and all—is situated within the confines of the famous Greyville horse racing track. Having laid out courses from Capetown to the northern reaches of Zimbabwe, Robert Grimsdell must surely go down as one of the African continent's most important golfing figures.

Notable Courses: Maritzburg CC; **Royal Durban GC; Royal Johannesburg CC, East Course;** Sishen GC; The Wanderers GC

Frances Griscom (USA)

The daughter of a shipping magnate who lent the original Merion Cricket Club enough land from his estate to add a second nine, Frances "Pansy" Griscom (1879–1973) was somewhat ahead of her time, being an able trapshooter,

the first known Philadelphia woman to own a car, and a Red Cross ambulance driver in France during World War I. She took up golf in 1897 when her brother gave her a set of clubs and within months reached the semifinals of the **U.S. Women's Amateur**. She again reached the semis in 1898 and, after a first-round exit in 1899, won her only national title in 1900 when she routed Margaret Curtis 6 and 5 at Shinnecock Hills.

A. H. Groom (UK/Japan)

Arthur H. Groom, a British tea merchant, came to Japan on business in 1868 and, taking a liking to both the undeveloped country and a local woman, elected to settle in Kobe. As both a keen mountain climber and golfer, he soon took to exploring the cooler heights of nearby Mt. Rokko and eventually, in 1902, got together with one or two Anglo friends to lay out a rudimentary, sand-greened golf course there. The soon-to-be Kobe GC was Japan's first, making A. H. Groom the Japanese game's father and his mountain retreat its place of birth.

Jack Grout (USA)

An Oklahoman by birth, Jack Grout is best known as the Scioto CC head pro who taught a young Jack Nicklaus how to play the game in the early 1950s. Less known is that Grout had previously worked with Henry Picard in Hershey, Pennsylvania, and that as a younger man, he'd worked at Ft. Worth's Glen Garden CC, where he often played with two of the club's up-and-coming ex-caddies, Ben Hogan and Byron Nelson. The winner of one early PGA Tour event (the 1947 **Spring Lake Invitational**), Grout later taught Raymond Floyd and also authored the not-so-subtly titled *Let Me Teach You Golf As I Taught Jack Nicklaus* (Atheneum, 1975).

Kathy (Baker) Guadagnino (USA)

Raised in South Carolina, Kathy Baker (b. Albany, New York, 3/20/1961) was the surprise winner of the 1985 **U.S. Women's Open** on the Upper course at Baltusrol GC, defeating Judy Clark by three strokes. Perhaps because she would only win once more on the LPGA Tour (at the 1988 **San Jose Classic**), Baker is sometimes portrayed as a flukish champion, but such a characterization ignores an impressive pre-Open record. For Baker (who later played under her married name of Guadagnino) was the 1979 **PGA National Junior**, 1980 **Western,** and 1979 and 1982 **Eastern Amateur** champion, as well as an **NCAA** individual titleist (1982) and a two-time All-American at the University of Tulsa. Also a 1982 Curtis Cup player and twice the low amateur in the U.S. Open prior to her victory, she has more recently worked as a teaching pro in Boca Raton, Florida.

Jesse Guilford (USA)

Nicknamed "Seige Gun," Manchester, New Hampshire's Jesse P. Guilford (1895–1962) was a golfer far ahead of his time, playing a game built almost entirely around power, of which he possessed more than his fair share. Widely recognized as golf's longest hitter of the early 1920s, Guilford won numerous amateur events around New England beginning in 1910, when he took his first **New Hampshire** title at age 14. He first appeared in the U.S. Amateur four years later at Vermont's Ekwanok CC, then reached the semifinals at Merion in 1916. Though unable to repeat this performance over the ensuing five years, Guilford finally claimed the **Amateur** crown in 1921, soundly beating another famously long hitter, Robert Gardner, 7 and 6 at the St. Louis CC.

Guilford was a three-time Walker Cup player (1922–26) who, in the words of Francis Ouimet, "revolutionized the game of golf" by seeing "the value of hitting the ball as far as he could." Ouimet further went on to cite Guilford's all-around skills, noting that "his short game was as good as that of any of the greats of his era."

Ralph Guldahl (USA)

Born: Dallas, Texas, 11/22/1911 **Died:** Sherman Oaks, California, 6/11/1987

The son of Hungarian immigrants, Texan Ralph Guldahl turned professional in 1930 and enjoyed some early suc-cess, finishing second at the 1933 U.S. Open at Chicago's North Shore GC when a missed five-footer at the 72nd left him one stroke behind amateur Johnny Goodman. In the mid-1930s, mired in a horrific slump, Guldahl worked as a carpenter on the Warner Brothers lot in Hollywood. But by the latter half of the decade, he was, if one heavily values Major championship play, arguably the finest golfer in the world.

Guldahl's Major record from 1936 to 1939 remains, to this day, terribly impressive. At the **Masters** he finished second in 1937 and '38, then won it in 1939, coming home in 33 on Sunday to edge Sam Snead by one. At the **U.S. Open,** Guldahl won in 1937 at Oakland Hills, twice shooting 69 to set a new record of 281, thus prompting Robert Trent Jones' controversial makeover of the course prior to its next Open in 1951. In 1938 he defended his title at Cherry Hills, this time closing with a 69 to run away from Dick Metz by six. Perhaps better suited to medal than match play, he wasn't much of a factor at the PGA, but in the era's "other" Major, he won three consecutive **Western Opens** from 1936 to 1938, the last by seven strokes over Snead in St. Louis. Only once an entrant in the British Open (while traveling with the 1937 Ryder Cup team), Guldahl finished 11th in his links golf debut at redoubtable Carnoustie.

As compelling as the tall and powerful Guldahl's run was, his disappearance from the top ranks after 1940 is at least as interesting. Stories abound of his losing his game literally overnight, partially as a result of analyzing his swing for the first time while writing a book. Thus having made his money and tired of the incessant travel, Guldahl essentially left the Tour near the start of the war, though he did appear in a total of six Masters or U.S. Opens after it.

PGA Tour Wins (16): 1936, '37 & '38 Western Open; **1937 & '38** U.S. Open; 1939 Greensboro; **1939 Masters**
Ryder Cup: 1937

1930-1949

	30	31	32	33	34	35	36	37	38	39
Masters					-	-	-	2	T2	1
US Open	T39	T32	T58	2	T8	T40	T8	1	1	T7
British	-	-	-	-	-	-	-	T11	-	-
PGA	-	-	-	-	-	-	-	T17	T17	T17

	40	41	42	43	44	45	46	47	48	49
Masters	T14	T14	T21				48	-	T35	-
US Open	T5	T21					MC	T55	T32	22
British							-	-	-	-
PGA	T3	T9	-			-	-	-	-	-

Bing Crosby, Scotty Chisholm, and Ralph Guldahl

Watts Gunn (USA)

Three years younger than Bobby Jones, Macon, Georgia, native Watts Gunn (1905–1994) followed in his friend's footsteps, playing out of the Atlanta Athletic Club and attending Georgia Tech where, in 1927, he would ride a string of seven consecutive birdies to the **NCAA** individual title. It had been two years earlier, however, that Gunn had hit the national stage, qualifying into match play of the U.S. Amateur at Oakmont at age 20. In a year in which all matches were contested over 36 holes, Gunn quickly fell 3 down in his opener against one V. L. Bradford before reeling off an eye-popping 15 consecutive holes to win 12 and 10. He then dusted off 1922 champion Jess Sweetser 11 and 10 in the second round before eventually losing 8 and 7 to Jones in the first final ever played between members of the same club. Twice a Walker Cup participant and the 1928 **Southern Amateur** champion, Gunn left the national golfing stage after his college graduation in 1930, depriving it of one of its most talented and exciting performers.

Sophie Gustafson (Sweden)

A successful player on the Women Professional Golfers European Tour in the mid-1990s, Sophie Gustafson (b. 12/27/1973) began playing full time in America in 1999. Her greatest success to date came when she won twice in 2000, including the last **Women's British Open** without LPGA Major championship status. Single-win, top-20 money seasons followed in 2001 and '03, bracketing a disappointing '02 in which her money rank fell to 57th. A powerful driver of the golf ball capable of hitting a lot of greens, Gustafson has been a regular selection to the European Solheim Cup team, playing all four events between 1998 and 2003.

Watts Gunn

H

Fred Haas (USA)

Portland, Arkansas, native Fred Haas (1916–2004) was twice a **Southern Amateur** winner (1934 and '37) and the 1937 **NCAA** champion, all while attending Louisiana State. He didn't turn pro until 1945 but would then enjoy a long career that, in total, included five PGA Tour victories. The NCAA title had helped earn him a spot on the losing 1938 Walker Cup team and upon being selected for the 1953 Ryder Cup, Haas became the first man to represent America in both events—an interesting statement on the dichotomy between amateur and professional golf prior to World War II. Though his Tour wins were largely nondescript, the first holds an everlasting place in golf history. For by winning the 1945 **Memphis Open** (while still an amateur), Haas will forever be remembered as the man who ended Byron Nelson's record 11-win streak.

Jay Haas (USA)

A collegiate star who won the 1975 **NCAA** individual title (and was a Walker Cup pick) while at Wake Forest, Jay Dean Haas (b. St. Louis, Missouri, 12/2/1953) has enjoyed an uncommonly long run of success on the PGA Tour, finishing among the top 90 money winners every year but one since 1977. During this span he managed nine official victories (spread out from 1978 to 1993) while also making two appearances each in the Ryder and Presidents Cups. Perhaps most impressively, with his distinctive slow takeaway and improved putting stroke, Haas remained highly competitive—indeed, played some of his best golf—at a late age, being one of Hal Sutton's two captain's picks for the 2004 Ryder Cup after turning 50. The nephew of 1968 Masters champion Bob Goalby, Haas comes from a golfing family, with brother Jerry (an ex-Tour player) coaching at Wake Forest and son Bill a former U.S. Amateur semifinalist and Walker Cup player.

Eddie Hackett (Ireland)

Dublin-born Eddie Hackett (1910–1997) hardly ranks among the greatest of Irish golfers, yet he has left as grand a legacy as any Joe Carr, Christy O'Connor, or Harry Bradshaw. After a successful club pro career that included posts in Belgium, South Africa, and Portmarnock, Hackett turned to golf course design as a second calling, eventually emerging as Ireland's most highly acclaimed architect.

He began building courses in the early 1960s and would ultimately design or remodel roughly 100 layouts, all on the Emerald Isle. Like many a lesser talent, Hackett's name benefited from modest remodeling jobs at famous courses (Ballybunion, Royal Dublin, Portmarnock, etc.) but unlike some, he also left a handful of very fine original layouts as well. Two of his best appeared in the early 1970s, the Waterville GC (where Hackett fashioned a nearly 7,200-yard seaside links) and Connemara, a wonderfully isolated track laid out across stoney terrain in the far west.

Notable Courses: Carne GL; Connemara GC; Donegal GC; **Waterville GC**

Walter Hagen (USA)

Born: Rochester, New York, 12/21/1892 **Died:** Traverse City, Michigan, 10/6/1969

The great Walter Charles Hagen may or may not rank as the finest American golfer who ever lived, such judgments hinging largely upon whether one prefers consistent, well-rounded excellence to stunning, almost epical flashes of brilliance. But there can be little doubt that from the perspective of the modern touring professional, who plays for millions each week and is universally treated like a king, Sir Walter was definitely the most important.

Growing up in Rochester, Hagen learned the game as a caddie and ultimately chose it over a potential career in professional baseball—the anticipated success of which varies from Hagen's version (a sure thing) to that of historians (a longshot, at best). Regardless, golf was fortunate to have him, for in addition to winning numerous tournaments, Hagen was among the first to recognize the financial windfall available in exhibitions, clinics, and various other ancillary enterprises. It was Hagen who pioneered the concept of the exhibition tour, traveling the world over (often with his trick-shooting pal Joe Kirkwood) to demonstrate his skills for hefty fees. Of course, Hagen also used the carrot of exhibitions as an ace in the hole, casually suggesting to opponents he was trailing that they might join him on a lucrative tour upon winning the event in question—which, inevitably, they wouldn't once allowing their thoughts to wander to the grand paydays ahead.

Stories of Hagen's high living abound, though in his later years he admitted that many examples (e.g., showing up at the first tee still in his rumpled evening clothes) were put-ons utilized both for marketing purposes and to distract opponents. So, perhaps, were many of his brasher statements ("Okay boys, who's gonna finish second?"), though Hagen's confidence in his abilities and penchant for delivering in the clutch were both 100 percent real. He was also exceedingly generous (turning over his entire £100 winner's check to his 16-year-old caddie at the 1929 Open Championship, for example) and, more important, a powerful force for social change. The latter was particularly true in class-conscious Great Britain where he and his fellow pros were generally barred from entering the clubhouse at most events. So excluded at the 1920 Open Championship, Hagen proceeded to eat and change his shoes in his rented Austin-Daimler—which his driver parked, naturally, right in front of the Royal Cinque Ports clubhouse. Three years later, upon finishing second at Royal Troon, Hagen was invited inside for the trophy presentation. Politely refusing, he instead invited the large gallery to join him where he was always welcome—at the local pub—and left behind him a very quiet ceremony indeed.

As a player Hagen's entire style was unorthodox, his stance inappropriately wide, his swing handsy and full of sway. He was, by most accounts, a long enough hitter, but his driver in particular was prone to truly spectacular flights of misbehavior. Of course Hagen was also, by universal acclaim, one of golf's all-time great recovery artists, his ability to find the putting surface from parts unknown often breaking the hearts of more orthodox opponents. His short game too was world class (particularly from sand), and his putting—in which he held supreme confidence—was even better. Much of Hagen's ability to walk his highly entertaining golfing tightrope came from having a keen understanding of his own game, for he grasped better than anyone that six or seven bad shots per round were an inevitability, allowing him never to dwell on them but simply to focus upon finding the best route back to civilization.

Hagen first entered the golfing spotlight at the 1913 U.S. Open where, as a complete unknown, he tied for fourth, three shots out of the historic Ouimet-Vardon-Ray play-off. Entering the next year's **Open** at Chicago's Midlothian CC, he commenced with a sterling 68 and never looked back, slipping past Chick Evans (who closed 71-70) by one while routing the rest of the field by seven. Hagen also won consistently among the handful of other important tournaments contested during the World War

Walter Hagen, circa 1930s, Olympia Fields

I era, claiming **Metropolitan Open** titles in 1916, '19, and '20, the **Western Open** in 1916 (and later four more times during the 1920s and '30s), the **North & South** in 1918, and, on only a slightly lesser scale, the **Shawnee Open** of 1916. Thus when he defeated perennial runner-up Mike Brady in a play-off for the first postwar **U.S. Open** in 1919, Hagen became the first American professional to walk away from his club affiliations, making his living entirely from playing golf.

Britain first saw Hagen in 1920 when he and Jim Barnes defeated Abe Mitchell and George Duncan in a prominent exhibition prior to the Open Championship. In the main event, however, he stumbled badly and finished next-to-last, though a victory at the **French Open** before returning home at least salvaged the trip financially. Hagen's first **Open Championship** came two years later at Royal St. George's, where a closing 72 was just enough to edge Duncan (who bogeyed the last for a 69) and Barnes by a single stroke. He finished second in 1923 (when he missed holing out from a bunker at the 72nd to tie, having had the flagstick pulled), then beat Reg Whitcombe by one at

Hoylake in 1924 for his second **Open** title. By the end of the decade, and now in his late 30s, Hagen closed his British account with back-to-back wins in 1928 (beating Sarazen by two at Royal St. George's) and 1929 (routing the field by six at Muirfield), becoming the only American save Tom Watson to claim the title more than three times.

Despite his successes in the national Opens, however, Hagen's true forte was match play, as his unsurpassed record in the **PGA Championship** proves conclusively. He first claimed the PGA title in 1921 (its fourth playing), beating Barnes 3 and 1 at New York's Inwood CC. He would later lose a memorable 1923 final to Sarazen at Pelham (on the 38th hole) before launching his unprecedented streak of four consecutive victories from 1924 to 1927, at the conclusion of which his career record in the event stood at 35-3. Not surprisingly, he also towered on the Ryder Cup stage, claiming a 7-1-1 career record as the Playing Captain of the first five American teams. Hagen also made further match-play history in 1926's "Battle of the Century," a 72-hole contest with Bobby Jones in which the Haig unceremoniously thumped the American icon 12 and 11. Two years later, however, he got a taste of his own medicine when, prior to the Open Championship at Royal St. George's, he was humiliated by the imposing Archie Compston in a similar match (played this time for £750) by the almost unbelievable margin of 18 and 17. Typically undaunted, Hagen righted the ship in time to win the Claret Jug two weeks later, leaving the wealthy but Major-less Compston nearly forgotten in third.

It is unlikely that anyone ever employed gamesmanship more effectively than Walter Hagen, yet he did so with such a mischievous delight that few opponents seemed genuinely to mind. From secretly slipping Sarazen an expensive tie from a fictitious blonde fan (tempting the Squire to search the gallery for her throughout their 1922 challenge match) to laughing off the pressure of a championship-winning putt at the 72nd ("Nobody ever beat *me* in a play-off"), the Haig was always playing the angles and gaining an edge.

In the end his record would include 11 Major championship victories (third all-time), a total which might easily be recalculated to 16 in deference to his five Western Open titles, certainly one of America's three most important events of the pre-Masters era. Yet despite so glowing a ledger, it will always be more for his style and color that Walter Hagen will be best remembered.

There has never been another golfer like him.

PGA Tour Wins (44): 1914 & '19 U.S. Open; 1916, '19 & '20 Metropolitan; 1916, '21, '26, '27 & '32 Western Open; 1918, '23 & '24 North & South; **1922, '24, '28 & '29 British Open; 1922, '24, '25, '26 & '27 PGA Championship;** 1923 Texas; 1931 Canadian Open and 4 Florida West Coast Opens
Intn'l Wins (3): 1920 French Open; 1924 Belgian Open
Ryder Cup: 1927–35 (c) (5) and 1937 Capt

1913-1937

	13	14	15	16	17	18	19	20	21	22	23	24	25
Masters													
US Open	T4	1	T10	7			1	11	T2	5	T18	T4	T5
British	-	-						53	T6	1	2	1	-
PGA				T3			-	-	1	-	2	1	1

	26	27	28	29	30	31	32	33	34	35	36	37
Masters									T13	T15	T11	-
US Open	7	6	T4	T19	T17	T7	10	T4	T58	3	T33	-
British	T3	-	1	1	-	-	-	T33	-	-	-	T26
PGA	1	1	T5	T3	-	T17	T17	-	T17	T33	-	

Marlene (Bauer) Hagge (USA)

A 2002 inductee into the LPGA Hall of Fame, Marlene Bauer (b. 2/16/1934) was a native of Eureka, South Dakota, whose father moved the family to Lakewood, California, as a means of fostering his young daughters' golfing careers. While older sister Alice was a fine player in her own right, it was Marlene who, with her mix of good looks and great talent, drew the lion's share of the attention. Her list of junior titles was a long one, headed by the 1949 double of the **Western Girls** and the inaugural **USGA Junior Girls**. The result was that at age 15 Bauer was chosen as the Associated Press's Woman Athlete of the Year.

In 1950, both Marlene (who was not yet 16) and Alice were among the 13 founding members of the LPGA, traveling to the tour's 15 events in a large motor home with their parents. Though Alice would remain winless, Marlene broke through in 1952, shortly after turning 18, with a win at the **Sarasota Open**. Second and third wins would follow by 1954, allowing Bauer's star to remain near the forefront of the Babe Zaharias/Patty Berg–dominated LPGA pack.

After beginning an eight-year marriage to prominent architect-to-be Bob Hagge (later known as Bob von Hagge), her career year came in 1956, a season in which she won eight times in 24 starts including three straight in late spring, the last being the **LPGA Championship**.

Though never again quite so regal, Hagge's play remained consistently good, with six more top-10 money rankings and a five-win campaign in 1965. Her last LPGA victory came in 1972, but Hagge proved herself a seemingly ageless player, continuing to compete well into the 1990s and making cuts as late as 1993, when she was 59.

LPGA Wins (26): 1956 Sea Island; 1956, '57 & '65 Babe Zaharias; **1956 LPGA Championship;** 1956 World Championship

1947-1974

	47	48	49	50	51	51	53	54	55	56	57	58	59	60
LPGA										-	1	T3	T17	5	10
US Open	T14	-	T6	T6	T4	T2	12	WD	T11	T3	T6	14	T3	T3

	61	62	63	64	65	66	67	68	69	70	71	72	73	74
LPGA	T13	T11	T19	T8	T7	T17	T17	19	4	25	19	T3	T24	T28
US Open	19	T8	T13	T7	T12	T25	T20	-	-	T26	T15	27	MC	T44

Paul Hahn (USA)

An unsuccessful PGA Tour player in the years following World War II, Charleston, South Carolina, native Paul Hahn (1918–1976) turned instead to entertaining, becoming a trick-shot artist of lasting repute. Using all manner of bizarre clubs, stances, accoutrements, and accomplices, he performed for crowds the world over with his pleasant banter and impressive skills. Paul Hahn hardly invented the trick-shot genre (for he was merely following in the footsteps of the great Joe Kirkwood) but he was certainly the preeminent practitioner of his time.

Gary Hallberg (USA)

A mid-1970s phenom at Wake Forest, Berwyn, Illinois, native Gary Hallberg (b. 5/31/1958) was the first four-time first-team All-American in history (a feat later matched by Phil Mickelson, David Duval and Bryce Moulder) as well as the 1979 **NCAA** champion and a two-time **North & South Amateur** winner. As a pro, Hallberg was Rookie of the Year in 1980, then enjoyed several strong seasons in the early 1980s with his biggest of three Tour wins, the **San Diego Open,** coming in 1983. Also a winner of events in France, Japan, and Argentina, Hallberg last cracked the Tour's top-100 money winners in 1994 but continues to compete on occasion, likely eying a run at the Champions Tour toward the end of this decade.

Jim Hallet (USA)

A hockey player who only turned seriously to golf when his alma mater, Bryant College, dropped the winter sport, Cape Cod's Jim Hallet (b. 3/30/1960) enjoyed several moments in the spotlight as an unheralded amateur at the 1983 Masters where he opened with a 68 and spent Friday hanging around the lead while paired with Arnold Palmer and Seve Ballesteros. The possessor of an unusually strong grip that mandated a Bobby Locke–like draw on his full shots, Hallet turned professional the following year and looked to be on his way to a promising PGA Tour career before a recurring wrist injury forced his early retirement in 1993.

Bob Hamilton (USA)

Former **Indiana Amateur** and **Open** champion Bob Hamilton (b. 1916) joined the PGA Tour in 1944, just in time to capture the **PGA Championship** (the only Major to hold any events between 1942 and 1945) at Spokane's Manito G&CC. En route the Evansville native would beat Harold "Jug" McSpaden in the quarter-finals, then shock Byron Nelson (not to mention the rest of the golfing world) one up in the final. Though never a top-shelf star, Hamilton would prove himself more than a fluke, winning four more times on Tour, finishing third in the 1946 Masters, reaching the PGA semifinals in 1952 and playing in the 1949 Ryder Cup. His career sidetracked by burns suffered in a small plane crash, Hamilton would enjoy one further highlight by becoming the youngest person ever to shoot his age with a remarkable 59 on June 4, 1975.

Todd Hamilton (USA)

A native of Galesburg, Illinois, former University of Oklahoma All-American Todd Hamilton (b. 10/18/1965) is perhaps not the most surprising winner of the **Open Championship** in recent memory—but only because Ben Curtis, who preceded him as champion in 2003, was even less heralded. In truth, Hamilton's supposed anonymity was a relative thing, for despite little success in America, he was in fact a 14-time winner in Japan and Asia, his primary base of operations since 1992. Coming off a season which saw him win four times and rank third in the Japanese Order of Merit, Hamilton successfully played his way through the PGA Tour Qualifying Tournament in late 2003 (his eighth attempt), then wasted little time in landing his first Tour victory by finishing birdie-birdie to take March's **Honda Classic** by one over Davis Love III.

Hamilton would not land another top-10 finish prior to the Open Championship but at Royal Troon, opening rounds of 71-67-67 saw him a surprising 54-hole leader, standing one ahead of Ernie Els and two up on Phil Mickelson and Retief Goosen, perhaps the three hottest players in the world. Though closing with a solid 69, Hamilton bogeyed the 72nd to allow Els into a four-hole play-off, then surprised many by making four straight pars to become an unlikely—but not *least* likely—Open champion.

Shelly Hamlin (USA)

An LPGA Tour campaigner for more than 25 years, Shelly Hamlin (b. San Mateo, California, 5/28/1949) put together a solid, if unspectacular, record during her first two decades as a professional. But after a 1991 bout with breast cancer placed her career in obvious jeopardy, she made a comeback worthy of both Ben Hogan and Hollywood, not only returning to competitive golf but winning her second and third career titles (at the **Phar-Mor** and **ShopRite** events) in 1992 and '93. Years earlier, as a talented West Coast amateur, Hamlin also represented the United States on victorious Curtis Cup teams in 1968 and '70.

Hee-Won Han (South Korea)

A fine amateur who captured 48 titles in the United States and throughout Asia, Seoul native Hee-Won Han (b. 6/10/ 1978) turned professional in 1998, winning twice on the LPGA of Japan tour the following year. Coming to America full-time in 2001, she was named the LPGA's Rookie of the Year despite going winless and finishing 70th on the money list. She rocketed up to 14th place the following year, however, before really breaking through in 2003 with two wins (at **Wykagyl** and the **Wendy's Championship**) and fourth place in official earnings. A bit of a streaky sort, Han is capable of great iron play, resulting in numerous greens hit and, at times, lots of birdies.

Frank Hannigan (USA)

A high-profile leader of the USGA during his seven-year term as executive director (1983–89), Staten Island, New York, product Frank Hannigan (b. 1931) brought a wider-than-usual range of golfing interests to the organization, presiding over the establishment of a fine rare book reprint program, pushing the organization to bring the U.S. Open back to Shinnecock Hills, and penning a seminal article for *Golf Journal* on A. W. Tillinghast that did much to spark modern interest in classic course architecture. Since leaving the USGA in 1989, however, he has become what one might call the loyal opposition, joining ex-presidents Frank "Sandy" Tatum and Grant Spaeth (not to mention most of the world's top players) in criticizing the organization's recent abandonment of equipment governance, as well as other policies with which he has found fault. Hannigan is today a freelance writer, as well as one of the game's most astute and independent observers.

Gil Hanse (USA)

Cornell-educated Gil Hanse (b. Panama City, Florida, 8/ 12/1963) followed in the footsteps of his first architectural employer, Tom Doak, by utilizing the William Frederick Dreer Award to spend a year in the British Isles studying the classic links. Also interning with the venerable firm of Hawtree & Son, Hanse returned to the States to work on several of Doak's early designs before striking out on his own in 1993.

A superior builder of natural-looking bunkers, Hanse initially established himself as a premier restorationist, performing work at places like Merion, Kittansett (Massachusetts), Plainfield (New Jersey) and Fenway (New York), the latter two jobs being especially well received. He also completed a uniquely impressive assignment by laying out a new links for Scotland's Crail Golfing Society (the seventh oldest golf club in the world) in 1998. Being only the third American ever to design a course in golf's homeland, Hanse was soon awarded a series of new domestic designs running from New England to Alabama to California, a carefully crafted body of work which has served to springboard him into the upper echelon of what might be termed "thinking man's design."

Notable Courses: Capstone Club, Alabama; Inniscrone GC, Pennsylvania; Rustic Canyon GC, California; Tallgrass GC, New York

Beverly Hanson (USA)

A native of Fargo, North Dakota, Beverly Hanson won the 1950 U.S. Women's Amateur at Atlanta's East Lake CC (6 and 4 over Mae Murray), then competed on a victorious Curtis Cup team before turning pro in time to join the LPGA Tour in late June of 1951. A mid-season arrival of this sort seldom generates much attention but Hanson's certainly did, for she won her very first start, the prestigious Eastern Open in Reading, Pennsylvania—defeating no less than the legendary Babe Zaharias.

Over the decade to follow, Hanson would emerge as one of the tour's more consistent winners, capturing 15 titles (including a career-high four in 1959) and a pair of Major championships. The first of these came in 1955 at the inaugural LPGA Championship in Indianapolis, an event which featured a bizarre (and short-lived) format requiring the two 54-hole stroke play leaders to compete in an 18-hole match-play final. Three strokes better than Louise Suggs after 54, Hanson prevailed in the head-to-head contest 4 and 3. In 1958 she added the Titleholders in more traditional style (beating Betty Dodd at the Augusta CC) as well as the Lawton Open (Oklahoma), resulting in Hanson's only Vare Trophy and the number one spot on the year's money list.

LPGA Wins (15): 1954 & '60 Orange Blossom; 1955 LPGA Championship; 1956 Western Open; 1958 Titleholders

Chick Harbert (USA)

Long-hitting Dayton, Ohio, native Melvin R. "Chick" Harbert (1915–1992) won the 1939 Trans-Mississippi Amateur and, having spent most of his life in Michigan, four of that state's Opens, the first (1937) while still an amateur. As PGA Tour player he claimed seven titles, the biggest, by a wide margin, being the 1954 PGA Championship. Clearly skilled at match play, Harbert had already reached the PGA final twice, losing in 1947 (on his home turf in Detroit) to Jim Ferrier 2 and 1, then in 1952 at Louisville's Big Spring CC where a hooked drive at the 36th handed the title to Jim Turnesa. But in 1954, Harbert narrowly squeaked by Jerry Barber and Tommy Bolt to reach the final, then rode a 29-hole stretch played in eight

under par to a 4 and 3 win over Walter Burkemo. A Ryder Cup player in 1949 and a playing captain in 1955, Harbert had a 2-0 record (both in singles) on a pair of winning teams. He also played an extremely important administrative role on the PGA's Tournament Committee during the late 1940s when player dissatisfaction with the PGA of America as a governing body first took serious root.

President Warren Harding (USA)

By most accounts President Warren G. Harding (1865–1923) ranks among our most golfing of presidents and was easily considered the most avid prior to Dwight Eisenhower's postwar arrival. Capable (though not always) of playing in the low 80s, Harding actually was a member of the USGA Executive Committee while in office (1921–23) and presented Jim Barnes with his victor's trophy after the 1921 U.S. Open at suburban Maryland's Columbia CC. After his death (by heart attack) during an official 1923 visit to San Francisco, Harding's love of the game was saluted when that city named its 1925 municipal facility Harding Park in his honor.

Ernest Hargreaves (UK)

A working-class youth from Leeds, England, Ernest Hargreaves (b. 1913) joined the ranks of notable caddies at the 1929 Open Championship when his charge, the inimitable Walter Hagen, proceeded first to win the event, then to hand the 16-year-old Hargreaves the entirety of his £100 first-place check. This splendid debut was soon followed by 20 plus years working—both on the bag and off—for three-time Open Champion Henry Cotton, the greatest of all war-era British pros. Hargreaves outlived each of his illustrious bosses and, late in his own game, wrote about both in a pleasant autobiography, *Caddie in the Golden Age* (Partridge, 1993).

Bob Harlow (USA)

A combination salesman, journalist, administrator and promoter, Newburyport, Massachusetts, native Bob Harlow was one of the key players in the development of American professional golf. A graduate of the University of Pennsylvania, he began his professional life as a writer but by 1922 was making most of his living as Walter Hagen's personal manager, the man responsible for the Haig's extensive exhibition schedule. In 1929, Harlow managed the traveling American Ryder Cup team and that same year was hired as the PGA's Tournament Bureau Manager, the organization's first significant step toward transformation into the present-day PGA Tour.

Harlow's tenure with the PGA was tempestuous, ending and restarting on several occasions, but on his watch the organization grew. A master of promotion, he drove the Tour to new heights, pushing for a year-round schedule, wining and dining the media, and corralling sponsors. Also an entrepreneur on a personal level, Harlow continued to manage Hagen (and Joe Kirkwood), write a syndicated golf column, and start a small paper, *Golf News*. The PGA required him to abandon the paper but much later, in 1947, Harlow would give it another shot, this time creating the long-running *Golf World*. A genuine visionary to whom the modern, highly paid professional owes much, Harlow passed away in 1954, fully 34 years before he would be inducted, as the father of the PGA Tour, into the World Golf Hall of Fame.

Butch Harmon (USA)

Claude "Butch" Harmon Jr. (b. 1943), son of the 1948 Masters champion, grew up at places like Winged Foot and Seminole, eventually playing the PGA Tour from 1969 to 1971 and winning the 1971 **B.C. Open** (the year before it became an official Tour event). Soon turning to teaching full time, Harmon worked at King Hassan's famous Royal Rabat GC (Dar-es-Salam, Morocco), then made several stops in Iowa and Texas before striking it big in the 1990s as one of America's elite instructors. His most famous charge was the young Tiger Woods, who incorporated Harmon's advice into the swing which made him, for a time, as dominant a player as the game has ever seen. Much attention has been paid to Woods' relative struggles since their breakup, and Harmon still retains a stable of players that includes Adam Scott, Darren Clarke, Justin Leonard, and many more.

Claude Harmon (USA)

A top player who primarily entered only Major championships, Eugene Claude Harmon (1916–1989) for many years lived a club professional's dream existence, spending summers at Winged Foot and winters at Seminole, and setting one of golf's longer-standing course records at the latter with a sizzling 60 in 1948. That same year Harmon would become the first Georgia native to claim the **Masters,** his lone PGA Tour win but hardly a shocker given that he was also three-time semifinalist at the PGA and a third-place finisher at the 1959 U.S. Open at Winged Foot. The father of three professional sons (including the above-profiled Butch), Harmon was well known as a man deeply

interested in discussing the many technical aspects of the golf swing, leading Jimmy Demaret once to claim: "I'm overgolfed. I just had lunch with Claude Harmon."

Paul Harney (USA)

Arguably the most nationally competitive player to come out of frigid New England since Francis Ouimet, Worcester, Massachusetts, product Paul Harney (b. 7/11/1929) was a fine collegiate player at Holy Cross before joining the PGA Tour in the mid-1950s. Standing 5'11" but weighing only 140 pounds, he was recognized among the game's longest hitters (generally placed behind only the gargantuan George Bayer) while winning a total of six Tour events and missing the three-way play-off for the 1963 U.S. Open at Brookline by a single stroke.

In his initial professional years, Harney traveled far and wide, actually winning the 1956 **Egyptian Match Play** title over the great Bobby Locke. But by the early 1960s, he settled into a California club job, limiting his PGA Tour appearances to eight winter events per year. Remarkably, even in this part-time role, Harney managed to win back-to-back **Los Angeles Opens** in 1964 and '65 and, at age 42, the 1972 **San Diego Open,** his final Tour victory.

Chandler Harper (USA)

Both the youngest (18) and oldest (56) state champion in Virginia history and one-time mentor to future PGA Tour star Curtis Strange, Portsmouth native Chandler Harper (1914–2004) was a seven-time Tour winner, including the 1950 **PGA Championship.** On that occasion, playing at the Scioto CC in Columbus, Ohio, Harper nipped Jimmy Demaret 2 and 1 in the semifinals before taking out upstart Henry Williams Jr. in the final 4 and 3. In 1954 Harper would set a then-72-hole scoring record of 259 in winning the **Texas Open,** closing with three consecutive 63s. Of course, this was accomplished at San Antonio's Brackenridge Park where one year later Mike Souchak would shoot his unforgettable 257, a 72-hole mark which would stand for over four decades. Harper was also a member of the victorious 1955 Ryder Cup team.

Donald Harradine (UK)

The stepson of a golf professional, Donald Harradine (b. 1911) was preparing to follow a similar career path when, through a family connection, he was hired to redesign a course at Switzerland's Ragaz Spa in 1930. Taking a liking to the resort, he settled in as its golf pro while also developing an architectural practice that saw no contracts in his native Britain but extensive work throughout Continental Europe. All told, Harradine would complete more than 40 new designs and countless remodelings, working right up into the 1980s. The best known of his works, the 1964 Glyfada GC, is generally rated as Greece's best.

H. M. Harriman (USA)

Herbert M. Harriman was an exceptionally affluent New York railroad man who will forever hold the distinction of being the first American-born player to win the **U.S. Amateur.** This he accomplished at Chicago's Onwentsia Club in July of 1899, first dispatching with C. B. Macdonald in the semifinals 6 and 5, then a widely favored Findley Douglas 3 and 2 in the final. Harriman also won the inaugural **Metropolitan Amateur** in 1899, but had the tables turned dramatically upon him the following spring when a visiting Harry Vardon took on the best ball of Harriman and Douglas over 36 holes in Atlantic City, thrashing them by the ignominious margin of 9 and 8.

A. W. Harrington (UK/USA)

Arvin W. Harrington, an attorney by trade, was the ringleader of a small band of Scottish immigrants from Albany, New York, who summered in the Green Mountain town of Dorset, Vermont, late in the nineteenth century. All available evidence suggests that with Harrington as their leader, this group founded the Dorset Field Club in 1886, their nine-hole golf course utilizing much the same site over which the club continues to play today. The 1886 date is especially important, for it came roughly 18 months prior to the founding of the St. Andrew's GC of Yonkers, New York, making Dorset the oldest continuously operating golf club in the United States.

Padraig Harrington (Ireland)

A primary contender for Colin Montgomerie's title as Europe's best player, Dublin native Padraig Harrington (b. 8/31/1971) has been projected for greatness since sweeping the **Irish Closed** and **Open Amateurs** in 1995 and participating on three Walker Cup teams (1991–95). He began his professional career by winning the 1996 **Spanish Open,** finishing 11th in that season's Order of Merit and only just losing Rookie of the Year honors to Denmark's Thomas Björn. Winless eighth- and 29th-place finishes followed but since 1998 Harrington has finished no worse than seventh, including back-to-back seconds (both behind South Africa's Retief Goosen) in 2001 and '02.

A solid tee-to-green player and an excellent putter, Harrington has thus far won nine times in Europe, his biggest successes coming at the 2001 **Volvo Masters** and the 2003 **Deutsche Bank,** and he has, of late, become a fixture among the top 10 of the World Rankings. Detractors will point out that Harrington has also finished second on a stout 20 occasions in Europe, a number which may suggest some difficulty in closing the deal. On the upside, however, with back-to-back seconds at the 2003 and '04 Players Championships and a 2004 play-off loss to Sergio Garcia at Westchester representing his best finishes, Harrington broke through for his first PGA Tour victory at the 2005 **Honda Classic** (defeating Vijay Singh in a play-off), an important benchmark for any world-class player. He has also logged five top-10 finishes in 20 Major championship starts since 2000 and acquitted himself adequately under the stifling pressure of the Ryder Cup, going 7-4-1 during three appearances from 1999 to 2004. Not surprisingly, he has also represented Ireland in every **World Cup** since 1996, teaming with Paul McGinley to win the team title in 1997.

John Harris (UK)

Born into a family golf construction business that included Wentworth and Sunningdale on its résumé, England's John Harris (1912–1977) followed World War II service as a naval commander by partnering with C. K. Cotton in a 1950s architectural firm. By the 1960s, however, he was on his own, working worldwide in occasional partnership with five-time Open champion Peter Thomson and American Ron Fream, designing or redesigning several hundred courses in more than 30 countries.

Though seldom working in Britain, Harris' portfolio suggests he was talented enough to have ventured abroad more by choice than necessity, a point supported by his involvement with such attractive jobs as the Eden course at the Royal Hong Kong GC (which comprises the majority of the club's composite "championship" layout) or Royal Canberra in the Australian Capital Territory. Harris was also well known for making his hazards plainly visible, believing that they should represent, in effect, the golfer's strategic guideposts.

Notable Courses: Royal Canberra GC; Tobago GC, Trinidad & Tobago; Wairakei International GC, New Zealand

Labron Harris Jr. (USA)

The son of the golf coach at Oklahoma State, Labron Harris Jr. (b. Stillwater, 9/27/1941) starred for the Cowboys in the early 1960s, winning the 1962 **U.S. Amateur** at Pinehurst where he beat, among others, R. H. Sikes,

Homero Blancas, Billy Joe Patton, and, in the final, Downing Gray. He appeared on a victorious 1963 Walker Cup team (compiling a 3-1 record, including a singles victory over Michael Bonallack) before turning professional in 1964. A big man at 6'4" and 200 pounds, Harris proceeded to enjoy only limited success over slightly more than a decade, winning once and never placing higher than 36th on the money list.

Robert Harris (UK)

A talented Scot from Dundee who learned his golf at Carnoustie, stockbroker Robert Harris (1882–1959) resided for much of his life around London, playing primarily at the Woking GC in Surrey. Widely considered to be of championship timber, he first reached the final of the British Amateur in 1913 at St. Andrews, only to fall 6 and 5 to the world-beating Harold H. Hilton. Ten years later at Deal, he again reached the last match, but again was dismissed by a legendary opponent, Roger Wethered, 7 and 6. Then age 41, Harris was largely written off as over the hill, yet in 1925 at Westward Ho!, he improbably reached the **Amateur** final one last time—and promptly took the full measure of poor Kenneth Fradgley, routing him by a then-record 13 and 12.

Harris was selected as a playing captain for three of the first four Walker Cups, and it was at the inaugural match in 1922 that his illness on the eve of competition forced journalist Bernard Darwin into the lineup, Darwin cementing his legend by defeating 1910 U.S. Amateur champion W. C. Fownes Jr. 3 and 1. In his later years, Harris would pen *Sixty Years of Golf* (Batchworth, 1953), a traditionalist manifesto chronicling the changes that had overtaken the game during the previous six decades. With its eyewitness profiles of so many early greats, *Sixty Years* is a rare but indispensable title today.

Robert Bruce Harris (USA)

As a golf course architect active prior to World War II, Robert Bruce Harris (1896–1976) can in some sense be considered a product of the Golden Age. The majority of his designs, however, came in the 1950s and '60s, when his prominent firm was centered largely in the Midwest. Having operated several courses during the Depression, Harris generally built with an emphasis on inexpensive maintenance. He was also a driving force in the founding of the American Society of Golf Course Architects in 1946, serving as the organization's first president.

Dutch Harrison (USA)

Born: Conway, Arkansas, 3/30/1910 **Died:** St. Louis, Missouri, 6/19/1982

The practice of citing golfers, often not yet 30, as the "Best Player Never to Win a Major" is an annoyingly silly modern phenomenon. The idea of noting great players who have failed to break through over an entire *career*, however, is another matter altogether. And unfortunately for the "Arkansas Traveler," Mr. Ernest Joseph "Dutch" Harrison, his name must figure prominently on any such list.

Another product of the caddie yard, Harrison initially spent two years playing left-handed before turning around and was 29 before achieving his first PGA Tour victory, but then demonstrated great longevity by claiming 17 more titles over a span of 19 years. His biggest wins were the 1949 **Canadian Open** (by four over Jim Ferrier) and the 1953 **Western Open,** where he beat Ed Furgol, Fred Haas, and Lloyd Mangrum by the same margin. In Major championship play, however, "close" was Harrison's best—and not even so very often at that. A 1939 trip to the semifinals was his best performance in the PGA Championship, while a fourth-place tie in 1954 represented his Masters peak. He was part of the third-place logjam at the 1960 U.S. Open but probably came nearest to the summit 10 years earlier at Merion where a fourth-place finish belies the fact that a closing 76 caused him to miss the famous Hogan-Fazio-Mangrum (won by Hogan) by a single stroke. Later a dominant Senior player, Harrison appeared on two Ryder Cup teams, going 2-1 overall.

PGA Tour Wins (18): 1939 & '54 Bing Crosby; 1939 & '51 Texas; 1949 Canadian Open; 1953 Western Open
Ryder Cup: 1947 & '49 (2)

1936-1960

	36	37	38	39	40	41	42	43	44	45	46	47	48
Masters	-	-	-	-	T31	-	T7				T37	T29	T13
US Open	T36	T32	-	T25	DQ	T7					T10	T13	T35
British	-	-	-	-							-	-	-
PGA	-	-	-	T3	T33	T33	T17		-	T17	T9	-	T33

	49	50	51	52	53	54	55	56	57	58	59	60
Masters	T23	WD	T57	-	-	T4	-	-	MC	-	-	-
US Open	MC	4	T47	T33	T14	-	-	T17	MC	T23	-	T3
British	-	-	-	-	-	-	-	-	-	-	-	-
PGA	-	-	-	T33	T17	T9	T33	-	-	-	-	-

Michael Harwood (Australia)

Standing 6′4″ and weighing 185 pounds, Sydney's Michael Harwood (b. 1/8/1959) had little more than wins in Fiji and Western Samoa under his belt prior to upsetting Greg Norman at the 1986 **Australian PGA,** his final-round 64 denying the Shark a third straight PGA title. Heading off to Europe, Harwood then enjoyed a strong turn-of-the-decade run, logging Order of Merit rankings of 14th, 6th and 12th from 1989 to 1991 while claiming five official victories. The two biggest came in 1990: the **Volvo PGA** (where he beat Nick Faldo and John Bland by one at Wentworth) and the **Volvo Masters** played at Valderrama. His final European title came at the 1991 **European Open,** where he bested Lyle and Ballesteros roughly a month after finishing second to Ian Baker-Finch in the Open Championship at Royal Birkdale. Unable to maintain such form into his late 30s, however, Harwood only once bettered 117th in the Order of Merit after 1991.

Coburn Haskell (USA)

A resident of Cleveland by the early 1890s, Boston-born Coburn Haskell (1868–1922) was the man primarily responsible for the single greatest leap in golf equipment technology, the rubber ball. Recognizing the inconsistencies of the old gutta-percha models, Haskell (along with partner Bertram Work) patented a new ball in 1898 which consisted of a core of wrapped elastic thread encased in a thin layer of plastic, the surface of which was imprinted with an early version of today's dimples as an aerodynamic aid. Though the "Haskell" did not catch on immediately, Walter Travis played one during his 1901 U.S. Amateur victory in Atlantic City, providing the necessary boost to jumpstart its popularity in America. In Britain a great debate raged, with giants like Vardon and J. H. Taylor stridently supporting its banishment. The ever-traditional John Low headed the R&A Rules Committee that recommended just such action but the broader R&A never acted on the recommendation. Sandy Herd then used a Haskell to claim his lone Open Championship (in 1902 at Hoylake) and the gutty was quickly on its way to oblivion.

Hassan Hassanein (Egypt)

By far the finest golfer yet produced by the Arab world—and likely to remain that way for some time—Hassan Hassanein (1915–1956) began as a barefoot caddie at the long-defunct Heliopolis Sporting Club and worked his way up to world-class professional status. In winning 10 of 11 **Desert Opens** from 1946 to 1956, he clearly established himself as his nation's best. But unlike subsequent challengers such as Cherif el-Sayed Cherif or Mohamed Said Moussa, Hassanein was a force to be reckoned with internationally as well. Indeed, while capturing four consecutive **Egyptian Open** titles from 1949 to 1952, he defeated all manner of high-class players including Max Faulkner, Alf Padgham, John Jacobs and the fine Belgian Flory Van Donck. He also won the 1951 **Egyptian Match Play,** defeating no less than Norman von Nida in the final. Further, Hassanein competed successfully in Europe, winning the 1949 **Italian Open** and the 1951 **French Open** and finishing 17th at the 1953 Open Championship at Carnoustie. He was even invited, on three occasions, to compete in George S. May's World Championship of Golf, the game's richest tournament, played just outside of Chicago from 1943 to 1957. One of golf's more overlooked performers, Hassanein died tragically at age 41 in a kerosene stove explosion.

Theodore Havemeyer (USA)

Known as the "Sugar King" for his chairmanship of the American Sugar Refining Company, Theodore A.

Havemeyer (1838–1897) was one of American golf's true founding fathers, a man whose own personal wealth and prestige played an integral part in the game's crucial early growth upon these shores. Havemeyer discovered golf at age 50 while vacationing in Pau, France, and was immediately determined to bring it to his summer home at fashionable Newport, Rhode Island. Assembling a group that included neighbors John Jacob Astor and Cornelius Vanderbilt, Havemeyer led the purchase of acreage on foggy Brenton Point, as well as the design and construction of a nine-hole course, the Newport GC.

In 1894, the club moved to the nearly adjacent tract upon which it presently lies, with Havemeyer representing it at the December 22nd New York meeting at which the USGA was founded. Despite the domineering presence of Charles Blair Macdonald, Havemeyer was elected as the organization's first president, celebrating this honor by donating a $1,000 silver trophy to be awarded each year to the national amateur champion. [Note: This original Havemeyer Trophy burned in a 1925 fire that claimed the clubhouse of Bobby Jones' East Lake CC and was soon replaced by the present version.] A great sportsman who was always on hand to congratulate the winners and commiserate with the losers, Havemeyer was known for underwriting operating expenses out of his own pocket, staring down a threatened player boycott when John Shippen broke the color line at the 1896 U.S. Open, and generally utilizing his tact, intelligence and goodwill to great effect during those early, fledgling days.

Arthur Havers (UK)

A tall and powerful man, Norwich, England's Arthur Gladstone Havers (1898–1981) was the lone Briton to stem the growing dominance of the Americans in the Open Championship between George Duncan's win in 1920 and the arrival of the home cavalry—in the form of Henry Cotton—in 1934. Havers was, by many accounts, rather an inconsistent sort capable of some truly wretched stretches. Yet from 1914 (when he qualified as a long, lanky 16-year-old) through Cotton's initial triumph, he rose to the occasion often enough to log 10 top-10 finishes at the **Open Championship,** including his great 1923 triumph at Troon, by one over Walter Hagen. Though seldom a winner of anything else substantial at home, Havers did prove himself a capable match player in America, defeating Bobby Jones over 36 holes and Gene Sarazen over 72 while touring, in 1924, as the reigning Open champion.

Fred Hawkins (USA)

Antioch, Illinois, native Fred Hawkins (b. 1923) played for some 18 seasons on the PGA Tour beginning in 1947, amassing exactly one victory (the 1956 **Oklahoma City Open**) and 19 second-place finishes. One of those runners-up was at the 1958 Masters when he tied Doug Ford, just a single shot behind Arnold Palmer. He also twice reached the quarter-finals of the PGA Championship and was the sole American to win his singles match during the disastrous 1957 Ryder Cup match at Lindrick.

F. G. Hawtree (UK)

A greenkeeper-turned-architect, Ealing, England's Frederic G. Hawtree (1883–1955) jumpstarted his career when, in 1922, he joined forces with five-time Open Champion and general golfing icon J. H. Taylor. Though their relationship was, in fact, very much a precursor to the sort of marketing-oriented design teams so common today (with Taylor charming clients and attending openings, while Hawtree handled the operational nuts and bolts), it is likely that their partnership grew out of more than simple business expediency. In class-stratified Britain, both Taylor and Hawtree were strong believers in affordable public golf, something which seldom seemed a high priority for most of the game's well-established hierarchy.

All told, the firm of Hawtree & Taylor was responsible for the design or redesign of over 100 courses. Hawtree himself was the owner of one of these, the Addington Court GC, which became the first privately owned daily-fee facility in Great Britain. While Taylor would ease into retirement during World War II, Hawtree kept the firm very much alive, partnering with his son Fred W. and staying at least somewhat active right up until his death.

Frederic W. Hawtree (UK)

The son of architect F. G., Bromley-born Fred W. Hawtree (b. 1916) was educated at Oxford and captured by the Japanese during World War II. Following his repatriation, Hawtree replaced the retired J. H. Taylor as his father's partner and embarked on a design career that would last right up until 1980. Geographically more wide-ranging than his father, Fred W. built courses across the Continent and as far away as Iran, El Salvador and South Africa, in addition to maintaining a busy U.K. practice. He has also made several substantial contributions as an historian/writer, most notably in authoring *Colt & Co.* (Cambuc Archive, 1991), a revealing look at the life of H. S. Colt and his various design partners. More recently, Hawtree edited *Aspects of Golf Course Architecture 1889–1924* (Grant, 1998), a collection of hard-to-find essays on golf design by many of Britain's finest early practitioners.

Upon retiring, Fred W. turned the family business over to his son Martin, keeping alive the longest continuously operating golf design firm in history.

Dale Hayes (South Africa)

The son of 1939 South African Amateur champion Otway Hayes, Pretoria native Dale Hayes (b. 7/1/1952) came along at essentially the same time—and with much the same expectations—as countryman Bobby Cole. In Hayes' case, he had pocketed national amateur titles in **South Africa, Germany** and **Brazil,** as well as a **World Junior Championship,** and he certainly found early professional success at home, winning the **South African PGA** in 1974, '75 and '76. He also won the 1976 **South African Open** (in a playoff over John Fourie at Houghton CC) though by this time he was already established as a top-shelf star on the European Tour.

A fast-swinging and aggressive player, Hayes' European career featured five top-4 Order of Merit rankings between 1973 and 1978, a period that saw him capture five official victories. Oddly, all were national Opens: the **Spanish** (1971 and '79), the **Swiss** (1975), the **Italian** (1978), and Hayes' crowning moment, the 1978 **French,** in which his 19-under-par total finished a stunning 11 shots ahead of second-place Seve Ballesteros. Hayes tried the PGA Tour in 1976 and '77 but with little to show for his efforts soon returned full time to Europe. In 1981 he retired to a South African club job where, with the exception of some European appearances in 1985, he has mostly remained.

Mark Hayes (USA)

A two-time All-American and U.S. Amateur runner-up while at Oklahoma State, Stillwater native Mark Hayes (b. 7/12/1949) went on to enjoy a solid PGA Tour run from the mid-1970s through the early '80s, winning three times and placing as high as 11th on the money list in 1976. In that season he won twice, at the **Byron Nelson** and in **Pensacola,** though his 1977 victory at the **Players Championship** (in its first year at the windblown Sawgrass CC) would prove Hayes' professional high point and help land him a spot on the 1979 Ryder Cup team. Despite shooting an Open Championship record 63 in 1977 at Turnberry, Hayes was occasionally afflicted with a balky putter, never worse than at the 1979 Bing Crosby where four putts from 7 feet at the 69th cost him a three-shot lead and landed him in a play-off with Lon Hinkle, which he lost.

Sandra Haynie (USA)

A member of the LPGA Hall of Fame, Ft. Worth native Sandra Haynie (b. 6/4/1943) won the 1957 **Texas Publinx** at age 14 and later captured two **Texas Amateurs** before joining the Tour in 1961, at age 18. A year later she became a rare teenage professional winner by capturing the **Austin Civitan Open,** then backed it up with a victory at the **Cosmopolitan Open** a week later. Five more titles would follow before Haynie claimed her first Major, the 1965 **LPGA Championship,** defeating Clifford Ann Creed by five at Las Vegas' Stardust CC. Thus staking her place among the best, Haynie proceeded to log an impressive 11 consecutive seasons (1965–1975) among the top five money earners, while winning at least twice in all but one of those years.

Though named Player of the Year in 1970, and a winner for three consecutive weeks in the spring of 1971, Haynie's peak didn't arrive until 1974 when her career-high six victories included both her second **LPGA Championship** and the **U.S. Women's Open.** The latter came in LaGrange, Illinois, and was won, by a single stroke, with birdies at the 71st and 72nd, making Haynie the first woman since Mickey Wright to take the two cornerstone Majors in a single season. Amazingly, despite such credentials, she would finish the year ranked third on the money list, and was beaten out for Player of the Year by JoAnne Carner.

Inducted into the Hall of Fame in 1977, Haynie played in only 17 events over the next four seasons due to injuries and business commitments. She would return for a full slate from 1981 to 1983, however, proving her continued competitiveness in 1982 with two wins, second place on the money list, and a fourth career Major at the **du Maurier,** where she defeated young Beth Daniel by one at Toronto's St. George's G&CC. A second-place finish at the 1983 LPGA Championship would prove Haynie's last run at a Major and with the exception of a full schedule in 1989, she has played sparingly ever since.

LPGA Wins (42): 1965 & '74 LPGA Championship; 1971 Dallas Civitan; 1973 Orange Blossom; **1974 U.S. Women's Open;** 1982 Rochester; **1982 du Maurier**

1961-1984

	61	62	63	64	65	66	67	68	69	70	71	72
Dinah												
LPGA	12	-	T9	T5	1	7	6	6	WD	T6	T3	-
US Open	-	T21	T2	5	T12	T5	T4	T23	T13	T2	T15	T14
du Maur												

	73	74	75	76	77	78	79	80	81	82	83	84
Dinah											T16	T6
LPGA	T11	1	2	T12	-	-	-	-	T18	T7	2	T37
US Open	WD	1	6	-	-	-	-	-	T10	T2	T21	T47
du Maur			T3	-	-	-	-	-	5	1	T5	-

Clayton Heafner (USA)

An army sergeant before pursuing golf professionally, Charlotte, North Carolina, product Clayton Heafner (1914–1960) spent 16 seasons on the PGA Tour, winning four times and finishing strongly in several Major championships. His biggest victory, by far, came at the 1948 **Colonial,** where he beat Ben Hogan and Skip Alexander with a 272 total that remained a tournament record for 30 years. He made a fine showing at the 1949 U.S. Open at Medinah, finishing one back of winner Cary Middlecoff, but it was in 1951, at Oakland Hills, that his best Open opportunity presented itself. Entering the final round tied with Ben Hogan only two behind leader Bobby Locke, Heafner shot a splendid 69 over perhaps the toughest Open course in history, overtaking Locke and looking very much a winner—until Hogan returned his still-talked-about 67 to win by two. A first-ballot Hall of Famer were there a wing for famous tempers, Heafner was reportedly the only man ever to withdraw upon hearing his name mispronounced during first-tee introductions, simply returning to his car, tossing his clubs in the trunk, and driving on to the next stop.

Jerry Heard (USA)

Northern California product Jerry Heard (b. Visalia, 5/1/1947) was a highly successful PGA Tour player during the early 1970s, winning four times from 1971 to 1974 and thrice cracking the top-10 money winners. Obviously not bothered by the switch to Bermudagrass, Heard twice won the **Florida Citrus Open,** though his biggest victory came at the 1972 **Colonial,** where he beat Fred Marti by two. Unfortunately, Heard was struck by lightning (along with Lee Trevino and Bobby Nichols) at the 1975 Western Open in Chicago, and though he was soon pronounced fit—even winning once more in 1978—he was never again quite the same world-class player. Always considered something of a free spirit, Heard has since made a name for himself by hawking offbeat game improvement products.

Jay Hebert (USA)

Though their careers were similar in many ways, Junius Jay Hebert (b. St. Martinville, Louisiana, 2/14/1923) was perhaps the better half of the only pair of brothers ever to capture professional national championships in America. Having enlisted in the Marine Corps during World War II, Hebert was wounded at Iwo Jima before returning home and attending Louisiana State University. He turned professional in 1948 but didn't try the PGA Tour full time until 1956, eventually winning all seven of his Tour titles between 1957 and 1961. His two 1957 victories, the **Bing Crosby** and the **Texas Open,** were not insignificant, but his shining hour wouldn't arrive until the 1960 **PGA Championship** when, in the event's third turn at stroke play, he defeated Jim Ferrier by one at the Firestone CC. A fine tee-to-green player whose putting, by his own admission, was seldom a strength, Jay Hebert played on victorious Ryder Cup teams in 1959 and '61 and also captained a winner 10 years later in St. Louis.

Lionel Hebert (USA)

Five years younger than brother Jay, Lafayette, Louisiana-born Lionel Hebert (1928–2000) nonetheless won his half of the family's dual **PGA Championships** sooner, capturing the title—the last contested at match play—at Ohio's Miami Valley GC in 1957. On this occasion, Lionel defeated 1953 champion Walter Burkemo in the semifinals, then overcame a self-called early penalty stroke to beat Dow Finsterwald in the final 3 and 1. Though not quite as successful overall as Jay, Lionel came close, winning five PGA

Tour titles and competing on the disappointing 1957 Ryder Cup team that crashed and burned at Lindrick. He was also an influential man with the PGA, twice serving as vice president and chairman of the old Tournament Committee. Like Jay, he too attended Louisiana State University.

Genevieve Hecker (USA)

Described in 1903 as "a slender, blue-eyed girl ... with a great mop of beautiful golden hair," Genevieve Hecker (1883–1960) gained great fame by taking back-to-back **U.S. Women's Amateur** titles, first at Baltusrol in 1901 (5 and 3 over Lucy Herron), then at The Country Club of Brookline (4 and 3 over Louisa Wells). A winner of four **Metropolitan Amateur** titles, Hecker pioneered women's golf in general, penning a series of instructional articles for the original *Golf* magazine in 1902 and campaigning to enhance women's access to many male-only courses. She made a lasting contribution by authoring *Golf for Women* (Baker & Taylor, 1904), a largely instructional volume and the first of its type to achieve a significant foothold in the marketplace. She occasionally is identified under her married name of Genevieve Hecker Stout.

Harold Henning (South Africa)

Born: Johannesburg, South Africa, 10/3/1934 **Died:** Miami Beach, Florida, 1/1/2004

Harold Henning is credited with more than 50 international victories, though many of these were accomplished on smaller tours against admittedly lesser competition. One of four Johannesburg golfing brothers, the stylish Henning was more a straight-ball hitter than a powerhouse, with his real equalizers being a fine short game and a deadly pendulum-style putting stroke.

A two-time **South African Open** champion and regular winner around Europe by the early 1960s, Henning played frequently in Great Britain where, in 1963, he won the then-enormous sum of £10,000 for making a hole-in-one during an event at Moor Park. He later enjoyed a 1965 **World Cup** victory with Gary Player in Madrid, then returned regularly to America where he had previously enjoyed only marginal success. His game was more polished by the late 1960s, allowing Henning to record one official PGA Tour victory at the 1966 **Texas Open** and to be Charlie Sifford's sudden-death victim at the 1969 Los Angeles Open. A regular participant in the Open Championship, Henning twice tied for third, initially in 1960 (four back of Kel Nagle), then in 1970 (two out of the Nicklaus-Sanders play-off). He also finished an impressive sixth in 1983, at age 48, having won the **Dutch Open** two years earlier.

Also a four-time **South Africa PGA** and three-time **Swiss Open** winner, Henning actually quit the game entirely in 1972, though he was back at it by the end of the decade in preparation for a successful run on the American Champions Tour beginning in 1984. Though never a household name throughout his 40 plus competitive years, Henning certainly ranks among South Africa's all-time best.

Intn'l Wins (52): 1957 & '62 South African Open; 1957 Italian Open; 1960, '64 & '65 Swiss Open; 1965 German Open; 1965, '66, '67 & '72 South African PGA; 1981 Dutch Open
PGA Tour Win (1): 1966 Texas
Champions Tour Wins: 3 (1985–1991)

Fred Herd (UK/USA)

The younger brother of the more famous Sandy, St. Andrews' Fred Herd (1874–1954) emigrated to America during the last years of the nineteenth century, taking a professional position in Washington Park, Illinois. Though never a prime contender in the Open Championship back home, he was, at least once, able to hang with the best in America, winning the 1898 **U.S. Open** at the Myopia Hunt Club by seven over future two-time champion Alex Smith. This was the first occasion of the championship being played over 72 holes, making Myopia (which had only nine in play at this time) a particularly odd choice of venue. This was also an era when golf pros were still viewed as low-class hired hands and drunkards, the latter stereotype dramatically reinforced when Herd was required to put up a deposit on the value of the championship trophy for fear that he might hock it to purchase alcohol. Perhaps not surprisingly, he returned to England early in the new century.

Sandy Herd (UK)

Born: St. Andrews, Scotland, 4/22/1868 **Died:** London, England, 2/18/1944

Often referred to as the "fourth member" of the great Triumvirate, Alexander "Sandy" Herd was indeed a top talent who, statistically speaking, would have won three Open Championships had Vardon, Taylor and Braid not been in the picture. But the great men were, of course, thus leaving Herd with a still-solid ledger that featured a lone **Open** title in 1902, as well as 12 top-four finishes and several reasonably competitive entries (e.g., 2nd in 1920 and 10th in 1921) when he was well into his 50s. His span of 54 years between first and last Open appearances is a remarkable record, particularly when one notes that Arnold Palmer will not reach it at the Masters, where he ceased to be competitive decades ago and never had to qualify!

Aside from the Open, Herd was twice a winner of the prestigious *News of the World* match play, which he took in 1906 at Hollinwell and 1926 at Mid-Surrey. Here again longevity was the story, for at Mid-Surrey Herd was an astounding 58 years old, setting a major tournament record for seniority that, with Sam Snead having failed to break it, may stand forever. Herd was also reported to have won numerous smaller events (few of which have been meaningfully documented) and to have participated in several old-fashioned challenge matches, most notably the 1905 "International Foursome" in which he and fellow Scot James Braid were defeated soundly by the English team of Vardon and Taylor. On a lesser note, Herd is generally credited with being the first man to utilize a preshot waggle as a means of relaxation, an innovation perhaps rued by modern five-hour golfers everywhere.

In assessing Herd's career, at least relative to the Triumvirate, it would be an oversight not to note that in winning his Open Championship in 1902, he was the only player in the field using the new Haskell ball, which would be proven, in short time, to provide substantial advantages. Herd might perhaps be credited with having the foresight and/or guts to employ the new invention while the others still refused, but at the end of the day the advantage gained must at least somewhat temper his one splendid victory over his otherwise superior rivals.

Fred Herreshoff (USA)

A long-hitting New Yorker whom H. B. Martin once called "as fine a sportsman as ever lived," Fred Herreshoff (b. 1888) contended at the highest reaches of American amateur golf for many years without ever quite scaling its peak. Not that he didn't come close, for Herreshoff initially reached the final of the U.S. Amateur at the ripe old age of 16, losing in 1904 to H. Chandler Egan at Baltusrol, 8 and 6. He would be a far more experienced 23 in his second final appearance, this time coming out on the short end of one of golf's most famous finishes. Six down at lunch to the great British amateur Harold Hilton, Herreshoff battled all the way back in the afternoon to force extra holes, whereupon Hilton's badly sliced approach to the 37th kicked off a wooded hillside and down onto the green, unnerving Herreshoff whose ensuing bogey made Hilton the only Briton ever to claim the American title. Fred Herreshoff would take one important victory during his career, however, beating four-time U.S. Amateur champ Jerome Travers 4 and 3 to win the 1910 **Metropolitan Amateur** at New Jersey's Morris County GC.

Davy Herron (USA)

A graduate of Princeton, S. Davidson "Davy" Herron (1899–1956) was a strong, stocky fellow best known for defeating Bobby Jones 5 and 4 in the final of the 1919 **U.S. Amateur,** played over his home course, the Oakmont CC. This event is considered notable both for Herron's being the first player to win a USGA title at his home club and for the sporting way in which Jones quietly absorbed his defeat—perhaps the first sign of the maturation so vital to his future greatness. Herron did enjoy several other prominent successes—for he was twice the **Pennsylvania Amateur** champion (defeating Max Marston 5 and 3 for his first title in 1920) as well as a member of the second American Walker Cup team, which won narrowly at St. Andrews in 1923.

Charles Hezlet (Ireland)

Though perhaps less famous than his illustrious sister May, Lieutenant Colonel Charles Owen Hezlet (1891–1965) was a high-caliber player in his own right. A man of grand stature who, despite a terribly wide stance, was a prodigious hitter, Hezlet won **Irish Open Amateur** titles in 1926 and '29 and reached the final of the 1914 British Amateur at Troon, where he lost to J. L. C. Jenkins 3 and 2. He played in three Walker Cups from 1924 to 1928 (the first Irishman to appear) and served in both major wars, earning a DSO during World War I.

May Hezlet
(UK/Northern Ireland)

Born in the British outpost at Gibraltar, May Hezlet (1882–1978) was the most talented of three golfing sisters raised in Northern Ireland and a key figure in the development of the game on the Emerald Isle. A strong, dark-haired young woman, Hezlet lost in the final of the **1898 Irish Ladies** championship when she was 15, then came back to win the event a year later, defeating friend and rival Rhona Adair 5 and 4 at Royal County Down. One week later the **British Ladies** was held on the same site with Hezlet (having turned 17 in the interim) again emerging victorious, thus becoming the youngest-ever winner of either championship and the first player to win both. She would later add to her ledger two more **British Ladies** (in 1902 at Deal and 1907 back at Royal County Down) and one runner-up (1904 at Royal Troon), as well as four additional **Irish Ladies** in five years, between 1904 and 1908.

A more frequent winner than sisters Violet and Frances, May drew the lion's share of publicity, increasing it further through her frequent contributions to *Golf Illustrated* and

The Irish Golfer. She also authored a landmark book, *Ladies' Golf* (Hutchinson, 1904), the first women's instructional volume published in the British Isles.

Betty Hicks (USA)

Betty Hicks (b. Long Beach, California, 11/16/1920) was a trailblazer among American women golfers, winning the 1941 **U.S. Women's Amateur** at The Country Club of Brookline, being named the AP's Woman Athlete of the Year, and, after a volunteer stint in the Coast Guard, jumping aboard the fledgling Women's Professional Golf Association (forerunner to the LPGA) in 1944. Winning the **All-American Open** that same year, Hicks served as the WPGA's first president while making her living barnstorming the country as a paid clinician for Wilson Sporting Goods. She also twice finished second at the U.S. Women's Open, both times losing to Babe Zaharias (1948 and '54) by fairly wide margins. Hicks was equally instrumental in the 1950 founding of the LPGA, though by then she was concentrating on teaching and never won an official Tour event. She did, however, find time not only to get her bachelor's degree from San Jose State but also to become a licensed pilot and flying instructor, the author of two books, and a certified junior college teacher in California.

Helen Hicks (USA)

A native of Cedarhurst, New York, Helen B. Hicks (1911–1975) initially came to light as an amateur, winning the **Canadian Ladies** title in 1929 (and finishing second the next year), the **Eastern** in 1931, and the **Metropolitan** in both 1931 and '33. In the **U.S. Women's Amateur** she had been the qualifying medalist in 1929 but took until 1931 to reach the final, where she faced five-time winner and three-time defending champion Glenna Collett Vare at the CC of Buffalo. Peaking at the right time, Hicks ended Mrs. Vare's run with a 6 and 5 victory, a level of play she could not repeat in the 1933 final when Virginia Van Wie eliminated her at Chicago's Exmoor CC 4 and 3. Hicks was also a participant in the inaugural Curtis Cup in 1932, winning her foursomes match with Van Wie and defeating Enid Wilson in singles.

One of the first women to turn professional, Hicks became *the* first to ink an equipment endorsement contract when she signed on with Wilson in 1934, earning her keep by staging clinics all around the country. Further, history records her as the first woman ever to play in a men's professional event, entering the South Australian Centenary Open (and shooting a first-round 78) while touring Down Under with Gene Sarazen in 1936. Past her playing prime by the time of the LPGA's founding, Hicks never won an official post-1950 event. She did, however, claim the 1937 **Women's Western Open** (the first professional to do so) as well as the 1940 **Titleholders Championship**.

Chako Higuchi (Japan)

Though perhaps not possessing as strong an international record as her countrywoman Ayako Okamoto, Japan's Hisako "Chako" Higuchi (b. 10/13/1945) was a 2003 inductee into the World Golf Hall of Fame, and not without good reason. Higuchi was a standard-bearer among Japanese women professionals, actually founding the Japanese LPGA Tour and, in recent years, serving as its commissioner. She was also Japan's first female to play competitively abroad as well as the first of what has become a tidal wave of talented Asian players to hit the LPGA Tour. All told, Higuchi claimed 72 titles worldwide, including five that carried the LPGA's sanction. Of course, three of these were actually played in Japan and a fourth in England. But the fifth, the 1977 **LPGA Championship**, was played in the decidedly American locale of North Myrtle Beach, South Carolina, where Higuchi's three-shot victory over Pat Bradley, Sandra Post, and Judy Rankin made her the first Japanese to win on the American tour and only the fourth foreigner (behind France's Catherine LaCoste, Canada's Sandra Post, and Uruguay's Fay Crocker) to claim an LPGA Major.

Dave Hill (USA)

For better or worse, James David Hill (b. Jackson, Michigan, 5/20/1937) will long be remembered far more for his outspokenness than his golf game; an unfortunate legacy perhaps, but one which he surely brought upon himself. Hill's most famous criticisms were leveled at the host of the 1970 U.S. Open, Minnesota's Hazeltine National GC, where despite finishing solo second (six back of a blazing Tony Jacklin), Hill suggested, in several colorful ways, that the Trent Jones-designed layout would be better off as a farm. For this he was fined and in many quarters criticized—but Hazeltine was substantially redesigned by the time it would next hold an Open in 1991. Hill also raised eyebrows with his book *Teed Off* (Prentice-Hall, 1977), a tell-all profile of PGA Tour life that must surely have resulted in numerous chilly receptions on the practice tee.

Lost in all of this, however, was Hill's considerable talent, a fine reservoir of shotmaking skill honed by an incessant, Hogan-like practice regimen. Though never able to capture a Major championship, Hill was a 13-time winner over a 16-year stretch (1961–76), including **Memphis Classics** in 1967, '69, '70, and '73. In 1969, his best year, he won three times during the spring and summer, finished second on the money list, and won the Vardon Trophy for lowest scoring average. Hill was three times a Ryder Cup player, with provocative comments from him and others making 1969 a particularly contentious match.

PGA Tour Wins (13): 4 Memphis Classics
Champions Tour Wins: 6 (1987–89)
Ryder Cup: 1969, '73 & '77 (3)

Mike Hill (USA)

Accruing a substantially more modest PGA Tour résumé than brother Dave, Jackson, Michigan, native Mike Hill (b. 1/27/1939) was also less controversial. It took him three tries to gain his PGA Tour card in the late 1960s and once aboard, his biggest of three career wins came early, at the 1970 **Doral Open** where he beat Jim Colbert by three. Though Mike's tour ledger pales in comparison to Dave's, his Champions Tour record has been most impressive, including a stellar 18 titles and almost $9 million won since 1990.

Opal Hill (USA)

An educated woman with a degree in nursing, Newport, Nebraska, native Opal Hill (1892–1981) took up golf only as a means of getting exercise in the face of a life-threatening illness, a lingering kidney infection sparked by complications from childbirth. Soon Hill was good enough to win her hometown **Kansas City Championship** not once but nine times, eventually moving up to capture the 1928 **North & South Amateur**, three **Western Amateurs** (1929, '31, and '32), two **Western Opens** (1935 and '36), and three **Trans-Mississippis** (1928, '29 and '31). She also recorded a 2-3-1 record while participating in the first three Curtis Cup matches.

Following the death of her attorney husband, however, Hill broke dramatically with the norms of the day and turned professional in 1938, determined to earn a living from playing golf. Though faced with few events in which to play, Hill, Helen Hicks, Babe Zaharias, and several others supplemented their meager tournament incomes with clinics, exhibitions, and small-scale endorsement deals. By the time the LPGA Tour came into being in 1950, Opal Hill was well past her playing prime but her role as one of its 13 founders was posthumously honored.

Arthur Hills (USA)

Among the more popular of America's modern golf course architects, Michigan State–educated Arthur Hills (b. 1930) has been responsible for more than 300 designs and rede-

signs since entering the field full time in 1966. Originally based in Ohio, Hills has enjoyed great success in his home region, with nearly 50 new Midwestern designs to his credit. However, he has also branched out with nearly the same number of completed projects in Florida, a representative presence throughout the rest of the South, and odd designs as far away as Japan and Thailand.

Perhaps because of his expansive staff of design associates, it is debatable as to just what might constitute Arthur Hills' architectural style, with various looks having appeared in different locations at different times. Similarly, the firm's designs have found a unique sort of favor with magazine ratings panels, frequently gaining attention at opening, yet landing precious few long-term positions among those holy grails of design success, the national Top 100s.

Notable Courses: Bighorn GC, California; Bonita Bay GC, Marsh Course, Florida; The Champions, Kentucky; GC of Georgia, Lakeside Course

Harold Hilton (UK)

Born: West Kirby, England, 1/12/1869 **Died:** Westcote, England, 3/5/1942

Harold Horsfall Hilton was a giant of turn-of-the-century British golf, following John Ball Jr. as the next great Hoylake amateur in the early 1890s and remaining a top-flight campaigner right up to the onset of World War I. Standing only a lean 5′7″, Hilton utilized a fast swing and enormous body action to generate needed distance, getting up on his toes through impact and carrying the club extremely loosely at the top, neither technique being widely associated with consistent and reliable hitting. Thus never an elite ball-striker, he possessed a fine and innovative short game and, more than anything, a vast reservoir of applied golfing intellect and competitive fire.

A four-time **British Amateur** winner, Hilton performed the odd feat of first taking two **Open Championships,** initially claiming the Claret Jug in 1892 at Muirfield when closing rounds of 72-74 were enough to overcome a poor start, resulting in a three-shot win over John Ball, Sandy Herd and Jack Kirkaldy. Then in 1897, with the Triumvirate just entering its dominance, Hilton closed with 75 to edge James Braid by one on his home links at Hoylake.

An Amateur finalist in 1891, '92, and '96 (losing to John Laidlay, Ball, and Freddie Tait, respectively), Hilton couldn't quite get over the bar until the dawn of the new century, finally claiming the title with an 8 and 7 rout of James Robb in 1900 at Royal St. George's. By now Tait (the one opponent Hilton genuinely feared) and Ball were off fighting the Boers, making his defense of the trophy just a little bit easier—though Hilton was still pressed to the limit by John L. Low before prevailing on the 36th green of the 1901 final.

There followed a lull in Hilton's play, largely owing to poor health but perhaps, some have speculated, due to difficulties adjusting to the new rubber ball. By 1910 he was back in the semifinals and the following year he reached what might well be called his competitive peak, initially capturing his third Amateur title at Prestwick by clipping E. A. Lassen 4 and 3 in the final. Then it was onto the Open Championship at Royal St. George's where a 304 total left him one stroke shy of the famous Vardon-Massy play-off. Finally Hilton made a long-awaited trip across the water to compete in the **U.S. Amateur** at Apawamis where he was qualifying medalist, beat two-time winner Jerome Travers in the quarter-finals, and jumped out to a six-hole lunchtime lead in the final against young American Fred Herreshoff. The stubborn Herreshoff clawed his way back,

however, ultimately forcing a 37th hole where Hilton's badly sliced approach ricocheted off a wooded hillside and down onto the putting surface, resulting in a routine par and the championship.

Becoming the first man to take the British and American titles in the same year gave Hilton a piece of immortality, and he further helped his cause with a fourth and final **British Amateur** triumph in 1913 at St. Andrews, dismissing Robert Harris 6 and 5 in the final. Also a four-time winner of the **Irish Amateur,** Hilton later served as the first editor of *Golf Monthly* and, eventually, held a similar position at *Golf Illustrated*. He also authored *My Golfing Reminiscences* (James Nisbet, 1907) and cowrote the classic *The Royal and Ancient Game of Golf* (Golf Illustrated, 1912) with Garden Smith.

Major Amateur Wins (7): 1892 & '97 British Open; 1900, '01, '11 & '13 British Amateur; 1911 U.S. Amateur

1887-1922

	87	88	89	90	91	92	93	94	95	96	97	98	99	00
US Am	-	-	-	-	-	-	-	-	-	-	-	-	-	-
Brit Am	T9	-	T9	T5	2	2	T17	T5	T17	2	T9	T9	T5	1
British	-	-	-	-	-	1	T8	WD	WD	23	1	3	T12	T16

	01	02	03	04	05	06	07	08	09	10	11	12	13	14
US Am	-	-	-	-	-	-	-	-	-	-	1	T17	-	-
Brit Am	1	T5	T33	T5	T33	T125	T9	T33	T17	T3	1	T9	1	T17
British	4	T6	T24	WD	WD	-	-	-	WD	-	T3	-	WD	WD

Jimmy Hines (USA)

Among the more overlooked players in American history, Mineola, New York, native Jimmy Hines (1905–1986) won a total of nine PGA Tour events between 1933 and 1945 while logging at least 10 top-10 finishes every year from 1934 to 1939, plus 17 more in 1945. Described by Herbert Warren Wind as "brilliant but erratic" and known for his narrow, pigeon-toed stance, Hines enjoyed his best season in 1936 when he won the season-opening **Los Angeles Open** (over Henry Picard and Jimmy Thompson by four), then the following week's **Riverside Open,** and, later, the second of his three **Glens Falls Opens**. He also won back-to-back **Metropolitan Opens** in 1937 and '38 at the Forest Hill Field Club and the old Fresh Meadow CC, respectively. Hines' final win, the 1945 **Tacoma Open,** fell between a pair of historic events: a record-setting 14-shot victory by Ben Hogan at the Portland Open and Byron Nelson's 13-shot payback in Seattle.

Lon Hinkle (USA)

San Diego State graduate Lon Hinkle (b. Flint, Michigan, 7/17/1949) was one of the PGA Tour's top players for several years during the late 1970s, finishing as high as third on the money list (1979) and winning three times, including the 1979 **Bing Crosby** and **World Series of Golf**. A large man capable of generating substantial power, Hinkle appeared poised to break through in a big way in 1980 when he stood among the final-round leaders at both the U.S. Open and the PGA Championship, only to finish third—with fine views of dramatic Jack Nicklaus victories—in each. Though his time near the top would not be long, Hinkle earned a special place in golf history at the 1979 U.S. Open at Inverness when his decision to shorten the new par-5 eighth hole by driving down the adjacent 17th fairway led to the overnight planting of a 30-foot Black Hills Spruce tree by the USGA—the "Hinkle Tree."

Simon Hobday (South Africa)

One of professional golf's great characters of the last three decades, South Africa's Simon Hobday (b. Mafeking, 6/23/1940) was a cattle rancher prior to turning professional in 1969, having previously represented Zambia in the 1966 World Amateur Team competition. A truly elite ball-striker, Hobday claimed six victories over nearly 15 years of competing both in Europe and South Africa, the most significant being the 1971 **South African Open** at Mowbray GC, where he held off a charging Gary Player to win by one. Hobday was also the 1976 **German Open** champion and, closer to home, a back-to-back winner of the old **Rhodesian Open** in 1976 and '77.

An entertaining (if occasionally eccentric) sort, Hobday reportedly practiced every day of his 50th year in preparation for the American Champions Tour. The time certainly proved well spent, for he was a five-time winner between 1993 and 1995, capturing the 1994 **U.S. Senior Open** (by one over Jim Albus and Graham Marsh) and pocketing over $4 million in total winnings.

Scott Hoch (USA)

A former Walker Cup player, U.S. Amateur finalist (where he lost to John Cook in 1978) and two-time All-American at Wake Forest, Scott Mabon Hoch (b. Raleigh, North Carolina, 11/24/1955) has ridden a solid tee-to-green game to a long and fruitful career on the PGA Tour, claiming 11 wins and over $18 million in nearly 25 years of campaigning. Of particular note is the fact that he played virtually all of his best golf after turning 40, with his top money rankings coming in 1996, '97, and 2001, the last at age 46. Hoch has also demonstrated truly remarkable consistency, failing to crack the top 40 money winners only once—in an injury-affected 1992 season—between 1982 and 2002.

Unfortunately not all memories of Hoch are pleasant, for his defining moment may well be the two-foot clinching putt that he missed during sudden death at the 1989 Masters, allowing Nick Faldo to win with a birdie on the second extra hole. Hoch also achieved a degree of infamy in Great Britain—if not among purists everywhere—when, in 1995, he called St. Andrews the "worst piece of mess" he'd ever seen. That same year, however, saw Hoch enjoy the unique experience of being paired with three U.S. presidents (Clinton, Ford, and Bush) at the Bob Hope—a round he later described, not without humor, as "slow."

PGA Tour Wins (11): 2001 Western Open; 2003 Doral
Intn'l Wins (6):
Walker Cup: 1979 **Ryder Cup:** 1997 & 2002 (2) **Presidents Cup:** 1994–98 (3)

Karl Hoffman (Germany)

The unquestioned father of golf course design in Germany, Karl Hoffman was a trained building architect and engineer who began both laying out and reconstructing courses in his homeland in the aftermath of World War I. In 1924 he assisted the colorful Tom Simpson in designing Germany's period standard, the Bad Ems GC, and soon enjoyed a virtual architectural monopoly throughout the country. He took on his eventual successor, Bernhard von Limburger, as a partner during the 1930s, endured a forced sabbatical from design work during World War II, then completed a modest number of new projects following the cessation of hostilities before passing away during the 1950s.

Ben Hogan (USA)

Born: Dublin, Texas, 8/13/1912 **Died:** Ft. Worth, Texas, 7/25/1997

It is possible (though only that) that there have been better ball-strikers than Ben Hogan, and conceivable (if that) that someone, somewhere, has outworked him. But when it comes to demonstrating the mix of grit, determination, and, above all, perfection of technique necessary to be a golfing champion, there was—and likely only will be—one William Ben Hogan.

The Hogan legend began in tiny Dublin, Texas, where he was born, before moving east to Ft. Worth following his father's suicide in 1922. Like most professionals of his era, Hogan discovered golf through caddying, a vocation he took up not out of interest but rather because it paid better than most other work available to an uneducated 12-year-old. In the caddie yard at Ft. Worth's Glen Garden CC, he met another up-and-comer, one Byron Nelson, who at the time was infinitely more popular and successful, giving the shy-yet-pugnacious Hogan an early yardstick with which to measure himself. Deciding to make golf his career, Hogan began a practice regimen that would one day become golf's gold standard, and despite standing barely over 5'7" and weighing only 130 pounds, soon developed into one of the game's longest hitters.

He did not, however, become one of its greatest players, for his early stabs at professional competition saw him well behind not only Nelson but also fellow Texans Lloyd Mangrum, Jimmy Demaret, and Ralph Guldahl, among many others. Yet Hogan persevered, failing in several competitive attempts but continually improving through his tireless, unending training. By the late 1930s, bolstered by the promise of financial backing from Henry Picard if things really got bleak, he finally gained a foothold, then took his first win partnered with Vic Ghezzi at the 1938 **Hershey Four-Ball**. Despite frequent problems with a

Three of the stars in the 1940 Miami $10,000 Open golf tournament finger
stacks of the silver dollars that will be awarded as prize money.
Left to right are Willie Klein, Horton Smith, and Ben Hogan.

hook, Hogan rose substantially in the final prewar years, winning four times in 1940, then five and six times in 1941 and '42, respectively.

During the war he served as a lieutenant in the Army Air Corps, finding little time to compete but a fair amount for practice. Discharged in 1945 and well aware of the enormous recent success enjoyed by the 4F Byron Nelson (winner of a combined 26 events in 1945–46), a determined Hogan roared back with five victories late that season, including an epic performance at the **Portland Open (Oregon)** in which his record-setting 261 total routed the second-place Nelson by 14! But this joyous moment proved fleeting; two weeks later, an inspired Nelson shot 259 to reset the record at the Seattle Open.

In 1946 Nelson, who was now on the verge of retirement, won six more times but was finally usurped, Hogan taking center stage all to himself with a robust 13 victories. But even in this sustained triumph there was further disappointment, for Hogan lost the Masters by three-putting the 72nd green from 12 feet and missed the Nelson-Mangrum-Ghezzi play-off at the U.S. Open by repeating the gaffe, this time from 18 feet. Still, he emerged from 1946 with a PGA Championship and status as the game's number one star and, perhaps, with something more: his vaunted "Secret." Claiming to have discovered a mysterious magic move that summer, Hogan—who fully understood the psychology of gaining a competitive edge—now utilized a swing that had, apparently, become hook-proof,

his longstanding nemesis buried beneath a succession of high, powerful and extremely accurate fades.

Over the next two seasons, this much-analyzed swing produced 17 more wins, including a memorable stretch at Riviera in which he claimed the 1947 and '48 **Los Angeles Opens** and the 1948 **U.S. Open,** the latter with a tournament record 276. The three victories over a single course in 18 months was unprecedented, leading Hogan's friend Jimmy Demaret to christen the California club "Hogan's Alley."

Riviera would again be central to the Hogan story two winters later, but only after he had nearly been killed in a February 2, 1949, car accident while driving in western Texas with wife Valerie. Initially thought to be crippled, Hogan's comeback stands among the most inspiring in sports, being memorialized by a major motion picture *(Follow The Sun)* and by the creation of the golf writers' Ben Hogan Award (for remaining "active in golf despite a physical handicap or serious illness"). Thus it was with great uncertainty that Hogan hobbled onto Riviera for the 1950 Los Angeles Open less than a year after the crash, yet he proceeded to shoot 73-69-69-69 for 280 and, amazingly, apparent victory. Perennial rival Sam Snead was still on the course, however, and managed to finish birdie-birdie to ruin a perfect storyline and force an 18-hole play-off. Delayed a week by weather and logistics, the play-off eventually went to Snead 72-76 but Hogan's comeback was little short of astonishing.

Equally so was the run he put together over the next four seasons, playing a sharply abbreviated schedule to accommodate legs that would never regain their pre-accident strength. Required to carefully wrap his limbs before each round and soak them extensively afterward, Hogan proceeded to win the **U.S. Open** in 1950, '51, and '53, the **Masters** in 1951 and '53, and the **Open Championship** in 1953, a dominant stretch that, when linked to his last pre-accident run, added up to nine Major championship victories in 16 starts.

The 1950 U.S. Open win at Merion (in a play-off over Lloyd Mangrum and George Fazio) remains forever memorialized by Hy Peskin's photo of Hogan's 1-iron approach to the 72nd. Equally memorable was the successful 1951 title defense at the newly modernized Oakland Hills, when a final-round 67 "brought the monster to its knees." It was in 1953 that Hogan truly achieved immortality by becoming the only man ever to take the Masters, U.S. Open, and Open Championship in the same season, the latter win being of particular note as it came during his one and only visit to golf's oldest championship. Being introduced to links golf at Carnoustie, the toughest layout in the Open rota, Hogan's steadily improving rounds of 73-71-70-68 left him four strokes clear of the field, forever staking "the Wee Ice Mon's" place on the timeless Scottish golf landscape.

Increasingly bothered by physical problems and ample post-accident putting difficulties, Hogan tried in vain to win the title he most coveted, a fifth U.S. Open, right up through 1960. He would come remarkably close, suffering heartbreak in 1955 at Olympic (when Jack Fleck birdied the 72nd to catch him, then won the play-off) and 1960 at Cherry Hills, when the now-47-year-old Hogan hit the first 34 greens of the 36-hole finale before spinning his wedge approach to the par-5 71st back into a pond, drowning his hopes once and for all.

Fittingly, Hogan's last victory came in 1959 at his hometown **Colonial National Invitational,** an event created by his longtime friend Marvin Leonard and which Hogan won an unmatched five times. Equally fittingly, his last competitive appearance came in 1971 at the Champions International in Houston, a tournament hosted by Hogan's pals Jimmy Demaret and Jack Burke Jr. He was by this time a living legend, the famed Hogan Mystique having grown to mythic proportions, fueled by its central character's avoidance of the spotlight and supposed gruffness.

What drove the legend, of course, was something beyond wins and losses. It was the uniquely powerful way in which Hogan struck the ball, generating a machine-like accuracy that, well into his 50s, still held onlookers in awe. His career numbers, sensational as they are, do not clearly establish Ben Hogan as golf's greatest-ever player, but few who witnessed these demonstrations firsthand believe that anyone has ever been better. Indeed when Nicklaus reached his prime and was considered a legitimate contender, Hogan's old friend Tommy Bolt summed things up with his usual directness, saying "All I know is that Nicklaus watches Hogan practice, and I never heard of Hogan watching Nicklaus practice." Henry Cotton, for his part, assessed Hogan's genius differently, calling him simply, "as tough a golfer as ever trod a links."

Amen.

PGA Tour Wins (64): 1940, '42 & '46 North & South; 1940 Greensboro; 1942, '47 & '48 Los Angeles; 1946 & '47 Phoenix; 1946 Texas; 1946, '47, '52, '53 & '59 Colonial; 1946 & '48 Western Open; **1946 & '48 PGA Championship;** 1947 & '51 World Championship; **1948, '50, '51 & '53 U.S. Open;** 1949 Bing Crosby; **1951 & '53 Masters,** 1953 British Open; and 3 Asheville Opens & 3 Miami Intn'l Four Balls

Ryder Cup: 1947 (c) & '51 (2); 1949 Capt

1934-1967

	34	35	36	37	38	39	40	41	42	43	44	45	46	47	48	49	50
Masters	-	-	-	-	T25	9	T10	4	2				2	T4	T6	-	T4
US Open	MC	-	MC	-	MC	T62	T5	T3					T4	T6	1	-	1
British	-	-	-	-	-	-							-	-	-	-	-
PGA	-	-	-	-	-	T9	T5	T5	T5		-	-	1	T33	1	-	-

	51	52	53	54	55	56	57	58	59	60	61	62	63	64	65	66	67
Masters	1	T7	1	2	2	T8	MC	T14	T30	T6	T32	38	-	T9	T21	T13	T10
US Open	1	3	1	T6	2	T2	-	T10	T8	T9	T14	-	-	-	-	12	T34
British	-	-	1	-	-	-	-	-	-	-	-	-	-	-	-	-	-
PGA	-	-	-	-	-	-	-	-	-	MC	-	-	-	T9	T15	-	-

Sir Ernest Holderness (UK)

Born in Lahor, India, Sir Ernest William Elsmie Holderness (1890–1968) was, by all reports, the sort of British civil servant one sees in movies: shy and unassuming, highly conscientious and dedicated first to the satisfactory completion of his colonial tasks. Golf, we are told, came second, shoehorned into weekends and summer evenings, with competitive play reserved strictly for holidays. A compelling and romanticized picture it is, but one made more so by Holderness' wonderful results, namely winning **British Amateurs** in 1922 and '24 (at Prestwick and St. Andrews) and establishing himself, along with Cyril Tolley and Roger Wethered, as one of the nation's elite nonprofessionals.

A Walker Cup player in 1923, '26 and '30, Holderness won the first four **President's Putter** competitions (1920–23) of the Oxford and Cambridge Golfing Society, as well as a fifth in 1929, events which, in those early years, drew fields nearly comparable to the national Amateur. A rock-steady player with little flash, Holderness was described by Longhurst as having "that simple and, in the best sense, elementary sort of style that enables a man to leave his clubs for a year or two in the attic and, on retrieving them, to play from memory." Which, given a full-time government career in the Home Office, was apparently necessary.

Marion Hollins (USA)

One of the most important golfing women of the first half of the twentieth century, East Islip, New York, native Marion Hollins (1892–1944) was an exceptional athlete and the daughter of the first president of New York's Metropolitan Golf Association, making her ascent in the world of competitive golf hardly a surprise. Defeated in the final of the U.S. Women's Amateur at age 22 by Gladys Ravenscroft, Hollins contented herself with **Metropolitan Amateur** wins in 1913 and '16 (plus a later title in 1924) before finally taking the **Women's Amateur** in 1921 in Deal, New Jersey, ending the reign of Alexa Stirling, the three-time champion, with a 5 and 4 win.

Hollins had big plans that extended far beyond playing golf. In 1923, she spearheaded the establishment of Long Island's Women's National GC (today's Glen Head CC) before heading west to help Samuel Morse develop the Cypress Point Club. By the late 1920s, she had moved north to Santa Cruz, where she developed her own recreational community, Pasatiempo. Riding the economic highs of the Roaring '20s and the lows of the Depression, Hollins eventually passed away in Pacific Grove of cancer at age 51.

Helen (Gray) Holm (UK)

One of Scotland's top World War II–era women, Glasgow native Helen Holm (1907–1971) was twice a **British Ladies** champion, first in 1934 (when she defeated 17-year-old Pamela Barton 6 and 5 at Royal Porthcawl), then again in 1938 (4 and 3 over Elsie Corlett at Burnham and Berrow). Particularly tall and a long, rhythmic swinger of the club, Holm participated in three Curtis Cup matches (1936, '38, and '48), captained several other international teams, and won five **Scottish Ladies** titles between 1930 and 1950.

Gene Homans (USA)

Though hardly a household name, Englewood, New Jersey-born Eugene V. Homans (1909–1965) became an indelible part of golfing history at the 1930 U.S. Amateur played at the then-Merion Cricket Club in Ardmore, Pennsylvania. Having defeated Lawson Little in the quarter-finals and Charlie Seaver in the semis, Homans became the unfortunate man to stand between the great Bobby Jones and his inevitable winning of the Grand Slam. The final was, in the words of Herbert Warren Wind, "a dull contest, an irritating, drawn-out anticlimax" that saw Homans concede the 29th hole to lose 8 and 7.

A Princeton graduate, Homans was not without some genuine highlights on his résumé, having won the 1930 **North & South** (over the great Canadian Sandy Somerville) and the 1928 **Metropolitan Amateur** (over Maurice McCarthy Jr. 4 and 3 at Fenway GC). He was also selected to the 1928 Walker Cup team, though he ultimately did not participate.

Richard Hooper (UK/Kenya)

A British expatriate who for many years resided in Kenya, Richard Hooper authored one of postwar golf's scarcest books, *The Game of Golf in East Africa* (W. Boyd, 1953), an omnibus volume chronicling the game's development in Kenya, Uganda, and Tanganyika (Tanzania). Though a fascinating representation of colonial life, the book's true significance is its rarity, a circumstance brought about by Hooper's having buried the last 500 copies in his garden just before fleeing the Mau Mau uprising of the mid-1950s.

Bob Hope (USA)

Truly an international show business legend, Leslie Townes "Bob" Hope (1903–2003) was born in Eltham, England before moving to Cleveland, Ohio, at age four. Eventually to become a dominant personality of stage and screen, Hope was also a great friend to golf, playing avidly and well (his low handicap was four) and famously remarking that "Golf is my profession, show business is how I pay the bills." By lending his name to the old Palm Springs Desert Classic, he gave both the tournament and desert golf an immense boost, also helping (along with his friend Bing Crosby) to give the game a new level of celebrity chic. Hope also wrote *Confessions of a Hooker: My Lifelong Love Affair With Golf* (Doubleday, 1985), a *New York Times* bestseller for 53 weeks. He died, at age 100, at his Toluca Lake, California, estate, just yards from the Lakeside GC, one of several at which he had long been a member.

Joe Horgan (USA)

Though never enjoying the lasting fame of men like "Big" Crawford and "Fiery" Carey, New Yorker Joe Horgan may have logged more time on high-profile bags than any caddie in the game's history. He began, innocently enough, in 1893 at the nation's first public course, Van Cortlandt Park, but within two years was looping for Horace Rawlins when the young English émigré won the first U.S. Open at Newport. In subsequent seasons, Horgan was a regular with such national champions as Findlay Douglas, Beatrix Hoyt, Willie Anderson, Genevieve Hecker, George Duncan, and even a pair of all-time legends, Walter Hagen and a visiting Harry Vardon. What a great shame that *he* didn't get around to writing a book before passing away in 1953.

J. P. Hornabrook (New Zealand)

Generally considered A. D. S. Duncan's successor as New Zealand's top amateur, John P. Hornabrook beat the pros in the **New Zealand Open** in 1937 and '39, while also capturing the national **Amateur** in 1935, '36, and '39, the latter occasion making him the first man since Duncan to win both titles in a single year. Blessed with remarkable natural talent, Hornabrook is far better recalled for his pleasant, almost cavalier attitude than for any real dedication to the game. That he loved playing has never been questioned, yet one story has him falling asleep during the 1936 Amateur Foursomes (in which he stayed awake long enough to win in 1937 and '38) and period accounts make frequent reference to his generally succeeding in spite of himself.

Reg Horne (UK)

London native Reginald W. Horne (b. 1908) burst upon the British golfing scene rather suddenly by winning the *News of the World* match-play title at Walton Heath in 1945. Cited by Leonard Crawley as a "magnificent striker of the ball," Horne won only a handful of relatively minor events beyond the match play, though he very nearly captured the 1947 Open Championship at Hoylake, finishing a single stroke behind winner Fred Daly. That stroke (and perhaps another) was lost at the 70th where an otherwise perfect 4-wood second to the par 5 came up a foot short, finding a bunker. Even so, Daly had to birdie the last from 35 feet to win, making Horne one of the harder-luck losers of the postwar era.

Tommy Horton (UK)

Following a long and distinguished line of Jersey golfers, St. Helens' product Thomas Alfred Horton, M.B.E. (b. 6/16/1941) won a handful of British events before the 1971 founding of the European Tour, as well as the 1970 **South African Open** (at Royal Durban) and several mid-1970s African titles of lesser pedigree. His 1974 victory at the **Penfold Tournament** came in the final edition of that event, though this and three additional Tour wins pale in comparison to his triumph at the 1978 **British Masters,** a one-stroke defeat of Dale Hayes, Graham Marsh and Brian Waites. Where the modest-hitting Horton has truly excelled, however, is as a European senior, capturing an impressive 22 of that tour's titles between 1992 and 2000.

S. V. Hotchkin (UK/South Africa)

Colonel Stafford V. Hotchkin (1876–1953), a career military man and one-time Conservative MP, first got involved in golf architecture upon purchasing his home course, Woodhall Spa, in 1920. His renovation of this 1905 Harry Vardon layout turned a good golf course into a great one and led Hotchkin to form his own design and construction firm. He spent the late 1920s touring South Africa, where he built or remodeled several of that nation's elite courses, before returning home to partner with fellow ex-soldiers Sir Guy Campbell and C. K. Hutchison. When the threesome went their separate ways during the mid-1930s, Hotchkin retired to Woodhall Spa where he served as club secretary until his death.

Notable Courses: Humewood CC, South Africa; Maccauvlei GC, South Africa; **Woodhall Spa GC**

C. R. Howden (UK/New Zealand)

A native of Edinburgh, Charles Ritchie Howden (b. 1838) has historically been referred to as the father of New

Zealand golf, enjoying the rare experience of actually launching the country's links fortunes twice. Initially, Howden was the driving force behind the Dunedin GC, an 1871 facility of his own design on the South Island that, upon Howden's business-related return to Britain, expired late in the decade. But by 1892 Howden was back and giving it a second go, this time forming the Otago GC that, after an 1895 expansion, remains in business today as New Zealand's oldest golf course.

Charles Howell III (USA)

Considered one of professional golf's top young prospects, Augusta, Georgia, native Charles Howell III (b. 6/20/1979) brought an impressive résumé onto the PGA Tour, dating back to his selection as AJGA Player of the Year in 1996. At Oklahoma State, the lean, hard-swinging Georgian was the 2000 **NCAA** Champion, the consensus collegiate Player of the Year, and a two-time first-team All-American. Such a record has not always guaranteed professional success, of course, but with a 2002 victory (at the **Michelob Championship**), over $8.6 million in career earnings and a 2003 Presidents Cup selection, Howell is certainly off to a good start. Still, potential stars are ultimately judged on their ability to win golf tournaments and with only the single victory in his first 145 Tour starts, Howell still has some work to do. But it's early yet.

David Howell (UK)

Closing in on age 30, England's David Howell (b. Swindon, 6/23/1975) has had an up-and-down go of it over nine seasons on the PGA European Tour, winning once (at the 1999 **Dubai Desert Classic**) but never finishing higher than 14th in the Order of Merit. He has, however, played his best golf of late, particularly since 2003 when two years of consistent effort resulted in a first Ryder Cup appearance in 2004. Also a winner at the 1998 **Australian PGA,** Howell is an average ball-striker from tee to green but a skilled man with a putter in his hand. Age-wise, at least, he is just entering his prime.

Beatrix Hoyt (USA)

Though born in Westchester County, Beatrix Hoyt (1880–1963) was playing out of Long Island's Shinnecock Hills GC by the time she emerged, at age 16, as the first dominant player in American women's golf. This she did by capturing three consecutive **U.S. Women's Amateurs,** first in 1896 at New Jersey's Morris County GC, then in '97 at

Massachusetts' Essex County Club, and finally, in '98, at the luxurious Ardsley Club on the eastern slopes of the Hudson River. Though perhaps not as skilled as her more advanced British counterparts, Hoyt used a full, aggressive swing (despite the restrictive women's attire of the period) and was generally considered to be far ahead of her American female competition and largely the equal of all but the best males.

Hoyt would sweep medalist honors in the Amateur's qualifying stage every year from 1896 to 1900, but she was upset in the first round in 1899, then reached the semifinals in 1900 where she lost to eventual three-time winner Margaret Curtis. Hoyt then promptly retired from competitive golf at the ripe old age of 21, leaving a threepeat legacy which has been equaled (by Alexa Stirling, Glenna Collett, Virginia Van Wie and Juli Inkster) but never exceeded.

Hsieh Min Nam (Taiwan)

Another in Taiwan's bumper crop of post-1960 professionals, Hsieh Min Nam first made international noise as an amateur when he captured medalist honors at the 1964 **World Amateur Team Championship,** at Rome's Olgiata CC. Maximizing an already successful visit, he then won the **Italian Amateur** before returning home. Turning professional soon thereafter, Hsieh would go on to establish himself as a regional force, winning numerous local events and finishing 1971 as the Asia circuit's top-ranked player. The following year, he would make history by teaming with Lu Liang Huan to capture a rain-shortened **World Cup** at Royal Melbourne, arguably the most surprising victory in the event's more than 50 years of competition.

Hsieh Yung Yo (Taiwan)

With frequent experience representing Taiwan in World Cup play, Hsieh Yung Yo was a regular winner on the Asia circuit during the 1960s and early '70s, finishing as that tour's top-ranked player on four separate occasions. Seemingly a collector of regional national titles, Hsieh won Open championships in **Korea** (1961 and '63), **Thailand** (1965 and '69), **Taiwan** (1967 and '68), **Singapore** (1968), the **Philippines** (1970) and, most impressively, three consecutive times in **Hong Kong** (1963–65). He also appeared in the Masters from 1970 to 1972, rather respectably tying for 29th on his first visit.

Bob Hudson (Canada/USA)

Long before the PGA of America tried to market Great Britain as our enemy in order to hit the financial jackpot with the Ryder Cup, Canadian-born Oregon fruit packer Bob Hudson took a more Samuel Ryder–like stance, making the first postwar match (1947) possible by footing the bill for the financially strapped British team to sail over on the Queen Mary. That the match was played in Portland is thus not so odd as it might otherwise seem, such a concession being a minor price to pay for keeping the entire series alive. Two years later, when the Americans packed off to Ganton, Hudson again stepped up, shipping a massive cache of food supplies to help the players through Britain's postwar rationing. A modest controversy erupted as the gesture was perceived by many Britons as arrogant, though in the end the food was shared by both teams, all of whom surely appreciated Hudson's continuing generosity.

Brian Huggett (UK)

Brian George Charles Huggett, M.B.E. (b. Porthcawl, 11/13/1936), Wales' finest golfer during the long years between Dai Rees and Ian Woosnam, won approximately 17 events of European Tour caliber, though only three came after the official founding of the Tour in 1971. Among his earlier titles of note were the 1962 **Dutch** and 1963 **German Opens,** though it was really a third-place at the 1962 Open Championship at Troon that announced the 5′6″ Huggett's arrival to the golfing world. A tie for second would follow in the 1965 Open at Royal Birkdale and that would have to do until the Welshman scored two important victories, the 1968 *News of the World* match play (beating John Panton in the final) and perhaps his biggest triumph, the 1970 **British Masters.** In this latter event, at Royal Lytham & St. Anne's, Huggett's winning score of 293 was an improbable +9, yet five clear of his nearest pursuer, David Graham, and nine ahead of Peter Oosterhuis. Even more impressively, Huggett's closing 65 beat the entire field by five and was the sole sub-70 round of the week under what obviously were severe conditions.

After 12 years of competitive retirement, Huggett joined the European Senior tour in 1992, winning 10 titles in eight seasons. He was also one of his era's more active Ryder Cup players, appearing in six matches between 1963 and 1975 and compiling a respectable 9-10-6 record on teams which went 0-5-1. He then returned to the scene of his British Masters triumph, Royal Lytham, to captain a losing team in 1977.

Intn'l Wins (17): 1962 Dutch Open; 1963 German Open; 1967 Volvo PGA; 1968 PGA Match Play; 1970 British Masters; 1974 Portuguese Open
Ryder Cup: 1963; 1967–75 (6); 1977 Capt

Lawrence Hughes (USA)

Chillicothe, Missouri, native Lawrence Hughes (1897–1976) was the product of solid golf design bloodlines, his father having worked construction for Donald Ross in the early years of the Golden Age. Entering the design field full time after World War II, Hughes' break came in 1946 when golfer/entrepreneur Johnny Dawson brought him aboard to design several desert courses in the Southwest, a previously unsuitable landscape that Dawson—acutely aware of underground aquifers—was prepared to develop. Hughes' first such layout, San Diego's Stardust CC, is no longer, but such subsequent endeavors as the Palm Springs area's Thunderbird, La Quinta, and Eldorado CCs and the famous Club de Golf Mexico all stand as monuments to his work.

Bernard Hunt (UK)

One of England's top professionals for two decades beginning in the early 1950s, Bernard John Hunt, M.B.E. (b. Atherstone, 2/2/1930) won with great consistency during the 1960s, both at home and on the Continent. Recognized for a short, rather ungainly backswing and the sort of steady, safe approach that sometimes leads to winning more money than titles, he was a strong iron player and a steady putter—all in all a fine recipe for longevity.

Though a winner of national Opens in **Belgium, Germany, France, Egypt** and **Brazil,** Hunt's two biggest triumphs came in the **British Masters,** first at Little Aston in 1963, then at Portmarnock two years later. On the great stage of the Open Championship, however, Hunt's record was a bit less shiny, yielding four top-five finishes between 1955 and 1965 but no real chances to actually win the Claret Jug.

A model of sportsmanship and comportment, Hunt made eight Ryder Cup appearances, the most memorable of which, unfortunately, came at Wentworth in 1953 when a famously missed 3-foot par putt at the last cost him—and Great Britain—a chance at victory. Hunt would also captain a pair of losing sides in 1973 and '75.

Intn'l Wins (24): 1957 Belgian Open; 1961 German Open; 1963 & '65 British Masters; 1967 French Open
Ryder Cup: 1953, 1957–69 (8); 1973 & '75 Capt

David Hunter (USA)

A little-known player with no recorded wins of significance, David Hunter nonetheless made golfing history at the 1909 U.S. Open when his opening 68 over the old Englewood (New Jersey) CC course made him the first player ever to break 70 in the national championship. Of course, eventual winner George Sargent would set a new tournament record total of 291 and Tom McNamara would add a 69, so conditions might well be described as favorable. Hunter, by the way, proceeded to self-destruct in round two with a full-bodied 84, ultimately finishing 23 strokes behind Sargent.

Robert Hunter (USA)

Terre Haute, Indiana, product Wiles Robert Hunter (1874–1942), a graduate of Indiana University, was one of golf's all-time most curious characters. A career academician and a political radical, Hunter wrote a number of books dedicated to leftist causes including the highly influential *Poverty*, a 1904 treatise that is considered a classic of its genre. Ironically Hunter, whose own roots were middle class, would marry an enormously wealthy woman and thus was living on her family's expansive farm when he ran for Connecticut's governorship on the Socialist ticket.

Eventually moving west, Hunter naturally took a position teaching at the University of California at Berkeley where—once again in apparent opposition to his radical politics—he continued developing a longstanding interest in golf course design. He soon penned *The Links* (Scribner's, 1926), a classic architectural volume written, so far as we know, without a moment's actual experience building a golf course. In the mid-20s, Hunter was instrumental in bringing Dr. Alister MacKenzie to California, and within a short time joined forces with MacKenzie in a design partnership. Though Hunter's precise role in the operation may forever be debated, he nonetheless received codesign credit for such layouts as Cypress Point, the Valley Club of Montecito, and Marin County's Meadow Club, all genuine MacKenzie classics.

Willie Hunter (UK/USA)

England's William I. Hunter (1892–1968), son of the golf professional at Royal Cinque Ports, was a fine post–World War I amateur whose misfortune it was to come along at a time dominated by Wethered, Tolley, and Holderness. Nonetheless, despite being a relatively short hitter, Hunter captured the 1921 **British Amateur** at Hoylake where he drubbed Allan Graham 12 and 11 in the final. That same year he drew a great measure of attention in America by defeating Bobby Jones in a quarter-final match at the U.S. Amateur, played at the St. Louis CC. Hunter appar-

ently liked what he saw of the United States, for soon after losing his British title to Holderness in the 1922 semifinals at Prestwick, he emigrated to Southern California and, after a bit of amateur competition, became a professional. He would eventually serve for 28 years at Los Angeles' Riviera CC, where his son Mac also proved a fine player, defeating a 17-year-old Arnold Palmer in 1946 to win the U.S. Junior Amateur.

Dr. Michael Hurdzan (USA)

Among golf course architecture's more educated practitioners, West Virginia native Dr. Michael Hurdzan (b. 1943) holds B.A. and B.S. degrees from Ohio State and a Masters and a Ph.D. from the University of Vermont. Having worked as a teenager for Ohio–based architect Jack Kidwell, Hurdzan opened a business that included course construction among its services while pursuing his postgraduate degrees. He only became a full-time architect after receiving his Doctorate, eventually becoming Kidwell's partner in 1976.

Working in recent years with Dana Fry, Hurdzan has produced several high-profile designs, including Ontario's Devil's Paintbrush and Devil's Pulpit courses, and the Naples National GC in Florida. An expert on environmental issues, he authored the influential *Golf Course Architecture* (Sleeping Bear, 1996) and also possesses one of the world's finest private golf libraries.

Pat Hurst (USA)

Californian Pat Hurst (b. San Leandro, 5/23/1969) initially came to attention by winning the 1986 **USGA Junior Girls**, backed it up with **NCAA** individual and team titles at San Jose State in 1989, then added a flourish by capturing the 1990 **U.S. Women's Amateur** at Canoe Brook. Despite such glowing credentials, however, Hurst worked as a teaching pro and played in various smaller venues before eventually reaching the LPGA Tour in 1995. Once on the big stage, however, she debuted with a splash, being named Rookie of the Year, then improving her money ranking from 49th to 19th over three seasons. She is a three-time career winner whose finest moment came at the 1998 **Dinah Shore** when she edged Helen Dobson to claim her first Major championship. Not surprisingly, Hurst's two weakest post-rookie seasons came in 1999 and 2002—both on the heels of giving birth—with returns to top form soon following. She participated on Solheim Cup teams in 1998, 2000, and '02.

John Huston (USA)

With seven wins in more than 15 PGA Tour seasons, John Huston (b. Mt Vernon, Illinois, 6/1/1961) might be considered something of a journeyman—but if so, then he is a journeyman who, when the stars are right, can uncork some of the hottest golf imaginable. The most obvious example came in at 1998's **Hawaiian Open** where, with rounds of 63-65-66-66, Huston broke the Tour record for lowest 72-hole score in relation to par with a 28-under total of 260. It was a record that had stood for 43 years, though with today's unchecked equipment, it was rebroken by Joe Durant just three seasons later. Other prime examples of a hot Huston must include his 61s at the 1996 Memorial Tournament and 2002 Buick Challenge, his closing 65 (with birdies at three of the last four holes) to win the 2000 **Tampa Bay Classic,** and the final-round 62 with which he overtook Mark O'Meara to win the 1992 **Walt Disney World Classic.** Though not an especially long driver of the golf ball, the Auburn-educated Huston stands well above average in greens hit and is clearly able to make enough putts to convert so many birdie opportunities.

Charles Hutchings (UK)

Devon-born Charles Hutchings (b. 1849) was one of the **British Amateur's** oldest champions, at age 53, when he won on his home links at Hoylake in 1902—and one cannot help but surmise that his beating a much younger field with the new rubber (or "Haskell") ball did much to launch the much-maligned "Bounding Billy" to British prominence. Hutchings is also noteworthy for helping to design Deal's old Prince's GC, a classic links upon which Gene Sarazen won the 1932 Open Championship but which expired during World War II.

C. K. Hutchinson (UK)

An outstanding athlete who excelled particularly at golf, Cecil Key Hutchison (1877–1941) hailed from East Lothian and was educated at Eton before becoming one of the United Kingdom's better amateur players. A classic Victorian-era military man, he was a member of the Coldstream Guards, served in both the Boer War and World War I (where he did time in a German POW camp) and left the service with the rank of Major. As a golfer, he was a fine competitor, winning numerous local events, frequently representing Scotland internationally, and losing the 1909 British Amateur at Muirfield (his home course) to Robert Maxwell with a heartbreaking bogey at the last.

Following World War I, Hutchison entered the field of golf course design by helping James Braid to build the famous 36 holes at the Gleneagles Hotel. During the 1920s he went into partnership with Colonel S. V. Hotchkin and Sir Guy Campbell, forming a high-profile firm responsible for such designs as the West Sussex (aka Pulborough) and Ashridge GCs, and some renovative work at North Berwick and Woodhall Spa. On his own, Hutchison also made alterations to Ganton and Turnberry's Ailsa course, among others.

Horace Hutchinson (UK)

Born: London, England, 5/16/1859 **Died:** London, England, 7/28/1932

Though his name may not stand the tallest to contemporary readers, there have been few more important figures in the development of golf as we know it than Mr. Horatio Gordon "Horace" Hutchinson. Born in London but raised primarily in Devon, Hutchinson learned the game at Royal North Devon, England's oldest seaside course which, to date him a bit, came into being when Horace was five. By 13 he was a strong player, and his capturing of the 1875 club medal at age 16 automatically made Hutchinson one of the youngest club captains in golfing history (a club protocol long since amended). It is also worth noting that his frequent caddie was a local lad named John Henry Taylor, an employee of the Hutchinson household who would himself have a thing or two to say about the course of golf history.

Saddled with a long, flippy-wristed swing, Hutchinson may not have been counted a stylist, but he hit it long, was well thought of as a putter, and was cited by Bernard Darwin as the best scrambler he'd ever seen. As such, Hutchinson was good enough to play at Oxford and, more memorably, to win back-to-back **Amateur Championships** in 1886 and '87. On the first occasion, at St. Andrews, he dispatched Henry Lamb 7 and 6, but it would be his second victory, at Hoylake, that represented his competitive peak. For there he won the last two holes of his semifinal match against the elder John Ball to set up a final against eventual eight-time champion John Ball Jr., which Hutchinson took one up.

More than his playing, however, it was Hutchinson's writing that most dramatically affected golf—and being some 17 years older than Darwin, he initially had the field largely to himself. All told, he would author or edit no less than 14 golf books, several of which stand as all-time classics. For introductory and instructional purposes, there were *Hints on the Game of Golf* (William Blackwood, 1886) and *Golf: The Badminton Library* (Longmans,

Green 1890), both of which have enjoyed modern reprints. For the budding fields of agronomy and course design, there was *Golf Greens and Green Keeping* (Country Life, 1906), while the stunning *British Golf Links* (J. S. Virtue, 1897) was the first book to graphically profile the finest courses. Finally, as a lifetime retrospective there was the classic *Fifty Years of Golf* (Country Life, 1919), an historical treasure trove reprinted by the USGA in 1985.

Among his many golfing achievements, Hutchinson was the first Englishman to be elected captain of the R&A (in 1908), and he also experimented—far ahead of his time—with an elongated driver whose swing weight was accordingly lessened, presaging modern equipment trends by a good 70 years. Hutchinson was generally perceived as somewhat aloof, and his friend Darwin acknowledged that he was "not always understood by those with no excessive power of understanding." However Darwin, equally noted that he could "think of no one more attractive and picturesque, with more varied interests or a more interesting mind."

Jock Hutchison (UK/USA)

Born: St. Andrews, Scotland, 6/6/1884 **Died:** Chicago, Illinois, 9/28/1977

Jock Hutchison joined the hundreds of Scottish golfers emigrating to America in the early 1900s, working at New York's St. Andrews and Pittsburgh's Allegheny CC before settling in for many years at Chicago's Glen View Club. A fast and decidedly nervous player, Hutchison established himself among the elite of American golfers prior to World War I, finishing fifth at the 1911 U.S. Open in Chicago, then second to the high-flying Chick Evans in 1916 at Minikahda. Hutchison also was runner-up at the first PGA Championship in 1916, losing to Jim Barnes (another British transplant) one down at New York's Siwanoy CC.

Denied several good years by the event cancellations of World War I, Hutchison enjoyed a fine run in its aftermath, tying for third at the 1919 U.S. Open, then for second in 1920, a year in which he won his first **Western Open** (at Olympia Fields) and also defeated the vastly underrated Douglas Edgar one up at Flossmoor CC to take the **PGA Championship.** The following summer it was off to his native St. Andrews where, after much practice in advance of the event, Hutchison became the first "American" (albeit a Scottish-born one) to win the **Open Championship,** routing a young Roger Wethered by nine strokes in a 36-hole play-off. The event was also notable for an equipment controversy, Hutchison's deeply scored irons being closely examined and, in later years, banned from tournament play.

Approaching 40, Hutchison finished fourth while defending his title in 1922 and third at the next year's U.S. Open, rounding out his best competitive period. An ageless sort who won **PGA Seniors** titles in 1937 and '47 and frequently shot his age, Hutchison gained further fame by serving (along with his contemporary Fred McLeod) as honorary starter at Masters tournaments right up into the 1970s, the two octogenarians representing the last surviving links to Scotland's incalculable contribution to the early American game.

PGA Tour Wins (14): 1920 & '23 Western Open; **1920 PGA Championship;** 1921 North & South; **1921 British Open**

1908-1928

	08	09	10	11	12	13	14	15	16	17	18
US Open	T8	T23	T8	T5	T23	T16	WD	T8	2		
British	-	-	-	-	-	-	-				
PGA									2		

	19	20	21	22	23	24	25	26	27	28
US Open	T3	T2	T18	T8	3	T3	27	-	22	T41
British		-	1	4	-	-	-	-	-	-
PGA	T5	1	T9	T5	-	T17	-	-	-	T5

Bill Hyndman (USA)

An ageless and particularly stylish player, Glenside, Pennsylvania, native William Hyndman III (b. 12/25/1915) must rank among the very best players never to win either the U.S. or British Amateur championships, though he certainly came close. In 1955, for example, Hyndman beat Hillman Robbins in the semifinals of the U.S. Amateur before running into a red-hot E. Harvie Ward, losing 9 and 8 in the final. In the 1959 British Amateur final, played at Royal St. George's, Hyndman lost 3 and 2 to future PGA Tour player and Commissioner Deane Beman. Ten years later he again reached the British final, this time losing to five-time champion Michael Bonallack at Hoylake, 3 and

2. A year later, both Hyndman and Bonallack would return to the final (a first) at Royal County Down GC, with the Englishman again winning, this time by a more substantial 8 and 7.

On the positive side of the ledger, the Penn State–educated Hyndman did win the 1961 **North & South Amateur** (over Dick Chapman) and the 1968 **Trans-Mis-** sissippi, played in several Masters and U.S. Opens, and appeared on five Walker Cup teams between 1957 and 1971, the last at age 55. He also won the **USGA Senior Amateur** in 1973, then became the oldest-ever winner of a USGA championship when he captured the same title in 1983, at age 67.

I

Trevor Immelman
(South Africa)

The product of a golfing family, Cape Town native Trevor Immelman (b. 12/16/1979) joined the top ranks of the European Tour in 2003. During the early season swing through his homeland, Immelman broke through for his first official European victory in the **South African Open,** a storybook sudden-death win at the course upon which he learned the game, the Erinvale GC. Claiming the Sunshine Tour's Order of Merit with a follow-up triumph at the **Dimension Data Pro-Am** and two subsequent runners-up, he would later team with Rory Sabbatini to win the **World Cup** at Kiawah Island, finishing the year 14th in the European Order of Merit.

A former **South African Amateur** and **U.S. Public Links** champion, Immelman has since become the first since Gary Player to successfully defend the **South African Open,** later claiming a second 2004 European Tour win at the **Deutsche Bank-SAP Open,** where he edged Padraig Harrington by one. The owner of a sound and reliable swing, Immelman looks a genuine up-and-comer on the international stage.

Juli (Simpson) Inkster
(USA)

Juli Inkster's Hall of Fame career has been played out over nearly a quarter-century, dating back to her four consecutive selections as an All-American (1979–82) at San Jose State when still known by her maiden name of Simpson. Even more impressively, during her final three college years, she swept consecutive **U.S. Women's Amateur** titles, the first woman to complete the hat trick since Virginia Van Wie some 48 years previous.

Inkster (b. Santa Cruz, California, 6/24/1960) qualified for the LPGA Tour in August of 1983 and proceeded to win the **SAFECO Classic** in only her fifth start, placing an impressive 30th on the money list despite entering only eight events. Technically still a rookie, she would win twice in 1984 with both events—the **Dinah Shore** and the **du Maurier Classic**—being Majors, a never-before-achieved first-year double that cinched Rookie of the Year honors. What followed was a decade of consistently high-class golf broken only twice for childbirth (1990 and '94), a stretch which saw Inkster establish herself as a rock-solid player with 12 more wins (including a second **Dinah Shore** in 1989) and three top-10 money finishes, the best being third in 1986.

Several leaner years followed in the mid-1990s, perhaps the inevitable result of focusing upon her growing family. But near millennium's end, at a late-30s juncture where many players begin cutting back, Inkster took a great leap forward, winning 10 times and finishing no worse than sixth on the money list between 1997 and 2000. At the center of this rush was a career-best 1999, a five-win campaign that included the two Majors (the **LPGA Championship** and the **U.S. Women's Open**) which Inskter needed to follow Pat Bradley as the second woman to complete the modern career Grand Slam. In 2000, she would notch three more victories including a defense of her **LPGA Championship,** and while 2001 saw a drop to 22nd on the money list, 2002 featured a second **U.S. Women's Open** victory, highlighted by a closing 66 to beat the world's best, Annika Sorenstam, at Prairie Dunes.

Now in her mid-40s, Inkster still finished fifth on the 2003 money list while winning twice, including the **Corning Classic** where her closing 62 was the lowest final-round score ever shot by an LPGA tournament winner. Relatively tall at 5'7", Inkster is lean and not overly powerful, yet her well-rounded game has shown precious few weaknesses. With 30 career wins, seven Major championships and an impressive measure of longevity, she has well-earned the Hall of Fame status that was conferred upon her in 1999—and she may not be done yet.

LPGA Wins (30): 1984 & '98 Dinah Shore; 1984 du Maurier; 1992 Wykagyl; 1997, '98 & 2000 Samsung WC; 1999 Welch's; **1999 & 2002 U.S. Women's Open; 1999 & 2000 LPGA Championship;** 2003 Corning
Curtis Cup: 1982 **Solheim Cup:** 1992, 1998–2003 (5)

1978-2004

	78	79	80	81	82	83	84	85	86	87	88	89	90	91
Dinah						-	1	T19	T5	T17	T12	1	T11	T30
LPGA	-	-	-	-	-	-	T7	T25	T3	T9	T61	T65	MC	9
US Open	T23	MC	-	MC	T29	-	T27	MC	T69	T40	T8	-	MC	MC
dM/Brit*		-	-	-	-	-	1	T43	T22	T39	T16	-	MC	T36

	92	93	94	95	96	97	98	99	00	01	02	03	04
Dinah	9	T40	-	T16	T19	T16	T24	T6	T17	T15	T19	T11	T28
LPGA	9	T65	T14	T47	T5	T53	T16	1	1	T15	T4	T37	T6
US Open	2	T39	T18	T37	T4	T14	MC	1	T23	T12	1	8	T58
dM/Brit*	3	T52	MC	3	T12	T5	T14	3	T5	MC	MC	T41	T25

*du Maurier replaced by the Women's British Open in 2001.

Mitchell Innis (UK)

Gilbert Mitchell Innis was a top-flight pre-Open Championship golfer for whom accounts are great but records are sketchy. What is well established is his occasional partnership with Young Tom Morris in challenge matches, and it is reported that in their primes the pair could find no takers, despite wagering £100 against £80. Widely considered James Fairlie's primary competition for supremacy among Scotland's period amateurs, Innis won medals all across the countryside and is reported, in one year, to have finished either first or second in each of the 22 competitions he entered.

Seiichi Inouye (Japan)

After years of assisting Japanese design patriarch Kinya Fujita, Seiichi Inouye went solo in the years following World War II, establishing himself as Japan's premier modern-era golf architect. Considered highly knowledgeable in areas of agronomy and greens construction, he is credited with completing more than 35 designs, nearly all in his home country. For faraway Western observers, the Musashi CC and Oarai GC (where Fujita reportedly provided some input) are likely the best-known entries.

Ann Irvin (UK)

Though not overly large of stature, Lancashire's Ann Irvin (b. 1944) was a fine British amateur of the 1960s and early '70s, her record of success dimmed only by occasional bouts with ill health or diminished interest. A four-time Curtis Cupper between 1962 and 1976, she took **English Ladies** titles in 1967 and '74 and the **British Open Stroke Play** (today's Women's British Open) in 1969. Curiously, the era's most coveted title, the **British Ladies Amateur,** managed to evade Irvin for many years, her nearest miss coming in 1969 when she grabbed an early 4-hole lead over Catherine LaCoste in the final at Royal Portrush before eventually losing 2 and 1. In 1973 Irvin's ship finally came in when her victory at Carnoustie denied Michelle Walker a third straight triumph.

Hale Irwin (USA)

A product of Joplin, Missouri, Hale S. Irwin (b. 6/3/1945) was a two-sport star at the University of Colorado, taking the 1967 **NCAA** individual golf title and being twice selected All-Big Eight as a football defensive back. An academic All-American, Irwin ultimately chose golf, primarily because he stood only 6'0" and weighed 180 pounds—and the choice proved a wise one, for with well over 65 professional victories in more than 35 years of competing, he has enjoyed one of the longest and most successful careers of the modern era.

A highly reliable player whose simple, arms-oriented swing perhaps requires less intricate timing, Irwin's widely acknowledged skill with long irons helped make his game ideal for tougher courses; thus it is no surprise to find victories at places like Riviera, Harbour Town, Butler National, and Pebble Beach dotting his record. These skills also propelled him to his most famous triumphs, three **U.S. Open** titles won in 1974, '79, and '90. On the first occasion Irwin merely survived when, facing perhaps the toughest Open setup of the modern era, he won at Winged Foot with a +7 total of 287. Five years later at Inverness, he held a commanding six-shot lead through 63 holes, then stumbled through his final nine to hold off Gary Player and Jerry Pate by two. But his most dramatic Open win was surely at Medinah in 1990 when, at age 45, he closed with a fine 67 to force a play-off with upstart Mike Donald, then claimed victory with a birdie at the 19th hole after both men shot 74 over the initial 18. Irwin has quietly posted a solid record in the other Majors as well, recording four consecutive top 5s at the Masters from 1974 to 1977 and three top 10s at the Open Championship in only 11 starts. Of course, his most embarrassing moment also took place in Britain when, during the 1983 Open at Royal Birkdale, he whiffed a 6-inch tap-in during the third round and ultimately lost the title to Tom Watson by one.

Though it has been frequently overlooked, Irwin also enjoyed a great deal of success overseas, largely before such globetrotting became fashionable. He won, for example, back-to-back **World Match Play** titles at Wentworth in 1974 and '75, defeating Gary Player and Al Geiberger in successive finals. He also took PGA titles in **Australia** (1978) and **South Africa** (1979), the Japanese **Bridgestone Open** (1981), and the **Brazilian Open** (1982), giving him the rare achievement of victories on all six inhabited continents. Irwin's 13-5-2 career Ryder Cup ledger, one of the best of his time, is further evidence of his international competitiveness.

A hint of the future was visible in Irwin's remarkable post-40 golf, for he claimed four more PGA Tour wins during his fifth decade, and in his last Ryder Cup appearance halved Bernhard Langer in the final 1991 match to clinch an American victory at Kiawah Island. Clearly among golf's more athletically inclined, Irwin continued this graceful aging right onto the Champions Tour where he has set a unique standard of greatness, claiming 40 titles (including the 1998 and 2000 **U.S. Senior Opens**) and nearly $26 million in prize money in less than nine full seasons.

PGA Tour Wins (20): 1971, '73 & '94 Heritage; **1974, '79 & '90 U.S. Open;** 1975 Western Open; 1976 Los Angeles; 1983 & '85 Memorial; 1984 Bing Crosby; 1990 Westchester
Intn'l Wins (8): 1974 & '75 World Match Play; 1978 Australian PGA; 1979 South African PGA
Champions Tour Wins: 40 (1995–2004)
Ryder Cup: 1975–81 & '91 (5) **Presidents Cup:** 1994

1966-1995

	66	67	68	69	70	71	72	73	74	75	76	77	78	79	80
Masters	-	-	-	-	-	T13	MC	-	T4	T4	T5	5	8	T23	MC
US Open	T61	-	-	-	-	T19	T36	T20	1	T3	T26	T41	T4	1	T8
British	-	-	-	-	-	-	-	-	T24	9	T32	T46	T24	6	-
PGA	-	-	-	-	T31	T22	T11	T9	WD	T5	T34	T44	T12	MC	T30

	81	82	83	84	85	86	87	88	89	90	91	92	93	94	95
Masters	T25	MC	T6	T21	T36	MC	-	-	-	-	T10	47	T27	T18	T14
US Open	T58	T39	T39	6	14	MC	MC	T17	T54	1	T11	T51	T62	T18	MC
British	-	-	T2	T14	-	-	-	-	-	T53	T57	T19	-	-	-
PGA	T16	T42	T14	T25	T32	T26	-	T38	-	T12	T73	T66	T6	T39	T54

Eleven of the top touring pros, all entered in the 1955 Titleholders Tournament, pose before the start of the LPGA Clinic at the Augusta Country Club: *(left to right)* 1st row: Patty Berg, Louise Suggs, Carol Bowman, Joyce Ziske, Vonnie Colby, Bonnie Randolph. 2nd row: Pat O'Sullivan, Alice Bauer Hagge, Marilyn Smith, Fay Crocker, and Marlene Bauer. (Historic Golf Photos)

J

Reid Jack (UK)

Scotland's Robert Reid Jack (b. 1924) enjoyed a brief but impressive run in the mid-1950s, winning the **Scottish Amateur** in 1955, then the **British Amateur** in '57, the latter by defeating American army sergeant Harold Ridgley in the final. Also a fifth-place finisher in the 1959 Open Championship at Muirfield, Jack may best be remembered for a pair of Walker Cup matches he played in 1957 and '59 (his only two appearances) against American Billy Joe Patton. In the former, at Minikahda, he lost after Patton roared back from a five-hole lunchtime deficit, but in the latter, at Muifield, Reid would gain a measure of revenge, handling the oft-wild Patton 5 and 3.

Tony Jacklin (UK)

The son of a truck driver in Scunthorpe, England, Tony Jacklin, C.B.E. (b. 7/7/1944) may not have put up career numbers to match the likes of the Triumvirate, Henry Cotton, or Nick Faldo, but in his particular place and time, Jacklin's performances in several prominent events served to make him a timeless British golfing hero.

A professional since 1962, Jacklin's first important win came at the 1967 **British Masters,** by which time he had already taken several lesser titles in New Zealand and South Africa. Playing frequently in America as well, he won the 1968 **Jacksonville Open** and in so doing became the first Englishman in 42 years to claim a PGA Tour title. But even with this growing résumé, few were ready to predict victory at the 1969 **Open Championship** at Royal Lytham & St. Annes, where Jacklin's rock-steady total of 280 bettered Bob Charles by two to capture the Claret Jug. The wildly popular win represented the end of a dark time in British golf, for no homebred had taken the title since Max Faulkner in 1951, and Jacklin became a national icon virtually overnight.

Hardly content to rest on his laurels, Jacklin then made further history by braving heavy winds and a controversial Hazeltine National GC to win the 1970 **U.S. Open,** surprising the Americans with rounds of 71-70-70-70, for a 281 total that left the field a distant seven shots in arrears. It was truly stunning stuff and a splendid high point in postwar British golf, for in addition to holding both national Opens, Jacklin was now the first Briton to take the American title since Ted Ray in 1920. He further backed his fine play with several strong continental victories over the next two seasons, an epic outgoing 29 during the first round of the 1970 Open Championship at St. Andrews and a second win at the **Jacksonville Open** in 1972.

Jacklin's peak, however, met a bloody end later that season at the Open Championship at Muirfield, where he came up the 71st fairway tied with Lee Trevino, but with Trevino laying three in greenside rough and Jacklin sitting two just 30 yards shy of the putting surface. Trevino proceeded to chip in, a rattled Jacklin took three putts for a six, and what seemed a third Major title was gone in a snap. Jacklin would later win four events in South America, occasionally contend in America (e.g., second to Tom Watson at the 1977 Bing Crosby), and, much later, take two titles on the Champions Tour but, for all intents and purposes, as a world-class player he was finished.

Jacklin did, however, make an enormous mark as a four-time Ryder Cup captain, losing narrowly at PGA National in 1983, then gaining the first British/European victory since 1957 at The Belfry in 1985. He further burnished his résumé when two years later his troops became the first ever to win the Cup on American soil (at Muirfield Village), then retained it in his final go-round with a 1989 tie, once again at The Belfry. A 2-1-1 captain's ledger seems a suitable legacy for a man whose own Cup playing record was 13-14-8, no small accomplishment on teams whose overall record was 0-6-1.

Intn'l Wins (12): 1967 & '73 British Masters; 1970 Trophée Lancôme; 1971 Benson & Hedges; 1972 & '82 Volvo PGA; 1973 Italian Open; 1979 German Open
PGA Tour Wins (4): 1969 British Open; 1970 U.S. Open
Champions Tour Wins: 2 (1994–95)
Ryder Cup: 1967–79 (7); 1983–89 Capts

1963-1975

	63	64	65	66	67	68	69	70	71	72	73	74	75
Masters	-	-	-	-	-	T22	MC	T12	T36	T27	MC	MC	MC
US Open	-	-	-	-	-	-	T25	1	MC	T40	T52	MC	MC
British	T30	-	T25	T30	5	T18	1	5	3	3	T14	T18	-
PGA	-	-	-	-	-	-	T25	MC	-	-	T46	T55	-

Katherine (Harley) Jackson (USA)

Fall River, Massachusetts, native Kate Harley (1881–1961) initially won the **U.S. Women's Amateur** in 1908, defeating Mrs. T. H. Polhemus 6 and 5 in the final at Chevy Chase, Maryland, to conquer the smallest field of entrants (41) in the twentieth century. Six years later, under her married name of Mrs. Arnold Jackson, she took a second national **Amateur** at Long Island's Nassau CC, getting up and down for bogey at the last to edge young Elaine Rosenthal one up. Mrs. Jackson was also the **Eastern Amateur** champion of 1914 and the **Massachusetts Women's** winner in 1917, as well as a participant in an informal international match in 1913 pitting American women against a team from Great Britain and Canada.

John Jacobs (UK)

Lindrick, England's John Robert Maurice Jacobs, O.B.E. (b. 1925) has seen and done it all in postwar British golf, initially making his bones as a fine tournament player during the 1950s when he won, among other things, the 1957 **Dutch Open** and the 1957 **South African PGA**. Jacobs was a Ryder Cup player in 1955 and twice a losing captain, first at The Greenbrier in 1979, then two years later at Walton Heath, where the Americans fielded perhaps the strongest international team ever assembled. He is also justifiably famous as one of the game's best teachers, having worked with numerous professionals, run golf schools both at home and abroad, and written several books including *Practical Golf* (Quadrangle, 1972) and *Golf Doctor* (Stanley Paul, 1979).

Perhaps Jacobs' most visible contribution to the game took place in the early 1970s when he was appointed Tournament Director-General of the British PGA, officially marking the separation of touring pros from their club-bound brethren. Integrating a variety of existing national opens and sundry other events into a unified schedule marked the beginning of the modern European Tour, a process which continued vigorously after Jacobs handed the rains over to Ken Schofield in 1975.

John Jacobs (USA)

The younger brother of former PGA Tour player Tommy, long-hitting John Jacobs (b. Los Angeles, California, 3/18/1945) remains, in his late 50s, one of American golf's more colorful characters. An elite junior player in Southern California, Jacobs had greatness predicted of him from the beginning—before he quit USC to fight in Vietnam, and certainly before enjoying himself, perhaps too much, amidst the softer sides of life. Always quick to a drink or a horserace, Jacobs never became a serious factor on the PGA Tour, instead playing literally the world over, winning several titles in the Far East during the 1980s and early '90s. He would eventually qualify to play the Champions Tour in 1996, where his fan-friendly demeanor and colossal drives quickly found favor. A five-time winner (including the 2003 **Senior PGA Championship**), Jacobs once cited Walter Hagen as his ideal playing partner because "my friends say we would have a heck of a twosome."

Tommy Jacobs (USA)

An elite junior player in the years following World War II, Tommy Jacobs (b. Denver, Colorado, 2/13/1935) joined the PGA Tour in 1957 and enjoyed a solid run through the mid-1960s, consistently earning top-60 money while totaling four official victories. A 1965 Ryder Cup pick, Jacobs fired a then-record-tying 64 in the second round of the 1964 U.S. Open at Congressional, ultimately finishing second when his 70-76 finish in debilitating heat was overtaken by Ken Venturi's famous 66-70 close. Jacobs came even closer at the 1966 Masters where his even-par 288 total landed him in a three-way play-off with Jack Nicklaus and Gay Brewer—but his solid play-off 72 lost to Nicklaus by two. There is, of course, a certain irony to Tommy's achieving far more as a player than his gifted younger brother

John, but such is the unpredictability of golf. Quitting the Tour in the late 1960s, Jacobs retired to a professional job at San Diego's La Costa Resort.

Peter Jacobsen (USA)

Long one of the PGA Tour's most popular players, Peter Erling Jacobsen (b. Portland, Oregon, 3/4/1954) has perhaps garnered more attention for his performing skills — both as a musician and an imitator of famous swings — than he has for his golf. This does not, however, represent any disparagement of the latter, for Jacobsen is a seven-time Tour winner who banked most of his $7.3 million before purses really got huge.

A three-time All-American at the University of Oregon, Jacobsen took more than three full seasons to gain his first win (the 1980 **Buick-Goodwrench Open**) and actually scored the majority of his titles in a pair of two-win seasons, 1984 and '95. During 1995 his victories came back-to-back, at the **Bing Crosby** and the **San Diego Open**, leading to a seventh-place money ranking and a season-ending appearance in his second Ryder Cup. Largely written off over the next seven years (a stretch in which he five times failed even to crack the top 125), Jacobsen closed out his full-time PGA Tour days in style, winning the 2003 **Greater Hartford Open** at age 49. He then spent 2004 splitting time between the PGA and Champions Tours, logging four top-10 finishes in his first five starts on the latter, including a victory at the **U.S. Senior Open**.

Fredrik Jacobson (Sweden)

After struggling just to retain playing privileges on the European Tour during the late 1990s, Fredrik Jacobson (b. Gothenburg, 9/26/1974) has since emerged as one of the blossoming talents in international golf. For after new-millennium Order of Merit finishes of 25th, 38th, and 30th, Jacobson exploded in 2003, first closing with 65-63-64 to win the **Hong Kong Open**, then later adding wins at the **Portuguese Open** and the **Volvo Masters**. In between, he found time to tie for fifth at his first U.S. Open and sixth at the Open Championship, all of which added up to fourth place on the Order of Merit and a good deal of buzz both at home and abroad. A somewhat quieter 2004 may have tempered expectations a bit, but with an outstanding putting stroke and a willingness to travel, Jacobson still has a chance to become an international star.

Thongchai Jaidee (Thailand)

Though diminutive Sukree Onsham was Thailand's first prominent golf professional, former army paratrooper Thongchai Jaidee (b. Lopburi 11/8/1969) is surely its best, coming into the international spotlight by qualifying into the U.S. Open (and tying for 74th) in 2001. Earlier, Jaidee had won the amateur championships of **Thailand, Singapore,** and **Pakistan** as well as several regional professional titles. He has since claimed three further Asian victories (including the 2003 **Volvo Masters**) and, most important, the European Tour's 2004 **Malaysian Open,** making him the first Thai player to win on a non-Asian tour. The victory earned Jaidee, of all things, a diplomatic passport from the Thai government designed to expedite his future international travel.

Louis James (USA)

Among the least likely of **U.S. Amateur** champions, Chicagoan Louis N. James (b. 1882) was the last man to qualify — off a shaky 94 — in 1902, the first year to require clearing a medal-play hurdle to reach a 64-man match-play field. The heavy favorite, two-time defending champion Walter Travis, was knocked off in the opposite bracket by Eben Byers, whom the 19-year-old James would ultimately face in the final. There, playing over a Glen View GC layout so rain-ravaged as to mandate the use of only nine holes, the hometown hero upset Byers 4 and 2, scarcely to be heard from, on a national level, ever again.

Mark James (UK)

After winning the **English Amateur** in 1974, Mark Hugh James (b. Manchester, 10/28/1953) turned professional and joined the European Tour in 1976, going on to claim 18 titles while establishing himself, along with Sam Torrance, as the best in the United Kingdom after the Faldo-Lyle-Woosnam triumvirate of the 1980s. Well known for both his wit and occasional bad temperament, James employed a short, powerful swing that was light on aesthetics but strong on reliability, affording him seven top-10 finishes on the Order of Merit, including a career-best third in 1979. He also set a Tour record by being fined £1,500 for generally boorish behavior during the 1979 Ryder Cup and once, due to injury, closed out an Italian Open round one-handed to post a spectacular 111.

But petulance and indiscretions aside, there is little doubt that James could play, with his first European win, a 1978 triumph at the old *News of the World* match play, proving stronger than the standard debut. Like most top British players, James collected his share of European national titles including two **Irish** and **Spanish Opens,** and one each in **Italy, Tunisia,** and **Morocco.** He also captured the 1986 **Benson & Hedges** event (in a three-way play-off with Lee Trevino and Hugh Baiocchi) and the 1990 **British Masters** (by two over David Feherty). Though never truly a threat to win an Open Championship, James certainly proved himself competitive, four times finishing among the top 5—but never closer than four off the winning score.

Despite his misadventures in 1979, James would ultimately represent Britain in seven Ryder Cups before serving as captain in 1999 at Brookline, where America's record-setting comeback triggered the great celebration controversy following Justin Leonard's clinching putt. James also represented England in World Cup play on nine occasions, and claimed his first Champions Tour victory—the **Senior Players Championship**—in 2004.

Intn'l Wins (18): 1978 PGA Match Play; 1979 & '80 Irish Open; 1982 Italian Open; 1986 Benson & Hedges; 1988 & '97 Spanish Open; 1990 British Masters
Champion Tour Win: 1 (2004)
Walker Cup: 1975 **Ryder Cup:** 1977–81, 1989; '95 (7); 1999 Capt

Betty Jameson (USA)

Born in Norman, Oklahoma, but raised in San Antonio, Betty Jameson (b. 5/19/1919) blossomed early as a golfer, winning the **Texas Public Links** title at age 13 and the 1934 **Southern Amateur** at 15. Truly a prodigy, Jameson possessed physical and course management skills well beyond her years, enabling her to win four straight **Texas Ladies** titles beginning at age 16, as well as two **Trans-Mississippis,** two **Western Amateurs,** and, ultimately, back-to-back **U.S. Amateurs** in 1939 (at Wee Burn) and 1940 (at Pebble Beach).

Having also claimed the 1942 **Western Open** while still an amateur, Jameson turned professional in 1945 and was one of the LPGA's 13 founding members in 1950. All told, she is credited with 12 professional victories, though three, the 1947 **U.S. Women's Open,** the 1948 **Tampa Open,** and the 1949 **Texas Open,** predate the existence of the Tour. Interestingly, her U.S. Open title came in the event's second year, with Jameson having lost the inaugural (which was contested at match play) 5 and 4 to Patty Berg in Spokane. But in 1947 at North Carolina's Starmount Forest CC, Jameson shot 295—the first recorded case of a woman breaking 300 for 72 holes—to run away by six.

Educated at the University of Texas, Jameson was far from the typical single-minded athlete, maintaining a lifelong interest in art that saw her happily into retirement as a painter. A Hall of Famer in 1951, she has also left the LPGA a lasting legacy by establishing an award for the player with the lowest annual scoring average, donating the trophy named for her childhood hero (and later good friend) Glenna Collett Vare.

LPGA Wins (12): 1942 & '54 Western Open; 1947 U.S. Women's Open; 1948 Tampa; 1952 World Championship; 1955 Babe Zaharias
Major Amateur Wins (7): 1934 Southern; 1937 & '40 Trans-Miss; 1939 & '40 U.S. Women's Amateur; 1940 & '42 Western Amateur

1947-1960

	47	48	49	50	51	52	53	54	55	56	57	58	59	60
LPGA									10	3	T9	T3	T15	20
US Open	1	3	T17	10	T14	T2	4	T14	T9	T7	DQ	5	T15	T12

Also won Western Opens as listed above.

Don January (USA)

A smooth, timeless swinger capable of winning PGA Tour events more than two decades apart, Donald Ray January (b. Plainview, Texas, 11/20/1929) starred on three consecutive national championship teams at North Texas State (1950–52) before serving in the Air Force, then joining the PGA Tour. Winning the 1956 **Dallas Open** by holing a bunker shot at the 72nd, January ultimately claimed 10 official victories, a number which might have been larger had he not frequently headed home after amassing $50,000–$60,000 in winnings, regardless of the month.

January's biggest triumph came in the 1967 **PGA Championship** at Denver's Columbine CC, where he defeated Don Massengale in a play-off, perhaps making up for a heartbreaking play-off loss to Jerry Barber at the 1961 PGA after Barber holed putts of 20, 40, and 60 feet on the final three greens to tie. By his early 40s January chose to give up the grind entirely, beginning a career as an architect that floundered when course development tanked during the mid-1970s recession. With little else to do, January returned to the Tour and, at age 45, won the 1970 **Texas Open,** then followed it up with the **Tournament of Champions** the following winter. Showing uncommon form for such an age, he was chosen for the 1977 Ryder Cup team, becoming the oldest American to participate to that point.

For all of January's accomplishments on Tour, modern readers will more readily recall his superb run in the early days of the Champions Tour, for January was its leading money winner three of its first five seasons, amassing a total of 22 wins and $4.3 million. History will also show him as the winner of the Champions' first official event, 1980's **Atlantic City International.**

PGA Tour Wins (10): 1967 PGA Championship; 1975 Texas
Ryder Cup: 1965 & '77 (2)

Lee Janzen (USA)

Since joining the PGA Tour in 1990, former Florida Southern Division II All-American Lee Janzen (b. Austin, Minnesota, 8/28/1964) has established himself as rather an intriguing player. Janzen's game features little of the power exhibited by most of golf's modern stars, yet he has managed eight Tour wins and more than $11 million in earning over a 15-year span. Further, two of his eight victories have been **U.S. Opens,** with the first coming in 1993 at Baltusrol, when Janzen's record-tying 272 total defeated Payne Stewart by two. Five years later at San Francisco's Olympic Club, he would become the 14th man to win more than one Open by again defeating Stewart, this time coming from five back with a closing 68, the largest final-round comeback since Johnny Miller at Oakmont some 25 years previous.

With two U.S. Opens raising expectations, it is not unnatural to wonder if perhaps the rest of Janzen's career hasn't quite measured up. To suggest this, however, would be to ignore an impressive record of consistency, for he has seldom fallen out of the top-60 money winners while thrice finishing among the top 10. He was also a winner at the 1994 **Buick Classic** and 1995 **Players Championship** and appeared in the 1993 and '97 Ryder Cups.

Dan Jenkins (USA)

An American sportswriting institution, Dan Jenkins (b. Ft. Worth, Texas, 12/2/1929) played golf at hometown Texas Christian University before turning to journalism full time, first with the *Fort Worth Press,* then the *Dallas Times-Herald.* Being, as he himself might say, smart enough to have been born in Ft. Worth, Jenkins became friendly with local hero Ben Hogan, hardly a career handicap given Hogan's general reticence with outsiders. Jenkins moved on to *Sports Illustrated* in 1962, then later to *Golf Digest* and *Playboy,* all the while spinning his own unique brand of irreverent, yet traditionalist humor. Equally adept as an over-the-top novelist, Jenkins penned the golf-oriented *Dead Solid Perfect* (Atheneum, 1974) as well as *You Gotta Play Hurt* (Simon & Schuster, 1991), an amusing tale that partially touches the Royal & Ancient game. He has twice had his magazine work anthologized and has written one nonfiction golf book, *Sports Illustrated's The Best 18 Golf Holes in America* (Delacorte, 1966).

J. L. C. Jenkins (UK)

Glasgow's J. L. C. Jenkins (b. 1883) was a largely undocumented figure who, playing out of Troon, won the final **British Amateur** before the first World War (1914) by defeating Charles Hezlet 3 and 2 at Royal St. George's. A reference to his subsequent departure from the top ranks was provided, once again, by Darwin who called Jenkins "a fine, confident and attacking golfer and a masterly iron player, who, but for a wound in the war, would, I think, have been a more prominent player in later years."

Ruth Jessen (USA)

The **Pacific Northwest Amateur** titleist in 1954 and '55, Seattle native Mary Ruth Jessen (b. 11/12/1936) was also **Women's Intercollegiate** champion in 1956 before turning professional later that same year. Destined to become an 11-time winner on the LPGA Tour, Jessen first broke through at the 1959 **Tampa Open** and peaked with a five-win 1964 that witnessed no sudden hot streaks, just five victories in five different months all across the country. Unfortunately, Jessen was soon waylaid with all manner of physical ailments and operations, including cancer surgery in 1968. Thus her final victory at the 1971 **Sears World Classic** held great significance, capping a courageous comeback that resulted in Jessen's receipt of the Ben Hogan Award, not to mention a then-record $60,000 purse.

Miguel Angel Jiménez (Spain)

Malaga's Miguel Angel Jiménez (b. 1/5/1964), he of the modern-day ponytail, can arguably be called Spain's best contemporary player, Sergio Garcia not withstanding. A very straight driver of the ball who, when on his game, can rank among the best in greens-in-regulation, Jiménez has won 11 times on the European Tour since 1992, including the national Opens of **Belgium,** the **Netherlands,** and **Portugal,** the 1998 **Trophée Lancôme** and the 1999 **Volvo Masters,** the last claimed with a closing 65 that nipped Bernhard Langer, Padraig Harrington, and Retief Goosen by two.

Though somewhat off form at the dawn of the millennium, Jiménez rocketed back to the spotlight in 2004 when he won four times by summer's end, including the **Johnnie Walker** in Thailand, the **BMW Asian Open** in Shanghai and the **BMW International** in Munich. This return to form led to a 2004 Ryder Cup selection and figures to presage several more strong years on the international stage and, perhaps, an addition or two to his seven previous World Cup appearances. Jiménez has also enjoyed strong finishes on the PGA Tour, tying Ernie Els for second in the 2000 U.S. Open (some 15 shots behind Tiger Woods) and losing a play-off to Woods at the 1999 WGC-American Express event, played in his hometown of Malaga.

Intn'l Wins (11): 1992 Belgian Open; 1994 Dutch Open; 1998 Trophée Lancôme; 1999 Volvo Masters; 2004 Johnnie Walker; 2004 Portuguese Open
Ryder Cup: 1999 & 2004 (2)

Per-Ulrik Johansson (Sweden)

Though yet to finish a season higher than 97th on the PGA Tour money list, Uppsala native Per-Ulrik Johansson (b. 12/6/1966) is recognizable to many Americans for the reversed fashion in which he wears his Hogan-style cap—a look once described by Peter Alliss as resembling "a U boat commander." A former roommate of Phil Mickelson on Arizona State's 1990 NCAA championship team, Johansson has certainly found greater success on the European Tour, claiming four top-20 finishes in the Order of Merit and five official victories between 1991 and 1997. Tops on this list were back-to-back **European Opens** in 1996 and '97, the latter by a resounding six strokes over Peter Baker at the K Club in Dublin. A three-time World Cup player and a Ryder Cup pick in 1995 and '97, Johansson came to America full time in 2001 but has thus far struggled to find his place.

Chris Johnson (USA)

Former two-time University of Arizona All-American Chris Johnson (b. Arcata, California, 4/25/1958) is a nine-time winner on the LPGA Tour who has logged three top-10 money rankings (1986, '87, and '97) in over 20 years of competition. Her finest season came in 1997 as she neared 40, for in addition to finishing fourth in money, Johnson was twice a winner, including the **LPGA Championship** where she defeated Leta Lindley in sudden death at Delaware's Dupont CC. She has twice won the **Welch's** event in Tucson (1984 and '91) and was a Solheim Cup player in 1998.

Hootie Johnson (USA)

Though the legendary Clifford Roberts surely cast a longer shadow, no Masters tournament chairman has been as controversial as South Carolina banker William "Hootie" Johnson (b. 1931). Ironically, the issue which has placed Johnson so squarely in the national limelight—the all-male nature of the Augusta National GC—is one in which he seems an unlikely combatant, having established a long record of progressive beliefs and actions in a part of the country not always embracing of such. But faced with threats of boycotts to protest the club's constitutionally protected right to choose its own membership, Johnson chose to take the most contentious path, allowing an issue upon which he was legally untouchable to grow far larger than necessary.

While history figures to see Johnson as the winner of that battle, it may not favor him so much when it comes to the Augusta National golf course. On Johnson's watch alterations have taken place that, prior to the generous cutting of Sunday pins in the 2004 Masters, have materially lessened the event's renowned final-nine drama. Perhaps more importantly, such changes have largely been antithetical to the roughless, highly strategic design created by Bob Jones and Dr. Alister MacKenzie, a particular disappointment at a club that claims so passionately to honor their memories. Decisions to cancel the lifetime tournament exemption afforded past champions (since amended after player outcry) and to cease automatic invitations to all PGA Tour winners have raised further questions as to Johnson's commitment to the event's traditions and legacies.

Harrison Johnston (USA)

As might befit a man who was shell-shocked during World War I, St. Paul, Minnesota, native Harrison R. "Jimmy" Johnston (1896–1969) occasionally battled his nerves in high-level tournament play, yet he was a gutsy competitor who defeated Francis Ouimet and Tommy Armour in back-to-back years at the U.S. Amateur. Described by H. B. Martin as possessing "one of the soundest of golf swings," Johnston thoroughly dominated his home turf in Minnesota, capturing the state's **Amateur** title six times in succession during the 1920s. He would also win the 1924

Western Amateur, though his greatest triumph surely came at the 1929 **U.S. Amateur** at Pebble Beach, an event more frequently recalled both for Bobby Jones' first-round elimination and 45-year-old H. Chandler Egan's stunning run to the semifinals.

Less remembered still might be Johnston's near defeat of Jones in the 1930 British Amateur at St. Andrews, the first leg of the immortal Grand Slam. Standing 4 down with 5 to play in the round of 16, Johnston fought his way back to force Jones to hole a tricky eight footer at the last green—and how differently might history read had *that* putt not fallen?

Johnston was also a Walker Cup player in 1924, '28, and '30, going a combined 5-0, including a 5 and 4 singles victory over defending British Amateur champion Cyril Tolley at Royal St. George's in 1930.

Tony Johnstone (Zimbabwe)

A native of Bulawayo who grew up with future superstar Nick Price, Tony Johnstone (b. 5/2/1956) has long been recognized as one of golf's great shortgame specialists. A 16-time winner in Southern Africa (including the 1984 and '93 **South African Opens** and the 1989 and '98 **South African PGAs**), Johnstone spent most of his career laboring on the European Tour where he won six times between 1984 and 2001, placed seventh in the Order of Merit in 1992, and finished among the top 60 on 14 occasions. His second **South African PGA** victory was particularly memorable as he defeated the much younger Ernie Els by two at the Houghton GC. Three years later, at age 44, he proved his continuing competitiveness by requiring only 101 putts to defeat Robert Karlsson at the 2001 **Qatar Masters.** With Price living abroad and thus seldom competing, Johnstone has been the mainstay of Zimbabwe's recent international teams, participating in seven World Cups over an eight-year span between 1994 and 2001.

Bobby Jones (USA)

Born: Atlanta, Georgia, 3/17/1902 **Died:** Atlanta, Georgia, 12/18/1971

Though immortalized for an epic run of golf that took place during his 20s, Atlanta's Robert Tyre "Bobby" Jones Jr. was very likely, with a possible nod to work-in-progress Michelle Wie, the greatest child prodigy in the history of American golf. Learning to swing by mimicking East Lake CC's Carnoustie-born professional Stewart Maiden, Jones won the club's junior title by age nine, was shooting in the 70s at 11 and driving a ball 250 yards by 14—an ability which at least partially explains his reaching the quarter-finals (with two matches won) of the 1916 U.S. Amateur at

Merion at this very age. That same summer he took the **Georgia Amateur** crown, then at 15 won the first of three **Southern Amateurs,** beating one Louis Jacoby 6 and 4 at Birmingham's Roebuck Springs GC.

With golf's growing popularity tied to the coverage it received in newspapers and early magazines like *The American Golfer,* the name of the young Georgia phenom gained almost household status well before Jones had actually won anything outside his home region. This had advantages during wartime, however, as Jones spent the summer of 1918 barnstorming as one of the "Dixie Kids," a Red Cross fund-raising group composed of himself, Perry Adair, the reigning Women's Amateur champion (and Jones' childhood friend) Alexa Stirling, and Chicago's Elaine Rosenthal. That people around the country would pay to observe a group of teenage amateurs play speaks volumes as to the degree of young Bobby's growing fame.

After the war he finished runner-up at the U.S. Amateur at Oakmont (losing to Davy Herron 5 and 4 in the final) and second at the Canadian Open, where he trailed record-setting winner Douglas Edgar by a full 16 shots. By now age 17, Jones proceeded to endure three more seasons in which the 1920 and '22 **Southern Amateurs** were his only substantial titles, and victory in national championship events eluded him. His youthful temper was generally cited as the cause, particularly after he tore up his scorecard in disgust during the third round of his Open Championship debut, at St. Andrews in 1921. Such struggles would not normally be a catastrophe for a young man barely 20, but popular expectation laid a far heavier burden on Jones. Indeed, he would later write that following his semifinal loss to eventual champion Jess Sweetser at the 1922 U.S. Amateur, "the thorn was beginning to rankle in earnest."

Though struggling on the links, Jones had little difficulty in the classroom, graduating from hometown Georgia Tech in 1922, then taking a degree in English Literature at Harvard (1924) and attending Emery University law school. While thus becoming perhaps the best-educated competitive golfer ever, Jones' playing schedule was necessarily affected by his academic commitments. Indeed, it has been noted that of the 13 years in which he competed on a national level, he was enrolled as a full-time student—either in high school or higher institutions—for nine of them, and he was forced to skip the 1923 Walker Cup matches at St. Andrews because he would not have been able to return to Harvard in time for final exams.

In any event, Jones' years of frustration finally ended at the 1923 **U.S. Open** at New York's Inwood CC, but not without a struggle. Having all but blown it with a bogey, bogey, double bogey finish at the end of regulation, he counted himself fortunate to end up in a play-off with Bobby Cruickshank, a contest he won with a fabled 2-iron approach to the 18th which carried a fronting pond before settling six feet from the pin. Thus the floodgates were open at last, and what followed—12 more Major titles over seven subsequent seasons—would represent a run unmatched even by the great Nicklaus.

In 1924 there came the **U.S. Amateur** (won 9 and 8 over George Von Elm back at Merion), a title Jones would defend the following summer at Oakmont by beating his longtime friend Watts Gunn 8 and 7. But it would be in 1926 that Jones recorded the heretofore unachieved feat which he believed, at the time, to be his ultimate success: winning both the **U.S.** and **British Opens** in the same season. At home this meant a one-stroke victory over Joe Turnesa at Ohio's Scioto CC. In England, Jones' Open Championship triumph was perhaps more stirring, won with a famous short-iron approach from a fairway bunker at the 71st which allowed him to edge Al Watrous by two at Royal Lytham & St. Anne's.

The following July saw Jones successfully defend his **Open Championship** by a robust six strokes over Aubrey Boomer and Fred Robson, an especially sweet victory as it took place at St. Andrews, site of his 1921 debacle. He would not enter the British Amateur on this visit but did claim the **U.S. Amateur** at Minikahda in something very close to peak form, easily disposing of stalwarts Harrison Johnston (10 and 9) and Francis Ouimet (11 and 10) before vanquishing two-time champion Chick Evans in the final, 8 and 7.

The next two years witnessed only single Major titles, though Jones would supplement his 1928 **U.S. Amateur** victory (a 10 and 9 rout of Phil Perkins at Brae Burn) with a second-place finish at the U.S. Open, losing a 36-hole play-off to Johnny Farrell by a single stroke at Olympia Fields. He would come back to win the **Open** the next year, however, holing a famously curling 12-footer for par at the 72nd to force a play-off with Al Espinosa at Winged Foot. After generously requesting a late start to accommodate the Catholic Espinosa's Sunday morning obligation, Jones then whipped him by an eye-popping 23 strokes! A first-round upset loss to Johnny Goodman in the U.S. Amateur at Pebble Beach ended Jones' 1929 campaign prematurely, but that disappointment would soon be buried amidst the joyous tumult of 1930.

The famous Grand Slam year actually began with a runner-up finish at the Savannah Open, a minor footnote quickly forgotten by the start of May's **British Amateur** at St. Andrews. There Jones struggled in early matches with Cyril Tolley and Harrison Johnston, barely escaped a semifinal encounter with George Voigt, then rose up to beat the talented Roger Wethered 7 and 6 to capture the title. Three weeks later, over the 7,078-yard links at Hoylake, he opened with a record 70, eventually coming home in 291 to win the **Open Championship** by two over Leo Diegel and Macdonald Smith. Now it was back to the States and the **U.S. Open** at Interlachen, where a third-round 68 highlighted a 287 performance that was enough to again beat Smith by two, a victory well recalled for Jones' second-round approach to the par-5 ninth which skipped across an intervening pond, allowing him to make birdie. And lastly on to Merion for a **U.S. Amateur** which, save for its historical implications, was largely devoid of drama, as Jones simply tore through the field, routing Gene Homans 8 and 7 in the final to claim what his faithful chronicler O. B. Keeler would nickname the "Impregnable Quadrilateral," the unique and timeless Grand Slam.

A worn-out Jones retired from competitive play immediately thereafter, primarily to practice law but also to make a series of instructional golf films (for which he received $120,000 and promptly pitched his amateur status) and, a bit later, to develop the Augusta National Golf Club. Considering it little more than a friendly gathering, Jones frequently entered the club's spring invitational tournament (soon to be known as the Masters) with his best finish being a tie for 16th in 1938. He also proved himself a fine and insightful writer, authoring numerous magazine pieces as well as three excellent books, *Down the Fairway* (Minton, Balch, 1926), *Golf Is My Game* (Doubleday, 1960), and *Bobby Jones on Golf* (Doubleday, 1966).

When wartime came, the 40-year-old Jones (who greatly disliked "Bobby" and was "Bob" to his friends) enlisted in the Army Air Corps, actually landing at Normandy on D-day plus one. In the years ahead he would be afflicted by a rare and crippling spinal ailment known as syringomyelia, the disease eventually paralyzing both his arms and legs. Though confined to a wheelchair, he would make an emotional return to St. Andrews in 1958 to receive the Freedom of the City medal in a poignant ceremony, for with his rare blend of talent, charm, integrity and humility, Jones was a golfer every bit as popular in the game's birthplace as he was in America.

As a gentleman, a scholar, and a career amateur who tamed his own youthful impetuousness to scale the game's greatest heights, Bobby Jones was an American hero like no other. Upon his death in 1971, play was stopped at St. Andrews and flags lowered to half-mast in his honor.

Major Amateur Wins (15): 1920 & '22 Southern; **1923, '26, '29 & '30 U.S. Open; 1924, '25, '27, '28 & '30 U.S. Amateur; 1926, '27 & '30 British Open; 1930 British Amateur**
Walker Cup: 1922, '24, '26, '28 (c) & '30 (c) (5)

1916-1930

	16	17	18	19	20	21	22	23	24	25	26	27	28	29	30
US Open	-			-	T8	T5	T2	1	2	2	1	T11	2	1	1
US Am	T5			2	T3	T5	T3	T9	1	1	2	1	1	T17	1
Brit Am				-	T17	-	-	-	-	T5	-	-	-	1
British				-	WD	-	-	-	-	1	1	-	-	1

Brian Jones (Australia)

Like American Brian Watts, Sydney's Brian Jones (b. 9/12/1951) is a man who found great success in Japan when it did not seem to be forthcoming elsewhere. Moving there at age 22, he married a Japanese woman and settled in for a nearly two-decade run that produced 10 Japan Tour victories as well as three **Indian Opens** (1972, '73, and '77), one **Malaysian Open** (1978), and other sundry titles in Australia and New Zealand. A favorite of Japanese galleries, Jones failed to qualify for the Champions Tour upon turning 50 but has since played in Europe, winning his first Senior Tour event in 2002.

Ernest Jones (UK/USA)

Ernest Jones (1887–1965) might well have emerged as a world-class tournament player had he not lost a leg fighting in France during World War I. Retaining a remarkable degree of skill despite his disability, Jones would spend 15 years teaching the game at the Chislehurst GC in Kent before emigrating to the United States in 1924. Quickly establishing himself as an elite instructor, Jones worked out of a Manhattan studio, then later at two clubs developed by 1921 U.S. Women's Amateur champion Marion Hollins, New York's Women's National GC (today's Glen Head CC) and the Pasatiempo GC in Santa Cruz, California. His philosophy was effectively summed up by a most prominent student, Dr. Alister MacKenzie, who wrote that his teacher believed "that if one gets a correct mental picture of swinging the club head like a weight at the end of a string the necessary body movements will automatically adjust themselves." Jones wrote two instructional volumes, *Swinging into Golf* (Nicholson & Watson, 1946) and the very popular *Swing the Clubhead* (Dodd, Mead, 1952).

Grier Jones (USA)

The 1968 **NCAA** champion at Oklahoma State and 1969 PGA Tour Rookie of the Year, Grier Jones (b. Wichita, Kansas, 5/6/1946) was a steady top-50 money winner through much of the 1970s. His best season came in 1972 when he claimed two of his three career victories, the first being the **Hawaiian Open** where a final-round 64 caught third-round leader Bob Murphy before Jones won a playoff. Jones was on the other side of such a turnabout, however, at the 1978 Inverrary Classic when Jack Nicklaus memorably birdied the last five holes (twice chipping in) to relegate him to second. Bothered by back and hand problems during his Tour days, Jones is now the golf coach at Wichita State.

Rees Jones (USA)

The younger of architectural icon Robert Trent Jones' two sons, Rees Jones (b. Montclair, New Jersey, 1941) majored in history at Yale, then studied landscape architecture at Harvard's Graduate School of Design before beginning a nine-year hitch with his father's firm in 1965. Having wet his feet in all aspects of the design business, Rees struck out on his own in 1974, and while high-level solo success was not immediate, it certainly arrived by the middle of the 1980s. The designer of more than 75 new courses, Jones is also one of the few big-name modern architects who performs alterations of older layouts (often erroneously marketed as "restorations") in anything resembling a 50-50 ratio. Indeed, perhaps his single biggest career boost came from the high-profile renovation of The Country Club in advance of the 1988 U.S. Open, and he has, to date, altered the sites of six additional Opens, five PGAs, three Ryder Cups and one Walker Cup.

Perhaps based upon this remodeling portfolio, Jones has, since the early 1990s, landed a variety of big-budget new projects throughout the United States, several of which generally creep into the lower half of the popular top-100 magazine rankings. Unlike his father and brother, however, Rees has seldom worked abroad.

Notable Courses: Atlantic GC, New York; GC at Briar's Creek, South Carolina; Nantucket GC, Massachusetts; Ocean Forest GC, Georgia

Robert Trent Jones (UK/USA)

Born: Ince, England, 6/20/1906 **Died:** Ft. Lauderdale, Florida, 6/14/2000

Arguably the most recognizable name in the history of golf course architecture, Robert Trent Jones was born in Lancashire but emigrated with his family to Rochester, New York, in 1909. A talented young golfer who occasionally caddied for Walter Hagen at the CC of Rochester, he elected not to pursue a playing career after developing a stomach ulcer, instead turning his attention to the field of course design. In this Trent Jones was surely the first man ever to tailor his education strictly toward a golf architectural career, studying agronomy, engineering, and landscape architecture at Cornell (as well as drawing at RIT) in a self-designed program that did not lead to a degree.

It did, however, produce a few local design projects, one of which, the Midvale G & CC, exposed his work to the flamboyant Canadian designer Stanley Thompson, who took Jones on as a partner forthwith. Their association lasted from 1930 to 1938, a period in which money became so tight that Thompson actually sailed off to Rio de Janeiro in search of work. Following World War II, however, golf construction came back to life and the now-solo Trent Jones was ideally positioned to capitalize.

Quantifying the magnitude of his postwar work is no easy task, for it encompassed more than 450 projects in 42 American states and 23 countries, including such far-flung places as Japan, the Philippines and Morocco, as well as most of Europe and the Caribbean. Jones also performed renovations to at least nine U.S. Open sites (as well as to Augusta National), work ranging from a minor touch-up at Winged Foot to a famously thorough rebunkering at Oakland Hills. He also built several original layouts that would serve as Major venues (including Hazeltine National, Bellerive and Firestone) or host other internationally prominent events (e.g., Ryder Cup venues Valderrama and Missouri's Old Warson CC).

For better or worse, Trent Jones' greatest impact on the game likely came from the style of his designs: big, brawny, palpably difficult and with an obvious aesthetic all their own. His oft-cited philosophy of "a hard par or an easy bogey" is familiar to all architectural aficionados, as are his grand, heavily contoured greens, runway-like tees and fairway-pinching bunkers. It was a style of design that was not quite penal and surely not strategic, leading Trent himself to dub its challenge "Heroic."

Though it certainly served him well, Jones' philosophy has fallen somewhat out of favor over the last 30 years, as trend-setting designers like Pete Dye led the game back toward shorter, more strategically intricate courses. Consequently many of Trent's more famous works do not hold the same cachet they once did, leaving California's Spyglass Hill GC as his only design currently appearing among the top 50 in either major American rankings.

Notable Courses: Ballybunion GC, Cashen Course, Ireland; **Firestone CC, South Course, Ohio; Hazeltine National, Minnesota; Mauna Kea GC, Hawaii; Peachtree GC (with Bobby Jones), Georgia; Spyglass Hill GC, California; Valderrama GC, Spain**

Robert Trent Jones Jr. (USA)

The older of architect Robert Trent Jones' two sons, "Bobby" (b. Montclair, New Jersey, 1939) graduated Yale and initially gave Stanford Law School a try before electing instead to pursue the field of golf design. He joined his father's firm in 1960, eventually taking full responsibility for its active West Coast office in Palo Alto, California. In 1972 he ventured out on his own, with the ensuing 30 years yielding more than 175 new designs in 38 countries, on all six golfing continents. Indeed, the worldwide

reach of the firm is quite remarkable, including, for example, five Australian designs, five in China, four in Malaysia, five in the Caribbean, more than 15 throughout Western Europe, and, last but surely not least, Russia's first 18-hole course, the Moscow CC.

One reason for this worldwide success is that Bobby is hardly your run-of-the-mill, golf-centric architect, having long been committed to furthering international relations and environmental interests. He was, in fact, a part of the American delegation to the 1975 Helsinki Accords on human rights, and has enjoyed personal relationships with foreign dignitaries and heads of state. He has also placed particular emphasis on blending his courses into their surrounding landscapes, a fine example being at Pebble Beach's Links at Spanish Bay, where a barren, rocky site was made to look very much like the surrounding area's famous sand dunes-covered landscape.

Notable Courses: Kensington G&CC, Florida; The Links at Spanish Bay (with T. Watson & S. Tatum), California; **The Prince GC, Hawaii;** Sugarloaf GC, Maine

Rosie Jones (USA)

Over the course of 20 LPGA Tour seasons, Rosie Jones (b. Santa Ana, California, 11/13/1959) has proven herself one of her era's better players, claiming 13 official victories, six top-10 money finishes and a solid 18 seasons ranked among the top 30. Though a native Californian, Jones has gravitated toward colder climates, attending Ohio State and later enjoying particular success in upstate New York, where she has twice won both the **Corning Classic** and **Rochester International.** A highly accurate ball-striker with a deft putting stroke, Jones lacks only a Major championship on her résumé, something of an oddity as she has logged 24 top-10 Major finishes including solo seconds at the 1984 U.S. Women's Open, the 1990 LPGA Championship, and the 2000 du Maurier. Though now in her mid-40s, Jones still remains near the top of her game, winning twice in her fifth decade, regularly placing among the top 10 money winners and tying for third at the 2003 LPGA Championship—so that elusive Major may yet fall within reach.

LPGA Wins (13): 1987 State Farm; 1988 Samsung WC; 1991 & '98 Rochester; 1996 & '97 Corning; 2001 Wykagyl
Solheim Cup: 1990, 1996–2003 (6)

Steve Jones (USA)

Over the course of nearly 20 years (and eight victories) on the PGA Tour, former University of Colorado star Steve

Jones (b. Artesia, New Mexico, 9/27/1958) has twice taken center stage in the golfing world. The first occasion came in 1989 when he started the season on fire, winning back-to-back at the **Tournament of Champions** and the **Bob Hope,** then adding the **Canadian Open** several months later to finish eighth on the money list, his only career foray into the top 10.

Jones' second, more memorable peak came in 1996 when he became the first sectional qualifier since Jerry Pate in 1976 to win a **U.S. Open,** defeating Tom Lehman and Davis Love III by one at ever-difficult Oakland Hills. Here again Jones showed an ability to ride a hot streak, adding the **Phoenix** and **Canadian Opens** in 1997 before cooling down noticeably by decade's end.

The 6′4″ Jones has battled various physical problems throughout his career, from serious injuries suffered to his left ring finger in a 1991 dirt bike accident to surgeries for an irregular heartbeat (2002) and an ailing right elbow (2003).

Stuart Jones (New Zealand)

A native of Hastings on the North Island, Stuart Gwyn Jones (b. 1925) possessed the sort of simple, highly consistent swing that allowed him to compete for many years, helping to establish him as New Zealand's best postwar career amateur. Originally a Rugby star, Jones was badly burned by a geyser in 1947 and soon took to golf, developing into a scratch player in less than two years and claiming his first **New Zealand Amateur** title in 1955. To this he would add six more national titles (the last in 1971 at age 46) while becoming the backbone of New Zealand's international teams, missing only one World Amateur Team Championship from 1958 to 1972. Also the winner

of the 1967 **Canadian Amateur,** Jones proved himself competitive with the professionals on several occasions, including a 1965 victory over a field that included both Peter Thomson and Kel Nagle.

José Jurado (Argentina)

Buenos Aires native José Jurado (1899–1971) was a golfing pioneer in the truest sense, for while early British professionals ventured out to parts unknown with the psychological might of the world's biggest empire (both golfing and otherwise) behind them, Jurado traveled thousands of miles to challenge the British golf monolith on its own turf. He was not, however, without ammunition. As his homeland's first great player, Jurado won the **Argentine Open** seven times and was, in Longhurst's summation, "a brilliant golfer."

Jurado contended several times at the Open Championship beginning in 1928 at Royal St. George's, where he trailed two-time winner Walter Hagen by one through 54 holes, then blew up with a closing 80 to finish joint sixth. His golden opportunity, however, came three years later at Carnoustie where rounds of 76-71-73 in difficult conditions stood him three ahead of the pack through 54. He then reached the 71st tee with nine strokes left to win but proceeded to top a 4-iron into the burn and take six. Then, even more sadly, he laid up at the par-5 72nd in the erroneous belief that par would still put him in a play-off when, in fact, a birdie was needed and there he was, alone in second, one behind the victorious Tommy Armour.

A dapper and engaging little man, Jurado was both a fan favorite and a landmark player, for he was surely the first man from outside the English-speaking world to climb within site of golf's competitive summit.

Golf does its bit for the Red Cross, at Nassau, Bahamas in 1941. *Left to right,* Gene Sarazen; Tom Walsh; Bobby Jones; the Duchess of Windsor; Walter Hagen; the Duke of Windsor, who umpired the 36-hole two-day match; and Tommy Armour. Jones and Armour won, 3 and 2.

K

Lorie Kane (Canada)

A fine amateur from Prince Edward Island, Lorie Kane (b. Charlottetown, 12/19/1964) joined the LPGA Tour full time on her second try in 1997 and has since been a consistent money winner, finishing no worse than 15th on the money list in each of her first seven seasons. She enjoyed three of her four career victories in 2000, with the later two (the **New Albany Classic** and Japan's **Mizuno Classic**) coming in sudden death over Mi Hyun Kim and Sophie Gustafson. Kane also won the 2001 **Takefuji Classic** with a closing 66 to defeat Annika Sorenstam—though Sorenstam would return the favor a year later, beating Kane in the same event in sudden death.

Robert Karlsson (Sweden)

A world-class free spirit who makes eccentric fellow Swede Jesper Parnevik look normal by comparison, colorful Robert Karlsson (b. St. Malm, 9/3/1969) has meditated, acupunctured and fasted his way to five wins on the European Tour since 1995. Standing 6′5″, Karlsson is Europe's tallest competing professional, yet he possesses a surprisingly compact swing that is widely considered among the Continent's purest. Indeed, though little known in America, Karlsson might be viewed as something of an underachiever, narrowly missing a spot on the 1999 Ryder Cup team but only once cracking the top 10 in the Order of Merit. A 2001 World Cup player, Karlsson has certainly shown flashes of being able to compete with the best, a fine example being a rare American appearance at the 1999 Los Angeles Open where he very quietly finished ninth.

Shunsuke Kato (Japan)

The most successful of Japan's contemporary golf course architects, Shunsuke Kato has been responsible for more than 70 design projects, the vast majority at home with a select handful in Korea, Taiwan, and mainland China. Kato's style is largely a modern one, but he is surely among the toughest contemporary designers to assess. For with available land so limited, a huge percentage of his work has been performed on mountainous, heavily treed terrain—land which cannot readily be employed for agricultural or residential purposes. The massive amounts of earthmoving thus required can succeed in making a golf course a reality, but seldom with anything resembling a natural, harmonious look.

A capable marketer, Kato has authored a large and attractive (if perfunctory) volume, *What Makes a Good Golf Course Good* (Ueno Shoten, 1991) which offers both Japanese and English text.

Oliver Kay (New Zealand)

The daughter of a transplanted Scottish greenkeeper in Whangerai, Oliver Kay (b. 1909) was the first top female player produced by New Zealand, a stocky, powerful girl who could tee-to-green it with many male players of her day. Kay's record was impressive from a young age, taking her first **New Zealand Ladies Amateur** title in 1930 at age 21, then adding additional wins in 1933 and '37 (the latter under her married name of Mrs. G. W. Hollis). In stroke play, Kay was virtually unbeatable on her home turf, capturing the nation's **Mellsop Cup** an overwhelming nine consecutive times between 1926 and 1934, plus one last postwar victory in 1946. However, Kay's biggest wins likely were the two **Australian Ladies** titles that she claimed in 1933 and '36, making her the second New Zealander to take the Australian crown and the only one to win it twice.

Stephen Kay (USA)

A native of New York City, Stephen Kay (b. 1951) was educated at Syracuse and Michigan State before beginning a golf architecture career in 1977 by working for Michigan designer William Newcomb. Returning to New York in 1983, he soon made a name for himself by restoring and renovating a number of established area courses including Pelham, Rye, Knollwood, Seawane, and Westchester CCs, among many others. Among his new designs, Blue Heron Pines (New Jersey) and the Links of North Dakota have both garnered critical acclaim, though perhaps neither is as noteworthy as his 1986 layout for the Royal Bhutan GC, a nine-hole design situated in a tiny and remote Himalayan kingdom.

O. B. Keeler (USA)

Marietta, Georgia, native Oscar Bane Keeler (1882–1950), a railroad clerk turned Atlanta *Journal* sportswriter, will forever hold a place in the lore of golf as the close friend, confidant, and chronicler of the great Bobby Jones. Becoming a writer in almost perfect lockstep with the 14-year-old Jones' breakthrough win at the Georgia Amateur, Keeler would spend the next 16 years covering the Immortal Bobby's rise to prominence, traveling over 120,000 miles with him in the process. The only man believed to have witnessed all 13 of Jones' Major championships, Keeler was also responsible for nicknaming his 1930 Grand Slam the "Impregnable Quadrilateral."

As a book writer, Keeler is best remembered for coauthoring Jones' *Down the Fairway* (Minton, Balch, 1927), one of the most acclaimed golf volumes ever written. He also penned *The Boy's Life of Bobby Jones* (Harper's, 1931) as well as his own entertaining story *The Autobiography of An Average Golfer* (Greenberg, 1925). Of Keeler, Jones would later say "the play and the result were as personally his as mine," and that "There is no way to measure the worth of such a companion when one is in the midst of a taxing endeavor." A great icon of the grand old days of sports journalism, O. B. Keeler is today enshrined—like Jones—in the Georgia Golf Hall of Fame.

Herman Keiser (USA)

An occasional PGA Tour player during the late 1930s, Springfield, Missouri's Herman Keiser (1914–2003) spent 30 months at sea with the U.S. Navy during World War II before returning to try competitive golf full time. All told, Kaiser would win five official Tour events, highlighted by his unquestioned shining hour, the 1946 **Masters**. In this first postwar event, Keiser's 69-68-70 start gave him a five-stroke lead going into the final round, before a closing 76 ended with a potentially fatal three-putt at the 72nd green. The player with a chance to catch him was his friend Ben Hogan, whose fine approach to the last left a 12-footer for 68 and a one-shot victory. Hogan, as historians are wont to recall, also three-putted, and Herman Keiser was shortly donning his Green Jacket.

Homer Kelley (USA)

A native of Bennington, Kansas, Homer Kelley (1907–1983) was working as an engineering aide in Seattle when, in 1941, he set about understanding the physics of the *entire* golf swing. Some 28 years later, satisfied that he had completed his task, he penned *The Golfing Machine* (Star System, 1969), easily the most complicated book of golf instruction ever written and certainly one of its most controversial. Breaking the swing down in terms of angles, force vectors, and the like, it enjoyed a brief flash of fame when its walking demonstrator, the young Bobby Clampett, showed the capacity for some truly awe-inspiring ball-striking. Kelley, however, passed away in 1983; Clampett fell irretrievably from golf's top shelf a year later; and *The Golfing Machine* exists today only as a cult classic.

Edwina Kennedy (Australia)

A career amateur in an era where such is increasingly rare, Sydney's Edwina Kennedy (b. 6/10/1959) is a tall, strong woman who has proven herself capable of competing with most men on equal terms. A four-time **Australian Junior** champion (1976–79) and regular plunderer of the pickings in New South Wales, Kennedy's greatest moment came on her 19th birthday when she defeated England's Julia Greenhalgh one up at the Hollingwell GC to become the first Australian winner of the **British Ladies** title. A 1980 **Canadian Ladies** crown soon followed, and in 1981 the USGA granted Kennedy its first-ever special exemption into the U.S. Women's Open. Oddly, it took Kennedy until 1986 to win her own **Australian Ladies** title, when she defeated Elizabeth Maxwell 5 and 4 at The Grange.

Ralph Kennedy (USA)

A New York–based businessman, Ralph Kennedy (1883–1961) holds the verifiable record for most courses played in a lifetime with a lofty total of 3,625. He started relatively slowly, not playing his thousandth course until his 50th birthday. But with business soon taking him more regularly around the country, Kennedy reached his two-thousandth only eight years later, cruising relatively easily to his title thereafter. The great traveling trick-shotter Joe Kirkwood once estimated that he'd played over 6,000 courses worldwide which, even with ample room for error or exaggeration, would still place him far ahead of Kennedy. But Kennedy's path was clearly documented (indeed he was profiled in *National Geographic*), and he certainly can be credited with giving impetus to the concept.

Cristie Kerr (USA)

Presently in her late 20s, Cristie Kerr (b. Miami, Florida, 10/12/1977) has paid her dues on the LPGA Tour since turning professional at age 18, initially burdened by great expectations after a junior career that included thrice being selected an AJGA All-American and once the organization's Player of the Year (1995). A former low amateur in the 1996 U.S. Women's Open and Curtis Cup participant, Kerr qualified for the LPGA Tour in 1997 but finished no better than 47th on the money list—without a win—in her first three seasons.

Thereafter she undertook a major physical fitness plan which resulted in the loss of 45 pounds, as well as greater strength and athleticism. The immediate result was a 15th-place finish in 2000; then, after slipping to 28th the next year, a 12th-place ranking as well as her first victory (the **Longs Drugs Challenge**) in 2002. A winless but not-unsuccessful (13th-place) 2003 followed before 2004 saw something of a breakout, with victories at the **Takefuji, ShopRite,** and **State Farm Classics,** and the sort of consistently fine play that speaks of quality. At the very least, Kerr now ranks among the elite of the LPGA's American-born players, with her best golf likely dead ahead.

Harry Kershaw (Australia)

From the unfortunate list of great talents who died too young to fully exhibit them comes Harry Kershaw (1940–1961), widely hailed as one of Australia's best-ever prospects but sadly killed in a car crash at age 21. Perhaps a bit of an eccentric (he played the game in workman's boots instead of spikes), Kershaw was a precocious sort who reportedly won the Marrickville GC club title at age 15 off a spectacular 61! Though not eligible for most Australian competitions due to a mandatory two-year apprenticeship rule, he did manage one colossal victory, the 1959 **New South Wales Open,** which he won while still a teenager from a field which included von Nida, Devlin, and Nagle.

Tom Kidd (UK)

Precious little record exists regarding St. Andrews caddie-turned-professional Tom Kidd, though he is known to have been a long hitter who played in several prominent challenge matches of the day. Further, it is recorded that he traveled to a professional event at Wemyss in 1874 by riding in the back of Willie Fernie's donkey cart along with Bob Martin, Tom Kirk and a 14-year-old Andra Kirkaldy. No great story there, except for the fact that he was doing so as the reigning **Open** champion, having made history in 1873 not only by winning the Claret Jug over the Old Course (by one over Jamie Anderson) but also by ending Young Tom Morris' unprecedented four-win streak in the process. Though surely celebrated at the time of his victory, Kidd reportedly was back among the caddie ranks—and donkey carts—shortly thereafter, a decidedly common occurrence in those very different times.

Mi Hyun Kim (South Korea)

Riding a modern wave of Koreans onto the LPGA Tour, 5′1″ Mi Hyun Kim (b. Inchon, 1/13/1977) thus far stands second only to Se Ri Pak in American success. A dominant amateur and Korean Ladies Professional player at home, Kim came to the United States in 1999, immediately won twice (at the **State Farm Rail** and **Betsy King Classics**), finished eighth on the money list and was selected Rookie of the Year. She followed this with a single win in 2000 and back-to-back titles in 2002 (never falling below eighth on the money list) before a disappointingly winless 2003 saw her slip to 20th and have her cuts-made streak snapped at 61. Nonetheless, showing somewhat better form in 2004 and currently only in her late 20s, this solid tee-to-greener would appear to enjoy a bright future.

Judy Kimball (USA)

Sioux City, Iowa, product Judy Kimball (b. 6/17/1938) surprised a number of people when she turned professional, for while her amateur and University of Kansas collegiate records were good, they included no major victories whatsoever. Yet Kimball's self-confidence was quickly justified, for the first of her three career victories came in her rookie year of 1961 (at Minneapolis' **American Women's Open**) while the second was a Major title, the 1962 **LPGA Championship,** where she beat Shirley Spork by four at Las Vegas' old Stardust CC. Kimball remained a regular among the top 20 money winners throughout the 1960s before falling back into the pack by the early 1970s.

Betsy King (USA)

One of the finest players of her time, Betsy King (b. Reading, Pennsylvania, 8/13/1955) might well be considered something of a late bloomer. Despite being low amateur at the 1976 U.S. Women's Open and a star of Furman's 1976 NCAA championship team, she won no major amateur titles and, owing to something of a reverse pivot in her swing, took more than six full seasons on the LPGA Tour to claim her first professional win. When she finally did break through, however, it would be with a vengeance, winning three times in a banner 1984 which also featured a first-place finish on the money list and the LPGA's Player of the Year award.

Thus began a truly wonderful run of 12 world-class seasons during which the Pennsylvanian won 30 times officially (plus the 1985 **Women's British Open**) and never finished outside of the top 10 on the money list. The first of King's six career Major championships came at the 1987

Dinah Shore, when a holed bunker shot at the 70th set up a sudden-death victory over Patty Sheehan. The second, a victory in the 1989 **U.S. Women's Open,** came at Michigan's Indianwood G & CC during a career year that included five additional wins, more money, and Player of the Year titles. Though 1990 would see only three victories, two were Majors: a second **Dinah Shore** in March and successful defense of her **Women's Open** crown at the Atlanta Athletic Club in July, where she again nipped Sheehan, this time by one. Multiwin seasons followed in 1991 and '92 while 1993, despite yielding only one title, saw a third Player of the Year award and money crown, plus a second Vare Trophy.

Though only once among the top 10 since 1995, King has experienced several post-40 bright spots including a third **Dinah Shore** title in 1997 and two victories (the **Hawaiian Open** and the **Corning Classic**) in 2000. Widely recognized for her charitable works, King owns 34 career victories and was inducted into the LPGA Hall of Fame in 1995.

LPGA Wins (34): 1985 Safeway; 1985, '86 & '88 State Farm; 1987 Welch's; **1987, '90 & '97 Dinah Shore; 1989 & '90 U.S. Women's Open;** 1989 Samsung WC; 1990 & '91 Wykagyl; 1991 & 2000 Corning; **1992 LPGA Championship**
Solheim Cup: 1990–98 (5)

1976-2000

	76	77	78	79	80	81	82	83	84	85	86	87	88
Dinah								T52	T24	T7	4	1	T35
LPGA	-	-	T49	MC	T27	T38	T21	T11	T7	T44	MC	2	T24
US Open	T8	MC	T20	MC	MC	T21	T25	T32	T5	T8	T3	T4	T12
du Maur				T26	-	T38	T12	T25	3	MC	T3	7	T19

	89	90	91	92	93	94	95	96	97	98	99	00
Dinah	T4	1	T11	56	T2	T48	T11	MC	1	T61	77	MC
LPGA	8	T5	7	1	T4	T17	T11	T14	T53	T37	T69	T23
US Open	1	1	T28	T16	T7	T6	T3	MC	T28	MC	T47	T46
du Maur	T2	T10	T6	T28	2	T4	T5	MC	T3	3	-	T23

Sam King (UK)

Englishman Sam King (b. 1911) established himself as a professional prior to World War II, undoubtedly losing several of his best competitive years to the hostilities. A short hitter who enjoyed the rather paradoxical advantage of not having much distance to lose with age, King remained competitive into his 50s despite the rise of some young British talent during the 1960s. The product of a working-class background, King had an enviable nine top 10s in the Open Championship and four top-5s, though it was really only in 1959 at Muirfield, when he led eventual winner Gary Player by four through 54 holes before closing with 76, that he enjoyed a real chance to win.

King Hassan II (Morocco)

By far the most golf-inclined royal of the second half of the twentieth century, King Hassan II (1929–1999) followed in the spike-clad footsteps of his country's colonial-era leader, the golf-crazy Pasha of Marrakesh. Like the Pasha, Hassan built courses, including nine-holers at two of his palaces and other full-sized facilities (such as the well-known Royal Rabat GC) designed to promote tour-ism. He also created the lucrative 1970s Moroccan Grand Prix Pro-Am and, from 1987 to 2002, the Moroccan Open, a regular stop on the European Tour. Unlike Belgium's King Leopold II, who developed golf for strictly economic reasons, King Hassan played the game avidly, though not, we are told, with any particular proficiency. He did, however, retain popular teacher Butch Harmon as his personal instructor long before Harmon's current Tiger Woods–based fame.

King James II (UK)

Though not known to be a golfer himself, King James II of Scotland (1430-1460) was the first to take an editorial position on the popular game, issuing a famous 1457 decree stating that "the futeball and golfe be utterly cryed downe and not be used." This was not simply some tennis lover speaking but rather a monarch who, due to seemingly endless strife with England, needed his populace to be focused on archery and more practical items employable in defense of the realm. Similar decrees would follow from his two successors, most notably James IV (1473–1513) who in 1491 stated: "It is statute and ordained that in na place of the realme there be used Fute-ball, Golfe, or uther sik unprofitable sportis" as such things were deemed contrary to "the commoun good of the Realme and defense thereof." To what degree such decrees were actually followed, however, is not entirely certain, and James IV was known to play the game following the signing of a "perpetual peace" between Scotland and England in 1502.

King James VI (UK)

The son of Mary, Queen of Scots, King James VI (1566–1625) may well be the most important Royal in the history of golf, for when he came south in 1603 to assume the thrones of both England (as James I) and Scotland, he brought his clubs and an entourage of players. He soon appointed one William Mayne of Edinburgh as royal clubmaker and, in 1618, granted James Melvill a monopoly for the manufacture of golf balls in attempts at minimizing their importation from Holland. James IV also decreed that sport and recreation would no longer be banned on Sundays for those pious souls who had "first done their duties to God," and it is a widely held belief that he jumpstarted the world's oldest golf club outside of Scotland by recognizing, in 1608, the Society of Blackheath Golfers. His sons Henry and Charles were avid players as well.

King Leopold II (Belgium)

At a glance it does seem a bit incongruous to find 10 golf clubs granted royal titles in Belgium, a small country with little more than 50 courses in total. But such is the legacy of King Leopold II (1835–1909), a financially astute monarch who recognized the value of extensive trade with Great Britain—and the role in procuring such trade that a spate of attractive golf courses might play. Thus it is no coincidence that British architectural luminaries such as Harry Colt, Willie Park Jr., and Tom Simpson worked extensively in Belgium, building courses for a monarch who didn't even play. His successor King Albert was equally non-participatory, but Albert's son and successor King Leopold III was perhaps the most skilled golfing monarch in history, several times competing in major amateur events and often playing to scratch.

Dorothy Kirby (USA)

Mary Dorothy Kirby (b. 1/15/1920) hailed from West Point, Georgia, winning four **Georgia Ladies** titles beginning with an improbable victory in 1933 at age 13. She was the **Southern Amateur** champion at 17, a U.S. Women's Amateur finalist (losing to Betty Jameson) at 19, the **North & South** winner at 23, and eventually suffered a second loss in the national final (this time to fellow Georgian Louise

Suggs) in 1947. A semifinalist in 1949, Kirby finally won the **Amateur** in 1951, edging Claire Doran 2 and 1 at St. Paul's Town and Country Club to end 18 years of frustration. A four-time Curtis Cup player from 1948 to 1954, Kirby also tied for second with Babe Zaharias at the 1949 Titleholders Championship, two strokes behind fellow amateur Peggy Kirk.

Ron Kirby (USA)

A native of Beverly, Massachusetts, Ron Kirby (b. 1932) was a trained agronomist who entered the field of course design during the 1960s when hired to oversee construction of American and British courses for Robert Trent Jones. By the early 1970s, he'd gone into partnership with Georgian Arthur Davis and Gary Player, later working for Jack Nicklaus' firm in Europe before returning Stateside in 1992 to practice on his own. Overall Kirby has been involved in projects in more than a dozen countries, with his calling card surely being 1997's Old Head Golf Links, a spectacular clifftop layout located on a sandstone peninsula in southwestern Ireland.

Andrew Kirkaldy (UK)

Born: Denhead, Scotland, 3/18/1860 **Died:** St. Andrews, Scotland, 4/16/1934

Andrew "Andra" Kirkaldy stands among the all-time great characters of the game, a large, dour Scot known far more for speaking his mind—generally quite amusingly—than for his considerable playing skills. On this score Darwin noted that "He acquired the reputation of a wit, but many of his supposed witticisms were, as I imagine, uttered in solemn and deadly earnest." Kirkaldy's swing was shorter than the period norm (perhaps average by today's standards) and decidedly quick, but he is frequently held among the very best players never to win an Open Championship.

Having begun competing with professionals no later than age 14, Andra certainly gave the Open a number of chances, finishing eight times in the top 5 between 1879 and 1899. His closest call, without question, came in 1889 at Musselburgh when he tied with Willie Park Jr., then lost a 36-hole play-off by five. He also finished tied for second in 1879 and '91, on the second occasion playing bridesmaid to his brother Hugh. Andra was also among the last to regularly play high-stakes challenge matches, his most prominent, perhaps, being the 8 and 7 victory he scored against Park (over 72 holes) in the aftermath of the Open loss.

Though a St. Andrean through and through, Andra twice ventured afar, once to fight in Egypt in 1882, and once for a short-lived professional job in England. He eventually replaced Old Tom Morris as professional to the R&A in 1910, holding the position until his death. Andra also wrote a somewhat overlooked autobiography *Fifty Years of Golf: My Memories* (T. Fisher Unwin, 1921) but will best be remembered for his spoken words—once, for example, famously deriding Muirfield "an old water meadow." He might best be portrayed, however, by a favorite story of Darwin's wherein Andra holed a putt at St. Andrews' 16th to go dormy in a challenge match against Andrew Scott, then "raced to the next tee calling aloud in a formidable voice, 'The door's locked noo.'"

Hugh Kirkaldy (UK)

The younger brother of the legendary Andra, St. Andrean Hugh Kirkaldy (1865–1897) was considerably less outspoken and generally viewed as the lesser player—though he managed to win the **Open Championship** (no small equalizer) in 1891 at St. Andrews. Hugh would follow his triumph with a tie for second in 1892, then a tie for third (with Andra) in 1893, proving his victory no fluke. Described by Darwin as "a grand, slashing player," Hugh was long in ill health and died young, at age 32. To this day the old wooden putter that he used in winning his Open hangs in the clubhouse at England's Rye GC where it is, in fact, *the* President's Putter for which Oxford and Cambridge golfers, old and young, compete each winter.

Oswald Kirkby (USA)

Never having reached as far as the semifinals of the U.S. Amateur, the name of Oswald Kirkby is not quickly recalled at the national level. But playing out of New Jersey's old Englewood GC, Kirkby was a force in his own region, winning three of four war-interrupted **Metropolitan Amateurs** between 1914 and 1919, and losing in two other finals to four-time national champion Jerome Travers. Kirkby's 1914 victory is likely his most memorable as he beat the legendary Walter Travis 4 and 2 over his home layout at Englewood. He also won three **New Jersey Amateurs** between 1912 and 1916.

Joe Kirkwood (Australia/USA)

Born: Canterbury, Australia, 3/22/1897 **Died:** Burlington, Vermont, 10/29/1970

One of the more entertaining characters in golf history, Joe Kirkwood became a legend as a trick-shot artist, initially performing for injured World War I soldiers on a lark, then later traveling on extended tours with master showman Walter Hagen. Having largely invented the craft, Kirkwood's repertoire of shots was staggering, utilizing all manner of freakish clubs, stances and gimmickry, though in the end the entire show was, of course, predicated on nothing beyond his great ball-striking talent.

Lost in most assessments of Kirkwood, however, was his playing ability which, especially in his youth, was quite exceptional. Already the holder of several course records, Kirkwood blasted onto the national scene by winning the 1920 **Australian Open** utilizing only seven clubs and breaking Ivo Whitten's tournament record by a stunning 12 shots. He also won the 1920 **New Zealand Professional** title and, by some reports, the 1920 **Australian PGA,** though no records were apparently kept at this time and Kirkwood did not specifically mention it in his autobiography *Links of Life* (privately published, 1973).

Moving on to America in the early 1920s, Kirkwood was highly successful, winning 13 PGA Tour titles including a combined seven in 1923 and '24, three of which came in succession during the later year. With exhibitions earning vastly more money than was offered by Depression-era tournament purses, however, Kirkwood frequently elected to concentrate more on worldwide jaunts with Hagen or Sarazen, seriously competing only occasionally. He retained his skills for many years, however, and in 1948, Kirkwood and his son, Joe Jr., became the first father-son pair to make the cut in the U.S. Open, finishing 28th and 21st respectively.

PGA Tour Wins (13): 1924 Texas; 1933 North & South; 1933 Canadian Open
Intn'l Wins (3): 1920 Australian Open

1920-1948

	20	21	22	23	24	25	26	27	28	29	30	31	32	33	34	35	36	37
Masters															-	-	T29	-
US Open	-	T33	T13	T12	T22	T45	-	MC	T41	T19	-	-	T23	T9	T12	-	-	-
British	-	T6	T20	4	-	T14	T24	4	-	-	-	T25	-	T14	T4	MC	-	MC
PGA	-	-	-	T5	-	-	-	-	-	T17	T3	T17	T17	-	-	-	-	-

Tom Kite (USA)

Some 10 years into his PGA Tour career, Tom Kite (b. McKinney, Texas, 12/9/1949) was described by Peter Alliss as "easily the best golfer in the world amongst those that hardly ever win a tournament." Kite would, of course, go on to capture 19 PGA Tour titles (16 after the time of Alliss' writing) establishing himself as one of the better players of his time and, as of 2004, a Hall of Famer.

A youthful pupil of legendary teacher Harvey Penick, Kite joined fellow Penick disciple Ben Crenshaw on University of Texas teams that won back-to-back national titles in 1971–72, with Kite and Crenshaw sharing the NCAA individual crown in 1972. Kite was runner-up to Lanny Wadkins at the 1970 U.S. Amateur and a constant threat in most major amateur events of the period, ultimately playing on a losing Walker Cup side in 1971.

As observed by Alliss, Kite's professional career got off to a slow start in terms of wins but certainly not in other ways, for he was selected Rookie of the Year in 1973, ranked 25th on the money list in 1974, then would finish no worse than 20th (with two first places) over the next 15 seasons. By the mid-1980s the wins were finally coming, frequently against strong fields on tough golf courses. The 1989 **Players Championship** (in which he edged Chip Beck by one) was the closest thing to a Major until the 1992 **U.S. Open** at Pebble Beach. Here Kite battled severe winds to post a superb closing 72, hanging on for a two-stroke victory over Jeff Sluman. The following year he blitzed the **Bob Hope Desert Classic** with a 35-under-par 325 total, a tournament record that still stands—by five shots!—to this day.

Such aggressive scoring, however, was not the Kite norm as he was far more the sort to hit fairways and greens, chip it close when he didn't and struggle a bit with the putter thereafter. As such he was a player whose great consistency frequently placed him around the lead, with victories often coming by simply hanging in while others around him were collapsing. Competitive golf, after all, is not about how but rather how many—and Tom Kite has managed to score less than most of the field for more than 30 years.

PGA Tour Wins (19): 1983 Bing Crosby; 1984 Doral; 1986 Western Open; 1989 Players Championship; **1992 U.S. Open;** 1993 Los Angeles
Champions Tour Wins: 7 (2000-2004)
Walker Cup: 1971 **Ryder Cup:** 1979–89 & '93 (7) and 1997 Capt

1971-1998

	71	72	73	74	75	76	77	78	79	80	81	82	83	84
Masters	T42	T22	-	-	T10	T5	T3	T18	5	T6	T5	T5	T2	T6
US Open	-	T19	-	T8	-	-	T27	T20	-	MC	T20	29	T20	MC
British	-	-	-	-	-	T5	-	T2	T30	T27	-	MC	T29	T22
PGA	-	-	-	T39	T33	T13	T13	-	T35	T20	T4	T9	T67	T34

	85	86	87	88	89	90	91	92	93	94	95	96	97	98
Masters	MC	T2	T24	44	T18	T14	56	-	MC	4	MC	MC	2	38
US Open	T13	T35	T46	T36	T9	T56	T37	1	MC	T33	T67	T82	T68	T43
British	T8	MC	T72	T20	T19	MC	T44	T19	T14	T8	T58	T27	T10	T38
PGA	T12	T26	T10	T4	T34	T40	T52	T21	T56	T9	T54	MC	5	MC

Beverly Klass (USA)

One of the stranger stories in the history of women's golf, Tarzana, California, native Beverly Klass (b. 11/8/1956) was a prodigious preteen talent, running away with a national Pee-Wee tournament by a ridiculous 65 shots. With visions of millions undoubtedly dancing in his head, her father Jack forced her to turn pro at age nine—which is only slightly more absurd than the fact that playing in four LPGA Tour events during the summer of 1967, she actually made a cut, cashing a check for $131. The LPGA, perhaps protecting some lesser players' egos as much as its competitive integrity, soon passed a rule barring those under 18 from competing and Klass was reinstated as an amateur, only to return in 1976 for a more legitimate try. This time she lasted 13 seasons, winning a quasi-official event called the **Women's International Satellite** in 1977 and several times finishing second. Now a teaching professional in Florida, Klass is perhaps sports' all-time example of immature parents imposing their own dreams upon the lives of their children.

Emilee Klein (USA)

Santa Monica, California, and Arizona State product Emilee Klein (b. 6/11/1974) arrived on the LPGA Tour in 1995 with the shiniest of credentials including two

All-American selections in two seasons, individual and team **NCAA** titles in 1994, a 1994 Curtis Cup appearance, and a bucket full of amateur victories from coast to coast. Following a rookie season that saw her finish 40th on the money list, Klein looked very much the future star upon winning the **Ping Welch's Championship** and the **Women's British Open** (not yet a Major) on back-to-back 1996 weekends. However, while never out of the top 60 over nine full seasons, Klein has not quite lived up to that standard, winning only once more (at the 2001 **Michelob Light Classic**) and logging only three top-10 finishes in 31 subsequent Major championship starts.

George Knudson (Canada)

Though the talented Mike Weir will surely overtake him, Winnepeg's George Knudson's eight PGA Tour wins remain, for the moment, the most ever logged by a Canadian player. Possessing one of the most widely admired swings of his time, Knudson (1937–1989) won the old **Coral Gables Open** during his rookie year of 1961, then proceeded to finish among the Tour's top 60 money winners from 1962 to 1972. His biggest victories were the 1967 **New Orleans Open** (by one over Jack Nicklaus) and the 1968 **Phoenix** and **Tucson Opens,** though he perhaps drew more attention with a second–place tie at the 1969 Masters (just one back of George Archer) than anything else.

At home Knudson won four **Canadian PGAs** between 1964 and 1977 and was a mainstay of his nation's 1960s **World Cup** teams, capturing medalist honors in 1966 in Tokyo, then teaming with Al Balding to win Canada's first title in Rome in 1968. Curiously, he never managed a victory in the Canadian Open, and this perhaps was one of the few failures to bother him. By many accounts Knudson was not wholly dedicated to golf, enjoying skiing and other activities, and certainly never ranking among the game's more ardent practicers.

Carin (Hjalmarsson) Koch (Sweden)

Twice a second-team All-American at the University of Tulsa, former **Swedish Junior** champion Carin Koch (b. Kungalv, 2/23/1971) has enjoyed mixed success on the LPGA Tour, managing only one top-10 money ranking (eighth in 2002) and two victories (the 2001 **Corning Classic** and the 2005 **Corona Morelia**) over nine seasons. A relatively short-but-accurate ball-striker who hits a large number of greens, Koch (née Hjalmarsson) is one of Europe's top female players, thrice seeing Solheim Cup action (2000–03) where her 17th-hole, cup-clinching birdie against Michele Redman in 2000 was a notable highlight.

Gary Koch (USA)

The **Florida State Open** winner at age 16 and **USGA Junior Boys** champion a year later, Gary Koch (b. Baton Rouge, Louisiana, 11/21/1952) starred at the University of Florida and won the 1973 **Trans-Mississippi Amateur** before qualifying for the PGA Tour in 1975. Though his ensuing professional career might be considered something of a disappointment, he did manage six Tour victories ranging from the 1976 **Tallahassee Open** to the 1988 **Las Vegas Invitational.** Like many Florida natives raised on Bermudagrass, Koch's performance on his home ground has always exceeded his success elsewhere, with four of his six titles coming in-state. He has, since 1990, been a familiar voice as a TV commentator and has recently begun playing some events on the Champions Tour.

Chuck Kocsis (USA)

A tremendous young talent in the years before World War II, Newcastle, Pennsylvania, native Charles R. Kocsis (b. 1913) won the 1936 **NCAA** individual title while at the University of Michigan, yet it can be argued that he accomplished even greater feats while earlier attending Redford (Michigan) High School. In 1930, he qualified into the U.S. Amateur at Merion at the age of 17—and defeated none other than Francis Ouimet in the first round. The following year, Kocsis captured the first of his three **Michigan Open** titles, an impressive feat for an 18-year-old—but an absolutely astounding one when we consider that he defeated the reigning British Open champion, Tommy Armour, in a play-off to do so.

In such a light it seems amazing that Kocsis never won a U.S. Amateur, though he came close in 1956 when E. Harvie Ward defended his 1955 crown by beating the then-43-year-old Kocsis in the final 5 and 4 at Chicago's Knollwood Club. Despite little in the way of nationally prominent wins, Kocsis was twice low amateur in the U.S. Open and once at the Masters. He was also selected for Walker Cup action in 1938, '49, and '57, a testimonial to the longevity of his game.

Takaaki Kono (Japan)

Raised adjacent to Japan's venerable Hodogaya CC, Takaaki Kono (b. 1940) began as a caddie before developing into one of Japan's finest players during the late 1960s and early '70s. Along with his younger brother Mitsutaka, Kono enjoyed fine success in his own region, winning the 1968 **Japan Open,** the 1969 and '71 **Malaysian Opens** (the latter with a record 269 total at the Royal Selangor GC) and the 1972 **Singapore Open.** He also captured the 1968

Brazilian Open and generally garnered enough international notice to appear in five Masters Tournaments, his best finish being a tie for 12th in 1970.

Bill Kratzert (USA)

Bill Kratzert (b. Quantico, Virginia, 6/29/1952) came from a golfing family, his father serving as a club professional for some 40 years while his sister Cathy has enjoyed a long LPGA Tour career (generally under her married name of Gerring). Bill was the **Indiana Open** champion at age 17 and a two-time All-American at the University of Georgia before turning pro in 1974 and joining the PGA Tour in 1976. All told he would win four Tour titles while once cracking the top 10 money winners (eighth in 1978). Falling permanently from the top 100 by the late 1980s, he has since done television work while occasionally playing the Champions Tour.

Ted Kroll (USA)

A three-time Purple Heart winner during World War II, Ted Kroll (1919–2002) actually turned professional prior to the war but saw precious little action. One prewar event in which he did play, however, was the 1941 U.S. Open at Colonial, to which he hitchhiked all the way from his hometown of New Hartford, New York, in order to compete. Finally joining the PGA Tour full-time in 1949, Kroll went on to record eight official victories, including the 1962 **Canadian Open** and the 1956 **World Championship of Golf,** a lucrative event whose $50,000 prize went a long way (along with wins in **Tucson** and **Houston**) to making Kroll that season's leading money winner. A Ryder Cup selection from 1953 to 1957, Kroll also was well-known as a teacher, sought out by fellow professionals in times of trouble.

Matt Kuchar (USA)

Following the Georgia Tech legacy of Bobby Jones and David Duval, Matt Kuchar (b. Winter Park, Florida, 6/21/1978) established himself as one of the better American amateurs of the 1990s, capturing the **U.S. Amateur** title in 1997 by a 2 and 1 margin over Joel Kribel at Chicago's Cog Hill G & CC. As a college sophomore he scored a rare one-two punch, finishing 21st at the Masters and 14th at the U.S. Open, fueling all manner of talk about abandoning his education for a crack at the pros. Remaining in school, however, Kuchar was twice named a first-team All-American, played on the 1999 American Walker Cup team and captured the 1998 Fred Haskins award as the collegiate Player of the Year.

Remarkably, even after graduating (and despite obvious endorsement opportunities) Kuchar elected to take a job in the financial services industry and remain an amateur—for a time. Toward the end of 2000, he finally turned professional and, after a substantial dry spell, came out of nowhere to win the 2002 **Honda Classic.** He would, however, slip to 182nd on the money list in 2003 before showing modest improvement throughout much of 2004.

Candie Kung (Taiwan/USA)

A young Taiwanese player for whom stardom seems likely, Candie Kung (b. Kaohsiung, 8/8/1981) was a three-time AJGA All-American and the organization's 1999 Player of the Year before being twice named a collegiate All-American at USC and winning the 2001 **U.S. Public Links.** Turning pro later that year, Kung debuted on the LPGA Tour in 2002, going winless but placing a steady 36th on the money list. Having thus wet her feet, Kung then exploded in 2003, winning three times (her first at Hawaii's **Takefuji Classic**), notching eight top 10s, and finishing an impressive sixth in money winnings. Though failing to match such lofty numbers in 2004, Kung remains a solid all-around player with few apparent weaknesses—and very likely the finest woman player ever born in Taiwan.

Alec Kyle (UK)

Scotland's Alexander Thompson "Alec" Kyle (b. 1907) falls among those whose competitive peaks were lost to wartime, though he did manage to win the last prewar **British Amateur** in 1939, defeating Colonel Anthony Duncan 2 and 1 at Hoylake. Kyle later extended his career effectively, appearing in Walker Cups in 1938, '47, and '51. His 1938 singles victory over Fred Haas closed out the visiting Americans, giving Britain its first-ever Walker Cup triumph. Fittingly, the match was played at St. Andrews.

L

Arthur Lacey (UK)

The product of a golfing family (his brother Charles finished third in the 1937 Open Championship at Carnoustie), Arthur Lacey (1904–1979) was a professional from Buckinghamshire, England, who managed a solid prewar playing record. In addition to capturing two **Belgian Opens** (1931 and '32) and a **French Open** (1932), he was twice a Ryder Cup player (1933 and '37) and once a captain, shepherding a losing squad in 1951 at Pinehurst. In America, Lacey is perhaps more readily remembered as the rules official who denied Arnold Palmer relief from an embedded ball at the 66th hole of the 1958 Masters, sparking a longstanding controversy as to whether Palmer properly announced his intention to play a second ball (on which the committee ultimately awarded him a par three) as the rules require.

Catherine Lacoste (France)

The daughter of the great tennis champion René LaCoste and golfing star Simone Thion de la Chaume, Paris-born Catherine LaCoste (b. 6/27/1945) proved herself able to escape the shadow of her illustrious upbringing, becoming, for a time, perhaps the finest woman golfer in the world. She first came to prominence at age 19, teaming with Claudine Cros and Brigitte Varangot to carry France to victory in the 1964 **World Amateur Team Championship.** LaCoste then claimed several smaller amateur events (including shooting a stunning 66 in the 1966 Astor Trophy at Prince's) before routing Varangot 8 and 6 to capture the 1967 **French Open Amateur.** She then trooped off somewhat anonymously to America where in rather a huge upset (at least from the U.S. perspective), her 294 total at The Homestead made her the youngest-ever winner of the **U.S. Women's Open** (a record since lowered by Se Ri Pak) and the event's only amateur champion.

Remarkably, LaCoste's best season still lay ahead. After winning the American **Western Amateur** and the **French Closed** title in 1968, she proved nearly invincible in 1969, taking the **French Open** and **Closed,** the **Spanish Ladies,** the **British Ladies** (coming from 4 down to defeat Ann Irvin in the final), and, to complete a Grand Slam of

sorts, the **U.S. Women's Amateur.** Soon after, LaCoste got married and retired from competitive golf, returning for long enough in the 1970s (as Mrs. LaCoste de Prado) to win two more **French** and **Spanish** titles.

Generally viewed as the finest driver and long iron player since Babe Zaharias, LaCoste certainly ranks among the elite female golfers, and it is interesting to ponder what additional heights she might have achieved had she opted for a long professional career in the American style.

Major Amateur Wins (3): 1967 U.S. Women's Open; 1969 British Ladies; 1969 U.S. Women's Amateur; 4 French Open Ladies & 3 Spanish Ladies

Ky Laffoon (USA)

One of golf's all-time great eccentrics, Ky Laffoon (b. Zinc, Arkansas, 12/23/1908) was a mostly–World War II professional who won 10 times on the PGA Tour between 1933 and 1946. His biggest victory was perhaps the 1935 **Phoenix Open,** where he defeated Craig Wood by four at the Phoenix CC. In 1934 he set a then-record for 72 holes with a score of 266 at Denver's unofficial Park Hill Open. He also was selected in 1935 for Ryder Cup play and a year later was tied for the U.S. Open lead through 54 holes before closing with 74 to finish tied for fifth. His playing career thus summarized, let the stories begin.

Laffoon was of the Lefty Stackhouse/Ivan Gantz school of temperament, but by most accounts he was considerably more subtle about it, not simply bashing himself into submission but rather creatively taking his frustration out upon his clubs. He was known, for example, to heap all manner of physical abuse on his putters, with one (likely apocryphal) story recalling his actually shooting an offending club before burying it in a greenside bunker. We shouldn't dismiss this account too hastily, as Pete Dye has recalled playing with Laffoon during the 1940s when Ky brought along a rifle to do a bit of rabbit hunting on the more richly stocked holes.

Like Lee Elder in later years, Laffoon spent some time hustling with the legendary Titanic Thompson, making him privy to all manner of tricks and shenanigans. On the Tour, he became famous for grinding the leading edge of his irons by dragging them along the highway at speed, causing sleeping traveling companions to awaken in a panic, seeing only a shower of sparks immediately outside their window. There were also, we are told, occasions where Laffoon's putter, somehow escaping its due discipline at the site of its failings, was tied to the rear bumper and dragged all the way to the next Tour stop.

Yet through all of this, Ky Laffoon was widely respected by his peers both as a player and a teacher. Reportedly strong enough to tear a deck of playing cards in half, Laffoon's impact on the game should probably be better remembered—but then again, this was a man who reportedly declined to play in one Western Open because the clubhouse was situated too far from the parking lot.

PGA Tour Wins (10): 1935 Phoenix
Ryder Cup: 1935

Renton Laidlaw (UK)

Edinburgh-born Renton Laidlaw has spent time covering sports in virtually every available medium, beginning as a writer for the Edinburgh *Evening News*, then branching part-time into radio with the BBC. For a quarter-century (from 1973 to 1998) he wrote for the London *Evening Standard*, the last few years spent overlapping with television work done for America's fledgling Golf Channel. Dedicated full time to the Golf Channel's PGA European Tour coverage since 1998, Laidlaw's smooth, knowledgeable voice has become famous in the United States, often broadcasting from such far-flung locales as Hong Kong, Dubai, and South Africa—frequently in successive weeks.

John Laidlay (UK)

Haddington, Scotland's John Ernest Laidlay (1860–1940) must rank among golf's all-time most underappreciated men, based simply on the fact that it was he who pioneered the overlapping grip which predominates modern golf—a technique that, due mostly to the overwhelming popularity of one subsequent user, will be forever known as the "Vardon grip."

Laidlay was also one of the elite players of his day, a winner, by his own count, of 139 career medals and a man universally grouped with John Ball and Horace Hutchinson as the three finest amateurs of the late nineteenth century. Laidlay won the **British Amateur** twice, first in 1889 at St. Andrews (where he beat Leslie Balfour-Melville 2 and 1), then two years later when it took 20 holes to dispatch Harold Hilton, also at St. Andrews. Perhaps more impressively, he reached the semifinals for seven consecutive years

between 1888 and 1894, a record of consistency not even approached by Ball, Hutchinson, or anyone else. Laidlay also made regular forays into the Open Championship, scoring four top-10 finishes including a pair of fourths and, in 1893 at Prestwick, a solo second.

Stylistically, Laidlay is often characterized as iconoclastic, though Darwin took pains to point out that while his stance (with ball positioned well forward, off his left foot) was indeed odd, "the swing itself was sound and normal enough." A passable driver of the ball, Laidlay was universally hailed both for the splendor of his approach play and his skill on the greens, the latter accomplished with an ancient putting cleek retained from his boyhood.

Henri de Lamaze (France)

Though the quality of his domestic competition is certainly up for debate, there can be no denying that the record of amateur Henri de Lamaze (b. 1918) is an impressive one. Between 1947 and 1971, he won the **French Closed Amateur** a remarkable 14 times while also holding his own against presumably more skilled foreigners, taking the **Open Amateur** crown on 11 occasions. Considered a steady player and an excellent putter, de Lamaze also won national Amateurs in **Italy** (1955), **Spain** (1950–52), **Belgium** (1953), and **Portugal** (1952), as well as the 1955 **Spanish Open,** though his best international performance likely came at the 1966 British Amateur at Carnoustie. Reaching the semifinals for the first time at age 48, de Lamaze was eliminated by 18-year-old Bobby Cole, the eventual champion, but not without a fight, losing 3 and 2.

Al Laney (USA)

A native of Pensacola, Florida, Al Laney (1895–1988) was among the last of the old-time sportwriters, primarily covering golf and tennis over a long and distinguished career, a good deal of which was spent in Europe with the Paris *Herald* (today's *International Herald Tribune*). Laney was especially observant of the lively inter-war European sporting scene, where he and O. B. Keeler were the only American writers to witness firsthand the first two legs of Bobby Jones' 1930 Grand Slam. By the mid-1930s he was back in New York where he would remain with the *New York Herald Tribune* until its close in 1968. A member of the International Tennis Hall of Fame, Laney's primary golfing monument is *Following the Leaders* (Ailsa, 1991), a charming retrospective of the game's greats completed in the 1970s, but not published until some three years after his death.

Bernhard Langer (Germany)

Coming from a country whose past golfing interest had been at best lukewarm, the success of Bernhard Langer (b. Anhausen, 8/27/1957) has been little short of astounding. After taking up the game at age seven and turning professional at 18, Langer not only battled a lack of prime competition and coaching but also a much-discussed bout with the "yips," an affliction normally reserved for players of a somewhat richer vintage. But Langer persevered, utilizing all manner of alternative putting grips (he ultimately switched to the long club in 1996) and a Hall of Fame iron game to claim his place among the world's best. Further, as a devotee of physical fitness—and perhaps because he didn't have much of a putting game to lose—Langer has remained at the top for as long as any contemporary player, very nearly two full decades.

Langer has mostly confined himself to the European Tour (averaging only 10 American appearances a year) where he has amassed a remarkably consistent record, finishing 16 times among the top 10 in the Order of Merit, including first place twice (1981 and '84) and second on an additional four occasions. Since hitting his stride in 1980, he has never been out of the top 40, save for 2003 when he spent the majority of the season in the United States. During this stretch Langer has won an even 40 times in Europe, an obviously grand mark which includes four-win campaigns in 1984 and '97, three in 1983 and '95, and not less than 11 two-win seasons dating back to 1981.

Given this impressive Continental record then, it is perhaps ironic that Langer's two greatest victories both took place in America at the **Masters**. In 1985, his 282 total was two shots better than Raymond Floyd, Seve Ballesteros, and Curtis Strange, making Langer only the second European (behind Ballesteros) to claim the coveted Green Jacket. Eight years later, in 1993, he took his second when his 277 total was four better than Chip Beck. Almost equally impressive was a 2004 run which saw him contend, at age 46, right into the closing holes before achieving a gutsy tie for fourth. Surprisingly, Langer's overall record in the American Majors has been modestly disappointing, amounting to ten top 10s (versus 16 missed cuts) in 57 starts. But like most Europeans, his greatest focus has long been on the Claret Jug and there he has many times been close, finishing second to Bill Rogers in 1981 at Royal St. George's, joint second to Ballesteros in 1984 at St. Andrews, and third (joint or solo) on four more occasions in 1985, '86, '93 and, at age 43, in 2001.

Though Langer's European successes are too numerous to recount, several have been of some historic note. In 1980, for example, his triumph at the **British Masters**—a five-stroke rout of Brian Barnes—made him the first German ever to capture a European Tour event. His victory at the following year's **German Open** perhaps held even greater sentimental value, for it was the first time that a native had ever claimed the national title in an event that dates to 1911.

Even with his induction into the World Golf Hall of Fame in 2002, it remains difficult to adequately state Bernhard Langer's importance to the development of modern international golf. It was the coming of Langer and Ballesteros that trumpeted a new and vibrant European Tour in the late 1970s, making it something more than a British-dominated affair and helping to give the game far greater spectator relevance across the Continent.

Sadly, the definitive image of Langer for many will be his missed 6-foot putt on the last green of the 1991 Ryder Cup at Kiawah Island, his resultant halving of the final match with Hale Irwin allowing America to retain the cup with a 14-14 tie. Overall, however, Langer's Ryder Cup record of 21-15-6 is more than respectable and he generally outperformed his teams, which accumulated only a 4-5-1 record in the years of his appearances. He also captained Europe's victorious team in 2004.

PGA Tour Wins (3): 1985 & '93 Masters; 1983 Heritage

Intn'l Wins (58): 1980 British Masters; 1981, '82, '85, '86 & '93 German Open; 1983 & '97 Italian Open; 1984 French Open; 1984 & '92 Dutch Open; 1984, '87 & '94 Irish Open; 1984 & '89 Spanish Open; 1986 Trophée Lancôme; 1987, '93 & '95 Volvo PGA Championship; 1991 & '97 Benson & Hedges; 1991 Hong Kong Open; 1994 & 2002 Volvo Masters

Ryder Cup: 1981–97 & 2002 (10); 2004 Capt

1976-2004

	76	77	78	79	80	81	82	83	84	85	86	87	88	89	90
Masters	-	-	-	-	-	-	MC	-	T31	1	T16	T7	T9	T26	T7
US Open	-	-	-	-	-	-	MC	-	-	MC	T8	T4	MC	T59	MC
British	MC	-	MC	-	T51	2	T13	T56	T2	T3	T3	T17	70	80	T48
PGA	-	-	-	-	-	-	-	-	-	T32	MC	T21	MC	T61	MC

	91	92	93	94	95	96	97	98	99	00	01	02	03	04
Masters	T32	T31	1	T25	T31	T36	T7	T39	T11	T28	T6	T32	MC	T4
US Open	MC	T23	MC	T23	T36	DQ	MC	MC	-	MC	T40	T35	T42	-
British	T9	T59	3	T60	T24	WD	T38	MC	T18	T11	T3	T28	MC	-
PGA	MC	T40	MC	T25	-	76	T23	-	T61	T46	MC	T23	T57	T66

William Langford (USA)

Austin, Illinois-born William Boice Langford (1887–1977) took up golf under the worst of circumstances, as a recuperative effort following a childhood bout with polio. He would go on to become a top-flight amateur, playing on three NCAA championship teams (1906–08) at Yale before earning a Masters degree in mining engineering at Columbia University. He then spent several years working for American Park Builders in Chicago before teaming up in 1918 with another engineer, Theodore J. Moreau, to form an independent course design firm which would operate prolifically well into the 1930s.

Langford claimed to have worked on over 250 courses in his career, with the clear majority being in the Midwest and Florida. From a design perspective, he is best known for his dramatically elevated green complexes, many of which were flanked with deep, grass-faced bunkers in a style reminiscent of Seth Raynor and Charles Banks. Also a great supporter of public golf, Langford owned and operated several Chicago-area daily-fee facilities and served for many years on the USGA's Public Links Committee.

Notable Courses: Culver Acadamies GC, Indiana; Harrison Hills CC, Indiana; Key West GC, Florida (NLE); Lawsonia GC, Links Course, Wisconsin; Texarkana CC, Arkansas; Wakonda C, Iowa

John Langley (UK)

Something of a boy wonder, England's John Douglas Algernon Langley (b. 1918) was British Boys champion at age 17 and awarded a Blue (the British equivalent of an American varsity letter) immediately upon enrolling at Cambridge. He was one of the youngest Walker Cuppers ever in 1936; then, after losing several prime years to the war, a considerably more experienced player during subsequent appearances in 1951 and '53. Never getting so far as the semifinals of the British Amateur, however, Langley eased out of competitive golf in the mid-1950s.

Lang Willie (UK)

Perhaps the most famous of a colorful crop of nineteenth-century St. Andrews caddies, Lang Willie supplemented his income by helping Allan Robertson and Old Tom Morris with the manufacture of feather golf balls, and by teaching. A tall man with more than a passing familiarity with the bottle, he would stop at nothing to convince his charges that they were improving under his knowing hand, often replying with a wonderfully noncommittal "Jist surprisin'!" when asked to define a newcomer's progress.

A frequent teacher of the game to the faculty of St. Andrews University, Lang Willie was known to scoff at their efforts by observing that "Learning Latin and Greek is all very fine, but you need *brains* to be a golfer."

Albert Lasker (USA)

Advertising executive and philanthropist Albert Lasker was a classic self-made American millionaire of the Roaring '20s, reinventing his business with the advent of radio commercials and building for himself a spectacular Lake Forest, Illinois, estate known as Mill Road Farm. Lasker's relevance to golfers lies in his hiring of William Flynn to design the most impressive private estate course ever built, a 6,915-yard monster that included more than 110 bunkers and carried a USGA rating of 76.32. Likely tough enough to host a U.S. Open even today, the golf course was subdivided after World War II, but not before Bobby Jones was heard to call it one of the three best layouts in the entire country.

E. A. Lassen (UK)

A product of Bradford in West Yorkshire, E. A. "Bertie" Lassen had little upon his résumé when he surprised observers by defeating H. E. Taylor to capture the 1908 British Amateur at Royal St. George's. In describing Lassen, Bernard Darwin wrote that "He was a fine putter and played the game with a cold, inhuman concentration not easy to combat." Lassen reached the Amateur final once more in 1911, losing to Harold Hilton but proving that his previous success, in Darwin's words, "was no fluke." He was also runner-up in the 1913 French championship.

Robert "Red" Lawrence (USA)

White Plains, New York, native Robert F. "Red" Lawrence (1893–1976) got his start in the field of golf design by working for Walter Travis during the 1919 building of the Westchester CC, and then was hired by William Flynn to supervise construction of several Golden Age layouts in Florida. Chief among these were 36 outstanding holes (now-deceased) at the Boca Raton Hotel, a legendary period club to which Lawrence latched on as greenkeeper during the doldrums of the Depression.

Not until after World War II did Lawrence enter the design business full time, initially in Florida and then, after 1958, in Arizona. Though he counted more than 25 new designs in his portfolio, Lawrence will surely be best remembered for the groundbreaking Desert Forest GC, a

1962 layout in Carefree that remains a fixture in all national Top 100s. Frequently tagged as the "Pine Valley of the West," Desert Forest features numerous forced carries to naturally contoured "island" fairways, presaging modern desert design by a good 20 years.

W. G. Lawrence (USA)

William G. Lawrence, who learned the game at the ancient French resort town of Pau, is today only a footnote in golf history, having won the first attempt at an American national championship in 1894 at his home club in Newport, Rhode Island. Lawrence carded a 36-hole score of 188, enough to defeat Charles Blair Macdonald by one—that is, until C. B. complained of a stone wall costing him two strokes *and* argued that any true amateur championship had to be played at match play, not medal. The resulting debate did much to spark the founding of the USGA, which held what is now regarded as the first "official" national championship (won by Horace Rawlins) a year later.

Paul Lawrie (UK)

Though largely a journeyman on the European Tour, Scotland's Paul Stewart Lawrie, M.B.E. (b. Aberdeen, 1/1/1969) achieved a measure of immortality by winning an epic **Open Championship** upon a badly tricked-up Carnoustie layout in 1999. That event will forever be recalled for Jean Van de Velde's heartbreaking seven at the last, creating a three-way, four-hole play-off with Lawrie and American Justin Leonard. Yet while Van de Velde clearly let things get away, Lawrie must equally be credited for playing some inspired golf, carding a brilliant closing 67 before making clutch birdies at the last two play-off holes to claim victory. Contrary to the view in America (where he has been largely unsuccessful), Lawrie has not disappeared altogether since 1999, notching European wins in 2001 and 2002 to bring his career total to five.

Henry Leach (UK)

Henry Leach was an editor of Britain's venerated magazine *Golf Illustrated*, a position which provided him a solid platform as both a journalist and author. All told, Leach penned three original volumes, the best of which, *The Happy Golfer* (Macmillan, 1914), represents a fascinating and much-overlooked survey of pre–World War I golf around the world. His most recognized contribution, however, would actually be a project that he edited, *Great Golfers in the Making* (Methuen, 1907). A compilation of autobiographical recollections originally contributed to *Golf Illustrated* by, quite literally, every great golfer of the day, *Great Golfers* is a rare and genuine classic, thankfully reprinted by the USGA in 1988.

David Leadbetter (UK/Zimbabwe)

Regardless of one's feelings about golf's many self-promoting "swing gurus," there can be little doubt that the most successful—in terms both of marketing and elite players taught—has been David Leadbetter (b. 1952). A native of Sussex, England, but raised primarily in Zimbabwe, Leadbetter turned professional at age 18 but never enjoyed substantial success as a player, instead making his name as a teacher by developing three of the more precise swings in modern golf, David Frost, Nick Price and Nick Faldo. With TV appearances and golf academies literally around the globe, Leadbetter has certainly topped a competitive marketplace—and looking at the before-and-after records of his top charges, his status has merit. For as Nick Price has stated: "[David] has an incredible knack of being able to look at a player, see how he's trying to swing the club, and then help him to swing it more efficiently."

Stephen Leaney (Australia)

Primarily a European and Australasian player during his first decade as a professional, Perth's Stephen Leaney (b. 3/10/1969) has been a consistent winner in those locales since 1995. In addition to a pair of **Victorian Opens** at home, he has won the national Opens of **Morocco** (1998) and the **Netherlands** twice (1998 and 2000), plus the 2002 **Linde German Masters**. Following an impressive second-place finish at the 2003 U.S. Open at Olympia Fields and a subsequent Presidents Cup appearance, Leaney began playing in the United States on a semiregular basis in 2004.

Joe Lee (USA)

One of golf design's more popular men, Oviedo, Florida-born Joseph L. Lee (1922–2003) was drawn into the design business by his friend Dick Wilson while working as an assistant golf professional in Ohio. Returning to Florida, Lee handled construction for a number of Wilson designs, including a now-defunct 1957 project in Havana. The two became full partners by the end of the decade with Lee having a hand in a great many of Wilson's trademark 1960s designs, such as La Costa, Cog Hill (No. 4), Bay Hill and the Blue Monster at Doral.

Following Wilson's death in 1965, Lee went into solo practice, ultimately becoming even more prolific than his celebrated mentor. Though Florida, where he worked on more than 80 courses, would forever be his primary stomping ground, Lee completed post-Wilson designs or alterations in 15 states and seven countries, with the Bahamas, Venezuela and Portugal all providing regular work. Though a fine player himself, Lee's focus was on building courses that were manageable for the average player, layouts with bunkers that looked more dangerous than they played, modest green contours and a minimum of flashy features.

All told, Joe Lee was involved with over 250 design projects, though one—the Trophy Club in Ft. Worth, Texas—must truly stand out. This was the legendary Ben Hogan's sole venture into golf course design, a joint 1976 effort with Lee in which Hogan, by all accounts, was deeply involved. The project was only a modest success, however, leaving Hogan to return to clubmaking and Lee to produce many more layouts of somewhat greater repute.

Notable Courses: Pine Meadow GC, Illinois; Stonehenge GC, Tennessee; Walt Disney World Resort, Palm Course, Florida

Herbert Leeds (USA)

An 1877 graduate of Harvard, Boston native Herbert Corey Leeds (1854–1930) is justifiably famous as the architect of one of America's great early championship venues, Massachusetts' Myopia Hunt Club, which hosted four U.S. Opens between 1898 and 1908. Something of a sporting all-rounder, Leeds starred in both football and baseball during college, dedicated several years of his life to sailing in far off corners of the world, and wrote books both on yachting and card games. Not taking up golf until age 40, he soon became a scratch player and top Boston-area competitor and visited the great links of Scotland in 1902. Clearly enjoying some fine social connections, Leeds also built courses for four of the East's most distinguished early clubs: the Palmetto Club (Aiken, South Carolina), the Essex County Club (Manchester, Massachusetts), the Kebo Valley Club (Bar Harbor, Maine) and the Bass Rocks GC (Gloucester, Massachusetts). He also served on the USGA Executive Committee in 1905.

Arthur Lees (UK)

A native of Sheffield in Yorkshire, Arthur Lees (1908–1991) was solidly dependable from tee to green and exceptional once within pitching range. A four-time Ryder Cup player

during the somewhat lean (for Britain) years of 1947–55, Lees had won the **Irish Open** before the war (1939) and would twice claim the old **Penfold Tournament** (1951 and '53) after it. His biggest win, by a wide margin, was the 1947 **British Masters** at Little Aston, and he would later maintain a degree of celebrity by serving for many years as professional at Sunningdale.

Peter Lees (UK/USA)

After serving as greenkeeper at Royal Mid-Surrey GC (where he helped the club's professional, five-time Open champion J. H. Taylor, remodel the links), Peter W. Lees (1868–1923) was brought to America in 1914 by Charles Blair Macdonald to supervise construction of his epic Lido GC, in Lido Beach, New York. Lees' "defection" caused a bit of controversy in England but as it turned out, he was in the United States to stay, eventually building additional courses for several Golden Age architects and even designing a few of his own, most notably New York's Hempstead CC in 1921.

Arthur Le Fevre (Australia)

Long-hitting Arthur Le Fevre (1887–1957) was a World War I veteran who served as professional at Royal Melbourne for 26 years. A golf course architect on the side, he helped to oversee construction of the club's new 1926 design (as planned by Dr. Alister MacKenzie) but was probably most celebrated as a clubmaker of the highest caliber. Somewhat forgotten, however, are Le Fevre's playing skills for in addition to winning countless regional events, he performed the relatively rare double of taking the **Australian Open** and **PGA** in the same season, 1921.

Harold G. Legg (USA)

A dominant force in early Midwestern golf, Yale graduate H. G. Legg won an impressive 10 **Minnesota Amateur** titles between 1905 and 1923, including six straight from 1908 to 1913. He was also the first amateur to win the state's **Open** (in 1925 at Interlachen) as well as a five-time **Trans-Mississippi** champion, the first four in succession from 1909 to 1912. Legg's biggest victory, however, was likely the prestigious **Western Amateur** in 1919, where he defeated Richard Bockenkamp 2 and 1 at Sunset Hill CC in St. Louis.

Cobie Legrange
(South Africa)

Once touted as the next in a line of fine young South Africans prepared to challenge Gary Player's supremacy, Boksburg native Cobie Legrange (b. 1942) showed flashes of brilliance during his 20s, particularly in 1964 when he took the **Wills Masters** in Australia (with Nicklaus and Palmer both in the field) as well as the prestigious **British Masters** at Royal Birkdale. After appearing at the Masters in 1965 and '66, he would again take the **British** version in 1969, a year in which he also tied for 11th at the Open Championship at Royal Lytham & St. Annes. Runner-up to Player in the South African Open in both 1966 and '68, Legrange frequently battled a nervous condition in which he had difficulty taking the club smoothly away from the ball going back. Though he ultimately won 12 times in South Africa, this odd affliction surely cost him a chance at carving a more lasting legacy.

Tom Lehman (USA)

Something of a late developer among modern touring pros, former University of Minnesota star Thomas Edward Lehman (b. Austin, Minnesota, 3/7/1959) initially struggled through hard times on the PGA Tour between 1983 and 1985. After heading off to Asia, South Africa, and similarly remote locales for the rest of the decade, he returned to win Player of the Year honors on the Nationwide Tour in 1991.

Thus requalified for the PGA Tour, Lehman recommenced in 1992 and never looked back, winning five titles and more than $14 million, and never finishing worse than 33rd on the money list from 1992 to 2001. He won the **Memorial Tournament** in 1994 and **Colonial** a year later, setting the stage for a Player of the Year 1996, which saw Lehman finish first on the money list and log victories at the **Open Championship** and, at season's end, the **Tour Championship.** His British triumph came at Royal Lytham & St. Annes and featured a record third-round 64, after which a closing 73 was enough to beat Ernie Els and Mark McCumber by two. The following year would yield only an international win (at the prominent **Loch Lomond Invitational**), yet with a tie for fourth at the Heritage Classic, Lehman unseated Fred Couples from the number one spot in the World Ranking—only to be uprooted himself, by Greg Norman, one week later.

A powerful ball-striker who favors a low, ever-reliable draw, Lehman was a Major championship contender throughout much of the 1990s, seven times finishing among the top-6 from 1992 to 1998. Since year 2000, however, he has remained winless and, since 2002, has fallen

from the top-60 money winners for the first time since returning to America.

Lennart Leinborn (Sweden)

Amateur Lennart Leinborn (b. 1919) didn't reach his golfing peak until the age of 40, having only taken up the game upon becoming too old to seriously compete at ice hockey. Obviously a good athlete, he established himself clearly as one of his region's best by winning the **Scandinavian Open Amateur** in 1957, '60 and '63, as well as his homeland's **Closed** title in 1958, '61 and '64. He regularly represented Sweden internationally beginning in 1953.

Cecil Leitch (UK)

Generally viewed as the first great woman golfer of the twentieth century, Silloth, England's Charlotte Cecilia Pitcairn "Cecil" Leitch (1891–1977) was a palpably strong player whose attacking style with both woods and irons was frequently said to resemble that of a man. Leitch first came to prominence in 1908 upon reaching the semifinals of the British Ladies at St. Andrews at age 17 and by 1914, with war looming, ascended the throne by defeating Gladys Ravenscroft 2 and 1 at Hunstanton for her first **British** title. At war's end she promptly won the first two **British Ladies** to be played (1920 and '21), strongly reasserting her dominance and supporting the assumption that at least two or three more titles had fallen irretrievably into the abyss.

Leitch's 1921 victory marked a milestone in women's golf for it was in this final (played at Turnberry) that she defeated the heretofore little-known Joyce Wethered, a marvelous talent who would return the favor by downing Leitch in the following year's final at Prince's. In the main, Wethered would ultimately be judged the better player, partly due to winning her four British Ladies in fewer attempts and partly because she also defeated Leitch in the 1925 final on the 37th hole at Troon (as well as in the sixth round at Royal Portrush in 1924). Also, rather backhandedly, Leitch's fourth title came in 1926, a year when Wethered was not in the field. More important than who won, however, was the effect that the Leitch-Wethered rivalry had on women's golf in Britain, attracting fans of both genders and thus taking the sport onto the front pages from its previous status as little more than an afterthought.

Leitch's overall record was impressive for in addition to her four British Ladies, she was five times the **French** champion (1912, '14, '20, '21 and '24), twice the **English** winner (1914 and '19) and once the **Canadian** titleist (1921). This latter occasion marked a particular high for it was here that Leitch set what is believed to be an all-time record when, in the 36-hole final, she defeated one M. M'Bride by the ungodly margin of 17 and 15.

Tony Lema (USA)

Born: Oakland, California, 2/25/1934 **Died:** Lansing, Illinois, 7/24/1966

A native of San Francisco, the colorful Anthony David Lema grew up something less than wealthy, caddying and working as an assistant professional at the famed San Francisco GC. Following a stint in the U.S. Marine Corps during the Korean War, he made his PGA Tour debut in 1958, initially finding slim pickings before capturing some smaller events in 1961 and '62. It was during the latter season that he earned his famous nickname, "Champagne Tony," after making good on a promise to buy the press a case of the bubbly should he win the **Orange County Open.** In 1963 Lema's game took a quantum leap forward as he finished fourth on the money list and very nearly won the Masters, coming up a single shot shy when Jack Nicklaus holed a long one at the 72nd to win.

Though he would ultimately total 11 Tour wins, Lema's shining hour came in 1964 at St. Andrews where, having never even seen a links golf course previously (and being wagered at 66-1), he rode the advice of local caddie Tip Anderson and a marvelously adaptable short game to finish five ahead of Jack Nicklaus and win the **Open Championship.** The victory was considered a stunning display of power and finesse, and marked Lema a world-class player, as did his four additional wins in America that same season.

Interestingly, though few of Lema's wins were of what one might today consider "quality," his record in Major championships and two Ryder Cups (where he was 8-1-2) and the remarkable power and elegance of his game had people widely ranking him among the world's elite at the time of his death in a 1966 plane crash. His charismatic personality and great popularity with the press may have influenced such assessments, of course, but looking back, it really is difficult not to believe that had he lived, further greatness would have visited Tony Lema.

PGA Tour Wins (11): 1964 British Open
Intn'l Wins (2): 1961 & '62 Mexican Open
Ryder Cup: 1963 & '65 (2)

1956-1966

	56	57	58	59	60	61	62	63	64	65	66
Masters	-	-	-	-	-	-	-	2	T9	T21	T22
US Open	T50	-	-	-	-	-	MC	T5	20	T8	T4
British	-	-	-	-	-	-	-	-	1	T5	T30
PGA	-	-	-	-	-	-	WD	T13	T9	T61	T34

Grace Lenczyk (USA)

A postwar flash who burned brightly for several years, Newington, Connecticut's Grace Lenczyk (b. 1927) captured a rare triple in 1948: the **Women's Intercollegiate** title (playing for Stetson University), the **Canadian Ladies** (which she would defend successfully the following year), and the **U.S. Women's Amateur** at Pebble Beach, where she defeated Helen Sigel 4 and 3 in the final. Lenczyk was also a Curtis Cup participant on winning sides in 1948 and '50 as well as a four-time **Connecticut Ladies** champion. A powerful ball-striker from a family of fine players, Lenczyk lost interest in competing nationally by the early 1950s.

Justin Leonard (USA)

Former University of Texas All-American Justin Charles Garrett Leonard (b. Dallas, Texas, 6/15/1972) is something

of a throwback to the stars of yesteryear, driving the ball no great distance yet succeeding with a wide range of alternative weaponry which includes top shotmaking skills, an elite wedge game, and one of the more effective putting strokes on the PGA Tour. Leonard was much touted during an amateur career wherein he won the 1992 **U.S. Amateur** (8 and 7 over Tom Scherrer at the Muirfield Village GC), took back-to-back **Southern** and **Western Amateurs** (1992 and '93), and appeared on the 1993 Walker Cup team.

With such a pedigree, success on the Tour was widely expected and Leonard has largely delivered, winning eight events in nine full seasons, beginning with the 1996 **Buick Open.** The following year he would win twice, first at the **Kemper Open,** then at the **Open Championship** at Royal Troon where a splendid final-round 65 was the only sub-70 round turned in by a contending player. Becoming the youngest winner of the Claret Jug since a 22-year-old Seve Ballesteros in 1979, Leonard also finished second at the PGA Championship (at Winged Foot) and made his first of two Ryder Cup appearances. A victory at the 1998 **Players Championship** solidified Leonard's top-shelf status. While 1999 proved a rare winless season, it was hardly without drama. At the Open Championship, for example, he was given second life after Jean Van de Velde's infamous seven at the 72nd hole but was defeated by Paul Lawrie in the ensuing three-way play-off. Two months later, it was Leonard's 45-foot putt on the 17th green of The Country Club that clinched a dramatic come-from-behind American Ryder Cup victory, the hasty celebration of which led to a rush of international controversy.

Leonard made some substantial swing changes in 2001, a move which slowed him briefly before victories and top-20 money rankings in 2002 and '03 seemed to right the ship. However, a play-off loss to Vijay Singh at the PGA Championship was the sole highlight of 2004, a disappointing campaign which saw only two top-10 finishes over its first eight months.

Stan Leonard (Canada)

Along with Al Balding, Vancouver's Stan Leonard (b. 2/2/1915) stood atop Canada's postwar field of professionals, claiming eight **Canadian PGA** titles between 1940 and 1961, playing nine times in the World Cup, and winning four events on the American PGA Tour. With World War II raging during the later half of his 20s, Leonard got a relatively late start and was one of the Tour's oldest first-time winners when he captured the 1957 **Greater Greensboro Open** at age 42. Similarly, he was 45 at the time of his biggest triumph, the 1960 **Western Open,** which required a play-off to defeat Art Wall. Though never part of a winning **World Cup** team, Leonard fared quite well individually, taking medalist honors in 1954 at Montreal's Laval-sur-Lac and tying Peter Thomson in 1959 at Royal Melbourne. Leonard never won a Canadian Open (though he was low Canadian on eight occasions) and his best Major championship finishes were ties for fourth at the 1958 and '59 Masters.

Patricia Lesser (USA)

Though born in New York City, Patricia Lesser (b. 8/13/1933) grew up in Seattle where she developed into a top golfing talent at a young age. In 1950 she won the second **USGA Junior Girls** title (defeating a 15-year-old Mickey Wright in the final) and the **Western Junior,** then was low amateur in the U.S. Women's Open in 1951 and '53. Taking **Pacific Northwest** titles in 1952 and '53 (plus a later win in 1965), Lesser was also the 1953 **Women's Intercollegiate** champion while playing for Seattle University. A pair of Curtis Cup appearances in 1954 and '56 actually bracketed Lesser's best season, for she won both the **U.S. Women's**

Amateur (7 and 6 over Jane Nelson at Charlotte's Myers Park CC) and the **Western Amateur** (at Olympia Fields) in 1955. She later married John Harbottle in 1957 and their son, John III, is a contemporary golf course designer.

Thomas Levet (France)

Once upon a time, Arnaud Massy put French golf on the map by winning the 1907 Open Championship, and though Jean Van de Velde very nearly repeated the feat in 1999, it is now Thomas Levet (b. Paris 9/5/1968) who stands the best chance of becoming France's second international star. A three-time **French PGA** champion between 1988 and 1992, Levet actually spent 1994 playing the PGA Tour (the first Frenchman ever to do so) but, finding little success, returned to Europe thereafter. His first official win, the 1998 **Cannes Open,** made him the first Frenchman to claim a significant victory on his home soil since Jean Garaialde's triumph at the 1969 French Open, though Levet generally enjoyed only limited success until the start of the new millennium.

Having never finished better than 69th in the Order of Merit, Levet jumped all the way to 19th in 2001, then very nearly won the Open Championship the following year, closing with a splendid 66 before losing to Ernie Els in a four-man, four-hole play-off. In 2004, a closing 63 sparked a one-stroke victory at the **Scottish Open** at Loch Lomond, thus gaining late entry to the following week's Open Championship at Royal Troon, where Levet was consistently around the lead before tying for fifth. Shortly thereafter he became France's first-ever Ryder Cup player, an accomplishment that, in addition to his five World Cup appearances between 1998 and 2003, allows the engaging Levet to safely be called his nation's best golfer in nearly a century.

Wayne Levi (USA)

The background of Wayne Levi (b. Little Falls, New York, 2/22/1952) offers little to suggest a professional golf career, for he hails from frigid upstate New York and attended the State University at Oswego, whose athletic program competes at the NCAA's division III level. So, starting from the bottom, Levi diligently worked his way up, initially claiming events like the 1973 **New Hampshire Open** before qualifying for the PGA Tour in 1977. In 1979 he captured his first win, the **Houston Open,** and then put together a run of six more titles between 1980 and 1985, including the 1982 **Hawaiian Open** where, demonstrating the fad of the day, he became the first player to win a PGA Tour event using an orange golf ball. Three consecutive winless seasons followed, though 1989, with a 16th-place money ranking, saw something of a return to form.

Regardless, few would have predicted Levi's magnificent 1990, which saw him win four times (at **Atlanta,** the **Western Open, Hartford** and the **Canadian Open**), claim Player of the Year honors and finish second on the season's money list. Such success, however, would prove short-lived, for after being selected for the 1991 Ryder Cup team, Levi never again cracked the top 60 and is today a quiet presence on the Champions Tour.

PGA Tour Wins (12): 1990 Western Open; 1990 Canadian Open
Champions Tour Wins: 2 (2003–2004)
Ryder Cup: 1991

Bruce Lietzke (USA)

For more than two decades, University of Houston product Bruce Alan Lietzke (b. Kansas City, Missouri, 7/18/1951) was perhaps the most envied man on the PGA Tour, never entering more than 25 events in a single season, yet winning 13 times and banking over $6 million in prize money. A dedicated family man, Lietzke generally skipped most of the summer season to be with his brood, missing numerous U.S. Opens and only thrice journeying to Britain for the Open Championship. Yet after each absence Lietzke resurfaced, remaining ultra-reliable with his steady left-to-right action, a cross-handed putting stroke (before such things had gained fashion), and a keen competitive sense.

Obviously a man who felt particularly at home on certain courses, Lietzke won twice at the **Tucson Open,** the **Canadian Open,** the **Byron Nelson,** and **Colonial,** with the sole blemish on his career perhaps being the absence of a Major championship. Granted his chances were lessened by playing in fewer than half of the Majors contested during his career, yet even when he did play Lietzke never seriously challenged for a victory. Indeed, with the exception of a second-place finish (well back of John Daly) at the 1991 PGA Championship, a tie for fourth at the 1981 PGA was his best Major effort.

Still playing a characteristically light schedule, Lietzke has, not surprisingly, proved himself an able senior as well, winning seven times on the Champions Tour since 2001, including the 2003 **U.S. Senior Open.**

PGA Tour Wins (13): 1978 & '82 Canadian Open; 1980 & '92 Colonial; 1981 San Diego; 1981 & '88 Byron Nelson
Champions Tour Wins: 7 (2001–2003)
Ryder Cup: 1981

W. T. Linskill (UK)

Though born in England, W. T. Linskill (1855–1929) spent most of his life at St. Andrews; thus we are hardly surprised to find him as the man who introduced golf to Cambridge upon enrolling there in 1873. He was also the primary facilitator of the Oxford vs. Cambridge match (which began in 1878) and he was later a founding member of the Oxford & Cambridge Golfing Society. Linskill, it is recorded, had a "double-jointed" backswing in the vein of John Daly and was apparently a less-than-serious academician. Indeed, graduation seemed scarcely to be on his agenda and, according to Darwin, "umtrammelled by any nonsensical rules as to date of matriculation, he continued to play for Cambridge until 1883."

John Lister (New Zealand)

A native of the South Island city of Temuka, John Lister (b. 3/9/1947) was the first native Kiwi to have a serious go at the PGA Tour, a roughly 10-year run that began in 1971. He came to America following a successful 1970 campaign in Europe (winning the **Ulster Open** and logging four top-10 finishes in eight starts) and on the heels of a 1971 **New Zealand PGA** title won at Mt. Maunganui with a stunning 30-under-par total of 262. A fine long-iron player whose short game only began to catch up as his career developed, Lister generally struggled in America, save for a victory in the 1976 **Quad City Open.** With two further **New Zealand PGAs** on his résumé, Lister showed a great deal of determination in opting to struggle abroad when he was clearly capable of winning regularly at home.

Karl Litten (USA)

A former civil engineer in both Ohio and Florida, Karl Litten (b. 1933) changed careers in 1968 when he joined the golf course design firm of Robert von Hagge. Litten eventually went solo in 1979, though it would take eight years—and the signing-on of Gary Player as a consulting partner—before a substantial volume of new design work was obtained. Litten's list of American projects is limited but he did gain international attention by constructing 1987's Emirates GC, a genuine desert oasis that hosts the PGA European Tour's annual Dubai Desert Classic. In 1992, Litten built a second 18 (the Dubai Creek GC) for the affluent Middle Eastern nation.

Lawson Little (USA)

Born: Newport, Rhode Island, 6/23/1910 **Died:** Pebble Beach, California, 2/1/1968

Though anyone born in Newport would seem ideally suited for the affluent world of pre–World War II amateur golf, William Lawson Little Jr. actually resided in California during the majority of his competitive years. A broad, patently strong man, Little was initially recognized as a power hitter, a player who could overwhelm a course with his length off the tee. He also possessed a deft greenside touch and, after a series of lessons with Tommy Armour, eventually added an iron game to match.

Little's initial forays onto the national scene seemed disappointing relative to his obvious talents, for while he beat Johnny Goodman in the second round of the 1929 U.S. Amateur (after Goodman's shocking first-round upset of Bobby Jones), he would lose early to Gene Homans in 1930, fail to qualify altogether in 1931, and be eliminated immediately by Johnny Fischer in 1932. But in 1933, fortified by experience and his work with Armour, Little reached the semifinals at Ohio's Kenwood CC (losing to eventual champion George Dunlap) and from then on became, in Longhurst's memorable words, "with the exception of Jones himself, the most formidable amateur golfer the game has seen."

At the 1934 Walker Cup, Little and Johnny Goodman routed the glamour team of Wethered and Tolley 8 and 6 before Little bounced Tolley at singles 6 and 5. On the same trip, Little won the **British Amateur** at Prestwick in remarkable fashion, annihilating James Wallace in the final by the record margin of 14 and 13. Clearly on his game, Little shot 66 in the morning round and was 10 strokes beneath level fours for 23 holes, a performance described by Darwin as "one of the most terrific exhibitions in all golfing history." Back home things were almost anti-climactic when Little routed David Goldman 8 and 7 in September to capture the **U.S. Amateur,** completing what in Jones' wake was christened the "Little Slam."

In 1935 Little returned to Britain and defended his title—but only just, barely holding off a tenacious (if physically overmatched) Dr. William Tweddell after Little had jumped out to an early five-hole lead. He escaped with victory when Tweddell missed a 20-footer to tie at the 36th, then returned home to defeat Walter Emery 4 and 2 to defend the **U.S. Amateur,** giving Little an unprecedented (and since unmatched) back-to-back sweep of both national titles. He also finished sixth in the 1935 Masters, leaving little doubt as to his ability to compete at the highest level.

Yet after turning professional in 1936, Little's career proved solid but hardly spectacular, producing eight PGA Tour victories, seven of which came between 1936 and 1942. Success at the 1936 **Canadian Open** was followed by 1940 victories in **Los Angeles** and, most important, at the **U.S. Open,** where Little defeated Gene Sarazen by three in a play-off at Canterbury. In assessing Little's record, however, we must recall that World War II deprived him of his peak years (ages 30–36) in both tournament and Ryder Cup play. It must further be noted that even rusty and at age 38, Little did manage to win once after the war, at **St. Petersburg** in 1948.

In a curious footnote, Little was also largely responsible for the 14-club rule under which all golfers today compete, his use of as many as 26 during the halcyon days ruffling the feathers of the governing bodies—as well as, we can assume, those of his caddies.

PGA Tour Wins (8): 1936 Canadian Open; 1940 Los Angeles; 1940 U.S. Open; 1941 Texas
Major Amateur Wins (4): 1934 & '35 British Amateur; 1934 & '35 U.S. Amateur
Walker Cup: 1934

1934-1952

	34	35	36	37	38	39	40	41	42	43	44	45	46	47	48	49	50	51	52
Masters	-	6	T20	T19	T10	T3	T19	8	T7				T21	T14	T40	T23	9	6	-
US Open	T25	-	-	MC	T38	T42	1	T17					T10	T31	MC	MC	MC	MC	MC
British	-	T4	-	-	-	MC							10	-	T32	-	-	-	-
PGA	-	-	-	-	-	-	-	-	-		-	-	T17	-	T33	T33	-	T17	T33

Sally Little (South Africa)

Upon joining the LPGA Tour in the early 1970s, the foreign status of South Africa's Sally Little (b. Cape Town 10/12/1951) was decidedly more of a novelty than it would be today. The former **South African Match-** and **Stroke-Play** champion initially struggled, her first five years in America yielding no wins and a top money ranking of 33rd in 1972. But Little persevered, finally breaking through at the 1976 **Ladies Masters** (where a holed 75-foot bunker shot at the last beat fellow international Jan Stephenson by one), then cracking the top 10 money winners in 1977.

What followed was a five-year run from 1978 to 1982 which included 13 official wins, her first Major title (the 1980 **LPGA Championship**), money rankings no worse than eighth, and a victory at the 1982 **Dinah Shore**—the final edition *before* the Dinah was granted Major status. In 1983, however, Little would be slowed by abdominal and knee surgeries, injuries that would ultimately prevent a return to top form. She would win only once more in the years ahead, though the victory would be a big one: a one-shot triumph over Laurie Davies at the 1988 **du Maurier Classic.**

An American citizen for more than 20 years, Little hasn't played anything resembling a full tournament slate since 1992.

LPGA Wins (15): 1980 LPGA Championship; 1982 Dinah Shore; **1988 du Maurier**

Gene Littler (USA)

A native of San Diego, Hall of Famer Gene Alec Littler (b. 7/21/1930) didn't travel far and wide to claim a box full of amateur medals. He instead attended hometown San Diego State and won only one major prize, the 1953 **U.S. Amateur,** where he defeated Dale Morey one up at the Oklahoma City CC. The following winter he entered the PGA Tour's **San Diego Open** as an amateur and, playing at the Rancho Santa Fe CC, proceeded to win the tournament by four. So armed, Littler turned professional and enjoyed quick success, winning three times each in 1955 and '56 while finishing fifth and sixth on the Tour money list. Thereafter it was generally more of the same with a total of 29 wins claimed between 1954 and 1975 and a remarkable 25 appearances among the top 60 money winners in 26 seasons.

The lone exception came in 1972 when Littler was diagnosed with cancer of his lymph glands and underwent surgery. Particularly in those less medically advanced days, retirement was pretty well expected, yet Littler was back on Tour by season's end and, despite now being in his early 40s, went on to win four more titles. Some of this longevity (which further extended through eight career wins on the Champions Tour) was undoubtedly due to his golf swing, a much-celebrated mechanism that represented the very picture of natural motion, sound mechanics, and sublime tempo. Nicknamed "Gene the Machine" because of it, Littler seemed able to consistently hit superb shots with little apparent effort, drawing comparisons to Sam Snead for his ease of motion and Ben Hogan for his precision.

The one blemish on Littler's record was the fact that he claimed only a single professional Major championship, that being the 1961 **U.S. Open** at Oakland Hills, where his 281 total edged Bob Goalby and Doug Sanders by one. He would, however, come agonizingly close on two subsequent occasions, first losing an 18-hole play-off at the 1970 Masters to Billy Casper, then seeing a four-stroke final-nine lead slip away at the 1977 PGA Championship at Pebble Beach, eventually losing to Lanny Wadkins on the third hole of sudden death.

PGA Tour Wins (29): 1954 San Diego; 1955 Los Angeles; 1955, '59 & '69 Phoenix; 1956 Texas; **1961 U.S. Open;** 1965 Canadian Open; 1971 Colonial; 1975 Bing Crosby; 1975 Westchester and 3 Tournament of Champions
Champions Tour Wins: 8 (1983–1989)
Walker Cup: 1953 **Ryder Cup:** 1961–71 & '75 (7)

1956-1979

	54	55	56	57	58	59	60	61	62	63	64	65	66
Masters	T22	T22	T12	MC	-	T8	MC	T15	4	T24	T13	T6	T44
US Open	2	15	T34	T32	4	T11	MC	1	T8	T21	T11	T8	T48
British	-	-	-	-	-	-	-	-	MC	-	-	-	-
PGA	-	-	-	T33	-	10	T18	T5	T23	T34	T33	T28	T3

	67	68	69	70	71	72	73	74	75	76	77	78	79
Masters	T26	T43	T8	2	T4	-	T17	T39	T22	T12	T8	T24	T10
US Open	MC	-	MC	T12	T37	-	T18	MC	T49	T50	-	T35	MC
British	-	-	-	-	-	-	-	T18	MC	T32	-	-	-
PGA	T7	T30	T48	T4	T75	-	MC	T28	T7	T22	2	MC	T16

Harold Lloyd (USA)

Perhaps the greatest (and certainly the wealthiest) of America's famed silent-movie stars, Nebraska-born Harold Lloyd (1893–1971) was also an avid golfer, playing in Los Angeles at the Riviera CC and, more impressively, in his own backyard. For Lloyd included a golf course on his Beverly Hills estate, Greenacres, a property widely considered the most opulent ever built by a movie star. Popular lore has erroneously credited the nine-hole, par-32 layout (christened "Safety Last" after a popular Lloyd film) to Dr. Alister MacKenzie when it was in fact created by George Thomas' able sidekick Billy Bell. Lloyd several times hosted top players like Armour, Von Elm, Kirkwood and Hagen on his private nine and maintained a cache of solid gold golf balls to award to anyone setting a course record. Eddie Loos, who fired a cool 28 in 1927, was one known winner.

Joe Lloyd (UK/USA)

One of so many fine nineteenth-century players from Hoylake, England, Joe Lloyd (b. 1870) lived the life of a jet-setter during the era of steamships, serving as the summer professional at Massachusetts' venerable Essex County Club and wintering in the Pyrenees at Pau, France. Known as "The General," Lloyd actually designed a long-lost nine at Pau for Russia's Grand Duke Michael, though he is surely better known—at least in America—for winning the 1897 **U.S. Open** at the Chicago GC by one over the soon-to-be dominant player of the era, Willie Anderson. Remarkably, Lloyd's margin of victory came from making a three at the club's old 466-yard closer, no mean feat in the era of gutta-percha.

Jane Lock (Australia)

Sydney native Jane Lock, M.B.E. (b. 10/19/1954) didn't take up golf until age 16 but was shortly beginning streaks of five **Victorian** and three **Australian Junior** titles in succession. Highly competitive at the adult level while still underage, Lock lost back-to-back national titles on the final hole in 1973 and '74 before taking the **Australian Ladies** crown in 1975, making her the rare player to hold national adult and junior titles simultaneously. She defended the **Ladies** crown in 1976 and took it a third time in 1979, this time beating the formidable Edwina Kennedy 4 and 3 at Royal Adelaide. Remaining an amateur until 1981, Lock defeated Spanish star Marta Figueras-Dotti to capture that season's **Canadian Ladies** and soon thereafter turned pro, joining the LPGA Tour and becoming a top-30 money winner until a wrist injury retired her back to Australia in 1986.

Bobby Locke (South Africa)

Born: Germiston, South Africa, 11/20/1917 **Died:** Johannesburg, South Africa, 3/9/1987

Often hailed around the world as the greatest putter who ever lived, Arthur D'Arcy "Bobby" Locke began swinging a club at age four, taking a serious interest five years later after watching British amateur Cyril Tolley play an exhibition in Johannesburg. In those days a far leaner fellow than the portly man we would later come to know, Locke was playing to scratch by age 16 and was South Africa's finest player by 18, taking the nation's **Amateur** and **Open**

titles in 1935, then repeating the feat in 1937. In the meantime, however, a job in the mining business had sent him to Great Britain in 1936, allowing Locke to compete in that summer's Open Championship at Hoylake and the 1937 event at Carnoustie, finishing as low amateur in both.

Electing to turn professional in 1938, Locke soon claimed his third **South African Open,** beginning a remarkable stretch from 1938 to 1955 wherein he won the event every time he entered, a run of seven more titles that would ultimately give him a career total of nine. Perhaps even more amazing, Locke at one point went for more than 20 years without losing a 72-hole stroke-play event on South African soil! Of course, he also established himself in Europe, where he took the 1938 **Irish Open** before the onset of war returned him home, to fly in the South African Air Force. Back to Britain in 1946, he won three times (the last title being the prestigious **British Masters**) and garnered the first of three Vardon Trophies for leading the Order of Merit.

Late that year, Locke hosted Sam Snead in a series of 16 exhibition matches played around South Africa. Though Snead obviously arrived the established favorite, Locke stunned the great American by winning the series handily with an impressive 12-2-2 record. Arriving in the States for the 1947 season duly fortified, Locke proceeded to demonstrate that this "man from the jungle" could beat more than just Snead, winning five official PGA Tour events plus the **Canadian Open,** tying for 14th in his first Masters and ranking second on the American money list. All told, Locke spent nearly three years on the PGA Tour, winning an impressive 11 times in 59 starts (18.6 percent), finishing second on 10 occasions, and winning the 1948 **Chicago Victory** tournament by 16 shots, a margin that remains a Tour record to this day. Though happy competing in America, Locke ceased playing the PGA Tour in 1949 for a very good reason: After he withdrew from several tournaments following a victory in the **Open Championship** in England, the PGA of America responded, in their infinite wisdom, by banning Locke from Tour events for life. It was, from all appearances, a greedy and/or xenophobic move—one characterized by Gene Sarazen as "the most disgraceful action by any golfing organization in the past 30 years."

The ban was lifted two years later, but by this time Locke was in Britain regularly winning **Open Championships.** His 1949 title had come at Royal St. George's, where he had routed Ireland's popular Harry Bradshaw by 12 in a 36-hole play-off. Locke defended his title in 1950 at Royal Troon (by two over Roberto de Vicenzo), then in 1952 beat his primary rival, Australian Peter Thomson, by one at Royal Lytham & St. Annes. After Thomson took three straight Claret Jugs from 1954 to 1956, Locke returned once more, at age 39, to take his fourth and final title at St. Andrews in 1957, beating Thomson by three. Notably, Locke was very nearly disqualified after the completion of play when it was discovered that he'd failed to correctly replace his marked ball on the final green. As he'd needed only two putts from five feet to win, however, the R&A elected to let his victory stand.

During these high-flying years, Locke also claimed his second and third Vardon Trophies (1950 and '54), another **British Masters** (1954), several more European national Opens and, undoubtedly on a stopover, the 1954 **Egyptian Open**. Though highly competitive right into his early 40s, Locke's run ended abruptly in 1960 when, en route to Johannesburg to see his newborn daughter, his car was hit by a train, nearly killing him, diminishing the sight in his left eye, and, it seems, causing bouts of erratic behavior that would plague him in the years ahead.

Several words are surely in order regarding Bobby Locke's utterly unique style, for no championship-caliber golfer ever played the game quite like him. For one thing, he hit every shot with a hook—not a draw!—which required him to aim so far right that today, after decades of tree growth, many classic American courses might well prove unplayable for him. He was widely believed even to hook

his putts, something that the great student of that craft George Low Jr. (not to mention one or two laws of physics) clearly disputed. Nonetheless, Locke's closed-stance prowess was legendary, allowing him early in his career to ignore pin placements altogether, simply firing shots into the center of greens, secure in the knowledge that he could regularly hole numerous longer putts for birdies.

In the end, Locke's records in South Africa, Britain, and Europe were rich and complete. Only in America, where the PGA stupidly sent him packing, has there ever been any doubt as to his status among the greatest golfers that have ever played the game.

PGA Tour Wins (15): 1947 Houston; 1947 Canadian Open; 1948 Phoenix; **1949, '50, '52 & '57 British Open**

Intn'l Wins (64): 1935, '37, '38, '39, '40, '46, '50, '51 & '55 South African Open; 1938, '39, '40, '46, '50 & '51 South African PGA; 1938 Irish Open; 1939 Dutch Open; 1946 & '54 British Masters; 1952 & '53 French Open; 1954 Swiss Open; 1954 German Open

1936-1960

	36	37	38	39	40	41	42	43	44	45	46	47	48
Masters	-	-	-	-	-	-	-				-	T14	T10
US Open	-	-	-	-	-	-					-	T3	4
British	T8	T17	T10	T9							T2	-	-
PGA	-	-	-	-	-	-	-		-		-	T33	-

	49	50	51	52	53	54	55	56	57	58	59	60
Masters	T13	-	-	T2	-	-	-	-	-	-	-	-
US Open	T4	-	3	WD	T14	5	-	-	-	-	-	-
British	1	T6	1	8	T2	4	-	1	T16	T29	-	
PGA	-	-	-	-	-	-	-	-	-	-	-	-

Robert Lockhart (UK/USA)

John Reid, owner of one very important Yonkers, New York, pasture, is generally spoken of as the "father of American golf," but without the help of his childhood friend Robert Lockhart, the story of the game's Stateside growth would read quite differently. For it was Lockhart, a Dunfermline native and an import/export man by trade, who routinely returned to Scotland on business, and it was he who ordered the now famous six clubs and two dozen gutta-percha balls from Old Tom Morris' St. Andrews shop that got the American game rolling. Ironically, Lockhart's name is frequently overlooked because he was not in attendance on February 22, 1888, when Reid opposed his friend John B. Upham in what history has long (erroneously) called the first golf match played on U.S. soil. Lockhart was, however, voted in as the St. Andrew's GC's

first active member, and later cited in a letter written by founding member Harry Tallmadge as "the person responsible for introducing golf in the United States."

Peter Lonard (Australia)

One of Australia's stronger contemporary players, 6'0", 225-pound Peter Lonard (b. Sydney 7/17/1967) has twice given the touring life a shot, having repaired to a club job in Australia between 1994 and 1997 after struggling on his first go-round. Then, having recovered from a bout with the mosquito-borne Ross River Fever, Lonard topped the 1997 Australasian Order of Merit with a win at the **Australian Masters** and has split time in Europe and the United States ever since. Lonard won, then successfully defended, the **Australian Open** in 2003 and 2004 and scored a major breakthrough abroad by capturing the PGA

Tour's **Heritage** event in early 2005, greatly solidifying his place on the international stage.

Henry Longhurst (UK)

Born: Bromham, England, 3/18/1909 **Died:** London, England, 7/23/1978

Along with the legendary Bernard Darwin and Herbert Warren Wind, Mr. Henry Carpenter Longhurst stands as one of three giants of twentieth-century golf writing. The son of a retail merchant in Bedfordshire, Longhurst was himself a fine player, captaining the team at Cambridge and counting among his notable victories the 1936 **German** Amateur. Embarking on a Fleet Street golf-writing career by penning monthly pieces for a long-defunct sheet called *Tee Topics*, he caught a great break when the *Sunday Times* came in need of a golf correspondent, with additional work soon following for the *Tatler* and the *Evening Standard*. Longhurst himself mentioned missing only one week in 340 for the *Tatler*, but his streak of 21 consecutive *years* of Sundays for the *Times* must rank among golf's greatest longevity records.

Also a regular in golf magazines on both sides of the Atlantic, Longhurst was a true television pioneer, participating in the BBC's rudimentary first live golf broadcasts in the late 1940s and, much later, becoming a favorite of American viewers with his annual coverage of the often-pivotal 16th hole at the Masters. A character of epic proportion, Longhurst coined the phrase "the tradesman's entrance" for putts falling in from the side of the hole—a trifling example of the wit he constantly displayed.

A fascinating diversion was Longhurst's two-year stint in the world of politics, serving as a Conservative wartime MP. Perhaps most interesting was his travel which, for both golf and other reasons, took him quite literally around the world. Few were the places of consequence that Longhurst failed to visit, and his extensive wanderings were chronicled in several fascinating volumes, which seldom bore more than passing references to golf. Indeed it is interesting to note that of the many titles carrying Longhurst's name, only *Golf* (J. M. Dent, 1937) represents a full-length manuscript focused exclusively on the game. The good half-dozen anthologies of his extensive magazine and newspaper work, however, serve as a lasting memorial, not just to Longhurst's incomparable talents but to a British epoch which he so richly symbolized.

Eddie Loos (USA)

Little remembered today, Eddie Loos (b. 1899) was a top professional during the 1920s, one of many talented players historically buried beneath the massive presence of Jones, Hagen and Sarazen. Born in New York City, Loos learned the game at the nation's first public golf course, Van Cortlandt Park, where he developed one of the sweetest swings of his era. At 17 he was runner-up in the Pennsylvania Open at a time when he was so impoverished as to spend one tournament night sleeping in a bunker beside the 16th green. At 19 he won the prestigious **Eastern Open** at Shawnee, PA, establishing his name on a national level. Later winning two more titles today recognized by the PGA Tour, he also teamed with a young Leo Diegel to engineer a high-profile upset of Harry Vardon and Ted Ray during their 1920 exhibition tour in Chicago.

Nancy Lopez (USA)

The book on Nancy Lopez (b. 1/6/1957) was certainly open for all to read well before her 1978 arrival on the LPGA Tour: Born in Torrance, California; took up the game at age eight, coached by her father Domingo; won the **New Mexico Women's Amateur** at age 12, the **USGA Junior Girls** at 15 and 17, and the **Mexican Amateur** at 17; **AIAW National Champion** and All-American at the University of Tulsa; **Western** and **Trans-Mississippi Amateur** winner and Curtis Cup player at 19; and perhaps most impressive, a second-place finish as an 18-year-old amateur at the 1975 U.S. Women's Open in Atlantic City. Yes, it was all there in black and white. Yet perhaps because of the lesser status of women's golf among the mainstream sports media, so sterling a record was, at the very least, underreported, making Lopez's eye-popping arrival in the professional ranks all the more striking.

Joining the LPGA Tour full time in 1978, Lopez proceeded to win an astounding nine times in 26 starts, beginning with back-to-back titles in **Sarasota** and **Los Angeles,** and driven by a record-setting five in a row (including the **LPGA Championship**) in May and June. Wins in England and Malaysia closed out the year and cemented for Lopez an unprecedented triple crown: the LPGA's Rookie of the Year, Player of the Year, and Vare Trophy. Perhaps mindful of a sophomore slump, Lopez began 1979 with a quick defense of her **Los Angeles** title, then proceeded to tack on seven more victories, resulting in the second of four Player of the Year awards and another Vare Trophy. All told, Lopez would, over two seasons, win 17 of 44 starts, a clip that even a peaking Tiger Woods would envy.

It is only because of this incredible standard that the ensuing 14 years—which included 30 wins, two major championships and two further Player of the Year awards—might somehow be viewed as anything less than superb, and it is well worth noting that this 14-year record, entirely divorced from 1978 to 1979, would have qualified for the LPGA's exclusive Hall of Fame entirely on its own. It contained, for example, 10 multi-win seasons, five years with three victories or more, 156 top-10 finishes, and 10 top-10 money rankings. At its peak was a five-win 1985, wherein Lopez claimed her third Player of the Year, her second **LPGA Championship** (by a resounding eight shots!) and an astonishing 21 top-10 finishes in 25 starts. It might also be noted that thrice during these years Lopez missed substantial amounts of time giving birth, or the overall numbers would be higher still.

Since the late 1990s, Lopez has scaled back her schedule considerably, with her last highly competitive season being 1997. That year she won her 48th career title (the **Chick-fil-A**) and made one final run at the sole championship conspicuously absent from her résumé, the U.S. Women's Open. Playing some of her best-ever Major championship golf, the 40-year-old Lopez became the only woman ever to complete all four Open rounds in the 60s, yet still finished second, an agonizing one stroke behind Britain's Alison Nicholas.

In assessing the Hall of Fame career of Nancy Lopez, however, we must look far beyond the straight numerical ledger. For more than anything else, Lopez, with her appearance, personality, fan friendliness, and pure Hollywood-style star power, provided the same sort of boost to the LPGA that Babe Zaharias and Mickey Wright had offered decades earlier. Lopez's explosive arrival drew previously unknown attention to the women's game, a circumstance that may have led to petty jealousy on the part of some players but served ultimately to raise the financial rewards for all.

LPGA Wins (48): 1978 & '79 Wykagyl; **1978, '85 & '89 LPGA Championships;** 1978, '80 & '81 Rochester; 1980 & '92 State Farm; 1981 Welch's; 1981 Colgate Dinah Shore; 1984 Samsung WC
Solheim Cup: 1990

1974-1997

	74	75	76	77	78	79	80	81	82	83	84	85
Dinah										T6	T16	T11
LPGA	-	-	-	-	1	T10	T19	T5	T35	T21	T14	1
US Open	T18	T2	MC	2	T9	T11	T7	WD	T7	-	T35	T4
du Maur						2	T6	T2	T9	WD	T8	-

	86	87	88	89	90	91	92	93	94	95	96	97
Dinah	-	T33	T5	T18	MC	T30	MC	T8	T9	T3	T15	T23
LPGA	-	T28	T24	1	T14	-	T18	T25	WD	T18	T18	T37
US Open	-	T21	T12	2	T19	-	T16	T7	T35	T28	MC	2
du Maur	-	T21	T45	9	-	-	-	-	T22	-	T2	-

Joe Louis (USA)

Very likely the greatest heavyweight boxer that ever lived, Lafayette, Alabama, native Joe Louis Barrow (1914–1981) was also a talented golfer, regularly playing in the low 70s at his peak and participating in whatever competitive fields he could get into (including George S. May's World Championship of Golf, where he was invited "on his boxing record"). Highly sensitive to the plight of black golfers barred from most PGA Tour events, he took to sponsoring his own tournament, the Joe Louis Open, played at Detroit's Rackham Park. In addition to putting up the $1,000 purse himself, Louis also paid the entry fees of many impoverished black pros, who only made up a portion of the event's mixed field. He also became full-time sponsor to long-hitting Ted Rhodes (then just a talented ex-caddie from Nashville) and it was Louis whose exclusion from the 1952 San Diego Open began drawing widespread attention to the PGA of America's infamous "Caucasians-Only" clause.

Though reportedly frustrated that he couldn't get his own game polished enough to beat a professional field,

Louis certainly did all he could to advance the cause of other black golfers. It is perhaps fitting then that his son, Joe Louis Barrow Jr., today serves as the national director of First Tee, the city-oriented national program designed to bring minority youth into the game.

Davis Love III (USA)

The son of a prominent teaching professional, Davis Milton Love III (b. Charlotte, North Carolina, 4/13/1964) first gained attention in the early 1980s as a prodigiously long hitter at the University of North Carolina, where he was three times chosen an All-American. Reining in some power to produce a more consistent swing, Love arrived on the PGA Tour in 1986 and finished 77th on the money list—his worst result in a nearly 20-year career that has seen him regularly within the top 10 and, on five occasions, among the top 5.

His first win came at the 1987 **Heritage Classic** where his one-shot victory over Steve Jones truly proved a harbinger, for fully five of Love's 18 Tour victories have come at the Heritage—no small testimonial as Harbour Town Links is well known as a shotmaker's layout where length is of little advantage. Love has also twice won the **Players Championship,** first in 1992 (by four over a group that included Faldo, Watson and Baker-Finch), then again in 2003 when his Sunday 64 in windy conditions was widely hailed as one of the finest closing rounds in recent memory. Also a two-time winner at the **Bing Crosby** (2001 and '03) and the **International** (1990 and 2003), Love's shining hour came in 1997 when he captured his only Major championship, the **PGA** at Winged Foot. Beating Justin Leonard by five, his 66-71-66-66 performance shattered all records for the club's previously fearsome West Course and came within two of Steve Elkington's all-time tournament mark.

Beyond Winged Foot, however, the Majors have been a mixed blessing for Love. On the positive side he has, since 1995, been a remarkably consistent performer on the game's biggest stages, recording an impressive 17 top-10 finishes in 40 starts. On the negative, he has not always held up under golf's most withering pressure, missing a short putt at the 72nd green to lose the 1996 U.S. Open by

a single stroke and frequently backsliding at those crucial late moments when the great champions find a way to push forward. He has, however, managed a respectable 9-12-5 mark over six Ryder Cup appearances and, in the less-pressurized setting of the **World Cup,** claimed four straight victories with Fred Couples from 1992 to 1995.

Love has also endured tragedy during his career, first when his father died in a 1988 plane crash, then in the suicide of his brother-in-law, who had embezzled vast sums from Love's bank account. Yet these and a series of recent physical problems have done little to stem his consistently fine play, with a four-win 2003 proving perhaps his finest year ever. Now entering his 40s, Love's ledger of titles and massive earnings is impressive—but can he win that second or third Major that would vault him well up the ladder among the game's elite?

PGA Tour Wins (18): 1987, '91, '92, '98 & 2003 Heritage; 1992 & 2003 Players Championship; 1996 San Diego; **1997 PGA Championship;** 2001 & '03 Bing Crosby
Walker Cup: 1985 **Ryder Cup:** 1993–2004 (6) **Presidents Cup:** 1994–2003 (5)

1986-2004

	86	87	88	89	90	91	92	93	94	95	96	97	98	99	00	01	02	03	04
Masters	-	-	MC	-	-	T42	T25	T54	MC	2	T7	T7	T33	2	T7	MC	T14	T15	T6
US Open	-	-	MC	T33	-	T11	T60	T33	T28	T4	T2	T16	MC	T12	MC	T7	T24	MC	MC
British	-	MC	MC	T23	MC	T44	MC	MC	T38	T98	MC	T10	8	T7	T11	T21	T14	T4	T5
PGA	T47	MC	-	T17	T40	T32	T33	T31	MC	MC	MC	1	T7	T49	T9	T37	T48	MC	MC

George Low Jr. (USA)

George Low Jr. (1912–1995) was among the last of a dying breed, a one-time touring pro who spent most of his life as an old-fashioned hustler, running with folks like President Eisenhower and Frank Sinatra and gaining a cultish reputation as the greatest putter in the world. The son of a well-known Scottish-American club professional, Low liked to point out that like most highly successful men, he never owned an overcoat—for those who could afford to always wintered in warmer climates. Low wasn't stingy with his putting expertise for those willing to pay, and no less than Arnold Palmer credited him with great help in winning the 1960 Masters. Relatively late in life, Low committed his thoughts to paper in *The Master of Putting* (Atheneum, 1983), a fine little book that, like the master himself, exists largely off of golf's mainstream radar screen.

George Low Sr. (UK/USA)

The father of putting wizard George Low Jr., the elder Low (1874–1950) emigrated from his native Carnoustie to

America in the late 1890s and quickly finished second (albeit by 11 shots) at the 1899 U.S. Open at the Baltimore CC. Though this would represent Low's competitive peak, he soon embarked on a professional career that saw him occupy some of the era's finest golf shops, including Dyker Meadow, Ekwanok, Baltusrol, Huntingdon Valley, and, eventually, Florida's Belleview-Biltmore. Also golf instructor to presidents Taft and Harding, Low was an occasional course architect, briefly teaming with Englishman Herbert Strong in the mid-1920s and codesigning New Jersey's Echo Lake CC with Donald Ross in 1913.

John L. Low (UK)

One of golf's most important Victorian-age personalities, Scotland's John Laing Low (1869–1929) had well-established credentials as a player, thrice contending deep into the British Amateur. In 1897 and '98, he lost semifinal matches that required extra holes, falling to James Robb at the 21st in the former and to eventual champion Freddie Tait at the 22nd in the latter. Then in 1901, Low reached the final against the great Harold Hilton, relying upon superior putting to take the match to the home green before ultimately losing one down.

A Cambridge man, Low was a founder, in 1897, of the Oxford & Cambridge Golfing Society and served as its captain or secretary for some 20 years. He was also longtime head of the R&A's Rules Committee, a robust body that, near the turn of the century, recommended the banning of the new American rubber-cored ball (a recommendation subsequently ignored by the R&A at large). Low was also a writer, serving on the staffs of the *Pall Mall Gazette* and the *Athletic News* and authoring two milestone books, *F. G. Tait: A Record* (James Nisbet, 1900)—the game's first first-ever biography—and *Concerning Golf* (Hodder & Stoughton, 1903), golf's first traditionalist manifesto. Low also held great sway in architectural circles after performing a landmark redesign of the Woking GC, a much-publicized reworking largely responsible for the advent of the sort of strategic architecture that would so epitomize golf's upcoming Golden Age.

Though Low's hardline defense of golf's traditional values has caused him to occasionally be painted as stiff or intransigent, Bernard Darwin more accurately described John Low the man when he wrote: "No one could blend in more perfect proportion a proper seriousness with friendliness and conviviality."

Eddie Lowery (USA)

Ten-year-old Eddie Lowery achieved lasting fame at the 1913 U.S. Open by caddying for local favorite Francis Ouimet during Ouimet's celebrated upset of British legends Harry Vardon and Ted Ray. Though even casual golf fans have likely seen the image of the plucky Lowery struggling to keep up with the statuesque Ouimet, few realize that the caddie grew up to play an important role in the game, becoming a member of the R&A, helping to organize the Bing Crosby Pro-Am and employing several prominent amateurs at his highly successful San Francisco auto dealership. It was Lowery, for example, who introduced local prospect Ken Venturi to his longtime mentor Byron Nelson. However, it was also Lowery who employed both Venturi and E. Harvey Ward as car salesmen, a position that did little to harm Venturi but ended up costing Ward a year's eligibility when the USGA ruled that Lowery had provided him with expense money in violation of his amateur status.

Fidel de Luca (Argentina)

Though never on a par with Argentina's elite threesome—de Vicenzo, Jurado, and Cerda—Fidel de Luca (b. 1921) was a four-time winner of his national **Open** (1954, '60,

'61, and '72) who also competed with some success in Europe (winning the 1958 **German Open**) and appeared in the 1962 Masters. De Luca's biggest achievement, however, was accomplished well outside the spotlight when, in 1979, he became the oldest player to win a national title by taking the **Brazilian Open** at age 58—an event he had previously claimed some 23 years previous, in 1956.

Laddie Lucas (UK)

Generally viewed as the best left-hander in the history of British golf, Sandwich, England's Percy Belgrave "Laddie" Lucas (b. 1915) was an equally distinguished man off the course, winning the DSO and DFC for his wartime wing commander service in the RAF, serving as a member of Parliament and writing four books, three of them nongolfing. On the links he was one of that all-too-familiar class: the world-beating junior player who, for reasons often unknown, never quite achieves a corresponding level of greatness on the adult stage. Lucas did, however, win numerous regional events as well as the 1949 **President's Putter,** and he was twice selected for Walker Cup teams, remaining on the sidelines in 1936 at Pine Valley but teaming with Leonard Crawley to rout Harvie Ward and Smiley Quick at St. Andrews in 1947. Lucas also captained the 1949 squad, which was soundly beaten at Winged Foot.

Lu Liang Huan (Taiwan)

Likely the best—and certainly the best-known—of Taiwan's rush of 1960s golfers, "Mr. Lu" (b. 1936) came to international fame at the 1971 Open Championship at Royal Birkdale when his dogged pursuit of Lee Trevino resulted in a second-place finish, one shot in arrears. Though Westerners might have considered this showing a lightning bolt, observers of the Far Eastern circuit knew better, for Lu had by this time already captured national opens in **Hong Kong, Taiwan,** the **Philippines** and **Thailand,** and twice ranked first in the region's Order of Merit. He was, in fact, an exempted player in the Royal Birkdale field and had already made two of his eventual four appearances at the Masters.

In the aftermath of his Open splash, Lu took advantage of a spate of Western opportunities, capturing the 1971 **French Open** at Biarritz (by two over Roberto de Vicenzo and Vicente Fernandez) and the 1972 **Panama Open.** He also very nearly beat eventual runner-up Jack Nicklaus in the opening round of the 1971 Piccadilly Match Play at Wentworth before making history, a year later, by teaming with Hsieh Min Nam to capture the rain-shortened 1972 **World Cup** at Royal Melbourne. He is today a prominent teacher, businessman and golf course architect, with nearly all of his work confined to the Far East.

Hilary (Homeyer) Lunke (USA)

With double majors in economics and psychology, followed by a Masters degree in sociology, Hilary Lunke (b. Edina, Minnesota, 6/7/1979) must surely be among the best-educated professionals in modern golf. On the course (and playing under her maiden name of Homeyer) she was a four-time All-American at Stanford as well as a seven-time contestant in the U.S. Women's Amateur. As a professional, she failed to record a top-10 finish in an abbreviated rookie season of 2002, setting the stage for the most dramatic first win imaginable: the 2003 **U.S. Women's Open,** captured in a thrilling 18-hole play-off with Kelly Robbins and Angela Stanford. At the final green, Stanford rolled in a 17-foot birdie putt to draw even, only to lose when Lunke, facing the greatest pressure of her life, coolly curled in a 15-footer of her own.

Michael Lunt (UK)

Birmingham's Michael Stanley Randle Lunt (b. 1935) came from fine golfing stock, his father Stanley having won the English Amateur in 1934. Michael matched that feat in 1966 when he came from 5 down on the 25th tee to win, making the Lunts the only father-son combination ever to claim the title. More frequently, however, he bore the very real misfortune of having to chase that greatest of modern English amateurs Michael Bonallack, though Lunt did carry the day at the 1963 **British Amateur,** becoming the first homebred to win the crown with a visiting American Walker Cup team in the field since Roger Wethered in 1923. A year later at Ganton, he very nearly defended, but stumbled down the stretch against Gordon Clark, ultimately losing at the 39th. Lunt competed in four successive Walker Cup matches from 1959 to 1965, amassing a disappointing overall record of 2-8-1.

Harold Lusk (New Zealand)

A diversely talented man, Auckland's Harold Butler "H. B." Lusk (1877–1961) was a career academician who as an athlete is best remembered as a world-class cricketer. Yet Lusk also won the 1910 **New Zealand Amateur** (played over his home links in Christchurch) and, in the words of Kiwi golf's centennial historian G. M. Kelly, was "the Bernard Darwin of New Zealand golf," his "classic, graceful prose" consistently filling the lead article in that nation's *Golf Illustrated* from the magazine's 1927 debut until just before Lusk's 1961 passing.

Mark Lye (USA)

Today a highly visible commentator on cable TV, Vallejo, California, native Mark Lye (b. 11/13/1952) was a three-time All-American at San Jose State before turning professional. Initially unable to qualify for the PGA Tour, he went abroad, winning twice and claiming the Australian Order of Merit title in 1976. Fully qualified in America the following year, Lye enjoyed a solid run from 1979 through 1985, always finishing among the top 75 money winners and winning once, at the 1983 **Bank of Boston Classic,** where his closing 64 beat John Mahaffey, Jim Thorpe, and Sammy Rachels by one.

Sandy Lyle (UK)

Though considerably less a threat in recent years, Alexander Walter Barr "Sandy" Lyle, M.B.E., enjoyed a run of 1980s accomplishments impressive enough to rank him a firm second, behind only Nick Faldo, among Britain's best players of the last 30 years. Though not overly large at 6'0", the English-born but Scottish-blooded Lyle (b. Shrewsbury, 2/9/1958) was certainly among the longest hitters in professional golf, not only shortening par 5s and long par 4s in the usual manner but gaining great advantage by ripping his much-safer 1-iron nearly as far as most of his competitors hit their drivers. A skilled enough putter to capitalize on his other talents, Lyle, it seems, lacked only a touch of that burning desire necessary to make a great talent a truly great player.

Nonetheless his record was impressive. After tearing through English amateur play in a brief but dominant run, Lyle turned professional in 1977, won on Africa's Safari Tour in 1978, then exploded onto the European Tour in 1979 with three victories (including a head-to-head triumph over Ballesteros at the **Scandinavian Open**) and the top spot in the Order of Merit. His record in the Order from 1979 to 1985 read 1st, 1st, 3rd, 2nd, 5th, 4th, and 1st, with the last year representing his European peak. For in addition to besting Ian Woosnam at the 1985 **Benson & Hedges,** Lyle broke through to become the first Scot since Jock Hutchison in 1921 to win the **Open Championship,** capturing the Claret Jug (despite a botched chip at the last) with a 282 total at Royal St. George's.

By this time Lyle was turning his attention to America, twice winning in **Greensboro** and once in **Phoenix,** but also becoming the first foreign-born winner of the **Players Championship,** a title he claimed (in sudden death over Jeff Sluman) in 1987. A year later, Lyle enjoyed his second scaling of the Major mountaintop when a marvelous approach from a fairway bunker at the 72nd led to birdie and a one-shot victory over Mark Calcavecchia at the

Masters, making Lyle the first Briton ever to claim the coveted Green Jacket.

By 1989, however, Lyle's form had slipped badly, causing an end to his streak of five consecutive Ryder Cup appearances. Never again a winner in America, he has claimed three further victories in Europe, but never seriously approached his world-class performance of the 1980s.

PGA Tour Wins (6): 1985 British Open; 1987 Players Championship; **1988 Masters**

Intn'l Wins (18): 1981 French Open; 1984 Italian Open; 1984 Trophée Lancôme; 1985 Benson & Hedges; 1988 British Masters; 1988 World Match Play; 1992 Italian Open; 1992 Volvo Masters

Walker Cup: 1977 **Ryder Cup:** 1979–87 (5)

1974-1998

	74	75	76	77	78	79	80	81	82	83	84	85	86
Masters	-	-	-	-	-	-	48	T28	-	MC	-	T25	T11
US Open	-	-	-	-	-	-	MC	MC	-	-	-	-	T45
British	T75	-	-	MC	MC	T19	T12	T14	T8	T64	T14	1	T30
PGA	-	-	-	-	-	-	-	MC	-	-	-	-	-

	87	88	89	90	91	92	93	94	95	96	97	98
Masters	T17	1	MC	MC	MC	T37	T21	T38	MC	MC	T34	MC
US Open	T36	T25	MC	MC	T16	T51	T52	-	-	-	-	-
British	T17	T7	T46	T16	DQ	T12	MC	13	T76	T55	MC	T18
PGA	-	-	-	-	T16	MC	T56	T69	T39	-	-	-

George Lyon (Canada)

Born: Richmond, Ontario, 9/27/1858 **Died:** Toronto, Ontario, 5/11/1938

An excellent all-around athlete, Ontario's George Lyon did not take up golf until age 37 when his days as a world-class cricketer were dwindling, yet within three years he was the 1898 **Canadian Amateur** champion. To say that Lyon then gained a stranglehold over the title is an understatement of the highest order, for he claimed further wins in 1900, '03, '05, '06, '07, '12, and '14, a total of eight triumphs (twice by 12 and 11 margins) and a record which, given the modern rewards incumbent to professional play, will likely stand forever. Lyon was also known to compete in the U.S. Amateur (finishing runner-up to Eben Byers in 1906) and he finished second in the 1910 Canadian Open, four strokes behind professional Daniel Kenny.

Looking for a competitive venue as he grew older, Lyon helped to found the Canadian Senior's Golf Association and was 10 times its champion between 1918 and 1930. Utilizing one of the flattest swings ever seen on a top-quality player, he remained a capable scorer very late in life, beating his age regularly. Lyon also represents a wonderful golfing footnote, having won the gold medal at the 1904 Olympics (defeating H. Chandler Egan 3 and 2 in St. Louis), the occasion of golf's last appearance in the games. Though age 45 at the time, the ever-athletic Lyon is reported to have walked the length of the clubhouse dining room on his hands in celebration.

M

Vernon Macan (Ireland/Canada)

An Irishman with a law degree from the University of London, Dublin-born Arthur Vernon Macan (1882–1964) emigrated to Canada in 1908, spending two years in Quebec, then moving west to British Columbia. A fine amateur golfer, he competed both in his home province (winning the **B.C. Amateur** in 1912 and '13) and across the border in the United States, where he captured both the **Washington State** and **Pacific Northwest Amateurs** in 1913. He designed his first course, British Columbia's Royal Colwood G&CC, soon thereafter, but World War I arrived (during which Macan lost the lower part of his left leg in combat), postponing any large-scale architectural work until the 1920s. Though also retaining his government law job, Macan went on to design a number of well-received courses on both sides of the border, continuing in the field right up until his death.

Notable Courses: Alderwood CC, Oregon (NLE); Columbia-Edgewater CC, Oregon; Royal Colwood G&CC, British Columbia

Norman MacBeth (UK/USA)

Having learned his golf at Royal Lytham & St. Annes, Norman MacBeth (1879–1940) lived both in England and India before emigrating to America at the age of 24. Eventually settling in Los Angeles, he became a figure of great importance in the area's early golfing development, establishing himself as a leading player (winning the **Southern California Amateur** in 1911 and '13) and, eventually, designing several significant courses. MacBeth's first known taste of golf architecture came in 1911 when he assisted several club members in laying out the present Los Angeles CC's first course, soon building both the Midwick and San Gabriel CCs on his own before joining the Red Cross during World War I. In later years, MacBeth would aid Dr. Alister MacKenzie in remodeling the Redlands CC, though he is perhaps best remembered for his 1918 design at Los Angeles's Wilshire CC, whose 426-yard, creek-menaced finisher ranks among golf's more unique and challenging holes to this day.

Notable Courses: St. Andrews GC, California (NLE); San Gabriel CC, California; Wilshire CC, California

Charles Blair Macdonald (Canada/USA)

Born: Niagara Falls, Ontario, 11/14/1855 **Died:** Southampton, New York, 4/23/1939

One who can genuinely carry the title "father of American golf," Charles Blair Macdonald was a tall, barrel-chested man whose superb mix of know-how, leadership, commitment to doing things right, outsized ego, and a clear streak of arrogance fairly mirrored the personality of his adopted country, the United States. And adopted is indeed an accurate word, for while Macdonald lived nearly his whole life in America, he was actually born to a Scottish father and Canadian mother just across the border in Ontario. He did, however, grow up in Chicago before pursuing his higher education at St. Andrews University where, surrounded by men like Old Tom Morris and David Strath—and regularly playing with Young Tom—he fell utterly in love with the royal and ancient game.

Upon returning to Illinois in 1875, Macdonald endured what he later referred to as "The Dark Ages," a 17-year stretch in which his closest run at golf was the beating of makeshift balls around an abandoned army training ground. Eventually, through little more than his considerable force of will, C.B. wrangled up enough local interest to found the Chicago GC, building a nine-hole course in suburban Belmont in 1892. Expanded a year later, this would become America's first 18-hole facility, though the Chicago GC itself would soon move out to Wheaton, where C.B. would construct a newer and better layout in 1895.

That same autumn, Macdonald became the first official **U.S. Amateur** champion by defeating Charles Sands 12 and 11 in Newport, Rhode Island—a victory not without some controversy. For a year earlier, he had joined a field of competitors in an initial attempt at an American national championship, also at Newport. Though absolute in his belief (not infrequently stated) that he was the finest golfer in the land, C.B. finished second in that first event, then managed to get the results nullified by disputing a two-stroke penalty and arguing that a "true" championship was decided at match play, not medal. A month later, at New York's St. Andrew's GC, Macdonald was again defeated—at match play—in another "national" event, this time blaming his loss on a hangover and further stating that without a national governing body, such events were irrelevant anyway. But from such petulance, it seems, can come good things, and largely as a result of C.B.'s grumbling, the USGA was soon born.

By 1900, after moving to New York to accept a partnership in the brokerage firm of C. D. Barney & Co., Macdonald became enamored with the idea of building America's first truly great course, a layout which would replicate (and perhaps even improve upon) the classic holes of the British Isles. The result, after years of organizing, site searching, and planning, was Southampton, New York's National Golf Links of America, a track whose strategic excellence likely influenced the evolving field of golf architecture more than any design before or since. Layouts at Sleepy Hollow, Piping Rock, the Greenbrier, and the St. Louis GC were soon to follow, though Macdonald was quickly relying more upon the abilities of his construction foreman and hand-picked protégé, Seth Raynor, than his own efforts in the field. A prominent exception came in 1917 at New York's Lido GC, perhaps the most ambitious golf design ever undertaken as it involved the importing of some two million cubic yards of sand to fill a site that had previously been largely underwater. The result, some $800,000 dollars later, was a masterpiece, an American links described by Bernard Darwin as being "the finest course in the world." It would, however, flounder during the Depression before expiring altogether during World War II.

His reputation as a master architect secure, Macdonald was seldom really active in the discipline, and it can be fairly suggested that of the 15 or so projects upon which his name appears, Raynor was actually the primary designer of at least half. C.B., it seems, was perfectly content to remain in Southampton, autocratically overseeing the National while commissioning portraits and statues of himself—paid for, not incidentally, out of the members' dues. A true and dedicated amateur, Macdonald never accepted payment for his design work and largely expected the rest of America's golfers to similarly embrace

his traditional values. Lest anyone be uncertain as to precisely what they were, he laid them out clearly in his autobiography *Scotland's Gift— Golf* (Scribner's, 1928), one of the game's essential volumes and a fitting memorial to one of its most colorful, bombastic, and critically important figures.

Notable Courses: Chicago GC, Illinois (BO); The Lido GC, New York (NLE); Mid Ocean Club, Bermuda; National GL of America, New York; Piping Rock GC, New York; The Course at Yale, Connecticut

Willie MacFarlane (UK/USA)

Born: Aberdeen, Scotland, 6/29/1890 **Died:** Miami Beach, Florida, 8/15/1961

A quiet, amiable man who served as professional at several New York area clubs from 1912 through 1935, Scottish immigrant Willie MacFarlane is remembered for winning the 1925 **U.S. Open** at Worcester CC in a 36-hole play-off over Bobby Jones. Simply reaching the play-off required a bit of doing, for with a 1-foot putt to tie at the 72nd, MacFarlane found his ball in a divot deep enough that he required a mid-iron in order to hole it. He then trailed Jones by as many as four during the play-off before completing the final nine in 33 to capture the title.

Interestingly, MacFarlane is often portrayed as having been largely disinterested in tournament competition, and it is true that he only appeared in six PGA Championships and never once returned to Britain to enter the Open Championship. Yet his 21 official PGA Tour titles tie him for 27th all-time and, as he was already 26 when the record-keeping began, he likely won several (if not many) more titles which will forever remain uncounted.

MacFarlane twice claimed Pennsylvania's prestigious **Shawnee Open** (1925 and '28) and New York's **Westchester Open** (1924 and '30), as well as the nationally prominent **Metropolitan Open**, first in 1930 (when it was played at the old Fairview CC in Elmsford), then in 1933 at Winged Foot. With an enviably smooth swing and disposition, MacFarlane stayed competitive well into his 40s, winning four times after turning 44. However, like Harry Cooper, Tommy Armour, and others, MacFarlane could never represent America in the Ryder Cup due to his British birth.

PGA Tour Wins (21): 1925 U.S. Open; 1930 & '33 Metropolitan

1912-1934

	12	13	14	15	16	17	18	19	20	21	22	23
Masters												
US Open	T18	WD	WD	T35	-	-	-	-	T8	-	WD	-
British	-	-	-						-	-	-	-
PGA					T3			-	T17	-	-	T5

	24	25	26	27	28	29	30	31	32	33	34
Masters									6		
US Open	-	1	T20	T18	T14	T27	T43	-	MC	-	-
British	-	-	-	-	-	-	-	-	-	-	-
PGA	T9	-	-	-	T9	-	-	T9	-	-	-

A. F. MacFie (UK)

Though not known historically as a great player, Allan Fullarton MacFie is recorded as the first **British Amateur** champion (1885), a not altogether legitimate title as the event was recognized retroactively rather than advance-billed as such. Further, MacFie benefited from playing over his home course at Hoylake (he owned a private putting green adjacent to the links) and from what surely must be unique in the annals of championship golf: a bye in the semifinals. Still, he did polish off no less than Horace Hutchinson 7 and 6 in the final, which removes any suggestion of having backed into the title. Never again a factor on the national stage, MacFie was nonetheless hailed by Darwin as: "a very good player, beautifully accurate if without any great power, knowing just what he could do and attempting no more, and a most deadly putter."

Ada MacKenzie (Canada)

In many ways a trendsetter, Toronto-born Ada Charlotte MacKenzie (1891–1973) came from a golfing family but starred in several sports while a student, thrice winning the Athlete of the Year award at Toronto's Havergal College. Golf, of course, was one of the rare games that a woman might competitively pursue as an adult in those early years and so MacKenzie did, dominating Canadian play between the wars with five **Open Ladies** victories (1919, '25, '26, '33, and '35) as well as five **Closed** titles (1926, '27, '29, '31, and '33). Predictably, MacKenzie was nearly invincible in her home province, winning the **Ontario Ladies** on nine occasions, and her aura was cast so large over the Canadian sporting scene that in 1933 she was named Female Athlete of the Year by the Canadian Press. She also enjoyed great longevity, winning numerous national and provincial senior events, and her last title, the

1969 **Ontario Seniors**, came a remarkable 50 years after her first.

Despite such a record, Ada MacKenzie is equally historic for her endeavors off the course where, like Marion Hollins in America, she forged impressively ahead in a man's world. MacKenzie was not of the idle rich, maintaining jobs first as a sports instructor at Havergal, then with the Canadian Bank of Commerce. She later created and financed the Ladies Golf and Tennis Club of Toronto in 1924 (North America's only surviving ladies-only golf club), in addition to founding and operating her own sports apparel company from 1930 to 1959.

Dr. Alister MacKenzie (UK/USA)

Born: Normanton, England, 8/30/1870 **Died:** Santa Cruz, California, 1/6/1934

Perhaps the most famous name in the history of golf course design, Dr. Alexander "Alister" MacKenzie was of Scottish blood, though born and raised near Leeds, England. A graduate of Cambridge with degrees in medicine, natural science, and chemistry, MacKenzie served in the Boer War, where he keenly observed the camouflage techniques employed by Afrikaner soldiers to outflank their more regimented British opponents. Surviving the hostilities intact, he then returned to Leeds and took up medical practice.

An avid golfer starting in his late 20s, MacKenzie's first recorded involvement with architecture came in 1907 when he aided the visiting H. S. Colt in the design of Leeds' new Alwoodley GC. Soon afterward, he began working solo, with another local layout, 1909's Moortown, drawing praise. In 1914 he further advanced his name by winning *Country Life* magazine's contest for the best design of a hypothetical par 4, a high-profile competition judged by no less than Bernard Darwin, Horace Hutchinson, and Herbert Fowler. The victorious submission was an elaborate triple-fairway creation, which C. B. Macdonald would later employ for his 18th hole at New York's late Lido GC.

At the outbreak of World War I, MacKenzie initially served as a surgeon, then was transferred to the Royal Engineers where he helped to develop groundbreaking camouflage techniques widely employed by the British military. By this time a partner with Colt and C. H. Alison in one of golf's most prominent architectural firms, the doctor returned from the war walking very much to his own beat, reportedly even bidding against his "partners" on certain desirable projects.

Perhaps it is fitting that MacKenzie found his true glory working abroad, unencumbered by Colt and Alison and very much in demand after publishing *Golf Architecture* (Simkin, Marshall, Hamilton, Kent, 1920), a how-to volume in which he famously codified 13 rules of successful course design. His first great ventures were in Australia and New Zealand in 1926, where he provided plans for the design or alteration of nearly a dozen courses, including a new 18 at Royal Melbourne and the addition of bunkering, on a massive scale, at Kingston Heath. A brief visit to South America yielded four projects in Argentina (including Buenos Aires' famous Jockey Club) before MacKenzie settled full time in America. There, between 1927 and his 1934 death, he would complete more than 20 projects, with household names like Cypress Point, Crystal Downs, and Augusta National (with Bobby Jones) heading the list, and genuine classics like Pasatiempo, the Valley Club of Montecito, and the thoroughly altered Sharp Park bolstering it.

During these years MacKenzie resided primarily in Santa Cruz, California, in a modest home adjacent to Pasatiempo's sixth fairway. As in Australia (where he had employed Alex Russell), MacKenzie entered into architectural "partnerships" with Oklahoman Perry Maxwell and fellow Californian Robert Hunter, seldom sharing a course's actual design but guaranteeing that someone at least nominally associated with him would oversee its construction in his absence.

All told, MacKenzie was involved in more than 110 projects on four continents, a design legacy and geographic range matched by very few. A marketing man's dream with his Scottish accent, plus-fours or kilt, and a fondness for the bottle, he was a stubborn and dogmatic advocate of strategic, "pleasurably thrilling" golf. His layouts generally featured prominent bunkering and heavily contoured greens, a minimum of rough and forced carries, and the most natural-looking features he could create where nature itself had failed to provide. In a field where the assessing of skills is largely subjective, calling anyone "the best" is a shaky proposition. Yet few will argue that in a comparison of any architect's finest designs — say, his top

five — Dr. Alister MacKenzie would prove an extremely difficult man to beat.

Notable Courses: **Augusta National GC, Georgia; Cypress Point C, California; Crystal Downs CC, Michigan; The Jockey C, Red Course, Argentina; Pasatiempo GC, California; Royal Melbourne GC, West Course, Australia; Sharp Park GC, California (BO); Valley C of Montecito, California**

Lee Mackey (USA)

Birmingham, Alabama, professional Lee Mackey was a complete unknown entering the 1950 U.S. Open at Merion, but his stunning opening-round 64 quickly turned him into something of a household name. Backtracking thoroughly to a Friday 81, Mackey went on to finish 25th at 297 and was never heard from on the national level again.

Mona MacLeod (Australia)

Mona MacLeod (1893–1953) was born in Penshurst, the daughter of a 15-year captain at the Royal Melbourne GC. Of modest proportion, she was nonetheless an excellent athlete, not taking up golf until adulthood, yet developing a swing that is still rated among the finest ever in Australia. Competitively, she carved her place by winning four **Australian Ladies** titles between 1921 and 1932, the last at match play (4 and 2) over Mrs. Alex Russell. MacLeod was also three times runner-up during this period and was later a participant on, and/or captain of, numerous international or interstate teams. Widely seen as a woman of modesty and character, she was, by most accounts, the most important woman in prewar Australian golf.

John Mahaffey (USA)

A two-time All-American and the 1970 **NCAA** champion at the University of Houston, John Drayton Mahaffey (b. Kerrville, Texas, 5/9/1948) arrived on the PGA Tour in 1971 with high expectations. Never a long hitter, he was numbingly accurate and a cool competitor, establishing himself among the Tour's top-60 earners every year (save for an injury-shortened 1977) for roughly two decades. He was also a regular winner, collecting 10 victories between 1973 and 1989, including a memorable 1978 **PGA Championship** at Oakmont, which he won in a sudden-death playoff with Tom Watson and Jerry Pate. Previously Mahaffey had experienced heartbreak in back-to-back U.S. Opens, first losing a Monday play-off to Lou Graham at Medinah in 1975, then being vanquished by Pate's famous 72nd-hole

5-iron at the Atlanta Athletic Club in 1976, having earlier stood five strokes ahead after 63 holes.

In this light, Mahaffey's Oakmont triumph proved a popular one, in addition to serving as something of an igniter, for fully eight of his victories came in its aftermath, including one at **Pleasant Valley** the following week. Two more titles would come at the **Bob Hope Desert Classic** (1979 and '84), though Mahaffey's biggest post-PGA victory would easily be the 1986 **Players Championship**, which he won by two over Larry Mize. More recently, Mahaffey has experienced an injury-riddled Champions Tour career.

PGA Tour Wins (10): 1978 PGA Championship; 1986 Players Championship
Champions Tour Wins: 1 (1999)
Ryder Cup: 1979

Ted Makalena (USA)

Hawaiian club pro Ted Makalena (1943–1968) made history in 1966 when he became the first "outsider"—that is, a player without any status whatsoever on the PGA Tour—to win a sanctioned Tour event, defeating Billy Casper and Gay Brewer by three at the Waialae CC to claim the **Hawaiian Open**. He had actually won this event five times in the years prior to its joining the Tour, as well as virtually every other title in Hawaiian golf. Emboldened by his victory, Makalena embarked on a PGA tour career in 1967 and finished eighth at the 1968 Bob Hope Desert Classic. A popular man in the islands, Makalena died tragically, in a swimming accident, in September of 1968.

H. S. Malik (India)

Owing to the British Raj, the history of golf in India is a long one, with Royal Calcutta, for example, being the world's oldest golf club outside of the British Isles (est. 1829). For nearly a century, however, the Indian game was strictly a province of the British, with native Indians excluded from clubs and prominent tournament play. The man most responsible for ending these practices was Sardar H. S. Malik, who took up the game while studying at Oxford and, within a short time, was both on scratch and, in 1914, the first Indian to earn his golfing Blue at a British university. Malik taught the game to his brother I.S., and, because H.S. spent a good deal of time in Britain, it remained for the younger sibling to actually break the game's color line back home. H.S. did make a similar form of history on his own, however, by competing in the 1921 British Amateur and Open Championship, though we note that qualifying was rather less arduous at the time.

I. S. Malik (India)

Like his older brother H.S., I. S. Malik was a Sikh whose tall turban surely cut quite the noticeable figure on pre-war golf courses. Taught the game by his trailblazing sibling, I.S. holds several Jackie Robinson–like distinctions, not the least of which was being the first native to compete in the All-Indian Amateur Golf Championship, a venerable British-run event dating to 1892. In addition to thrice finishing runner-up there (1945, '47, and '48), I.S. was the first Indian member of the Royal Calcutta GC, as well as the father of Ashok Malik, himself a talented player who would take the All-India title five times. Though actually having followed his older brother's lead, I. S. Malik is nonetheless widely viewed as the father of Indian golf.

Meg Mallon (USA)

Though not as big a winner as contemporaries like Beth Daniel, Laura Davies, or Betsy King, former Ohio State star Meg Mallon (b. Natick, Massachusetts, 4/14/1963) has enjoyed a very solid career featuring 18 wins, four Major championships, and eight top-10 finishes on the LPGA Tour's official money list. After three quiet years at the start of her career, Mallon blossomed in a remarkable 1991 that saw her claim four titles, two of them Majors. In late June she captured the **LPGA Championship**, defeating Pat Bradley by one stroke at the Bethesda CC (Maryland). Then, only two weeks later, she slipped by Bradley again at the **U.S. Women's Open**, defeating the Hall of Famer by two at venerable Colonial CC. Curiously, both women would end the season with four victories, yet despite two of Mallon's being Majors, Bradley, who won the money title and the Vare Trophy, was named Player of the Year.

Mallon would enjoy further multiple-win seasons in 1993, '96, '99, and 2000, with the latter, which included a one-shot victory at the **du Maurier** and third place on the money list, likely standing out the farthest. She then fell from the top 10 in 2001, beginning a comparatively dry spell that saw money rankings of 19th, 20th and 12th, only two victories, and, turning 40 during 2003, perhaps the start of the inevitable decline. But like so many LPGA stars before her, Mallon responded to this milestone with some of her best-ever golf, roaring through a three-win 2004 that included back-to-back triumphs at the **U.S.** and **Canadian Women's Opens**, the former her fourth Major championship. Whether she can maintain such a pace well into her fifth decade remains to be seen, but the engaging Mallon has certainly gotten off to a good start.

LPGA Wins (18): 1991 LPGA Championship; 1991 & 2004 U.S. Women's Open; 1991 Samsung WC; 1993 Welch's; 2000 Rochester; **2000 du Maurier**
Solheim Cup: 1992–2003 (7)

1986-2004

	86	87	88	89	90	91	92	93	94	95	96	97	98	99	00	01	02	03	04
Dinah	-	-	-	-	T9	T30	5	T49	T11	T16	T2	MC	T16	2	3	T28	T36	T36	T48
LPGA	-	-	T61	T29	T20	1	T26	T45	T11	T15	T10	T22	T6	T11	T17	T17	T12	T27	16
US Open	MC	-	T44	MC	T9	1	4	21	T6	2	T19	T43	MC	T5	T2	T30	T22	MC	1
dM/Brit*	-	-	-	T59	MC	T23	T13	T64	T4	T12	4	T30	T4	T66	1	MC	T8	T37	MC

*du Maurier replaced by the Women's British Open in 2001.

Roger Maltbie (USA)

A top Northern California amateur and San Jose State star during the early 1970s, five-time PGA Tour winner Roger Maltbie (b. Modesto, 6/30/1951) made a major splash during his rookie season of 1975, capturing **Quad Cities** and the old **Pleasant Valley** event back-to-back. The following season he won Jack Nicklaus's inaugural **Memorial Tournament** in memorable style: On the third hole of sudden death with Hale Irwin, Maltbie's hooked approach at the par-4 17th hit an out-of-bounds stake and kicked back onto the green. Given new life, Maltbie promptly birdied the 18th for an impressive third victory. A twice-repaired shoulder slowed him for several years but, in 1985, Maltbie returned to win the **Westchester Classic** and the **World Series of Golf**, the latter's coveted 10-year exemption being worth far more than its first-place money.

In recent years, Maltbie has declined serious competition on the Champions Tour in favor of TV work. Always known as one of golf's more fun-loving personalities, his laid-back reputation was heavily boosted in 1975 when, after his victory at Pleasant Valley, Maltbie proceeded to leave the $40,000 winner's check in a nearby restaurant, where it likely remains on display still.

Pier Mancinelli (Italy)

The only Italian to become internationally known as a golf course designer, Pier Luigi Mancinelli lived a fascinating twentieth-century life. Originally a music student, he became a squadron commander in the Italian air force during World War II before defecting to the Allies near the close of hostilities. Returning to school and becoming a civil engineer, Mancinelli next spent eight years in East Africa building roads, before returning home to join the company that built the well-known Olgiata CC outside of Rome. After a brief spell with the World Bank, Mancinelli went into golf architecture full time, ultimately designing courses in Europe, Brazil, the Ivory Coast, and even a now-deceased layout in pre-revolution Iran, while also renovating France's Golf de Saint-Nom-La-Bretêche, longtime site of the Trophée Lancôme.

Tony Manero (USA)

Though born in New York City, Tony Manero (1905–1989) grew up in Westchester County where he caddied at Elmsford's Fairview CC, also the spawning ground of Major champions Tom Creavy, Jim and William Turnesa, and Johnny Farrell. Manero was a solid player but hardly thought of among the elite, an impression perhaps boosted by two huge beatings he endured in early PGA Championships, first at the hands of Walter Hagen 11 and 10 in 1927, then, a year later, in the opening round by Leo Diegel 10 and 8. But Manero's game would eventually improve enough for him to win eight PGA Tour events and appear on the 1937 Ryder Cup team, the latter achievement based largely upon his greatest triumph, the 1936 **U.S. Open**.

This was the year the Open visited Baltusrol's less-heralded Upper course, an occasion when "Lighthorse" Harry Cooper had already posted a record-setting 284 and looked every bit the winner until Manero charged home late with a spectacular 67 to steal the title by two. Manero drew great support over the closing holes from his playing partner and good friend Gene Sarazen—enough support, actually, that several members of the observing media filed a complaint with the USGA accusing Sarazen of giving Manero advice. An hour-long meeting was held before it was resolved that Manero's victory would stand.

Lloyd Mangrum (USA)

Born: Trenton, Texas, 1/8/1914 **Died:** Apple Valley, California, 11/17/1973

Yet another war-era star from Texas, Lloyd Eugene Mangrum never looked (and seldom acted) the part of the genteel professional golfer, instead resembling a riverboat gambler with his neatly parted hair and pencil-thin mustache and living a less-refined life than many of his competitors. Part of this may well have been due to his World War II military service, which saw him wounded at the Battle of the Bulge and the recipient of two Purple Hearts, after which the niceties of golfing life perhaps seemed a bit less relevant.

Aside from injuries, the war was also an impediment to Mangrum's golf career in terms of timing, for he had just won three PGA Tour events in 1942 and looked very much like an imminent world-beater when packed off to fight. Mangrum recovered successfully from his wounds, however, and most dramatically made his first postwar victory his lone Major championship, the 1946 **U.S. Open**. Playing at Cleveland's Canterbury CC, a closing 72 left him tied with both Byron Nelson and Vic Ghezzi at 284, mandating an 18-hole play-off that, most amazingly, saw the three remain tied with equal 72s. Another 18 ensued and this time Mangrum came from behind with three late birdies to post another 72, enough to beat both of his competitors by a single shot.

Frequently successful during the winter Western swing, Mangrum dominated in the **Los Angeles Open** (taking four titles from 1949 to 1956) as well as twice winning both the **Bing Crosby** and the **Tucson Open**. He also took two **Western Opens**—borderline Major championships in those days—and made a minor fortune by winning three **All-American Opens** and the 1948 **World Championship of Golf**, all lucrative events played at Chicago's Tam O'Shanter CC where Mangrum also happened to be the club's touring professional. The Tour's leading money winner in 1951, Mangrum was never out of the top 10 from 1946 through 1954, claimed Vardon Trophies (for lowest scoring average) in 1951 and '53, and amassed a 6-2 record in the four Ryder Cups from 1947 through 1953, serving as playing captain in the last. Most impressively, his career total of 36 official victories remains 12th all-time on the PGA Tour at the time of this writing.

Like most elite players, Mangrum seemed able to elevate his game in time for the two Major championships he valued the most, the Masters and the U.S. Open. At Augusta he finished second to Jimmy Demaret in 1940, then added six top-4 finishes between 1948 and 1956, having already set the course record of 64 in 1940. At the Open, in addition to his popular 1946 victory, Mangrum added five more top-5s including a loss in the 1950 three-way play-off at Merion, actually standing a chance of derailing Ben Hogan's epic post-accident victory until being penalized for illegally marking his ball at the 16th. Only an occasional participant at the Open Championship, Mangrum was perhaps not a man given to match play either, for his record was somewhat less accomplished at the PGA.

Hailing from a town located less than 80 miles from Ft. Worth, Mangrum maintained a rivalry with Hogan that was not entirely friendly. But that, to a large degree, was simply Mangrum, a tough, hard-living man who surely wasn't going to be intimidated by the frequently daunting "Hogan Mystique."

PGA Tour Wins (36): 1946 U.S. Open; 1948 & '53 Bing Crosby; 1948 Greensboro; 1948 World Championship; 1949, '51, '53 & '56 Los Angeles; 1952 & '53 Phoenix; 1952 & '54 Western Open; 3 All-American Opens
Ryder Cup: 1947–51 & 1953 (c) (4)

Lloyd Mangrum, 1947

1937-1957

	37	38	39	40	41	42	43
Masters	-	-	-	2	T9	WD	
US Open	MC	-	T56	T5	T10		
British	-	-	-				
PGA	-	-	-	-	T3	T9	

	44	45	46	47	48	49	50
Masters			T16	T8	T4	T2	6
US Open			1	T23	T21	T14	T2
British			-	-	-	-	-
PGA		-	T33	T5	T17	T3	T5

	51	52	53	54	55	56	57
Masters	T3	6	3	T4	7	T4	T28
US Open	T4	T10	3	T3	-	-	MC
British	-	-	T24	-	-	-	-
PGA	T9	T17	-	-	-	-	-

Ray Mangrum (USA)

The older and less-celebrated brother of Lloyd, tall, skinny Ray Mangrum was runner-up to Henry Picard at the 1936 North & South Open and winner of the **Miami Open** a year later. He would eventually capture five PGA Tour events (including an 18-hole play-off victory over Ben Hogan in the 1946 **Pensacola Open**) and tie for fourth at the 1935 U.S. Open at Oakmont and sixth at the 1936 Masters. Originally considered a rising star, Ray Mangrum's love of gambling—on all things, golfing and otherwise—is generally blamed for his failure to achieve world-class status.

Carol Mann (USA)

It has never been easy to ignore Hall of Famer Carol Mann (b. Buffalo, New York, 2/3/1941), for at 6'3" she is surely the tallest great woman golfer in history. But beyond her height, Mann was also an oversized talent, tallying 38 LPGA wins over 21 seasons, nine top-10 money rankings, the seasonal money title in 1969, and a Vare Trophy in 1968.

Curiously, Mann won only one Major championship, the 1965 **U.S. Women's Open** at New Jersey's Atlantic City

CC, where she recovered from an opening-round 78 to defeat Kathy Cornelius by two. As it came on the heels of a victory at the **Carling Open** a week earlier, and represented the third win in an obviously up-and-coming career, one might well have bet the farm on Mann's prospects of winning several more Major titles—but there it was.

Nonetheless, the Open did kick off a stretch of 11 years wherein Mann won 37 times and only twice finished worse than eighth on the money list. Her peak season came in 1968 when she won 10 times and captured the Vare Trophy with a 72.04 scoring average, then an all-time record. Surprisingly, such numbers would not be enough to win Player of the Year, which instead went to Kathy Whitworth who also won 10 times. The following year, Mann came back with nine more victories and the money title—and still failed to dislodge Whitworth (who tallied only seven wins) from Player of the Year honors. Mann's last great season was a four-win 1975, though she would continue playing a relatively full schedule until retiring at the close of 1981.

LPGA Wins (38): 1964 Western Open; **1965 U.S. Women's Open**; 1966 Peach Blossom; 1969 & '75 Dallas Civitan; 1972 Orange Blossom

1961-1977

	61	62	63	64	65	66	67	68	69	70	71	72	73	74	75	76	77
LPGA	T18	T4	T6	35	3	T17	4	-	T2	16	T7	T16	T15	15	5	T20	-
US Open	T14	18	T13	-	1	2	T20	T3	T26	8	T15	T9	MC	T2	MC	-	T17

Ellis Maples (USA)

The son of longtime Pinehurst greenkeeper and Donald Ross construction supervisor Frank Maples, Ellis Maples (1909–1985) logged substantial experience as a greenkeeper, golf professional, and course builder (for both Ross and William Flynn) before going into golf architecture full time in 1953. Over approximately 30 years, his firm would design or redesign more than 70 courses, exclusively in the U.S. Southeast. Not surprisingly, the majority of these projects fell within his native North Carolina, including Pinehurst No. 5, the Grandfather G & CC, the CC of North Carolina (with Willard Byrd), and Forest Oaks CC, longtime site of the PGA Tour's Greater Greensboro Open. His son Dan followed in his footsteps, building more than 30 new courses primarily within the Southeast including The Pit, a novel Pinehurst-area public layout routed through an old sand quarry.

Bill Marr (UK)

Perhaps the walking embodiment of every stereotype— good and bad—ever applied to caddies, Bill Marr was a

North Berwick looper whose legend has long outlived his earthly tenure. A drunk of epic proportion, he was apparently capable of working effectively in the morning but was often staggeringly intoxicated after lunch. Consequently, he would frequently make it out as far as the Quarry hole (today's sixth) before stumbling down the interceding slope and passing out, leaving his hopefully fit player to fend for himself over the remaining 12 holes.

Dave Marr (USA)

Born: Houston, Texas, 12/23/1933 **Died:** Houston, Texas, 10/5/1997

One of the funniest and most obliging men ever to pick up a golf club, Dave Marr was the son of a golf pro and cousin of two-time Major champion Jack Burke Jr., a golfing pedigree that was furthered by caddying in his youth for players like Tommy Bolt. Turning pro in 1953, Marr was one of a cadre of dedicated assistants following Claude Harmon between Winged Foot and Seminole before eventually trying the PGA Tour in 1960. There he found several years worth of success, winning three times and remaining amidst the top 60 money winners right through 1968. Never a long hitter, he fared surprisingly well in Major championships, tying for second at the 1964 Masters and fourth at the 1966 U.S. Open. In between, however, came Marr's greatest triumph, a two-stroke victory (over Billy Casper and Jack Nicklaus) at the 1965 **PGA Championship** in Ligonier, Pennsylvania.

By 1973 Marr was making his living in the TV tower where he would ultimately establish himself as an entertaining presence on both sides of the Atlantic. Cited by Dan Jenkins as "the only Tour pro who ever picked up a dinner check," Marr's humor was legendary to those in the golf world, always making him great company. In the 1964 Masters, for example, Marr was paired in the final round with Arnold Palmer, who was far out in front and destined to win by six. Viewing the short 12th as his one potential stumbling point, Palmer aimed to take Rae's Creek out of play by swinging particularly hard at his short iron before losing sight of the ball in midair. "Did it get over?" Palmer asked nervously. "Hell Arnold," Marr shot back, "your *divot* got over."

Sadly, Marr lost an ongoing battle with stomach cancer in 1997.

Graham Marsh (Australia)

A promising cricketer until a broken arm led him to golf, Graham Marsh, O.B.E. (b. Kalgoorlie, 1/14/1944) was prepared for a career as a mathematics teacher until a victory in the 1967 **Western Australia Amateur** prompted him to try professional golf. A classic tee-to-greener with a highly reliable swing, Marsh followed the examples of men like Thomson, Devlin, and Crampton, pursuing his trade overseas where the pickings were clearly more plentiful.

Marsh has truly been a globetrotting player, winning the national Opens of eight countries (though not, strangely enough, Australia) and significant European Tour events such as the **Trophée Lancôme** (1977), the **Benson & Hedges International** (1976 and '80), the **European Open** (1981), and, most prominently, the 1977 **World Match Play**, where he defeated Raymond Floyd 5 and 3 at Wentworth. A winner of the **Australian PGA** and several other significant events at home, Marsh came to America just often enough to prove he could win, taking the 1977 **Heritage Classic** by one over Tom Watson and appearing in seven Masters. Nowhere, however, has he been more successful than in Japan, where his roughly 30 career wins (including three **Suntory Opens** and two **Chunichi Crowns**) have given him rather an iconic status. Indeed, the only real mark against Marsh's record is that he was seldom a serious factor in Major championship play, but given his ball-striker's style, this might well be viewed more as an aberration than a weakness.

More recently, Marsh has finally found his way to America on a regular basis, capturing six Champions Tour titles (including the 1997 **U.S. Senior Open**) and over $8.3 million in winnings. Also an active golf course architect, Marsh has built courses on four continents with an especially deep Asian portfolio.

PGA Tour Win (1): 1977 Heritage
Intn'l Wins (55): 1970 & '72 Swiss Open; 1972 German Open; 1973 Scottish Open; 1976 & '80 Benson & Hedges; 1977 Trophée Lancôme; 1977 World Match Play; 1979 & '85 Dutch Open; 1982 Australian PGA
Champions Tour Wins: 6 (1995–99)

Max Marston (USA)

A high-profile amateur of the Golden Age, Buffalo, New York–born Maxwell R. Marston (b. 1892) made his first U.S. Amateur appearance at Ekwanok in 1914, losing in the first round, one down, to eventual champion Francis Ouimet. A year later, at the CC of Detroit, Marston reached the semifinals where he again lost to the eventual winner, this time Robert Gardner, whose chance came at the 37th hole after Marston missed a two-footer for victory at the 36th.

Marston served in the Navy during World War I and, upon returning, took up golf in earnest. He won a **New Jersey Amateur** title in 1919, then moved to Philadelphia where he played out of Pine Valley and proceeded to capture three straight **Pennsylvania Amateurs** between 1921 and 1923. It was during the latter year, at Chicago's Flossmoor CC, that Marston finally broke through in the **U.S. Amateur**, initially upsetting Bobby Jones in the second round, then defeating Francis Ouimet in the semifinals and Jess Sweetser in an epic 38-hole final. Also a loser in the Amateur final in 1933, Marston played on the first three Walker Cup teams (1922–24), then returned once more in 1934, compiling an overall record of 5-3.

Paula Martí (Spain)

Daughter of the prominent Spanish painter Juan Martí, Paula Martí (b. Barcelona, 1/29/1980) appears to possess both the game and the glamour to make it big in women's professional golf. Still in her mid-20s, the attractive former Spanish national champion has some experience in America, having played college golf at the University of Florida. Since turning pro in late 2000, however, she has played mostly in Europe where she won the 2002 LET Order of Merit after finishing sixth in 2001. A two-time winner in Europe, Martí made her biggest noise at the 2002 Women's British Open (an LPGA Major championship) by tying for second, two shots behind Karrie Webb. Though not yet committed to playing full time in the States, Martí would seem to possess all the ingredients necessary for high-profile stardom.

Bob Martin (UK)

St. Andrews caddie/professional Bob Martin (b. 1848) was clearly one of the better players of his day, as two victories and eight top-5 finishes at the **Open Championship** indicate. Yet for all of his apparent skill, his two Open titles can fairly be stamped among the luckiest of all time. In 1876, in a furiously mismanaged St. Andrews event, there came a famous incident wherein a protest was filed against David Strath for allegedly hitting into the group ahead at the 17th when two fives would win him the title. Though he got his five there (with no advantage gained from the supposed infraction), Strath took six at the last, tying him with Martin and setting up a play-off, pending the result of the protest. Inexplicably, the tournament committee refused to issue a ruling until Monday, raising the prospect of Strath participating in a play-off, which might then be declared null and void a day later. He refused to play and Martin was awarded the title. At St. Andrews again some nine years later, in one of the less-discussed meltdowns of Open history, David Ayton came to the 71st some five strokes clear of the field and promptly took an 11, allowing Martin to capture his second Claret Jug by one over Archie Simpson and two over the crestfallen (we assume) Ayton.

Dean Martin (USA)

Legendary comedian, singer, and actor Dean Martin (1917–1995) was one of Hollywood's most avid golfers, once joking that he "only played golf on days that end in Y." He was a daily presence at Los Angeles's Riviera and Bel-Air CCs (playing a highly capable game) and for three years hosted the PGA Tour's Dean Martin Tucson Open. Along with then-partner Jerry Lewis, Martin starred in the 1953 movie *The Caddie,* a comedy partially filmed at Riviera that featured appearances by Hogan, Snead, and Demaret, among others. Later, disappointed at the poor rebuilding of Bel-Air's greens, he became involved with the ill-fated development of the Beverly Hills CC, a 1965 project slated for a small mesa in the Santa Monica mountains, which was eventually abandoned after $22 million had been poured into the ground.

H. B. Martin (USA)

Harry Brownlaw "Dickey" Martin was a prominent golf writer of the Golden Age, perhaps less famous than Grantland Rice or O. B. Keeler, but certainly on par with the rest of the field. Covering the game primarily for the New York *Globe,* Martin was also a prolific author as well as confidant and ghost writer for Walter Hagen, particularly in the Haig's earlier years. Martin's lasting legacy to the game is *Fifty Years of American Golf* (Dodd Mead, 1936), a wonderfully detailed history and one of the American game's truly essential volumes. He passed away in 1959.

Miguel Angel Martin (Spain)

Miguel Angel Martin (b. Huelva, 5/2/1962) is best known for his dismissal from the 1997 Ryder Cup team by captain Seve Ballesteros for refusing to take a physical in order to prove his injured wrist sound. Many believed that Ballesteros simply wanted his friend and Ryder Cup veteran Olazábal added to the team at any cost and saw Martin—a three-time European Tour winner but no better than 17th in the Order of Merit—as a cheap and convenient sacrifice. Though Martin's third win, the **Moroccan Open**, came in 1999, his career has been in steady decline since the dismissal, most recently finding him playing events on Europe's minor-league Challenge Tour.

Shigeki Maruyama (Japan)

Known for his pleasant demeanor and ever-present smile, Shigeki Maruyama (b. Chiba, 9/12/1969) has, in his mid-30s, established himself as the most successful Japanese player ever on the PGA Tour. This he accomplished rather quickly, debuting full time in America in 2000, then winning an event in each of the next three seasons (most notably the 2002 **Byron Nelson Classic**) while never finishing worse than 37th on the money list. Maruyama also gained no small measure of fame by carding a stunning 58 during qualifying for the 2000 U.S. Open, a record score recorded over the par-71 Woodmont CC in Rockville, Maryland.

Despite such American success, it has largely been on the international stage where Maruyama has proven his mettle, dating back to his selection for the 1998 Presidents Cup following a four-win 1997 season in Japan. Playing at Royal Melbourne, Maruyama surprised everyone by going 5-0 overall: 2-0 with each of his foursomes partners (Joe Ozaki and Craig Parry), then a 3 and 2 singles winner over John Huston during the International team's 20½ to 11½ rout. He has since returned to the Presidents Cup in 2000 and represented Japan in each of the last five World Cups, while regularly contending throughout the PGA Tour season.

Debbie Massey (USA)

A native of Grosse Pointe, Michigan, Debbie Massey (b. 11/5/1950) put together a fine mid-1970s amateur record that included the 1972 and '75 **Western Amateurs,** the 1975 **Eastern,** and three straight **Canadian Amateurs** from 1974 through 1976. Finally turning professional in her late 20s, she was the LPGA Tour's 1977 Rookie of the Year after winning the late-season **Mizuno Classic** in Osaka, Japan, and remained among the top 25 money winners for several years. Curiously, Massey consistently demonstrated a penchant for playing her best golf overseas, for two of her three official LPGA victories were claimed in Japan and she won back-to-back **Women's British Open** titles (well before they became official American events) in 1980 and '81. Bothered by injuries and illness, she retired from the Tour in 1995.

Arnaud Massy (France)

Born: Biarritz, France, 7/6/1877 **Died:** Etretat, France, 4/16/1950

Had Jean Van de Velde managed to close the deal at the 1999 Open Championship, there might at least be some room for discussion, but as things stand now Arnaud Massy remains, nearly a century after his prime, France's greatest-ever golfer. A native of Biarritz, Massy learned the game by caddying, looping for many visiting Britons at the popular coastal resort, including the great Horace Hutchinson. Discovered by one Everard Hambro, he was shepherded off to North Berwick where he apprenticed to Ben Sayers and took quickly to Scottish life, marrying a local girl and becoming, over time, a surprisingly popular player with British galleries.

Described by Darwin as "a really glorious striker of the ball, having not only great power but the greatest delicacy of touch on and round the green," the big, broad-shouldered Massy became a regular in the Open Championship beginning in 1902, finishing an impressive fifth in 1905 at St. Andrews. A year later it was sixth at Muirfield plus a victory at the inaugural **French Open** at La Boulie. And then a breakthrough: a victory over all the top British players at a lucrative tournament at **Cannes** in early 1907. His confidence soaring, Massy proceeded that summer to become the first foreigner ever to capture the **Open Championship,** initially taking medalist honors during qualifying, then riding the steadiest of golf in windy conditions to a two-stroke victory over J. H. Taylor at Hoylake. A frequent top-10 Open finisher right up until World War I, Massy very nearly won the Claret Jug again in 1911 at Royal St. George's, reaching a 36-hole play-off with Vardon before conceding in frustration, standing 5 down at the 35th.

Consistently a great putter, Massy claimed several smaller events in Britain and remained competitive on the Continent for many years, winning the **French Open** as late as 1925 (at age 48) and becoming the only man ever to take the inaugural editions of three national Opens with the 1910 **Belgian** and 1912 **Spanish** titles. He also led France's "Four Mousquetaires" (Jean Gassiat, Louis Tellier, and Etienne Lafitte) to their sweep of a visiting American team in 1913, joined with Archie Compston to beat Bobby Jones and Watts Gunn at a 1926 exhibition in America, and served as personal professional to the golf-mad Pasha of Marrakech. Massy further authored a very popular book entitled simply *Golf* (Lafitte, 1911), initially published in France but later becoming the only French golfing volume ever to be re-issued in English.

Perhaps more highly strung than his British counterparts (Darwin cited him as being "a little too palpably in high or low spirits"), Massy retired to northern France where he passed away in relative poverty at age 72.

Intn'l Wins (15): 1906, '07, '11 & '25 French Open; **1907 British Open;** 1910 Belgian Open; 1912, '27 & '28 Spanish Open

Margie Masters (Australia)

Swan Hill native Margaret Anne Masters (b. 10/24/1934) was a powerful ball-striker who completely dominated her home state's golf in the late 1950s and early '60s, winning the **Victorian Ladies** title five times from 1957 through 1963. She was also the 1958 **Australian Ladies** champion and, obviously comfortable playing abroad, a national champion of **New Zealand** (1956), **South Africa** (1957), and **Canada** (1964). Perhaps mindful of such overseas success, Masters turned professional at age 31, becoming the first Australian to play the LPGA Tour full time. Though likely just a shade past her prime, Masters took Rookie of the Year honors in 1965 and was a steady top-20 money winner into the early 1970s. More notably, her victory at the 1967 **Quality Chekd Classic** in Waco, Texas (where she edged no less than Mickey Wright, Kathy Whitworth, and Carol Mann) made her the first Australian woman ever to win a professional golfing event.

Thomas Mathison (UK)

An Edinburgh writer who later became a minister in both northern England and Scotland, Thomas Mathison was born sometime before 1720 and died in June of 1760, having penned one of golf's most historic writings, *The Goff* (subtitled "An "Heroi-comical Poem in Three Cantos"), which was first published in 1743. Though hardly the initial written work to reference golf, *The Goff* was the first to be dedicated exclusively to it, describing the game and its prominent people in a rambling verse that has shed much light on a variety of historical figures. Reprinted several times in the modern era, it was also reissued in 1763 and 1793, with the second edition bearing a quite remarkable dedication to "All the Lovers of Goff in Europe, Asia, Africa, and America"—a line which gives historians cause to think if ever there was one.

Billy Maxwell (USA)

One of several future PGA Tour players to star in the early 1950s at North Texas State, Billy Maxwell (b. Abilene, Texas, 7/23/1929) was also the 1951 **U.S. Amateur** champion, defeating both Deane Beman and Harvie Ward en route to a 4 and 3 final victory over Joseph Gagliardi at Pennsylvania's Saucon Valley CC. Despite being handicapped by a lack of length, Maxwell joined the Tour in 1954 and proved himself a steady competitor, remaining among the top 60 money winners from 1957 through 1967, claiming seven victories and logging several top-5 finishes in Major championships. A play-off loser (to Doug Ford) at the 1957 Western Open, Maxwell's biggest wins came in 1961 at the **Palm Springs Classic** (forerunner to the Bob Hope) and at **Hartford**, the latter in a memorable seven-hole play-off with Ted Kroll. Also a member of a victorious 1963 Ryder Cup team (where he went 4-0), Maxwell began playing the Champions Tour in 1981, but saw only modest success.

Perry Maxwell (USA)

A successful banker by trade, Princeton, Kentucky-born Perry Duke Maxwell (1879–1952) took up the game of golf circa 1909 and was soon smitten enough to lay out a nine-hole course on his farm in Ardmore, Oklahoma. Following his wife's death in 1919, the financially comfortable Maxwell turned to architecture full time, touring established courses throughout the South and East to study firsthand a level of design not yet apparent in the Southwest. One of his earliest projects was the redesign and expansion of his own layout, a track that, with the addition of the region's first grass putting greens, would gain some measure of fame as the Dornick Hills G&CC.

Maxwell's career received an enormous boost in the early 1930s when he partnered for a time with Dr. Alister MacKenzie, playing an active role in such designs as Crystal Downs and the University of Michigan GC. Presumably influenced by MacKenzie, Maxwell would himself become known for his rolling, heavily contoured putting surfaces, leading numerous famous clubs to hire him for greens modifications—though ironically, much of his 1930s work for Augusta National actually involved *softening* MacKenzie's original contouring.

Among Maxwell's most recognizable works are the original nine holes at Prairie Dunes CC (Kansas) and six-time Major championship site Southern Hills CC in Tulsa, the latter being home to Oklahoma's first bentgrass greens. Responsible for roughly 120 design or redesign projects overall, Maxwell was slowed by the amputation of his right leg in 1946, and he ultimately turned his practice over to son Press before passing away in 1952.

Notable Courses: Dornick Hills G&CC, Oklahoma; Old Town C, North Carolina; **Prairie Dunes CC (9), Kansas;** Southern Hills CC, Oklahoma

Press Maxwell (USA)

The son of Golden Age architect Perry, James Press Maxwell (b. 1916) began a career in golf design soon after graduating from high school by helping with the construction of Augusta National and three-time U.S. Open site Southern Hills. During World War II he was a highly decorated pilot, flying a remarkable 81 combat missions before performing special search-and-rescue work for Yugoslavia's Marshall Tito, from whom he received a special award. Once back in the United States, he rejoined his ailing father, supervising the firm's first postwar designs before ultimately taking it over after Perry's death in 1952. Continuing to operate largely in the Midwest, Press would go on to build more than 30 new layouts, including San Antonio's Pecan Valley CC (site of the 1968 PGA Championship) and more than a dozen in his adopted home state of Colorado. His most acclaimed work, however, was surely the seamless addition of a second nine to his father's masterpiece, the famous Prairie Dunes CC in Hutchinson, Kansas.

Robert Maxwell (UK)

Much like his English contemporary Jack Graham, Edinburgh's Robert Maxwell (b. 1876) was a reserved man made uncomfortable by the rush of the tournament crowd. He was, however, a top-flight talent of whom Darwin stated: "A beautiful player he was not, but he was immensely strong and accurate, and I think few today realize what a very great and formidable golfer he was."

As evidence of this, we turn first to Maxwell's dual **British Amateur** titles, won in 1903 and '09 at Muirfield, where he was a member. In the former he laid waste to Horace Hutchinson in the final 7 and 5, while in the latter he required a 3-4 finish to edge C. K. Hutchison at the last. Maxwell's résumé offers several more tidbits, including an original 1897 Amateur debut which saw him eliminate the two finest players of his era, John Ball and Harold Hilton, in a single day, a semifinal finish in the 1902 Amateur, and a fourth-place finish at the 1902 Open Championship (only two shots behind champion Sandy Herd). Perhaps most impressive, however, was Maxwell's 5-2 head-to-head record versus Ball during the annual "international" matches between England and Scotland, a remarkable accomplishment given the great dominance normally shown by the eight-time Amateur champion.

Bob May (USA)

Yet another former junior phenom from California, Lakewood native Bob May (b. 10/6/1968) qualified into the 1985 Los Angeles Open at age 16, the then-youngest person ever to play his way into a PGA Tour event. Later a three-time All-American at Oklahoma State, May's relatively nondescript professional career took place primarily overseas until 2000, when he came out of nowhere to challenge Tiger Woods at the PGA Championship. Closing with three straight 66s, May took Woods to a thrilling three-hole play-off, which Tiger survived by a single stroke. May has since played more regularly in the United States, but has been bothered by back problems since 2001.

George May (USA)

Illinois businessman George S. May (1891–1962) was a millionaire before ever turning to golf, but with his gift for promotion, his presence proved a great catalyst for the PGA Tour. May's purview was Chicago's old Tam O'Shanter CC, a tough (though none too strategic) golf course that he owned and where he staged for nearly two decades a series of "All-America" and "World Championship" tournaments on back-to-back August weekends — carnival-like events that were simply too lucrative for most top pros to pass up. Indeed, it has been noted that from 1952 through 1957, the PGA Tour's leading money winner was invariably the same man who won May's World Championship of Golf, his purses being that disproportionately large.

A born promoter, May spiced up his event with door prizes, trick-shot artists, cheap tickets, and free parking, well aware that he could make a killing on concessions to more than recover his investment. Such an approach bothered more than one traditionalist (including Ben Hogan, who frequently stayed away) yet on the whole made May's events a highlight of the golfing calendar.

Numerous innovations have been attributed to May (perhaps erroneously), including the construction of on-course grandstands and the use of radios to immediately convey players' scores. Another first associated with the World Championship was television, for the 1954 event was the premier golf tournament to be broadcast live across the country, ending, to May's good fortune, with Lew Worsham famously holing a 104-yard approach to the 72nd to beat Chandler Harper by one. Clearly a progressive thinker, May included women's and amateur divisions in his events and regularly invited black players such as Bill Spiller and Ann Gregory at a time when the PGA of America was doing all in its power to keep them excluded.

Dick Mayer (USA)

Growing up in affluent Greenwich, Connecticut, Dick Mayer (1924–1989) was a strong all-around athlete who initially established his golfing credentials by winning the 1947 **New York Amateur** title. Turning pro in 1950, he was reasonably successful on the PGA Tour, winning several minor events and placing third in a U.S. Open, all by mid-decade. It was in 1957 that Mayer would become a household name, initially due to a play-off victory over Dr. Cary Middlecoff at the **U.S. Open** at Inverness. After draining a clutch nine-footer at the 72nd hole, it looked like Mayer might win the title outright until Middlecoff caught him late, but the play-off was seldom close, ending 72-79. Later that season, Mayer compounded his good fortune by winning George May's **World Championship of Golf**, a huge $50,000 payday that guaranteed him first place on the Tour's official money list. Never quite the same player following a year of lucrative exhibitions, Mayer did finish fourth at the 1959 Masters, then won the last of his seven Tour titles by pitching in from 35 yards at the 72nd to claim the 1964 **New Orleans Open**.

Billy Mayfair (USA)

Phoenix native Billy Mayfair (b. 8/6/1966) launched his national amateur career by winning the 1986 **U.S. Public Links**, then was named 1987 collegiate Player of the Year at Arizona State, before adding the 1987 **U.S. Amateur**, 4 and 3 over Eric Rebmann at Florida's Jupiter Hills Club. Joining the PGA Tour in 1988, Mayfair has enjoyed 15 consecutive seasons among the top 125 money winners and taken five titles, the biggest being the 1995 **Western Open**, the 1995 **Tour Championship**, and the 1998 **Los Angeles Open** (in sudden death over Tiger Woods). Known for his looping, slice-like putting stroke, Mayfair's game is based far more on accuracy than distance, a situation that has perhaps hindered him at Augusta (where he has only once bettered 32nd in nine appearances) but served him well at the U.S. Open (three top 10s since 1999). Quite capable of going low, Mayfair owns a piece of the Tour's nine-hole scoring record in the form of a seven-birdie, one-eagle 27 posted at the 2002 Buick Open in Grand Blanc, Michigan.

Maurice McCarthy
(Ireland/USA)

After emigrating to the United States from County Cork at age 15, Maurice McCarthy (1875–1938) worked primarily as a teaching pro, both for country clubs and at the New York outlet of the A. G. Spalding sporting goods chain. McCarthy began designing golf courses around the turn of the century, largely as a sideline and almost exclusively within the Northeast region, his highest profile work fashioned in Hershey, Pennsylvania, where he built a total of four courses for the famous chocolateer Milton Hershey. While some estimates have McCarthy responsible for over 100 design or redesign projects, nowhere near that many have ever been documented.

Mark McCormack
(USA)

Described in 1990 by *Sports Illustrated* as "the most powerful man in sports," lawyer-turned-business manager Mark McCormack (1930–2003) actually began his Cleveland-based International Management Group over a handshake agreement with Arnold Palmer in 1960. Later representing Jack Nicklaus, Gary Player, and literally scores of others, McCormack's company (now called IMG) set the standard for the lucrative marketing of golfers and other athletes, developing an impressive client list and a reputation for manipulating both clients and the sports themselves for maximum profit. In golf, IMG provided us with early television programming *(Big Three Golf);* one significant event (The World Match Play Championship); the present-day World Golf Ranking (designed as a tool to market ex-client Greg Norman); and the recent IMG Academies, a Florida youth training program that offers accredited private schooling to young athletes endeavoring to skip a normal childhood altogether.

It can be debated whether McCormack's involvement has, on the whole, left the sporting world a better place, but he certainly did prove that the money—*big* money—was there for the taking.

Max McCready
(Ireland)

Samuel Maxwell McCready (1918–1981) was born in Belfast but, owing to military and business commitments, saw a good deal more of the world than just Ireland. A powerful ball-striker (as most of the top period Irish amateurs seem to have been), McCready grabbed an important piece of history in 1949 by winning the **British Amateur** over two-time U.S. champion Willie Turnesa at Portmarnock, the sole occasion when the championship was played outside of Britain. McCready was also a Walker Cupper in 1949 and '51 and, primarily due to the geographic demands of a career in the cigar business, won the **Jamaican Amateur** in 1948. He would later reside for a number of years in South Africa.

Mark McCumber (USA)

A native Floridian playing a Bruce Lietzke–style left-to-right game, Mark McCumber (b. Jacksonville, 9/7/1951) came largely out of nowhere when he won the 1979 **Doral Open** in only his 12th PGA Tour start. Having grown up adjacent to Jacksonville's Hyde Park GC, McCumber was well-schooled on the state's signature Bermudagrass, resulting in five of his 10 career wins coming inside Florida. McCumber was particularly steady from 1983 through 1989 when he won six times and only once fell below 50th on the money list. It was also during this window when he came closest to winning a Major championship, tying for second at the 1989 U.S. Open at Oak Hill, one back of repeat winner Curtis Strange. Seven years later he enjoyed a similar finish in Britain, two behind Tom Lehman at the 1996 Open Championship.

McCumber is another who seems to find success in familiar places, winning twice at **Doral,** the **Western Open,** and the **Anheuser-Busch Classic.** Essentially a part-time player since winning the **Tour Championship** in 1994, McCumber joined the Champions Tour in 2001 where he is thus far winless. Also a practicing golf course architect and occasional TV commentator, McCumber's firm built the TPC at Heron Bay, which served as a short-lived host of the PGA Tour's Honda Classic.

PGA Tour Wins (10): 1979 & '85 Doral; 1983 & '89 Western Open; 1988 Players Championship
Ryder Cup: 1989

John McDermott (USA)

Born: Philadelphia, Pennsylvania, 8/12/1891 **Died:** Yeadon, Pennsylvania, 8/2/1971

The story of John J. McDermott (called Jack by contemporaries, but not by history) ranks at once among golf's most thrilling and frightening, for McDermott was America's first great homebred star and equally its most tragic. A Philadelphia youth who learned the game through caddying, he first came to prominence by defeating four-time U.S. Open champion Willie Anderson by one to capture the 1910 **Philadelphia Open.** He then lost in a three-way play-off to Alex Smith when the decidedly larger U.S. Open visited the Philadelphia Cricket Club that summer, confidently vowing that he would put matters right a year later. This the upstart McDermott did, defeating Mike Brady and George Simpson in another three-way play-off at the Chicago GC to make history as the first native-born **U.S. Open** champion. The following year he proved his triumph no fluke by defending at the old CC of Buffalo, beating Tom McNamara by two while also becoming the first player to break par in a 72-hole event.

Though McDermott failed to qualify after crossing the ocean for the 1912 Open Championship, he returned to Britain in 1913 and finished fifth at Hoylake, 11 shots behind J. H. Taylor but the best-ever result by an American. He also routed Mike Brady by seven in taking the 1913 **Western Open** and further compounded his dominance with an eight-shot triumph at that year's **Shawnee Open**, leaving the visiting Harry Vardon and Ted Ray 13 and 14 shots in arrears, respectively. Unfortunately McDermott earned the undying ire of many by insulting the British legends during his acceptance speech, though evidence suggests that his words were more ill-considered than deliberately affronting. The USGA considered rejecting his U.S. Open entry in response, though in the end their deliberations were moot as McDermott failed in his attempt at a threepeat, finishing four strokes out of the seminal Vardon-Ray-Ouimet play-off.

By 1914, McDermott's life began veering dramatically off course, perhaps due in part to the lingering effects of the Shawnee incident. Losing much of his money in bad investments, he then arrived late for the Open Championship, sailing back to America without playing. His demeanor growing increasingly introverted, McDermott later blacked out in his Atlantic City CC pro shop, then suffered a complete mental breakdown in 1915. Committed to a lunatic asylum, he would live another 56 years without ever being released, though contrary to some reports he did play golf on occasion, even making brief local competitive overtures. But mentally stable McDermott wasn't, and he remained institutionalized right up until his death, just shy of his 80th birthday.

J. J. McDermott, 1913 Western Open champion

1909-1914

	09	10	11	12	13	14
US Open	T49	2	1	1	8	T9
British	-	-	-	-	T5	-

Peter McEvoy (UK)

London-born Peter McEvoy (b. 1953) was one of the United Kingdom's top career amateurs of the modern era, winning back-to-back **British Amateur** titles in 1977 and '78 (only the fifth man to do so) and reaching the semifinals and final as late as 1986 and '87. Also the low amateur in the 1979 Open Championship at Royal Lytham & St. Annes, McEvoy has represented his country in all manner of international competitions, not the least of which were five Walker Cups between 1977 and 1989, where he managed an overall record of 5-11-2. He enjoyed consider-

ably more success as team captain, however, leading his squads to only the fifth and sixth Great Britain and Ireland victories in the event's history in 1999 and 2001, at Nairn and Georgia's Ocean Forest GC, respectively. McEvoy also appeared in the 1978, '79, and '80 Masters.

Michelle McGann (USA)

Winner in 1987 of both the **USGA Junior Girls** and the AJGA's Player of the Year award, Michelle McGann (b. West Palm Beach, Florida, 12/30/1969) joined the LPGA

Tour at 18, eventually enjoying a strong three-year run in the mid-1990s. Indeed, the tall, fashionable Floridian won an impressive seven times during this stretch, while finishing 7th, 8th, and 12th on the money list. Unfortunately, due to a loss of confidence and occasional difficulties with diabetes, it has been something of a struggle ever since, with 31st-place in 2000 being McGann's best recent effort.

Jerry McGee (USA)

A regular on the PGA Tour from 1967 through 1981, Jerry McGee (b. New Lexington, Ohio, 7/21/1943) was a four-time winner as well as a Ryder Cup player in 1977. His wins all came in the latter half of the '70s, including two—the **Kemper Open** and the **Greater Hartford**—in 1979. Four times in the top 20 on the money list, McGee has more recently battled injuries during a winless Champions Tour career.

Garth McGimpsey (Ireland)

Clearly Ireland's finest contemporary amateur, Ulsterman Garth McGimpsey (b. 1955) has represented his country internationally more than 125 times and captured 14 championships, including multiple wins in the **North, East,** and **West of Ireland** titles (the South, inexplicably, remaining beyond his grasp). Employed as a sporting goods distributor in Bangor, McGimpsey's greatest individual moment came in 1985 when he won the **British Amateur** at Royal Dornoch, routing Graham Homewood 8 and 7. Largely as a result he was selected to the 1985 Walker Cup team, then chosen again in 1989 when his valuable point-and-a-half aided in Great Britain and Ireland's first-ever Cup win on American soil, at Peachtree GC in Atlanta. McGimpsey twice appeared at the Masters (missing cuts in 1986 and '87) and returned to the Walker Cup in 1991, later captaining the Great Britain and Ireland squad to victory—its third straight—at Ganton in 2003. He has since been reappointed captain for the 2005 match in Chicago.

Paul McGinley (Ireland)

With three wins and only a single top-10 finish in the Order of Merit (eighth in 2001) in 13 years of campaigning, Dublin native Paul McGinley (b. 12/16/1966) has enjoyed the quintessential journeyman's career on the PGA European Tour. He did, however, enjoy one magnificent moment in the sun when his 10-foot putt to halve Jim Furyk clinched the 2002 Ryder Cup for Europe—an experience McGinley enjoyed so much that he played in 10 straight

summer events to garner enough qualifying points to return to the biennial matches in 2004. He has also been a World Cup regular, representing Ireland on nine occasions since 1993.

Barbara McIntire (USA)

One of America's top postwar amateurs, Toledo, Ohio, and Rollins College product Barbara McIntire (b. 1935) began her national career with back-to-back seconds at the USGA Junior Girls in 1951 and '52, also making an appearance in the U.S. Women's Amateur at age 15 (where she beat an aging Glenna Collett Vare). She took her first **U.S. Amateur** in 1959 (over Joanne Goodwin 4 and 3 at Congressional), sailed across in 1960 to beat Ireland's Philomena Garvey for the **British Ladies** title, then claimed a second American championship in 1964 by defeating Joanne Gunderson 3 and 2 at Prairie Dunes. Despite such success, McIntire's most impressive moment came years earlier, in an event that she failed to win. At the 1956 U.S. Women's Open, she scored a dramatic eagle at the 72nd to tie Kathy Cornelius, ultimately losing an 18-hole play-off by seven in her attempt to become the first amateur ever to capture the Open crown. A Curtis Cup stalwart from 1958 through 1966 and then again in 1972, McIntire also captained victorious teams in 1976 and '98, and was six times a winner of the prestigious **North & South.**

Major Amateur Wins (9): 1957, '60, '61, '65 '69 & '71 North & South; 1959 & '64 U.S. Women's Amateur; 1960 British Ladies
Curtis Cup: 1958–66 & '72 (6); 1976 & '98 Capts

Mary McKenna (Ireland)

The best of Ireland's modern female amateurs, Dublin native Mary McKenna (b. 4/29/1949) is the all-time leader among the British and Irish side in Curtis Cup appearances with nine, an uninterrupted run stretching from 1970 through 1986. Not surprisingly, she also dominated the **Irish Ladies** championship, which she won seven times (while thrice finishing runner-up) during a 15-year span from 1968 through 1972. Representing Ireland internationally, first as a player and then as a captain, McKenna journeyed occasionally to America and regularly to England to compete against stronger fields with mixed results. Though several times making deep runs in both country's larger amateur events, she never won a national title outside of Ireland. She was, however, the low amateur in both the 1977 and '79 Women's European Open.

Sam McKinlay (UK)

A native of Glasgow, Samuel Livingstone McKinlay (b. 1907) was a semifinalist twice in the Scottish Amateur (1927 and '29) and once in the British (1947), and also participated on a losing Walker Cup side in 1934, at St. Andrews. A short hitter with splendid skills around the greens, McKinlay became even better-known as the golf columnist for the Glasgow *Herald*, a position he occupied for more than 40 years. A collection of his writings, *Scottish Golf and Golfers* (Ailsa, 1992), was published as he reached his mid-80s.

Jim McLean (USA)

One of the biggest names in contemporary golf instruction, Jim McLean has enjoyed more playing success than many prominent teachers, being named All-American at the University of Houston (where he teamed with John Mahaffey, Bruce Lietzke, and Fuzzy Zoeller) and competing successfully over the years in all four major USGA events: the Junior, the Amateur, the Open, and the Senior Open. McLean has also made the cut at the Masters and, earlier, won three **Pacific Northwest Amateurs** and one **Pacific Coast** title. As a teacher he has produced more than 20 books and videos and has worked with players like Hal Sutton, Tom Kite, Bernhard Langer, and Sergio Garcia, among many others.

Fred McLeod (UK/USA)

Born: North Berwick, Scotland, 4/25/1882 **Died:** Washington, D.C., 5/8/1976

A childhood friend of fellow North Berwick native Willie Anderson, Fred McLeod was an established amateur in Scotland before turning professional and heading to America in 1903. A mere wisp of a man at 5'4" and 120 pounds, McLeod was nonetheless a highly competitive player best known for his short game, particularly his special skill at escaping bunkers with something resembling a 9-iron.

Playing the limited tournament schedule of his day, McLeod established himself as a contender early on, routinely landing top-five finishes in the U.S. and Western Opens and winning some smaller, long-forgotten titles. His great moment came in the 1908 **U.S. Open** at Boston's Myopia Hunt Club where, in an 18-hole play-off, he defeated Carnoustie's Willie Smith by six to win the national title, weighing in at only 108 pounds at event's close. Remarkably, he would then miss by a single shot the three-way play-offs that would later settle the next Opens of 1910 and '11.

Though a runner-up to Jim Barnes at the second PGA Championship in 1919, and at the 1907 and '08 Western Opens, McLeod did manage to twice win the **North & South Open** at Pinehurst, in 1909 and 1920. The extent of his victory ledger beyond these nationally prominent events, however, can only be guessed at due to a lack of official records prior to the founding of the PGA of America in 1916.

McLeod took the professional position at Maryland's Columbia CC in 1912 and retained it for an astounding 55 years before retiring in 1967. As an added bonus for his members, he managed to tie for second (albeit nine behind winner Jim Barnes) at age 39 when the club hosted the 1921 U.S. Open. Retaining a functional swing well into his 90s, McLeod joined fellow expatriate Scot Jock Hutchison as honorary starters at the Masters from 1963 until 1976.

1903-1926

	03	04	05	06	07	08	09	10	11	12	13	14
Masters												
US Open	T26	T29	19	T35	T5	1	T13	4	4	T13	T39	T3
British	-	-	-	-	-	-	-	-	-	-	-	-
PGA												

	15	16	17	18	19	20	21	22	23	24	25	26
Masters												
US Open	T8	T24			8	13	T2	-	-	T40	-	MC
British						-	-	-	-	-	-	7
PGA		-			2	-	T5	-	T5	T17	-	T17

Tom McNamara (USA)

Originally from Boston, Tom McNamara (1882–1939) was the first native-born American to seriously challenge the competitive reign of the immigrant (or visiting) Britons that had previously maintained a stranglehold over the U.S. Open. Unfortunately, McNamara was never able to do more than challenge for the title, finishing second on three occasions. In 1909, he led at Englewood, New Jersey, after a third-round 69 but closed with 77 to lose to George Sargent by four, then closed with a 69 in 1912 but failed to catch Johnny McDermott (the first homebred winner) at the CC of Buffalo. McNamara's most heartbreaking defeat, however, must surely have been 1915 at Baltusrol when Jerome Travers played the closing six in one-under-par to edge him by a stroke. Repeatedly a bridesmaid, McNamara even finished second in the 1917 Open Patriotic Tournament—a U.S. Open substitute similar to the USGA-sponsored Hale America Open that appeared during World War II. Also a runner-up in the 1911 Western Open, McNamara did, at least, have the satisfaction of winning back-to-back **North & South Opens** at Pinehurst in 1912 and '13.

Mark McNulty (Zimbabwe)

Though Nick Price is without question the finest player ever produced by Zimbabwe, it is at least worth noting that his contemporary Mark McNulty (b. Bindura, 10/25/1953) has actually won a larger number of events worldwide, some 50 to 42. Price, of course, is a three-time Major champion and a World Golf Hall of Famer so there is really no comparison, but McNulty's career numbers do stand to make him one of the finest international players of his era.

A dominant force in Southern Africa in the early 1980s, McNulty also enjoyed four solid seasons on the European Tour before splitting the years from 1982 to 1985 between Africa and America—though only 1985 produced any high-level success. Returning full time to Europe in 1986, McNulty proceeded to play some of his finest golf, finishing in the top 10 in the Order of Merit for the next five seasons, including second place in 1987 and '90. The former year, in fact, might well be seen as his best, for McNulty won the second of his four **German Open** titles, the prestigious **British Masters** (by one over Ian Woosnam at Woburn), and, back home, his first of two **South African Opens**. He would also enjoy a resurgence at age 43, finishing fifth in the 1996 Order of Merit and winning thrice. His last official win came at the 2001 **South African Open**, where a 20-foot birdie putt at the last defeated young Justin Rose, though McNulty very nearly became the oldest winner in European Tour history when he tied for second at the 2003 European Open just three months shy of his 50th birthday.

Twice a Presidents Cup choice and an eight-time World Cupper, McNulty lacks only a great presence in the Majors on his résumé. He has managed only two top-10 finishes in more than 50 Major starts and even his best, a tie for second at the 1990 Open Championship, fell a full five shots behind winner Nick Faldo. One of the era's finest putters, McNulty was forced to take up Irish citizenship in 2003 (having a grandmother who was born there) to escape the declining political situation in Zimbabwe. He has recently spent a bit of over-50 time on the American Champions Tour, thus far winning thrice and earning well over $1 million.

Intn'l Wins (50): 1980, '87, '90 & '91 German Open; 1986 Portuguese Open; 1987 British Masters; 1987 & 2001 South African Open; 1993 South African PGA; 1996 Dutch Open; 1996 Volvo Masters; 3 Zimbabwe Opens
Champions Tour Wins: 3 (2004)
Presidents Cup: 1994 & '96 (2)

Jug McSpaden (USA)

Born: Rosedale, Kansas, 7/21/1908 **Died:** Kansas City, Kansas, 4/22/1996

Harold "Jug" McSpaden (so nicknamed due to a prominent jaw, *not* a propensity for the bottle) is perhaps best remembered as one of the Gold Dust Twins, a title bestowed upon him and his good friend Byron Nelson in recognition of their vast mid-1940s winnings. McSpaden, of course, was not quite the player Nelson was, and his rise to the top was considerably more measured. He first appeared on Tour in 1929 and played through four winless seasons, though his 11 official victories between 1933 and 1943 (and several others not recognized today) certainly represented a run of solid golf. Tops among these triumphs was the 1939 **Canadian Open** (a five-shot victory over Ralph Guldahl), though wins in **San Francisco** (1935), **Miami** (1938), and **Houston** (1938) were all recorded against representative fields.

McSpaden reached his peak in 1944 when, after being turned down for military service due to asthma, he won five times, beginning with the season-opening **Los Angeles Open** and ending with the **Minneapolis Four Ball** (where he partnered with Nelson). On paper, his one-win 1945 might thus seem a disappointment, but this was Lord Byron's magical year, the season in which Nelson would win an unfathomable 18 times. McSpaden's 13 runner-ups then simply established him as the best of the mortals, a field left far behind by a man who seemed to be playing an entirely different game.

McSpaden would never win again after 1945 and would retire without ever claiming a Major championship, compelling the obvious question: Was he just a good player who reached his peak at a time when fields were substantially war-reduced, or a genuine top-shelf talent overshadowed by the presence of Nelson at the very height of his powers?

PGA Tour Wins (17): 1939 Canadian Open; 1944 Los Angeles; 1944 Phoenix

1927-1948

	27	28	29	30	31	32	33	34	35	36	37
Masters								T7	T19	T15	32
US Open	-	MC	-	-	-	T40	WD	-	MC	T18	T20
British	-	-	-	-	-	-	-	-	-	-	-
PGA	-	-	-	-	-	-	-	-	-	T5	2

	38	39	40	41	42	43	44	45	46	47	48
Masters	T16	T12	T17	T9	T18				T29	T4	33
US Open	T16	T9	T12	T7					WD	-	T12
British	-	-							-	-	-
PGA	T17	T33	T3	T9	T9		T5	T17	T3	T33	-

Rocco Mediate (USA)

Though occasionally plagued by back troubles during a nearly 20-year career, former Florida Southern star Rocco Mediate (b. Greensburg, Pennsylvania, 12/17/1962) is a five-time PGA Tour winner who has banked more than $11 million, consistently finishing among the top 50 money winners when healthy. A straight hitter of only moderate power, Mediate's first win came at the 1991 **Doral Open** (over Curtis Strange in a play-off), and he counts two victories at the **Greater Greensboro Open** among his four additional titles. Sidelined for much of 1994–95 with a ruptured disk, Mediate had earlier taken to using the long putter to ease the stress on his back, becoming the first Tour player to win with the oversized club at Doral. Mediate's best Major championship finishes have come relatively late: a fourth at the 2001 U.S. Open and a sixth at the 2002 PGA.

Bill Mehlhorn (USA)

Born: Elgin, Illinois, 12/2/1898 **Died:** Miami, Florida, 4/3/1989

"Wild" Bill Mehlhorn was one of golf's great prewar characters, though today his name is surely better recalled than many of his deeds. A native of suburban Chicago, Mehlhorn was considered one of the elite ball-strikers of his day but a man forever battling himself on the greens. The roots of his nickname are uncertain, though most accounts point to Leo Diegel as its originator and Mehlhorn's favored oversized cowboy hats as its source. A man who in his early professional years made his way around the country by giving golf lessons and selling subscriptions to *Golf Illustrated,* Mehlhorn was also considered a superior bridge player who made plenty of money at a card table.

On the golf course Mehlhorn was streaky, a man capable of posting extremely low numbers (including a then-record 72-hole total of 271 at the 1929 El Paso Open) if his putter was cooperating. Though never a Major champion, he did manage a **Western Open** win (by eight shots over Al Watrous) in 1924 in addition to some 19 other PGA Tour titles between 1923 and 1930. It is especially noteworthy that from 1926 to 1929 Mehlhorn won 16 times, a number far in excess of those posted during the same period by Johnny Farrell (13), Tommy Armour (11), Leo Diegel (11), Gene Sarazen (10), or Walter Hagen (9), the top-ranked stars of the day.

Mehlhorn was a member of the first Ryder Cup team in 1927, as well as the 1921 and '26 squads that competed against Great Britain informally. He was also a fine designer of clubs, having pioneered our weight-concentrated modern style of iron and, by his own account, the concept of numbering them. He was also, again in his own words, "the world's worst putter."

But dull he was not.

PGA Tour Wins (20): 1923, '28 & '29 Texas; 1924 Western Open; 1929 Metropolitan
Ryder Cup: 1927

1919-1948

	19	20	21	22	23	24	25	26	27	28	29	30	31	32	33
Masters															
US Open	WD	T27	-	4	T8	3	T15	T3	5	T49	T55	T9	T4	T35	-
British	-	-	-	-	-	-	-	T8	MC	9	T30	-	-	-	-
PGA	T17	T9	-	-	-	T17	2	-	T17	T17	T9	T17	T9	-	-

	34	35	36	37	38	39	40	41	42	43	44	45	46	47	48
Masters	WD	T35	-	T33	-	-	-	-							
US Open	T37	-	-	T52	-	-	-	-							
British	-	-	-	-	-	-									
PGA	T17	-	T3	T33	-	-	-	2							

Steve Melnyk (USA)

A native of Brunswick, Georgia, who starred at the University of Florida, Steve Melnyk (b. 2/26/1947) put together one of the more impressive amateur records of his time, winning the **U.S. Amateur** in 1969 (by five over Vinny Giles at Oakmont), then completing the rare modern double by capturing the **British Amateur** (3 and 2 over Jim Simons) at Carnoustie in 1971. A Walker Cup player in both of those years, Melnyk was also three times an All-American at Florida prior to a modest professional career, followed by a long and ongoing turn in the broadcast booth.

James Melvill (UK)

In 1618, James Melvill and his partner William Berwick were granted a 21-year monopoly over the sale of golf balls in Britain by King James I. In retrospect, this designation seems purely a money-making move all around, for Melvill and Berwick appear nowhere in ancient records as active ballmakers, the King enjoyed granting monopolies as a way to generate funds for the crown, and, at a more legitimate level, it was felt that the monopoly might limit the currency finding its way to Holland for the purchase of featheries. The arrangement was eventually struck down in court in 1629 when Melvill, a man of questionable character, was convicted of threatening William and Thomas Dickson, prominent ballmakers from Leith, and of illegally confiscating their property.

Lauri Merten (USA)

A native of Waukesha, Wisconsin, Lauri Merten (b. 7/6/1960) played most of her junior golf in Arizona and was twice named an All-American at Arizona State. A winner of one LPGA Tour event in each of her first two seasons (1983 and '84), she then fell into an eight-year victory drought that ended with a banner 1993 when her nearly $400,000 in winnings (sixth on the money list) exceeded her entire career total to date. Included in 1993 was her third and final victory, a one-stroke triumph over Donna Andrews and Helen Alfredsson at the **U.S. Women's Open**, as well as a runner-up finish (one back of Patty Sheehan) at the LPGA Championship.

Dick Metz (USA)

A somewhat underrated player today, Dick Metz (1909–1993) was a winner of 10 official PGA events (plus at least four more not historically recognized) and a man whose longevity as a competitor was notable. The survivor of a serious car accident in 1936, he would, in 1939, win four times and tie for seventh at the U.S. Open in Philadelphia. All told, Metz's style seemed particularly well-suited for the Open, ringing up nine top-10 finishes there, most notably in 1938 when he led Ralph Guldahl by four through 54 holes at Cherry Hills, only to close in 79 and lose by six. Selected to play in the cancelled 1939 Ryder Cup, Metz would later develop a strong reputation as a teacher, writing *The Graduated Swing Method* (Scribners, 1981) to go with two shorter volumes dating from 1940.

PGA Tour Wins (10):
Ryder Cup: 1939

Patricia Meunier-Lebouc (France)

France's finest international female player since Catherine LaCoste, Patricia Meunier-Lebouc (b. Dijon, 11/16/1972) is a two-time winner on the LPGA Tour, with the second being a Major, the 2003 **Dinah Shore**, where she edged top-ranked Annika Sorenstam by one. A former **French Ladies** champion with lots of international experience, Meunier-Lebouc was a six-time winner on the Ladies European Tour (including **English**, **Irish**, **Austrian,** and **French Opens**) before adding roughly one-half of the LPGA schedule to her slate in 2001. A solid tee-to-green player who is obviously capable of closing, Meunier-Lebouc figures to enjoy a good deal more American success, should she elect to play here full time.

Shaun Micheel (USA)

Six-year PGA Tour veteran and former Indiana University star Shaun Micheel (b. Orlando, Florida, 1/25/1969) may well have illustrated the future of Major championship golf with his stunning win at the 2003 **PGA Championship**, for with the USGA and R&A having dropped the ball regarding equipment, the extreme playing conditions deemed necessary to keep par a relevant number (and the expanded element of luck introduced therein) are bound to produce more and more unlikely winners. Micheel, for his part, played beautifully at Oak Hill, very nearly holing his 175-yard 7-iron approach at the 72nd to clinch victory. But if we are indeed in an age where players with comparatively little pedigree can routinely win Majors, Micheel—with but a single third-place finish in 163 prior starts, and but a single top-10 since—can surely stand at the vanguard.

Phil Mickelson (USA)

The title "Best Player Never to Win a Major Championship" is largely a specious one, a space-filler generally thrown about by those unable to come up with more pertinent or interesting storylines. Yet in the case of San Diego's Philip Alfred Mickelson (b. 6/16/1970), whose 0-for-46 Major streak included 17 top-10 finishes and nine visits to the top 5, such a title was beginning to gain genuine relevance—that is until his thrilling victory at the 2004 **Masters** removed the gorilla from his back and sent the cognoscenti scrambling to figure out who next to saddle with this silly designation.

In the left-handed Mickelson's case, golf stardom seemed likely from the very start, for after hitting his first shots at 18 months, he developed into a dominant junior player, then the rare four-time first-team All-American at Arizona State. In 1989 and '90 he became the first man since Scott Simpson to claim back-to-back **NCAA** individual titles, and in the latter year the first since Jack Nicklaus to take the NCAA and **U.S. Amateur** in the same season (beating Manny Zerman 5 and 4 at Denver's Cherry Hills CC). Then in 1991, Mickelson put the finishing flour-

ish on his payless days by becoming the last amateur to win a PGA Tour event, the 1991 **Tucson Open**, where he edged Bob Tway and Tom Purtzer by one.

As a professional things continued down this pleasant path, with Mickelson's record of consistently fine play matching anyone's. He began with two victories (at hometown **San Diego** and **The International**) during his first full season of 1993, peaked with four wins in both 1996 and 2000, and, prior to a slumping 2003, logged at least one Tour title every year, save 1996. Further, he has never finished lower than 38th on the money list and finished second four times, including three consecutive seasons from 2000 through 2002.

Despite this nearly unparalleled level of year-to-year success there were problems. The long-hitting Mickelson frequently drew criticism for his aggressiveness, costing himself vital strokes by routinely attempting to force the action where a bit of discretion was required. Similarly, though known as a fine putter, there was the odd tendency not only to miss short ones but to occasionally blow up with three and even four putts, placing great pressure on his vaunted (and often spectacular) short game. These problems seemed to crescendo in 2003 when, after so many Major disappointments (including a dramatic 72nd-green loss to Payne Stewart at the 2002 U.S. Open), Mickelson went winless and fell from the top 30 for the first time in his career.

Faced with the very real possibility that his best days might prematurely be behind him, Mickelson played superbly in 2004, quieting many critics by winning the **Bob Hope Desert Classic**, then silencing them all with his stunning triumph at the Masters. There, trailing Ernie Els in the late going, Mickelson—looking noticeably more confident and in control—fired a sizzling 31 on the final nine, ultimately beating Els with an 18-foot birdie putt on the 72nd green. A very popular winner, Mickelson was barely done celebrating when he experienced another Major championship heartbreak, three-putting from four feet at the 71st green to lose the 2004 Open at USGA-damaged Shinnecock Hills. Yet there he was a month later, resiliently battling back to finish third in the Open Championship at Royal Troon (one shot out of the Els–Todd Hamilton play-off), then adding a competitive tie for sixth at August's PGA.

This, in a nutshell, is Phil Mickelson, always around the lead, capable of winning or losing in epic style, and, very likely, remaining an elite professional competitor—with moments of both exhilaration and great heartbreak—for several more years to come.

PGA Tour Wins (23): 1993, 2000 & '01 San Diego; 1996 Byron Nelson; 1996 World Series; 1998 Bing Crosby; **2004 Masters;** 3 Tucson Opens & 3 San Diego Opens
Walker Cup: 1989 & '91 (2) **Ryder Cup:** 1995-2004 (5) **Presidents Cup:** 1994–2003 (5)

1990-2004

	90	91	92	93	94	95	96	97	98	99	00	01	02	03	04
Masters	-	T46	-	T34	-	T7	3	MC	T12	T6	T7	3	3	3	1
US Open	T29	T55	MC	-	T47	T4	T94	T43	T10	2	T16	T7	2	T55	2
British	-	T73	-	-	MC	T40	T40	T24	79	MC	T11	T30	T66	T59	3
PGA	-	-	-	T6	3	MC	T8	T29	T34	T57	T9	2	T34	T23	T6

Gerald Micklem (UK)

Burgh Heath, England's Gerald Hugh Micklem, C.B.E. (1911–1988) was something of an ageless amateur, a good thing given that his late 20s and early 30s were spent with the Brigade of Guards in World War II. An Oxford man and a stockbroker by trade, Micklem never won the British Amateur (his best effort being a semifinal appearance in 1946), but he was twice **English Amateur** champion, a long and successful competitor at the President's Putter, and a four time Walker Cup player between 1947 and 1955. He also captained losing teams in 1957 and '59, at Minikahda and Muirfield, respectively.

Far beyond his playing résumé, Micklem's greatest influence on golf was surely as one of the game's most devoted postwar servants. He was, for example, a prominent member of the R&A, sitting on virtually all its important committees at one time or another, and exercising particular influence on causes such as worldwide standardization of the golf ball. Micklem's list of titles and organizations served is lengthy and while his stature in British golf certainly requires no outside ratification, it is well worth noting that he is one of only a handful of foreigners ever to be awarded the USGA's Bobby Jones Award for sportsmanship in golf, which he won in 1969.

Dr. Cary Middlecoff (USA)

Born: Halls, Tennessee, 1/6/1921 **Died:** Memphis, Tennessee, 9/1/1998

Once referred to by Bobby Jones as "a voluntarily unemployed dentist," Dr. Cary Middlecoff was indeed a DDS who, after winning an unprecedented four straight **Tennessee Amateur** titles (1940–43) and the 1945 **North & South Open** (the only amateur ever to do so), proceeded to fill more than 12,000 teeth during 18 months of postwar military service. Upon being discharged, Middlecoff passed on a 1947 Walker Cup invite and instead turned professional, embarking on a career that saw him claim some 40 PGA Tour victories (eighth all-time) and emerge as the leading money winner for the decade of the 1950s.

A man wholly dedicated to understanding and perfecting the golf swing, Middlecoff was a highly intelligent player who, to his detriment, developed a reputation as one of the Tour's slowest performers. A long and accurate driver of the ball, his time was wasted mostly on the putting green, and he didn't help his reputation by such stunts as deliberately hitting a ball onto the Pennsylvania Turnpike before withdrawing from the 1953 U.S. Open at Oakmont, a move for which he would later apologize.

Despite such idiosyncrasies, Middlecoff was a player of the highest caliber, finishing among the top 10 money winners (while claiming 23 official titles) from 1949 through 1956. He thrice won six times in a season (1949, '51, and '55), took the Vardon Trophy for lowest scoring average in 1956, and, in the trivial realm, co-holds the Tour record for participating in the longest sudden-death play-

Dr. Cary Middlecoff, 1955

off, he and Lloyd Mangrum ultimately calling it a tie after 11 extra holes at the 1949 **Motor City Open.**

Though the winner of a **Western Open,** two **Bing Crosby Pro-Ams,** and the aforementioned North & South title, Middlecoff's high moments came in the form of two **U.S. Open** victories and one **Masters** title. The Opens came in 1949 and '56, the former by a single shot over Clayton Heafner and Sam Snead at Medinah, the latter by one over Julius Boros and Ben Hogan at Oak Hill. His 1955 Masters victory also came at Hogan's expense, only this time in a runaway, Middlecoff riding a second-round 65 to a seven-shot victory. There were several near misses as well, including a second and third at the Masters (1948 and '56), a final-round loss to Doug Ford in the PGA Championship (1955), and, closest of all, a play-off loss to Dick Mayer in the 1957 U.S. Open at Inverness,

Middlecoff blowing up to a 79 after a fine closing 68 had bought his share of the tie.

Retired by back problems in 1963, Middlecoff spent 18 years as a prominent TV broadcaster, offering more forthright commentary than would find favor in today's "everything is great" world of golf coverage. He also committed much of his extensive golf knowledge to paper in the form of several books, the most prominent being *Cary Middlecoff's Master Guide to Golf* (Prentice-Hall, 1960) and *The Golf Swing* (Prentice-Hall, 1974).

PGA Tour Wins (40): 1945 North & South; **1949 & '56 U.S. Open;** 1950 & '53 Houston; 1951 Colonial; **1955 & '56 Bing Crosby; 1955 Masters;** 1955 Western Open; 1956 Phoenix; 3 Motor City Opens

Ryder Cup: 1953, '55 & '59 (3)

1946-1962

	46	47	48	49	50	51	52	53	54	55	56	57	58	59	60	61	62
Masters	T12	T29	2	T23	T7	T12	11	T27	T9	1	3	MC	T6	2	MC	MC	T29
US Open	-	MC	T21	1	T10	T24	T24	WD	T11	T21	1	2	T27	T19	T43	MC	MC
British	-	-	-	-	-	-	-	-	-	-	-	14	-	-	-	-	-
PGA	-	-	-	-	-	-	T5	T17	T3	2	-	-	T20	T8	T29	T11	T15

Angel Miguel (Spain)

Madrid native Angel Miguel (b. 1929) was the younger of Spain's pioneering golfing brothers, and with a compact swing that somewhat resembled Hogan, he was also the more successful. Competing both on the Continent and in Britain throughout the 1950s and '60s, Angel amassed 10 titles of note including the 1961 and '64 **Spanish Opens,** the 1954, '56, and '64 **Portuguese Opens,** and the national Opens of **France** and the **Netherlands** in 1956 and '65, respectively. He also finished fourth in the 1957 Open Championship and appeared in five Masters, tying for 25th in 1959. The Miguels frequently played in other Spanish-speaking countries during the winter months, with Angel finding further success at the Opens of **Mexico** (1959) and **Argentina** (1962). He also enjoyed the unique experience of partnering with Sebastian in the 1958 **World Cup** in Mexico City, with Angel claiming medalist honors while the brothers finished second as a team.

Sebastian Miguel (Spain)

Eight years older than brother Angel, Sebastian Miguel (b. 1921) was a more even-tempered player whose performances were steadier but less likely to result in victory. His only notable triumphs were local, coming in the 1954, '60, and '67 **Spanish Opens** and the 1959 **Portuguese**

Open, though his record at the Open Championship was commendable (four top-10 finishes) and he was invited to three Masters. A modest, straight hitter with a reliable short game, Sebastian, who led the Spanish ascent from the humble beginnings of the caddie ranks, deserves a tip of the cap from men like Angel Gallardo, Antonio Garrido, and, later, Seve Ballesteros for showing it was possible and for serving as a fine golfing ambassador for his country.

Marion Miley (USA)

A tragic and largely forgotten figure in American golf, Lexington, Kentucky's Marion Miley (1914–1941) was a long-hitting talent who once consistently outdrove the powerful Babe Zaharias during an exhibition match. A six-time winner of the **Kentucky Ladies** title between 1931 and 1938, Miley won back-to-back **Trans-Mississippi** crowns in 1935 and '36, **Western Amateur** titles in 1935 and '37 (the latter in a 7 and 6 rout of Betty Jameson), back-to-back **Southern Amateurs** in 1938 and '39, and reached the semifinals of the 1938 U.S. Women's Amateur. Also a member of the victorious 1938 Curtis Cup team, Miley was just the sort of charismatic player who would have played well in women's professional golf had she lived long enough to see its arrival. Sadly, she was shot and killed in a robbery in 1941, a rarity among competitive golfers who seem seldom to have died violent deaths.

Alice Miller (USA)

Born in the central California town of Marysville, Alice Miller (b. 5/15/1956) played collegiate golf at Arizona State where she was a member of the 1975 AIAW national champions. After joining the LPGA Tour full time in 1979, Miller enjoyed a strong run during the first half of the 1980s, finishing 7th, 11th, and 3rd on the money list between 1983 and 1985, a period when she would claim seven of her eight career victories. Her peak year was 1985, which she began by capturing her lone Major championship, the **Dinah Shore** (by three over Jan Stephenson), before adding wins at the **S&H Classic**, the **McDonald's Championship**, and **Mayflower**, plus an unofficial victory at the season-ending **Mazda Champions**. Never again among the top-40 money winners, Miller did claim one final victory in 1991 at the **Jamie Farr Toledo Classic** before falling permanently from the top 75.

Johnny Miller (USA)

San Francisco native John Laurence Miller (b. 4/29/1947) first came to the golf world's attention by winning the 1964 **USGA Junior Boys**, then compounded that tenfold by qualifying for the 1966 U.S. Open (played at his hometown Olympic Club) at age 19 and finishing a thoroughly impressive eighth. By this time Miller was also an All-American at Brigham Young, paving the way for him to turn pro and join the PGA Tour in 1969.

Tall and lean, the dashing Miller possessed a long and aggressive swing capable of great accuracy, which at his peak enabled him to attack the hole as one of the finest iron players the game has known. A compelling golfer of great style, Miller's sole weakness was his putting, a challenge surmounted in earlier years with alignment help from caddie Andy Martinez (a tactic later outlawed) but which eventually left him a modern successor to the nerve-ridden Snead or Hogan.

Though a heartbreaking loser at the 1971 Masters (which he led through 68 holes before being overtaken by Charles Coody), Miller logged victories at the 1971 South-

ern Open and the 1972 **Heritage** before breaking through in historic fashion at the 1973 **U.S. Open** at Oakmont. Trailing by six shots through 54 holes, he proceeded to uncork one of the greatest rounds in golf history, a near-perfect 63, which vaulted him over a dozen men to a one-stroke victory over John Schlee.

So established, Miller simply exploded in 1974, winning his first three starts (the **Bing Crosby, Phoenix,** and **Tucson**) in a powerful display that set the table for an eight-win, money-leading, Player of the Year season. He came back in 1975 to win four more times and finish second on the money list, once again dominating the West Coast swing (and particularly the desert) by repeating at **Phoenix** and **Tucson**, then adding another victory at the **Bob Hope**. Though 1976 saw a slip to 14th in money, it began with still more desert success, including a third straight **Tucson** triumph and a repeat at the **Bob Hope**. Then in July, Miller took his second Major title at the **Open Championship**, his final-round 66 sparking a 279 total that ran away (by seven) from Jack Nicklaus and a 19-year-old Spaniard named Severiano Ballesteros.

Thereafter, however, the luster began steadily to dim as Miller battled minor physical problems, a bit of indifference, and perhaps an aversion to much of what came with being the best, resulting in a winless stretch that saw him plunge as low as 111th on the money list in 1978. A comeback of sorts followed with a win in 1980 (the **Inverrary Classic**), then two more in 1981 (at **Tucson**—naturally—and **Los Angeles**) before a renewed lack of confidence, particularly in his putter, brought Miller irreversibly back to the pack. An inspirational, lightning bolt victory at the 1994 **Bing Crosby** proved that even at 46 Miller could still strike it with the best. But afflicted by a terminally ill putting stroke, he passed on the Champions Tour upon turning 50, instead remaining in the TV booth where his candid commentary mixes great insight with a touch of the off-the-wall.

PGA Tour Wins (25): 1972 & '74 Heritage; **1973 U.S. Open;** 1974, '87 & '94 Bing Crosby; 1974 Westchester; **1976 British Open;** 1981 Los Angeles; 1982 San Diego; 4 Tucson Opens

Intn'l Wins (4): 1979 Trophée Lancôme

Ryder Cup: 1975 & '81 (2)

1966-1986

	66	67	68	69	70	71	72	73	74	75	76
Masters	-	T53	-	-	-	T2	MC	T6	T15	T2	T23
US Open	T8	MC	-	T42	T18	T5	7	1	T35	T38	10
British	-	-	-	-	-	T47	T15	T2	10	T3	1
PGA	-	-	-	-	T12	T20	T20	T18	T39	MC	-

	77	78	79	80	81	82	83	84	85	86
Masters	T35	T32	MC	T38	T2	MC	T12	MC	T25	T28
US Open	T27	T6	MC	MC	T23	T45	MC	T4	8	T45
British	T9	MC	T56	T65	T39	T22	-	T31	-	MC
PGA	T11	T38	-	T68	MC	T32	T30	WD	MC	WD

Mary Mills (USA)

Similar to Andy North on the men's side, Mary Mills (b. 1/19/1940) was a player whose game seems to have been especially well-suited to Major championship play, for fully three of her eight career LPGA Tour victories came on the game's biggest stages. The first (and her debut professional triumph) was the 1963 **U.S. Women's Open** in Cincinnati, where Mills was the only woman to break par, finishing three ahead of Sandra Haynie and Louise Suggs. The following year it was the **LPGA Championship**, where she managed to overcome a peaking Mickey Wright by two at the event's then-regular home, the old Stardust CC in Las Vegas. Finally, Mills captured her second **LPGA Championship** in 1973, slipping past Betty Burfeindt by one at Massachusetts' Pleasant Valley CC. Having previously dominated amateur golf in her native Mississippi (where she won eight straight **Ladies** titles between 1954 and 1961) and claimed the LPGA Rookie of the Year award in 1962, Mills tour success was hardly surprising—but not many players can claim 38 percent of their professional victories to be Major championships.

Gloria Minoprio (UK)

In no way a serious contender in championship play, the eccentric Gloria Minoprio holds the distinction of being the first woman to play a major British event (the 1933 English Ladies) in slacks. In addition to her black slacks, she wore a black tunic and black toque—a sort of high-fashioned Gary Player. Of course, Minoprio also had the habit of playing with only one club (her "caddie" carrying a second in case of damage to the indispensable first). Minoprio was defeated in her opening match yet the effects of her appearance were lingering, for as Enid Wilson later wrote: "Had she arrived in the nude, the effect on the officials and other competitors then present could not have been more profound."

Abe Mitchell (UK)

Born: East Grinstead, England, 1/19/1887 **Died:** St. Albans, England, 6/11/1947

One of a handful of candidates for the "best player never to win the Open Championship" moniker, popular Abe Mitchell competed successfully as both an amateur and a professional in an era when class divisions generally regulated players permanently to one field or the other. A flat-footed swinger who relied on a pair of immensely powerful hands to generate his fabled length, he joined George

Duncan and Archie Compston among Britain's top post-Triumvirate players of the 1920s.

Prior to turning pro, Mitchell twice made deep runs at the British Amateur, losing in the 1910 semifinals at Hoylake to homestanding John Ball, then suffering a heartbreaking loss to Ball in the 1912 final by missing a 4-foot clincher at the 36th, then losing at the 38th. By 1913 Mitchell was a pro, finishing fourth on the occasion of Vardon's sixth title at the 1914 Open Championship, then dropping the game, like everyone else, for service in World War I. Back in peacetime, he and George Duncan would tie for a faux Open Championship, the **Victory Open**, and in 1920 Mitchell looked good for the real thing when leading by six through two rounds, only to balloon to an 84 in the third en route to a disappointing fourth-place finish. In one final gasp at age 46, Mitchell stood tied for the lead through 54 holes in 1933 until a closing 79 ultimately placed him seventh.

Though unable to capture the Claret Jug, Mitchell did manage the rare (and long-forgotten) feat of winning in America, claiming the 1924 Miami Open by five over Bobby Cruickshank. This highly legitimate victory, though far more prominent than many "official" wins of the period, remains unrecognized today by the PGA Tour. The aura of xenophobia also dogged Mitchell at the 1922 Southern Open in Nashville where, following a deadlock in a 36-hole play-off, he defeated Leo Diegel over three additional holes—only to have his crown stripped days later on the rather lame grounds that the players had agreed to continue play without the tournament committee's approval.

Mitchell generally fared better in match play, however, for he was three times champion of the *News of the World* event (second only to the British Open in importance), winning at Walton Heath in 1919, Mid-Surrey in 1920, and Wentworth in 1929. In the unofficial international match of 1926, he trounced expatriate Jim Barnes 8 and 7, then proceeded to stand out during the 1929, '31, and '33 Ryder Cups, mounting an overall record of 4-2. Indeed, Abe Mitchell's legacy will forever be a part of the Ryder Cup—quite literally—for as a close friend and private professional to Samuel Ryder, it is Mitchell's figure that is sculpted atop the famous trophy.

William Mitchell (USA)

The son of a greenkeeper, Salem, Massachusetts, native William Mitchell (1912–1974) initially followed in his father's footsteps, working as a superintendent and operating a New Hampshire turfgrass farm for a number of years. Prior to World War II, he assisted Connecticut-based architect Orrin Smith on several projects around New England. After the war, he formed a design and construction firm with his brothers Henry and Samuel before going solo by the mid-1950s. All told, Mitchell would design or redesign over 300 courses, the vast majority along the Eastern seaboard. A representative sampling of new designs would include 36 holes at the CC of New Seabury (Massachusetts), 27 at Old Westbury (New York), and a popular 36 at Quinta do Lago on the Portuguese Algarve. The list of clubs upon which Mitchell performed renovations—particularly in the New York City area—includes Shinnecock Hills, Old Oaks, Gardiner's Bay, and Glen Head, among others.

Tomekichi Miyamoto (Japan)

Born outside of Kobe very near Mt. Rokko, site of Japan's first golf course, Tomekichi Miyamoto (b. 1902) learned the game by caddying there, then eventually distinguished himself as that nation's first significant professional. Though matched against obviously lean fields, Miyamoto was six times the **Japan Open** champion (the last in 1940) as well as the winner of countless lesser events scarcely recorded. He also broke ground by becoming the first Japanese player to compete abroad when he and "Jack" Yasuda participated in the 1929 Hawaiian Open. Miyamoto also led a team of six Japanese players that toured the American mainland during 1935, playing exhibition matches against teams of American pros.

Larry Mize (USA)

Augusta, Georgia, native and ex-Georgia Tech star Larry Hogan Mize (b. 9/23/1958) carved himself an indelible place in **Masters** history in 1987 when his 140-foot chip-in on the second hole of sudden death snatched apparent victory from Greg Norman, giving Mize his lone Major championship. While there is always an element of fortune to such things, nobody can accuse Mize of lucking into victory, for he birdied the 72nd hole to force the play-off, which initially included Seve Ballesteros as well.

For Mize, this was easily his career peak, not simply for the Green Jacket but also because his sixth-place finish on the 1987 money list would be his only career visit to the top 10. An extremely accurate driver of the ball, Mize's steady play did keep him comfortably among the top 125 for 20 consecutive seasons (1982–2001), a period during which he would claim all four of his official Tour victories. He was also a Ryder Cup player in 1987, going 1-1-2 on the first-ever American team to lose on its home soil.

Tomekichi Miyamoto at Pinehurst

Alexander M'Kellar (UK)

Noted in historical volumes like *The Golfer's Handbook* as "The Cock o' the Green," Edinburgh resident Alexander M'Kellar bore the wholly subjective rank of the world's most enthusiastic golfer, a particularly difficult claim to verify since he was not a player of competitive record, and he died in 1813. Still, stories abound of his endless hours spent on the Bruntsfield Links, practicing his putting by lamplight, and playing alone when winter's chill scared off the rest of humanity. Such tales have surely grown with time, of course, but rare is the truly avid golfer who cannot relate to M'Kellar's legendary lifestyle.

Jack M'Lean (UK)

Often listed under the anglicized spelling "McLean," Glasgow native John "Jack" M'Lean (1911–1961) was twice low amateur in the Open Championship, twice a winner of the **Irish Amateur,** and, closer to home, three times the **Amateur** champion of Scotland. M'Lean was also selected to the Walker Cup team in 1934 and '36 and therein lies his greater claim to fame. During the 1936 trip to Pine Valley, the British team also entered the U.S. Amateur at Garden City GC, where M'Lean became the third (and thus far last) Briton to reach the final of the American championship. Standing one up through 33 holes, he might well have won it, save for birdies at the 36th and 37th by the eventual champion Johnny Fischer.

John Montague (USA)

John "Mysterious" Montague (1906–1972) was one of golf's all-time most curious characters, a fine talent who debuted on the Los Angeles golfing scene, seemingly out of nowhere, in 1930. A powerful man who may well have been the game's longest hitter, Montague appeared to be of independent means, joining Lakeside GC, spending vast sums of money, and running with Bing Crosby, Gary Cooper, and others of Hollywood's golfing elite. Despite cultivating a reputation as one of the finest players in America, Montague confined himself only to private money matches, never venturing into any public events. He also refused to do interviews and went to great lengths to avoid being photographed, frequently relieving photographers of their cameras forcibly, then compensating them with cash.

Eventually the reason for such wariness became apparent: Montague was actually one LaVern M. Moor, a native of Syracuse, New York, who was wanted for a robbery and murder. He was returned to New York where he stood trial, beating the rap after celebrities like Crosby and Oliver Hardy testified on his behalf. Though many considered the verdict a travesty, Montague returned to Los Angeles where he became a prominent trick-shot artist and professional at the old California CC. Where exactly his early spending money had come from may never be known, but Montague's skills as a hustler—beating capable players with only a rake, a bat, and a shovel—saw him through later life in relative style.

Russell Montague (USA)

A native New Englander and Harvard-educated attorney, Russell W. Montague (b. 1852) moved to White Sulphur Springs, West Virginia for health reasons, owning an attractive homestead in the Allegheny Mountains. Here in 1884, Montague, his visiting nephew, and three Scottish neighbors laid out a short nine-hole course, the Oakhurst Links, which stands today as the oldest clearly documented golf course in the United States. Oakhurst is never mentioned ahead of New York's St. Andrew's, however, because Montague's holes were abandoned near the turn of the century, whereas St. Andrew's endured. Fully restored in the early 1990s, Oakhurst is back in business as a 2,235-yard layout whose occasionally crossing fairways must be negotiated with hickory and gutta-percha—a unique throwback to golf as it once was.

Colin Montgomerie (UK)

One of the most consistently successful players of his era, Scotland's Colin Stuart Montgomerie, M.B.E. (b. Glasgow, 6/23/1963) was a dominant force on the worldwide scene from 1990 to 2002, never ranking worse than sixth in the European Tour Order of Merit and finishing first an unprecedented seven consecutive seasons between 1993 and 1999. During these halcyon years, the extremely accurate but not terribly long Montgomerie accumulated 21 European wins as well as the occasional lucrative title in Africa (e.g., the 1996 **Million Dollar Challenge**) while often challenging in the Major championships, where he logged seven top-10 finishes in 27 starts.

Montgomerie, alas, has not yet claimed that elusive Major championship, though he has come agonizingly close. In the 1992 U.S. Open at Pebble Beach, for example, he finished early and at even-par in extreme conditions, looking for all the world a winner until Tom Kite rattled home at two-under to beat him. Two years later, when the Open returned to Oakmont, there was a three-way play-off loss to Ernie Els, then another second to Els in the 1997 Open at Congressional, this time after a three-putt bogey at the tough 71st. But hardest to swallow, perhaps, was a loss to Steve Elkington in the 1995 PGA Championship at Riviera where Monty holed a clutch 20-footer at the 72nd to force a play-off, only to have Elkington beat him with nearly the same putt on the first hole of sudden death.

Though a disappointment in the Majors, Montgomerie has delivered wonderfully on the high-pressure Ryder Cup stage, claiming an overall record of 19-8-5 and a singles mark of 5-0-2, the latter including wins over Scott Hoch, Payne Stewart, Lee Janzen, Ben Crenshaw, and David Toms. Further, his list of European wins (mostly against legitimately strong international fields) amply demonstrates his status as one of the game's premier players of the last 15 years. In addition to Montgomerie's Major disappointments, however, detractors will note that unlike countrymen Nick Faldo, Sandy Lyle, Ian Woosnam, and even Lee Westwood, he has never won in America, this despite making more than 100 Stateside starts. Sadly, one factor in this lack of success has been the moronic heckling he has received, a circumstance that is only likely to worsen following a high-profile rules infraction at the 2005 Indonesian Open.

Intn'l Wins (36): 1989 Portuguese Open; 1993 Dutch Open; 1993 Volvo Masters; 1994 Spanish Open; 1994 & '95 German Open; 1995 Trophée Lancôme; 1996 Dubai; 1996, '97 & 2001 Irish Open; 1998, '99 & 2000 Volvo PGA; 1998 British Masters; 1999 Benson & Hedges; 1999 Loch Lomond; 1999 World Match Play; 2000 French Open; 2002 Volvo Masters
Walker Cup: 1985 & '87 (2) **Ryder Cup:** 1991–2004 (7)

1990-2004

	90	91	92	93	94	95	96	97	98	99	00	01	02	03	04
Masters	-	-	T37	T52	MC	T17	T39	T30	T8	T11	T79	MC	T14	MC	MC
US Open	-	-	3	T33	T2	T28	T10	2	T18	T15	T46	T52	MC	T42	
British	T48	T26	MC	MC	T8	MC	MC	T24	MC	T15	T26	T13	82	WD	T25
PGA	-	-	T33	MC	T36	2	MC	T13	T44	T6	T39	DQ	MC	MC	70

Janice Moodie (UK)

One of Scotland's top contemporary players, Janice Moodie (b. Glasgow, 5/31/1973) attended San Jose State where she won 12 intercollegiate events and was four times an All-American, while also representing Great Britain and Ireland in the 1994 and '96 Curtis Cups. Joining the LPGA Tour in 1998, Moodie finished 36th on the money list as a rookie, then proceeded to rank no worse than 22nd through 2002 (with single victories in 2001 and '02) before slipping to a winless 46th in 2003. She also represented Europe in the Solheim Cup in 2000 and '03.

Orville Moody (USA)

Perhaps with Hollywood's recent infatuation with golf-themed movies, someone will see fit to bring the remarkable story of Orville Moody (b. Chickasha, Oklahoma, 12/9/1933) to the big screen. Moody, after all, walked away from a scholarship at the University of Oklahoma in 1953 to join the Army, rising to the rank of staff sergeant over 14 years while also winning two **Army** golf titles and, when posted abroad, three **Korean Opens**. In 1967 he elected to give the PGA Tour a shot, then scarcely survived a fruitless rookie season in 1968. But things changed in a hurry at the 1969 **U.S. Open** at Houston's Champions Club where a rock-steady Moody shot 281 and, as the other challengers fell away, emerged victorious, by a single stroke, over Deane Beman, Al Geiberger, and Bob Rosburg.

Though something of a stunner at the time, Moody's victory is really not so perplexing as his superior ball-striking was perfectly suited to Open conditions, an event which traditionally minimizes his gravest weakness, the putter. Remarkably, Moody never again won on the PGA Tour, three-putting away a golden opportunity at the 1973 Bing Crosby and largely disappearing altogether by the

late 1970s. Though he did manage overseas victories in Hong Kong, Morocco, and Australia, Moody's greatest overall success came—with the advent of the long putter—on the Champions Tour, where he won 11 times between 1984 and 1992 (including the 1989 **U.S. Senior Open**) and pocketed nearly $4 million.

Ossie Moore (Australia)

Oswald "Ossie" Moore (b. 1958) won the 1981 **Australian Amateur** in comfortable style (8 and 7 over C. Lindsay at Royal Adelaide), then turned professional in 1982 to relative success. Though never a winner beyond Australasia, Moore can claim the 1986 **Victorian Open** among his triumphs, as well as the 1986 **Queensland PGA** and the 1989 **Australian Match Play**, where he defeated Peter Fowler. A four-time participant in the Open Championship, Moore's best finish was joint 44th in 1987. He is currently familiar to golf viewers worldwide for his TV work on the Australasian Tour.

Frank Moran (UK)

Perhaps the most underrated of all of Britain's great golf writers, Scotland's Frank Moran, M.B.E., went to work for Edinburgh's *The Scotsman* in 1911 and for more than 50 years covered the game, penning regular news pieces as well as weekly columns. Similar to Bernard Darwin in his ability to weave the history and ambience of the game into his copy, Moran also authored two books, the revealing *Golfer's Gallery* (Oliver & Boyd, 1946)—written "to provide an escapist corner among the war news"—and the *Book of Scottish Golf Courses* (Scottish Country Life, 1939), a nearly impossible title to locate today.

Michael Moran (Ireland)

Perhaps nearly forgotten outside of his native Ireland, Michael "Dyke" Moran (1886–1918) was unquestionably that nation's top professional in the years before World War I. He was the **Irish Professional** champion every year from 1909 to 1913, and in that final campaign tied Harry Vardon for third at the Open Championship at Hoylake, despite shooting an outlandish 89 in the third round.

Born immediately adjacent to the Royal Dublin GC, Moran learned the game while caddying there in his youth. Though not allowed to actually play the links, the story goes that he would sneak on at odd hours, using the layout's drainage dikes for cover between presumably rushed shots. Whether this truly was the source of his nickname we shall likely never know, but in apparent tribute, the word "dyke" remains a part of the Irish golfing lexicon (as a synonym for birdie) to this day. Sadly, Moran died in France near the end of the Great War at age 32, ending what surely would have been a record-setting domestic career and a noteworthy international one.

Gus Moreland (USA)

Once described as "the best amateur competitor I ever played against" by Byron Nelson, Gus Moreland (1911–1998) was a native of Dallas who, at his peak, was widely considered the best amateur in the Southwest. He won three straight **Texas Amateurs** between 1931 and 1933, back-to-back **Trans-Mississippi Amateurs** in 1932 and '33 (the latter over Lawson Little at The Broadmoor), and the 1932 **Western Amateur**. Also the champion of **Mexico** in 1934 and **Illinois** in 1940, Moreland more than held his own against big-name competition, beating both Nelson and Ben Hogan while all were still teens, tying for second with Gene Sarazen at the 1932 Texas Open and finishing seventh in the 1933 U.S. Open. Moreland was undefeated as a Walker Cup player in 1932 and '34 and appeared in the inaugural Masters in 1934. He also carried a unique nickname, "Gus the Walker," which came from his habit of moving briskly alongside a putt he believed was on its way in. Presumably he wasn't wrong too often as LPGA Hall of Famer Betsy Rawls once called Moreland "the most remarkable putter I ever saw."

Dale Morey (USA)

Though never a U.S. Amateur champion, Indiana native Dale Morey (b. 1919) was one of America's top competitors during the 1950s and '60s, capturing more than 260 events, including the 1953 **Western Amateur**, the 1950 and '64 **Southern Amateurs**, the 1964 **North & South**, and, a decade later, **U.S. Senior Amateurs** in 1974 and '77. A former high school basketball star, Morey appeared in 27 U.S. Amateurs and came terribly close to victory in 1953, when he birdied the 34th and 35th holes to draw even in his final match with Gene Littler, only to lose to a Littler birdie at the last. Briefly a professional during the 1940s, Morey soon regained his amateur status, later appearing on Walker Cup teams in 1955 and '65.

Dr. Gil Morgan (USA)

Though determined to pursue a career in golf, Gil Morgan (b. Wewoka, Oklahoma, 9/25/1946) first secured his doctorate in optometry before turning professional, then joined the PGA Tour full time in 1974. Utilizing a simple, repetitive swing, Morgan established himself as one of the Tour's most consistent earners as well as a seven-time winner, his two biggest titles coming in 1978 at the **Los Angeles Open** (beating Jack Nicklaus by two) and the lucrative **World Series of Golf**, the latter contributing heavily to a second-place finish on the year's money list. Morgan would again win in **Los Angeles** in 1983, this time after opening the season a week earlier with a play-off victory over Curtis Strange and Lanny Wadkins at the **Tucson Open**.

Morgan's only real slip was in 1986 and '87, when rotator cuff surgery affected parts of both seasons. Long healed by the mid-1990s, he began a second career on the Champions Tour in 1996, where he has captured some 23 victories and more than $19 million in winnings (second only to Hale Irwin) at the time of this writing. Morgan also participated on winning Ryder Cup teams in 1979 and '83.

Wanda Morgan (UK)

Lymm, England's Wanda Morgan (b. 3/22/1910) was a premier player in the decade before World War II, winning the **British Ladies** in 1935 at Royal County Down (3 and 2 over 18-year-old Pam Barton) after having lost in the 1931 final to Enid Wilson, 7 and 6 at Portmarnock. A fine tee-to-green player whose putting was less a strength, Morgan also took **English** titles in 1931, '36, and '37, as well as all manner of lesser regional wins. She was a part of the first three Curtis Cup matches but could manage only a disappointing 0-5-1 overall record, and later renounced her amateur status upon becoming a sales representative for a sporting goods concern.

Sloan Morpeth
(New Zealand/Australia)

A native of Auckland, Sloan Morpeth (1897–1973) was one of New Zealand's top amateurs of the World War I era, winning three national **Amateur** titles (1920, '27, and '29) plus one **New Zealand Open** (1928). By 1929 he was living in Australia, winning the **Victorian Amateur** and serving in several administrative capacities, including secretary of the Australian Golf Union, the executive committee of the Victorian Golf Association and team manager on several overseas excursions with Australia's best. A tall, popular man, Morpeth eventually turned to golf course architecture, remodeling the Commonwealth GC (where he once served as manager) and designing or redesigning such layouts as the Peninsula CC and Portsea GC during the 1960s. His wife Susie was also a significant figure, winning back-to-back Australian Ladies titles (1930 and '31) as well as five Victorian Amateur championships.

James Morris (UK)

The second son of Old Tom Morris, James Oglivie Fairlie "J.O.F." Morris (1852–1906) was named after Colonel James Fairlie who had brought Old Tom to Prestwick and was so instrumental in the establishment of the Open Championship. Though overshadowed by the heroic doings of his older brother and father, James was himself a fine player who finished third in the 1878 Open at Prestwick and frequently partnered with Old Tom after Young Tom's tragic death. A third son, who was born a cripple, remained far removed from golf while Old Tom's nephew Jack was a prominent professional who served at Hoylake for a record 60 years.

Old Tom Morris (UK)

Born: St. Andrews, Scotland, 6/26/1821 **Died:** St. Andrews, Scotland, 5/24/1908

In a game that treasures its past more than any other, there is no greater golfing legend than Old Tom Morris. Described in 1928 by Charles Blair Macdonald as "the Grand Old Man of golf, the philosopher and friend of all youthful, aspiring golfers" and, earlier, by Horace Hutchinson as "the High Priest of the hierarchy of professional golf," Morris's presence *was* St. Andrews to many a Victorian-era visitor.

The son of a letter carrier, Morris initially intended to become a carpenter but instead hired on as an apprentice to an earlier St. Andrews legend Allan Robertson. In this capacity Morris developed his skills as both a club- and feather ball-maker and as a player. On the business side, his relationship with Robertson became strained when Morris began using the new gutta-percha ball (an invention Robertson correctly viewed as a threat to his livelihood), leading Old Tom to accept Colonel James Fairlie's offer to become keeper of the green at Prestwick in 1851. On the playing side, it is generally accepted that once Morris became capable of beating the supposedly undefeated Robertson, Allan would only partner with Tom and never play against him. An imposing team they were too, winning their most famous challenge, an 1849 contest against Musselburgh's Dunn brothers, two up after trailing the 108-hole match four down with eight to play.

Due to poor documentation, the game's steady evolution, and a relative scarcity of period tournaments, we cannot say much by way of comparing Old Tom even to Harry Vardon, never mind to modern players. What indisputable records do exist, however, are the results of early **Open Championships** where, against admittedly limited fields, Old Tom established himself as the top competitor of his day. Already 39 at the time of the Open's 1860 inception, Morris was defeated by Willie Park Sr. in the inaugural event, then promptly came back to win three of the next four, plus a fourth title in 1867. Generally chased by the elder Park, Morris's victories were all hard fought, save for a 13-shot romp in 1862. Though usurped toward decade's end by his own son Tom Jr., Old Tom would continue competing at the Open for many years, his last entry coming in 1896 at age 75 — though there was, we must recall, no qualifying in those days.

Eventually returning to St. Andrews as professional and keeper of the green in 1865, Morris remained the town's most prominent presence well into the twentieth century. Operating from his shop adjacent to the 18th green, he became golf's central figure, manufacturing clubs, teaching, presiding over tournaments, and, more than anything, spreading the game's gospel in a singularly appealing manner. Old Tom was also one of the game's most prolific early architects in an era when earthmoving was essentially nonexistent, laying out at least 60 highly natural courses, including early versions of Prestwick, Westward Ho!, and Carnoustie. Though precious little of his work remains, his impact on early designers was incalculable, with a list of architects directly influenced by him necessarily including Macdonald, Colt, Fowler, MacKenzie, Tillinghast, Ross, and Tom Simpson, among others.

Old Tom seemed destined to live forever, for he was still a gentle force upon the golfing scene well into his 80s. His 1908 death, at 87, was the result of falling down the stairs inside the R&A clubhouse and was mourned throughout the golfing world. With his profound impact as a player, equipment maker, teacher, administrator, greenkeeper, architect, and general booster, Old Tom may well have been the single most important individual in the history of the game.

Young Tom Morris (UK)

Born: St. Andrews, Scotland, 4/20/1851 **Died:** St. Andrews, Scotland, 12/25/1875

The first son of Old Tom Morris, Young Tom, or Tommy, was golf's first true superstar, a player whose pure physical talents were, by all indication, vastly beyond his competition in a manner historically experienced by precious few. A powerful ball-striker whose strength was a great advantage given the plethora of bad lies in those early days, Young Tom won his first recorded tournament against professionals at age 16 at Perth, defeating Willie Park Sr. and Bob Andrew in a play-off. That same year he finished fourth in the Open Championship, five shots behind his victorious father, who was then taking the last of his four championship belts.

A year later, at 17, Young Tom was the champion golfer of 1868, playing three rounds over Prestwick's 12 holes in 157 to finish two ahead of Bob Andrew. The following summer he improved, lowering his total to a record 154 while also breaking 50 over his third loop, a number that may not sound special until we note that it is hardly above level fours. Notably it was his father, playing remarkable golf in his late 40s, who finished second at 157, likely the only time a father and son will ever finish 1-2 in a Major championship.

Tommy's shining hour, however, came in 1870 at Prestwick when he shot a stunning record score of 47-51-51—149, lowering his previous mark by five shots and leaving Bob Kirk and Davie Strath tied for second, some 12 shots in arrears. The reader may first do well to imagine a modern player standing 12 up after 36 holes—a virtual inconceivability—but an even more telling statistic is this: Tommy's 149 score would not be bettered for the duration of the event's 36-hole days (1892), and then remained the 36-hole record right through 1908, fully six years into the rubber-ball era and an astounding 38 years after it was set.

Per tournament rules, Young Tom's three consecutive wins resulted in his taking permanent possession of the championship belt, supposedly (though not likely) the cause of the 1871 event being cancelled. When the tournament returned in 1872, however, it was Young Tom's name that would first be engraved on the new Claret Jug, winning his fourth straight title by three shots over Davie Strath despite a dramatically higher 36-hole total of 166. With the event's departure from Prestwick in 1873, Tommy slipped to level third on his home links at St. Andrews, then to second, two shots behind Mungo Park, the following year at Musselburgh.

By this time, it has been suggested, Young Tom may have been experiencing some modest health problems, the cause of this minor slippage in form. True or false, such became irrelevant when, in September of 1875, his wife and infant died during childbirth. From there forward Tommy turned more to the bottle than golf before passing away on Christmas day, romantically reported as the result of a broken heart but, according to a post-mortem examination, actually resulting from a burst artery in his right lung.

1866-1874

	66	67	68	69	70	71	72	73	74
British	9	4	1	1	1		1	T3	2

Jay Morrish (USA)

Golf course architect Jay Morrish (b. 1936) made more than the usual number of stops along the career road, working for Robert Trent Jones, George Fazio, Desmond Muirhead, and, finally, Jack Nicklaus. During his 10-year stint with the Golden Bear, Morrish was involved in numerous Nicklaus designs while simultaneously moonlighting with associate Bob Cupp in a venture known as Golforce. Finally, in 1983, he joined former British Open champion Tom Weiskopf in a long-term partnership that yielded memorable results.

Together Morrish and Weiskopf produced 23 new designs, any number of which have received national attention. Two in particular, Ohio's Double Eagle Club and the Canyon course at Arizona's Forest Highlands, frequently appear in published top-100 rankings with several others having previously held positions on such lists. A third major success came in an unlikely locale: with their 1992 design of the famous Loch Lomond GC, Morrish and Weiskopf became the first American architects ever to build a course in Scotland. Though several of Morrish's independent redesign projects have met with mixed reviews, his solo work at Arizona's Boulders Resort (36 holes) has received universally high acclaim.

Notable Courses: The Boulders GC (36), Arizona; **Double Eagle Club, Ohio; Forest Highlands GC, Canyon Course, Arizona; Loch Lomond GC, Scotland;** Shadow Glen GC, Kansas

Alex Morrison (USA)

Though scarcely known among today's golfers, Alex Morrison (1896–1986) was perhaps the most prominent instructor of the golf-mad 1920s and for years thereafter, working in Los Angeles and Palm Springs and, for a time, operating a New York City teaching studio and a driving range beneath the 59th Street Bridge. Morrison began teaching by accident while working at the Los Angeles CC (he was forced to instruct a beginner when no one else was available) and quickly found it to his liking. Though counting two-time Major champion Henry Picard among his followers, Morrison's teachings were considered somewhat radical, his points of emphasis being the maximization of centrifugal force to generate power while anchoring the swing by pointing one's chin just behind the ball from start to finish. Never a member of the PGA, Morrison wrote frequent pieces for Grantland Rice's *American Golfer* magazine and was a pioneer in the use of photography in golf instruction. His brother Fred was a touring professional who, though less celebrated, won the lucrative Agua Caliente Open in 1932.

J. S. F. Morrison (UK)

Having worked primarily after World War II and lacking much of the cachet of H. S. Colt, C. H. Alison, or Dr. Alister MacKenzie, Deal native John Stanton Fleming Morrison (1892–1961) is often thought of as the "other" partner in Colt's famous course design firm. Yet Morrison was a highly accomplished man, playing cricket, soccer, and golf at Cambridge, serving in the Royal Flying Corps during World War I, and pairing with some impressive partners in high-profile amateur events. He won, for example, the Worplesdon Foursomes with Joyce Wethered and the Halford-Hewitt Cup, on five occasions, with the redoubtable Henry Longhurst.

As a designer, Morrison worked far more directly with Colt than did the globetrotting Alison, frequently collaborating with the firm's legendary founder during his later years. Morrison also oversaw most of the company's European projects, playing a major role in a number of Dutch, French, and German designs. He also teamed with Sir Guy Campbell to rebuild and expand Deal's famous Prince's GC after the war and, working solo, performed remodeling work at places like Sunningdale, the Berkshire, Royal Lytham & St. Annes, and Royal Cinque Ports, among others. Morrison also made one foray into the literary world, editing *Around Golf* (Arthur Barker, 1939), a fine anthology of period British golf writing.

Mohamed Said Moussa (Egypt)

Mohamed Said Moussa (b. 1933) learned the game of golf as a caddie at the Heliopolis GC and was only 22 years old when he defeated Egyptian golfing icon Hassan Hassanein in the old **Desert Open**, played over sand greens on the long-defunct Maadi Sporting Club course near Cairo. Ultimately Moussa would go on to represent Egypt more than a dozen times in World Cup play and, despite the presence of Cherif el-Sayed Cherif, win the **Egyptian Open** with roughly equal regularity. Clearly established as the best post-Hassanein player in the Arab world, Moussa was prohibited by travel restrictions from regularly competing in Europe, instead taking up residence at the Alexandria Sporting Club as head professional.

Desmond Muirhead (UK/USA)

Long one of golf course architecture's most eccentric and controversial figures, Norwich, England, native Gordon Desmond Muirhead (1923–2002) was trained in architecture and engineering at Cambridge and in horticulture at the Universities of British Columbia and Oregon. The son of a fine Scottish player, Muirhead himself was a less-than-avid golfer who drifted into course design as an offshoot of his expanding career as a community planner. Despite a penchant for publicly eschewing all that was traditional, he built a number of mainstream courses in Florida and around Palm Springs before eventually teaming up with Jack Nicklaus in the early 1970s, an alliance that included the joint design of Ohio's Muirfield Village GC.

Following a non-golf decade spent living in Australia, Muirhead returned to the United States in the mid-1980s, unleashing a string of "symbolic" designs (i.e., holes shaped like mythological figures and the like) for which he was widely ridiculed. Indeed, the noted architect Tom Doak has written that Muirhead's "success in the business is the ultimate proof that salesmanship is more important than golfing knowledge." In an interesting retrenchment, however, Muirhead later teamed with British caddie Tip Anderson to write *How to Play the Old Course* (Newport Press, 2000), a detailed guide to the hallowed ground that he once so loudly mocked.

Notable Courses: Aberdeen GC, Florida; Mission Hills CC, Dinah Shore Course, California; Stone Harbor GC, New Jersey

Lionel Munn (Ireland)

Usually acclaimed as the first really great Irish golfer, Londonderry native Lionel Munn (b. 1887) was the first homebred to make a consistent stand in the **Irish Open Amateur**, winning three straight titles from 1909 to 1911. He was also a four-time **Closed Amateur** champion (1908, '11, '13, and '14) and in 1911 added the **South of Ireland** title, giving him a sweep of the nation's three biggest prizes in that single season. Like so many men of the day, Munn enlisted to fight following the outbreak of World War I and, though he survived the conflict, his game was never of truly championship caliber thereafter.

Joseph Murdoch (USA)

The late Joseph S. F. Murdoch, a Philadelphian who passed away in March of 2000, was very likely the world's foremost postwar golf book collector, amassing over 3,000 volumes in his personal library. As a founder of America's Golf Collectors Society, Murdoch published several important books on both collecting and the literature of golf. His decidedly rare *The Library of Golf 1743–1966* (Gale Research, 1968) was a first attempt at cataloging roughly 900 prominent books, but his later collaboration with book dealer Richard Donovan, *The Game of Golf and The Printed Word 1566–1985* (Castalio, Endicott, 1985) represents easily the most thorough bibliography of golf literature ever assembled.

Bob Murphy (USA)

Brooklyn native Bob Murphy (b. 2/14/1942) enrolled at the University of Florida as a baseball player but when injuries slowed that pursuit, he turned his attention fully toward golf. In 1965 he won the first of the USGA's ill-fated stroke-play experiments at the **U.S. Amateur**, edging Bob Dickson by one at Tulsa's Southern Hills CC. The following spring he was the **NCAA** individual champion, paving the way for a PGA Tour career that began with back-to-back victories at the **Philadelphia** and **Thunderbird Classics** and a first-year money record of over $105,000.

Never a long hitter but famously accurate, Murphy went on to win a total of five Tour events, the last and biggest being the 1986 **Canadian Open** at Glen Abbey where he beat Greg Norman by three. With a career in the TV booth in the offing, he was first talked into pursuing the Champions Tour full time by Lee Trevino and, overcoming problems with arthritis, proceeded to win 11 titles and more than $8.5 million before settling into the tower.

Albert Murray (UK/Canada)

The younger brother of the well-known Canadian professional Charles, Albert Murray (1887–1974) was born in Nottingham, England, before emigrating with his family at a young age. Beginning as a caddie, he learned clubmaking from the respected professional George Cumming before serving as his brother's assistant at Westmount GC and the Royal Montreal GC, then held several head jobs of his own. A smaller and less gregarious sort than Charles, Albert won the 1908 **Canadian Open** in an impressive performance, which saw him hit every fairway over four rounds. He won again in 1913 (this time by six over Nicol Thomson and Jack Burke Sr.), and it is an interesting footnote that both victories came over a highly familiar Royal Montreal layout. He also won the **Canadian PGA** in 1924.

Charles Murray (UK/Canada)

Canada's first top-flight professional competitor, Charles Murray (1880–1938) was, like younger brother Albert, born in England (Birmingham) before emigrating as a youth. Getting his start as a caddie at the Toronto GC, he eventually became chief assistant to the famed George Cumming before branching out on his own, eventually settling at Royal Montreal (North America's oldest golf club) in 1904. Remaining there until his unexpected death in 1938, the outgoing Murray soon established himself as a leading player, riding a quick, compact swing to **Canadian Open** titles in 1906 and 1911, while also losing in a play-off with a pair of elite players, Douglas Edgar and Tommy Armour, in 1920. Never out of the top six during 11 pre–World War I Opens, Murray also took the inaugural **Canadian PGA** title in 1912.

N

Kevin Na (South Korea/USA)

Potentially one of golf's compelling stories in the years ahead, Seoul native Kevin Na (b. 9/15/1983) came to Southern California with his family at age eight, eventually developing so quickly that he elected to turn professional following only his junior year at Diamond Bar High School. Such an unprecedented move drew criticism in many quarters, particularly when Na failed to qualify for the PGA Tour and packed off to the relative obscurity of the Asian circuit for the 2002 season.

But well beyond the American limelight, Na performed wonderfully, finishing fourth in the Asian Order of Merit and stunning everyone with a closing 66 to win the season-ending **Volvo Masters**. A subsequent 40th-place Order of Merit ranking in 2003 can be misleading, as Na spent several months away from Asia trying his hand at the European Tour, where he managed a joint sixth at the lucrative Dubai Desert Classic. Following the 2003 season, he successfully qualified for 2004 PGA Tour membership where his best finish to date is a tie for fourth at the Honda Classic. Currently the Tour's youngest player, Na's learning curve and long-term potential appear steep, making him an obvious player to watch in the years ahead.

Kel Nagle (Australia)

A former apprentice carpenter who grew up poor during the Depression, Kelvin David George Nagle (b. Sydney, 12/21/1920) rose to stand among Australia's all-time greatest golfers, not only winning numerous championships but helping to grow the Australian game with his great personal popularity. Like many a period player, Nagle's competitive aspirations were derailed by World War II but in its aftermath he was quickly back at Sydney's Pymble GC, shortening his backswing and preparing for that first big victory, which finally came in 1949 at the **Australian PGA**.

Though he would, in the ensuing years, win titles in Asia, Europe, and North America and amass staggering regional numbers that included one **Australian Open**, six **Australian PGAs**, seven **New Zealand Opens,** and seven **New Zealand PGAs,** Nagle truly established himself as a world-class player with his victory in the 1960 **Open Championship** at St. Andrews. There, on the occasion of the event's Centennial, he holed a clutch 10-footer at the 71st, then routinely parred the last to hold off a hard-charging Arnold Palmer and capture the Claret Jug. With five more top-5 Open finishes over the next six years (including a second to Palmer in 1962), Nagle proved his victory no fluke, and he very nearly equaled it at the 1965 U.S. Open, tying Gary Player over 72 holes in St. Louis before losing by three strokes in a play-off.

Nagle regularly represented Australia internationally, but never more proudly than when he twice teamed with his good friend Peter Thomson to capture the **World Cup**, first in 1954 in Montreal, then five years later when the event came to Royal Melbourne. He enjoyed another important triumph in Canada in 1964 by again turning back Palmer to capture the **Canadian Open**, his lone PGA Tour victory.

A regular winner of senior events in the days before the Champions Tour, Nagle was also the victim of one of golf's more amusing mistakes at the 1968 Alcan Tournament in England. On that occasion, playing partner Christy O'Connor mistakenly marked Nagle's front-nine total of 35 in place of his ninth-hole score. Thus when Nagle signed the incorrect card, his total suddenly ballooned 31 strokes, from 71 to 105.

PGA Tour Wins (1): 1964 Canadian Open
Intn'l Wins (31): 1949, '54, '58, '59, '65 & '68 Australian PGA; 1959 Australian Open; **1960 British Open;** 1961 French Open; 1961 Swiss Open; 1961 Hong Kong Open; 7 New Zealand Opens, 7 New Zealand PGAs, 7 New South Wales PGAs, 4 ACT Opens & 3 Western Australia Opens

1951-1971

	51	52	53	54	55	56	57	58	59	60	61
Masters	-	-	-	-	-	-	-	-	-	MC	MC
US Open	-	-	-	-	-	-	-	-	-	-	T17
British	T19	-	-	-	T19	-	-	-	-	1	T5
PGA	-	-	-	-	-	-	-	-	-	-	-

	62	63	64	65	66	67	68	69	70	71
Masters	MC	T35	T21	T15	MC	T31	T30	-	-	-
US Open	-	MC	MC	2	T34	T9	T52	MC	T12	-
British	2	4	45	T5	T4	T22	T13	9	T32	T11
PGA	-	-	-	T20	MC	-	-	-	-	-

Tommy Nakajima (Japan)

Tsuneyuki "Tommy" Nakajima (b. Kiryu City, 10/10/1954) was the **Japanese Amateur** champion at age 18 before turning professional in 1976, quickly establishing himself as one of that nation's top competitors both at home and abroad. Though a winner of six Japanese titles over his first two seasons, Nakajima's domestic peak came in 1985–86 when he won a combined 11 times, taking the **Japan Open** in both years and becoming the first home-born winner of the lucrative **Dunlop Phoenix** title. He added further **Japan Open** titles in 1990 and '91, his career total of four placing him behind only Jumbo Ozaki among modern players.

Though competing primarily in the Far East for many years now, Nakajima was impressive during early appearances in several Grand Slam events, notably at the Open Championship where he tied for 17th in 1978 and 8th in 1986. Unfortunately it is the former occasion that British fans best recall, mostly for a third-round disaster at St. Andrews' famous 17th where, lying inches short of the green in two, Nakajima putted his ball into the Road bunker and took four to escape, his eventual nine causing the ancient hazard to be rechristened the "Sands of Nakajima." Remarkably, this calamity took place only months after he had set another record for futility by taking a 13 on the par-5 13th at Augusta National during the 1978 Masters, as high a score as has ever been recorded in the event's seven-decade history.

Pete Nakamura (Japan)

A three-time winner of the **Japan Open**, Torakichi "Pete" Nakamura (b. 1915) was perhaps more responsible than anyone for that nation's post–World War II golf boom. The spark was not so much domestic, however, as international, for in the 1957 **World Cup** at Kasumigaseki, Nakamura teamed with Koichi Ono to capture the team title, defeating the Americans (Sam Snead and Jimmy Demaret), the South Africans (Gary Player and Harold Henning), and the Australians (Peter Thomson and Bruce Crampton) in the process. Nakamura also claimed the individual crown by a resounding seven shots, a clean sweep that quickly grabbed the attention of Japanese sports fans. By the early 1960s, with the game growing rapidly, Nakamura smartly broadened his résumé to include golf course architecture, allowing him to capitalize on this boom which saw Japan's total number of courses explode from less than 100 to well over 2,000 today.

Jim Nelford (Canada)

A native of Vancouver, British Columbia, Jim Nelford (b. 6/28/1955) was twice an All-American at Brigham Young while playing with future PGA Tour regulars Mike Reid, John Fought, and Pat McGowan. After winning the **Canadian Amateur** in 1975 and '76 and the **Western Amateur** in '77, Nelford was a regular on Tour from 1978 to 1985, drawing attention for his technique of playing right-handed while putting lefty. Though never a Tour winner, he did team with Dan Halldorson to lead Canada to its second **World Cup** title in 1980 in Bogotá, before having his career interrupted by a serious 1985 water-skiing accident in which he nearly lost his right arm. Though he succeeded in fighting his way back to the Tour by 1987, Nelford was never again a serious factor, eventually turning to a career in television.

Byron Nelson (USA)

A product of the same Glen Garden CC caddie yard that produced Ben Hogan, John Byron Nelson, Jr. (b. Ft Worth, 2/4/1912) was the polar opposite of the dour young Hogan, his courtly manners and pleasing personality winning over outsiders from an early age. Nelson's golfing talents were

Harold "Jug" McSpaden and Byron Nelson

similarly impressive and considerably more advanced than Hogan's—and not simply because he beat his smaller rival, in a play-off, in Glen Garden's 1927 caddie tournament. Quitting school early, Nelson prepared himself for a career in golf, though his main reason for playing was decidedly different from the norm. Where most young players wanted to build their fortunes by winning as many championships as possible, Nelson's goal, never wavering, was simply to amass enough money to buy himself a ranch.

After winning the 1930 **Southwestern Amateur** and failing to qualify for match play at the 1931 U.S. Amateur (three-putting 13 times on unfamiliar bentgrass greens), Nelson turned professional in late 1932 but found little immediate success. His first PGA Tour–recognized victory, in fact, wouldn't come until the 1935 **New Jersey Open**, claimed while working as an assistant at Ridgewood CC. The following year it was the far more prestigious **Metropolitan Open** (played at Quaker Ridge GC) and by 1937 Nelson was off and running, winning his first **Masters** that spring by riding an opening 66 to a two-shot victory over Ralph Guldahl.

In 1939, as war was breaking out in Europe, Nelson ascended to the summit of American golf, winning first in **Phoenix**, then later at the **North & South** and the **U.S.** and **Western Opens**. In the U.S. Open (played at Philadelphia CC) he closed with a fine 68 to finish tied with Craig Wood and Denny Shute. Shute disappeared after

an 18-hole play-off with 76 while Nelson and Wood both carded 68s, necessitating another 18 during which Nelson holed a full 1-iron to eagle the 4th and ultimately triumphed by three. Also finishing runner-up in the PGA Championship at New York's old Pomonok CC (when Henry Picard blocked an apparent tap-in victory with a stymie at the 36th, then holed a 20-footer to win at the 37th), Nelson completed his stellar season by claiming the Vardon Trophy.

The following year, 1940, was relatively undistinguished save for coming back to win the **PGA Championship** in Hershey, Pennsylvania, beating Guldahl in the semis and Sam Snead in the final, both one up. Nelson also took the 1942 **Masters** when his 280 total tied with Hogan, and a six-under-par run over an 11-hole stretch allowed him to claim one of golf's more dramatic play-offs 69-70. Later that year Nelson was turned away by the military for a condition known as "free bleeding" (his blood failing to coagulate quickly enough) but his winning nevertheless ceased when professional golf essentially ground to a halt until early 1944.

By this time, however, Nelson was reaching peak form, winning eight events in 1944, then roaring through golf's greatest-ever statistical season in 1945, a peerless epic that saw him claim an incredible 18 victories in 31 starts, seven second-place finishes, and, from early March through early August, a streak of 11 straight wins, perhaps the most unbreakable record in all of sports. Detractors have long pointed out several factors that might mitigate these accomplishments, primarily that fields were undeniably shorter during wartime. But a telling statistic is that in stroke play, Nelson's average margin of victory was 6.3 shots, a remarkable number that might suggest dominance over any field.

In 1946, with everyone back in the lineup, Nelson won eight more times, including the one top event that he'd been missing, the **Los Angeles Open**. Thus at season's end he made good on his longstanding promise and retired to his Roanoke, Texas ranch, playing only in occasional events thereafter. One of note was his final American victory at the 1951 **Bing Crosby** (by three over Cary Middlecoff). A second came in 1955 when his good friend Eddie Lowery (of Francis Ouimet caddying fame) invited Nelson to join him in trying to qualify for the Open Championship at St. Andrews. Having only once entered the world's oldest event (finishing fifth at Carnoustie when visiting with the Ryder Cup team in 1937), Nelson accepted, qualified, then finished 12th. The next week, in his final competitive outing, he won the **French Open** at La Boulie, then retired for good.

Byron Nelson won a total of 52 official PGA Tour events (fifth all-time) and five Major championships, the latter number unquestionably suppressed by the wartime cancellation of eight American events at the very peak of his career. Similarly, he retired at the ripe old age of 34, still very much in form but tired of the touring life. If travel conditions and higher purses had matched those of our modern era, how many more events might Nelson have won had he played until, say, age 40? And how many more Majors might he have entered, à la Hogan, had there been a better awareness of their long-term historical importance?

Nelson did continue competing at the Masters and remained quite active both as a broadcaster and a teacher, playing a major role in the careers of both Ken Venturi and Tom Watson. This is hardly surprising, however, given that Nelson's own swing—built around a full shoulder turn, remarkable left-side extension, and an aggressive driving of the lower body—was the model for much of what would be considered ideal in the modern era (not to mention the PGA Tour's current logo). Arguably the finest long iron player of all time, Nelson also drove the ball with exceptional accuracy and plenty of length, with only his putting falling anywhere near "average" in description.

Above all, Byron Nelson has long stood out as one of golf's finest gentlemen, an extraordinarily modest and kind man who, when playing exhibitions, would always inquire as to what the course record was and who held it—for if the answer was the club's resident professional, it was Lord Byron's rule never, ever to break it.

PGA Tour Wins (52): 1936 Metropolitan; **1937 & '42 Masters;** 1939 & '45 Phoenix; 1939 North & South; **1939 U.S. Open;** 1939 Western; 1940 & '44 Texas; **1940 & '45 PGA Championship;** 1941 & '45 Greensboro; 1945 Canadian Open; 1946 Los Angeles; 1946 Houston; 1951 Bing Crosby
Intn'l Win (1): 1955 French Open
Ryder Cup: 1937 & '47 (2); 1965 Capt

1934-1955

	34	35	36	37	38	39	40	41	42	43	44
Masters	-	T35	T13	1	5	7	3	2	1		
US Open	MC	T32	MC	T20	T5	1	T5	T17			
British	-	-	-	5	-	-					
PGA	T17	-	-	T5	T5	2	1	2	T3		2

	45	46	47	48	49	50	51	52	53	54	55
Masters		T7	T2	T8	T9	T4	T8	T24	T29	T12	T10
US Open		T2	-	-	MC	-	-	-	-	-	T28
British		-	-	-	-	-	-	-	-	-	12
PGA	1	T5	-	-	-	-	-	-	-	-	-

Larry Nelson (USA)

Among modern golf's Major champions, few at the age of, say, 20 would have seemed less likely to achieve great golfing success than Ft. Payne, Alabama, native Larry Gene Nelson (b. 9/10/1947). This is because at 20 Nelson had never played the game, only taking it up after returning from military service in Vietnam. Obviously something of a natural, he studied Ben Hogan's seminal *Five Lessons: The Modern Fundamentals of Golf* intently, broke 100 his first time on the course, and was bettering 70 within a year. As a measure of his inexperience, Nelson's successful trip through the 1974 Tour qualifier was only the second 72-hole event in which he had ever played.

Standing 5'9" and weighing 150 pounds, Nelson employed one of golf's smoothest and most repetitive swings, allowing him to play with great consistency, especially off the tee. He advanced steadily up the money list over his first four seasons before breaking through for two 1979 victories, the **Inverrary Classic** and, in a play-off with Ben Crenshaw, the **Western Open**. Nelson would eventually total 10 PGA Tour victories, of which three would prominently stand out. In the 1981 **PGA Championship**, playing near his longtime residence in Atlanta, Nelson beat Fuzzy Zoeller by three to capture his first Major championship. He grabbed his second at the 1983 **U.S. Open** at Oakmont where, seven strokes back after 36 holes, a third-round 65 put him dead in the hunt. Following a late-round rain delay on Sunday, Nelson holed a 65-foot birdie putt at the 16th to steal the momentum, ultimately defeating Tom Watson by one. Finally, in 1987, Nelson beat Lanny Wadkins on the first hole of sudden death to win his second **PGA**, an event made particularly memorable by the PGA of America's decision to play it over their own South Florida facility in early August, resulting in extreme heat and dead greens. Nelson would also win twice at **Walt Disney World** and twice at his hometown **Atlanta Classic**, the latter, in 1988, being his final Tour victory.

Also a four-time winner in Japan, Nelson was a Ryder Cup pick in 1979, '81, and '87, winning an unprecedented nine straight matches in the first two events before going 0-3-1 during the 1987 loss at Dublin, Ohio. His syrupy swing aging nicely, Nelson eventually joined the Champions Tour in 1998 where he has enjoyed great success, winning 18 times to date while cashing checks worth more than $15 million.

PGA Tour Wins (10): 1979 Western Open; **1981 & '87 PGA Championships; 1983 U.S. Open**
Champions Tour Wins: 18 (1998–2004)
Ryder Cup: 1979, '81 & '87 (3)

1976-1992

	76	77	78	79	80	81	82	83	84	85	86	87	88	89	90	91	92
Masters	-	-	-	T31	T6	MC	T7	MC	5	T36	T36	MC	T33	MC	48	55	DQ
US Open	T21	T54	MC	T4	T60	T20	T19	1	MC	T39	T35	MC	T62	T13	T14	T3	MC
British	-	-	-	-	T12	-	T32	T53	T64	T55	MC	T48	T13	MC	-	-	-
PGA	T34	T54	T12	T28	MC	1	MC	T36	MC	T23	MC	1	T38	T46	MC	MC	T28

Liselotte Neumann (Sweden)

A two-time **Swedish Amateur** champion, Liselotte Neumann (b. Finspang, 5/20/1966) burst onto the American golfing scene by winning the 1988 **U.S. Women's Open** as an LPGA Tour rookie, defeating Patty Sheehan by one stroke at the Baltimore CC. The win, which caught many Stateside observers by surprise, would lead to a 12th place finish on the season's money list as well as Rookie of the Year honors. Five decidedly leaner campaigns would soon follow, with just one Tour win (the 1991 **Mazda Japan Classic**) and not a single top-20 money ranking. But beginning in 1994, Neumann pushed her game to a different level, crashing the top 10 in four of the next five seasons and winning 10 times, including the 1994 **Women's British Open**, which, unfortunately, had not yet been elevated to Major championship status.

Neumann's U.S. numbers, of course, must be judged in the context of her being an international player who frequently teed it up overseas. During these peak years, for example, she also captured events in Europe, Australia, and Japan and has recorded 12 WPGET/LET wins overall. Combine those with 13 LPGA titles and six Solheim Cup appearances and Liselotte Neumann stacks up squarely as one of the best international players of her time.

LPGA Wins (13): 1988 U.S. Women's Open; 1994 Women's British Open; 1996 Welch's; 1998 Safeway
Intn'l Wins: (12)
Solheim Cup: 1990–2000 (6)

Jack Neville (USA)

Growing up in Oakland, California, St. Louis native Jack Neville (1891–1978) developed into a talented competitive golfer, winning a record five **California State Amateurs** and the 1914 **Pacific Northwest** title. Though also a member of the second Walker Cup team in 1923, Neville is best remembered for teaming with Douglas Grant to design the original Pebble Beach GL in 1916, and he was also responsible for laying out the back nine at the nearby Pacific Grove GL, as well as an early redesign of today's Del Monte GC. In an odd footnote, Neville also played a key role in the creation of Los Angeles's Bel-Air CC, for when land intended for the club's second nine became unusable, it was Neville who demonstrated the accessibility of an alternative tract by driving a ball across a 150-foot-wide canyon with a putter. Today's back nine, routed through the previously ignored Stone Canyon, was the result.

Remaining a real estate salesman for the Del Monte Properties Company for many years, Neville also helped future USGA president Frank "Sandy" Tatum to toughen up Pebble Beach prior to the 1972 U.S. Open, giving him the rare opportunity to fine tune his own design more than 50 years after its inception.

Jack Newton (Australia)

An outstanding cricketer and rugby player as a youth, Jack Newton (b. Sydney, 1/30/1950) had his promising golf career cut abruptly short in 1983 when, in evening darkness, he accidentally walked into an airplane propeller at Sydney Airport, losing both his right arm and right eye and suffering serious internal injuries. Though he today plays recreational golf one-handed and does regular TV work Down Under, there was a time when Newton, a larger-than-life character in the classic Australian mode, sat nearly on top of the golfing world.

In 1975, he fired a record-tying 65 in the third round of the Open Championship at Carnoustie, then stumbled late in the finale to finish 72 holes tied with Tom Watson. The ensuing 18-hole play-off was a rainy, nip-and-tuck affair that saw the players reach the last all square before Newton's 2-iron approach found sand, with the resulting bogey costing him the championship. In brighter days, he gained his lone PGA Tour win by defeating Mike Sullivan in sudden death at the 1978 **Buick Open**, then followed it a year later with his biggest title, the 1979 **Australian Open**, where he edged Greg Norman and Graham Marsh by one. Newton's second-place finish at the 1980 Masters (four behind Ballesteros) was also noteworthy, as was a 1974 victory in the old *News of the World* match play, then on its last legs.

Though dealt a staggeringly bad break, Newton today remains philosophical about it, saying "When I started out in life my ambition was to win an Australian Open and a British Open...and I got pretty close."

Alison Nicholas (UK)

Born, like Ireland's May Hezlet, at the British outpost of Gibraltar, England's Alison Nicholas, M.B.E. (b. 3/6/1962) is one of professional golf's smallest players at 5'0". Yet for nearly 15 seasons she has ranked among the best on the Ladies European Tour, finishing as high as fifth in the Order of Merit while also managing several successful forays to America. Her crowning moment, to be sure, came at the 1997 **U.S. Women's Open** in Cornelius, Oregon, where a 10-under-par performance was enough to win by one, ending the great Nancy Lopez's last real shot at winning the Open. Twice claiming LPGA victories in 1995 and once more in 1999, Nicholas has also won six titles in Europe (including three consecutive **Praia d'El Ray Euro-**

pean **Cups** from 1997 to 1999) and earlier events in Australia and Malaysia. Involved in every Solheim Cup to date, Nicholas played in the first six matches before serving as the European vice-captain in 2003.

Gilbert Nicholls (UK/USA)

One of the great unsung players of all time, Folkstone, England's Gilbert Nicholls (1878–1950) followed his older brother Bernard first to Cannes and then to the United States in pursuit of golf's greenest pastures. Initially aiming only to be as good as his brother (the sole man to beat Vardon head-to-head during King Harry's 1900 American tour), Gilbert eventually shot past not only Bernard but everyone else, becoming, for a period, this country's finest player. In 1917, no less than Grantland Rice noted that "In a thirty-six-hole match at match play he would be the favorite against any golfer in America."

Nicholls' problem was simply one of timing, for his peak playing years came not only before golf emerged into the 1920s sporting spotlight but also, for the most part, before the 1916 founding of the PGA of America. Because today's PGA Tour acknowledges as official only select events played after the PGA's founding, Nicholls is credited with exactly five victories, though in reality he took more than 50. His 1911 and '15 **Metropolitan Open** titles, for example, are not counted, nor are his 1911 and '14 wins at the **North & South Open** (wherein he defeated both Donald Ross and two-time U.S. Open champion Johnny McDermott, respectively). Of course, Nicholls would have carved a lasting place for himself had he ever won a U.S. Open, and in hindsight it seems most remarkable that he didn't. Nicholls was five times among the top-5 finishers and twice runner-up, first in 1904 at Glen View (five behind the streaking Willie Anderson), then in 1907 when a closing 79 allowed Alex Ross to beat him by two in Philadelphia.

A prodigiously long hitter and a snappy dresser whose style Walter Hagen supposedly emulated, Nicholls held numerous prestigious club jobs (including Deepdale, Boca Raton, and Seminole) and was also highly successful as a clubmaker, first in partnership with his brother, then later with Cuthbert Butchart. Also the last man to play with Willie Anderson before the four-time U.S. Open champion suddenly passed away, Gilbert Nicholls must surely rank as the most important forgotten figure in the history of American golf.

Bobby Nichols (USA)

A standout football and basketball prospect in high school, Louisville, Kentucky, product Bobby Nichols (b. 4/14/1936) was forced to concentrate on golf after a severe car accident precluded him from ever again pursuing those more physical games. Impressed with both Nichols' recovery and his golfing skills, legendary Texas A&M (later Alabama) coach Bear Bryant offered him a football scholarship when none were available for golf, a fine gesture that Nichols at least somewhat repaid by winning the 1956 Southwest Conference championship.

Turning professional in 1959 and joining the PGA Tour in 1960, Nichols immediately began an enviable 16-year streak of top-60 money finishes, during which he won 11 official events. The biggest, by far, was the 1964 **PGA Championship** where his three-stroke victory over Arnold Palmer and Jack Nicklaus may not have been so popular, for it came at the Columbus CC in Nicklaus's hometown. Nichols would later add the 1973 **Westchester Classic** to his ledger and, at age 38, the 1974 **San Diego** and **Canadian Opens**, the latter being his final Tour victory.

A Ryder Cup player in 1967 (where he sported a fine 3-0-1 record), Nichols served for a number of years as the head professional at Ohio's Firestone CC while also competing on tour. In 1986 he began a modest Champions Tour run that saw him win one title and well over $1 million.

PGA Tour Wins (11): 1962 &'65 Houston; **1964 PGA Championship**; 1973 Westchester; 1974 San Diego; 1974 Canadian Open

Champions Tour Win: 1 (1986)

Ryder Cup: 1967

Jack Nicklaus (USA)

There are several criteria to be considered in attempting to rank golf's all-time greats but if the number of Major championship victories is the method of choice, then the clear standout—both now and for the foreseeable future—is one Jack William Nicklaus (b. 1/21/1940) of Columbus, Ohio. Even if one discounts Nicklaus's two **U.S. Amateur** titles (as seems entirely fair in the postwar era), his professional total of 18 Grand Slam victories stands five ahead of Bobby Jones and fully nine clear of the leading active competitor Tiger Woods (whose own three Amateurs must also be discounted). In short, when it comes to regularly claiming golf's grandest prizes, Nicklaus has simply had no peer.

Though it may surprise those who recall his portlier early years, Nicklaus, the son of a Columbus pharmacist, was an excellent all-around athlete, starring in basketball and giving up several other sports only when they began to conflict with golf. As a golfer he was clearly special, learning the game at the venerable Scioto CC under the tutelage of Jack Grout, qualifying for the U.S. Amateur at age 15, winning the **Ohio Open** at 16 (including a third-round 64) and the **National Jaycees** title at 17 before matriculating at hometown Ohio State University. There he claimed the full roster of national amateur wins including the **North & South** (1959), the **Trans-Mississippi** (1958 and '59), the **Western** (1961), the **NCAA** individual title (1961), and, most important, a pair of **U.S. Amateurs** in 1959 and '61. There was also a runner-up finish at the 1960 U.S. Open (two behind Arnold Palmer), some talk of selling insurance and remaining an amateur, then, in 1961, the inevitable jump to the professional ranks and, in 1962, the PGA Tour.

To recount all 73 of Nicklaus's victories (second all-time) or even his 18 professional Majors would fill a volume of its own, so suffice to say, by way of summary, that his dominance of the pro game was thorough and, with the briefest of nods to Palmer, relatively immediate. He defeated Palmer in a play-off (on Arnold's home turf at Oakmont) for the 1962 **U.S. Open** while finishing third on the money list as a rookie, then proceeded to rank either first or second for 13 of the next 15 seasons (the exceptions being third in 1969 and, inexplicably, ninth in 1970). Brushing aside the wildly popular Palmer was not without its problems, however, and the upstart Nicklaus was initially saddled with unflattering nicknames generally centered upon his weight. By mid-decade, however, he had slimmed down, donned the "Golden Bear" commercial persona, and gotten very seriously to work.

As a student of golf history who idolized Bobby Jones, Nicklaus was focused primarily on accumulating Major titles and his early years reflected this, for in 1963 he took both the **Masters** (by one over Tony Lema) and **PGA Championship**, while in 1964 he finished solo or joint second at the Masters, the Open Championship, and the PGA. More Green Jackets came in 1965 (in a record-setting nine-shot romp) and '66 (a play-off triumph over Gay Brewer and Tommy Jacobs), and in the latter year he completed the career Grand Slam—at age 26—by claiming a one-shot **Open Championship** victory over Doug Sanders and Dave Thomas at Muirfield.

By this time, Nicklaus was a worldwide phenomenon, having taken the first of his six **Australian Opens** in 1964 and being widely marketed (along with Palmer and Player) by Mark McCormack as the centerpiece of golf's "Big Three." A tremendously long hitter, he ranked with Nelson and Armour among the greatest long-iron players ever—though in Jack's case there was the particular advantage of using them mostly for second shots on par 5s. Hitting everything with a soft, high fade he was as solid a tee-to-greener as the game has seen (especially under pressure), and though his short game was never considered elite, it was certainly not the weakness that some liked to suggest. As a putter, Nicklaus was generally viewed as being "above average"—but when the pressure of the closing holes mounted, not even Locke could be called his better.

Married young and a father of five, Nicklaus seemed always to have his priorities well arranged, and it can safely be said that his maturity—both on and off the course—was as potent a weapon as anything else in his considerable arsenal. Seeming always to maintain his focus in the biggest events, he marched inexorably onward, taking a second **U.S. Open** at Baltusrol in 1967 (his record 275 beating Palmer by four); winning a second **Open Championship** in 1970 (beating Doug Sanders in a play-off at St. Andrews after Sanders famously missed a three-foot clincher at the 72nd); and completing a second career Grand Slam at the 1971 **PGA**.

Given such remarkable proficiency in the Majors (where 18 second-place finishes would supplement his career win total), at least one run at a true, singe-season Grand Slam seemed inevitable. Nicklaus's best chance came in 1972, when he began by winning both the **Masters** and the **U.S. Open**, the latter highlighted by a famous pin-rattling 1-iron to the par-3 71st at Pebble Beach. Then, in the Open Championship at Muirfield, he trailed leader Lee Trevino by six after 54 holes before mounting an heroic charge, going out in 32 before missed six-footers at the 15th and 16th saw him home in 66, a single stroke too many—and so went his chance of making the 1972 PGA championship the most watched tournament in golf history.

Three years later Nicklaus took multiple Majors for the fourth time, initially winning his record fifth Green Jacket when a famous 45-foot putt at the 70th held off both Tom Weiskopf and a hard-charging Johnny Miller. In August it was the **PGA** at Firestone, a win that was followed by a nearly three-year drought before a 69-69 finish provided a two-shot victory in a memorable 1978 **Open Championship** at St. Andrews.

By this time, however, there was a serious challenger. While the mid-1970s rush of Miller had been effectively beaten back, in Tom Watson there was a man who, like Trevino a decade earlier, seemed to have Nicklaus's number. Well-chronicled Watson triumphs at the 1977 Masters and, most famously, the '77 Open Championship at Turnberry suggested that Jack's time had finally come, an idea given great credibility by a winless, 12-event 1979 that saw Nicklaus plummet to 71st in Tour winnings. But the Golden Bear proceeded to roar back in June of 1980 at the **U.S. Open**, with an opening 63, a record total of 272, and a two-stroke win (over Japan's Isao Aoki) at Baltusrol. As a final exclamation point, he traveled up to Rochester in August and gave another superb performance, taking the **PGA** at Oak Hill by a full seven strokes.

In 1982 at Pebble Beach, Watson denied Nicklaus his most coveted prize, a fifth U.S. Open title, with his dramatic chip-in at the 71st, and thereafter Jack's performance genuinely began to slip. He managed 10th on the money list during a winless 1983, then 15th in '84 and 43rd—at age 45—in 1985. But in April of 1986, the 46-year-old Nicklaus mounted his most memorable charge of all, clos-

Jack Nicklaus

ing with a stunning 65 to claim his sixth **Masters**, defeating Greg Norman (who bogeyed the 72nd) and Tom Kite by one. One of golf's grandest-ever triumphs, it would prove the most fitting swan song imaginable—though Nicklaus would actually contend once more at Augusta some 12 years later at age 58, a title that, had he won it, would have meant the certain end of competitive golf, for there would surely have been nothing left for us to see.

During these later years, Nicklaus became a 10-time winner on the Champions Tour (including the 1991 and '93 **U.S. Senior Opens**), one of the world's most prolific course designers, and a courageous voice regarding the dangers of unchecked equipment technology. Whatever his ancillary successes may be, they will always take a backseat to a uniquely great record that saw him stand among the modern game's leaders for winning efficiency (claiming 14.7 percent of his Tour starts before age 50) and the ability to raise his game for the Majors (15.6 percent during the same period). Perhaps more important, Nicklaus the sportsman has represented golf with a measure of class that harkens back to men like Vardon, Jones, and Nelson, setting the supreme example for on-course decorum and sportsmanship.

In the 1969 Ryder Cup matches at Royal Birkdale, for example, Nicklaus faced then–Open Champion Tony Jacklin in the final singles match, with the proceedings all knotted at 15½ points per team. All square coming to the final green, Nicklaus coolly holed a tricky four-footer for par, then immediately conceded Jacklin's shorter putt for a half, averting what surely would have been an ugly victory had Jacklin missed, while still allowing the Americans to retain the cup. It was a move typical of Jack Nicklaus, a man who has surely burned for victory as much as any golfer who ever lived, yet accepted his defeats with a graciousness and class that served to elevate an entire world's perception of the game.

PGA Tour Wins (73): 1962, '67, '72, & '80 U.S. Open; 1963, '65, '66, '72, '75 & '86 Masters; 1963, '71, '73, '75 & '80 PGA Championship; 1964 Phoenix; **1966, '70 & '78 British Open;** 1967, '72 & '73 Bing Crosby; 1967 & '68 Western Open; 1967 & '72 Westchester; 1969 San Diego; 1970 & '71 Byron Nelson; 1972 & '75 Doral; 1974, '76 & '78 Players Championship; 1975 Heritage; 1976 World Series; 1977 & '84 Memorial; 1982 Colonial; 5 Tournament of Champions, 4 Sahara Invitationals, 3 Portland Opens & 3 Walt Disney Invitationals

Intn'l Wins (11): 1964, '68, '71, '75, '76, '78 Australian Open; 1970 World Match Play

Champions Tour Wins: 10 (1990–1996)

Walker Cup: 1959 & '61 (92) **Ryder Cup:** 1969–77 & '81 (6); 1983 & '87 Capts **Presidents Cup:** 1998 & 2003 Capts

1958-1998

	58	59	60	61	62	63	64	65	66	67	68	69	70	71
Masters	-	MC	T13	T7	T15	1	T2	1	1	-	T5	T23	8	T2
US Open	T41	-	2	T4	1	-	T23	T32	3	1	2	T25	T51	2
British	-	-	-	-	T34	3	2	T12	1	2	T2	T6	1	T5
PGA	-	-	-	-	T3	1	T2	T2	T22	T3	-	T11	T6	1

	72	73	74	75	76	77	78	79	80	81	82	83	84	85
Masters	1	T3	T4	1	T3	2	7	4	T33	T2	T15	WD	T18	T6
US Open	1	T4	T10	T7	T11	T10	T6	T9	1	T6	2	T43	T21	MC
British	2	4	3	T3	T2	2	1	T2	T4	T23	T10	T29	T31	MC
PGA	T13	1	2	1	T4	3	MC	T65	1	T4	T16	2	T25	T32

	86	87	88	89	90	91	92	93	94	95	96	97	98
Masters	1	T7	T21	T18	6	T35	T42	T27	MC	T35	T41	T39	T6
US Open	T8	T46	MC	T43	T33	T46	MC	T72	T28	MC	T27	T52	T43
British	T46	T72	T25	T30	T63	T44	MC	MC	MC	T79	T44	T60	-
PGA	T16	T24	MC	T27	MC	T23	MC	MC	MC	T67	MC	T60	-

Tom Nicoll (UK/USA/Japan)

Though little is recorded of the life of Scottish-born professional-turned-architect Tom Nicoll, it is known that he attended Madras College in the town of St. Andrews before joining the flood of turn-of-the-century golfing immigrants to the United States. Having built several courses in California prior to World War I (including an early version of the historic Burlingame CC), Nichol went to Manila to design and run a course for the American government, then eventually moved on to Japan where he was one of a handful of early Westerners who helped popularize the game there. He returned to California sometime after the war, eventually retiring there.

Frank Nobilo (New Zealand)

Like most upwardly mobile golfers from Australia or New Zealand, Auckland's Frank Nobilo (b. 5/14/1960) became an international player out of necessity, establishing himself first at home (with **New Zealand PGA** wins in 1985 and '87), then in Europe, and eventually, by the late 1990s, in America. A solid ball-striker with a much-admired swing, Nobilo was remarkably consistent in Europe between 1988 and 1996, winning five times and finishing between 14th and 38th in the Order of Merit. Though his earnings peaked in 1993, his biggest wins came at the 1991 **Trophée Lancôme**, the 1995 **BMW International**, and the 1996 **Deutsche Bank**, the last a lucrative event in which Nobilo's closing 64 edged Colin Montgomerie by one.

Having cracked the PGA Tour's top 125 as a visitor in 1996, Nobilo came aboard full time in 1997 and soon won his sole American title, a play-off victory over Brad Faxon at the **Greater Greensboro Open**. He also captured the **Hong Kong** and **Mexican Opens** that year which, combined with a 23rd-place finish on the American money list, went a long way toward landing Nobilo on his third straight Presidents Cup team. Also a perennial World Cupper for New Zealand, Nobilo has recently gone into television work after shoulder surgery and significant back problems affected his ability to compete.

Greg Norman (Australia/USA)

Among the most striking and exciting golfers ever to play the game, Queensland's Gregory John Norman (b. Mt Isa, 2/10/1955) may not rank as highly as Tom Watson, Seve Ballesteros, or Nick Faldo on most all-time lists, yet he was arguably golf's most captivating figure between the reigns of Jack Nicklaus and Tiger Woods. A typically sports-oriented Australian youth, Norman only took up golf after caddying for his low-handicap mother at age 16 and worked his way down to scratch within two years. Pondering a career in the Australian Air Force, Norman instead turned professional after winning the **Queensland Junior** title. After working briefly in Sydney and for a longer stint at the Royal Queensland GC, he apprenticed for the man who would be his primary teacher, the well-known Charlie Earp.

By 1976 Norman was ready to compete around Australia—so ready, in fact, that he won his fourth start, Adelaide's **West Lakes Classic**, over a strong professional field. Like many an ambitious Aussie before him, Norman spent the next three years playing largely abroad, taking five titles in Europe and Asia as well as four more in his homeland. By 1979 he was beginning to approach the game's highest levels when a missed putt of 4 feet at the 72nd cost him the **Australian Open**. But with a work ethic to match his raw talent, Norman continued his steady improvement and took the national title for the first time the following year, by one over Brian Jones at The Lakes GC in Sydney. The victory led to an invitation to the Masters and it was at Augusta in 1981 that America got its first look at a player whose attacking style, charisma, and white-blond hair made for ideal golf television. Norman would finish fourth in his Masters debut, entertaining the media with tales of shark hunting that, inevitably, spawned his famous "Great White Shark" nickname. Three months later he added joint fourth at the PGA Championship in Atlanta, and a new international star was born.

Generally considered the longest straight driver in history, Norman soon began playing regularly in America, where his aggressiveness and larger-than-life personality ticketed him as the logical heir apparent to Palmer, Nicklaus, and Watson. Frequently he seemed capable of living up to the hype, such as the summer of 1984 when, within a five-week span, he won twice (at the **Kemper** and **Canadian Opens**), lost to Tom Watson in a play-off for the Western Open, and endured an 18-hole play-off loss to Fuzzy Zoeller in the U.S. Open at Winged Foot. This, of course, was one of the modern era's most memorable

Greg Norman, 1986

Opens with Norman blowing his approach to the 72nd into a grandstand before ultimately holing a 50-foot putt for par. Back in the fairway, thinking that Norman had made birdie, Zoeller waved the white towel of surrender—but on Monday it would be Norman who yielded when Fuzzy took the play-off with a sparking 67.

The loss at Winged Foot led to some talk—at that time largely misplaced—of Norman as a choker, and his unique "Saturday Slam" of 1986 hardly helped. In that remarkable season, Norman indeed led all four Majors after 54 holes, yet won only the **Open Championship**, his most crushing defeat coming at the PGA where Bob Tway holed a famous bunker shot at the 72nd for victory. Such a loss can only happen once in a lifetime, one might assume, but at the 1987 Masters Norman endured another notorious lightning bolt when Larry Mize drained a 45-yard pitch to snatch victory on the second hole of sudden death. Three years later David Frost would hole a bunker shot at the last to edge Norman in New Orleans, and then, barely a month later, Robert Gamez would beat him at Bay Hill by actually holing a full 176-yard 7-iron at the last!

The gods, then, were not always with him, but Norman often generated his own misery, including a badly blocked 4-iron at the 72nd which cost him a play-off with Nicklaus at the 1986 Masters, a disappointing 76 in a much-anticipated third-round duel with Nick Faldo at the 1990 Open Championship, and, the saddest of them all, the final-round 78 that eviscerated a seemingly insurmountable six-shot lead, allowing Faldo to win the 1996 Masters with a closing 67.

But if Norman is to be vilified for these losses, he must also be credited with some of modern golf's greatest work. In 1990, for example, he closed the **Doral Open** with a scorching 62, then won in a play-off by eagling the first extra hole—a 12-under-par total for 19 holes. Even more impressive were rounds played during his two Major titles, the 1986 and '93 **Open Championships**. In 1986, after opening with a weather-induced 74, Norman uncorked an almost unbelievable second-round 63 in dismal conditions, a round that stood only three putts at both the 17th and 18th away from perhaps being the greatest ever played. Then in 1993, he stormed home at Royal St. George's with a near-perfect closing 64 to beat Nick Faldo by two, a round described by Gene Sarazen as "the most awesome display of golf I have ever seen."

A fitness devotee, Norman retained his world-class skills well into his 40s, winning twice in 1997 at age 42 and taking his own homeland event, the **Greg Norman Holden Invitational**, a year later. Today he rides herd over Great White Shark Enterprises, a highly successful international business conglomerate, while receding slowly from the competitive scene. But whatever critics may say regarding his career, two Open Championships, more than 80 wins worldwide, 29 top-10 finishes in Major championships, and a record 331 total weeks ranked as the number-one player in the world add up to a large and impressive legacy, particularly when judged against the field as opposed to a generalized sense of expectations. Further, no player between Nicklaus and Woods has loomed larger over the game, or brought more excitement and epic struggle to its playing fields.

PGA Tour Wins (20): 1984 & '92 Canadian Open; **1986 & '93 British Open;** 1988 Heritage; 1990, '93 & '96 Doral; 1990 & '95 Memorial; 1994 Players Championship; 1995 & '97 World Series

Intn'l Wins (61): 1979 & '83 Hong Kong Open; 1980, '85, '87, '95 & '96 Australian Open; 1980 French Open; 1980, '83 & '86 World Match Play; 1980 & '82 Benson & Hedges; 1981 & '82 British Masters; 1984 & '85 Australian PGA; 1988 Italian Open; 1994 Johnnie Walker; 6 Australian Masters, 4 New South Wales Opens & 3 Martini Intn'ls

Presidents Cup: 1994–2000 (4)

1977-2000

	77	78	79	80	81	82	83	84	85	86	87	88
Masters	-	-	-	-	4	T36	T30	T25	T47	T2	T2	T5
US Open	-	-	T48	-	T33	-	T50	2	T15	T12	T51	WD
British	MC	T29	T10	MC	T31	T27	T19	T6	T16	1	T35	-
PGA	-	-	-	-	T4	T5	T42	T39	MC	2	70	T9

	89	90	91	92	93	94	95	96	97	98	99	00
Masters	T3	MC	MC	T6	T31	T18	T3	2	MC	MC	3	T11
US Open	T33	T5	MC	-	MC	T6	2	T10	MC	-	MC	MC
British	T2	T6	T9	18	1	T11	T15	T7	T36	-	6	-
PGA	T12	T19	T32	T15	2	T4	T20	T17	T13	-	MC	MC

Moe Norman (Canada)

Born: Kitchener, Ontario, 7/10/1929 **Died:** Kitchener, Ontario, 9/4/2004

Ontario's Murray "Moe" Norman was long widely known as one of golf's most fascinating, eccentric, and, above all, overlooked characters, a man whose legend caught up with his utterly unique talents all too late in life. A successful Canadian amateur of the mid-1950s, Norman can only be viewed as a golfing genius, a man whose bizarre, self-taught technique (stance ultra-wide, clubs gripped in his palms, a pronounced sway with almost no leg action) utterly destroyed convention, yet produced almost superhuman results. For decades, in fact, those who saw him play cited Norman as the finest striker of a golf ball they'd ever witnessed. Lee Trevino said as much, and Tom Watson observed that "He may be the most commanding ball striker in the game, ever."

Unfortunately, this unique genius was lacking several ingredients necessary to achieve golfing superstardom. A reliable putting stroke was an obvious one but more important, Moe Norman was at the very least highly eccentric and, more likely, appears to have been something of a functional autistic. As a result, his on-course behavior, while sometimes entertaining to fans, frequently was a distraction to his fellow players, particularly on the PGA Tour where Norman paid a brief visit during the late 1950s. Poorly dressed, constantly talking, and thoroughly unable to deal with crowds or the media, this remarkably talented misfit soon returned to the much smaller Canadian Tour, then ultimately made his living as a hustler before becoming a paid spokesman for several equipment companies during the 1990s.

For the record, Moe Norman did win the **Canadian Amateur** in 1955 and '56, and the **Canadian PGA** title in 1966 and '74. Perhaps most impressive, he was twice invited to the Masters as an amateur, appearing in 1956 and '57 but neither time making the cut. Not a bad playing legacy, but as anyone who saw him strike a golf ball can attest, Norman's competitive record failed to reflect even a fraction of one of golf's purest talents.

Tim Norris (USA)

A former two-time All-American at Fresno State, local product Tim Norris (b. 10/20/1957) spent only a few short years on the PGA Tour, yet he carved his place in history at the 1982 **Greater Hartford Open** when his rounds of 63-64-66-66 (259) represented the first time anyone had broken 260 in a Tour event since Mike Souchak's record 257 in 1955. Though impressively routing Ray Floyd and Hubert Green by six shots, this would prove Norris's only official Tour triumph. He is presently the men's golf coach at Kansas State University.

Andy North (USA)

For those who believe that the extreme playing conditions imposed by the USGA at the U.S. Open generate a peculiar form of golf for which a certain few players simply have a knack, a primary case in evidence is Andy North. North (b. Thorpe, Wisconsin, 3/9/1950) claimed exactly three victories during a roughly 20-year PGA Tour career, two of which were **U.S. Opens**.

The first came at Denver's Cherry Hills CC in 1978 when, playing his standard brand of smart, steady golf, North found himself leading the championship by four through 67 holes. Arriving at the 18th still two ahead, he laid up safely short of the 480-yard finisher in two, proceeded to drop the ensuing pitch into a greenside bunker, then gathered himself enough to get up and down, to edge Dave Stockton and J. C. Snead by one. North's second title came some seven winless seasons later, when he arrived at Detroit's Oakland Hills CC in 1985 as a largely overlooked competitor. Once again his fairways-and-greens, error-free style stood him in good stead, and his one-under-par 279 total proved just good enough to win by one.

A fine all-around athlete forced to concentrate on golf after high school knee problems sidelined him in football and basketball, the 6′4″ North initially went on to become a three-time All-American at the University of Florida and win the 1971 **Western Amateur** champion before turning pro. His "other" Tour win came at the 1977 **Westchester Classic**, and he was also both a Ryder Cupper (1985) and a **World Cup** winner (with John Mahaffey) in 1978. Primarily a TV broadcaster today, North is in many ways a golfing curiosity, though anyone capable of twice flourishing within the U.S. Open cauldron has certainly earned his place in history.

Dick Nugent (USA)

A 1958 graduate of the University of Illinois, Dick Nugent (b. 1931) spent six years working for architect Robert Bruce Harris before teaming up with another Harris apprentice, Ken Killian, in 1964. Their resulting firm was a major one around Chicago, contributing a good number of new designs (including 1989 PGA Championship site Kemper Lakes) while also performing unsubtle modernizations of numerous area classics. Upon the 1983 dissolution of Killian & Nugent, Nugent pioneered the use of computers in his solo designs while at least occasionally departing from the old firm's established style. Most prominent in this regard was his design for The Dunes Club, a New Buffalo, Michigan, layout routed over terrain at least somewhat reminiscent of Pine Valley.

Lorena Ochoa (Mexico)

Already the finest female golfer her nation has ever produced, eight-time **Mexican** champion Lorena Ochoa (b. Guadalajara, 11/15/1981) joined the LPGA on the heels of an all-time great American collegiate career. Twice named NCAA Player of the Year during a two-year stint at the University of Arizona, Ochoa made history by winning eight consecutive collegiate events during 2001–02, though surprisingly, she could only twice finish second in the NCAA Championship. Turning professional in 2002, she proceeded to win three times on the Futures Tour, with the resulting number-one money ranking automatically qualifying her for the LPGA circuit in 2003. Though her debut was a winless one, Ochoa finished ninth in earnings and was named Rookie of the Year, setting the table for a 2004 season that saw her first two victories (at the **Franklin American Championship** and the **Wachovia Classic**) and a level of consistently high play clearly exceeded only by Annika Sorenstam and a resurgent Meg Mallon. Though not the longest of hitters, with greater maturity and an improved ability to close when in contention, the machine-like Ochoa certainly possesses the potential to achieve superstardom.

Christy O'Connor (Ireland)

A living legend of Irish golf, Galway's Christy O'Connor (b. 12/21/1924) was a farmer's son who learned the game as a caddie before turning professional in 1951. Initially he only competed in Ireland, a fact that bears a certain irony for despite a long and prolific career, O'Connor never managed to win an Irish Open. He did, however, take the old **Carrolls International** four times between 1964 and 1972, a modest title to be sure, but O'Connor's winning of it did much to expand the game's popularity on his home soil.

Blessed with a long and wonderfully rhythmic swing, O'Connor was both a superb ball-striker and a pleasure to watch, that is until he reached the putting surface where an entirely different sort of battle was undertaken. That he never won an Open Championship is still mourned by his surviving legions, particularly as he was many times close. Indeed, he appeared among the top six finishers on seven occasions between 1958 and 1969, including third in 1961, second in 1965 (two behind Peter Thomson), and his closest call, a tie for third in 1958, when a bogey off a bunkered tee shot at the 72nd kept him out of the Thomson–Dave Thomas play-off.

O'Connor did, however, enjoy much success in Britain, claiming three titles that ranked only behind the Open in prestige: the 1957 *News of the World* match play at Turnberry and the 1956 and '59 **British Masters**, the latter of which came over amateur Joe Carr during one of the event's rare visits to Portmarnock. O'Connor also twice won the Vardon Trophy for leading the pre–European Tour Order of Merit (1961 and '62) and finished second on seven further occasions during the 1960s. Internationally, he appeared in 15 **World Cups** (teaming with Harry Bradshaw to claim Ireland's first victory in 1958 in Mexico City) and also set a Ryder Cup record by playing in 10 consecutive matches between 1955 and 1973, a mark later broken by Nick Faldo.

Known affectionately in Ireland as "Himself" in deference to his golfing stature and immense popularity, O'Connor will forever be grouped with that nation's two other postwar stars Harry Bradshaw and Fred Daly. The debate over who was best is an endless one, though O'Connor's great longevity certainly made him a much larger presence in the contemporary conscience.

Intn'l Wins (26): 1956 & '59 British Masters; 1957 PGA Match Play; 4 Carrolls Intn'l & 3 Gallaher Ulster
Ryder Cup: 1955–73 (10)

Christy O'Connor Jr. (Ireland)

The nephew (not the son) of his renowned namesake, Christy O'Connor Jr. (b. Galway, 8/19/1948) managed a three-decade career on the European Tour that saw him regularly rank among the top 50 in the Order of Merit, climbing as high as seventh in 1975. In that year he collected two of his four career wins (at the **Martini International** and the **Irish Open**), though his biggest title was certainly the 1992 **British Masters** where he defeated Tony Johnstone in sudden death at Woburn. Today a senior player both in Europe and America, Christy Jr. will long be remembered for his 230-yard 2-iron to the 18th green at the Belfry which, upon finishing 3 feet from the cup, cemented a Ryder Cup tie for the European side (and retention of the cup) in 1989.

Lew Oehmig (USA)

A legend in his home state of Tennessee, Lewis W. Oehmig starred at the University of Virginia during the late 1930s, then returned home to dominate Tennessee amateur golf as nobody has before or since. It is not so much Oehmig's record of eight **Tennessee Amateur** titles that impresses as much as the time frame in which they were won, a span of 34 years that included wins in five separate decades. Though never a U.S. Amateur champion, Oehmig did capture the **U.S. Senior Amateur** in 1972 and '76 and captained a victorious American Walker Cup team in 1977, at Shinnecock Hills.

Brett Ogle (Australia)

A talented junior and amateur in his native Australia, Sydney's Brett Ogle (b. 1962) qualified for the PGA Tour in late 1992, then won in only his second start at the 1993 **Bing Crosby**. A long hitter but a decidedly shaky putter, Ogle proved the Crosby to be no accident by beating Davis Love III by one at the 1994 **Hawaiian Open**, giving him two Tour victories in less than a year. Already a winner of several notable titles in his homeland, including the 1990 **Australian PGA**, Ogle was soon beset by both personal and (further) putting problems and stayed away from competitive golf for a time before ultimately retiring in 2001.

Mac O'Grady (USA)

Minneapolis native Mac O'Grady (b. 4/6/1951) may be golf's finest example of the adage that nothing takes the place of persistence. Originally playing under his given name of Phil McGleno, O'Grady went through PGA Tour qualifying school an astounding 17 times before finding success in the mid-1980s, winning twice and earning over $1 million. His first win, at the 1986 **Greater Hartford Open**, came in a play-off over Roger Maltbie after O'Grady's closing 62 made up huge ground. The following winter he held off a star-studded field to claim the **Tournament of Champions** at La Costa, before fading slowly but steadily from the top ranks.

An eccentric and often volatile personality who was suspended from the Tour for six weeks in 1986, O'Grady claims equal proficiency left-handed as right and actually pursued a new-millennium comeback from the left side, renaming himself Mac O'Grady II. For several years in the early 1990s he gained a following as an instructor, but he has thus far chosen to pass on the Champions Tour in favor of a semi-secluded life in Palm Springs.

Ayako Okamoto (Japan)

Though never a Major champion, Ayako Okamoto (b. Hiroshima, 4/2/1951) managed to carve out quite a career for herself over 12 full seasons on the LPGA Tour, logging 17 career wins, eight top-10 money rankings, and a Player of the Year award in 1987. After single wins in 1982 and '83, Okamoto soared to third place on the 1984 money list with three victories. From 1986 through 1988, she claimed nine more titles, four of which came during a career-best 1987 which featured an impressive 17 top-10 finishes in 24 total starts.

If Okamoto failed to win that elusive Major, it certainly wasn't from lack of competitive play, for during one 1983–91 run she notched 20 top-10 finishes in 35 Majors, including three solo seconds in four du Maurier Classics and five top-3 finishes in six years at the LPGA Championship. Okamoto scaled back her schedule considerably in her late 40s and though not quite a Hall of Famer, her 60 victories worldwide surely make her Japan's finest-ever female competitor.

LPGA Wins (17): 1982 Welch's; 1983 Rochester; 1984 Women's British Open; 1987 Samsung WC; 1989 Corning

Clarence Olander (South Africa)

Amateur Clarence Olander stood among South Africa's golfing elite during the 1930s, winning the national **Amateur** in 1932, '34, and '36, the last in memorable fashion at Royal Cape when, standing 7 down through 21 holes against Maurice (Bobby) Bodmer, he stole the 22nd by pitching in from off the green to launch a grand comeback. That same season Olander recorded a rare double by also winning the **South African Open** (contested over the same course) after handling Johnny Robertson in a 36-hole play-off, 146-151. Olander also captured seven straight **South African Border** titles from 1927 through 1934, claimed numerous regional victories, and failed to defend his Amateur title in 1937 only through the great misfortune of meeting a young Bobby Locke in the final.

José Maria Olazábal (Spain)

Born and raised adjacent to a golf course where much of his family worked, José Maria Olazábal (b. Fuenterrabia, 2/5/1966) was a golfing prodigy, traveling to the United Kingdom often enough to become the only player ever to win **British Boys**, **Youths**, and **Amateur** titles—the latter over Colin Montgomerie at Formby in 1984. Also claiming **Spanish** and **Italian Amateurs**, Olazábal turned professional in 1985 and soon began a 10-year run that saw him win 15 titles in Europe and finish seven times among the top 7 in the Order of Merit. He also made selective ventures to America where, in 1990, he loudly introduced himself with a 12-shot victory at the **World Series of Golf**, torching Firestone CC with an opening-round 61, then tacking on three straight 67s for a record 262 total.

Olazábal made further international noise in 1994 by winning the **Masters**, finishing 69-69 to overtake Tom Lehman and follow his friend and mentor Seve Ballesteros as the second Spaniard to don the Green Jacket. A second win at the **World Series** capped his 1994 season. In the interim, a victory over Ernie Els and Bernhard Langer at the **Volvo PGA** helped cement his position among the world's best. By 1995, however, Olazábal was suffering foot pain so great that he withdrew from the Ryder Cup and was soon confined to his bed. After being initially misdiagnosed as an arthritic condition, the problem was eventually traced to his back. After extensive therapy, Olazábal

returned in 1997 to win the **Turespaña Masters** in just his third start. The following season saw only one win (at the **Dubai Desert Classic**) but in 1999 Olazábal surprised everyone by outdueling another sentimental favorite, Greg Norman, to win his second **Masters**, an emotional triumph for a man who'd watched the event from a horizontal position just four years earlier.

Olazábal has further made his presence felt in the Ryder Cup where a sterling 15-8-5 career mark includes an amazing 11-2-2 record in foursomes/four-ball when teamed with Ballesteros. The pair particularly excelled during Europe's breakthrough "road" victory at Muirfield Village (1987) and subsequent retention of the Cup at The Belfry two years later. Similar to Ballesteros, and to some degree the new Spanish star Sergio Garcia, Olazábal can be an erratic sort whose occasionally wild driving is offset by some marvelous powers of recovery. With an aggressive, accelerating move through the hitting area (which perhaps keeps his clubhead on-line fractionally longer), he can be a very accurate iron player—a handy skill to have given some of the places he's been known to drive the ball.

PGA Tour Wins (6): 1990 & '94 World Series; **1994 & '99 Masters;** 2002 San Diego
Intn'l Wins (21): 1986 European Masters; 1988 Belgian Open; 1989 Dutch Open; 1990 & 2000 Benson & Hedges; 1990 Irish Open; 1990 Trophée Lancôme; 1994 Volvo PGA; 1998 Dubai; 2001 French Open
Ryder Cup: 1987–91, '93, '97 & '99 (6)

1984-2004

	84	85	86	87	88	89	90	91	92	93	94
Masters	-	MC	-	MC	-	T8	13	2	T42	T7	1
US Open	-	-	-	T68	-	T9	T8	T8	MC	MC	MC
British	MC	T25	T16	T11	T36	T23	T16	T80	3	MC	T38
PGA	-	-	-	MC	-	MC	T14	MC	MC	T56	T7

	95	96	97	98	99	00	01	02	03	04
Masters	T14	-	T12	T12	1	MC	T15	4	T8	30
US Open	T28	-	T16	T18	WD	T12	MC	T50	MC	-
British	T31	-	T20	T15	MC	T31	T54	MC	MC	-
PGA	T31	-	MC	MC	MC	T4	T37	69	T51	MC

Porky Oliver (USA)

Born: Wilmington, Delaware, 9/6/1916 **Died:** Wilmington, Delaware, 9/20/1961

Though he made several prewar PGA Tour appearances, Edward "Porky" Oliver established himself as one of America's top touring professionals in the years following

World War II, winning eight times and contending regularly in all three American Major championships. At the Masters, the corpulent and very popular Oliver finished second—five distant of a streaking Hogan in 1953. The pair met again in the 1946 PGA Championship final, with Oliver leading by three at lunch before Hogan shot 30 going out, ultimately winning 6 and 4. But it was at the U.S. Open where Oliver would suffer his greatest heartbreak, being disqualified from playing off with Gene Sarazen and Lawson Little in 1940 after he and five other players were ruled to have gone out ahead of their appointed tee times. The players had done so attempting to beat an anticipated rainstorm and though Sarazen and Little both argued for Oliver's inclusion in the play-off, their appeals were denied.

While Oliver also finished second at the 1952 U.S. Open, tied for third in 1947, and was widely portrayed as a luckless runner-up sort, his list of victories was not unimpressive, including the 1940 **Bing Crosby** and **Phoenix Open** and the 1941 **Western Open** where he defeated both Hogan and Byron Nelson at the Phoenix CC. He also played on victorious Ryder Cup teams in 1947, '51, and '53 and was selected to be the nonplaying captain in 1961. Sadly, Oliver was terminally ill with cancer by the time of the event, forcing his withdrawal.

Peter O'Malley (Australia)

A former **Australian Junior** and **New Zealand Amateur** champion, Peter O'Malley (b. Bathurst, 6/23/1965) was considered one of the finest prospects ever to emerge from New South Wales upon turning pro in 1987. Playing primarily in Europe, he has been, if not a world beater, consistent and successful with 11 top-60 finishes in the Order of Merit and three victories since 1989. His first win, the 1992 **Scottish Open** at Gleneagles, featured an amazing final-round 62 that included a closing five holes played in 7 under par, enough to nip Colin Montgomerie by two. Despite ranking among the best tee-to-greeners in Europe, O'Malley has a relatively paltry record in Major championship competition, largely because he has scarcely entered those played in America. At the Open Championship, his best finish, by leaps and bounds, was a tie for eighth in 2002.

Mark O'Meara (USA)

While the notion of underrating a man with a U.S. Amateur title and 14 PGA Tour victories might seem strange, there is little doubt that Mark Francis O'Meara (b. Goldboro, North Carolina, 1/13/1957) greatly advanced his place in history by adding to that ledger, at age 41, the 1998 **Masters** and **Open Championship**. In the former, O'Meara closed with back-to-back birdies, his last on a dramatic putt, to defeat Fred Couples and David Duval by one. Then in July, O'Meara's final-round 68 at Royal Birkdale drew him even with upstart Brian Watts, setting the stage for a four-hole play-off which O'Meara won by two strokes. To cap off this middle-age Player of the Year performance, O'Meara soon defeated close friend Tiger

Ed "Porky" Oliver, 1941 Western Open champion

Woods in the final of the **World Match Play** at Wentworth one up for a third world-class triumph.

Nineteen years earlier, while a student at Long Beach State, O'Meara first gained national attention by ending John Cook's defense of his **U.S. Amateur** title in an 8 and 7 final rout at Canterbury CC. His ensuing professional career has been long and fruitful, for in addition to 16 Tour wins and two Majors, O'Meara has banked over $13.5 million in official money, only once finishing outside of the top 45 between 1984 and 1999. The 1995 **Canadian Open** was likely his biggest non-Major title, though O'Meara has scored a remarkable five victories at the **Bing Crosby**, the last, 1997's one-shot triumph over both Tiger Woods and David Duval, being particularly impressive.

A four-time Ryder Cup selection, O'Meara has long felt at home playing overseas, claiming victories on five continents. In 2004 he proved himself one very competitive 47-year-old by beating Woods and Ernie Els, among others, in capturing the **Dubai Desert Classic**, one of the European Tour's stronger-fielded events.

PGA Tour Wins (16): 1985, '89, '90, '92 & '97 Bing Crosby; 1995 Canadian Open; 1997 San Diego; **1998 Masters; 1998 British Open**

Intn'l Wins (8): 1997 Trophée Lancôme; 1998 World Match Play; 2004 Dubai

Ryder Cup: 1985, '89, '91, '97 & '99 (5)

1981-2004

	81	82	83	84	85	86	87	88	89	90	91	92
Masters	-	-	-	-	24	48	T24	T39	T11	MC	T27	T4
US Open	MC	58	-	T7	T15	T41	MC	T3	MC	MC	MC	MC
British	T47	-	-	-	T3	T43	T66	27	T42	T48	T3	T12
PGA	T70	-	MC	T25	T28	MC	MC	T9	MC	T19	MC	MC

	93	94	95	96	97	98	99	00	01	02	03	04
Masters	T21	T15	T31	T18	T30	1	T31	MC	T20	MC	T8	T27
US Open	MC	MC	-	T16	T36	T32	MC	T51	MC	T18	T35	-
British	MC	-	T49	T32	T38	1	MC	T26	T42	T22	T65	T30
PGA	MC	-	T6	T26	T13	T4	T57	T46	T22	MC	MC	MC

Sukree Onsham (Thailand)

Standing only 5'3" and weighing 110 pounds, Sukree Onsham (b. 10/28/1943) bears the dual distinction of being Thailand's first internationally competitive professional as well as the game's smallest-ever player of prominence. Onsham was never much of a winner on the Far East circuit, yet his consistently competitive play was enough to get him invitations to the Masters in 1970 and '71 (both missed cuts), and he was also a three-time World Cup participant. He remains active around the Asian Senior Tour to this day.

Peter Oosterhuis (UK)

Europe's premier player for several years after Tony Jacklin's cooling down, London native and 1967 Walker Cupper Peter Arthur Oosterhuis (b. 5/3/1948) finished first in the European Tour's Order of Merit from 1971 through 1974—a record that remained intact until Colin Montgomerie topped the Order for seven straight years during the 1990s. Throughout this productive period, the 6'5" Oosterhuis claimed nine official victories, including back-to-back **French Opens** in 1973 and '74, the 1974 **Italian Open,** and the 1973 **Volvo PGA** at Wentworth, where his 280 total bested Dale Hayes and Donald Swaelens by three. Focusing his attention mostly on America by the mid-1970s, Oosterhuis achieved some steady success before winning the 1981 **Canadian Open** at Glen Abbey, where his 280 total edged course designer Jack Nicklaus, Bruce Lietzke, and Andy North by one.

Oosterhuis was also a regular contender in Major championships, perhaps not so surprisingly at the Open Championship (where he finished second in 1974 and joint second—one behind Tom Watson—in 1982) but also at the Masters where, in 1973, he held a three shot 54-hole lead before ultimately sharing third, the best result yet recorded by a British player. Oosterhuis was also an especially dangerous opponent in Ryder Cup play, accumulating a 14-11-3 record over six consecutive matches (1971–81), all of which were won handily by the Americans. His 6-2-1 singles record was particularly impressive as he counted among his victims Gene Littler, Johnny Miller, J. C. Snead, and, on two occasions, Arnold Palmer!

An especially talented player on and around the greens, Oosterhuis was a shrewd competitor who has since become one of television's more skilled and knowledgeable commentators.

Maureen Orcutt (USA)

Though prominent as a groundbreaking *New York Times* sports reporter from 1937 onward, New York–born Maureen Orcutt (b. 1907) was also an elite amateur golfer, capturing roughly 65 events of prominence over a seemingly endless career that still saw her winning club events during the 1990s! A long and aggressive type with recovery skills of the Walter Hagen style, Orcutt began competing seriously at age 11—that is, if winning her mother's clubs from her in an 18-hole match can truly be called "serious."

In 1926 she won the first of 10 **Women's Metropolitan Amateurs**, with her last coming an incredible 43 years later in 1968. In the interim she claimed three straight **North & South Amateurs** (1931–33), back-to-back **Canadian Ladies** (1930 and '31), and a record seven **Eastern Amateurs**, as well as senior events (including two **U.S. Senior Women's Amateurs**) in profusion. Curiously

Orcutt never quite made it at the U.S. Women's Amateur, losing in the final in both 1927 and '36 (the latter to England's Pam Barton at Canoe Brook CC). She was, however, a mainstay of prewar Curtis Cup teams, participating in the first four matches from 1932 to 1938.

As a measure of Orcutt's remarkable longevity, one need only open virtually any issue of *Golf Illustrated* or *The American Golfer* from the late 1920s and early '30s to find her youthful image splashed across their pages, competing—often successfully—in one glamorous locale or another.

Pat O'Sullivan (USA)

Ten times the **Connecticut Women's Amateur** champion between 1947 and 1968, Patricia O'Sullivan (b. 1927) appeared on the losing 1952 Curtis Cup team and captured **North & South** titles in 1950, '51, and '53. Her great claim to fame, however, was a seemingly unlikely victory—while still an amateur—in an LPGA Major championship, the 1951 **Titleholders**, where her 301 total at the Augusta (Georgia) CC defeated a field that included Patty Berg, Louise Suggs, and the great Babe Zaharias. Also a two-time **Eastern Amateur** winner, O'Sullivan (who later played under the married name of Lucey) eventually turned professional, though she found only limited success on the LPGA Tour.

Komyo Otani (Japan)

Often referred to as "the father of Japanese golf," English-educated Komyo Otani was the man primarily responsible for bringing the great British architect C. H. Alison to Japan in late 1930, a visit that resulted in the creation of several of that nation's elite layouts and changed its golfing landscape forever. Having already toured many of the world's great courses with writer Chozo Ito in 1925, Otani would later design several layouts of his own, including the postwar Tokyo GC, site of the 2001 Japan Open.

Francis Ouimet (USA)

Born: Brookline, Massachusetts, 5/8/1893 **Died:** Newton, Massachusetts, 9/2/1967

As long as golf is played in America, the name of Francis de Sales Ouimet will remain in the limelight, for it was Ouimet's spectacular upset of Britain's Harry Vardon and Ted Ray at the 1913 **U.S. Open** that jump-started the game's soon-to-be-enormous popularity on these shores. Ouimet was little more than a kid at the time of his victory, a 20-year-old amateur who, history tells us, entered

the Open largely because it was played at The Country Club of Brookline, an old-money club located across the street from his middle-class home. Yet the notion that Ouimet came completely out of left field to steal the title is largely romanticized fiction. He was, in fact, a fine area player who earlier in 1913 had been eliminated from the U.S. Amateur by eventual champion Jerome Travers after finishing second (behind Chick Evans) in medal qualifying. Ouimet had also won the 1913 **Massachusetts Amateur**, noteworthy because during his semifinal match against John G. Anderson, he stood two down with six to play before winning with a run of six consecutive threes, an almost unheard of barrage given the equipment of the day.

But the U.S. Open was another game entirely, particularly after an outgoing 43, followed by a double bogey at the 64th, appeared to dash Ouimet's final-round hopes entirely. But with all seemingly lost, he managed, quite remarkably, to play the final six holes in 2 under par and draw even, mandating an 18-hole play-off with Vardon and Ray the next morning. For Ouimet the pressure was so great as to not exist at all, for what chance did he have against the reigning British Open champion Ray and the utterly immortal Vardon? He was, we can be sure, pleased simply to remain in contention when the threesome all turned in 38, but then he was out in front with a birdie at the 10th and doggedly hanging on. By the 17th, Ray was gone but Vardon stood only one back, until a bunkered tee shot cost him a five and Ouimet rolled home a 15-footer for birdie, effectively clinching victory. In the end, his even-par 72 not only won the title, it actually defeated the Britons' *best ball,* and America had itself a new sport splashing across its front pages.

Perhaps because it might detract from the longshot storyline, Ouimet seldom receives enough credit for the rest of his golfing career. He was, for example, the **U.S. Amateur** champion of 1914 (ending Travers' reign with a 6 and 5 rout in Manchester, Vermont) as well as that season's **French** champion. He took both the 1917 **Western Amateur** and the 1920 **North & South**, and his joint fifth in defense of his Open title in 1914 at Midlothian was more than respectable. He also enjoyed great longevity, reaching eight more semifinals at the U.S. Amateur but bearing the great misfortune of having to deal with Bobby Jones in his prime. It is no coincidence then that following Jones' 1930 retirement, a 39-year-old Ouimet promptly captured his second **Amateur** title in 1931 at Chicago's Beverly CC. He was also a popular competitor in the United Kingdom where, after a rocky start in 1914, he got as far as the semifinals of the British Amateur, losing 3 and 2 to Roger Wethered in 1923.

Though involved in a famous amateur-status wrangle (over his employment in the sporting goods business) with the USGA, Ouimet participated in the first eight Walker Cup matches, amassing a 9-5-2 overall record and twice serving as playing captain. He was then chosen nonplaying captain for four more matches that, given the war interruption, took his involvement up through 1949. Having made many friends in Britain during these years, Ouimet received the extraordinarily high honor of being selected the first non-British captain of the R&A in 1951.

1913-1932

	13	14	15	16	17	18	19	20	21	22
US Open	1	T5	T35	-			T18	-	-	-
US Am	T9	1	T9	-			T5	2	T9	T9
Brit Am	-	T33						-	T65	-
British	-	*						-	-	-

	23	24	25	26	27	28	29	30	31	32
US Open	T29	-	T3	-	-	-	-	-	-	-
US Am	T3	T3	-	T3	T3	T17	T3	T17	1	T3
Brit Am	T3	-	-	T9	-	-	-	T3	-	-
British	-	-	-	-	-	-	-	-	-	-

*Result unverified—made cut but finished outside top 30.

Francis Ouimet at the U.S. Amateur, Beverly Hills Country Club, Chicago, Illinois

Simon Owen (New Zealand)

At times battling Bob Charles for the rank of New Zealand's best golfer, Simon Owen (b. 12/10/1950) was the winner of more than 10 events in his native region and two European Tour titles, most notably the 1974 **German Open** where he beat Peter Oosterhuis in a play-off. Owen, however, will be best remembered for going head-to-head with eventual winner Jack Nicklaus at the 1978 Open Championship at St. Andrews, actually taking the lead through 69 holes before a bad-bounce bogey at the 70th, combined with a clutch Nicklaus birdie, ultimately left him tied for second. He also reached the final of that season's prestigious World Match Play Championship at Wentworth, where he was beaten 3 and 2 by Isao Aoki. More recently, after running away with an over-50 event in New Zealand, Owen sold his farm to finance an assault on the European Senior Tour, a raid which has thus far yielded one victory and, one hopes, enough money to eventually buy back the homestead.

Charles Owens (USA)

Winter Haven, Florida, native Charles Owens (b. 2/22/1930) had a cup of coffee on the PGA Tour in the early 1970s, an extended military career forcing too late a start to achieve any real success. The founding of the Champions Tour a decade later brought new life, however, and the 6'3" Owens made good, particularly in his career year of 1986 when he won twice and finished eighth on the money list with over $200,000. Owens attracted significant publicity at this time, both for playing on a fused left knee and, quite remarkably, for utilizing a crosshanded grip on every shot. He was also a pioneer in the use of the long putter, having designed the original "Slim Jim" that served as forerunner to many of today's extended models.

Dinah Oxley (UK)

An outstanding junior player who took the **British Girls** title at age 14, Surrey's Dinah Oxley (b. 10/17/1948) also added **English** (1965) and **French** (1969) junior crowns to her résumé before moving on to the adult ranks. This Oxley did most memorably in 1970 when she scored, at age 21, the fine double of winning both the **English** and **British Ladies Amateurs**, then repeated as **English** champion the following summer. A four-time Curtis Cup participant between 1968 and 1976, Oxley was a majestic ball-striker who clearly looked Britain's best until the talented Michelle Walker came along some four years behind her. Oxley was, for some time, club secretary at Worplesdon GC, longtime home of the famed Worplesdon Foursomes.

Joe Ozaki (Japan)

The youngest of Japan's three famous golfing brothers, Naomichi "Joe" Ozaki (b. Tokushima, 5/18/1956) has long been overshadowed by the epic success of brother Jumbo, yet has put together a fine international career in his own right. The winner of 31 titles at home (including the 1999 **Japan Open**), Joe also competed regularly on the PGA Tour in the latter half of the 1990s, placing 66th on the money list in 1995 and tying for second at the 1997 Buick Open. Twice in the top 10 at the Players Championship (1993 and '95), Joe has yet to record a top-10 result in a Major championship, though he has rarely appeared in the Masters or U.S. Open. Standing 5'8" and weighing 160 pounds, he is a bit less physically imposing than Jumbo and hits the ball noticeably shorter.

Jumbo Ozaki (Japan)

Without question, Japan's greatest-ever domestic golfer is former professional baseball prospect Masashi "Jumbo" Ozaki (b. Tokushima, 1/24/1947), whose 6'2", 200-pound frame is likely as memorable among Japanese golfers as his mind-boggling total of 111 homeland victories. Though competing almost exclusively on a tour that offers limited competition compared to that found in America or Europe, Ozaki's numbers and longevity remain impressive. He has, for example, won five **Japan Opens** and six **Japan PGAs**, led the domestic money list on 11 occasions between 1973 and 1998, represented his country internationally for nearly a quarter-century, and been selected for the 1996 Presidents Cup at age 49 (though he was replaced by brother Joe upon declining the invitation). Perhaps most impressive of all, he remained among the top 20 players in the official World Ranking until age 52, easily the oldest man to retain that lofty position.

Of course, one knock on the World Ranking is that it rates players from lesser tours unduly well, and many have questioned Jumbo's status based on his only once having won abroad—and the 1972 **New Zealand PGA** is seldom confused with the U.S. Open. Also, while the long-hitting Ozaki has scored well in the handful of lucrative Japanese events frequented by Western players, a record of only three top 10s in 44 Major championship starts (plus 18 missed cuts) hardly stacks him among the international elite.

It's a shame that Jumbo, a colorful and exciting player, didn't choose to play in the West more frequently, but with the vast riches to be earned by a top player in Japan, he likely never felt the need.

P

Larry Packard (USA)

A former landscape architect and postwar apprentice to Robert Bruce Harris, Edward Lawrence Packard (b. 1912) was extremely active during the 1960s and '70s, designing or redesigning as many as 300 courses, primarily in the Midwest. As seems the birthright of former Harris assistants, his redesign efforts were centered largely around Chicago and included modernizing such Golden Age classics as Bob O'Link, Olympia Fields, and Northmoor, among others. Packard favored heavily undulating greens as well as the occasional double-dogleg par 5, and is perhaps best known for his 63 holes at the Innisbrook Resort in Tarpon Springs, Florida.

Alf Padgham (UK)

Caterham, England's Alfred Harry Padgham (1906–1966) was the possessor of one of his era's finest swings, a short but eminently smooth motion that drew praise from all quarters. Sporting a huge set of hands, Padgham was a superior ball-striker whose putting stroke only caught up once he began to swing the blade rather uniquely, with arms extended as if playing a chip. The winner of many smaller titles and events that expired long before the record-keeping of the European Tour began, he was the *News of the World* match-play champion in 1931 and '35 as well as the winner of the **Irish** (1932), **German** (1934), and **Dutch** (1938) **Opens**.

For all of that, Padgham's career year came in 1936, when he won the now-defunct **Silver King** and *News Chronicle* tournaments as well as his lone **Open Championship**, a one-shot victory over Jimmy Adams at Hoylake that was sealed by a dramatic birdie at the 72nd. By most accounts, it was now Padgham's putting that put him over the top, with his peculiar method ranking him, at least temporarily, among the best in memory. It must also be noted that he was four more times among the top five at the Open, including a second at Muirfield in 1935. He also made one noble postwar run, at age 42, in the 1948 contest, trailing the leaders by two through 54 holes before running out of gas with a closing 77. Curiously, for a man who'd twice won at match play in the

News of the World, Padgham was a clean 0-6 in three Ryder Cup appearances.

Intn'l Wins (15): 1931 & '35 PGA Match Play; 1932 Irish Open; 1934 German Open; **1936 British Open;** 1938 Dutch Open
Ryder Cup: 1933–37 (3)

Estelle (Lawson) Page (USA)

Though born in East Orange, New Jersey, Estelle Lawson (1907–1983) lived much of her life in North Carolina where she largely dominated pre- and postwar golf proceedings, capturing the **Carolina States** women's championship nine times between 1932 and 1949. She managed nearly an equal performance at Pinehurst's prestigious **North & South Amateur**, a more national event at which she won a record seven victories from 1935 to 1945. Later to marry Julius Page, Lawson was hardly just a regional phenomenon, for she made it to the semifinals of the **U.S. Women's Amateur** on five occasions, pushing through to the final in 1937 and '38. On the first occasion she routed an 18-year-old Patty Berg 7 and 6 at the Memphis CC to claim the title, only to be clipped 6 and 5 by Berg at Illinois' Westmoreland CC a year later. A Curtis Cup player in 1938 and '48, Page would almost certainly have appeared in all four interceding matches, which were cancelled due to the war.

Se Ri Pak (South Korea)

Thirty times an amateur winner (and six times as a professional) in her native Korea, Se Ri Pak (b. Daejeon, 9/28/1977) came to the United States full time for the 1998 season and caught fire, winning four times, finishing second on the money list, and fairly breezing to Rookie of the Year honors. Even more remarkable, her first two LPGA victories were both Majors, starting with May's **LPGA Championship** where she defeated Donna Andrews and Lisa Hackney by three. Seven weeks later, in Kohler, Wisconsin, Pak became the youngest-ever **U.S. Women's Open** winner in the longest tournament in women's golf history, defeating amateur Jenny Chuasiriporn on the second hole of sudden death after the two deadlocked in a full 18-hole play-off. Six days later Pak won again at the **Jamie Farr Kroger Classic** (where her second-round 61 set an all-time LPGA record) and, two weeks further on, yet again at the **Giant Eagle Classic**. Perhaps the most amazing thing about her breakout year was that Pak somehow lost out to a Major-less Annika Sorenstam in Player of the Year balloting.

Save for an oddly winless 2000, Pak seldom broke stride over the next five seasons, winning 17 times and consistently logging second- or third-place money finishes, an overall level of performance second only to Sorenstam. She also added two more Majors to her ledger (the 2001 **Women's British Open** and 2002 **LPGA Championship**) and played impressively consistent golf, notching 17 and 20 top-10 finishes in 2002 and '03, respectively. Perhaps the most impressive element to this performance was

Pak's age, for her consistency tended to belie someone so young, and her LPGA Championship made her the youngest woman ever to win four Major titles. However...

With only a single win (at **Kingsmill**) through most of 2004, Pak is, at present, something less than the dominant force of six years ago. Further, she faces the very real possibility of being passed by blossoming stars such as Grace Park, Lorena Ochoa, and Cristie Kerr, all of whom have been climbing at impressive speed. With Pak's proven talent, however, an equally likely scenario sees further maturity and the ironing out of some management and business issues placing her back among the elite for many years to come.

LPGA Wins (22): 1998 & 2002 LPGA Championships; 1998 U.S. **Women's Open;** 1999 Samsung WC; **2001 Women's British Open;** 2003 Safeway

1997-2004

	97	98	99	00	01	02	03	04
Dinah	-	-	T13	T15	T11	T9	T15	T16
LPGA	-	1	T7	T3	T39	1	T46	T17
US Open	T21	1	T14	T15	2	5	50	T32
dM/Brit*	-	T41	T13	T7	1	T11	2	T21

*du Maurier replaced by the Women's British Open in 2001.

Anne-Marie Palli (France)

Though seldom a major factor on the LPGA Tour, Ciboure, France's Anne-Marie Palli (b. 4/18/1955) was a dominant amateur around Europe during the 1970s, claiming the **British Girls** crown in 1973 as well as multiple national titles in **Spain,** the **Netherlands, Morocco,** and, of course, **France.** With four **French Ladies Closed** titles (between 1972 and 1976) under her belt, she joined the LPGA Tour in 1979, eventually scoring a pair of wins but logging only one top-10 Major championship finish (a tie for ninth at the 1990 LPGA Championship) in nearly 60 starts. Palli has continued competing in America into her late 40s, though she hasn't cracked the top 100 money winners since 1992.

Arnold Palmer (USA)

The son of a Latrobe, Pennsylvania, golf course superintendent and professional, Arnold Daniel Palmer (b. 9/10/1929) may not have been the post–World War II era's best golfer but he was very likely its most important, his aggressive, fan-friendly style going a long way toward rekin-

dling the game's American popularity following the doldrums of Depression and war.

Having developed a skilled and powerful style by his mid-teens, Palmer had seen little competition outside of Western Pennsylvania prior to receiving a golf scholarship to Wake Forest, ultimately dropping out after his close friend and teammate Buddy Worsham was killed in a car accident. Palmer then spent three years in the Coast Guard before returning briefly to amateur golf, where his biggest previous splash had been reaching the semifinals of the 1948 and '49 North & South Amateurs. Perhaps a bit more mature now, Palmer stepped up in the 1954 **U.S. Amateur** at the CC of Detroit where he beat Frank Strafaci and Frank Stranahan en route to the final, then claimed the title with a 1-up victory over 1937 **British Amateur** champion Robert Sweeny Jr.

Though blessed with enough confidence for any battle, Palmer's early forays on the PGA Tour hardly suggested him as the likely heir to the Hogan throne. But in 1957 he won four times and crept up to fifth place on the money list, setting the stage for a three-victory 1958 breakthrough that saw him claim the first of four Tour money titles. The key to 1958 was Palmer's first Major championship, a **Masters** victory that included a bit of controversy when Arnold apparently took five at the par-3 12th, later to have it ruled a three when tournament officials opted to accept his version of a disagreement over an imbedded ball ruling and the subsequent playing of a second.

A "quiet" 1959 followed (three wins and a return to fifth on the money list) before Palmer hit his peak, a four-year run from 1960 through 1963 that included 29 victories, five of his seven Major championships, two Vardon Trophies (1961 and '62), two Player of the Year awards (1960 and '62), and money finishes of 1st, 2nd, 1st, and 1st. In 1960 in particular, Palmer at times looked unbeatable, claiming four victories before the **Masters**, then taking the Green Jacket by a single stroke with dramatic birdies at the 71st and 72nd. Two months later at the **U.S. Open**, he further enhanced his reputation for final-round charges by famously driving the par-4 opener at the Cherry Hills CC en route to a closing 65 and a two-stroke victory over an amateur named Jack Nicklaus. With a professional Grand Slam potentially in the offing, Palmer tore off to his first Open Championship at St. Andrews and with a closing 68 found himself only one behind Australian Kel Nagle with Nagle facing a 10-footer for par at the 71st. But Nagle coolly holed his putt, routinely parred the last, and Palmer (who later finished seventh in the PGA Championship) was left alone in second.

He returned to Britain the following year and this time was successful at Royal Birkdale, his one-stroke victory over Dai Rees greatly helping to reestablish the **Open Championship's** prominence in modern golf, a status lost when most American pros had stopped coming over after the war. A year later, Palmer claimed his third **Masters** in a play-off with Gary Player and Dow Finsterwald before defending his British title brilliantly, his record-setting 276 total standing six shots better than Nagle and fully 13 ahead of third-place finishers Brian Huggett and Phil Rodgers. It was also during this eight-win 1962 that the first sign of trouble appeared, specifically at the U.S. Open where, playing in his native Pennsylvania, Palmer was defeated in a play-off by the 22-year-old Nicklaus, now a dangerous young professional.

With seven victories (including the prestigious **Los Angeles** and **Western Opens**) in 1963, Palmer held Nicklaus off one final time in the money race, though Jack's wins at both the Masters and the PGA suggested the changing of the guard. A final victory at the 1964 **Masters** still positioned Arnold prominently among the game's elite, but as Nicklaus got his professional sea legs, the issue was soon settled. Palmer would still win with some regularity (a dozen more titles during the 1960s) but his next few seasons were largely defined by an epic meltdown in the 1966 U.S. Open at Olympic, where he squandered a seven-stroke lead with nine to play and ultimately lost an 18-hole play-off to Billy Casper, perhaps a fitting cap to the largest final-round collapse in Major championship history.

Arnold Palmer

By the late 1960s and early '70s, Palmer's skills were in a noticeable, though hardly catastrophic decline. His aggressive swing and trademark contorted follow-through were, by some accounts, actually hitting the ball straighter but his short game and putting were regressing markedly. If Palmer's game was slipping, however, his wallet certainly wasn't, for Arnold was the first top athlete to be represented by Mark McCormack, thus tying him into all manner of commercial enterprises, both golfing and non-golfing alike. He established himself as a big-name golf course designer (working on more than 300 projects worldwide) and later engaged in a Champions Tour career, which may well have been motivated more by a sense of obligation than a genuine desire to play. He also served as the USGA's primary spokesman for a number of years, then inexplicably turned on the organization by doing paid endorsements for a nonconforming driver in a move as baffling (for an affluent man) as it was bizarre.

Backtracking some four decades, however, there can be little doubt that Palmer's charisma and style married beautifully with golf's first ventures into television, resulting in a much-needed shot of popularity for the game at a crucial time. Though Walter Hagen did more to improve the lot of American golf pros, the half-joking notion that a quarter of every dollar earned by modern players is owed to Arnold Palmer is not without some validity, his impact on the game's commercial viability having surely represented at least that much.

Though usurped by Nicklaus, Palmer's overall record—62 PGA Tour wins (fourth all-time), seven Major championships, four Masters titles in seven years, and a 22-8-2 record in six Ryder Cups—more than qualifies for iconic status. Not surprisingly then, he has retained a large measure of his popularity decades past the point of competitive viability, a favor he has repaid to his legions of fans by making multiple farewell appearances at the Masters right into the new millennium.

PGA Tour Wins (62): 1955 Canadian Open; 1957 & '61 San Diego; 1957 & '66 Houston; **1958, '60, '62 & '64 Masters;** 1960, '61 & '62 Texas; **1960 U.S. Open;** 1961, '62 & '63 Phoenix; 1961 & '63 Western Open; **1961 & '62 British Opens;** 1962 Colonial; 1963, '66 & '67 Los Angeles; 1969 Heritage; 1971 Westchester; 5 Bob Hope Desert Classics, 3 Thunderbird Classics & 3 Tournament of Champions

Intn'l Wins (10): 1964 & '67 World Match Play; 1966 Australian Open; 1971 Trophée Lancôme; 1975 Spanish Open; 1975 Volvo PGA

Champions Tour Wins: 10 (1980–88)

Ryder Cup: 1961, '63 (c), '65, '67, '71 & '73 (6); 1975 Capt

1953-1978

	53	54	55	56	57	58	59	60	61	62	63	64	65
Masters	-	-	T10	21	T7	1	3	1	T2	1	T9	1	T2
US Open	MC	MC	T21	7	MC	T23	T5	1	T14	2	T2	T5	MC
British	-	-	-	-	-	-	-	2	1	1	T26	-	16
PGA	-	-	-	-	-	T40	T14	T7	T5	T17	T40	T2	T33

	66	67	68	69	70	71	72	73	74	75	76	77	78
Masters	T4	4	MC	26	T36	T18	T33	T24	T11	T13	MC	T24	T37
US Open	2	2	T59	T6	T54	T24	3	T4	T5	T9	T50	T19	MC
British	T8	-	T10	-	12	-	T6	T14	-	T16	T55	7	T34
PGA	T6	T14	T2	WD	T2	T18	T16	MC	T28	T33	T15	T19	MC

Johnny Palmer (USA)

Though dramatically overshadowed by the unrelated Arnold's arrival some 10 years behind him, Eldorado, North Carolina's Johnny Palmer (b. 1918) was very much the successful player both at home and abroad, winning seven official PGA Tour titles, plus the 1954 **Mexican Open.** His biggest victory in terms of prestige was the 1947 **Western Open,** where his score of 270 edged Bobby Locke and Porky Oliver by one. In terms of money, however, Palmer's 1949 18-hole play-off victory over Jimmy Demaret at George S. May's **World Championship of Golf** paid a cool $10,000, astronomical money in those postwar days. Also a winner of the 1952 **Canadian Open** (by a stout 11 strokes) and the 1954 **Colonial,** Palmer appeared in one Ryder Cup match (1949) and was immortalized by a popular set of irons bearing his name.

Sandra Palmer (USA)

Ft. Worth, Texas, native Sandra Palmer (b. 3/10/1943) was something of a late arrival to the center stage, succeeding around the fringes with four **West Texas Amateur** titles, the 1963 **Texas Women's Amateur,** and a runner-up at the 1961 Women's Intercollegiate while playing for North Texas State. Her 1964 debut on the LPGA Tour was thus less-heralded than some others, and it would, in fact, be eight long seasons before Palmer logged her first official tour win. These early campaigns were hardly unsuccessful, however, as Palmer was never worse than 31st on the money list and broke into the top 10 in 1968, '69, and '70.

Palmer finally won in 1971 (at both the **Sealy Classic** and the **Heritage Open**) and was off and running, enjoying a full decade of top-10 money rankings (1968–77) and a 16-year stretch that would include all 19 of her official wins, two of which were Major championships. The first of these was the 1972 **Titleholders**, where she beat Mickey Wright and Judy Rankin at Pine Needles. The second came during her peak year of 1975, in which Palmer won the **U.S. Women's Open** (by four at the Atlantic City CC), the-not-yet-Major **Dinah Shore**, and both the tour money title and Player of the Year honors. All told, Palmer would man-age 11 wins from 1973 to 1977 before dropping from the top 25 in 1983, then returning to 14th in 1986 behind her final victory, the **Mayflower Classic**. She fell permanently from the top 100 in 1990.

LPGA Wins (19): 1972 Titleholders; 1975 Dinah Shore; **1975 U.S. Women's Open**

1964-1986

	64	65	66	67	68	69	70	71	72	73	74	75
Dinah												
LPGA	T24	T19	T21	T10	35	83	3	T12	T12	T8	3	T6
US Open	-	T15	T17	T23	T21	T32	T4	T37	T19	T6	T37	1
du Maur												

	76	77	78	79	80	81	82	83	84	85	86
Dinah								T30	T16	MC	T10
LPGA	T33	T7	T17	WD	T10	T10	T10	T16	T17	T47	T28
US Open	2	T8	T34	T2	MC	T29	T18	-	-	T39	T44
du Maur				T19	T10	WD	T9	T58	-	MC	T17

Also won Titleholders, as listed above.

John Panton (UK)

Though in some ways a big fish in a small pond, Pitlochry's John Panton, M.B.E. (b. 1916) shared Scottish professional golfing dominance with Eric Brown for roughly two decades after World War II, winning the **Scottish Professional** title eight times, with sundry smaller victories adding up well beyond that number. Though only six times a champion of what might be considered European Tour–caliber events, Panton did count among his victories the 1956 *News of the World* match play as well as the 1951 **Daks Tournament**. He was never in a position to win the Open Championship but did twice crack the top-five, first taking solo fifth in 1956 at Hoylake (when he was low Briton), then tying for fifth in 1959 at Muirfield. A husky sort known for his superior iron play, Panton thrice represented Britain in Ryder Cup play, going a disappointing 0-5 in 1951, '53, and '61.

Grace Park (South Korea)

One of the bright young stars in women's golf, South Korean native Grace Park (b. Seoul, 3/6/1979) moved to Arizona at age 12 and proceeded to dominate the American amateur game like few others. A six-time AJGA All-American and two-time Player of the Year, Park won a total of 55 junior, collegiate, and amateur events and, in a spectacular 1998, was named an All-American at Arizona State while becoming the first player since Patty Berg (in 1938) to sweep the **Western, Trans-Mississippi,** and **U.S. Women's Amateurs** in a single season. In 1999, Park finished eighth in the U.S. Women's Open while still an amateur, then joined the Futures Tour where she won five times in 10 starts, was named Player of the Year, and, playing on a sponsor's exemption, finished second in the Safeway LPGA Championship.

Surprisingly, Park did not tackle the LPGA Tour with great ease, winning once in both 2000 and '01 but finishing no better that 19th and 23rd on the money list. Single wins would also follow in 2002 and '03 as her play improved considerably, with a sixth-place ranking in the former and third (behind 19 top 10s in 26 starts) in the latter. Having lost a play-off to Annika Sorenstam at the 2003 LPGA Championship, Park broke through for her first Major at the 2004 **Dinah Shore**, rolling in a 6-foot birdie atop Aree Song's dramatic 72nd-hole eagle to win by one.

A player whose style matches her considerable talent, Grace Park remains a full notch behind Annika Sorenstam at the time of this writing. Still just in her mid-20s, however, she is one of a small handful of young stars who, with a bit more maturity, should figure among the favorites to ultimately ascend the Sorenstam throne.

Mungo Park (UK)

The fifth son of farmer James Park of Musselburgh, Scotland, Mungo Park (1835–1904) was a talented player who has forever lived in the shadow of his older brother Willie and his nephew, the legendary Willie Park Jr. Mungo did, however, enjoy one triumphant moment by winning the 1874 **Open Championship** on his home Musselburgh Links, a victory made sweeter by the fact that he beat four-time champion Young Tom Morris to do so. As an habitual traveler who frequently made his living as a sailor, Mungo missed a good deal of his playing prime while at sea, entering most of his Open Championships relatively late in his competitive life.

A skilled club- and ballmaker in the family tradition and an occasional course architect, Mungo was also one of the earliest Scottish pros to take up employment in England, working at Alnmouth and West Cumberland. When he passed, an old friend sent an obituary to the British magazine *Golfing*, which recalled an evening past when "the moonlight was playing on the bosom of the great North Sea and all was calm and sweet. We were fighting the day's battles o'er again, when Mungo, in all seriousness remarked to me: 'I hope when I dee that they'll bury me under this seat, so I can heer ye a' talking gowf.'"

Mungo Park II (UK/Argentina)

The fourth son of Willie Park Sr. and nephew of Mungo, Musselburgh's Mungo II (1877–1960) was himself a fine player who engaged in several notable challenge matches in addition to learning the club- and ballmaking business. In 1897 he traveled to New York to run a fledgling branch of the family business. The store was closed in 1898, and he soon became professional at Dyker Meadow in Brooklyn and, in the winter, at the Galveston (Texas) CC. He moved back to help Willie Jr. with his development at Huntercombe in 1901 but in 1904 demonstrated the wanderlust known to have inhabited his namesake by moving to Argentina, where he became pro at the Buenos Aires GC, a three-time **Argentine Open** winner, and, eventually, a prolific course designer. Like many Britons gone abroad, Young Mungo returned to England to serve during World War I, then briefly repaired to Argentina before heading to America to work with Willie's booming design business. Thus it was Mungo who shepherded a mentally declining Willie back to Scotland in 1924 before completing the firm's American projects, eventually retiring back to Musselburgh in 1936.

Willie Park Jr. (UK)

Born: Musselburgh, Scotland, 5/24/1864 **Died:** Edinburgh, Scotland, 5/24/1925

The son of the eponymous four-time Open Champion and clubmaker extraordinaire, Willie Park Jr. grew up in the seaside town of Musselburgh, where the famous racecourse-encircled links has seen golf played for several hundred years. His was an upbringing conducive to golfing greatness, for in addition to his father, his uncle Mungo sported a sparkling résumé, as did brothers Frank, Jack, and young Mungo, and close boyhood friend Willie Dunn Jr.—all fine players and future professionals.

Young Willie twice reached the pinnacle of nineteenth-century golf, winning the 1887 **Open Championship** at Prestwick, then recapturing the Claret Jug two years later on his home turf at Musselburgh, where he defeated the outspoken Andra Kirkaldy in a 36-hole play-off. Though perhaps something of an erratic ball-striker, he possessed a blue-chip short game, the foundation of which was his universally acclaimed talent with the putter. In those days of rough, unmanicured greens, he was known to practice his stroke for as long as 12 hours, believing that properly grooved, it could overcome even the wildest drives and approaches. Most frequently it did, gaining Park a grand reputation and leading him to coin the timeless phrase, "A man who can putt is a match for anyone."

Curiously, despite so fine a playing record, Young Willie is perhaps best remembered for an event he lost, a 72-hole challenge match played in 1899 against six-time Open champion Harry Vardon. The challenge—for a then enormous £100-a-side—had been issued by Park in 1898, but it took the better part of a year, and considerable wrangling, before the match was actually played. In the event, however, the negotiations may have been more exciting than the game, for Vardon, two up following the first 36 holes at North Berwick, simply took off upon returning to his home course Ganton, ultimately routing Park 11 and 10.

A bit of an iconoclast, Young Willie operated outside of the professional herd, always running an independent business and never, during his adult life, seeking employment in service to a club. He was also of a competitive nature and held immense confidence in his own game, going so far as to issue an open challenge to play anyone, anywhere, at any time, for any amount of money. As Park is believed to have been the only professional to regularly stake himself in such challenges (as opposed to wagering money put up by wealthy backers), this was no easy boast.

Such confidence traveled nicely into the business world where Park carved his niche as golf's entrepreneurial pioneer. Taking over the family equipment company from his father in the early 1890s, he expanded it both within the United Kingdom and to America, using his name, a reputation for quality, and countless design innovations to achieve widespread success. His major advances included the convex shaping of a driver's clubface, a forerunner of today's lob wedge known as the "lofter," an offset putter, and a diamond-mesh pattern for the cover of a golf ball, the latter placing him nearly a decade ahead of his time in grasping the aerodynamics of ball flight.

Not surprisingly, Young Willie also broke ground in the field of golf literature, becoming the first professional ever to author a book, *The Game of Golf* (Longmans, Green, 1896). That this prized volume included a landmark chapter on course design is fitting, for in addition to his other accomplishments, he is generally accepted as having been the first golf architect—that is, the first to organize his practice into a full-fledged business, codify his design beliefs in writing, and, perhaps most important, create standards of strategy and sophistication soon to be followed by a generation of celebrated architects.

Park's Old course at Sunningdale has long been considered his calling card though at Huntercombe he once again started a trend, launching what is believed to have been the world's premier real estate/golf venture. The first of the great British architects to venture abroad, Park made three trips to the United States, the last a seven-year stay from 1916 to 1923. During these visits he built or rebuilt more than 50 courses, the modern standard bearers of which are Long Island's Maidstone Club and the North course at Olympia Fields.

Willie Park Sr. (UK)

Well known as a premier ball- and clubmaker in the old Scottish town of Musselburgh, Willie Park Sr. (1833–1903) was also one of the leading players of his day, claiming a piece of immortality by winning the first **Open Championship** in 1860 at Prestwick, defeating his primary period rival Old Tom Morris by two. Park would again beat Morris by two in 1863 (following a pair of Morris victories in the interim), then clip his own brother David by an identical margin for his third win in 1866. Eleven years later in 1875, at age 42, Willie would finally match both Old and Young Tom with four Open titles by beating Bob Martin, once again at Prestwick.

Park was considered an excellent putter, a skill he clearly passed along to his talented son Willie Jr. Yet he was perhaps better recognized for his powerful driving, a part of his game that intimidated, among others, Allan Robertson, who never responded to Park's advertised challenges for a £100 match. Old Willie was also a pioneer architect, building at least 35 somewhat primitive courses in the United Kingdom and Ireland, joining Old Tom and

Tom Dunn as the first men to actively design courses beyond what might be considered their native ground.

A true pillar of golf's early development, Willie Park Sr. remains a bit underappreciated solely because of the monumental status accorded his celebrated, namesake son.

Sam Parks Jr. (USA)

Born across the border in Ohio but raised in Pittsburgh, Sam Parks Jr. (1909–1997) took his first golf lessons from Gene Sarazen before starring for the University of Pittsburgh, then turning professional. Primarily a club pro, Parks took full advantage of the 1935 **U.S. Open's** visit to nearby Oakmont CC by playing countless practice rounds, his local knowledge helping him to a 299 total and a surprise two-shot victory over Jimmy Thomson. Largely because this was Parks' sole PGA Tour victory, he is frequently dismissed as a flukish winner. Yet as a regular player on the old winter tour, he had already been invited to the first Masters in 1934 and played in 16 overall, plus 13 U.S. Opens, and the 1935 Ryder Cup matches. While winning the Open proved a singular occurrence, the suggestion that Parks was somehow out of his league simply is not supported by fact.

Jesper Parnevik (Sweden)

The son of Sweden's most popular comedian, Stockholm's Jesper Bo Parnevik (b. 3/7/1965) has long been identified by his upturned baseball cap and drainpipe slacks, as well as such additional eccentricities as the eating of volcanic dust to help clean his digestive system. Beyond all of this color, Parnevik also represents a bit of history, for he was the first Swedish man to reach the highest levels of international golf, not only winning four times in Europe but taking on the American PGA Tour with equal success.

Parnevik experienced four solid (if unspectacular) European campaigns before a five-shot victory over Payne Stewart at the 1993 **Scottish Open** keyed a 17th-place finish in that season's Order of Merit. Unlike many who might have chosen to polish their European résumé a bit longer, Parnevik immediately began splitting time with the PGA Tour in 1994, initially playing less than 20 American events a year while also winning the 1995 and '98 **Scandinavian Masters** and the 1996 **Trophée Lancôme** at home, and placing second at both the 1994 and '97 Open Championships. But 1997 also saw him 12th on the American money list and by 1998 he'd become a regular Tour winner, first at that season's **Phoenix Open**, then in 1999 at **Greensboro**, in 2000 at the **Bob Hope** and the **Byron Nelson**, and in 2001 at the **Honda**. Having already represented Sweden in the 1994 and '95 World Cups, Parnevik became an obvious Ryder Cup choice from 1997–2002, though his growing commitment to the American Tour meant that he, like Sergio Garcia, would generally have to be a captain's pick.

By late 2001, however, Parnevik's game had slipped a bit, consigning him to 63rd and 118th on the 2002 and '03 Tour money lists. A 40th-place finish in 2004 brightened his fortunes a bit, but we must wonder if, as he approaches 40, we have already seen the affable Swede's best golf.

Craig Parry (Australia)

Stockily built at 5'6" and weighing 175 pounds, Craig David Parry (b. Sunshine, 1/12/1966) utilizes an over-the-top cutter's swing as well as the long putter—neither to the delight of purists—but his worldwide record over nearly two decades certainly speaks for itself. A winner of 19 international events, including national Opens in **Germany**, **Italy**, and **Japan** and the 1992 **Australian PGA**, Parry claimed his largest-ever title at the 2002 **WGC-NEC Invitational** (the old World Series of Golf) in Seattle, his 65-66-65 finish helping him to cruise home by four.

Known as Popeye for his powerful forearms, Parry has long been the typical Australian pro, playing what lucrative events he can at home, then heading off to either Europe or America for the rest of the year. Ironically, Parry had only just refocused on Europe, after 10 winless campaigns in America, when the WGC victory came along. Though he followed it up with only 16 Stateside appearances in 2003, he once again made noise in America in 2004 by winning the **Doral Open** in dramatic fashion, holing a full 6-iron at Doral's famous 18th on the first hole of sudden death to defeat a luckless Scott Verplank in remarkable style.

PGA Tour Wins (2): 2002 World Series; 2004 Doral
Intn'l Wins (19): 1989 German Open; 1991 Scottish Open; 1991 Italian Open; 1992 Australian PGA; 1997 Japan Open
Presidents Cup: 1994–98 (3)

The Pasha of Marrakech (T'hami el Glaoui) (Morocco)

One of golf's more intriguing characters was T'hami el Glaoui (1879–1956), the Pasha of Marrakech during Morocco's colonial era and a confirmed lover of the game. Frequently playing in plus-fours (was there a stranger sight traipsing about the North African desert?), the Pasha built the Marrakech Royal GC in 1920, piping in water from the nearby Atlas Mountains for purposes of maintenance.

Any suggestion that either the Pasha or the condition of his course was of a high golfing caliber would seem absurd, yet no less than Winston Churchill played with him there on several occasions prior to World War II.

Jerry Pate (USA)

The injury-shortened career of Jerome Kendrick Pate (b. Macon, Georgia, 9/16/1953) raises an interesting historical question: Which will be longer remembered, Pate's hitting one of the great shots of all time to win a U.S. Open or diving into a lake to celebrate a far lesser triumph?

Pate first drew national attention while attending the University of Alabama by winning the 1974 **U.S. Amateur** (2 and 1 margin over John Grace at Ridgewood CC), appearing in the Walker Cup the following year. He then became a household name during his rookie year on the PGA Tour by catching John Mahaffey over the final nine holes of the 1976 **U.S. Open** at the Atlanta Athletic Club, ultimately taking a one-shot lead to the 72nd. After driving into the light rough, Pate faced a 194-yard approach over water with the alternative of laying up and likely settling for a play-off. With typical Pate confidence he went for it, drilled a 5-iron within 2 feet of the pin, and won the Open by two.

One month later, a final-round 63 led to a follow-up victory (over Jack Nicklaus) at the **Canadian Open**, which in turn was backed by a win in the 1977 **Phoenix Open**, plus 1977 and '78 **Southern Open** titles. Then in 1981, Pate again fronted the sports page when, upon ending a drought with a victory at the **Memphis Classic**, he made good on a Saturday promise and dove into a greenside lake in celebration. Never one to shy away from good publicity, the amiable Pate then followed his 1982 victory at the **Players Championship**—the first edition to be played at Pete Dye's famed TPC at Sawgrass—not only by going for another swim but by also tossing both Dye and PGA Tour Commissioner Deane Beman into the drink before him.

Unfortunately Pate's skyrocketing career was soon cut short by major shoulder problems from which he could never fully recover, limiting him to eight career wins and a single Ryder Cup appearance. On a PGA Tour frequently accused of lacking personality, Pate's loss was palpable, for his skill, affability, and aesthetically unequaled swing combined to make him a first-rate drawing card. At times Pate seemed unable to win as frequently as his considerable talent appeared to suggest, and his failures (e.g., a third-round 87 in the 1976 Open Championship) were occasionally epic. But with that magical swing, a spate of top-10 Major championship finishes, and the kind of cool confidence that greatness feeds on, a healthy Jerry Pate seemed destined to rank among the finest players of his era.

1975-1984

	75	76	77	78	79	80	81	82	83	84
Masters	37	-	T14	T18	T41	T6	T5	T3	-	-
US Open	T18	1	MC	T16	T2	MC	T26	MC	MC	-
British	-	80	T15	60	T25	T16	T19	DQ	-	-
PGA	-	T4	5	T2	T5	T10	T11	T9	T23	MC

Steve Pate (USA)

Long known as "Volcano" for his explosive temper, former UCLA star Steve Pate (b. Ventura, California, 5/26/1961) has seen peaks and valleys in his long career, finishing as high as sixth on the PGA Tour's money list in 1991 and as low as 274th in an injury-shortened 1996. By 1999 he'd climbed all the way back to 13th, then had to return to the Tour's Qualifying Tournament to reacquire playing privileges by 2003. Throughout this odyssey, Pate managed to win six Tour events (including the 1988 and '92 **San Diego Opens**) and play in the 1991 Ryder Cup, while suffering injuries with causes ranging from car accidents to tripping on a dock, and finally a second auto collision en route to the '91 Ryder Cup banquet. Never dull, Pate has long been a threat to win anytime he's rolling and an apparition whenever he's not.

Billy Joe Patton (USA)

A flashy and charismatic player, North Carolina's William Joseph Patton (b. 4/19/1922) was twice the low amateur at both the Masters (1954 and '58) and the U.S. Open (1954 and '57), as well as a three-time **North & South Amateur** winner (1954, '62, and '63) and a two-time **Southern Amateur** champion (1961 and '65). A powerful player with an extremely quick swing, he was occasionally wild off the tee but a master of the unlikely recovery, making him ideal for the match play inherent to the Walker Cup. Indeed, in five playing appearances between 1955 and 1965, Patton ran up an overall record of 11-3 (including a 5-2 mark in singles play) before serving as the American captain in 1969.

Unfortunately, despite such credentials, Patton is generally best remembered for his failure to win the 1954 Masters after leading the field at the halfway mark. Paired with Ben Hogan on Sunday, Patton aced the par-3 sixth and still held the lead upon reaching the 13th fairway. There he elected to go for the green in two, dumped his wooden approach into the creek bed, left his third shot in the hazard, and ultimately made seven. A watery bogey at the 15th compounded his misery, leaving Patton to finish a disappointingly memorable third.

Corey Pavin (USA)

As the star of a UCLA team that included future PGA Tour players Duffy Waldorf, Steve Pate, Jay Delsing, and Tom Pernice Jr., Corey Pavin (b. Oxnard, California, 11/16/1959) certainly arrived on the professional scene with a strong upside. But at 5'9" and weighing only 155 pounds, his relative lack of length was held out as cause for concern. Pavin's resultant success—14 PGA Tour wins, a U.S. Open, and $14 million in career winnings—would certainly illustrate that though a profound advantage, great length still wasn't everything. But then again, few modern American players have possessed Pavin's all-around shotmaking skills or general reliability with a putter.

After a 1983 season spent winning overseas, Pavin arrived on Tour polished and ready, finishing 18th on the 1984 money list and winning the **Houston Open** as a rookie. He would improve to sixth place in 1985 and though not always in the top 10, failed to crack the top 50 only once during the next 11 seasons. Not surprisingly, his game was particularly well-suited to older courses, which required more well-rounded shotmaking, and it is no coincidence that he won twice at Riviera, Colonial, and, to a lesser degree, Waialae. Ditto for his performance at San Antonio's Oak Hills CC where, during the 1988 **Texas Open**, Pavin's 259 made him only the fifth player in Tour history to break 260, running away to an eight-shot victory.

His competitive peak unquestionably came in 1995, however, when a 225-yard 4-wood at the 72nd finished 5 feet from the hole, clinching his sole Major championship, the **U.S. Open** at Shinnecock Hills. Beginning the final round three behind leader Greg Norman, Pavin's closing 68 came, not surprisingly, on a golf course far more suited to creative play and shotmaking than many of the USGA's more monotonous Open venues. It also marked Pavin's peak in a more literal way as he would drop to 18th on the money list the following season, then fall primarily outside of the top 100 thereafter.

Perhaps due to his early experience overseas, Pavin never confined himself strictly to American competition, winning 10 full-field events around the world, including victories in Asia, New Zealand, and Europe. His creative game obviously being well-suited to match play, Pavin also built a strong 8-5 record during three Ryder Cup appearances.

PGA Tour Wins (14): 1985 & 96 Colonial; 1994 & '95 Los Angeles; **1995 U.S. Open**

Intn'l Wins (10): 1983 German Open; 1983 South African PGA; 1993 World Match Play

Walker Cup: 1981 **Ryder Cup:** 1991–95 (3) **Presidents Cup:** 1994 & '96 (2)

1985-1999

	83	84	85	86	87	88	89	90	91	92	93	94	95	96	97	98	99
Masters	-	-	T25	T11	T27	T42	50	-	T22	3	T11	T8	T17	T7	T43	T41	MC
US Open	MC	-	T9	MC	WD	MC	-	T24	T8	MC	T19	MC	1	T40	MC	MC	T34
British	-	T22	T39	MC	MC	T38	-	T8	MC	T34	T4	MC	T8	T26	T51	MC	MC
PGA	-	T20	T6	T21	MC	T17	MC	T14	T32	T12	MC	2	MC	T26	-	MC	T10

Eddie Pearce (USA)

His name long synonymous with high golfing expectations unattained, Ft. Myers, Florida, native Eddie Pearce (b. 3/16/1952) racked up an impressive early résumé, including victories at the 1968 **USGA Junior Boys**, the inaugural **Independent Insurance Agent Junior Classic** (1969), and the 1971 **North & South Amateur**. That same year he also challenged at the stroke-play U.S. Amateur in Wilmington, Delaware, losing by three when Canadian Gary Cowan holed a 9-iron to eagle the 72nd. Twice an All-American (though not first team) at Wake Forest, Pearce left school early, enjoying the spoils of a national golf shoe commercial before ever winning an event. He would experience a moment or two in the professional spotlight—finishing second to Jack Nicklaus at the 1974 Hawaiian Open and Bob Murphy at the 1975 Inverrary—but Pearce ultimately disappeared quietly from the Tour, still winless, by the end of the decade. A brief comeback in the early 1990s proved short-lived.

Calvin Peete (USA)

The game's first black star, Calvin Peete (b. Detroit, Michigan, 7/18/1943) has lived one of the most unique lives in the history of professional golf. One of 19 children raised in poverty in central Florida, Peete initially made his living as a traveling salesman whose customers were migrant workers in remote locales who seldom got to shop in big-city stores. He first tried golf in Rochester, New York, at age 23 and nine years later found himself, quite remarkably, on the PGA Tour.

Despite a left elbow permanently bent from a childhood accident, Peete became well known as a ball-striker and legendary for his accuracy off the tee, leading the Tour's fairways-hit category for an amazing 10 straight seasons between 1981 and 1990. More important, he parlayed these skills into wins, capturing 12 titles between 1979 and 1986 and thrice finishing among the top four on the money list. Twice a winner both in **Milwaukee** and at the **Anheuser-Busch**, Peete's biggest victory came at the 1985 **Players Championship**, where he earned a coveted 10-year exemption by defeating D. A. Weibring by three.

Occasionally bothered by a bad back during his 40s, Peete later had a budding Champions Tour career curtailed by a variety of health problems. Much earlier in his career, he'd found himself facing a different sort of obstacle: being ineligible to join the PGA of America, not because of his skin color but simply because he lacked a high school diploma. Thus upon passing the GED exam, and with several million dollars already in the bank, Peete commented dryly: "Now that I have my diploma, I expect a whole world of opportunity to open up for me."

PGA Tour Wins (12): 1985 Players Championship
Ryder Cup: 1983 & '85 (2)

Dave Pelz (USA)

A mainstay of modern instruction, short-game specialist Dave Pelz played golf at Indiana University, where regular losses to a fellow Big Ten player named Nicklaus led him to choose science over the prospect of a professional career. After serving as a NASA research scientist for 14 years, however, Pelz began, in 1975, to research the physics of golf, experimenting with club design before evolving into a teacher of putting, chipping, and pitching recognized the world over. A popular instructor of both touring pros and average players, he has written three definitive books on his subject and regularly highlights instructive programming on American cable television.

Harvey Penick (USA)

A golfer of no small talent, Harvey Morrison Penick (1904–1995) became golf professional at his hometown Austin CC (Texas) when he was 18 years of age, a title he would retain for fully 50 years. Though a strong enough player to qualify for the 1928 U.S. Open, Penick knew that his strength lay far more in teaching, in which capacity he worked with such stars as Ben Crenshaw, Mickey Wright, Kathy Whitworth, Betsy Rawls, and Tom Kite, as well as with thousands of far less-gifted amateurs. Already well known within the profession, his name took on international importance rather late in life with the publication of *Harvey Penick's Little Red Book* (Simon & Schuster, 1992), a collection of brief lessons and hints drawn from his private notebook of several decades. As the largest-selling sports volume of all time, the *Little Red Book* spawned several popular sequels both before and after Penick's death in the spring of 1995.

Toney Penna (Italy/USA)

A name familiar to all who recall the not-so-old days of fine persimmon drivers, clubmaker Antonio "Toney" Penna was born (1908) in Naples, Italy, but initially made a name for himself playing on the American PGA Tour. The 5′6″ Penna was a six-time winner in the years after World War II (most notably at the 1948 **North & South Open** at Pinehurst) whose best Major championship finish was a joint third at the 1938 U.S. Open at Cherry Hills CC.

Penna's true fame would come as a club designer, a field he fairly dominated by creating nearly every famous model produced by MacGregor from the late 1930s until leaving to start his own company in 1966. The list includes all of the famous Tommy Armour woods and irons of yesteryear, the company's entire Ben Hogan line, the ageless Tommy Armour putter, and the groundbreaking MacGregor MT Irons, all among the most sought after items of their time. It has been stated that both Hogan and Jack Nicklaus won virtually all of their biggest titles using Penna-designed clubs—not a bad item to have on one's résumé.

Frank Pennink (Netherlands/UK)

Though born in the Netherlands city of Delft, John Jacob Frank Pennink (1913–1983) lived nearly all of his life in Britain, where he established himself as a fine junior golfer, a three-year player at Oxford, and a two-time **English Amateur** champion (1937 and '38). Also a member of the victorious 1938 Walker Cup team (where he took a woeful beating, 12 and 11, in his singles match with Bud Ward), Pennink retired from competitive play after the war, only to become involved in nearly every other aspect of golf.

As an administrator, he served on several committees of the R&A and was president of the English Golf Union in 1967. As a writer he was perhaps even more prolific, serving as golf correspondent for the *Sunday Express* and the *Daily Mail* and authoring three prominent books, *Homes of Sport: Golf* (Peter Garnett, 1952), *Golfer's Companion* (Cassell, 1962), and *Frank Pennink's Choice of Golf Courses* (A. & C. Black, 1976). But it was as an architect that Pennink likely left his greatest legacy, occasionally partnering with C. K. Cotton, often working solo, and eventually being responsible for new courses in at least 20 countries, as well as renovations to such famous British tracks as Royal Liverpool, Royal Lytham & St. Annes, Royal St. Georges, and Saunton.

Notable Courses: Olgiata CC (27) (with C. K. Cotton), Italy; **Noordwijk GC, Netherlands; Royal Selangor GC, New course, Malaysia; Saunton GC, West Course, England;** Vilamoura GC, Portugal; **Woburn G & CC (36) (with C. K. Cotton), England**

Dottie Pepper (USA)

On a contemporary LPGA Tour dominated by foreign-born players, Dottie Pepper (b. Saratoga Springs, New York, 8/17/1965) spent most of the 1990s as America's last, best hope for competitiveness. Following an All-American career at Furman, Pepper (who played under the married name Mochrie from 1988 to 1995) joined the LPGA Tour full time in 1988 and truly hit stride from 1991 to 1996, when she won 12 events and finished no worse than fifth on the money list. Amidst this consistent excellence, 1992 might be considered her peak as it included Pepper's first Major, the **Dinah Shore** (won in sudden death over Juli Inkster), as well as three additional wins, the LPGA's Player of the Year award, and a Vare Trophy.

After a lull in 1997, Pepper rejoined the top 10 money winners from 1998 to 2001, with an obvious highlight being a second **Dinah Shore** title in 1999, when her record 19-under-par total ran away from Meg Mallon by six. Freely demonstrating the sort of patriotic fervor happily exploited by both promoters and the media, Pepper has welcomed the pressure incumbent to international team play, logging an impressive 13-5-2 record in six Solheim Cup appearances. However, plagued by shoulder problems during 2002, she eventually opted for surgery, clawed her way back to 14th on the money list in 2003, and then announced her competitive retirement at the end of 2004.

LPGA Wins (17): 1992 & '99 Dinah Shore; 1993 Samsung WC; 1995 Welch's; 1996 Rochester
Solheim Cup: 1990–2000 (6)

1984-2004

	84	85	86	87	88	89	90	91	92	93	94
Dinah	-	-	-	-	T7	T66	T11	2	1	T30	T19
LPGA	-	-	-	-	T45	T39	T53	T22	T5	T30	T11
US Open	T22	T55	78	T12	T3	T5	T3	T5	T6	T17	T12
dM/Brit*	-	-	-	-	T35	T18	T27	T6	T20	4	T14

	95	96	97	98	99	00	01	02	03	04
Dinah	T11	T23	T11	T9	1	2	T2	-	T51	T24
LPGA	T6	T26	T37	MC	T19	T23	T17	-	T67	T70
US Open	T13	MC	T14	T11	T14	WD	3	WD	WD	-
dM/Brit*	T12	-	T27	T14	T34	-	MC	-	T24	-

*du Maurier replaced by the Women's British Open in 2001.

Phil Perkins (UK/USA)

Thomas Philip Perkins (b. 1904) emerged from the English Midlands with a splash, winning the 1927 **English Amateur** at Little Aston, then the 1928 **British Amateur** at Prestwick, the latter in convincing 6 and 4 fashion over Roger Wethered. Perkins, according to Longhurst, "took golf more 'seriously' than was then perhaps the fashion," which was a diplomatic way of saying that he was a slow player. So slow, in fact, that during his unsuccessful attempt to defend the Amateur in 1929, a following group requested to play through on the grounds that Perkins' match had fallen two clear holes behind.

As a Walker Cupper in 1928, Perkins faced Bobby Jones in the top singles match and suffered a massive 13 and 12 defeat. Two weeks later, the pair met again in the final of the U.S. Amateur at Brae Burn, with the rampaging Jones again winning handily, 10 and 9. Despite such beatings, Perkins was apparently quite smitten by America, emigrating shortly thereafter, turning professional, and, in 1932, very nearly winning the U.S. Open. Shooting 289 at New York's old A. W. Tillinghast–designed Fresh Meadow CC, he looked sure to be playing off the next day with Bobby Cruickshank until Gene Sarazen, completing his famous "28 holes in 100 strokes" closed with a 66 to beat the both of them.

Arthur Perowne (UK)

Twice a semifinalist in the British Amateur, Arthur Herbert Perowne (b. 2/21/1930) was a native of Norwich, England, where he won the **Norfolk Amateur** some 11 times. A farmer by trade, he played on his first Walker Cup team in 1949 at age 19, then followed it up with appearances in 1953 and '59. Considered by many to be too amiable a gentleman to scale the competitive heights, Perowne drifted away from the national scene following his final Walker Cup performance.

Alf Perry (UK)

A winner of several now-deceased events in the 1930s, Coulsdon, England, native Alfred Perry (1904–1974) remains prominent in British golfing history based primarily on his splendid win at the 1935 **Open Championship** at Muirfield, a four-stroke triumph over Alf Padgham that featured record-setting rounds of 69-75-67-72. This victory, while clearly well earned, seems highly illustrative of just how powerful an asset confidence can be to one's game, for as Darwin wrote: "I never saw a man less frightened of winning... At last he needed a five and a six to win. It might have been a moment for caution. Narrowly skirting the bunkers at each hole, scorning the safe line, he hit two colossal, full-blooded cracks with wooden clubs to the heart of the last two greens and strode cheerfully to the clubhouse."

Though Perry's only other run at an important title ended in a final-round loss to Cotton at the 1932 *News of the World* PGA Match Play, he appeared in three Ryder Cups between 1933 and 1937, going 0-3-1 in one British victory followed by two losses.

Kenny Perry (USA)

In one sense Kentucky native James Kenneth Perry (b. Elizabethtown, 8/10/1960) can be viewed as one of the PGA Tour's more consistent players, for he has finished among the top 100 money winners every season since 1987, never even coming close to losing his exempt status. Conversely, he might also be seen as a decidedly streaky sort, for Perry's career has witnessed two distinct and noteworthy highs. The first came in the mid-1990s when, after seven seasons finishing between 93rd and 44th, he strung together consecutive seasons of 26th, 21st, and 13th, which included wins at the 1994 **New England Classic** and the 1995 **Bob Hope**. After cooling off toward the end of the decade, Perry returned to the top 30 in 2001 and '02, then soared once again in 2003, when back-to-back wins at **Colonial** and **Memorial**, a third triumph at the **Greater Milwaukee**, and top 10s in three Major championships landed him in a career-best sixth place. Though never a Major winner, the former Western Kentucky star did come close—and on his home turf—in the 1996 PGA Championship at Valhalla CC, where his bogey at the 72nd allowed Mark Brooks into a play-off, which Brooks promptly won in sudden death.

Frank Phillips (Australia)

Moss Vale, Australia, native Frank Phillips (b. 1932), a long-hitting, gallery-friendly sort, was a popular player in his native country throughout the 1950s and '60s. On two occasions he scaled Oz's highest golfing mountain, capturing **Australian Opens** in 1957 (by one over Ossie Pickworth and Gary Player at Kingston Heath) and 1961 (by two over Kel Nagle at Victoria). Having tied the tournament record of 270 in 1965, he might well have won it a third time too—until Gary Player's total of 264 (which featured a pair of 62s!) routed him by six. Also a five-time winner of the **New South Wales Open**, Phillips got around Asia enough to capture the national Opens of the **Philippines** (1960), **Singapore** (1961), and **Hong Kong** (1966), and partnered with Nagle on Australia's behalf in the 1958 World Cup.

Henry Picard (USA)

Born: Plymouth, Massachusetts, 11/28/1906 **Died:** Charleston, South Carolina, 4/30/1997

An elite American professional in the decade before World War II, Henry G. Picard won more PGA Tour events between 1930 and 1941 than anyone not named Sam Snead—and Snead himself only had him by one. A tall man whose graceful swing was often pronounced ideal, Picard's career total of 26 wins (20th all-time) is frequently overshadowed by Major victories in the 1938 **Masters** and the 1939 **PGA Championship**. In the former, a score of 285 was enough to beat Ralph Guldahl and Harry Cooper by two, but the latter was a more involved story. For here, playing Byron Nelson in the final at New York's old Pomonok CC, Picard came to the 36th, a short drive-and-pitch, one down. When Nelson skipped his approach to three feet, the title appeared settled but Picard followed by knocking his even closer—and laying Byron dead with a stymie in the process. On they went to sudden death where Picard got a free lift in the rough after a radio truck ran over his ball, wedged on and holed a 20-footer for a dramatic—and fortunate—victory.

Picard twice captured both the **North & South** and the **Metropolitan Opens**, took Mexico's colorful and lucrative **Agua Caliente Open** in 1935, and appeared on Ryder Cup teams in 1935 and '37. He also earned a nice footnote in golf history, having saved the fledgling career of a young and unpolished Ben Hogan by offering financial backing when Hogan's early fortunes were at their bleakest. Picard also secured Hogan an invite to the 1938 Hershey Four-Ball (a longshot that proved the Hawk's first-ever Tour win), then recommended the Texan for the Hershey CC job when he himself abandoned it for Canterbury in 1940. As a result, Hogan, in a rare moment of public sentiment, dedicated his first book, *Power Golf*, to "Henry Picard, an outstanding player, an outstanding teacher and an outstanding man."

PGA Tour Wins (26): 1934 & '36 North & South; 1935 & '39 Metropolitan; **1938 Masters; 1939 PGA Championship;** 3 Tournament of the Gardens Opens

Ryder Cup: 1935 & '37 (2)

1932-1951

	32	33	34	35	36	37	38	39	40	41	42	43	44	45	46	47	48	49	50	51
Masters			T23	4	T9	T33	1	8	T7	-	T15				T25	T6	T25	T21	T14	-
US Open	-	-	T47	T6	T5	T10	T7	T12	T12	T26					T12	MC	-	-	T12	T24
British	-	-	-	6	-	T15	-	-							-	-	-	-	-	-
PGA	T9	T9	-	T33	T9	T5	T3	1	T9	T33	-		-	-	-	-	-	-	T3	T17

Ossie Pickworth (Australia)

A fabulously colorful character of the sort so woefully lacking in modern professional golf, Sydney's Horace Henry Alfred "Ossie" Pickworth (1918–1969) remains the only man ever to capture three consecutive **Australian Opens**, doing the trick in 1946 (at Royal Sidney), '47 (at Royal Queensland), and '48 (at Kingston Heath). He would later grab a fourth title in 1954 when he routed Norman von Nida by eight at Kooyonga, but it is likely 1948 that is best remembered, coming, as it did, in a play-off against expatriate Jim Ferrier. Prior to the play-off, Ferrier stirred things up by recalling how Pickworth had caddied for him before the war—a bit of nostalgia/gamesmanship that seemed irrelevant when Pickworth beat him by three.

A jovial, rotund man who always played with a cigarette in his mouth and at great speed, the free-spirited Pickworth was, to say the least, a relaxed sort. In addition to his Open successes, he won three **Australian PGAs**, the 1950 **Irish Open** (during his one trip to Europe), and a prominent 1950 exhibition match against Bobby Locke on Royal Melbourne's famed West course, in which Locke shot 65—and lost by two. Pickworth also dominated the now-defunct **Ampol** tournament, winning it so often (six times between 1947 and 1953) that the company's bosses claimed it would be cheaper simply to appoint Ossie to Ampol's board of directors.

A remarkable talent who, by acclamation, ranks with the elite fairway wood players of all time, Pickworth teamed with Peter Thomson to land Australia third in the inaugural 1953 World Cup, ultimately retiring to a hotel that he purchased with money won in a lottery. After surviving several heart attacks, Pickworth passed away all too young at age 52, and golf had lost one of its most engaging competitors.

Manuel Piñero (Spain)

Though generally seen as Seve Ballesteros's second in the great wave of modern Spanish players, Badajoz native Manuel Piñero (b. 9/1/1952) accumulated rather a strong record in his own right, winning nine European Tour events between 1974 and 1985, finishing four times in the Order of Merit top 5, twice playing in the Ryder Cup (1981 and '85), and appearing in the 1978 Masters. Though wins at three **Madrid Opens** surely struck close to his heart, Piñero's biggest win was likely the 1977 **Volvo PGA** (where he beat Peter Oosterhuis and Tom Watson at Royal St. George's), with the 1982 **European Open** running a solid second. Also twice the **Swiss Open** champion (1976 and '81), Piñero's two Ryder Cup appearances resulted in an impressive 6-3 record, and while some may write off several foursomes victories simply to being partnered with Ballesteros, singles wins over Jerry Pate and Lanny Wadkins cannot be dismissed so easily. Piñero was not, by any measure, all the player Seve was, but as his nine **World Cup** appearances (including the individual title in 1982) serve to indicate, he certainly ran a clear second among Spanish golfers of the period.

Woody Platt (USA)

John Wood "Woody" Platt (1899–1959) was one of the Northeast's leading amateurs beginning just before 1920 and continuing on for nearly 40 years. A young man of what today might be called upper-middle-class means,

Platt skipped college entirely and focused on golf, soon defeating Francis Ouimet in 38 holes to reach the semifinals of the 1919 U.S. Amateur at age 20, where he was summarily dismissed by eventual champion Davy Herron, 7 and 6. Though this was Platt's only appearance in such rarified air, he was forever a factor on his home turf, winning a total of seven **Philadelphia Amateurs** between 1920 and 1942 and a **Pennsylvania Amateur** in 1935. His lone national title came at the inaugural **USGA Seniors** in 1955.

Far beyond these victories, however, Platt is best remembered for an unprecedented flash of greatness that took place well outside of the limelight. Playing a friendly round at Pine Valley during the 1940s, Platt birdied the first, holed a 7-iron for eagle at the second, then aced the par-3 third. When a 30-foot birdie putt fell at the long par-4 fourth, Platt, an astonishing six under par through four holes, repaired to the adjacent clubhouse for a drink—and never returned to the fifth tee.

Gary Player (South Africa)

Generally viewed as the most successful international golfer of all time, Gary Jim Player (b. Lyndhurst, 11/1/1935) has logged nearly 12 million globetrotting miles in the course of claiming some 163 professional titles on six continents. It is an impressive record indeed for a man who started out not as part of golf's gilded gentry but rather as the working-class son of a gold miner, who was additionally hindered by a limited frame, standing all of 5'7" and weighing 150 pounds in his prime. Such challenges can only be overcome with hard work and dedication, and few golfers have ever demonstrated more of these qualities than Player, a workout and diet disciple who certainly followed Ben Hogan's approach of digging his game "out of the dirt." Player also made up for his slightness by perhaps swinging more aggressively at the ball than any of golf's great modern players, seldom finishing in balance and often "walking through" the shot when his momentum carried his right foot forward into the upswing.

Developing his game while working for the well-known Johannesburg pro Jock Verwey (whose daughter he would later marry), Player turned professional at age 18 and won his first significant event, the 1955 **East Rand Open**, two years later. Even then he was already traveling far and wide, for the record shows that he defeated fellow South African Harold Henning 5 and 4 to claim the long-defunct **Egyptian Match Play** title during that same season. In 1956 Player won the first of his incomparable 13 **South African Opens** while also claiming his first titles in Britain (the **Dunlop Tournament**) and in Australia (the **Ampol**). The following year he made his initial foray onto the American circuit where he would shortly become the first foreign player to make a long-term impact. From that time forward, Player's annual round-the-world golfing odyssey was in full flight.

The first of his nine career Major titles came at the 1959 **Open Championship** at Muirfield, but not without some excitement. Needing four at the 72nd for 66 and a sure victory, Player instead closed with a disastrous six, then had to wait around, distraught, until Flory van Donck and local pro Fred Bullock also staggered home, giving him the title. A second Claret Jug came in 1968 at Carnoustie, where an eagle at the 68th helped defeat Bob Charles by two. Player's third Open title, in 1974 at Royal Lytham & St. Annes, was particularly memorable, for coming to the 71st with a comfortable lead, he hit his approach into knee-deep rough, miraculously found his ball just before his allotted five minutes expired, and scraped out a five. He then blew his approach through the 72nd green where, forced to play left-handed due the close proximity of the clubhouse, he backhanded it on and two-putted to beat Peter Oosterhuis by four.

Player also enjoyed early Major success in America, capturing his first **Masters** title in 1961 at age 25, when after rounds of 69-68-69, a closing 74 slipped him past Arnold Palmer (who double-bogeyed the 72nd) and hard-closing amateur Charles Coe. He would later win two more Green Jackets in 1974 and '78, the former by two over Dave Stockton and Tom Weiskopf, the latter in epic style with a closing 64 (featuring a back-nine 30) to beat Hubert Green, Rod Funseth, and Tom Watson by one. Having switched to a sweeping putting stroke after years of utilizing a familiar, closed-stance jab, Player then reeled off consecutive wins at the **Tournament of Champions** and the **Houston Open**, becoming only the 11th man in PGA Tour history to claim three straight victories. The jab stroke, however, would shortly return.

At the **PGA Championship**, Player's 1962 win at Aronimink (by one over Bob Goalby) was especially important, for it came at a time when he'd been fighting a minor slump. He also put up a remarkable fight at the 1969 event in Dayton, Ohio, finishing only one behind winner Raymond Floyd despite frequent harassment from spectators claiming to protest South Africa's policy of apartheid. His winning of the 1972 title at Oakland Hills is perhaps even better remembered, however, due to a 9-iron approach from deep rough at the 70th, which carried a fronting lake and finished 4 feet from the hole, sealing the victory. Player also became only the third man (after Sarazen and Hogan) to complete the career Grand Slam by taking his only **U.S. Open** title in 1965, at St. Louis's Bellerive CC. This time an 18-hole play-off was necessary to polish off Australia's Kel Nagle by three (71-74), but the win was made equally memorable by Player's donating his entire $26,000 purse to American junior golf and cancer research, which, after paying his caddie $2,000, left him with a financial loss for the week.

Gary Player

Plainly South Africa's best after Locke's 1960 car accident, Player represented his country in an impressive 16 **World Cups**, taking the team title (with Harold Henning) in 1965 in Madrid and grabbing individual honors both there and at the 1977 contest in Manila. He would also claim a total of seven **Australian Opens**, as well as several prominent titles in South America, the most notable being the 1974 **Brazilian Open** in which he shot a second-round 59, the first time 60 had ever been bettered in a national championship.

Less of a force by the early 1980s, Player's perennial dedication to proper conditioning made him an ideal candidate for the Champions Tour, where he won a total of 19 events, including the 1987 and '88 **U.S. Senior Opens**. He also took **Senior British Open** titles in 1988, '90, and '97, the latter at age 61. The following year he claimed his final Champions Tour victory as well as becoming the oldest man ever to make the cut at the Masters (finishing 46th), having set a similar record at the 1995 Open Championship at 59. Finally, Player also holds a splendid record for long-term consistency, having won at least one recognized professional title for 27 consecutive years, at least a decade longer than his nearest competitor.

For all of his greatness, Player will in many ways be best remembered for tangential things: his dedication to diet and exercise, his penchant for wearing black golf attire (to absorb the sun's heat), his great competitive drive, and his wonderfully courtly demeanor, the latter tinged with an oddly offsetting touch of ego. Accusations of twice violating golf's rules (by no less than Tom Watson and Ken Venturi) only add to the unique Player makeup, though at the end of the day, more than 185 total wins, nine Major championships, and those 12 million miles traveled clearly establish Gary Player as one of golf's all-time greats.

PGA Tour Wins (24): 1959, '68 & '74 British Open; 1961, '74 & '78 Masters; 1962 & '72 PGA Championship; 1963 San Diego; **1965 U.S. Open;** 1970 Greensboro

Intn'l Wins (141): 1956, '60, 1965-69, '72, 1975-77, '79 & '81 South African Open; 1957 Australian PGA; 1958, '62, '63, '65, '69, '70 & '74 Australian Open; 1965, '66, '68, '71 & '73 World Match Play; 1969, '79 & '81 South African PGA; 1975 Trophée Lancôme
Champions Tour Wins: 19 (1985–98)
Presidents Cup: 2003 Capt

1956-1985

	56	57	58	59	60	61	62	63	64	65	66	67	68	69	70
Masters	-	T24	MC	T8	T6	1	T2	T5	T5	T2	T28	T6	T7	T32	3
US Open	-	-	2	T15	T19	T9	T6	T8	T23	1	T15	T12	T16	T48	T44
British	4	T24	7	1	7	MC	MC	T7	T8	MC	T4	T3	1	T23	MC
PGA	-	-	-	-	-	T39	1	T8	T13	T33	T3	-	-	2	T12

	71	72	73	74	75	76	77	78	79	80	81	82	83	84	85
Masters	T6	T10	-	1	T30	T28	T19	1	T17	T6	T15	T15	MC	T21	T36
US Open	T27	T15	12	T8	T43	T23	T10	T6	T2	MC	T26	MC	T20	T43	-
British	T7	T6	T14	1	T32	T28	T22	T34	T19	MC	MC	T42	MC	MC	MC
PGA	T4	1	T51	7	T33	T13	T31	T26	T23	T26	T49	MC	T42	T2	MC

Sir Hugh Playfair (UK)

A former Major in the Indian army, Sir Hugh Lyon Playfair (1786–1861) was an avid golfer and one of the great benefactors of the town of St. Andrews, where he had attended the university. Elected mayor in 1850 (as well as captain of the R&A in 1856), Playfair was the man primarily responsible for cleaning up the town from a mid-century state of dilapidation that seriously threatened its very existence. He was also the primary mover behind both the present R&A clubhouse and its smaller predecessor and, perhaps most important, the man most responsible for building up sea-eroded land along the right side of today's first fairway, allowing for the establishment of duel fairways (albeit mostly to double greens) and the routing of the Old Course as we know it today.

Ralph Plummer (USA)

After starting his golfing life in the caddie yard at Ft. Worth's Glen Garden CC just a few years ahead of two kids named Hogan and Nelson, Ralph Plummer (1900–1982) worked as a golf professional in the early 1920s, then as an architect (under John Bredemus) until well into the 1930s. Following a postwar stint spent resurrecting abandoned courses, Plummer finally began the solo designing of new courses in the early 1950s. Working predominantly in Texas, his most famous layout might well be the Cypress Creek course of the Champions GC, site of the 1969 U.S. Open and several recent PGA Tour Championships. In truth, however, Major championship golf has seldom visited Texas and *not* seen the fruits of Plummer's labor, for he also built the Blue course of the Dallas Athletic Club (site of the 1963 PGA) and made alterations to Colonial (1941 U.S. Open) and Dallas's Northwood CC (1952 U.S. Open). Plummer even reconnected with the Glen Garden crowd, building the Preston Trail GC (former site of the Byron Nelson Golf Classic) and, with Trent Jones and Lawrence Hughes, the Shady Oaks CC (longtime home of the retired Ben Hogan).

Notable Courses: Champions GC (Cypress Creek), Texas; Preston Trail GC, Texas; Tryall G & Beach C, Jamaica

Dan Pohl (USA)

During the earlier years of his PGA Tour career, ex-Arizona Wildcat Danny Joe Pohl (b. Mt. Pleasant, Michigan, 4/1/1955) was widely recognized as one of golf's very longest hitters, a smooth-swinging powerhouse who led the Tour's long driving stats in the first two years they were kept. By 1987, however, his game had evolved enough to claim the Vardon Trophy for the Tour's lowest scoring average, a remarkable metamorphosis indeed.

But the Vardon notwithstanding, Pohl's best had already come in 1986 when his fifth-place money finish featured his only two career wins, first at **Colonial** (in a play-off over Payne Stewart), then later at the **World Series of Golf.** He would also appear in the 1987 Ryder Cup, going 1-2 in the first-ever American loss on home soil. Curiously, Pohl's best results in Major championships came during his less-refined early days when he finished third at the 1981 PGA and the 1982 U.S. Open and lost a play-off to Craig Stadler for the 1982 Masters. Beginning in the late 1980s Pohl's career was beset by injuries of all types, with surgeries to his back, neck, and both knees effectively ending his days as a competitive touring pro.

Don Pooley (USA)

University of Arizona graduate Sheldon George "Don" Pooley Jr. (b. Phoenix, 8/27/1951) was a classic PGA Tour journeyman over his 20 plus year career, winning once, in 1980, at the **B.C. Open**, then gaining a victory of real importance at the 1987 **Memorial**. Remarkably, Pooley was also the Vardon Trophy winner (for lowest scoring average) during a winless 1985, which saw him finish an incongruous 46th on the money list. Even more remarkably, he won $1 million by acing the 17th hole at Bay Hill during the 1987 Bay Hill Classic when the attention-drawing prize was offered only on the final day. Pooley later achieved consistently better results on the Champions Tour, where he won the 2002 **U.S. Senior Open** in a dramatic five-hole sudden-death play-off with Tom Watson, as well as nearly $5.8 million in prize money since 2002.

Martin Pose (Argentine)

Following in the footsteps of José Jurado, Martin Pose (b. 1911) was the second world-class player produced by Argentina, capturing his own national **Open** in 1933, '39, and '50, as well as numerous other events around South America including the inaugural **Brazilian Open** in 1945. Where Pose stepped ahead of his regional contemporaries, however, was by competing successfully in Europe, particularly during 1939 when he won the **French Open** at Le Touquet. Shortly thereafter he suffered a disappointing fate at the Open Championship at St. Andrews when, at least peripherally still in contention through the 70th, he blew himself to bits with a disastrous eight at the Road hole, including a two-stroke penalty for grounding his club in the roadside grass that was, he abruptly discovered, technically considered part of the hazard.

Sandra Post (Canada)

Obviously something of a prodigy, Oakville, Ontario's Sandra Post (b. 6/4/1948) began winning **Canadian Girls** titles at age 15, stringing together consecutive victories between 1964 and 1966 while establishing herself as Canada's first legitimate top-shelf prospect in the professional golf era. In 1968 Post became the first Canadian to

regularly play the LPGA Tour, quickly justifying the expectations by winning Rookie of the Year honors. Further, her first title was that year's **LPGA Championship** where an 18-hole play-off was required to defeat the great Kathy Whitworth by seven. The victory established Post as the LPGA's youngest-ever Major champion at 20 years and 20 days, a record that still stands today.

Unfortunately, back problems would cause her to struggle for a number of years thereafter, particularly in the early 1970s when she did little more than remain among the top 60 money winners. But starting so young, Post had a bit of time on her side, and by the late 1970s—battle-hardened but still not yet 30—she rallied to win the 1978 **Dinah Shore** and the **Lady Stroh's Open**. Her best season came in 1979 when she repeated at the **Dinah**, then added two more victories to finish second on the LPGA money list. As the Dinah Shore did not enjoy Major championship status until 1983, Post's career ledger reflects eight overall victories and a single Major, a strong record if not, perhaps, all that some might initially have forecast.

Johnny Pott (USA)

A member of a 1955 national championship team at LSU, long-hitting Johnny Pott (b. Cape Girardeau, Missouri, 11/6/1935) was a five-time winner on the PGA Tour, as well as a three-time Ryder Cup selection from 1963 through 1967 (though he did not actually appear in the 1965 match). A steady money winner who remained top-60 exempt from 1958 through 1967, Pott's biggest victory came at the 1968 **Bing Crosby** where he took a sudden-death play-off from Billy Casper and Bruce Devlin. He also won twice in 1960, at the **Dallas** and **West Palm Beach Opens**.

Ian Poulter (UK)

Thus far best recognized around the world for his offbeat fashion and wild hair styles, Hitchin, England's young Ian Poulter (b. 1/10/1976) has established himself as an up-and-comer in European golf, winning the **Italian Open** (as well as the Tour's Rookie of the Year award) in 2000 and capturing at least one title every year since. In 2003 he climbed to fifth in the Order of Merit by winning twice, first going wire-to-wire at the **Wales Open**, then closing with 66 to edge Colin Montgomerie at the **Nordic Open** in Copenhagen. With a 2004 victory at the Volvo Masters Andalucia, Poulter's continued solid play qualified him for his first Ryder Cup appearance and the chance—at least in practice rounds, perhaps—to show off his spectacular Union Jack golf slacks Stateside.

Renee Powell (USA)

Following closely behind Althea Gibson, Renee Powell (b. Canton, Ohio, 5/4/1946) was the second black player on the LPGA Tour, joining in 1967 and competing actively for 13 years. Having previously been several times junior and national champion of the minority-dominated United Golf Association, Powell never won an LPGA event, though she spent seven seasons among the top 60 money winners and managed to make a living. Powell, in fact, was not the golfing pioneer in her family, for her father Bill—frustrated by being denied access to public courses after having served his country in World War II—became the first black to design, build, and operate his own facility (Canton's Clearview GC) in 1946.

Jo Anne Prentice (USA)

Though never a dominant amateur, Alabama native Jo Anne Prentice (b. Birmingham, 2/9/1933) was a top-30-caliber player on the LPGA Tour from the late 1950s to the mid-1970s, winning six times in the process. Her best season came in 1974 when she won twice at age 42, the first victory coming at the not-yet-Major **Dinah Shore**, where she defeated Sandra Haynie and Jane Blalock in sudden death. Setting the stage, however, was Prentice's first-round 71, a 1-under-par effort accomplished amidst a massive desert sandstorm, a round frequently cited among the LPGA's all-time bad-weather best.

Webster Prentice (UK/South Africa)

James A. Webster Prentice (1885–1915) was a native of Edinburgh, Scotland, who emigrated to South Africa in approximately 1905. There he followed in the footsteps of Douglas Proudfoot (a man who'd also learned his golf in Edinburgh) by dominating the **South African Amateur**, winning in 1908, '09, '11, and '13. This last occasion (on which he cruised to a 10-shot victory over Stuart MacPherson) was especially important, for Prentice also captured the 1913 **South African Open**, making him the first to claim both national titles in a single season. Eventually killed—in his competitive prime—while fighting in World War I, Prentice's name became legend in South Africa after his will left the then-substantial sum of £60 to underwrite an ambitious and long-running junior golf program.

Phyllis Preuss (USA)

A native of Detroit who played out of Pompano Beach, Florida, Phyllis "Tish" Preuss was one of America's top female amateurs during the 1960s, winning the 1964 and '67 **North & South**, the 1963 and '67 **Eastern**, the 1968 **Southern**, three **Doherty Invitationals** (1962, '71, and '76), and two **Broadmoor Invitationals** (1971 and '78), in addition to playing on all five Curtis Cup teams from 1962 to 1970. Unfortunately, Preuss is also remembered for a record of futility set during the final of the 1961 U.S. Women's Amateur in Tacoma, Washington, where Anne Quast stampeded her to 12 down at lunch, ultimately winning by a massive 14 and 13 margin. Occasionally competing against the pros, Preuss was the low amateur at the 1963 and '68 U.S. Women's Opens.

Charles Price (USA)

In the eyes of many, Charles Price (1925–1994) falls right behind Herbert Warren Wind as America's number two postwar golf writer. A top-flight amateur player, Price made his bones as a chronicler of tournaments by playing coast-to-coast with the PGA Tour during the winter/spring of 1947–48, traveling with old friend Lew Worsham. By the late 1940s, Price had joined Bob Harlow's *Golf World*, though he would later come to greater fame as the first editor of *Golf Magazine* and, later still, as a writer for *Golf Digest*.

A native of Washington, D.C., Price authored a small but distinguished body of books, the most prominent being *The World of Golf* (Random House, 1962), an entertaining historical overview of the game from its beginnings. Garnering comparable acclaim was *The American Golfer* (Random House, 1964), an anthology of vintage articles from the eponymous Golden Age magazine, as selected by Price. His last full work, *A Golf Story* (Atheneum, 1987) covered the growth of Augusta National and the Masters while *Golfer-at-Large* (Atheneum, 1982) represents the lone published anthology of his magazine work.

Elizabeth Price (UK)

A leading British amateur in the years after World War II, London native Elizabeth Price (b. 1/17/1923) reached a total of six English or British Ladies finals, losing the first five but emerging dramatically victorious in the last, the 1959 **British Ladies** at The Berkshire. On that occasion,

Price trailed Belle McCorkindale two down through the 34th, managed to square things at the last, then won on the 37th, removing, one imagines, a rather large monkey from her shoulders. Six times a Curtis Cup player from 1950 to 1960, the short but extremely consistent Price later sold Dunlop sporting goods before serving, for many years, as a golf correspondent for the *Daily Telegraph*.

Nick Price
(South Africa/Zimbabwe)

Though of English parentage, Nicholas Raymond Leige Price (b. 1/28/1957) was born in Durban, South Africa, and raised in Zimbabwe. A fine all-around athlete as a youth, he first came to prominence upon winning the 1974 **Junior World** in San Diego, eventually turning professional in 1977. For three years Price played primarily in Europe, where he claimed only one title (the 1980 **Swiss Open**) while working his way steadily up the Order of Merit. Then in 1982 he very nearly leapfrogged the pack at the Open Championship, looking a sure winner until surrendering four shots over the final six holes to lose to Tom Watson by one.

Joining the PGA Tour in 1983, Price experienced the odd scenario of winning the lucrative **World Series of Golf** (by two over Jack Nicklaus), yet finishing 104th on the year's money list. Thereafter followed a stretch of six seasons in which his only three victories came at the 1985 **Trophée Lancôme** and lesser events in South Africa and Australia. Price's golf was hardly terrible during this period, for his average ranking on the American money list was a bearable 49th, and he only just lost the 1988 Open Championship at Royal Lytham & St. Annes when Ballesteros closed with a spectacular 65 to clip him by two. This relative lack of success eventually turned Price back to his childhood friend, instructor David Leadbetter, whose tutelage resulted in a more reliable swing and a 22nd place on the American money list in 1990.

What followed thereafter was one of the hottest runs in modern golf history, for after winning twice in 1991 (at the **Byron Nelson** and the **Canadian Open**) and reaching seventh-place in earnings, Price captured the 1992 **PGA Championship** by three shots at St. Louis's demanding Bellerive CC. His confidence soaring, he then rose to the top of the World Ranking by claiming four American titles in 1993, including the **Players Championship** (by five over Bernhard Langer) and three successive starts at **Hartford**, the **Western Open**, and **Memphis**. But it was in 1994 that Price truly peaked, for in addition to winning at the **Honda, Colonial,** and the **Canadian Open** and defending his title at the **Western**, he became the first man since Tom Watson in 1982 to capture consecutive Majors, winning the **Open Championship** at Turnberry and the **PGA** at Southern Hills. In the former, Price battled Jesper Parnevik down the stretch before a birdie at 16 and a 55-foot eagle putt at 17 gave him a one-shot victory. At the PGA, however, a streaking Price was simply untouchable, firing a tournament record 269 to rout Corey Pavin by six. Topping the money list twice, Price was the PGA Tour Player of the Year in both seasons.

His fortune thus made as he neared age 40, the sincere and extremely popular Price soon backed off a bit, spending more time with his family and suffering through the 1997 death of his longtime caddie Jeff Medlin from leukemia. He continued winning the odd event in America as well as several titles back in Southern Africa (including his three **Zimbabwe Opens**), and in his late 40s, Price still remains a threat to contend any time he tees it up, as a tie for fifth at the 2003 U.S. Open indicates.

In this context it is interesting to note that like Tom Watson, Price has an uptempo swing, the sort that has long been considered ill-suited to playing longevity. But equally like Watson, Price has superb, unvarying rhythm, and as Leadbetter observed, "if the arms and body work in 'sync', it's difficult to swing the club *too* fast." When on his game, as he was in the mid-1990s, there have been few more "locked-in" players, for Price has been the consummate marksman, picking apart courses with his laser-like accuracy in a manner reminiscent of another compact swinger, Ben Hogan.

PGA Tour Wins (18): 1983 World Series; 1991 Byron Nelson; 1991 & '94 Canadian Open; **1992 & '94 PGA Championship;** 1993 Players Championship; 1993 & '94 Western Open; 1994 & 2002 Colonial; **1994 British Open;** 1997 Heritage
Intn'l Wins (24): 1980 Swiss Open; 1985 Trophée Lancôme; 1997 South African PGA; 3 Million Dollar Challenges & 3 Zimbabwe Opens
Presidents Cup: 1994–2003 (5)

1978-2004

	78	79	80	81	82	83	84	85	86	87	88	89	90	91
Masters	-	-	-	-	-	-	MC	-	5	T22	T14	MC	-	T49
US Open	-	-	-	-	-	T48	-	MC	-	T8	2	MC	-	T19
British	T39	-	T27	T23	T2	MC	T44	MC	-	T8	2	MC	T25	T44
PGA	-	-	-	-	-	T67	T54	5	MC	T10	T17	T46	T63	-

	92	93	94	95	96	97	98	99	00	01	02	03	04
Masters	T6	MC	T35	MC	T18	T24	MC	T6	T11	MC	T20	T23	T6
US Open	T4	T11	MC	T13	-	T19	4	T23	T27	MC	T8	T5	T24
British	T51	T6	1	T40	T44	MC	T29	T37	MC	T21	T14	T28	T30
PGA	1	T31	1	T39	T8	T13	T4	5	MC	T29	MC	-	-

Phillip Price (UK)

Largely a journeyman during his first eight seasons on the European Tour, Welshman John Phillip Price (b. Pontypridd, 10/21/1966) climbed to 15th in the Order of Merit in 1998, then to 8th in 2000, and 10th in 2003. Twice a winner of the **Portuguese Open** (1994 and 2001), Price also captured the 2003 **European Open** by making birdie at the 72nd hole to edge Mark McNulty and Alastair Forsyth by one. A year earlier, Price achieved his lifelong goal of making the Ryder Cup team, with his 3 and 2 singles defeat of Phil Mickelson securing an important point in Europe's three-point triumph at The Belfry.

Ron Prichard (USA)

After graduating from Middlebury College and serving a two-year hitch in the United States Army, Ron Prichard entered the golf design business by joining architect Joe Finger's firm in 1968. He would later work with Desmond Muirhead as well as Robert von Hagge and Bruce Devlin before setting out on his own in 1983. While Prichard has completed a number of original designs (including the PGA Tour's TPC at Southwind), he is perhaps better known for his restorative skills, with a particular expertise in the work of Donald Ross. Among Prichard's higher-profile restorations have been Aronimink (Pennsylvania), Charles River and The Orchards (Massachusetts), Beverly (Illinois), Wannamoisett and Metacomet (Rhode Island), and the reconstruction of the long-abandoned third nine at the William Flynn–designed Huntingdon Valley (Pennsylvania).

Otto Probst (USA)

Colonel R. Otto Probst (1896–1986) was a South Bend, Indiana, engineer who took to the collecting of golf books and other memorabilia during the early 1920s and went on to establish the world's largest golf library. Worldwide in his acquisitive scope, Probst once purchased the famous Clapcott Collection from a British dealer for £350, a fair piece of change at the time but a priceless bargain in hindsight. Probst's collection exceeded 1,600 titles by the onset of World War II and continued growing thereafter. It would eventually be outsized by the library of the late Joseph Murdoch—but Murdoch, who lived until 2000, had a far larger body of published titles from which to choose.

Douglas Proudfoot (South Africa)

Douglas C. Proudfoot (1860–1930) was a native of Port Elizabeth on the Eastern Cape but had the splendid golfing fortune of living for nearly two decades in Edinburgh, allowing him learn the game at Bruntsfield and perfect his skills at St. Andrews, North Berwick, and the like. Returning to South Africa in 1888, he proceeded to dominate that nation's **Amateur** championship to a degree that shall likely never be equaled, winning eight consecutive times from 1893 to 1902 (the 1900 and '01 events being cancelled due to the Boer War). A popular man revered for the accuracy of his iron play, Proudfoot was also four times champion of the **Natal** before retiring to Durban, where he died in 1930.

Penny Pulz (Australia)

The daughter of Czechoslovakian immigrants, Penelope "Penny" Pulz (b. Melbourne, 2/2/1953) joined Jan Stephenson as the first Australian women to regularly play the LPGA Tour since Margie Masters in the mid-1960s. A colorful and quotable sort, Pulz first became interested in golf by watching it on television while bedridden with a childhood case of meningitis. Though not quite the player that Stephenson was, Pulz survived 18 seasons in America while winning twice, at the 1979 **Corning Classic** and the 1986 **Tucson Open**, the latter title sparked by a career-best closing 64.

Jackie (Liwai) Pung (USA)

The finest woman player thus far produced in the Hawaiian Islands, Jackie Pung (b. Honolulu, 12/13/1921) was a four-time **Hawaiian** champion before scoring big on the mainland with a victory at the 1952 **U.S. Women's Amateur** in Portland, Oregon. Though already 31 years old, the stocky and long-hitting Pung turned pro shortly thereafter, joining the LPGA Tour in 1953. She made a great start, winning twice as a rookie (in Palm Springs and New Jersey) and just missing out at the U.S. Open where, at the CC of Rochester, she tied Betsy Rawls through 72 holes, only to lose by six shots in the play-off.

A popular and colorful player given to entertaining fans by dancing the hula, Pung will sadly be remembered not for her great skills, but rather for falling victim to one of golf's sorriest clerical errors. At the 1957 U.S. Women's Open at Winged Foot, she again dueled with Rawls, this time winning by a single stroke with a score of 298. But in her excitement, Pung signed a card that, though totaling up correctly to 72, mistakenly showed a 5 instead of a 6 for the fourth hole. The rules being clear, USGA officials could only disqualify her, though at least Pung's financial loss ($1,800) was alleviated by a generous Winged Foot membership who took up a collection and presented her with a check for $3,000.

A winner of only one event thereafter, Pung retired from the Tour in 1964, returning to Hawaii for a career as a teaching professional.

Tom Purtzer (USA)

Long admired for possessing one of golf's smoothest, yet most powerful swings, Arizona State graduate Tom Purtzer (b. Des Moines, Iowa, 12/5/1951) initially struggled for a place on the PGA Tour before settling in for a long and profitable run. All told, Purtzer won five times on Tour, including the 1977 **Los Angeles Open**, the 1984 **Phoenix Open**, the 1991 **Colonial** and his biggest title, the 1991 **World Series of Golf** (in sudden death over Davis Love III and Jim Gallagher Jr.). Never climbing quite high enough to reach the Ryder Cup, Purtzer joined the Champions Tour in 2002 where he has since won twice.

Babe Ruth *(right)* acts as a referee on the first day of play in the International Four Ball Tournament at the Miami Country Club. Willie Klein is putting with, from left to right, Walter Hagen, Johnny Farrell, and Willie MacFarlane looking on.

Smiley Quick (USA)

A gregarious, confident sort of whom Herbert Warren Wind once observed "He did not suffer from an inferiority complex," Lyman "Smiley" Quick (1907–1979) was a well-known Midwestern amateur in the immediate aftermath of World War II. Clearly 1946 was his competitive peak, winning the **Amateur Public Links** before losing in the final of the U.S. Amateur at Baltusrol by missing a short putt at the 37th hole. Quick was also low amateur at the '46 U.S. Open and appeared in the following year's Walker Cup at age 40. He turned pro soon thereafter but enjoyed only limited success and in later years was known to hustle with the likes of Titanic Thompson.

Ronan Rafferty
(Northern Ireland)

A former teenage prodigy, Ronan Patrick Rafferty (b. Newry, 1/13/1964) was the **British Boys** champion at age 15 and a Walker Cup player—the youngest ever, breaking Jimmy Bruen's record—at 17. Given the overwhelming projections of greatness born therein, there are those who might consider Rafferty's professional career somewhat disappointing, though after a bit of a slow start, the talented Irishman has actually acquitted himself rather nicely.

Nineteenth in the Order of Merit by his third European Tour season (1984), Rafferty put together seven subsequent top-20 campaigns, reaching an undeniable peak in 1989 when his three victories (including the **Volvo Masters**) slipped him just ahead of José Maria Olazábal for first place overall. Though four wins (including **Swiss** and **Austrian Opens**) followed between 1990 and 1993, Rafferty's form was inconsistent throughout the mid-1990s prior to being beset by a series of injuries toward millennium's end. A winner of several lesser titles in Australia and the 1982 **Venezuelan Open**, Rafferty's Major championship record includes few entries in the American Majors, and only 9th- and 11th–place finishes at the Open Championship. His lone Ryder Cup appearance came, not surprisingly, in 1989.

Judy (Torluemke) Rankin (USA)

A prodigious teenage talent, St. Louis product Judy Rankin (b. 2/18/1945) won the **Missouri Amateur** in 1959 at age 14, then turned heads with a low amateur finish in the 1960 U.S. Women's Open a year later, throwing in semifinal appearances at the 1960 and '61 USGA Junior Girls for good measure. Joining the LPGA Tour while still only 16, Rankin finished an impressive 41st on the 1962 money list, then improved to 33rd, 13th, 9th, and 7th in the years immediately to follow. Though her first win didn't come until the 1968 **Corpus Christi Civitan Open**, Rankin hit a memorable stride in the 1970s when, between 1970 and 1977, she recorded eight straight top-10 money finishes and an imposing 23 victories. A four-win 1973 was impressive (with its accompanying Vare Trophy and second-place money ranking) but Rankin's unquestioned summit came in 1976 and '77, which included six and five wins, respectively, as well as consecutive money titles, Vare Trophies, and Player of the Year honors.

Amazingly Rankin never won a Major championship, though she did twice capture titles that would later be granted Major status (the 1976 **Dinah Shore** and 1977 **Peter Jackson du Maurier**). Pushed from her perch by Nancy Lopez during 1978 and '79, Rankin battled back problems into an early 1980s retirement but has since built a solid second career for herself as a broadcaster of both men's and women's events. She also served as the American Solheim Cup captain in 1996 and '98.

LPGA Tour Wins (26): 1976 Dinah Shore; 1977 Orange Blossom; 1977 du Maurier
Solheim Cup: 1996 & '98 Capts

1962-1981

	62	63	64	65	66	67	68	69	70	71	72	73	74	75	76	77	78	79	80	81
LPGA	34	T35	T13	T24	-	-	-	9	T14	T7	T24	T11	T6	T20	2	T2	3	T10	T25	67
US Open	T26	34	-	T10	7	T11	T9	MC	MC	MC	T2	T5	MC	9	T17	T10	T53	T26	WD	T48
du Maur																		T5	-	T30

Henry Ransom (USA)

Houston native Henry Ransom (1911–1980) spent a number of years as a club pro before trying the PGA Tour during the late 1940s. Possessed with a quick, streaky swing, he was capable of producing low numbers when things were right, for example taking the 1948 **Illinois PGA** by making eight birdies over the last 11 holes. Though the winner of numerous regional events, Ransom claimed only four official Tour titles, the largest being the 1950 **World Championship of Golf** where he won a princely $11,000 by defeating Chick Harbert in an 18-hole play-off.

John Rattray (UK)

A surgeon from Edinburgh, John Rattray was a Freemason and a member of the Gentlemen Golfers of Leith (later the Honourable Company of Edinburgh Golfers) at the time of the organization's founding in 1744. As the club's first captain (a position won in competition), he carved his place in posterity as a signatory to the first rules of golf, a document for which the Gentleman Golfers were entirely responsible. Rattray won a second captaincy in 1745 but thereafter had his playing career sidelined by a bit of political intrigue. As a doctor who came to the aid of Jacobite troops during the rebellion of 1745, he was twice imprisoned by government forces, only to be saved at least once (and likely twice) by his fellow clubmember Duncan Forbes, an anti-Jacobite with clout—proving that golf clubs, as much as politics, can make for strange bedfellows.

Gladys Ravenscroft (UK)

A big, strong, and good-natured woman, England's Gladys Ravenscroft (1888–1960) took the 1912 **British Ladies** at Turnberry, then became only the second Briton to also win the **U.S. Women's Amateur** (after Dorothy Campbell) with a 1913 triumph in Wilmington, Delaware. To accomplish this she had to first defeat the 1913 British champion Muriel Dodd in the semifinals, then narrowly slip past Marion Hollins two up in the final. Though also the **French** champion of 1912 and a finalist at the 1919 English Ladies, Ravenscroft seldom competed at the highest levels thereafter, instead dominating the game in her native Cheshire where she was seven times ladies champion.

Horace Rawlins (UK/USA)

Isle of Wight native Horace Rawlins (1876–1940) enjoys a hallowed place in American golfing lore as the first official **U.S. Open** champion, though his legacy is somewhat grander than the actual level of his skills. Having emigrated to America in 1895 at age 19 to work as William Davis's assistant at the Newport CC (Rhode Island), Rawlins decided to enter the inaugural 1895 event only because Newport hosted it, then beat an 11-man field by two with a 36-hole total of 173. A year later at Shinnecock Hills, he defended his title well, finishing runner-up, some three strokes behind James Foulis. The Open fields quickly expanded, however, leaving Rawlins (who eventually represented prominent clubs such as New York's Wykagyl and Vermont's Ekwanok) to find his more rightful place among the second tier.

Betsy Rawls (USA)

Though born in Spartanburg, South Carolina, Elizabeth Earle Rawls (b. 5/4/1928) made her golfing name in Texas, taking up the game at age 17 while living in Arlington and winning the state's **Ladies Amateur** (as well as the **Women's Trans-Mississippi**) in 1949. A Phi Beta Kappa graduate of the University of Texas who studied golf under Harvey Penick, Rawls repeated her state title in 1950 and supplemented it with an impressive runner-up finish at the U.S. Women's Open, albeit nine shots behind runaway winner Babe Zaharias in Wichita.

Rawls turned professional in time to join the fledgling LPGA Tour in 1951, the first step in a Hall of Fame career that included 55 wins (fifth all-time) and eight Major championships. At the heart of this record lay four **U.S. Women's Open** titles, the first won as a rookie when she bested Louise Suggs by five at Atlanta's Druid Hills CC. Rawls next claimed the 1953 title in an 18-hole play-off over Jackie Pung at the CC of Rochester, an ironic precursor to 1957 when the popular Ms. Pung should have won by a single stroke at Winged Foot but signed an incorrect scorecard, allowing runner-up Rawls to take her third title. The fourth Open followed in 1960 in more traditional fashion: a one-stroke victory over Joyce Ziske at Worcester (Massachusetts) CC.

A winner of events literally throughout the country, Rawls was impressively consistent, sporting 15 consecutive seasons (1951–65) with at least one victory. She also put together several extraordinary seasons, winning five times in 1957, eight in 1952, and on a stunning 10 occasions (in a 30-event season) in 1959, a career year which included taking both the Vare Trophy and the money title.

The rare player of lasting dominance not to have at least some of their game built around power, Rawls was considered the consummate LPGA shotmaker in addition to possessing an elite short game. Claiming her last win in 1972, she retired in 1975 to take up the position of LPGA Tournament Director, then later broke a minor gender barrier by serving on the rules committee of the men's U.S. Open in 1980.

LPGA Wins (55): 1951, '53, '57 & '60 U.S. Women's Open; 1952 & '59 Western Open; 1954, '56, '57 & '58 Tampa; 1956 & '57 Peach Blossom; 1958 Orange Blossom; 1959 & '60 Babe Zaharias; **1959 & '69 LPGA Championship;** 1964 & '70 Dallas Civitan

1950-1970

	50	51	52	53	54	55	56	57	58	59	60
LPGA						-	23	14	13	1	3
US Open	2	1	7	1	4	T19	13	1	6	7	1

	61	62	63	64	65	66	67	68	69	70
LPGA	3	T14	T6	T5	T19	T10	T31	7	1	T26
US Open	2	T21	T11	22	T26	MC	T15	T36	T20	T14

Also won Western Opens as listed above.

Ted Ray (UK)

Born: Grouville, England, 3/28/1877 **Died:** Watford, England, 8/28/1943

A native of the Channel Islands, Edward "Ted" Ray was one of golf's most unforgettable figures, a bear of a man who was seldom seen on the links without his trademark pipe and trilby hat. A colossally long hitter, Ray was never one to be cheated out of his cuts, swinging hard enough to occasionally send the trilby flying and developing a strong enough set of recovery skills to avoid being crucified by his misses. He was also considered a talented man around the greens and, given an amiable (if somewhat tempestuous) personality, was highly popular with fans, club members, and his fellow players.

Ray's great failing in life was simply being born at the wrong time, for with the exception of his victory at the 1912 **Open Championship** at Muirfield, he was constantly overshadowed by the legendary dominance of the Triumvirate. While the cumulative psychological effect of losing to Messrs. Vardon, Taylor, and Braid may well have slowed him, the oft-suggested notion that Ray would have won several more Opens had the great threesome never existed doesn't stand up to scrutiny. If one removes the Triumvirate from the record book entirely, only once more does Ray's name find the Claret Jug, in 1913 when he finished second to J. H. Taylor at Hoylake. There is only one place where the Triumvirate—and *only* the Triumvirate—greatly hindered Ray: the **News of the World** match play where he lost in the final to Braid in 1903 and '11 and Vardon in 1912.

If Ray is thus perhaps a touch overrated, he does bear the great distinction of joining Vardon and Tony Jacklin

Edward "Ted" Ray

as the only Britons to win both the Open Championship and the **U.S. Open,** taking the latter at Inverness while touring America in 1920. Ray, of course, had joined Vardon as a victim of the upstart Francis Ouimet at the 1913 U.S. Open, likely making this victory (which came when Vardon ran out of gas down the stretch) particularly satisfying. The win was equally memorable for Ray's gargantuan tee shots, most notably at Inverness's late lamented seventh, a 316-yard dogleg-left across a deep swale that he attempted to drive (and subsequently birdied) all four days.

The British captain for the first official Ryder Cup match in 1927, Ray was truly a colorful sort and a man known not to suffer fools nearly as well as the eternally obliging Vardon. Indeed, his trademark words came in response to a plebian sort inquiring as to how he might generate more power with his fault-ridden swing, a common question to which Ray replied simply: "Hit it a bloody sight harder, mate!"

1899-1927

	99	00	01	02	03	04	05	06	07	08	09	10	11	12	13
US Open	-	-	-	-	-	-	-	-	-	-	-	-	-	-	T2
British	T16	13	T12	9	23	T12	T11	T8	T5	3	6	T5	T5	1	2

	14	15	16	17	18	19	20	21	22	23	24	25	26	27
US Open	-	-	-		-		1	-	-	-	-	-	-	T27
British	T10						3	T19	*	T12	*	2	30	T29

*Results unverified—made cut but finished outside top 30.

Seth Raynor (USA)

Born: Manorville, New York, 5/7/1874 **Died:** West Palm Beach, Florida, 1/23/1926

Princeton graduate Seth J. Raynor, primarily a surveyor by trade, was well on his way to a quietly successful life in Southampton, New York, when fate—in the form of Charles Blair Macdonald—intervened. In need of a surveyor to help construct his prized National Golf Links of America in 1907, Macdonald hired Raynor, ultimately becoming so enamored of his skills as to utilize them at Piping Rock, Sleepy Hollow, and The Greenbrier, then making him a full design partner in 1915.

The result was a series of classic Golden Age designs that included The Lido, The Creek, Deepdale, Yale University, and several others that bear Macdonald's name but often were built largely by Raynor. At the same time, Raynor was also taking on solo commissions, with his design skills and access to C.B.'s society connections resulting in a thriving national practice. Quite apart from the specter of Macdonald, Raynor's designs for such affluent clubs as Shoreacres (Illinois), Camargo (Ohio), Fishers Island (New York), and Yeamans Hall (South Carolina) rank among the elite of the Golden Age and are still widely studied today.

Raynor's design style is especially worthy of note, for he generally followed Macdonald's practice of replicating several classic holes, adapting them to fit the particulars of each specific site. Consequently, much of the fun of a Raynor layout is to examine its particular Redan, Biarritz, or Alps and compare them with so many of the architect's other interpretations. Raynor also favored a quasi-geometric aesthetic, with many of his greens and bunkers being somewhat squarish in shape.

Though largely overlooked by modern golfers until recent years, Raynor's work has been highly influential to designers like Pete Dye and has found great favor among the various contemporary course rankings. His style also lived on, albeit briefly, in the work of his eventual partner Charles Banks who, following Raynor's untimely death, pursued a solo career specializing, as his ads directly stated, "in the Raynor type of courses."

Notable Courses: Camargo C, Ohio; Fishers Island C, New York; Lookout Mountain GC, Georgia; Mountain Lake C, Florida; **Shoreacres, Illinois;** Waialae CC, Hawaii; **Yeamans Hall C, South Carolina**

Charles Redhead (Ireland/New Zealand)

Though largely unheard of in much of the golfing world, the wonderfully named Charles H. Redhead (1874–1944) was a man of enormous importance in the history of New Zealand golf. A native of Ireland and a solid amateur player, Redhead retired from a government engineering job in the early 1920s, moving to New Zealand in 1924. Finding that nation's courses to be either painfully boring or overly penal, he completely redesigned his home club at Roturua employing the strategic style then in vogue in both Britain and America. His initial work finding great favor, Redhead was off on a second career, ultimately laying out at least 10 new courses and renovating roughly 20 others, with nearly all of New Zealand's best period layouts (save Titirangi) coming under his able hand.

Dai Rees (UK)

Born: Barry, Wales, 3/31/1913 **Died:** Barnett, England, 11/18/1983

Few will argue that before the ascension of Ian Woosnam to the world stage, the finest golfer ever produced by Wales was one David James "Dai" Rees, C.B.E. The son of a golf professional, Rees seemed a timeless player, establishing himself internationally in the late 1930s and still winning major British titles into the 1960s. His total of 21 such victories seems particularly impressive when one considers how relatively few period events there were to enter—a far cry from today's never-ending carousel of lucrative professional golf.

Rees stepped into the limelight at age 23 when he defeated Ernest Whitcombe to capture the *News of the World* match play in 1936, then followed it up with a Ryder Cup singles victory over Byron Nelson at Southport & Ainsdale in 1937. Fittingly, he would, over the next 25 years, be associated more closely with these two events than any other for in the *News*, British golf's second most prominent event, Rees would claim further titles in 1938, '49, and '50 and demonstrate his Sam Snead–like longevity by reaching the final in 1969, some 33 years after his initial win. In the Ryder Cup he played in a total of nine matches (the last four as captain) and would easily have outdistanced Nick Faldo's record 11 had World War II not intervened, canceling four more.

Though Rees won **Irish, Belgian,** and **Swiss Opens** and the prestigious **British Masters** in 1950 and '62, he, like so many others, never quite broke through in the Open Championship. His best opportunity came in 1954 when he reached the 72nd tied with Peter Thomson, then lost with a bogey when his 4-iron approach ran through the green. In 1946 he entered the final round tied with eventual winner Sam Snead before a disappointing 80 dropped him back to fourth, and in 1961, at age 48, he closed with a solid 72 but lost by one to Arnold Palmer, who matched him shot-for-shot.

One reason for Rees's great longevity was his smooth, compact swing, a repetitive mechanism that, on a man 5'7", had limited room to vary. He was also an excellent putter and one of the few users of the 10-finger grip among top twentieth-century players. Rees played only rarely outside of Europe and spent many years as professional at the South Herts GC, where he followed in Harry Vardon's illustrious footsteps.

Intn'l Wins (21): 1936, '38, '49 & '50 PGA Match Play; 1948 Irish Open; 1950 & '62 British Masters; 1954 Belgian Open; 1956, '59 & '63 Swiss Open; 1959 Volvo PGA
Ryder Cup: 1937–53, 1955–61 (c) (9)

Victor Regalado (Mexico)

In a modern golfing world fully stocked with fine international players, Tijuana's Victor Regalado (b. 4/15/1948) remains the only native of Mexico ever to win a PGA Tour event, the 1974 **Pleasant Valley Classic**. Easily his homeland's best player by his early 20s, Regalado qualified for the PGA Tour in 1972 and enjoyed several top-60 seasons, six second-place finishes, and two appearances at the Masters before eventually returning to his childhood course, the Tijuana CC, as director of golf.

Alexander Reid (UK/Australia)

A merchant and insurance man in the Scottish port of Leith, Alexander Reid emigrated so early (1821) that his new home, Tasmania, was still known as Van Diemen's Land at the time of his arrival. Reid soon opened a farm on 2,000 Clyde River Valley acres and erected a golf course either in 1822 or, more likely, upon returning from a visit home to Scotland in 1842. Either way, his rudimentary, sheep-dotted layout remains in play today (as the Bothwell GC) and, though somewhat altered, bears the great distinction of being the oldest single-site course known to exist outside of Scotland.

John Reid (UK/USA)

Curiously enough, John Reid (1840–1916), a native of Dunfermline, Scotland, and the generally accepted "father of American golf" never actually played the game prior to that fateful February 22, 1888, when he and John B. Upham first tested their primitive three-hole course in Reid's Yonkers, New York cow pasture. But in receipt of clubs and balls ordered directly from Old Tom Morris by his friend Robert Lockhart, Reid certainly took to the game with a vengeance, enticing friends and neighbors to play during that first summer and forming the new St. Andrew's GC (apostrophe added) in November of 1888.

Though a preponderance of evidence now suggests that Vermont's Dorset Field Club (1886) and Pennsylvania's Foxburg CC (1887) actually predate St. Andrew's as America's oldest continuously operating golf clubs, Reid's place in history remains secure. For in addition to guiding St. Andrew's through three early moves, he was one of the nine founders of the USGA in 1894 and remained a cornerstone of the nation's fledgling golfing community for more than two decades.

Mike Reid (USA)

A two-time All-American and teammate of future PGA Tour players John Fought, Jim Nelford, and Pat McGowan at Brigham Young, Mike Reid (b. Bainbridge, Maryland, 7/1/1954) enjoyed a solid amateur career that included being the surprise leader of the 1976 U.S. Open after the opening round. Nicknamed "Radar" for his uncanny accuracy, Reid was a notoriously short hitter who relied upon first-class skills with fairway woods and long irons to regularly rank among the Tour's leaders in greens in regulation.

It has been suggested that such players win lots of money but few tournaments, a theory that Reid would appear to bear out. He was an automatic presence among the Tour's top 125 throughout the 1980s but took 11 seasons to gain his first victory, the 1987 **Tucson Open**. Reid would also capture the 1990 **Casio World Open** in Japan, though his biggest win was surely the 1988 **World Series of Golf** where, unbothered by Firestone CC's traditional emphasis on length, he defeated Tom Watson on the first hole of sudden death. Alas, Reid is equally recalled for being overtaken on the final holes of the 1989 PGA Championship by Payne Stewart after self-destructing at the 70th and 71st holes.

Wilfrid Reid (UK/USA)

A native of Bullwell, England, Wilfrid Reid (1884–1973) moved to Edinburgh at age 14 where he learned club- and ballmaking from Tommy Armour's father Willie. Coached a bit by the great Harry Vardon, he developed into a talented player with a fine swing who, after tying for 16th at the 1913 U.S. Open, emigrated to the States in 1915. Club stops at Seaview, DuPont, Detroit, Seminole, Beverly, the Broadmoor, and others followed, and Reid would ultimately list two British kings, Winston Churchill, and President Warren Harding among his pupils.

Having laid out several courses in France and England before emigrating, Reid expanded his architectural interests in America, with the majority of his documented work done in Michigan, in tandem with fellow club pro (and ex–Donald Ross construction man) William Connellan. Reid also helped to lay out San Francisco's short-lived Lakeside G&CC (the forerunner to today's Olympic Club), but his most prominent lasting designs were both in the Detroit area: the stylish and quirky Indianwood G&CC (a two-time U.S. Women's Open site) and Plum Hollow G&CC, site of the 1947 PGA Championship.

Johnny Revolta (USA)

Born: St. Louis, Missouri, 4/5/1911 **Died:** Palm Springs, California, 3/3/1991

Though his success would be somewhat shorter lived, former caddie Johnny Revolta was one of the few players capable of consistently going toe-to-toe with Sam Snead and Henry Picard during the latter half of the 1930s. Officially credited with 18 PGA Tour victories, Revolta, an acknowledged master of the short game, was first heard from with a win at the 1933 **Miami Open**, then claimed two more titles in 1934. But it was in 1935 that he truly arrived, winning five times, including both the **Western Open** and his lone Major championship, the **PGA**, where he got up-and-down seven times from bunkers during a first-round victory over Walter Hagen before eventually defeating 40-year-old Tommy Armour 5 and 4 for the title.

Revolta would win seven more events over the next three seasons, including four titles in 1938, and he managed a 2-1 record on winning Ryder Cup teams in 1935 and '37. After World War II deprived him of several prime years, he scaled back his competitive schedule consider-

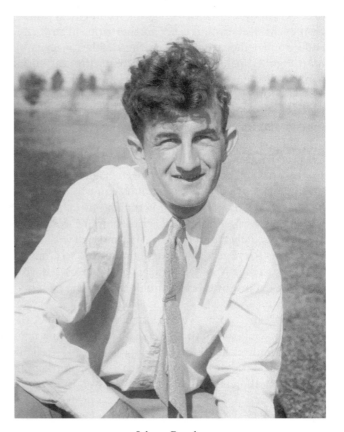

Johnny Revolta

ably, repairing to his long-time position at the Evanston GC (Illinois) (where he became one of America's most sought-after teachers) and wintering in Palm Springs. Though he won the 1944 **Texas Open** and returned to Major championship play in the early 1950s, Revolta never again revisited his prewar form that, at its peak, saw him defeat the best ball of Gene Sarazen and Tommy Armour in one early 1930s exhibition.

PGA Tour Wins (18): 1935 Western Open; **1935 PGA Championship;** 1944 Texas

Ryder Cup: 1935 & '37 (2)

1928-1956

	28	29	30	31	32	33	34	35	36	37	38	39	40	41	42
Masters							T18	T13	25	T13	T18	T31	T27	-	-
US Open	MC	-	-	-	-	T15	T8	T36	T14	T28	T16	T22	T16	WD	
British	-	-	-	-	-	-	-	-	-	T31	-	-			
PGA	-	-	-	-	-	T9	T9	1	T17	T17	T17	T9	T33	-	-

	43	44	45	46	47	48	49	50	51	52	53	54	55	56
Masters				-	T42	-	T39	-	T42	13	58	T60		
US Open				-	-	-	-	-	T19	40	MC	T29		
British				-	-	-	-	-	-	-	-			
PGA		-	T9	-	T33	-	-	-	-	-	-	T9		

Ted Rhodes (USA)

Though Bill Spiller led the cause and Charlie Sifford pioneered playing the PGA Tour full time, the first black to actually participate in a Tour event was Ted Rhodes (1916–1969) at the 1946 Los Angeles Open. A native of Nashville, Rhodes, a long-hitting former caddie, also played in the 1948 U.S. Open at Riviera (firing an opening-round 70) and taught the game to Joe Louis and Lee Elder, among many others. Largely sponsored by Louis, Rhodes played primarily on the minority-oriented United Golf Association tour where his dominance was so great that some estimates have him winning 150 titles. Better documented are his four **Negro National Open** victories in 1949, '50, '51, and '57, and an impressive 1948 win at the **Ray Robinson Open**, a Caribbean event in which Rhodes recorded a red-hot 62. A smoother and more conventional player than Sifford, Rhodes never got the chance to test himself against the best, for he was too old to compete seriously by the time the color lines had fallen.

Grantland Rice (USA)

Born: Murfreesboro, Tennessee, 11/1/1880 **Died:** New York, New York, 7/13/1954

Surely the most famous sportswriter in American history, Henry Grantland Rice attended Vanderbilt University, played a bit of semi-pro baseball, then joined the staff of the Nashville *Daily News*—as sports editor!—in 1901. From there it was onto the Atlanta *Journal*, the Cleveland *News*, back to Nashville, and eventually, in 1911, up to New York for his first big-time gig at the *Evening Mail*.

In the years to follow, Rice's personage would take on almost mythic proportions, for he seemed to be at every major event, establishing close personal relationships with everyone from Ty Cobb to Babe Zaharias. His column, *The Sportlight*, would become among the most widely syndicated in history while his penchant for reeling off original lines of poetic verse—which he tended to dismiss modestly, though they numbered more than 6,000 in total—would earn him lasting footholds in the American lexicon. "It's not whether you win or lose, it's how you play the game," for example, comes from his poem "Alumnus Football," and it was Rice who nicknamed the Fighting Irish's 1924 football backfield the "Four Horsemen of Notre Dame."

A remarkably popular man, Rice was an avid golfer who used a good deal of his ink covering Zaharias, Walter Hagen, Bobby Jones, and the game's other period stars. He would also serve for a number of years as editor of *The American Golfer* and authored several golf-oriented texts, the most famous likely being the amusing *Duffer's Handbook of Golf* (Macmillan, 1926). Rice's final book was his autobiography, *The Tumult and the Shouting* (A. S. Barnes, 1954), an all-encompassing retrospective that recounted a life so unique as to remain, some 50 years later, the very symbol of the grand sporting era in which it was lived.

Skee Riegel (USA)

Prior to World War II, Pennsylvanian Robert H. "Skee" Riegel (b. New Bloomfield, 11/25/1914) was a solid player with little beyond the 1935 **Southern Amateur** title upon his résumé. But in 1946 Riegel got the postwar era rolling with the first of back-to-back **Trans-Mississippi** titles, then reached his career peak in 1947 when he defeated Johnny Dawson 2 and 1 at Pebble Beach to win the **U.S. Amateur.** Also the 1948 **Western Amateur** champion, Riegel appeared on victorious Walker Cup teams in 1947 and '49, then finished as low amateur in the 1949 U.S. Open. Finally electing to turn professional in his mid-30s, he very nearly scored a Major victory when his 282 total led the 1951 Masters late on Sunday, only to be overtaken in the closing moments by Ben Hogan's final-round 68.

Chris Riley (USA)

San Diego native Chris Riley (b. 12/8/1973) has won only once on the PGA Tour (the 2002 **Reno-Tahoe Open**), yet managed to earn a spot on the 2004 Ryder Cup team with his consistently solid play, particularly during 2003. A former four-time All-American at UNLV and 1995 Walker Cup participant, Riley neither overpowers the ball nor ranks among the Tour's leaders for hitting greens in regulation. He is, however, a consistently fine putter who has steadily climbed the money list, from 112th in 1999 to 23rd in both 2002 and '03. Now in his early 30s, is he on the verge of becoming a regular winner or have we seen his best?

Polly Riley (USA)

San Antonio native Polly Ann Riley was a career amateur who, in a splendid footnote of golfing history, won the LPGA Tour's first official event, the 1950 **Tampa Open.** This would be Riley's sole victory against a professional field but among amateurs she was dangerous, winning the **Western** in 1950 and '52, the **Trans-Mississippi** in 1947, '48, and '55, and the **Southern** on a record six occasions. On the national level, Riley was runner-up in the 1953 U.S. Women's Amateur, when Mary Lena Faulk beat her 3 and 2 at the Rhode Island CC, and was also that rare amateur to contend seriously at the U.S. Women's Open, tying for second (albeit six behind winner Betsy Jameson) in 1947.

Riley was reported to have won roughly 100 events during her career in addition to competing in all four Curtis Cups from 1948 through 1954 and captaining a victorious team in 1962. In another pleasant footnote, Riley beat Babe Zaharias on three of the five occasions they went head-to-head, including a 10 and 9 pasting in the fi-

nal of the 1948 **Texas Women's Open**, the most lopsided loss ever suffered by the greatest of all women athletes. Riley passed away in 2002.

José Rivero (Spain)

In a career started by a much-publicized £2,500 loan from the Spanish Golf Federation, Madrid's José Rivero (b. 9/20/1955) enjoyed a two-decade run on the European Tour, which would ultimately include four wins and seven appearances among the top 25 in the Order of Merit. Rivero's best stretch came from 1984 to 1988, when he was only once out of the top 13, a period in which he took the 1987 **French** and 1988 **Monte Carlo Opens**, the latter head-to-head against Mark McNulty and Seve Ballesteros at Mont Agel. These high-flying years also saw Rivero selected to the 1985 and '87 Ryder Cup teams and he would eight times represent Spain in the **World Cup**, teaming with José Maria Cañizares to win the 1984 event in Rome on his first try. Strictly a European player, Rivero has amassed not a single win elsewhere and has never appeared in an American Major, though he has finished as high as third at the Open Championship (1985).

James Robb (UK)

Dunfermline native James Robb (b. 1878) attended Madras College at St. Andrews, though he would reside for most of his life in Prestwick. A winner of the **British Amateur** in 1906 (beating C. C. Lingen 4 and 3 at Hoylake), he was also twice a loser in the final (to A. J. Travers Allan in 1897 and Harold Hilton in 1900) as well as a semifinalist in 1898 and 1902. Hardly an aesthetically pleasing player, Robb reportedly drove the ball neither long nor straight but more than covered for his shortcomings once on the putting surface. For as Darwin wrote: "His name is not often mentioned when great putters are enumerated, but I am very sure it ought to be. Having regard to his record I doubt if there has been one better."

Hillman Robbins Jr. (USA)

Air Force Lieutenant Hillman Robbins Jr. (1932–1981) was in active service during 1957 when he made his lone Walker Cup appearance (at Minikahda), then, only two weeks later, defeated Dr. Frank "Bud" Taylor 5 and 4 to capture the **U.S. Amateur** at The Country Club of Brookline. Previously, he had visited the semifinals of the Amateur in 1955 (losing to Bill Hyndman at the CC of Virginia), won the 1956 **North & South Amateur,** and been the 1954 **NCAA** individual champion while playing at hometown

Memphis State. Robbins was widely viewed as a top PGA Tour prospect when he turned professional in 1958, but once again the oddsmakers were mistaken.

Kelly Robbins (USA)

A former NCAA Co-Player of the Year (with Annika Sorenstam) and two-time All-American at the University of Tulsa, nine-time LPGA Tour winner Kelly Robbins (b. Mt. Pleasant, Michigan, 9/29/1969) enjoyed a run of four world-class seasons from 1994 through 1997, finishing no worse than eighth on the money list while winning five times, the largest being the 1995 **LPGA Championship**. Robbins fell from the top 10 in 1998 (despite two more victories) but has since remained solid, generally remaining among the top 30 in earnings and continuing to maintain a regular spot on the American Solheim Cup team (1994–2003). Now in her mid-30s, Robbins still remains capable of competing at the highest level, as her play-off loss at the 2003 U.S. Women's Open indicates.

Clifford Roberts (USA)

Charles DeClifford Roberts (1894–1977) is a certified golf legend, a primary name in discussions of Augusta National and the Masters, and *the* name in any conversation regarding the benefits of the "benevolent despot" approach to golf club management. Hardly the native-born blueblood that many might think, Roberts came from a farm in the southeastern Iowa town of Morning Sun, eventually finding great success as an investment banker in New York, where he met Bobby Jones in the 1920s. While Jones held an artistic vision for Augusta National, it was Roberts who handled the financial side—no easy task when developing a national golf club at the height of the Depression.

Soon thereafter, Roberts would come to fame as the chairman of the Masters, forever being cited for his fussiness and perceived grouchiness—but the tournament, after all, did not become America's most revered golfing event simply by happenstance. Further, Roberts demonstrated a great understanding of what Bobby Jones and Dr. Alister MacKenzie had intended in building the Augusta National layout, writing in 1976 that "It has been proven, at least to our own satisfaction, that those who patronize the Masters get more pleasure and excitement watching great players make birdies than bogies. It would be easy to set up the Augusta National so that no one could break 80 on it. But, if this were done, we doubt if the players would like it. And we are certain such a policy would be unpopular with the patrons."

Loren Roberts (USA)

Soft-spoken Loren Lloyd Roberts (b. San Luis Obispo, California, 6/24/1955) is a classic example of the success that can be achieved in golf through hard work and patience. A relative latecomer to the idea of competing professionally, he attended college and worked as an assistant professional in his hometown for several years before trying the PGA Tour, and, even then, he was five times back to qualifying school before finally latching on in 1987. What followed, however, has been a long and successful run, including 16 straight appearances among the top 100 money winners, more than $13 million in winnings, eight Tour victories, and an impressive mid-40s stretch that has seen him claim four of his eight career top 10s in Major championships.

Twice a winner at **Bay Hill** (1994 and '95) and at the **Greater Milwaukee Open** (1996 and 2000), Roberts also has victories at the 1996 **Heritage** and the 1999 **Byron Nelson** on his résumé, as well as a heartbreaking play-off loss to Ernie Els at the 1994 U.S. Open. Widely known as one of golf's best putters, Roberts only perfected his technique after switching to a mallet head and—very much against prevalent theory—a slightly wristier stroke in 1988.

Allan Robertson (UK)

Born: St. Andrews, Scotland, 9/11/1815 **Died:** St. Andrews, Scotland, 9/1/1859

It has long been said—almost surely apocryphally—that the reason for the creation of the Open Championship in 1860 was to determine the suddenly vacant title of golf's best player, the idea being that there had been no issue prior to the death of Allan Robertson in 1859. This, like many legends that have sprouted up around old Allan, seems a bit exaggerated, though what evidence there is certainly ranks Robertson among the very best of his time.

Coming from a long line of ball- and clubmakers, Allan was certainly the revered figure around St. Andrews in the mid-nineteenth century, and it was to his shop that Tom Morris Sr. came to learn at the foot of the master. Though they would have a well-documented falling out over the new gutta-percha ball in the late 1840s (Allan seeing it as a threat to his status as *the* feathery maker), Robertson and the elder Morris would continue to partner in many a foursomes match, most notably in a famous 108-hole contest in 1849 against Musselburgh's Dunn brothers, which the St. Andreans won despite trailing 4 down with eight to play. Other matches were considerably less chronicled but if Old Tom and Allan were ever beaten, there seems little substantive record to say where, when, or precisely by whom.

Allan's singles career, on the other hand, perhaps showed a bit more flash than substance, for despite being billed in various places as "undefeated," ample record exists of losses to Old Tom, Willie Dunn Sr. and a handful of others. Old Tom perhaps confirmed this with his famous recollection that "I could cope wi' Allan mysel' but never with Tommy" (in reference to his son), and if Robertson didn't avoid big money matches with Morris, he certainly dodged Willie Park Sr. who challenged him in print.

Immensely popular in the "auld grey toon" despite such legerdemain, the short, stocky Robertson retains a number of firsts in golf history. He was, for example, the first real golf professional and greenkeeper, as well as the first man to break 80 over the Old Course (shooting 79 less than a year before his death). He was also the first golf course architect in that he initiated the 1848 widening of the Old Course that included the construction of many of its famous double greens. Even more important, it was Robertson who built the green complex of the Road 17th, probably the most famous, feared, and dramatic hole anywhere on earth.

Belle (McCorkindale) Robertson (UK)

Argyll's Isabella "Belle" McCorkindale, M.B.E. (b. 4/11/1936) has been Scotland's longest-running female amateur show, her longevity perhaps spurred on by the desire to finally win a British Ladies Amateur, an event in which McCorkindale lost in the final as early as 1959. When the six-time **Scottish** champion eventually did break through in 1981, however, it was a near thing, blowing a 5 up lead (with only five to play!) before eventually winning—with a grand sigh of relief—at the 20th. If taking the **Amateur** at age 45 seems impressive, however, consider that the by-then Mrs. Robertson had previously captained Curtis Cup teams in 1974 and '76 when selected to play in her sixth and seventh matches in 1982 and '86, making her the first ex-captain ever to return to active play in the event's history.

David Robertson Jr. (UK/Australia)

The older brother of St. Andrews' legendary Allan Robertson, David Robertson Jr. is not recorded as having been either a feathery ballmaker or a high-level competitor, though he was certainly a capable player before emigrating to Sydney, Australia, in 1848. Some reports have him "introducing" the game Down Under at that time but these cannot be correct, for Alexander Reid in Tasmania and James Graham in Melbourne were clearly playing on

Australian soil before Robertson had left St. Andrews. What is clear, however, is that Robertson had a son named Allan who, during World War I, rather belatedly presented the Royal Sydney GC with a collection of ancient clubs and balls, which reportedly had belonged to his namesake uncle Allan and grandfather David Sr. This priceless collection includes 26 feathery balls, 10 wooden clubs, and 8 irons, with several of the clubs possessing the telltale "nick" indicative, we are told, of the great Allan's favor and usage.

Ted Robinson (USA)

An established land planner who didn't take up golf course design until middle age, Ted Robinson (b. 1923) would ultimately lay out nearly 100 courses, the majority in his native California. He was particularly active in the Palm Springs area, where he completed approximately 20 projects beginning in the mid-1970s. Known primarily for his man-made waterfalls, Robinson teamed with Greg Norman for a handful of designs in the early 1990s.

Fred Robson (UK)

A native of Shotten, England, Fred Robson (1885–1952) was, in his youth, a very fine player, pushing J. H. Taylor to the brink in the final of the 1908 *News of the World* match play and coming home tied for fifth at the 1910 Open Championship. Nearly two decades later, in his early 40s, he found a second great rush of Open form, tying for second (six behind Bobby Jones) in 1927, then for fourth in both 1928 and 1930. Yet despite such brushes with greatness, Robson became more famous as a teacher, actually being appointed full-time coach (as opposed to the rotating position of captain) to the Walker Cup team. He also developed a reputation as a superior clubmaker, working from his shop at the Addington where he was for many years the pro.

Constantino Rocca (Italy)

Bergamo's Constantino Rocca (b. 12/4/1956) is Italy's most famous golfer to date, though this celebrity perhaps stems less from his five European Tour victories than it does from his memorable play-off loss to American John Daly in the 1995 Open Championship at St. Andrews. Reaching the 72nd hole one off the lead, Rocca uncorked a powerful drive to a point just shy of St. Andrews 18th green. But just when the tying birdie seemed assured, he fluffed his chip badly—only to hole the ensuing 60-footer to force the losing play-off!

Rocca began his golfing life as a caddie, then a caddie master, before turning pro at age 24. A dominant player in Italy by the mid-1980s, he reached the top 50 in the European Order of Merit in 1990 and remained there throughout the decade to follow, placing in the top 10 in 1993, '95, and '96. Though his résumé includes wins at the 1993 **French Open** and 1996 **Volvo PGA**, Rocca's greatest triumph likely came at the 1997 **European Masters** when his dazzling final-round 62 slipped past Robert Karlsson and Scott Henderson by one. Italy's first-ever Ryder Cup player (where he amassed a fine 6-5 record between 1993 and 1997) and a 10-time World Cupper, Rocca has seen his form slip, only once cracking the Order of Merit's top 150 since 2000.

John D. Rockefeller (USA)

The quintessential American capitalist, John Davison Rockefeller (1839–1937) made his fortune with the Standard Oil trust, then parlayed it into this country's most prominent economic and philanthropic dynasty. Frequently cited as the world's richest man, Rockefeller was also a devoted golfer who hired William Flynn to build nine reversible holes on his Pocantico Hills, New York, estate. He also drew great attention each winter by playing precisely eight holes each morning (excluding Sundays) at the old Ormond Beach GC, a facility owned by the company of his deceased former Standard Oil partner Henry Flagler. Rockefeller believed strongly in the health benefits of golf (he played sans cart, after all) and lived 97 years to prove them.

Phil Rodgers (USA)

An advanced golfing talent at a young age, the 5'8" (and occasionally somewhat portly) Philamon Webster Rodgers (b. San Diego, California, 4/3/1938) spent one year at the University of Houston, winning all three collegiate events he entered, including the 1958 **NCAA** individual title. After service in the Marines he joined the PGA Tour in 1961, then won both the **Los Angeles Open** (by nine strokes!) and the **Tucson Open** in 1962. Legitimately compared to an equally young Jack Nicklaus, Rodgers seemed destined for greatness, yet despite two further titles in 1966 (at the **Doral** and **Buick Opens**), would ultimately claim only five Tour victories overall. A regular contender in both the U.S. and British Opens, Rodgers finished a strong third in each during 1962, then lost the latter in a play-off to New Zealand's Bob Charles a year later. Remarkably, he was never selected to play in the Ryder Cup.

Largely inactive as a competitor by the late 1970s, Rodgers himself stated that it was his personality that pre-vented him from becoming a truly great champion. Still, he developed a sterling reputation both as a designer of clubs (especially wedges) and as a teacher, particularly of the short game. In a widely publicized move, no less than Jack Nicklaus went to him for greenside help during 1979, coming away with an added versatility that helped spark stunning 1980 Major championship wins at the U.S. Open and the PGA.

Chi Chi Rodriguez (USA)

One of golf's more recognizable and popular players for more than 40 years, Puerto Rico's Juan "Chi Chi" Rodriguez (b. Rio Piedras, 10/23/1935) was an eight-time winner on the PGA Tour, yet was far better known for his showmanship and on-course antics. Initially those antics (which included dropping his hat over the hole and dancing around it following a made birdie putt) ruffled some fellow competitors' feathers; thus they were later refined into Rodriguez's patented swordfighting routine, which has delighted crowds for decades. As a player he was the epitome of the self-taught ex-caddie who began by beating tin cans with a guava tree stick, showing great doses of creativity, a sand game second only to Gary Player's, and almost unbelievable power off the tee. Indeed, during his early years, he frequently outdrove the Tour's longest hitters despite standing 5'7" and weighing 110 pounds.

Rodriguez's biggest wins came at the 1964 **Western Open** (beating Arnold Palmer by one at Chicago's old Tam O'Shanter CC) and the 1972 **Byron Nelson Classic** (when he defeated Billy Casper in sudden death). But upon turning 50 he found a remarkable second life on the Champions Tour, capturing an impressive 22 titles and more than $7.6 million beginning in 1985. Along with legends like Nicklaus, Palmer, and Trevino, Rodriguez's fan-friendly game was a boon to the senior circuit, helping it gain life in a competitive TV market. His contributions there, however, pale in comparison to the millions he has raised for his Florida-based Chi Chi Rodriguez Youth Foundation, an organization dedicated to helping at-risk inner-city kids.

Bill Rogers (USA)

A former star at the University of Houston, 1973 Walker Cupper William Charles Rogers (b. Waco, Texas, 9/10/1951) enjoyed several solid seasons on the PGA Tour in the late 1970s, landing his first win at the 1978 **Bob Hope Desert Classic**. A year later, though winless in America, he finished sixth on the money list and captured the prestigious **World Match Play** title in England, defeating Isao Aoki in the final. Then, in 1981, all hell broke loose.

Rogers initially won the **Heritage Classic**, then, toward season's end, added the **World Series of Golf** and the **Texas Open**. In the interim, he tied for second at the U.S. Open (losing out to David Graham's splendid final-round 67 at Merion) and traveled to Royal St. George's, where he captured the **Open Championship** by four over Bernhard Langer. Finally, on a late-season visit Down Under, he claimed both the **New South Wales Open** and the prestigious **Australian Open**, the latter by a single stroke over a young Greg Norman at the Victoria GC. All told, Rogers' 1981 ranked among the strongest worldwide seasons of its time and fully justified the Ryder Cup and Player of the Year selections soon to follow.

A tall, exceedingly lean man known best for a smooth putting stroke, Rogers was now 30 years old and, one might guess, looking at his best years dead ahead. Yet he fell from 5th to 27th on the money list in 1982, then down to 42nd a year later. A 1983 win in **New Orleans** might have stemmed the decline yet by his own admission, Rogers' attitude toward the game was changing. He fell out of the top 100 in 1984, slipped all the way to 239th in 1988, and retired from the Tour prior to 1989.

Douglas Rolland (UK)

A cousin of James Braid and a stonemason by trade, Elie native Douglas Rolland (1860–1914) was one of nineteenth-century British golf's more interesting characters. Though apparently not overly dedicated to the game, Rolland was a great natural talent, his innate skills enhanced by a massive and powerful physique that saw him drive the ball heretofore unseen distances. Darwin referred to him as "one of the uncrowned kings of golf" and was almost wildly enamored with Rolland's talent and style, further noting that "Wherever he went he was loved, admired and forgiven—an irreclaimably dashing dog that nobody could withstand."

One well-documented aspect of Rolland's career was a £50 challenge match he took up in 1883 against John Ball Jr., played over their respective home courses at Earlsferry and Hoylake. Rolland went 9 up at Earlsferry before going on to win 11 and 10, then bested Ball again the next day by coming from 5 down with six to play to win 1 up. Perhaps even more interesting, Darwin relates that "on the day on which he had to play the second half of his match against John Ball, he ought to have attended a summons in a local Court in Scotland, due to an affair of gallantry. Since he could not be in two places at once he went to Hoylake and thought it prudent thereafter to stay in England. That is why until 1894, when the Open Championship was played for the first time on an English course, Sandwich, his name is not to be found among the competitors."

This account does not entirely square with Rolland's tying for second at the 1884 Open Championship at Prestwick, but he does appear to be wholly absent thereafter until 1894 at Royal St. George's, where he reemerged to again finish second, this time five behind J. H. Taylor. Darwin's version may also explain Rolland's reported move to the United States for several years, though he would eventually return to England where he died in Farnborough, Hampshire, at age 54.

Barbara Romack (USA)

Californian Barbara Romack (b. Sacramento, 11/16/1932) enjoyed a strong amateur run during the mid-1950s, the highlight being her defeat of the legendary Mickey Wright in the final of the 1954 **U.S. Amateur** at Pittsburgh's Allegheny CC. Also a finalist in 1958 (losing to Anne Quast), Romack counted victories in the **North & South** (1952) and **Canadian** (1953) **Amateurs** on her résumé, as well as a runner-up at the 1955 British Women's Amateur, where she lost 7 and 6 to Jessie Valentine at Royal Portrush. Also a Curtis Cupper from 1954 through 1958, Romack turned professional after the 1958 match and played the LPGA Tour for roughly 15 seasons, winning only once, at the **Rock City Open** in 1963.

Eduardo Romero (Argentina)

The son of a Cordoba, Argentina, club professional, Eduardo Romero (b. 7/17/1954) has been a dominant force in his native South America for three decades, capturing more than 85 titles—though few of great note beyond their region. Curiously, like Tony Cerda a half-century earlier, Romero has *not* dominated the **Argentine Open** (winning only once, in 1989) but he has managed six **Argentine PGA** titles as well as a **Mexican Open** in 1998.

Only an occasional visitor to the United States, Romero has enjoyed some real success in Europe, claiming eight wins and nine top-20 rankings in the Order of Merit since 1989. His first European title came at the 1989 **Trophée Lancôme** (by one over Langer and Olazábal), and he would later claim the national Opens of **Spain** and **France** in 1991 and **Italy** in '94. Also a two-time winner of the **European Masters** (1994 and 2000), Romero's second Masters victory was a powerful 10-shot runaway over Thomas Björn. Perhaps most impressive, Romero has played some of his best golf in his late 40s, taking the **Scottish Open** and ranking fifth in the Order of Merit during a 2002 season in which he turned 48. Romero has also represented Argentina 14 times in World Cup play since 1983, including six straight events from 1999 to 2004.

President Franklin D. Roosevelt (USA)

Though physically unable to play the game in later life, President Franklin Delano Roosevelt (1882–1945) does carry a unique golfing distinction, for he is surely the only president ever to design a golf course. The layout in question was an early nine-holer on Campobello Island, a famously rustic retreat located just across the Maine/New Brunswick border, where Roosevelt's New York–based family regularly summered. While there is little dispute as to the course's lineage, there is equally little information as to its playing specifics as it ceased to exist in or about 1935.

Jennifer Rosales (Philippines)

The winner of five straight **Philippines Ladies Amateur** titles (1994–98), Manila native Jennifer Rosales (b. 9/17/1978) played collegiate golf at USC, where she was the 1998 **NCAA** individual champion. Joining the LPGA Tour in 2000, the colorful Rosales has made steady progress, climbing from 79th and 87th on the money list in her first two seasons to 30th and 32nd in 2002 and '03. She claimed her first Tour victory (the **Chick-fil-A**) early in 2004, then nearly scored a Major breakthrough at the U.S. Women's Open when rounds of 70-67-69 gave her a three-shot 54-hole lead, only to finish fourth after a disappointing final-round 75. A strong ball-striker who hits a large number of greens, Rosales presently ranks behind such young LPGA stars as Grace Park, Lorena Ochoa, Cristie Kerr, and Se Ri Pak. But with her game continuing to climb as she enters her late 20s, she clearly holds the potential to join their ranks in the near future.

Bob Rosburg (USA)

Well known to contemporary viewers for more than two decades of television work, Stanford-educated Bob Rosburg (b. San Francisco, California, 10/21/1926) utilized the 10-finger grip and an ungainly looking swing, yet rode a Hall of Fame putting stroke and a keen competitive edge to great golfing heights. All told, Rosburg would win six times on the PGA Tour, placing no worse than 26th in money through 1959 and claiming the Vardon Trophy in 1958. In 1959 he captured what was easily his biggest victory, the **PGA Championship**, when he closed 68-66, yet still trailed by one until Jerry Barber bogeyed both the 71st and 72nd holes, handing Rosburg the title.

With the exception of a win at the 1961 **Bing Crosby**, Rosburg virtually vanished from the Tour for the next de-

cade, reappearing rather dramatically at the 1969 U.S. Open, where only a missed short putt at the 72nd prevented him from playing off with Orville Moody. In 1971 he tied for third when the Open returned to Merion, two strokes out of the famous Nicklaus-Trevino play-off. Then 45, he surprised everyone once more by defeating Lanny Wadkins to capture the 1972 **Bob Hope Desert Classic**, before suffering two declining years and retiring in 1975.

Justin Rose (South Africa/UK)

Few golfers have ever splashed onto the scene more lustily than did 17-year-old amateur Justin Rose (b. 7/30/1980), when he hung around the lead of the 1998 Open Championship for four days, ultimately holing a thrilling pitch at the 72nd to tie for fourth place. Born in Johannesburg but raised in England, Rose surprised everyone by turning professional the very next day, then proceeded to endure a long and rough initiation when he finished 197th and 122nd on the 1999 and 2000 Orders of Merit, respectively, looking sadly overmatched in the process.

But in 2001 he returned to his native land to open the European Tour season with back-to-back second-place finishes at the Alfred Dunhill (the South African PGA) and the South African Open, and suddenly he was back in the game. Though he wouldn't win in 2001, Rose rocketed up to 33rd on the Order of Merit, then jumped all the way to ninth in 2002 behind quality wins at the **Alfred Dunhill** and the **British Masters**, while also claiming lesser titles in South Africa and Japan.

By 2003 Rose was splitting his time almost evenly between Europe and the United States, finishing fifth in that year's U.S. Open at Olympia Fields and looking very close to arriving center stage. Failing to win throughout 2004 has perhaps slowed that process, particularly after finishing tied for 22nd at the Masters despite leading at the halfway mark. But with his combination of strong talent and a cool, polished attitude, the 24-year-old Rose must still be viewed as a potential star of the near future.

Elaine Rosenthal (USA)

The daughter of an affluent Illinois businessman and philanthropist, Chicagoan Elaine Rosenthal was a narrow loser to Katherine Harley in the final of the 1914 U.S. Women's Amateur at Long Island's Nassau CC. Though never again so close to the national title, Rosenthal did shine in what for her was surely the next best thing, the **Western Amateur**, which she won in 1915, '18, and '25. Also the 1917 **North & South Amateur** champion, Rosenthal is perhaps best recalled as the decidedly non-Southern member of 1918's "Dixie Kids," a Red Cross fund-raising tour featuring herself, Bobby Jones, Perry Adair, and the reigning Women's Amateur champion Alexa Stirling. Chaperoned by Rosenthal's mom, the foursome toured the eastern half of the country all summer, raising more than $150,000 toward wartime relief efforts.

Alec Ross (UK/USA)

That Alexander "Alec" Ross (1881–1952) is far less remembered than his older brother Donald is due solely to the timeless publicity reaped from designing golf courses as opposed simply to winning ancient tournaments. Raised in the famous Scottish golf town of Dornoch, Alec emigrated to America in 1900 (two years behind his brother), where he became the professional at Boston's Brae Burn CC, wintering as Donald's assistant at Pinehurst. Clearly the family's best player, Alec won the 1907 **U.S. Open** in Philadelphia (beating Gilbert Nicholls by two) as well as six straight **Massachusetts Opens** and, years later, the **Swiss Open** in 1923, '25, and '26. Perhaps more impressive than any of these titles, however, was Alec's six victories in Pinehurst's famous **North & South Open**, one of the very few period events of a truly national scope. Alec beat Donald in the tournament's 1902 inaugural, then added further titles in 1904, '07, '08, '10, and '14. He was also twice runner-up—both times to Donald—in 1905 and '06.

Donald Ross (UK/USA)

Born: Dornoch, Scotland, 11/23/1872 **Died:** Pinehurst, North Carolina, 4/26/1948

Among the most famous of Golden Age golf course designers, Donald James Ross was born and raised in Dornoch, Scotland, but spent several years living at St. Andrews where, like C. B. Macdonald before him and A. W. Tillinghast after, he fell under the influence of Old Tom Morris. Becoming well-versed in Old Tom's principles of sound course architecture, Ross returned home and served for seven years as Royal Dornoch's professional and greenkeeper. Eventually, having been invited to Boston by a vacationing Harvard professor, Ross emigrated to America in 1899.

His first job Stateside was at the Oakley Country Club in Watertown, Massachusetts, where he soon met James Walker Tufts, the developer of Pinehurst. Almost immediately Ross had found himself a winter job—a seasonal position that he would retain for nearly half a century. In addition to teaching and overseeing maintenance of the Pinehurst courses, Ross also found time to establish himself as a fine player (he finished fifth in the 1903 U.S. Open

Donald Ross presents prizes to the winners of the Annual Father and Son Golf Tournament at Pinehurst.

at Baltusrol) and to begin in earnest his true calling as an architect.

It has been wrongly overestimated that Ross designed as many as 600 courses in his career, though the actual number of just over 400 is certainly impressive enough. Ross's detractors have long accused him of laying out many courses from afar, using topographical maps to create drawings from which a third party—perhaps skilled, perhaps not—completed actual construction. As there certainly exists an obvious discrepancy between such high-profile classics as Seminole and Pinehurst No. 2 and many of Ross's lesser-known works, this argument likely holds some merit. For as Pete Dye once wrote of Ross: "He designed so many golf courses, but there are probably only twenty of them that ever had that strategy. Those are the ones built by his construction crews."

Because of such variance in the final product, references to alleged Ross design trademarks are largely unsupportable. However, one consistent aspect of his actual, hands-on work was an attention to green positioning and contouring nearly unique in American history, resulting in green complexes that favor thoughtful approaches and, above all, an imaginative short game. Consequently, Ross's designs are seldom spectacular, instead offering the sort of subtle, ground-level challenges often invisible on a course map and frequently requiring multiple playings (with different pin placements) to be fully appreciated.

During the Golden Age, Ross maintained several regional offices and utilized the extensive help of associates, including Walter Hatch and James McGovern. Consequently, his work was largely concentrated in certain areas, including North Carolina (more than 40 projects), Florida (about the same), Massachusetts (50+), and northern New England (35+). In addition, he occasionally reached the far West (one California design, three in Colorado), regularly found Canada (at least 11 projects), and even twice visited the then-rich man's playground of Havana, Cuba.

Ringing endorsements of Ross's work are the more than 100 American national championships that have been contested over his courses, and even after decades of often noxious alteration, he sports more layouts ranked among the national top 50 (eight) than any other architect. The defacing of classic courses by green committees and ill-suited architects takes on greater relevance in Ross's case, for it was in response to such desecrations that the Donald Ross Society—the first organization dedicated to the preservation of a Golden Age architect's work—was formed.

Notable Courses: Aronimink GC, Pennsylvania; East Lake GC, Georgia; Inverness C, Ohio; Oak Hill CC, East Course, New York; Oakland Hills CC, South Course, Michigan; Pinehurst Resort & CC, No. 2 Course, North Carolina; Plainfield CC, New Jersey; Salem CC, Massachusetts; Seminole GC, Florida; Wannamoisett CC, Rhode Island

MacKenzie Ross (UK)

Edinburgh native Phillip MacKenzie Ross (1890–1974), the son of a fine amateur golfer, learned the game at Musselburgh and was himself a keen competitor. Following a six-year military stint during World War I, he managed to latch on with golf architect Tom Simpson in a construction capacity, eventually becoming a partner in the new firm of Simpson & Ross by the mid-1920s. Handling much of the outfit's fieldwork, Ross was the driving force behind a number of courses generally credited to Simpson, including Belgium's Royal GC des Fagnes and a 1930 redesign/expansion of the Royal Antwerp GC.

Ross would, however, make a major name for himself after World War II, primarily by resurrecting the Turnberry Hotel's vaunted Ailsa course from the devastation of wartime service as an RAF base, turning it into the three-time Open Championship venue that we know today. He also built Scotland's Southerness GC about this time and redesigned the Forest course at Le Touquet in 1958.

Notable Courses: Estoril GC, Portugal; Southerness GC, Scotland; Turnberry Hotel GC, Ailsa Course, Scotland

Mason Rudolph (USA)

Clarksville, Tennessee, native Mason Rudolph (b. 5/23/1934) made history in 1950 when, at age 16, he became both the youngest-ever participant in the U.S. Open and the youngest winner of the USGA Juniors Boys title. Later playing at Memphis State, Rudolph added the 1956 Western Amateur and was a U.S. Amateur semifinalist and a Walker Cup player in 1957. He then began a 21-year PGA Tour career that included five victories, a Rookie of the Year award in 1959, and a Ryder Cup appearance in 1971. In 1965 Rudolph managed his best Major championship finish, a fourth-place at the Masters behind only the Big Three of Nicklaus, Palmer, and Player. In retirement he oversaw Vanderbilt University's golf program, which now hosts an annual Mason Rudolph Invitational in his honor.

Erik Runfelt (Sweden)

One of the more important figures in the history of Swedish golf, Erik G. W. Runfelt (1893–1978) can fairly be called that nation's first truly fine player, having won a total of 10 Swedish Open Amateurs between 1911 and 1938. Also a four-time Closed Amateur winner and a five-time Scandinavian Amateur champion, Runfelt later served as secretary of the Swedish Golf Union as well as editor of its magazine, *Svensk Golf*, for approximately two decades. Remaining competitive for many years, he captured 13 Swedish Seniors titles, including 11 straight beginning in 1944.

Paul Runyan (USA)

Born: Hot Springs, Arizona, 7/12/1908 Died: Palm Springs, California, 3/17/2002

Distance has always been a central component of golfing greatness, with few of the game's all-time elite being anything less than long hitters. Yet if ever there was a man to prove that shortness can be overcome, it was Hall of Famer Paul Runyan. Long known as "Little Poison," Runyan was a top player throughout the 1930s, winning 29 official PGA Tour events while being outdriven by nearly everyone.

Indeed, Runyan was so short that legend (and perhaps little more) holds that on the 18th at Merion, fearing the inability to carry 200 yards over the famed quarry from the blue markers, he pitched his first shot down to a lower tee from where the carry became manageable. True or not, the story is highly illustrative, for despite (or perhaps because of) such shortcomings, Paul Runyan had one of the greatest short games in history.

All but one of Runyan's wins came during the 1930s, and fully 15 came in 1933–34, the latter year including both a **Metropolitan Open** and his first Major title, the **PGA Championship**, where he beat Craig Wood at the 38th hole at Buffalo's Park CC. A second Major, also the **PGA**, would follow in 1938 at Pennsylvania's Shawnee CC, and it was perhaps here that so much of Runyan's lasting reputation was built. By all accounts, the then-26-year-old Sam Snead drove at least 30 yards past the underdog Runyan

all day, yet in the end Runyan beat Snead badly, the final margin being 8 and 7.

Runyan posted a number of high finishes at the Masters and the U.S. Open, and long after World War II put an end to his PGA Tour career, he was successful competing in the handful of national and international seniors events that predated the organized Champions Tour. He also became something of a household name among teachers, holding positions at several prestigious American clubs. Especially well thought of as a fixer of putting strokes, Runyan was still giving lessons at age 93 when he died of pneumonia in Palm Springs.

PGA Tour Wins (29): 1930 & '35 North & South; 1934 Metropolitan; **1934 & '38 PGA Championships;** 4 Westchester Opens

Ryder Cup: 1933 & '35 (2)

1928-1952

	28	29	30	31	32	33	34	35	36	37	38	39	40
Masters							T3	7	T4	T19	4	T16	T12
US Open	63	-	-	-	T12	DQ	T28	T10	T8	T14	T7	T9	49
British	-	-	-	-	-	*	-	-	-	-	-	-	
PGA	-	-	-	T9	T17	T5	1	T5	T33	T9	1	T5	T5

	41	42	43	44	45	46	47	48	49	50	51	52	
Masters	T35	3				-	-	-	-	-	-	-	
US Open	T5					21	T6	T53	-	T25	T6	T22	
British						-	-	-	-	-	-	-	
PGA	T33	-		-	-	-	-	-	-	T33	-	-	

*Result unverified—made cut but finished outside top 30.

Alex Russell (Australia)

Geelong, Victoria's Alex Russell (1892–1961) is best known as Dr. Alister MacKenzie's chief design collaborator during (and after) the famous architect's two-month visit Down Under in 1926. However, any suggestion that he owes the lion's share of his fame to MacKenzie is not a fair one, for the Cambridge-educated Russell was well established before the good doctor's visit, having won the 1924 **Australian Open** and finished second in that same season's Australian Amateur. Further, as a member of Royal Melbourne, Russell had already supplied a remodeling plan for the club's existing 18 well before MacKenzie came on the scene.

Russell (along with greenkeeper Mick Morcum) would eventually oversee construction of a MacKenzie plan for Royal Melbourne in 1926, having been named the doctor's post-visit "partner" specifically to fulfill such a role. Beyond completing several MacKenzie works, Russell am-

ply demonstrated his own architectural skills by building Royal Melbourne's East course in 1932 and New Zealand's classic links test, the Paraparaumu Beach GC, in 1949. In addition, he was the actual designer of two well-known facilities often erroneously credited to MacKenzie, Yarra Yarra (on the Melbourne sandbelt) and Western Australia's Lake Karrinyup — the confusion likely arising from Russell's having worked under the business name of "MacKenzie & Russell, Golf Course Architects."

Peter Ryde (UK)

Just over a half-century ago, 37-year-old Peter Leighton Ryde, avid golfer and more-than-capable golf writer, faced perhaps the most daunting task in the history of the game: replacing the retiring Bernard Darwin as golf correspondent for the *Times*. That Ryde did so—and held the post for roughly 30 years—speaks volumes as to the caliber of his work. Aside from simply filling the shoes that largely invented golf writing, Ryde produced several outside projects of lasting importance, the most notable being *The Shell International Encyclopedia of Golf* (Ebury, 1975), a mammoth, comprehensive volume (coauthored with Donald Steel) which no less than Herbert Warren Wind has called "one of the few indispensable golf books." In addition, Ryde edited *Mostly Golf* (A&C Black, 1976), the first and perhaps best posthumous anthology of the great Darwin's work.

Samuel Ryder (UK)

Though informal matches between teams from the United States and Great Britain had taken place in 1921 and '26, it wasn't until wealthy British seed merchant Samuel Ryder (1858–1937) donated his eponymous cup that the event took on a regular, structured form. A latecomer to golf, Ryder was personally coached by English star Abe Mitchell (whose likeness stands atop the cup) and envisioned the biennial event as creating "a cordial, friendly and peaceful feeling throughout the whole civilized world." Sadly, the event's current American and European organizers have veered far from Ryder's ideals in their jingoistic marketing of the event, manufacturing conflict in the desire to cash in on such sophomoric drivel as "The War at the Shore" (1991) and the like. Regrettably, it took the tragic events of September 11, 2001, to restore some civility, a modest resurfacing of Samuel Ryder's values that hopefully will trump organizational greed in the long run.

Cargie Rymill (Australia)

Adelaide native Herbert L. "Cargie" Rymill (1870–1951) came from affluence and did not even take up golf until his early 30s, yet he managed to establish himself as a leading authority on golf course design in a turn-of-the-century Australia largely devoid of legitimate experts. Though carrying a bit of C. B. Macdonald–like self-importance and completing relatively few projects, Rymill does hold the distinction of having worked on Adelaide's four most important courses, most notably the highly ranked Kooyanga, which was his personal pride and joy.

Grantland Rice presents a winner's check of $1,500 to Byron Nelson for the Fourth Annual Augusta National Golf Tournament, Augusta, Georgia, April 4, 1937. *Left,* Ralph Guldahl, and *right,* Ed Dudley.

S

Sandy Saddler (UK)

Standing only 5′4″, Alexander C. "Sandy" Saddler (b. 1935) was a native of Forfar, Scotland, who came to great attention as a young amateur by tying John Panton in a professional event at Carnoustie, then losing an 18-hole play-off by a single shot. Considered one of the toughest competitors of his time, Saddler was selected to the three Walker Cup sides from 1963 to 1967, going 3-5-2 overall but 3-1-2 in singles, the two halves coming against no less than Charlie Coe and Deane Beman, both in 1963.

Jarmo Sandelin (Finland/Sweden)

Though now a citizen of Sweden, Jarmo Sandelin (b. 5/10/1967) is a native of Imatra, Finland, and thus qualifies as that nation's finest competitive golfer to date. Long hitting, extroverted, and the possessor of one of golf's flashier wardrobes, Sandelin perhaps gained more fame for accusing Mark O'Meara of cheating at the 1998 Trophée Lancôme than for anything accomplished with his clubs, though he did register five European Tour wins between 1995 and 2002 and appeared in the 1999 Ryder Cup. That was a season in which he finished a career-best ninth in the Order of Merit and won both the **Spanish** and **German Opens,** a peak of form which seems rather distant now after finishing 100th in both 2001 and '03 and showing little improvement in '04.

Anne (Quast) Sander (USA)

A native of Everett, Washington, Anne Quast Sander (b. 1937) has been America's finest postwar woman golfer to forego the money of the LPGA and retain her amateur status. A prodigious talent from day one, Quast entered her first **U.S. Women's Amateur** at 14, making her a seasoned veteran by the time she won the 1958 contest (3 and 2 over Barbara Romack) as a Stanford University history major, age 20.

A mechanical but highly reliable player, Quast would add further **U.S. Amateur** titles in 1961 and '63 (along with runner-up finishes in 1965, '68 and '74) to a ledger that came to include **Western Amateur** wins in 1956, '61, and '88, **North & South** titles in 1982 and '83, a fourth-place finish at the 1973 U.S. Women's Open, and eight Curtis Cup appearances spread over 32 years (1958–90). Still very much competitive in her mid-40s, Quast waited until 1980 (when she had long since added Sander) to become the 10th woman to win both the U.S. and **British Amateurs,** later adding on four **US Senior Women's Amateurs** (1987, '89, '90, and '93).

It is certainly worth noting that Quast came along in a postwar period well stocked with talented players, a field that included Barbara McIntire, Canada's Marlene Stewart Streit, and, perhaps the largest presence of all, Joanne Gunderson Carner. That Carner and Quast both hailed from Washington State added spice to the mix, and their private rivalry seemed even more fitting when one compared Carner's outgoing personality and long, attacking game with Quast's quieter, more regimented approach.

Major Amateur Wins (9): 1956, '61 & '88 Western Amateur; 1958, '61 & '63 U.S. Women's Amateur; 1980 British Ladies; 1982 & '83 North & South

Curtis Cup: 1958–62, '66, '68, '74, '84 & '90 (8)

Doug Sanders (USA)

Cedartown, Georgia's George Douglas Sanders (b. 7/24/1933) is memorable for many golf-related things, from having the shortest backswing ever seen on a top professional, to his colorful Jimmy Demaret–like wardrobe, to his tragic missed putt at the 72nd that cost him the 1970 Open Championship. Less remembered, however, was a consistently high standard of play that saw Sanders contend in several other Majors, rank among the PGA Tour's top 25 money winners for a solid decade, and, most important, claim 20 official Tour victories between 1956 and 1972.

Having attended the University of Florida, Sanders came to the national stage as that rare postwar amateur to win a major professional event, in this case the 1956 **Canadian Open** where he defeated Dow Finsterwald in a play-off. Turning professional soon thereafter, Sanders was an established Tour presence by the end of the decade, taking the **Western Open** in 1958, five additional titles in 1961, and three more in the year following. He was also a prominent factor in Major championships, tying for 2nd at the 1959 PGA (one behind Bob Rosburg), the 1961 U.S. Open at Oakland Hills (one back of Gene Littler), and the 1966 Open Championship at Muirfield (one behind Jack Nicklaus). Despite such disappointment, Sanders' greatest heartbreak indeed came in 1970 at St. Andrews when he three-putted at the last (including the above-mentioned miss from but a yard) to allow Nicklaus into a play-off, then lost by one the following day when Jack matched his 18th-hole birdie by driving the green and two-putting. This would prove to be the 37-year-old Sanders' last run at a Major, and his miss at the 72nd remains one of modern golf's more famous disasters.

Sanders was a colorful personality who entertained many a crowd and dazzled with his unique backswing, left arm scarcely getting past parallel, the shaft struggling to reach vertical, all at blindingly quick speed. Sanders claimed this distinctive move was a product of trying to keep the ball in play as a youth, when losing them was beyond his financial range. Such a technique would surely be "coached" away today—but then modern professional golf doesn't have too many players or personalities that resemble Doug Sanders.

PGA Tour Wins (20): 1956 Canadian Open; 1958 Western Open; 1961 Colonial; 1963 & '66 Greensboro; 1965 & '67 Doral
Champions Tour Win: 1 (1983)
Ryder Cup: 1967

1957-1973

	57	58	59	60	61	62	63	64	65	66	67	68	69	70	71	72	73
Masters	T31	-	-	T29	T11	T33	T28	-	T11	T4	T16	T12	T36	-	-	-	MC
US Open	-	MC	-	T46	T2	T11	T21	T32	T11	T8	T34	T37	-	-	T37	MC	-
British	-	-	-	-	-	-	MC	11	MC	T2	T18	34	-	2	T9	4	T28
PGA	-	-	T2	T3	3	T15	T17	T28	T20	T6	T28	T8	MC	T41	MC	T7	-

Charles Sands (USA)

Charles Sands, who was vastly better known as a lawn tennis player, bears the distinction of being the first man to win an Olympic gold medal in golf, a feat he accomplished at the Paris games of 1900. His victory came by one stroke over Great Britain's equally anonymous Walter Rutherford at the racetrack-enclosed Golf de Compiégne course, an 1896 layout that still remains in play just north of the city. Golf would only make one more Olympic appearance, in 1904, when Canadian George Lyon won the gold in St. Louis.

Gene Sarazen (USA)

Born: Harrison, New York, 2/27/1902 **Died:** Marco Island, Florida, 5/13/1999

By virtue of living until the ripe old age of 97, Gene Sarazen (born Eugenio Saraceni) was the longest-running act in the golf business, the primary accomplishments of his great career having taken place in an age so far removed from Tiger Woods and Ernie Els as to seem almost a different game. To put it in perspective, Jack Dempsey was the heavyweight champion when Sarazen won his first Major championship, and two more Grand Slam titles had been added to the Sarazen résumé before Lou Gehrig even be-

gan his legendary consecutive-games streak for the New York Yankees.

As timeless and vaunted as the Sarazen record was to become, however, it remains interesting to note that nearly all of his most important titles came in two brief clusters spread a decade apart. The first began in 1922 when the little-known ex-caddie closed with a record final-round score of 68 to win the **U.S. Open** at Chicago's Skokie CC, edging Bobby Jones and a 43-year-old Scot named John Black by one. When many thought this victory a fluke, Sarazen proved otherwise by adding that summer's **PGA Championship** at Oakmont, defeating Emmet French 4 and 3 in a final that hinged on a crucial rub of the green: At the par-5 27th, standing all square, French's second shot hit the base of the flagstick on the fly and caromed back into a bunker, giving Sarazen both the hole and the momentum.

Shortly thereafter, he challenged British Open champion Walter Hagen to a 72-hole "World Championship of Golf," which was duly contested at Oakmont and the brand new Westchester Biltmore CC (today's Westchester CC) with Sarazen ultimately winning 3 and 2. The final victory of this first great rush was the successful defense of his **PGA** title the following year at New York's Pelham CC, where he again beat Hagen, once more having fortune smile upon him at a key moment. For on the 38th hole of their epic final, Sarazen's attempt to drive across a sharp dogleg was headed out-of-bounds before ricochet-

Gene Sarazen measures a proposed 8-inch golf cup, of which he was
one of the most famous sponsors.

ing back to fairway's edge, from where he pitched stiff for a winning three.

Having thus reached the game's highest level, Sarazen then fell into a nine-year decline during which, by his own admission, he paid too much attention to lucrative exhibition tours, attempting to turn his natural draw into a fade and the excitement of Roaring '20s affluence, the result being occasional victories but no further Major championships. His primary successes during this phase came during his South Florida winters, for he would eventually claim 13 victories in the Sunshine State (plus one in the Bahamas), including four straight **Miami Opens** from 1926 through 1929.

Sarazen's second great run came in the early 1930s when, following the stock market crash of 1929, he felt some driving financial incentive. His first big triumph came at the 1932 **Open Championship,** an event he had faithfully entered ever since failing to qualify (with an inglorious 75-85 performance) on his maiden visit in 1923. At that time he vowed to Bernard Darwin that "I'll be back even if I have to swim across," and though it was more often the *Aquitania* that brought Sarazen over, his 283 at the old Prince's GC was enough win the 1932 event by five. He then returned Stateside for an even more impressive display, for the 1932 **U.S. Open** was played at New York's old Fresh Meadow CC, where Sarazen once served as club professional and had lost to Tommy Armour in the final of the 1930 PGA. This time he found himself seven shots off the Open lead through 44 holes, then birdied the 45th, returned an inward 32, and followed it up with a

spectacular closing 66. The result was a three-shot triumph over Bobby Cruickshank and a final 28 holes famously played in an even 100 strokes.

Sarazen added a third **PGA** title in 1933 (defeating Willie Goggin 5 and 4 at Milwaukee's Blue Mound CC) before making even more history in 1935 at the second playing of the **Masters.** Trailing the popular Craig Wood by three strokes with only four to play, he proceeded to tie things up with a single stroke, holing a 235-yard 4 wood for a two at the par-5 15th, a shot that, some 70 years later, still ranks among the game's most famous. Thus all square, Sarazen cruised to a five-shot victory in the following day's 36-hole play-off.

Though his best golf was behind him now, Sarazen remained at least occasionally competitive for years, losing the 1940 U.S. Open in a play-off to Lawson Little and appearing at both the Masters and the Open Championship well into his golden years. His final moment of brilliance came at the 1973 Open at Royal Troon where, at age 71, he aced the famed Postage Stamp eighth in round one, then holed a bunker shot to birdie it the next day.

A world traveler throughout his career, Sarazen spent a number of summers tending to his Connecticut farm (hence his longtime nickname "The Squire") and later settled year-round on Marco Island, Florida. He remained prominent during the 1960s in his role of cohost for *Shell's Wonderful World of Golf* and was still traveling to a Japanese tournament that bore his name well into his 80s. As a player, an innovator (he is generally credited with inventing the sand wedge), and a direct link to the Golden Age of American golf, Gene Sarazen was truly the very last of a late, lamented breed.

PGA Tour Wins (39): 1922 & '32 U.S. Open; 1922, '23 & '33 PGA Championship; 1925 Metropolitan; 1930 Western Open; **1932 British Open; 1935 Masters;** 5 Miami Opens & 3 Florida West Coast Opens
Intn'l Wins (2): 1936 Australian Open
Ryder Cup: 1927–37 (6)

1920-1958

	20	21	22	23	24	25	26	27	28	29	30	31	32
Masters													
US Open	T30	17	1	T16	T17	T5	T3	3	T6	T3	T28	T4	1
British	-	-	-	-	*	-	-	-	2	T8	-	T3	1
PGA	-	T5	1	1	T9	T33	T9	T5	T3	T5	2	T3	-

	33	34	35	36	37	38	39	40	41	42	43	44	45
Masters		-	1	3	T24	T13	5	T21	T19	T28			
US Open	T26	2	T6	T28	T10	10	T47	2	T7				
British	T3	T21	-	T5	MC	-	-						
PGA	1	T9	T17	T33	T17	T5	T33	T5	T3	-		-	T17

	46	47	48	49	50	51	52	53	54	55	56	57	58
Masters	-	T26	T23	T39	T10	T12	WD	T38	T53	WD	T49	MC	MC
US Open	MC	T39	MC	MC	T38	T35	T33	MC	WD	-	-	MC	MC
British	-	-	-	-	-	-	T17	-	T17	-	WD	-	T16
PGA	-	T9	T9	T33	-	T17	-	T33	-	T17	T9	-	MC

*Result unverified—made cut but finished outside top 30.

George Sargent (UK/USA)

A former assistant to Harry Vardon at Ganton, Dorking native George Sargent (1882–1962) emigrated first to Canada, then on to America where he served as professional at several fine clubs including, for many years, East Lake. Sargent was also a capable player, winning the first **U.S. Open** he entered, in 1909 at New Jersey's old Englewood CC. There he closed with 71 to carry the day by four, later confirming his ability by tying for third in 1914 at Midlothian and fourth in 1916 at Minikahda. Sargent also won the 1912 **Canadian Open** (by three over Jim Barnes) after finishing runner-up there to Albert Murray in 1908. A charter member (and future president) of the PGA of America, he is also generally credited with being the first man to utilize film as an instructional aid.

Vivien Saunders (UK)

Sutton, England's Vivien Saunders, O.B.E. (b. 11/24/1946) was a British Women's Amateur finalist in 1966 (losing to Elizabeth Chadwick at Ganton) and a Curtis Cup player in 1968. Turning professional a year later, she enjoyed some success in Australia and Britain, with her most notable triumph being the 1977 **Women's British Open,** a then-fledgling event still far shy of Major championship status. A well-known writer and teacher in the United Kingdom, Saunders was also the first European player to qualify for the LPGA Tour (with only mixed results) in 1969.

Ben Sayers (UK)

Born: Leith, Scotland, 6/23/1856 **Died:** North Berwick, Scotland, 3/9/1924

The colorful and diminutive Ben Sayers, born in Leith but forever linked with North Berwick, was among the last of a dying breed: the old-fashioned British professional whose living was made far more from teaching, club-making, and high-profile challenge matches than standard tournament competition. This is not to suggest that Sayers wasn't a regular Open Championship competitor, for, in fact, he played for more than 40 years in succession, tying for second (one back of Jack Burns) at St. Andrews in 1888 and solo third the following year, four out of the Willie Park Jr.–Andrew Kirkaldy play-off at Musselburgh.

As a teacher Sayers gained great repute with the British aristocracy and traveled to both the United States and Monte Carlo, the latter to instruct several golfing royals. Such associations could only serve to build his equipment business, which began strictly with golf balls in the mid-1870s but soon branched out to cover all manner of clubs, eventually flourishing more after Ben's death (when run by his son) than it ever did during his lifetime. No less than Jack Nicklaus special-ordered a Ben Sayers putter in 1959 and the company still goes strong—albeit preparing to produce in China—at the time of this writing.

Sayers was probably most famous for his height, an unimposing 5′3″. Until the age of 16, he was trained as an acrobat, the root, we assume, of his occasional cartwheels following the holing of an important putt. Most such displays took place during challenge matches in which he frequently engaged as a single or in partnership with his brother-in-law David Grant or his good friend Andra Kirkaldy. Sayers won more than his share of these well-documented contests, though he perhaps is better recalled for a comment he made after a surprise loss, opining that "It's no' possible, but it's a fact." Such confidence was further expressed (if not altogether backed up) prior to an Open Championship at Muirfield when Sayers promised "Give me a wind and I'll show you who'll be champion." But clearly Wee Ben won the Open a bit less frequently than the Scottish winds blew.

Adam Scott (Australia)

One of the top young players in the world today, two-time **Australian Junior** champion Adam Scott (b. Adelaide, 7/16/1980) seems, at the tender age of 25, to be bound for greatness. An intelligent young man with a powerful swing rather reminiscent of Tiger Woods, Scott enjoyed four top-10 finishes in 11 starts as a European Tour rookie in 2000, then won the **Dunhill Championship** (the old South African PGA) and finished 13th on the Order of Merit in 2001. The following year saw even further advancement as Scott scored two runaway victories, first in **Qatar** (where his –19 total won by six) and then at the **Scottish PGA** (by an extraordinary 10 shots), pushing him to seventh on the Order of Merit. A single win at the **Scandinavian Masters** was his lone 2003 European victory, but by now Scott was splitting time in America where he scored his first PGA Tour victory in September at the inaugural **Deutsche Bank Championship,** beating Rocco Mediate by four.

Though still working on several aspects of his game, Scott entered 2004 on track for stardom, and his prospects leaped forward with a victory at the 2004 **Players Championship,** the biggest "non-Major" title in golf. Playing the famed TPC at Sawgrass, Scott overcame a horrendously hooked approach at the 72nd by scrambling for a gutsy bogey—just enough to hold off a hard-charging Padraig Harrington by one. That two weeks later, as an obvious favorite, he shot an opening-round 80 and missed the cut at the Masters points to the need for greater consistency, a quality that often comes with added maturity. A subsequent win at the **Booz Allen Classic** righted the ship, however, and reminded us that in a golfing world where talented youngsters are often hyped beyond any degree of reality, Adam Scott appears to be progressing at a pace well suited to long-term stardom.

Lady Margaret Scott (UK)

The daughter of the Earl of Eldon, Lady Margaret Scott (1875–1938) can rightly be recalled as the first superstar of women's golf. A tall, graceful and attractive young lady who used a 10-finger grip and John Daly–like backswing, she was widely rated the best player in the land before the playing of the first **British Ladies** championship in 1893—and her performance there did little to alter the perception, as she cruised easily through four matches, routing Issette Pearson 7 and 5 in the final. The following year at Littlestone it was more of the same, plowing through the field before again defeating Pearson, this time 3 and 2. Only in 1895 was Scott pushed, actually trailing in her semifinal match before eventually dispatching a Ms. E. Lythgoe 5 and 4 at Royal Portrush.

In the late Victorian world in which Lady Margaret was raised, such things as professional golf—or really any sort of career for a woman—were nonexistent. Thus she retired, undefeated, soon after her third title and settled into married life as Lady Margaret Hamilton-Russell, never even beginning to capitalize on a game, style, and appearance that today would generate millions.

Hon. Michael Scott (UK/Australia)

Born of the same noble golfing family that spawned Lady Margaret, The Hon. Michael Scott (1878–1959) emigrated near the turn of the century to Australia where he became a successful dairy farmer. A member of Royal Melbourne, he proceeded to utterly dominate early golf Down Under, winning four **Australian Amateurs** between 1905 and 1910, the first **Australian Open** in 1904, and a second, more controversial Open title in 1907. On the latter occasion, Scott apparently accidentally teed his ball outside the markers on Royal Melbourne's 12th hole during the third round and a protest was lodged. The committee ruled in Scott's favor, stating that no real advantage was gained but more likely basing their decision on the fact that his margin of victory was a convincing eight strokes.

The controversy, which included appeals to the R&A, raged on for months and was never adequately resolved.

Scott returned to England before World War I and, with two **French Amateur** titles under his belt, was selected for Walker Cup duty in 1924, at the age of 46. There, playing at Garden City, he made a significant splash, first teaming with the unrelated Robert Scott to defeat Bobby Jones and William C. Fownes Jr. one up in foursomes, then taking full measure of Jess Sweetser in singles 7 and 6. Yet with all of this on his résumé, the long-hitting Scott is likely best remembered as the oldest-ever winner of the **British Amateur,** a title he captured in 1933—at age 55—by defeating Dale Bourn at Hoylake 4 and 3.

Syd Scott (UK)

Englishman Sidney Simeon Scott (b. 1913) was one of Great Britain's better professionals in the early postwar years, finishing runner-up at the 1954 Open Championship at Royal Birkdale and going 0-2 at the 1955 Ryder Cup match at Palm Springs. Also solo fourth at the 1959 Open at Muirfield, he was later a fine senior player, losing the world senior title to Sam Snead in 1964.

Ed Seay (USA)

A graduate of the University of Florida and an ex-U.S. Marine, Ed Seay (b. 1938) began a career in golf design in the mid-1960s working for North Carolina–based architect Ellis Maples. Though he would briefly practice solo in the early 1970s, the overwhelming majority of his work has come beneath the umbrella of Arnold Palmer, where Seay has worked on over 200 designs, both domestic and international, that carry the Palmer name. Seay does have one very notable solo project to his credit, however: Florida's Sawgrass CC, which hosted five Players Championships preceding the event's 1982 move to the famous TPC at Sawgrass.

Charles Seaver (USA)

The son of 1908 **Trans-Mississippi Amateur** champion Everett Seaver and father of Hall of Fame baseball pitcher Tom, Charles Seaver (b. 1911–2004) grew up in Southern California and starred in football and golf at Stanford in the early 1920s. While still in school, Seaver won the **California** and **Northern California Amateurs,** completing a rare triple by adding the **Southern Cal** title the following year. On the national level, he won both of his matches during a lone 1932 Walker Cup appearance, an American rout at The Country Club in Brookline.

Beyond these accomplishments, Seaver's name pops up in two rather interesting places. First, he and his father bore the unique distinction of joining Dr. Alister MacKenzie in the first foursome ever to play Cypress Point, in 1928. Later, on a more public stage, it was Seaver whom Gene Homans edged one up in the semifinals of the 1930 U.S. Amateur, winning Homans the right to face Bobby Jones in the latter's Grand Slam–winning final match. "I got to play Bobby Jones three other times," Seaver later lamented, "but not the most important time."

Lally Segard (La Vicomtesse de Saint-Sauveur) (France)

Few top players have performed under more names than this petite but highly talented Frenchwoman (b. Paris, 4/4/1921), who initially made waves under her maiden name of Lally Vagliano, later under a married moniker of Lally Segard, and, most memorably, under her title as La Vicomtesse de Saint-Sauveur. With a long, powerful swing and a keenly attacking style, Mrs. Segard (the shortest choice) enjoyed remarkable longevity, performing internationally for more than 30 years after claiming the **British Girls** title in 1937. Though her total of four **French Open** and five **French Closed** victories was surely limited by the interruption of World War II, Segard remained a dominant force around the Continent thereafter, taking Ladies titles in **Italy** (1949 and '51), **Switzerland** (1949 and '65), **Luxembourg** (1949), and **Spain** (1951). Most important, she also captured the 1950 **British Ladies,** beating Jessie Valentine 3 and 2 at Royal County Down.

Perhaps of comparable importance to her playing success was Segard's long-term effect on French women's golf, for the great postwar star Brigitte Varangot was her direct protégé and both Claudine Cros and Catherine LaCoste followed closely in her championship wake. Additionally, her family donated the Vagliano Trophy, competed for biennially by Great Britain, Ireland, and a team from Continental Europe.

Hope Seignious (USA)

Though little noted as a player, Hope Seignious (1919–1968) was a genuine golfing trailblazer, one of the first women to renounce her amateur status as well as the first known to have been hired as a club professional, joining Milwaukee's North Shore CC in 1944. Seignious was also the driving force behind the founding of the Women's Professional Golf Association during that same year, an organization designed to create a women's professional tour in line with the popular men's edition. With Betty

Hicks, Betty Jameson, Helen Dettweiler, and others on board, Seignious scored one major blow by enlisting the help of a Spokane, Washington, civic group to create the U.S. Women's Open in 1946, an event not taken over by the USGA until some seven years later. In general, the WPGA was an unstable entity, largely financed by Seignious's own money and that of her father, a prosperous cotton broker. With things looking bleak in 1949, the organization was officially disbanded and replaced by the new LPGA, with former PGA Tour manager Fred Corcoran brought aboard to inject some excitement, and Seignious packing off to North Carolina to run a trucking business.

Peter Senior (UK/Australia)

Born to a British military family then residing in Singapore, Peter Senior (b. 7/31/1959) was raised in Brisbane and has represented only Australia in international play. A fine ball-striker who joined the European Tour at age 20, Senior has won 18 times in Australia, four in Europe, and twice in Japan, with his homeland titles including the 1989 **Australian Open** and **PGA,** the 1991 and '95 **Australian Masters,** and a pair of **Johnnie Walker Classics** in 1989 and '91. In Europe where he has finished as high as seventh in the Order of Merit (1987), his biggest wins are his most recent, the 1990 **European Open** (where Senior edged Ian Woosnam by one at Sunningdale) and the 1992 **Benson & Hedges International.**

Interestingly, nearly all of these larger victories came after Sam Torrance solved Senior's longstanding putting woes by converting him to the long or "broomstick" style of club. For Senior, who had previously both putted and *chipped* cross-handed, the move was a godsend, taking a stalled career to places—and financial winnings—previously unthinkable. It is also worth noting that despite possessing the tee-to-green skills so well suited to Major championships, Senior has only once played at the Masters (tying for 42nd) and the U.S. Open (missing the cut) and has never bettered a tie for 44th at the PGA Championship. He has, however, twice cracked the top 10 at the Open Championship, finishing level fourth in 1993 and sixth in 1988.

Intn'l Wins (25): 1989 Australian PGA; 1989 Australian Open; 1992 Benson & Hedges
Presidents Cup: 1994 & '96 (2)

Major P. G. Sethi (India)

Major P. G. "Billoo" Sethi was one of India's earliest indigenous stars, following I. S. Malik and playing alongside his son Ashok. Sethi joined the younger Malik as the second five-time winner of the venerable **All-India Amateur Golf Championship** by capturing titles in 1959, '61, '62, '70 and '72, a feat later to be matched by Vikramjit Singh, mostly in the 1970s. A strong, powerful player, Sethi also ventured abroad to compete, reaching the third round of the 1960 U.S. Amateur where he was eliminated by eventual runner-up Robert W. Gardner. Perhaps most important, in between Peter Thomson's unsurprising victories in the first and third **Indian Opens** (1964 and '66), Sethi did his nation proud by capturing the 1965 event as an amateur, opening with a pair of 68s before winning by a glorious seven strokes.

Sewsunker Sewgolum (South Africa)

One of golf's all-time most fascinating stories, Sewsunker "Papwa" Sewgolum (1929–1978) was born to Indian parents living in Durban, South Africa, and, being darkly complected, was largely unable to play professionally in his homeland due to apartheid. An ex-caddie of limited educational background, Sewgolum bore another curious distinction, being one of the very few golfers ever to successfully play all of his shots cross-handed. Despite such handicaps, Sewgolum proved his mettle frequently, traveling to friendlier arenas such as the Netherlands, where he quite remarkably won the **Dutch Open** in 1959, '60, and '64. Sadly, he will likely be best remembered in South Africa for winning the 1963 **Natal Open** at the Durban CC, then having to receive his trophy in a driving rain when the club refused him admittance to its segregated clubhouse.

Geoff Shackelford (USA)

A Southern Californian who played collegiate golf at Pepperdine University, historian/writer/architect Geoff Shackelford (b. 9/23/1971) established himself by his mid-20s as a leading proponent of traditionalist values in the corporate-run world of modern American golf. As an author, Shackelford has penned nine architecture-related volumes, most notably the attractive *Golden Age of Golf Design* (Sleeping Bear, 1999) and *Grounds for Golf* (Thomas Dunne, 2003). He also authored the controversial *Future of Golf in America* (iUniverse, 2004), a state-of-the-game address that called on the carpet both equipment manufacturers and the USGA for conduct dangerously detrimental to the game. A frequent contributor to major publications both domestic and international, Shackelford also codesigned the award-winning Rustic Canyon GC (Moorpark, California) in 2002.

Ronnie Shade (UK)

The son of an Edinburgh club professional, Ronald David Bell Mitchell Shade, M.B.E. (1938–1986) was one of Scotland's finest postwar amateurs, a mechanical swinger of tremendous accuracy whose stock-in-trade was hitting more greens than virtually all of his competition. After finishing runner-up in 1962, Shade reeled off an impressive five successive **Scottish Amateur** titles while also pocketing three wins at the **English Amateur Stroke Play** and a single triumph (1968) in the **Scottish** equivalent. His record was surprisingly disappointing at the British Amateur, however, his only appearance past the quarters being a 3 and 2 final-round loss to the streaking young South African Bobby Cole in 1966 at Carnoustie. A stalwart of all four Walker Cup teams between 1961 and 1967, Shade turned professional at age 30 and enjoyed several good years, remaining among the top 60 in the European Order of Merit into the mid-1970s.

Andy Shaw (UK/New Zealand)

Born in Troon, Andrew J. Shaw (b. 1898) learned the game as a youth, reportedly with coaching from men like Harry Vardon and James Braid. In 1919, he emigrated to New Zealand where he soon added polish to his powerful, right-to-left long game. By 1926 Shaw was a **New Zealand Open** champion and in 1929 his winning score of 299 was the first sub-300 total since A. D. S. Duncan's record 295 in 1910 — a standard whose days were now numbered. In 1930, in windy conditions, Shaw began the Open with rounds of 69-68, staking himself to an astounding 15-shot lead. When all was said and done, his 284 stood 18 clear of the field and shattered Duncan's mark by 11 strokes, a new record that would stand for 19 years. All told, Shaw would win seven **New Zealand Opens** and defeat both Walter Hagen and Gene Sarazen in exhibition matches on his home turf. In today's era of jet travel and a thriving European/World Tour, he would, one suspects, be a well-known star.

Bob Shearer (Australia)

Joining Bruce Crampton as one of only two men to win the **Australian Amateur** (1969), **Australian Open** (1982), and **Australian PGA** (1983), Bob Shearer (b. Melbourne, 5/28/1948) overcame several health problems to capture 19 titles in his homeland as well as two European events (the 1975 **Madrid Open** and the '75 **Piccadilly Medal Play**) and one second-tour event in the United States (the 1982 **Tallahassee Open**). Widely respected for his long driving and overall shotmaking skills, Shearer can take particular pride in his Australian Open title, for he won it by four over Payne Stewart and Jack Nicklaus on an Australian GC layout that Nicklaus himself designed. All told, Shearer may have made a bit less of an impact around the world than many expected, though as an over-50, he won four events on the European Senior Tour between 1998 and 2001.

Patty Sheehan (USA)

The daughter of a longtime college ski coach, Patricia Leslie Sheehan (b. Middlebury, Vermont, 10/27/1956) was initially one of America's highest-rated junior skiers before switching seriously to golf during her teens. Once dedicated, her amateur record was impressive, beginning with four straight **Nevada Amateurs** from 1975 through 1978 and back-to-back **California** titles in 1978 and '79. Losing in the final of the 1979 U.S. Women's Amateur to Carolyn Hill, Sheehan rebounded the following year to win the **AIAW** individual title playing for San Jose State and to appear on a victorious Curtis Cup team, for which she won all four of her matches.

An outgoing player whose colorful dress and style were popular with fans, Sheehan finished 11th on the 1981 LPGA Tour money list in her first full season, then moved up to fourth in 1982, beginning a streak of 12 top-eight finishes that would extend all the way through 1993. During this remarkably consistent period, she claimed 31 of her 35 career victories, four of her six Major championships, one Player of the Year award (1983), and one Vare Trophy (1984). Her Major victories began at the 1983 **LPGA Championship** at Kings Island, Ohio, and continued with an epic defense of the crown in '84, running away from Beth Daniel and Pat Bradley by a gargantuan 10 strokes. During those same years, Sheehan was also enduring great disappointment at the U.S. Women's Open, finishing second in both 1983 and '88, then suffering the hardest defeat imaginable in 1990 when she led the event by a colossal nine strokes after 36 holes before stumbling home to lose to Betsy King by one. Sheehan would finally make amends at Oakmont in 1992, however, when her 4-under-par 280 tied with Juli Inkster, and her Monday 72 took the ensuing play-off by two strokes. A third **LPGA Championship** then followed in 1993.

Sheehan left the top tier in the mid-1990s, initially falling to 13th, 14th, and 12th on the money list from 1994 through 1996 before easing her way steadily from the limelight by the end of the decade. Even during these downward years she managed to claim two more Major titles, a second **U.S. Open** in 1994 and, finally, a **Dinah Shore** (by one over Kelly Robbins and Meg Mallon) in 1996.

Perhaps due to her skiing background, Sheehan possessed a great deal of strength in her 5'3" frame, and her short game and bunker play were widely viewed as first class. A participant in the first four Solheim Cup matches, she logged a career 5-7-1 record on teams that went 3-1, then split a pair of matches as the American captain in 2002 and '03. An LPGA Hall of Famer, Sheehan has long been known for her work with troubled youth, particularly her funding of a home for wayward teenage girls in northern California.

LPGA Wins (35): 1983 Corning; **1983, '84 & '93 LPGA Championship;** 1989, '90, '92 & '95 Rochester; **1992 & '94 U.S. Women's Open;** 1993 Safeway; **1996 Dinah Shore;** 3 Sarasota Classics, 3 Inamori Classics & 3 Safeco Classics
Curtis Cup: 1980 **Solheim Cup:** 1990–96 (4); 2002 & '03 Capts

1976-1997

	76	77	78	79	80	81	82	83	84	85	86
Dinah								T30	T8	T7	T38
LPGA	-	-	-	-	-	MC	DQ	1	1	T38	2
US Open	MC	MC	MC	MC	-	T6	T29	T2	T5	T12	T44
du Maur				-	T28	6	11	T5	T8	T10	T22

	87	88	89	90	91	92	93	94	95	96	97
Dinah	2	T63	T23	T11	T3	T3	T12	T19	T43	1	63
LPGA	T7	MC	7	T5	T64	T7	1	T7	T3	T10	MC
US Open	T21	2	T17	2	T15	1	6	1	T10	T14	T9
du Maur	MC	T23	T4	2	MC	T13	-	T11	T25	-	-

John Shippen (USA)

Born: Washington, D.C., 12/5/1879 **Died:** Newark, New Jersey, 5/20/1968

The son of a black Presbyterian pastor, John Shippen represents one of the most remarkable stories in the history of American golf. Raised from the age of nine on Long Island's Shinnecock Indian reservation (where his father was sent to minister), Shippen helped to build the original Shinnecock Hills GC and was taught the game by the club's first professional, Willie Dunn. Demonstrating great proficiency, Shippen was encouraged by the membership to enter when the club hosted the 1896 U.S. Open, only to face a threatened boycott by many of the field's not-so-progressive professionals. To his undying credit, USGA President Theodore Havemeyer told the pros what they could do with their boycott and on game day everybody played. Amazingly, Shippen's first-round 78 was tied for the lead but a second-round 81 (including an 11 at the par-4 13th) doomed him to a tie for fifth with H. J. Whigham.

Interestingly, Shippen was long believed to have been half American Indian, apparently an alibi provided by Havemeyer in staring down the boycott. Even so, his hiring by Philadelphia's Aronimink CC at age 19 must surely represent among the most progressive personnel moves in the history of the game, making Shippen the first minority to serve as a head professional at a major American club, likely by more than half a century! He would later play, less eventfully, in five more U.S. Opens and serve as professional at New Jersey's Shady Rest GC (the nation's first predominately black club) for 36 years.

Dinah Shore (USA)

A well-known singer, actress, and television host, Frances Rose "Dinah" Shore (1916–1994) may not have enjoyed the golfing stature of Bing Crosby or Bob Hope, but her 1972 founding of an eponymous LPGA golf tournament in the Palm Springs desert likely had a bigger impact on the ladies' tour than Crosby, Hope, or any other celebrity ever had on the mens'. The initial Colgate Dinah Shore, for example, offered a total purse of $110,000 in a year when neither the LPGA Championship nor the U.S. Women's Open was bettering $50,000. Such money combined with Shore's celebrity status made the event an instant centerpiece of the LPGA Tour, and it received Major championship status in 1983. Rancho Mirage's Mission Hills CC, permanent home of the event, eventually renamed the host course after Shore following her 1994 death.

Denny Shute (USA)

Born: Cleveland, Ohio, 10/25/1904 **Died:** Akron, Ohio, 5/13/1974

An outstanding player primarily during the 1930s, Herman Densmore "Denny" Shute was a 15-time winner on the PGA Tour despite entering far fewer events than many of his brethren. His first important victory came at the 1930 **Los Angeles Open** when he defeated Bobby Cruickshank and Horton Smith by four. Three years later, while traveling abroad with the Ryder Cup team, Shute won his first Major at the **Open Championship** at St. Andrews, riding four straight 73s into a play-off with countryman Craig Wood, which Shute won by two. His best finish at the Masters was a tie for fifth in 1935, while at the U.S. Open he was seven times among the top 10, finishing second in 1941 and losing in a three-way play-off to Byron Nelson and Craig Wood in 1939 in Philadelphia.

Shute's luck ran a bit better in the **PGA Championship**, however, an event he would win in 1936 and '37 and remain the last man to claim back-to-back until Tiger Woods in 1999 and 2000. In 1936 at Pinehurst, Shute bounced Bill Mehlhorn in the semis before closing out long-hitting Jimmy Thomson on the 34th hole of the final with an eagle. In '37, he caught a break when Jug McSpaden missed a four-footer at the 36th to win, opening the door for Shute to triumph with a par at the 37th.

A quiet, focused, and well-liked man, Shute gained a bit of unwanted notoriety in 1939 when his entry into the PGA was refused because his entry fee arrived a day late. A threatened boycott by other stars got Shute into the field, of course, but the story is highly illustrative for those who might assume the PGA of America's preoccupation with money to be strictly a modern thing.

PGA Tour Wins (15): 1930 Los Angeles; 1930 Texas; **1933 British Open; 1936 & '37 PGA Championship**
Ryder Cup: 1931, '33 & '37 (3)

1926-1951

	26	27	28	29	30	31	32	33	34	35	36	37	38
Masters									T13	5	T11	T13	WD
US Open	T43	T48	T6	T3	T25	T25	T14	T21	T43	T4	10	T10	T11
British	-	-	-	-	-	-	-	1	20	-	-	14	-
PGA	-	-	-	T17	T9	2	T17	-	T3	T9	1	1	T9

	39	40	41	42	43	44	45	46	47	48	49	50	51
Masters	15	-	18	WD				T25	20	32	T45	T35	T47
US Open	3	-	2					MC	MC	-	MC	T31	MC
British	-							-	-	-	-	-	-
PGA	T9	-	T5	T17		-	T5	-	-	-	T33	T9	T17

Dick Siderowf (USA)

Arguably the finest career amateur ever produced in Connecticut, stockbroker Richard L. Siderowf separated himself from a field of strong regional players largely on the strength of having twice won the **British Amateur** (1973 and '76), while reaching the semifinals in 1975. Though never advancing further than the quarter-finals of the U.S. Amateur (and tying for sixth, during the ill-fated stroke-play experiment in 1966), Siderowf was the low amateur at the 1968 U.S. Open and a four-time Walker Cup selection between 1969 and 1977, as well as captain of the victorious 1979 team. His overall Cup playing record was 4-8-2, but included a 4 and 2 singles victory over the powerful Michael Bonallack at Brookline in 1973. He also won four **Metropolitan Amateur** titles between 1968 and 1974.

Charlie Sifford (USA)

Widely viewed as the Jackie Robinson of golf, Hall of Famer Charles Luther Sifford (b. Charlotte, North Carolina, 6/22/1922) fought through the barriers of a racially stratified society and the infamous "Caucasians Only" clause of the PGA of America to become, in 1961, the first full-time black player on the PGA Tour. Having learned the game as a caddie in North Carolina, Sifford, who once served as jazz singer Billy Eckstine's personal pro, followed the earlier trailblazing done by Bill Spiller and Ted Rhodes and was himself a none-too-young 39 when the big chance came.

Though his competitive record seems almost secondary in importance, the fact is that Sifford managed to win twice, in 1967 at **Hartford** and 1969 at the **Los Angeles Open**. The latter proved particularly fitting, for aside from coming in Sifford's adopted hometown, the L.A. event had long stood among the game's less restricted, having included both Rhodes and Spiller in its field during the postwar 1940s. Also a six-time winner of the **Negro National Open,** Sifford has emerged as rather the complex personality over the years, an inevitable by-product of having lived a life that few in today's golf world can truly understand.

Jay Sigel (USA)

A top junior player in the early 1960s, R. Jay Sigel (b. Bryn Mawr, Pennsylvania, 11/12/1943) initially attended the University of Houston before transferring, after a conversation with Arnold Palmer, to Wake Forest. Sigel, however, was not a world beater at Wake and upon graduating chose a career in the insurance business rather than golf. He continued to compete in prominent amateur events, however, and eventually found his stride in the late 1970s. Two **Porter Cups** (1975 and '81) and a pair of **Sunnehanna Amateurs** (1976 and '78) got him rolling, setting the stage for the 1979 **British Amateur** at the Hillside GC where a 3 and 2 victory over fellow Wake Forest grad Scott Hoch claimed the title.

From then on it was all roses, beginning with an 8 and 7 final victory over Virginian David Tolley to capture the 1982 **U.S. Amateur** at The Country Club in Brookline. A year later, future PGA Tour player Chris Perry was the victim as Sigel became only the eighth player to take back-to-back **Amateurs,** this time at Chicago's North Shore GC. **Mid Amateur** titles came in 1983, '85, and '87, as did several more regional victories, all of which set the stage for Sigel to finally turn pro in 1993, in time to win eight times on the Champions Tour.

Sigel will be best remembered as an amateur, however, particularly for appearing on winning Walker Cup sides in 1977, '83, '85, and '93, serving as playing captain for the middle two matches.

Dan Sikes (USA)

The recipient of a law degree from the University of Florida, Jacksonville native Dan Sikes (1930–1987) won the 1957 **U.S. Public Links** title before joining the PGA Tour in 1961. A six-time Tour winner, he followed the pattern of many native Floridians by claiming half of his titles on the familiar Bermudagrass of the Sunshine State. His peak seasons came in 1967 and '68 when he finished fifth and eighth on the money list and won four times, most notably at his hometown **Jacksonville Open** in 1967. Sikes experienced a particularly strange run of luck at the 1967 Westchester Classic when he initially withdrew before the second round (play was subsequently washed out, along with his withdrawal), then played poorly enough the next morning to easily miss the cut (until *that* round too was washed away), then, on his third opportunity, fired a course record 62, which allowed him not only to see the weekend but to ultimately tie for second, one back of Jack Nicklaus. Sikes was also a Ryder Cup player in 1969.

R. H. Sikes (USA)

A native of Paris, Arkansas, and a graduate of the state's university at Fayetteville, Richard H. Sikes (b. 3/6/1940) was a two-time **U.S. Public Links** champion (1961 and '62), a U.S. Amateur runner-up (to Deane Beman in 1963), the 1963 **NCAA** individual champion, and a 1963 Walker Cupper prior to joining the PGA Tour in 1964. His professional future certainly seemed bright upon winning the lucrative **Sahara Invitational** as a rookie, but his game proved itself unable to sustain such heights for the long term. Sikes would win once more at the 1966 **Cleveland Open** and managed to hang around well into the 1970s, but never as a top-level competitor.

Bryan Silk (New Zealand)

Bryan Silk (b. 1910) was a contemporary and schoolmate of New Zealand's dominant World War II–era amateur J. P. Hornabrook and a three-time winner of the nation's **Amateur** title in 1934, '37, and '47. A strongly built, steady player, his full-time job as an accountant clearly demanded more attention than was ideal for top-caliber golf, leading Hornabrook to observe that "if Bryan Silk could have played golf as a professional, he would have become one of the greatest players in the world." As it was, Silk competed in the national Open well into the 1960s and made a strong name for himself representing New Zealand internationally for years.

Brian Silva (USA)

A native of Framingham, Massachusetts, Brian Silva (b. 1953) initially studied and taught agronomy and turfgrass management, eventually working for the USGA Greens Section in the early 1980s. In 1983, he shifted gears, pursuing a career as a golf course architect by going into partnership with veteran Geoffrey Cornish, their firm later adding partner Mark Mungeam in 1995.

One of Silva's earlier works, Cape Cod's Captains GC, received acclaim as one of the nation's first high-end public courses, and several additional Massachusetts designs have garnered similar praise. It can be argued that Silva's major contemporary prominence lies in his restorative work to the designs of Golden Age standard bearers Donald Ross and Seth Raynor, with a résumé that counts Ross's Seminole, Biltmore Forest, and Augusta CC and Raynor's Lookout Mountain, Mountain Lake, and Everglades Club among its marquee entries. Silva gained further attention with his original design of Chattanooga's Black Creek GC, a 2000 layout built in the unique Seth Raynor/Charles Blair Macdonald style.

Notable Courses: Black Creek GC, Tennessee; Captains GC, Massachusetts

Golem Silverio (Philippines)

Considered by some the finest talent in the not-so-well documented history of Filipino golf, Luis "Golem" Silverio won the 1966 **Philippines Open** at the Wack Wack GC while still in school, only the second amateur to take the Open title. For this success he became the second Filipino (after Ben Arda) to be invited to the Masters, appearing, with limited success, in both 1966 and '67. Given the fluctuations in native talent and the paucity of Western stars visiting the Philippines, career ledgers there can be misleading. In addition to Silverio's win as an amateur, some mention must be made of professionals Celestino Tugot and Larry Montes who won the national Open 6 and 13 times respectively—the latter cleaning up in and around wartime when the competition was severely limited.

Jim Simons (USA)

Butler, Pennsylvania, native and Wake Forest graduate Jim Simons (b. 5/15/1950) caused quite a stir in 1971 when, while still an amateur, a third-round 65 gave him a two-stroke 54-hole lead in the U.S. Open at Merion. A closing 76 left him tied for fifth, but the Open served as a fine centerpiece to a year that included a runner-up finish at the British Amateur (losing 3 and 2 to Steve Melnyk at Carnoustie) and selection to the Walker Cup team. A year later the two-time All-American turned pro and, after several years of adjustment, won thrice on the PGA Tour, first in **New Orleans** in 1977, then later at the **Memorial Tournament** (1978) and the **Bing Crosby** (1982). Simons retired after the 1988 season to pursue a stock brokerage business, making only rare appearances on the Champions Tour upon becoming eligible in 2000.

Archie Simpson (UK)

Little is recorded of Earlsferry, Scotland's Archie Simpson, a contemporary of Andrew Kirkaldy and Ben Sayers who was twice second in the Open Championship (in 1885 at St. Andrews and 1890 at Prestwick) and five times among the top-5 overall. Having played in an era when all but the champions went largely undocumented, Simpson "had by all accounts a most beautiful swing" according to Darwin who, like most historians, never had the chance to see him play.

Jack Simpson (UK)

Jack Simpson clearly has been more celebrated by history than his brother Archie, rather an oddity as Jack's single appearance in the top five at the **Open Championship** hardly matches Archie's five visits. To the victor goes the spoils, however, and indeed Jack's sole top-five was a win, capturing the Claret Jug in 1884 at Prestwick, by two over Willie Fernie and Douglas Rolland. A stonemason by trade, Jack was described by Darwin as "a mighty driver and a most dashing player," though it is apparent that he, like contemporaries Bob Martin and Tom Kidd, was one of Scotland's old-fashioned professionals, playing for prize money but dissolving back into blue-collar working lives when the contest was complete.

Scott Simpson (USA)

Scott Simpson (b. San Diego, California, 8/17/1955) is a prominent example of a player whose game has been particularly well suited to the severe conditions of the **U.S. Open,** winning the title in 1987 and regularly contending for years thereafter, including ties for sixth in 1988 and '89 and a solo second in 1991, when he lost an 18-hole playoff at Hazeltine National GC to Payne Stewart.

A two-time **NCAA** individual champion and All-American (1976 and '77) at USC and a Walker Cup player in 1977, Simpson has enjoyed wide-ranging professional success, winning seven times on the PGA Tour as well as on multiple occasions in Japan and Europe. His first victory came at the 1980 **Western Open** at Chicago's Butler National GC (a distinctly U.S. Open-style course) and he later added wins at **Westchester** (1984) and **Greensboro** (1987). His crowning moment took place at the 1987 Open at the Olympic Club when, trailing 54-hole leader Tom Watson by one, Simpson played the closing nine in a splendid 32 strokes, his resulting 68 overtaking the heavily favored Watson by one. Simpson would later add victories at **Atlanta** (1989), the **Byron Nelson Classic** (1993), and **San Diego** (1998) before slipping from exempt status at the end of the millennium. He becomes eligible for the Champions Tour in late 2005.

Tom Simpson (UK)

Cambridge-educated as an attorney, England's Thomas G. Simpson (1877–1964) was a scratch golfer and member of both the Oxford & Cambridge Golfing Society and the Woking GC in Surrey. His interest in course design developed largely upon observing the then-radical redesign performed upon Woking by club members John L. Low and Stuart Patton, and by 1910 Simpson was closing his law practice and turning full time to architecture. He joined forces with Walton Heath designer Herbert Fowler to form a prominent firm that would, after World War I, add J. F. Abercromby and A.C.M. Croome to the masthead. With Fowler handling most of the outfit's British work, Simpson spent a good deal of time on the Continent, especially in France where his designs at Chantilly, Morfontaine, Chiberta, and Hardelot stand among that nation's best.

During the late 1920s, Simpson aligned himself with the young MacKenzie Ross, primarily undertaking projects within the United Kingdom. A man of great wealth, he traveled around Britain in a chauffeur-driven Rolls-Royce, sporting cloak, sunglasses, and a beret. Despite such flighty trappings, he was very much the old-school type when it came to design, spending long hours supervising construction work and holding up the Old Course at St. Andrews as the only place where one might truly come to understand the medium. He also coauthored, with H. N. Wethered, *The Architectural Side of Golf* (Longmans, 1929), a period standard featuring a fine collection of Simpson's sketches and tri-color hole maps.

Having retired from the field at the start of World War II, Simpson repaired to his Hampshire estate where he died in relative seclusion at age 87.

Notable Courses: G de Chantilly, France; Club de Campo de Malaga, Spain; Mittelrheinischer GC (aka Bad Ems), Germany; G de Morfontaine, France; Royal Antwerp GC, Belgium

Sir W. G. Simpson (UK)

An Edinburgh attorney by trade, Sir Walter G. Simpson was hardly a life-long golfer/writer in the mold of Bernard Darwin or Horace Hutchinson. In 1887 he penned what can well be considered the game's first truly exceptional text, *The Art of Golf* (David Douglas, 1887), a magnificently written overview that included the first photographs ever utilized to demonstrate proper swing

technique. Sadly, with the exception of a chapter contributed to Horace Hutchinson's *Golf: The Badminton Library* and one or two stray articles, the wittily sarcastic Simpson wrote little more about golf, joining him with Patric Dickinson as men from which we dearly would have loved more.

Joey Sindelar (USA)

A three-time All-American and member of a 1979 National Championship team at Ohio State, Horseheads, New York, native Joey Sindelar (b. 3/30/1958) enjoyed a long and successful run on the PGA Tour, only twice finishing outside the top 125 from 1984 through 2003. He was also a six-time winner during this period, the largest conquest being the 1988 **International** in which he defeated Steve Pate and Dan Pohl by four points under the modified Stableford system. With nearly $7.5 million in winnings, Sindelar looked well on his way into the sunset before coming out of nowhere to capture the 2004 **Wachovia Championship** in Charlotte, beating a strong field that included a late-charging Tiger Woods. This popular victory, at age of 47, came some 14 years and 370 starts since Sindelar's last Tour triumph.

Vijay Singh (Fiji)

In a perfect world, Vijay Singh (b. Lautoka, 2/22/1963) would be one of the game's true folk heroes, a man of color who worked his way up from absolute oblivion to the highest stratum of the professional golfing ranks. He has done so with obvious ability and a legendary work ethic, yet despite his myriad accomplishments, Singh remains among the least popular/most misunderstood players in contemporary golf.

Singh learned the game from his father, an airplane technician, and played his way through various golfing backwaters on his way up, once serving as a club pro in Borneo and claiming as his first professional victory the **Malaysian PGA Championship.** Through the late 1980s he collected titles in places many Westerners didn't know even held tournaments, winning events like the **Nigerian** and **Ivory Coast Opens** and European Challenge Tour events such as the **El Bosque.** By 1990 he had cracked the top 20 in the European Order of Merit (rising as high as sixth in 1994) and soon his attentions were set on America, where in 1995 he won at **Phoenix** and **Westchester** and finished ninth on the money list.

A powerfully reliable ball-striker with one of the game's truly dedicated practice regimens, Singh initially battled putting problems before switching to various models of the long stick. Subsequently, his big breakthrough came

Vijay Singh hoists the PGA trophy after his 1998 win.

earners, always ranking among the top five in money and topping the list in 2003. His elite status had already been further cemented in 2000 when his 278 at Augusta was enough to hold off Ernie Els to win the **Masters** by three, a grand triumph that Singh unfortunately dulled with an off-color comment as he left the club on Sunday evening.

And therein lies Singh's problem, for while he is undoubtedly correct in feeling that the press has at times treated him unfairly, he is often his own worst enemy in providing them with ammunition. His comments that Annika Sorenstam didn't belong in the field at the 2003 Colonial, for example, represented the views of many Tour members and were not without merit, for Sorenstam got in without qualifying and came from a tour that itself is gender exclusive. Yet Singh's assertions that he hoped she wouldn't make the cut came off mean-spirited enough to give the writers a field day, resulting in his being tarred and feathered from coast to coast. Such incidents have also given the press reason to return to an allegation of cheating made against him at the 1985 Indonesian Open, a scorecard-altering charge that he today denies but which resulted in a two-year ban from the Asian Tour nonetheless.

Now in his early 40s, Singh remains very much at the top of his game, enjoying a sensational 2004 that included a remarkable nine wins, PGA Tour Player of the Year honors, overtaking Tiger Woods for the world number one ranking, claiming his third Major championship (the **PGA** at Whistling Straits), and even a return to the short putter. Certainly the world's hottest golfer at the time of this writing, Singh has come a long way from Fiji. And Borneo.

PGA Tour Wins (24): 1993 & '95 Westchester; 1997 Memorial; **1998 & 2004 PGA Championship; 2000 Masters;** 2003 Byron Nelson; 2004 Bing Crosby; 2004 Canadian Open
Intn'l Wins (21): 1992 German Open; 1994 Trophée Lancôme; 1997 South African Open; 1997 World Match Play
Presidents Cup: 1994–2003 (5)

at Seattle's Sahalee CC in the 1998 **PGA Championship,** an event in which he'd previously managed top-five finishes in 1993 and '96. At Sahalee, Singh strung together rounds of 70-66-67-68 to beat Steve Stricker by two for his first Major championship, then proved the victory no fluke by taking the following week's **International,** vaulting him to second-place on the money list. Since that time he has become one of the Tour's most prolific winners and

1989-2004

	89	90	91	92	93	94	95	96	97	98	99	00	01	02	03	04
Masters	-	-	-	-	-	T27	MC	T39	T17	MC	T24	1	T18	7	T6	T6
US Open	-	-	-	-	MC	-	T10	T7	T77	T25	T3	T8	T7	T30	T20	T28
British	T23	T12	T12	T51	T59	T20	T6	T11	T38	T19	MC	T11	T13	MC	T2	T20
PGA	-	-	-	T48	4	MC	MC	T5	T13	1	T49	MC	T51	8	T34	1

Carole Jo Skala (USA)

A native of Eugene, Oregon, Carole Jo Skala (b. 6/13/1938) competed under numerous monikers, from her maiden name of Kabler to married names of Skala, Callison, and Callison Whitted. It was under the first two that she achieved her highest success, winning the 1955 **USGA Jun-** ior **Girls,** the 1968 **Trans-Mississippi,** and seven straight **Oregon Ladies Amateurs** from 1955 through 1961. After taking several years off to begin raising her children, Skala reappeared as the 1968 **Trans-Mississippi** champion and by 1970, at age 32, was trying her luck on the LPGA Tour. Eventually winning four times, Skala's peak year came in 1974 when she took the **Peter Jackson Classic** (forerunner to the du Maurier) and two other titles, finishing eighth on the money list.

Jeff Sluman (USA)

Standing 5'7" and weighing 140 pounds, Rochester, New York, native Jeff Sluman (b. 9/11/1957) has never been among the more physically imposing men on the PGA Tour, but he has certainly stood among its most consistent players. Over two full decades, in fact, the diminutive Florida State graduate has never finished worse than 93rd on the money list, placing as high as 14th in 1992, averaging 36th from 1990 to 2003, and pocketing nearly $15 million in total winnings in the process.

Of course, earning big money and winning tournaments do not always walk hand-in-hand, and Sluman's victory ledger has indeed been a curious one. His first title came at the 1988 **PGA Championship** at Oklahoma's Oak Tree GC, an event in which he rode a hot putter to come from three back in overtaking Paul Azinger with a final-round 65. Thus apparently poised for stardom, Sluman proceeded to go the next 8-plus years without a victory, looking for all the world like a solid player who had simply caught lightning in a bottle. The drought was broken in 1997 at **Tucson,** however, and Sluman has since added four more titles over six seasons, including two **Greater Milwaukee Opens.** Though performing at an admirable level well into his 40s, he has seldom been a big factor in Major championships, recording only seven top-10 finishes in 68 starts.

Alex Smith (UK/USA)

The oldest of the three Carnoustie-born Smith brothers (there were five total) who emigrated to America near the turn of the last century, Alex (1872–1930) enjoyed little documented success in his homeland but was an immediate factor in early U.S. Open play, finishing second (seven behind Fred Herd) at the Myopia Hunt Club in 1898. After losing a play-off to the great Willie Anderson when the Open returned to Myopia in 1901, Smith soon added a fourth in 1903 at Baltusrol, then a third runner-up at Myopia (once again to Willie Anderson) in 1905. In 1906 his time finally came when, at Chicago's Onwentsia Club, he shattered Anderson's previous **Open** record with a score of 295, seven shots better than his brother Willie and 10 ahead of Laurie Auchterlonie. Smith added two more third-place finishes in 1908 and '09 before capturing his second **Open** title at the Philadelphia Cricket Club in 1910, this time in a three-way play-off over his other brother MacDonald and a very young Johnny McDermott. He would also add an improbable tie for fifth some 11 years later at age 49.

Beyond this great national championship record, Smith also captured a pair of **Western Opens** in 1903 and '06, as well as four **Metropolitan Opens** beginning with the inaugural in 1905. Throughout these competitive years, he served as professional at a number of fine clubs, holding positions in New York, Chicago, Southern California, and Florida among his many stops. Smith is also credited with inventing the phrase "Miss 'em quick" to describe his own speed/frustration on the putting green.

Frances "Bunty" (Stephens) Smith (UK)

Britain's first great postwar female, Frances "Bunty" Smith (1924–1978) won the **British Ladies** twice, first in 1949 at Harlech, then again in 1954 at Ganton. A runner-up in 1951 and '52 (the latter in 38 holes to Moira Paterson at Royal Troon), Smith was also three times the **English** champion (1948, '54, and '55) as well as the **French** winner of 1949.

A wonderfully consistent player whose powers of concentration during key moments were universally hailed, Smith put together one of the United Kingdom's all-time best Curtis Cup records, going 7-2-1 overall and 4-0-1 in singles in the five matches played during the 1950s. Most critical were her 1956 and '58 victories over American Polly Riley, for both times their match came to the last with the overall team contest hanging in the balance. On both occasions (first at Prince's GC, then at Brae Burn near Boston), Smith executed crucial iron shots to defeat Riley one up and two up, securing, respectively, a victory and a tie for the British women. Riley would gain some measure of revenge when the two squared off as nonplaying captains in 1962, and Smith would again taste defeat (though by a close margin) when leading the 1972 squad. Always actively engaged with the game, Smith was serving as president of the Ladies Golf Association at the time of her death.

Garden Smith (UK)

A talented writer and painter, the curiously named Garden G. Smith (1860–1925) is perhaps best remembered as an early editor of Britain's *Golf Illustrated*, a position he held for a decade beginning in 1898. As a writer, he was responsible for authoring three books, the best likely being *The World of Golf* (A. D. Innis, 1898). Smith also shared cowriting credit with Harold Hilton (despite actually penning only one of 12 chapters) for *The Royal & Ancient Game of Golf* (Golf Illustrated, 1912), a grand, ornate, and decidedly rare volume that features sections contributed by a variety of well-known period names.

Horton Smith (USA)

Born: Springfield, Missouri, 5/22/1908 **Died:** Detroit, Michigan, 10/14/1963

Widely viewed as one of the great putters of all time, Horton Smith burst onto the scene during the winter tour of 1928–29, winning an improbable eight times in nine starts and becoming a household name at the young age of 20. That Smith could never duplicate such a performance is hardly surprising—for how many have managed even one?—but he would go on to capture 22 more PGA Tour titles as well as two Major championships, the 1934 and '36 **Masters**. The former, of course, was the event's debut, then rather quaintly known as the Augusta National Invitation, and Smith's rock-steady 70-72-70-72 was enough to defeat frequent bridesmaid Craig Wood by one. Following Sarazen's 4-wood heroics in 1935, Smith again claimed the Green Jacket in 1936 when a closing 72 was enough to overtake Lighthorse Harry Cooper, once again winning by a single stroke.

Though perhaps not on par with his career-opening heroics, Smith's Masters titles fell within a 1934–37 stretch that saw him claim a total of 11 victories, including wins in California and Florida and his second **North & South Open** in 1937. He also bore a fine record in the other Majors, tying for fourth at the 1930 Open Championship at Hoylake and finishing third at both the 1930 and '40 U.S. Opens, the latter when a closing 69 left him one shy of the Lawson Little-Gene Sarazen play-off at Canterbury.

Developing a long, flowing swing from that which had once stretched just to reach three-quarters and playing with a casual, almost indifferent air, the tall and angular Smith seemed ideally suited for a long run in the competitive arena. Having never fully recovered from an early wrist injury, however, he instead opted for the security of a job at the Detroit GC beginning in 1946, making only sporadic PGA Tour appearances thereafter. Perhaps because of this—to borrow the words of his articulate contemporary Henry Cotton—"golfers of today in America do not give him quite the place he earned."

PGA Tour Wins (30): 1929 & '37 North & South; **1934 & '36 Masters**
Ryder Cup: 1929–37 (5)

1927-1952

	27	28	29	30	31	32	33	34	35	36	37	38	39
Masters								1	T19	1	T19	T22	T26
US Open	T44	T28	10	3	T27	T55	T24	T17	T6	T22	T36	T19	15
British	-	-	T25	T4	T11	-	T14	-	-	-	10	-	-
PGA	-	-	T17	T5	T5	T17	T17	-	T5	T5	T9	T5	T5

	40	41	42	43	44	45	46	47	48	49	50	51	52
Masters	T47	T19	5				T21	T22	34	T23	T12	T32	T30
US Open	3	T13					MC	WD	MC	T23	MC	MC	T15
British							-	-	-	-	-	-	-
PGA	T33	T9	-	-	-	-	-	T33	T17	-	-	T33

Macdonald Smith (UK/USA)

Born: Carnoustie, Scotland 3/18/1892 **Died:** Los Angeles, California, 8/31/1949

The youngest of the three golfing Smith brothers who emigrated to America (leaving two more back in Carnoustie), sweet-swinging Macdonald ranks high among the greatest players who never claimed a Major championship—a remarkable occurrence given his many quality victories and overall golfing talent. His career actually consisted of two separate and distinct periods, for he competed heavily in his early 20s before World War I, then reappeared a full decade later to achieve greater stardom during golf's Golden Age. Because the PGA Tour chooses not to recognize most events won prior to the PGA of America's 1916 founding, history frequently overlooks Smith's victories at the 1912 **Western** and 1914 **Metropolitan Opens**—perhaps not truly Majors but, without any question, among the elite events in America during these pre-PGA and Masters years.

Still, Smith's "official" record is impressive enough, with two more **Western Opens** won in 1925 and '33, additional **Metropolitans** in 1926 and '31, a **Canadian Open** in 1926 and four **Los Angeles Opens** won between 1928 and 1934. Despite this pile of top-class victories, however, there is no getting around Smith's inability to win both the U.S. and British Opens, especially when we consider that he finished within three shots of the lead in these events on

Robert T. Jones Sr. presents Horton Smith (*right*) a check for $1,500 as the winner
of the 1934 Masters Golf Tournament.

a combined 10 occasions. Without reciting this litany in too much detail, we can note his loss (to brother Alex) in a three-way play-off at the 1910 U.S. Open, second–place finishes to Bobby Jones at both Opens during the immortal one's Grand Slam year of 1930, and, most disappointing of all, a final-round 82 at the 1925 Open Championship at Prestwick, which turned a five-stroke lead into a three-stroke defeat.

But such disappointments aside, one cannot help but marvel at the longevity of Smith's genuinely competitive years, a circumstance driven by a silky, elegant swing that was frequently cited as the best of its period. Due to his British birth, Smith was ineligible to represent the United States in Ryder Cup play where, one senses, his record might have been formidable.

PGA Tour Wins (24): 1925 North & South; 1912, '25 & '33 Western Open; 1926 Texas; 1926 Canadian Open; 1914, '26 & '31 Metropolitan; 1928, '29, '32 & '34 Los Angeles; 4 Long Island Opens

1910-1936

	10	11	12	13	14	15	16	17	18	19	20	21	22	23
Masters														
US Open	T2	-	-	T4	WD	T37	-	-	-	-	-	-	-	T20
British	-	-	-	-	-						-	-	-	3
PGA							-			-	-	-	-	-

	24	25	26	27	28	29	30	31	32	33	34	35	36
Masters											T7	-	-
US Open	T4	T11	T9	T18	T6	T23	2	T10	T14	T19	T6	T14	4
British	T3	4	-	-	-	T15	T2	T5	2	-	T4	T17	-
PGA	-	-	-	-	-	-	-	-	-	-	-	-	-

Margaret Smith (USA)

Selected to the 1956 Curtis Cup team, Margaret "Wiffi" Smith (b. Redlands, California, 1937) made the most of her trip abroad, routing the great Philomena Garvey 9 and 8 in singles while separately winning the **French** and **British Ladies** titles, the latter in another rout, 8 and 7 over fellow American Mary Janssen at Sunningdale. Living in California, Mexico, and Michigan, Smith enjoyed a fine run of amateur triumphs including the 1953 **Mexican Ladies,** 1954 **USGA Junior Girls,** 1955 **North & South** and **Tam O'Shanter World Amateurs,** and the 1956 **Trans-Mississippi.** She never succeeded in capturing the U.S. Women's Amateur, however, reaching the semifinals in 1953 and the quarters in the two years immediately to follow.

An enthusiastic yet easygoing player, the long-hitting Smith turned professional in late 1956, enjoying immediate LPGA Tour success that saw her claim eight victories between 1957 and 1960. A two-time winner in 1957, Smith's best season came in 1960 when her three official victories included a third straight triumph at the **Peach Blossom Open,** and she also finished a career-best sixth place at the U.S. Women's Open. Soon after, her career was cut short by injury and illness, but Smith's accomplishments over a memorable half-decade were undeniably impressive.

Marilynn Smith (USA)

Topeka native Marilynn Smith (b. 4/13/1929) was the **Kansas Women's Amateur** champion from 1946 through 1948, then the **Women's Intercollegiate** winner while playing for the University of Kansas in 1949. Turning professional soon thereafter, Smith was a founding member of the LPGA who began competing during the organization's 15-event opening season of 1950, though it would take her until 1954 to find the winner's circle at the **Ft. Wayne Open.** For the next 17 seasons, however, she was a consistent force, winning 21 official events between 1954 and 1972 while amassing a long run of top-20 money finishes (including ten top 10s) throughout the 1960s and early '70s. Her biggest wins came in back-to-back years (1963 and '64) at the **Titleholders Championship,** on both occasions defeating the legendary Mickey Wright who was then at the peak of her powers.

Always a popular personality and one of the tour's great early ambassadors, Smith served as president of the LPGA from 1957 to 1960 and was instrumental in founding the organization's teaching division in 1959. Also organizing the first women's senior golf event (the Marilynn Smith Founders Classic) in the late 1980s, Smith broke ground on television as well, becoming the first woman to broadcast men's professional tournaments in 1973 at the U.S. Open and Colonial.

LPGA Wins (21): 1963 & '64 Titleholders; 1963 & '65 Peach Blossom; 1966 & '67 Orange Blossom; 1967 Babe Zaharias

Martin Smith (UK)

Eric Martin Smith (1908–1951), whom Longhurst described as "a happy-go-lucky golfer with a long flowing swing," was one of the more unexpected **British Amateur** champions on record, defeating John de Forest for the 1931 title at Westward Ho! on the 36th hole. Only 22 and a recent graduate of Cambridge, Smith was the very definition of a longshot, but as Longhurst further observed "when there came to him a chance which he might assume would not come again, he took it like a man."

Captain W. D. Smith (UK)

Captain William Dickson "Dick" Smith (b. 1918) was a native of Glasgow who first came onto the golfing radar screen by winning the **Indian Amateur** in 1945, defeating that nation's first significant native player, Sardar I. S. Malik 6 and 5 in the final. Smith returned home to Britain during the later half of the 1950s and eventually added a **Scottish** and two **Portuguese Amateurs** to his ledger, the former helping to land him on the 1959 Walker Cup team where he lost to Jack Nicklaus in singles 5 and 4. Smith's finest accomplishment, however, must surely be his tie for fifth at the 1957 Open Championship at St. Andrews, an amateur finish that would not be bettered until 17-year-old Justin Rose improbably tied for fourth at Royal Birkdale in 1998.

Willie Smith (UK/USA/Mexico)

Much closer in age to older brother Alex than younger sibling Macdonald, Carnoustie's Willie Smith (1872–1915) was a regular contender at the U.S. Open around the turn of the last century, finishing six times among the top five between 1898 and 1908. His peak was a victory in 1899, a runaway 11-shot triumph at the Baltimore CC that would stand as the **Open's** record margin for more than a century, until bettered by Tiger Woods' epic 15-shot rout at Pebble Beach in 2000. Also the winner of the first **Western Open** in 1899, Willie initially served as professional at Shinnecock Hills and Midlothian, then moved on to the brand-new Mexico City CC in 1907. Apparently happy in his pioneering role south of the border, Smith was killed during the country's 1915 revolution upon refusing to abandon the clubhouse when it came under rebel attack.

Steve Smyers (USA)

A graduate of the University of Florida, Washington, D.C., native Steve Smyers (b. 1953) played on the Gators' 1973 National Championship squad that included future PGA Tour regulars Andy Bean and Gary Koch. After graduating, he spent eight years working with Florida–based architect Ron Garl before opening his own company, Fairway Design International, in 1983. Not the sort of designer to churn out a dozen courses per year while claiming to dedicate himself fully to each project, Smyers has produced a relatively steady flow of well-received layouts, both in the United States and abroad. His first major success was Indiana's Wolf Run GC (1989), though England's Chart Hills GC (done jointly with Nick Faldo), Florida's Southern Dunes, and an extensive redesign of Orlando's famous Isleworth CC have received comparable degrees of praise. Very much at home with strategic variety, small greens, and extensive bunkering (one par 3 at Wolf Run boasts 13!), Smyers has completed projects on five continents while continuing to compete as a talented amateur player.

Notable Courses: Chart Hills GC, England; Old Memorial GC, Florida; Southern Dunes GC, Florida; Wolf Run GC, Indiana

Des Smyth (Ireland)

Though never approaching superstardom, Des Smyth (b. Drogheda, 2/12/1953) has carved out a remarkably long and fruitful career on the European Tour, thrice cracking the Order of Merit top 10, becoming that rare player to win in four separate decades and, with his victory at the 2001 **Madeira Island Open,** ranking as the Tour's oldest-ever winner (at age 48) of an official event.

Interestingly, among Smyth's biggest victories was his very first, the final playing of the old *News of the World* match play, in which he defeated Nick Price at Fulford in 1979. Though perhaps not the event it was during the halcyon days gone by, few titles bore a greater historical pedigree—and Smyth will forever carry the honor of being its last champion. Like many Irishmen a formidable player in the wind, Smyth is a six-time **Irish PGA** winner and twice a Ryder Cup selection (1979 and '81). As of 2003, he has been plying his trade, thus far with middling success, on the American Champions Tour.

J. C. Snead (USA)

Forever known as the nephew of the legendary Sam, Jesse Carlyle Snead (b. Hot Springs, Virginia, 10/14/1940) was a fine all-around athlete who originally pursued a baseball career with the Washington Senators. Failing that, he turned to golf but took four years to find his way onto the PGA Tour, then three more before notching his first win at the 1971 **Tucson Open.** Two weeks later he added another at **Doral,** ultimately going on to claim eight Tour titles, including back-to-back triumphs at **San Diego** in 1975 and '76. Also a winner of the 1973 **Australian Open** during a stray venture Down Under, Snead appeared in three Ryder Cup matches (1971–75), amassing an unassailable 9-2-0 record that included singles wins over Tony Jacklin (then near his peak), Brian Barnes, Christy O'Connor, and perennial Cup stalwart Peter Oosterhuis. The long-hitting J. C. may have lacked his uncle's overall greatness but he at least possessed a bit of his longevity, for his final win came at the **Westchester Classic** in 1987, when at age 47 he defeated Seve Ballesteros in sudden death.

Sam Snead (USA)

Born: Hot Springs, Virginia, 5/27/1912 **Died:** Hot Springs, Virginia, 5/23/2002

In a golf world inhabited largely by big-city bluebloods, British immigrants, and a smattering of pioneer types from Texas, Samuel Jackson Snead, a hillbilly from high among the Allegheny Mountains, definitely broke the mold. A well-built and especially supple man, Snead came into the golfing spotlight in the mid-1930s with as smooth and natural a swing as might be imagined, a flowing, ageless move that would remain world-class functional into his 60s. A tremendously powerful striker of the ball, he would eventually claim some 82 PGA Tour titles between 1936 and 1965 (first all-time) and an estimated 135 total victories, the latter including unofficial events, various four-balls, and regional titles.

Snead got his first look at the Tour in 1936 but began playing seriously in 1937, quickly making his presence felt by winning five times as rookie in California, Minnesota, Florida, and the Bahamas. He did not, however, win at Michigan's Oakland Hills CC, the site of the '37 U.S. Open, where a 283 total came within one of the previous Open record, yet lost by two to a streaking Ralph Guldahl. For a rookie it was a performance to be proud of—but it also started a pattern of U.S. Open heartbreak that would haunt Snead throughout his otherwise-great career.

Even as he became the Tour's top money winner in 1938 and '39, Player of the Year in 1949, a four-time Vardon Trophy winner (1938, '49, '50, and '55), and seven-time Ryder Cup player, the Open became Snead's annual nightmare, a place where the entire golfing world expected him to find some new method of avoiding victory. In 1939, arguably his best opportunity, he came to the 72nd at the Philadelphia CC needing only a five to beat Byron Nelson, Craig

Sam Snead driving off the tenth tee at the Oakland Hills Golf Club course, June 10, 1937.

Wood, and Denny Shute but took two to escape a greenside bunker, then three-putted for a humiliating eight and fifth place. Eight years later in St. Louis, Snead holed an 18-footer for birdie at the 72nd to shoot 282 and force a play-off with Lew Worsham. The next day, with the players all even at the 18th and Snead facing a short putt for par, Worsham suddenly called for a measurement. The tape confirmed that Snead was slightly away but rattled by what he saw as rank gamesmanship, Sam missed. Worsham, needless to say, then tapped in for the victory. Snead also endured a one-shot loss to Cary Middlecoff in 1949 at Medinah and, in 1953, entered the final round at Oakmont one behind Ben Hogan, then stumbled home with a 76 to finish second, six back.

In truth, Snead's early years saw frustration in all of his Major championship entries until he finally broke through in the 1942 **PGA Championship** at New Jersey's Seaview CC, defeating Jim Turnesa (an Army corporal supported by a reported 7,000 of his fellow soldiers from nearby Fort Dix) 2 and 1 in the final. It was then off to the Navy for wartime service, after which Snead received the then-princely sum of $10,000 to journey to South Africa for 16 exhibition matches with Bobby Locke, a series in which Sam's record was a harrowing 2-12-2. Still, his best years were those following the war, beginning with a six-win 1946 that included taking the **Open Championship** on his only visit to St. Andrews. This victory came by four over Bobby Locke and Johnny Bulla, and while British golf was only

just beginning to recover from the ravages of wartime, Snead hardly helped matters by calling the Open "just another tournament" and coming off as the stereotypical ugly American.

Though he had won a combined 11 times in 1945–46, Snead found himself afflicted with the dreaded "yips" in 1947, his putting knocking his entire game from its lofty perch for nearly two years. He would eventually switch putters, then converted to croquet-style in the mid-1960s, a technique soon banned by the USGA, which chose to disallow straddling the line. Thereafter Snead utilized his famed "side-saddle" method that found him using a croquet-like motion only with the putter outside of his right leg, his stooped posture leading Jimmy Demaret to observe that he "looked like he was basting a turkey."

Putting woes or not, Snead won six times in 1949 and 11 times in 1950, though it was certainly not coincidence that this surge came in the aftermath of Hogan's car accident and throughout his long recovery. Snead took Player of the Year honors for 1949, when his victories included his first **Masters** (by three over Bulla) and second **PGA** (beating Johnny Palmer 3 and 2 in Richmond, Virginia), but rightfully felt slighted upon losing the 1950 award to Hogan, whose comeback U.S. Open victory was as epic as it gets, but also his only win of the year.

By the mid-1950s, Snead's game was past its peak and he moved into an especially remarkable stage of his career, a 20-year stretch in which he remained steadfastly among the Tour's top 125 money winners (ranging from 16th in 1963 to 104th in 1967), ultimately winding down with a 49th-place finish in 1974 at age 62. Amazingly, he was still genuinely competitive in his seventh decade, sitting only one off the 54-hole lead at the 1973 Los Angeles Open (he finished joint seventh), then returning a year later to finish second, some 37 years after first competing in the event.

Ever the competitor—if not a bit of a hustler—Snead was notably tough in match play, reaching the final of the pre-1958 PGA five times (winning thrice) and collecting a 10-2-1 record over seven Ryder Cups. He was also both a playing and nonplaying Ryder Cup captain, the latter in 1969 when he was reportedly upset at Nicklaus' sportsmanlike concession to Jacklin at the last, allowing the match to end in a tie.

Snead would live to within days of his 90th birthday, holding court at The Greenbrier and returning to the golfing limelight each spring as an honorary starter at the Masters. Even in his late years, with mind and body both surprisingly agile, he could be difficult to get a handle on, generally gracious, yet a bit cagey to the last. Once portrayed as the amiable country rube, Snead was often just playing along with the press's stereotypical notions, perhaps at the suggestion of his one-time business manager Fred Corcoran. In the end Snead *was* truly different, as a person, as a competitor, and as an athlete. His physical talents—with or without a U.S. Open—bore a sublime naturalness and almost surreal longevity that observers of the game are lucky to see once in a lifetime.

PGA Tour Wins (82): 1937, '38, '41 & '50 Bing Crosby; 1938, '46, '49, '50, '55, '56, '60 & '65 Greensboro; 1938, '40 & '41 Canadian Open; 1941 & '50 North & South; **1942, '49 & '51 PGA Championship;** 1945 & '50 Los Angeles; **1946 British Open;** 1948 & '50 Texas; **1949, '52 & '54 Masters;** 1949 & '50 Western Open; 1950 Colonial; 5 Miami Opens, 5 Palm Beach Round-Robins, 3 St. Petersburg Opens & 3 Dallas Opens
Ryder Cup: 1937, 1947–55 & '59 (c) (7); 1969 Capt

1937-1974

	37	38	39	40	41	42	43	44	45	46	47	48	49
Masters	18	T31	2	T7	T6	T7				T7	T22	T16	1
US Open	2	T38	5	T16	T13					T19	2	5	T2
British	T11	-	-							1	-	-	-
PGA	T9	2	-	2	T5	1		-	-	T17	T17	T5	1

	50	51	52	53	54	55	56	57	58	59	60	61	62
Masters	3	T8	1	T16	1	3	T4	2	13	T22	T11	T15	T15
US Open	T12	T10	T10	2	T11	T3	T24	8	MC	T8	T19	T17	T38
British	-	-	-	-	-	-	-	-	-	-	-	-	T6
PGA	T17	1	T33	T17	T9	T17	T5	T9	3	T8	T3	T27	T17

	63	64	65	66	67	68	69	70	71	72	73	74	
Masters	T3	MC	MC	T42	T10	42	MC	T23	MC	T27	T29	T20	
US Open	T42	T34	T24	-	-	T9	T38	MC	-	-	T29	WD	
British	-	-	MC	-	-	-	-	-	-	-	-	-	
PGA	T27	-	T6	T6	-	T34	T63	T12	T34	T4	T9	T3	

Ed Sneed (USA)

Though Roanoke, Virginia, native Ed Sneed (b. 8/6/1944) was a four-time winner on the PGA Tour and a 1977 Ryder Cup player, he is surely best remembered for the great disappointment of the 1979 Masters, an event he lost in a three-way play-off with Tom Watson and Fuzzy Zoeller (the winner) after surrendering a three-stroke lead with bogies at the final three holes. Once upon a time Sneed had struggled mightily just to subsist on the Tour, eventually breaking through when, after winning the 1973 **New South Wales Open** in Australia, he flew to San Francisco, Monday qualified for the **Kaiser International,** and went on to claim his first U.S. victory by defeating John Schlee in a play-off.

Karsten Solheim (Norway/USA)

A native of Bergen, Norway, Karsten Solheim (1911–2000) moved to America as a child, eventually becoming a successful design engineer with General Electric. In his spare time he began creating putters utilizing a revolutionary form of heel and toe weighting, the huge success of which led him eventually to expand into a full-fledged equipment manufacturing concern. Perhaps Solheim's greatest innovation was the perimeter weighting of irons, making off-center shots achieve decidedly better results than those found with a traditional blade. Also a pioneer in both the investment casting of clubs and the custom fitting of average players (through standard production of varied lofts and lies), his Ping Eye 2s became the largest selling irons in the history of the game.

Solheim ruffled some feathers in the late 1980s when he sued the USGA over their ruling that the square grooves of his Eye 2s were too close together and thus illegal. When the suit was settled out of court in 1990, the USGA agreed to grandfather all past Ping irons to save the company a potentially sticky recall situation but it was Solheim who caved the most, agreeing to manufacture future irons to meet the governing body's guidelines. A strong supporter of women's golf, Solheim guaranteed the perpetuation of his name by founding the Solheim Cup, the distaff answer to the Ryder Cup, in 1990.

Sandy Somerville (Canada)

One of Canada's greatest-ever amateurs, London, Ontario's Charles Ross "Sandy" Somerville (1903–1991) was a 1924 graduate of the University of Toronto where he starred at football and hockey in addition to golf. Opting for a career in life insurance over the then-less-lucrative life of a professional, Somerville captured a record six **Canadian Amateurs** between 1926 and 1937, also finishing runner-up on four occasions. He was also the first Canadian to win the **U.S. Amateur,** something he accomplished in 1932 at the Baltimore CC by routing Jesse Guilford 7 and 6 in the semifinals, then slipping past 1937 champion Johnny Goodman in the final. Somerville made a good run at joining Dick Chapman and E. Harvie Ward as the only men to win the U.S., Canadian, and British Amateurs in 1938 when he reached the British semifinals at Troon, but there he fell shy, losing 2 down to Cecil Ewing.

Also a competitor in the inaugural Masters in 1934 (where he tied for 43rd), Somerville was a tall and powerful man, though it was his exacting iron play and aggressive style that are recalled sooner than any prodigious length. A member of both the Canadian Golf and Sports Halls of Fame, he was also voted Canada's Golfer of the Half-Century in 1950 before serving many years in a variety of administrative capacities.

Aree Song (Thailand/Korea)

Now beginning her professional career while still in her teens, Aree Song Wongluekiet (b. Bangkok, 5/1/1986) be-

came the youngest USGA champion in history when she won the 1999 **Junior Girls** title in Owings Mills, Maryland, at the tender age of 13. Prior to turning 14, she was invited (along with twin sister Naree) to appear in the 2000 Dinah Shore—and rather improbably tied for 10th! Since those explosive debuts, Aree has gone on to become the youngest semifinalist in U.S. Women's amateur history (14), finished 13th in a second professional event (the 2000 Safeway LPGA Championship), made the cut in three more Dinah Shores, been medalist in the 2002 World Amateur Team Championship, and finished as low amateur in the 2002 U.S. Women's Open—all before her 17th birthday.

Obviously one of the finest young talents the game has produced, Song elected, following a tie for fifth at the 2003 Women's Open, to forego college entirely and move directly into the professional ranks. Armed with a special age-limit exemption from LPGA Commissioner Ty Votaw, she made her professional Tour debut in March of 2004 and, in just her third start, eagled the 72nd hole but just missed forcing a play-off with Grace Park at the year's first Major, the Dinah Shore. Whether Song will continue to improve into her 20s remains to be seen but at age 19, she has clearly proven herself capable of competing with the finest players in the world. And sister Naree, who toils on the Futures Tour at the time of this writing, may not be far behind.

Annika Sorenstam (Sweden)

Presently building an eloquent case for the title of Greatest Women Golfer Ever, Annika Sorenstam (b. Stockholm, 10/9/1970) was an elite junior prospect of the late 1980s before coming to America to compete for the University of Arizona. An **NCAA** individual champion, Co-Player of the Year and two-time All-American, Sorenstam captured the **World Amateur** title in 1992 before turning professional and taking Rookie of the Year honors on Europe's WPGET in 1993.

It is today interesting to note that while Sorenstam successfully qualified for the LPGA Tour on her first try, it wasn't exactly easy, as her 28th-place finish at the 1993 Qualifying Tournament gained her only nonexempt status for the 1994 season. Though not a winner in this debut campaign, she did log three top-10 finishes in 18 starts and 39th spot on the money list, enough to land Rookie of the Year honors. Sorenstam's breakout season came in 1995 when she claimed her first LPGA win at the **U.S. Women's Open** (by one over Meg Mallon at The Broadmoor), then added two further victories as well as first place on the money list, her first Player of the Year award, and the Vare Trophy. Save for finishing third in money, 1996 virtually repeated this checklist (including a successful defense of her **U.S. Open** crown at the Pine Needles Lodge) before 1997–98 saw a combined 10 victories, back-to-back money titles, and two more Player of the Year awards. While the millennium ended with Sorenstam being temporarily nudged aside by Australian Karrie Webb, Annika's 1999–2000 total of seven victories and fourth- and second-place money rankings could hardly be called a slump.

By 2001, Webb had cooled a bit while Sorenstam had reached cruising speed, racking up Mickey Wright–like numbers in a spectacular run that is now at four years and counting. Between 2001 and 2003, for example, Sorenstam would win a total of 25 tournaments (including a stunning 11—in only 23 starts—in 2002), claim three consecutive Player of the Year awards, and earn two more Vare Trophies (2001 and '02). In addition to dominating week-to-week play at a level not seen since Nancy Lopez's heyday, Sorenstam also took home five Major championships during this period, including back-to-back victories at the 2001 and '02 **Dinah Shores,** a sudden-death triumph over Grace Park at the 2003 **LPGA Championship,** and the 2003 **Women's British Open** at Royal Lytham & St. Annes, the latter completing the career Grand Slam. Further, Sorenstam's Vare-winning scoring average of 2001 was a record 69.42, a number she would improve substantially to 68.71 during her dazzling 2002. This latter season also would close with two non-LPGA victories in Australia, not quite enough to match Wright's single-season record of 13 official wins but a relevant footnote just the same.

Despite so remarkable a run of excellence, Sorenstam generally drew more attention for her playing, on a sponsor's exemption, in the PGA Tour's 2003 Colonial tournament—the first appearance by a woman in an official Tour event since Babe Zaharias qualified into the 1945 Los Angeles and Tucson Opens. Surviving a media frenzy that seemed oblivious to the fact that she hadn't actually *earned* her spot, Sorenstam held up beautifully, narrowly missing the cut with rounds of 71-75 but impressing widely with both her play and her exceptional grace under extreme pressure. The following week upon returning to the LPGA Tour, she promptly fired a first-round 62 at the Kellogg-Keebler Classic—an impressive number, yet nothing compared to the epic 13-under-par 59 she'd shot at the 2001 Standard Register Ping.

A rock-solid all-around player with no weaknesses to her game, Sorenstam is hardly huge at 5'6", yet consistently ranks among the LPGA's longest hitters. She is equally strong from the fairway, regularly standing among the leaders in greens-in-regulation, and has demonstrated herself more than capable of holing the putts needed to win consistently. A mainstay of the European Solheim Cup squad from 1994 forward, Sorenstam sports an overall record of

Annika Sorenstam 2001 (Historic Golf Photos)

16-8-3 for teams that have gone 2-4 during her six years of competition.

Having been inducted into the Hall of Fame in 2003, Sorenstam, presently in her mid-30s, has so rapidly ascended the LPGA career victory list that only Kathy Whitworth (88) and Mickey Wright (82) now stand ahead of her. Though a bit of work remains to equal Wright's 13 Major championship titles, it can be reasonably argued that Sorenstam needn't match her long-retired rival stride-for-stride to be judged golf's best-ever female. But should she manage to do so anyway—in this era of far deeper fields and talent-mitigating equipment—the now-legendary Swede's claim to the top spot will be absolutely beyond reproach.

LPGA Wins (56): 1995 & '96 U.S. Women's Open; **1995, '96 & 2002 Samsung WC;** 1998 & 2000 **Wykagyl;** 2000 & '01 **Welch's;** 2001 & '04 **Safeway;** 2001 & '02 Dinah Shore; 2003 & '04 LPGA Championship; 2004 Corning; 2003 Women's British Open; **3 Michelob Light**
Solheim Cup: 1994–2003 (6)

1992-2004

	92	93	94	95	96	97	98	99	00	01	02	03	04
Dinah	-	-	T24	T2	T8	T8	T7	T7	T17	1	1	2	T13
LPGA	-	-	-	10	T14	3	T30	T16	T12	5	3	1	1
US Open	T64	-	-	1	1	MC	T41	MC	T9	T16	2	4	2
dM/Brit	-	-	T22	T45	T6	MC	2	-	3	T32	MC	1	T13

*du Maurier replaced by the Women's British Open in 2001.

Ramon Sota (Spain)

Though frequently recalled first as Seve Ballesteros's uncle, Pedreña native Ramon Sota (b. 4/23/1938) was a more-than-capable international player who finished 10th on the inaugural European Tour Order of Merit (1971) at a time when Continental players were still thought little match for their British counterparts. Another of Spain's self-taught ex-caddies, Sota bore the hallmark of the impoverished golfer—an inventive short game—but needed vast practice on his driving and long-iron play before claiming an impressive eight national Opens: the **Spanish** (1963), **Portuguese** (1963, '69, and '70), **French** (1965), **Dutch** (1966 and '71), and **Italian** (1971). Sota made a largely unsuccessful mid-1960s trip to America but did manage six career appearances at the Masters, including an impressive tie for sixth in 1965, the highest finish yet recorded by a Continental player. His **French Open** victory included a record-shattering 62 at St.-Nom-la-Bretèche, and Sota was also a regular in the World Cup, thrice ranking in the top four individually.

Mike Souchak (USA)

Long-hitting Pennsylvanian Mike Souchak (b. Berwick, 5/10/1927) was a football star at Duke University who be-

gan playing PGA Tour events in 1953. He is remembered, of course, for setting an all-time Tour scoring record that would stand for 46 years, a lights-out 60-68-64-65 performance at the 1955 **Texas Open,** with his 257 total trouncing Fred Haas by seven. Even over a relatively easy A. W. Tillinghast-designed Brackenridge Park GC, these numbers were stunning, but none more so than Souchak's opening-round back nine, an 8-under-par 27. As a raw number this total has never been beaten, though Billy Mayfair's 27 at the 2001 Buick Open represented nine strokes under par and thus might rank slightly better.

Lost in recollections of this legendary scoring explosion, however, is the fact that Souchak was no one-hit wonder, winning 15 PGA Tour events between 1955 and 1964, including the 1956 **Agua Caliente Open** in Tijuana and the 1959 **Western Open,** a one-shot triumph over Arnold Palmer. Souchak also fared well in Major championship play, particularly at the U.S. Open where he tied for third in 1959 and '60 and fourth in 1961. He also tied for fourth and fifth at the Masters (in 1955 and '62, respectively), and finished level fifth at the PGA Championship in 1959. Twice a Ryder Cup player, Souchak compiled an admirable 5-1 record during American victories in 1959 and '60.

PGA Tour Wins (15): 1955 & '64 Houston; 1955 Texas; 1956 Colonial; 1959 Western Open; 1960 San Diego; 1961 Greensboro
Ryder Cup: 1959 & '61 (2)

1953-1967

	53	54	55	56	57	58	59	60	61	62	63	64	65	66	67
Masters	-	-	T4	T17	MC	T14	T25	T16	T28	T5	T11	T9	T35	T33	-
US Open	MC	MC	T10	T29	MC	MC	T3	T3	T4	T14	T32	-	MC	MC	-
British	-	-	-	T8	-	-	-	-	-	-	-	-	-	-	-
PGA	-	-	-	T9	T8	T5	T12	T45	T39	T23	T13	T15	MC	T20	

Dan Soutar (UK/Australia)

Emigrating to Australia in 1903 at the behest of his childhood friend Carnegie Clark, Carnoustie product Daniel

Gordon Soutar (1882–1937) soon won the 1903 **Australian Amateur,** then, after turning pro, the second **Australian Open** in 1905 at Royal Melbourne. Though also a winner of the first three **Australian PGAs** (1905–07), plus a fourth title in 1910, Soutar suffered the fate of finishing seven times the Open runner-up, including five straight solo seconds from 1906 through 1910.

Soutar's importance to Australian golf was not so much as a player, however, as it was spreader of the gospel. This he did largely as an instructor, first at Royal Sydney, then later at the Marrickville, Luera and Manly GCs, the latter stop producing a prodigiously talented youngster named Joe Kirkwood as well as future Australian legends Jim Ferrier and Ossie Pickworth. In addition, Soutar authored the nation's first known golf book, *The Australian Golfer* (Angus & Robertson, 1906), and covered the game for the Sydney *Sun* during the 1920s. Soutar can also fairly be called Australia's first practicing golf course architect, for he laid out numerous early courses both there and in New Zealand, his most famous undoubtedly being the pre-Alister MacKenzie version of Melbourne's famous Kingston Heath GC.

Angelo Spagnola (USA)

The winner of *Golf Digest's* Worst Avid Golfer contest, Fayette City, Pennsylvania, grocery store manager Angelo Spagnola fired an eye-popping 257 at the TPC at Sawgrass in Ponte Vedra Beach, Florida, on June 19, 1985. This score may be somewhat misleading, however, for Spagnola used a robust 66 of those shots at the famous 145-yard island-green 17th, dunking 24 shots in the water before opting to putt his ball all the way down the cart path, behind the green, and across the footbridge onto the putting surface. "I could have taken a lot of strokes off my overall score if I had tried to go around the hole fifteen balls earlier," Spagnola observed afterward, proving once again the timeless value of sound course management.

Marley Spearman (UK)

Née Marley Baker (b. 1/11/1928) but known in her playing days as Spearman (and later Mrs. Harris), this former dancer was for a time Britain's best woman golfer, taking back-to-back **British Ladies** titles in 1961 and '62 and the **English** championship in 1964. Her interest in the game spawned by a promotional lesson taken while shopping at Harrod's, Spearman was a regular English international for a decade, and a three-time Curtis Cup selection, going 2-2-2 overall in 1962 and '64 after being unable to participate in 1960.

Bill Spiller (USA)

While Charles Sifford was the first black to play full-time on the PGA Tour, it was Tishomingo, Oklahoma, native Bill Spiller (1913–1988) who did much of the groundwork that made Sifford's trailblazing possible. A graduate of all-black Wiley College in Texas, Spiller was a fine all-around athlete who didn't take up golf until age 29. Having moved to Los Angeles in 1938, he soon became a top regional competitor, playing out of the public Sunset Fields GC and developing his game to the point of readying himself for a run at the PGA Tour.

Sadly, that chance never came. Spiller did play in several Tour events, most notably shooting 68 during the 1948 Los Angeles Open at Riviera. Faced with the "Caucasians Only" clause so doggedly preserved by the PGA of America, his greatest accomplishments weren't made on the golf course but rather in the legal battle simply to gain access to it. A courageous, outspoken and intelligent man, Spiller first filed suit against the PGA in 1948, then petitioned California Attorney General Stanley Mosk whose subsequent banning of the organization from playing restricted events in the Golden state led to the "Caucasians Only" rule's swift demise. Calvin Peete thanked Bill Spiller publicly for his sacrifices. For far too many others in the world of golf, however, his is largely a forgotten name.

Sandra Spuzich (USA)

When Indianapolis's Sandra Spuzich (b. 4/3/1937) won the 1982 **Corning** and **Mary Kay Classics,** she set, on each occasion, a new record as the oldest winner of an LPGA tournament, both at age 45. JoAnne Carner and Beth Daniel would subsequently break the record but just the fact that Spuzich held it, combined with her victory in the 1966 **U.S. Women's Open** (where she edged Carol Mann by one at Hazeltine National), must establish Spuzich among the more overlooked pros of her time. All told she won seven events during a career that began in 1963, consistently finishing among the top 40 money winners and peaking with fifth- and sixth-place finishes in 1968 and '69, respectively.

Lefty Stackhouse (USA)

Atoka, Oklahoma, product Wilburn Artist "Lefty" Stackhouse (1909–1973) resides in that pantheon of golfing lunatics whose temper vastly exceeded all other recordable aspects of their games. Along with Ivan Gantz, Stackhouse stands immortal for stories of equipment destruction and self flagellation that would make a professional wrestler blanch. A fairly talented player who logged sixth- and seventh-place finishes in the Western Open, Stackhouse was also an alcoholic who once passed out at the ninth green of a tournament, only to wake up all alone in the deserted clubhouse many hours later. No less than

Ben Hogan told of witnessing Stackhouse shredding his own hands in thorny rosebushes after hooking a tee shot, and he was widely reported to have flattened himself several times with a powerful left fist. Lost in such wild stories, of course, were some substantial accomplishments, particularly as a teacher where he helped, among others, Babe Zaharias and Betty Jameson. Stackhouse is known to have played an exhibition with Tommy Armour and Bobby Cruickshank when he was just 16, regularly driving it past both professionals. Apparently he managed to avoid doing himself great bodily harm on at least that one occasion.

Hollis Stacy (USA)

Another of the "horses for USGA-set-up courses" crowd, Savannah, Georgia's Hollis Stacy (b. 3/16/1954) was an elite amateur who, prior to attending Rollins College, became the first player ever to capture three consecutive **USGA Junior Girls** titles (1969–71). Then, throughout a fine professional career that included 18 LPGA victories, Stacy burnished her reputation as a tough-course specialist by winning three **U.S. Women's Opens,** the first coming in 1977 at the infamous Hazeltine National GC, where she defeated Nancy Lopez by two. She then defended her crown in 1978 in Indianapolis, her +5 total enough to edge JoAnne Carner and Sally Little by one. Adding a solo second in the 1980 event, Stacy eventually captured her third Open in 1984 at the Salem CC (Massachusetts), where her 290 total (+2) beat Rosie Jones by two.

Surrounding this propensity for national championships, however, has been a strong overall career that, between 1977 and 1983, included 15 additional victories, money rankings no worse than 11th, and a fourth Major, the 1983 **du Maurier Classic.** Stacy continued to play a fairly full slate of LPGA events through 2000, though seldom contending at the highest level. A popular and entertaining player, her final win came at the 1991 **Crestar-Farm Fresh Classic.**

LPGA Wins (18): 1977, '78 & '84 U.S. Women's Opens; 1977 State Farm; **1983 du Maurier**

1970-1986

	70	71	72	73	74	75	76	77	78	79	80	81	82	83	84	85	86
Dinah														T35	28	T13	T14
LPGA	-	-	-	-	-	T7	T29	MC	T9	T47	T10	T12	T7	T11	20	T25	T28
US Open	MC	MC	MC	T23	T14	MC	T23	1	1	T15	2	T10	T49	T32	1	MC	T11
du Maur										T11	T38	T7	T16	1	16	T10	MC

Craig Stadler (USA)

Following in the footsteps of Gene Littler, Phil Rodgers, and Mickey Wright, Craig Robert Stadler (b. San Diego, California, 6/2/1953) grew up playing at San Diego's La Jolla CC where he won, among other things, the 1971 **Junior World** title. Attending USC, Stadler captured the 1973 **U.S. Amateur** at Inverness (in the event's blessed return to match play) and, after debating an early run at the professional life, stuck around long enough to be named All-American in 1974 and '75.

It took the long-hitting Stadler three seasons to get his sea legs on the PGA Tour but by the early 1980s he ranked among the elite, cracking the top-10 money winners four times between 1980 and 1984. His banner year, bar none, was 1982 when an early win in **Tucson** paved the way for a run at the **Masters,** where Stadler led by five through 67 holes before making three bogies, then three-putting the last to end up in a play-off with Dan Pohl. Par was good enough to win the first play-off hole, however, and with a Major under his belt, Stadler later added his second **Kemper Open** and the **World Series of Golf,** taking the season money title in the process.

Stadler won 13 PGA Tour events overall (as well as overseas titles in Japan, Europe, and South America), the last five following a six-year drought in the late 1980s. Nicknamed "The Walrus" for his rotund physique and drooping mustache, he would not immediately seem the type to remain highly competitive with gathering age. His victory at the 1996 **Los Angeles Open** came at 42, however, and was later thoroughly trumped by a win at the 2003 **B.C. Open,** where a final-round 63 made Stadler (then just past 50) the oldest player since Art Wall in 1975 to win an official Tour event.

Beyond his Masters victory, Stadler's record in Major championship play has not, perhaps, been all that he would have liked, and he may well be best remembered for his combustible temper. Despite the grumbling and the disgusted tossing of clubs, Stadler has long been known as one of the game's more honest, amiable, and obliging men.

PGA Tour Wins (13): **1982 Masters;** 1982 & '92 World Series; 1984 Byron Nelson; 1994 San Diego; 1996 Los Angeles
Intn'l Wins (4): 1985 European Masters
Champions Tour Wins: 7 (2003–04)
Walker Cup: 1975 **Ryder Cup:** 1983 & '85 (2)

1977-1996

	77	78	79	80	81	82	83	84	85	86
Masters	-	-	T7	T26	T43	1	T6	T35	T6	MC
US Open	-	-	MC	T16	T26	T22	T10	WD	MC	T15
British	-	-	-	T6	MC	T35	T12	T28	MC	WD
PGA	-	6	MC	T55	MC	T16	T63	T18	T18	T30

	87	88	89	90	91	92	93	94	95	96
Masters	T17	3	MC	T14	T12	T25	T34	MC	MC	T29
US Open	T24	T25	-	T8	T9	T33	T33	MC	-	-
British	T8	T61	T13	MC	T101	T64	-	T24	MC	T44
PGA	T28	T15	T7	T57	T7	T48	MC	T19	T8	MC

Louis Stanley (UK)

The longtime golf correspondent for the British magazine *The Field*, Louis T. Stanley (b. 1912) was a remarkably prolific writer, authoring an amazing 74 books in his lifetime, many about automobile racing or popular figures in British society. He did, however, pen some 16 golf volumes, most of them instructional in nature. *A History of Golf* (Weidenfeld & Nicholson, 1991) would be an obvious exception, while the *Field* anthologies, *Green Fairways* (Methuen, 1947) and *Fresh Fairways* (Methuen, 1949), are perhaps the best examples of his craft.

Donald Steel (UK)

An important figure in British golf for more than four decades, Donald Steel (b. 1937) is something of a throwback to the golfing renaissance men of yesteryear, having been involved in virtually every aspect of the Royal & Ancient game. A fine all-around athlete, he was a scratch golfer who played at Cambridge and won a multitude of amateur events, including, on three occasions, the Oxford & Cambridge Golfing Society's **President's Putter** played annually at Rye.

Shortly after graduation, Steel became the golf correspondent for London's *Sunday Telegram*, a position he would hold for the better part of 30 years. Also a regular contributor to *Country Life*, he has edited several books, though his most important literary contributions surely came from his own talented pen in the form of *Classic Golf Links of England, Scotland, Wales & Ireland* (Pelican, 1992) and the invaluable *Encyclopedia of Golf* (Viking, 1975), the latter written jointly with Peter Ryde.

Also a golf course architect, Steel initially worked with C. K. Cotton's firm before opening his own practice in the late 1980s. Since that time, he has laid out a number of courses both at home and abroad, while also performing renovations on a number of the United Kingdom's championship facilities. Ironically, his highest-profile design likely lies in Canada, at Ontario's Red Tail GC, whose green complexes have been cited among the best built in the postwar era.

Notable Courses: Red Tail GC, Canada; St. Andrews, Strathtyrum Course, Scotland

Jan Stephenson (Australia)

Jan Stephenson (b. Sydney, 12/22/1951) ranks as the LPGA Tour's all-time sex symbol, a justly earned status given her provocative clothing, obvious beauty, and a willingness to pose for magazine and calendar shots in positions well designed to highlight it. Beyond all the glitz—which, truth be told, was a public relations bonanza for the women's game—was a world-class talent who perhaps has not always received her just due as a player.

A dominant amateur in New South Wales from an early age, Stephenson claimed three **Australian Junior** titles and one **Australian Open** (1973) before packing off to America in 1974. Though the winner of that season's LPGA Rookie of the Year award (and four titles over the next six years), Stephenson wouldn't reach her competitive peak until 1981–87, a period in which she logged 12 LPGA victories, including three Major championships: the 1981 **du Maurier Classic** (by one over Nancy Lopez and Pat Bradley), the 1982 **LPGA Championship** (by two over JoAnne Carner), and the 1983 **U.S. Women's Open** (by one over Carner and Patty Sheehan). All Stephenson lacked for the career Grand Slam was the Dinah Shore, an event where she thrice finished in the top five, including a solo second in 1985.

Surpassed only by Karrie Webb among Australian women professionals, Stephenson's career was often affected by strange off-the-course events and injuries. Yet her full, aggressive swing and fine wooden play carried her far, resulting, despite the occasional controversy, in a career record that stands among the stronger LPGA ledgers of her time.

LPGA Wins (16): 1981 du Maurier; 1982 LPGA Championship; 1983 Welch's; **1983 U.S. Women's Open**

1974-1989

	74	75	76	77	78	79	80	81	82	83	84	85	86	87	88	89
Dinah										T20	T31	2	T5	T11	T10	T42
LPGA	-	T29	-	T14	T15	T6	T19	T34	1	T11	T20	T25	T33	-	T15	WD
US Open	T44	T36	T17	T4	T20	T26	T57	T29	WD	1	T27	T12	T11	MC	5	DQ
du Maur						-	22	1	T7	T5	T13	MC	T22	MC	T4	WD

Captain John C. Stewart (UK)

Army Captain John Campbell Stewart (b. 1832) of the 51st Highlanders was a native of the wonderfully named Scottish town of Fasnacloich and lived, for his day, rather an eventful life. Through military postings, he spent time in the Crimea and putting down the Indian Mutiny, establishing himself as an elite pre–Open Championship golfer when granted extended time at home. A winner of many golfing medals, he is reported to have once halved a match with the great Allan Robertson after standing three down with four to play. Better documented, however, is Stewart's chief claim to fame, teaming with fellow Blackheath member George Glennie to win James Fairlie's **Great Golf Tournament** of 1857, a forerunner to the Open Championship.

Payne Stewart (USA)

Born: Springfield, Missouri, 1/30/1957 **Died:** Mina, South Dakota, 10/25/1999

William Payne Stewart came from a golfing family, his father having won the Missouri Amateur and Senior and participated in the 1955 U.S. Open. Payne was an All-American at Southern Methodist but, upon failing to earn his PGA Tour card directly out of school, played the Asian tour (with wins in India and Indonesia) in 1980 and '81. By 1982 he was back in the States and winning, first at **Quad Cities,** then, in 1983, at **Walt Disney World**. Though a big money earner (including a third-place ranking in 1986), Stewart would not win again until 1987, when a three shot victory at **Bay Hill** led him to donate the entire $108,000 first-place check to a local hospital in memory of his father, who had died of cancer two years earlier to the day.

With a powerful, reliable swing to support one of golf's best tee-to-green games, Stewart seemed a likely contender for Major championship honors and in 1989 he broke through, receiving a bit of help on the closing holes from a fading Mike Reid before capturing the **PGA Championship** at Chicago's Kemper Lakes GC. Two years later he grabbed an even bigger prize, his decisive birdie at the 16th helping to defeat former champion Scott Simpson in a Monday play-off for the 1991 **U.S. Open** at Hazeltine National GC. Stewart would then go into a modest mid-30s decline before very nearly winning another Open in 1998, a final-round 74 at the Olympic Club leaving him a single shot behind winner Lee Janzen. A last, singular gasp from a man now over 40? Hardly, for in 1999 Stewart won the **Bing Crosby** early, then captured a truly memorable **U.S. Open** at Pinehurst by holing a 15-foot par putt at the 72nd to edge playing partner Phil Mickelson by one.

We will never know how much more greatness Payne Stewart had left, for he was tragically killed in 1999 when a private jet in which he was traveling depressurized midflight, winging automatically onward in macabre fashion until crashing, upon running out of fuel, in rural South Dakota. Aside from his friends on the PGA Tour, Stewart was widely eulogized by several top European players against whom he had competed so vigorously in five Ryder Cups, his loss genuinely felt on both sides of the Atlantic.

PGA Tour Wins (11): 1989 & '90 Heritage; **1989 PGA Championship;** 1990 Byron Nelson; **1991 & '99 U.S. Open;** 1999 Bing Crosby

Intn'l Wins (7): 1991 Dutch Open

Ryder Cup: 1987–93 & '99 (5)

1981-1999

	81	82	83	84	85	86	87	88	89	90
Masters	-	-	T32	T21	T25	T8	T42	T25	T24	T36
US Open	-	-	-	MC	T5	T6	MC	T10	T13	MC
British	T57	-	-	T64	2	T35	T4	T7	T8	T2
PGA	-	MC	MC	MC	T12	T5	T24	T9	1	T8

	91	92	93	94	95	96	97	98	99	
Masters	-	MC	T9	MC	T41	MC	-	-	T52	
US Open	1	T51	2	MC	T21	T27	T28	2	1	
British	T32	T34	12	MC	T11	T44	59	T42	T30	
PGA	T13	T69	T44	T62	T13	T69	T29	MC	T57	

Wayne Stiles (USA)

The first recorded works of Boston-born architect Wayne E. Stiles (1884–1953) were nine-hole courses in Brattleboro, Vermont, and Nashua, New Hampshire, both of which opened in 1916. By the early 1920s, with real estate costs low and golf's popularity soaring, Stiles' workload picked up, resulting in a good 15 solo projects completed by 1924, when he formed a partnership with Cornell-educated landscape architect John Van Kleek. The firm maintained offices in Boston, New York, and St. Petersburg, Florida, with Stiles primarily handling the northern operation and Van Kleek the southern.

Over the next seven years, Stiles & Van Kleek would be responsible for more than 20 courses, the majority located in central Florida or New England, and many of which remain in play, relatively intact, today. The northern layouts, which were clearly the product of Stiles' hand, tend to feature aggressive bunkering and relatively small greens and are generally routed naturally across their landscapes, having required little significant earthmoving.

The collapse of the Florida land boom, then the onset of the Depression, dissolved the Stiles & Van Kleek partnership, though Stiles continued working solo, on and off, for a number of years.

Notable Courses: Cranwell Resort & GC, Massachusetts; Pasadena CC, Florida (BO); Radium CC, Georgia; Taconic GC, Massachusetts

Alexa Stirling (USA)

Atlanta native Alexa Stirling (1897–1977) was a childhood friend and playing partner of Bobby Jones, the two of them learning the game at East Lake CC under the watchful eye of Carnoustie transplant Stewart Maiden. Like Jones,

Stirling was nationally competitive at a young age, taking her first **Southern Amateur** in 1915, then repeating in 1916 before adding a third title three years later. Her big breakthrough, however, came at the 1916 **U.S. Women's Amateur** when, at age 19, she defeated Mildred Caverly 2 and 1 for the championship in Waverly, Massachusetts. With the succeeding two events cancelled due to World War I,

Alexa Stirling

Stirling had to wait until 1919 to defend her title, something she accomplished by beating Mrs. W. A. Gavin 6 and 5 in Shawnee, Pennsylvania. She then made it three straight with a 5 and 4 win over Dorothy Campbell Hurd in Cleveland in 1920. Though never again an Amateur winner, Stirling did reach the final twice more, losing to Marion Hollins 5 and 4 in 1921 and Edith Cummings 3 and 2 in 1923.

Also a winner of one **Metropolitan Amateur** and the 1920 and '34 **Canadian** titles (having moved north after getting married), Stirling is equally remembered for touring the eastern United States during the summer of 1918 with Jones, Perry Adair, and Chicago's Elaine Rosenthal as the "Dixie Kids," playing wartime fundraising exhibitions for the American Red Cross.

Dave Stockton (USA)

Californian Dave Stockton (b. San Bernardino, 11/2/1941) has never been one of golf's more powerful hitters, owing to the effects of a broken back suffered during his youth. He has succeeded, however, partly due to fine course management and coolness under fire and, in larger measure, because of that greatest of equalizers, a sublime putting stroke.

After graduating from USC and joining the PGA Tour in 1964, Stockton endured three seasons of struggle before breaking through with a two-shot victory at the 1967 **Colonial.** From there he enjoyed a solid decade of top-60 money winnings (including five years inside the top 20) and nine further victories, two of which came in the 1970 and '76 **PGA Championships.** On the earlier occasion, at Tulsa's Southern Hills CC, Stockton had to survive both a late charge from Arnold Palmer and overwhelming summer heat to win by two. Then in 1976 at Congressional, he came from arrears to lead down the stretch, then hole a 13-foot par putt at the 72nd to edge Don January and Ray Floyd by one. Stockton is perhaps equally well-remembered for a non-Major victory, the 1974 **Los Angeles Open,** when he fired a 235-yard 3-wood to 12 feet on Riviera's famed 18th to make birdie and defeat John Mahaffey and an astounding 61-year-old Sam Snead by two.

The 1976 PGA would be Stockton's final Tour victory, though he would later enjoy great success on the Champions Tour where he won 14 times (including the 1996 **U.S. Senior Open**) and more than $11 million. A two-time Ryder Cup player in 1971 and '77, he returned to captain the overhyped but nonetheless exciting victory at Kiawah Island in 1991.

PGA Tour Wins (10): 1967 Colonial; **1970 & '76 PGA Championships;** 1974 Los Angeles
Champions Tour Wins: 14 (1992–96)
Ryder Cup: 1971 & '77 (2); 1991 Capt

1968-1982

	68	69	70	71	72	73	74	75	76	77	78	79	80	81	82
Masters	-	18	T5	T9	T10	T14	T2	T26	-	T39	MC	MC	T26	T31	-
US Open	T9	T25	-	MC	MC	T39	T40	T43	MC	MC	T2	T36	T51	MC	T45
British	-	-	-	T11	T31	-	-	-	-	-	-	-	-	-	-
PGA	T17	T35	1	T40	T40	T12	T26	MC	1	T31	T19	T35	MC	T43	MC

Eustace Storey (UK)

Edward Francis "Eustace" Storey (b. 1901) was a strong player of the sort given to constantly tinkering with his swing. A former team captain at Cambridge, his high competitive watermark came in the 1924 British Amateur at St. Andrews when, at age 23, he was beaten in the final 3 and 2 by Ernest Holderness. This performance earned Storey the first of his three Walker Cup appearances (1924–28) during which he amassed a 1-5 record, the one being a singles win over Roland McKenzie at St. Andrews in 1926.

Charlie Stowe (UK)

Charles Stowe (1909–1976) was a native of Staffordshire and a member of Britain's first victorious Walker Cup team, which defeated the Americans in 1938 at St. Andrews. Though a loser in foursomes with Alec Kyle, Stowe brought home an important point in singles when he beat Chuck Kocsis 2 and 1. A powerful and decidedly streaky player, Stowe faired less well against American Frank Stranahan, to whom he lost both in singles at the 1947 Walker Cup (Stowe's second, and last, appearance) and in the final of the 1948 British Amateur at Royal St. George's.

Frank Strafaci (USA)

A product of Brooklyn's public Dyker Beach GC, Frank Strafaci (1916–1988) was the best of four talented brothers who might be considered the city's answer to Westchester's talented Turnesas. During the years just before and after World War II, Strafaci dominated New York–area play, taking a record seven **Metropolitan Amateur** titles and five **Long Island Amateurs,** along with back-to-back **North & South** victories (1938 and '39) and the 1935 **U.S. Public Links.** Strafaci made surprisingly little impact in the U.S. Amateur, however, his deepest run being to the 1949 quarter-finals where he was eliminated by William Turnesa. Oddly, he and Willie (the sole career amateur among the seven Turnesas) only met twice in major competition, the other occasion being the final of the 1938 **Met Amateur,** which Strafaci took 3 and 1 at Ridgewood. Among Strafaci's other high-profile Met Am victims were 1940 U.S. Amateur winner Dick Chapman (1939 at Nassau CC) and future Masters and PGA champion Doug Ford (1946 at Essex County).

Frank Stranahan (USA)

The son of R. A. Stranahan, founder of Champion spark plugs, Frank Stranahan (b. Toledo, Ohio, 8/6/1922) grew up extraordinarily wealthy, yet possessed the desire and work ethic of the hungriest man. Tall and athletic, he was the forerunner of today's highly fit golfers, so fanatically dedicated to conditioning that he carried free weights in his bags when on the road. As a youngster he played at Inverness, taking lessons from Byron Nelson, and though his swing would end up quite a bit more mechanical than Lord Byron's, his confidence and competitiveness eventually saw him through to great things.

Stranahan first crept into the national spotlight by taking the **Trans-Mississippi Amateur** in 1941, then later claimed the 1946 **Western** and **Mexican** titles. He would truly stand front and center in a regal 1947 that included finishing joint 2nd at the Masters, then tying for 13th at the U.S. Open and 2nd at the Open Championship—the finest run of Major championship golf by an amateur since Bobby Jones. In 1948 he would capture three national amateur titles, winning his second **Mexican,** his first **Canadian,** and, most important, the first of two **British,** defeating England's Charles Stowe 5 and 4 at Royal St. George's. Following **Western** and **North & South Amateur** wins in 1949, Stranahan again took the **British** title in 1950 (routing fellow American Dick Chapman 8 and 6 at St. Andrews) and very nearly claimed the U.S. Amateur as well, losing on the 39th hole to Sam Urzetta in a tremendous final. That same year Stranahan tied for ninth

Frank Stranahan, 1948 USGA Amateur Championship, Memphis Country Club

in the Open Championship, and in 1953 achieved a four-way tie for second during Ben Hogan's famous Carnoustie victory. Not surprisingly, he was also a Walker Cup regular, competing from 1947 through 1951 with a combined record of 3-2-1.

Unfortunately, Stranahan's personality ruffled many a feather, leading him often to be held in lesser esteem than his on-the-course abilities might have merited. Indeed, following his wondrous 1947 Masters showing, Augusta National rescinded his invitation to the 1948 edition for etiquette violations and being verbally abusive to a club employee, actually yanking him from the course during a practice round. Nonetheless, Frank Stranahan's Major Championship ledger and his ability to claim several late-1940s PGA Tour events as an amateur were truly remarkable—though perhaps no more so than his inability to win a U.S. Amateur or his somewhat limited record after turning professional in 1954.

Major Amateur Wins (10): 1941 Trans-Miss; 1946, '49 & '52 North & South; 1946, '49, '51 & '52 Western Amateur; 1948 & '50 British Amateur

Walker Cup: 1947–51 (3)

1946-1960

	46	47	48	49	50	51	52	53	54	55	56	57	58	59	60
Masters	20	T2	-	T19	T14	T32	T19	T15	T43	T15	T22	MC	MC	T34	-
US Open	T45	T13	T41	MC	T46	T42	MC	-	MC	-	-	-	T10	MC	T49
US Am	T17	T17	T5	T33	2	T129	T9	T65	T9						
Brit Am	T9	T9	1	T5	1	T33	2	T33	T9						
British	-	T2	T23	13	T9	T12	T37	T2	T29	-	12	T19	-	-	-

Curtis Strange (USA)

The son of a golf pro, Virginia's Curtis Northrup Strange (b. Norfolk, 1/30/1955) put together a sterling amateur record during the mid-1970s, winning **Eastern** and **Western Amateurs,** two **North & Souths,** and the 1974 **NCAA** championship, while also being selected All-American and NCAA Player of the Year at Wake Forest. Seemingly destined for PGA Tour success, Strange initially struggled for two seasons before winning the 1979 **Pensacola Open** and placing 21st on the money list, the beginning of an 11-year run that would include 17 official victories, three money titles and multiple Player of the Year selections.

Strange claimed four titles from 1980 through 1984 but it was in 1985 that his stock soared, as he won three times—at the **Honda, Las Vegas,** and the **Canadian Open**—and finished first on the money list. The following year witnessed a mild step back (one win and 32nd in earnings) before 1987 saw three more victories (including his second **Canadian Open** and the **World Series of Golf**) and the first of back-to-back money titles. Even with such success, however, Strange's career-best campaign was surely 1988, wherein he won at **Hartford,** the **Memorial,** and the **Nabisco Championship,** as well as his first Major, the **U.S. Open,** at The Country Club of Brookline. There, having missed the 72nd green with a 7-iron, he got up-and-down from a deep bunker to force a play-off with Nick Faldo, ultimately winning the Monday contest by four.

Surprisingly, Strange would experience only one more Tour win, but it was a big one: the defense of his **Open** crown in 1989 at Oak Hill CC in Rochester. Once again it was his steady, methodical golf that carried the day, defeating Chip Beck, Mark McCumber, and Ian Woosnam by a single stroke while making Strange the first since Ben Hogan in 1951 to claim back-to-back Open titles. Though he briefly challenged for a threepeat in 1990 at Medinah, Strange ended that season 53rd on the money list, ultimately departing the top 100 permanently in 1996.

Solidly put together at 5'10" and 180 pounds, Strange was never among the Tour's longer hitters, instead relying upon a simple right-side-dominant technique to become one of its most consistent ball-strikers. Strange segued into television broadcasting during the late 1990s, bowing out in mid-2004 in apparent preparation for a 2005 venture onto the Champions Tour.

PGA Tour Wins (17): 1980 Westchester; 1985 & '87 Canadian Open; 1987 World Series; 1988 Memorial; **1988 & '89 U.S. Open**
Intn'l Wins: (4)
Walker Cup: 1975 **Ryder Cup:** 1983–89 & '95 (5); 2002 Capt

1976-1996

	76	77	78	79	80	81	82	83	84	85	86
Masters	T15	-	-	-	MC	T19	T7	MC	T46	T2	T21
US Open	-	-	-	-	T16	T17	T39	T26	3	T31	MC
British	MC	-	-	-	-	-	T15	T29	-	-	T14
PGA	-	-	T58	-	T5	T27	T14	86	MC	MC	MC

	87	88	89	90	91	92	93	94	95	96
Masters	T12	T21	T18	T7	T42	T31	WD	T27	9	MC
US Open	T4	1	1	T21	MC	T23	T25	4	T36	T27
British	-	T13	T61	MC	T38	MC	-	-	MC	T72
PGA	9	T31	T2	MC	WD	MC	MC	T19	T17	T26

Mike Strantz (USA)

A 1978 graduate of Michigan State and former Tom Fazio design associate, Mike Strantz (1955–2005) garnered large helpings of attention after going out on his own (under the suitable name Maverick Golf Course Design) in 1987. Certainly less prolific than his former employer, Strantz was one of the few modern architects who actually *did* handle only one project at a time, allowing an attention to detail uncommon in today's design game. A skilled artist, he relied heavily on sketches made in the field, resulting in dramatically conceived holes that rank, by any measure, among the most visually exciting in golf. The cornerstone of Strantz's work was a series of high-profile new designs in Virginia and the Carolinas, as well as a critically acclaimed renovation of the Shore Course at California's Monterey Peninsula CC. He died in June 2005.

Andrew Strath (UK)

The older of St. Andrews' famous golfing brothers for whom a fearsome bunker at the Old Course's famed 11th hole is forever named, Andrew Strath (1836–1868) was a fine player who won the **Open Championship** in 1865 at Prestwick, defeating Willie Park Sr. by two. He had previously finished third in the 1860 inaugural contest, fourth in 1863, and second in 1864, making his victory a logical culmination rather than any sort of surprise. Also well known as a clubmaker, Andrew was a frequent participant in high-profile challenge matches, splitting, for example, a pair of 1862 contests with Old Tom Morris over 36 holes at St. Andrews, and defeating Willie Park Sr. over 36 holes during that same year. Like brother David, Andrew would die young, though a third sibling, George, would survive longer, serving as professional at Troon before leading the wave of late nineteenth-century Scottish golfing immigrants to the United States.

David Strath (UK)

Four years younger than brother Andrew, St. Andrean David Strath (1840–1879) was widely considered the better player, though he was forever damned—like so many others—for failing to win an Open Championship. He might well have had his Claret Jug in 1876 at St. Andrews but for a closing six which set him in an apparent tie with Bob Martin—and then the fun started. A protest was filed against Strath for allegedly hitting into the group ahead at the 17th, a claim that the Committee, in an act of remarkable weakness, stated itself unwilling to resolve until after the scheduled play-off. Strath, rightly arguing that he had no intention of joining a play-off which might well be nullified the following day anyway, refused to play and Martin was awarded his first Open title.

A close friend of Young Tom Morris, Strath made five appearances among the Open's top-five, including second place (behind Young Tom) in 1870 and '72. Moving to North Berwick soon after the controversial loss to Martin, he died in 1879 during a trip to Australia.

Ron Streck (USA)

An Oklahoma native who attended his hometown University of Tulsa, Ron Streck (b. 7/17/1954) was largely a journeyman on the PGA Tour, making the top 125 every year from 1978 through 1985 and winning only twice, but each occasion in some style. The first time, at the 1978 **Texas Open,** he earned a place in history by shooting a 36-hole record 63-62 on the weekend to beat Hubert Green and Lon Hinkle by one—after getting up-and-down from a bunker at his 36th hole just to make the cut! Three years later, he fired a third-round 62 at the 1981 **Houston Open** to move three ahead of Hale Irwin and Jerry Pate, only to be declared a 54-hole winner when incessant rains made it impossible to continue.

Marlene (Stewart) Streit (Canada)

The assigning of superlatives in a book such as this is largely a subjective thing, the "best ofs" and "greatest sinces" nearly all being judgment calls. But here we have a prominent exception, for Alberta's Marlene Stewart Streit (b. Cereal, 3/9/1934) is, without question, the finest woman golfer ever produced by Canada. Indeed, her record of achievement is staggering, beginning with 11 **Ontario Ladies** titles (her first taken at age 16) and working through to the 2003 **U.S. Senior Women's Open** where, at 69, she became the oldest winner of a USGA title.

Among her lesser-noticed achievements, Streit was the American **Women's Intercollegiate** champion in 1956 while playing for Rollins College. Of course, by this time she had already captured the 1953 **British Ladies** (defeating Ireland's Philomena Garvey 7 and 6 at Royal Porthcawl) and three **Canadian Ladies** championships, so a victory against a small field of collegians was perhaps of little consequence. That same year, however, she would also become the first Canadian to win the **U.S. Women's Amateur** (defeating JoAnne Gunderson 2 up at Indianapolis CC), in addition to recording her first of two victories at Pinehurst's **North & South** event. When, in 1963, she claimed the **Australian Ladies** crown, Streit became the only player of either gender ever to have won the Canadian, U.S., British, and Australian titles.

Domestically her record was dominant to the point of monotony as Streit won 11 **Canadian Ladies** titles between 1951 and 1973 and nine **Canadian Closed** crowns between 1950 and 1969. She was also low amateur at the Peter Jackson/du Maurier LPGA Tour stop on four occasions (also accomplishing the feat twice in the U.S. Women's Open), was selected five times as Canadian Female Athlete of the Year, and represented Canada in more international events (as both player and captain) than can possibly be listed. This dominance has carried over to senior play where beyond the 2003 U.S. Senior Women's' Open, she won two additional American titles (1985 and '94) and four **Canadian Seniors** (1987, '88, '90, and '93).

Standing barely over 5'0", Streit has relied on a compact, repetitive swing to produce an enviable tee-to-green game, as well as that rare brand of competitive fire that makes one continue to burn for victories long after most are content to rest on their laurels. She has also distinguished herself as a representative of old-fashioned golfing ideals, taking prize money won in a 1965 *Shell's Wonderful World of Golf* match and starting her own fund to help top Canadian juniors with their travel expenses.

Major Amateur Wins (4): 1953 British Ladies; 1956 U.S. Women's Amateur; 1956 & '74 North & South; 11 Canadian Ladies, 3 U.S. Senior Women's' Open & 4 Canadian Senior Ladies

Steve Stricker (USA)

A former All-American at the University of Illinois, Edgerton, Wisconsin, product Steve Stricker (b. 2/23/1967) has had an up-and-down career on the PGA Tour. After getting his card in 1992, Stricker climbed steadily for five straight years, peaking in 1996 when he finished fourth on the money list and won twice, first at the **Kemper Open,** then at the **Western Open,** where his eight-shot triumph seemed to suggest the brightest of futures—a feeling supported by a late-season third at the Tour Championship.

Unfortunately, Stricker has been terribly inconsistent since, finishing as high as 13th on the money list in 1998 and as low as 189th in 2003. In 2001 he finished 30th despite gaining his third career victory, the lucrative **WGC-Match Play** event played at Australia's Metropolitan Club. A tallish man with great rhythm and a fine, balanced swing, Stricker surely hopes to put it all together once more as he reaches his late 30s, for he has proven already that the raw talent is there.

Herbert Strong (UK/USA)

After working his way up to the professional's job at prestigious Royal St. George's GC in Kent, Ramsgate native Herbert Strong (1879–1944) emigrated to America to take the professional position at New York's Apawamis Club in 1905. He would make some design alterations to the historic course during his stay, though not to the extent that he would alter his next stop, Queens' Inwood CC, eventual site of the 1921 PGA Championship and the 1923 U.S. Open.

With a growing reputation in the booming New York market, Strong soon turned to architecture full time, completing several area projects, the most notable of which was the quirky Engineers GC, site of the 1919 PGA and the 1920 U.S. Amateur. Over the next two decades, he landed projects from Maine to Havana, and as far west as suburban Detroit, all the while earning a reputation as an on-site designer who did his own surveying and supervision of construction before moving on. Though two-time U.S. Open site Canterbury CC in Cleveland is likely Strong's highest-profile layout, he closed his career with a pair of links-like Florida designs of note, Ft. Pierce's much-altered Indian Hills G&CC and the better-known Ponte Vedra Club, intended site of the cancelled 1939 Ryder Cup matches.

Notable Courses: Canterbury CC, Ohio; Engineers GC, New York; Ponte Vedra C, Ocean Course, Florida; Saucon Valley CC, Old Course, Pennsylvania

Alexander Stuart (UK)

Though we today find only limited references to this Oxford contemporary of Horace Hutchinson, Alexander Stuart was rated by Darwin as among Britain's eight finest players at the mid-1880s onset of the Amateur Championship. While citing Stuart's "smooth and graceful style," Darwin considered him among the bottom three of the eight, and it is true that Stuart only once went so far as the semifinals, losing there in 1888 to eight-time champion John Ball. Though he left competitive golf early, it will be noted that Hutchinson considered Stuart nearly the equal of the period's best (Ball, John Laidlay, and himself)—but then Stuart and Horace were schoolmates, and the Old School ties are, of course, well-nigh unbreakable.

Mary Stuart (Mary, Queen of Scots) (UK)

As golf was, prior to the invention of the inexpensive gutta-percha ball, primarily the province of the affluent, it hardly surprises that two of its earliest female practitioners were royalty: the first wife of King Henry VIII, Catherine of Aragon (1485–1536) and that most famous of Scottish leaders, Mary, Queen of Scots (1542–1587). Mary's affinity for the game is illustrated by her being famously chided for playing it within days of the murder of her husband, Lord Darnley. This certainly indicates golf's status within the royal house, of course, though one tends to wonder just how many other women were actively taking to the links in the mid-1500s.

Karen Stupples (UK)

Prior to 2004, England's Karen Stupples (b. Dover, 6/24/1973) was a somewhat anonymous professional who played collegiate golf at Florida State, represented Great Britain and Ireland in the 1996 and '98 Curtis Cups, and struggled to find her way on the LPGA Tour. After two trips through the Tour Qualifying Tournament and five competitive seasons, she had yet to place better than 35th on the money list or joint third in a single event. In 2004 that all changed, beginning with a scorching season-opening victory at the **Welch's/Fry's Championship** where Stupples began with a 63, then added 66-66-63 for a 22-under-par total and a five-shot victory. Later that summer she not only won her first Major championship but did so on her home turf, firing 65-70-70-64 at Sunningdale to claim the **Women's British Open,** her 19-under-par total matching Dottie Pepper's record for the lowest Major score in LPGA history. Playing full time in America, Stupples' ability to go very low could mark her as an up-and-coming star.

John R. Stutt (UK)

Scotsman John R. Stutt (1897–1990) is primarily famous as the man who constructed many of the nearly 200 golf courses designed or redesigned by five-time Open champion James Braid, a pretty fair legacy. In the background, Stutt also built courses for other architects (most notably J. S. F. Morrison), was among the first to mechanize his construction crews, invented one of the first turf aerating machines, and, ultimately, designed a fair number of courses entirely on his own. Followed into the business by his son John H., Stutt perhaps remains a bit unsung, for given Braid's well-documented reluctance to travel, he surely did more than the average construction man when working, essentially unsupervised, in the field.

Louise Suggs (USA)

Blessed with a quiet personality that did little to court the spotlight, Mae Louise Suggs (b. 9/7/1923) is somewhat underrated in golf's female hierarchy, for her career record takes a back seat to very, very few. Born in Atlanta and raised in suburban Lithia Springs, Suggs was introduced to golf at age 10 by her father, an ex-professional baseball player who designed and built his own course. Possessing a classic, smooth and powerful swing, Suggs became one of the dominant amateurs of her era, initially winning the **Georgia Women's** title in 1940 and '42 (the former at age 16), then later adding two **Southern Amateurs** (1941 and '47), three **North & Souths** (1942, '46 and '48), and three **Doherty Invitationals** (1945, '46, and '48), to her ledger.

Suggs' profile became a national one in 1946 when she claimed the **Western Amateur** and, playing against the professionals, the **Western Open,** a rare double that she promptly repeated the following season. Suggs also beat the then-small field of pros at the 1946 **Titleholders,** making her victory at the 1947 **U.S. Women's Amateur** (two up over Dorothy Kirby at Michigan's Franklin Hills CC) hardly unexpected. She then traveled to Britain with the victorious 1948 Curtis Cup team and became only the second American to take the **British Ladies** title, defeating Jeanne Donald one up at Royal Lytham & St. Annes.

With few amateur mountains left to conquer, Suggs turned professional in 1948 and was among the 13 founders of the LPGA a year later. Having already proven herself against the pros, her success on the fledgling tour seemed virtually assured, and she did indeed amass 58 victories (fourth all-time) and 11 Major championships, the latter including four **Titleholders** and four **Western Opens.** She was also twice a winner of the **U.S. Women's Open** and by startling margins, defeating Babe Zaharias by an eye-popping 14 shots in 1949 in Landover, Maryland, then taking Marlene Hagge and Betty Jameson by seven in 1952 in Philadelphia.

President of the LPGA from 1955 to 1957 and an inaugural inductee into the organization's Hall of Fame in 1967, Suggs scaled back her schedule in the early 1960s, though she continued to appear in sporadic events as late as 1984. The holder of numerous LPGA records long since broken, she does maintain one gender-related accomplishment that, though largely overlooked, will remain forever in the record books. In 1961 Suggs won the **Royal Poinciana Invitational,** a mixed-gender event whose field included Sam Snead and Dow Finsterwald. The catch was that the tournament was largely a promotional affair and was played over a par-3 course in Palm Beach. Both men and women played from the same tees, however, making Suggs the first (and thus far only) woman to defeat the men professionals on a genuinely equal basis.

Professional/LPGA Wins (58): 1946, '54, '56 & '59 Titleholders; 1946, '47, '49 & '53 Western Open; 1949 & '52 U.S. Women's Open; 1953 & '54 Peach Blossom; 1954 & '61 Sea Island; 1954 & '58 Babe Zaharias; **1957 LPGA Championship;** 1959 & '62 Orange Blossom; 1959, '60 & '61 Dallas Civitan; 3 All-American Opens & 3 Triangle Round Robins
Curtis Cup: 1948

1947-1969

	47	48	49	50	51	52	53	54	55	56	57	58
LPGA									2	T8	1	T9
US Open	4	-	1	3	2	1	10	3	T2	T7	T3	2

	59	60	61	62	63	64	65	66	67	68	69
LPGA	3	2	T2	-	T2	T17	T15	8	12	T28	T10
US Open	2	T9	4	T4	T2	-	8	T33	T4	T29	T8

Also won Western Opens and Titleholders, as listed above.

Hideyo Sugimoto (Japan)

A former caddie at the elegant Kawana Hotel, Hideyo Sugimoto (b. 1938) became one of Japan's top players during the 1960s, thrice appearing in the World Cup and narrowly missing out on the 1966 individual title when, playing in Tokyo, he lost a two-stroke lead by double-bogeying the last, then lost to George Knudson in a play-off. Despite this disappointment, Sugimoto was, for a time, a force around Asia, winning **Japan Opens** in 1964 and '69, as well as national Opens in **Taiwan** (1969), the **Philippines** (1972), and **Malaysia** (1973). He was also a Masters invitee in 1967 and '68, tying for 35th on his second visit.

Van Tassel Sutphen (USA)

Philadelphian William G. Van Tassel Sutphen (1861–1945) was well known as a turn-of-the-century science fiction author, though his involvement with golf was also a deep one. In addition to writing or editing five golf-oriented books (including the historic *Harper's Official Golf Guide 1901*), Sutphen served as editor of the original *Golf* magazine, penned numerous articles and managed much of J. H. Taylor's 1900 American Tour. Taylor himself considered Sutphen to be of major importance in golf's Stateside development, citing "his love for the game" and "his advocacy of its merits through the medium of his voluminous writings."

Hal Sutton (USA)

There was a time when Shreveport, Louisana's Hal Evan Sutton (b. 4/28/1958), the latest "next Nicklaus" in a long line, appeared to have a chance at actually becoming the real thing. An All-American at hometown Centenary College where he won 14 collegiate titles, Sutton was the 1980 NCAA Player of the Year as well as the winner of the North & South Amateur (1980) and two **Western Amateurs** (1979 and '80). Twice a Walker Cupper (1979 and '81), Sutton took the 1980 **U.S. Amateur** at the CC of North Carolina (9 and 8 over Bob Lewis Jr.) and ran away with medalist honors at the **World Amateur Team** event, winning by nine. There was talk of Sutton following in the footsteps of Bob Jones, and he indeed went briefly to work for his affluent oilman father before deciding instead to turn professional in 1981.

Joining the PGA Tour full time in 1982, Sutton quickly set about earning his keep with Rookie of the Year honors, a late win at **Walt Disney World,** and 11th place on the money list. Then in 1983, he stepped up to Nicklaus–like status by finishing first on the money list and taking Player of the Year honors with victories at the **Players Championship** and the **PGA Championship,** the latter an impressive one-shot win over the Golden Bear himself at Riviera. Two wins (along with seventh- and sixth-place money rankings) followed in 1985 and '86 before Sutton slipped into a 10-year decline that was not so much terrible as it was inconsistent, with only a single victory (the 1995 **B.C. Open**) and money winnings ranging from 23rd in 1989 to a dismal 185th in 1992.

But turning 40 and little in need of money, Sutton suddenly found his form in 1998, launching a four-season renaissance that included six wins and top-six money finishes from 1998 through 2000. Most impressively, after stating that his fellow Tour players shouldn't be so intimidated by the young Tiger Woods, Sutton backed up his words by defeating Woods at the 2000 **Players Championship** in a memorable head-to-head battle. Always the consummate ball-striker, Sutton was selected to his third and fourth Ryder Cup teams in 1999 and 2002, then served as captain of the disappointing 2004 team that endured a record defeat at Oakland Hills.

PGA Tour Wins (14): 1983 & 2000 Players Championship; **1983 PGA Championship;** 1986 Memorial; 1999 Canadian Open
Walker Cup: 1979 & '81 (2) **Ryder Cup:** 1985, '87, '99 & 2002 (4); 2004 Capt **Presidents Cup:** 1998 & 2000 (2)

1981-2004

	81	82	83	84	85	86	87	88	89	90	91	92
Masters	MC	-	T27	MC	T31	MC	MC	MC	MC	MC	-	MC
US Open	MC	T19	6	T16	T23	T4	T31	64	T29	MC	MC	-
British	T47	MC	T29	MC	-	-	T11	MC	-	-	-	-
PGA	-	T29	1	T6	T65	T21	T28	T66	MC	T49	T7	MC

	93	94	95	96	97	98	99	00	01	02	03	04
Masters	-	-	MC	MC	-	-	MC	10	36	-	-	-
US Open	-	-	T36	-	T19	-	T7	T23	T24	MC	-	-
British	-	-	-	-	-	-	T10	MC	-	MC	MC	-
PGA	T31	T55	MC	MC	MC	T27	T26	MC	T44	T60	T39	MC

Donald Swaelens (Belgium)

Though not quite on a par with Flory van Donck, Donald Swaelens (1935–1975) remains the second-best golfer produced by Belgium, having established himself as one of Continental Europe's best in the pre-Ballesteros world of the 1960s and early '70s. Swaelens' best season came in 1967 when he won three times, including the **German Open** at Krefeld, but there was not yet an official European Order of Merit to be measured against. Thus his formal European Tour peaks came with 15th-place finishes in 1973 and '74, the former highlighted by a runner-up finish to Peter Oosterhuis at the Volvo PGA at Wentworth and the second best ranking among Continental players. In 1974 Swaelens managed his best Open Championship finish, joint seventh, at Royal Lytham & St. Annes.

Robert Sweeny Jr. (USA/UK)

Amateur Robert Sweeny (1911–1983) was born in Pasadena, California, yet lived most of his life in Britain, graduating from Oxford and winning the Distinguished Flying Cross while serving in the RAF during World War II. Called by Leonard Crawley "one of the finest swingers of the golf club one could wish to see," Sweeny competed on both sides of the Atlantic, his high watermark coming in 1937 when he defeated Ireland's Lionel Munn 3 and 2 to capture the **British Amateur** at Royal St. George's. A member of the R&A, Sweeny very nearly won the first post-war Amateur as well, losing a hard-fought final to another Irishman, Jimmy Bruen, at Royal Birkdale. In America, Sweeny ran more as a bridesmaid, losing in the final of the 1954 U.S. Amateur to Arnold Palmer and twice finishing second at the Metropolitan Amateur, in 1948 and '57. He

was also selected as a reserve for the 1947 British Walker Cup but did not compete.

Jess Sweetser (USA)

Born: Cobb, Kentucky, 4/18/1902 **Died:** Washington, D.C., 5/27/1989

Born the same year as Bobby Jones and raised in St. Louis, the hugely talented Jess W. Sweetser was widely considered a worthy challenger for the young Georgian, particularly as he reached competitive maturity earlier, capturing both the **U.S.** and **British Amateurs** prior to Jones. Sweetser won the 1920 **NCAA** individual title while a student at Yale (another nice touch, Jones being, at least for his graduate work, a Harvard man) and then crashed through at Brookline in 1922, beating Chick Evans 3 and 2 in the final to capture the U.S. Amateur. And here again Sweetser's success seemed directly tied to Jones, for he soundly paddled young Bobby 8 and 7 in the semifinal, playing some of what Jones later referred to as "the most devastating golf ever seen in our national amateur."

Jones would, of course, overtake Sweetser by the middle of the decade, with the remainder of his career being the stuff of lore. Before being dislodged from his pedestal, Sweetser came agonizingly close to defending his Amateur crown (losing in the 1923 final to Max Marston, on the 38th hole), won a pair of **Metropolitan Amateurs** (1922 and '25), and battled the flu to capture the 1926 **British Amateur** at Muirfield. Not surprisingly, Sweetser was also a Walker Cup stalwart, appearing in the first five editions plus a sixth in 1932, and captaining two victorious squads in 1967 and '73. Curiously, he also holds the distinction of being the only man ever to win a Walker Cup match in extra holes, defeating C. V. L. Hooman in the competition's first-ever round of singles. It seems that upon finishing 36 holes all square, and uncertain as to proper protocol, the pair simply played on with Sweetser winning at the 37th. Every match thereafter was officially deemed a halve.

Nancy (Roth) Syms (USA)

A native of Elkhart, Indiana, who grew up primarily in Florida, Nancy Roth Syms (b. 1939) won five **Florida Ladies** titles between 1960 and 1968 as well as three straight **Eastern Amateurs** (1964–66), two **Southern Amateurs** (1964 and '66), two **Broadmoor Invitationals** (1972 and '75), three **Doherty Invitationals** (1963, '64, and '66), and the 1963 and '66 **North & South Amateurs**. Though never a winner of the U.S. Women's Amateur, Syms did capture the **British Ladies** crown in 1975 (beating Suzanne Cadden 3 and 2 at St. Andrews) and appeared in the 1964, '66, and '76 Curtis Cups. Captaining the American team in 1980, Syms also scored a relatively late playing triumph by winning the 1978 **Trans-Mississippi** title.

T

President William H. Taft (USA)

Of the 27th President William Howard Taft (1857–1930) golf historian H. B. Martin once wrote: "Taft was a golfer at heart and did not play it merely as a means of keeping his weight down—although this was something to be considered in his case." A large and jovial man, there are perhaps more images of Taft playing the game than any other pre–World War II president, partially because he played often and over many different venues and partially, one guesses, because his size made him particularly photogenic on the links. Though widely reported as a decent player who often came around in the 80s, he is well remembered for a decidedly gruesome 27 recorded—mostly within one very deep bunker—on the par-4 17th at the Kebo Valley GC in Bar Harbor, Maine.

T. Suffern Tailer (USA)

Thomas Suffern Tailer (1867–1928) was a prominent New York banker and sportsman who divided his time between Manhattan and fashionable Newport, Rhode Island, where he was a member at the famed Newport CC. Unhappy with that course's growing obsolescence in the face of new equipment technology, Tailer decided simply to build his own layout, commissioning C. B. Macdonald and Seth Raynor to design nine holes on land immediately adjacent to the Newport CC property. Completed in 1920, Tailer's Ocean Links was open to any member of Newport and would gain great fame by hosting his annual Gold Mashie tournament, an invitational featuring many of the day's top amateurs competing over 72 holes. Counting Francis Ouimet and Jesse Guilford among its champions, the Ocean Links was eventually sold off by Tailer's widow following his unexpected death in 1928.

Freddie Tait (UK)

Born: Edinburgh, Scotland, 1/11/1870 **Died:** Koodoosberg, South Africa, 2/4/1900

Though dying young, and as a military hero, certainly burnishes the legend, Frederick Guthrie Tait remains, more than a century after his death, one of the most celebrated figures in the history of amateur golf. The son of a professor of natural philosophy at Edinburgh University, Tait was a tall, strong man, an excellent all-around athlete, and a highly engaging personality. In his early golfing days he was tremendously long but also a bit wild, his recovery skills, quite necessarily, being of an elite caliber. Later, as he learned to throttle back a bit, he became, to use a modern analogy, the Greg Norman of his day—the very longest *and straightest* of hitters.

Tait's list of golfing accomplishments, though limited to the last decade of the nineteenth century, is somewhat overwhelming. At the top of the ledger is his seven-year run at the **British Amateur** from 1893 through 1899, which began with three straight semifinal appearances in which he was set back, in succession, by Johnny Laidlay, Mure Fergusson, and John Ball. But in 1896, Tait was finally ready, and his dash to the title left no stone unturned, vanquishing, in order, Laidlay, Ball, Horace Hutchinson, and, in the final, the great Harold Hilton, who found himself on the short end of an 8 and 7 verdict. After poor putting derailed Tait's 1897 defense, he roared back to recapture the title at Hoylake in 1898, defeating Mure Fergusson 7 and 5 in the final. Finally in 1899, Tait again reached the final, but this time lost a heartbreaker to Ball at the 37th.

Tait was also a regular participant in the Open Championship where, during these same years, he was thrice leading amateur and, from 1896 through 1899, finished 3rd, 3rd, 5th, and 7th. He reportedly played the Old Course in 72 in 1894 and, we are told, an unimaginable 69 in 1897. In addition to setting similar scoring records at places like Muirfield and Carnoustie, he was a winner of numerous medals and trophies, including the prestigious **St. George's Challenge Cup**, which he claimed in 1896, '98, and '99 while serving a military posting nearby.

Unfortunately, it would be this military career that would be Tait's undoing, for as a member of the Black Watch (and a graduate of Sandhurst), he shipped off to South Africa to fight the Boers in October of 1899. Carrying the rank of lieutenant, Tate was killed in early February while leading a charge at Koodoosberg Drift, a death as lamented as any in the history of golf. Later in 1900, he would be accorded a unique posthumous honor when his great friend John L. Low penned *F. G. Tait: A Record* (J. Nisbet, 1900), an altogether splendid account and, not incidentally, the first biography of a golfer ever written.

Harry Tallmadge (USA)

New Yorker Henry O. "Harry" Tallmadge (1862–1948) was several years younger than the other founding members of the St. Andrew's GC of Yonkers, New York, allowing him to relate a good deal of the club's history to interested writers long after men like John Reid and Robert Lockhart were gone. But Tallmadge was no youthful hanger-on; in addition to playing a prominent role at St. Andrew's, it was he who organized and hosted the December 22, 1884, New York dinner that resulted in the founding of the USGA. Serving as the fledgling organization's first secretary, Tallmadge also arranged for the 1895 visit of two-time Open Championship winner Willie Park Jr., a tour which, like Vardon's five years later, did much to spread the gospel in the New World.

Frank "Sandy" Tatum (USA)

Hopefully not the last of a dying breed, Frank "Sandy" Tatum (b. 1/10/1920) is that rarest of creatures in contemporary golf, an experienced, knowledgeable leader who represents the game's finest time-honored values, not accepting carts, $200 greens fees, and 360-yard tee shots as somehow representing "progress." A Phi Beta Kappa graduate of Stanford, a Rhodes Scholar, and a Bay Area golf icon, Tatum was the 1942 **NCAA** individual medalist and a winner of the **Danish Amateur**, though his great service to golf came as a USGA Executive Committee member from 1972 through 1980, serving as the organization's president during the latter two years. A close friend and frequent playing partner of Tom Watson, Tatum has more recently championed the renovation of San Francisco's famed Harding Park GC while still speaking out—apparently to deaf New Jersey ears—on the critical problems facing the modern game.

J. H. Taylor (UK)

Born: Northam, England, 3/19/1871 **Died:** Northam, England, 2/10/1963

One of the most beloved, important, and, above all, talented golfers of his or any other time, John Henry Taylor grew up close to the links at Royal North Devon (aka Westward Ho!), where he began caddying at age 11. Also employed as a domestic in the service of Horace Hutchinson's father, Taylor eventually intended a military career but was turned down by both the army and the navy multiple times for poor eyesight and flat feet. He was further rejected in attempts at becoming a police officer (being one inch too short at 5'8") and so on to golf it was, his initial glory coming after defeating the renowned Andra Kirkaldy 4 and 3 in an 1890 challenge match played at Winchester and Burnham & Berrow.

Taylor first made noise in the **Open Championship** of 1893 by commencing with a sensational 75 over the old Prestwick links, though a rain-battered second-round 89 soon removed him from the heart of the fray. The following year, however, with the event making its initial venture outside of Scotland, he arrived to stay, posting rounds of 84-80-81-81 at England's Royal St. George's to finish five clear of colorful runner-up Douglas Rolland. With his win, Taylor became the first non-Scot to claim the Claret Jug, a fact hardly lost upon the Scottish professionals, some of whom had boycotted his initial appearance in 1893. Thus the old guard poised for revenge when the Open returned to St. Andrews in 1895, yet J. H. was undaunted. Recovering from a poor opening-round 86, he shot 78-80 and a strong closing 78 (the only contender to break 80) to successfully defend his title by four over Sandy Herd and 10 over Kirkaldy, both St. Andrews' natives.

Taylor then was king of the hill, but for how long? In the spring of 1896, he played a challenge match at Ganton against that club's up-and-coming young professional Harry Vardon. Taylor went in with confidence befitting a two-time Open winner, yet in his own words suffered a long day of Vardon "remorselessly knocking all the conceit out of me," ultimately losing 8 and 7. Thus the first seeds of the Triumvirate were sown, with Vardon also claiming that summer's Open Championship by defeating Taylor in a 36-hole play-off at Muirfield. James Braid would arrive with a second-place finish (behind amateur Harold Hilton) the following year at Hoylake, and thereafter the battle was on for career supremacy among the game's three British titans.

Taylor matched Vardon with three Open titles when he won in 1900 at St. Andrews, later catching both of his rivals at four by claiming the 1909 title with a fine 295 score at Royal Cinque Ports. Once again falling behind after

J. H. Taylor

earlier at Hoylake where, had the 36 holes of qualifying figured in, he would have won!

One component to Taylor's longevity, perhaps, was the simplicity of his swing, a short, decidedly flat-footed motion relying more on arm and hand strength (of which he had much) and less on the intricate timing of countless moving parts. He was a remarkably straight hitter who, having grown up in the wind at Westward Ho!, was capable of hitting it very low and was frequently cited for his length directly into a gale. His greatest strength, however, was surely his approach game, for Taylor was deadly accurate with the equivalent of today's short irons, able to hit them high or low at will. He was also rated a better putter than either Vardon or Braid.

In the limited field of tournaments open to professional golfers of the era, Taylor twice won British golf's second largest event, the **News of the World** match play (1904 and '08), as well as national Opens in **France** (1908 and '09) and **Germany** (1912). He also finished second to Vardon at the 1900 U.S. Open, an event entered while making his own less-famous exhibition tour of America.

Despite such a record, the reverence in which J. H. Taylor was held stemmed even more from his nonplaying endeavors, particularly his strong support of artisan golfing societies. Further, Taylor's leading role in founding the British PGA in 1901 led Andra Kirkaldy to observe that he "has done more for the professional golfers of this country than any Labour leader or Union secretary ever did for the men under him." Taylor was also active in golf course architecture, teaming with Frederic G. Hawtree in a successful design firm that specialized in public-access facilities. His greatest accomplishment, however, may well have been educating himself enough in his adult life (after leaving school at age 11) to pen years worth of golf articles for the *News of the World*, as well as his fine autobiography *Golf: My Life's Work* (Johnathan Cape, 1943) without the aid of a ghost writer. Elected president of Royal North Devon at age 86, Taylor lived his final years in a hillside house overlooking the links before eventually passing at age 91.

Braid won in 1910 at St. Andrews and Vardon took the 1911 event at Royal St. George's, Taylor drew even for the final time at Hoylake in 1913 when his 304 total in dreadful wind and rain ran away from the field, routing Ted Ray by eight. Interestingly, Taylor very nearly failed to qualify for this event, holing a 6-foot putt at the last to claim the final spot.

Vardon, of course, would settle things for posterity with his sixth Claret Jug in 1914, though after World War I, with the Triumvirate all in their late 40s, it was Taylor who would remain the most competitive, actually tying for sixth as late as 1925 (at age 54) after finishing fifth a year

Intn'l Wins (10): 1894, '95, 1900, '09 & '13 British Open; 1904 & '08 PGA Match Play; 1908 & '09 French Open; 1912 German Open
Ryder Cup: 1933 Capt

1893-1920

	93	94	95	96	97	98	99	00	01	02	03	04	05	06
US Open	-	-	-	-	-	-	-	2	-	-	-	-	-	-
British	T10	1	1	2	T10	4	4	1	3	T6	T9	T2	T2	2

	07	08	09	10	11	12	13	14	15	16	17	18	19	20
US Open	-	-	-	-	-	-	T30	-	-	-			-	-
British	2	T7	1	T14	T5	T11	1	2						12

Reg Taylor (South Africa)

A native of Johannesburg, Reginald Carden Taylor (b. 1927) was one of postwar South Africa's elite amateurs, and certainly its most impressive if measured in terms of overseas competition. Indeed, Taylor was successful the world over, capturing the **German Open Amateur** in 1958, the **Canadian Amateur** in 1962, and, reaching his mid-40s, the **French Open Amateur** in 1970. At home, he resides upon that short list of players who've won both the **South African Open** and **Amateur**, the former coming in 1954 at East London, the latter in 1956 at Durban. Perhaps most impressive, however, was a second-place finish at the 1955 Open at Zwartkop, where Taylor came within one stroke of denying Bobby Locke his ninth South African title, in the process winning his second Freddie Tait Trophy, awarded to the low amateur in each year's Open field.

Louis Tellier (France/USA)

Famous are the many Britons who emigrated to America to pursue club professional positions in the early 1900s, but largely overlooked is one prominent Frenchman who did the same, Louis Tellier. Of course, the diminutive Tellier, who possessed enough game to join Arnaud Massy, Jean Gassiat, and Etienne Lafitte as French golf's "Four Mousqueteers," may simply have been ducking World War I when he held positions at Canoe Brook, the Country Club, and Brae Burn between 1914 and 1921. Regardless, he competed frequently in America, first at the historic 1913 U.S. Open (where he tied for fourth with Walter Hagen, three back of the historic Vardon-Ray-Ouimet play-off), then logging further top-five finishes in 1915 and '19. As an early member of the PGA of America following the organization's founding in 1916, Tellier played in a number of events that would later be recognized by the PGA Tour, winning the **Massachusetts Open** in 1921. Sadly, he died of his own hand, hanging himself from a tree on the Brae Burn course that same year.

Rachel (Hetherington) Teske (Australia)

A former four-time **New South Wales Junior** champion and **Open Amateur** winner, Rachel Teske (b. Port Macquarie, 4/23/1972) has enjoyed a steady ascent since joining the LPGA Tour in 1997, debuting at 53rd on the money list (while still playing under her maiden name of Hetherington) before reaching as high as 11th, 9th and 7th from 2001 through 2003. An eight-time Tour winner, Teske has twice won in consecutive weeks (in 1999 and 2003) and—perhaps equally rarely—twice taken play-off victories over Annika Sorenstam (the 1999 First Union Betsy King and the 2002 Ping Banner Health). Her Major championship record, however, is a mixed one, featuring only two top-10 finishes in 24 starts, though both of those (ties for second at the 2001 Dinah Shore and third at the 2003 LPGA Championship) have come recently. Now in her mid-30s (and again playing under her maiden name), the consistently sound Ms. Hetherington has certainly established herself as a world-class player, but does she enough game to become a Major champion?

Doug Tewell (USA)

Originally recruited to Oklahoma State as a basketball player by coach Henry Iba, Doug Tewell (b. Baton Rouge, Louisiana, 8/27/1949) eventually worked as a club professional before joining the PGA Tour in 1975. After several lean years he hit stride in the late 1970s, finishing among the top 100 money winners 13 of 14 times from 1977 to 1989. A notably accurate ball-striker who epitomized the phrase "fairways and greens," Tewell claimed all four of his Tour victories between 1980 and 1987. His first came at the 1980 **Heritage Classic** where he bested Jerry Pate in a play-off, though more memorable, perhaps, was a 1986 **Los Angeles Open** victory that featured a 66-63 finish (and a seven-shot runaway) at venerable Riviera.

Finding the top 100 only once after 1989, Tewell was ready for the Champions Tour upon becoming eligible in 2000, to date claiming eight victories and banking nearly $9.6 million in earnings.

Alan Thirlwell (UK)

A native of Newcastle, Englishman Alan Thirlwell (b. 8/8/1928) was one of Britain's top postwar amateurs, his degree of success inhibited only by a mediocre short game and the looming presence of Michael Bonallack. Considered a top tee-to-greener, Thirlwell won back-to-back **English Amateurs** in 1954 and '55, and very likely would have won a third in 1963 had Bonallack not enjoyed one of the great scrambling days on record, getting up-and-down 22 times in 36 holes during the final. A Walker Cupper in 1957, Thirlwell also suffered disappointment in his lone trip to the British Amateur final in 1958, losing to Joe Carr 3 and 2 in an exciting match at St. Andrews. He remained highly competitive into his 40s, however, knocking Bonallack from the 1969 English Amateur and, most impressively, reaching the British Amateur final in 1972 at age 44, where he lost to Trevor Homer at Royal St. George's.

Dave Thomas (UK)

Though born in Newcastle, England, Dave Thomas (b. 8/16/1934) grew up in Wales where for a time he looked every bit the successor to Dai Rees as a Welshman capable of reaching international heights. A powerful man, Thomas was a long, straight driver in the Greg Norman mold, capable of overwhelming many a course, and tales of his majestic tee shots abound. He was not, however, a highly skilled wedge player—a serious weakness when one is routinely facing little more than pitches for their approach.

Consequently, Thomas never won on the large scale predicted for him, though he did manage 14 significant titles in the United Kingdom and on the continent, the largest being the 1963 *News of the World* match play at Turnberry. Also the winner of the 1966 **Penfold Tournament** plus national Opens in **Belgium** (1955), the **Netherlands** (1958), and **France** (1959), Thomas twice came agonizingly close at the Open Championship, first losing a 36-hole play-off to Peter Thomson at Royal Lytham & St. Annes in 1958 (Thomson's fourth title), then closing beautifully with 69-69 at Muirfield in 1966, only to finish one back of a peaking Jack Nicklaus. He also tied for fifth at St. Andrews in 1957.

Afflicted with back and eye problems—could a golfer think of two less desirable maladies?—Thomas eased off of the competitive scene by the early 1970s, though he remained a presence as a golf course architect (partnering with Peter Alliss) for many years.

Intn'l Wins (14): 1955 Belgian Open; 1958 Dutch Open; 1959 French Open; 1963 PGA Match Play
Ryder Cup: 1959, 1963–67 (4)

George Thomas Jr. (USA)

Born: Philadelphia, Pennsylvania, 10/3/1873 **Died:** Beverly Hills, California, 2/23/1932

Among golf's great architects, there can be little doubt that when judging in a worldly context, the most accomplished individual, by a wide margin, was one George Clifford Thomas Jr. The first-born son of an affluent Philadelphia-area banking family, Thomas was a genuine military hero, serving as a pilot during World War I and surviving three major crashes. He was also one of the finest hybridizers of commercial roses in history (creating at least 40 new species), a highly successful dog trainer (his English Setter winning Best of Breed awards at the 1901 and '03 Westminster shows), and, after moving to California, an accomplished fisherman and yachtsman.

Thomas's greatest legacy, however, remains his all-too-brief practice of golf course design, a strictly recreational pursuit for which he never accepted compensation. Having come of golfing age in Philadelphia circles that included such gifted architects as A. W. Tillinghast, Hugh Wilson, and George Crump, Thomas's first major project was 1908's Whitemarsh Valley CC, built upon his family's Chestnut Hill estate. After moving to Beverly Hills in 1919, he aided in Herbert Fowler's 1921 redesign of the Los Angeles CC before embarking on a mid-1920s stretch that saw Thomas complete all 10 of his original West Coast designs, including his celebrated "triumvirate": the Bel-Air CC, a complete 1927 rebuild of the Los Angeles CC, and his unquestioned masterpiece, Riviera. Sadly, several comparable facilities either no longer exist or, in the cases of Ojai and La Cumbre, have been altered into oblivion. Thomas also authored *Golf Architecture in America* (Times-Mirror, 1927), a visually splendid volume that can arguably be called the finest book ever written on the subject.

An impressively philanthropic sort, the story—perhaps apocryphal—goes that when the city of Los Angeles ran out of funds during his 1923 expansion of its courses at Griffith Park, Thomas actually donated the money required to complete the project. He also provided an enormous boost to the career of William P. "Billy" Bell, his frequent construction foreman/collaborator who, following Thomas's 1932 death, would go on to build roughly 75 courses of his own.

Notable Courses: Bel-Air CC, California; Fox Hills CC (36), California (NLE); La Cumbre CC, California (BO); **Los Angeles CC, North Course, California;** Ojai Valley Inn & CC; **Riviera CC, California**

A. C. "Titanic" Thompson (USA)

Born: Rogers, Arkansas, 11/30/1892 **Died:** Euless, Texas, 5/19/1974

One of the few well-known golfers to run with the likes of Arnold Rothstein, Nick the Greek, and Al Capone, Alvin Clarence Thomas (aka "Titanic Thompson") was by trade a professional gambler, spending much of his life moving from place to place in search of the richest games and the biggest suckers. He was also, as it happened, a highly talented golfer and thus did a good deal of his fleecing on the fairways. He never competed in any "legitimate" settings and he certainly never won any tournaments that might appear in anyone's record books, yet stories of his golfing deeds abound.

Thompson, we are told, would make bets allowing his opponent to hit two or three balls all the way around, choosing his best each time. The match would remain close for a while, with Thompson possibly even trailing. But eventually the pigeon, getting a far greater physical workout than he was used to, would tire and it was all over. Or Thompson would lay a hose on a wet putting green before its cutting, creating an invisible trough, then bet some unsuspecting sort that he could hole three out of five from distance by simply putting it down the trough. He routinely won bets by playing left-handed, the catch being that he was a natural lefty who'd later mastered the game right-handed—but who knew?

His nickname came from a loser in a Missouri pool hall who suggested Titanic "because he's sinking everybody"—or was it simply due to his sky's-the-limit bets? A third version—that he'd earned the name by escaping the doomed ocean liner dressed as a woman—is colorful but way off base; he was in Missouri in the spring of 1912. One thing that is known is that Damon Runyon really did base Sky Masterson, the famous womanizing gambler in *Guys and Dolls,* on Thompson. It is also pretty clear that stories of his having Hogan-like ability on the links are somewhat exaggerated. What Thompson could do, likely as well as anyone in history, was accurately assess the odds so that his bets (golfing and otherwise) were generally won before the competition even started. Failing an accurate calculation, he simply cheated.

Once in Texas, Thompson spotted a man hopelessly trying to flip a playing card for distance. Recognizing a sure thing, he bet the floundering soul $50 that he couldn't flip the card over a nearby cigarette machine. The man accepted, rolled the card into a ball, and tossed it over the machine with room to spare. Thompson just shrugged and smiled. "You run into one of those guys every once in a while."

Carol Semple Thompson (USA)

The rare golfer whose game truly has improved with age, Pennsylvanian Carol Semple Thompson (b. Sewickley, 10/27/1948) is the all-time champion of Curtis Cup participation, playing in a remarkable 12 matches between 1974 and 2002 and amassing a record total of 18 victories, including the 2002 clincher at Pittsburgh's Fox Chapel GC. The low amateur in four U.S. Women's Opens, Thompson won the 1973 **U.S. Amateur** (one up over Anne Quast Sander at Montclair, New Jersey), then lost her title defense in the 1974 final to Cynthia Hill. Her summer wasn't a total loss, however, for after traveling across to Porthcawl, Thompson defeated Angela Bonallack in the **British Ladies** final to become only the ninth player to claim both national amateur titles. Also the winner of the 1976 and '87 **North & South Amateurs**, the 1986 **Trans-Mississippi**, and the USGA's contemporary **Mid-Amateur** title in 1990 and '97, Thompson further solidified her dominance by winning four consecutive **U.S. Senior Women's Amateurs** from 1999 through 2002.

Leonard Thompson (USA)

A fine basketball prospect who instead chose to play collegiate golf at Wake Forest, Laurinburg, North Carolina, product Leonard Thompson (b. 1/1/1947) went on to become a three-time winner on the PGA Tour, remaining an exempt player throughout most of the 1970s. Capable of shooting low numbers when things were going right, he fired a course-record 62 at Glen Abbey during the 1981 Canadian Open, several years after carding a 29 on Pinehurst No. 2's back nine in 1977. Perhaps most impressively, Thompson came back from five consecutive years outside the top 100 to win the 1989 **Buick Open** at age 42. He has also won thrice on the Champions Tour since becoming eligible in 1997.

Nicol Thompson (UK/Canada)

As the oldest of Canada's famous golfing brothers, Nicholas "Nicol" Thompson (1880–1954) was actually born in the tiny Scottish town of Ecclefechan before emigrating to Ontario with his family in 1882. A fine player at a young age, the stocky, powerful Thompson became professional at the Hamilton G&CC at age 17, a post he would retain for nearly half a century. Widely considered a great competitor, he claimed only a single national title (the 1922 **Canadian PGA**) but was also hailed as one of that nation's finest teachers and equipment manufacturers, his line of products including an inexpensive golf ball called the Shur-Putt.

Curiously, those outside of Canada likely remember Nicol as something of a footnoted partner in brother Stanley's famous architectural firm, but this characterization is not altogether fair. For while Stanley certainly earned his place among the great designers of the Golden Age, Nicol had earned his stripes with several solo projects of his own prior to coming aboard.

Stanley Thompson (Canada)

One of five brothers who would all achieve measures of fame as professional or top-flight amateur golfers, Stanley Thompson (1893–1953) was exposed to the design work of one great British architect, H. S. Colt, by caddying at the Toronto GC as a youth, then many more by visiting classic British courses during and immediately after his service in World War I. Turning to architecture full time once back in Canada, Thompson initially labored in relative anonymity before completing his landmark layout at Jasper National Park for the Canadian National Railway in

1926. Called by the occasionally effusive Dr. Alister MacKenzie "the best [course] I have ever seen," it was soon followed in 1929 by the Banff Springs GC, quite possibly the most spectacularly scenic course in the entire world. His reputation as a highly strategic designer with an exceptional eye for natural beauty thus firmly established, Thompson was off and running.

A large, flamboyant figure with twin loves of drinking and womanizing, Thompson's design method was once described by his former protégé Robert Trent Jones as "walk a property to get the feel of it, never taking a note, then sit back with a bottle of scotch and a good cigar and design the course." It was a method that served him well over the course of an estimated 145 projects, a disproportional percentage of which were situated in his home province of Ontario. Not strictly confined to Canada, Thompson did several designs in the northern United States as well as several hard-to-verify projects in Florida. Better documented, however, were visits he made to South America and Jamaica during the doldrums of the Depression, trips that resulted, among other projects, in Rio de Janeiro's spectacular Gavea G&CC, completed in 1932.

A man who built golf courses on the same grand scale upon which he lived life, Stanley Thompson was a mentor to future architects Trent Jones, Geoffrey Cornish, and Howard Watson, among others. Inducted posthumously into the Canadian Golf Hall of Fame, he died en route to Bogotá, Colombia, where he planned to undertake several new designs.

Notable Courses: Banff Springs Hotel GC, Alberta; Cape Breton Highlands GL, Nova Scotia; Capilano G&CC, British Columbia; Gavea G&CC, Brazil; Jasper Park Lodge GC, Alberta; Seigniory C, Quebec

Hector Thomson (UK)

A native of Scotland's well-known golfing town of Machrihanish, Hector Thomson (b. 1913) started young, winning the **British Boys** title in 1931, then **Irish Amateurs** in 1934 and '35, and the **Scottish Amateur** in 1935. His shining moment, however, would come in 1936 when he took on Australian Jim Ferrier in the final of the **British Amateur** at St. Andrews. Clinging to a 1-up lead at the last, and with Ferrier on the home green in birdie range, Thomson thrilled the obviously partisan crowd by stopping his approach a mere five inches from the hole, promptly being conceded the championship. Not surprisingly, Thomson (who was also a fine piano player) appeared in the 1936 and '38 Walker Cup matches, with his singles victory in the latter over Johnny Goodman playing a big part in Britain's first-ever cup victory.

Jimmy Thomson (UK/USA)

Strong, stocky Jimmy Thomson (b. 1908) gained great fame during the Golden Age as golf's longest hitter, routinely pounding it well over 300 yards, regularly driving par 4s, and reaching Oakmont's 595-yard 12th in two during the 1935 U.S. Open. A native of North Berwick, Scotland, Thomson emigrated to America with his family in 1921, then followed in the footsteps of his father, a pro who served at the CC of Virginia, Tennessee's Holston Hills, and Maryland's Burning Tree, among others.

An early bloomer, Thomson qualified to play in the 1925 U.S. Open at age 16, then the youngest player ever to do so. Later, he became highly popular on the PGA Tour, playing and traveling with many of the Golden Age's elite despite not truly counting among their numbers. He did, however, capture the 1934 **Centenary Open** in Melbourne, Australia, defeating a field that included the best local talent plus such imports as Sarazen, Diegel, Kirkwood, Shute, and Macdonald Smith. His finest win in America came at the 1938 **Los Angeles Open** when he beat Johnny Revolta by four at Griffith Park. In Major championship play, Thomson finished second at the 1935 U.S. Open, losing by two to local hero Sam Parks Jr. after bogeying the final four holes. He also lost the 1936 PGA Championship final at Pinehurst, by a 3 and 2 margin to Denny Shute.

A naturalized American, Thomson served in the U.S. Coast Guard—at no young age—during World War II.

Mabel Thomson (Canada)

Though universally acclaimed as Canada's first great female golfer, New Brunswick's Mabel Thomson (1874–1940) came along prior to the founding of today's Maritime Golf Association, making records of her early regional play sketchy at best. What is far better documented, however, is her national championship ledger, which began with a victory at the 1902 **Canadian Ladies** (later to be classified as the Closed title after the 1913 arrival of a true Open event), then took flight with four victories in succession from 1905 through 1908.

A pleasant and popular competitor who was equally talented on a tennis court, Thomson's greatest strength was her long game, particularly her driving, which relied upon a low, sweeping draw to achieve great distance. Of course, Thomson faced only limited competition during her peak years, and it was a lingering ankle injury—not the arrival of some great challenger—that ended her dominance. Yet her record of four consecutive titles would be exceeded only once prior to the Closed event's discontinuation in 1969 (by the great Marlene Streit's astounding seven straight wins from 1950 through 56), leaving

Thomson's place in Canadian golf history a widely honored one.

Peter Thomson (Australia)

Though the Triumvirate had each accomplished the feat decades earlier, Peter William Thomson, C.B.E. (b. 8/23/1929) will forever be recorded as the first modern player to win five **Open Championships**, a number that, when compared to the totals of such luminaries as Nicklaus (3), Ballesteros (3), Faldo (3), and even Thomson's great rival Bobby Locke (4) seems almost mystical. True, Thomson's dominance came largely in a period when the American's weren't traveling, effectively meaning that if he beat Locke, he was well on his way to victory. But such criticism, while perhaps partially valid, ignores the fundamental fact that American golf was hardly at *its* peak of greatness during the late 1950s; even if our stars had flocked to Britain en masse, who among this pre-Palmer/Nicklaus crowd are we so sure was Thomson's better?

A native of the Melbourne suburb of Brunswick, the young Thomson was a fine athlete who, growing up across the road from the Royal Park GC, eventually turned away from a career as an industrial chemist to head full time into golf. Though never an especially long hitter, he possessed a smoothly compact swing that was highly reliable, particularly fine iron skills, great senses of distance and improvisation, and, most important, an utterly unflappable nature.

So armed, Thomson claimed his first significant title at the 1948 **Victoria Amateur**, a noteworthy win largely because he beat no less than Doug Bachli 6 and 4 in the final. Turning professional a year later, he quickly established his credentials with a victory at the 1950 **New Zealand Open** (an event he would ultimately win nine times), then boosted them enormously with a four-shot victory over the nation's top player, Norman von Nida, at the 1951 **Australian Open**.

Thomson's first visit to the Open Championship saw him home sixth at Royal Portrush in 1951, setting the stage for a seven-year run in which he never finished worse than level second. In 1952 he was a single stroke behind Locke at Royal Lytham & St. Annes, then joined a group of four runners-up the next year when Hogan tamed Carnoustie in his lone Open visit. But with Hogan choosing not to defend, the floodgates opened in 1954 when Thomson beat Locke, Dai Rees, and Syd Scott by one at Royal Birkdale. The next year it was a two-shot triumph over Johnny Fallon at St. Andrews, followed, in 1956, by a three-shot victory at Hoylake over Belgium's Flory van Donck, making Thomson the first since Scotland's Bob Ferguson in the early 1880s to claim the Claret Jug three years in succession. The streak was stopped by Locke at St. Andrews

in 1957 with a record-tying 279 (Thomson finishing second) but Thomson came back to win again at Royal Lytham in 1958, this time by four in a 36-hole play-off with Dave Thomas of Wales. He then endured a stretch of six years which saw him between 5th and 24th, before rallying for his fifth title in 1965 at Royal Birkdale, beating a stronger field that included Nicklaus, Palmer and defending champion Tony Lema, among other Americans.

Thereafter, in 14 more attempts at equaling Vardon's sixth Open crown, Thomson's best result was level third in 1969, during Tony Jacklin's historic victory at Royal Lytham. It is well worth noting, however, that in 1957 Locke was very nearly disqualified when, an hour after the fact, it was realized that he had improperly replaced his marked ball at the 72nd green. Given that he'd needed only two putts from five feet to win, the R&A elected to ignore the infraction and uphold Locke's victory. Had they ruled otherwise, however, Thomson would not only have had his sixth Open title but also—had future events been uninfluenced by so bizarre a turnabout—an unprecedented five victories in succession, from 1954 through 1958.

Without question, Thomson's remarkable record at the Open has tended to overshadow the rest of his playing career, but nearly 80 wins internationally—including the Open titles of **Australia** (thrice), **Spain**, **Italy**, **Hong Kong** (thrice) and **Germany**—are nothing to scoff at. Further, Thomson didn't simply visit Britain for the Open but rather was a regular force on the British circuit, claiming four *News of the World* match plays between 1954 and 1967, a pair of **British Masters** in 1961 and '68, and multiple wins at several other prominent stops. Additional international prestige came from teaming with his friend Kel Nagle to win the **World Cup** in 1954 and '59, the latter on home soil at Royal Melbourne. Thomson was also instrumental in developing the Asian Tour during the 1960s, his support giving the circuit (particularly the Hong Kong and Indian Opens) greatly enhanced credibility. However, his dislike of American courses, the larger golf ball, and, it seems, most things Yankee led him only rarely to play in the States—though he did win the 1956 **Byron Nelson** (in a play-off with Cary Middlecoff and Gene Littler) and finished fourth in that year's U.S. Open at Oak Hill CC. Of course, this antipathy toward the American game didn't stop Thomson from coming over in his mid-50s to raid the Champions Tour, taking 11 titles in less than two seasons, including a stunning nine victories in 1985.

Thomson has never been your average single-minded golf pro, his interests running the gamut from music and literature to politics and the rehabilitation of drug addicts. He ran in the Victorian State elections of 1982 (narrowly losing) and was heavily involved with the administration of the Australian PGA for many years. He is also a writer of no mean talent, having covered the game in many forums while also authoring several volumes, including *This Wonderful World of Golf* (Pelham, 1969) and *Classic Golf*

Holes of Australia (Lothian, 1988), and contributing to the splendid *World Atlas of Golf* (Mitchell Beazley, 1976). Golf architecture also appears on his résumé, with the Capital GC, the National GC, and the new Moonah Links (home of the Australia Golf Union) representing his firm's most noted projects.

Beyond his many talents, Thomson has long been recognized as a focused, principled, and decidedly funny man. Indeed, when he arrived at Royal Lytham & St. Annes for round one of the 1958 Open Championship as a three-time winner, he was stopped by a security guard who didn't recognize him. Unsure if he was anything more than a spectator, the guard asked simply: "What are you?"

"Presbyterian," Thomson replied, and went on to win his fourth Open.

PGA Tour Wins (6): 1954, '55, '56, '58 & '65 British Open; 1956 Byron Nelson

Intn'l Wins (74): 1951, '67 & '72 Australian Open; 1959 Spanish Open; 1959 Italian Open; 1960, '65 & '67 Hong Kong Open; 1960 German Open; 1961 & '68 British Masters; 1954, '61, '66 & '67 PGA Match Play; 9 New Zealand Opens, 4 Indian Opens, 3 Victorian Opens, 3 Daks Tournaments & 3 Yorkshire Evening News

Champions Tour: 11 (1984–85)

1951-1971

	51	52	53	54	55	56	57	58	59	60	61
Masters	-	-	T38	T16	T18	-	5	T23	DQ	-	T19
US Open	-	-	T26	MC	-	T4	T22	-	-	-	MC
British	T6	2	T2	1	1	1	2	1	T23	T9	7
PGA	-	-	-	-	-	-	-	-	-	-	-

	62	63	64	65	66	67	68	69	70	71
Masters	-	-	-	-	-	-	-	MC	-	-
US Open	-	-	-	-	-	-	-	-	-	-
British	T6	5	T24	1	T8	T8	T24	T3	T9	T9
PGA	-	-	-	-	-	-	-	-	-	-

Jim Thorpe (USA)

Jim Thorpe (b. Roxboro, North Carolina, 2/1/1949) was the ninth of 12 children who grew up in a home directly adjacent to the Roxboro CC, where his father served as greenkeeper. Standing a powerful 6'0", Thorpe was a star fullback at Morgan State before concentrating on golf where he became, after Calvin Peete, the game's second black star. Tutored a bit by his older brother Chuck (himself briefly a PGA Tour player), big Jim won his playing privileges in 1976, failed badly, then made it for keeps in 1979. Several mediocre seasons followed but by 1983 he reached 46th on the money list, and in 1985 he rocketed up to fourth, claiming his first win by beating Jack Nicklaus in **Milwaukee**. Thorpe would later lose in sudden death to amateur Scott Verplank at the Western Open (though he took home the first-place purse) before closing the season with the first of back-to-back **Tucson Open** titles, an event then contested at match play.

An extremely strong man with a tight, muscular swing, Thorpe was a fine tee-to-green player who routinely performed well in the U.S. Open and other "ball-striking" tournaments, though he occasionally struggled a bit around the greens. An engaging and entertaining sort who

kept fit as he reached 50, Thorpe seemed the ideal candidate for Champions Tour success, and he has in fact won 11 titles and over $11 million since 1999.

A. W. Tillinghast (USA)

Born: North Philadelphia, Pennsylvania, 5/7/1874 **Died:** Toledo, Ohio, 5/19/1942

The only child of well-to-do parents in the Philadelphia suburb of Frankford, Albert Warren Tillinghast followed few of the educational and professional conventions incumbent to his economic class. Indeed, Tillinghast misspent his youth in all manner of social and antisocial ways, running with a street gang, dropping out of several schools, and skipping college altogether. Thankfully, prior to becoming a genuine menace to society, the young Tilly discovered the game of golf which, in effect, saved him.

Ultimately becoming a fine amateur player (he finished 25th in the 1910 U.S. Open and competed in numerous U.S. Amateurs), Tillinghast took advantage of his family affluence by visiting the British Isles in 1896 where, at St. Andrews, he became friendly with that most legendary of golfing icons, Old Tom Morris. Whether Old Tom, himself a most prolific architect, had an influence on Tilly's eventual design style is not known but the association helped to instill in the young American an abiding sense of the game's roots and traditions that would be everlasting.

Back in the United States, the then–34-year-old Tillinghast received his first design commission in Shawnee-on-Delaware, Pennsylvania, in 1909, where Mr. Charles Worthington, a family friend, had undertaken the construction of a riverfront resort. When this layout (which occupied the site of today's Shawnee Inn & Golf resort) proved successful, Tillinghast's attentions turned to architecture full time. By 1915 he was a national designer, completing projects as far afield as Florida, Texas, and California. By the early 1920s, with his duel 36-hole masterpieces at Baltusrol (a redesign) and Winged Foot up and going, he had, without question, "made it." Indeed, by the mid-1930s, Tilly had completed the design or reconstruction of 11 of today's top 100 American courses, making him, by his own supportable claim, "The Dean of American-Born Architects."

In addition to architecture, however, Tillinghast's other contributions to the game can stand toe-to-toe with anybody's. He was, for example, an excellent agronomist heavily involved with the founding of the USGA's Green Section. He was also, despite so poor an education, an engaging and prolific writer who served for several years as editor of the splendid magazine *Golf Illustrated*. As author of two golf-related works of fiction, *Cobble Valley Yarns* (Philadelphia Printing, 1915) and *The Mutt and Other Golf Yarns* (privately printed, 1925), he might best be described—charitably—as a poor man's P. G. Wodehouse. His countless magazine pieces on architecture, the game's history, and its prominent personalities became a veritable treasure trove when finally assembled, in three volumes, between 1995 and 2001.

Tillinghast was also a character of epic proportions, being driven to his New York City office from his New Jersey home in a chauffeured limousine, dressing in three-piece suits (even on site), and drinking with the best of them. Never one to produce detailed maps, he was the epitome of the in-the-field designer, generally traipsing through the outback, bottle in hand, directing his troops. His results were usually of a grand proportion, full-sized tests with deep, prominent bunkering and an uncommonly fine appearance, the famed "Tillinghast Polish."

As with many affluent Americans, the combination of the Depression and some ill-conceived investments brought Tilly to his economic knees in the early 1930s. Sipping from the WPA trough, he was able to complete one large-scale commission when he designed four new courses (and redesigned a fifth) at New York's Bethpage State Park, but eventually he would be reduced to touring the country on the PGA of America's tab, advising clubs on how many bunkers they might remove to ease mainte-

nance costs. Eventually settling in Los Angeles, Tilly shared a short-lived design partnership with Billy Bell before moving to his daughter's home in Ohio, where he died in 1942.

Notable Courses: **Baltimore CC, Maryland**; **Baltusrol GC (36), New Jersey**; **Bethpage State Park GC, Black Course, New York**; Brook Hollow CC, Texas; Fenway GC, New York; **Quaker Ridge GC, New York**; **Ridgewood CC, New Jersey**; San Francisco GC, California; Somerset Hills CC, New Jersey; **Winged Foot GC (36), New York**

Albert Tingey (UK)

Little-known Albert Tingey was the head professional at Fontainebleau (France) when World War I started, causing him to make a perilous escape to England that saw him arrive with little more than his life. Soon, however, he was teaming up with fellow pro Charles Mayo to push the idea of the "Niblick Brigade," suggesting that any bachelor professionals not already conscripted should enlist for service as a single unit. Ultimately some 26 pros did so, including Open champion-to-be George Duncan. The Triumvirate was, by a wide margin, too old for service but each did their part, Vardon working on a Totteridge farm, Braid in a munitions factory, and Taylor for the Red Cross. They also played countless exhibitions in aid of one wartime charity or another, an altogether more pleasant way to help the national effort.

Esteban Toledo (Mexico)

A former professional boxer who grew up impoverished in the border town of Mexicali, Esteban Toledo (b. 9/10/1962) is the first Mexican-born golfer to make a significant impact on the PGA Tour since Victor Regalado in the early 1970s. Though his only victory of note came abroad in the 2000 **Mexican Open**, Toledo has finished four times among the Tour's top 100 money winners and counts a tie for second at the 2002 Buick Open as his career-best finish.

Cyril Tolley (UK)

Incarcerated in a German POW camp during World War I, London-born Cyril James Hastings Tolley (1895–1982) emerged during the 1920s as a kingpin—along with Roger Wethered and Ernest Holderness—of British amateur golf. Among the three, it was the long-hitting Tolley who struck first, winning a spirited match against a comparable bomber, America's Robert Gardner, in the 1920 **British Amateur** final at Muirfield. Having squandered a 3-up lead with four to play, Tolley righted himself to win with a birdie at the 37th where, according to a story related by Longhurst, "having equipped himself with a five pound note for his caddie in the event of victory, he handed it over before he stepped up to the putt."

An Oxford man, Tolley cut quite the figure on the links, attired in plus-fours and, like his countryman Ted Ray, perennially smoking a pipe. Though not so much a factor in the Amateur for most of the 1920s, Tolley remained a force elsewhere, claiming both the 1924 and '28 **French Opens** against largely professional fields. By 1929, however, he was again in top form at home, beating J.N. Smith 4 and 3 at Royal St. George's for his second **Amateur** crown. In many quarters, however, Tolley is even better remembered for a match he lost in the 1930 Amateur at St. Andrews, a windswept fourth-round contest against Bobby Jones who was then pursuing leg one of his Grand Slam. An exceedingly close affair in which the lead changed hands not less than six times, Jones would ultimately win at the 19th when Tolley fell victim to a stymie, settling a contest still considered among the best ever played.

Tolley's swing, which Longhurst described as "full, smooth, supple, unhesitating and in every sense 'classical'," allowed him to compete far longer than most, and he actually returned to the Amateur semifinals at age 55, losing to eventual champion Frank Stranahan. A participant in six of the first eight Walker Cup matches (missing 1928 and '32), Tolley remains today one of British golf's great amateur legends.

David Toms (USA)

A former **Junior World** and **PGA Junior** champion and an All-American at LSU, David Wayne Toms (b. Monroe, Louisiana, 1/4/1967) failed to crack the top 100 during his first four seasons on the PGA Tour before hitting his stride in the latter half of the 1990s. A win at **Quad Cities** jumped him up to 49th in 1997 but it was in 1999, when he won at the **International** and the **Buick Challenge** and finished 10th on the money list, that Toms truly arrived.

A fine iron player who wins more by a succession of good shots than a sudden flash of great ones, Toms proceeded to join the ranks of the elite in 2001 by finishing third on the money list, winning at **New Orleans**, defending a 2000 title at the **Anheuser-Busch**, and, in between, claiming his first Major championship, the **PGA** at the Atlanta Athletic Club. There he shot 66-65-65 to hold the 54-hole lead, then came to the 72nd only one ahead of playing partner Phil Mickelson. With a poor lie and water fronting the long par-4 green, Toms coolly elected to lay up, wedged his third to 12 feet and calmly sunk the putt for the victory. Though winless in 2002, Toms still played well enough to finish fourth in money, then came back in 2003 with an eighth-place campaign, which included victories at **Memphis** and the inaugural **Wachovia Classic**, the latter despite making an eight on the 72nd hole!

A Ryder Cup selection in 2002 and '04 (when he successfully defended his **Memphis** title after recovering from wrist surgery), Toms has thus far enjoyed solid Major championship results, tying for fourth at the 2000 Open Championship, fifth at the 2003 U.S. Open, and twice cracking the top 10 at the Masters, in addition to his PGA title.

PGA Tour Wins (10): 2001 PGA Championship
Ryder Cup: 2002 & '04 (2) **Presidents Cup:** 2003

Sam Torrance (UK)

Few contemporary golfers have been better groomed for the life of a touring pro than Scotland's Samuel Robert Torrance, M.B.E. (b. Largs, 8/24/1953), who was coached by his father from a young age, quit school at 13 to pursue the game full time, and turned professional at 16. By 17 he was competing internationally, though he would not win an official European Tour event until age 23.

All told, the long-hitting Torrance would claim 21 European victories, five **Scottish Professional** titles, the odd win in South America and Africa, and the 1980 **Australian PGA**. His biggest win at home was perhaps the 1995 **British Masters**, though a 1984 **Benson & Hedges International** title wasn't far behind. He was also the champion of five different European nations over the years, including a **French Open** title (over Bernhard Langer) in 1998 at age 44. What holds Torrance back a bit in comparison with his British contemporaries was an uneven record in the Open Championship, where he never stood a real chance to win and only once finished in the top five, a fifth in 1981 at Royal St. George's.

Torrance represented Scotland in 11 World Cups and, more impressive, played in eight Ryder Cups, also captaining the European team's fine 2002 victory at The Belfry.

Intn'l Wins (22): 1980 Australian PGA; 1981 & '95 Irish Open; 1982 Spanish Open; 1982 & '83 Portuguese Open; 1984 Benson & Hedges; 1987 & '95 Italian Open; 1995 British Masters; 1998 French Open
Ryder Cup: 1981–95 (8); 2002 Capt

Tony Torrance (UK)

Edinburgh native Thomas A. "Tony" Torrance (b. 1891) was a mainstay of British Walker Cup sides in the late 1920s and early '30s. A winner of the **Irish** (1925) and **German** (1929) **Amateur** titles, Torrance competed against America five times between 1924 and 1934, including a playing captaincy in 1932. As Britain went 0-5 during these years, Torrance's 3-4-1 personal record stands up nicely—particularly since his three victories were singles contests against Chick Evans, Francis Ouimet, and Max Marston. Ouimet in particular must have been impressed, for Torrance hammered him 7 and 6 in 1930, then halved the great American in a 1932 rematch played on Ouimet's home turf, The Country Club of Brookline.

Bob Toski (USA)

Haydenville, Massachusetts, native Bob Toski (b. 9/18/1927), all 5′7″ and 125 pounds of him, was a long-hitting force on the mid-1950s PGA Tour, winning a total of seven official events between 1953 and 1958. His best year by far was 1954 when he took four titles including George S. May's lucrative **World Championship of Golf**, whose $50,000 prize guaranteed Toski first place on the season's money list. Retiring from the Tour in the early 1960s, Toski went on to become one of modern golf's first highly publicized teachers, producing several books and videos and reportedly giving more than 100,000 lessons.

Peter Townsend (UK)

England's Peter Townsend (b. Cambridge, 9/16/1946) was considered one of Britain's top postwar prospects during the mid-1960s when he won major junior and amateur events and performed admirably in a 1965 Walker Cup tie. A focused, aggressive player, Townsend turned pro soon thereafter and was off to South Africa where, during his first winter, his game fell apart in a manner unexpected in one so young. But where others have packed it in Townsend persevered, regaining form enough to win the 1967 **Dutch Open** and the 1968 **Volvo PGA** and to make Ryder appearances in 1969 and '71. A willing traveler, Townsend tried the PGA Tour briefly in the late 1960s (finishing 42nd at the 1969 Masters) before enjoying his best European seasons in the early 1970s, finishing three times in the Order of Merit top 10 between 1971 and 1974. He also won events in Australia, South America, and Africa, though at the end of the day Townsend's professional career cannot be said to have lived up to the lofty heights initially predicted for it.

William Townsend (USA/Mexico)

An American businessman from Louisville, Kentucky, William Townsend headed a small group of foreigners responsible for debuting the game of golf in Mexico. This they did in 1897, with a rudimentary nine holes laid out over barren, sandy terrain in a place called Puehla, a small suburb situated some 45 minutes (by donkey cart!) southwest of Mexico City. Several years later, as the game grew in popularity, a more modern layout and clubhouse were needed, leading to the construction of today's Mexico City CC.

Jerome Travers (USA)

Born: New York, New York, 5/19/1887 **Died:** East Hartford, Connecticut, 3/30/1951

Having opened his *Travers' Golf Book* (Macmillan, 1913) with the words "I started playing golf on my father's country estate...," it goes without saying that Jerome Dunstan Travers was a member of New York's privileged upper class. He was also, by any definition, a superbly talented amateur whose only real failing was a lack of commitment to the game. Despite an often blasé approach, he was something of a child prodigy, getting instruction from eventual two-time U.S. Open champion Alex Smith at the Nassau CC and winning that club's prestigious invitational event—over Walter Travis—at age 17.

In an era when length was not as important as all-around skill, Travers was considered an inconsistent driver of the ball, but he was a world-class recovery artist, an excellent putter, and the owner of a splendid, even-tempered disposition. Thus ideally suited for match play, Travers was a terror in the two events he most frequently entered, winning four **U.S.** and five **Metropolitan Amateurs**, all between 1906 and 1914.

His first two national titles came back-to-back in 1907 and '08, the latter taken at Garden City GC where he again beat a homestanding Travis in a close semifinal, then blew away Max Behr in the final 8 and 7. For the next three seasons, Travers' commitment to his social life exceeded his interest in golf and he was seldom a factor in the latter rounds of most events. By 1912, however, he was rededicated and at his career peak, winning his third **Amateur** title at the Chicago GC by battering hometown favorite Chick Evans into submission 7 and 6. In 1913 he again defended successfully, returning to Garden City to beat John Anderson in the final, 5 and 4. Interestingly, in three of the four years in which Travers won the U.S. Amateur, he also claimed the Metropolitan title, proving that when his heart was in it, Jerome Travers was one very tough opponent.

Much like the great English champion John Ball, Travers' sparkling amateur ledger was enhanced tenfold by the addition of a single Major victory against the pros, in this case the 1915 **U.S. Open** at Baltusrol. Contested over the club's long-deceased pre-Tillinghast 18, this event went right down to the wire when Boston-based professional Tom McNamara posted a score of 298, requiring of Travers a sub-par final nine for victory. Though he drove out-of-bounds at the 10th, he managed still to steal a four, played the remaining eight holes in the requisite one-under figures and took the Open by a single shot. Likely worn down from the competitive grind—or perhaps simply losing interest—Travers did not even return in 1916 to defend his title, effectively marking his retirement from competitive golf.

So many years later, it is sometimes difficult to appreciate just how important a player Jerry Travers was in the history of American golf. Doing frequent battle with archrival Walter Travis, the nation's first domestic superstar, Travers was widely viewed as being nearly invincible during his peak years, possessing, in the words of H. B. Martin, "indomitable courage, [an] ability to outgame his opponent in match play, and a nerve that had never been known to fail in a crisis." When fully engaged, he was a competitor of the highest order, for according to Herbert Warren Wind, "Like most rich men's sons who have played a sport well, Travers could afford to play the game as if his next meal depended on winning." And by the Depression it would, for Travers ultimately died a pauper.

Major Amateur Wins (10): 1906, '07, '11, '12 & '13 Metropolitan; 1907, '08, '12 & '13 U.S. Amateurs; 1915 U.S. Open

Jerome Travers

1903-1916

	03	04	05	06	07	08	09	10	11	12	13	14	15	16
US Open	-	-	-	-	T25	-	-	-	-	-	T27	-	1	-
US Am	T17	T17	T17	T5	1	1	-	-	T5	1	1	2	T9	-
Brit Am	-	-	-	-	-	-	T125	-	-	-	-	T125		
British	-	-	-	-	-	-	WD	-	-	-	-			

Walter Travis
(Australia/USA)

Born: Maldon, Australia, 1/12/1862 **Died:** Denver, Colorado, 7/31/1927

Though truly a seminal factor in the development of American golf, Walter John Travis was actually born in the Victorian mining town of Maldon, Australia. Emigrating to New York in 1886, he didn't even take up golf until age 35, surely the latest start of a championship career in the game's history. Playing his first tentative rounds at Queens' old Oakland GC in 1897, Travis improved quickly and, certainly benefiting from the smaller fields of the day, found himself nationally competitive within a year.

A decidedly short hitter, Travis built his game around two fundamental strengths: He was both laser-straight and, without much question, the finest putter of his day. Consequently, he was a semifinalist at the U.S. Amateur in 1898 and '99, on both occasions being eliminated by Findlay Douglas. By 1900, however, buoyed by greater competitive maturity and the added bonus of playing over his home course at Garden City, Travis first took medalist honors before routing A. G. Lockwood 11 and 10 in the semis, then defeating Douglas 2 up in the final to claim his first **Amateur** title. He then defended his crown in 1901 in Atlantic City, again leading the qualifiers and this time vanquishing Douglas in the semifinals (at the 38th hole) before beating Walter Egan 5 and 4 in the final. As an important footnote, Travis won this title using the new rubber or "Haskell" ball that would, in a very short time, change the game forever.

By 1902 Travis was 40 years old—nearly twice the age of some of his amateur competitors—and a third-round upset victim to eventual runner-up Eben Byers at Chicago's Glen View Club. But the next year "The Old Man" (as the press had taken to calling him) had his revenge by beating Byers 5 and 4 in the final, to regain his crown at Long Island's Nassau CC. Though not foreseeable at the time, this would be Travis's last victory in the Amateur, but by no means his last important title. Many consider his most significant win to have taken place in 1904 when he defeated long-hitting Ted Blackwell at Royal St. George's, becoming the first foreigner ever to capture the **British Amateur**. En route, Travis disposed of future champion James Robb as well as established legends Harold Hilton and Horace Hutchinson, though his triumph would perhaps best be remembered for the center-shafted putter he utilized—the Schenectady—which was subsequently banned by the R&A. Was this move merely sour grapes, as some have suggested? Suffice to say that the occasionally surly Travis was no more enamored with the British golf establishment than it was with him. Anything beyond that is purely speculation.

Not generally inclined toward playing with the professionals, Travis entered the first of his six U.S. Opens in 1902, and then only because it was being played at Garden City. Surprising many, he came back from a pair of opening 82s with 75-74 to tie for second, six back of Laurie Auchterlonie. His best subsequent finish, however, was a tie for seventh in 1909.

Back amongst the amateurs, there were multiple triumphs in two of the era's most prominent events, the old **North & South** (which Travis won in 1904, '10, and '12) and the **Metropolitan**, where he first broke through in 1900 and '02, then later added middle-age victories in 1909 and '15. This last occasion saw a 53-year-old Travis beat four-time U.S. Amateur champ Jerome Travers en route to the final, then vanquish John G. Anderson by holing a dramatic 40-foot putt at the last green. Immediately afterward, he announced his retirement from competitive golf, ending one of the most remarkable careers the game has ever witnessed.

An intelligent and well-rounded man, Travis's immense contributions to golf's growth hardly ended with winning championships. In 1905 he founded *The American Golfer*, an influential publication that he presided over for a number of years. He also authored the famous instructional volume *Practical Golf* (Harper's, 1901) and coauthored (with 1904 Open Championship winner Jack White) a rare booklet, *The Art of Putting* (Macmillan, 1904). Travis also was one of America's first big-name golf course architects, injecting a trend-setting dose of strategic elements into projects that included the Westchester CC, Vermont's Equinox GL, and the original nine at Sea Island, Georgia. Long affected by a declining bronchial condition, Travis passed away in Denver—where his doctors had sent him to live out his days—at age 65.

Major Amateur Wins (11): 1900, '02, '09 & '15 Metropolitan; 1900, '01 & '03 U.S. Amateur; 1904, '10 & '12 North & South; 1904 British Amateur

1898-1915

	98	99	00	01	02	03	04	05	06	07	08	09	10	11	12	13	14	15
US Open	-	-	-	-	T2	T15	-	T11	-	-	T22	T7	-	-	T10	-	-	-
US Am	T3	T3	1	1	T9	1	T9	T5	T3	T5	T3	T5	T9	T17	T9	T5	T3	-
Brit Am	-	-	-	-	-	-	1	-	-	-	-	-	-	-	-	-	-	-
British	-	-	-	-	-	-	MC	-	-	-	-	-	-	-	-	-	-	-

Lee Trevino
(USA)

If professional golf is, as many have claimed, a dull game populated by a race of flat, clone-like individuals, then for nearly 40 years the antidote to its sameness has been Dallas product Lee Buck Trevino (b. 12/1/1939). A Mexican-American who grew up decidedly poor, Trevino left school early and spent four years in the U.S. Marine Corps before turning to golf full time, eventually becoming an assistant professional in El Paso.

Having developed his game in all manner of high-stakes matches but seldom in real, organized competition,

Trevino genuinely had little idea how good he was prior to winning $600 with a tie for 54th at the 1966 U.S. Open. Entering again in 1967, he found far greater success at Baltusrol, his rounds of 72-70-71-70 claiming fifth place, behind men named Nicklaus, Palmer, January, and Casper. Emboldened, Trevino stayed on Tour the rest of the season and finished 45th on the money list, then became a household name the following summer when he took his **U.S. Open** ascendancy that final big step, claiming the title at Rochester's Oak Hill CC. Becoming the first man ever to break 70 in all four rounds, Trevino's 275 total equaled Nicklaus' record of a year earlier while comfortably beating Jack by four.

Lee Trevino

Now Trevino was in the big time, a darling of both the media and galleries with his constant line of banter, pleasant demeanor, and a game that, though hardly an aesthetic pleasure, was deadly efficient. Famous as a low fader of the ball, Trevino was a first-rate iron player and as good an all-around shotmaker as has appeared in the modern era. His unorthodox motion actually bore several similarities to Hogan's vaunted swing, maintaining a low arc angle through the impact area and, by hitting against his left arm, keeping the clubhead on-line far longer than the norm. It was a game which might not have looked the part but was, in fact, ideal for Major championship golf—except, perhaps, at Augusta, where the perceived need for a high, right-to-left flight pattern caused Trevino to not even enter the Masters on more than one occasion.

A frequent winner who finished among the Tour's top 10 money earners from 1968 to 1975 and 1978 to 1980, Trevino left an everlasting mark during the summer of 1971 when, over 23 days, he won the national Opens of **America**, **Canada**, and **Great Britain**. In the United States, his 69-69 close at Merion forced a tie with Nicklaus, at whom he playfully tossed a rubber snake on the first tee of their Monday play-off before shooting 68 to win by three. Then it was on to Canada where sudden death was required to

dispatch Art Wall, and finally to Britain where a 278 total at Royal Birkdale was enough to hold off Taiwan's tenacious Lu Liang Huan by one. Combining this success with three additional PGA Tour wins, Trevino was an easy choice for PGA Player of the Year, while also taking his second of five Vardon Trophies.

The following season, 1972, saw Nicklaus, with Masters and U.S. Open victories already in his pocket, arrive at Muirfield in pursuit of the Grand Slam. But in the end the **Open Championship** came down to Trevino and Tony Jacklin, a victory Trevino seemingly snatched from the jaws of defeat by chipping in for birdie at the 71st, having already holed out twice from off the green late in the third round. A one-shot victory over Nicklaus at the 1974 **PGA Championship** represented Trevino's fifth Major title, though his performance would slip somewhat over the following three seasons after being struck by lightning at the 1975 Western Open in Chicago. Remarkably, he still managed to record at least one victory during every year of the 1970s, then returned to the second spot on the money list with a three-win 1980. A grand exclamation point was added when Trevino rode a hot putter to an unexpected four stroke triumph at the 1984 **PGA Championship**, defeating Gary Player and Lanny Wadkins at 44.

A six-time competitor in Ryder Cup play, Trevino amassed a 17-7-6 overall record, including a 6-2-2 record at singles. He also twice finished runner-up at the World Match Play in England, while adding such significant overseas titles as the **Benson & Hedges International** (1978), the **Trophée Lancôme** (1978 and '80), and the prestigious **British Masters** (1985). By his late 40s, Trevino dabbled in what seemed an obvious career course—television—before rolling onto the Champions Tour in 1990 where, in nine seasons, he proceeded to match his PGA Tour total of 29 victories, including the 1990 **U.S. Senior Open**. A Hall of Famer since 1981, Trevino is no longer a full time competitor, yet remains one of golf's most fascinating and engaging personalities.

PGA Tour Wins (29): 1968 & '71 U.S. Open; 1971, '77 & '79 Canadian Open; **1971 & '72 British Open**; 1973 Doral; **1974 & '84 PGA Championship**; 1976 & '78 Colonial; 1980 Players Championship

Intn'l Wins (10): 1975 Mexican Open; 1978 Benson & Hedges; 1978 & '80 Trophée Lancôme; 1985 British Masters

Champions Tour Wins: 29 (1990–98)

Ryder Cup: 1969–75, '79 & '81 (6); 1985 Capt

1966-1991

	66	67	68	69	70	71	72	73	74	75	76	77	78
Masters	-	-	T40	T19	-	-	T33	T43	-	T10	T28	-	T14
US Open	T54	5	1	MC	T8	1	T4	T4	MC	T29	-	T27	T12
British	-	-	-	T34	T3	1	1	T10	T31	T40	-	4	T29
PGA	-	-	T23	T48	T26	T13	T11	T18	1	T69	MC	T13	T7

	79	80	81	82	83	84	85	86	87	88	89	80	91
Masters	T12	T26	MC	T38	T20	43	T10	47	MC	MC	T18	T24	T49
US Open	T19	T12	MC	MC	-	T9	MC	T4	MC	T40	MC	-	MC
British	T17	2	T11	T27	5	T14	T20	T59	T17	MC	T42	T25	T17
PGA	T35	7	DQ	-	T14	1	2	T11	-	MC	MC	MC	MC

Kirk Triplett (USA)

One of the PGA Tour's more reliable players, Kirk Triplett (b. Moses Lake, Washington, 3/29/1962) has been a fixture among the top 100 money winners since 1992, with a peak performance of 11th in 2000. That was the year he captured his first career win at the **Los Angeles Open**, holding off a charging Jesper Parnevik to finally claim victory in his 266th career start. A second title would come at the 2003 **Reno-Tahoe Open**, but Triplett is far better known for his great money-winning consistency, with well over $11 million banked at the time of this writing. A former University of Nevada star and veteran of the Australian, Asian, and Canadian tours, Triplett is not a long hitter despite standing 6'3" but keeps the ball very much in play and hits a large number of greens. He is also noted for his 1960s-style bucket cap, a relative rarity on Tour today.

Ty Tryon (USA)

After making the cut at the PGA Tour's Honda Classic at age 16, Orlando's Ty Tryon (b. 6/2/1984) turned pro at 17 and proceeded to surprise the golfing world by successfully playing his way through 2001 Qualifying School, enabling him to join the PGA Tour full time in 2002—or so he thought, until the Tour retroactively established a minimum playing age of 18. Becoming an official Tour member following his June birthday, Tryon was already sidelined by mononucleosis and missed much of the season, allowing him to compete in 2003 on a medical exemption. So armed, he proceeded to make four cuts in 21 starts and lose his status, relegating him to the 2004 Nationwide Tour where he is currently attempting to restart his teetering career.

Vincent Tshabalala (South Africa)

A black South African from Johannesburg, auto mechanic Vincent Tshabalala (b. 3/16/1942) was, like all others of color, essentially denied the opportunity to compete in his homeland. With financial help from Gary Player and others, Tshabalala made occasional trips abroad, including two mid-1970s excursions onto the European Tour, the first (1976) resulting in a shocking victory in only his second event, the **French Open**. Playing over venerable Le Touquet, Tshabalala shot 69-70-66-67 to beat a strong field that saw Ballesteros, Hobday, Coles and Torrance all among its top 10 finishers. Denied subsequent entry into the South African Open, however, Tshabalala turned down an invitation to represent that country in the World Cup and soon had his playing career curtailed by a back injury. He returned to Europe during the 1990s where he enjoyed solid earnings on the Senior Tour.

William Tucker (UK/USA)

An experienced professional and greenkeeper, Redhill, England's William Tucker (1871–1954) emigrated to America in 1895 to take up employment at New York's St. Andrew's GC. Together with his brother Samuel, he would manufacture fine handmade clubs for many years while, in the meantime, also designing a "new" course (later to be modified by James Braid, in absentia) when St. Andrews moved to its present site in 1897. After several further pro-greenkeeper stops, William eventually formed a design business with his son William Jr. during the early 1920s, maintaining offices in New York, Los Angeles and Portland, Oregon. Though lacking in marquee Golden Age projects, Tucker was responsible for the first nine holes built at Southampton's exclusive Maidstone Club in 1896, as well as for a unique agronomical project of the period: putting down the first turf at New York's legendary Yankee Stadium in 1923.

James Walker Tufts (USA)

Charlestown, Massachusetts, native James Walker Tufts (1835–1902) made a late nineteenth-century fortune in the manufacture of soda fountains, eventually taking his money and his ill health and developing a planned convalescent resort in the North Carolina sandhills town of Pinehurst. That Tuft's facility soon morphed from a non-profit health farm to a leading American golf center owes to several factors, though the initial playing of the game was done independently by guests, with little assist from management. No golfer himself, Tufts could certainly see the possibilities and soon built a rudimentary nine (1898), which was expanded to 18 by 1900. He then brought Donald Ross aboard as his golf professional in 1901 and the resort's development began in earnest, with the establishment of drawing-card tournaments (the famed North & South events) preceding an ultimate expansion to 90 holes, and beyond.

Richard Tufts (USA)

Though born into a family of obvious privilege, James Walker's grandson Richard S. Tufts (1889–1980) took the ball and ran with it, becoming an important presence in the world of postwar America golf. Harvard educated, Tufts was a fine player but concentrated far more on the game's administrative side, serving in virtually every important position that the Carolinas Golf Association and the USGA had to offer, including the latter's presidency in 1956–57. He was also a close friend of Donald Ross, and took over as Pinehurst's in-house architect after Ross's death, rebuilding a war-abandoned No. 4 course and providing Ellis Maples with input on No. 5. A great supporter of amateur golf, Tufts captained the victorious 1963 Walker Cup team, and he also authored two small but significant volumes, *The Principles Behind the Rules of Golf* (privately published, 1960) and *The Scottish Invasion* (Pinehurst, 1962).

Alfred H. Tull (UK/USA)

A native Englishman raised both in Canada and the United States, A. H. Tull (1897–1982) initially joined his brother William in a golf construction business, which operated primarily in the Northeast, building courses designed by such luminaries as A. W. Tillinghast, Walter Travis, and Devereux Emmet. Emmet, in particular, took a liking to Tull and hired him in 1924, making him a full partner five years later. Following his mentor's 1934 passing, Tull went into solo practice, working primarily in his familiar Northeast but also venturing occasionally down the Eastern seaboard and into the Caribbean. He would also perform alterations (not necessarily substantial) to a large complement of New York–area Golden Age courses, including Canoe Brook (North), White Beeches, Pelham, Apawamis, and Maidstone, among many others.

Notable Courses: Bethpage State Park, Yellow Course, New York; Concord Hotel GC, International Course, New York

Peter Tupling (UK)

Though an **English Boys** champion and 1969 Walker Cup player, Sheffield's Peter Tupling (b. 1950) never made much of a splash on the European Tour, his best Order of Merit finish being 17th in 1974. But until 2003 Tupling held a unique position in the game's record book, for in the 1981 **Nigerian Open** he posted a 72-hole score of 255, golf's all-time competitive record. In point of fact, Tupling did so on a 6,000-yard course with flat, oiled sand greens, and he needed to birdie four of the last five holes just to win the tournament! Thus while his record was really sort of an apples-and-oranges proposition in comparison to those posted on the world's more established tours, the question of its legitimacy was ultimately rendered moot by Tommy Armour III's 254 at the PGA Tour's 2003 Texas Open.

Sherri Turner (USA)

A 1979 All-American at Furman University, Sherri Turner (b. Greenville, South Carolina, 10/4/1956) enjoyed seven strong years on the LPGA Tour between 1984 and 1990, finishing no worse than 41st on the money list and winning thrice. Her career year came in 1988 when she won for the first time at the **LPGA Championship** (edging Amy Alcott by one at Kings Island, Ohio) then added a second victory the following week at the **Corning Classic** en route to 17 top-10 finishes and first place on the money list. The following year she would take the **Hawaiian Open** and place 10th in money, hardly bad but the first step in a slide that would see her fall to 115th by 1991. Though twice back inside the top 50 near the millennium, Turner failed to claim another victory after 1989 and fell, perhaps permanently, from the top 100 once again in 2003.

Jim Turnesa (USA)

Several are the families that have seen multiple children achieve international fame in the game of golf, but not even California's fabled Espinosas can match the exploits of the seven Turnesa brothers of Elmsford, New York. Jim (1909–1971) was the fourth oldest of the bunch, all sons of a poor Italian immigrant who had walked the 26 miles from Manhattan to Elmsford before finding work constructing, then later maintaining, the old Fairview CC.

One of many Golden Age stars to emerge from Fairview's caddie yard (a list which also included Johnny Farrell, Tom Creavy, and Tony Manero), Jim won only two official PGA Tour events but they were both significant: the 1952 **PGA Championship** and the 1959 **Metropolitan Open**. At the PGA in Louisville, Kentucky, he came from 3 down at lunch to defeat Chick Harbert with a tie-breaking par at the 36th, the victory perhaps making up for past PGA final-round losses of brothers Joe (1927) and Mike (1948), plus his own to Sam Snead at Seaview in 1942. Often cited as the family's best ball-striker, Jim also made a single Ryder Cup appearance in 1953, winning his singles match as the beneficiary of a famous missed putt by Peter Alliss.

Joe Turnesa (USA)

The tallest Turnesa brother and the first to achieve national fame, Joe (1901–1991) captured the first of his 14 PGA Tour victories in 1924 at the **Augusta Open**. He would later win the inaugural **Metropolitan PGA** title in 1926, recapturing that event twice more in 1930 and '32. Widely viewed as the most accomplished of the brothers, he is nonetheless recalled more for several famous second-place finishes, the first being a one-stroke loss to

Gene Sarazen at the old Grassy Sprain CC in the 1925 Metropolitan Open. The following year disappointment came on a larger stage when Joe led Bobby Jones by as many as four during the final round of the U.S. Open at Ohio's Scioto CC, only to slip to a 77 and another one-stroke loss. Then in 1927 he reached the final of the PGA Championship at Cedar Crest CC in Dallas and led Walter Hagen through 31 holes before the Haig pulled one of his patented comebacks to win the match (and his record-setting fourth consecutive title) 2 and 1.

With seven PGA Tour wins between 1925 and 1927, Joe was a logical choice for the first two Ryder Cup teams, and he is also recalled for occasionally putting one-handed. He eventually settled at Long Island's Rockville Links Club where he served as pro for two decades.

PGA Tour Wins (14): 1925 Texas; 3 Metropolitan PGAs
Ryder Cup: 1927 & '29 (2)

Mike Turnesa (USA)

Though seldom remembered as quickly as brothers Joe (older) and Jim (younger), Mike Turnesa (1907–2000) was himself a six-time PGA Tour winner over 18 competitive seasons, his victories including the 1933 and '41 **Westchester Opens** and the 1949 **Metropolitan PGA**. Like Joe, however, Mike is sooner recalled for his near misses, several accumulated against two of golf's greatest-ever players. In the 1942 Hale America Open (a USGA-sponsored U.S. Open replacement event), he finished second to Ben Hogan at Chicago's Ridgemoor CC and was later routed by Hogan 7 and 6 in the final of the 1948 PGA in St. Louis. He also lost a tremendous second-round match to eventual champion Byron Nelson at the 1945 PGA, standing two up through 32 holes before Nelson finished with two birdies and an eagle to advance in what would ultimately be the ninth of his record 11 straight victories.

Also a veteran of the inaugural Masters tournament (along with brother Joe) in 1934, Mike later served for more than 40 years as professional at Elmsford's prestigious Knollwood CC.

William Turnesa (USA)

The youngest member of the Turnesa clan, "Willie the Wedge" (1914–2000) took a decidedly different golfing path, first attending Holy Cross College at the urgings of his brothers (who paid his tuition) and then remaining a career amateur. This scarcely stopped him from achieving great fame, however, beginning with **Westchester Amateur** titles in 1933, '36 and '37 and a **Metropolitan Amateur** in 1937. In 1938 he went national, capturing his first **U.S. Amateur** at Oakmont when he routed B. Patrick Abbott 8 and 7 in a match that reportedly saw him get up-and-down all 13 times he was bunkered!

World War II ate into several of Willie's prime competitive years but he returned in 1947 to capture a long-remembered **British Amateur** at Carnoustie, his 3 and 2 victory over countryman Dick Chapman being called by Leonard Crawley "one of the greatest finals in the history of British Golf." Willie then capped his national career by beating fellow New Yorker Ray Billows 2 and 1 to win the 1948 **U.S. Amateur** in Memphis. He also appeared on Walker Cup teams in 1947, '49, and '51 (serving as playing captain on the latter) and is widely considered to have had among the greatest short games of all time.

It is perhaps worth noting the career paths of the other three Turnesa brothers. Phil, the oldest, remained close to the nest, spending many years teaching at the Elmwood CC. Frank, the next in line, worked at White Plains' Metropolis CC and was considered the family's best teacher. Doug, the youngest of the professionals, taught for many years at the old Briar Hall CC in Briarcliff Manor.

Ed Tutwiler (USA)

Edgar M. Tutwiler Jr. (1920–1988) reached a late competitive peak as an amateur, playing on the 1965 and '67 Walker Cup squads in his middle 40s, as well as captaining the 1975 team. A successful automobile dealer, Tutwiler had earlier won his native **West Virginia Amateur** 12 times between 1939 and 1963, generally doing pitched battle with the state's other great amateur, Bill Campbell, throughout. Campbell, however, got the last laugh on the national stage, edging Tutwiler one up for the 1964 U.S. Amateur title at Cleveland's Canterbury GC in the only appearance of either man in the national final.

Bob Tway (USA)

A three-time All-American and the 1981 **NCAA** Player of the Year at Oklahoma State, Robert Raymond Tway (b. Oklahoma City, 5/4/1959) was an amateur with glowing credentials who took four years to earn full time playing privileges on the PGA Tour. Thus a 45th-place money ranking during his 1985 debut was impressive, yet it offered little hint of the breakout year that was to follow in 1986. After his first career victory in a rain-shortened **San Diego Open** (via sudden death over Bernhard Langer), Tway then added hard-fought victories at the **Westchester** and **Atlanta Classics**, setting the stage for his lone Major title, the **PGA Championship**. Playing at famed Inverness, Tway trailed Greg Norman by four shots through 64 holes, yet managed to creep back to even by the 72nd tee. Then,

in one of the era's more dramatic moments, he holed out for birdie from a greenside bunker to win, the first of several career daggers to be shot through Norman's competitive heart.

Little did we know, however, that we had just seen Tway's best, for over the next 15 years, despite remaining a consistent top-60 money winner with victories at **Memorial**, **Las Vegas**, and the **Heritage**, he seldom resembled the world beater that so dominated 1986. But in a curious turn, a 44-year-old Tway arose to put together his second-best season in 2003, beating Brad Faxon in sudden death for the **Canadian Open** and finishing an impressive 13th on the money list. A tall man at 6'4" yet never an especially long hitter, Tway has obviously aged well and might be marked down as a Champions Tour player to watch near decade's end.

Dr. William Tweddell (UK)

A native of Whickham, England, Dr. William Tweddell (b. 1897) was that truest of amateurs, a practicing medical man who generally played golf only on weekends and holidays. This scarcely stopped him from winning the 1927 **British Amateur**, however, a feat accomplished with relative ease (7 and 6 over D. E. Landale) following a tougher victory over Roger Wethered in the semis. Like many in this peculiar game, however, Dr. Tweddell is perhaps better remembered for a match in which he did not triumph, for in 1935, nearing 40 and not in the fullest of health, he again reached the final, this time at Royal Lytham & St. Annes against defending champion Lawson Little. Thoroughly overmatched off the tee, the doctor initially fell 5 down, cut it to 3 by lunch, then won the 25th through 27th to draw square. Little took the 32nd and 33rd but Tweddell, showing uncommon guts, rallied to win the 35th, ultimately losing only when a 20-footer to tie slipped by at the last. A future captain of the R&A (1961–62), Tweddell also captained two Walker Cup teams, playing in a 1928 loss at the Chicago GC, then directing 1936's drubbing at Pine Valley from the sidelines.

H. J. Tweedie (UK/USA)

A native of Hoylake, England, where he competed as a youth against the great John Ball, Herbert James "H. J." Tweedie emigrated to America with his brother L. P. in 1887, the both of them settling in to manage the A. G. Spalding sporting goods store in Chicago. As friends of Charles Blair Macdonald, the Tweedies were members of the original Chicago GC in Belmont, choosing to remain there when C. B. lead the rest of his flock on to Wheaton in 1895. For the stragglers, H. J. built a new layout on the old site, then went on to design several other prominent Chicago-area courses including, in 1898, the Midlothian CC, site of Walter Hagen's first U.S. Open championship in 1914.

Howard Twitty (USA)

A two-time All-American at Arizona State, Phoenix product Howard Twitty (b. 1/15/1949) finished third, behind co-champions Ben Crenshaw and Tom Kite, at the 1972 NCAA championships. After playing abroad for two seasons (winning the 1975 **Thailand Open**), the 6'5" Twitty returned to America full time in 1976, settling in for a long PGA Tour run that largely achieved only journeyman's status but did include three victories. His final title, the 1993 **Hawaiian Open**, came in his mid-40s, and Twitty has more recently played semi-regularly on the Champions Tour.

U

Sam Urzetta (USA)

Rochester, New York, product Sam Urzetta (b. 1926) was initially known as a basketball star, first in high school, then at St. Bonaventure University in Olean, New York. But by the late 1940s the former caddie had developed into a high-class amateur golfer, winning the **New York State** title in 1948, then capturing the 1950 **U.S. Amateur** by defeating the favored Frank Stranahan over a record 39 holes in Minneapolis. Also a successful Walker Cup player in 1951 and '53, Urzetta eventually turned professional and was good enough to play in four Masters and five PGA Championships, despite working full time at the Rochester CC.

Mrs. Francis Ouimet shared the honors with her husband at Woodland Country Club, Auburndale, Massachusetts, as the new Amateur Golf champ returned home from Chicago, September 7, 1931.

V

André Vagliano (France)

Though perhaps better known as the father of 1950 British Ladies champion Lally Vagliano (aka the Vicomtesse de Saint-Sauveur), André Vagliano (1896–1971) was France's leading Golden Age amateur, winning the nation's **Closed** title in 1923, '24, '26, '30, and '31, while also capturing the more prestigious **Open Amateur** in 1929. Much a sportsman in the old-fashioned, affluent mold, Vagliano donated the eponymous trophy that is awarded to the winners of a biennial match pitting women amateurs from Great Britain and Ireland against their counterparts in Continental Europe.

Jessie (Anderson) Valentine (UK)

Scotland's Jessica Anderson, M.B.E. (b. Perth, 3/18/1915) initially established herself under her maiden name before marrying George Valentine during the war. A former **British Girls** winner in 1933 and a six-time **Scottish** champion between 1936 and 1956, she won her first adult title (the 1935 **New Zealand Ladies**) while touring Down Under, then added the **French** crown in 1936. But Valentine is best recalled as a three-time winner of the **British Ladies**, first in 1937 at Turnberry, then after the war in 1955 (routing American Barbara Romack at Royal Portrush) and '58 (over Elizabeth Price at Hunstanton). Another whose career record was greatly diminished by seven years of international conflict, Valentine appeared in seven Curtis Cups from 1936 through 1958 (missing only 1948), a number that could well have gone as high as 11 without wartime cancellations.

William K. Vanderbilt (USA)

The grandson of Cornelius "Commodore" Vanderbilt, William K. (1849–1920) spent his working days overseeing the family's railroad interests but generated his success as a yachtsman and general sportsman all on his own. Though never portrayed as a serious or highly skilled golfer, his significance to the game is nonetheless substantial, for it was Vanderbilt and friends Duncan Cryder and Edward Mead who, while vacationing in Biarritz during the winter of 1890–91, had the previously unseen game demonstrated for them by professional Willie Dunn Jr. Enthralled, they returned to the States determined to build what they thought would be America's first course, the very early (but not quite first) Shinnecock Hills GC. A generation later, Vanderbilt's son William Kissam II (1878–1944) would leave an important mark of his own, converting part of his Long Island estate into the original Deepdale GC, a now-defunct C. B. Macdonald/Seth Raynor design that was among the finest American courses built in the 1920s.

Jean Van De Velde (France)

Born in Mont de Marsan, Jean Van de Velde (b. 5/29/1966) will forever be remembered for his tragic loss at the 1999 Open Championship at Carnoustie where, leading by three at the 72nd tee, he proceeded to make triple bogey seven, then lose a four-hole play-off to Paul Lawrie (the eventual winner) and Justin Leonard. However, the former **French Youth** and **Amateur** champion did not go to pieces following his disaster, instead rallying to join the PGA Tour in 2000 where he twice finished as high as second, at Tucson and Reno-Tahoe (the latter in a four-hole play-off loss to Scott Verplank). A Ryder Cup player in 1999, Van de Velde returned home to Europe in 2002 but has been battling knee problems ever since.

Flory Van Donck (Belgium)

Before there was Seve Ballesteros or Bernhard Langer, Continental golf had little to debate as to the identity of its best-ever player, for the answer was clearly Belgium's Flory van Donck (b. Tervueren, 6/23/1912). A tall, stylish man best known for a toe-in-the-air putting stroke à la Isao Aoki, van Donck racked up a remarkably dominant record on the Continent from the last of the prewar years right on through the 1950s, capturing a formidable 22 national Open titles and countless domestic Belgian events.

Van Donck was 19 times a **World Cup** participant, claiming medalist honors in 1960 at Portmarnock, losing in a 1955 play-off at Columbia, Washington, and setting a record as the event's oldest competitor (67) in 1969. South American wins in the 1954 **Uruguayan** and 1957 **Venezuelan Opens** further burnish the international record.

Skeptics will note that van Donck's European wins came in an era when there was only limited interaction between Continental players and their superior British counterparts. Fair enough. But van Donck also managed an admirable record in the Open Championship, claiming nine top-10 finishes (including runner-ups in 1956 and '59) and firing a Championship-record 65 in the third round in 1950 at Royal Troon. He was also twice a finalist in the *News of the World* match play and recorded two British victories during a banner 1953 campaign, which saw him win the Vardon Trophy (the period Player of the Year standard) and tie Norman von Nida's record for wins in a European season with seven.

Van Donck's only weakness then was one of timing, for he played in era of relative European anonymity, long before a seat at the Ryder Cup table could be offered to a player from Belgium. Consequently, though well known in Great Britain, he represents little more than an odd-sounding name to many less-knowledgeable Americans.

Intn'l Wins (31): 1936, '37, '46, '51 & '53 Dutch Open; 1938, '47, '53 & '55 Italian Open; 1939, '46, '47, '53 & '56 Belgian Open; 1953 & '56 German Open; 1953 & '55 Swiss Open; 1954, '57 & '58 French Open; 1955 Portuguese Open

Lawrence Van Etten (USA)

A native of Kingston, New York, Lawrence E. Van Etten (1865–1951) held both engineering and law degrees from Princeton but used only the former professionally, laying out ever-proliferating residential subdivisions around the New York metropolitan area near the turn of the century. A fine amateur golfer, he inevitably turned to course design, building early layouts for well-known clubs including New Jersey's Deal GC and New York's Knollwood CC, both in 1898. Remarkably, two courses that he built in 1905, Pelham Bay Park and New Rochelle's venerable Wykagyl CC, though substantially dressed up, still retain a good deal of Van Etten's original routings.

John Van Kleek (USA)

A landscape architect who initially partnered with Boston-based Wayne Stiles to form a prominent 1920s design team, John Van Kleek operated the firm's St. Petersburg, Florida, office, where he was primarily responsible for a number of Southern projects, including two prominent Florida courses that are no longer, the Holly Hill CC (of Davenport) and Sebring's Kenilworth Lodge GC. Following the firm's Depression-era breakup, Van Kleek performed some of his most memorable design work as a solo act, using WPA funds to build or rebuild seven of New York City's municipal courses, with his 36 holes at Pelham Bay Park (18 renovated, 18 new) featuring several of the wildest green complexes ever built in the United States. He passed away in 1957.

Virginia Van Wie (USA)

Chicago's Virginia Van Wie (b. 1909) was a frail and sickly youth who turned to golf mostly as a means of gaining exercise. Obviously well suited to the game, she developed into a tremendously long hitter and was competing nationally by age 16. Reaching the final of the U.S. Women's Amateur in 1928, Van Wie soon discovered that as ready as she might be, two-time champion Glenna Collett was that much more so, the result being a dramatic 13 and 12 loss at The Homestead. Van Wie returned to the final in 1930 and again it was Collett who sent her packing, though this time the margin was a more palatable 6 and 5. But by 1932, Van Wie was an irresistible force and for three straight years she captured the **Amateur** title, first avenging her 1928 embarrassment by routing Collett 10 and 8 at Salem, then dispatching Helen Hicks and Dorothy Traung at Exmoor and Whitemarsh Valley, respectively. The possessor of one of the period's most envied swings, Van Wie also appeared in the first two Curtis Cups (1932 and '34) before retiring after her third Amateur triumph.

Brigitte Varangot (France)

Brigitte Varangot (b. 1940) hails from Biarritz, where she followed in the golfing footsteps of championship players such as Arnaud Massy and Jean Gassiat. Utilizing a reliable three-quarter swing made possible by a strong, stocky physique, Varangot first served notice by winning the **British Girls** in 1957, then claimed **French Girls** titles in 1959, '60, and '61. A protégé of the famous Vicomtesse de Saint-Sauveur (Mrs. Segard), Varangot joined with Catherine LaCoste and Claudine Cros to make French women's golf an international force during the 1960s, herself capturing six **French Open** titles and five **Closed** ones. Even more impressive, however, were Varangot's three triumphs in the **British Ladies** championship, which proved her abilities against stronger competition and also came on golf courses — Royal County Down (1963), St. Andrews (1965), and Walton Heath (1968) — vastly different in style from those of her parkland French upbringing.

Harry Vardon (UK)

Born: Grouville, England, 5/9/1870 **Died:** London, England, 3/20/1937

A century before there was Tiger Woods, there was Harry Vardon.

The name, of course, is legendary, attached to trophies, the game's predominant grip, and a record of six Open Championship victories that has been challenged but never equaled. Despite such marquee status, the mists of time have managed to obscure a man known to his contemporaries as the Greyhound, blurring both the enormity of his accomplishments and the remarkable impact he exerted upon nearly every aspect of the game.

A product of the English Channel island of Jersey, Vardon (whose given name was actually Henry) burst loudly onto the golfing scene by winning **Open Championships** in 1896, '98 and '99, a stretch in which, according to Darwin, he "went up and down the country trampling opponents like some relentless Juggernaut." An extended tour of the United States followed in 1900, netting both international fame and, in a 1-2 finish with J. H. Taylor, a **U.S. Open** title. But then, following an epic fourth **Open** win in 1903 at Prestwick, Vardon was struck down by the scourge of the day, tuberculosis. Fully eight months would be spent at the Mundesley Sanatorium, and though he made a courageous entry into the 1904 Open (amazingly leading at the halfway mark before finishing fifth) the evidence clearly suggests that Vardon was never again in the fullest of health.

By 1910, his fellow members of golf's great Triumvirate, J. H. Taylor and James Braid, had equaled or exceeded Vardon's four Claret Jugs, but despite turning 40, the Greyhound wasn't finished. Fighting a balky putting stroke brought about by his sickness, Vardon equaled Braid by claiming his fifth **Open Championship** at Royal St. George's in 1911—a feat soon matched by Taylor, at Hoylake, in 1913. Then with war looming and the end of their era at hand, Vardon captured that immortal sixth title at Prestwick in 1914, defeating Taylor by three and setting a mark that, despite the best efforts of Peter Thomson and Tom Watson, stands tall to this day.

Curiously, the roots of Vardon's prodigious talent remain somewhat obscured, for while his own recollections certainly indicate some youthful proficiency, precisely when or how his almost mystical skills blossomed remains essentially undocumented. What is clear is that his swing—a rather upright move with a decidedly bent left arm—was typical among early Channel Island golfers and bore little in the way of individual innovation. Also well known is that blessed with conspicuously large hands, Vardon experimented at length before settling upon the same overlapping grip used by the fine English amateur

Harry Vardon on his home course at Totteridge

J. E. Laidlay some 30 years earlier—a grip also employed by J. H. Taylor but forever named, as all golfers know, after Vardon.

But if his swing wasn't revolutionary, Vardon's playing style surely was, primarily in the extraordinary smoothness of his tempo. While others expended great energy to propel the old gutta-percha ball along, Vardon seemed scarcely to raise a sweat as he rhythmically, almost casually, ripped it past nearly everyone. Of similar impact was the manner in which Vardon comported himself, for he was quiet, focused, and unfailingly gracious; a man who, in the words of 1925 British Amateur champion Robert Harris, "did not appear to know he was great." Further, Vardon was immensely popular among his fellow professionals and was, in fact, very close friends with his chief rivals, Taylor and Braid. Even the prickly Andra Kirkaldy, whose career was blackmarked by never beating Vardon, was an unabashed fan, noting "He could laugh with the best of us; the most genial of men."

With such talent and magnetism, it is hardly surprising that Vardon's visits to America—particularly the 1900 tour on behalf of the A. G. Spalding Company—played an enormous role in sparking golf's growth in the New World. All told, Vardon estimated that he traveled over 20,000 miles and played some 88 matches on this first visit, en-thralling audiences and battering the competition (he lost only once in head-to-head matches) across the continent.

So just how good a player was Harry Vardon? Darwin answered this question rather succinctly by stating: "I cannot believe that anyone ever had or ever will have a greater genius for hitting a golf ball than Harry Vardon." And far more recently, Herbert Warren Wind, a man hardly given to wild rhetoric, wrote that "there has surely never been a better golfer than Harry Vardon."

Comparing Vardon to today's long-hitting stars, of course, is a thorny question. Was his competition up to snuff? Did the primitive equipment of the era make it easier for the top talents to distance themselves from the field? And how much must his illness be factored in, for without it a total of perhaps 10 Open Championships seems not only reasonable but downright likely—a flight of golfing excellence almost inconceivable by modern standards.

Still, the numbers as they stand—what Vardon actually accomplished—are extraordinary. His competitive years stretched from 1895 through 1914, during which time he entered 20 Open Championships (many at less than full strength), winning six times and taking four seconds. During this same span, he won more than one-third of the documented tournaments in which he played and finished first or second in more than half. At his pre-illness peak, just before the turn of the century, he once won a mind boggling 17 of 22 events entered—and finished second in the other five. Thus when we consider that Vardon won only three of the 18 match-play events in which he competed, then remove the relatively lackluster performances of his illness-plagued years, we find a man who,

when healthy, came as close to stroke-play invincibility as the game will ever see.

Also significant were his three attempts at the U.S. Open, the first of which he won at the Chicago Golf Club in 1900. Returning in 1913, he came agonizingly close to "defending" at The Country Club, losing the famous three-way play-off (along with fellow Jerseyman Ted Ray) to the teenage Francis Ouimet. Yet it was Vardon's final attempt, a 1920 second-place tie at Inverness, that was perhaps the most stirring. For there, at the improbably old age of 50, he held a four-shot lead with seven to play before a freak windstorm erupted, derailing this final storybook challenge in a rush of fatigue and bad luck.

Retiring from competition, Vardon repaired to the South Herts Golf Club in Totteridge where, despite in-consistent health, he played, taught, and designed golf courses right up until his death in 1937. Though obviously not the player he once was, Vardon could, as late as age 60, still provide inspired flashes. Indeed, 1949 Walker captain Laddie Lucas has written of playing with him at South Herts in 1930, one day after the Greyhound's return from a long convalescent stint. Not having swung a club in six weeks and too tired to last more than 11 holes, Vardon still managed to hobble around the opening nine in a stunning 29 strokes. "Every drive and every iron flew dead straight," Lucas reported, "no fade, no draw. I never saw this straightness again."

Nor has golf seen another Harry Vardon, a man who might or might not have beaten Hogan, Nicklaus, or Woods at their games, but was the absolute master of his own.

Intn'l Wins (9): 1896, '98, '99, 1903, '11 & '14 British Open; 1900 U.S. Open; 1911 German Open; 1912 PGA Match Play

1893-1920

	93	94	95	96	97	98	99	00	01	02	03	04	05	06
US Open	-	-	-	-	-	-	-	1	-	-	-	-	-	-
British	T23	T5	T9	1	6	1	1	2	2	T2	1	5	T9	3

	07	08	09	10	11	12	13	14	15	16	17	18	19	20
US Open	-	-	-	-	-	-	T2	-	-	-			-	T2
British	T7	T5	T26	T16	1	2	T3	1						T14

Tom Vardon (UK/USA)

The younger brother of Harry, Channel Islander Tom Vardon (1874–1938) has been largely overlooked by historians despite finishing among the top five at the Open Championship from 1902 to 1904 (including a second, six behind Harry, in '03) and losing in the final of the 1905

News of the World match play to James Braid. Though Tom was known to occasionally caddie for Harry when not in contention himself, it was actually his success as a professional on the mainland that spurred Harry to get serious about the game in the first place. Tom also struck out on his own by emigrating to America (a prospect Harry considered but ultimately declined) where he both competed and served as a club pro, most notably at Chicago's Onwentsia Club and Minnesota's White Bear Yacht Club. He also became a part-time golf course architect, building, by some estimates, as many as 50 courses in the upper Midwest before passing away in Minneapolis in 1938.

Ken Venturi (USA)

San Francisco's Ken Venturi (b. 5/15/1931) has experienced a career the likes of few others, reaching dazzling peaks and disheartening valleys that even Hollywood might consider a bit too far-fetched if presented in movie script form. A highly talented Bay Area amateur, Venturi was runner-up in the inaugural USGA Junior Boys in 1948, then starred on the victorious 1953 Walker Cup team for which he won his singles match over one J. C. Wilson 9 and 8.

Initially considering a Bob Jones–like amateur career, Venturi took to selling cars for San Francisco dealer Eddie Lowery, then suffered an epic defeat at the 1956 Masters when his four-stroke 54-hole lead was eviscerated by a final-round 80 (under, we must note, extremely windy conditions) to lose to Jack Burke Jr. by one. It was a loss that no mortal could soon forget, but for Venturi there was more Augusta pain in store, specifically two years later when he looked to be in the final-round driver's seat after Arnold Palmer apparently made 5 at the par-3 12th. But in a controversy that lingers still, Masters officials opted to accept Palmer's version of a disagreement over an imbedded ball ruling and the subsequent playing of a second ball, retroactively giving Arnold a three, a blow from which Venturi could not recover. That Palmer defeated Venturi again at the 1960 Masters—this time winning with birdies at the 71st and 72nd—only added to the frustration.

But by now, Venturi had established himself as one of golf's top professional talents, a superb iron player with plenty of length and an outstanding short game whose money winning ranked as high as third in 1958 and second in 1960. He claimed 10 official victories during this period

and appeared well on his way to the greatness many (including Byron Nelson and Ben Hogan) had predicted of him when physical, marital, and swing problems combined to derail him badly during the early 1960s. Always resilient, however, Venturi came back, rebuilding his game completely and setting up one of sport's truly epic triumphs.

After having to qualify for the 1964 **U.S. Open** at Congressional, Venturi rode a splendid third-round 66 into contention, trailing Tommy Jacobs by two. Unfortunately he was also suffering from heat prostration in the blistering 100-degree weather and was advised by the tournament physician not to continue. But in a performance later lionized in Frank Gifford's book *Gifford on Courage* (Evans, 1976), Venturi not only played, he shot a remarkable 70, staggering home—quite literally—to defeat Jacobs by four. Winning twice more that season, Venturi was named Player of the Year and was back on top of the world—but yet again, his success would be short-lived.

By October he began to mysteriously lose the feeling in his hands, a situation which became nearly unbearable in cold or wet weather. Eventually diagnosed with carpal tunnel syndrome and bound by the limited medical knowledge of the day, Venturi had little choice but to undergo surgery on both wrists, the diciest of propositions for a golfer. Yet once more he rose from the ashes, coming back to win the 1966 **Lucky International**, an event rather fittingly played over his boyhood course at San Francisco's Harding Park.

Venturi's hands were never quite the same after surgery, however, and by the late 1960s he was effectively finished, beginning a long and popular stint in the television booth that finally ended with his retirement in 2002. Venturi also served as captain of the winning Presidents Cup team in 2000.

PGA Tour Wins (14): 1958 Phoenix; 1959 Los Angeles; 1960 Bing Crosby; **1964 U.S. Open**
Ryder Cup: 1965 **Presidents Cup:** 2000 Capt

1953-1967

	53	54	55	56	57	58	59	60	61	62	63	64	65	66	67
Masters	T16	-	-	2	T13	T4	MC	2	T11	T9	T34	-	MC	16	T21
US Open	MC	-	-	T8	T6	T35	T38	T23	-	-	-	1	MC	T17	T28
British	-	-	-	-	-	-	-	-	-	-	-	-	-	-	-
PGA	-	-	-	-	-	T20	T5	9	T37	T51	-	T5	-	T15	T11

Scott Verplank (USA)

One of the great collegiate golfers of his time, Scott Verplank (b. Dallas, Texas, 7/9/1964) was a four-time All-American at Oklahoma State, the 1986 **NCAA** individual

champion, the 1984 **U.S. Amateur** champion (defeating Sam Randolph 4 and 3 at Oak Tree GC), and both a Walker Cup player and **Western Amateur** winner in 1985. Even more memorably, he became the first amateur in nearly three decades to win a PGA Tour event, defeating Jim

Thorpe in sudden death at the 1985 **Western Open** at Chicago's Butler National GC.

In this context then, Verplank's professional career has been perhaps a shade disappointing, though the phrase is certainly relative when discussing a man with four Tour victories and over $13 million earned. Verplank's primary problem has been two elbow surgeries, which have caused him either to miss extensive time or, alternatively, to achieve impressive standards of futility, such as his famous 1991–92 stretch where he made two cuts in 39 starts.

But Verplank is nothing if not determined and with his health once again solid, he has emerged, since the late 1990s, as a truly fine player, winning in 2000 and 2001 (the latter a **Canadian Open**), notching four top-25 money rankings and being selected to the Ryder Cup team in 2002. Though now reaching his 40s, Verplank may well have some strong years left ahead of him, for his game has never been about power, and hitting fairways and greens at a high clip tends to keep one relevant for a good long while.

Bobby Verwey (South Africa)

The son of 1948 and '49 South African PGA winner Jock Verwey and brother-in-law to Gary Player (who married his sister Vivienne), Johannesburg's Bobby Verwey (b. 1/21/1941) was a four-time winner in his native South Africa, three of which came during a banner 1968. Also a regular on the European Tour during the late 1970s, Verwey did manage to win a PGA Tour event back in 1966, the now-defunct **Almaden Open** (for which he was invited to the 1967 Masters), and twice represented South Africa in World Cup play (1978 and '80). He later became a highly successful money winner upon joining the European Senior Tour in 1992.

Roberto de Vicenzo (Argentina)

Of the handful of golfers whose careers are best remembered for a single tragic moment, popular Roberto de Vicenzo (b. Buenos Aires, 4/14/1923) remains the group's poster boy. Playing in the 1968 Masters, de Vicenzo closed—on his 45th birthday, no less—with a dazzling 65 to finish in a tie with Bob Goalby, necessitating an 18-hole Monday play-off. However in signing his scorecard, de Vicenzo failed to notice that his playing partner Tommy Aaron had mistakenly marked his birdie at the 71st as a par. Thus while the card's total of 65 was correct, the error was freely admitted to by Aaron, and although the presence of television cameras left zero doubt as to de Vicenzo's correct score, the rules clearly dictated that he be credited with an incorrect 66. With that, Goalby was an unpopular champion and de Vicenzo was officially placed

second, handling the entire disaster with remarkable grace and muttering his famous words, "What a stupid am I."

An unfortunate aspect of this sorry incident is that it has long overshadowed one of golf's greatest international careers and one of its more interesting biographical stories. For de Vicenzo was not the product of money but rather of lower-income parents bearing no connection to golf whatsoever. He discovered the game in that most traditional of ways, as a caddie, and developed his skills by playing with his brothers, four of whom also pursued professional careers. He claimed his first of nine **Argentine Open** titles in 1944 but quickly realized that competitive opportunities in South America were limited, necessitating that he pack off to Britain or America on a regular basis.

For the better part of four decades, the seemingly ageless de Vicenzo traveled the world, amassing a record of tournament wins that surely exceeds that of any professional golfer in raw numbers (the 165 presented below actually representing the *lowest* estimate), though many of his titles came in remote events of limited international relevance. An extremely long hitter who spent much of his career battling a balky putter, de Vicenzo won at least 40 national Opens in at least a dozen countries, including virtually every South and Central American nation that offered one. He was also the winner of nine official PGA Tour titles and numerous events on what would today be considered the European Tour, with his crowning achievement coming at the 1967 **Open Championship** at Hoylake. Having previously assembled as strong an Open record as any modern non-winner (including a second, two behind Locke, in 1950), de Vicenzo rode a third-round 67 to a slim lead over Player and Nicklaus, then closed with a solid 70 for one of the more popular non-British victories on record.

De Vicenzo eventually became a long-term force in senior golf, claiming both the **U.S.** and **World Senior** titles in 1974. He also won the inaugural **U.S. Senior Open** in 1980 at Winged Foot, ironically on the same East course that witnessed golf's *other* great scorecard disaster, Jackie Pung's clerical error at the 1957 U.S. Women's Open. A perennial presence at the **World Cup**, de Vicenzo appeared on 19 occasions, including four for Mexico between 1956 and 1961. He was the individual winner in 1962 at his hometown Jockey Club in Buenos Aires and teamed with Antonio Cerda to win the Cup's inaugural event in 1953 in Montreal.

PGA Tour Wins (10): 1957 Colonial; 1966 Byron Nelson; **1967 British Open**; 1968 Houston
Intn'l Wins (165): 1950 Dutch Open; 1950 Belgian Open; 1950, '60 & '64 French Open; 1951, '53 & '55 Mexican Open; 1964 German Open; 1966 Spanish Open; 9 Argentine Opens, 7 Argentine PGAs & 5 Brazilian Opens
Champions Tour Wins: 2 (1980–84)

1948-1972

	48	49	50	51	52	53	54	55	56	57	58	59	60
Masters	-	-	T12	T20	-	-	-	-	T17	-	MC	-	-
US Open	-	-	-	T29	-	-	-	-	T27	T8	MC	-	-
British	T3	3	2	-	-	6	-	-	3	-	-	-	T3
PGA	-	-	-	-	T9	-	T9	-	-	-	-	-	-

	61	62	63	64	65	66	67	68	69	70	71	72
Masters	T22	T33	-	-	-	T22	T10	2	MC	MC	T9	T22
US Open	-	-	-	-	-	-	-	T24	-	-	-	-
British	-	-	-	3	4	T20	1	T10	T3	T17	T11	-
PGA	-	-	-	-	-	-	-	-	-	-	-	-

Ellsworth Vines (USA)

Following in the nineteenth-century footsteps of England's Lottie Dod, Los Angeles's Henry Ellsworth Vines Jr. (1911–1994) was a Grand Slam tennis champion (1931 and '32 U.S. Opens, 1932 Wimbledon) before turning to golf in the late 1930s. Standing 6'2" and weighing only 143 pounds during his tennis days, Vines seldom achieved a comparable standard of greatness on the links but was a regular competitor on the PGA Tour after turning pro in 1942. Though never a winner of an official Tour event, he was six times a runner-up and a semifinalist in the 1951 PGA Championship at Oakmont.

Randall Vines (Australia)

Though perhaps not reaching the lofty heights that some initially predicted for him, Brisbane's Randall Vines (b. 1945) posted some very low numbers in his day, initially venturing forth to claim overseas national Opens in **Switzerland** (1967), **Thailand** (1968), and **Hong Kong** (1968), plus a remarkable 17-shot victory at the 1968 **Tasmanian Open**. A lean 140-pound man who could hit it a long way, Vines did take back-to-back **Australian PGAs** in 1972 and '73 but in the end proved unable to carry his successes onto the world's larger stages.

George Voigt (USA)

New Yorker George Voigt was a highly regarded international competitor during the Depression years, who was once described by Henry Longhurst as "an American amateur of almost professional quality." A three-time Walker Cupper (1930, '32, and '36) who flogged Sir Ernest Holderness 10 and 8 in a 1930 singles match, Voigt is best recalled for very nearly ending Bobby Jones' 1930 Grand Slam bid before it got rolling. In their British Amateur semifinal match at St. Andrews, Voigt stood two up with five to play before driving it out-of-bounds at the 14th, then into the Principle's Nose at the 16th, before ultimately losing at the last when his approach trickled back into the Valley of Sin. On the positive side of the ledger, Voigt won three straight **North & South Amateurs** (1927–29) when the event was at its peak, defeating Gene Homans, Johnny Dawson, and William C. Fownes Jr., respectively.

George Von Elm (USA)

Growing up at a time when Chicago was still considered "the West," Utah-born and Southern California–raised George Von Elm (1901–1961) was America's first national **Amateur** champion to hail from beyond the Rockies. His great moment of triumph came in the 1926 final at Baltusrol where, in an exciting match that went to the 35th hole, Von Elm edged Bobby Jones 2 and 1 to break what otherwise would have been a run of five straight American titles for Jones. At a glance, the win might seem flukish, particularly since Jones had sent Von Elm packing from the two previous U.S. Amateurs. But it was really only Jones who kept Von Elm from grabbing many more titles, and who wrote of 1926: "I had beaten [Von Elm] at Merion and at Oakmont, and the Lord knows that nobody is going to keep beating on a golfer like George Von Elm."

A handsome man of German descent, Von Elm was equally capable at stroke play, tying for third in the 1926 Open Championship (where Jones was again to win, this time at Royal Lytham & St. Annes) and tying Walter Hagen for fourth at the 1928 U.S. Open at Olympia Fields. Von Elm's best shot at a professional Major championship came in 1931 when, with the retired Jones out of the way, he birdied the 72nd hole to tie Billy Burke for the U.S. Open at Inverness. A 36-hole play-off ensued, and again

Von Elm birdied the last to force a tie, necessitating yet another 36. This time a final birdie wasn't in the offing and Burke won, by a single stroke, the longest U.S. Open on record.

Von Elm also claimed **Pacific Northwest** titles in 1921 and '22, took the **Trans-Mississippi** crown in 1921, and appeared in three Walker Cups matches (1926–30) with his only loss coming in 1930's foursomes, when he and George Voigt lost to the imposing team of Cyril Tolley and Roger Wethered, two down.

Robert von Hagge (USA)

One of the game's more colorful modern characters, Robert von Hagge (b. 1930) was the son of a Midwestern greenkeeper and course builder who, by the time he was 17, had experience in most every aspect of the golf business. A fine player, he briefly tried the PGA Tour after graduating from Purdue University, then worked as a club professional before taking a swing (unsuccessfully) at an acting career in Hollywood. He also gained some degree of early celebrity by marrying the LPGA's first glamour girl, Marlene Bauer, in 1950—an especially noteworthy occurrence since he divorced her older sister Alice to do so.

Von Hagge entered the golf design business in 1955, when hired by Dick Wilson, and eventually formed his own firm in 1962. Perhaps due to his Hollywood past, he soon took on flamboyant trappings that might today seem bizarre, such as the reported touring of sites in a gold lamé cape and the addition of "von" to a last name which had previously only been Hagge. Though hardly unsuccessful as a solo designer, his fortunes really soared after taking on popular Australian Bruce Devlin as a partner in 1968, with the pair combining to design more than 75 courses worldwide over the next 20 years. Following Devlin's 1987 departure for the Champions Tour, von Hagge formed a new firm with several younger designers and still remains active at the time of this writing.

Notable Courses: Bay Point Y&CC, Lagoon Legend Course, Florida; Crandon Park GC, Florida; Eagle Vail GC, Colorado; El Conquistador Hotel & C, Puerto Rico (BO)

Bernhard von Limburger (Germany)

A three-time **German Amateur** champion during the first half of the 1920s, Leipzig native Bernhard von Limburger (1901–1981) learned the game while spending time in Scotland as a youth. A well-educated man with a doctorate in law, von Limburger chose never to pursue the bar, instead starting the German-language magazine *Golf,* which would eventually become the official publication of the German Golf Union. His involvement with course design began in 1925 (though in a rudimentary way) and he had completed 10 layouts prior to going into partnership with Karl Hoffman, Germany's first successful architect, shortly before the outbreak of World War II. Not overly proud of his earliest works, von Limburger joked that it was just as well that many had fallen on the east side of Germany's postwar partition, as they were soon built over and thus gone without lasting documentation.

With Karl Hoffman passing away soon after the war, von Limburger quickly became Germany's leading architect, gaining commissions for courses on American military bases as well as for numerous civilian projects. He would complete more than 70 postwar designs, the most noteworthy being Garlstedter Heide (aka Club Zur Vahr), a thickly wooded layout near Bremen widely rated among the best in Europe.

Notable Courses: GC Hubbelrath; Krefelder GC; **Club Zur Var**

Norman von Nida (Australia)

One of Australian golf's all-time most colorful characters, Sydney native Norman George von Nida (b. 2/14/1914) moved with his family to Brisbane at a young age, learning golf as a caddie at the Royal Queensland Golf Club. At 15, skinny and undernourished, he drew the plum assignment of looping for the great Walter Hagen in an exhibition match against Australian trick-shot artist Joe Kirkwood, a job for which Hagen slipped the young von Nida the then-enormous sum of £5. Motivated to follow in Hagen's illustrious footsteps, von Nida practiced diligently and developed his game, eventually winning the **Queensland Amateur** in 1932 and the state's **Open** (where he beat a heavily favored Jim Ferrier) in 1935.

In 1936 Gene Sarazen visited Brisbane, offering to play anybody for any amount of money. The black beret-wearing von Nida found a backer willing to put up £50, took up the challenge, and defeated the Squire two up, reportedly shooting 67. Sarazen advised von Nida to head for Europe if he was serious about competing professionally, and following the war he took this sage advice. As such, von Nida was something of a pioneer, for while other Australians had emigrated seeking golf-related jobs, he was the first to go abroad simply to compete, with intentions of returning Down Under at season's end.

Though forays to America (which included five Masters appearances between 1950 and 1962) were largely unsuccessful, von Nida did splendidly in Britain, claiming numerous events from 1946 to 1948, including seven titles in 1947, a record unbroken by anyone on the modern European Tour. He was even more impressive at home winning three **Australian Opens** (1950, '52, and '53) as well as four **PGAs** and seven **Queensland Opens**. Though terribly disappointed at never winning the Open Championship (his best finish being a tie for third in 1948), von Nida took it upon himself to groom the young Peter Thomson, in whom he saw—quite correctly, as it turned out—the makings of Australia's first world-beater.

After his retirement from competitive play, von Nida took a professional job at Malaysia's Royal Selangor Golf Club, then later taught at Jack Nicklaus' Muirfield Village GC before retiring back to Australia in the late 1980s.

Intn'l Wins (45): 1946, '48, '50 & '51 Australian PGA; 1948 British Masters; 1950, '52 & '53 Australian Open

Erzsebet von Szlavy (Hungary)

More or less by default, Budapest-born Erzsebet von Szlavy (b. 1902) remains timelessly enshrined as Hungary's best-ever female golfer, having won that nation's **Ladies** title some 15 times in 18 years between 1922 and 1939. Though never a factor in any of the game's bigger events, she did enjoy some international success, taking the **Austrian Ladies** on four occasions (1927–29 and 1936), the **Czech** title just as often (1932, '33, '35, and '37), and the larger **German Ladies** title in 1926. As golf in Hungary has slowed to little more than a trickle, von Szlavy's domestic records may well last longer than Byron Nelson's 11 consecutive wins.

W

Lanny Wadkins (USA)

A streaky player with one of golf's better up-tempo swings, Jerry Lanston "Lanny" Wadkins (b. Richmond, Virginia, 12/5/1949) staked his claim early, making waves in the 1966 U.S. Amateur at age 16, then later winning the **Amateur** title (then still contested at stroke play) in 1970 by one over Tom Kite at Oregon's Waverly CC. Also a winner of the **Western** (1970) and two **Southern Amateurs** (1968 and '70), and twice an All-American at Wake Forest, Wadkins starred on two Walker Cup teams (1969 and '71) before joining the PGA Tour in late 1971.

He started fast, finishing 10th and 5th on the 1972 and '73 money lists while winning thrice, then suffered through three winless seasons in which he failed to better 57th in earnings. But in 1977 Wadkins arrived for good, finishing third on the money list and winning his first Major, the **PGA Championship,** at Pebble Beach. Benefiting from Gene Littler's late struggles, Wadkins found himself in sudden death with the 47-year-old San Diegan, barely staying alive by holing a long par putt on the first extra hole before closing Littler out at the third.

Shortly thereafter he would win the **World Series of Golf,** kicking off a 15-year run that, though sometimes inconsistent, would include 16 more wins, five top-10

money rankings, and 13 top-10 Major championship finishes in 54 starts. He was particularly effective at the Masters (thrice tying for third between 1990 and 1993) and at the PGA (solo or joint second in 1982, '84 and '87) and also tied for second at the 1986 U.S. Open. Long known for posting impressively low scores when hot, Wadkins shot 263 in winning the 1982 **Phoenix Open,** 267 at Firestone in the 1977 **World Series,** and an eye-popping 264 over a dried-out Riviera at the 1985 **Los Angeles Open,** a record which still stands today.

By the mid-1990s Wadkins' play had dropped off considerably, and though he would win a single Champions Tour event during 2000, he has spent most of his post-50 years as a prominent television announcer. Lanny's younger brother Bobby, though never a winner, also earned a good living on the PGA Tour for more than 20 years before finally claiming a Champions Tour victory in 2001.

PGA Tour Wins (21): 1973 Byron Nelson; **1977 PGA Championship;** 1977 World Series; 1979 & '85 Los Angeles; 1979 Players Championship; 1987 Doral; 1988 Colonial
Intn'l Wins: 4
Champions Tour Win: 1 (2000)
Walker Cup: 1969 & '71 (2) **Ryder Cup:** 1977, '79, '83–93 (8); 1995 Capt

1971-1993

	71	72	73	74	75	76	77	78	79	80	81	82
Masters	-	T19	T29	-	-	-	-	T18	T7	MC	T21	T33
US Open	T13	T25	T7	T26	T38	-	-	-	T19	MC	T14	T6
British	-	-	T7	T22	MC	-	-	MC	-	-	-	-
PGA	-	T16	T3	-	-	-	1	T34	70	T30	T33	2

	83	84	85	86	87	88	89	90	91	92	93
Masters	T8	MC	T18	T31	T12	T11	T26	T3	T3	T48	T3
US Open	7	T11	T5	T2	T36	T12	MC	T51	T63	MC	-
British	T29	T4	MC	-	T29	T34	T26	MC	T73	T45	MC
PGA	MC	T2	T10	T11	2	T25	MC	MC	T43	T40	T14

Cyril Walker (UK/USA)

Manchester, England, native Cyril Walker (1892–1948) is frequently portrayed as being among the least likely of

U.S. Open champions, not simply because he was a wisp of a man at 118 pounds (he was known to wear two pairs of plus-fours in order to look sturdier) but also due to the oft-written claim that after his 1924 triumph at Oakland

Hills, he was never again heard from on the competitive stage. The notion that Walker managed one flukishly great week, however, is flatly incorrect, for he won five more events recognized by today's PGA Tour and finished second on six further occasions, including twice behind Walter Hagen at the prestigious North & South Open (1923 and '24). It may also be worth noting that Walker's U.S. Open victory was over Bobby Jones, Bill Mehlhorn, and Walter Hagen, though he apparently failed to parlay it into any long-term financial security, dying penniless in 1948.

George Herbert Walker (USA)

Grandfather of the elder President George Bush, George Herbert Walker (1874–1953) was a fine player out of St. Louis who served as president of the USGA in 1920. A keen believer in international competition as well as a member of the USGA delegation that visited the R&A in 1920 to discuss modifications to the rules of golf, Walker developed plans for an international match open to any nation wishing to field a team, the prize being his donated trophy, the Walker Cup. With much of the golfing world mired in post–World War I economic doldrums, there were no takers to his initial 1920 offer. But following an informal match between British and American amateurs at Hoylake in 1921, the British announced that they would send a team to America to compete for the cup and the rest — including no further recruitment of additional participants — is history.

Mickey Walker (UK)

One of England's finest-ever professional prospects, Carol Michelle "Mickey" Walker, O.B.E. (b. 12/17/1952) looked for all the world a superstar on the way up, becoming the youngest modern-era winner of the **British Ladies** in 1971 (at age 18), then successfully defending the title a year later. In 1972 she also starred in the Curtis Cup and competed successfully abroad, winning the **Portuguese Ladies** as well as the American **Trans-Mississippi,** the latter making Walker the first British female since Pamela Barton in 1936 to take a major amateur title on U.S. soil. A 1973 **English Ladies** title rounded out an impressive early résumé.

With such a pedigree, Walker certainly seemed capable of being the first Briton to have an impact on the LPGA Tour, but such projections were soon proven faulty. After several disappointing years in which she only once came close to victory (a 1976 play-off loss to Sandra Palmer at the Jerry Lewis Classic), Walker returned home to the Ladies European Tour where she would win six times and twice finish runner-up in the early (non-Major championship) days of the Women's British Open. Though past her best by the advent of the Solheim Cup, she was selected as European team captain for the first four playings, from 1990 through 1996.

Art Wall (USA)

Born: Honesdale, Pennsylvania, 11/25/1923 **Died:** Scranton, Pennsylvania, 10/30/2001

A graduate of Duke University with a degree in business, Art Wall Jr. enjoyed a long and successful run on the PGA Tour, winning a total of 14 times over an impressive 22-year span. Though always competitive, Wall's game peaked at the end of the 1950s when he won twice in 1958, then four more times in 1959. The **Bing Crosby** was his first victory of that career season, serving to set up an epic **Masters** triumph that saw Wall come from six shots back with a closing 66 (including birdies on four of his last five holes) to overhaul both Arnold Palmer and Cary Middlecoff. At year's end, Wall was the Tour's leading money earner and Vardon Trophy winner, making him the obvious choice for Player of the Year honors.

A six-shot victory in the 1960 **Canadian Open** was Wall's last big title before entering a slow decline that saw him claim only two victories over the next 15 seasons. However in 1975, coming off 83rd- and 109th-place finishes on the money list, he reemerged to become the second oldest winner in PGA Tour history, edging Gary McCord to capture the **Greater Milwaukee Open** at age 51. A three-time Ryder Cup pick, Wall has always been considered one of golf's finest putters, yet he was clearly an elite iron player too, as his 40+ career holes-in-one will thoroughly attest.

PGA Tour Wins (14): 1959 Bing Crosby; **1959 Masters;** 1960 Canadian Open; 1964 San Diego

Ryder Cup: 1957, '59 & '61 (3)

1952-1968

	52	53	54	55	56	57	58	59	60	61	62	63	64	65	66	67	68
Masters	-	-	-	-	T34	MC	T6	1	-	-	MC	T21	MC	T45	MC	T49	T22
US Open	47	T26	MC	T16	MC	MC	-	WD	T43	-	T11	T40	-	-	-	T9	T50
British	-	-	-	-	-	-	-	-	-	-	-	-	-	-	-	-	-
PGA	-	-	-	-	T17	T33	T11	T25	T39	T5	T23	T8	-	-	-	-	-

Philip Walton
(Ireland)

A Dublin native who spent three years at the University of Oklahoma, Philip Walton (b. 3/28/1962) won major amateur titles in Ireland, Scotland, and Spain before joining the European Tour in 1983. His has been an up-and-down ride, peaking with a 13th-place finish on the 1995 Order of Merit but more frequently residing between 50 and 100. Though a **French Open** winner in 1990, Walton will surely best be remembered for 1995 when, in addition to winning the **Catalonia** and **English Opens,** he made his lone Ryder Cup appearance at Rochester's Oak Hill CC — and promptly won the Cup for Europe by defeating Jay Haas one up in the penultimate singles contest.

Fred Wampler
(USA)

Indiana native Fred Wampler Jr. (1923–1985) was an honored Air Force pilot during World War II before returning to Purdue University, where he won three straight **Big Ten** titles and the 1950 **NCAA** individual championship. Two years later he began playing the PGA Tour, capturing his lone official victory at the 1954 **Los Angeles Open** where he defeated Jerry Barber and Chick Harbert at the old Fox Hills GC. By the early 1960s Wampler was holding down a full-time club job, eventually serving 17 years at the Denver CC, where he was dominant regional player and senior champion. He died, following a long battle with leukemia, in 1985.

Charlie Ward (UK)

Birmingham native Charles Harold Ward (b. 1911) holds the rather odd distinction of being perhaps the only English professional whose game benefited from the horrors of World War II, for he spent much of the war stationed at an RAF post near Torquay where he had ample opportunity to polish his short game during his down time. Consequently Ward emerged from the conflict as one of the world's best from 50 yards and in, enabling him to win several prominent postwar titles. The biggest was the 1949 **British Masters** at St. Andrews, but Ward's overall steady play earned him Vardon Trophies (for leading the Order of Merit) in 1948 and '49 and Ryder Cup appearances from 1947 through 1951. A slight man with a quick, lashing swing, Ward was a notoriously short hitter who, by the 1950s,

steadily became overmatched by the younger, longer breed.

E. Harvie Ward (USA)

Born: Tarboro, North Carolina, 12/8/1925 **Died:** Pinehurst, North Carolina, 9/4/2004

Though his run at the top was a relatively short one, most knowledgeable observers considered E. Harvie Ward Jr. to have been the best of a strong crop of post–World War II American amateurs. A North Carolinian who won the 1949 **NCAA** individual title while attending Chapel Hill, Ward played with a relaxed easiness that was the envy of all, his swing bearing the same balance and syrupy tempo as contemporary stars like Jerry Pate or Ernie Els.

Blessed with such obvious talent, Ward charged across the Atlantic in 1952 to capture the **British Amateur** in his very first try, handling quirky old Prestwick as well as talented fellow American Frank Stranahan in the final, 7 and 5. He returned in 1953 to very nearly defend his title at Hoylake, trumping Arthur Perowne in the semis before losing a heartbreaker to the great Irishman Joe Carr on the 36th green of the final.

Though he also won the 1948 **North & South** and the 1954 **Canadian,** Ward took surprisingly long to claim his most coveted prize, the **U.S. Amateur.** After eight unsuccessful tries he broke through in 1955 at the CC of Virginia by routing Stranahan 9 and 8 in the final, playing seven under level fours. A year later, he successfully defended this crown by edging 1957 Walker Cupper Joe Campbell in the semis, then defeating the Michigan star Chuck Kocsis in the final at Chicago's Knollwood Club.

A three-time Walker Cup player himself (1953, '55, and '59), Ward made his living as a salesman at Eddie Lowery's San Francisco car dealership while regularly notching top-20 finishes in the Masters and U.S. Open. His best such effort came in 1957 at Augusta, when he stood in contention going the final nine before bogeys at the 11th and 12th eventually landed him in fourth place. Soon thereafter, the USGA, citing expense money provided by Lowery, stripped Ward of his amateur status for a year. Though the governing body was certainly acting in accordance with their rules, the suspension failed to acknowledge the patently obvious: had Lowery simply given Ward a raise in salary the whole thing would have been legal. Instead, he spent 12 months on the competitive sidelines and never truly returned to his former glory. For as Ward later said himself, "After I was banned, I kind of let my game go to hell. I never really got [it] back after that."

1948-1960

	48	49	50	51	52	53	54	55	56	57	58	59	60
Masters	T50	-	T35	T35	T21	14	T20	T8	T34	4	MC		
US Open	-	-	-	T39	-	MC	MC	T7	47	T26	T37	MC	
US Am	T65	T9	T65	T17	T17	T17	T33	1	1	T9	T9	T9	
Brit Am	-	-	-	-	1	2	-	-	-	-	-	-	-
British	-	-	-	-	-	-	-	-	-	-	-	-	-

Marvin Ward (USA)

In the relatively quiet golfing years that immediately preceded America's entry into World War II, Olympia, Washington, native Marvin H. "Bud" Ward (1913–1968) stood tall in a somewhat lean field, winning the 1939 and '41 **U.S. Amateurs** (after losing in the '37 semifinals), the 1941 **Pacific Northwest,** as well as **Western Amateurs** in 1940, '41, and, later, 1947. His 1939 U.S. Amateur came at the expense of New Yorker Ray Billows, 7 and 5, at Chicago's North Shore GC. Two years later, at Nebraska's Omaha Field Club, he took his second national crown over B. P. Abbott, 4 and 3. Ward then expanded his success after the war, beating professional fields to claim three successive **Pacific Northwest Opens** and frequently ranking as first or second low amateur at the Masters and the U.S. Open. He also appeared in the two Walker Cups that bracketed the war (1938 and '47), taking full account of Frank Pennink, 12 and 11, in the former contest.

Pat Ward-Thomas (UK)

One of the world's leading golf writers during his postwar tenure with *The Guardian* and *Country Life*, Cheshire native Pat Ward-Thomas (1913–1982) wrote with a pleasant, highly knowledgeable and very honest style. While rich samplings of his work appeared in the anthology *The Long Green Fairway* (Hodder & Stoughton, 1966), he is equally well remembered as the driving force behind the seminal *World Atlas of Golf* (Mitchell Beazley, 1976), a first-class survey of the world's great courses that included such luminary contributors as Herbert Warren Wind, Charles Price, and Peter Thomson. Ward-Thomas' most fascinating work, however, was surely his autobiography *Not Only Golf* (Hodder & Stoughton, 1981), for it detailed both his being shot down as an RAF pilot during World War II and the subsequent establishment of an improvised golf course for POWs within the fences of Stalag Luft III. Ultimately it would be Ward-Thomas' account of this golfing adventure, mailed to Henry Longhurst, that would begin opening the doors that enabled his celebrated writing career.

Tom Wargo (USA)

A former auto worker and bartender who taught himself to play golf at age 25, Marlette, Michigan, native Tom Wargo (b. 9/16/1942) is a classic rags-to-riches story made possible by the Champions Tour. Having developed into a solid club pro by the 1980s, Wargo joined the Champions in 1993 and soon got everyone's attention with a victory at the **PGA Seniors' Championship.** Three more Champions titles followed in 1994, '95, and 2000, adding up to nearly $7 million in winnings as of this writing. Wargo also won the **Senior British Open** at Royal Lytham & St. Annes in 1994.

Laurie Waters (UK/South Africa)

A youthful assistant to Old Tom Morris at St. Andrews, Lawrence Buddo "Laurie" Waters (1875–1960) was plagued by ill health in his teens and thus followed the common advice of the day, emigrating to one of Great Britain's warmer holdings, in this case South Africa. Though not much more than a quiet, well-liked apprentice in the Old Country, Waters would become, perhaps improbably, an iconic figure in the history and development of golf in southern Africa.

His primary career was that of a club professional, and over the better part of 35 years he held two plum jobs, first at the Royal Johannesburg CC, then up north, at Rhodesia's Royal Salisbury GC. Waters was also a notable player, winning a total of four **South African Opens,** including the first and second official titles, played over 36 holes in 1903 and '04. His last win came at age 45 in 1920, so while depth of field is not an unreasonable question, Waters clearly had some staying power. He also served for many years as South Africa's first noteworthy golf course architect, with his best-known design being the West course at Royal Johannesburg. His name has also been long associated with the nation's finest course, the Durban CC, though in this case Waters only served as a consultant to the club's primary designer George Waterman.

Al Watrous (USA)

Though born in the New York suburb of Yonkers, eight-time PGA Tour winner Al Watrous (1899–1983) lived for most of his professional life in Michigan, where he established himself as a regional powerhouse, capturing nine **Michigan PGA** titles and six **Michigan Opens.** Never a long hitter, Watrous' reliable swing and fine putting stroke saw him to one title of international importance, the 1922 **Canadian Open,** where he edged Mike Kerrigan by one at the Mt. Bruno GC in Quebec. Though a successful participant in the first two Ryder Cup matches (as well as the unofficial international match of 1926), Watrous is equally recalled for falling victim to one of Bobby Jones' most memorable shots, at the 1926 Open Championship at Royal Lytham & St. Anne's. Standing level at the 71st, Jones managed a splendid 170-yard approach out of sandy country, making three a possibility where five had been looming. Unnerved, Watrous promptly three-putted and finished second.

Denis Watson (Zimbabwe)

A native of Salisbury in what was then called Rhodesia, Denis Watson (b. 10/18/1955) was one of those far-flung players who packed off for the European and American PGA Tours sooner rather than later, arriving in America full time in 1981 at age 26. Though his career was riddled by significant injuries to nearly every key part of the golf swing (wrist, elbow, shoulder, and back), Watson did enjoy one overwhelming season when, in 1984, he won the **Buick Open,** the **World Series of Golf,** and the **Las Vegas Invitational,** finished fourth on the money list and narrowly lost out (to Tom Watson) for Player of the Year honors. The following year saw a dip to 48th and an unfortunate occurrence at the U.S. Open where, during the first round, Watson waited half a minute for a putt to fall in off the lip, drawing a two-stroke penalty for creating an undue delay—then ultimately losing the championship to Andy North by a single shot. Battling injuries all the way, Watson only once more saw the top 100 on the Tour money list (43rd in 1987). He becomes eligible for the Champions Tour in 2005.

Howard Watson (Canada)

A native of Dresden, Ontario, Howard Watson (1907–1992) began a career in golf course design with the great architect Stanley Thompson, then with Thompson's disciple Robert Trent Jones. Though hardly decorated on the scale of either of these men, Watson would go on to become one of Canada's more prolific designers, laying out dozens of courses, primarily in Quebec and Ontario, right up into the early 1970s.

Tom Watson (USA)

Kansas City, Missouri, native Thomas Sturges Watson (b. 9/4/1949) came to the game young, his scratch-playing father placing a club in his hands at age six. Growing up under the watchful eye of Stan Thirsk at the Kansas City CC, Watson developed into a four-time **Missouri Amateur** champion, but never finished better than fifth at the U.S. Amateur (still in the silliness of its stroke-play phase) and was comparatively quiet while playing for Stanford University. He did, however, measure up nicely in the classroom, for Watson was never on a golf scholarship and his degree, fully earned, came in the field of psychology.

Joining the PGA Tour in 1972, Watson initially found it rough going, eventually being labeled a "choker" by ever-insightful writers who, to be sure, had themselves broken 100 on at least one or two occasions. Watson did, however, need to "learn how to lose in order to learn how to win," several times blowing solid leads, most obviously at the 1974 U.S. Open at Winged Foot where a 54-hole advantage went up in smoke with a closing 79. Instead of being crushed by this defeat, however, Watson the psychologist bounced back vigorously, taking his first Tour victory only weeks later at the **Western Open** when his closing 69 made up a six-stroke deficit. Further, his Open loss had resulted in an invitation to work with the legendary Byron Nelson, whose ensuing instruction likely aided Watson's confidence every bit as much as his swing.

In 1975 Watson finished ninth at the U.S. Open after leading with a record 36-hole total of 135, but he more than made up for this disappointment three weeks later in Scotland by scoring his Major breakthrough in the **Open Championship** at Carnoustie. This was Watson's first entry in the Open and he won it in exciting style, first by holing a 15-foot birdie putt at the 72nd to tie Australian Jack Newton (with Nicklaus, Johnny Miller, and Bobby Cole but one back), then with a brave four on the 18th hole of their play-off to edge Newton by one.

Though a landlocked Midwesterner with nothing in his background to suggest a particular aptitude for links golf, Watson became the unquestioned modern master of the Open Championship, winning a total of five Claret Jugs in nine years, each at a different venue. His second title was surely the most dramatic, for it came in a classic duel with Nicklaus at Turnberry in 1977, a contest hailed by some as the most exciting Major championship ever played. Paired together for the third round, Watson and Nicklaus both fired scorching 65s to run out to a joint lead, three ahead of Ben Crenshaw. In the finale, their record-setting play continued with Watson trailing until he holed a gargantuan putt from the fringe at the 69th to draw even, then went ahead with a birdie at the par-5 71st when Nicklaus missed a tricky four-footer to match. With Jack in the gorse off the last tee, Watson ripped a 7-iron approach to two feet for the apparent clincher, but could only look on admiringly as Nicklaus somehow hacked his second onto the green, then drained a 35-foot putt to suddenly make Watson's knee-knocker interesting. But arguably the best putter in golf, Watson duly sunk it to claim an epic victory.

The third Claret Jug came in 1980 at Muirfield, where a third-round 64 staked him to a four-stroke lead, a margin he maintained over Trevino with a closing 69. Two years later at Royal Troon it was more a matter of steady play, first waiting out a hot opening 36 from Bobby Clampett (who ultimately faded to a tie for 10th), then posting a final-round 70 and looking on as a young Nick Price staggered home with four late bogeys, allowing Watson to prevail by one. Finally, he took his fifth Open the following year at Royal Birkdale, sealing it with a fine 2-iron approach at the 72nd to beat Hale Irwin and Andy Bean, again by one.

Though in contention on several subsequent occasions, Watson was never to capture that elusive, Vardon-equaling sixth Open title, coming closest in 1984 at St. Andrews (before a final-round disaster at the Road hole left him two behind Ballesteros), and in 1989 at Royal Troon (where he finished two shots out of the Calcavecchia-Grady-Norman play-off). Curiously, just like Vardon, Watson never managed to win at St. Andrews, though he certainly enjoyed success at America's golfing shrine, Augusta National, posting nine top-5 finishes at the **Masters,** including wins in 1977 and '81. In 1977 he defeated Nicklaus by two in a pitched battle won largely with an 18-foot birdie putt at the 71st, the victory foreshadowing the pair's splendid encounter at Turnberry three months later. In 1981 the margin of victory was again two shots, this time over Nicklaus and Johnny Miller.

Watson's most memorable victory, however, came in 1982 at the **U.S. Open,** the title that he clearly coveted the most, being played on this occasion at Pebble Beach, a layout familiar from his Stanford days. Fittingly, it once again came down to a Watson-Nicklaus duel, with Jack in the clubhouse at 284 and Watson needing pars at the 71st and 72nd for a tie. Things suddenly appeared dicey when

his 2-iron at the famous 17th found deep rough just left of the green, though in the end it was all just a setup for more fireworks. For in one of the era's most famous shots, Watson promptly holed the chip, then added another birdie at the last to deny Nicklaus a record fifth Open, winning by two.

All told, the Watson ledger is a highly impressive one, particularly between 1974 and 1984. During these 11 years, he won 36 PGA Tour titles in 226 starts (15.9 percent) as well as eight Major championships in 42 attempts (19 percent). He won the money title five times (1977–80 and '84), consecutive Vardon Trophies from 1977 through 1979, and PGA Player of the Year honors on six occasions (1977–80, '82, and '84). He also rang up a 10-4-1 record over the course of four career Ryder Cup appearances, then captained a victorious team in 1993.

Always a fast swinger of the club, Watson survived on his superior rhythm, though in his prime he did let the occasional wild one fly. He possessed superb recovery and short-game skills, however, and at his peak was one of the finest putters—particularly inside 5 feet—that the game has ever seen. Oddly, his talents would undergo a complete reversal in his late 40s, his putting skills heading dramatically south while his ball-striking improved to a near-elite consistency. He ended a nine-year winless drought with an emotional 1996 victory at Jack Nicklaus' **Memorial Tournament** (where else?) and later proved his longevity by winning the 1998 **Colonial** at age 48 before heading for the lucrative pickings of the Champions Tour. Watson also spent much time and money promoting efforts to cure Lou Gehrig's disease once his longtime caddie Bruce Edwards became afflicted, ultimately passing away during the spring of 2004.

PGA Tour Wins (39): 1974, '77 & '84 Western Open; 1975, '78, '79 & '80 Byron Nelson; **1975, '77, '80, '82 & '83 British Open;** 1977 & '80 San Diego; 1977 & '78 Bing Crosby; **1977 & '81 Masters;** 1979 & '82 Heritage; 1979 & '96 Memorial; 1980 & '82 Los Angeles; 1980 World Series; **1982 U.S. Open;** 1998 Colonial; 4 Tournament of Champions

Intn'l Wins (4): 1984 Australian Open; 1992 Hong Kong Open
Champions Tour Wins: 6 (1999–2003)
Ryder Cup: 1977, '81, '83 & '89 (4); 1993 Capt

1972-1997

	72	73	74	75	76	77	78	79	80	81	82	83	84
Masters	-	-	-	T8	T33	1	T2	T2	12	1	T5	T4	2
US Open	T29	MC	T5	T9	7	T7	T6	MC	T3	T23	1	2	T11
British	-	-	-	1	MC	1	T14	T26	1	T23	1	1	T2
PGA	-	T12	T11	9	T15	T6	T2	T12	T10	MC	T9	T47	T39

	85	86	87	88	89	90	91	92	93	94	95	96	97
Masters	T10	T6	T7	T9	T14	T7	T3	T48	T45	13	T14	MC	4
US Open	MC	T24	2	T36	T46	MC	T16	MC	T5	T6	T56	T13	64
British	T47	T35	7	T28	4	MC	T26	MC	MC	T11	T31	-	T10
PGA	T6	T16	T14	T31	T9	T19	MC	T62	5	T9	T58	T17	MC

Willie Watson (UK/USA)

William Watson came to America in 1898 to work with his fellow Scot Robert Foulis in building the original nine holes at Minnesota's Minikahda Club, site of the 1916 U.S. Open. He then stayed on for several years as the club's pro-greenkeeper while wintering at the Hotel Green in Pasadena, California, where, during his initial season, he laid out one of the better resort nines of the period. His design career continued intermittently until after World War I, when he took up full-time residence in California and became one of that golf-crazed region's busier architects.

Though his work is among the least documented of the Golden Age, Watson's West Coast portfolio features several important projects, including, in 1924, the original 36 holes of San Francisco's Olympic Club, half of which, the world-class Ocean course, landslided into oblivion within a few short winters. Another lost California gem was 1921's Flintridge CC, a barranca-filled track located near Pasadena. Among his still-extant works, Orinda (outside of Oakland) and Midwestern layouts such as Interlachen and Olympia Fields have long garnered substantial attention.

Notable Courses: Belvedere GC, Michigan; **Interlachen CC, Minnesota;** Olympia Fields CC, No. 2 Course, Illinois (NLE); **The Olympic C (36-18 NLE), California;** Orinda CC, California

DeWitt Weaver (USA)

The son of the famous Texas Tech football coach by the same name, Danville, Kentucky, native DeWitt Weaver (b. 9/14/1939) played quarterback at Southern Methodist before eventually turning seriously to golf. Though not especially large, Weaver was a notably long hitter, possibly to the detriment of his overall scoring. He was a regional force in his adopted home state of Georgia but enjoyed only modest success on the PGA Tour, winning the 1972 **Southern Open** as well as a short-lived but intriguing event, the 1971 **U.S. Professional Match Play,** in which he eliminated Julius Boros, George Archer, Bruce Crampton, and Doug Sanders. Weaver later played the Champions Tour, claiming a single victory in 1991.

Karrie Webb (Australia)

Though several others enjoyed regional success in the days before jet travel and substantial prize money made coming to America a viable option, there is little doubt that Queensland's Karrie Webb (b. Ayr, 12/21/1974) is the finest international female player yet produced by Australia. As a youngster of obvious talent, Webb wasted little time competing as an amateur, instead turning professional at age 19 (after winning the 1994 **Australian Women's Stroke Play**) and heading off to both Europe and the American Futures Tour. Selected Rookie of the Year on the WPGET in 1995 (where she won the not-yet-Major **Women's British Open**), Webb qualified for the LPGA Tour in time for the 1996 season.

Getting out of the gate fast, Webb logged top-10 finishes in her first six starts, including a win at her second, the **HealthSouth Inaugural.** From there it was onto three more victories, first place on the money list, and an easy selection as the LPGA's Rookie of the Year. The following two seasons, if slightly less successful, could hardly be called a failure, with a total of five more wins (including another **Women's British Open**) and money rankings of second and fourth. But in 1999 Webb hit a stride that would make her, for a time, the premier woman player in the world, winning six times (including her first Major championship, the **du Maurier**), notching an impressive 22 top-10 finishes in 25 starts, and taking both the money title and, with a then-record scoring average of 69.43, the Vare Trophy. Proving it was no fluke, Webb then came back with an even better year in 2000, repeating her money and Vare honors while winning seven times, including two more Major championships. The first came in March at the **Dinah Shore,** where Webb's 14-under-par 274 total routed Dottie Pepper by 10 shots. Four months later in Libertyville, Illinois, she added her first **U.S. Women's Open** in another runaway, her 282 total besting Meg Mallon and Cristi Kerr by five.

In the three seasons to follow, however, Webb experienced a modest decline of form, winning only six events in total and seeing her money ranking slip to 3rd, 5th, and 11th. In 2001 this drop-off might well have been attributed to focusing heavily on the Majors, for she successfully defended her **U.S. Women's Open** title at Southern Pines and also claimed her first **LPGA Championship** in Wilmington, Delaware, defeating Laura Davies by two to become the sixth (and youngest) woman to claim an LPGA career Grand Slam. Further, with one of her two 2002 victories being in the now fully knighted **Women's British Open** (her third), Webb became the proud holder of the so-called Super Slam, having won all five Majors available during her career.

But by 2003 Webb had fallen further back among the mortals, still playing well enough to win once but generally operating deep within Annika Sorenstam's broad wake. A similar performance in 2004 suggested that while she is still undeniably a world-class player, Webb has, at present, been passed by several younger stars of the Grace Park, Lorena Ochoa, and Se Ri Pak variety.

LPGA Wins (30): 1995, '97 & 2002 **Women's British Open;** 1999 & 2002 Rochester; **1999 du Maurier; 2000 Dinah Shore; 2000 & '01 U.S. Women's Open; 2001 LPGA Championship**

1996-2004

	96	97	98	99	00	01	02	03	04
Dinah	T5	29	T7	3	1	T2	7	T21	3
LPGA	T41	T9	T4	MC	T9	1	T4	T56	T39
US Open	T19	4	T31	7	1	1	MC	MC	T16
dM/Brit*	T2	T27	T14	1	T7	T15	1	T3	-

*du Maurier replaced by the Women's British Open in 2001.

Bobby Weed (USA)

One of many modern architects who began their design careers working for the legendary Pete Dye, Bobby Weed (b. 1955) was also the first greenkeeper at one of Dye's landmarks, the TPC of Sawgrass, before becoming a consultant, then in-house designer for the PGA Tour. In this capacity he laid out several prominent TPC courses in conjunction with well-known players, including the TPC at Summerlin (with Fuzzy Zoeller), the TPC at The Canyons (Raymond Floyd), and the TPC at Tampa Bay (Chi Chi Rodriguez), as well as redesigning the TPC at River Highlands, site of the Greater Hartford Open. Known as a traditionalist who builds his courses "by hand," Weed has also made a name for himself with restorations/renovations of several Golden Age classics, including the Ponte Vedra Club's Ocean course and Timuquana CC, both in Florida. He has also continued, on occasion, to collaborate with his former mentor Dye.

Notable Courses: GC at Glen Mills, Pennsylvania; TPC at Summerlin, Nevada; World Golf Village, Slammer & Squire Courses, Florida

Harry Weetman (UK)

Oswestry, England's Harry Weetman (1920–1972) might well be viewed as a British forerunner of Seve Ballesteros, attacking the ball aggressively, hitting it miles (often terribly off-line), then recovering marvelously, all the while becoming a fan favorite despite a personality that might soothingly be called "quirky." And though Weetman was no Seve in terms of victories, he was certainly among the best of Britain's early postwar pros, twice winning the *News of the World* match play (1951 and '58) and the **British Masters** (1952 and '58). He was also the 1957 **German Open** champion and a four-time winner of the old **Penfold Tournament** (1957, '58, '60, and '62).

Unfortunately, like several of his British contemporaries, Weetman's record in the ultimate test, the Open Championship, was not so favorable, his best finish being a joint fifth at St. Andrews in 1955. He also enjoyed only limited success at the Ryder Cup, appearing in all seven matches from 1951 through 1963 but amassing a disappointing 2-11-2 record. One of his wins, however, was truly an epic, roaring back from four down with six to play to edge Sam Snead one up during the heartbreaking 1953 British loss at Wentworth. Weetman also logged one of the most impressive scores ever recorded anywhere, a scorching 58 over his 6,090-yard home course at Croham Hurst in 1956. He died sadly, and well before his time, in a 1972 car accident.

Mike Weir (Canada)

Arguably Canada's greatest-ever golfer, Sarnia, Ontario's Michael Richard Weir (b. 5/12/1970) plays the game left-handed, an approach he considered altering before asking Jack Nicklaus' advice in a childhood letter and being told to stick with what came naturally. His confidence boosted, Weir became a solid junior player, then a second-team All-American at Brigham Young and a star on the Canadian Tour before beginning full-time American play in 1998. That season saw a disappointing 131st-place finish on the PGA Tour money list but in 1999 Weir rocketed all the way to 23rd, a run highlighted by an ideal first win, the **Air Canada Championship** in Vancouver. He then claimed the 2000 **WGC-American Express** event at Spain's Valderrama GC, followed by the season-ending 2001 **Tour Championship,** a thriller featuring a four-man play-off that included Ernie Els, Sergio Garcia, and David Toms.

In this light 2002 was a minor disaster, a winless season that saw Weir plummet from 11th to 78th on the money list. But with a renewed commitment, 2003 proved the pleasant Canadian's breakthrough year, first with early wins at the **Bob Hope** and the **Los Angeles Open,** then with a dramatic victory at the **Masters.** Around the Augusta lead all week, the red-hot Weir fired a bogey-free 67 on Sunday, only to end up playing off with Len Mattiace who had bogied the 72nd for 65. Mattiace, however, found the woods on the first play-off hole, allowing Weir to win, rather anticlimactically, with a bogey. Adding ties for third at the U.S. Open and seventh at Augusta's PGA Championship, Weir proved his winter/spring play to be no fluke—a point further driven home by his defense of the **Los Angeles** title in 2004, in an exciting back-nine duel with Shigeki Maruyama.

A fine putter and a wizard around the greens, Weir has already appeared in the 2000 and '03 Presidents Cup and began what figures to be a long line of World Cup appearances in 2000.

Tom Weiskopf (USA)

Standing 6′3″ and blessed with what has been universally hailed as one of the finest swings in golf, Thomas Daniel Weiskopf (b. Massillon, Ohio, 11/9/1942) has loomed large over the game since first entering the spotlight in the early 1960s. An obvious talent, Weiskopf claimed the **Western Amateur** at age 20, starred (two years behind Jack Nicklaus) at Ohio State, and the eventually won 16 PGA Tour titles—yet he is equally recalled for a temperament that at times appeared to border on the irrational.

Weiskopf joined the PGA Tour full time in 1965 and by his second season was a fixture among the top 30 money winners, seldom falling from the top 20 until late in the 1970s. Winning at **San Diego** and Michigan's **Buick Open,** he pushed all the way to a career-best third in 1968, a position he would revisit in 1973 and '75. Two more wins came in 1971, then another in 1972 (plus the prestigious **World Match Play** at Wentworth), setting the stage for one of modern professional golf's best-ever worldwide seasons in 1973.

The winning began in May with a one-shot victory over Bruce Crampton and Jerry Heard at **Colonial,** then continued a month later with back-to-back titles at the **Kemper Open** and the **Philadelphia Classic.** June saw perhaps a disappointing third at the U.S. Open (where Johnny Miller's famous final-round 63 rendered all chal-

lenges moot) but July provided Weiskopf's all-time peak, a three-stroke win over Miller and Neil Coles in the **Open Championship** at Royal Troon. Before the month was out he made it a remarkable five wins in eight weeks by adding a two-shot triumph at the **Canadian Open,** then tacked on an unofficial victory at the **World Series of Golf** (under its old four-man format) and a final international title at the **South African PGA.**

Though six more Tour victories remained in Weiskopf's future, he would never again approach his 1973 level of dominance, an outgrowth, he quite rationally explained, of lacking the single-minded desire to win possessed by most of the all-time greats. Still, it is disappointing that so skilled a man failed to win more than a single Major, though his overall record (five top-4 U.S. Open finishes during the 1970s and four seconds at the Masters) was certainly competitive enough. But in the end there always seemed to be the blowup or the odd behavior: backhanding his ball up the 18th fairway at the 1966 Canadian Open before withdrawing; making a 13 at Augusta National's famed 12th in 1980 by repeatedly dunking pitch shots into Rae's Creek; complaining to the press regarding the sort of marker used by his amateur playing partner during the 1996 U.S. Senior Open, and so on.

With 1986 rotator cuff surgery curtailing his Tour career, Weiskopf would later dabble on the Champions Tour during the 1990s, winning four events including the 1995 **U.S. Senior Open.** His primary interest, however, has become golf course architecture, first in a highly successful partnership with Jay Morrish, more recently on an equally flourishing solo basis.

PGA Tour Wins (16): 1968 San Diego; 1973 Colonial; **1973 British Open;** 1973 & '75 Canadian Open; 1978 Doral; 1982 Western Open

Intn'l Wins (4): 1972 World Match Play; 1973 South African PGA; 1981 Benson & Hedges

Ryder Cup: 1973 & '75 (2)

1965-1984

	65	66	67	68	69	70	71	72	73	74
Masters	-	-	-	T16	T2	T23	T6	T2	T34	T2
US Open	T40	-	T15	T24	T22	T30	MC	8	3	T15
British	-	-	-	-	-	T22	T40	T7	1	T7
PGA	-	T72	-	MC	T44	MC	T22	T62	T6	WD

	75	76	77	78	79	80	81	82	83	84
Masters	T2	T9	T14	T11	T41	MC	-	T10	T20	T35
US Open	T29	T2	3	T4	T4	37	-	T39	T24	-
British	15	T17	T22	T17	MC	T16	-	T60	T45	-
PGA	3	T8	T58	T4	MC	T10	T27	MC	T30	MC

Jack Westland (USA)

A prominent Republican congressman from 1953 through 1965, Everett, Washington, native Alfred John "Jack" Westland (1904–1982) was elected to the House shortly after becoming the oldest-ever winner of the **U.S. Amateur,** a feat he accomplished at hometown Seattle GC in 1952 when, at age 47, he defeated Al Mengert 3 and 2. Previously, Westland had appeared on the national stage as a final-round loser in the 1931 Amateur to Francis Ouimet, as winner of the 1933 **Western Amateur,** and as a member of victorious Walker Cup teams in 1932 and '34. Largely embracing only regional competition for the next two decades, he took three straight **Pacific Northwest Amateurs** from 1938 through 1940 (plus a fourth title in 1951) before the 1952 Amateur victory drew him back into the limelight. A 1953 Walker Cup appearance and a victorious nonplaying captaincy in 1961 followed, both taking place while Westland served in Congress.

Lee Westwood (UK)

It has certainly been an up-and-down ride for Lee John Westwood (b. Worksop, 4/24/1973), a talented young Englishman once hailed in the late 1990s as Europe's answer to Tiger Woods. And though such comparisons often appear silly both during and after the fact, Westwood's late-1990s run in Europe and abroad did little to suggest them altogether absurd. Despite coming along at the peak of Colin Montgomerie's powers, Westwood won an impressive 15 European Tour events between 1996 and 2000, steadily climbing the Order of Merit with placings of 6th, 3rd, 3rd, 2nd and, in 2000, the 1st-place finish, which ended Montgomerie's unprecedented seven-year run at the top. Adding to Westwood's growing credentials was a victory at the 1997 **Australian Open**, as well as his ability to win relatively early in America (at the 1998 **New Orleans Classic**), something the formidable Montgomerie has never been able to accomplish.

Yet after Westwood's stunning six-win 2000 (which included a 38th-hole victory over Montgomerie at the **World Match Play**) he endured a baffling loss of form that saw him go winless internationally while plummeting to 52nd and 75th on the Order of Merit in 2001 and '02. Obviously frustrated by what seemed an early end to a potentially great career, Westwood did a spell with instructor David Leadbetter, and in 2003 he seemed on his way back, putting together an uneven season but one that included badly needed wins at the **BMW International** and the **Dunhill Links.** A fairly long hitter and a very skilled putter, Westwood seems at least to be headed back in the right direction, though a relatively quiet 2004 continues to leave his long-term prospects somewhat up in the air.

Intn'l Wins (25): 1997 Australian Open; 1997 Volvo Masters; 1998 Scottish Open; 1999 Dutch Open; 2000 World Match Play
PGA Tour Win: (1)
Ryder Cup: 1997–2002 & 2004 (4)

H. N. Wethered (UK)

An avid if not altogether top-class player, Herbert Newton Wethered (1869–1955) is famous for two golf-related things: fathering the champion amateur siblings Joyce and Roger and authoring two well-known volumes, *The Perfect Golfer* (Methuen, 1931) and *The Architectural Side of Golf* (Longmans, 1929), the latter a joint production with course designer Tom Simpson. Born to the leisure class, Wethered was largely an artist by profession and the several additional titles that he authored generally related to art, history, or literature. There is little evidence to indicate that he was the driving force behind his children's greatly developed skills (the modern athletic parent he wasn't), yet it is difficult to imagine a man who clearly knew so much of the game not being at least somewhat contributory to their resounding successes.

Joyce Wethered (UK)

Born: Brook, England, 11/17/1901 **Died:** London, England, 11/18/1997

It is hardly surprising that, having ended the overwhelming dominance of Cecil Leitch and later come out of retirement to vanquish the great American champion Glenna Collett, England's Joyce Wethered was considered, in her time, the greatest woman golfer ever. What might surprise, however, is that for many the qualifying adjective "woman" wasn't necessary, for no less than Bobby Jones called Wethered the finest golfer—male or female—that he had ever seen, noting "I have not played golf with anyone who made me feel so utterly outclassed." Three-time Open Champion Henry Cotton backed up such praise by adding that "I do not think a golf ball has ever been hit, except perhaps by Harry Vardon, with such a straight flight."

The daughter of H. N. and sister of Roger, Joyce Wethered stood long and lean at 5′10″, allowing her to develop exceptional power while remaining, as Cotton suggests, impressively accurate. Her swing was considered the ideal of its day, built around its much-envied gracefulness and a remarkable sense of balance. She was also an impressively mature player as her competitive arrival indicates, for Wethered was all of 19 when she came out of left field to beat the indomitable Leitch 2 and 1 at Sheringham, capturing the 1920 **English Ladies** championship. She then proceeded to take this event for four

Joyce Wethered

more years in succession, seldom being seriously tested and winning her finals by margins ranging from 7 and 6 to 12 and 11. As Wethered then proceeded to retire (for a while), her five-for-five dominance of the English title could not have been any fuller.

Leitch initially held her ground in the larger British Ladies, however, defeating Wethered in the 1921 final at Turnberry 4 and 3. But a year later, with Joyce hitting peak form, the favor was returned in a 9 and 7 rout at Prince's, and two years hence, in 1924, Wethered easily took her second **British** title at Royal Portrush, defeating Mrs. Cautley 7 and 6. This set the stage for an epic 1925 event at Royal Troon during which Wethered first played 15 semifinal holes in level fours to defeat the reigning American champion and presumed challenger to her throne, Glenna Collett, 4 and 3. In the final she was again matched with the now 34-year-old Leitch and in one of Britain's most memorable matches, Wethered prevailed on the 37th hole.

In 1925, before turning 24, she retired from active competition, stating that "I have simply exercised a woman's prerogative of doing something without the slightest regard for what anybody else thinks and because I want to please myself." But four seasons later, when the **British Ladies** was again played at St. Andrews, Wethered returned to the fray, lured back both by the Old Course and the chance to do battle once more with Glenna Collett. Both favorites found their way through to one of women's golf greatest-ever finals, a match viewed by some 10,000 spectators who saw Collett stand 5 up through 11 before Wethered charged back after lunch, playing the outward half in 35 and ultimately winning at the Road hole 3 and 1.

From there on Wethered was retired permanently, becoming the golf manager at London's Fortnum & Mason department store and competing only in the **Worplesdon Foursomes,** an event she won eight times including once with Bernard Darwin as her partner. Her amateur status jeopardized by her new employment, Wethered tossed it entirely in 1935 when she toured America, playing 53 exhi-

bitions including matches with Gene Sarazen and Walter Hagen. In 1936 she met and married baronet Sir John Amory (becoming Lady Heathcote Amory) and re-retired largely to the happy pastime of gardening. Wethered did keep playing recreationally, however, and served as president of the English Ladies Golf Union once the R&A reinstated her amateur status in 1954.

Roger Wethered (UK)

Son of H. N. and older brother of Joyce, England's Roger Henry Wethered (1899–1983) was himself an elite performer, generally grouped with Cyril Tolley and Ernest Holderness as Britain's best during amateur golf's shining hour, the 1920s. That Roger won "only" a single British Amateur seems, of course, a valid concern, yet an examination of his record suggests a really fine career—albeit one slightly tainted, perhaps, by the expectations associated with the family name.

Then again, such expectations would have been inevitable even had his name been Churchill after the Open Championship of 1921 where, while still an undergraduate at Oxford, he lost to Scottish expatriate Jock Hutchison in a 36-hole play-off at St. Andrews. It was a truly splendid showing for so young a man, particularly on the final day when closing rounds of 72-71 made up lots of ground. As has been widely recounted, Wethered incurred a one-stroke penalty for inadvertently stepping on his ball during the third round, an oddity that has led to some "He would have won the Open if..." sort of thinking. Not true, of course, for there were vastly too many shots left to be played, not the least of which was his pitch to the 72nd that came up shy, found the Valley of Sin, and resulted in a crucial bogey. It is interesting, too, to note that Wethered apparently had to be persuaded to remain at St. Andrews for the play-off, having committed to a cricket match at home on the following day. He stayed, of course, but lost by nine.

Wethered's **British Amateur** title came in 1923 at Deal, where he routed the veteran campaigner Robert Harris 7 and 6 in the final. There were several more close calls during a good late-decade run, including a semifinal appearance in 1927 (where he lost to Dr. Tweddell) and trips to the final in 1928 and '30. The former resulted in a 6 and 4 loss to Phil Perkins at Prestwick while the latter was of particular note, Wethered's 7 and 6 loss to Bobby Jones representing the first leg of the invading American's legendary Grand Slam. That same year Roger served as playing captain of the homestanding Walker Cup team, one of his five appearances in the biennial competition. Given the one-sided nature of the event in those years, his overall record of 5-3-1 was actually quite impressive, especially with two of the losses being singles contests with the indomitable Jones.

Wethered's Achilles' heel was an occasionally erratic driver, a deficiency that his superb iron play and daft recovery skills could not always overcome. Longhurst likened the weakness to Vardon's post-tuberculosis putting, observing that "Just as Vardon missed occasionally and 'unaccountably' from one yard, so did Wethered from time to time unloose a tee shot which earned the awe of the spectators for its splendid inaccuracy."

Wethered had been scheduled to serve as captain of the R&A in 1939, but waited until 1946 owing to the war. Some 26 years later, when the town of St. Andrews memorialized Bobby Jones following his 1972 death, Wethered, as the senior captain in attendance, gave the eulogy.

H. J. Whigham (UK/USA)

Born: Tarbolton, Scotland, 12/24/1869 **Died:** Southampton, New York, 3/17/1954

A Scottish native educated at Oxford, Henry James Whigham would go on to become, without question, one of the great renaissance men of American golf. Initially drawn across the Atlantic (at the behest of C. B. Macdonald) to demonstrate the proper playing of the game at the 1893 Chicago World's Fair, he returned two years later to teach English and economics at nearby Lake Forest College. During what amounted to a three-year stay, he lectured at numerous Midwestern colleges, served as drama critic for the Chicago *Tribune,* and aided in the design of nine holes at the famous Onwentsia Club. Perhaps most memorably, he also won the second and third **U.S. Amateur** championships in overwhelming style, defeating J. G. Thorp 8 and 7 at Shinnecock Hills in 1896, then routing W. R. Betts 8 and 6 at the Chicago GC a year later.

An accomplished writer who authored several books on international affairs, Whigham grabbed another piece of golfing history by penning *How to Play Golf* (Herbert S. Stone, 1897), the first instructional book written on this side of the Atlantic. Following his journalistic inclinations, he then left America in 1898 to cover the Spanish-American and Boer Wars, as well as China's Boxer Rebellion and other international events. Returning to the States in 1907 to help Macdonald design the National Golf Links of America, Whigham eventually married C. B.'s daughter Frances, became editor of *Town & Country* magazine, and reported on both politics and golf for more than two decades.

Charles Whitcombe (UK)

The middle of Somerset's three golfing brothers, Burnham-born Charles Albert (1895–1978) was generally ranked as the best of the Whitcombes, owing both to the widely admired accuracy of his game and a very solid tournament record. He won, for example, the *News of the World* match-play title in 1928 and '30 (defeating a young Henry Cotton on each occasion), the **Irish Open** in 1930, and not less than four of the more significant British professional events of the 1920s. Throughout his long career, however, he was seldom able to do much at the Open Championship, his best chance coming in 1935 at Muirfield when a closing 76 left him in third, five behind winner Alf Perry. He also finished fifth in 1922 at Royal St. George's.

Given that brother Ernest won roughly as many important titles, perhaps what distinguished Charles was his Ryder Cup record, where he appeared in the first six matches (the last two as playing captain), then served as nonplaying captain for the second postwar match in 1949. Also picked for the cancelled 1939 contest, Charles sported a 3-2-4 overall record, which included an 8 and 6 singles rout of Johnny Farrell in 1929.

Ernest Whitcombe (UK)

Though often spoken of as the least-successful of the three Whitcombe brothers, senior sibling Ernest R. (1890–1971) put together a record that hardly sings of inferiority. The winner of at least eight substantial titles at home and on the Continent, his biggest victory was surely the 1924 *News of the World* match play at St. George's Hill—an event he would return to the final of in 1936, at age 46. Also a winner of the **Dutch Open** (1928), the **French Open** (1930), and a pair of **Irish Opens** (1928 and '35), Ernest's record at the Open Championship largely mirrored that of brother Charles, with his one great chance coming in 1924 at Hoylake when the great Walter Hagen nipped him by one. Where Ernest surely fell shy, however, was in the Ryder Cup, where he appeared thrice (1929, '31, and '35) and managed only a 1-4-1 record.

Reg Whitcombe (UK)

The youngest of the three golfing Whitcombes, Reginald Arthur (1898–1957) is a fine example of just how effectively winning the Big One enlivens one's résumé. For taken as a whole, Reg's record in major professional events scarcely matches brother Ernest, never mind the higher-rated Charles. But in addition to an **Irish Open** (1936) and two **Penfold** titles (1934 and '47), Reg managed to land the grand prize, capturing the 1938 **Open Championship** by two over Jimmy Adams, on a final day besieged by a legendary gale at Royal St. George's. Something of a late bloomer, Reg might have *really* enhanced his Open record with a bounce or two, for he also finished second in 1937 (two behind Cotton) and level third in 1939, trailing Dick

Burton by four. Curiously, Whitcombe's only Ryder Cup appearance came before this fine run, when he lost at singles to Johnny Revolta in 1935, though he was also selected for the cancelled 1939 match.

Donna (Horton) White (USA)

A native of Kinston, North Carolina, the then-Donna Horton (b. 4/7/1954) initially attended UNC-Greensboro before graduating from the University of Florida in 1976. While in Gainesville, she lost to Beth Daniel in the final of the 1975 U.S. Amateur (3 and 2 at Massachusetts' Brae Burn CC) but came back a year later to defeat Marianne Bretton 2 and 1 at Sacramento's Del Paso CC to capture the **Amateur** title. A mainstay of the 1976 Curtis Cup team, Horton joined the LPGA Tour during 1977 where, as Donna White, she played for 14 seasons, winning three times (twice in Florida) and taking home close to $1 million.

Jack White (UK)

Pefferside, Scotland's John "Jack" White (1873–1949) was the nephew of the famous North Berwick professional Ben Sayers and is remembered as the first player to break 300 at the **Open Championship,** a feat accomplished when his closing 69 gave him 296 and a one-shot win over James Braid in 1904 at Royal St. George's. Though three previous top-5 finishes might suggest that White's victory was coming due, we must recall that he competed at the height of the Triumvirate's awesome powers. In fact, in winning, he joined Sandy Herd, Harold Hilton, and Arnaud Massy as the only men to break the Vardon-Taylor-Braid stranglehold over the Claret Jug between 1894 and 1912.

Considered among the very finest putters of his day, White was one of the first to apply any technical innovation on the greens, allowing his elbows to hinge outward in order to keep the clubface square throughout and hitting the ball firmly off the toe on short, substantially breaking putts. Not surprisingly, he teamed with that great American putter Walter Travis to pen *The Art of Putting* (Macmillan, 1904), the first book to be dedicated strictly to the use of the blade.

Robert White (UK/USA)

St. Andrean Robert White (1874–1959) emigrated to America at age 20, where he spent several decades working as pro-greenkeeper at such places as Boston's Myopia Hunt Club, Chicago's Ravisloe CC, and New York's Wykagyl CC. Well thought of as a teacher, White also took to laying out courses on the side, his efforts adding up to more than 20 original designs over roughly a 40-year span. Likely his best was today's Pine Lakes International (née Ocean-Forest GC), a deluxe Golden Age club that was the first of the more than 100 currently gracing the modern hotbed that is Myrtle Beach, South Carolina. A charter member of the PGA of America in 1916, White was also a founding member of the American Society of Golf Course Architects in 1946.

Notable Courses: Pine Lakes International GC, South Carolina; Shorehaven GC, Connecticut; Skytop Lodge GC, Pennsylvania

Ronnie White (UK)

In golf there are, from time to time, players whose pure, unadulterated ball-striking skill is so impressive that it seems hardly to matter if those talents vastly outdistance the amount of championship hardware accumulated in their trophy case. And though World War II stands as a partially mitigating circumstance, Wallasey, England's Ronald James White (b. 1921) was surely one such man. His reputation for immaculate tee-to-green play was well established by his late teens, though because of the war, White didn't take his place among Britain's elite amateurs until the end of the 1940s. Even then he only sporadically entered national events, resulting, all told, in only one **English Amateur** title (1949) to show for it. Yet White's reputation preceded him to the degree that no less than Bobby Locke considered him the world's best amateur during the early 1950s, and he was selected to five consecutive Walker Cup teams from 1947 through 1955, accumulating an overall 6-4 record that included singles wins over heavyweights Willie Turnesa, Charlie Coe, and Dick Chapman.

Nelson Whitney (USA)

New Orleans' resident Nelson Whitney was both a prominent player and a member of the USGA Executive Committee, the latter during 1920–21. His competitive record within his home region bore few period equals, particularly in the **Southern Amateur,** which he won on five occasions between 1907 and 1919. Among these wins two stand out: a 1908 victory (4 and 3) over two-time U.S. Amateur champion H. Chandler Egan and a 13 and 12 whitewash of a teenage Perry Adair, both in Memphis. Whitney was also a **Trans-Mississippi Amateur** winner in 1919, and it is a good bet that had the Walker Cup come into existence a few years earlier, he would have been a regular participant. Whitney passed away in 1948.

Ivo Whitton (Australia)

A native of Melbourne, Ivo Harrington Whitton (1893–1967), Australia's most celebrated amateur, was actually a frustrated cricketer who turned to golf only after failing to make real strides at that "other" British game. He ultimately became a stylish player, known for his machine-like precision from tee and fairway, a marvelous short game when needed, and a fedora-like felt hat, which accompanied him through all of his many titles. Perhaps most notably, he generally played with only six clubs: a two-wood, a putter and four irons of varying lofts.

It is not unreasonable to surmise that Whitton's great tee-to-green consistency made him particularly well suited to medal play, as his five **Australian Open** titles easily outdistanced a pair of **Australian Amateurs.** After his initial Open victory (1912) raised some controversy over an apparently friendly ruling on an unplayable lie, Whitton set matters straight by defending his crown in 1913 with a 302 total that broke the tournament record by four. He would later add victories in 1926 and '29 (both at Royal Adelaide) and finally 1931, at the old Australian GC, his record total of five standing until broken by Gary Player in 1970. It is well worth noting, however, that Whitton was denied six additional chances—all during his competitive prime—by the event's wartime cancellation from 1914 through 1919.

Whitton's Australian Amateurs came back-to-back in 1922 and '23, and he was also a finalist in 1913 and '26. In addition, he won multiple state amateur titles in **Victoria** (five) and **Queensland** (three), while also recording a single triumph in **New South Wales.** Later an important administrator who represented Australia on the Rules Committee of the R&A, Whitton left a record of amateur accomplishment that, in these days of lucrative professionalism, seems likely to remain unequaled for quite some time.

Kathy Whitworth (USA)

With the prominent exception of Sam Snead, no American golfer has ever maintained world-class form for as long as Monohans, Texas, native Kathrynne Ann Whitworth (b. 9/27/1939), a feat that allowed her to amass career records for victories, Player of the Year awards, and Vare Trophies that few will ever match. Having attended Odessa Junior College and won the 1957 and '58 **New Mexico Women's Amateur,** the tall (5'9") and lean Whitworth turned professional in time to join the LPGA Tour in 1959, at age 19.

Her initial forays were not unsuccessful, for she finished 26th, 11th and 17th on the money list over her first three seasons, but Whitworth remained winless until the summer of 1962 when she finally broke through at the **Kelly Girls Open** in Ellicott City, Maryland. The following year she blossomed, winning an impressive eight times—a number made really quite remarkable when we recall that 1963 represented Mickey Wright's career peak, in which she set the all-time single-season victory record of 13. Whitworth only claimed a single title (compared to Wright's 11) in 1964 but by 1965, with Wright easing into semi-retirement, Whitworth added eight more triumphs and largely stepped into the number one spot, her stranglehold upon it growing as Wright steadily receded from the scene.

From 1965 through 1969, Whitworth won 42 times in 147 starts (28.6 percent), easily her best clip in a career that, overall, saw her win some 12 percent of the time. She also claimed four of five Player of the Year awards and Vare Trophies during this period, as well as four of her six career Majors: the **Titleholders Championship** in 1965 and '66, and both the **Western Open** and the **LPGA Championship** in 1967. Whitworth would then continue at a lesser, yet decidedly strong pace in the early 1970s, adding 16 more wins between 1971 and 1973, as well as three more Player of the Years and two further Vares. The 1971 and '75 **LPGA Championships** rounded out her Major ledger.

Widely rated as both a first-class shotmaker and one of the very best putters of her time, Whitworth was a highly determined player who soldiered on into her early 50s, in the end remaining competitive as much on guile and guts as any great reservoir of remaining skill. In 1982, a victory at the **Lady Michelob Classic** was her 83rd, passing Mickey Wright as the LPGA's all-time winningest player—though Whitworth graciously (and correctly) stated that regardless, Wright remained the greatest woman golfer of them all. In July of 1984, Whitworth crossed the final hurdle when a victory at the **Rochester International,** her 85th, moved her ahead of Sam Snead as the winningest American golfer of all time.

Unfortunately for Whitworth, in addition to longevity and a page full of victories, she shares one other point in common with Snead: the failure to win a U.S. Open. Like Snead, Whitworth was frequently close, eight times finishing among the top 5, though her highest-ever placing, second in 1971, saw her fully eight shots behind JoAnne Carner at Pennsylvania's Kahkwa CC. In point of fact, Whitworth's overall record in the Majors must be viewed as disappointing, for in winning only 6.3 percent of those that she entered (six for 95), she actually saw her game diminish substantially under the brightest spotlight.

With her career total of 88 victories and an obvious place in the LPGA Hall of Fame, Whitworth was a natural choice to captain the first two American Solheim Cup teams in 1990 and '92. Though a family emergency necessitated her replacement in the latter match, the 1990 squad's 11½–4½ inaugural victory in Orlando certainly proved a fitting way to end one of women's golf all-time great careers.

LPGA Wins (88): 1965, '68, '69, '70 & '74 Orange Blossom; **1967 Western Open;** 1965 & '66 Titleholders; 1967, '71 & '75

LPGA Championship; 1968 & '73 Dallas Civitan; 1977 Dinah Shore; 1984 Rochester; 3 Raleigh Golf Classics, 3 Southgate Opens & 3 Lady Carling Opens, Maryland
Solheim Cup: 1990 & '92 Capts

1959-1984

	59	60	61	62	63	64	65	66	67	68	69	70	71
Dinah													
LPGA	T18	T11	17	T4	T6	T3	4	T10	1	2	T6	2	1
US Open	T32	T9	16	T10	T5	9	T18	T5	T15	T5	3	T4	2
du Maur													

	72	73	74	75	76	77	78	79	80	81	82	83	84
Dinah											T2	T10	
LPGA	T12	3	T10	1	T17	10	T33	MC	MC	-	T21	-	-
US Open	T19	T29	T4	6	MC	T10	T34	T40	MC	3	T29	DQ	T10
du Maur								T26	T14	T25	T38	T21	T19

Also won Western Opens and Titleholders, as listed above.

Michelle Wie (USA)

In more than 160 years of recorded golf, it is doubtful that anyone—with the possible exception of Bob Jones—has had as large an impact on the game at so early an age as young Michelle Sung Wie. A native of Honolulu, Wie (b. 10/11/1989) began playing golf at age four and was capable of breaking par by age 10, the year she made history as the youngest-ever qualifier for the USGA Women's Public Links. Always tall for her age and capable of generating remarkable power, Wie won the **Hawaiian Women's Stroke Play** title at age 11, then got her first real national attention by qualifying for the LPGA Tour's 2002 Takefuji Classic at age 12—the youngest player ever to win a spot in an LPGA field.

Though missing the cut on that occasion, Wie came back in 2003 to try to qualify for the PGA Tour's Hawaiian Open—a seemingly over-the-top move that proved at least marginally realistic when she shot 73, finishing 47th in a field of 97. Two months later, entered on a sponsor's exemption, the now-6'0" Wie played in an LPGA Major championship, the Dinah Shore, and shocked the golfing world by finishing ninth. Further, a stunning third-round 66 actually put her squarely in contention, and she played in Sunday's final pairing before a closing 76 dropped her back. After so remarkable a display, a **Women's Public Links** title in June seemed almost expected (though at 13 she was easily the event's youngest winner), as did a 39th-place finish at the U.S. Women's Open.

Wie began 2004 by turning whatever few heads weren't already staring intently in her direction by appearing in the PGA Tour's Hawaiian Open on a sponsors exemption, then shooting 72-68 to miss the cut by a single stroke. Not taken seriously by most astute observers beforehand, her unbelievable performance left little doubt that the legend was, to an impressively high degree, very real—and that she had surpassed a slumping Tiger Woods as the hottest commodity in golf. After a fourth-place finish at March's 2004 Dinah Shore, a starring performance on a victorious Curtis Cup team and a tie for 13th at the U.S. Women's Open, speculation has rapidly turned to if and when Wie might turn professional, for she has clearly proven herself a world-class player despite not yet being old enough to drive.

To date, Wie's game has been primarily based on power as pound for pound she may be the greatest driver of the golf ball in history. The rest of her arsenal, though obviously of a high standard, is slightly less developed, a point that could suggest future pitfalls, but just as easily might indicate great potential for significant improvement. Bobby Jones, the record book tells us, went to the U.S. Amateur quarter-finals at age 14, yet failed to win his first Major championship for seven full years. To what degree Wie can follow in Jones' footsteps remains to be seen, but the prospect of watching this almost freakish talent blossom is the most compelling story in golf today.

Dave Williams (USA)

Though coaching college golf is generally far more about recruiting and motivating than actually teaching anything concrete, a handful of men have done it noticeably better than the competition, none more so than the University of Houston's legendary Dave Williams (1918–1998). For Williams won an unprecedented 16 national titles between 1952 and 1987, including a modern record of five straight from 1956 through 1960, then six out of seven between 1964 and 1970. Though considered a relative novice regarding golf technique, Williams could surely recruit, with players like Fred Couples, John Mahaffey, Bruce Lietzke, Fuzzy Zoeller, Steve Elkington, and even Nick Faldo (though only for one year) developing their games under his supervision. Williams was also something of an innovator, leading the trend away from two-school duel matches and towards the more cost-effective and competitive multiteam stroke-play events. He also believed in keen competition among his own players; indeed Mahaffey was the NCAA individual champion in 1970, yet he only appeared in roughly half of Houston's matches because his daily qualifying scores weren't always strong enough. Oklahoma State's Mike Holder, Wake Forest's Jesse Haddock and others have also seen great success, but nothing to approach the record of Dave Williams.

Harry Williams (Australia)

A nearly forgotten tragedy of Australian golf, Harry Williams (1915–1961) was an eccentric, a lefthander, perhaps mentally ill, and certainly, according to those who saw him play, as talented an amateur as Australia has ever produced. A native of Melbourne, he twice won the **Australian Amateur,** first in 1931 at the improbably young age of 16, then again in 1937. In between he finished second to Gene Sarazen in the 1936 Australian Open, later passing up a lucrative offer from Sarazen to travel to America and turn pro.

An utterly dominant local player who won the **Victorian Amateur** five times, Williams was lionized for decades by contemporary competitors such as Norman von Nida and Jim Ferrier. Unfortunately, an unstable sort from the start, he abruptly walked away from tournament golf at age 24, entering a life of dead-end jobs, shady associates, and the occasional appearance on one of Melbourne's public golf courses. Despite coming from an affluent family, he died penniless, and at his own hand, at age 46.

Dick Wilson (USA)

Though thoroughly associated with the modern, postwar era of golf course design, Philadelphia-born Louis Sibbett "Dick" Wilson (1904–1965) possessed a pedigree rooted in the ultra-classical. Following a football career at the University of Vermont, Wilson returned home to join the construction crew that handled William Flynn's 1925 redesign of Merion, eventually signing on with the firm of Toomey & Flynn full time.

Wilson formed his own Florida-based design company shortly after the war, hiring associates such as Joe Lee and Robert von Hagge, and soon established himself as the prime challenger to Robert Trent Jones atop the American architectural heap. His style, if not as aesthetically pleasing as his Golden Age predecessors, was certainly functional, with elevated green complexes, extensive bunkering, and enough yardage—at least from the tips—to make any of his courses a challenge. Wilson's base of operation and timing were perfect, for with golf's postwar explosion in Florida, he was able to fill out his résumé with such Sunshine State designs as Pine Tree, Doral's Blue Monster, and the old JDM CC (now known as BallenIsles), site of the 1971 PGA Championship. But Wilson also built famous courses in the West (San Diego's La Costa CC), the Midwest (36 holes each at Cog Hill and NCR), the Northeast (Laurel Valley and Deepdale), Canada (45 holes at Royal Montreal), South America, the Bahamas, and even Cuba.

Dick Wilson was not above taking on the occasional modernization job, though in hindsight he might well have wished that he hadn't. His grassing over of some of William Flynn's splendid bunkering at Miami Beach's Indian Creek CC and his general dismembering of several of golf's most unique holes at Los Angeles' Bel-Air have perhaps turned attention disproportionally away from an otherwise well-received body of original work.

Notable Courses: Cog Hill GC, No. 4 Course, Illinois; Deepdale CC, New York; Doral CC, Blue Course, Florida; **Laurel Valley GC, Pennsylvania;** Meadow Brook C, New York; **NCR CC, South Course, Ohio;** Pine Tree CC, Florida

Enid Wilson (UK)

Derbyshire's Enid Wilson (b. 3/15/1910) was an icon of British golf, first as a premier player, then as a journalist of great standing following her retirement. Initially making noise as the 1925 **British Girls** champion, Wilson finished runner-up in the 1927 **English Ladies** before winning the title in 1928 and '30. Thus fully warmed up, she proceeded to make history by following Lady Margaret Scott and Cecil Leitch as only the third woman to capture three consecutive **British Ladies** titles, first routing Wanda Morgan at Portmarnock in 1931, then beating Clementine Montgomery and Diana Plumpton in '32 and '33, at Saunton and Gleneagles, respectively.

Though a relatively early retiree from the competitive scene, Wilson did participate in the inaugural 1932 Curtis Cup match (scoring a singles victory over Helen Hicks) and several times entered the U.S. Women's Amateur, reaching the semifinals in 1931 and '33. Following the war (wherein her left eye was damaged during the 1941 blitz), she became a well-known golf writer, covering the ladies' game for the *Daily Telegraph*, authoring an engaging book, *A Gallery of Women Golfers* (Country Life, 1961), and generally presiding as a knowledgeable and supportive chronicler of the game.

Hugh Wilson (USA)

A Princeton graduate and an insurance broker by trade, Philadelphian Hugh Irvine Wilson (1879–1925) was a capable amateur golfer assigned the task of designing a new course for his home club, Merion, in 1910. In preparation, Wilson took an extended trip to the United Kingdom to visit the classic courses and proved himself a quick study, for upon returning home he designed a splendidly strategic course that, with modifications to five holes in 1925, would go on to host four U.S. Opens and remains today a consensus choice among the 20 finest courses in the world.

Wilson's health, however, was never the strongest and he would die at a young age in 1925. By that time, he had added a Merion's shorter West course, public layouts in suburban Phoenixville (nine holes) and for the city of Philadelphia at Cobb's Creek, and the original Bay course at Seaview CC near Atlantic City. Not brought to fruition was a plan for a design partnership with his close friend William Flynn, the potential fruits of which remain tantalizingly on display in Merion's five altered holes (the first, and numbers 10-13) which were, to a large degree, a collaboration between the two.

President Woodrow Wilson (USA)

The 28th president, Woodrow Wilson (1856–1924) was a lifetime golfer, having developed his love for the game during his student, teaching, and administrative days at Princeton. Despite such enthusiasm, however, Wilson ranked among the less-talented of White House players, seldom breaking 100 and, swinging with virtually no follow-through, hitting a slice of sometimes epic proportion. Indulging regularly while in office, Wilson was in the midst of a friendly 1915 foursome at the Chevy Chase CC when he received word of the sinking of the Lusitania, which catapulted the United States into World War I.

Herbert Warren Wind (USA)

Born: Brockton, Massachusetts, 8/11/1916 **Died:** Bedford, Massachusetts, 5/30/2005

The dean of American golf writers, Herbert Warren Wind graduated from Yale University in 1937, then journeyed to England to earn a Masters degree at Cambridge in 1939. Fascinated by golf after seeing such stars as Francis Ouimet, Gene Sarazen, and Walter Hagen play during his youth, Wind became fully addicted to the game while in Britain, attending the 1938 Walker Cup matches at St. Andrews and meeting the great Bernard Darwin.

Wartime saw Wind stationed in both China and, during the occupation, Tokyo. Upon returning Stateside, he landed a job writing profiles for the *New Yorker* while also researching and writing his first book, the epic *Story of American Golf* (Farrar, Strauss, 1948). An enduring classic that has been reprinted as recently as 2000, this masterpiece opened numerous literary doors, paving the way for famous biographical collaborations with Gene Sarazen and Jack Nicklaus, as well as with Ben Hogan for the instructional epic *The Modern Fundamentals of Golf* (A. S. Barnes, 1957). Another period work, *The Complete Golfer* (Simon & Schuster, 1954) showed Wind as a most astute editor, for a half-century later, this remains among the very best anthologies of golf material ever assembled.

Blessed with a pleasant, informative style that is at once extremely learned yet relaxed and highly accessible, Wind gained great fame as a writer and editor in the early years of *Sports Illustrated*, then for his expansive essays on all aspects of golf upon returning to the *New Yorker* in 1962. Two anthologies of Wind's magazine work can be deemed essential, *Herbert Warren Wind's Golf Book* (Simon & Schuster, 1971) and *Following Through* (Ticknor & Fields, 1985) as they represent, quite simply, the best that American golf writing has ever had to offer.

Bo Wininger (USA)

Chico, California, native Francis G. "Bo" Wininger (1922–1967) was a star collegian at Oklahoma State before playing the PGA Tour during the 1950s and early '60s. The winner of six Tour events overall, Wininger was most successful in New Orleans, where he won the **New Orleans Open** in 1962 (by two over Bob Rosburg), then defended the title in 1963 (by three over Rosburg and Tony Lema). He also finished second in the Canadian Open in 1957 and '59, with his best Major championship finish being fourth, three shots behind Dave Marr, at the 1965 PGA Championship.

Tom Winton (UK)

The son of a professional and clubmaker in Montrose, Scotland, Tom Winton (1871–1944) moved to London in his mid-20s, then emigrated to America at the start of World War I, ostensibly to do construction work for Willie Park Jr. When Park's business proved too light to support him, Winton latched on as superintendent for the

Westchester County (New York) Parks Commission, in which capacity he built several public courses for the county, in addition to picking up additional commissions from Massachusetts to as far south as Virginia. Though his designs clearly were tempered somewhat for municipal play, Winton did utilize the occasional deep bunker or steeply elevated green.

Gerry de Wit (Netherland)

Far and away the most successful of Dutch golfers, Wassenaar native Gerard de Wit (b. 1918) thoroughly dominated that country's closed events in the years after World War II, winning both the **National Closed Championship** and the **Closed PGA** a remarkable 14 times each. Skeptics will point out that even with a home-field advantage, de Wit never managed to win so much as a single Dutch Open (though he did lose thrice in play-offs) and their point is well taken. But de Wit did appear in three Masters (1962–64) and on at least one occasion gave cause to think him internationally competitive, beating Byron Nelson head-to-head in a 1963 episode of *Shell's Wonderful World of Golf*.

P. G. Wodehouse (UK)

In a game where attempts at literary humor often seem stale or forced, Sir Pelham Grenville "P. G." Wodehouse, K.B.E. (1881–1975) stands out as a terribly obvious exception. Wodehouse was a talented all-around man with a pen, writing over 70 novels, 300 short stories, and some 500 essays and articles, but what directly concerns us are the several dozen short stories that revolved, most hilariously, around golf. The majority were published in two volumes, *The Clicking of Cuthbert* (Herbert Jenkins, 1922) and *The Heart of a Goof* (Herbert Jenkins, 1926), both of which were released in America, with different titles, shortly thereafter. A more complete volume, which included the remaining few stories that would comprise the whole of Wodehouse's golfing repertoire, was published decades later as *The Golf Omnibus* (Barrie & Jenkins, 1973).

Liv (Forsell) Wollin (Sweden)

Before there was a prominent national junior program to produce the likes of Liselotte Neumann, Helen Alfredsson and Annika Sorenstam, Swedish women's golf existed largely in the form of Liv Wollin (b. 4/17/1946), a 10-time winner of the nation's **Closed Ladies** titles as well as a World Amateur Team player for 10 consecutive years.

Though regional competition was not yet at its steepest, Wollin also won seven **Scandinavian Open Amateurs** between 1963 and 1972, as well as scattered foreign titles including those of **Portugal** (1967) and **Morocco** (1972). Though unquestionably a pioneering figure, Wollin's place has largely been overtaken by the impressive international success enjoyed by the recent generation of world-class Swedish professionals.

Guy Wolstenholme (UK/Australia)

Leicester, England, native Guy Wolstenholme (1931–1984) first came to notice in the latter half of the 1950s as an elite British amateur, winning the **English** and **German** titles twice and playing on losing Walker Cup teams in 1957 and '59. Turning professional in 1960, he enjoyed a solid if unspectacular career on what was not yet officially the European Tour, winning national Opens in **Denmark, Kenya,** and the **Netherlands,** the **Volvo PGA,** and additional events in Japan and Australia. Apparently smitten with what he found Down Under, Wolstenholme resettled in Australia during the mid-1960s, going on to represent that country in international play by 1971. He also won a record four **Victorian Opens** (1971, '76, '78 and '80) with the middle two coming in sudden death over Graham Marsh and Arnold Palmer, respectively. The father of three-time British Walker Cup player Gary, Guy Wolstenholme lost a long and arduous battle with cancer in 1984.

Craig Wood (USA)

Born: Lake Placid, New York, 11/18/1901 **Died:** Palm Beach, Florida, 5/8/1968

Perhaps as popular a player among his peers as has ever teed it up, Craig Ralph Wood came out of Lake Placid, New York, to make a major splash in golf during the game's prewar Golden Age. The son of a timber company foreman, Wood was big, blond, and exceptionally powerful, yet he also possessed the sort of refined skills that led to 21 victories on the PGA Tour between 1928 and 1944. As a glamour figure golf has seen few grander, for Wood married a beautiful New York heiress and lived the jet-set life when jet-setters traveled by Packard. Yet he was universally hailed as the ultimate non-celebrity, a down-to-earth man who routinely helped younger players and remained modest to the core. Indeed, Sam Snead once called him "the nicest guy I think I've ever seen."

On the links, Wood was a long and superbly straight driver of the ball, an earlier version of Greg Norman. And beyond the driving, blond hair, and gregarious lifestyles, the Wood-Norman similarities hold one more unfortunate component, for Craig Wood was among the unluckiest golfers of all time. Like Norman, Wood lost all four Major championships in play-offs. At the Masters, he was the victim of Gene Sarazen's miraculous double eagle, his seemingly insurmountable three-shot lead vanishing in a heartbeat before Sarazen beat him over 36 holes the next day. At the U.S. Open it was Byron Nelson holing a 1-iron during their 1939 play-off, after he and Wood had tied over the initial extra 18. In Britain Wood had largely himself to blame, driving into the Swilcan Burn to commence a 1933 Open Championship play-off at St. Andrews, ultimately losing to Denny Shute by five strokes. And then, inevitably, there was the 1934 PGA Championship. Facing his own former assistant Paul Runyan in the final, Wood hit his second shot on the first play-off hole, a par 5, to just 9 feet while Runyan needed a deflection off of a car tire just to lie 60 yards short in the fairway. Runyan wedged to a foot, Wood missed, and Runyan closed him out on the 38th.

As his 21 titles testify, however, Wood also knew how to win and in 1941, at age 39, he finally broke through to become the first man ever to capture the **Masters** and the **U.S. Open** in the same season, the former by three over Byron Nelson, the latter by the same margin over Denny Shute. By this time, however, any Grand Slam aspirations had died amidst the wartime cancellation of the Open Championship, with the conflict soon removing most big-event play from what little remained of Wood's prime.

After serving as the golf professional at Winged Foot during the war years, Wood would ultimately retire to the Bahamas and Florida, outliving his wife and dying childless in 1968.

PGA Tour Wins (21): 1933 Los Angeles; 1940 Metropolitan; **1941 Masters; 1941 U.S. Open;** 1942 Canadian Open
Ryder Cup: 1931–35 (3)

1925-1949

	25	26	27	28	29	30	31	32	33	34	35	36	37
Masters										2	2	T20	T26
US Open	T51	-	46	MC	T16	T9	-	T14	3	DQ	T21	T66	T36
British	-	-	-	-	-	-	-	-	2	-	-	-	-
PGA	-	-	-	-	T5	-	-	T17	-	2	-	T3	T17

	38	39	40	41	42	43	44	45	46	47	48	49
Masters	T34	6	T7	1	T23				WD	T53	T43	34
US Open	-	2	4	1					MC	-	MC	T27
British	-	-								-	-	-
PGA	-	-	T17	T17	T5		T9	-	-	-	-	T33

Tiger Woods (USA)

And then there was Tiger Woods.

In an era when many felt that enhanced equipment, a deeper talent pool, and the reduced incentive brought on by massive purses made another Nicklaus or Hogan an impossibility, Cypress, California, native Eldrick "Tiger" Woods (b. 12/30/1975) proved the skeptics wrong. The son of a retired army Green Beret who introduced him to the game as soon as he could walk, Woods appeared on Mike Douglas' television program at age two, having a putting contest with legendary comedian Bob Hope. But unlike many showcased juniors, Woods' early skills continued to blossom, and from 1991 through 1993 he established himself as the first-ever three-time winner of the **USGA Junior Boys** title, also appearing in the 1992 Los Angeles Open on a sponsor's exemption (and missing the cut) at age 16. Coming of age, he smoothly adjusted his game to the amateur ranks where from 1994 through 1996 Woods made more history as the first man since Bobby Jones to win three **U.S. Amateur** titles—and the only one ever to claim three in succession. His third and final victory, a memorable come-from-behind triumph over University of Florida star Steve Scott, came shortly on the heels of a 1996 **NCAA** individual title, won while playing for Stanford.

Turning professional soon thereafter, Woods finished joint 60th in his first start, the Greater Milwaukee Open, then promptly won twice (at **Las Vegas** and **Walt Disney World**) to successfully avoid the PGA Tour's dreaded Qualifying Tournament and to justify the faith of sponsors who'd armed him with $60 million in endorsement deals prior to hitting his first professional shot. Yet in hindsight, the investments in Woods seemed natural for, aside from his ability to win, he brought a powerful, aggressive style to the game, overpowering golf courses with

Tiger Woods

his immense length, covering any mistakes with a stunning short game, and holing enough putts to keep the whole show moving. Further, Woods brought an entirely new demographic to the game, being a rich mix of Black, Indian, Asian, and Caucasian, a pedigree that he has admirably downplayed simply as "Caublasian." Golf's popularity—at least on television—skyrocketed during Tiger's ascent, making him a godsend for a PGA Tour short on interesting personalities.

In April of 1997, Woods made history as the first minority golfer to win a Major championship by taking the **Masters** with a record 270 total, routing Tom Kite by 12. This breakthrough was the centerpiece of a four-win, Player of the Year season that firmly established him among the game's elite. A disappointing 1998 followed (one win, fourth place on the money list) as Woods' friend Mark O'Meara dominated the year's play but by 1999, with some swing alterations orchestrated by teacher Butch Harmon, Woods was back in top form. Indeed, that summer he

became the first player since Johnny Miller in 1974 to win eight Tour events in a season, easily claiming both the Vardon Trophy and Player of the Year, awards he would monopolize straight on through 2003.

But if 1999 had been a great year, 2000 proved an epic. For after finishing fifth at the Masters, Woods was literally a field of one in the **U.S. Open** at Pebble Beach, his record-tying 272 beating the pack by a mind-boggling 15 shots while breaking the Major championship margin-of-victory record of 13, set by Old Tom Morris in 1864. A month later he journeyed to St. Andrews where his 19-under-par 269 total won the **Open Championship** by 12, establishing Woods as the fifth (and youngest) man to complete the career Grand Slam. Finally, in August, though hardly playing his best, Tiger fought off a spirited challenge from upstart Bob May to win the **PGA Championship** in a three-hole play-off, making him only the second player in history (after Ben Hogan in 1953) to win three professional Majors in a single season. With six additional Tour victories thrown in for good measure, it was a very good year.

Though 2001 would not add up quite so impressively, it was history-making nonetheless, for by edging Duval to win his second **Masters,** Woods became the only player ever to hold golf's four Major championships simultaneously. The result, in addition to some splendid trophy-filled photo ops, was a rash of media hype attempting to label it a Grand Slam—which, quite obviously, it wasn't. It was, however, the single most impressive feat in the history of competitive golf which, one hopes, might stand up well enough on its own.

A year later Woods claimed his third Green Jacket and by now, not surprisingly, was at least as intimidating to his fellow competitors as Nicklaus or Hogan had ever been, winning with an unspectacular final-round 71 as the likes of Els, Phil Mickelson, and Retief Goosen appeared to stumble all over themselves attempting to clear his path. When Woods took a relatively unexciting victory at the **U.S. Open** at New York's Bethpage State Park in June (beating Mickelson by three), a real Grand Slam seemed perhaps in the offing. But at the Open Championship, trailing halfway leader Els by two, Woods fired an inglorious third-round 81 in extreme conditions to end such aspirations, at least for another year.

And then a funny thing happened. Following a so-so (read Major-less) 2003 that began with arthroscopic knee surgery, Woods found himself mired in his first professional slump, a serious affair that saw him spraying shots all over the golf course, remaining competitive only through his splendid grit and spectacular short game. A rabid press speculated on the cause: his breakup with Butch Harmon perhaps, or maybe his engagement and subsequent marriage to Swedish model/au pair Elin

Nordegren. It all made for terribly interesting viewing in 2004 and painted a large question mark over Woods' otherwise rosy competitive future.

For some, the prospect of a non-dominant Tiger is both disappointing and commercially ominous, taking away materially from professional golf's marketability. For others, who recall the perceived arrogance of his early years (e.g., refusing to sign golf balls to be donated to a charity fundraiser), Tiger's prospective demise is not unwelcome. His play-off victory at the 2005 **Masters** certainly showed Woods capable of rising once again, though at present his game far more resembles the wildly scrambling antics of an in-his-prime Ballesteros than the awesomely powerful,

ultra-precise machine that was the turn-of-the-century Tiger.

PGA Tour Wins (40): 1997, 2001 & '02 Masters; 1997 Byron Nelson; 1997, '99 & 2003 Western Open; 1999 & 2003 San Diego; 1999, 2000 & '01 Memorial; **1999 & 2000 PGA Championship;** 1999, 2000 & '01 World Series; 2000 Bing Crosby; **2000 & '02 U.S. Open; 2000 British Open;** 2000 Canadian Open; 2001 Players Championship; 2003 & '04 WGC-Match Play; 4 Bay Hill Invitationals & 3 WGC-American Express
Intn'l Wins (7): 1998 & 2000 Johnnie Walker
Walker Cup: 1995 **Ryder Cup:** 1997–2004 (4) **Presidents Cup:** 1998–2003 (3)

1995-2004

	95	96	97	98	99	00	01	02	03	04
Masters	T41	MC	1	T8	T18	5	1	1	T15	T22
US Open	WD	T82	T19	T18	T3	1	T12	1	T20	T17
British	T68	T22	T24	3	T7	1	T25	T28	T4	T9
PGA	-	-	T29	T10	1	1	T29	2	T39	T24

Ian Woosnam (UK)

Though born on the English side of the border in Owestry, Ian Harold Woosnam, M.B.E. (b. 2/2/1958) came from Welsh parents and learned his golf on a course (Llanymynech) that has three holes in England and 15 in Wales. A shortish fellow at just a shade under 5′5″, his days spent baling hay on the family farm turned Woosnam into a stocky, powerful man who was in no way overmatched by the game's longer hitters.

Hailed as one of Europe's top young prospects of the early 1980s, Woosnam initially cut his teeth on the off-season African Safari Tour, then hit his stride on the European Tour in 1982, commencing a 16-year run in which he was only once out of the top 12 in the Order of Merit, and twice number one (1987 and '90). All told he has won 31 European events as of this writing, including the national Opens of six nations, the 1994 **British Masters** (by four over Seve Ballesteros), and the 1997 **Volvo PGA** (by two over Nick Faldo, Ernie Els, and Darren Clarke). Woosnam also holds the distinction of winning the **World Match Play** at Wentworth in three different decades, taking titles in 1987 (one up over Sandy Lyle), 1990 (4 and 2 over Mark McNulty), and 2001 (2 and 1 over Padraig Harrington). He has represented Wales 14 times in World Cup play.

A regular presence toward the top of Major championship leaderboards from the mid-1980s on, Woosnam gained great fame by becoming the fourth straight British winner of the **Masters** in 1991 when he outdueled José Maria Olazábal and 41-year-old Tom Watson in an old-fashioned Augusta thriller. All three players needed pars at the 72nd to finish –11, but while Olazábal bogeyed and Watson took six, Woosnam smartly drove his ball left, into the wide open practice fairway, and won the Green jacket with a simple four.

Unfortunately, Woosnam gained Major championship notice of a different kind during the final round of the 2001 Open Championship at Royal Lytham & St. Annes. Tied for the lead through 54 holes, he proceeded to move ahead with a tap-in birdie at the par-3 opener, only to be penalized two strokes upon the discovery of a 15th club in his bag on the second tee. Woosnam, to his credit, admirably hung together, recovering from the colossal caddie blunder with a gutsy 71 to ultimately tie for third.

Intn'l Wins (36): 1982 Swiss Open; 1987, '90 & '96 Scottish Open; 1987 Hong Kong Open; 1987 & '93 Trophée Lancôme; 1987, '90 & 2001 World Match Play; 1994 British Masters; 1996 Johnnie Walker; 1996 German Open; 1997 Volvo PGA
PGA Tour Wins (2): 1991 Masters
Ryder Cup: 1983–97 (8)

1982-2002

	82	83	84	85	86	87	88	89	90	91	92
Masters	-	-	-	-	-	-	MC	T14	T30	1	T19
US Open	-	-	-	-	-	-	-	T2	T21	T55	T6
British	T80	MC	T64	T16	T3	T8	T25	T49	T4	T17	75
PGA	-	-	-	-	T30	MC	WD	6	T31	T48	-

	93	94	95	96	97	98	99	00	01	02
Masters	T17	T46	T17	T29	T39	T16	T14	T40	MC	MC
US Open	T52	MC	T21	T79	MC	MC	-	-	-	-
British	T50	MC	T47	MC	T24	T55	T24	T68	T3	T37
PGA	T22	T9	MC	T36	MC	T29	MC	MC	T51	MC

Lew Worsham (USA)

Virginian Lew Worsham (1917–1990) was a former caddie who came up the old-fashioned way, ultimately winning six times on the PGA Tour, twice in memorable fashion. Perhaps the most unforgettable came at the 1953 edition of the highly lucrative **World Championship of Golf**, played outside of Chicago. There at the 72nd hole, a 410-yard creek-fronted par 4, Worsham needed a birdie to catch fellow Virginian Chandler Harper, but instead proceeded to knock his 104-yard wedge shot directly into the hole, winning the title and $25,000. The other unforgettable event had taken place six years earlier, when Worsham faced Sam Snead in a play-off for the **U.S. Open** at the St. Louis CC. With the players still level through 17 holes and Snead preparing to stroke a short putt for par at the 18th, Worsham suddenly requested a measurement. USGA rules chief Ike Grainger called for a tape measure and confirmed that Snead was indeed slightly away. Rattled by the entire process, however, Snead missed, allowing Worsham to tap in and capture his lone Major championship.

Ben Wright (UK/USA)

Few voices were more familiar to international golf fans during the 1980s and '90s than that of John Bentley-Wright (b. 1932), known, since his journalistic debut in 1954, simply as Ben Wright. A former golf correspondent and/or regular contributor to the *Daily Dispatch*, the *Daily Mirror*, *Sports Illustrated*, *Golf World* (UK) (of which he was a founder), the London *Financial Times*, and the BBC, among others, Wright's popularity exploded in America after taking up residence on CBS's PGA Tour broadcasts during the mid-1970s. His was a significant on-air presence, pumped up a bit by famed producer Frank Chirkinian who, it can be fairly said, often utilized Wright's marvel-

ous style and Britishness over his deep and abiding knowledge of the game. Seldom one to shy away from an honest opinion, Wright got in trouble in 1995 when repeating comments made to him by potential LPGA Tour sponsors regarding lesbianism, and recalling an interview he'd done with Hall of Famer JoAnne Carner regarding challenges peculiar to the female golf swing. In the ensuing media frenzy, he found himself branded a sexist—and rather quickly sacked by CBS.

Since that time Wright has busied himself with freelance writing, a bit of golf course design, and the authoring of *Good Bounces & Bad Lies* (Sleeping Bear, 1999), a detailed and engaging retrospective of his life in golf.

Bill Wright (USA)

A native of Seattle, Washington, Bill Wright quietly made history when, more than three decades ahead of Tiger Woods, he became the first black to win a USGA championship, capturing the **U.S. Amateur Public Links** in 1959. Wright's 3 and 2 victory came over Frank H. Campbell at Denver's Wellshire GC and was hardly proven a fluke as the Western Washington graduate would later play in occasional PGA Tour and Senior tour events, as well as four U.S. Senior Opens.

George Wright (USA)

Known in his day as America's first great baseball player, Yonkers, New York, native George Wright (1847–1937) eased into retirement by founding the nation's first sporting goods firm, Wright & Ditson. In addition to playing a major role in the development of several other sports (importing, for example, the first tennis racquets to this country), Wright made history by organizing and playing in

Boston's first golf outing, a nine-hole experiment over a makeshift Franklin Park course in 1890. Though this and a subsequent game at Revere Beach failed to catch mainstream Boston's eye, Wright remained a prominent area booster (and supplier) once golf did take off in the early 1890s. Long a friend and supporter of Francis Ouimet (who worked for Wright at the time of his seminal 1913 U.S. Open victory), George Wright was posthumously honored when the city of Boston named their fine Donald Ross-designed municipal course after him in 1938. Interestingly, Wright once claimed to have hit golf balls with an unnamed Scotsman at New York's St. George Cricket Club as early as 1863, though no corroborative evidence apparently exists to back up this assertion.

Mickey Wright (USA)

Determining an all-time greatest woman golfer is no simple task, for early candidates such as Glenna Collett or Joyce Wethered played less frequently and in weaker fields, making their handful of results largely ill-suited for comparison with most modern players. Yet for virtually all of the postwar field, a broad body of hard data is available, with the numbers—and a good deal more—telling only one story: that the greatest woman player of them all was San Diego's Mary Kathryn "Mickey" Wright.

The daughter of a sports-minded attorney who wanted a son he planned to name Michael, Wright (b. 2/14/1935) was introduced to golf at age 11. A quick study and a diligent worker, she improved rapidly enough to reach the final of the second **USGA Junior Girls** as a 15-year-old in 1950 (losing to Patricia Lesser) before capturing the title two years later, defeating Barbara McIntire at the Monterey Peninsula CC. A highly intelligent young woman with many non-golf interests, Wright packed off to study psychology at Stanford University where, at age 19, she reached the final of the 1954 U.S. Women's Amateur (losing to Barbara Romack 4 and 3 in Sewickley, Pennsylvania) and tied for fourth—easily the low amateur—in the U.S. Women's Open at Salem CC.

Turning professional in 1955, Wright went winless in her first season before becoming a top-five money earner and occasional winner by 1957. She then took her first big jump in 1958, claiming both the **LPGA Championship** and **U.S. Women's Open** by wide margins, beating Fay Crocker and Louise Suggs by six and five shots, respectively. Three additional wins left Wright with a Tour-leading five, a number she would nearly match the following year with a successful defense of her **Open** crown, plus three further titles. With six more wins and another **LPGA Championship** in 1960, Wright was now among the elite of the women's game, yet as the next four years would indicate, the golfing world hadn't seen anything yet.

For Wright now kicked off a run that, pound for pound, must rank with any four-year stretch in the game's history. Each season she led the Tour in victories, racking up 10, 10, 13, and 11 from 1961 through 1964, claiming 42 percent of the events in which she entered, and comfortably holding first place on the money list throughout. She was also the Vare Trophy winner all four years while adding a total of eight Major titles to her list—a striking number that becomes even more so when we realize that she actually managed *two* career Grand Slams just within this four-year window!

By 1965, however, Wright was slowed by serious foot problems, the desire to complete her discontinued education and, apparently, a bit of fatigue from the nomadic touring life. Returning to college, she entered only 11 events that season (winning two) before coming back to claim 15 more victories in 55 starts between 1966 and 1968. A single-win 1969 followed and thereafter Wright was strictly a part-time player, only once entering as many as 11 tournaments for the duration of her career. Still, despite growing physical ailments and a dwindling schedule, she remained capable of competing with the best, actually taking her 82nd win—in sneakers—at the 1973 **Dinah Shore** and very nearly making it 83 before losing a 1979 play-off to Nancy Lopez at the Coca Cola Classic.

Perhaps the most remarkable thing about Wright was her personality, for unlike most top players she was shy, highly introverted and generally ill-suited—at least by common definition—to top-flight competition. Her physical problems were equally a handicap and likely prevented her from amassing a record that stars of today's rather more competitive tour could only dream of approaching. But Wright was blessed with several rare qualities, not the least of which was a golf swing separately cited by both Ben Hogan and Byron Nelson as the most fundamentally sound they'd ever seen. At 5'9" she also had uncommon height, as well as arms strong enough to play many full shots (including her long irons) more in the manner of a man. Considered every bit as long as the late Babe Zaharias, Wright was universally rated a far better shotmaker and, in the main, simply a better all-around player.

And then there are the numbers. Wright shot 62 in Midland, Texas, in 1964 (it would be 27 years before an LPGA player would equal it) and her 13 wins in 1963 remain the tour record. Yet these and other singular achievements pale in comparison to several career statistics, such as: Wright won nearly 27 percent of the LPGA events in which she started during her legitimately competitive years, roughly 4 percent better than Annika Sorenstam has thus far managed and a number never matched once the tour had full fields and a complete schedule. She further raised this yield to nearly 32 percent during her best decade (1958–67), a standard that we shall likely never witness again. But perhaps most impressive is a simple comparison with Kathy Whitworth, whose 88 career wins is the all-time American professional record, bettering Wright by six. It took Wright 19 seasons (336 starts) to reach number 82, while ironwoman Whitworth required 32 full seasons (733 starts) to achieve her 88. At least between these two players then, there was simply no contest.

LPGA Wins (82): 1957, '58, '60, '62 & '63 Sea Island; **1958, '60, '61 & '63 LPGA Championship; 1958,** '59, '61 & '64 U.S. **Women's Open;** 1958, '63 & '65 Dallas Civitan; **1961 & '62 Titleholders;** 1961 & '63 Orange Blossom; **1962, '63 & '66 Western Open;** 1963 Babe Zaharias; 1964 Peach Blossom; 1973 Dinah Shore; 5 Sea Island Opens, 3 Jacksonville Opens & 3 Mickey Wright Invitationals

1955-1972

	55	56	57	58	59	60	61	62	63	64	65	66	67	68	69	70	71	72
LPGA	T14	4	T11	1	8	1	1	8	1	2	-	2	5	10	T8	-	T15	-
US Open	16	9	T22	1	1	5	1	T4	-	1	-	3	WD	2	T13	37	T3	T6

Also won Western Opens and Titleholders, as listed above.

Dudley Wysong (USA)

A product of McKinney, Texas, the unforgettably named H. Dudley Wysong (1939–1998) enjoyed one great moment in the Monterey sun, defeating Ireland's Joe Carr in the semifinal of the 1961 U.S. Amateur at Pebble Beach, only to get routed 8 and 6 in the final by Jack Nicklaus. As a professional, Wysong also finished second at the 1966 PGA Championship (four shots back of winner Al Geiberger), though he did win twice on Tour at the 1966 **Phoenix Open** and the 1967 **Hawaiian Open,** the latter in sudden death over Billy Casper.

Y

Bert Yancey (USA)

The story of Chipley, Florida, native Albert Winsborough "Bert" Yancey (1938–1994) ranks among golf's saddest, for here was a man of unquestioned talent and desire who was afflicted with a disease not yet understood by medical science during his prime playing years. A former West Point cadet, Yancey's intensity was such that he built miniature models of Augusta's greens to best prepare himself, each year entering what he called his "pre-Masters fog." But at West Point Yancey had suffered what was diagnosed as a nervous breakdown, and he was later afflicted by several bouts of bizarre behavior while on Tour. Eventually he was found to be manic depressive—the proper diagnosis of which likely did little to help as the drugs required to maintain an even mental keel made his hands unsteady, badly damaging his putting stroke.

But despite so massive a handicap, Yancey still managed a solid professional record, winning a total of seven PGA Tour events, including the 1970 **Bing Crosby,** where he defeated Jack Nicklaus by one. His Major championship record was similarly strong, finishing third at the 1968 U.S. Open at Oak Hill (behind Trevino and Nicklaus) and fifth at the 1973 Open Championship at Troon. Not surprisingly it was at the Masters that Yancey fared best, finishing third in 1967 and '68 and fourth in 1970.

Yancey was widely considered an excellent teacher, and in later years, improved medicines allowed him to compete, with marginal success, on the Champions Tour. Unfortunately Yancey's sad story came to an even sadder end when he died of a heart attack just moments before teeing off at a Champions event in Park City, Utah, in 1994.

Charlie Yates (USA)

Atlanta-born Charles R. Yates (b. 9/9/1913) went to college at hometown Georgia Tech where he won **NCAA** individual titles in 1934 and '35. A two-time **Georgia Amateur** champion (1931 and '32) and the 1935 **Western Amateur** winner, Yates' selection to his second Walker Cup team in 1938 provided a trip to St. Andrews and, more importantly, the chance to enter the **British Amateur** at Troon—which he promptly won, 3 and 2, over Cecil Ewing. A genial man whose powerful game was not always stylish, Yates was a good friend of Bobby Jones and a longtime member of Augusta National, for many years overseeing the press tent during the Masters.

Charlie Yates

Z

Babe (Didrickson) Zaharias (USA)

Born: Port Arthur, Texas, 6/26/1914 **Died:** Galveston, Texas, 9/27/1956

Probably the finest female athlete in history, Babe Zaharias—much like Jim Thorpe—seemed almost freakishly gifted, excelling to so high a degree in so many different sports that one wonders if there was something genuinely different in her genetic makeup. Born to Norwegian immigrants, the then–Mildred Ella Didriksen grew up primarily in Beaumont, eventually taking on the nickname "Babe" after Ruth and changing the spelling of her last name to Didrickson to emphasize her Norwegian ancestry. A high school star in baseball, tennis, swimming, volleyball, and especially basketball, she actually left school early to go to work for a Dallas insurance company that fielded athletic teams in a number of A.A.U.-sponsored sports. There she proved herself surely the finest female softball and basketball player yet seen and also took a serious interest in track and field, where her excellence achieved levels heretofore unimagined. At the 1932 Los Angeles Olympics, for example, she was limited to three events and took two gold medals and a silver. These results paled in comparison to her performance at that year's National Women's A.A.U. Track Meet, however, where the Babe landed six gold medals and three world records in a single afternoon, winning the national team championship for her club despite being its sole participant in the competition!

Making her Depression-era living largely as a barnstorming athlete, the publicity-savvy Babe only turned seriously to golf during the mid-1930s after receiving encouragement from her friend, the great sportswriter Grantland Rice. By 1935 she was the **Texas Women's** champion and, having demonstrated that she could play, soon had her amateur status revoked by the USGA, primarily for her money-making endeavors in other sports. With no ladies professional tour on which to compete, however, Babe was relegated to events like the celebrity division of the 1938 Los Angeles Open where she met her husband-to-be, professional wrestler George Zaharias.

Prior to marrying Zaharias, Babe had long been unpopular among her athletic peers, widely considered a braggart and subject to all manner of criticism and innuendo, including the patently absurd suggestion that anyone so athletically gifted must, in fact, have been a male. Thus something of a social misfit, her life, demeanor, and popularity (at least with galleries) improved noticeably after the marriage, as did her golf game. A prodigiously long hitter whose full, athletic swing produced drives comparable to those of an average male professional, the now–Mrs. Zaharias was capable of overpowering courses in the Tiger Woods style, though the rest of her game required some time to approach comparable proficiency.

Nonetheless, she won the **Western Open** both as a professional and, in 1945, as a reinstated amateur, later beating the pros in the 1947 **Tampa Open** and **Titleholders** as well. Zaharias also made history in 1945 by earning a spot among the men (through 36-hole qualifying) at the PGA Tour's Los Angeles and Tucson Opens, actually making the 36-hole cut at the former with a score of 157. Her amateur run of 1946–47, however, was no less impressive, resulting in victories at the 1946 **U.S. Women's Amateur,** the 1947 **British Ladies** (the first American to win that prestigious title), and a purported streak of 17 straight tournament wins that, in reality, appears to have been more like 13.

Offered big money by Hollywood for a series of golf films, Zaharias once again turned professional (this time by choice) in 1947, hired Fred Corcoran as her manager, and became a founding member of the LPGA in 1949. Clearly the fledgling organization's star attraction, the Babe joined women like Patty Berg, Betsy Rawls, and Louise Suggs on the marquee, yet set herself apart by winning an astounding 31 official tournaments in only 69 career starts (44.9 percent). She also managed the little-remembered feat of taking all three 1950 events that are today recognized as Major championships of the period, including the **U.S. Women's Open** (by nine over Betsy Rawls), the **Titleholders** (by eight over amateur Claire Doran), and the **Western Open** (5 and 3 over Peggy Kirk at Denver's Cherry Hills CC).

Sadly, the only thing that could stop Babe Zaharias was her health, a fact brought pointedly home when, after feel-

Babe Zaharias

U.S. Women's Open in Peabody, Massachusetts. Publicly Zaharias was energized and talking of playing for 20 more years, but by early 1955 the cancer had returned, now beyond the point of operability. Enduring a great deal of pain and very little golf near the end, she passed away at age 42 in September of 1956.

Assessing Zaharias's place as a player is not altogether easy, for while she was at times utterly dominant, her game was somewhat unpolished and occasionally streaky. Further, while Berg, Rawls, Suggs, and a handful of others could certainly play, the depth of fields against which Zaharias ran up her huge record is a legitimate question. Of course, they weren't so very different from the early-1960s fields that would soon be dominated by Mickey Wright, the lone woman generally conceded to have clearly been the Babe's better.

Zaharias's place as a pioneer, however, is unquestioned. For whatever elements of ego or marketing bravado may at times have tainted her persona, the Babe endured innumerable slights and indignities simply for being a superior woman athlete in an era when such was frowned upon. By fighting through all of this to achieve not only success but status as a national hero, she single-handedly paved the way for generations of female competitors to follow. Even today, a half-century later, nobody has ever equaled the Babe.

ing aches and pains for several months, she was diagnosed with cancer and underwent an immediate colostomy in April 1953. Back to competitive golf only 14 weeks later, she surprisingly won five more tournaments in 1954, including a stunning 12-shot victory over Betty Hicks in the

Professional/LPGA Wins (41): 1940, '44, '45 & '50 Western Open; 1947, '50 & '52 Titleholders; 1948, '49, '50 & '51 World Championship; **1948, '50 & '54 U.S. Women's Open;** 1955 Peach Blossom; 4 All-American Opens & 3 Tampa Opens

Major Amateur Wins (4): 1946 Trans-Miss; 1946 U.S. Women's Amateur; 1947 North & South; 1947 British Ladies; 3 Broadmoor Invitationals

1948-1955

	48	49	50	51	52	53	54	55
LPGA								-
US Open	1	2	1	3	-	-	1	-

Also won Western Opens and Titleholders, as listed above.

Kermit Zarley (USA)

Long referred to as "the pro from the moon" after being so named by a jocular Bob Hope, Seattle native Kermit Zarley (b. 9/29/1941) was an **NCAA** individual and team champion at the University of Houston before joining the PGA Tour in 1963. A consistent money winner with one of the Tour's more enviable swings, Zarley generally remained among the top 60 money earners until the late 1970s, and was a three-time winner, most notably at the

1970 **Canadian Open** where he beat Gibby Gilbert by three. Upon reaching 50, he was also a regular competitor on the Champions Tour in the early 1990s, winning once.

Walter Zembriski (USA)

Mahwah, New Jersey, native Walter Zembriski (b. 5/24/1935) enjoyed several shining moments on the Champions Tour during the late 1980s, one of those classic late-blooming stories that have given the Tour a bit of added color. A former caddie and self-taught player, and the only public-course player ever to win the Metropolitan section's prestigious **"Ike"** amateur title (at Winged Foot, in 1964), Zembriski appeared briefly on the PGA Tour in 1967 and later qualified for the 1978 and '82 U.S. Opens. Playing Florida minitours while making money as a construction worker, Zembriski finally hit the jackpot with the establishment of the Champions Tour, winning a total of three events, leading the 1985 U.S. Senior Open through two rounds (he finished fourth), and banking over $3 million. In a sport that loves to trumpet so-called everymen who make good, Walter Zembriski comes about as close as any to being the real thing.

Lian-wei Zhang (China)

Lian-Wei Zhang (b. Zhuhai, 5/2/1965) made history in 2003 when he became the first Chinese player to win a European Tour event, his 72nd-hole birdie at the **Caltex Masters** (played in Singapore) providing the margin of victory over a heavily favored Ernie Els. Little known in the West, Zhang has toiled at least part time on the European circuit since 1995 and is a 10-time winner in Asia, most notably taking back-to-back **Macao Opens** in 2001 and '02, the latter over a hard-charging Nick Price in sudden death. Given Zhang's solid résumé and Augusta National's marketing acumen, it is hardly surprising that he became, in 2004, the first Chinese player to be invited to the Masters, missing the cut by a single stroke. As Zhang is fast approaching 40 at the time of this writing, however, it will likely fall to another to become China's first top-shelf international player.

Larry Ziegler (USA)

St. Louis product Larry Ziegler (b. 8/12/1939) was a three-time winner on the PGA Tour and one of the game's longer hitters during the 1970s. He also endured what must surely be a unique experience in the modern history of the Tour, winning his first title at the 1969 **Michigan Classic** only to be told at the presentation ceremony that the sponsor had gone bankrupt (he was later paid by the Tour). Ziegler repaired to the Champions Tour in the early 1990s where he won twice before retiring.

Fuzzy Zoeller (USA)

One of professional golf's most engaging and popular players since the late 1970s, long-hitting Frank Urban "Fuzzy" Zoeller (b. New Albany, Indiana, 11/11/1951) first drew attention at the 1976 Quad Cities Open when he tied Bob Goalby's 15-year-old record by carding eight consecutive birdies en route to a first-round 63. Though bothered from time to time by recurring back problems dating back to a high school basketball injury, Zoeller won a total of 10 times on the PGA Tour, his first title coming at the 1979 **San Diego Open** by a comfortable five strokes. Having already established himself as a rising star, Zoeller then proceeded to win the 1979 **Masters,** given new life when Ed Sneed missed several key putts down the stretch, then defeating both Sneed and Tom Watson with a birdie on the second hole of sudden death.

Further wins would follow at **Colonial** (1981) and both the **Heritage** and **Las Vegas** in 1983, a year in which Zoeller would finish a career-best second on the money list. Then came 1984 and the **U.S. Open** at Winged Foot, the lingering memory of which was Zoeller, believing he'd just been beaten by Greg Norman's long putt at the 72nd, waving the white towel of surrender from back in the fairway. But Norman's putt, it turned out, had been for par, resulting in a Monday play-off that saw Zoeller trounce the Shark with a flawless round of 67 for his second Major title.

Within months there would be back surgery, then an impressive comeback, to 15th on the money list in 1985, then to 13th, with his final three Tour wins, in 1986. But by his late 30s, with his back constantly an issue, Zoeller experienced an inevitable decline, eventually falling as low as 114th in 1992 before one final surge during 1994 produced a final fifth-place finish.

Unfortunately, Zoeller returned to the limelight in a less flattering way in 1997 when his racially insensitive comments regarding Tiger Woods' breakthrough victory at the Masters ignited a media firestorm of epic proportion. Incessantly castigated by the press, Zoeller apologized and was generally supported by fans and fellow players, with Vijay Singh speaking for many by stating that "Fuzzy got *really* screwed" by the media overkill.

A fan favorite at every stop, the former University of Houston player was a much-awaited arrival on the Champions Tour in 2002, where he has won two events and over $8.1 million at the time of this writing.

PGA Tour Wins (10): 1979 San Diego; **1979 Masters;** 1981 Colonial; 1983 & '86 Heritage; **1984 U.S. Open;** 1986 Bing Crosby
Ryder Cup: 1979, '83 & '85 (3)

BIBLIOGRAPHY

The research involved in putting together *The Book of Golfers* has included a roster of literary sources large enough that I long ago gave up attempting to catalogue it. Still, I would be remiss not to cite the genuine importance of many older issues of *Golf World*, as well as those early gems *The American Golfer* and *Golf Illustrated* (both the U.S. and U.K. versions) among a list of relevant periodicals. Numerous old editions of the *New York Times* and *Los Angeles Times* also were invaluable, providing day-to-day details largely unobtainable anywhere else.

In terms of books, though many, many others were consulted, the following titles all proved themselves too valuable—in all manner of ways—not to receive mention:

Alliss, Peter. *The Who's Who of Golf*. London: Orbus, 1983.

Barkow, Al. *Gettin' to the Dance Floor*. New York: Atheneum, 1986.

Barkow, Al. *The History of the PGA Tour*. New York: Doubleday, 1989.

Browning, Robert. *A History of Golf*. London: J. M. Dent, 1955.

Cornish, Geoffrey S., and Ronald E. Whitten. *The Architects of Golf*. New York: HarperCollins, 1993.

Cotton, Henry. *This Game of Golf*. London: Country Life, 1948.

Darwin, Bernard. *The Darwin Sketchbook*. New York: Classics of Golf, 1991.

Darwin, Bernard. *Golf Between Two Wars*. London: Chatto & Windus, 1944.

Darwin, Bernard, et al. *A History of Golf in Britain*. London: Cassell, 1952.

Doak, Tom. *The Confidential Guide*. Chelsea, Mich.: Sleeping Bear, 1996.

Donovan, Richard E., and Joseph S. F. Murdoch. *The Game of Golf and the Printed Word 1566–1985*. Endicott, New York: Castalio, 1985.

Finegan, James W. *A Centennial Tribute to Golf in Philadelphia*. Philadelphia: Golf Assoc. of Philadelphia, 1996.

Gibson, William. *Early Irish Golf*. Naas: Oakleaf, 1988.

Glenn, Rhonda. *The Illustrated History of Women's Golf*. Dallas: Taylor, 1991.

Hagen, Walter. *The Walter Hagen Story*. New York: Simon & Schuster, 1956.

Harris, Robert. *Sixty Years of Golf*. London: Batchworth, 1953.

Hutchinson, Horace G. *Fifty Years of Golf*. London: Country Life, 1919.

Jarman, Colin M. *The Ryder Cup*. New York: McGraw Hill, 1999.

Kirkaldy, Andrew. *Fifty Years of Golf: My Memories*. London: T. Fisher Unwin, 1921.

Leach, Henry (editor). *Great Golfers in the Making*. London: Methuen, 1907.

Lewis, Peter N. *The Dawn of Professional Golf*. Tunbridge Wells: Hobbs & McEwan, 1995.

Martin, H. B. *Fifty Years of American Golf*. New York: Dodd Mead, 1936.

Murray, Francis. *The British Open*. London: Pavilion, 2000.

Pollard, Jack. *Australian Golf*. Sydney: Angus & Robertson, 1990.

Sarazen, Gene, with Herbert Warren Wind. *Thirty Years of Championship Golf*. New York: Prentice-Hall, 1950.

Shackelford, Geoff. *The Golden Age of Golf Design*. Chelsea, Mich.: Sleeping Bear, 1999.

Sommers, Robert. *The U.S. Open: Golf's Ultimate Challenge*. New York: Atheneum, 1987.

Steel, Donald, and Peter Ryde. *The Shell International Encyclopedia of Golf*. London: Ebury, 1975.

Stirk, David. *Golf: History & Tradition 1500–1945*. Ludlow, England: Excellent Press, 1998.

Taylor, J. H. *Golf: My Life's Work*. London: Johnathan Cape, 1943.

20th Century Golf Chronicle. Lincolnwood, Il.: Publications International, 1998.

Vardon, Harry. *My Golfing Life*. London: Hutchinson, 1933.

Ward-Thomas, Pat, et al., *The World Atlas of Golf.* London: Mitchell Beazley, 1976.
Wind, Herbert Warren. *The Story of American Golf.* New York: Farrar, Strauss, 1948.

Also worth noting is that longest running of annuals, *The Golfer's Handbook* (whose prewar records sections, in particular, were invaluable), as well as the contemporary media guides of the PGA, LPGA, and European Tours.

APPENDIX

All statistics current through August 2004.

Appendix A
Players

All-Time Player Rankings

Men's All-Time Rankings (Top 50)

Any attempt at ranking the entirety of men's competitive golf runs into several obvious hurdles, the primary one being that enormous changes in equipment, agronomy, depths of fields, prize money, and so on make cross-generational comparisons extremely difficult. Indeed, it is a challenge to effectively judge even Tiger Woods versus Tom Watson, never mind Woods versus Hogan, Jones, or Vardon. Further, the PGA and European Tours as we know them are largely modern entities, with 100 percent reliable record-keeping seldom dating earlier than 1970 in either case. Thus, while the PGA has retroactively recognized what are now deemed "official" victories dating back to 1916 (the year of the PGA of America's founding), virtually all of their older statistical records are, in effect, well-researched estimates. The numbers cited here then are deemed accurate enough to paint a clear picture, but should hardly be viewed as exact.

Two rather subjective qualifiers have been imposed with regard to eligibility. The first recognizes the fundamental change in the golf ball (from gutta-percha to rubber) near the turn of the last century, and thus disqualifies any player who never competed with the latter. Such a stipulation excludes only Young Tom Morris as a realistic contender for this list—and there is simply no way to accurately compare him to modern players anyway. Similarly, a golfer's accomplishments can be judged effectively only if he has played long enough to avoid having his numbers skewed by a particularly hot or cold period. Thus to be eligible, a candidate must turn 30 before the end of 2005—a standard that, though obviously crafted to include Tiger Woods, excludes not a single player with a reasonable case for inclusion.

A great deal of emphasis has been placed on Major championships in developing this list, for they are the single most consistent factor in the history of the competitive game. Though countless events have come and gone around them, the Majors have always been *the* most desired titles, places where the elite players always show up and the golf courses are, if not always great, at least of a high-level challenge. Thus they are easily the best separator of "the men from the boys."

Several statistics are frequently cited, the most common being winning percentage and major winning percentage. The reader will bear in mind that these numbers represent only official PGA Tour results accumulated during a player's legitimately competitive years and *not* over his entire career—lest his numbers be dragged downward by countless "ceremonial" starts (e.g., Arnold Palmer at Augusta). A more detailed description of these statistics appears in Major Tour Winning percentages.

Finally, a word about the timeless argument of ancient versus modern and its would-Vardon-really-still-measure-up strain of questioning. Though such debate obviously cannot be resolved, there seems an inherent logic to the assumption that men of elite talent would adjust to the conditions of the day, Vardon having made the switch from gutta-percha to rubber every bit as smoothly as our modern players have shifted from steel to graphite. Thus the notion that the stars of the past might somehow be outclassed today seems a specious one, for is there any reason to think that Woods would inherently take to hickory better than Vardon to graphite? Indeed, to some extent the opposite might even be true, for as A. W. Tillinghast once observed, the men of yore "had to know much more about hitting a golf ball in more ways with fewer clubs than the lads of today."

Note: Players marked with an asterisk are still within their legitimately competitive years.

1.   Jack Nicklaus (73 PGA Tour Wins, 18 Major Championships)

Winning percentage: 16.0%
Major percentage: 15.0%

The numbers say it all. Other than Hogan possibly being a better ball-striker, there is simply no serious criterion to suggest anyone but Nicklaus for number one. His 73 Tour wins trail only Snead and were accomplished against deeper fields. The length and consistency of his dominance are unmatched in the game's history. His performances under pressure have been legendary and his 18 professional Major championships exactly doubles the total accumulated by his closest professional pursuers (Hogan and Gary Player). Others have dominated for limited periods but when we examine the career-long record, it's no contest.

2. Ben Hogan (64 PGA Tour Wins, 9 Major Championships)

Winning percentage: 24.3%
Major percentage: 19.1%

Ranking Hogan over Bobby Jones is no snap decision, and one predicated primarily upon longevity. Specifically, Jones retired at age 28 citing burnout whereas Hogan, despite debilitating injuries to his legs, remained the world's best player right on into his 40s. Beyond this, one suspects that the quality of Hogan's competition was a bit deeper, and his statistical domination of men like Snead, Mangrum, Demaret, and Nelson (discounting the latter's war-era runaways) is most impressive. Further, Hogan was the most revered ball-striker of all time and a man who accomplished his feats despite the affects of his near-fatal car accident injuries. An undamaged Hogan might well have made a run at some of Nicklaus' numbers—but that, of course, is strictly a matter of conjecture.

3.   Bobby Jones (13 Major Championships)

Winning percentage: N/A
Major percentage: N/A

Jones' early retirement prevented him from amassing Nicklaus-like numbers, though his record is still imposing enough. His stretch of 13 Major championship victories in 21 starts (61.9%) between 1923 and 1930 has only been approached by Hogan (9 for 16, 56.3%, from 1946 through 1953) and will likely stand forever now that Tiger Woods (8 for 22, 36.4%, from 1997 through 2002) has failed to better it. The quality of Jones' amateur competition certainly cannot match the PGA Tour fields faced by later players but before casting too doubtful an eye, we must note that seven of Jones' 13 Majors came in U.S. and British Opens—so he can hardly be accused of running up his numbers against weak amateur fields.

4.   Tiger Woods* (40 PGA Tour Wins, 8 Major Championships)

Winning percentage: 24.4%
Major percentage: 25.0%

The living proof that we must evaluate an entire career and not just several hot years, Woods' recent slump allows us to rank him where so young a player duly belongs—for while tremendously impressive, his overall record has not yet matched those of the players above him. With regard to those close behind, however, Woods stands miles ahead of Walter Hagen at the same stage of their respective careers and ranks ahead of Harry Vardon based on achieving a similarly groundbreaking level of dominance against far deeper fields. Nearly matching overall and Major winning percentages speaks well to Tiger's remarkable consistency—at least until late 2003.

5.   Harry Vardon (7 Major Championships)

Winning percentage: N/A
Major percentage: 26.9%

The modern game's first great player, Vardon lacked only the large, well-lit contemporary stage upon which to establish an even grander legend. Prior to contracting tuberculosis, his dominance was astounding, including once winning 17 of 22 events entered, while finishing second in the other five. It is always difficult to relate a player of Vardon's era with those of today, but with ball-striking ability vastly beyond that of his peers, it is difficult not to imagine King Harry being an elite player in any period. A. W. Tillinghast, who saw them both, rated him ahead of Jones (and everyone else) in 1939.

6.   Walter Hagen (44 PGA Tour Wins, 11 Major Championships)

Winning percentage: 24.3%
Major percentage: 22.9%

Like Vardon, Walter Hagen's greatness is too often overlooked today, perhaps overshadowed by his famous personality and lifestyle. But Hagen won more events than any prewar player, had the highest overall and Major winning percentages of that era, and ranks second all-time behind Vardon for highest all-time Major percentage. He proved himself remarkably adaptable by winning four British Opens (only Tom Watson has matched this among Americans) and was perhaps the greatest match-play competitor in history. If Hagen's five Western Opens were counted as Majors, his total of 16 might have altered the young Nicklaus' view considerably.

7.   Bobby Locke (15 PGA Tour Wins, 4 Major Championships, 64 Intn'l Wins)

Winning percentage: 18.6%
Major percentage: 14.8%

Some will question rating Locke above his compatriot Gary Player, but the numbers bear this out. Locke, after all, won at a substantially higher clip on the game's biggest stages, especially during his three-year stretch in America where his winning percentage very nearly tripled what Player would manage 25 years later. He also claimed Majors at a 5.5% greater rate and went 20 plus years without losing a 72-hole stroke-play event in South Africa! Locke's postwar fields were certainly a bit lighter (particularly in Britain)—but not so much to draw Player even. Had he not been xenophobically banned in America, who knows how high Locke might have climbed? Being the consensus choice as "Best Putter Ever," of course, seldom hurt.

8.   Gary Player (24 PGA Tour Wins, 9 Major Championships, 141 Intn'l Wins)

Winning percentage: 7.1%
Major percentage: 10.1%

Player grades out ahead of men such as Snead and Nelson by winning consistently, all over the world, in Major and minor events, for longer than anyone else in golf history. Though hardly an elegant stylist, he was a world-class competitor who managed the relatively rare feat of raising his winning percentage substantially in Major championships. Winning the career Grand Slam also gains him a leg up on the five Americans just behind him, each of whom failed (by one) to do so.

9. Sam Snead (82 PGA Tour Wins, 7 Major Championships)

Winning percentage: 17.8%
Major percentage: 9.5%

There are some who consider Snead the best of all time, though any player who spends the majority of his career battling the yips seems a bit up against it in this regard. Snead's legendary failures at the U.S. Open also work against him, though his longevity, stunningly natural swing, and remarkable victory ledger guarantee him a spot in the top 10.

10. Tom Watson (39 PGA Tour Wins, 8 Major Championships)

Winning percentage: 8.1%
Major percentage: 9.9%

Another of those rare players whose winning percentage increased during Major championship play, Watson's 39 Tour victories were gathered against substantially stronger fields than those faced by Arnold Palmer and Byron Nelson. He ranks third (behind Woods and Nicklaus) among modern players in Major winning percentage and his five British Opens are a modern landmark. Had he won a PGA, he'd have moved up at least two spots.

11. Byron Nelson (52 PGA Tour Wins, 5 Major Championships)

Winning percentage: 20.1%
Major percentage: 12.2%

Though undeniably a golfer and gentleman of the very highest order, the fact is that exactly half (26) of Byron Nelson's official victories came during 1944 and '45, years when Hogan, Snead, and Demaret were largely out of action and Lloyd Mangrum completely so. Of course, Nelson also ceased playing full time at 34, leading us to wonder what more he might potentially have accomplished by sticking around—but again, such is strictly conjecture. What Nicklaus (and others) accomplished is fact.

12. Arnold Palmer (62 PGA Tour Wins, 7 Major Championships)

Winning percentage: 11.8%
Major percentage: 7.7%

Though Palmer's late 1950s/early 1960s numbers were striking, he accumulated them at a time when Hogan, Snead, and Cary Middlecoff were well into their decline, and largely before Nicklaus, Player, and Casper reached cruising speed. Like Watson, a win at the PGA would have altered Arnold's profile greatly.

13. Lee Trevino (29 PGA Tour Wins, 6 Major Championships)

Winning percentage: 7.2%
Major percentage: 8.7%

Though he maintained high-level form for nearly 20 years, Trevino was not as day-to-day dominant as several of the American players ranked above him. Palmer and the young Nicklaus might have faced slightly leaner fields, but Watson certainly didn't. A more competitive showing at Augusta (where Trevino never bettered 10th) would have helped.

14. Peter Thomson (6 PGA Tour Wins, 5 Major Championships, 74 Intn'l Wins)

Winning percentage: 5.7%
Major percentage: 14.7%

Thomson only briefly played in America, five of his six official victories actually being British Opens. Like Palmer, he scarcely dealt with Hogan or Snead (particularly in Britain) and four of his Opens were won before Nicklaus and Player became relevant. Still, Thomson is much underrated in America—but with only two top-10 finishes in 15 Stateside Major starts, this is perhaps not surprising.

15. Seve Ballesteros (9 PGA Tour Wins, 5 Major Championships, 78 Intn'l Wins)

Winning percentage: 6.0%
Major percentage: 7.0%

Though an utterly thrilling talent, Seve was, in the end, simply too wild to be dominant at *all* types of golf—as only five top 10s in a combined 31 U.S. Open and PGA entries indicate. His international record, of course, was top-shelf, but being widely bettered by Watson at the British Open limits his upside in this crowd.

16. Gene Sarazen (39 PGA Tour Wins, 7 Major Championships)

Winning percentage: 16.5%
Major percentage: 11.9%

Sarazen's longevity, competitiveness, and status as the first career professional Grand Slam winner are big pluses. Shallower fields and a steep decrease in winning percentage in the Majors work against him. For what it's worth, he probably enjoyed more prominent good breaks in Major championship play than anyone else.

17. Nick Faldo (9 PGA Tour Wins, 6 Major Championships, 30 Intn'l Wins)

Winning percentage: 4.3%
Major percentage: 9.5%

A true blue-chipper at his peak, Faldo finishes here largely on his relatively low overall winning percentage in America. He fared rather better overseas, of course, and nearly doubling his U.S. percentage in the Majors is quite impressive.

18. Willie Anderson (8 PGA Tour Wins, 4 Major Championships)

Winning percentage: N/A
Major percentage: N/A

As dominant in America (against significantly weaker fields) as his contemporary Vardon was in the United Kingdom, Anderson is extremely difficult to compare with modern players. Several of his longer-lived contemporaries (including Fred McLeod) rated him the equal of Hagen and Jones, but A. W. Tillinghast pegged him a shade lower, beneath both the Triumvirate and John Ball.

19. Henry Cotton (3 PGA Tour Wins, 3 Major Championships, 32 Intn'l wins)

Winning percentage: N/A
Major percentage: N/A

Britain and Europe's best between the Triumvirate and the modern era. Cotton's ledger suffered greatly by losing the prime years of his early thirties to World War II but he simply didn't compete enough elsewhere (only one American Major start before age 49) to rank higher.

20. Cary Middlecoff (40 PGA Tour Wins, 3 Major Championships)

Winning percentage: 12.6%
Major percentage: 7.0%

Back problems largely sidelined Middlecoff at age 42, lest he might have tacked a few more wins onto his résumé. Further, much of his success came against Hogan, Snead, Demaret, and Mangrum—no minor feat. A large decline in winning percentage during the Majors works against him, however.

21. James Braid (5 Major Championships)

Winning percentage: N/A
Major percentage: N/A

Another difficult man to rate against modern players, particularly since his inability to travel limited his Major championship play strictly to the British Open. Still, Braid's five Claret Jugs in 10 years (1901–10) has been matched only by Watson and is truly Hall of Fame stuff.

22. Jim Barnes (20 PGA Tour Wins, 4 Major Championships)

Winning percentage: 23.1%
Major percentage: 11.4%

Much overlooked is Long Jim Barnes, bettered only by Hagen among prewar American professionals and a winner of every Major championship available to him. Though his Major winning percentage was a relative disappointment, Barnes was already 30 years old when PGA Tour records became official in 1916, so he actually won quite a few more than the 20 victories credited.

23. Billy Casper (51 PGA Tour Wins, 3 Major Championships)

Winning percentage: 10.5%
Major percentage: 4.8%

A quiet performer whose overall consistency was bettered only by Nicklaus among his immediate contemporaries, Casper was the last player (save Nicklaus and Woods) to maintain a double-digit winning percentage throughout his relevant years. Only a large performance drop-off in the Majors holds him back.

24. Ernie Els* (13 PGA Tour Wins, 3 Major Championships, 38 Intn'l Wins)

Winning percentage: 8.4%
Major percentage: 6.1%

Els edges ahead of Greg Norman with three Majors won in 57% as many starts and better numbers across the board—and he's just now in his prime. Poised to climb a bit further if he maintains his current pace, Els' American winning percentage trails only Woods and Nicklaus in the modern era.

25. Greg Norman (20 PGA Tour Wins, 2 Major Championships, 61 Intn'l Wins)

Winning percentage: 7.9%
Major percentage: 2.9%

Norman probably has less to show for seemingly always being in contention than any player of his time. His winning percentage ranks a healthy fifth in the modern era, but his precipitous plummet in the Majors sets him back. The world's worst luck didn't help.

26. J. H. Taylor (5 Major Championships)

Winning percentage: N/A
Major percentage: N/A

Another apples-and-oranges ranking relative to modern stars, and only listed behind Braid because it took him 19 years to claim his five Claret Jugs compared to Braid's 10.

27. Raymond Floyd (22 PGA Tour Wins, 4 Major Championships)

Winning percentage: 3.9%
Major percentage: 5.0%

The most surprising thing about the ageless and highly competitive Floyd is the relative weakness of his winning percentages. His victory totals are substantial, but they took far more starts to attain than virtually all above him.

28. Tommy Armour (25 PGA Tour Wins, 3 Major Championships)

Winning percentage: 14.0%
Major percentage: 8.6%

In nearly a dead heat with Jimmy Demaret, Armour noses ahead based on his winning percentages—though given the slightly lesser fields of his era, even this is a near thing. Does teaching ability count?

29. Jimmy Demaret (31 PGA Tour Wins, 3 Major Championships)

Winning percentage: 11.2%
Major percentage: 6.7%

Like Walter Hagen, Demaret's skills are perhaps overshadowed by his splendid personality, for building his record against Hogan, Snead, and company was no mean accomplishment. A Major other than the Masters would have broadened the résumé.

30. John Ball (8 Major Amateur Wins, 1 Major Championship)

Winning percentage: N/A
Major percentage: N/A

The ultimate wild card in this deck, having built his record primarily in early British Amateurs. The discrepancies between amateur and professional fields were not so large then, however, and Ball did win the 1890 British Open to prove this.

31. Vijay Singh* (24 PGA Tour Wins, 3 Major Championships, 21 Intn'l Wins)

Winning percentage: 6.9%
Major percentage: 5.9%

Coming from well off the pace, Singh's relatively late charge has him climbing with a bullet as of this writing. Further Majors could vault him into the 20s quickly.

32. Nick Price (18 PGA Tour Wins, 3 Major Championships, 23 Intn'l Wins)

Winning percentage: 5.2%
Major percentage: 5.1%

Best recalled for winning three Majors in nine starts during a torrid early 1990s stretch, Price's earlier years were a shade less productive, dragging down his overall numbers accordingly.

33. Harold Hilton (5 Major Amateur Wins, 2 Major Championships)

Winning percentage: N/A
Major percentage: N/A

John Ball may have won eight British Amateurs but Hilton took four of them—plus a U.S. Amateur and, most impressively, two British Opens. Only a pronounced lull after the turn of the last century prevents him from ranking higher.

34. Johnny Miller (25 PGA Tour Wins, 2 Major Championships)

Winning percentage: 7.2%
Major percentage: 3.2%

At his best Johnny Miller legitimately challenged the Nicklaus throne, but an inability to sustain such play for a longer period costs him here. A disappointing winning percentage in the Majors doesn't help.

35. Hale Irwin (20 PGA Tour Wins, 3 Major Championships)

Winning percentage: 3.6%
Major percentage: 4.4%

The model of focused consistency, Irwin produced a limited winning percentage, yet rose up to claim three U.S. Opens. Also, though senior results are not highly relevant here, his ability to remain near the top of the Champions Tour at age 60 cannot be ignored.

36. Henry Picard (26 PGA Tour Wins, 2 Major Championships)

Winning percentage: 14.4%
Major percentage: 5.3%

An underrated player historically, Picard dominated the later half of the 1930s to a degree matched only by Snead, though the majority of his competitive years actually were postwar. Highly rated by his peers.

37. Roberto de Vicenzo (10 PGA Tour Wins, 1 Major Championship, 165 Intn'l wins)

Winning percentage: 8.3%
Major percentage: 2.9%

De Vicenzo enjoyed solid success in America for a man who made barely 120 PGA Tour starts. He remains best remembered for his Masters scorecard disaster instead of for winning the 1967 British Open at age 44, an impressive accomplishment.

38. Paul Runyan (29 PGA Tour Wins, 2 Major Championships)

Winning percentage: 11.5%
Major percentage: 5.1%

Another underrated character, perhaps because our first memory of him—as being a *short* hitter—hardly squares with a swaggering Hall of Fame image. There might be something to this, however, for both of Runyan's Majors were PGA Championships, where the nature of match-play made his shortness less of a handicap.

39. Ralph Guldahl (16 PGA Tour Wins, 3 Major Championships)

Winning percentage: 9.4%
Major percentage: 10.0%

Guldahl won 13 of his 16 official victories (including two U.S. Opens and a Masters) between 1936 and 1940. Had he returned to the Tour and continued at such a pace following World War II.... But he did neither.

40. Bernhard Langer* (3 PGA Tour Wins, 2 Major Championships, 58 Intn'l Wins)

Winning percentage: 1.8%
Major percentage: 2.8%

Langer climbs ahead of Horton Smith with his striking longevity, for while Smith enjoyed one great burst of success, Langer has forged consistently along for two decades. The low PGA Tour winning percentage is somewhat misleading as he seldom settled in long enough in America to get comfortable.

41. Horton Smith (30 PGA Tour Wins, 2 Major Championships)

Winning percentage: 9.6%
Major percentage: 3.9%

Another streaky sort, Horton Smith won 14 times between 1928 and 1930, then on 11 more occasions (including twice at Augusta) from 1934 through 1937. Some might rank him higher but a third Major or a greater winning percentage would be needed to make any great headway on this list.

42. Leo Diegel (30 PGA Tour Wins, 2 Major Championships)

Winning percentage: 19.7%
Major percentage: 6.3%

Diegel's numbers (particularly his off-the-charts winning percentage) would suggest a higher ranking, but sadly this was a man noted far more for a balky putting stroke and blowing numerous chances in Major championships. Both of his Majors, we note, came in the match-play PGA.

43. Lloyd Mangrum (36 PGA Tour Wins, 1 Major Championship)

Winning percentage: 10.8%
Major percentage: 2.6%

Some will argue that Mangrum was a better player than several above him, and this may well be true. But ranking ninth in winning percentage among postwar-era stars and claiming only one Major (despite finishing in the top 10 in 66.7% of his relevant Major starts) just leaves too much room for lesser talents to slip in.

44. Phil Mickelson* (23 PGA Tour Wins, 1 Major Championship)

Winning percentage: 7.9%
Major percentage: 2.4%

Ranked fourth among those still in their competitive prime, Mickelson's numbers are exceptional for the modern era—except in Major championships. Further success there and he's climbing quickly. Otherwise, he's a modern Leo Diegel.

45. Jock Hutchison (14 PGA Tour Wins, 2 Major Championships)

Winning percentage: 14.9%
Major percentage: 7.4%

Like Jim Barnes, Hutchison's official Tour victory total is artificially low; he was 32 years old and many times a winner when the record-keeping started. Hutchison was five times among the top three at the U.S. Open, where a victory would have changed his legacy substantially.

46. Jerome Travers (9 Major Amateur Wins, 1 Major Championship)

Winning percentage: N/A
Major percentage: N/A

Despite oscillating levels of competitive interest, Travers remains, according to the numbers, America's second greatest amateur, trailing only Bobby Jones. This, however, leaves plenty of room between him and the top.

47. Denny Shute (16 PGA Tour Wins, 3 Major Championships)

Winning percentage: 7.0%
Major percentage: 7.0%

Three Majors (a British Open and two PGAs) might suggest a higher ranking but Shute's long-term numbers place him here.

48. Lawson Little (8 PGA Tour Wins, 1 Major Championship, 4 Major Amateur Wins)

Winning percentage: 3.3%
Major percentage: 2.8%

A tough one to rate. As an amateur, Little played some of the best golf ever seen to that point, and as a professional he won the U.S. Open. However, the remainder of his career, though war-interrupted, must be seen as a modest disappointment.

49. Chick Evans (15 Major Amateur Wins, 1 Major Championship)

Winning percentage: N/A
Major percentage: N/A

Chick Evans won two U.S. Amateurs but is perhaps more noteworthy for consistently contending in professional fields that included men such as Hagen, Sarazen, and Barnes.

50. Walter Travis (11 Major Amateur Wins)

Winning percentage: N/A
Major percentage: N/A

America's first great player and *the* dominant amateur at the turn of the century. His inability to score a substantial victory over the pros, however, drops him behind both Travers and Evans, who did.

Women's All-Time Rankings (Top 25)

Ranking golf's all-time greatest women is actually somewhat easier than attempting to organize the men for two reasons. First, women's competitive golf developed far more slowly, the result being that every player considered for this list played in the rubber-ball era, the overwhelming majority with steel shafts. Further, the founding of the LPGA in 1949 resulted in fairly detailed records from 1950 onward, allowing us to make cross-generational statistical comparisons of a type rendered difficult when working with the PGA Tour's sometimes murky past. Readers will note, however, that even the LPGA's numbers are not quite exact and thus should again be viewed more as general indicators—though clearly more accurate ones than those on the men's side.

Once again, players must turn 30 before the end of 2005 to be eligible for this list, with Se Ri Pak being the only legitimate contender thus excluded.

Note: Players marked with an asterisk are still within their legitimately competitive years.

1. Mickey Wright (82 LPGA Wins, 13 Major Championships)

Winning percentage: 26.7%
Major percentage: 26.0%

Mickey Wright remains golf's best-ever female player—for now. Her 82 wins trail Kathy Whitworth's 88 but were accomplished in an amazing 56% fewer starts (372 vs. 837). Her 13 Major championships also rank second (behind Patty Berg's 15) but were completed in 42% fewer starts (50 vs. 86). Wright's overall and Major championship winning percentages remain unequaled (save for the short career of Babe Zaharias) and her 31.9% winning percentage between 1958 and 1967 betters any other 10-year run (by a stout 6%!) ever recorded in LPGA history. For the time being, she remains ahead of ....

2. Annika Sorenstam* (56 LPGA Wins, 7 Major Championships)

Winning percentage: 23.3%
Major percentage: 18.9%

With each passing year, 35-year-old Annika Sorenstam draws closer to Mickey Wright's illustrious perch—but will she reach it? Sorenstam stands some 30 victories behind Wright at present, yet some allowance must obviously be made for the greater quality of modern fields. While her eight Major championships also leave some work to be done, Sorenstam's winning percentage ranks behind only Wright and Babe Zaharias and is nearly 8% ahead of any contemporary competitor. If Annika can maintain her new millennium pace for just a bit longer, and tack on a few more Majors...

3. Babe Zaharias (31 Professional/LPGA Wins, 5 Major Championships)

Winning percentage: 44.9%
Major percentage: 35.7%

Likely the greatest woman athlete in history, Babe Zaharias is easily the hardest golfer to rate due to her untimely death at age 42. Though accomplished against clearly lesser fields, Zaharias' career winning percentages will likely stand as all-time landmarks. Further, her ability to qualify for the PGA Tour's 1945 Los Angeles and Tucson Opens remains a unique accomplishment among women, though the wartime nature of the fields cannot be totally ignored. Could Zaharias have continued such dominance into her later 40s against strengthening fields? Might her power-oriented game—which was never as refined as Wright's—actually have improved with greater experience? Unfortunately, what the Babe *might* have done is conjecture, whereas the accomplishments of Wright (and now Sorenstam) are a matter of record.

4. Joyce Wethered (4 Major Amateur Titles)

Winning percentage: N/A
Major percentage: N/A

Like Babe Zaharias, Joyce Wethered is a particularly difficult player to rank, for her dominance was relatively brief and accomplished against limited amateur fields—though her biggest victories did come against Cecil Leitch and Glenna Collett. Perhaps the most compelling points in her favor were the testimonials of Bobby Jones and Henry Cotton, whose glowing praise have helped lift the Wethered image to near mythic status. But Wethered's dominance was wedged into six competitive seasons, leaving us once again to speculate as to how her *potential* accomplishments might have measured up to the actual achievements of others.

5. Kathy Whitworth (88 LPGA Wins, 6 Major Championships)

Winning percentage: 12.0%
Major percentage: 7.6%

Kathy Whitworth's greatest strength has been durability, for her 837 career LPGA starts extended over nearly 40 years, during which she became the winningest American professional golfer of all time. Whitworth's relatively low winning percentage ranks 9th in Tour history, however, and a disappointing Major championship yield of 7.6% places only 13th. Still, Whitworth's 88 wins against generally stronger fields lifts her above such older contenders as Patty Berg and Louise Suggs.

6. Louise Suggs (58 LPGA Wins, 11 Major Championships)

Winning percentage: 18.0%
Major percentage: 14.6%

Louise Suggs' 58 wins rank fourth all time while her 11 Major championships place third. Indeed, she places strongly in all statistical categories including fourth in winning percentage and fifth in Major winning percentage. Remarkably, in Major championship play, Suggs scored top-10 finishes 71% of the time during her competitive years and was among the top five 47% of the time. She betters Patty Berg in nearly every statistical category while having faced perhaps slightly stronger competition.

7. Patty Berg (60 Professional/LPGA Wins, 15 Major Championships)

Winning percentage: 12.9%
Major percentage: 11.3%

Patty Berg's numbers are difficult to get a handle on as fully 22 of her career wins (and eight of her top-ranked 15 Majors) came prior to the founding of the LPGA, against fields of dubious quality. Still, her initial decade on the newly established Tour (1950–59) resulted in winning percentages that would stand up nicely in any generation.

8. JoAnne Carner (44 LPGA Wins, 2 Major Championships, 8 Major Amateur Wins)

Winning percentage: 11.0%
Major percentage: 4.9%

Of her 43 LPGA Tour victories, 42 came after JoAnne Carner's 30th birthday, this the result of her greatly extended amateur career. Carner's winning percentage of 11.0% was exceeded only by Nancy Lopez among a strong field of contemporaries, but a career total of only two Major championships (both U.S. Women's Opens) seems surprisingly low.

9. Nancy Lopez (48 LPGA Wins, 3 Major Championships)

Winning percentage: 12.2%
Major percentage: 6.0%

Though a total of only three Major championships might legitimately be viewed as disappointing, Nancy Lopez's 48 Tour wins rank behind only Sorenstam among players turning pro after 1960. Ditto her winning percentage of 12.2%, comfortably the best of her time. Skeptics may suggest that her career stats are ballooned by spectacular 1978-79 numbers, but Lopez would have qualified for the old LPGA Hall of Fame even with those two seasons omitted entirely.

10. Patty Sheehan (35 LPGA Wins, 6 Major Championships)

Winning percentage: 9.0%
Major percentage: 8.8%

Sheehan rates the best of the fine group of American pros who peaked during the mid to late 1980s, edging ahead of Pat Bradley, Juli Inkster, and Betsy King primarily on the strength of a winning percentage that bested them by 3.9%, 2.4%, and 4.1%, respectively. A career win total of 35, however, falls well shy of those ranked above her.

11. Betsy Rawls (55 LPGA Wins, 8 Major Championships)

Winning percentage: 10.4%
Major percentage: 10.3%

Like Louise Suggs, Rawls' career standing in wins (fifth) and Major championships (tied for fifth) is impressive. Unlike Suggs, however, Rawls' winning percentages fail to lift her clearly above the cadre of 1980s players—and their stiffer competition—that surround her.

12. Juli Inkster* (30 LPGA Wins, 7 Major Championships, 3 Major Amateur Wins)

Winning percentage: 6.6%
Major percentage: 9.1%

A late rush of success has pushed Inkster's career numbers from strong to a near-elite level. It's close, but her seventh Major championship (the 2002 U.S. Women's Open) and spectacular sweep of three straight U.S. Women's Amateurs (from 1980 through 1982) nose Inkser just ahead of Pat Bradley, whose career numbers (minus the Amateurs) are strikingly similar.

13. Pat Bradley (31 LPGA Wins, 6 Major Championships)

Winning percentage: 5.1%
Major percentage: 8.1%

Pat Bradley's career professional numbers rank nearly a dead heat with Juli Inkster's, and Bradley has recorded top-10 Major championship finishes far more frequently (47% to 32%). But Inkster has *won* 9.1% of her Major starts (to Bradley's 8.1%) and that, along with Inkster's historic amateur record, settles that.

14. Sandra Haynie (42 LPGA Wins, 4 Major Championships)

Winning percentage: 8.7%
Major percentage: 7.4%

An argument can be made that Sandra Haynie—with 42 wins and a winning percentage of 8.7%—should rank more competitively with several of the 1980s players placed above her. But Haynie's four Major titles (won against slightly lesser competition) work against her, as does the fact that her performance actually declined slightly on the game's biggest stages.

15. Betsy King (34 LPGA Wins, 6 Major Championships)

Winning percentage: 4.9%
Major percentage: 6.7%

Betsy King's six Major championships might suggest a higher ranking, and during her best decade (1984–93) she may in fact have been slightly better than Bradley or Inkster. Her winning percentages, however, suggest that on the whole, she played in many more events to achieve similar career totals.

16. Glenna Collett (18 major amateur wins)

Winning percentage: N/A
Major percentage: N/A

Like Joyce Wethered, Glenna Collett is difficult to rank based on the differences between Golden Age amateur competition and the modern professional game. Dominant at home (to the tune of six U.S. Women's Amateur titles), Collett's lone weakness was a failure to win the British Ladies, where she was twice beaten in the final (once by Wethered).

17. Karrie Webb* (31 LPGA Wins, 6 Major Championships)

Winning percentage: 15.7%
Major percentage: 17.0%

The verdict remains out on Webb who, until 2003, appeared destined to accompany Annika Sorenstam toward the very top of this list. Even with her recent slip in form, however, her career winning percentages continue to place her quite favorably all time—but have we already seen her best?

18. Amy Alcott (29 LPGA Wins, 5 Major Championships)

Winning percentage: 5.4%
Major percentage: 6.7%

One of the easier players to rank, Alcott's career numbers fall a clear notch behind those listed above her, and similarly ahead of those who follow in her wake.

19. Laura Davies* (20 LPGA Wins, 4 Major Championships)

Winning percentage: 5.8%
Major percentage: 5.6%

Britain's most successful female professional is one of the few players here to have logged substantial wins (25+) overseas. Still, her career LPGA totals lag somewhat behind Alcott in most categories, though her winning percentage is slightly higher.

20. Cecil Leitch (4 major amateur wins)

Winning percentage: N/A
Major percentage: N/A

It can be argued that with her main rival Joyce Wethered ranked fourth, Cecil Leitch belongs further up this list. But Wethered, by all accounts, was clearly the better player, and given Leitch's career numbers and lesser early competition, it becomes difficult to rate her ahead of anyone among the first 19.

21. Donna Caponi (24 LPGA Wins, 4 Major Championships)

Winning percentage: 4.0%
Major percentage: 6.3%

Caponi's victory totals cannot match Alcott and her winning percentage is 1.8% lower than Davies. Comparing her to amateurs Leitch and Campbell Hurd, however, is a crapshoot.

22. Dorothy Campbell Hurd (8 major amateur wins)

Winning percentage: N/A
Major percentage: N/A

Another whose limited period competition makes her hard to rate, Dorothy Campbell's status as the first woman to claim the British, American, and Canadian titles made her an elite player of her day. She must be ranked beneath Leitch, however, who proved herself able to battle Joyce Wethered on at least somewhat equal terms.

23. Catherine LaCoste (1 Major Championship/2 major amateur wins)

Winning percentage: N/A
Major percentage: N/A

Perhaps the finest woman golfer in the world in the late 1960s, LaCoste muddled her place in history by retiring shortly thereafter, leaving us to wonder what further heights she might have attained. She remains that rare athlete who may actually have retired *before* his/her prime!

24. Meg Mallon* (18 LPGA Wins, 4 Major Championships)

Winning percentage: 4.2%
Major percentage: 7.8%

Mallon climbs onto the list largely on the strength of winning the 2004 U.S. Women's Open, a fourth Major championship victory that places her equal to or better than five LPGA professionals ranked above her. Was this the beginning of a Juli Inkster-like early 40s rush or just one final peak?

25. Pam Barton (3 major amateur wins)

Winning percentage: N/A
Major percentage: N/A

Barton's untimely World War II death cut short a blossoming career that saw her become only the second woman to capture British and American Amateur titles in the same year (1936). By all accounts, she was destined for continuing greatness though once again, such talk is entirely speculative.

Major Tour Winning Percentages

Presenting career performance statistics for golf's greats poses a unique problem: Unlike virtually every other sport, the golfing elite frequently continue competing (at least part-time) long after their competitive peaks. Thus in order to make our comparisons valid, we must look primarily at what was achieved during the years in which a player remained genuinely near the top of his or her game. How is such a time frame determined? Unfortunately, as golfers age at widely differing paces, there can be no set formula. Thus we are reduced to making general determinations as to when a player ceased being "in his prime," then scaling down his numbers accordingly. There is, of course, an inherent degree of subjectivity to such a process, creating a margin of error that is further widened by the inexact nature of early PGA Tour records. Thus numbers presented here must be viewed mostly as general trends and guideposts; When player A wins 3% more often than player B, there is a substantial difference. When the margin is 0.3%, there really isn't.

Presented first are records illustrating PGA Tour and European Tour Winning percentages (tables A and B); that is, the percentage of total starts won by players during their legitimately competitive years. Table C provides worldwide Major winning percentages, a similar "batting average" but this time limited strictly to Major championship play. Table D then supplements these numbers with the percentage of top-10 finishes achieved in Major championships during these same years, a fine measure of who has regularly elevated their games on the biggest occasions.

With deeper fields, improved course conditioning, and unchecked equipment advances making it ever harder to win consistently, tables E, F, and G allow us to compare period players more directly, ranking winning percentages in three different eras: pre–World War II (1900–1939), post–World War II (1940–1970), and modern (1971–present). Finally, tables H and I provide the Tour's leading "extended" or full-career winning percentages; that is, for example, Jack Nicklaus' numbers right up through 2004, with, in his case, more than 130 "past-his-prime" starts factored in.

On the women's side, tables J, K, L and M provide winning percentages and Major winning percentages, then extended percentages for LPGA players dating to the organization's opening season of 1950.

Numbers presented here represent play through August 2004.

Note: Ties broken by extended percentage points (not shown) where applicable.

Table A
PGA Tour Winning Percentage*

(minimum 50 events)

Ranking	Player	Percentage		
1	Tiger Woods	40/164	=	24.4
2	Ben Hogan	64/263	=	24.3
3	Walter Hagen	44/181	=	24.3
4	Jim Barnes	21/91	=	23.1
5	Macdonald Smith	24/105	=	22.9
6	Byron Nelson	52/248	=	20.1
7	Leo Diegel	30/152	=	19.7
8	Bobby Locke	11/59	=	18.6
9	Sam Snead	82/460	=	17.8
10	Gene Sarazen	39/237	=	16.5
11	Jack Nicklaus	73/455	=	16.0
12	Willie MacFarlane	21/131	=	16.0
13	Jock Hutchison	14/94	=	14.9
14	Henry Picard	26/180	=	14.4
15	Tommy Armour	25/179	=	14.0
16	Harry Cooper	31/241	=	12.9
17	Cary Middlecoff	40/319	=	12.6
18	Arnold Palmer	62/524	=	11.8
19	Paul Runyan	29/253	=	11.5
20	Jimmy Demaret	31/278	=	11.2
21	Olin Dutra	10/91	=	11.0
22	Lloyd Mangrum	36/333	=	10.8
23	Bobby Cruickshank	17/159	=	10.7
24	Billy Casper	51/485	=	10.5
25	Bill Mehlhorn	20/192	=	10.4
26	Johnny Farrell	22/224	=	9.8
27	Horton Smith	30/313	=	9.6
28	Joe Kirkwood	13/138	=	9.4
29	Ralph Guldahl	16/171	=	9.4
30	Craig Wood	21/243	=	8.6
31	Ernie Els	14/167	=	8.4
32	Roberto de Vicenzo	10/121	=	8.3
33	Tom Watson	39/480	=	8.1
34	Jug McSpaden	17/213	=	8.0
35	Phil Mickelson	23/292	=	7.9
36	Greg Norman	20/254	=	7.9
37	Ken Venturi	14/186	=	7.5
38	Johnny Miller	25/345	=	7.2
39	Lee Trevino	29/401	=	7.2
40	Gary Player	24/340	=	7.1

*Ties were broken by extended percentage points (not shown) where applicable.

Table B
PGA European Tour Winning Percentage*

(minimum 50 events; 1970–present)

Ranking	Player	Percentage		
1	Seve Ballesteros	54/289	=	18.7
2	Graham Marsh	12/78	=	15.4
3	Greg Norman	17/119	=	14.3
4	Bernhard Langer	39/315	=	12.4
5	Ernie Els	19/157	=	12.1
6	Peter Oosterhuis	9/78	=	11.5
7	Nick Faldo	29/275	=	10.5
8	Ian Woosnam	31/344	=	9.0
9	Mark O'Meara	5/59	=	8.5
10	Colin Montgomerie	29/378	=	7.7
11	Sandy Lyle	18/255	=	7.1
12	Tony Jacklin	11/157	=	7.0
13	Mark McNulty	16/233	=	6.9
14	José Maria Olazábal	21/310	=	6.8
15	Lee Westwood	17/262	=	6.5
16	Vijay Singh	12/224	=	5.4
17	Bernard Gallacher	11/243	=	4.5
18	Padraig Harrington	9/212	=	4.3
19	Brian Barnes	9/222	=	4.1
20	Ratief Goosen	11/274	=	4.0
21	Mark James	18/452	=	4.0
22	Sam Torrance	21/534	=	3.9
23	Brian Huggett	5/133	=	3.8
24	Maurice Bembridge	7/196	=	3.6
25	Neil Coles	12/337	=	3.6

*Tiger Woods has won 20 of 53 European Tour events entered (37.8%) but 12 of those victories came in Major championships and WGC events recognized officially in Europe but played in the United States. The Masters, U.S. Open, and PGA became officially recognized by the European Tour in 1999 and are thus factored into players' totals from that point forward.

Ties were broken by extended percentage points (not shown) where applicable.

Table C
PGA Tour Major Winning Percentage*

(minimum 25 events)

Ranking	Player	Percentage		
1	Harry Vardon	7/26	=	**26.9***
2	Tiger Woods	8/32	=	**25.0**
3	Walter Hagen	11/48	=	**22.9**
4	J. H. Taylor	5/25	=	**20.0***
5	Ben Hogan	9/47	=	**19.1**
6	Jack Nicklaus	18/120	=	**15.0**
7	Bobby Locke	4/27	=	**14.8**
8	Peter Thomson	5/34	=	**14.7**
9	Byron Nelson	5/41	=	**12.2**
10	Henry Cotton	3/25	=	**12.0**
11	Gene Sarazen	7/59	=	**11.9**
12	Jim Barnes	4/35	=	**11.4**
13	Gary Player	9/89	=	**10.1**
14	Ralph Guldahl	3/30	=	**10.0**
15	Tom Watson	8/81	=	**9.9**
16	Nick Faldo	6/63	=	**9.5**
17	Sam Snead	7/74	=	**9.5**
18	Lee Trevino	6/69	=	**8.7**
19	Tommy Armour	3/35	=	**8.6**
20	Arnold Palmer	7/91	=	**7.7**
21	Jock Hutchison	2/27	=	**7.4**
22	Seve Ballesteros	5/71	=	**7.0**
23	Cary Middlecoff	3/43	=	**7.0**
24	Denny Shute	3/43	=	**7.0**
25	Jimmy Demaret	3/45	=	**6.7**
25	Vic Ghezzi	2/30	=	**6.7**
27	Leo Diegel	2/32	=	**6.3**
28	Ernie Els	3/49	=	**6.1**
29	Vijay Singh	3/51	=	**5.9**
30	Larry Nelson	3/57	=	**5.3**
30	Henry Picard	2/38	=	**5.3**
32	Paul Runyan	2/39	=	**5.1**
33	Nick Price	3/59	=	**5.1**
34	Raymond Floyd	4/80	=	**5.0**
34	Jack Burke Jr.	2/40	=	**5.0**
36	Julius Boros	3/61	=	**4.9**
37	Craig Wood	2/41	=	**4.9**
38	Billy Casper	3/62	=	**4.8**
39	Dave Stockton	2/43	=	**4.7**
40	Payne Stewart	3/65	=	**4.6**

*Technically, Vardon and Taylor are not eligible for tables B and C, as only British Open *victories* are counted as official PGA Tour starts. James Braid (22.7%), Olin Dutra (11.1%), and Tony Lema (5.6%) all would make this list had they played in the minimum number of events during their legitimately competitive years.

Ties were broken by extended percentage points (not shown) where applicable.

Table D
PGA Tour Percentage of Top-10 Major Finishes*

(minimum 25 events)

Ranking	Player	Percentage		
1	Harry Vardon	22/26	=	84.6
2	J. H. Taylor	21/25	=	84.0
3	Ben Hogan	39/47	=	83.0
4	Jack Nicklaus	73/103	=	70.9
5	Bobby Locke	19/27	=	70.4
6	Gene Sarazen	41/59	=	69.5
7	Henry Cotton	17/25	=	68.0
8	Walter Hagen	18/27	=	66.7
9	Jock Hutchison	18/27	=	66.7
9	Lloyd Mangrum	26/39	=	66.7
11	Byron Nelson	27/41	=	65.9
12	Macdonald Smith	17/28	=	60.7
13	Peter Thomson	20/34	=	58.8
14	Bill Mehlhorn	15/27	=	55.6
14	Ted Ray	15/27	=	55.6
16	Sam Snead	41/74	=	55.4
17	Tom Watson	44/81	=	54.3
18	Jim Barnes	19/35	=	54.3
19	Tiger Woods	17/32	=	53.0
20	Paul Runyan	20/39	=	51.3
21	Leo Diegel	16/32	=	50.0
21	Phil Mickelson	21/42	=	50.0
21	Henry Picard	19/38	=	50.0
21	Roberto de Vicenzo	17/34	=	50.0
25	Gary Player	44/89	=	49.4
26	Ernie Els	24/49	=	49.0
27	Harry Cooper	19/39	=	48.7
28	Bobby Cruickshank	16/34	=	47.1
29	Denny Shute	19/43	=	44.2
30	Johnny Farrell	18/42	=	42.9
31	Jim Ferrier	14/33	=	42.4
32	Jimmy Demaret	19/45	=	42.2
33	Arnold Palmer	38/91	=	41.8
34	Greg Norman	29/70	=	41.4
35	Nick Faldo	26/63	=	41.3
36	Tommy Armour	14/35	=	40.0
36	Ralph Guldahl	12/30	=	40.0
38	Craig Wood	16/41	=	39.0
39	Nick Price	22/59	=	37.3
40	Cary Middlecoff	16/43	=	37.2

*Ties were broken by extended percentage points (not shown) where applicable.

Table E
Winning Percentage — Pre-WWII-Era Players*

(1900–1939)

Ranking	Player	Percentage		
1	Walter Hagen	44/181	=	24.3
2	Jim Barnes	21/91	=	23.1
3	Macdonald Smith	24/105	=	22.9
4	Leo Diegel	30/152	=	19.7
5	Gene Sarazen	39/237	=	16.5
6	Willie MacFarlane	21/131	=	16.0
7	Jock Hutchison	14/94	=	14.9
8	Tommy Armour	25/179	=	14.0
9	Harry Cooper	31/241	=	12.9
10	Paul Runyan	29/253	=	11.5
11	Olin Dutra	10/91	=	11.0
12	Bobby Cruickshank	17/159	=	10.7
13	Bill Mehlhorn	20/192	=	10.4
14	Johnny Farrell	22/224	=	9.8
15	Horton Smith	30/313	=	9.6
16	Joe Kirkwood	13/138	=	9.4
17	Ralph Guldahl	16/171	=	9.4
18	Craig Wood	21/243	=	8.6
19	Jug McSpaden	17/213	=	8.0
20	Johnny Revolta	18/271	=	6.6

*Ties were broken by extended percentage points (not shown) where applicable.

Table F
Winning Percentage — Postwar-Era Players*

(1940–1970)

Ranking	Player	Percentage		
1	Ben Hogan	64/263	=	24.3
2	Byron Nelson	52/248	=	20.1
3	Bobby Locke	11/59	=	18.6
4	Sam Snead	82/460	=	17.8
5	Henry Picard	26/180	=	14.4
6	Cary Middlecoff	40/319	=	12.6
7	Arnold Palmer	62/524	=	11.8
8	Jimmy Demaret	31/278	=	11.2
9	Lloyd Mangrum	36/333	=	10.8
10	Billy Casper	51/485	=	10.5
11	Roberto de Vicenzo	10/121	=	8.3
12	Ken Venturi	14/186	=	7.5
13	Jack Burke Jr.	17/298	=	5.7
14	Gene Littler	29/586	=	4.9
15	Tony Lema	11/226	=	4.9
16	Jim Ferrier	18/374	=	4.8
17	Dutch Harrison	18/384	=	4.7
18	Doug Sanders	20/439	=	4.6
19	Mike Souchak	15/336	=	4.5
20	Tommy Bolt	15/372	=	4.0

*Ties were broken by extended percentage points (not shown) where applicable.

Table G
Winning Percentage — Modern-Era Players*

(1971–present)

Ranking	Player	Percentage		
1	Tiger Woods	40/164	=	**24.4**
2	Jack Nicklaus	73/455	=	**16.0**
3	Ernie Els	14/167	=	**8.4**
4	Tom Watson	39/480	=	**8.1**
5	Greg Norman	20/253	=	**7.9**
6	Phil Mickelson	23/292	=	**7.9**
7	Lee Trevino	19/401	=	**7.2**
8	Johnny Miller	25/345	=	**7.2**
9	Vijay Singh	20/291	=	**6.9**
10	Gary Player	24/350	=	**6.9**
11	Seve Ballesteros	9/151	=	**6.0**
12	David Duval	13/220	=	**5.9**
13	Nick Price	18/347	=	**5.2**
14	Sergio Garcia	5/99	=	**5.1**
15	Retief Goosen	4/89	=	**4.5**
16	Nick Faldo	9/211	=	**4.3**
17	Davis Love III	18/454	=	**4.0**
18	Raymond Floyd	22/571	=	**3.9**
19	Tom Weiskopf	16/418	=	**3.8**
20	José Maria Olazábal	6/159	=	**3.8**

*Ties were broken by extended percentage points (not shown) where applicable.

Table H
PGA Tour Extended Winning Percentage*

(minimum 50 events)

Ranking	Player	Percentage		
1	Macdonald Smith	24/105	=	**22.9**
1	Tiger Woods	40/175	=	**22.9**
3	Walter Hagen	44/195	=	**22.6**
4	Jim Barnes	21/97	=	**21.6**
5	Ben Hogan	64/298	=	**21.5**
6	Leo Diegel	30/152	=	**19.7**
7	Bobby Locke	11/59	=	**18.6**
8	Byron Nelson	52/283	=	**18.4**
9	Sam Snead	82/550	=	**14.9**
10	Willie MacFarlane	21/141	=	**14.9**
11	Jock Hutchison	14/99	=	**14.1**
12	Tommy Armour	25/189	=	**13.2**
13	Gene Sarazen	39/297	=	**13.1**
14	Henry Picard	26/200	=	**13.0**
15	Jack Nicklaus	73/589	=	**12.4**
16	Cary Middlecoff	40/324	=	**12.3**
17	Olin Dutra	10/91	=	**11.0**
18	Paul Runyan	29/278	=	**10.4**
19	Bill Mehlhorn	20/192	=	**10.4**
20	Harry Cooper	31/291	=	**10.1**
21	Lloyd Mangrum	36/363	=	**9.9**
22	Johnny Farrell	22/224	=	**9.8**
23	Jimmy Demaret	31/328	=	**9.5**
24	Ralph Guldahl	16/171	=	**9.4**
25	Billy Casper	51/555	=	**9.2**

*Ties were broken by extended percentage points (not shown) where applicable.

Table I
PGA Tour Extended Major Winning Percentage*

(minimum 25 events)

Ranking	Player	Percentage		
1	Tiger Woods	8/35	=	21.0
2	Walter Hagen	11/54	=	20.1
3	Ben Hogan	9/58	=	15.5
4	Peter Thomson	5/43	=	11.6
5	Jack Nicklaus	18/167	=	10.8
6	Henry Cotton	3/28	=	10.7
7	Jim Barnes	4/38	=	10.5
8	Bobby Locke	4/40	=	10.0
9	Byron Nelson	5/52	=	9.6
10	Ralph Guldahl	3/39	=	7.7
11	Tommy Armour	3/44	=	6.8
12	Tom Watson	8/119	=	6.7
13	Nick Faldo	6/90	=	6.7
13	Jock Hutchison	2/30	=	6.7
13	Tony Jacklin	2/30	=	6.7
13	Vic Ghezzi	2/30	=	6.7
13	Lee Trevino	6/90	=	6.7
18	Gary Player	9/145	=	6.2
19	Gene Sarazen	7/116	=	6.0
20	Ernie Els	3/50	=	6.0
21	Seve Ballesteros	5/85	=	5.9
21	Vijay Singh	3/51	=	5.9
21	Sam Snead	7/119	=	5.9
24	Leo Diegel	2/35	=	5.7
25	Cary Middlecoff	3/54	=	5.6

*Extended results incomplete for Harry Vardon, J. H. Taylor, James Braid, and Ted Ray.

Ties were broken by extended percentage points (not shown) where applicable.

Table J
LPGA Winning Percentage*

(minimum 50 events)

Ranking	Player	Percentage		
1	Babe Zaharias	31/69	=	44.9
2	Mickey Wright	81/303	=	26.7
3	Annika Sorenstam	52/223	=	23.3
4	Louise Suggs	50/278	=	18.0
5	Karrie Webb	31/198	=	15.7
6	Patty Berg	38/295	=	12.9
7	Se Ri Pak	22/171	=	12.9
8	Nancy Lopez	48/394	=	12.2
9	Kathy Whitworth	88/733	=	12.0
10	JoAnne Carner	43/390	=	11.0
11	Betsy Rawls	55/529	=	10.4
12	Patty Sheehan	35/391	=	9.0
13	Carol Mann	38/435	=	8.7
14	Sandra Haynie	42/482	=	8.7
15	Ayako Okamoto	17/242	=	7.0
16	Juli Inkster	30/455	=	6.6
17	Laurie Davies	20/343	=	5.8
18	Beth Daniel	33/571	=	5.8
19	Jane Blalock	27/470	=	5.7
20	Amy Alcott	29/536	=	5.4

*Results for Patty Berg, Louise Suggs, and Babe Zaharias cover LPGA—era (post–1949) only.

Ties were broken by extended percentage points (not shown) where applicable.

Table K
LPGA Major Winning Percentage*

Ranking	Player	Percentage		
1	Babe Zaharias	5/14	=	35.7
2	Mickey Wright	13/50	=	26.0
3	Annika Sorenstam	7/37	=	18.9
4	Karrie Webb	6/35	=	17.0
5	Louise Suggs	6/41	=	14.6
6	Se Ri Pak	4/28	=	14.3
7	Patty Berg	7/62	=	11.3
8	Betsy Rawls	8/78	=	10.3
9	Juli Inkster	7/77	=	9.1
10	Patty Sheehan	6/68	=	8.8
11	Pat Bradley	6/74	=	8.1
12	Meg Mallon	5/64	=	7.8
13	Kathy Whitworth	6/79	=	7.6
14	Sandra Haynie	4/54	=	7.4
15	Betsy King	6/89	=	6.7
16	Amy Alcott	5/75	=	6.7
17	Donna Caponi	4/63	=	6.3
18	Nancy Lopez	4/67	=	6.0
19	Betty Jameson	3/51	=	5.9
20	Laurie Davies	4/71	=	5.6

*Results for Patty Berg, Louise Suggs, and Babe Zaharias cover LPGA—era (post–1949) only.

Ties were broken by extended percentage points (not shown) where applicable.

Table L
LPGA Extended Winning Percentage*

(minimum 50 events)

Ranking	Player	Percentage		
1	Babe Zaharias	31/69	=	44.9
2	Annika Sorenstam	52/226	=	23.0
3	Mickey Wright	82/372	=	22.0
4	Louise Suggs	50/310	=	16.1
5	Karrie Webb	31/198	=	15.7
6	Se Ri Pak	22/171	=	12.9
7	Nancy Lopez	48/456	=	10.5
8	Kathy Whitworth	88/837	=	10.5
9	Patty Berg	38/369	=	10.3
10	Betsy Rawls	55/543	=	10.1
11	Carol Mann	38/464	=	8.2
12	Patty Sheehan	35/429	=	8.2
13	Sandra Haynie	42/526	=	8.0
14	JoAnne Carner	43/632	=	6.8
15	Ayako Okamoto	17/269	=	6.3
16	Juli Inkster	30/479	=	6.2
17	Laura Davies	20/343	=	5.8
18	Beth Daniel	33/590	=	5.6
19	Jane Blalock	27/491	=	5.5
20	Judy Rankin	26/487	=	5.3

*Results for Patty Berg, Louise Suggs and Babe Zaharias cover LPGA—era (post–1949) only.

Ties were broken by extended percentage points (not shown) where applicable.

Table M
LPGA Extended Major Winning Percentage*

(minimum 25 events)

Ranking	Player	Percentage		
1	Babe Zaharias	5/14	=	35.7
2	Mickey Wright	13/57	=	22.8
3	Annika Sorenstam	7/37	=	18.9
4	Karrie Webb	6/35	=	17.0
5	Louise Suggs	6/51	=	11.8
6	Betsy Rawls	8/80	=	10.0
7	Patty Berg	7/75	=	9.3
8	Juli Inkster	7/85	=	8.2
9	Meg Mallon	5/65	=	7.7
10	Patty Sheehan	6/80	=	7.5
11	Pat Bradley	6/93	=	6.5
12	Sandra Haynie	4/63	=	6.3
13	Kathy Whitworth	6/95	=	6.3
14	Betsy King	6/98	=	6.1
15	Donna Caponi	4/68	=	5.9
15	Betty Jameson	3/51	=	5.9
17	Laura Davies	4/71	=	5.6
18	Amy Alcott	5/94	=	5.3
19	Nancy Lopez	4/83	=	4.8
20	Hollis Stacy	4/96	=	4.2

*Results for Patty Berg, Louise Suggs, and Babe Zaharias cover LPGA—era (post–1949) only.

Ties were broken by extended percentage points (not shown) where applicable.

Major Championships

In our contemporary game, the phrase "Major championship" is universally taken to include the Masters, the U.S. Open, the British Open (the "Open Championship"), and the PGA—the modern professional Grand Slam. In Bobby Jones' day, however, when the PGA was young and the Masters didn't yet exist, an alternative version encompassed the two national Opens as well as the U.S. and British Amateurs, the Grand Slam won by Jones in 1930, but one for which no professional was eligible to compete.

Following are four tables covering all of the options. Table A provides an overall list, including all six events that have counted at one time or another. Table B details the modern professional version, while table C covers the more amateur-oriented Jones-era model. Finally, table D is purely a theoretical list utilizing the most prestigious "non-Major" event of the pre–Masters era (the Western Open) to give pre-war pros an even, four-event Grand Slam playing field with their modern brethren.

Notes:

A dash (—) indicates that a player was eligible to compete in the event but never won it.

The designation N/A (not applicable) indicates that the event did not exist during the player's legitimately competitive years or that the player wasn't eligible to compete in the event.

Table A
Major Championships (Total)

Player	Masters	US Open	British Open	PGA	US Amateur	British Amateur	Total
Jack Nicklaus	6	4	3	5	2	—	20
Bobby Jones	N/A	4	3	N/A	5	1	13
Walter Hagen	N/A	2	4	5	N/A	N/A	11
Tiger Woods	3	2	1	2	3	—	11
John Ball	N/A	—	1	N/A	—	8	9
Ben Hogan	2	4	1	2	N/A	N/A	9
Gary Player	3	1	3	2	—	—	9
Arnold Palmer	4	1	2	—	1	—	8
Tom Watson	2	1	5	—	—	—	8
Harold Hilton	N/A	—	2	N/A	1	4	7
Gene Sarazen	1	2	1	3	N/A	N/A	7
Sam Snead	3	—	1	3	—	—	7
Harry Vardon	N/A	1	6	N/A	N/A	N/A	7
Nick Faldo	3	—	3	—	—	—	6
Lee Trevino	—	2	2	2	—	—	6
Seve Ballesteros	2	—	3	—	—	—	5
James Braid	N/A	—	5	N/A	N/A	N/A	5
Lawson Little	—	1	—	—	2	2	5
Byron Nelson	2	1	—	2	—	—	5
J. H. Taylor	N/A	—	5	N/A	N/A	N/A	5
Peter Thomson	—	—	5	—	—	—	5
Jerry Travers	N/A	1	—	N/A	4	—	5
Willie Anderson	N/A	4	—	N/A	N/A	N/A	4
Jim Barnes	N/A	1	1	2	—	—	4
Raymond Floyd	1	1	2	—	—	—	4
Bobby Locke	—	—	4	—	—	—	4
Tom Morris Jr.	N/A	N/A	4	N/A	N/A	N/A	4
Tom Morris Sr.	N/A	N/A	4	N/A	N/A	N/A	4
Willie Park Sr.	N/A	N/A	4	N/A	N/A	N/A	4
Walter Travis	N/A	—	—	N/A	3	1	4
Jamie Anderson	N/A	N/A	3	N/A	N/A	N/A	3
Tommy Armour	—	1	1	1	—	—	3
Julius Boros	—	2	—	1	—	—	3
Billy Casper	1	2	—	—	—	—	3
Henry Cotton	—	—	3	—	—	—	3
Jimmy Demaret	3	—	—	—	—	—	3
Ernie Els	—	2	1	—	—	—	3
Chick Evans	N/A	1	—	N/A	2	—	3
Bob Ferguson	N/A	N/A	3	N/A	N/A	N/A	3
Ralph Guldahl	1	2	—	—	—	—	3
Hale Irwin	—	3	—	—	—	—	3
Cary Middlecoff	1	2	—	—	—	—	3
Larry Nelson	—	1	—	2	—	—	3
Francis Ouimet	—	1	—	N/A	2	—	3
Nick Price	—	—	1	2	—	—	3
Denny Shute	—	—	1	2	—	—	3
Vijay Singh	1	—	—	2	—	—	3
Payne Stewart	—	2	—	1	—	—	3

Table B
Major Championships (post–WWII)

Modern Era Grand Slam
(Professional Events Only)

Player	Masters	US Open	British Open	PGA	Total
Jack Nicklaus	6	4	3	5	18
Ben Hogan	2	4	1	2	9
Gary Player	3	1	3	2	9
Tom Watson	2	1	5	—	8
Tiger Woods	3	2	1	2	8
Arnold Palmer	4	1	2	—	7
Sam Snead	3	—	1	3	7
Nick Faldo	3	—	3	—	6
Lee Trevino	—	2	2	2	6
Seve Ballesteros	2	—	3	—	5
Peter Thomson	—	—	5	—	5
Raymond Floyd	1	1	—	2	4
Bobby Locke	—	—	4	—	4
Julius Boros	—	2	—	1	3
Billy Casper	1	2	—	—	3
Jimmy Demaret	3	—	—	—	3
Ernie Els	—	2	1	—	3
Hale Irwin	—	3	—	—	3
Cary Middlecoff	1	2	—	—	3
Larry Nelson	—	1	—	2	3
Nick Price	—	—	1	2	3
Vijay Singh	1	—	—	2	3
Payne Stewart	—	2	—	1	3

Table C
Major Championships (pre–WWII)

The Bobby Jones Grand Slam
(National Opens & Amateurs Only)

Player	US Open	British Open	US Amateur	British Amateur	Total
Bobby Jones	4	3	5	1	13
John Ball	—	1	—	8	9
Harold Hilton	—	2	1	4	7
Harry Vardon	1	6	N/A	N/A	7
Walter Hagen	2	4	N/A	N/A	6
James Braid	—	5	N/A	N/A	5
Lawson Little	1	—	2	2	5
J. H. Taylor	—	5	N/A	N/A	5
Jerry Travers	1	—	4	—	5
Willie Anderson	4	—	N/A	N/A	4
Tom Morris Jr.	—	4	N/A	N/A	4
Tom Morris Sr.	—	4	N/A	N/A	4
Willie Park Sr.	—	4	N/A	N/A	4
Walter Travis	—	—	3	1	4
Jamie Anderson	—	3	N/A	N/A	3
Henry Cotton	—	3	—	—	3
Chick Evans	1	—	2	—	3
Bob Ferguson	—	3	N/A	N/A	3
Francis Ouimet	1	—	2	—	3
Gene Sarazen	2	1	N/A	N/A	3

Table D
Major Championships (pre-1934)

The Pre-Masters Professional Grand Slam
(Western Open replacing Masters)

Player	US Open	British Open	PGA	Western	Total
Walter Hagen	2	4	5	5	16
Willie Anderson	4	—	—	4	8
Jim Barnes	1	1	2	3	7
Bobby Jones	4	3	N/A	—	7
Gene Sarazen	2	1	3	1	7
Harry Vardon	1	6	N/A	—	7
James Braid	—	5	N/A	—	5
Ralph Guldahl	2	—	—	3	5
J. H. Taylor	—	5	N/A	—	5
Tommy Armour	1	1	1	1	4
Jock Hutchison	—	1	1	2	4
Tom Morris Sr.	N/A	4	N/A	N/A	4
Tom Morris Jr.	N/A	4	N/A	N/A	4
Willie Park Sr.	N/A	4	N/A	N/A	4
Alex Smith	2	—	N/A	2	4
Jamie Anderson	N/A	3	N/A	N/A	3
Henry Cotton	—	3	—	—	3
Bob Ferguson	N/A	3	N/A	N/A	3
Johnny McDermott	2	—	N/A	1	3
Denny Shute	—	1	2	—	3
Macdonald Smith	—	—	—	3	3

Miscellaneous

World Golf Hall of Fame Members

Today's World Golf Hall of Fame (St. Augustine, Florida) opened in 1998, necessitating the inclusion of 71 players previously inducted into the former Hall of Fame (in Pinehurst, North Carolina) and the LPGA Hall of Fame. Consequently, all players with induction dates preceding 1998 are "grandfathered" members, recognized for their earlier selections.

The original Hall of Fame class of 1974—the *de facto* greatest players ever, up to that time—is worth noting and included: Patty Berg, Walter Hagen, Ben Hogan, Bobby Jones, Byron Nelson, Jack Nicklaus, Francis Ouimet, Arnold Palmer, Gary Player, Gene Sarazen, Sam Snead, Harry Vardon, and Babe Zaharias.

Men (Year of Induction)

United States — Players

Willie Anderson (1975)
Tommy Armour (1975)
Jim Barnes (1989)
Deane Beman (2000)
Tommy Bolt (2002)
Julius Boros (1982)
Jack Burke Jr. (2000)
Bill Campbell (1990)
Billy Casper (1978)
Harry Cooper (2002)
Ben Crenshaw (2002)
Jimmy Demaret (1983)
Leo Diegel (2003)
Chick Evans (1975)
Ray Floyd (1989)
Ralph Guldahl (1981)
Walter Hagen (1974)
Ben Hogan (1974)
Hale Irwin (1992)
Bobby Jones (1974)
Tom Kite (2004)
Lawson Little (1980)
Gene Littler (1990)
Lloyd Mangrum (1998)
Dr. Cary Middlecoff (1996)
Johnny Miller (1996)
Byron Nelson (1974)
Jack Nicklaus (1974)
Francis Ouimet (1974)
Arnold Palmer (1974)
Chi Chi Rodriguez (2002)
Paul Runyan (1990)
Gene Sarazen (1974)
Charles Sifford (2004)
Horton Smith (1990)
Sam Snead (1974)
Payne Stewart (2001)

Jerome Travers (1976)
Walter Travis (1979)
Lee Trevino (1981)
Tom Watson (1988)

United States — Others

Fred Corcoran (1975)
Bing Crosby (1978)
Joe Dey (1975)
Herb Graffis (1977)
Bob Harlow (1988)
Bob Hope (1983)
Robert Trent Jones (1987)
Harvey Penick (2002)
Clifford Roberts (1978)
Donald Ross (1977)
Karsten Solheim (2001)
Richard Tufts (1992)

United Kingdom

John Ball (1977)
Michael Bonallack (2000)
James Braid (1976)
Neil Coles (2000)
Henry Cotton (1980)
Nick Faldo (1997)
Harold Hilton (1978)
Tony Jacklin (2002)
John Jacobs (2000)
Tom Morris Jr. (1975)
Tom Morris Sr. (1976)
Allan Robertson (2001)
J. H. Taylor (1975)
Harry Vardon (1974)

South Africa

Bobby Locke (1977)
Gary Player (1974)

Australia

Greg Norman (2001)
Peter Thomson (1988)

Spain

Severiano Ballesteros (1997)

Argentina

Roberto de Vicenzo (1989)

Germany

Bernhard Langer (2002)

Japan

Isao Aoki (2004)

Zimbabwe

Nick Price (2003)

Fiji

Vijay Singh (2005)

Women (Year of Induction)

United States — Players

Amy Alcott (1999)
Patty Berg (1974)
Pat Bradley (1991)
Donna Caponi (2001)
JoAnne Carner (1985)

Beth Daniel (1999)
Marlene Hagge (2002)
Sandra Haynie (1977)
Dorothy Campbell Hurd (1978)
Juli Inkster (2000)
Betty Jameson (1951)
Betsy King (1995)
Nancy Lopez (1989)
Carol Mann (1977)
Judy Rankin (2000)
Betsy Rawls (1987)
Patty Sheehan (1993)
Louise Suggs (1979)
Glenna Collett Vare (1975)
Kathy Whitworth (1982)
Mickey Wright (1976)
Babe Zaharias (1974)

United States — Others

Judy Bell (2001)
Dinah Shore (1994)

Canada

Marlene Stewart Streit (2004)

United Kingdom

Joyce Wethered (1975)

Sweden

Annika Sorenstam (2003)

Japan

Chako Higuchi (2003)

All-Time Victory Leaders

PGA Tour*

Ranking	Player	Wins
1	Sam Snead	82
2	Jack Nicklaus	73
3	Ben Hogan	64
4	Arnold Palmer	62
5	Byron Nelson	52
6	Billy Casper	51
7	Walter Hagen	44
8	Dr. Cary Middlecoff	40
8	Tiger Woods	40
10	Gene Sarazen	39
10	Tom Watson	39
12	Lloyd Mangrum	36
13	Horton Smith	32
14	Harry Cooper	31
14	Jimmy Demaret	31
16	Leo Diegel	30
17	Gene Littler	29
17	Paul Runyan	29
17	Lee Trevino	29
20	Henry Picard	26
21	Tommy Armour	25
21	Johnny Miller	25
23	Gary Player	24
23	Macdonald Smith	24
25	Phil Mickelson	23

* Pre-1970 events recognized retroactively.

LPGA Tour*

Ranking	Player	Wins
1	Kathy Whitworth	88
2	Mickey Wright	82
3	Patty Berg	60
4	Louise Suggs	58
5	Annika Sorenstam	56
6	Betsy Rawls	55
7	Nancy Lopez	48
8	JoAnne Carner	43
9	Sandra Haynie	42
10	Babe Zaharias	41
11	Carol Mann	38
12	Patty Sheehan	35
13	Betsy King	34
14	Beth Daniel	33
15	Pat Bradley	31
16	Juli Inkster	30
16	Karrie Webb	30
18	Amy Alcott	29
19	Jane Blalock	27
20	Judy Rankin	26
21	Marlene Hagge	25
22	Donna Caponi	24
23	Se Ri Pak	22
24	Marilynn Smith	21
25	Laura Davies	20

* Pre-1950 events recognized retroactively.

PGA European Tour*

Ranking	Player	Wins
1	Seve Ballesteros	54
2	Bernhard Langer	40
3	Ian Woosnam	31
4	Nick Faldo	29
4	Colin Montgomerie	29
6	José Maria Olazábal	21
6	Sam Torrance	21
8	Tiger Woods	20
9	Ernie Els	19
10	Mark James	18
10	Sandy Lyle	18
12	Greg Norman	17
12	Lee Westwood	17
14	Mark McNulty	16
15	Neil Coles	12
15	Graham Marsh	12
15	Vijay Singh	12
18	Howard Clark	11
18	Bernard Gallacher	11
18	Retief Goosen	11
18	Tony Jacklin	11
18	M. A. Jiménez	11
23	Darren Clarke	10
24	Brian Barnes	9
24	Padraig Harrington	9
24	Peter Oosterhuis	9
24	Manuel Piñero	9

* Since 1970 only.

Ryder Cup Records*

United States

	Overall Winning %				Singles Winning %		
Ranking	Player	Record	Percentage	Ranking	Player	Record	Percentage
1	Gardner Dickinson	9-1-0	90	1	Tom Kite	5-0-2	100
2	Tony Lema	8-1-2	89	2	Chip Beck	3-0-0	100
3	Jack Burke Jr.	7-1-0	88	2	Dave Hill	3-0-0	100
4	Walter Hagen	7-1-1	88	2	Tom Lehman	3-0-0	100
5	Sam Snead	10-2-1	83	5	Craig Stadler	2-0-0	100
6	Al Geiberger	5-1-3	83	6	Larry Nelson	2-0-1	100
7	J. C. Snead	9-2-0	82	6	Tom Weiskopf	2-0-1	100
8	Tom Weiskopf	7-2-1	78	6	Al Geiberger	2-0-1	100
9	Gene Sarazen	7-2-3	78	9	Sam Snead	6-1-0	86
10	Dow Finsterwald	9-3-1	75	10	Gene Sarazen	4-1-0	80
10	Larry Nelson	9-3-1	75	11	Billy Casper	6-2-2	75
12	Julius Boros	9-3-4	75	11	Lee Trevino	6-2-2	75
13	Lloyd Mangrum	6-2-0	75	13	Jack Burke Jr.	3-1-0	75
14	Chip Beck	6-2-1	75	13	Walter Hagen	3-1-0	75
15	Gene Littler	14-5-8	74	13	Lloyd Mangrum	3-1-0	75
				13	J. C. Snead	3-1-0	75

continued

Great Britain/Europe

Overall Winning %					Singles Winning %			
Ranking	Player	Record	Percentage		Ranking	Player	Record	Percentage
1	Sergio Garcia	10-3-2	77		1	C. Montgomerie	5-0-2	100
2	Paul Way	6-2-1	75		1	Eric Brown	4-0-0	100
3	C. Montgomerie	19-8-5	70		1	Manuel Piñero	2-0-0	100
4	Manuel Piñero	6-3-0	67		1	Paul Way	2-0-0	100
5	J. M. Olazábal	15-8-5	65		5	Peter Oosterhuis	6-2-1	75
6	P. Harrington	7-4-1	64		6	Howard Clark	4-2-0	67
7	S. Ballesteros	20-12-5	63		6	J. M. Cañizares	2-1-1	67
8	Bernhard Langer	21-15-6	58		8	Nick Faldo	6-4-1	60
9	Lee Westwood	11-8-1	58		9	Bernhard Langer	4-3-3	57
10	Peter Oosterhuis	14-11-3	56		9	Bernard Gallacher	4-3-4	57
11	J. M. Cañizares	5-4-2	56		11	Ken Bousfield	2-2-0	50
12	Nick Faldo	23-19-4	55		11	Arthur Lees	2-2-0	50
13	Constantino Rocca	6-5-0	55		13	S. Ballesteros	2-4-2	33
14	Ian Woosnam	14-12-5	54		13	Sergio Garcia	1-2-0	33
15	Bernard Gallacher	13-13-5	50		13	Constantino Rocca	1-2-0	33
15	Howard Clark	7-7-1	50					
15	Darren Clarke	7-7-3	50					
15	Ken Bousfield	5-5-0	50					
15	Eric Brown	4-4-0	50					
15	Arthur Lees	4-4-0	50					

*Players must have participated in at least eight overall matches to be eligible. Percentages are tabulated strictly in terms of wins and losses, with halved matches not factored in. In cases where players with identical won-lost records have differing numbers of halves, the man with the lower number (having won a higher percentage of his overall starts) is ranked higher.

Miscellaneous Records

PGA Tour

Score	Player	Date/Tournament	Course
Low 72-Hole Score			
254 (−26)	Tommy Armour III	2003 Texas Open	La Cantera GC
256 (−28)	Mark Calcavecchia	2001 Phoenix Open	TPC Scottsdale
257 (−27)	Mike Souchak	1955 Texas Open	Brackenridge Park GC
Low 18-Hole Score			
59 (−13)	Al Geiberger	6/10/1977, Memphis Classic	Colonial CC
59 (−13)	Chip Beck	10/11/1991, Las Vegas Inv	Sunrise GC
59 (−13)	David Duval	1/24/1999, Bob Hope	PGA West GC (Palmer)
Low 9-Hole Score			
27 (−8)	Mike Souchak	2/17/1955, Texas Open	Brackenridge Park GC
27 (−7)	Andy North	8/29/1975, BC Open	En-Joie GC
27 (−9)	Billy Mayfair	8/12/2001, Buick Open	Warwick Hills G&CC

Wins	Player	Dates
Most Consecutive Victories		
11	Byron Nelson	March 8–11, 1945 — August 2–4, 1945
6	Ben Hogan	June 9–12, 1948 — August 19–22, 1948
6	Tiger Woods	August 26–29, 1999 — February 3–6, 2000*

*Three of Woods' victories were in non-full-field events.

Most Victories in a Calendar Year		
18	Byron Nelson	1945
13	Ben Hogan	1946
11	Sam Snead	1950

Career Grand Slam Winners

	Gene Sarazen	(1922 U.S. Open, 1922 PGA, 1932 British Open, 1935 Masters)
	Ben Hogan	(1946 PGA, 1948 U.S. Open, 1951 Masters, 1953 British Open)
	Gary Player	(1959 British Open, 1961 Masters, 1962 PGA, 1965 U.S. Open)
	Jack Nicklaus	(1962 U.S. Open, 1963 Masters, 1963 PGA, 1966 British Open)
	Tiger Woods	(1997 Masters, 1999 PGA, 2000 U.S. Open, 2000 British Open)

Youngest Winner

	Johnny McDermott	1911 U.S. Open (19 years, 10 months)
	Gene Sarazen	1922 Southern Open (20 years, 5 days)

Oldest Winner

	Sam Snead	1965 Greater Greensboro Open (52 years, 10 months, 8 days)
	Art Wall	1975 Greater Milwaukee Open (51 years, 7 months, 10 days)

Widest Margin of Victory

Strokes	Player	Year	Tournament
16	J. Douglas Edgar	1919	Canadian Open
16	Joe Kirkwood	1924	Corpus Christi Open
16	Bobby Locke	1948	Chicago Victory Championship

PGA European Tour (since 1970)

Score	Player	Date/Tournament	Course
Low 72-Hole Score			
258 (–14)	David Llewellyn	1988 Biarritz Classic	Biarritz GC
258 (–18)	Ian Woosnam	1990 Monte Carlo Open	Mont Agel GC
259 (–25)	Mark McNulty	1990 German Open	Frankfurt GC
Low 18-Hole Score			
60 (–12)	Jamie Spence	9/6/1992 Crans-sur-Sierre GC (European Masters)	
60 (–12)	Bernhard Langer	10/4/1997 Berliner G&CC (German Masters)	
Low 9-Hole Score			
27 (–9)	José Maria Cañizares	9/2/1978 Crans-sur-Sierre GC (Swiss Open)	
27 (–9)	Joakim Haeggman	10/19/1997 St. Andrews (Old) (Dunhill Cup)	

Wins	Player	Dates	
Most Consecutive Victories			
3	Nick Faldo	May 5–8, 1983 — May 19–22, 1983	
3	Seve Ballesteros	June 19–22, 1986 — July 3–7, 1986	
Most Victories in a Calendar Year			
6	Seve Ballesteros	1986	
6	Nick Faldo	1992	
6	Colin Montgomerie	1999	
6	Lee Westwood	2000	

Youngest Winner

Dale Hayes — 1971 Spanish Open (18 years, 290 days)

Oldest Winner

Des Smyth — 2001 Madeira Island Open (48 years, 34 days)

Widest Margin of Victory

Strokes	Player	Year	Tournament
11	Tony Jacklin	1974	Scandinavian Enterprise Open
11	Dale Hayes	1978	French Open
11	Ken Brown	1984	Glasgow Open
11	Colin Montgomerie	1989	Portuguese Open
11	Vijay Singh	1992	German Open

LPGA Tour

Score	Player	Date/Tournament	Course
Low 72-Hole Score			
258 (–22)	Karen Stupples	2004 Welch's/Fry's Championship	Dell Ulrich GC
Low 18-Hole Score			
59 (–13)	Annika Sorenstam	3/16/2001 Standard Register PING	Moon Valley CC
Most Consecutive Victories			
5	Nancy Lopez	May 12–14, 1978—June 16–18, 1978	
Most Victories in a Calendar Year			
13	Mickey Wright	1963	
Career Grand Slam Winners			
	Louise Suggs	(Titleholders 1946, Western Open 1946, LPGA 1947, U.S. Women's Open 1949)	
	Mickey Wright	(LPGA 1958, U.S. Women's Open 1958, Titleholders 1961, Western Open 1962)	
	Pat Bradley	(du Maurier 1980, U.S. Women's Open 1981, Dinah Shore 1986, LPGA 1986)	
	Juli Inkster	(Dinah Shore 1984, du Maurier 1984, LPGA 1989, U.S. Women's Open 1989)	
	Karrie Webb	(du Maurier 1999, Dinah Shore 2000, U.S. Women's Open 2000, 2001 LPGA, 2002 Women's British Open)	
	Annika Sorenstam	(U.S. Women's Open 1995, Dinah Shore 2001, LPGA 2003, Women's British Open 2003)	
Youngest Winner			
	Marlene Hagge	1952 Sarasota Open (18 years, 14 days)	
Oldest Winner			
	Beth Daniel	2003 Canadian Women's Open (46 years, 8 months, 29 days)	

Widest Margin of Victory

Strokes	Player	Year	Tournament
14	Louise Suggs	1949	U.S. Women's Open
14	Cindy Mackey	1986	Mastercard International

APPENDIX B
ARCHITECTS

The ranking of golf courses is an entirely subjective exercise in which such extraneous factors as an architect's reputation, aggressive marketing, a course's current maintenance standards, or, sadly, the degree of "hospitality" extended to visiting raters often creep annoyingly into the equation. Still, such ratings—flawed though they are—represent our sole method of quantifying the portfolios of the game's top designers. The tables that follow reflect recent rankings worldwide as well as specifically in the United States, Canada, Great Britain, Continental Europe, Australia, and South Africa. The number of courses ranked per country is roughly proportional to how many overall courses each possesses. Also, some additional statistics are included for the United States, the birthplace and runaway hotbed of the ratings game, and a place where, in addition to having so many courses, we can blend the results of two national rankings to greater effect.

In each table, architects are listed from those with the highest number of ranked courses to those with the lowest, as indicated in column two. Column three reflects the ranking of their top—rated ("highest") course while column four indicates the average position of all of their ranked courses combined ("average"), a statistic that gains greater relevance on the lists of 50 and 100. Architects have been given a ½ point in cases where credit must genuinely be split, often in the case of performing substantial redesigns of already existing courses.

Architects must have at least one full design (i.e., not two half—point redesigns) to qualify for inclusion, except as indicated.

Courses noted as "Omitted" are either of unknown origin or have too complex a design lineage to credit to a single architect.

Courses Ranked in World Top 25

(Golf Magazine)

Architect	# Ranked	Highest	Average
Dr. Alister MacKenzie	4½	2	12
Donald Ross	3	9	18.7
H. S. Colt	1½	3	7.5
George Crump	1	1	1
Tom Morris	1	3	9.5
William Flynn	1	4	4
Neville & Grant	1	7	7
Coore & Crenshaw	1	11	11
Hugh Wilson	1	14	14
William Fownes	1	15	15
MacKenzie Ross	1	17	17
A. W. Tillinghast	1	18	18
Tom Doak	1	19	19
C. B. Macdonald	1	20	20
Perry Maxwell	1	23	23
Tom Simpson	½	13	13

Omitted: St. Andrews (Old) and Royal County Down.

Courses Ranked in World Top 50

(Golf Magazine)

Architect	# Ranked	Highest	Average
Dr. Alister MacKenzie	6½	2	21.9
Donald Ross	4	9	24.5
A. W. Tillinghast	4	18	30
Perry Maxwell	2	23	22
Seth Raynor	2	29	30
Pete Dye	2	34	41
H. S. Colt	1½	3	7.5
Tom Simpson	1½	13	30
George Crump	1	1	1
Tom Morris	1	3	9.5
William Flynn	1	4	4
Neville & Grant	1	7	7
Coore & Crenshaw	1	11	11
Hugh Wilson	1	14	14
William Fownes	1	15	15
MacKenzie Ross	1	17	17
Tom Doak	1	19	19
C. B. Macdonald	1	20	20
Hawtree & Taylor	1	28	28
W. Laidlaw Purves	1	32	32
Willie Campbell	1	33	33
C. H. Alison	1	35	35
George Thomas	1	36	36
Jack Nicklaus	1	37	37
Willie Fernie	1	38	38
Sam Whiting	1	39	39
G. Ross & W. Pickeman	1	40	40
Willie Park Jr.	1	44	44
S. V. Hotchkin	1	46	46
David Harmon	1	49	49

Omitted: St. Andrews (Old), Royal County Down, and Carnoustie (Championship).

Courses Ranked in World Top 100

(Golf Magazine)
(minimum 2 ranked courses to qualify)

Architect	# Ranked	Highest	Average
A. W. Tillinghast	8	18	50.1
Dr. Alister MacKenzie	7½	2	29.8
Donald Ross	7	9	46.3
Pete Dye	7	34	62
Seth Raynor	5	29	53.2
R. T. Jones	4	77	82.8
William Flynn	3	4	62.7
C. H. Alison	3	35	63.3
Tom Fazio	3	83	86.7
H. S. Colt	2½	3	31
Perry Maxwell	2	23	32
George Thomas	2	36	47.5
Jack Nicklaus	2	37	52.5
Willie Park Jr.	2	44	52
Stanley Thompson	2	64	79.5
Herbert Fowler	2	76	79

Omitted: St. Andrews (Old), Royal County Down, Carnoustie (Championship), and Ganton.

Courses Ranked in South African Top 25

(South African Golf Digest)

Architect	# Ranked	Highest	Average
Gary Player	9	1	10.8
Robert Grimsdell	4	8	15.8
Peter Matkovich	2	6	14.5
R. T. Jones Jr.	1	7	7
C. M. Murray	1	10	10
C. H. Alison	1	11	11
S. V. Hotchkin	1	12	12
Jack Nicklaus	1	13	13
George Peck	1	15	15
Sid Brews	1	19	19
Tom Weiskopf	1	21	21
A. M. Copland	1	24	24

Courses Ranked in Australian Top 50*

(Australian Golf Digest)

Architect	# Ranked	Highest	Average
Peter Thomson	6	16	38.4
Graham Marsh	5	18	31
Dr. Alister MacKenzie	4½	1	3.8
Jack Nicklaus	3	7	28
Greg Norman	3	9	13
R. T. Jones Jr.	3	22	27.3
Alex Russell	3	1	22.5
Vern Morcum	2	30	32.5
Dan Soutar	1½	2	20.5
Sam Bennet	1½	19	21
Sloan Morpeth	1½	34	36
Von Hagge & Devlin	1	6	6
Michael Coate	1	10	10
John Harris	1	12	12
Cargie Rymill	1	13	13
David Graham	1	15	15
Eric Apperly	1	20	20
Tony Cashmore	1	24	24
David Anderson	1	25	25
Arnold Palmer	1	26	26
Al Howard	1	33	33
Victor East	1	37	37
C. H. Alison	1	41	41
Sam Berriman	1	45	45
Karl Litten	1	47	47

*Table actually includes 53 courses, counting Royal Melbourne's 36 holes as separate entries (*Golf Digest* ranks only the composite), adding the Moonah Links (home of the Australian Open that was too new for the last ranking), and including Kerry Packer's private Ellerston GC, which was also omitted. These additions are not counted in the average of their designers, Alex Russell, Peter Thomson, and Greg Norman, respectively.

Courses Ranked in European Top 50

(Golf World United Kingdom)

Architect	# Ranked	Highest	Average
R. T. Jones	9	1	18.9
Tom Simpson	5	4	22
Javier Arana	3	6	26.3
R. T. Jones Jr.	3	11	35.3
J. S. F. Morrison	3	12	17.3
H. S. Colt	3	20	25.7
Robert von Hagge	2	21	2
Frank Pennink	2	8	29
Peter Gannon	2	28	28.5
Bernhard von Limburger	2	34	36
Rafael Sundblom	1	3	3
Joe Lee	1	9	9
N. Coles & A. Gallardo	1	10	10
Cabell Robinson	1	13	13
Hubert Chesneau	1	14	14
Nick Faldo	1	16	16
Ture Bruce	1	19	19
Sir Guy Campbell	1	23	23
Sven Tumba	1	24	24
Gunnar Bauer	1	26	26
Bernhard Langer	1	27	27
Arthur Hills	1	33	33
Dave Thomas	1	35	35
Kurt Rossknect	1	37	37
Jim & George Fazio	1	39	39
D. Feherty & D. Jones	1	43	43

Courses Ranked in British Isles Top 50

(Golf World United Kingdom)

Architect	# Ranked	Highest	Average
H. S. Colt	9½	1 2	6.3
James Braid	5	12	33.6
Willie Park Jr.	3½	11	38
Herbert Fowler	3	18	35
Tom Morris	2½	15	33.3
S. V. Hotchkin	2	9	25
Sir Guy Campbell	2	31	42.7
Tom Simpson	1½	10	23
Mackenzie Ross	1	3	3
Hawtree & Taylor	1	5	5
Weiskopf & Morris	1	6	6
G. Ross & W. Pickeman	1	7	7
Kyle Phillips	1	13	13
W. Laidlaw Purves	1	16	16
Willie Fernie	1	20	20
Pat Ruddy	1	21	21
George Lowe	1	22	22
Eddie Hackett	1	23	23
R. Chambers & G. Morris	1	24	24
C. Barcroft	1	27	27
H. Finch-Hatton	1	33	33

Omitted: St. Andrews (Old), Royal County Down, Carnoustie (Championship), and Ganton.

Courses Ranked in Canadian Top 50

(SCOREGolf)

Architect	# Ranked	Highest	Average
Stanley Thompson	7	3	12.6
Tom McBroom	6½	8	29.3
Doug Carrick	5	20	33.8
Les Furber	3	16	25.7
Graham Cooke	2½	12	19.7
H. S. Colt	2	1	8
Dr. Michael Hurdzan	2	13	21
A. Vernon Macan	2	17	20.5
Jack Nicklaus	2	21	34
R. T. Jones Jr.	2	43	45.5
Willie Park Jr.	2	49	49.5
Bob Cupp	1½	9	25.5
Tom Fazio	1	2	2
Dick Wilson	1	7	7
Donald Steel	1	14	14
Rod Whitman	1	18	18
Jack Thompson	1	26	26
R. T. Jones	1	27	27
Norman Woods	1	30	30
Harvey Coombe	1	34	34
Ron Garl	1	39	39
Bill Newis	1	45	45

Courses Ranked in American Top 25

(combined *Golf Digest*/*Golf Magazine*)

Architect	# Ranked	Highest	Average
Donald Ross	5	6	15.6
A. W. Tillinghast	5	9	21.9
Dr. Alister MacKenzie	3	2	8.2
Perry Maxwell	2	14	19.8
William Flynn	2	3	20.1
Seth Raynor	2	18	26.3
George Crump	1	1	1.0
Neville & Grant	1	5	5.0
Henry Fownes	1	4	6.5
Hugh Wilson	1	8	7.5
C. B. Macdonald	1	12	15.5
Willie Campbell	1	11	16.0
Sam Whiting	1	16	20.0
Jack Nicklaus	1	18	20.5
Harry Collis	1	13	21.5
Coore & Crenshaw	1	7	22.5
George Thomas	1	22	24.0
Tom Doak	1	11	29.0
Willie Park	1	24	42.0
Pete Dye	0	28	—
Tom Fazio	0	37	—
C. H. Alison	0	40	—
George Fazio	0	42	—
R. T. Jones	0	43	—
Rees Jones	0	47	—
Dick Wilson	0	59	—
Weiskopf & Morrish	0	64	—

Courses Ranked in United States Top 50

(combined *Golf Digest*/*Golf Magazine*)

Architect	# Ranked	Highest	Average
Donald Ross	8	6	28.7
A. W. Tillinghast	7	9	26.4
Pete Dye	5	28	50.6
Dr. Alister MacKenzie	4	2	24.8
William Flynn	4	3	38.3
Seth Raynor	4	18	40.0
Tom Fazio	4	37	60.6
R. T. Jones	3	43	50.2
Perry Maxwell	2	15	19.8
George Thomas	2	22	27.5
Willie Park	2	24	49.0
George Crump	1	1	1.0
Neville & Grant	1	5	5.0
Henry Fownes	1	4	6.5
Hugh Wilson	1	8	7.5
C. B. Macdonald	1	12	13.5
Willie Campbell	1	11	16.0
Sam Whiting	1	24	20.0
Jack Nicklaus	1	18	20.5
Harry Collis	1	13	21.5
Coore & Crenshaw	1	7	22.5
Tom Doak	1	11	29.0
Devereux Emmet	1	29	30.5
John Bredemus	1	35	47.0
David M. Kidd	1	43	52.5
Willie Watson	1	36	58.5
Herbert Strong	1	46	60.0
Frederic Hood	1	50	64.0
C. H. Alison	1	40	67.5
George Fazio	1	42	71.5
Rees Jones	1	47	71.5
Weiskopf & Morrish	0	64	—
Dick Wilson	0	59	—

Courses Ranked in United States Top 100

(combined *Golf Digest*/*Golf Magazine*)
(minimum 2 ranked courses to qualify)

Architect	# Ranked	Highest	Average
R. T. Jones	12	43	77.8
Donald Ross	11	6	41.5
A. W. Tillinghast	11	9	46.8
Pete Dye	10	28	62.2
Tom Fazio	8	37	77.6
Dr. Alister MacKenzie	5	2	37.3
Seth Raynor	5	18	47.6
Jack Nicklaus	5	18	75.0
William Flynn	4	3	45.3
C. B. Macdonald	4	12	68.1
Rees Jones	4	47	86.3
Dick Wilson	4	59	86.0
George Thomas	3	22	50.7
George Fazio	2	42	79.8
Willie Park	2	24	44.0
Perry Maxwell	2	15	19.8
Coore & Crenshaw	2	7	54.5
C. H. Alison	2	40	81.3
Weiskopf & Morrish	2	64	73.0

Average Rank of Architect's Top 100 Courses

(combined *Golf Digest*/*Golf Magazine*)

All Ranked Courses*		Top Three Courses	
Perry Maxwell (2)	19.8	Dr. Alister MacKenzie	8.2
Dr. Alister MacKenzie (5)	37.3	Donald Ross	11.5
Donald Ross (11)	41.5	A. W. Tillinghast	18.9
Willie Park (2)	44.0	William Flynn	29.7
William Flynn (4)	45.3	Seth Raynor	34.8
A. W. Tillinghast (11)	46.8	Pete Dye	50.0
Seth Raynor (5)	47.6	George Thomas	50.7
George Thomas (3)	50.7	R. T. Jones	51.2
Coore & Crenshaw (2)	54.5	Tom Fazio	56.3
Pete Dye (10)	62.2	C. B. Macdonald	60.1
C. B. Macdonald (4)	68.1	Jack Nicklaus	60.2
Weiskopf & Morrish (2)	73.0	Rees Jones	82.0
Jack Nicklaus (5)	75.0	Dick Wilson	82.3
Tom Fazio (8)	77.6	Perry Maxwell	N/A
R. T. Jones (12)	77.8	Willie Park	N/A
George Fazio (2)	79.8	Coore & Crenshaw	N/A
C. H. Alison (2)	81.3	Weiskopf & Morrish	N/A
Dick Wilson (4)	86.0	George Fazio	N/A
Rees Jones (4)	86.3	C. H. Alison	N/A

*Total number of top 100 courses in parentheses.

Total U.S. Major/National Championships Held

(by architect)

Architect	Masters	US Open	PGA	Total	US Amateur	Others*	Total
Dr. A. MacKenzie	68	—	—	68	—	2	70
Donald Ross	—	19	13	32	17	57	106
A. W. Tillinghast	—	10	6	16	8	17	41
R. T. Jones	—	6	9	15	1	10	26
Henry Fownes	—	7	3	10	5	1	16
William Flynn	—	7	2	9	5	12	26
Perry Maxwell	—	3	4	7	2	8	17
Herbert Strong	—	3	3	6	4	3	13
Harry Collis	—	3	2	5	—	1	6
Pete Dye	—	—	3	5	3	6	14
Neville & Grant	—	4	1	5	4	2	11
Jack Nicklaus	—	—	5	5	3	2	10
Hugh Wilson	—	4	1	5	5	3	13
Devereux Emmet	—	1	3	4	4	5	13
C. B. Macdonald	—	4	—	4	6	6	16
Willie Park	—	2	2	4	1	1	6
Sam Whiting	—	4	—	4	2	—	6
Willie Campbell	—	3	—	3	5	6	14
George Thomas	—	1	2	3	1	3	7
H. J. Tweedie	—	2	1	3	2	1	6
Dick Wilson	—	—	3	3	—	3	6
C. H. Alison	—	1	1	2	3	3	8
William Davis	—	2	—	2	2	—	4
Willie Watson	—	1	1	2	—	4	6
John Bredemus	—	1	—	1	—	1	2
Tom Fazio	—	—	1	1	—	4	5
Seth Raynor	—	—	1	1	—	4	5
Rees Jones	—	—	—	0	—	1	1

*Includes U.S. Women's Open, U.S. Women's Amateur, U.S. Senior Open, Walker Cup, Curtis Cup, and Ryder Cup.

Appendix C
Writers

Complete Book Titles of Featured Writers

Titles are arranged chronologically and generally include only works penned predominantly by author. Only golf—oriented books of 50 or more pages are listed. Subsequent revised or abridged editions and reprints do not appear, nor do overseas editions of the same title.

Peter Allen

Famous Fairways, Stanley Paul, 164 pp., 1968.
Play the Best Courses: Great Golf in the British Isles, Stanley Paul, 264 pp., 1973.
The Sunley Book of Royal Golf, Stanley Paul, 160 pp., 1989.

Al Barkow

Golf's Golden Grind: The History of the Tour, Harcourt Brace, 310 pp., 1974.
Gettin' to the Dance Floor, Atheneum, 282 pp., 1986.
The History of the PGA Tour, Doubleday, 298 pp., 1989.
The Golden Era of Golf, St. Martin's, 314 pp., 2000.
Golf Legends of All Time, Publications Intn'l, 215 pp., 1997.
That's Golf, Burford, 257 pp., 2001.
Gene Sarazen and Shell's Wonderful World of Golf, Clocktower, 224 pp., 2003 (with Mary Ann Sarazen).

Innis Brown

How to Play Golf, American Sports, 128 pp., 1930.
Swinging into Golf, Whittlesey, 150 pp., 1937 (with Ernest Jones).

Robert Browning

(Numerous club handbooks are not included.)
The Stymie: A Miscellany of Golfing Humour and Wit, Fraser, Asher, 104 pp., 1910.
Super Golf, Simpkin, Marshall, 143 pp., 1919.
Moments with Golfing Masters, Methuen, 100 pp., 1932.
The Golfer's Catechism, H. O. Quinn, 88 pp., 1935.
Golf with Seven Clubs, W&G Foyle, 93 pp., 1950.
A History of Golf: The Royal and Ancient Game, J. M. Dent, 236 pp., 1955.
Golf in Cornwall, Golf Clubs Association, 87 pp., 1952.
Golf in Devon, Golf Clubs Association, 95 pp., 1952.
Golf in Essex, Golf Clubs Association, 83 pp., 1952.
Golf in Kent, Golf Clubs Association, 123 pp., 1952.
Golf in Somerset, Golf Clubs Association, 59 pp., 1952.
Golf in Gloucestershire, Golf Clubs Association, 53 pp., 1954.

Golf in Hants & Dorset, Golf Clubs Association, 163 pp., 1955.
Golf in Surrey, Golf Clubs Association, 191 pp., 1957.
Golf on the Lancs Coast, Golf Clubs Association, 56 pp., 1957.
Golf in Sussex, Golf Clubs Association, 103 pp., 1959.
Golf in Devon and Cornwall, Golf Clubs Association, 60 pp., 1970.

Patrick Campbell

How to Become a Scratch Golfer, Anthony Blond, 144 pp., 1963.
Patrick Campbell's Golfing Book, Blond & Briggs, 127 pp., 1972.

Robert Clark

Poems on Golf, Privately published, 78 pp., 1867.
Golf: A Royal and Ancient Game, R&R Clark, 284 pp., 1875.

Leonard Crawley

Playfair Golf Annuals (1950–54), Playfair, 176–240 pp., 1950–54.

Bernard Darwin

(Numerous club handbooks are not included.)
The Golf Courses of the British Isles, Duckworth, 253 pp., 1910.
Tee Shots and Others, Kegan Paul, 271 pp., 1911.
Golf from the Times, The Times, 141 pp., 1912.
Hints on Golf, Burberry's, 55 pp., 1912.
Present Day Golf, Hodder & Stoughton, 309 pp., 1921.
A Friendly Round, Mills & Boon, 142 pp., 1922.
A Round of Golf on the L&NER, London & Northeastern Railway, 127 pp., ca. 1925.
The Golf Courses of Great Britain, Johnathan Cape, 287 pp., 1925.
Green Memories, Hodder & Stoughton, 332 pp., c1928.
Second Shots, George Newnes, 178 pp., 1930.
Out of the Rough, Chapman & Hall, 336 pp., c1932.
Playing the Like, Chapman & Hall, 246 pp., 1934.
Rubs of the Green, Chapman & Hall, 260 pp., 1936..
Life Is Sweet Brother, Collins, 285 pp., 1940.
Pack Clouds Away, Collins, 288 pp., 1941.
Golf Between Two Wars, Chatto & Windus, 227 pp., 1944.
Golfing By–Paths, Country Life, 203 pp., 1946.
Every Idle Dream, Collins, 254 pp., 1948.
James Braid, Hodder & Stoughton, 196 pp., 1952.
A History of Golf in Britain, Cassell, 312 pp., 1952 (with Longhurst, Cotton, et al.)
Golf: The Pleasures of Life Series, Burke, 222 pp., 1954.
The World that Fred Made, Chatto & Windus 256 pp., 1955.
Mostly Golf, A&C Black 198 pp., 1976.
A Round with Darwin, Souvenir, 223 pp., 1984.
Darwin on the Green, Souvenir, 240 pp., 1986.
The Darwin Sketchbook, Classics of Golf, 384 pp., 1991.
The Happy Golfer, Flagstick, 264 pp., 1997.
Bernard Darwin on Golf, Lyons, 414 pp., 2003.

Patric Dickinson

A Round of Golf Courses, Evans Brothers, 159 pp., 1951.

Peter Dobereiner

The Game with the Hole in It, Faber & Faber, 142 pp., 1970.
The Glorious World of Golf, McGraw, Hill, 250 pp., 1973.
Stroke, Hole or Match? David & Charles, 192 pp., 1976.
For the Love of Golf, Stanley Paul, 256 pp., 1981.
Down the Nineteenth Fairway, Andre Deutch, 205 pp., 1982.
The Golfers, The Inside Story, Collins, 190 pp., 1982.
The Book of Golf Disasters, Stanley Paul, 179 pp., 1983.
Jacklin's Golf Secrets, Stanley Paul, 109 pp., 1983.
Golf à la Carte, Stanley Paul, 219 pp., 1991.

James Finegan

A Centennial Tribute to Golf in Philadelphia, Golf Assoc of Philadelphia, 519 pp., 1996.
Blasted Heaths and Blessed Greens, Simon & Schuster, 286 pp., 1996.
Emerald Fairways and Foam, Flecked Seas, Simon & Schuster, 287 pp., 1996.
All Courses Great and Small, Simon & Schuster, 288 pp., 2003.

Herb Graffis

The Golf Club Organizer's Hand-Book, Golfdom Magazine, 56 pp., 1931.
Golf Facilities, National Golf Foundation, 77 pp., 1949.
Planning the Professional's Shop, National Golf Foundation, 50 pp., 1951.
Esquire's World of Golf, Trident, 240 pp., 1965.
The PGA: The Official History of the Professional Golfer's Association of America, Crowell, 559 pp., 1975.

Bob Harlow

True Golf Facts, Pinehurst Outlook, 57 pp., 1940.

Horace G. Hutchinson

Hints on the Game of Golf, William Blackwood, 69 pp., 1886.
Golf: The Badminton Library, Longmans, Green, 495 pp., 1890.
Famous Golf Links, Longmans, Green, 199 pp., 1891.
Golfing: The Oval Series of Games, George Routledge, 120 pp., 1893.
After Dinner Golf, Hudson, 124 pp., 1896.
British Golf Links, J. S. Virtue, 331 pp., 1897.
A Golfing Pilgrim on Many Links, Methuen, 287 pp., 1898.
The Book of Golf and Golfers, Longmans, Green, 316 pp., 1899.
Aspects of Golf, J. W. Arrowsmith, 150 pp., 1900.
Bert Edward, the Golf Caddie, John Murray, 257 pp., 1903.
Golf Greens and Green Keeping, Country Life, 219 pp., 1906.
The New Book of Golf, Longmans, Green, 361 pp., 1912.
Fifty Years of Golf, Country Life, 229 pp., 1919.
The Lost Golfer, John Murray, 335 pp., 1930.

Dan Jenkins

Sports Illustrated's the Best 18 Golf Holes in America, Delacorte, 160 pp., 1966.
The Dogged Victims of Inexorable Fate, Little Brown, 298 pp., 1970.
Dead Solid Perfect, Atheneum, 234 pp., 1974.
You Gotta Play Hurt, Simon & Schuster, 353 pp., 1991.
Fairways and Greens, Doubleday, 247 pp., 1994.

O. B. Keeler

The Autobiography of an Average Golfer, Greenberg, 247 pp., 1925.
Down the Fairway, Minton,Balch, 239 pp., 1927, (with Bobby Jones).
The Boy's Life of Bobby Jones, Harpers', 308 pp., 1931.
Golf in North Carolina, North Carolina Department of Conservation & Development, 52 pp., ca. 1938.

Renton Laidlaw

Play Better Golf, Pelham, 121 pp., 1986.
The European Open: The First 10 Years, Birchgrey, 120 pp., 1988.
Golfing Heroes, Stanley Paul, 190 pp., 1991.

Al Laney

Following the Leaders, Ailsa, 169 pp., 1991.

Henry Leach

Great Golfers in the Making, Methuen, 299 pp., 1907.
The Spirit of the Links, Methuen, 314 pp., 1907.
Letters of a Modern Golfer to His Grandfather, Mills & Boon, 309 pp., 1910.
The Happy Golfer, Macmillan, 414 pp., 1914.

Henry Longhurst

(Numerous club handbooks are not included.)
Candid Caddies, Duckworth, 120 pp., 1935.
Golf, J. M. Dent, 303 pp., 1937.
Go Golfing, Duckworth, 105 pp., 1937 (with Archie Compston).
Golf Mixture, Werner Laurie, 203 pp., 1952.
A History of Golf in Britain, Cassell, 312 pp., 1952 (with Darwin, Cotton, et al.).
Round in Sixty-Eight, Werner Laurie, 173 pp., 1953.
Only on Sundays, Cassell, 259 pp., 1964.
Ryder Cup, 1965, Stanley Paul, 64 pp., 1965 (with Geoffrey Cousins).
Talking about Golf, Macdonald, 150 pp., 1966.
How to Get Started in Golf, Hodder & Stoughton, 92 pp., 1967.
Never on Weekdays, Cassell, 182 pp., 1968.
My Life and Soft Times, Cassell, 366 pp., 1971.
The Best of Henry Longhurst, Collins, 206 pp., 1979.
The Essential Henry Longhurst, Willow, 320 pp., 1988.

John L. Low

F. G. Tait: A Record, James Nisbet, 304 pp., 1900.
Concerning Golf, Hodder & Stoughton, 217 pp., 1903.

H. B. Martin

Golf Yarns: The Best Things About the Game of Golf, Dodd Mead, 85 pp., 1913.
Sketches Made at the Winter Golf League..., Publishers Typesetting, 102 pp., 1915.
Pictorial Golf, Dodd Mead, 243 pp., 1928.
What's Wrong with Your Golf Game, Dodd Mead, 240 pp., 1930.
Golf for Beginners, Modern Sports, 98 pp., 1930.
Great Golfers in the Making, Dodd Mead, 268 pp., 1932.
Fifty Years of American Golf, Dodd Mead, 423 pp., 1936.
How to Play Golf, Modern Sports, 98 pp., 1936.
St. Andrews Golf Club 1888–1938, Privately printed, 146 pp., 1938 (with A. B. Halliday).
The Garden City Golf Club 1899–1949, Privately printed, 67 pp., 1949.

Sam McKinlay

Scottish Golf and Golfers, Ailsa, 211 pp., 1992.

Frank Moran

Book of Scottish Golf Courses, Scottish Country Life, 127 pp., 1939.
Golfers' Gallery, Oliver & Boyd, 196 pp., 1946.

Joseph Murdoch

The Library of Golf 1743–1966, Gale Research, 314 pp., 1968.
Golf: A Guide to Information Sources, Gale Research, 232 pp., 1979.
The Game of Golf and the Printed Word 1566–1985, Castalio, 658 pp., 1985 (with R. Donovan).
The Murdoch Golf Library, Grant, 233 pp., 1991.

Charles Price

Golf Magazine's Pro Pointers and Stroke Savers, Harpers, 253 pp., 1960.
The World of Golf, Random House, 307 pp., 1962.
The American Golfer, Random House, 241 pp., 1964.
Sports Illustrated Book of Golf, Lippincott, 73 pp., 1970.
The World Atlas of Golf, Mitchell Beazley, 280 pp., 1976 (with Ward-Thomas, Wind, et al.).
Black's Picture Sports: Golf, A&C Black, 95 pp., 1976.
The Carolina Lowcountry, Birthplace of American Golf, Sea Pines, 76 pp., 1980 (with G. Rogers).
Golfer-at-Large, Atheneum, 241 pp., 1982.
A Golf Story, Atheneum, 161 pp., 1987.

Grantland Rice

The Winning Shot, Doubleday, Page, 258 pp., 1915 (with Jerome Travers).
The Duffer's Handbook of Golf, Macmillan, 163 pp., 1926.
The Bobby Jones Story, Tupper & Love, 303 pp., 1953.

Peter Ryde

The Shell International Encyclopedia of Golf, Ebury & Pelham, 480 pp., 1975 (with D. Steel).
Royal & Ancient Championship Records 1860–1980, R&A G.C. of St. Andrews, 535 pp., 1981.
Halford Hewitt: A Festival of Foursomes, Public Schools Golfing Society, 192 pp., 1984.

Geoff Shackelford

The Riviera Country Club: A Definitive History, Riviera CC, 196 pp., 1995.
The Captain, Captain Fantastic, 207 pp., 1996.
Masters of the Links, Sleeping Bear, 241 pp., 1997.
The Good Doctor Returns, Sleeping Bear, 162 pp., 1998.
The Golden Age of Golf Design, Sleeping Bear, 211 pp., 1999.
Alister MacKenzie's Cypress Point Club, Sleeping Bear, 189 pp., 2000.
The Art of Golf Design, Sleeping Bear, 191 pp., 2001 (with M. Miller).
Grounds for Golf, Thomas Dunne, 300 pp., 2003.
The Future of Golf in America, iUniverse, 139 pp., 2004.

Sir W. G. Simpson

The Art of Golf, David Douglas, 186 pp., 1887.

Garden G. Smith

Golf, Lawrence & Bullen, 104 pp., 1897.
The World of Golf, A. D. Innis, 330 pp., 1898.
Side Lights on Golf, Sisley's, 153 pp., 1907.
The Royal and Ancient Game of Golf, Golf Illustrated, 275 pp., 1912 (with H. Hilton).

Louis T. Stanley

Green Fairways, Methuen, 204 pp., 1947.
Fresh Fairways, Methuen, 220 pp., 1949.
Master Golfers in Action, Macdonald, 143 pp., 1950.
Style Analysis, Naldrett, 103 pp., 1951.
The Woman Golfer, Macdonald, 128 pp., 1952.
The Faulkner Method, Hutchinson, 62 pp., 1952 (with Max Faulkner).
This Is Golf, W. H. Allen, 192 pp., 1954.
The Golfer's Bedside Book, Methuen, 197 pp., 1955.
Fontana Golf Book, Collins, 127 pp., 1957.
Swing to Better Golf, Collins, 256 pp., 1957.
This Is Putting, W. H. Allen, 191 pp., c1957.
The Book of Golf, Max Parrish, 147 pp., 1960.
Golf With Your Hands, Collins, 256 pp., 1966.
Pelham Golf Year, Pelham, 443 pp., 1981 (with 2 subsequent editions).
St. Andrews, W. H. Allen, 216 pp., 1986.
A History of Golf, Weidenfeld & Nicolson, 218 pp., 1991.

Donald Steel

The Golfer's Bedside Book, Batsford, 240 pp., 1965.
The Golfer's Bedside Book, Batsford, 240 pp., 1971.
The Shell International Encyclopedia of Golf, Ebury & Pelham, 480 pp., 1975 (with P. Ryde).
Guiness Book of Golf Facts and Feats, Guiness, 256 pp., 1980.
Classic Golf Links of England, Scotland, Wales & Ireland, Pelican, 224 pp., 1992.

William G. van Tassel Sutphen

The Golfer's Alphabet, Harper's, 112 pp., 1898.
The Golficide and other Tales of the Fair Green, Harper's, 227 pp., 1898.
Harper's Official Golf Guide 1901, Harper's, 332 pp., 1901.
The Nineteenth Hole, Harper's, 190 pp., 1901.
The Official Golf Guide, Grafton Press, 372 pp., 1902.

Pat Ward-Thomas

Masters of Golf, Heinemann, 257 pp., 1961.
The Long Green Fairway, Hodder & Stoughton, 192 pp., 1966.
Shell Golfer's Atlas of England, Scotland and Wales, George Rainbird, 76 pp., 1968.
The World Atlas of Golf, Mitchell Beazley, 280 pp., 1976 (with Wind, Price, et al.).
The Royal and Ancient, R&A Golf Club, 124 pp., 1980.
Not Only Golf, Hodder & Stoughton, 206 pp., 1981.

Herbert Warren Wind

The Story of American Golf, Farrar, Strauss, 502 pp., 1948.
Thirty Years of Championship Golf, Prentice-Hall, 276 pp., 1950 (with Gene Sarazen).
The Complete Golfer, Simon & Schuster, 315 pp., 1954.
Tips from the Top, Prentice-Hall, 105 pp., 1955.
Tips from the Top: Book 2, Prentice-Hall, 105 pp., 1956.
Five Lessons, The Modern Fundamentals of Golf, A. S. Barnes, 127 pp., 1957 (with Ben Hogan).
On Tour with Harry Sprague, Simon & Schuster, 94 pp., 1960.
The Greatest Game of All, Simon & Schuster, 416 pp., 1969 (with Jack Nicklaus).
Herbert Warren Wind's Golf Book, Simon & Schuster, 317 pp., 1971.
The World Atlas of Golf, Mitchell Beazley, 280 pp., 1976 (with Ward-Thomas, Price, et al.).
Golf Quiz, Golf Digest, 248 pp., 1980.
Following Through, Ticknor & Fields, 414 pp., 1985.

P. G. Wodehouse

The Clicking of Cuthbert, Herbert Jenkins, 256 pp., 1922.
The Heart of A Goof, Herbert Jenkins, 314 pp., 1926.
Wodehouse on Golf, Doubleday, Doran, 844 pp., 1940.
The Golf Omnibus, Barrie & Jenkins, 467 pp., 1973.
Fore: The Best of Wodehouse on Golf, Ticknor & Fields, 259 pp., 1983.

Ben Wright

Good Bounces & Bad Lies, Sleeping Bear, 304 pp., 1999.
Speak Wright: The Literate Guide to the Game of Golf, Sleeping Bear, 165 pp., 2000.

ACKNOWLEDGMENTS

Without question, I must first thank my ever-supportive mother Roberta, who once again provided her superior editing skills — and must by now be dying for me to write about something that actually interests her.

Further thanks are extended to Wayne Wilson and his wonderful staff at the Amateur Athletic Foundation of Los Angeles, the Communications Department of the PGA Tour, my friend and golf consigliere Geoff Shackelford, and everyone at Sports Media Group, without whom this project could never have come to fruition.

Finally, like anyone interested in golf's long agos, I am greatly indebted to Horace Hutchinson, Bernard Darwin, and the game's other pre–World War I writers, without whose prose we would have little beyond faceless numbers with which to assess so many early players.